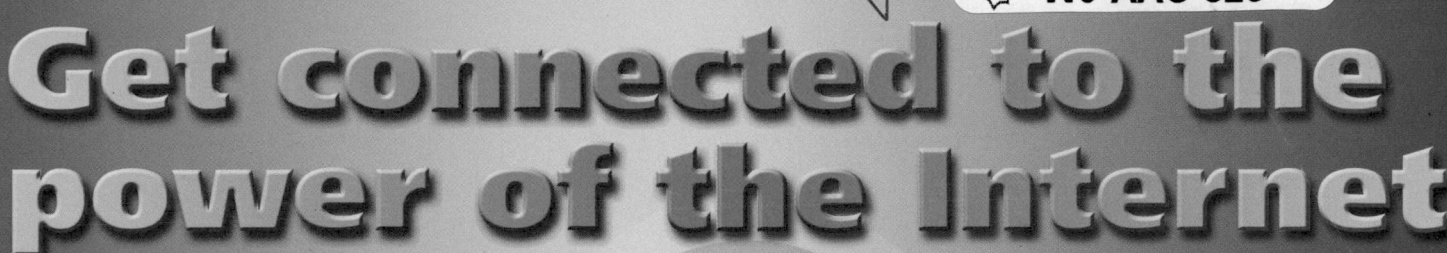

Get connected to the power of the Internet

McDougal Littell's online resources for students and parents provide motivating instruction, practice, and learning support.

eEdition Plus ONLINE

Visit classzone.com for eEdition Plus Online purchasing information and a free demo

This online version of the text encourages students to explore American history through interactive features.

- Animated maps and infographics
- Onscreen notetaking
- Links to online test practice

classzone.com

With a click of the mouse, students gain immediate access to this companion Web site to *Creating America.*

- Links correlated to the text
- Web Research Guide
- Self-scoring quizzes
- Interactive activities, games, and simulations
- Links to current events
- Test practice

Now it all clicks!™

 CLASSZONE.COM

McDougal Littell

W9-AAC-825

Creating America

A History of the United States

McDOUGAL LITTELL

Zitkala-Ša
Native American author

Benjamin Franklin
Author, printer, scientist, diplomat

Abigail Adams
Supporter of women's rights; married to President John Adams

Maya Lin
Designer of the Vietnam Veterans Memorial

Juan Seguín
A hero of the Texas Revolution

Amelia Earhart
Aviator; first woman to fly solo across the Atlantic Ocean

Ida B. Wells
Journalist and reformer who fought against discrimination

Abraham Lincoln
Sixteenth president of the
United States

Dr. Martin Luther King, Jr.
Civil rights leader

Harry S. Truman
Thirty-third president of the
United States

Creating America

A History of
the United States

Jesus Garcia

Donna M. Ogle

C. Frederick Risinger

Joyce Stevos

McDougal Littell
A DIVISION OF HOUGHTON MIFFLIN COMPANY

Senior Consultants

Jesus Garcia is Professor of Social Studies at the University of Nevada at Las Vegas. A former social studies teacher, Dr. Garcia has co-authored many books and articles on subjects that range from teaching social studies in elementary school to seeking diversity in education. Dr. Garcia served as President of the National Council for the Social Studies in 2004–2005.

Donna M. Ogle is Professor of Reading and Language Arts at National-Louis University in Evanston, Illinois, and is a specialist in reading in the content areas with an interest in social studies. She is past president of the International Reading Association. A former social studies teacher, Dr. Ogle is also Director of a Goals 2000 grant for Reading and Thinking in the Content Areas for four Chicago high schools. She developed the K-W-L reading strategy that is so widely used in schools.

C. Frederick Risinger is Director of Professional Development and Coordinator for Social Studies Education at Indiana University. He is past president of the National Council for the Social Studies. Mr. Risinger also served on the coordinating committee for the National History Standards Project. He writes a monthly column on technology in the social studies classroom for *Social Education.*

Joyce Stevos recently retired from 36 years of service to the Providence, Rhode Island, Public Schools. For 15 of those years, she was the social studies area supervisor and developed programs on Holocaust studies, the Armenian genocide, character education, voter education, and government and law. Currently, she is a Ph.D. candidate in education focusing on how youth develop a citizen identity.

Copyright © 2007 by McDougal Littell, a division of Houghton Mifflin Company. All rights reserved.

Maps on pages A1–A39 © Rand McNally & Company. All rights reserved.

Warning: No part of this work may be reproduced or transmitted in any form or by any means, electronic or mechanical, including photocopying and recording, or by any information storage or retrieval system without the prior written permission of McDougal Littell unless such copying is expressly permitted by federal copyright law. With the exception of not-for-profit transcription in Braille, McDougal Littell is not authorized to grant permission for further uses of copyrighted selections reprinted in this text without the permission of their owners. Permission must be obtained from the individual copyright owners as identified herein. Address inquiries to Supervisor, Rights and Permissions, McDougal Littell, P.O. Box 1667, Evanston, IL 60204.

Acknowledgments begin on page R97.

ISBN-13: 978-0-618-68977-4   ISBN-10: 0-618-68977-X

Printed in the United States of America
X 2 3 4 5 6 7 8 9 10 – DWO – 10 09 08 07 06

Consultants and Reviewers

Content Consultants

The content consultants reviewed the manuscript for historical depth and accuracy and for clarity of presentation.

Roger Beck
Department of History
Eastern Illinois University
Charleston, Illinois

David Farber
Department of History
University of New Mexico
Albuquerque, New Mexico

Cheryl Johnson-Odim
Department of History
Loyola University
Chicago, Illinois

Joseph Kett
Department of History
University of Virginia
Charlottesville, Virginia

Jack N. Rakove
Department of History
Stanford University
Stanford, California

Virginia Stewart
Department of History
University of North Carolina,
    Wilmington
Wilmington, North Carolina

Christopher Waldrep
Department of History
Eastern Illinois University
Charleston, Illinois

Nancy Woloch
Department of History
Barnard College
New York, New York

Multicultural Advisory Board

The multicultural advisers reviewed the manuscript for appropriate historical content.

Betty Dean
Social Studies Consultant
Pearland, Texas

Tyrone C. Howard
College of Education
The Ohio State University
Columbus, Ohio

Jose C. Moya
Department of History
University of California
    at Los Angeles
Los Angeles, California

Pat Payne
Office of Multicultural Education
Indianapolis Public Schools
Indianapolis, Indiana

Betto Ramirez
Former Teacher, La Joya, Texas
Social Studies Consultant
Mission, Texas

Jon Reyhner
Department of Education
Northern Arizona University
Flagstaff, Arizona

Ronald Young
Department of History
Georgia Southern University
Statesboro, Georgia

Consultants and Reviewers

Teacher Consultants

The following educators contributed activity options for the Pupil's Edition and teaching ideas and activities for the Teacher's Edition.

Paul C. Beavers
J. T. Moore Middle School
Nashville, Tennessee

Holly West Brewer
Buena Vista Paideia Magnet School
Nashville, Tennessee

Ron Campana
Social Studies Consultant
New York, New York

Patricia B. Carlson
Swanson Middle School
Arlington, Virginia

Ann Cotton
Ft. Worth Independent School
    District
Ft. Worth, Texas

Kelly Ellis
Hamilton Junior High School
Cypress, Texas

James Grimes
Middlesex County Vocational–
Technical High School
Woodbridge, New Jersey

Brent Heath
De Anza Middle School
Ontario, California

Suzanne Hidalgo
Serrano Middle School
Highland, California

Barbara Kennedy
Sylvan Middle School
Citrus Heights, California

Pamela Kniffin
Navasota Junior High School
Navasota, Texas

Tammy Leiber
Navasota Junior High School
Navasota, Texas

Lori Lesslie
Cedar Bluff Middle School
Knoxville, Tennessee

Brian McKenzie
Dr. Charles R. Drew Science
    Magnet School
Buffalo, New York

W. W. Bear Mills
Goddard Junior High School
Midland, Texas

Lindy Poling
Millbrook High School
Raleigh, North Carolina

Jean Price
T. H. Rogers Middle School
Houston, Texas

Meg Robbins
Wilbraham Middle School
Wilbraham, Massachusetts

Philip Rodriguez
McNair Middle School
San Antonio, Texas

Leslie Schubert
Parkland School
McHenry, Illinois

Robert Sisko
Carteret Middle School
Carteret, New Jersey

Marci Smith
Hurst-Euless-Bedford Independent
    School District
Bedford, Texas

James Sorenson
Chippewa Middle School
Des Plaines, Illinois

Nicholas G. Sysock
Carteret Middle School
Carteret, New Jersey

Lisa Williams
Lamberton Middle School
Carlisle, Pennsylvania

Michael Yell
Hudson Middle School
Hudson, Wisconsin

Teacher Panels
The following educators provided ongoing review during the development
of prototypes, the table of contents, and key components of the program.

Bill Albright
Wilson Southern Junior High School
Sinking Spring, Pennsylvania

Henry Assetto
Gordon Middle School
Coatesville, Pennsylvania

James Berry
Kennedy Middle School
Grand Prairie, Texas

Ralph Burnley
Roosevelt Middle School
Philadelphia, Pennsylvania

Mary Ann Canamar
Garner Middle School
San Antonio, Texas

Zoe Carter
San Jacinto Junior High School
Midland, Texas

Stephen Cicero
Butler Area Junior High School
Butler, Pennsylvania

Charles Crescenzi
Dover Intermediate School
Dover, Pennsylvania

Sharon McDonald
Cook Junior High School
Houston, Texas

Phil Mifsud
Roosevelt Middle School
Erie, Pennsylvania

Joel Mumma
Centerville Middle School
Lancaster, Pennsylvania

September Olson
Richardson Middle School
El Paso, Texas

Donald Roberts
Frick International Studies Academy
Pittsburgh, Pennsylvania

Mary Rogers
Brookside Intermediate School
Friendswood, Texas

Lucy Sanchez
John F. Kennedy High School
San Antonio, Texas

Steve Seale
Hamilton Middle School
Houston, Texas

Yolanda Villalobos
Dallas Independent School District
Dallas, Texas

Diane Williams
Hill-Freedman Middle School
Philadelphia, Pennsylvania

Lisa Williams
Lamberton Middle School
Carlisle, Pennsylvania

Student Board
The following students reviewed pages for the textbook.

Adam Backhaus
Parkland School
McHenry, Illinois

Ben Barney
Hamilton Junior High School
Cypress, Texas

Amanda Berrier
Lamberton Middle School
Carlisle, Pennsylvania

Debra Hurwitz
T. H. Rogers Middle School
Houston, Texas

Reginald Jones
Dr. Charles R. Drew Science
   Magnet School
Buffalo, New York

Brendon Keinath
Wilbraham Middle School
Wilbraham, Massachusetts

Daniel MacDonald
Carteret Middle School
Carteret, New Jersey

Cameron Mote
Serrano Middle School
Highland, California

Kim Nguyen
Sylvan Middle School
Citrus Heights, California

Arianna G. Noriega
De Anza Middle School
Ontario, California

Nicholas Tofilon
Burlington Middle School
Burlington, Wisconsin

Emmanuel Zepeda
Haven Middle School
Evanston, Illinois

Pontiac

George Washington

UNIT 2

Creating a New Nation 1763–1791

x

The Early Republic   1789 – 1844

UNIT 3

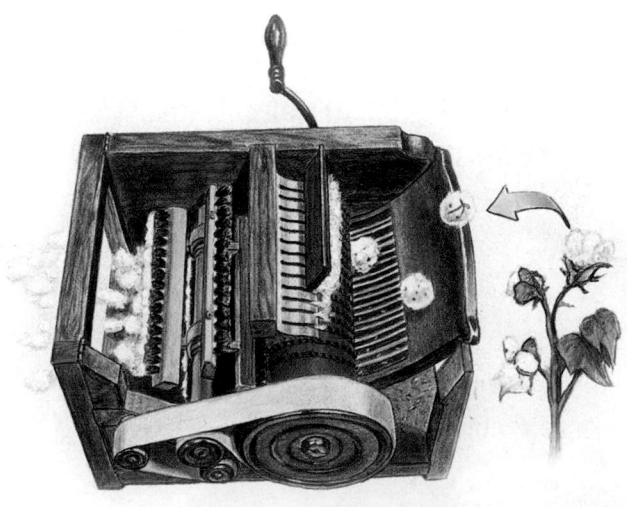

UNIT 4

A Changing Nation 1810 – 1860

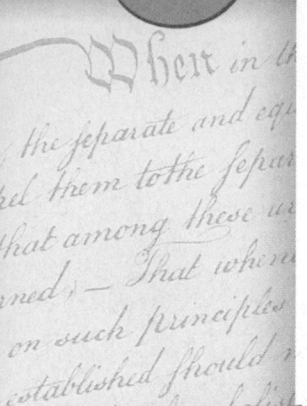

California gold miner

Frances Ellen Watkins Harper

xii

A Nation Divided and Rebuilt 1846 – 1877

UNIT 5

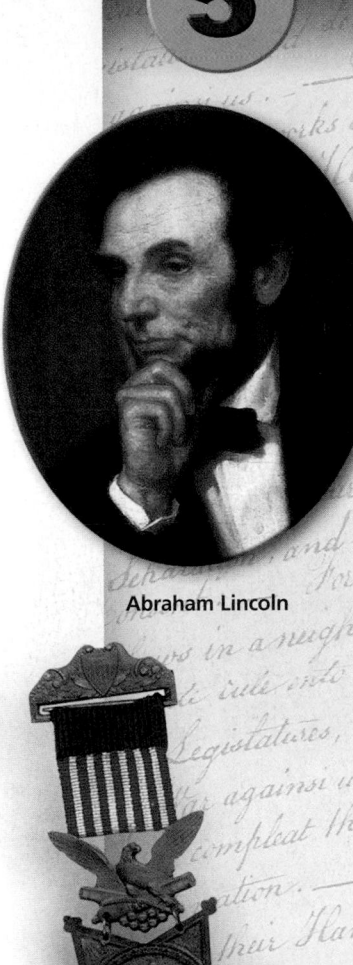

Abraham Lincoln

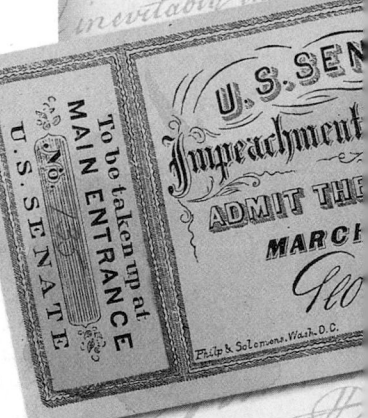

UNIT 6

America Transformed 1860 – 1914

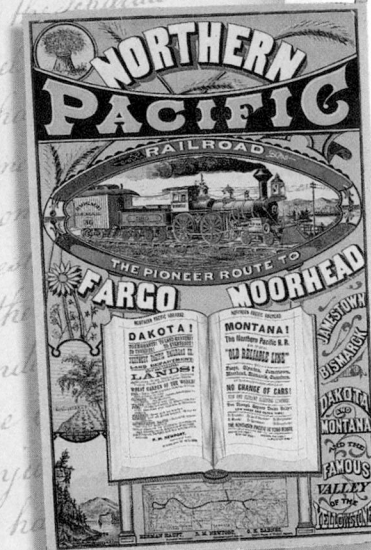

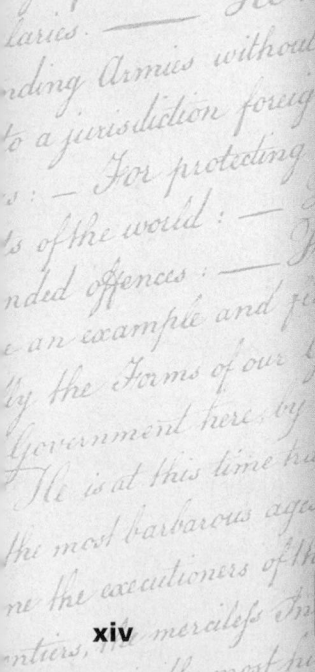

Immigrants approaching Ellis Island

xiv

Modern America Emerges 1880 – 1920   UNIT 7

Queen Liliuokalani

Tensions at Home and Abroad 1954 – PRESENT

UNIT 9

President John F. Kennedy

Buzz Aldrin

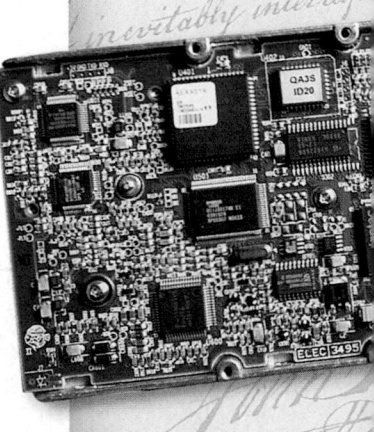

xvii

Features

Features

Voices from the Past

A VOICE FROM THE PAST

These, with the pictures, busts [sculptures of the head and shoulders], and prints (of which copies upon copies are spread everywhere), have made your father's face as well known as that of the moon.

Benjamin Franklin,
letter to his daughter Sally

Voices from the Past

A VOICE FROM THE PAST

Eliza made her desperate retreat across the river just in the dusk of twilight. The gray mist of evening, rising slowly from the river, enveloped her as she disappeared up the bank, and the swollen current and floundering masses of ice presented a hopeless barrier between her and her pursuer.

Harriet Beecher Stowe,
Uncle Tom's Cabin

A VOICE FROM THE PAST

Is it possible . . . that nine millions of men can make effective progress in economic lines if they are deprived of political rights? . . . If history and reason give any distinct answer to these questions, it is an emphatic *No.*

W. E. B. Du Bois,
The Souls of Black Folk

Voices from the Past

Visual Primary Sources for Assessment

Historical Maps

Charts and Graphs

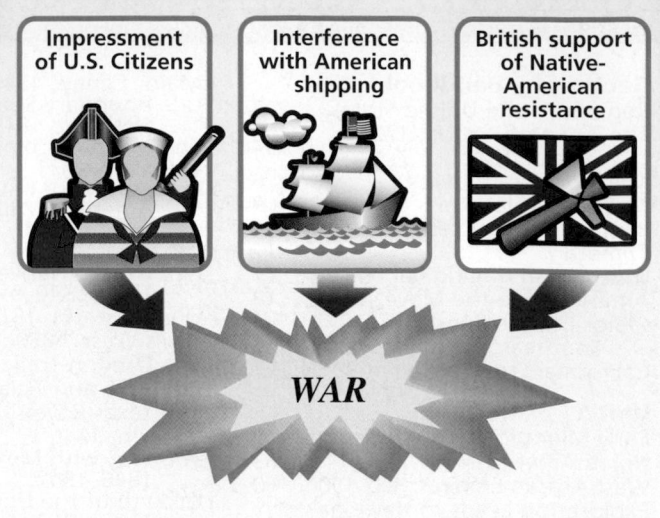

CONNECTIONS TO MATH

Military Deaths in the American Revolution

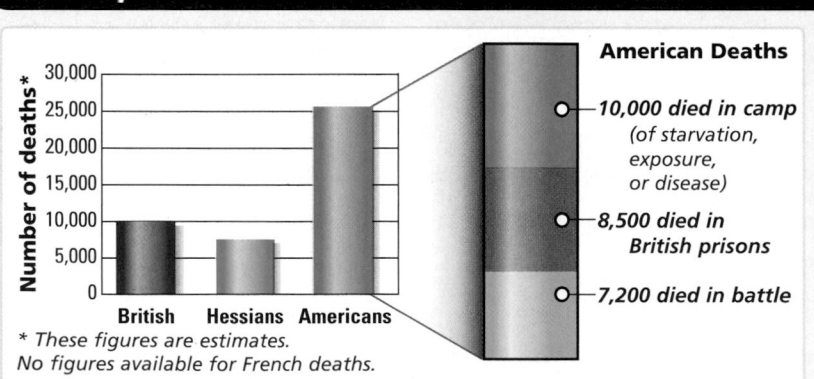

American Deaths

- 10,000 died in camp (of starvation, exposure, or disease)
- 8,500 died in British prisons
- 7,200 died in battle

British   Hessians   Americans

Number of deaths*

* These figures are estimates.
No figures available for French deaths.

Sources: *World Book Encyclopedia; An Outline History of the American Revolution*

Time Lines and Infographics

Time Lines

Infographics

The Rise and Decline of Feudalism

In feudalism, nobles offered to protect peasants from invaders. In return, the peasants farmed the nobles' lands.

Feudalism made people feel safe enough to travel. Trade increased and towns grew.

Then many peasants ran away to towns, where they could live more freely. Feudalism declined. Trade continued to grow.

THEMES of AMERICAN HISTORY

Imagine life in Jamestown, America's first permanent English settlement. The nation we inhabit now is a much different place than it was then, more than three centuries ago. Yet there are repeating themes—ideas and issues—in American history that tie the past and present together. This book focuses on nine significant themes in U.S. history. Understanding these themes will help you to make sense of American history.

Democratic Ideals

From the day they declared themselves citizens of a new nation, Americans have built their society around the principles of democracy. In a democracy, power lies with the people, and every individual enjoys basic rights that cannot be taken away. Throughout the nation's history, however, some Americans—mainly women and minorities—have had to struggle to gain their full rights. Still, the ideals of democracy remain the guiding principles of this land.

What right or freedom do you consider the most important? Why?

Citizenship

The citizens of the United States enjoy rights and freedoms found in very few other places in the world. Yet Americans know that with such freedoms come responsibilities and duties. Whether they stand in line to vote or spend a weekend to clean up a local river, Americans recognize that citizen participation is what keeps a democracy strong.

How do citizens that you know contribute to your community?

Dr. Martin Luther King, Jr.

Impact of the Individual

The history of the United States is the story not only of governments and laws but of individuals. Indeed, individuals have made the United States what it is today through their extraordinary achievements. American history provides a variety of examples of the impact of the individual on society in both the United States and the world.

Name several individuals who have an impact on American society today. What impact do they have?

Diversity and Unity

The United States has been a land of many peoples, cultures, and faiths. Throughout the nation's history, this blend of ethnic, racial, and religious groups has helped to create a rich and uniquely American culture. The nation's many different peoples are united in their belief in American values and ideals.

What things do you enjoy that came to the United States from other cultures?

Immigration and Migration

The movement of people has played a vital role in American history. The first Americans migrated from Asia thousands of years ago. Millions more have immigrated in the past five centuries. Even within the United States, large numbers of people have migrated to different regions of the country. However, movements to and within the United States have not always been voluntary. Africans were brought against their will to this country. Native Americans were forced from their homelands in order to make room for European settlers.

Why do you think people continue to immigrate to the United States?

A young Asian immigrant

Expansion

When the United States declared its independence from Great Britain, it was only a collection of states along the Atlantic Ocean. But the new country would not remain that way for long. Many Americans shared a sense of curiosity, adventure, and a strong belief that their destiny was to expand all the way to the Pacific Ocean. Driven by this belief, they pushed westward. Americans' efforts to increase the size of their nation is a recurring theme in early U.S. history.

Where do you predict that the exploration of space—the final frontier—will lead?

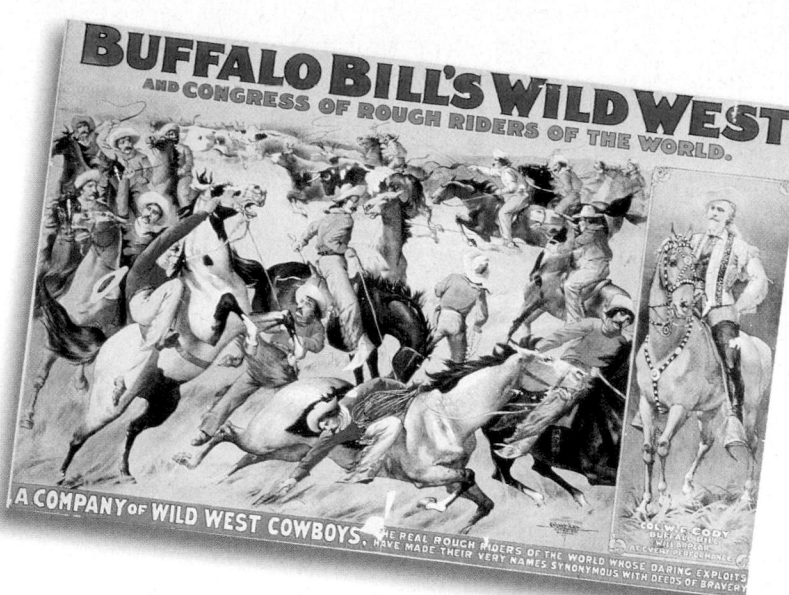

Poster for Buffalo Bill's Wild West show

America and the World

As the power and prestige of the United States have grown, the nation has played a much more active role in world affairs. Indeed, throughout the 20th century, the United States focused much of its energy on events beyond its borders. The nation fought in two world wars and tried to promote democracy, peace, and economic growth around the globe. As one of the world's political and economic leaders, the United States will continue to be a key player in world affairs throughout the new century.

What do you think the role of the United States in the world should be today?

Science and Technology

Americans have always been quick to embrace inventions and new ways of doing things. After all, this country was settled by people who turned away from old ways and tried new ones. In the past two centuries, new inventions, new technologies, and scientific breakthroughs have transformed the United States—and will continue to do so in the new century.

What recent inventions or innovations affect your life?

Economics in History

Economics has had a powerful impact on the course of U.S. history. For example, the desire for wealth led thousands to join the California Gold Rush in 1849. The nation as a whole has grown wealthy, thanks to its abundant resources and the hard work of its citizens. An important economic issue, however, has been how to make sure that all people have opportunities to share fully in the nation's wealth. This issue will continue to be important in the 21st century.

What do you think are the most exciting economic opportunities for Americans today?

Thomas Edison's first light bulb

STRATEGIES FOR TAKING STANDARDIZED TESTS

This section of the textbook helps you develop and practice the skills you need to study history and to take standardized tests. Part 1, **Strategies for Studying History,** takes you through the features of the textbook and offers suggestions on how to use these features to improve your reading and study skills.

Part 2, **Test-Taking Strategies and Practice,** offers specific strategies for tackling many of the items you'll find on a standardized test. It gives tips for answering multiple-choice, constructed-response, extended-response, and document-based questions. In addition, it offers guidelines for analyzing primary and secondary sources, maps, political cartoons, charts, graphs, and time lines. Each strategy is followed by a set of questions you can use for practice.

CONTENTS

Part 1: Strategies for Studying History

Reading is the central skill in the effective study of history or any other subject. You can improve your reading skills by using helpful techniques and through practice. The better your reading skills, the more you'll remember what you read. Below you'll find several strategies that involve built-in features of this textbook. Careful use of these strategies will help you learn and understand history more effectively.

Preview Chapters Before You Read

Each chapter begins with a two-page chapter opener and a one-page **Reading Strategy** feature. Study the materials to help you get ready to read.

1 Read the chapter and section titles and study the chapter-opening visual. Look for clues that indicate what will be covered in the chapter.

2 Preview the time line. Note the years that the chapter covers. What important events took place during this time period?

3 Study the **Interact with History** feature. Experience what it was like to live in the past by answering **What Do You Think?** questions.

4 Read the **Reading Strategy** feature (see page S3). **What Do You Want to Know?** and the note taking chart will help focus your reading.

CHAPTER 6

The Road to Revolution 1763–1776

Section 1
Tighter British Control

Section 2
Colonial Resistance Grows

Section 3
The Road to Lexington and Concord

Section 4
Declaring Independence

Angry confrontations between colonial protestors and British Red Coats became common as the colonies moved towards independence.

The bayonets, or blades, on the soldiers' gun were very dangerous in close combat.

The fife and drum corps played music to keep soldiers at a steady march. During battle, the drummers beat out orders and the fifers carried messages and stretchers.

Interact *with* History

The year is 1765. Your neighbors are enraged by Britain's demand that British troops be housed in American cities at American expense. Britain has never done this before. There are protests in many cities. You have to decide what you would do.

Would you join the protest?

What Do You Think?

- What is the best way to show opposition to policies you consider unjust?
- Is there anything to be gained by protesting? Anything to be lost?
- Does government have the right to make demands without consent of the people? Why or why not?

RESEARCH LINKS
CLASSZONE.COM
Visit the Chapter 6 links for more information about the American Revolution.

1763
Proclamation of 1763 becomes law.

1765
Stamp Act is passed.

1767
Townshend Acts are passed.

1769
Spanish begin to establish military posts and missions in California.

1770
Boston Massacre

1773
Boston Tea Party

1774
Intolerable Acts are passed; First Continental Congress meets.

1775
Battles of Lexington and Concord

1776
Declaration of Independence is signed.

USA World 1763

1763
Treaty of Paris ends Seven Years' War in Europe.

1765
Chinese forces invade Burma.

1769
Scotland's James Watt patents a steam engine capable of running other machines.

1772
Captain Cook explores the South Pacific.

1774
Reign of Louis XVI begins in France.

1776

156 CHAPTER 6

The Road to Revolution 157

Preview Sections Before You Read

Each chapter consists of three, four, or five sections. These sections focus on shorter periods of time or on particular historical themes. Use the section openers to help you prepare to read.

5 Study the sentences under the headings **Main Idea** and **Why It Matters Now**. These tell you what's important in the material that you're about to read.

6 Preview the **Terms & Names** list. This will give you an idea of the issues and personalities you will read about in the section.

7 Read **One American's Story** and **A Voice from the Past**. These provide one individual's view of an important issue of the time.

8 Notice how the section is divided into smaller chunks, each with a red headline. These headlines give you a quick outline of the section.

TERMS & NAMES

King George III — Stamp Act
Quartering Act — Patrick Henry
revenue — boycott
Sugar Act — Sons of Liberty

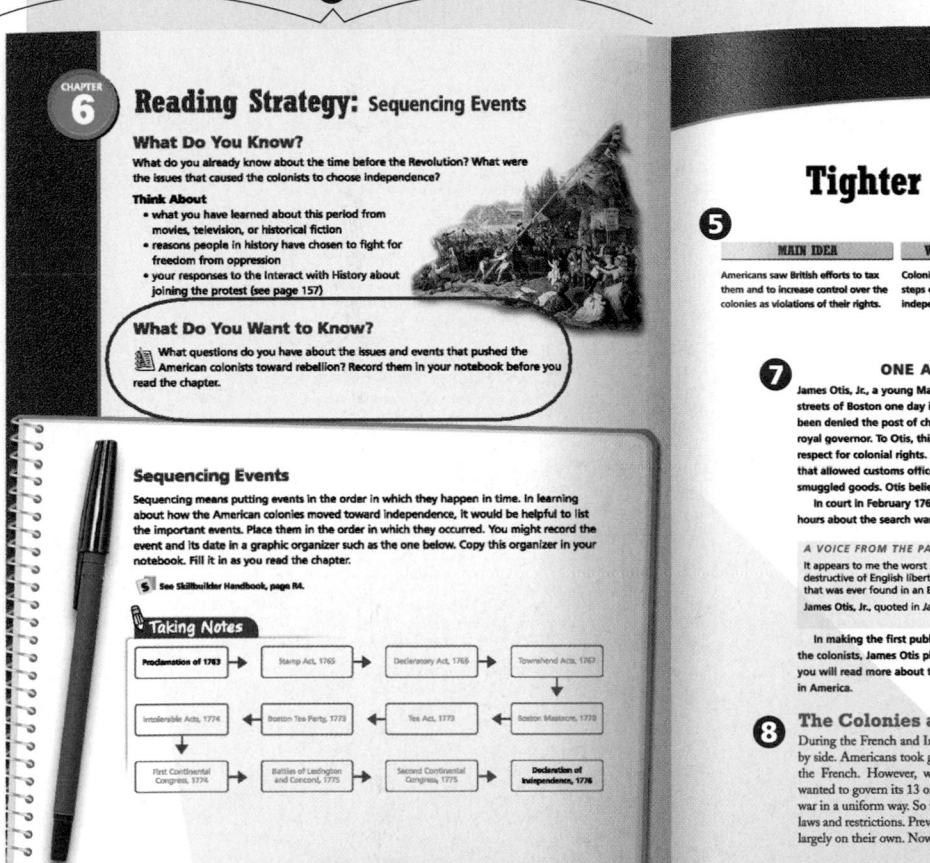

What Do You Want to Know?

What questions do you have about the issues and events that pushed the American colonists toward rebellion? Record them in your notebook before you read the chapter.

S3

STRATEGIES FOR TAKING STANDARDIZED TESTS

Use Active Reading Strategies As You Read

Now you're ready to read the chapter. Read one section at a time, from beginning to end.

1 Ask and answer questions as you read. Look for the **Reading History** questions in the margin. Answering these will show whether you understand what you've just read.

2 Try to visualize the people, places, and events you read about. Studying the pictures and any illustrated features will help you do this.

3 Read to build your vocabulary. Use the marginal **Vocabulary** notes to find the meaning of unfamiliar terms.

4 Look for the story behind the events. Read **Background** notes in the margin for additional information on people, places, events, and ideas.

Reading **History**

A. Summarizing
Who was upset by the Proclamation of 1763?

The first of Parliament's laws was the Proclamation of 1763. (See Chapter 5.) It said that colonists could not settle west of the Appalachian Mountains. Britain wanted this land to remain in the hands of its Native American allies to prevent another revolt like Pontiac's Rebellion.

The proclamation angered colonists who had hoped to move to the fertile Ohio Valley. Many of these colonists had no land of their own. It also upset colonists who had bought land as an investment. As a result, many ignored the law.

Reading **History**
A. Summarizing
Who was upset by the Proclamation of 1763?

British Troops and Taxes

King George III, the British monarch, wanted to enforce the proclamation and also keep peace with Britain's Native American allies. To do this, he decided to keep 10,000 soldiers in the colonies. In 1765, Parliament passed the **Quartering Act**. This was a cost-saving measure that required the colonies to quarter, or house, British soldiers and provide them with supplies. General Thomas Gage, commander of these forces, put most of the troops in New York.

Britain owed a large debt from the French and Indian War. Keeping troops in the colonies would raise that debt even higher. Britain needed more **revenue**, or income, to meet its expenses. So it attempted to have the colonies pay part of the war debt. It also wanted them to contribute toward the costs of frontier defense and colonial government.

In the past, the king had asked the colonial assemblies to pass taxes to support military actions that took place in the colonies. This time, however, Parliament voted to tax the Americans directly.

In 1764, Parliament passed the **Sugar Act**. This law placed a tax on sugar, molasses, and other products shipped to the colonies. It also called for strict enforcement of the act and harsh punishment of smugglers. Colonial merchants, who often traded in smuggled goods, reacted with anger.

Colonial leaders such as James Otis claimed that Parliament had no right to tax the colonies, since the colonists were not represented in Parliament. As Otis exclaimed, "Taxation without representation is tyranny!" British finance minister George Grenville disagreed. The colonists were subjects of Britain, he said, and enjoyed the protection of its laws. For that reason, they were subject to taxation.

Vocabulary
tyranny: absolute power in the hands of a single ruler

Britain Passes the Stamp Act

The Sugar Act was just the first in a series of acts that increased tension between the mother country and the colonies. In 1765, Parliament passed the **Stamp Act**. This law required all legal and commercial documents to carry an official stamp showing that a tax had been paid. All diplomas, contracts, and wills had to carry a stamp.

The colonial view of the hated stamp tax is shown by the skull and crossbones on this emblem (above); a royal stamp is pictured at right.

160

Even published materials such as newspapers had to be written on special stamped paper.

The Stamp Act was a new kind of tax for the colonies. The Sugar Act had been a tax on imported goods. It mainly affected merchants. In contrast, the Stamp Act was a tax applied within the colonies. It fell directly on all colonists. Even more, the colonists had to pay for stamps in silver coin—a scarce item in the colonies.

Colonial leaders vigorously protested. For them, the issue was clear. They were being taxed without their consent by a Parliament in which they had no voice. If Britain could pass the Stamp Act, what other taxes might it pass in the future? Samuel Adams, a leader in the Massachusetts legislature, asked, "Why not our lands? Why not the produce of our lands and, in short, everything we possess and make use of?" **Patrick Henry**, a member of Virginia's House of Burgesses, called for resistance to the tax. When another member shouted that resistance was treason, Henry replied, "If this be treason, make the most of it!"

The Colonies Protest the Stamp Act

Colonial assemblies and newspapers took up the cry—"No taxation without representation!" In October 1765, nine colonies sent delegates to the Stamp Act Congress in New York City. This was the first time the colonies met to consider acting together in protest. Delegates drew up a petition to the king protesting the Stamp Act. The petition declared that the right to tax the colonies belonged to the colonial assemblies, not to Parliament. Later, colonial merchants organized a **boycott** of British goods. A boycott is a refusal to buy.

Meanwhile, some colonists formed secret societies to oppose British policies. The most famous of these groups was the **Sons of Liberty**. Many Sons of Liberty were lawyers, merchants, and craftspeople—the colonists most affected by the Stamp Act. These groups staged protests against the act.

Not all of their protests were peaceful. The Sons of Liberty burned the stamped paper whenever they could find it. They also attacked customs officials, whom they covered with hot tar and feathers and paraded in public. Fearing for their safety, many customs officials quit their jobs.

The protests in the colonies had an effect in Britain. Merchants thought that their trade with America would be hurt. Some British political leaders, including

Reading **History**
B. Making Inferences Why did the colonists boycott goods?

Background
To voice their protests, the Sons of Liberty in Boston met under a huge, 120-year-old elm tree that they called the Liberty Tree.

Colonists protest the Stamp Act.

161

Background
To voice their protests, the Sons of Liberty in Boston met under a huge, 120-year-old elm tree that they called the Liberty Tree.

Review and Summarize What You Have Read

When you finish reading a section, review and summarize what you've read. If necessary, go back and reread information that was not clear the first time through.

5 Reread the red headlines for a quick summary of the major points covered in the section.

6 Study any charts, graphs, and maps in the section. These visual materials usually provide a condensed version of information in the section.

7 Review the pictures and note how they relate to the section content.

8 Complete all the questions in the **Section Assessment**. This will help you think critically about what you have just read.

---

immediately offered Massachusetts their support. They sent food and money to Boston. The committees of correspondence also called for a meeting of colonial delegates to discuss what to do next.

5 ### The First Continental Congress Meets

In September 1774, delegates from all the colonies except Georgia met in Philadelphia. At this meeting, called the **First Continental Congress**, delegates voted to ban all trade with Britain until the Intolerable Acts were repealed. They also called on each colony to begin training troops. Georgia agreed to be a part of the actions of the Congress even though it had voted not to send delegates.

The First Continental Congress marked a key step in American history. Although most delegates were not ready to call for independence, they were determined to uphold colonial rights. This meeting planted the seeds of a future independent government. John Adams called it "a nursery of American statesmen." The delegates agreed to meet in seven months, if necessary. By that time, however, fighting with Britain had begun.

Reading **History**
A. Evaluating
Why do you think the First Continental Congress was important?

Between War and Peace

The colonists hoped that the trade boycott would force a repeal of the Intolerable Acts. After all, past boycotts had led to the repeal of the Stamp Act and the Townshend Acts. This time, however, Parliament stood firm. It even increased restrictions on colonial trade and sent more troops.

By the end of 1774, some colonists were preparing to fight. In Massachusetts, John Hancock headed the Committee of Safety, which had the power to call out the militia. The colonial troops continued to train.

6

CAUSE AND EFFECT: Growing Conflict Between Britain and America		
DATE	BRITISH ACTION	COLONIAL REACTION
1763	Proclamation of 1763 issued	Proclamation leads to anger
1765	Stamp Act passed	Boycott of British goods; Stamp Act Resolves passed
1766	Stamp Act repealed; Declaration Act passed	Boycott ended
1767	Townshend Acts passed	New boycotts; Boston Massacre (March 1770)
1770	Townshend Acts repealed (April)	Tension between colonies and Britain reduced
1773	Tea Act passed	Boston Tea Party
1774	Intolerable Acts passed	First Continental Congress bans trade; militias organized
1775	Troops ordered to Lexington and Concord, Massachusetts	Militia fights British troops; Second Continental Congress; Continental Army established

SKILLBUILDER Interpreting Charts
1. What British action caused the first violence in the growing conflict between Britain and America?
2. How might the Intolerable Acts be seen as a reaction as well as an action?

171

When the British moved, so did Revere and Dawes. They galloped over the countryside on their "midnight ride," spreading the news. In Lexington, they were joined by Dr. Samuel Prescott. When Revere and Dawes were stopped by a British patrol, Prescott broke away and carried the message to Concord.

Lexington and Concord

At dawn on April 19, some 700 British troops reached Lexington. They found Captain John Parker and about 70 militiamen waiting. The British commander ordered the Americans to drop their muskets. They refused. No one knows who fired first, but within a few minutes eight militiamen lay dead. The British then marched to Concord, where they destroyed military supplies. A battle broke out at a bridge north of town, forcing the British to retreat.

Nearly 4,000 Minutemen and militiamen arrived in the area. They lined the road from Concord to Lexington and peppered the retreating redcoats with musket fire. "It seemed as if men came down from the clouds," one soldier said. Only the arrival of 1,000 more troops saved the British from destruction as they scrambled back to Boston.

Background
British losses totaled 273 soldiers compared to 95 militiamen.

Reading **History**
C. Drawing Conclusions
Why did Emerson call it the "shot heard 'round the world"?

Lexington and Concord were the first battles of the Revolutionary War. As Ralph Waldo Emerson later wrote, colonial troops had fired the "shot heard 'round the world." Americans would now have to choose sides and back up their political opinions by force of arms. Those who supported the British were called **Loyalists**. Those who sided with the rebels were **Patriots**. The conflict between the two sides divided communities, families, and friends. The war was on!

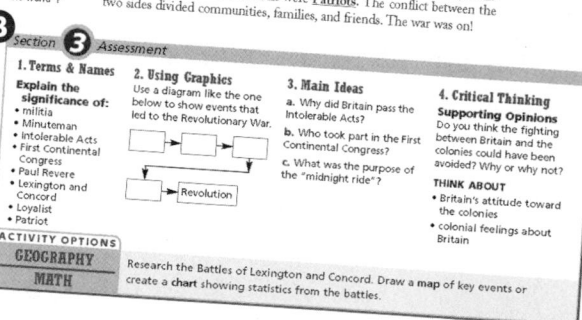

Now *and* **then**
PATRIOTS' DAY
The "shot heard 'round the world" is celebrated every year in Massachusetts and Maine. Patriots' Day, as it is called, is the third Monday of April. In Concord and nearby towns, modern-day Minutemen like those below reenact the battle that began the Revolution on April 19, 1775. The Boston Marathon is also run on Patriots' Day.

7

8 Section **3** Assessment

1. Terms & Names
Explain the significance of:
• militia
• Minuteman
• Intolerable Acts
• First Continental Congress
• Paul Revere
• Lexington and Concord
• Loyalist
• Patriot

2. Using Graphics
Use a diagram like the one below to show events that led to the Revolutionary War.

□ → □ → □
↓
□ → Revolution

3. Main Ideas
a. Why did Britain pass the Intolerable Acts?
b. Who took part in the First Continental Congress?
c. What was the purpose of the "midnight ride"?

4. Critical Thinking
Supporting Opinions
Do you think the fighting between Britain and the colonies could have been avoided? Why or why not?

THINK ABOUT
• Britain's attitude toward the colonies
• colonial feelings about Britain

ACTIVITY OPTIONS
GEOGRAPHY
MATH
Research the Battles of Lexington and Concord. Draw a map of key events or create a chart showing statistics from the battles.

The Road to Revolution **173**

Part 2: Test-Taking Strategies and Practice

Improve your test-taking skills by practicing the strategies discussed in this section. Read the tips on the left-hand page. Then apply them to the practice items on the right-hand page.

Multiple Choice

A multiple-choice question consists of a stem and a set of choices. The stem is usually in the form of a question or an incomplete sentence. One of the choices correctly answers the question or completes the sentence.

1 Read the stem carefully and try to answer the question or complete the sentence without looking at the choices.

2 Pay close attention to key words in the stem. They may direct you toward the correct answer.

3 Read each choice with the stem. Don't jump to conclusions about the correct answer until you've read all of the choices.

4 Think carefully about questions that include *All of the above* among the choices.

5 After reading all of the choices, eliminate any that you know are incorrect.

6 Use modifiers to help narrow your choice.

7 Look for the best answer among the remaining choices.

---

stem

1 1. At the beginning of the Revolution, (most) **2** Americans were

Most is a key word here. Replacing it with *all* or *some* changes the sentence and calls for a different answer.

3 choices
- A. united in support of the war.
- B. Patriots who wanted independence from Great Britain.
- C. against a war with Great Britain.
- D. Loyalists who supported the British point of view.

2. Which of the following weapons were first used effectively during World War I?
- A. airplanes
- B. machine guns
- C. tanks
- D. all of the above

4 If you select this answer, be sure that all of the choices are correct.

3. In June 1945, Germany was divided into four zones controlled by
- A. Great Britain, France, the United States, and Japan.
- B. Great Britain, France, the United States, and the Soviet Union.
- C. the Allied Powers.
- D. (all) of the countries of Europe.

5 You can eliminate **A** if you remember that the Allies were still at war with Japan in June 1945.

6 Absolute words, such as *all, never, always, every,* and *only,* often signal an incorrect choice.

7 Either **B** or **C** could be correct. The Allied Powers did control Germany after World War II. However, Great Britain, France, the United States, and the Soviet Union controlled the four zones. Therefore, **B** is the best answer.

answers: 1 (C), 2 (D), 3 (B)

Directions: Read the following questions and choose the *best* answer from the four choices.

1. New inventions that helped open the Great Plains to farming included

   A. the steel windmill.

   B. barbed wire.

   C. the spring-tooth harrow.

   D. All of the above

2. Which of the following statements *best* explains why, by the year 1500, there were hundreds of Native American groups with diverse religious beliefs, economies, and languages?

   A. The local environment influenced each group in different ways.

   B. Spiritual beliefs dictated many groups' distinct cultural growth.

   C. Contagious disease caused the people to form smaller groups.

   D. Trading practices led to the establishment of specialized cultures.

3. During the presidency of Thomas Jefferson, the United States was able to foster westward expansion when it acquired territory in what is known as

   A. Seward's Folly.

   B. the Missouri Compromise.

   C. the Kansas-Nebraska Act.

   D. the Louisiana Purchase.

4. In 1950, the United Nations Security Council voted to intervene after an act of aggression by which one of the following countries?

   A. Libya

   B. Great Britain

   C. the Democratic People's Republic of Korea

   D. the People's Republic of China

Primary Sources

Primary sources are materials written or made by people who took part in or witnessed historical events. Letters, diaries, speeches, newspaper articles, and autobiographies are all primary sources. So, too, are legal documents, such as wills, deeds, and financial records.

1 Look at the source line and identify the author. Consider what qualifies the author to write about the events discussed in the passage.

2 Skim the document to form an idea of what it is about.

3 Note special punctuation. Ellipses indicate that words or sentences have been removed from the original passage. Brackets indicate words that were not in the original. Bracketed words often are replacements for difficult or unfamiliar terms.

4 Carefully read the passage and distinguish between facts and the author's opinions. (That the groups of soldiers were wandering in all directions is a fact. The reasons for their wandering offered by Madison are her opinions.)

5 Consider for whom the author was writing. The intended audience may influence what and how an author writes.

6 Before rereading the passage, skim the questions to identify the information you need to find.

answers: 1 (D), 2 (B)

The Flight from the White House

Wednesday Morning, twelve o'clock. Since sunrise I have been turning my spy-glass in every direction, . . . but alas! I can see **3** only groups of military, wandering in all directions, as if there was **4** a lack of arms, or of spirit to fight for their own fireside.

Three o'clock. Will you believe it, my sister? we have had a battle, or skirmish, near Bladensburg, and here I am still, within sound of the cannon!. . . Two messengers covered with dust come to bid me fly. . . . At this late hour a wagon has been [found], and I have had it filled with plate and the most valuable portable articles belonging to the house. Whether it will reach its destination . . . or fall into the hands of British soldiery, events must determine. Our kind friend, Mr. Carroll, has come to hasten my departure, and is in a very bad humor with me, because I insist on waiting until the large picture of General Washington is secured. . . . It is done! and the precious portrait placed in the hands of two gentlemen of New York, for safe keeping. And now, dear sister, I must leave this house. . . . When I shall again write to you, or where I shall be tomorrow, I cannot tell!

The author is Dolley Madison, the wife of President James Madison. She personally oversaw the evacuation of the White House in 1814. **1**

—Dolley Madison, in a letter to her sister describing her flight from the White House in August 1814

5 This is a letter. If it were an official report to Congress, the style and content would be much different.

6 1. Dolley Madison's letter describes her preparations to flee the White House in advance of a British attack. In which war did this attack take place?

A. War of Jenkins' Ear

B. French and Indian War

C. Revolutionary War

D. War of 1812

2. Why might Dolley Madison be considered a good source of information on the British attack on Washington, D.C.?

A. She was the wife of President James Madison.

B. She was an eyewitness to the attack.

C. She helped her husband develop military policy.

D. She had intercepted British war plans.

Directions: Use this passage from a letter on conservation, written by President Theodore Roosevelt, and your knowledge of U.S. history to answer questions 1 through 3.

> In the east, the States are now painfully, and at great expense, endeavoring to undo the effects of their former shortsighted policy in throwing away their forest lands. Congress has before it bills to establish by purchase great forest reserves in the White Mountains and the Southern Appalachians, and the only argument against the bills is that of their great expense. New York and Pennsylvania are now, late in the day, endeavoring themselves to protect the forests which guard the headwaters of their streams. Michigan and Wisconsin have already had their good timber stript from their forests by the great lumber companies. But the western States, far more fortunate than their eastern sisters in this regard, can now reserve their forests for the good of all their citizens, without expense, if they choose to show the requisite foresight.
>
> —President Theodore Roosevelt, in a private letter in 1907

1. According to President Roosevelt, forests not yet damaged by timber companies could be set aside at no expense in the

   A. Midwest.

   B. East.

   C. South.

   D. West.

2. You can tell from this letter that President Roosevelt

   A. favored changing forests to farmland.

   B. was a good president.

   C. supported environmental protection.

   D. was an owner of a large lumber company.

3. Which one of the following statements from the letter is most strictly a fact?

   A. "Congress has before it bills to establish by purchase great forest reserves in the White Mountains. . . ."

   B. "New York and Pennsylvania are now, late in the day, endeavoring themselves to protect the forests. . . . "

   C. ". . . States are now painfully, and at great expense, endeavoring to undo the effects of . . . throwing away their forest lands."

   D. "But the western States, far more fortunate than their eastern sisters . . . can now reserve their forests. . . ."

Reprinted by permission of the publisher from "Letter to James Wilson," June 7, 1907, in *The Letters of Theodore Roosevelt, Volume 5,* edited by Elting E. Morison, Cambridge, Mass.: Harvard University Press. Copyright © 1951 by the President and Fellows of Harvard College.

Secondary Sources

Secondary sources are descriptions or interpretations of historical events made by people who were not at those events. The most common types of written secondary sources are history books, encyclopedias, and biographies. A secondary source often combines information from several primary sources.

1 Read titles to preview what the passage is about.

2 Look for topic sentences. These, too, will help you preview the content of the passage.

3 As you read, use context clues to help you understand difficult or unfamiliar words. (You can tell from the description of the battle in the previous sentences that the word *fiasco* must mean something like "disaster," "failure," or "blunder.")

4 As you read, ask and answer questions that come to mind. You might ask: Why would the Washington raid embarrass and anger Americans? Why did the Washington raid achieve little?

5 Before rereading the passage, skim the questions to identify the information you need to find.

1 The British Offensive

2 Ironically, Britain's most spectacular success began as a diversion from [its main] offensive [in the North]. A British army that had come up from Bermuda entered Chesapeake Bay and on August 24, 1814, met a larger American force . . . at Bladensburg, Maryland. The Battle of Bladensburg deteriorated into the "Bladensburg Races" as the American troops fled, virtually without firing a shot. The British then descended on Washington, D.C. Madison, who had witnessed **3** the Bladensburg fiasco, fled into the Virginia hills. His wife, Dolley, loaded her silver, a bed, and a portrait of George Washington onto her carriage before joining him. British troops ate the supper prepared for the Madisons and then burned the presidential mansion **4** and other public buildings in the capital. Beyond embarrassing and angering Americans, the Washington raid accomplished little, for after a failed attack on Baltimore, the British broke off the operation.

—Paul S. Boyer, et al., *The Enduring Vision*

5 1. Why do you think the authors refer to the Battle of Bladensburg as a "fiasco"?

A. because the American forces fled almost without a fight

B. because President Madison had to flee the White House

C. because it allowed the British to attack Washington, D.C.

D. because it was a famous victory for the British forces

2. What, according to the authors, did the British raid on Washington, D.C., accomplish?

A. It paved the way for the British capture of Baltimore.

B. It burned down all the public buildings in the city.

C. It helped the British offensive in the North.

D. It embarrassed and angered many Americans.

> Remember to be wary of choices that contain absolutes, such as *all, every,* or *only.*

answers: 1 (A), 2 (D)

For more test practice online . . .
TEST PRACTICE
CLASSZONE.COM

Directions: Use this passage and your knowledge of U.S. history to answer questions 1 through 3.

African-American Sailors

African Americans contributed greatly to the growth of maritime commerce in the United States. Beginning in colonial times, slaves, with their masters' permission, hired themselves out as sailors. Some served as translators on slave ships. Merchant ships also offered a means of escape for runaway slaves. A few escapees even took to the sea as pirates.

Seafaring was one of the few occupations open to free African Americans. They served on clippers, naval vessels, and whaling ships from the 1700s into the late 1800s. Federal crew lists from Atlantic seaports show that during this time African Americans made up 10 percent or more of sailors on American ships. Seafaring was an especially dangerous line of work for free blacks. They risked capture in southern ports, where they were often thrown in jail or sold into slavery.

1. What records show that African Americans made up 10 percent or more of sailors on American ships?

A. shipyard records

B. family bibles

C. federal crew lists

D. ships' logs

2. The passage implies that free and enslaved African Americans went to sea for all of the following reasons *except* to

A. escape slavery.

B. live as pirates.

C. earn wages as sailors.

D. discover new lands.

3. The author states that life was especially dangerous for free African-American sailors because

A. American prosperity depended on their work alone.

B. the worst jobs on board ship were always assigned to them.

C. they ran the risk of capture and enslavement in southern ports.

D. they were more likely than white sailors to contract scurvy.

Political Cartoons

Political cartoons are drawings that express views on political issues of the day. Cartoonists use symbols and such artistic styles as caricature—exaggerating a person's physical features—to get their message across.

1 Identify the subject of the cartoon. Titles and captions often indicate the subject matter.

2 Identify the main characters in the cartoon. Here, the main character is Horace Greeley, a candidate in the 1872 presidential election.

3 Note the symbols—ideas or images that stand for something else—used in the cartoon.

4 Study labels and other written information in the cartoon.

5 Analyze the point of view. How cartoonists use caricature often indicates how they feel. The exaggeration of Greeley's physical appearance—short and overweight—makes him appear comical.

6 Interpret the cartoonist's message.

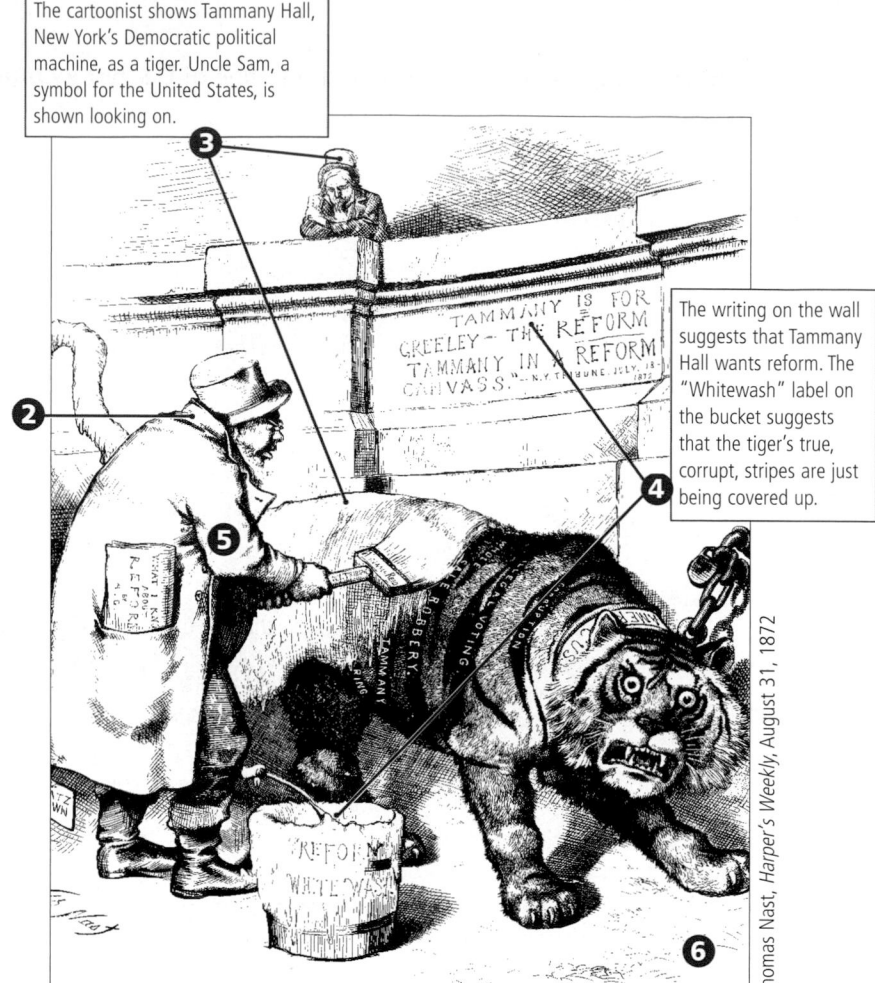

The cartoonist shows Tammany Hall, New York's Democratic political machine, as a tiger. Uncle Sam, a symbol for the United States, is shown looking on.

The writing on the wall suggests that Tammany Hall wants reform. The "Whitewash" label on the bucket suggests that the tiger's true, corrupt, stripes are just being covered up.

Thomas Nast, *Harper's Weekly*, August 31, 1872

1 "What are you going to do about it, if 'Old Honesty' lets him loose again?"

1. Based on the cartoon, what do you think was Horace Greeley's major issue in the 1872 presidential campaign?

   A. political reform

   B. states' rights

   C. abolition

   D. temperance

2. Which one of the following statements do you think *best* represents the cartoonist's point of view?

   A. Horace Greeley is an honest man.

   B. Tammany Hall supports political reform.

   C. Tammany Hall, regardless of Greeley's view, is still corrupt.

   D. Horace Greeley, like most Tammany politicians, is corrupt.

answers: 1 (A), 2 (C)

PRACTICE

For more test practice online . . .

TEST PRACTICE
CLASSZONE.COM

STRATEGIES FOR TAKING STANDARDIZED TESTS

Directions: Use the cartoon and your knowledge of U.S. history to answer questions 1 through 3.

Rollin Kirby, *New York World*, 1917

"That's my fight, too!"

1. The cartoon character is a symbol of

   A. Americans opposed to war.

   B. the president of the United States.

   C. old soldiers retired from the United States Army.

   D. the United States as a whole.

2. The "fight" in the cartoon caption refers to

   A. the War of 1812.

   B. World War II in Europe.

   C. World War II in the Pacific.

   D. World War I in Europe.

3. The cartoonist's point of view is *best* described by which of the following statements?

   A. The United States believes it has an obligation to join in this foreign war.

   B. Uncle Sam is too old and too late for every battle.

   C. The United States should stay out of other countries' wars.

   D. A country should equip its soldiers with the best weapons and other supplies.

Charts

Charts present information in a visual form. History textbooks use several types of charts, including tables, flow charts, Venn diagrams, and concept webs. The type of chart most commonly found in standardized tests is the table. It organizes information in columns and rows for easy viewing.

❶ Read the title and identify the broad subject of the chart.

❷ Read the column and row headings and any other labels. This will provide more details about the subject of the chart.

❸ Compare and contrast the information from column to column and row to row.

❹ Try to draw conclusions from the information in the chart. Ask yourself: What trends does the chart show?

❺ Read the questions, and then study the chart again.

Review difficult or unfamiliar words. Here, the term *nativity* means "place of birth."

❶ United States Population by Region and Nativity, 1890–1920

❷

	1890	1900	1910	1920
Northeast				
Total Population	17,407,000	21,047,000	25,869,000	29,662,000
% Native Born	78	77	74	77
% Foreign Born	22	23	26	23
North Central				
Total Population	22,410,000	26,333,000	29,889,000	34,020,000
% Native Born	82	84	84	86
% Foreign Born	18	16	16	14
South				
Total Population	20,028,000	24,524,000	29,389,000	33,126,000
% Native Born	97	98	97	97
% Foreign Born	3	2	3	3
West				
Total Population	3,134,000	4,309,000	7,082,000	9,214,000
% Native Born	76	79	79	82
% Foreign Born	24	21	21	18

❹

Source: *Historical Statistics of the United States*

Compare changes in population over time and contrast statistics among regions.

❸

❺ 1. The two regions with the highest percentage of foreign-born inhabitants are the

A. Northeast and the West.

B. West and the South.

C. South and the North Central.

D. North Central and the Northeast.

2. When did immigration to the Northeast peak?

A. between 1910 and 1920

B. before 1900

C. between 1900 and 1910

D. after 1920

answers: 1 (A), 2 (C)

Directions: Use the chart and your knowledge of U.S. history to answer questions 1 through 4.

Percentage of Population Free and Enslaved, by States and Territories, 1790

North		
State/Territories	Free	Enslaved
Connecticut	98.9	1.1
Delaware	85.0	15.0
Maine	100.0	0.0
Massachusetts	100.0	0.0
New Hampshire	99.9	0.1
New Jersey	93.8	6.2
New York	93.8	6.2
Pennsylvania	99.1	0.9
Rhode Island	98.6	1.4
Vermont	100.0	0.0

South		
State/Territories	Free	Enslaved
Georgia	64.5	35.5
Kentucky	83.1	16.9
Maryland	67.8	32.2
North Carolina	74.5	25.5
South Carolina	57.0	43.0
Virginia	60.9	39.1

Source: Inter-University Consortium for Political and Social Research

1. The state with the highest percentage of enslaved people was

   A. New Hampshire.

   B. North Carolina.

   C. Rhode Island.

   D. South Carolina.

2. Which of the following *best* describes most states in the North?

   A. The population was more than 98 percent free.

   B. More than 10 percent of the population was enslaved.

   C. Less than 60 percent of the population was free.

   D. The population was more than 20 percent enslaved.

3. Which statement about the percentage of enslaved people is true?

   A. It is much lower in the South.

   B. It is much higher in the South.

   C. There is no difference between the regions.

   D. There is a slight difference between the regions.

4. What economic factor *best* explains the population differences between the regions?

   A. The North focused on manufacturing.

   B. The North was wealthy enough to free enslaved people.

   C. The South focused on plantation agriculture.

   D. The South needed enslaved people for factory work.

Line and Bar Graphs

Graphs show statistics in a visual form. Line graphs are particularly useful for showing changes over time. Bar graphs make it easy to compare numbers or sets of numbers.

① Read the title and identify the broad subject of the graph.

② Study the labels on the vertical and horizontal axes to see the kinds of information presented in the graph. Note the intervals between amounts and between dates. This will help you read the graph more efficiently.

③ Look at the source line and evaluate the reliability of the information in the graph. Government statistics on education tend to be reliable.

④ Study the information in the graph and note any trends.

⑤ Draw conclusions and make generalizations based on these trends.

⑥ Read the questions carefully, and then study the graph again.

① High School Graduates, 1880–1920

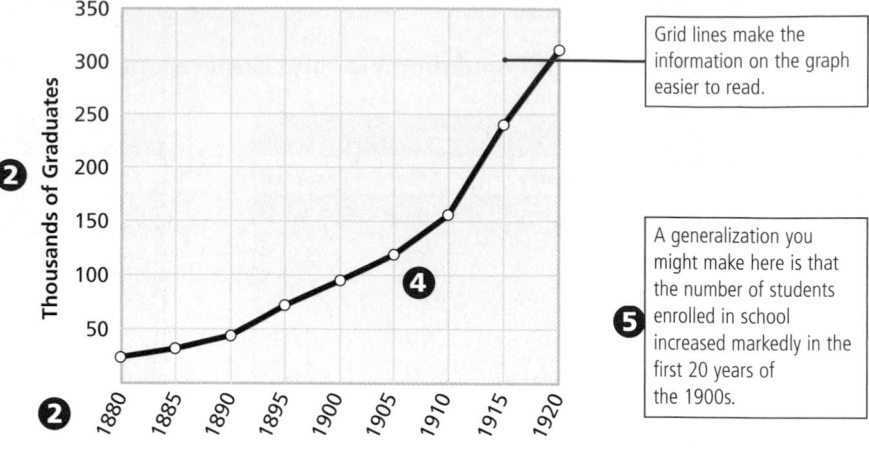

Grid lines make the information on the graph easier to read.

A generalization you might make here is that the number of students enrolled in school increased markedly in the first 20 years of the 1900s. **⑤**

③ Source: *Historical Statistics of the United States*

⑥ 1. How many students graduated from high school in 1905?

A. exactly 100,000

B. about 125,000

C. about 150,000

D. exactly 175,000

① Public Secondary School Enrollment, 1880–1920

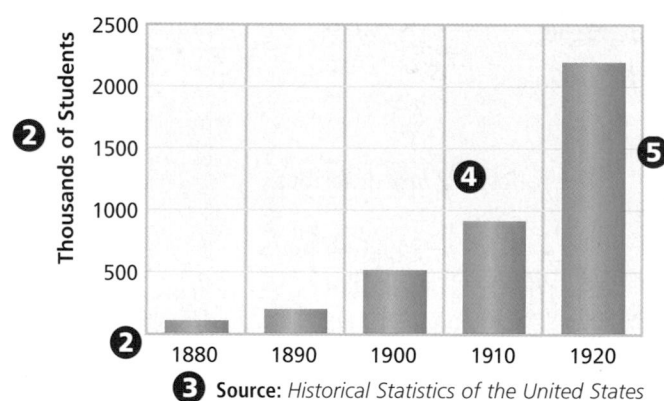

③ Source: *Historical Statistics of the United States*

⑥ 2. Which one of the following sentences do you think *best* describes the trend shown in the bar graph?

A. The number of students enrolled steadily increased.

B. The number of students enrolled showed little change.

C. The number of students enrolled rose and fell.

D. The number of students enrolled steadily decreased.

answers: 1 (B), 2 (A)

Directions: Use the graphs and your knowledge of U.S. history to answer questions 1 through 4.

Motor Vehicle Registrations, 1930–1960

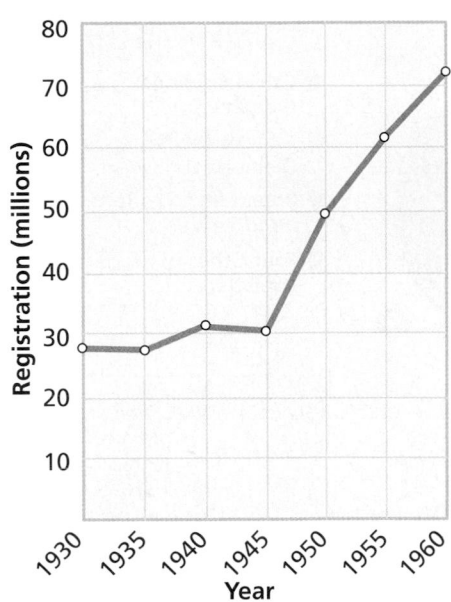

Source: *Historical Statistics of the United States*

Churches by Denomination, 1750

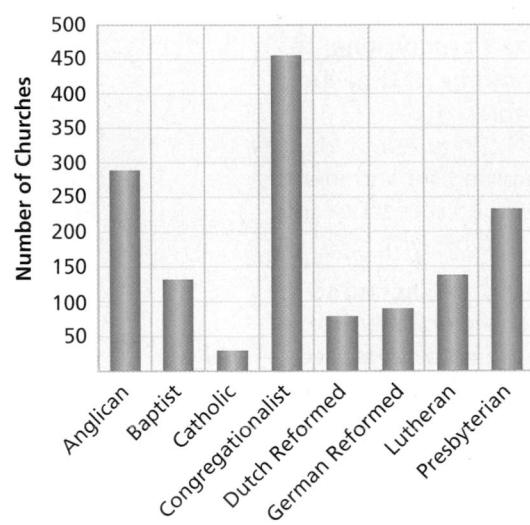

Source: Gilder Lehrman Institute of American History

1. In which time periods did motor-vehicle registrations decline?

    A. 1930 to 1935 and 1935 to 1940

    B. 1930 to 1935 and 1940 to 1945

    C. 1935 to 1940 and 1940 to 1945

    D. 1935 to 1940 and 1945 to 1950

2. Which one of the following would be another good title for this graph?

    A. The American Love Affair with the Automobile

    B. Industrial Decline After World War II

    C. The Automobile Industry During the Great Depression

    D. Automobiles Through the Ages

3. Which one of the following statements accurately reflects information in the graph?

    A. There were more Congregationalist churches than all other denominations combined.

    B. There were more Presbyterian churches than Anglican churches.

    C. The Baptists had the fewest churches.

    D. The Congregationalists had the most churches.

4. Which statement about religion in the colonies of the mid-18th century does the graph support?

    A. All of the colonists were Anglicans.

    B. By 1750, there were many religions in the colonies.

    C. The colonists of 1750 were not religious.

    D. Only immigrants from England established churches.

Pie Graphs

A pie, or circle, graph shows relationships among the parts of a whole. These parts look like slices of a pie. The size of each slice is proportional to the percentage of the whole that it represents.

1 Read the title and identify the broad subject of the pie graph.

2 Look at the legend to see what each of the slices of the pie represents.

3 Read the source line and note the origin of the data shown in the pie graph.

4 Compare the slices of the pie and try to make generalizations and draw conclusions from your comparisons.

5 Read the questions carefully and review difficult or unfamiliar terms.

6 Eliminate choices that you know are wrong.

1 **The Popular Vote in the 1924 Presidential Election**

Sometimes the information in the legend is shown as labels around the outside of the pie graph.
2

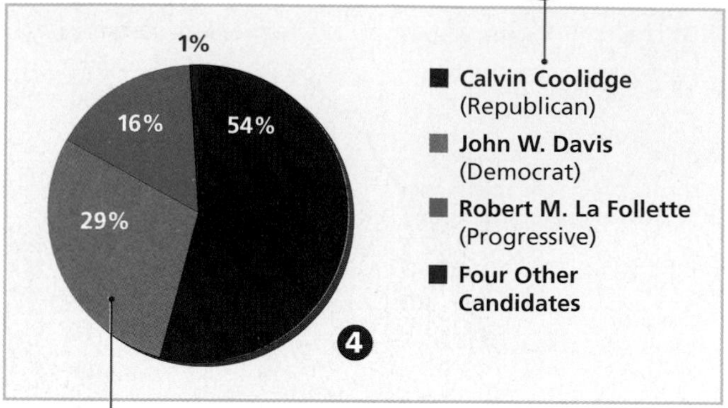

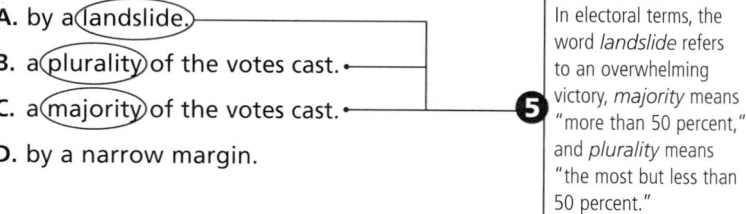

1%
16%
54%
29%

■ **Calvin Coolidge** (Republican)
■ **John W. Davis** (Democrat)
■ **Robert M. La Follette** (Progressive)
■ **Four Other Candidates**

4

3 **Source:** *Historical Statistics of the United States*

Remember that pie graphs show proportions, or percentages, of the whole, not absolute quantities.

1. In the 1924 presidential election, Calvin Coolidge won

   A. by a landslide.
   B. a plurality of the votes cast.
   C. a majority of the votes cast.
   D. by a narrow margin.

   5 In electoral terms, the word *landslide* refers to an overwhelming victory, *majority* means "more than 50 percent," and *plurality* means "the most but less than 50 percent."

2. Which party's candidate won the second largest share of the popular vote?

   A. the Democratic Party
   B. the Other Party
   C. the Progressive Party
   D. the Republican Party

   6 You can eliminate **B** because there is no political party named "Other."

answers: 1 (C), 2 (A)

Directions: Use the pie graphs and your knowledge of U.S. history to answer questions 1 through 4.

Distribution of Workers in the United States, 1850 and 1900

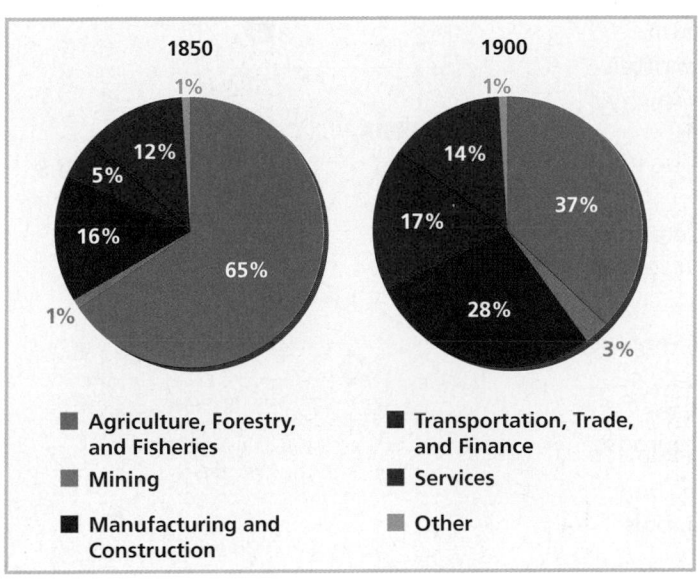

Source: *Historical Statistics of the United States*

1. In 1850, most people worked in

    A. agriculture, forestry, and fisheries.

    B. mining.

    C. services.

    D. transportation, trade, and finance.

2. In 1900, more people worked in manufacturing and construction than in

    A. agriculture, forestry, and fisheries.

    B. mining and agriculture, forestry, and fisheries combined.

    C. services and transportation, trade, and finance combined.

    D. transportation, trade, and finance.

3. Which occupation category showed an increase between 1850 and 1900?

    A. manufacturing and construction

    B. services

    C. transportation, trade, and finance

    D. all of the above

4. What helped to bring about the changes reflected in the two pie graphs?

    A. the passage of new immigration laws

    B. the growth of industry

    C. the decline of world agricultural markets

    D. all of the above

Political Maps

Political maps show countries and the political divisions within countries—states, for example. They also show the location of major cities. In addition, political maps often show physical features, such as rivers, seas, oceans, and mountain ranges.

1 Read the title to determine the subject and purpose of the map.

2 Read the labels on the map. This will reveal information about the map's subject and purpose.

3 Study the legend to find the meaning of symbols used on the map.

4 Look at the lines of latitude and longitude. This grid makes locating places much easier.

5 Use the compass rose or the North arrow to determine directions on the map.

6 Use the scale to estimate the distances between places shown on the map.

7 Read the questions, and then carefully study the map to determine the answers.

1 Alaska: Political

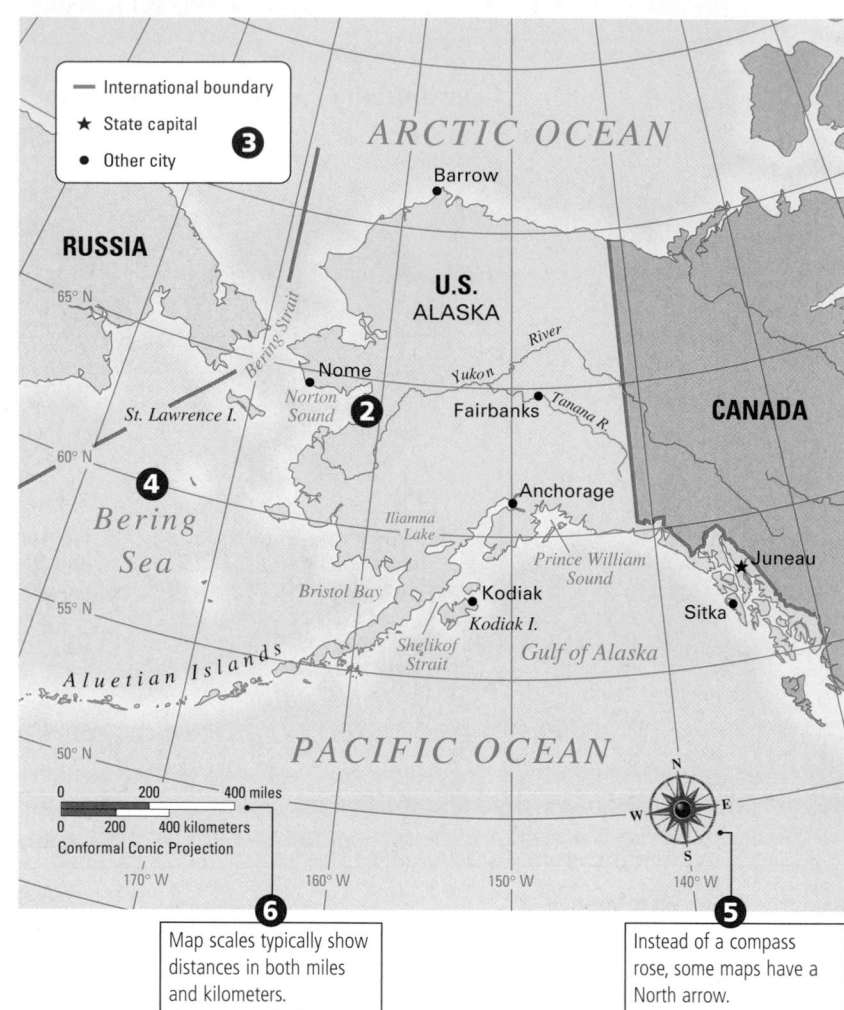

Map scales typically show distances in both miles and kilometers.

Instead of a compass rose, some maps have a North arrow.

7 **1.** Which one of the following cities is located closest to 65° N 150° W?

    A. Anchorage

    B. Barrow

    C. Fairbanks

    D. Nome

2. If you took an airplane trip from Juneau to Anchorage, in which general direction would you be traveling?

    A. north

    B. south

    C. east

    D. west

answers: 1 (C), 2 (D)

Directions: Use the map and your knowledge of U.S. history to answer questions 1 through 4.

San Francisco Bay Area

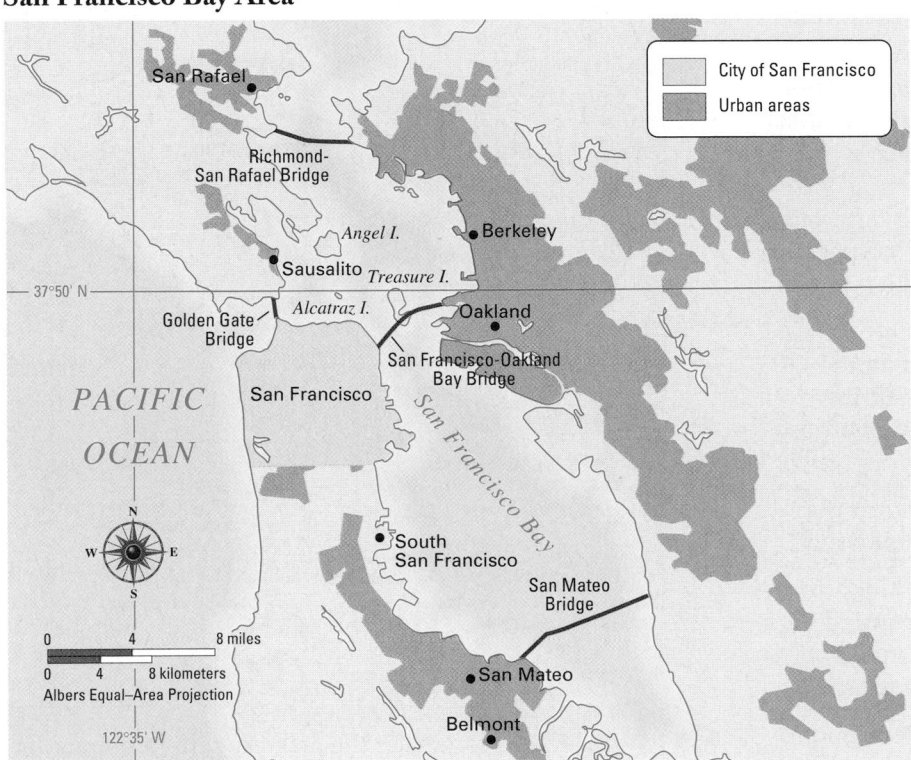

1. Which one of the following describes the location of Sausalito?

   A. north of 37° 50′ N latitude

   B. east of 122° 35′ W longitude

   C. west of Berkeley

   D. all of the above

2. About how far is San Rafael from San Mateo?

   A. 15 miles

   B. 30 miles

   C. 60 miles

   D. 120 miles

3. Which location would figure prominently in a history of immigration to the United States?

   A. Angel Island

   B. Golden Gate Bridge

   C. Treasure Island

   D. Belmont

4. Which one of the following place names does *not* reflect California's Spanish heritage?

   A. San Rafael

   B. Sausalito

   C. Alcatraz

   D. Oakland

Thematic Maps

A thematic map, or special-purpose map, focuses on a particular topic. The location of baseball parks, a country's natural resources, election results, and major battles in a war are all topics you might see illustrated on a thematic map.

1 Read the title to determine the subject and purpose of the map.

2 Examine the labels on the map to find more information about the map's subject and purpose.

3 Study the legend to find the meaning of the symbols and colors used on the map.

4 Look at the colors and symbols on the map and try to identify patterns.

5 Read the questions and then carefully study the map to determine the answers.

1 **Americans on the Move, 1970s**

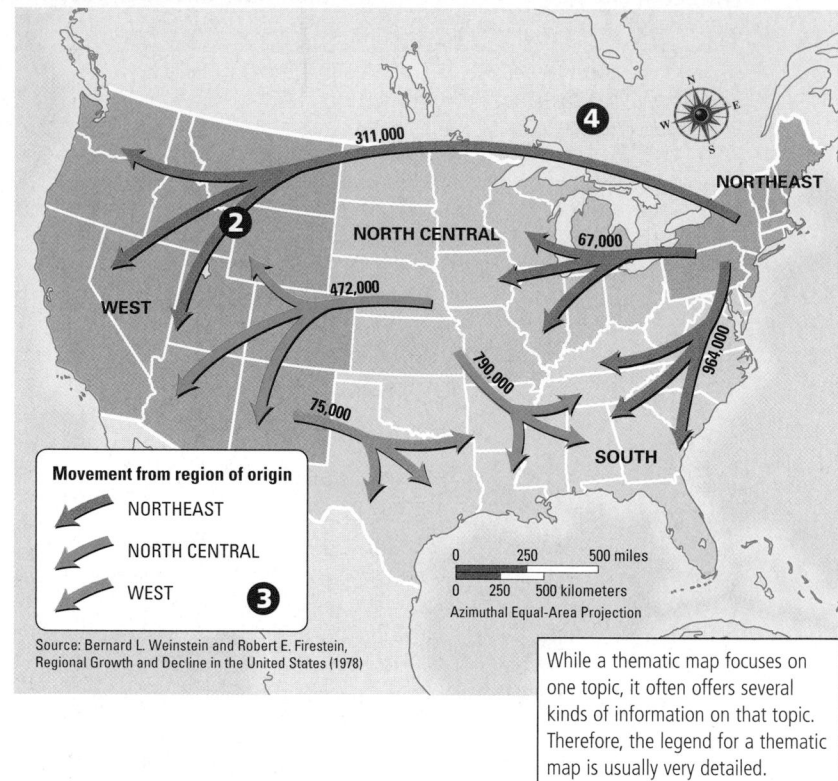

Movement from region of origin

NORTHEAST

NORTH CENTRAL

WEST **3**

Source: Bernard L. Weinstein and Robert E. Firestein, Regional Growth and Decline in the United States (1978)

While a thematic map focuses on one topic, it often offers several kinds of information on that topic. Therefore, the legend for a thematic map is usually very detailed.

5 **1.** Which region made the greatest gain in population because of people moving from one part of the country to another?

A. the South

B. the West

C. the North Central

D. the Northeast

2. The region that lost the most population from migration was the

A. North Central.

B. South.

C. Northeast.

D. West.

answers: 1 (A), 2 (C)

Directions: Use the map and your knowledge of U.S. history to answer the questions 1 through 4.

U.S. School Segregation, 1952

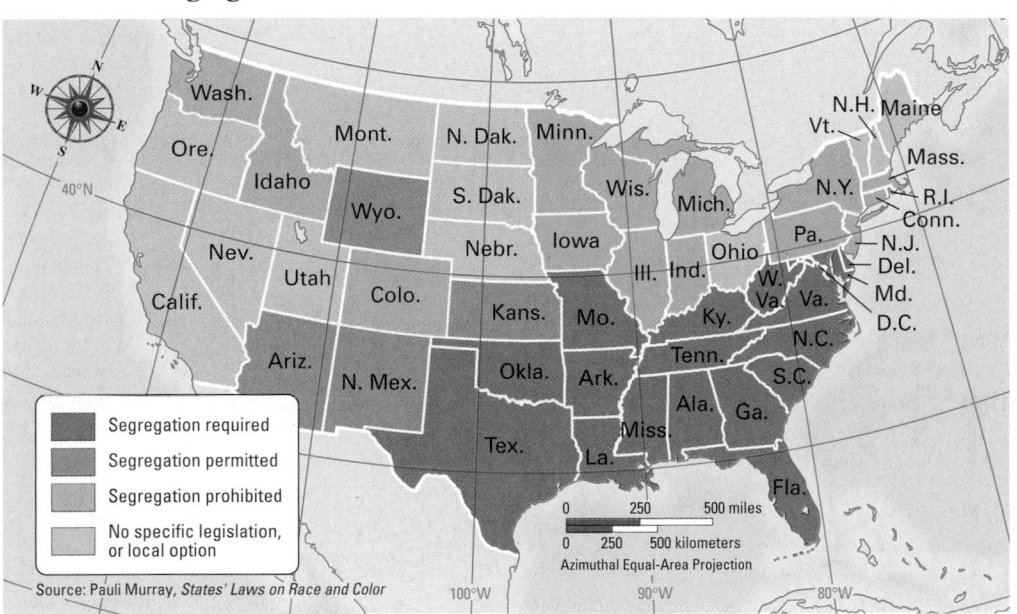

Segregation required
Segregation permitted
Segregation prohibited
No specific legislation, or local option

0   250   500 miles
0   250   500 kilometers
Azimuthal Equal-Area Projection

Source: Pauli Murray, *States' Laws on Race and Color*

1. In what region of the United States was segregation in schools most widespread?

   A. the Northeast

   B. the Midwest

   C. the South

   D. the West

2. In which of the following western states was segregation in schools prohibited?

   A. Arizona

   B. California

   C. Oregon

   D. Washington

3. What was the name given to laws passed by various states to separate the races?

   A. apartheid

   B. Jim Crow

   C. affirmative action

   D. emancipation

4. Which U.S. Supreme Court case struck down segregation in schools as unconstitutional?

   A. *Brown* v. *Board of Education*

   B. *Plessy* v. *Ferguson*

   C. *Hazelwood School District* v. *Kuhlmeier*

   D. *Williams* v. *Mississippi*

Time Lines

A time line is a type of chart that lists events in the order in which they occurred. In other words, time lines are a visual method of showing what happened when.

1 Read the title to discover the subject of the time line.

2 Identify the time period covered by the time line by noting the earliest and latest dates shown. On vertical time lines, the earliest date is shown at the top. On horizontal time lines, it is on the far left.

3 Read the events and their dates in sequence. Notice the intervals between events.

4 Use your knowledge of history to develop a fuller picture of the events listed in the time line. For example, place the events in a broader context by considering what was happening elsewhere in the world.

5 Note how events are related to one another. Look particularly for cause-effect relationships.

6 Use the information you have gathered from the above strategies to answer the questions.

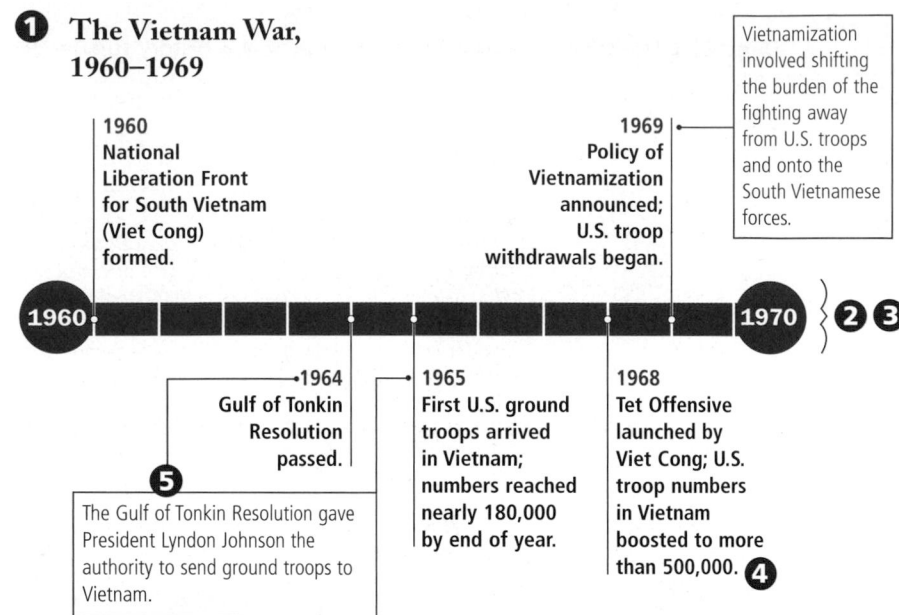

1 The Vietnam War, 1960–1969

1960 National Liberation Front for South Vietnam (Viet Cong) formed.

1969 Policy of Vietnamization announced; U.S. troop withdrawals began.

Vietnamization involved shifting the burden of the fighting away from U.S. troops and onto the South Vietnamese forces.

1964 Gulf of Tonkin Resolution passed.

1965 First U.S. ground troops arrived in Vietnam; numbers reached nearly 180,000 by end of year.

1968 Tet Offensive launched by Viet Cong; U.S. troop numbers in Vietnam boosted to more than 500,000. **4**

5 The Gulf of Tonkin Resolution gave President Lyndon Johnson the authority to send ground troops to Vietnam.

6 1. In what year was U.S. troop strength boosted to more than 500,000?

    A. 1964

    B. 1965

    C. 1968

    D. 1969

2. What event led to a reduction of U.S. troop strength in Vietnam?

    A. passage of the Gulf of Tonkin Resolution

    B. announcement of the policy of Vietnamization

    C. launch of the Tet Offensive

    D. formation of the Viet Cong

answers: 1 (C), 2 (B)

Directions: Use the time line and your knowledge of U.S. history to answer questions 1 through 3.

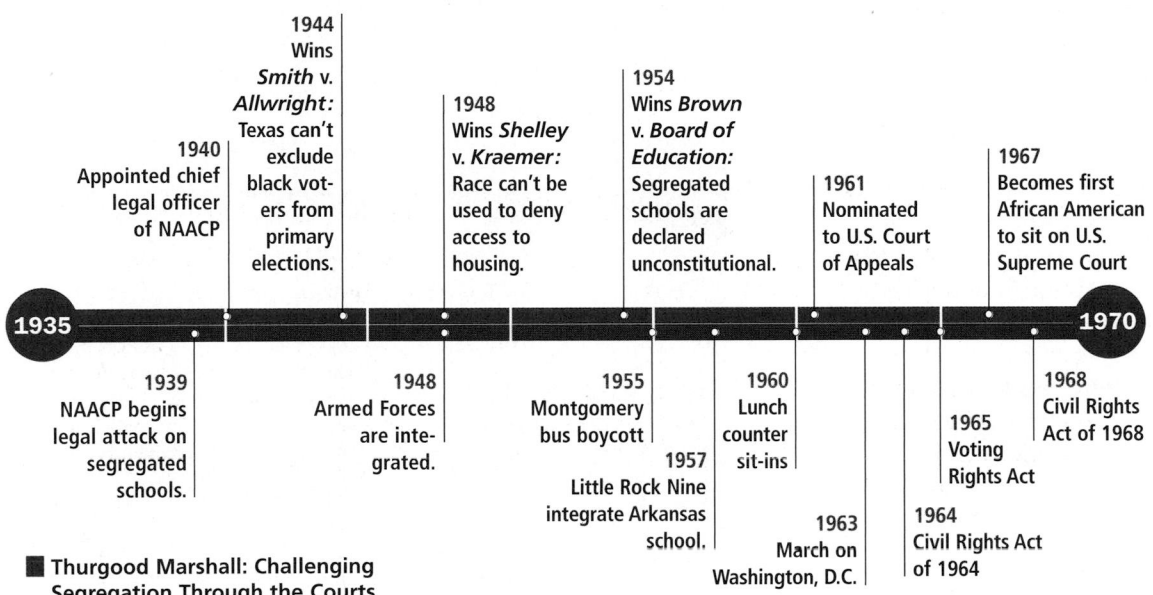

1935 ——————————————————————————————— 1970

1940
Appointed chief legal officer of NAACP

1944
Wins *Smith* v. *Allwright:* Texas can't exclude black voters from primary elections.

1948
Wins *Shelley* v. *Kraemer:* Race can't be used to deny access to housing.

1954
Wins *Brown* v. *Board of Education:* Segregated schools are declared unconstitutional.

1961
Nominated to U.S. Court of Appeals

1967
Becomes first African American to sit on U.S. Supreme Court

1939
NAACP begins legal attack on segregated schools.

1948
Armed Forces are integrated.

1955
Montgomery bus boycott

1957
Little Rock Nine integrate Arkansas school.

1960
Lunch counter sit-ins

1963
March on Washington, D.C.

1964
Civil Rights Act of 1964

1965
Voting Rights Act

1968
Civil Rights Act of 1968

■ **Thurgood Marshall: Challenging Segregation Through the Courts**

■ **Nonviolent Demonstration and Legislative Action**

1. In what year did the NAACP achieve a major victory in its goal to desegregate schools throughout the United States?

   A. 1939

   B. 1944

   C. 1954

   D. 1964

2. How many years after *Brown* v. *Board of Education* did Arkansas integrate a public school?

   A. three years

   B. five years

   C. seven years

   D. ten years

3. Thurgood Marshall was known as "Mr. Civil Rights" because he was

   A. a lawyer who successfully argued to end legal segregation in voting, housing, and education.

   B. the chief legal officer of the NAACP beginning in the late 1930s.

   C. the first African American appointed to the Supreme Court.

   D. an African-American lawyer and judge before the civil rights acts were passed.

Constructed Response

Constructed-response questions focus on various kinds of documents. Each document usually is accompanied by a series of questions. These questions call for short answers that, for the most part, can be found directly in the document. Some answers, however, require knowledge of the subject or time period addressed in the document.

1 Read the title of the document to discover the subject addressed in the questions.

2 Study and analyze the document. Take notes on what you see.

3 Read the questions and then study the document again to locate the answers.

4 Carefully write your answers. Unless the directions say otherwise, your answers need not be complete sentences.

1 Joseph Glidden's Patent

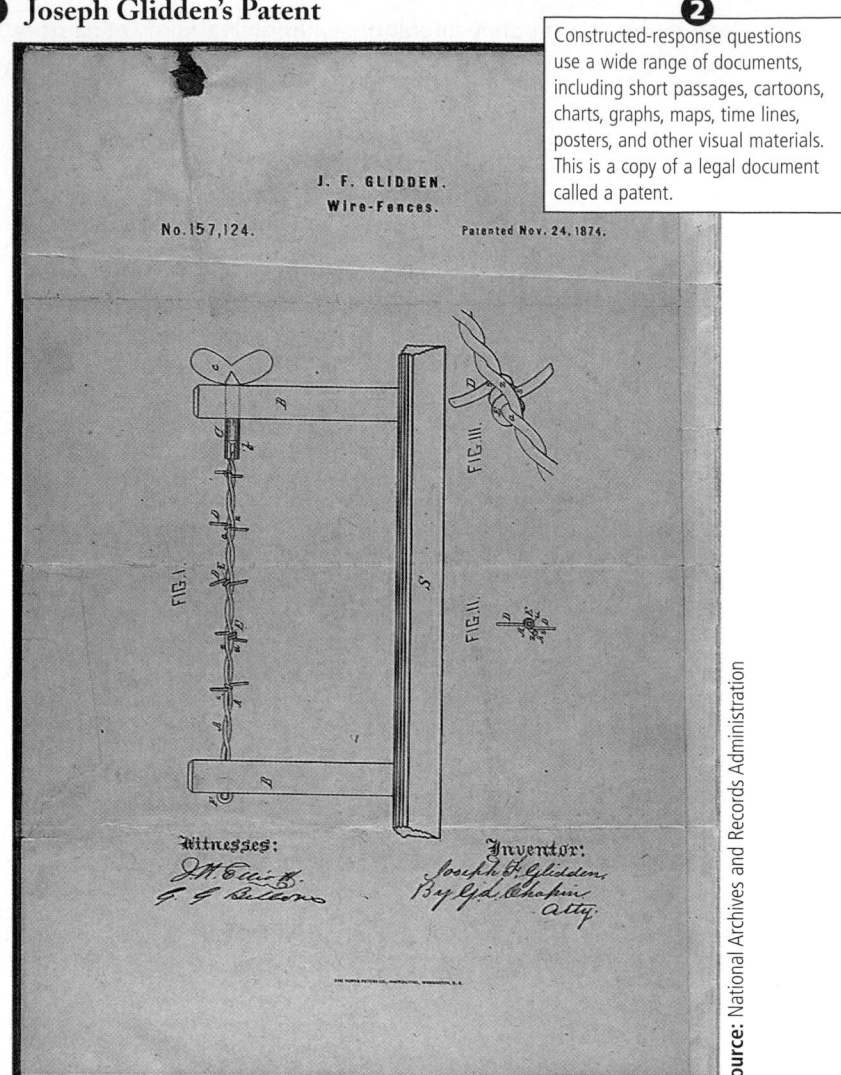

J. F. GLIDDEN.
Wire-Fences.
No. 157,124.　　Patented Nov. 24, 1874.

Witnesses:　　Inventor:

2 Constructed-response questions use a wide range of documents, including short passages, cartoons, charts, graphs, maps, time lines, posters, and other visual materials. This is a copy of a legal document called a patent.

Source: National Archives and Records Administration

3 **1.** What invention is illustrated on this patent?

4 *barbed wire fence*

2. What suggests that this is a legal document?

It is signed by witnesses and an attorney.

3. What other developments had a major impact on farming on the plains in the 1800s?

steel plows, reapers, threshers, dry farming

For more test practice online . . .

TEST PRACTICE
CLASSZONE.COM

Directions: Use the photograph below and your knowledge of U.S. history to answer questions 1 through 3. Your answers need not be complete sentences.

Exercise Desert Rock: Six Miles from Ground Zero

Troops of the Battalion Combat Team, U.S. Army 11th Airborne Division. Yucca Flats, Nevada, November 1, 1951.

Source: National Archives and Records Administration

1. What are the soldiers in the photograph looking at?

2. What major nonmilitary global conflict caused the United States to conduct tests like "Exercise Desert Rock"?

3. Name the 1963 agreement that ended aboveground tests like the one pictured here, and identify the two nations that signed it.

Extended Response

Extended-response questions, like constructed-response questions, usually focus on one kind of document. However, they are more complex and require more time to complete than typical short-answer constructed-response questions. Some extended-response questions ask you to present information from the document in a different form. Others require you to apply your knowledge of history to information contained in the document.

1 Read the title of the document to get an idea of the subject.

2 Study and analyze the document. Take notes on your ideas.

3 Carefully read the extended-response questions.

4 If the question calls for a graph or some other kind of diagram, make a rough sketch on scrap paper first. Then make a final copy of your drawing on the answer sheet.

5 If the question requires a written response, jot down ideas in outline form. Use this outline to write your answer.

1 **Carbon Dioxide Output of Average U.S. Single-Family Home**

Source	Pounds of Carbon Dioxide per Year
Space Heating	10,132
Air Conditioning	2,609
Water Heating	3,618
Refrigerator, Freezer	3,429
Cooking	935
Other Appliances	6,337
Lighting	2,460
Automobile	20,960

Source: Rocky Mountain Institute, 1999

3 1. Use the information in the chart to create a bar graph showing the annual carbon dioxide output of the average American single-family home.

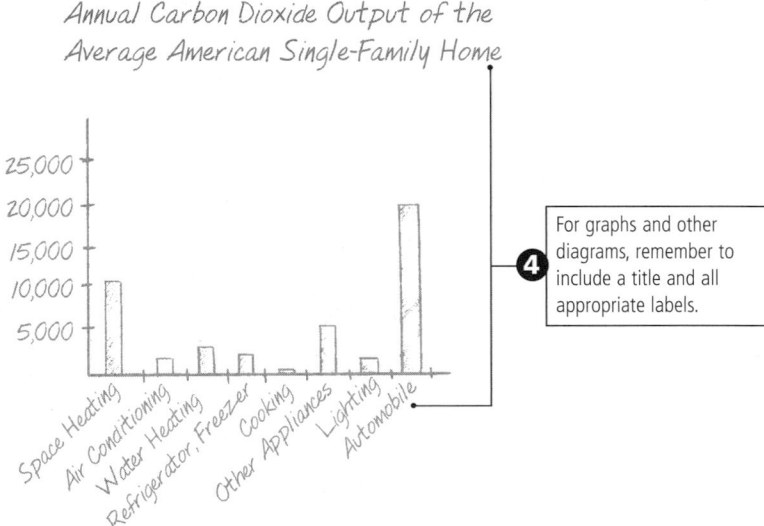

For graphs and other diagrams, remember to include a title and all appropriate labels.

3 2. Write a short essay discussing the steps that the typical American family could take to reduce its carbon dioxide output.

5 **Essay Rubric** The best essays will point out that families could reduce their carbon dioxide output by reducing their use of appliances and vehicles. Walking, carpooling, and taking public transportation would greatly reduce carbon dioxide output. So, too, would setting thermostats at a reasonable level to cut the use of heaters and air conditioners. Finally, replacing old appliances with newer, more efficient ones also would cut carbon dioxide emissions.

For more test practice online . . .

TEST PRACTICE
CLASSZONE.COM

Directions: Use the passage and your knowledge of U.S. history to make a chart like the one below. Complete the chart by providing the information requested at the end of the paragraph.

A Country Dividing

As the United States grew during the 1800s, Congress and the people argued about what form of government each new territory and state would have. The differences of opinion centered on one issue more than any other: slavery. Eventually, those sectional arguments led to the Civil War. The left side of the chart below lists three acts of Congress that addressed the issue of slavery in the West. Describe at least three provisions of each of these acts. (Note that the first provision of each act has been written for you.)

Act	Provisions
Missouri Compromise, 1820	**1.** Slavery was to be prohibited in the Louisiana territory north of the 36° 30' parallel. **2.** **3.**
Compromise of 1850	**1.** The territories of New Mexico and Utah were created without restrictions on slavery. **2.** **3.**
Kansas-Nebraska Act, 1854	**1.** Two new territories, Kansas and Nebraska, were created. **2.** **3.**

Document-Based Questions

A document-based question focuses on several documents—both visual and written. These documents often are accompanied by short-answer questions. You then use the answers to these questions and information from the documents to write an essay on a specified subject.

1 Carefully read the "Historical Context" to get an indication of the issue addressed in the question.

2 Note the action words used in the "Task" section. These words tell you exactly what the essay question requires.

3 Study and analyze each document. Think about how the documents are connected to the essay question. Take notes on your ideas.

4 Read and answer each of the document-specific questions.

Introduction

1 **Historical Context:** After the United States entered World War II, many men left their jobs to join the military. Millions of women stepped in to take their place in factories and offices.

2 **Task:** (Discuss) how life for women in the U.S. changed during World War II and (note) the gains that women made in the field of employment.

Part 1: Short Answer

Study each document carefully and answer the questions that follow.

3 **Document 1: Working Women During World War II**

Source: National Archives and Records Administration

4 **How does this image of women workers differ from the traditionally accepted image of the time?**

This image shows a woman in the nontraditional role of a factory worker. It also shows the woman as self-confident and physically strong.

Document 2: Women in the U.S. Work Force, 1940–1946

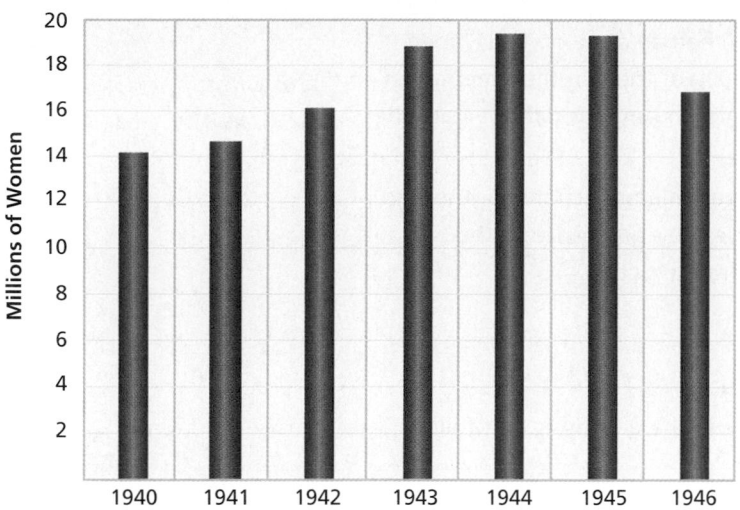

Source: *Historical Statistics of the United States*

What trends in women's employment does this graph show?

The graph shows a marked increase during the war years
with a decrease after the war's end.

Document 3: The Future of Women's Work

Despite the surge of women into heavy industry, markedly larger numbers of new women entrants into the wartime work force took up clerical and service jobs, . . . and there women's gains proved far more durable. The number of women factory operatives plummeted at war's end. . . . By 1947 the proportion of working women in blue-collar occupations was actually smaller than it had been at the war's outset. . . . The future of women's work lay not in the wartime heavy industries, . . . but in the [growing] service occupations, which within a decade of the war's conclusion eclipsed factory work as the nation's principal source of employment.

— David M. Kennedy, *Freedom from Fear*

In what jobs did women make the most long-lasting gains?

clerical and service jobs

❺ Part 2: Essay

Using information from the documents, your answers to the questions in Part 1, and your knowledge of U.S. history, write an essay that discusses how life for women changed during World War II and notes the gains that women made in employment. ❻

❺ Carefully read the essay question. Then write an outline for your essay.

❻ Write your essay. Be sure that it has an introductory paragraph that introduces your argument, main body paragraphs that explain it, and a concluding paragraph that restates your position. In your essay, include extracts or details from specific documents to support your ideas. Add other supporting facts or details that you know from your study of American history.

Sample Response The best essays will point out that the greatest change for American women during World War II was that many entered the work force for the first time (Documents 2 and 3) and that many took jobs that were not traditionally held by women (Document 1). Essays also should note that while many women took jobs traditionally held by men, more entered clerical and service jobs (Document 3). And while the number of women in industrial jobs declined after the war, the number in service jobs grew (Document 3).

Introduction

Historical Context: In 1775, Great Britain had an army of 48,647 men located throughout the world, about 8,000 of them in the Americas. A rebellion by the small group of 13 colonies in America did not scare the keepers of such a large colonial empire.

Task: Discuss how the colonists' beliefs and military actions contributed to their victory in the Revolution. Include the significance of the American alliances with European nations.

Part 1: Short Answer

Study each document carefully and answer the questions that follow.

Document 1: First Georgia Regiment of Infantry Continental Line, 1777

The hunting shirt, or rifle dress, shown here was recommended by George Washington in his general order of July 24, 1776. Declaring it a practical item to be given to the troops, he also claimed that ". . . it is a dress justly supposed to carry no small terror to the enemy, who think every such person a complete marksman."

Source: New-York Historical Society

What unusual military tactics did patriots like the man in the picture use to surprise and outsmart the British during the Revolution?

Document 1: *Uniforms of the American Revolution: 1st Georgia Regiment Continental Infantry, 1777, Private Field Dress,* Charles Lefferts. Watercolor, gouache on paper. Copyright © Collection of the New-York Historical Society.

Document 2: Philadelphia, September 12, 1777

> I close this paper with a short address to General Howe. . . . We know the cause which we are engaged in, and though a passionate fondness for it may make us grieve at every injury. . . . We are not moved by the gloomy smile of a worthless king, but by the ardent glow of generous patriotism. We fight not to enslave, but to set a country free, and to make room upon the earth for honest men to live in. In such a case we are sure that we are right; and we leave to you the despairing reflection of being the tool of a miserable tyrant.
>
> —Thomas Paine, *The American Crisis No. IV*

Although this excerpt is addressed to the British General Howe, how might it also have encouraged the colonists to continue their fight against the British?

Document 3: The Battle of Yorktown, 1781: Winning the American

Estimated American, French, and British Forces and Casualties		
Generals and Their Divisions	Forces	Casualties
General Washington (American colonies)	11,100	90
General Rochambeau (France)	7,800	250
General Cornwallis (Britain)	8,900	550

Estimated French and British Naval Strength*		
French and British Fleets	Ships	Guns on Board Ship
Admiral Graves (Britain)	25	1,450
Lieutenant General DeGrasse (France)	35	2,610

*Does not include small craft or transport ships

Source: U.S. Army Center of Military History

Revolution

What support was provided by the French in the Battle of Yorktown?

Part 2: Essay

Using information from the documents, your answers to the questions in Part 1, and your knowledge of U.S. history, write an essay that discusses how the colonists' beliefs and military actions contributed to their victory in the Revolution. Include in your essay the significance of American alliances with European nations.

The Landscape of America

The best place to begin your study of American history is with the geography of America. Geography is more than the study of the land and people. It also involves the relationship between people and their environment.

The United States is part of the North American continent. The United States ranks third in both total area and population in the world. It is filled with an incredible variety of physical features, natural resources, climatic conditions, and people. This handbook will help you to learn about these factors and to understand how they affected the development of the United States.

A timber company collects logs in the Northwest.

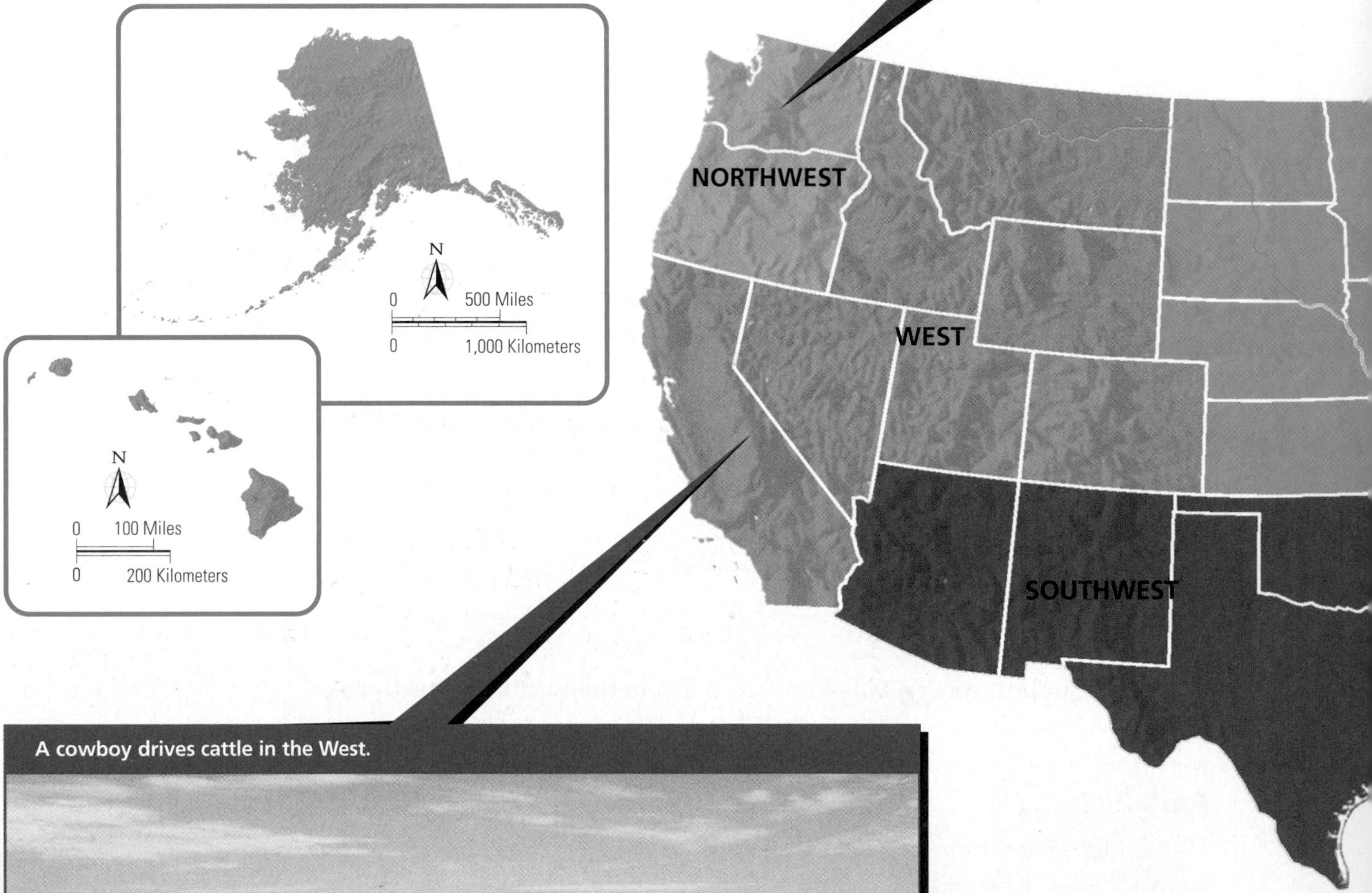

NORTHWEST

WEST

SOUTHWEST

0   500 Miles

0   1,000 Kilometers

0   100 Miles

0   200 Kilometers

A cowboy drives cattle in the West.

A combine harvests wheat in the Midwest.

TABLE OF CONTENTS

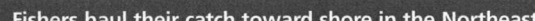

Fishers haul their catch toward shore in the Northeast.

NORTHEAST

MIDWEST

SOUTHEAST

Oranges are big business in the Southeast.

N

0   500 Miles

0   1,000 Kilometers

The Landscape of America **3**

Themes of Geography

One useful way to think about geography is in terms of major themes or ideas. These pages examine the five major themes of geography and show how they apply to Boston, Massachusetts. Recognizing and understanding these themes will help you to understand all the different aspects of geography.

Boston is located on the shores of the Atlantic Ocean.

Location

"Where am I?" Your answer to this question is your *location*. One way to answer it is to use *absolute* location. That means you'll use the coordinates of longitude and latitude to give your answer (see page 8). For example, if you're in Boston, its absolute location is approximately 42° north latitude and 71° west longitude.

Like most people, however, you'll probably use *relative* location to answer the question. Relative location describes where a certain area is in relation to another area. For example, Boston lies in the northeast corner of the United States, next to the Atlantic Ocean.

THINKING ABOUT GEOGRAPHY What is the relative location of your school?

Place

"What is Boston like?" *Place* can help you answer this question. Place refers to the physical and human factors that make one area different from another. Physical characteristics are natural features, such as physical setting, plants, animals, and weather. For example, Boston sits on a hilly peninsula.

Human characteristics include cultural diversity and the things people have made—including language, the arts, and architecture. For instance, Boston includes African Americans, as well as people of Irish, Italian, Chinese, and Hispanic ancestry.

THINKING ABOUT GEOGRAPHY What physical and human characteristics make where you live unique?

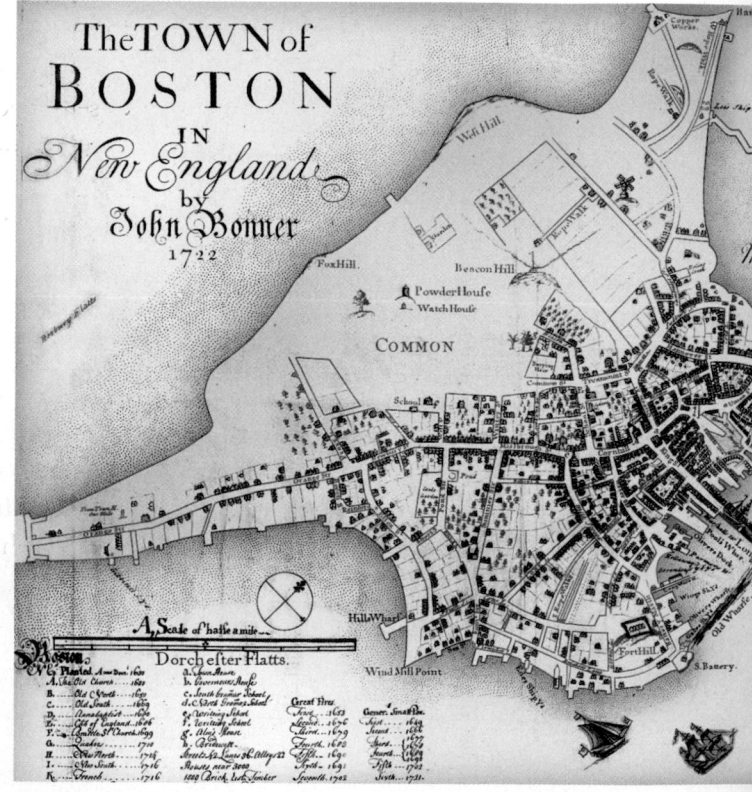

Boston has grown and changed since this 1722 map.

Region

Geographers can't easily study the whole world at one time. So they break the world into regions. A *region* can be as large as a continent or as small as a neighborhood. A region has certain shared characteristics that set it apart. These characteristics might include political division, climate, language, or religion. Boston is part of the northeast region. It shares a climate— continental temperate—with the cities of New York and Philadelphia.

THINKING ABOUT GEOGRAPHY What characteristics does your city or town share with nearby cities or towns?

Airplanes from Boston's
Logan International
Airport move people and
ideas around the globe.

People shop, eat, and
interact at Boston's
famous Quincy Market.

Movement

Movement refers to the shifting of people, goods, and ideas from one place to another. People constantly move in search of better places to live, and they trade goods with one another over great distances. Movement also causes ideas to travel from place to place. In recent years, technology has quickened the movement of ideas and goods.

Boston became known as the *Cradle of Liberty* because of the movement of ideas. The concepts of freedom and self-government that developed in Boston spread to the other colonies and helped to start the American Revolution.

THINKING ABOUT GEOGRAPHY What are some of the different ways you spread information and ideas?

Human-Environment Interaction

Human-environment interaction refers to ways people interact with their environment, such as building a dam, cutting down a tree, or even sitting in the sun.

In Boston, human-environment interaction occurred when officials filled in swampy areas to make the city larger. In other ways, the environment has forced people to act. For example, people have had to invent ways to protect themselves from extreme weather and natural disasters.

THINKING ABOUT GEOGRAPHY What are ways that people in your city or town have changed their environment?

Themes of Geography Assessment

1. Main Ideas

a. What is the relative location of your home?

b. What are three characteristics of the region in which you live?

c. What are at least three ways in which you have recently interacted with the environment?

2. Critical Thinking

Forming and Supporting Opinions Which aspect of geography described in these themes do you think has most affected your life? Explain.

THINK ABOUT

• ways that you interact with your environment

• how you travel from place to place

Map Basics

Geographers use many different types of maps, and these maps all have a variety of features. The map on the next page gives you information on a historical event—the War of 1812. But you can use it to learn about different parts of a map, too.

Types of Maps

Physical maps Physical maps show mountains, hills, plains, rivers, lakes, oceans, and other physical features of an area.

Political maps Political maps show political units, such as countries, states, provinces, counties, districts, and towns. Each unit is normally shaded a different color, represented by a symbol, or shown with a different typeface.

Historical maps Historical maps illustrate such things as economic activity, migrations, battles, and changing national boundaries.

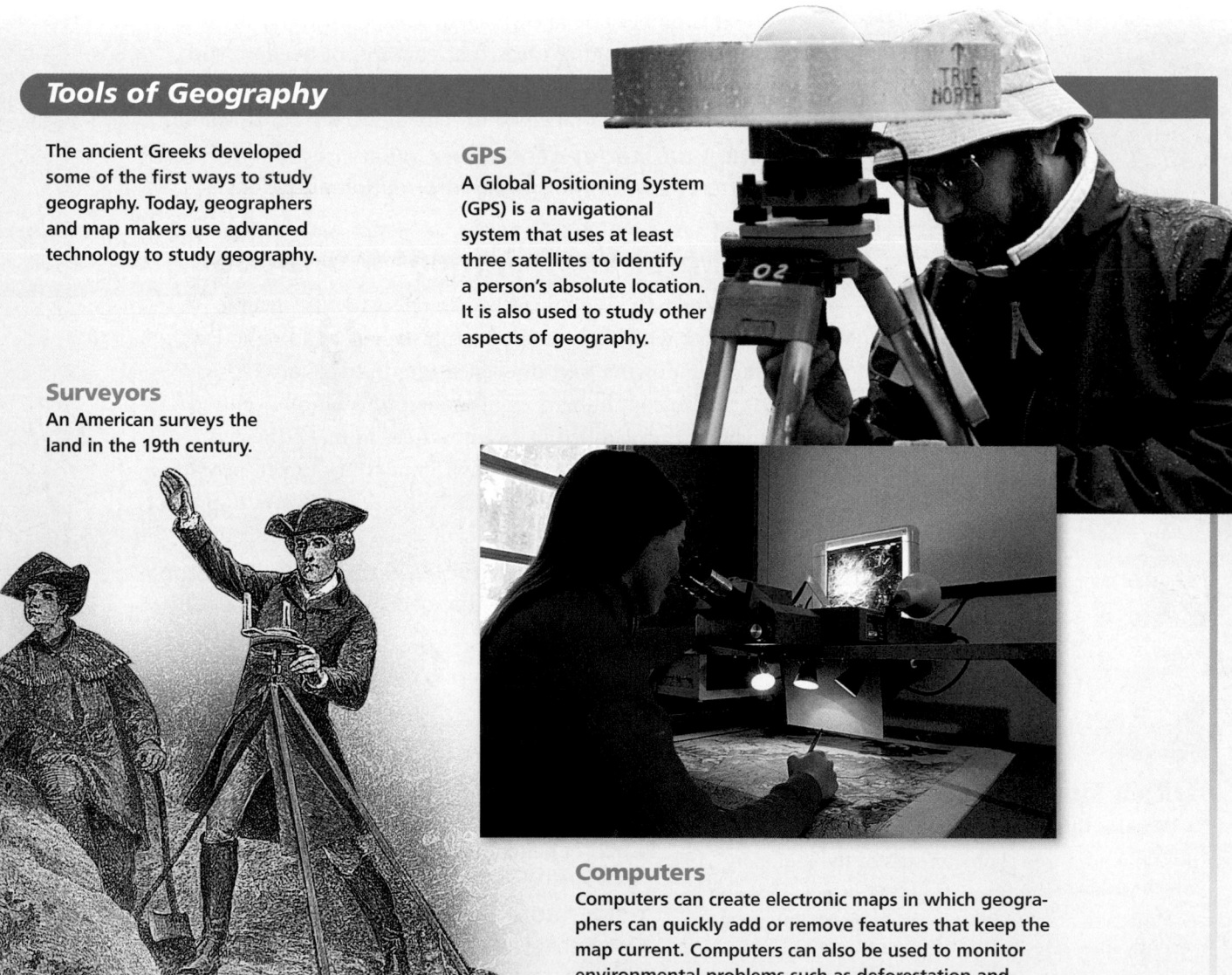

Tools of Geography

The ancient Greeks developed some of the first ways to study geography. Today, geographers and map makers use advanced technology to study geography.

Surveyors
An American surveys the land in the 19th century.

GPS
A Global Positioning System (GPS) is a navigational system that uses at least three satellites to identify a person's absolute location. It is also used to study other aspects of geography.

Computers
Computers can create electronic maps in which geographers can quickly add or remove features that keep the map current. Computers can also be used to monitor environmental problems such as deforestation and global warming.

Reading a Map

A **Lines** Lines indicate political boundaries, roads and highways, human movement, and rivers and other waterways.

B **Symbols** Symbols represent such items as capital cities, battle sites, or economic activities.

C **Labels** Labels are words or phrases that explain various items or activities on a map.

D **Compass Rose** A compass rose shows which way the directions north (N), south (S), east (E), and west (W) point on the map.

E **Scale** A scale shows the ratio between a unit of length on the map and a unit of distance on the earth. A typical one-inch scale indicates the number of miles and kilometers that length represents on the map.

F **Colors** Colors show a variety of information on a map, such as population density or the physical growth of a country.

G **Legend or Key** A legend or key lists and explains the symbols, lines, and colors on a map.

H **Lines of Longitude** These are imaginary, north-south lines that run around the globe.
Lines of Latitude These are imaginary, east-west lines that run around the globe. Together, latitude and longitude lines form a grid on a map or globe to indicate an area's absolute location.

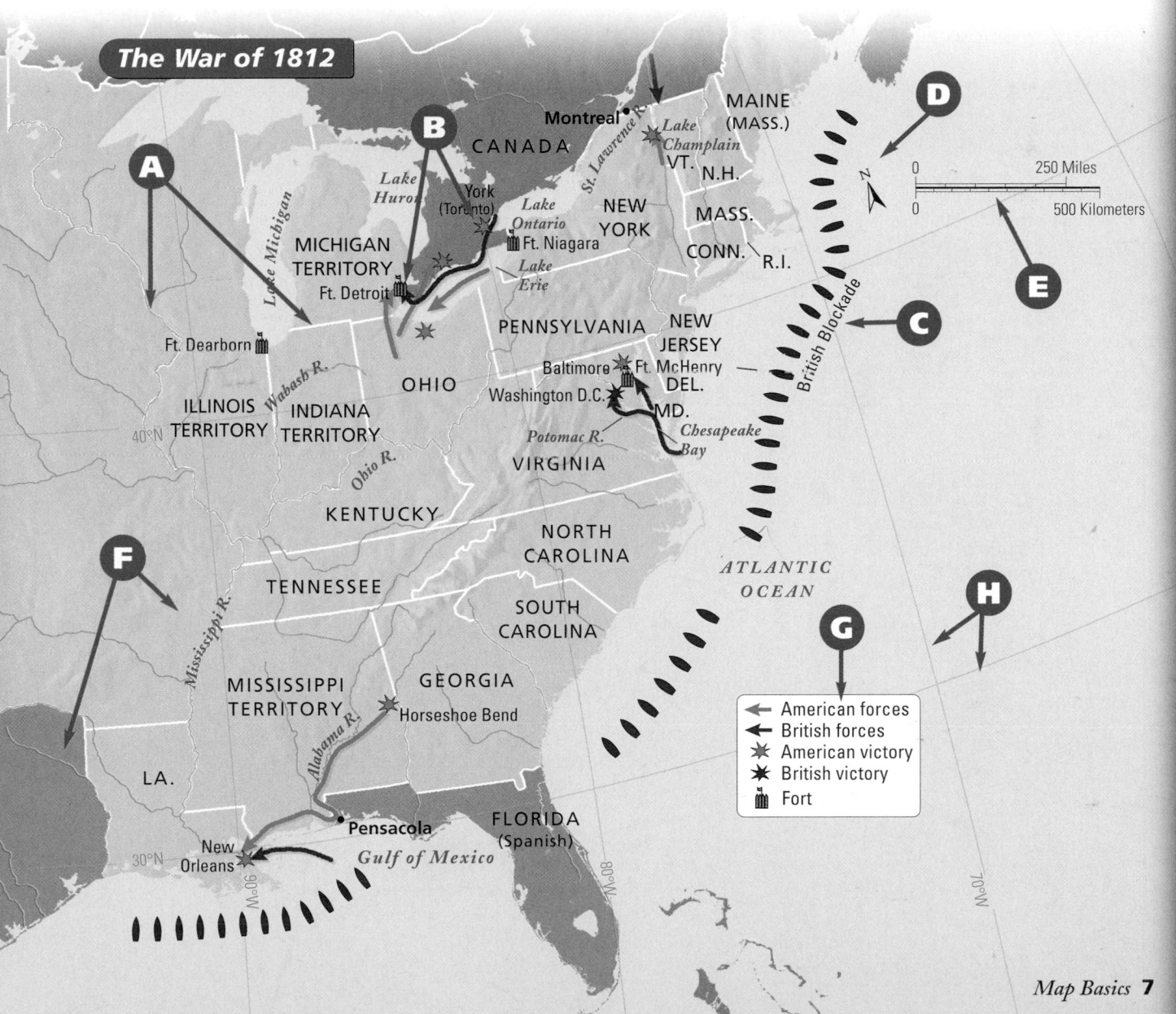

The War of 1812

Legend:
- ← American forces
- ← British forces
- ✳ American victory
- ✳ British victory
- ⛫ Fort

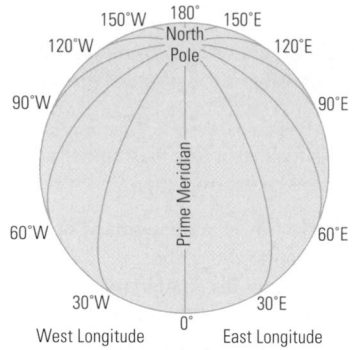

Longitude Lines (Meridians)

180°
150°W   150°E
North Pole
120°W   120°E
90°W   90°E
Prime Meridian
60°W   60°E
30°W   30°E
0°
West Longitude   East Longitude

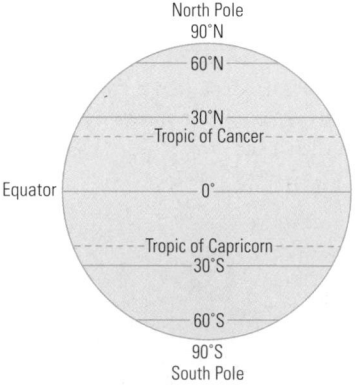

Latitude Lines (Parallels)

North Pole
90°N
60°N
30°N
Tropic of Cancer
Equator   0°
Tropic of Capricorn
30°S
60°S
90°S
South Pole

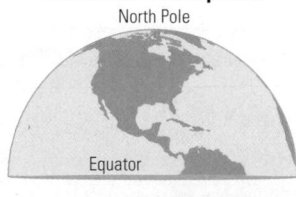

Northern Hemisphere
North Pole

Equator

South Pole
Southern Hemisphere

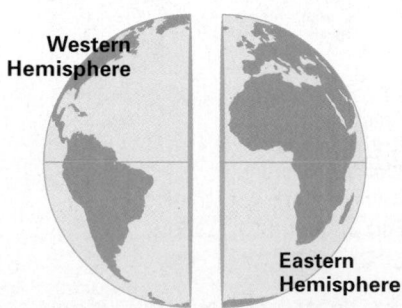

Western Hemisphere

Eastern Hemisphere

Longitude lines

- are imaginary lines that run north to south around the globe and are known as meridians
- show the distance in degrees east or west of the prime meridian

The prime meridian is a longitude line that runs from the North Pole to the South Pole. It passes through Greenwich, England, and measures 0° longitude.

Latitude lines

- are imaginary lines that run east to west around the globe and are known as parallels
- show distance in degrees north or south of the equator

The equator is a latitude line that circles the earth halfway between the North and South poles. It measures 0° latitude.

The tropics of Cancer and Capricorn are parallels that form the boundaries of the Tropics, a region that stays warm all year.

Latitude and longitude lines appear together on a map and allow you to pinpoint the absolute location of cities and other geographic features. You express this location through coordinates of intersecting lines. These are measured in degrees.

Hemisphere

Hemisphere is a term for half the globe. The globe can be divided into Northern and Southern hemispheres (separated by the equator) or into Eastern and Western hemispheres. The United States is located in the Northern and Western hemispheres.

Projections

A projection is a way of showing the curved surface of the earth on a flat map. Flat maps cannot show the size, shape, and direction of a globe all at once with total accuracy. As a result, all projections distort some aspect of the earth's surface. Some maps distort distances, while other maps distort angles. On the next page are four projections.

Mercator Projection

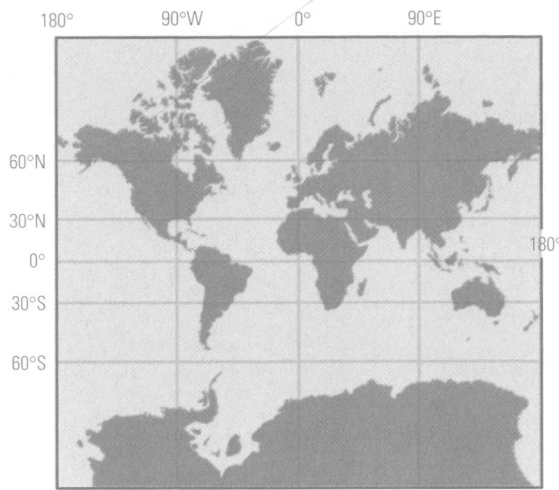

The Mercator projection shows most of the continents as they look on a globe. However, the projection stretches out the lands near the North and South poles. The Mercator is used for all kinds of navigation.

Azimuthal Projection

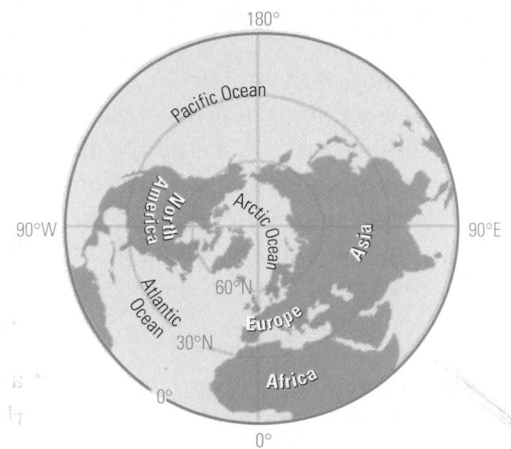

An azimuthal projection shows the earth so that a straight line from the central point to any other point on the map gives the shortest distance between the two points. Size and shape of the continents are also distorted.

Homolosine Projection

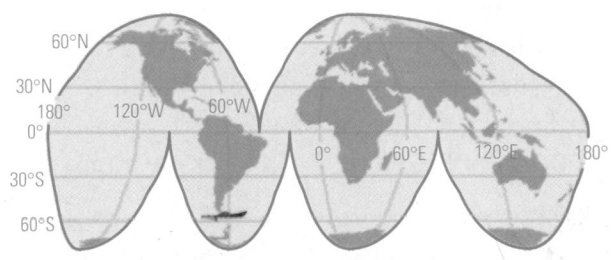

This projection shows the accurate shapes and sizes of the landmasses, but distances on the map are not correct.

Robinson Projection

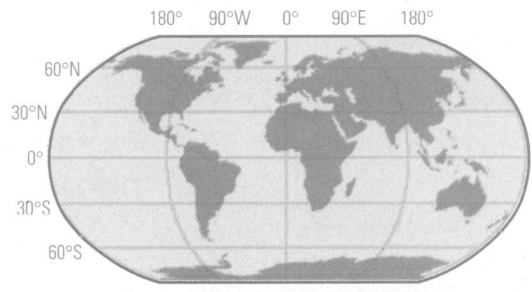

Textbook maps commonly use the Robinson projection. It shows the entire earth with nearly the true sizes and shapes of the continents and oceans. However, the shapes of the landforms near the poles appear flat.

Map Basics Assessment

1. Main Ideas

a. What is the longitude and latitude of your city or town?

b. What information is provided by the legend on the map on page 7?

c. What is a projection? Compare and contrast Antarctica on the Mercator and the Robinson projections.

2. Critical Thinking

Making Inferences Why do you think latitude and longitude are so important to sailors?

THINK ABOUT

• the landmarks you use to find your way around
• the landmarks available to sailors on the ocean

Physical Geography of the United States

From the heights of Mount McKinley (20,320 feet above sea level) in Alaska to the depths of Death Valley, California (282 feet below sea level), the geography of the United States is incredibly diverse. In between these extremes lie such varied features and conditions as scorching Arizona deserts, lush Oregon forests, freezing Vermont winters, and sunny Florida beaches. Physical geography involves all the natural features on the earth. This includes the land, resources, climate, and vegetation.

Flowers and brush cover the Coral Pink Sand Dunes in southern Utah.

Land

Separated from much of the world by two oceans, the United States covers 3,717,796 square miles and spans the entire width of North America. To the west, Hawaii stretches the United States into the Pacific Ocean. To the north, Alaska extends the United States to the Arctic Circle. On the U.S. mainland, a huge central plain separates large mountains in the West and low mountains in the East. Plains make up almost half of the country, while mountains and plateaus make up a quarter each.

An abundance of lakes—Alaska alone has three million—and rivers also dot the landscape. Twenty percent of the United States is farmed, providing the country with a steady food supply. Urban areas cover only about two percent of the nation. Refer to the map on the next page for a complete look at the U.S. landscape.

THINKING ABOUT GEOGRAPHY What is the land like around your city or state?

Resources

The United States has a variety of natural resources. Vast amounts of coal, oil, and natural gas lie underneath American soil. Valuable deposits of lead, zinc, uranium, gold, and silver also exist. These resources have helped the United States become the world's leading industrial nation—producing nearly 21 percent of the world's goods and services.

These resources have also helped the United States become both the world's largest producer of energy (natural gas, oil, coal, nuclear power, and electricity) and the world's largest consumer of it. Other natural resources include the Great Lakes, which are shared with Canada. They contain about 20 percent of the world's total supply of fresh surface water. Refer to the map on the next page to examine the nation's natural resources.

Oil drilled from Alaska helps power the nation's planes, trains, cars, and factories.

THINKING ABOUT GEOGRAPHY What are the different natural resources that you and your family use in your daily lives?

Land and Resources

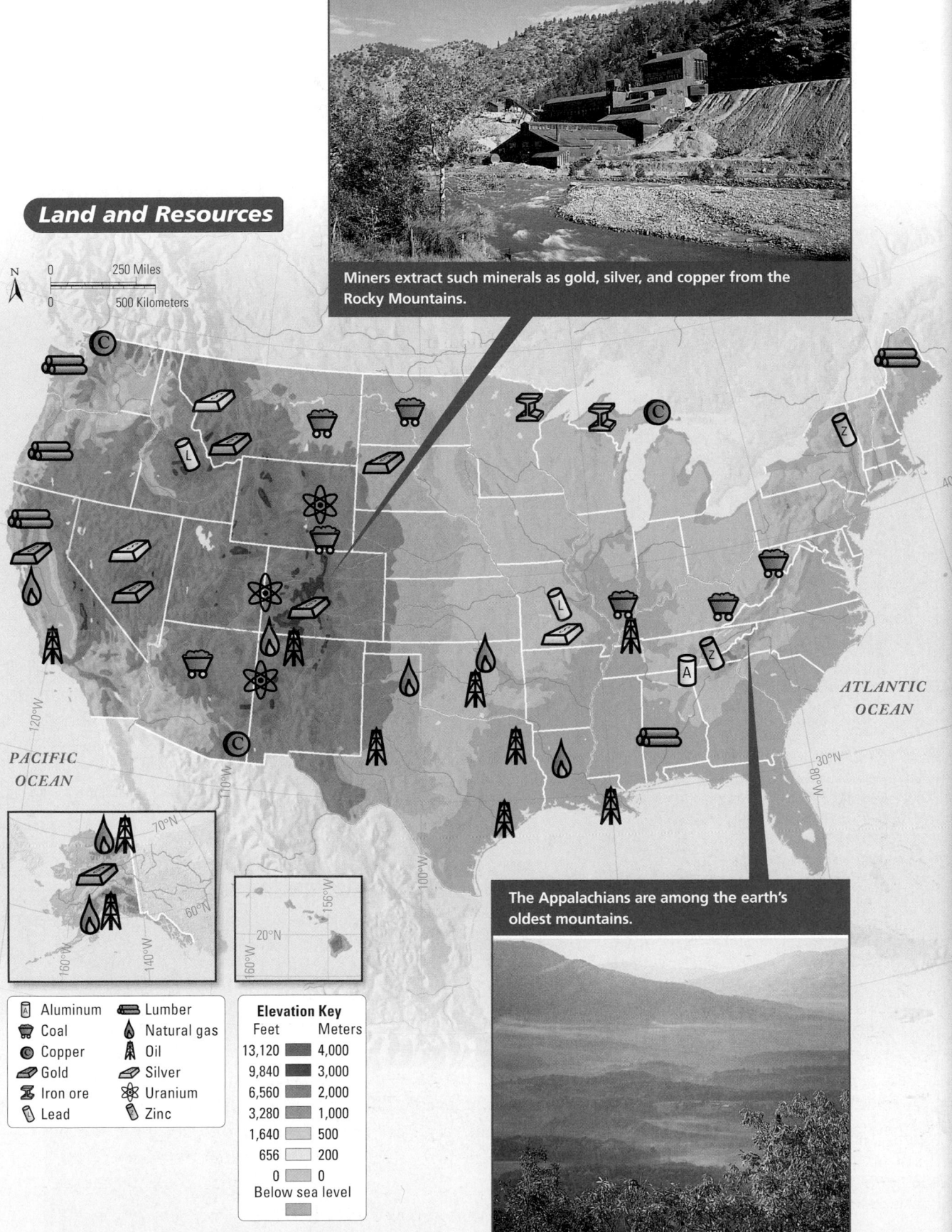

Miners extract such minerals as gold, silver, and copper from the Rocky Mountains.

The Appalachians are among the earth's oldest mountains.

PACIFIC OCEAN

ATLANTIC OCEAN

N

0   250 Miles
0   500 Kilometers

Ⓐ	Aluminum	🪵	Lumber
🛒	Coal	🔥	Natural gas
◉	Copper	🛢	Oil
▱	Gold	▱	Silver
⚡	Iron ore	✴	Uranium
🗋	Lead	🗋	Zinc

Elevation Key

Feet	Meters
13,120	4,000
9,840	3,000
6,560	2,000
3,280	1,000
1,640	500
656	200
0	0
Below sea level	

Physical Geography of the United States **11**

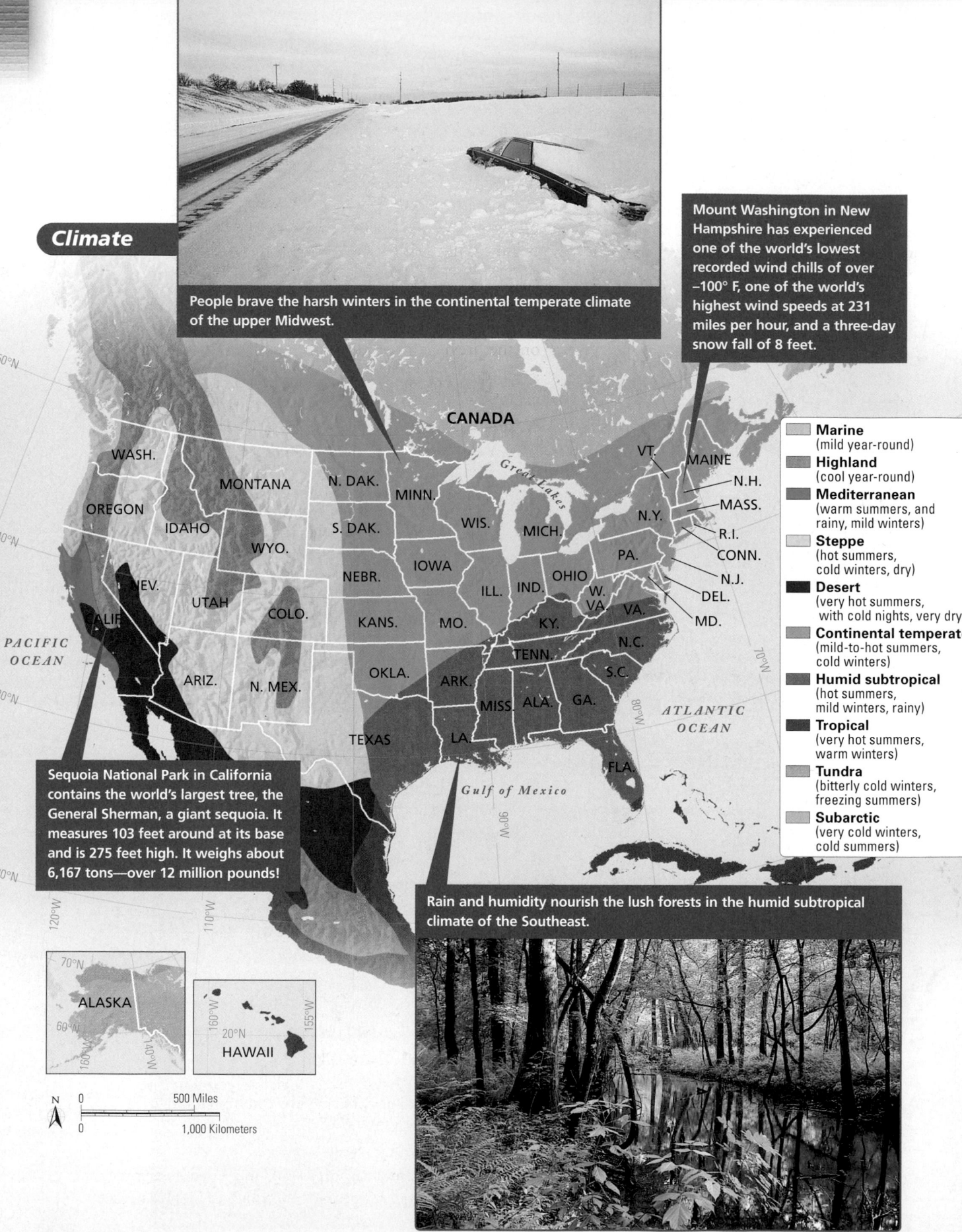

Climate

People brave the harsh winters in the continental temperate climate of the upper Midwest.

Mount Washington in New Hampshire has experienced one of the world's lowest recorded wind chills of over −100° F, one of the world's highest wind speeds at 231 miles per hour, and a three-day snow fall of 8 feet.

CANADA

Great Lakes

WASH.

OREGON

IDAHO

MONTANA

N. DAK.

S. DAK.

MINN.

WIS.

WYO.

NEV.

UTAH

COLO.

CALIF.

ARIZ.

N. MEX.

NEBR.

IOWA

KANS.

OKLA.

MO.

MICH.

ILL. IND.

OHIO

W. VA.

KY.

TENN.

ARK.

MISS. ALA.

TEXAS

LA.

N.Y.

PA.

VA.

N.C.

S.C.

GA.

FLA.

VT. MAINE

N.H.

MASS.

R.I.

CONN.

N.J.

DEL.

MD.

PACIFIC OCEAN

ATLANTIC OCEAN

Gulf of Mexico

50°N

40°N

30°N

20°N

120°W

110°W

90°W

80°W

70°W

Legend

- **Marine** (mild year-round)
- **Highland** (cool year-round)
- **Mediterranean** (warm summers, and rainy, mild winters)
- **Steppe** (hot summers, cold winters, dry)
- **Desert** (very hot summers, with cold nights, very dry)
- **Continental temperate** (mild-to-hot summers, cold winters)
- **Humid subtropical** (hot summers, mild winters, rainy)
- **Tropical** (very hot summers, warm winters)
- **Tundra** (bitterly cold winters, freezing summers)
- **Subarctic** (very cold winters, cold summers)

Sequoia National Park in California contains the world's largest tree, the General Sherman, a giant sequoia. It measures 103 feet around at its base and is 275 feet high. It weighs about 6,167 tons—over 12 million pounds!

Rain and humidity nourish the lush forests in the humid subtropical climate of the Southeast.

ALASKA

70°N

60°N

160°W

140°W

HAWAII

160°W

155°W

20°N

N

0   500 Miles

0   1,000 Kilometers

Tourists and residents bask in the sunshine of Waikiki Beach in Hawaii.

This mountainside burns with the autumn foliage of New Hampshire.

Climate

The United States contains a variety of climates. For example, the mean temperature in January in Miami, Florida, is 67° F, while it is 11° F in Minneapolis, Minnesota. Most of the United States experiences a continental climate, or distinct change of seasons. Some regional climatic differences include hot and humid summers in the Southeast versus hot and dry summers in the Southwest. Harsh winters and heavy snow can blanket parts of the Midwest, the Northeast, and the higher elevations of the West and Northwest. Refer to the map on the previous page to see the nation's climatic regions.

Human activities have affected the climate, too. For example, pollution from cars and factories can affect local weather conditions and may be contributing to a dangerous rise in the earth's temperature.

THINKING ABOUT GEOGRAPHY How would you describe the climate where you live?

Vegetation

Between 20,000 and 25,000 species and subspecies of plants and vegetation grow in the United States—including over 1,000 different kinds of trees. Climate often dictates the type of vegetation found in a region. For instance, cold autumns in the Northeast contribute to the brilliantly colored autumn leaves. Rain nourishes the forests in the Northwest and Southeast. The central plains, where rainfall is less heavy, are covered by grass. Cactus plants thrive in the dry southwestern deserts.

Along with natural vegetation, climate dictates the nation's variety of planted crops. For example, temperate weather in the Midwest helps wheat to grow, while warm weather nourishes citrus fruit in Florida and California.

THINKING ABOUT GEOGRAPHY What kinds of trees or plants grow in your region?

Physical Geography Assessment

1. Main Ideas

a. What are the different aspects of physical geography?

b. Which state contains the largest variety of climates?

c. What two states contain most of the country's oil resources?

2. Critical Thinking

Drawing Conclusions What do you think are the advantages of living in a country with diverse physical geography?

THINK ABOUT
• the different resources available in your region
• the variety of recreational activities in your region

Geographic Dictionary

volcano
an opening in the earth, usually raised, through which gasses and lava escape from the earth's interior

strait
a narrow strip of water connecting two large bodies of water

cape
a pointed piece of land extending into an ocean or lake

sea level
level of the ocean's surface, used as a reference point when measuring the height or depth of the earth's surface

bay
part of an ocean or lake partially enclosed by land

harbor
a sheltered area of water, deep enough for docking ships

(river) mouth
the place where a river flows into a lake or ocean

marsh
soft, wet, low-lying, grassy land that serves as a transition between water and land

island
a body of land surrounded by water

delta
a triangular area of land formed from deposits at the mouth of a river

flood plain
flat land near the edges of rivers formed by mud and silt deposited by floods

swamp
an area of land that is saturated by water

desert
a dry area where few plants grow

butte
a raised, flat area of land with steep cliffs, smaller than a mesa

oasis
a spot of fertile land in a desert, fed by water from wells or underground springs

"The story of my people and the story of this place are one single story."

—Taos Pueblo man

CHAPTER 1 The World in 1500

Beginnings–1500

Section 1
Crossing to the Americas

Section 2
Societies of North America

Section 3
Societies of West Africa

Section 4
Societies of Europe

Section 5
Early European Explorers

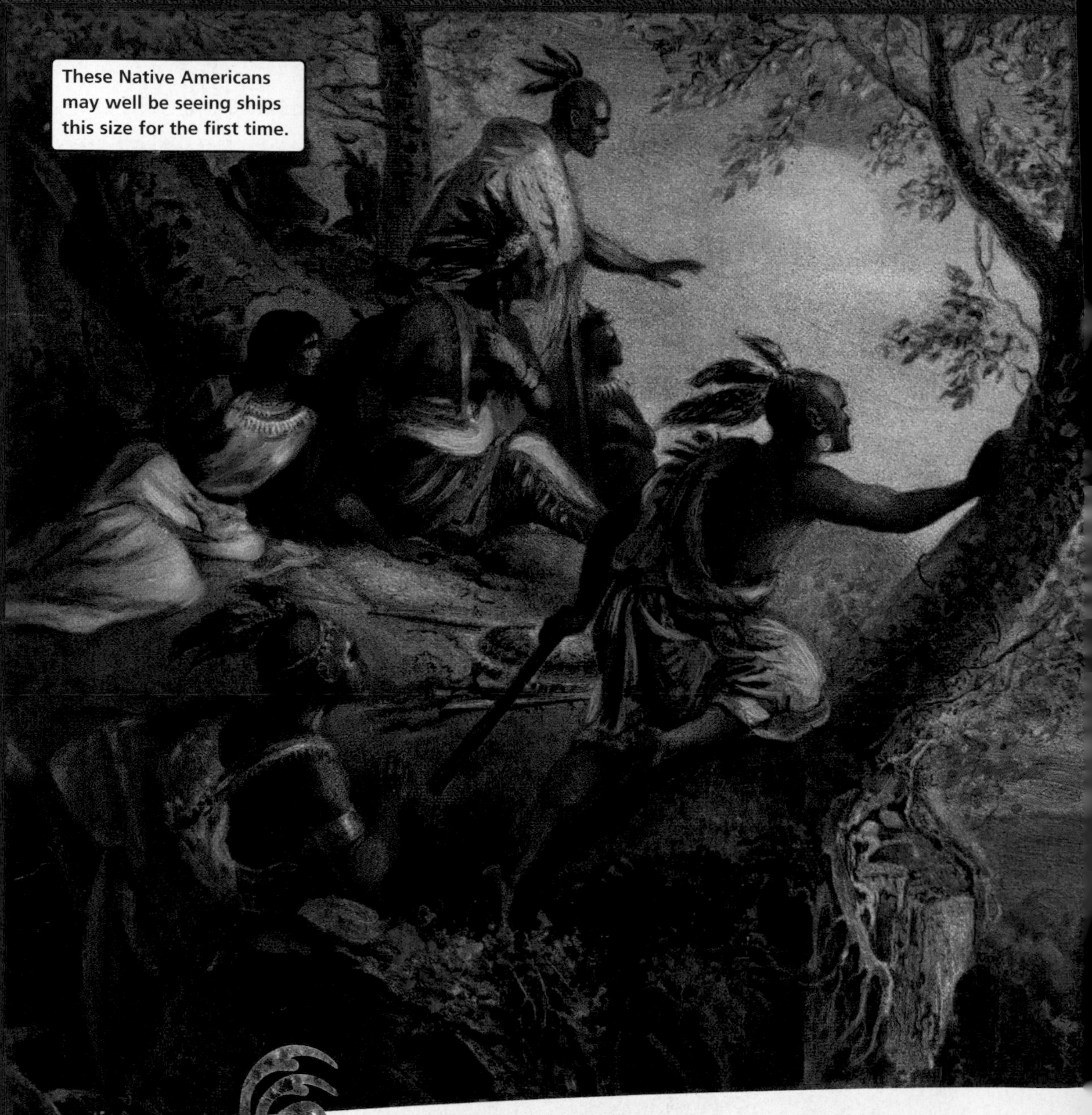

These Native Americans may well be seeing ships this size for the first time.

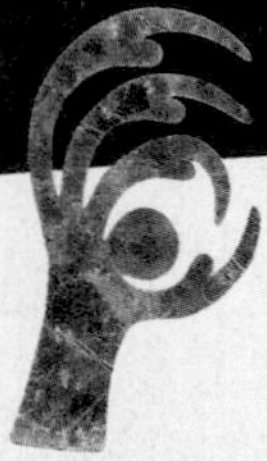

Americas
World

200 B.C.

400 B.C.–200 B.C.
Hopewell culture, which created this mica birdclaw, flourishes in the Midwest.

200s
The Maya are using hieroglyphic writing.

About 6 B.C.
Jesus of Nazareth is born. His teachings become the basis for Christianity.

476
Western Roman Empire ends. Over time, Europe splits into small kingdoms.

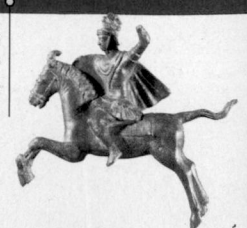

You are a Native American living on the northeastern coast of North America. One day you see a giant boat topped by strange white cloths. Men climb into smaller boats and row toward you. You have never seen men like this. They have pale skin and wear heavy, colorful clothing. You wonder what will happen when they land.

What happens when different societies meet?

What Do You Think?

- What can different societies learn from each other?
- What might they gain from each other?
- What positive and negative things might happen when they meet?

 **RESEARCH LINKS**
CLASSZONE.COM

Visit the Chapter 1 links for more information about the first Americans or European voyagers.

This European ship spent weeks at sea to reach the coast of North America.

800s
Maize is widely grown in what is now the southeastern United States.

1000
Viking Leif Erikson reaches what is now Newfoundland.

1100s
The city of Cahokia flourishes in what is now Illinois.

1200s
The Aztecs conquer much of central Mexico.

1492
The European explorer Columbus lands in the Americas.

A.D. 1500

Early 600s
Muhammad begins the religion of Islam in Arabia.

1096
Europeans begin the Crusades to capture the Holy Land from followers of Islam.

1324
Mansa Musa, emperor of Mali, travels to Islam's holy city. Word of his gold spreads to Europe.

Reading Strategy: Categorizing Information

What Do You Know?

What do you know about the history of the Americas, West Africa, and Europe? How advanced must a society be to build large structures like the ones at the right?

Think About

- what you know about other societies, such as Egypt, that built large structures
- what you've read in books
- your responses to the Interact with History about when different societies meet (see page 25)

AFRICA This Muslim mosque in Timbuktu, Mali, was built in the 1300s and 1400s.

EUROPE St. Peter's Basilica (a Christian church) in Vatican City, Italy, was built in the 1500s and early 1600s.

What Do You Want to Know?

What questions do you have about the past societies of the Americas, West Africa, and Europe? What do you want to know about how they met? Record those questions in your notebook before you read the chapter.

Categorizing Information

One way to make better sense of what you read is to categorize. To categorize is to sort information into groups. The chart below will help you record information about the societies of the Americas, West Africa, and Europe. As you read, look for information relating to the categories of trade, technology, religion, and art. Record that information on your chart.

 S See Skillbuilder Handbook, page R6.

Taking Notes

	Trade	Technology	Religion	Art
AMERICAS				
WEST AFRICA				
EUROPE				

Crossing to the Americas

MAIN IDEA	WHY IT MATTERS NOW	TERMS & NAMES
Ancient peoples came from Asia to the Americas and over time developed complex civilizations.	Archaeologists and other scientists continue to make new discoveries about these ancient people.	archaeologist domestication artifact civilization migrate irrigation culture Mound Builders

ONE AMERICAN'S STORY

For many years, Solveig Turpin has searched Texas for paintings that ancient people drew on rock walls. Turpin is an **archaeologist**. That is a scientist who studies the human past by examining the things people left behind. Turpin believes that one of the paintings she found shows a religious leader who turned himself into a panther.

A VOICE FROM THE PAST

This is the Shaman [religious leader] who transforms into the largest and most powerful animal here. . . . I like to call [the shamans] supramen because they were over everything.

Solveig Turpin, quoted in *In Search of Ancient North America*

Archaeologists make theories about the past based on what they learn from bones and artifacts. **Artifacts** are tools and other objects that humans made. Section 1 discusses some theories about early Americans.

Archaeologist Solveig Turpin wears a shirt displaying the rock paintings of ancient peoples as she discusses her work.

The First People in America

As many societies do, many Native Americans have stories explaining the origin of their people. Some believe the gods created their ancestors. Others believe their ancestors were born of Mother Earth. In contrast, scientists think that the first Americans **migrated**, or moved, here from Asia. But scientists disagree about how and when this move took place.

Some ancient people may have crossed a land bridge that joined Asia and North America during the last Ice Age. The Ice Age was a time of extreme cold that lasted for thousands of years. Glaciers trapped so much water that ocean levels dropped. A bridge of land, now called Beringia, appeared where the Bering Strait is now. (See map, page 28.) When the earth grew warm again, the glaciers melted and flooded Beringia. Some scientists who hold this theory believe the earliest Americans arrived

Taking Notes

Use your chart to take notes about the Americas.

	Trade	
AMERICAS		
WEST AFRICA		
EUROPE		

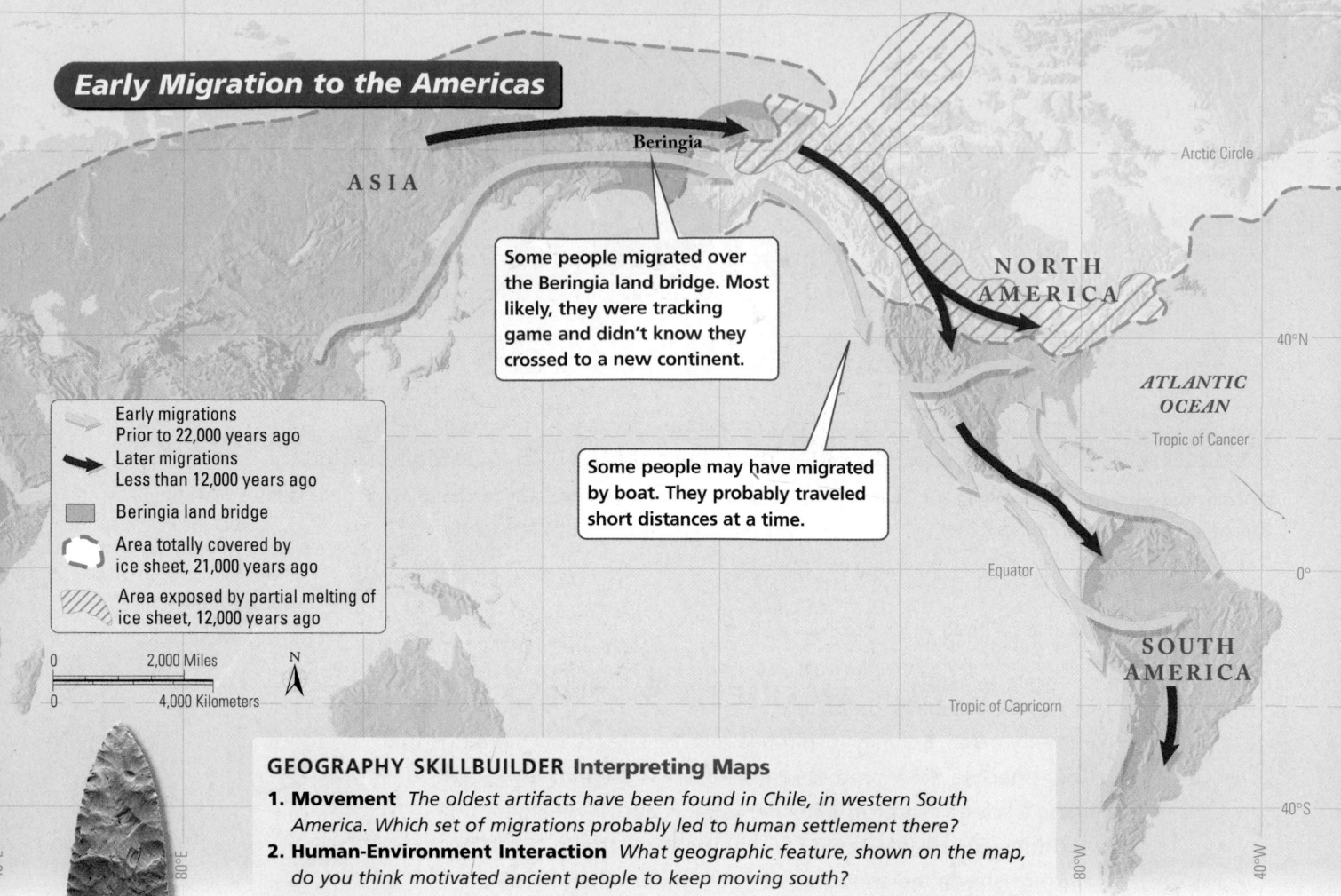

Early Migration to the Americas

ASIA

Beringia

NORTH AMERICA

Some people migrated over the Beringia land bridge. Most likely, they were tracking game and didn't know they crossed to a new continent.

Some people may have migrated by boat. They probably traveled short distances at a time.

ATLANTIC OCEAN

SOUTH AMERICA

Arctic Circle

40°N

Tropic of Cancer

Equator

Tropic of Capricorn

40°S

Early migrations
Prior to 22,000 years ago

Later migrations
Less than 12,000 years ago

Beringia land bridge

Area totally covered by
ice sheet, 21,000 years ago

Area exposed by partial melting of
ice sheet, 12,000 years ago

0   2,000 Miles
0   4,000 Kilometers

N

GEOGRAPHY SKILLBUILDER Interpreting Maps

1. **Movement** *The oldest artifacts have been found in Chile, in western South America. Which set of migrations probably led to human settlement there?*
2. **Human-Environment Interaction** *What geographic feature, shown on the map, do you think motivated ancient people to keep moving south?*

Ancient hunters used spear points such as this one, which is about 10,000 years old.

12,000 years ago. Other scientists believe humans came to the Americas much earlier. They have found artifacts in South America that tests show to be 30,000 years old. These scientists believe that people came to the Americas by many routes, over thousands of years. Some came by boat, sailing short distances from island to island. This theory may also change as scientists find more evidence of ancient Americans.

Agriculture Leads to Civilization

A **culture** is a way of life shared by people with similar arts, beliefs, and customs. The first Americans lived in hunting and gathering cultures. They hunted small animals, such as rabbits, and large animals, such as the woolly mammoth. They gathered wild seeds, nuts, and berries.

In time, people started to plant the seeds they found. This was the beginning of agriculture. About 5,000 years ago, humans began domestication. **Domestication** is the practice of breeding plants or taming animals to meet human needs. By trial and error, people in central Mexico learned which seeds grew the best crops. By selecting the right seeds, they improved the quality of maize, or corn, until its ears were large. Dried and stored for future use, corn became a main food source.

Knowledge of agriculture spread throughout the Americas. Having a stable food supply changed the way people lived. Once they no longer had to travel to find food, they built permanent villages. Farmers were able to produce large harvests, so that fewer people needed to farm.

Vocabulary
woolly mammoth: a hairy ancestor of the elephant, now extinct

<u>*Reading*</u>**History**
A. Drawing
Conclusions Why
would a culture
need to learn
agriculture before
it could develop a
civilization?

Some people began to practice other crafts, such as weaving or making pots. A few people became religious leaders.

Slowly, some cultures grew complex and became civilizations. A **civilization** has five features: (1) cities that are centers of trade, (2) specialized jobs for different people, (3) organized forms of government and religion, (4) a system of record keeping, and (5) advanced tools.

Early Mesoamerican Civilizations

About 1200 B.C., an advanced civilization arose in Mesoamerica, a region that stretches from central Mexico to present-day Nicaragua. For 800 years, a people called the Olmec thrived along the Gulf of Mexico. The Olmec set up a network of trade routes and constructed earthen mounds shaped like pyramids. They built large, busy cities like La Venta.

> ### A VOICE FROM THE PAST
> La Venta was not just an empty ceremonial spot visited by Olmec priests and nobles but a prosperous community of fishers, farmers, traders, and specialists, such as the artisans and the sculptors.
> **Rebecca González,** quoted in "New Light on the Olmec," *National Geographic*

Around 400 B.C., the Olmec abandoned La Venta and other cities. Scientists don't know why. By then, Olmec culture had spread along trade routes and influenced others. Later people in Mesoamerica adapted Olmec religious practices and carved designs inspired by Olmec art.

By A.D. 250, about 650 years after the Olmec vanished, the Maya had developed a great civilization. Their cities were in southern Mexico and Guatemala, where they built pyramid mounds topped by temples. From artifacts, archaeologists know that the Maya had an accurate yearly calendar. They were the first people in the Americas to create a number system using zero. Their written language used picture symbols.

By 900, the Maya had abandoned many of their cities. Scientists think that revolts, disease, or crop failures may have caused their society to fail.

Background
Mathematicians in India also developed the idea of using a symbol for zero. Traders later carried the idea from Asia to Europe.

The Hohokam and the Anasazi

During the Mayan period, an agricultural people inhabited the American Southwest. The Hohokam lived in what is now Arizona from about 300 B.C. to A.D. 1400. That desert region has little rain, so farming is difficult. But the Hohokam altered their dry environment. They dug hundreds of miles of canals to carry river water to their crops. The practice of bringing water to crops is called **irrigation.**

The Hohokam raised corn, beans, and squash. They also gathered wild plants and hunted animals. They traded widely—with people in Mexico, the Southwest, and California. Hohokam pottery and religious practices show the influence of Mesoamerican cultures, which they learned about through trade.

Ancient peoples of the American Southwest used images like this to communicate with each other. Such images are called petroglyphs.

The Mound Builders

During the 1700s, Europeans discovered several mysterious earthen mounds in what is now the American Southeast and Midwest. They believed a lost civilization had built the mounds. Historians now know that different Native American groups, known as the Mound Builders, built these structures. The builders may have used the mounds for burial tombs, as a tribute to their gods, or for some other religious purpose. One famous mound is the Great Serpent Mound in present-day Ohio. The Adena, Fort Ancient, or Hopewell cultures possibly built it. An aerial photograph of the Great Serpent Mound is shown below.

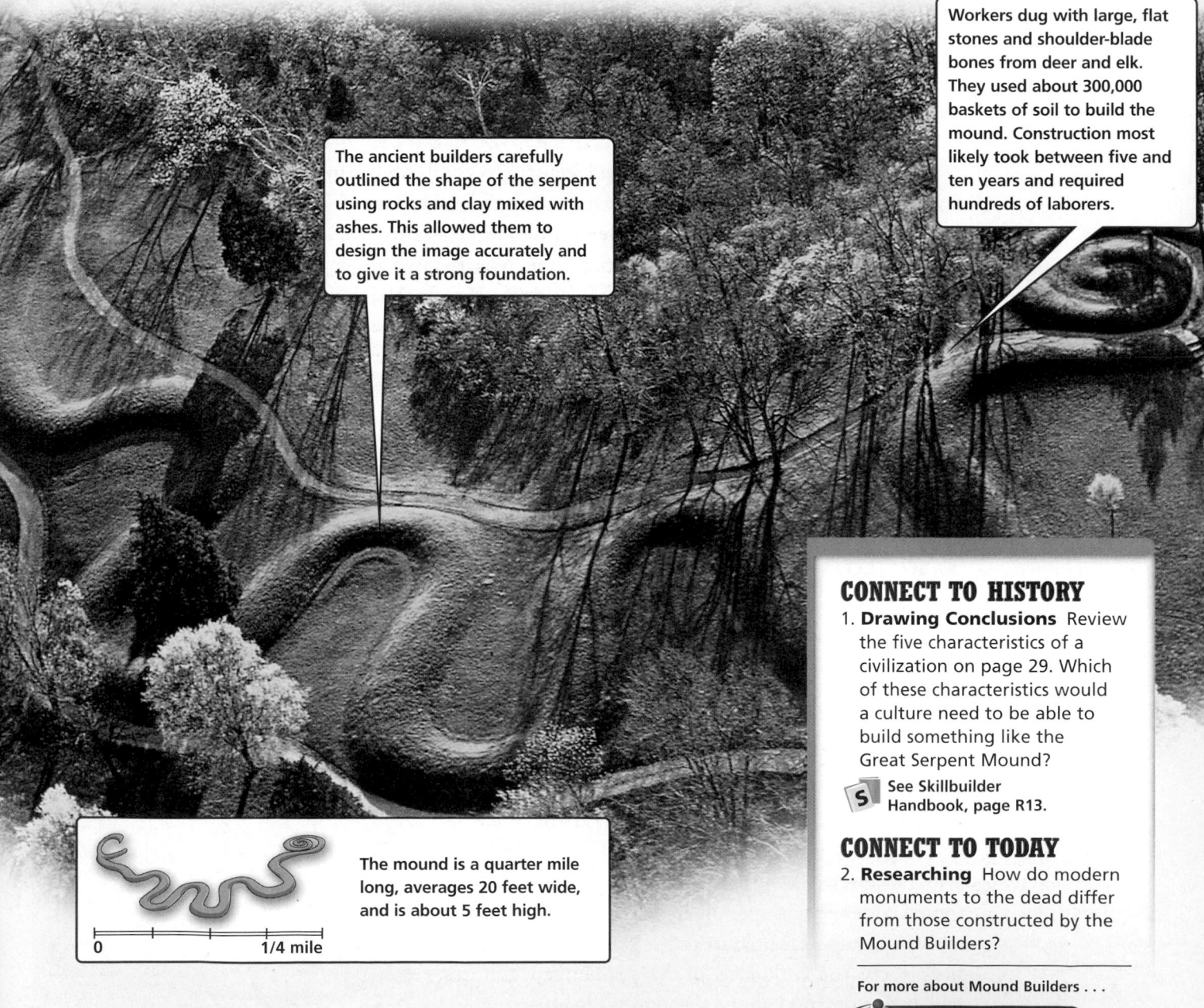

The ancient builders carefully outlined the shape of the serpent using rocks and clay mixed with ashes. This allowed them to design the image accurately and to give it a strong foundation.

Workers dug with large, flat stones and shoulder-blade bones from deer and elk. They used about 300,000 baskets of soil to build the mound. Construction most likely took between five and ten years and required hundreds of laborers.

The mound is a quarter mile long, averages 20 feet wide, and is about 5 feet high.

0   1/4 mile

CONNECT TO HISTORY

1. **Drawing Conclusions** Review the five characteristics of a civilization on page 29. Which of these characteristics would a culture need to be able to build something like the Great Serpent Mound?

   S See Skillbuilder Handbook, page R13.

CONNECT TO TODAY

2. **Researching** How do modern monuments to the dead differ from those constructed by the Mound Builders?

For more about Mound Builders . . .

RESEARCH LINKS CLASSZONE.COM

Beginning about A.D. 100, the Anasazi lived in the area where Utah, Arizona, Colorado, and New Mexico now meet. Scientists don't know their origin. Like the Hohokam, the Anasazi were mainly farmers who also traded widely.

The Anasazi built houses with hundreds of rooms and many stories. For protection, they placed some buildings against overhanging canyon walls. The 800-room Pueblo Bonito in Chaco Canyon, New Mexico, housed perhaps 1,000 people. In the 1500s, when Spanish explorers first saw these houses, they called them *pueblos*, meaning villages. Around 1300, drought or warfare caused the Anasazi to leave their homes.

The Mound Builders

In the eastern part of what is now the United States lived several groups of people called Mound Builders. The **Mound Builders** were early Native Americans who built large earthen structures.

The two oldest Mound Builder societies were the Adena and the Hopewell. Archaeologists know little about the Adena. The Hopewell, located in what is now the Midwest, lived from 400 B.C. to A.D. 400. Like the Hohokam, they grew corn. Artifacts show that they had a large trade network. It stretched from the Atlantic to the Rocky Mountains, and from the Great Lakes to Florida. Hopewell mounds served as burial sites. Their tombs contained jewelry and other gifts for the dead.

*Reading*History
B. Comparing
What other ancient American cultures built pyramid-shaped mounds?

The last group of Mound Builders, the Mississippians, lived from A.D. 800 to 1700. They built some of the first cities in North America. For example, Cahokia in Illinois has more than 100 mounds. One of them, Monks Mound, rises 100 feet and covers 16 acres. In some cities, the Mississippians built flat-topped, pyramid-shaped temple mounds.

By the 1700s, most of the Mississippians had died from diseases they caught from Europeans. But many Native American groups continued to thrive throughout the United States, as you will read in Section 2.

Section **1** Assessment

1. Terms & Names

Explain the significance of:
- archaeologist
- artifact
- migrate
- culture
- domestication
- civilization
- irrigation
- Mound Builders

2. Using Graphics

Use a chart like the one below to list ancient cultures of Mesoamerica and North America and their locations.

Ancient Culture	Location

Which of these cultures was closest to where you live?

3. Main Ideas

a. By what land bridge did some ancient people migrate to North America, and how was it created?

b. How did the development of farming lead to the growth of civilization?

c. How did trade help to spread culture?

4. Critical Thinking

Comparing How did the Hohokam and the Anasazi adapt to living in their environment?

THINK ABOUT
- Hohokam agriculture
- Anasazi dwellings

ACTIVITY OPTIONS

SCIENCE
LANGUAGE ARTS

Research the growing of corn. Draw a **diagram** of a corn plant with its parts labeled or write a **description** of how corn grows.

2
Societies of North America

MAIN IDEA	WHY IT MATTERS NOW	TERMS & NAMES
By 1500, a variety of Native American groups—each with a distinct culture—lived in North America.	Many Americans today claim one or more of these cultures as part of their heritage.	technology tundra kayak matrilineal slash-and-burn agriculture Deganawida Iroquois League

ONE AMERICAN'S STORY

Many Native Americans today work to save their culture. Haida artist Bill Reid took part in this effort. When he was a teenager in the 1930s, few Haida artists were making totem poles or other Haida crafts. Reid began to learn about Haida arts from his grandfather.

Reid studied Northwest Coast native arts and jewelry making. Soon he created gold jewelry with Haida designs and carved sculptures. When Reid died, his work was praised.

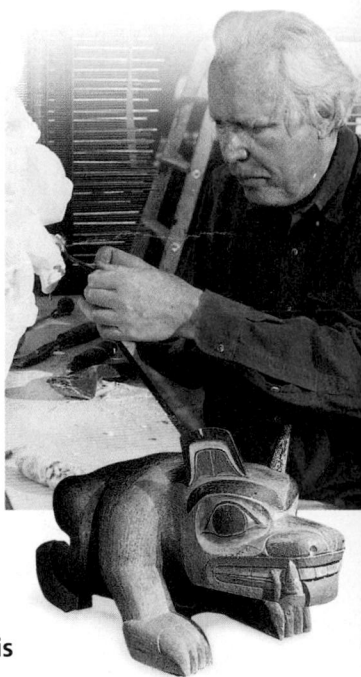

Creating sculptures of traditional designs was one way Bill Reid kept Haida culture alive.

> ### A VOICE FROM THE PAST
>
> Canada has lost one of its greatest artists. A descendant of a lineage of great Haida artists . . . , Bill Reid revived an artistic tradition that had survived only in museum collections.
>
> **Dr. George MacDonald,** at Bill Reid's memorial service, March 24, 1998

Written records and people like Reid have preserved knowledge of the cultures that flourished in the Americas when Europeans arrived. This section explains the diversity of Native American groups in 1500.

Taking Notes

Use your chart to take notes about the societies of North America.

	Trade
AMERICAS	
WEST AFRICA	
EUROPE	

Native American Diversity

By 1500, Native Americans had divided into hundreds of cultural groups, speaking perhaps 2,000 languages. One reason Native Americans were so diverse was that each group adapted to its own environment—whether subzero ice fields, scorching deserts, or dense forests.

Environment shaped each group's economy, technology, and religion. **Technology** is the use of tools and knowledge to meet human needs. In some regions, Native Americans based their economy on farming. In others, they relied on hunting or fishing. Different environments caused technology to vary. In coastal areas, farmers made tools from shells. In

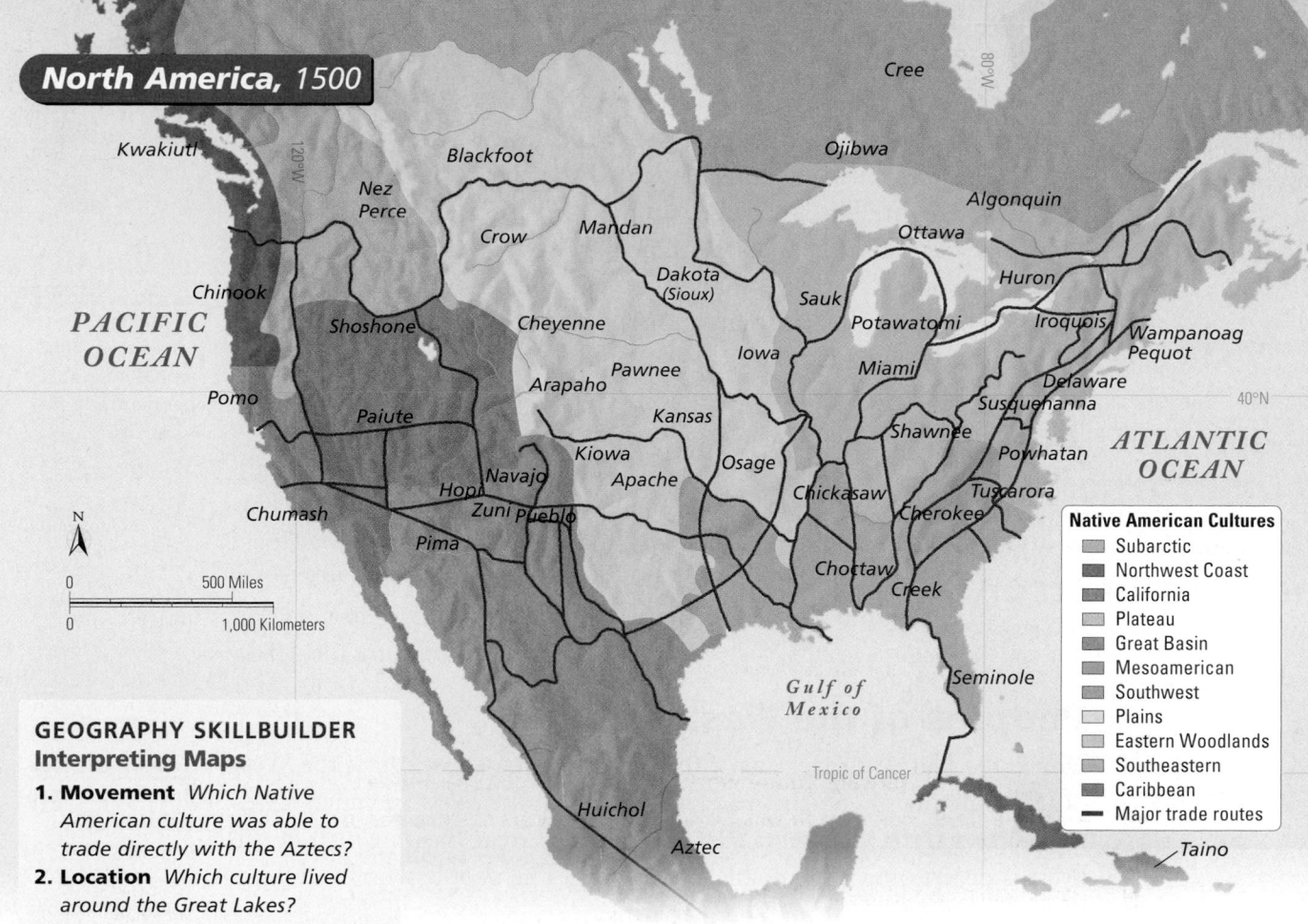

North America, 1500

Cree
Kwakiutl
Blackfoot
Ojibwa
Nez Perce
Algonquin
Crow
Mandan
Ottawa
Chinook
Dakota (Sioux)
Huron
PACIFIC OCEAN
Shoshone
Cheyenne
Sauk
Iroquois
Pomo
Potawatomi
Wampanoag
Pequot
Paiute
Arapaho
Pawnee
Iowa
Miami
Delaware
Susquehanna
40°N
Kansas
Shawnee
ATLANTIC OCEAN
Chumash
Kiowa
Osage
Powhatan
Hopi
Navajo
Apache
Tuscarora
Zuni Pueblo
Chickasaw
Cherokee
Pima
Choctaw
Creek
Gulf of Mexico
Seminole
Tropic of Cancer
Huichol
Aztec
Taino

Native American Cultures
- Subarctic
- Northwest Coast
- California
- Plateau
- Great Basin
- Mesoamerican
- Southwest
- Plains
- Eastern Woodlands
- Southeastern
- Caribbean
- Major trade routes

GEOGRAPHY SKILLBUILDER
Interpreting Maps
1. **Movement** Which Native American culture was able to trade directly with the Aztecs?
2. **Location** Which culture lived around the Great Lakes?

deserts, they used irrigation. Environment affected religion, too. Native Americans strongly believed that certain places were sacred—and that animals, plants, and natural forces had spiritual importance.

Although Native American groups had many differences, they all felt closely connected to nature, as shown in the following chant.

A VOICE FROM THE PAST
Earth's body has become my body
  by means of these I shall live on.
Earth's mind has become my mind
  by means of these I shall live on.
Navajo Blessing Way, quoted in *America in 1492*

In addition, trade linked Native Americans. Trading centers developed across North America, especially at points where two cultures met.

Peoples of the North and Northwest Coast

Background
The Inuit are also called the Eskimo.

The Aleut (uh•LOOT) and the Inuit (IHN•yoo•iht) were peoples of the far North. The Aleut lived on islands off Alaska, and the Inuit lived near the coast on tundra. **Tundra** is a treeless plain that remains frozen under its top layer of soil. Ice and snow cover the ground most of the year.

Because their climate was too cold for farming, the Inuit and Aleut were hunters. They paddled **kayaks**, small boats made of animal skins,

into icy seas to spear whales, seals, and walruses. They hunted these mammals for food, and they made seal and walrus skins into clothes. Some Inuit religious ceremonies honored the spirits of the whales and seals they caught. The Inuit also hunted such land animals as caribou. They made arrowheads and spear points from bones and antlers.

Farther south, Northwest Coast people also hunted sea mammals. But they mostly fished for salmon. Living by forests, Northwest Coast people used wood for houses, boats, and carved objects. They traded such coastal products as shells for items from the inland, such as furs.

Reading **History**
A. Making Inferences Why would inland people trade for seashells?

> *"The term [potlatch] comes from Chinook . . . and means 'to give.'"*
> Gloria Cranmer Webster,
> U'mista Cultural Centre

Northwest Coast groups such as the Kwakiutl (KWAH•kee•OOT•uhl) and Haida had a special ceremony—the potlatch. Individuals would give away most or all of their goods as a way to claim status and benefit their community. They held potlatches to mark life events, such as naming a child or mourning the dead.

Peoples of the West

Unlike the Native Americans of the Northwest Coast, those of the West did not rely mainly on the sea. The peoples of the West included tribes in California, the Columbia Plateau, and the Great Basin. Much of the West is desert or is not suitable for farming. The people who lived there existed mainly by hunting and gathering.

The men hunted deer, elk, antelope, rabbits, and birds. They also fished, especially for salmon that swam up the western rivers. Women gathered such wild foods as nuts, seeds, and berries. Many western groups moved with the seasons to collect food.

Reading **History**
B. Reading a Map On the map on page 33, locate the cultures of California, the Plateau, and the Great Basin. Notice why these three together are called the peoples of the West.

The women of some western tribes became expert weavers. Pomo women wove beautiful baskets that they used to gather and store food. They wove some baskets tightly enough to be watertight.

The peoples of the West had strong spiritual beliefs, often linked to nature. Some held ceremonies to ensure a large food supply. Others held dances to ask for rain, for plant growth, and for good hunting. Still others believed that their religious leaders could contact the spirit world.

The Aztec Calendar

This stone is the Aztec calender wheel. In the center is the sun god. Around it are symbols for the 20 days of the Aztec month. Three are enlarged below.

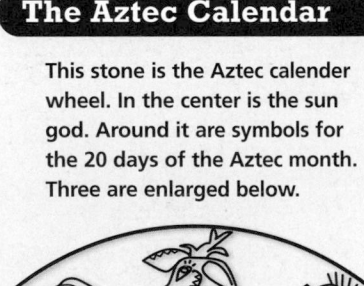

Peoples of Mexico

Far to the south, the Aztecs ruled a great civilization in what is now central Mexico. The origin of the Aztecs is unclear. They may have been hunters and gatherers like the Native Americans of the West. Sometime during the 1100s, they migrated into the Valley of Mexico.

In 1325, they began to build their capital city, Tenochtitlán (teh•NAWCH•tee•TLAHN), on islands in Lake Texcoco. Two things helped the Aztecs become a strong empire. First, they drained swamps and built an

irrigation system. This enabled them to grow plenty of food. Second, they were a warlike people who conquered most of their neighbors. The defeated people then had to send the Aztecs food and resources.

The Aztecs had a complex society. Rulers were the highest class. Priests and government workers ranked next. Slaves and servants were at the bottom. The Aztecs had elaborate religious ceremonies linked to their calendar and their study of the sun, moon, and stars. Many of their beliefs came from earlier Mesoamerican cultures.

The Aztecs' most important ritual involved feeding their sun god human blood. To do this, the Aztecs sacrificed prisoners of war by cutting out the person's heart while he was still alive. One reason the Aztecs fought so many wars was to capture prisoners to sacrifice.

Peoples of the Southwest

North of the Aztec, in what is now the American Southwest, lived the Pueblo people. Their ancestors were the ancient Hohokam and Anasazi. Like their ancestors, the Pueblo used irrigation to alter their desert region for farming. They lived in many-storied houses of adobe—dried mud bricks. These large buildings sometimes held an entire village.

Pueblo Indian farmers raised corn, beans, and squash. For meat, they hunted game and raised turkeys. Men did most of the farming, hunting, weaving, and building. Women ground the corn and cooked the food, repaired the adobe houses, and crafted pottery.

The Navajo and the Apache were nomadic, or wandering, hunter-gatherers who came to the region later than the Pueblo. For food, they relied mainly on game and on cactus, roots, and piñon nuts. Often, they traded these wild products for crops that the Pueblo had grown. Over time, the Navajo adopted farming and other Pueblo practices.

Peoples of the Great Plains

Farther north, the Great Plains is a flat grassland region stretching from the Mississippi River west to the Rocky Mountains. Today, most people think of Plains Indians on horseback, but originally they had no horses. The Spanish first brought horses to the Americas in the 1500s.

Some Plains groups were nomads. Others lived in villages by rivers, where land was easier to farm. In summer, entire villages set out to track bison. Hunting bison on foot was difficult, but Plains tribes used their environment to help them. Working together, the villagers stampeded the herd over a cliff, so the fall would kill or disable the animals. Plains Indians not only ate the bison's meat. They also made its hide into clothes and its bones into tools.

*Reading*History
C. Drawing Conclusions Why do you think the Navajo adopted farming?

Background Horses spread across North America through trade and by escaping from humans and wandering on their own.

daily *life*

KACHINA DANCES
Every year in summer the Hopi, Zuni, and other Pueblo Indians held a religious celebration. The ceremony called on the kachinas, or spirits of the ancestors. The Pueblo believed the kachinas had the power to bring a plentiful harvest. At the festival, masked dancers played the role of different kachinas. They danced and sang songs to bring rain in the year ahead. Today, the Pueblo also carve kachina dolls, shown below, as well as hold dances.

In winter such northern Plains groups as the Mandans and Pawnee lived in large circular lodges. Wooden beams held up the earthen walls. A hole at the top provided air, light, and an outlet for smoke from the fire. Buried partly underground, the earth lodge protected the people from the extreme cold and wind of the Plains climate.

Vocabulary
lodge: house

The spiritual beliefs of Plains tribes varied. Some felt a close tie to regional animals such as the bison or plants such as corn. Some honored sacred places, such as the Black Hills of South Dakota and Wyoming. Many Plains tribes held a ceremony called the Sun Dance, which involved making a vow and asking the Creator for aid.

Peoples of the Southeast

The Southeast, which stretches from east Texas to the Atlantic Ocean, has mild winters and warm summers with plentiful rainfall. The long growing season led the Choctaw (CHAHK•taw), Chickasaw (CHIHK•uh•SAW), and other southeastern groups to become farmers. As many other Native Americans did, they grew corn, beans, squash, and pumpkins.

*Reading*History
D. Analyzing Causes Why would a long growing season lead people to become farmers?

Women did most of the farming, while men hunted, fished, and cleared land. The men spent months in the forest tracking deer. In the Southeast, people traced their family ties through the women. Societies in which ancestry is traced through the mother are called **matrilineal**.

In southeastern villages, people gathered at a central square for public meetings and such religious ceremonies as the Green Corn Festival. Held once a year, this festival offered thanks for the corn harvest and also served as a kind of New Year's celebration. People cleaned their houses, threw away old pots, and settled quarrels as a sign of a fresh start for the year.

Peoples of the Eastern Woodlands

Many Native Americans in the Southeast and Eastern Woodlands played lacrosse using sticks like these. Modern Americans have adopted the game.

Like the Southeast, the Northeast had plenty of fish, game, and rain. But the climate was colder with snowy winters. Forests covered much of the region, so it is called the Eastern Woodlands. Most of the people living there spoke either an Iroquoian or Algonquian language.

Like all Native Americans, the Iroquois learned to live in their environment. They hunted wild game. They adapted the forest for farming by using slash-and-burn agriculture. In **slash-and-burn agriculture,** farmers chopped down and then burned trees on a plot of land. The ashes from the fire enriched the soil. When a field's soil became worn out, the farmer abandoned it and cleared a new field. The Iroquois lived in longhouses, bark-covered shelters as long as 300 feet. One longhouse held eight to ten families.

Background
Although it is a quick way to clear fields, slash-and-burn agriculture does cause environmental damage by destroying forests.

The Algonquin lived in wigwams, domelike houses covered with deerskin and slabs of bark. For protection, both the Iroquois and Algonquin surrounded their villages with high fences made of poles. Iroquois villagers often needed protection not only from the enemies of the Iroquois, but from each other. The Iroquois often raided neighboring villages for food and captives.

In the late 1500s, five northern Iroquois nations took the advice of a peace-seeking man named **Deganawida.** They stopped warring with each other and formed an alliance. This alliance of the Cayuga, Mohawk, Oneida, Onondaga, and Seneca was the **Iroquois League.** The League brought a long period of peace to the Iroquois. A council of leaders from each nation governed the League. They followed rules called the Great Law of Peace. The Iroquois were also a matrilineal society. If a leader did something wrong, the women of his clan could vote him out of office.

Across the Atlantic, the peoples of West Africa also adapted to their environment and engaged in trade. West Africa was the region from which most Africans were brought to the Americas. You will read about it in the next section.

AMERICA'S HISTORY MAKERS

DEGANAWIDA (THE PEACEMAKER)

Iroquois tradition honors Deganawida as the Peacemaker. Seeing how destructive warfare was for the Iroquois, Deganawida went from tribe to tribe and described his dream of peace. A poor speaker, he persuaded few warriors. Finally, an Iroquois chief named Hiawatha spoke for him. After long negotiations, the leaders of the warring nations made peace. However, Deganawida's own tribe, the Huron, did not join the League.

How did both Deganawida and Hiawatha lead the Iroquois toward peace?

Section 2 Assessment

1. Terms & Names

Explain the significance of:

- technology
- tundra
- kayak
- matrilineal
- slash-and-burn agriculture
- Deganawida
- Iroquois League

2. Using Graphics

Use a cluster diagram to record how Native Americans from each region adapted to their environment.

People of the North

Adapted to Environment

3. Main Ideas

a. What were some of the religious ceremonies of Native Americans?

b. How were the Pueblo like their ancestors, the Hohokam?

c. How did the formation of the Iroquois League benefit its member nations?

4. Critical Thinking

Drawing Conclusions
How did trade benefit both groups that took part in it?

THINK ABOUT

- who the Northwest Coast people traded with and what they exchanged
- what the Pueblo exchanged with nomadic groups

ACTIVITY OPTIONS

ART

LANGUAGE ARTS

Reread the Navajo chant on page 33. Draw an **illustration** to go with the chant or write additional **verses.**

The Iroquois Great Law of Peace

Setting the Stage The five nations of the Iroquois League created a constitution, called the Great Law of Peace, that had 117 laws and customs. These laws governed all aspects of life and war. In this excerpt, Deganawida introduces the Great Law by describing a tree that symbolizes the permanence and stability of the league. **See Primary Source Explorer** ◉

1 I am Deganawida and with the Five Nations' Confederate **Lords**[1] I plant the Tree of Great Peace. I plant it in your territory, **Adodarhoh,**[2] and the Onondaga Nation, in the territory of you who are Firekeepers.

   I name the tree the Tree of the Great Long Leaves. Under the shade of this Tree of the Great Peace we spread the soft white feathery down of the globe thistle as seats for you, Adodarhoh, and your cousin Lords.

   We place you upon those seats, spread soft with the feathery down of the globe thistle, there beneath the shade of the spreading branches of the Tree of Peace. There shall you sit and watch the Council Fire of the **Confederacy of the Five Nations,**[3] and all the affairs of the Five Nations shall be transacted at this place before you, Adodarhoh, and your cousin Lords, by the Confederate Lords of the Five Nations.

2 Roots have spread out from the Tree of the Great Peace, one to the north, one to the east, one to the south, and one to the west. The name of these roots is The Great White Roots and their nature is Peace and Strength.

   If any man or any nation outside the Five Nations shall obey the laws of the Great Peace and make known their disposition to the Lords of the Confederacy, they may trace the Roots to the Tree and if their minds are clean and they are obedient and promise to obey the wishes of the Confederate Council, they shall be welcomed to take shelter beneath the Tree of the Long Leaves.

A CLOSER LOOK

THE COUNCIL FIRE

The council fire of the Iroquois League was kept burning for about 200 years.

1. What do you think it would mean if the council fire were allowed to die?

A CLOSER LOOK

THE GREAT WHITE ROOTS

The roots of a tree help to anchor it in the ground, and they draw water and food from the soil.

2. Why might Deganawida say the nature of the roots is "Peace and Strength"?

1. **Lords:** chiefs.

2. **Adodarhoh:** the name of the office of the Onondaga chief.

3. **Confederacy of the Five Nations:** the Iroquois League.

Interactive Primary Source Assessment

1. Main Ideas

a. In what territory was the Tree of the Great Peace planted?

b. Where will the affairs of the Five Nations be conducted?

c. Where have the Tree's roots spread?

2. Critical Thinking

Making Inferences Were outsiders welcome to join the Iroquois League? Explain.

THINK ABOUT

• the phrase *they may trace the Roots to the Tree*

• the phrase *take shelter beneath the Tree*

Societies of West Africa

MAIN IDEA	WHY IT MATTERS NOW	TERMS & NAMES
The peoples of West Africa developed sophisticated kingdoms, trade networks, and artistic achievements.	It was from this region that many Africans were brought to the Americas.	Ghana Songhai Muslims Hausa Islam Yoruba Mali Benin

ONE AFRICAN'S STORY

King Tenkaminen (TEHN•kah•MEE•nehn) of the West African empire of **Ghana** was a powerful ruler. He grew rich by taxing gold traders who traveled through his land. In 1067, a geographer wrote a description of the royal court.

A VOICE FROM THE PAST

The king adorns himself . . . wearing necklaces round his neck and bracelets on his forearms. . . . Behind the king stand ten pages holding shields and swords decorated with gold.

al-Bakri, quoted in *The Horizon History of Africa*

Kumasi, a modern West African chief, wears gold to show his status.

West Africa was the homeland of many of the enslaved Africans who were brought to the Americas after 1500. You will read about West Africa in this section.

African Geography and World Trade

Africa is the world's second largest continent after Asia. (See the map on page 40.) Although Africa has a variety of land forms and climates, almost three quarters of it lies within the tropics. The equator runs east-west across the center of Africa. Dense rain forests stretch along the equator in central and western Africa. North and south of the rain forests are broad savannas, which are grassy plains with thorny bushes and scattered trees. Beyond the savanna in the North lies the Sahara, the world's largest desert. Beyond the savanna in the South lies the smaller Kalahari Desert.

By A.D. 1500, coastal ports had linked Africa with the rest of the world for many centuries. Ships from ports on the Mediterranean and the Red Sea carried goods to Arabia and Persia. On Africa's east coast, city-states carried on a brisk trade with ports across the Indian Ocean.

Taking Notes

Use your chart to take notes about West Africa.

	Trade	
AMERICAS		
WEST AFRICA		
EUROPE		

Like other parts of Africa, West Africa has rain forest along the equator and savanna to the north. The Niger River arcs across those grasslands and forests and then empties into the Atlantic Ocean. Along its northern edge, West Africa borders the Sahara.

Ghana Grows Wealthy

On a map, the Sahara appears to be a barrier between West Africa and the ports on the Mediterranean coast. But by A.D. 500, camel caravans led by eager merchants made regular journeys across the great desert. This connected West Africa to the wider world.

Ghana became the first West African kingdom to grow rich through trade. From the 700s to the mid-1000s, Ghana prospered by controlling the busy trade in gold and salt. Located on the southern edge of the Sahara, Ghana became a marketplace for traders going north and south in search of salt and gold. (Ancient Ghana was northwest of modern Ghana.) Salt was important because it helps the human body retain water in hot weather. Traders carried salt from the Saharan salt mines in the north. In Ghana's markets, they met other traders offering gold from the forests of West Africa.

Ghana's king benefited from this trade. He imposed taxes on all gold and salt passing through his kingdom. The taxes had to be paid in gold. The king also claimed all gold nuggets found in his kingdom. Ghana's king used the resulting wealth to pay for an army and build an empire.

Background
The camel is used in the desert because it can travel up to 10 days without water.

Reading **History**
A. Analyzing Causes Why did the king want taxes to be paid in gold and all gold nuggets to be given to him?

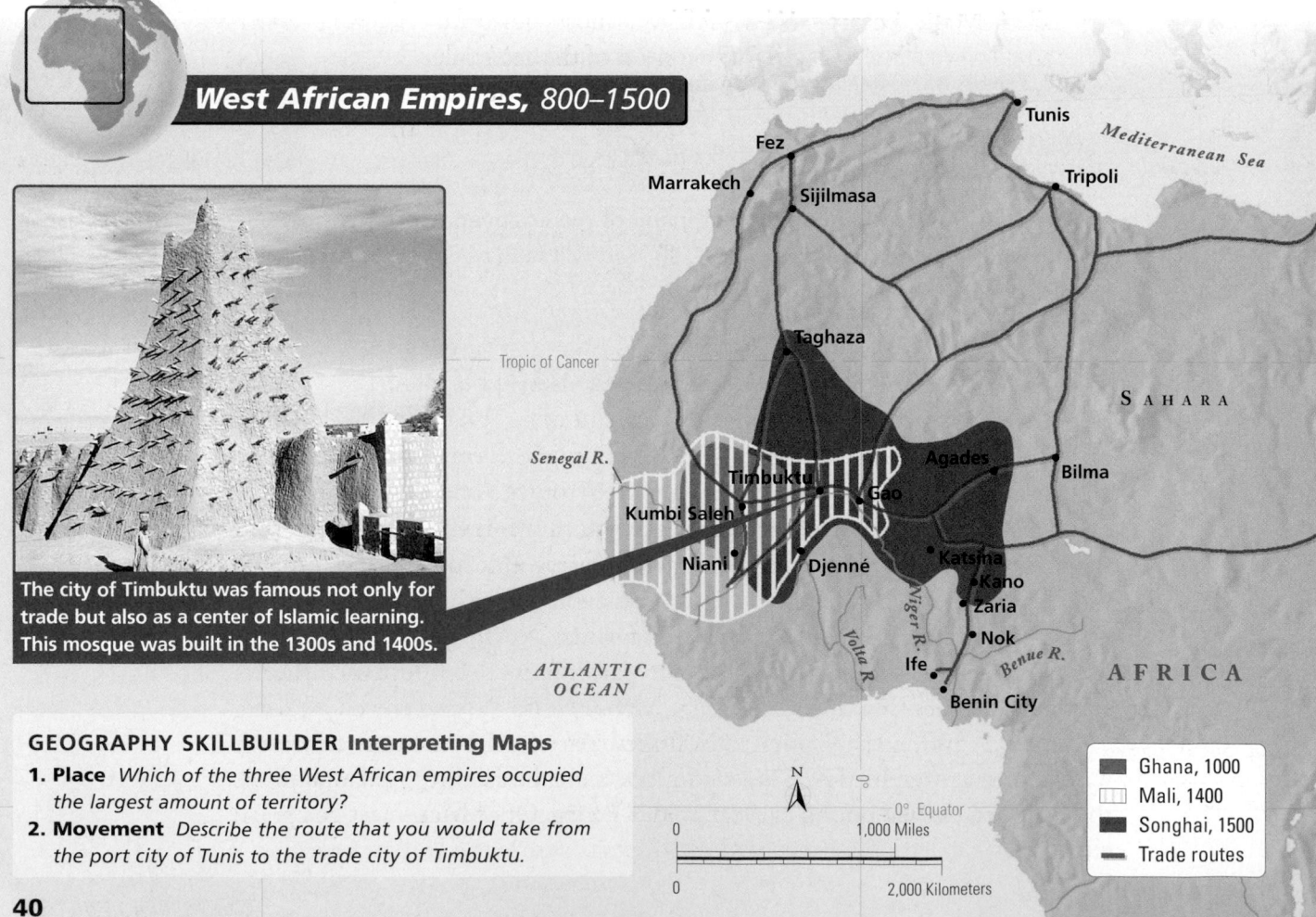

West African Empires, 800–1500

The city of Timbuktu was famous not only for trade but also as a center of Islamic learning. This mosque was built in the 1300s and 1400s.

Legend:
- ■ Ghana, 1000
- ▥ Mali, 1400
- ■ Songhai, 1500
- — Trade routes

GEOGRAPHY SKILLBUILDER Interpreting Maps

1. **Place** Which of the three West African empires occupied the largest amount of territory?
2. **Movement** Describe the route that you would take from the port city of Tunis to the trade city of Timbuktu.

Islam Enters Ghana

Many of the traders who came to Ghana from North Africa were Muslims. **Muslims** are followers of the religion of Islam. Founded by the prophet Muhammad in the 600s, **Islam** teaches that there is one God, named Allah. Muslims must perform such duties as praying five times a day and making a pilgrimage to the holy city of Mecca in Arabia. Muslim traders crossing the Sahara brought Islam from North Africa to West Africa. Ghana's rulers allowed those Muslims to build mosques, or houses of worship, in Ghana's capital, Kumbi Saleh. In time, Ghana's rulers employed Muslims as advisers.

Vocabulary
pilgrimage: a trip to a holy place

The Muslim empires of North Africa wanted to convert Ghana's people to Islam and to control Ghana's gold trade. In 1076, a Muslim army conquered Kumbi Saleh. This lessened Ghana's power. A number of local leaders took advantage of Ghana's weakness. They built up their own small states on the edges of the once mighty empire. Ghana never regained its former strength.

Over the next several centuries, more and more West Africans converted to Islam. In fact, many of the enslaved Africans who were brought to the Americas were Muslims.

Mali Replaces Ghana

By the 1200s, another West African kingdom had taken over most of Ghana's territory. This kingdom, called **Mali,** became West Africa's most powerful state. Its wealth also came from control of the gold-salt trade. But because it was located farther south than Ghana, Mali was better able to control the trade on the upper Niger River. (Ancient Mali stretched farther west than modern Mali and not as far north.)

Mali's first great ruler, Sundiata (sun•JAHT•ah), reigned from about 1230 to 1255. He came to power by crushing a cruel, unpopular leader. Sundiata's armies conquered many important trading cities. This made Mali's hold on trade stronger and made Mali more prosperous. Sundiata was a Muslim, but he did not force his people to accept Islam. Most of the people of Mali retained their traditional African beliefs.

A European mapmaker placed this picture of Mansa Musa on a map in 1375. It was drawn from his imagination.

Vocabulary
devout: very religious

Mali's other great leader was Mansa Musa (MAHN•sah moo•SAH), who was a devout Muslim. Mansa Musa came to the throne in 1312. Under his leadership, the empire became one of the largest in the world.

*Reading*History
B. Making Inferences How do you think the Egyptians reacted to Mansa Musa's caravan?

Mansa Musa is best remembered for making the Muslim pilgrimage to Mecca in 1324 and 1325. On his way to Mecca, he stopped in Cairo, Egypt. According to some stories, Mansa Musa entered the city leading a huge caravan that included 500 servants who waved staffs decorated with gold. Each of the 80 camels in his caravan struggled under the weight of a 300-pound sack of gold. The legend of Mali's wealth spread

all the way to Europe. This was one reason that Europeans began to trade with Africa about 150 years later.

On his return to Mali, Mansa Musa brought back many Muslim scholars, artists, and architects. They helped spread Islamic culture and learning throughout the empire. The city of Timbuktu (TIHM•buhk•TOO) in eastern Mali became a leading center of trade and Islamic learning. After Mansa Musa's death in 1337, Mali slowly grew weaker.

The Empire of Songhai

As Mali's power decreased, the **Songhai** (SAWNG•HY) people living at the Great Bend in the Niger River broke away from its control. In 1464, under the leader Sunni Ali, they began their own empire. Sunni Ali was a Muslim, but he also practiced the traditional Songhai religion.

Under Sunni Ali, the Songhai captured the great city of Timbuktu. Then they put the important trading city of Djenné (jeh•NAY) under siege and captured it after seven years. In addition to conquering territory, Sunni Ali set up an organized system of government.

After Sunni Ali died in 1492, conflicts arose. Some Muslims began a rebellion because they wanted Islam to be the only religion of Songhai. The leader of the revolt was Askia Muhammad, a devoted Muslim.

Askia Muhammad won his fight and became Songhai's second great ruler. For 35 years, he ably governed the empire. He chose capable officials who made the government run smoothly. He also expanded trade and set up an efficient tax system. Askia Muhammad used his wealth to build mosques and support Muslim scholars.

After Askia Muhammad's reign, several weak rulers succeeded him. Even when a strong ruler took the throne again, the empire faced problems. In spite of Songhai's wealth and learning, it lacked modern weapons. In 1591, a Moroccan fighting force from North Africa invaded Songhai with gunpowder and cannon. They easily defeated Songhai's soldiers, who were defending their empire with swords and spears.

AFRICAN HERITAGE

One way many African Americans show pride in their heritage is by wearing kente cloth. Kente cloth, shown below, is a colorful fabric woven by the Akan and Ewe people of Ghana.

Some African Americans celebrate the holiday of Kwanzaa in December. Based on traditional African harvest festivals, Kwanzaa lasts a week. Each day honors a value held by Africans: unity, self-determination, collective responsibility, cooperative economics, purpose, creativity, and faith.

Vocabulary
siege: surrounding a castle or city with an army until it surrenders

Reading **History**
C. Recognizing Effects How would Askia Muhammad's actions promote Islam in Songhai?

Other West African Kingdoms

As empires rose and fell in some parts of West Africa, small city-states arose in other parts of the region. The **Hausa** (HOW•suh) states emerged after A.D. 1000 in what is now northern Nigeria. Hausa city-states, such as Katsina and Kano, thrived on trade. Although the Hausa people shared a language, their city-states were independent of each other.

The **Yoruba** (YAWR•uh•buh) lived in the forests southwest of the Niger River. Ife and Oyo, the largest Yoruba states, had kings

who were considered to be partly divine. The Yoruba were mostly farmers, but they also had gifted artists, who carved wood and ivory and cast metal sculptures. Yoruba statues are still considered great art.

Another kingdom famous for its art was Benin. **Benin,** located in the delta of the Niger River, lay on main trade routes and prospered because of that. The capital, Benin City, was large and surrounded by thick, earthen walls. About 1600, a Dutch visitor compared Benin City to his home city of Amsterdam in Europe.

Reading **History**

D. Analyzing Points of View Do you think Dapper's view of Benin City is positive or negative? Explain.

A VOICE FROM THE PAST

The houses in this town stand in good order, each one close and evenly placed with its neighbor, just as the houses in Holland stand. . . . The king's court is very great. It is built around many square-shaped yards.

Olfert Dapper, quoted in *Centuries of Greatness*

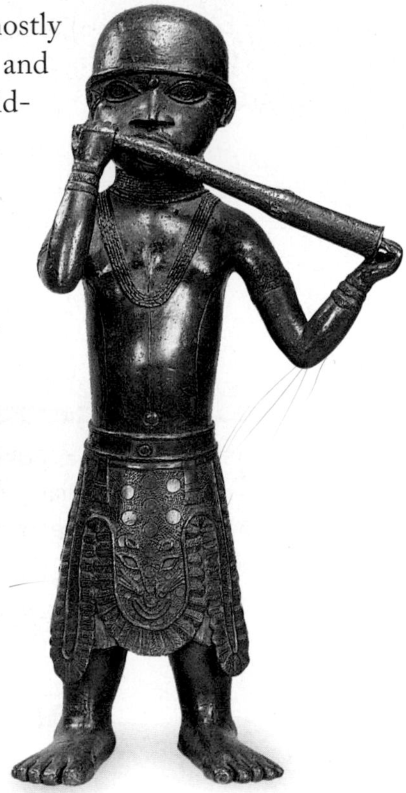

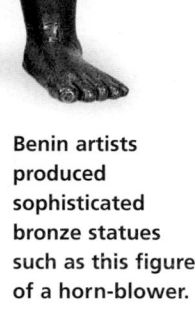

Benin artists produced sophisticated bronze statues such as this figure of a horn-blower.

In the late 1400s, Europeans reached Benin. Portuguese ships arrived, and the Portuguese set up a trade center near Benin City. Benin traders sold the Portuguese pepper, ivory, and leopard skins in exchange for copper and guns. In time, the Portuguese and other Europeans also began to trade for enslaved Africans. The Europeans who came to West Africa were not seeking information about its rich history or culture. They wanted a supply of laborers to work on large farms, called plantations. Chapter 2 explains more about plantations and slavery.

Trade was just one reason Europeans were sailing far beyond their lands. Social changes were also spurring them to explore the world. Those changes are discussed in Section 4.

Section 3 *Assessment*

1. Terms & Names

Explain the significance of:

- Ghana
- Muslims
- Islam
- Mali
- Songhai
- Hausa
- Yoruba
- Benin

2. Using Graphics

Compare the Ghana Empire and the Mali Empire using a Venn diagram like the one shown.

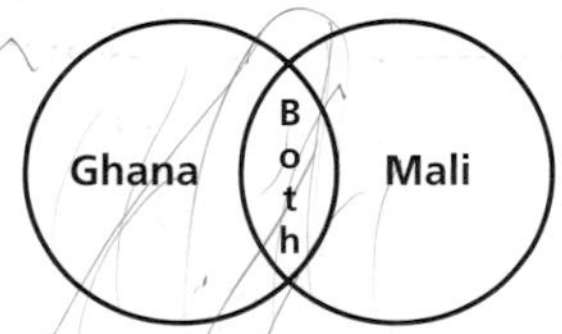

How was the influence of Islam different in each?

3. Main Ideas

a. How did Ghana's ruler benefit from controlling the gold-salt trade?

b. How did Islam spread within West Africa?

c. For what artistic achievements are the Yoruba and the people of Benin known?

4. Critical Thinking

Identifying Facts and Opinions Is the description of Benin City above mainly a statement of fact or opinion?

THINK ABOUT

- whether Dapper's statement can be proven by measurement or observation
- whether his statement expresses his own bias

ACTIVITY OPTIONS

SPEECH

GEOGRAPHY

Retell Mansa Musa's famous journey as an **oral history** or create a **map** that shows the route you think he took from Mali to Mecca.

Societies of Europe

MAIN IDEA	WHY IT MATTERS NOW	TERMS & NAMES
By 1500, Europe was going through a period of social change that sparked interest in learning and exploration.	The changes taking place in Europe led to the exploration of the Americas.	European Middle Ages feudalism manor system Crusades	Renaissance printing press Reformation profit

ONE EUROPEAN'S STORY

Ermentrude gathered up a chicken and five eggs and went to see the steward. He was the man who managed the land where she lived for its owners. Ermentrude and her husband, Bodo, were farmers who worked on a small piece of a large estate owned by someone else.

Ermentrude gave the chicken and eggs to the steward as part of her rent. Then she hurried home to weave cloth and cook supper.

Ermentrude lived in the early 800s, but her life was typical of the way many Europeans lived for centuries. This section explains that way of life and how it had changed by 1500.

The peasants in this 11th-century drawing are probably plowing land owned by someone else. European peasants like Ermentrude hardly ever left the manor where they lived.

Taking Notes

Use your chart to take notes about Europe.

	Trade
AMERICAS	
WEST AFRICA	
EUROPE	

Feudalism in Europe

Ermentrude lived in the **European Middle Ages,** which lasted from the late 400s, when the Western Roman Empire ended, to about the 1300s. (In some parts of Europe, the Middle Ages lasted to the 1400s.) The Romans used written laws and a mighty army to keep order. But over time, the empire grew weak. Germanic tribes from the east and north invaded the empire and contributed to its fall. The rough, uneducated Germanic tribes destroyed the strong Roman government and trade networks, and the tribes set up small kingdoms. With no trade, people stopped using money. They paid in goods, such as chickens and eggs.

Other groups also disrupted Europe. During the 800s to 1000s, Vikings swept down from the north. From their warships, they carried out lightning raids, looting villages and then racing back out to sea. To survive such difficult times, Europeans turned to feudalism. **Feudalism** is a political system in which a king allows nobles, or lords, to use lands

that belong to him. In return, the lords owe the king military service and protection for the people living on the land.

*Reading*History

A. Identifying Problems What problems were Europeans trying to solve with feudalism and the manor system?

Along with feudalism, Europeans developed the **manor system.** In this system, lords divided their lands into manors, or large estates, that were farmed mostly by serfs. Serfs were landless peasants who weren't allowed to leave the manor. In return for the serfs' work, the lord promised to protect them. The lords built heavily walled castles where people could go in times of danger.

The Roman Catholic Church also gained power during these uncertain times. Taking on the roles once filled by government officials, the Church collected taxes, aided the sick, and punished criminals. It became a powerful, unifying force throughout Europe.

Revival of Trade and Towns

By the 1000s, feudalism had brought more stability to society. As strong lords gained more control over their lands, long periods of peace and security followed. Merchants once again felt safe to travel. New farming methods, such as better ways to plant and plow fields, led to a food surplus. With more to eat, the population increased. More people meant more demand for goods, which spurred trade. Old towns near busy trade routes revived, and new towns grew up near manor houses and churches. Money came back into use.

Vocabulary
craftspeople: those who work in skilled trades

As the economy grew, many serfs ran away to towns. Some became craftspeople who practiced such trades as shoemaking. Others became merchants who sold the goods that craftspeople made. Merchants and craftspeople formed a new social class, the middle class. They had fewer riches, rights, and privileges than lords, but far more freedom than they had known as serfs.

Trade with the East

Trade increased, not only within Europe, but also with places outside Europe. Located on the Mediterranean, Italy had an advantage in this trade. Italian cities such as Venice traded with other port cities, such as Constantinople, located in what is now Turkey.

*Reading*History

B. Recognizing Effects What effect did the Crusades have on Italian trade?

War also spurred trade. Many European Christians were angry that Muslims held the Holy Land, where Jesus had lived. In 1096, European Christians launched the **Crusades,** a series of wars to capture the Holy Land. They ultimately failed to keep the Holy Land, but the Crusades changed European life. Italians supplied the ships that carried Crusaders to the Middle East. On the return trip, the ships brought Asian goods to Europe. These goods had traveled across the Indian Ocean and then overland to the Mediterranean.

STRANGE *but* True

PEPPER MILLIONAIRES
Europeans were desperate to get spices, such as pepper and cloves. Before refrigeration, meat often spoiled. Spices helped disguise the taste of rotten meat.

In the 1500s, just one shipload of spices could make a merchant wealthy for life. The average working person would have to work at least 1,000 years to earn as much as a merchant could earn from one load of pepper!

45

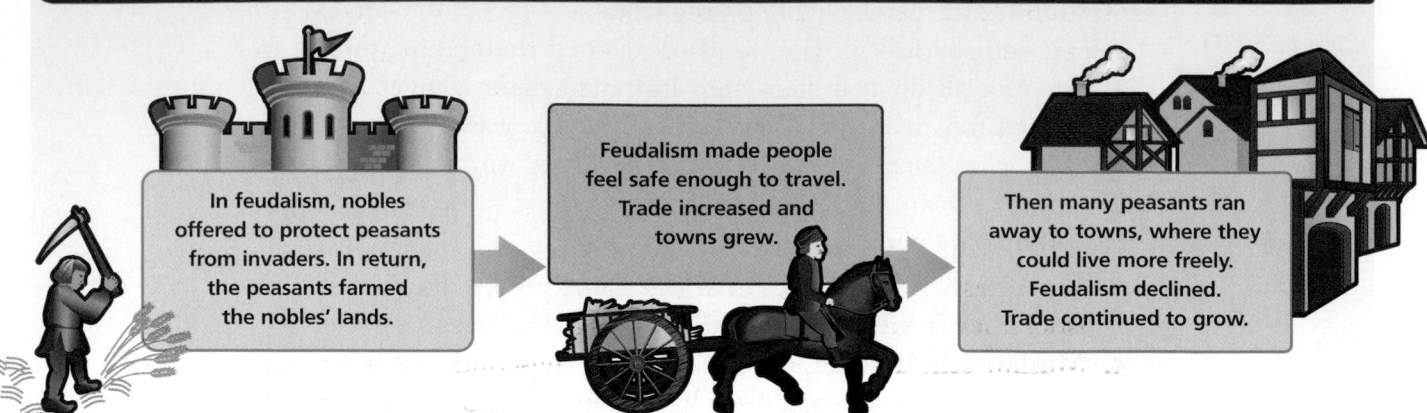

In feudalism, nobles offered to protect peasants from invaders. In return, the peasants farmed the nobles' lands.

Feudalism made people feel safe enough to travel. Trade increased and towns grew.

Then many peasants ran away to towns, where they could live more freely. Feudalism declined. Trade continued to grow.

After the Crusades, Italians continued to trade with Muslims in other Mediterranean cities.

An Italian merchant named Marco Polo also stirred European curiosity about distant lands. Polo had spent 24 years traveling in China and central Asia. A book written about Polo's travels described China's riches and wonders. It increased European interest in Asia.

The Decline of Feudalism

The growth of trade and towns weakened feudalism because so many serfs left the manors for town life. The power of the lords shrank because they had fewer people under their control. Beginning in 1347, a deadly disease also weakened feudalism. The bubonic plague swept across Europe, killing about one-fourth of the population and reducing the number of workers. Lords competed for the laborers who survived, so they began to pay wages to peasants, such as John of Cayworth.

A VOICE FROM THE PAST

John of Cayworth . . . ought to carry in autumn beans or oats for 2 days with a cart and 3 animals of his own, the value of the work being 12 denarii [about a penny]. And he shall receive from the lord each day 3 meals.

Contract of John of Cayworth, from *Readings in European History*

As feudal lords lost power, kings grew stronger. They won the support of townspeople because they could raise large armies to enforce order. In return, townspeople agreed to support their kings by paying taxes. The armies enforced order and imposed the king's authority over lesser lords. As countries became safer, trade flourished even more.

Reading **History**

C. Analyzing Causes What three causes led to the decline of feudalism?

The Renaissance and Reformation

Italy, which was thriving because of trade, became the birthplace of the **Renaissance**—a time of increased interest in art and learning. *Renaissance* is a French term meaning "rebirth." Lasting from the 1300s to 1600, the Renaissance spread from Italy throughout Europe.

Several forces led to this rebirth of learning. As feudalism weakened and the plague brought great suffering, Europeans began to question

what life meant. In their search for new answers, some people turned to old sources. They read the writings and studied the art of the Greeks and Romans. The classical Greeks and Romans lived from about 750 B.C. to A.D. 476. As a result of these studies, European ideas changed.

Vocabulary
philosophy: the study of the meaning of life

1. The Greeks had praised human achievement. European scholars began humanism, the study of human worth, ideas, and potential.
2. Classical education stressed such subjects as history, philosophy, and literature. Europeans spent more time studying those subjects.
3. From classical art, European artists learned to make art more realistic. They created some of the world's finest paintings and statues.
4. Muslim scholars had saved classical manuscripts about science. Also, Muslim mathematicians had invented algebra. Contact with Muslim societies influenced European science and mathematics.

Background
A printing press uses movable type—blocks of metal or wood that have raised characters. The Chinese invented movable type in about 1045. Gutenberg re-invented it.

A new invention helped spread Renaissance ideas. In about 1455, a German named Johannes Gutenberg invented the **printing press,** a machine that mechanically prints pages. People no longer had to copy books by hand. Printers could make hundreds of copies of a book cheaply and accurately. More people read, and ideas spread quickly.

By the early 1500s, Renaissance ideas and other forces weakened the Catholic Church. Many church leaders were corrupt. Some claimed to grant God's forgiveness for money. Martin Luther, a German monk, publicly posted 95 statements that criticized such practices. This began the **Reformation,** a movement to correct problems in the Church.

The Reformation split the Church into two groups—Catholics and Protestants. In time, Protestants divided into many different churches.

HISTORY *through* ART

This painting, _School of Athens_ by Raphael, shows many aspects of Renaissance art and culture.
- Like much Renaissance art, it looks more realistic than the art of the Middle Ages. (See page 44 for comparison.)
- It honors the Greek thinkers Aristotle and Plato, who are the two men in the center arch.
- It also honors Renaissance artists. Raphael himself is in the group to the right.

Why might Raphael have wanted to include himself in a painting with famous Greeks?

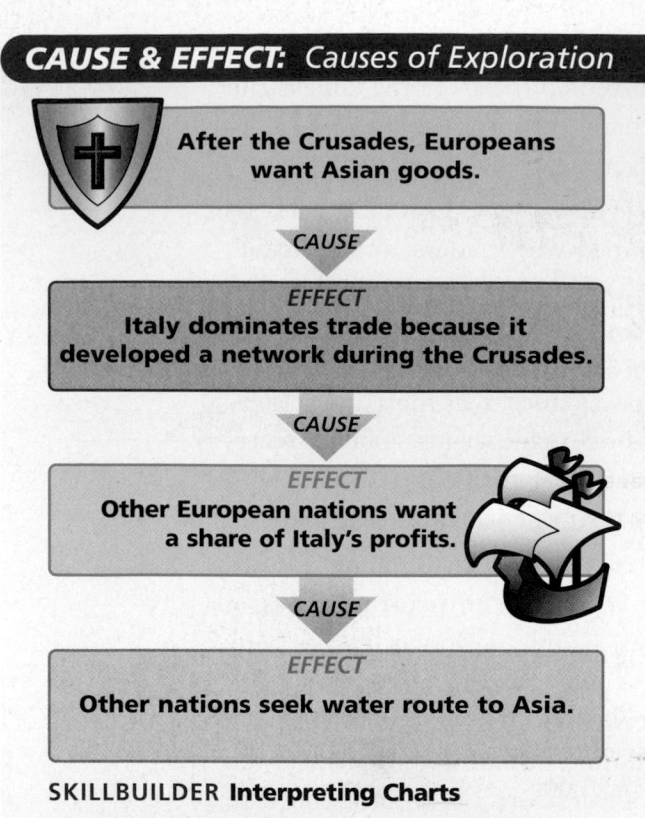

CAUSE & EFFECT: Causes of Exploration

After the Crusades, Europeans want Asian goods.

CAUSE

EFFECT
Italy dominates trade because it developed a network during the Crusades.

CAUSE

EFFECT
Other European nations want a share of Italy's profits.

CAUSE

EFFECT
Other nations seek water route to Asia.

SKILLBUILDER Interpreting Charts
What economic activity was the primary cause of exploration?

When European colonists came to America, they carried their religious disagreements and hopes for religious freedom with them.

Changes in Trade

The Renaissance period saw not only changes in learning and religion, but also in trade. As trade grew, Italian merchants needed to improve the way they did business. They began to use more exact ways of keeping track of a business's income and its costs. By subtracting the costs from the income, the merchants determined the **profit**.

Italian merchants made huge profits by trading in Asian goods. Because Italians had done business with Muslims for centuries, they had a special relationship. In addition to that, the Italians used military strength to control the trade on the Mediterranean—and didn't allow other Europeans to take part in it.

Merchants in other European countries envied the profits made by Italian merchants. As a result, other Europeans began to want a share of the rich trade in Asian goods. They had to find different routes to Asia from the ones controlled by the Italians and Muslims. Other European countries began to search for a non-Mediterranean water route to Asia, as you will read in Section 5.

Reading **History**
D. Making Generalizations
If a country tries to completely dominate trade in a certain area, how will other countries respond?

Section 4 Assessment

1. Terms & Names

Explain the significance of:
- European Middle Ages
- feudalism
- manor system
- Crusades
- Renaissance
- printing press
- Reformation
- profit

2. Using Graphics

On a chart like this one, list how the Renaissance changed art and learning.

Changes to Art and Learning
•
•
•
•

3. Main Ideas

a. What caused feudalism to develop?

b. What led to the revival of trade and towns?

c. How did Italy come to control European trade with Asia?

4. Critical Thinking

Contrasting How did the Renaissance differ from the European Middle Ages?

THINK ABOUT
- the economy
- how power was distributed
- the authority of the church

ACTIVITY OPTIONS

TECHNOLOGY

MUSIC

Design a **Web site** or compose a **song** advertising the great new Renaissance invention—the printing press.

Early European Explorers

MAIN IDEA	WHY IT MATTERS NOW	TERMS & NAMES
As Europeans searched for sea routes to Asia, Christopher Columbus reached the Americas.	Columbus's journey permanently linked the Americas to the rest of the world.	navigator Christopher Columbus caravel

ONE EUROPEAN'S STORY

Sailors seeking a route to Asia depended on the skill of their navigator. A **navigator** plans the course of a ship by using instruments to find its position. In the 1400s, Portugal had a famous prince called Henry the Navigator. Yet, Henry wasn't a navigator. He lived at Sagres, on the southwestern coast of Portugal. In this town, he began a school of navigation.

Henry decided to organize and pay for sailing expeditions to explore the Atlantic and the west coast of Africa. He was hoping to find African gold, to learn more about geography, and to spread Christianity. His ships traveled farther down the African coast than Europeans had ever gone. Because Henry sponsored the voyages, the English named him "the navigator." As you will read in this section, those voyages began Europe's age of discovery.

Henry the Navigator sponsored voyages that helped Portugal find a water route to Asia.

A Water Route to Asia

Under Prince Henry, the Portuguese developed an improved ship called the **caravel**. The caravel had triangular sails as well as square sails. Square sails carried the ship forward when the wind was at its back. Triangular sails allowed the caravel to sail into the wind. The caravel was better than other European ships of the time at sailing into the wind.

In January 1488, the Portuguese explorer Bartolomeu Dias (DEE•uhs) reached the southern tip of Africa. After sailing around it, he returned to Portugal at the urging of his crew. Portugal's king named the tip the Cape of Good Hope because he hoped they had found a route to Asia.

Ten years later, another Portuguese explorer, Vasco da Gama, followed Dias's route around the cape. He continued north along the eastern coast of Africa. Then he sailed east across the Indian Ocean to India. At last, someone had found an all-water route to Asia.

Taking Notes

Use your chart to take notes about European explorers.

	Trade	
AMERICAS		
WEST AFRICA		
EUROPE		

AMERICA'S HISTORY MAKERS

CHRISTOPHER COLUMBUS
1451–1506

Christopher Columbus's son Ferdinand wrote that his father "took to the sea at the age of 14 and followed it ever after."

Columbus's early voyages nearly cost him his life. When he was 25, pirates off the coast of Portugal sank his ship. Columbus survived by grabbing a floating oar and swimming to shore.

But he also learned a lot from sailing on Portuguese ships. The sailors taught Columbus about Atlantic wind patterns. This knowledge later helped him on his history-making voyage.

What character traits, shown in Columbus's early life, might have made him a good leader?

That route meant that the Portuguese could now trade with Asia without dealing with the Muslims or Italians. Portugal took control of the valuable spice trade. The merchants of Lisbon, Portugal's capital, grew rich. Spain and other European rivals wanted to take part in this profitable trade. They began to look for their own water routes to Asia.

Columbus's Plan

By the time of da Gama's voyage, an Italian sailor named **Christopher Columbus** thought he knew a faster way to reach Asia. Europeans had known for centuries that the earth is round. Columbus decided that instead of sailing around Africa and then east, he would sail west across the Atlantic. He calculated that it would be a short journey.

But Columbus made several mistakes. First, he relied on the writings of two people—Marco Polo and a geographer named Paolo Toscanelli—who were wrong about the size of Asia. They claimed that Asia stretched farther from west to east than it really did.

Second, Columbus underestimated the distance around the globe. He thought the earth was only two thirds as large as it actually is! Because of Polo and Toscanelli, Columbus thought that Asia took up most of that distance. Therefore, he believed that the Atlantic Ocean must be small. And a voyage west to Asia would be short.

In 1483, Columbus asked the king of Portugal to finance a voyage across the Atlantic. The king's advisers opposed the plan. They argued that Columbus had miscalculated the distance to Asia. They also reminded the king of the progress that Portuguese explorers had made sailing down the coast of Africa looking for a route to Asia. The advisers persuaded the king not to finance the voyage. So in 1486, Columbus turned to Portugal's rival, Spain.

Help from Spain's Rulers

Spain's rulers, King Ferdinand and Queen Isabella, liked Columbus's plan because they wanted a share of the rich Asian trade. As a strong Catholic, the Queen also welcomed a chance to spread Christianity. But there were also reasons not to support Columbus. First, a royal council had doubts about Columbus's calculations and advised Ferdinand and Isabella not to finance him. Second, the Spanish monarchs were in the middle of a costly war to drive the Muslims out of Spain. Third, Columbus was asking a high payment for his services.

The years of waiting had made Columbus determined to profit from his explorations. As a reward for his efforts, he demanded the high title

Reading **History**

A. Comparing Compare what happened after Portugal began to control the spice trade to what happened when Italy controlled it.

Background As you read in Section 4, Marco Polo's book about his travels had increased European interest in Asia.

Vocabulary **monarch:** a king or queen

Admiral of the Ocean Sea and a percentage of any wealth he brought from Asia. He also expected to be made the ruler of the lands he found.

Finally in January of 1492, the Spanish conquered the last Muslim stronghold in Spain. The Spanish monarchs could now afford to finance Columbus but still had doubts about doing so. Columbus left the palace to return home. But after listening to a trusted adviser, the king and queen changed their minds and sent a rider on horseback to bring Columbus back. He and the rulers finally reached an agreement.

Reading **History**

B. Drawing Conclusions Did this agreement give Columbus what he was asking for? Explain.

A VOICE FROM THE PAST

Your Highnesses . . . accorded me great rewards and ennobled me so that from that time henceforth I might . . . be high admiral of the Ocean Sea and perpetual Governor of the islands and continent which I should discover.

Christopher Columbus, letter to King Ferdinand and Queen Isabella

Preparing to sail, Columbus assembled his ships—the *Niña*, the *Pinta*, and the *Santa María*—at the port of Palos de la Frontera in southern Spain.

Setting Sail

At first, Columbus had trouble finding a crew. Then a respected local shipowner agreed to sign on as captain of the *Pinta*. Other crew members soon followed. About 90 men loaded the ships with enough food for one year, casks of fresh water, firewood, and other necessities.

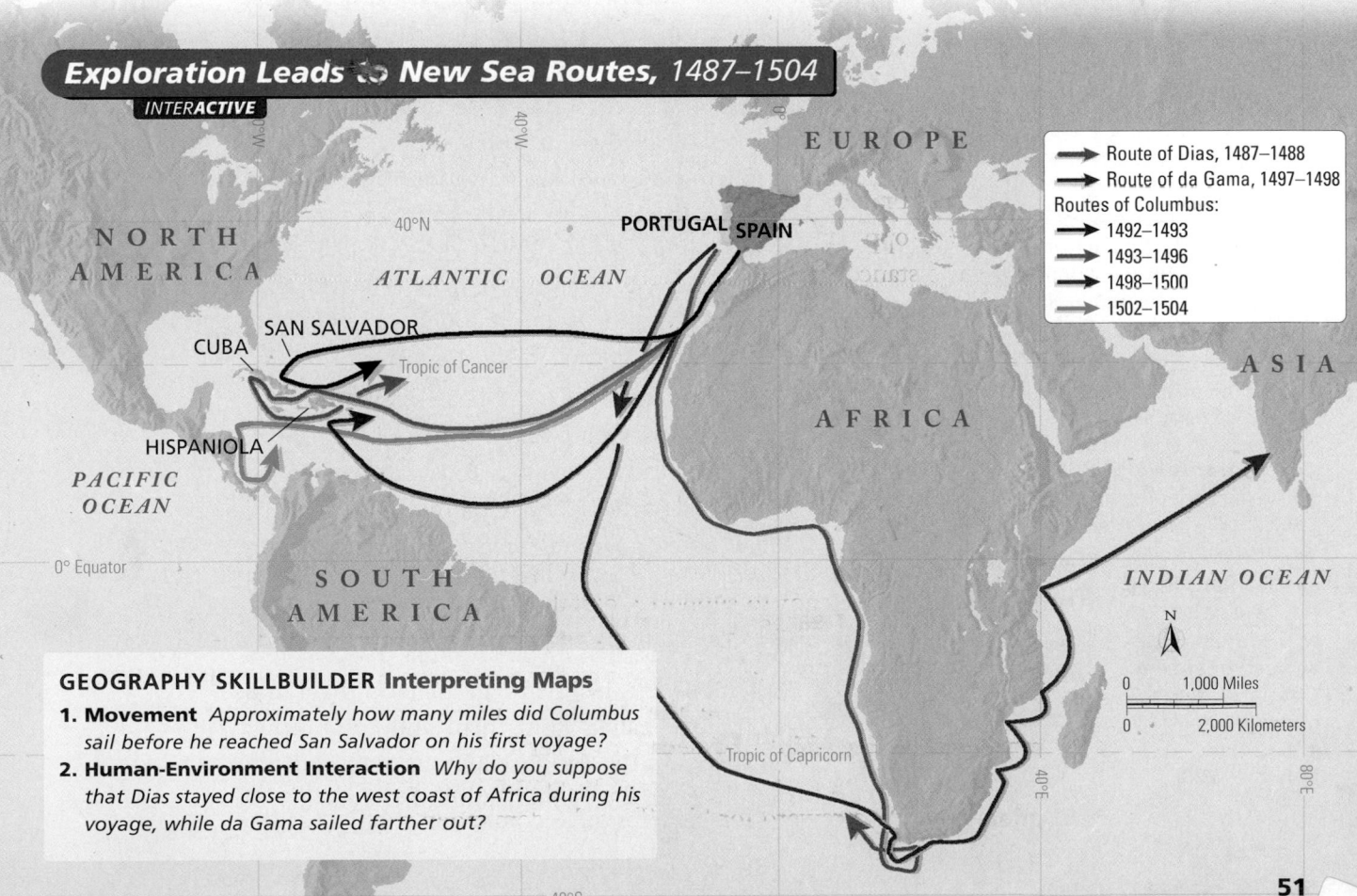

Exploration Leads to New Sea Routes, *1487–1504*

INTER**ACTIVE**

→ Route of Dias, 1487–1488
→ Route of da Gama, 1497–1498
Routes of Columbus:
→ 1492–1493
→ 1493–1496
→ 1498–1500
→ 1502–1504

EUROPE

PORTUGAL SPAIN

NORTH AMERICA

ATLANTIC OCEAN

ASIA

SAN SALVADOR

CUBA

AFRICA

HISPANIOLA

PACIFIC OCEAN

0° Equator

SOUTH AMERICA

INDIAN OCEAN

N

0   1,000 Miles
0   2,000 Kilometers

Tropic of Cancer

Tropic of Capricorn

GEOGRAPHY SKILLBUILDER Interpreting Maps

1. **Movement** *Approximately how many miles did Columbus sail before he reached San Salvador on his first voyage?*
2. **Human-Environment Interaction** *Why do you suppose that Dias stayed close to the west coast of Africa during his voyage, while da Gama sailed farther out?*

The tiny fleet of wooden ships glided out of the harbor on August 3, 1492. First they sailed southwest toward the Canary Islands off the northwest coast of Africa. From there, Columbus was relying on trade winds that blew toward the west to speed his ships across the ocean.

Once aboard ship, Columbus kept a log, or daily record of each day's sailing. In fact, he kept two logs. One he showed to his men and one he kept secret. Columbus's secret log recorded the truth about the journey.

> ### A VOICE FROM THE PAST
>
> [We] made 15 leagues [this] day and . . . [I] decided to report less than those actually traveled so in case the voyage were long the men would not be frightened and lose courage.
>
> **Christopher Columbus,** quoted in *Columbus and the Age of Discovery*

Reading **History**

C. Analyzing Causes What caused Columbus to decide to keep two logs?

By October 10, the men had lost both courage and confidence in their leader. They had been at sea for almost ten weeks and had not seen land for over a month. Afraid that they would starve if the trip went on longer, they talked of returning home. To avoid mutiny, Columbus and the crew struck a bargain. The men agreed to sail on for three more days, and Columbus promised to turn back if they had not sighted land by then. Two days later in the early morning hours of October 12, a sailor on the *Pinta* called out "Tierra, tierra" [Land, land].

Reaching the Americas

By noon, the ships had landed on an island in the Caribbean Sea. Columbus believed that he had reached the Indies, islands in Southeast Asia where spices grew. The islanders who greeted Columbus and his men were Taino (TY•noh) people, but Columbus mistakenly called them Indians.

Columbus named the island San Salvador. After unfurling the royal banner and flags, he ordered his crew to "bear witness that I was taking possession of this island for the King and Queen." Eager to reach the rich country of Japan, which he believed was nearby, he left San Salvador. He took six or seven Taino with him as guides. For the next three months, he visited several of the Caribbean islands.

Finally, he reached an island that he named Española, which we call Hispaniola today. (See map on page 51.) On that island, Columbus and his men found some gold and precious objects such as pearls. This convinced Columbus that he had reached Asia. He decided to return home, leaving 39 of his men on Hispaniola. Even before Columbus left, his men had angered the Taino people by stealing from them and committing violence. By the time Columbus returned ten months later, the Taino had killed the men.

Background
Today, the Indies are called the East Indies. The islands of the Caribbean are called the West Indies.

NATIVE AMERICAN VIEW OF COLUMBUS

In 1992, many Native Americans protested the 500th anniversary of Columbus's voyage. Suzan Shown Harjo, who is Cheyenne and Creek, explained why.

As Native American peoples in this red quarter of Mother Earth, we have no reason to celebrate an invasion that caused the demise [death] of so many of our people and is still causing destruction today.

The Spanish enslaved the Taino, who nearly all died from disease and bad treatment. This statue is one of the few Taino artifacts left from the 1500s.

In January 1493, he sailed back to Spain. Firmly believing that he had found a new water route to Asia, he wrote to Ferdinand and Isabella. The Spanish rulers called him to the royal court to report on his voyage. Neither Columbus nor the king and queen suspected that he had landed near continents entirely unknown to Europeans.

A French map-maker uses an instrument to learn his exact position on the globe.

An Expanding Horizon

Columbus made three more voyages to the Americas, but never brought back the treasures he had promised Spain's rulers. He also failed to meet Queen Isabella's other goal. She wanted Christianity brought to new people. When she learned that Columbus had mistreated and enslaved the people of Hispaniola, she became angry.

After the fourth voyage, Spain's rulers refused to give Columbus any more help. He died in 1506, still believing he had reached Asia and bitter that he had not received the fame or fortune that he deserved.

In time, the geographic knowledge Columbus brought back changed European views of the world. People soon realized that Columbus had reached continents that had been unknown to them previously. And Europeans were eager to see if these continents could make them rich.

*Reading*History
D. Making Inferences How did the Atlantic become a bridge connecting Europe, Africa, and the Americas?

For centuries, Europeans had seen the ocean as a barrier. With one voyage, Columbus changed that. Instead of a barrier, the Atlantic Ocean became a bridge that connected Europe, Africa, and the Americas. As you will learn in Chapter 2, Columbus's explorations began an era of great wealth and power for Spain. As Spain grew rich, England, France, and other European countries also began to send ships to the Americas.

Section 5 Assessment

1. Terms & Names

Explain the significance of:
- navigator
- caravel
- Christopher Columbus

2. Using Graphics

On a diagram like the one shown, list the effects of Columbus's voyages.

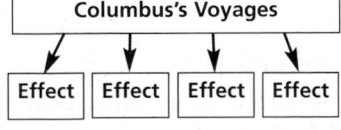

Columbus's Voyages

Effect | Effect | Effect | Effect

Which effects were negative and which were positive?

3. Main Ideas

a. Why was Prince Henry eager to find an all-water route to Asia?

b. Why did Spain's king and queen decide to support Columbus's first voyage?

c. Why was Columbus disappointed by the outcome of his four voyages to the Americas?

4. Critical Thinking

Analyzing Points of View Explain how each of the following people might have viewed Columbus's first voyage. Give reasons for their points of view.

THINK ABOUT
- Columbus
- Queen Isabella
- a Taino chief

ACTIVITY OPTIONS

GEOGRAPHY

MATH

Use the map on page 51. Create an enlarged **map** of Columbus's first voyage, or measure the distance of each voyage to list on a **table**.

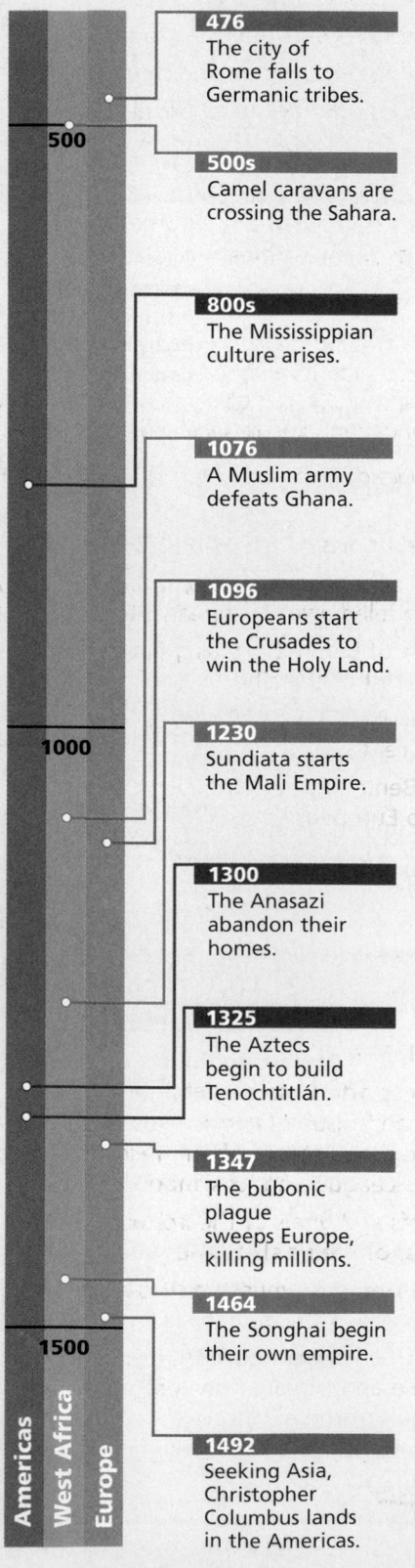

VISUAL SUMMARY

The World in 1500

476
The city of Rome falls to Germanic tribes.

500

500s
Camel caravans are crossing the Sahara.

800s
The Mississippian culture arises.

1076
A Muslim army defeats Ghana.

1096
Europeans start the Crusades to win the Holy Land.

1000

1230
Sundiata starts the Mali Empire.

1300
The Anasazi abandon their homes.

1325
The Aztecs begin to build Tenochtitlán.

1347
The bubonic plague sweeps Europe, killing millions.

1464
The Songhai begin their own empire.

1500

1492
Seeking Asia, Christopher Columbus lands in the Americas.

Americas West Africa Europe

TERMS & NAMES

Briefly explain the significance of each of the following.

1. migrate
2. civilization
3. technology
4. Iroquois League
5. Islam
6. feudalism
7. Crusades
8. Renaissance
9. navigator
10. Christopher Columbus

REVIEW QUESTIONS

Crossing to the Americas (pages 27–31)

1. What are two theories about migration to the Americas?
2. For what purposes did the Mound Builders construct earthen mounds?

Societies of North America (pages 32–38)

3. What enabled the Aztecs to become a strong empire?
4. How did the Iroquois League come about?

Societies of West Africa (pages 39–43)

5. What enabled Ghana, Mali, and Songhai all to grow rich?
6. Did Islam become more or less influential in West Africa from the 700s to the 1400s? Explain.

Societies of Europe (pages 44–48)

7. How did the manor system work during the Middle Ages?
8. How did the Crusades increase European interest in trade?

Early European Explorers (pages 49–53)

9. Why did non-Italian Europeans seek new trade routes to Asia?
10. How did Columbus miscalculate the distance to Asia?

CRITICAL THINKING

1. USING YOUR NOTES: CATEGORIZING INFORMATION

Using your completed chart, answer the questions below.

	Trade	Technology	Religion	Art
AMERICAS (Sections 1 and 2)				
WEST AFRICA (Section 3)				
EUROPE (Sections 4 and 5)				

a. What was one instance in which trade spread knowledge?
b. Which of the technologies that you listed are still used today?
c. What religions were practiced in each of the three regions?

2. ANALYZING LEADERSHIP

Do you think Columbus was a good leader or a bad one? Use details from the chapter to explain your answer.

3. THEME: DIVERSITY AND UNITY

How have Native Americans, Africans, and Europeans all influenced American culture? Give examples from your own experience.

4. MAKING GENERALIZATIONS

What types of goods are people most likely to seek through trade? Think about the trade goods mentioned in the chapter and why people wanted them.

5. APPLYING CITIZENSHIP SKILLS

Compare the Iroquois League to what you know of the U.S. government. How are they similar?

Interact *with* History

Think about the various encounters between societies mentioned in the chapter. What do you think happened when more Europeans came to the Americas and met Native Americans?

Use the map and your knowledge of U.S. history to answer questions 1 and 2.

Additional Test Practice, pp. S1–S33.

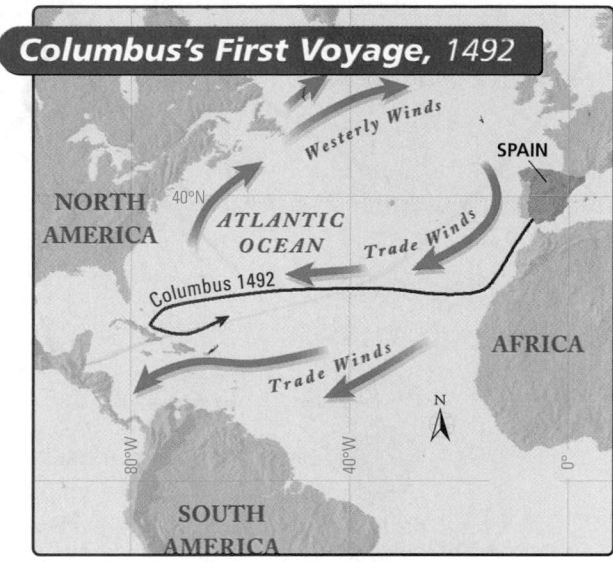

Columbus's First Voyage, 1492

NORTH AMERICA
40°N
ATLANTIC OCEAN
Westerly Winds
SPAIN
Trade Winds
Columbus 1492
Trade Winds
AFRICA
N
80°W
40°W
0°
SOUTH AMERICA

1. How did the winds affect Columbus's journey?
   A. The westerly winds across the Atlantic made the voyage faster.
   B. The trade winds across the Atlantic slowed down the voyage.
   C. The trade winds across the Atlantic made the voyage faster.
   D. The winds had little effect on Columbus's voyage.

2. If Columbus's route had been farther north, which of the following would have happened?
   A. The voyage would have taken less time.
   B. The voyage would have taken more time.
   C. The voyage would not have been different.
   D. The voyage would not have been possible.

This quotation from Olfert Dapper is about Benin City in Africa. Use this quotation and your knowledge of West Africa to answer question 3.

PRIMARY SOURCE

The houses in this town stand in good order, each one close and evenly placed with its neighbor, just as the houses in Holland stand . . . The king's court is very great. It is built around many square-shaped yards.

Olfert Dapper, *Centuries of Greatness*

3. The passage best supports which point of view?
   A. Benin City, and other African cities, should be unique, not modeled after European cities.
   B. The king's court of Benin City was great in contrast to the rest of the city.
   C. The design of Benin City made it an extremely valuable trade center.
   D. The design of Benin City was appealing in its resemblance to European cities.

TEST PRACTICE
CLASSZONE.COM

ALTERNATIVE ASSESSMENT

1. WRITING ABOUT HISTORY

Imagine you have been hired to write the **brochure** for a Native American exhibit at a museum.

- Choose a Native American group discussed in the chapter. Use library resources to learn more about the group.
- Highlight their economy, religion and spiritual beliefs, or arts and crafts in your exhibit. Write a description of the exhibit for your brochure that would encourage people to come.

2. COOPERATIVE LEARNING

Work with a group to create a radio program of Columbus's first voyage. Group members can find his log in the library, select parts to record, or create sound effects to play in the background.

INTEGRATED TECHNOLOGY

DOING INTERNET RESEARCH

Countries and alliances often use a symbol to represent who they are. The Iroquois League chose a tree as their symbol. Use the Internet and library resources to research the Iroquois League and its symbol.

- Research the beliefs and goals of the Iroquois League. Make a list of their beliefs and goals.
- Also search Native American museum sites and/or reservation sites in New York state.
- Describe why the tree was an appropriate symbol for the Iroquois League and explain how it represented the beliefs and goals of the alliance.

For more about the Iroquois League . . .

INTERNET ACTIVITY
CLASSZONE.COM

Create and Decode a Pictograph

Native Americans of the Southwest created thousands of images to communicate with each other. These images, known as pictographs, helped people recall certain events, ideas, or information. Even if the people who created them were no longer present, others could read the messages. Most images were painted or carved on the surfaces of rock. There are three types of pictographs: petroglyphs, petrograms, and geoglyphs. (See HELP DESK on the next page.)

ACTIVITY Create a pictograph that other students will decode, or figure out. Then, acting as an anthropologist, interview students in one other group about their pictograph.

TOOLBOX

Each group will need:

drawing paper or poster board

markers

regular and colored pencils

watercolor paints and brushes (optional)

an envelope

The Fremont culture carved this petroglyph. It is currently located in Dinosaur National Monument—most of which sits in northwestern Colorado.

STEP BY STEP

1 **Form a group of 4 or 5 students.** Together, think of a message to tell someone living in the future. What might you want future generations to know about your culture, or way of life? If you're having trouble coming up with a message, copy the chart below into your notebook. Write information for each category that you think would be interesting to future generations. Then choose one of these categories for your message.

Sports	
Politics	
Fashion	
Music	
Entertainment	
Weather	
Daily Life	

2 **Examine reference materials.** In the library or on the Internet, research Native American pictographs. Use the information you find to help start your project. (See HELP DESK on the next page.)

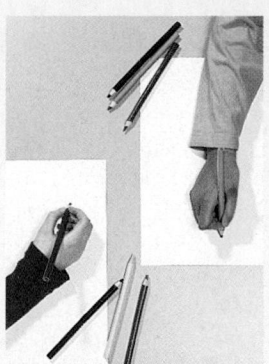

3 **Create your pictograph.** Communicate your message with symbols like the ones that you have researched. Sketch your pictograph on the drawing paper or poster board with a pencil first. Make the pictograph simple so that the decoders will understand your message. Remember to use symbols—not letters.

4 **Decorate your pictograph.** Use markers or watercolor paints to finish your pictograph. Also, record the translation of your pictograph in your notebook.

5 **Exchange your pictograph with another group of students.** Try to decode the message in the pictograph that the other group of students has given you. Write your translation and place it in your envelope. Give the envelope to the group whose pictograph you decoded.

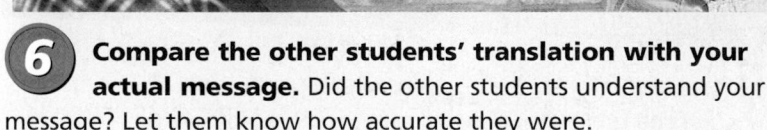

6 **Compare the other students' translation with your actual message.** Did the other students understand your message? Let them know how accurate they were.

WRITE AND SPEAK

Using the information in the pictograph that you decoded, write a description of the people who created the message. Use the symbols as well as the message itself to help you in your description. Explain to the class how you came to your conclusions.

 HELP DESK

For related information see Chapter 1, p. 29.

Researching Your Project

• *On the Trail of Spider Woman: Petroglyphs, Pictographs, and Myths of the Southwest* by Carol Patterson-Rudolph. Shows variety of actual pictographs.

• *21 Kinds of American Folk Art and How to Make Each One* by Jean and Cle Kinney. Explains process of making pictographs.

For more about pictographs . . .

 **RESEARCH LINKS**
CLASSZONE.COM

Did You Know?

Petroglyphs are images carved into a rock using stone tools. **Petrograms** are images painted on a rock. **Geoglyphs** are images formed on the ground by scraping away soil or by arranging stones to form an image.

REFLECT & ASSESS

• Which symbols in your pictograph were clear to the decoders? Which were not clear?

• What methods did you use to decode the messages of others?

• What did you learn about language and communication from doing this pictograph decoding activity?

CHAPTER 2

European Exploration of the Americas 1492–1700

Section 1
Spain Claims an Empire

Section 2
European Competition in North America

Section 3
The Spanish and Native Americans

Section 4
Beginnings of Slavery in the Americas

Ships in a harbor in Lisbon, Portugal, are preparing for a voyage of exploration.

Smaller boats ferry the crew to the sailing ships.

A crane loads supplies onto the ships, much like today.

1497
Cabot searches for Northwest Passage.

1521
Cortés conquers the Aztec Empire.

1535
Cartier leads expedition up St. Lawrence River.

1539–1542
Coronado, de Soto, and Cabrillo explore different parts of North America.

1565
Spanish found St. Augustine.

N. America
World · **1492**

1494
Spain and Portugal agree to Treaty of Tordesillas.

1534
English Parliament declares Henry VIII head of the English Church.

1542
King of Spain issues the New Laws for better treatment of Native Americans.

1588
English navy defeats Spanish Armada.

The year is 1510. You live in a European port town and have heard exciting tales about mysterious lands across the sea. You decide to join a voyage of exploration in search of fortune.

Would you join a voyage of exploration?

What Do You Think?

- What do you think led Europeans to explore distant lands?
- What reasons would make you want to join a voyage of exploration?
- What reasons would keep you from joining such a voyage?

RESEARCH LINKS
CLASSZONE.COM

Visit the Chapter 2 links for more information about exploration of the Americas.

1609
Hudson searches for Northwest Passage.

1626
Dutch buy Manhattan Island.

1680
Popé leads Pueblo Revolt and forces Spanish from New Mexico.

1700

1644
Manchus establish Qing Dynasty in China.

1651
English Parliament passes Navigation Act.

Reading Strategy: Finding Main Ideas

What Do You Know?

What comes to mind when someone uses the word *explorer*?
Why do you think people explored different territories?

Think About
- what you've learned about explorers from movies, school, or your parents
- reasons that people travel throughout the world today
- your responses to the Interact with History about joining a voyage of exploration (see page 59)

What Do You Want to Know?

 What questions do you have about exploration or the early colonization of the Americas? Write those questions in your notebook before you read the chapter.

Vasco Núñez de Balboa claims the Pacific Ocean for Spain.

Finding Main Ideas

To help you remember what you read, take notes about the events and ideas discussed in the chapter. Taking notes means writing down important information. The chart below lists the major events and ideas covered in the chapter. Use the chart to take notes about these important events and ideas.

S See Skillbuilder Handbook, page R3.

Taking Notes

Event/Idea	Notes
Exploration	
Establishing Colonies	
European Competition	
Columbian Exchange	
Origins of Slavery	

Spain Claims an Empire

MAIN IDEA	WHY IT MATTERS NOW	TERMS & NAMES
Spain claimed a large empire in the Americas.	The influence of Spanish culture remains strong in modern America.	Treaty of Tordesillas missionary mercantilism Amerigo Vespucci	*conquistador* Hernando Cortés Montezuma Francisco Pizarro

ONE EUROPEAN'S STORY

In 1493, the rulers of Spain and Portugal wanted Pope Alexander VI to decide who would control the lands that sailors from their countries were exploring.

In May 1493, Alexander VI issued his ruling. He drew an imaginary line around the world. It was called the Line of Demarcation. Portugal could claim all non-Christian lands to the east of the line. Spain could claim the non-Christian lands to the west. In this section, you will learn how Spain and Portugal led Europe in the race to gain colonies in the Americas.

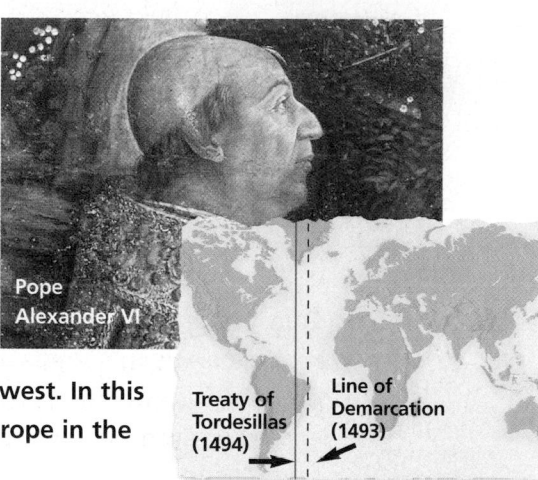

Pope Alexander VI

Treaty of Tordesillas (1494) ←

Line of Demarcation (1493) ←

Spain and Portugal Compete

King John II was unhappy with the pope's placement of the line. He believed that it favored Spain. So he demanded that the Spanish rulers meet with him to change the pope's decision. In June 1494, the two countries agreed to the **Treaty of Tordesillas** (TAWR•day•SEEL•yahs). This treaty moved the Line of Demarcation more than 800 miles farther west.

The change eventually allowed Portugal to claim much of eastern South America, which later became the Portuguese colony of Brazil. After making this agreement, Spain and Portugal increased their voyages of exploration in search of wealth, power, and glory.

European countries had three main goals during this age of exploration. First, they wanted to spread Christianity beyond Europe. Each expedition included **missionaries,** or people sent to convert the native peoples to Christianity. Second, they wanted to expand their empires. Third, they wanted to become rich.

By increasing their wealth, European countries could gain power and security. An economic system called **mercantilism** describes how

> **Taking Notes**
>
> Use your chart to take notes about exploring and establishing colonies.
>
> | Event/Idea | Notes |
> |---|---|
> | Exploration | |
> | Establishing Colonies | |
> | European Competition | |
> | Columbian Exchange | |
> | Origins of Slavery | |

Economics *in* History

Mercantilism

The main goal of mercantilism was to increase the money in a country's treasury by creating a favorable balance of trade. A country had a favorable balance of trade if it had more exports than imports. Colonies helped a country have the goods to maintain a favorable balance of trade.

For example, say Spain sold $500 in sugar to France, and France sold $300 in cloth to Spain. France would also have to pay Spain $200 worth of precious metals to pay for all the sugar. Spain would then have a favorable balance of trade because the value of its exports (sugar) was greater than the value of its imports (cloth). Spain would become richer because of the precious metals it received from France.

Sugar
$500

France

Spain

Cloth
$300

Gold & Silver
$200

CONNECT TO HISTORY

1. **Finding Main Ideas** Under mercantilism, what did a country need to do to become rich? Discuss the way colonies enriched a country according to mercantilism.

   See Skillbuilder Handbook, page R5.

CONNECT TO TODAY

2. **Making Inferences** Think about your own family budget. What do you think would happen if your family collected less money than it paid for goods for several years? Do you think this situation would be the same for a nation as it would for a family?

   For more about mercantilism . . .

   RESEARCH LINKS
   CLASSZONE.COM

Europeans enriched their treasuries. (See *Economics in History,* above.) Colonies helped nations do this in several ways. They provided mines that produced gold and silver. They also produced goods such as crops that could be traded for gold and silver. Finally, they served as a market for the home country. The search for riches spurred European exploration.

Vocabulary
colony: a region or people that is politically and economically controlled by another country

Europeans Explore Foreign Lands

After Columbus's first voyage, many explorers went to sea. **Amerigo Vespucci** (vehs•POO•chee) was one of the first. He was an Italian sailor who set out in 1501 to find a sea route to Asia. Vespucci realized that the land he saw on this voyage was not Asia. A German mapmaker was impressed by Vespucci's account of the lands, so he named the continent "America" after him.

Another famous explorer was the Spaniard Vasco Núñez de Balboa. Balboa heard Native American reports of another ocean. In 1513, he led an expedition through the jungles of Panama and reached the Pacific Ocean. Raising his sword, Balboa stepped into the surf and claimed the ocean and all the lands around it for Spain. (See page 59.)

Perhaps no explorer was more capable than the Portuguese sailor Ferdinand Magellan. He proposed to reach Asia by sailing west around South America. The Spanish king agreed to fund Magellan's voyage.

In 1519, Magellan set out from Spain with five ships and about 240

men. After a stormy passage around South America, Magellan entered the Pacific Ocean. For several months his crew crossed the Pacific, suffering great hardship. A member of the crew described what they ate.

A VOICE FROM THE PAST

We were three months and twenty days without . . . fresh food. We ate biscuit, which was no longer biscuit, but powder of biscuits swarming with worms. . . . We drank . . . water that had been putrid for many days.

Antonio Pigafetta, quoted in *The Discoverers*

*Reading***History**
A. Finding Main Ideas What were the main contributions of Vespucci, Balboa, and Magellan as explorers?

Eventually, Magellan reached the Philippines, where he became involved in a local war and was killed. But his crew traveled on. In 1522, the one remaining ship arrived back in Spain. The sailors in Magellan's crew became the first people to sail around the world.

The Invasion of Mexico

While Magellan's crew was sailing around the world, the Spanish began their conquest of the Americas. Soldiers called ***conquistadors*** (kahn•KWIHS•tuh•DAWRZ), or conquerors, explored the Americas and claimed them for Spain. **Hernando Cortés** was one of these *conquistadors*. He landed on the Central American coast with 508 men in 1519.

The Spanish arrival shook the Aztec Empire, which dominated most of Mexico. The Aztec emperor **Montezuma** feared that Cortés had been

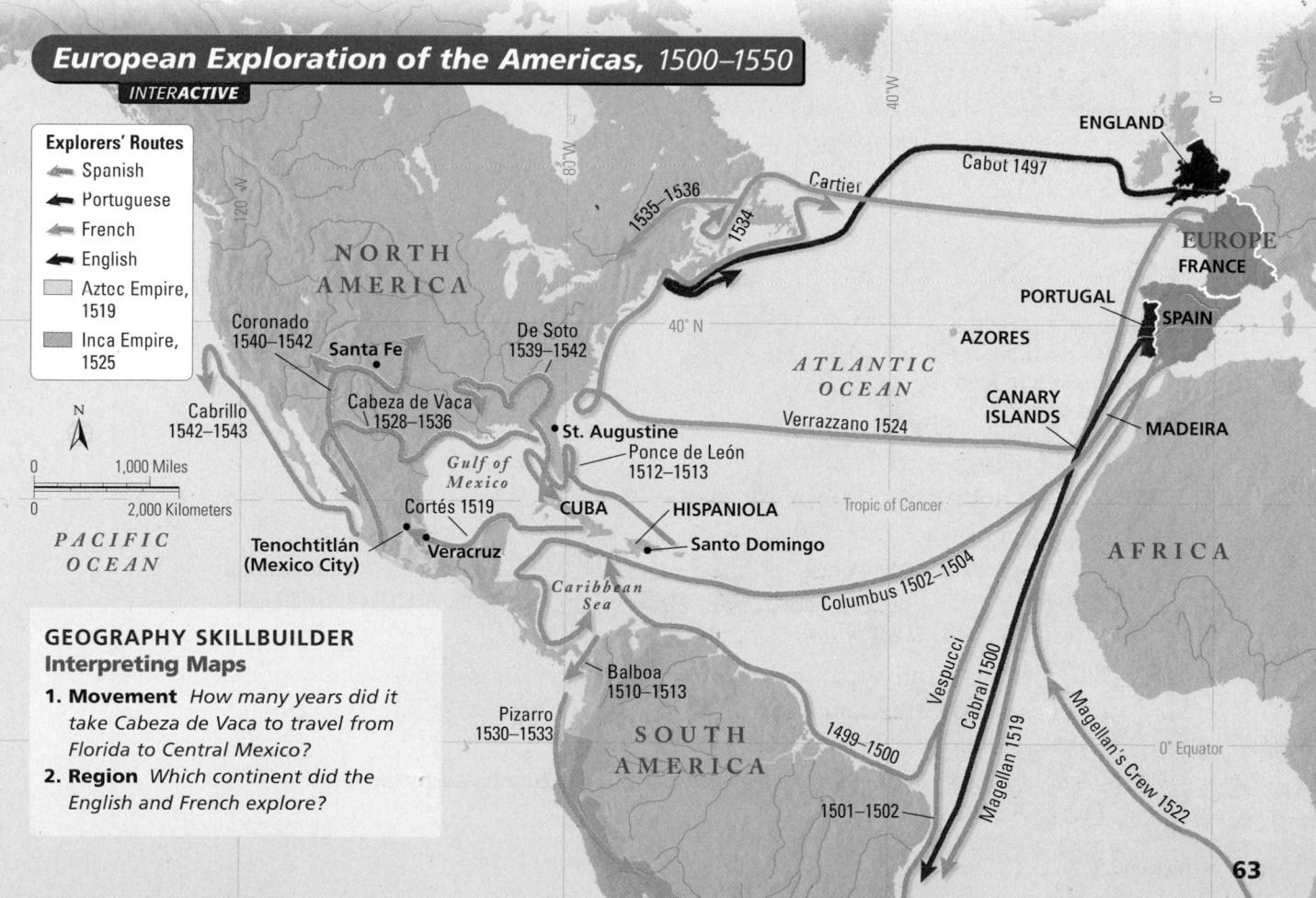

European Exploration of the Americas, *1500–1550*
INTER**ACTIVE**

Explorers' Routes
- Spanish
- Portuguese
- French
- English
- Aztec Empire, 1519
- Inca Empire, 1525

ENGLAND
Cabot 1497
Cartier
1535–1536
1534
NORTH AMERICA
EUROPE
FRANCE
PORTUGAL
SPAIN
AZORES
Coronado 1540–1542
Santa Fe
De Soto 1539–1542
40° N
ATLANTIC OCEAN
CANARY ISLANDS
MADEIRA
Cabrillo 1542–1543
Cabeza de Vaca 1528–1536
St. Augustine
Ponce de León 1512–1513
Verrazzano 1524
N
0   1,000 Miles
0   2,000 Kilometers
Gulf of Mexico
Cortés 1519
CUBA
HISPANIOLA
Tropic of Cancer
PACIFIC OCEAN
Tenochtitlán (Mexico City)
Veracruz
Santo Domingo
AFRICA
Caribbean Sea
Columbus 1502–1504
GEOGRAPHY SKILLBUILDER
Interpreting Maps
Balboa 1510–1513
Vespucci
Cabral 1500
Magellan's Crew 1522
1. **Movement** *How many years did it take Cabeza de Vaca to travel from Florida to Central Mexico?*
Pizarro 1530–1533
1499–1500
Magellan 1519
0° Equator
SOUTH AMERICA
2. **Region** *Which continent did the English and French explore?*
1501–1502

sent by an Aztec god to rule Mexico. Montezuma sent Cortés gifts—including two disks of solid gold and silver—to get him to leave. But the gifts only excited Spanish dreams of riches.

The Spaniards marched inland and formed alliances (agreements with friendly peoples) with the native peoples who hated Aztec rule. After a few months, Cortés reached the Aztec capital, Tenochtitlán (teh•NAWCH•tee•TLAHN). Montezuma received Cortés with great ceremony and housed the *conquistadors* in a magnificent palace. But Cortés took Montezuma captive and tried to rule the Aztec Empire by giving commands through Montezuma. The Aztecs rebelled.

The Aztecs surrounded the Spaniards and their allies in their head-quarters in Tenochtitlán. On the night of June 30, 1520, the Spaniards tried to sneak out of the city, but the Aztecs discovered them and vicious fighting broke out. About 800 Spaniards and more than 1,000 of their allies were killed that night. The Spaniards later called the event *La Noche Triste* (lah NAW•cheh TREES•teh)—the Sad Night.

Despite this defeat, the Spaniards and their allies regrouped. In May 1521, Cortés led his forces back to Tenochtitlán. At this point, the Spaniards got help from an invisible ally. Many Aztecs fell victim to an outbreak of smallpox, which severely weakened their ranks. The germs

Background
One of the people whom Cortés brought into his group was Malintzin. She was the daughter of a local chief and served as an interpreter for Cortés.

AMERICA'S
HISTORY MAKERS

HERNANDO CORTÉS
1485–1547

Hernando Cortés was born in Spain to a noble but poor family. In 1504, at the age of 19, he sailed to the Americas to seek his fortune. Although he became a wealthy land-owner in Cuba, he was not satisfied. "I have come to win gold," he said, "not to plow the fields like a peasant." His great chance came when he was picked to lead the expedition to Mexico. Strong-willed, shrewd, and cruel, Cortés succeeded against great odds.

MONTEZUMA
1466–1520

Montezuma, ruler of the Aztec Empire, rose to the throne in 1502. His words carried weight with his subjects.

According to Juan de Tovar, a Jesuit, "When he spoke, he drew the sympathy of others by his subtle phrases and . . . by his profound reasoning."

Montezuma lived in great luxury, receiving officials and commoners alike at his lavish palace. His subjects treated him almost as a god and were not allowed to look at him. Though brutal at times, he was said to be a just and effective ruler.

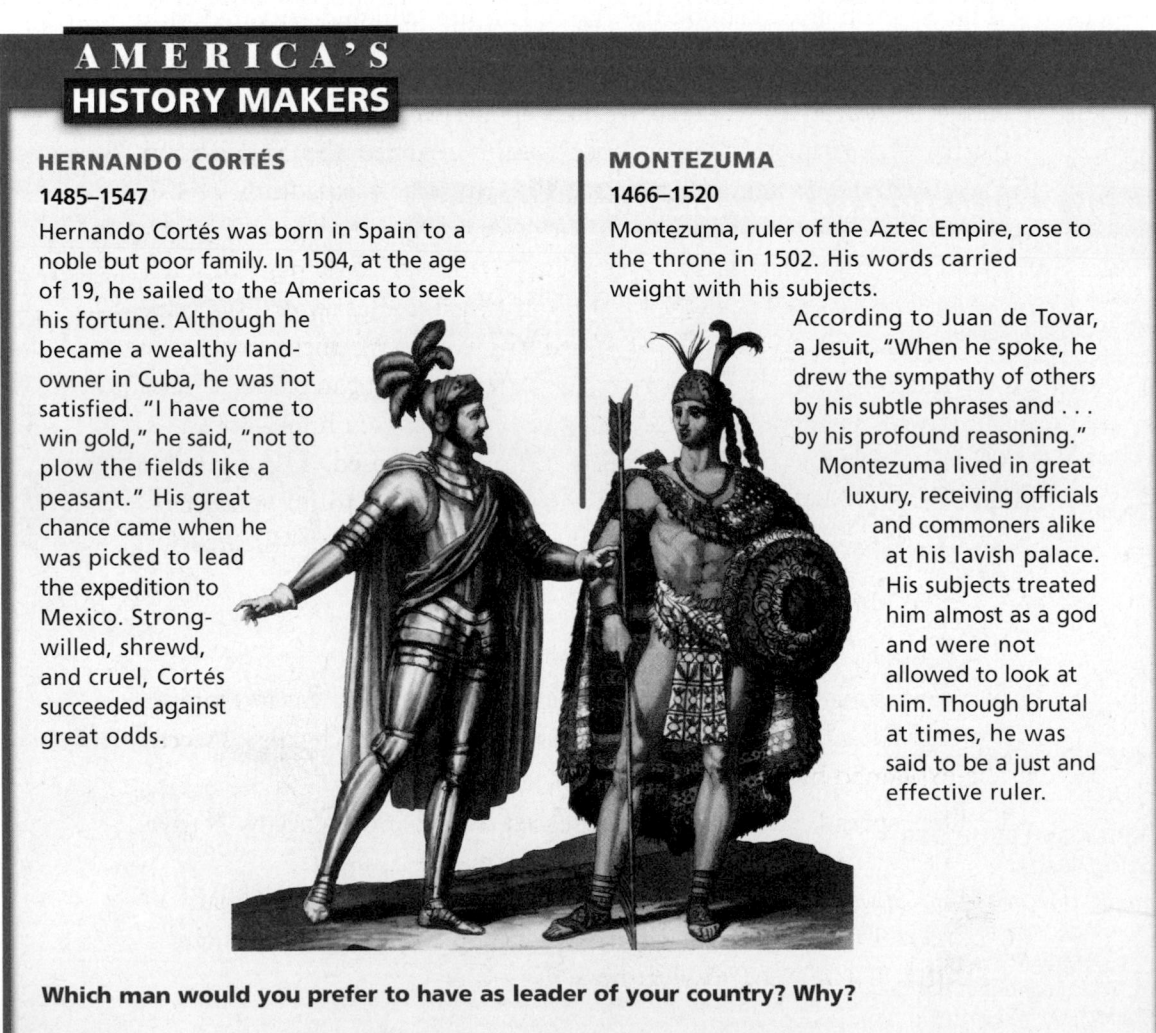

Which man would you prefer to have as leader of your country? Why?

that caused this disease had been brought to America by the Europeans.

Cortés placed Tenochtitlán under siege for three months. When Tenochtitlán finally fell, the Aztec Empire lay in ruins. An Aztec poet described the scene.

A VOICE FROM THE PAST

Broken spears lie in the roads; we have torn our hair in our grief. The houses are roofless now, and their walls are red with blood. . . . We have pounded our hands in despair against the adobe walls, for our inheritance, our city, is lost and dead.

Aztec poet, quoted in *Seeds of Change*

On the rubble of the Aztec capital, the Spanish built Mexico City. Over time, the populations and cultures of Spain and Mexico merged and produced a new society, that of the present-day nation of Mexico.

This Aztec mask represents Quetzalcoatl, the god that Montezuma feared had sent Cortés.

The Conquest of the Incan Empire

Reading History
B. Reading a Map
Use the map on page 63 to find the Incan Empire.

Despite the fall of the Aztecs, a people called the Inca still had a powerful empire centered in the Cuzco Valley in what is now Peru. By 1525, the Inca ruled a 2,000-mile-long territory in the Andes Mountains along the western coast of South America. The Inca also possessed much gold and silver.

Native American stories of Incan wealth reached the Spanish. In 1531, a *conquistador* named **Francisco Pizarro** led an expedition of 180 men into Peru. Like the Aztecs, the Incas feared that the Spanish might be gods. The Incan emperor Atahualpa (AH•tuh•WAHL•puh) ordered his troops not to fight. Then he went to meet the *conquistadors*. The Spanish attacked quickly. They killed thousands of Incas and took Atahualpa captive. In an attempt to free himself, the Incan emperor gave the Spanish a treasure of gold. The Spaniards strangled him anyway.

Reading History
C. Drawing Conclusions Why did the Incan Empire fall to the Spanish?

With Atahualpa dead, the Incan Empire collapsed. Having been ordered by Atahualpa not to fight, the Incas refused to defend themselves even after his death. Then Pizarro took control of this area for Spain. The Spanish called the area Peru.

Reasons for Spanish Victories

People have long been amazed that the great Aztec and Incan empires fell to such small groups of Spanish *conquistadors*. But Spanish success can be explained by four major reasons.

1. The spread of European diseases killed millions of Native Americans and weakened their resistance to conquest.
2. The Spanish were excellent soldiers and sailors. They also had superior weapons, such as guns, that helped them defeat much larger Native American armies.

Estevanico was a slave who helped the Spanish explore parts of North America. He was killed during Coronado's search for golden cities.

3. Spain made alliances with Native Americans who were enemies of the Aztecs and Incas.
4. The Spanish *conquistadors* acted brutally toward the Native Americans under their control.

Having conquered the major Native American empires in Central and South America, the Spaniards began to explore other parts of North and South America.

*Reading*History
D. Drawing Conclusions
What was the most important reason for the Spanish success in conquering territory in the Americas?

Other Spanish Explorers

The Spaniards hoped to collect treasures from North America as they had from Mexico and Peru. Rumors of golden cities kept Spanish hopes high. For example, a few men, including the Spaniard Álvar Núñez Cabeza de Vaca and Estevanico, a slave of North African descent, survived a shipwreck off the North American mainland. As the men wandered across the continent, they heard Native American stories about cities of gold. When they reached Mexico, Cabeza de Vaca and Estevanico thrilled the Spaniards with these rumors.

Between 1539 and 1542, three expeditions set out to find these cities. Francisco Vázquez de Coronado traveled through present-day Arizona and New Mexico. Hernando de Soto set out from Florida to explore the southeast. Juan Rodríguez Cabrillo sailed up the California coast. But all three failed to find the fabled cities of gold.

For a while, it seemed that the Spaniards would explore the Americas all by themselves. As you will read in the next section, however, the Spanish would soon face competition from other Europeans.

Section 1 Assessment

1. Terms & Names

Explain the significance of:
- Treaty of Tordesillas
- missionary
- mercantilism
- Amerigo Vespucci
- *conquistador*
- Hernando Cortés
- Montezuma
- Francisco Pizarro

2. Using Graphics

Review the section and find four events to place on a time line that shows how Spain built its empire.

Spain Builds an Empire

1492 — — — — — 1542

Which event do you think is the most important? Why?

3. Main Ideas

a. Why did Europeans explore different territories?

b. Why did Spain succeed in conquering so much of the Americas?

c. What was significant about the Magellan expedition?

4. Critical Thinking

Comparing What was similar about the conquests of Mexico and Peru?

THINK ABOUT
- the *conquistadors*
- the Incan and Aztec leaders

ACTIVITY OPTIONS

ART

LANGUAGE ARTS

Use the library or the Internet to find a photograph of an Aztec or Incan artifact. Create a **replica** or write a **description** of the object.

European Competition in North America

MAIN IDEA	WHY IT MATTERS NOW	TERMS & NAMES
Other European countries competed with Spain for control over territory in the Americas.	European culture has strongly influenced American culture.	Henry Hudson Jacques Cartier John Cabot Spanish Armada Giovanni da Samuel de Champlain Verrazzano New France

ONE EUROPEAN'S STORY

In 1609, the Englishman **Henry Hudson** sailed under the Dutch flag from Europe. He hoped to find a route to China. Arriving at the coast of present-day New York, he sailed up the river that now bears his name. Hudson described what he saw.

A VOICE FROM THE PAST

The land is the finest for cultivation that I ever in my life set foot upon, and it also abounds in trees of every description. The natives are a very good people; for, when they saw that I would not remain, they . . . broke [their arrows] in pieces and threw them into the fire.

Henry Hudson, quoted in *Discoverers of America*

Hudson did not find a passage to Asia, but he led another expedition in 1610, this time for the English. In Canada, he disovered a large bay, today called Hudson Bay. After enduring a harsh winter, his crew rebelled. They put Hudson, his young son, and several loyal sailors in a small boat and set them adrift. Hudson's party was never heard from again.

The Search for the Northwest Passage

Hudson's voyages showed that some European countries hoped to find a westward route to Asia as late as the 1600s. While Spain was taking control of the Americas, other Europeans were sending out expeditions to find the Northwest Passage, a water route through North America to Asia.

One of the first explorers to chart a northern route across the Atlantic in search of Asia was the Italian sailor **John Cabot**. In 1497, Cabot crossed the Atlantic Ocean to explore for the English. He landed in the area of Newfoundland, Canada. He was certain that he had reached Asia and claimed the land for England. The next year he set sail once more,

Taking Notes

Use your chart to take notes about European competition for colonies.

Event/Idea	Notes
Exploration	
Establishing Colonies	
European Competition	
Columbian Exchange	
Origins of Slavery	

hoping to reach Japan. He was never seen again. Even so, his voyages were the basis for future English colonies along North America's Atlantic shore.

In 1524, another Italian, **Giovanni da Verrazzano,** set out under the French flag to find the Northwest Passage. He explored the Atlantic coastline of North America, but there was no passage to be found.

France tried again between 1534 and 1536 with the voyages of **Jacques Cartier** (ZHAHK kahr•TYAY). Cartier traveled up the St. Lawrence River to the site of present-day Montreal. At that point, rapids blocked the way and ended his search for the Northwest Passage. It would be almost 75 years before the French would return to colonize the region.

*Reading*History
A. Reading a Map
Use the maps on pages 63 and 67 to see the areas Cabot, Hudson, Verrazzano, and Cartier visited.

Spain Responds to Competition

French and English claims to North America angered Spain, which had claimed the land under the Treaty of Tordesillas. The tensions between Spain, England, and France stemmed from religious conflicts in Europe, such as the Reformation, which you read about in Chapter 1. These conflicts also led to fighting in the Americas.

Florida was one of the battlegrounds between the Spanish and the French. In 1564, a group of French Protestants, called Huguenots (HYOO•guh•NAHTS), founded a colony called Fort Caroline. Before long, Spanish troops under the command of Pedro Menéndez de Avilés arrived in that area. "This is the armada of the King of Spain," he announced, "who has sent me [here] to burn and hang the Lutheran [Protestant] French." Menéndez built a fort, St. Augustine, a short distance away. Then he brutally massacred the French.

Vocabulary
armada: a fleet of warships

Spain and England Clash

Religious differences and the quest for national power also led to conflict between Spain and England. In 1558, Queen Elizabeth I, a Protestant, came to the English throne. Spain, which was Catholic, plotted to remove the Protestant queen. But Elizabeth fought to defend England and challenge Spain's power at sea.

Although England's navy was not as powerful as Spain's, the English fleet had many speedy ships with skillful sailors. Daring sailors, known as sea dogs, used these ships to attack the bulky Spanish sailing ships—called galleons—that brought gold and silver from the Americas.

Sir Francis Drake became the most famous of the sea dogs because of his bold adventures and attacks against the Spanish. In 1577, Drake began a three-year voyage that took him around the world. During this voyage,

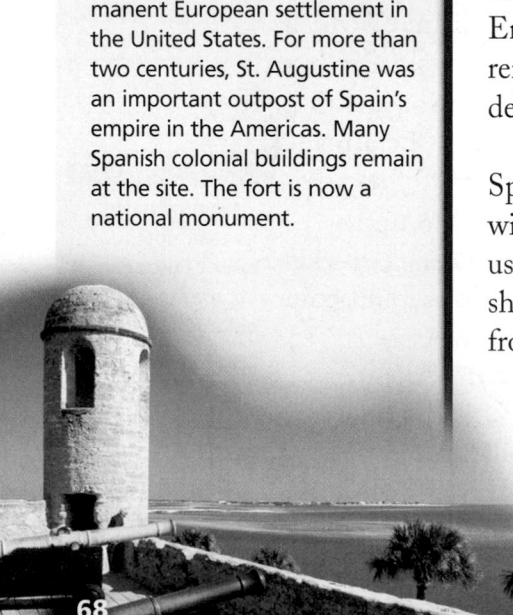

America's HERITAGE

ST. AUGUSTINE
The thick stone walls of the fort at St. Augustine (shown below) still stand guard over the Florida coast today. Founded in 1565, St. Augustine is the oldest permanent European settlement in the United States. For more than two centuries, St. Augustine was an important outpost of Spain's empire in the Americas. Many Spanish colonial buildings remain at the site. The fort is now a national monument.

The English navy used its smaller, quicker ships to defeat the larger, slower galleons of the Spanish Armada.

he raided Spanish ports and ships in South America. He stole great amounts of treasure from them. When he arrived home in 1580, he was a national hero. Not only had Drake and his men hounded the Spanish, but they were also the first Englishmen to sail around the world.

The Defeat of the Spanish Armada

The attacks of Drake and other sea dogs enraged Philip II, the Spanish king. Determined to teach the English a lesson, Philip sent the **Spanish Armada** to conquer England and restore Catholicism to that nation. This fleet, made up of 130 ships, set out for England in the summer of 1588.

The English and Spanish navies met in the English Channel, which separates England from the European continent. In their smaller but faster craft, the English darted among the Spanish warships, firing deadly rounds with their cannons. Confused and crippled, the armada was retreating when it was hit by a severe storm. With half of its ships destroyed, the armada barely made it home.

Spain was still quite strong after the defeat of the armada. It quickly rebuilt its navy and maintained its large colonial possessions. But Spain would never again be as powerful as it was in 1588.

Reading **History**

B. Drawing Conclusions Why was the defeat of the Spanish Armada important?

The English victory over Spain had two important effects. First, England remained independent and Protestant. Although England was less powerful than Spain, it had shown that it could defend itself. Second, Spain's image suffered. The world saw that Spain could be beaten. Other nations joined England in challenging Spain.

English adventurers like Drake continued to attack Spanish interests abroad. In addition, England challenged Spanish claims to lands in North America, such as California and Newfoundland. Even so, England took a cautious approach to overseas expansion. The English government refused to provide money to start colonies. Instead, private citizens had to provide the money for colonization. As a result, England did not establish a successful colony in America until after 1600.

The French and Dutch Seek Trade

France and the Netherlands were also looking for ways to gain wealth through exploration and colonization. At first, their goal in the Americas was to find the Northwest Passage to Asia. When that search failed, they began to focus on North America itself.

The Frenchman **Samuel de Champlain** (sham•PLAYN) explored the St. Lawrence River. In 1608, he founded a fur-trading post at Quebec. This post became the first permanent French settlement in North America. Champlain's activities opened a rich fur trade with local Native Americans. After a couple of decades, **New France,** as the colony was called, began to thrive.

At the same time, the Dutch were building a colony called New Netherland. It was located along the Hudson River in present-day New York. After Hudson's voyage up the river in 1609, the Dutch built Fort Nassau in 1614, near the site of the modern city of Albany.

In 1626, the Dutch bought Manhattan Island from Native Americans. The Dutch then founded the town of New Amsterdam on that site, where New York City is currently located. New Netherland was soon thriving from the fur trade with Native Americans.

These early French and Dutch colonies, however, were small compared to the large empire Spain was building in the Americas. You will read about the growth of Spain's American empire in the next section.

*Reading*History
C. Making Inferences Why do you think it took France and the Netherlands so long to set up colonies in the Americas?

Section **2** Assessment

1. Terms & Names

Explain the significance of:
- Henry Hudson
- John Cabot
- Giovanni da Verrazzano
- Jacques Cartier
- Spanish Armada
- Samuel de Champlain
- New France

2. Using Graphics

Use a chart like the one below to show how European nations competed for power.

England	
France	
Netherlands	
Spain	

3. Main Ideas

a. What were the English, French, and Dutch searching for in their early voyages of exploration?

b. How did England defeat the Spanish Armada?

c. Where did the French and Dutch set up their first American colonies?

4. Critical Thinking

Making Inferences Why do you think England founded colonies later than Spain did?

THINK ABOUT
- conditions in Spain and England
- the lands each country discovered

ACTIVITY OPTIONS

MUSIC
TECHNOLOGY

Research the life of one of the explorers discussed in this section. Compose a **song** or design a **Web page** about that person.

The Spanish and Native Americans

MAIN IDEA	WHY IT MATTERS NOW	TERMS & NAMES
Spanish rule in the Americas had terrible consequences for Native Americans.	The destruction of Native American cultures created social problems that continue today.	viceroyalty Popé *encomienda* plantation *hacienda* Bartolomé de Las Casas mission Columbian Exchange

ONE AMERICAN'S STORY

Huamán Poma, a Peruvian Native American, wrote to King Philip III of Spain to complain about the abuse the Spanish heaped upon Native Americans.

> ### A VOICE FROM THE PAST
> It is their [the Spanish] practice to collect Indians into groups and send them to forced labor without wages, while they themselves receive the payment.
> **Huamán Poma,** *Letter to a King*

In his letter, Poma asked the king to help the Native Americans and uphold the rule of law in Peru. If the king actually read the letter, it made no difference. Spanish colonists continued to mistreat Native Americans as the Spanish Empire expanded in the Americas.

A Spanish priest forces a Native American woman to work at a loom.

Spanish Colonies in the Americas

The Spanish Empire grew rapidly, despite efforts by other European countries to compete with Spain. By 1700, it controlled much of the Americas. Spain took several steps to establish an effective colonial government. First, it divided its American empire into two provinces called New Spain and Peru. Each province was called a **viceroyalty.** The top official of each viceroyalty was called the viceroy. He ruled in the king's name.

The Spanish also built new roads to transport people and goods across the empire. These roads stretched outward from the capitals at Mexico City and Lima. The roads helped Spain to control the colonies by allowing soldiers to move quickly from place to place. Roads also improved the Spanish economy because materials, such as gold and silver, could be transported efficiently to the coast and then to Spain.

Taking Notes

Use your chart to take notes about establishing colonies and the Columbian Exchange.

Event/Idea	Notes
Exploration	
Establishing Colonies	
European Competition	
Columbian Exchange	
Origins of Slavery	

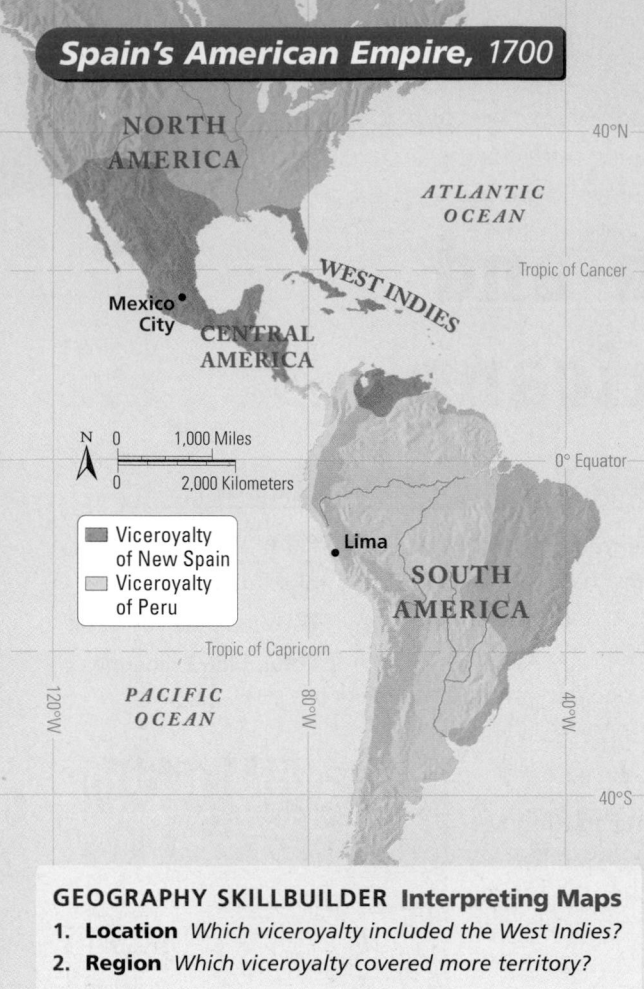

Spain's American Empire, 1700

NORTH AMERICA

40°N

ATLANTIC OCEAN

WEST INDIES

Tropic of Cancer

Mexico City

CENTRAL AMERICA

N

0   1,000 Miles
0   2,000 Kilometers

Lima

SOUTH AMERICA

0° Equator

■ Viceroyalty of New Spain
■ Viceroyalty of Peru

Tropic of Capricorn

PACIFIC OCEAN

120°W   80°W   40°W

40°S

GEOGRAPHY SKILLBUILDER Interpreting Maps
1. **Location** *Which viceroyalty included the West Indies?*
2. **Region** *Which viceroyalty covered more territory?*

Life in Spanish America

Spanish colonists received *encomiendas* to help them make the colonies productive. An **encomienda** was a grant of Native American labor. Hernando Cortés received a grant of more than 100,000 Native Americans to work his estate.

The Spanish rulers also created large estates, called **haciendas,** to provide food for the colony. *Haciendas* usually became large farms where Native Americans worked to grow cash crops, such as coffee and cotton. The *encomienda* and *hacienda* systems put much of the power and land in the hands of a few people.

The Spaniards made sure that people with Spanish backgrounds held power in the colonies. Spanish-born colonists such as Cortés made up the top layer of colonial society. Just below the Spanish were the Creoles—people of Spanish descent who were born in the colonies. The next step down the social order were the *mestizos. Mestizos* are people of mixed Spanish and Native American ancestry. The people with the least power and fewest rights were Native Americans and enslaved Africans.

Background
The problem of unequal wealth, especially in land, continues to trouble Latin American societies today.

The Role of the Church

The Catholic Church played an important role in Spanish colonial society. In places like New Mexico and California, the church built **missions,** settlements that included a church, a town, and farmlands. The goal of the missions was to convert Native Americans to Christianity. The missions also increased Spanish control over the land.

Missionaries helped the Native Americans to create a better supply of food. They also offered Native Americans protection against enemies. Many Native Americans learned how to read and write in the missions. Others developed skills such as carpentry and metalworking.

Over time, however, many Native Americans grew increasingly unhappy. The missionaries often worked them as if they were slaves. The missionaries also tried to replace Native American religions and traditions. As a result, some Native Americans ran away, while others rebelled. Some destroyed churches and killed missionaries.

In 1680, a man named **Popé** led the Pueblo Indians in a rebellion against the Spanish. His forces surrounded the Spanish settlement at

*Reading*History

A. Summarizing How did the Spanish missions change the lives of Native Americans?

Santa Fe, in present-day New Mexico, and forced the colonists to flee. Popé ordered the churches and other Spanish buildings to be destroyed. He then tried to revive native customs that had been lost under Spanish rule. But before long, attacks from neighboring tribes weakened Pueblo control. In 1692, the Spanish regained control of Santa Fe.

Sugar Plantations Develop

The Spanish also forced Native Americans to work on **plantations,** large farms that raised cash crops. These crops were usually exported to Europe. The most important crop was sugar.

Although sugar was in great demand in Europe, there was not much land there to grow it. The resulting demand led to the development of sugar plantations in the Americas. On his second voyage to the Americas, in 1493, Columbus brought sugar cane to Hispaniola, one of the Caribbean islands he had landed on in 1492. He found ideal conditions for sugar production there. Spanish planters soon expanded operations to the nearby islands that Spain colonized.

Sugar plantations required many workers, so the Spanish planters turned to native peoples, such as the Taino. Through *encomiendas,* the Spaniards forced thousands of Taino to work in the fields. The plantations thrived, but many of the Taino suffered and died.

The Abuse of Native Americans

Most Spaniards treated the Native Americans as little more than beasts of burden. According to Fray Toribio de Benavente, a Catholic missionary, the Spanish "do nothing but command. They are the drones who suck the honey which is made by the poor bees, the Indians."

Not all Spaniards approved of this treatment. One man in particular fought for better treatment of Native

Background
Other plantation crops included tobacco, cotton, cochineal (a dye), and cacao.

HISTORY *through* ART

Theodore de Bry created this picture, *Sugar: the greatest gift of the Old World to the New,* in the 1600s. It shows workers processing sugar in the Americas. Europeans brought sugar production to the Americas from the Mediterranean.

How does the picture help explain why the Europeans used slaves to make sugar?

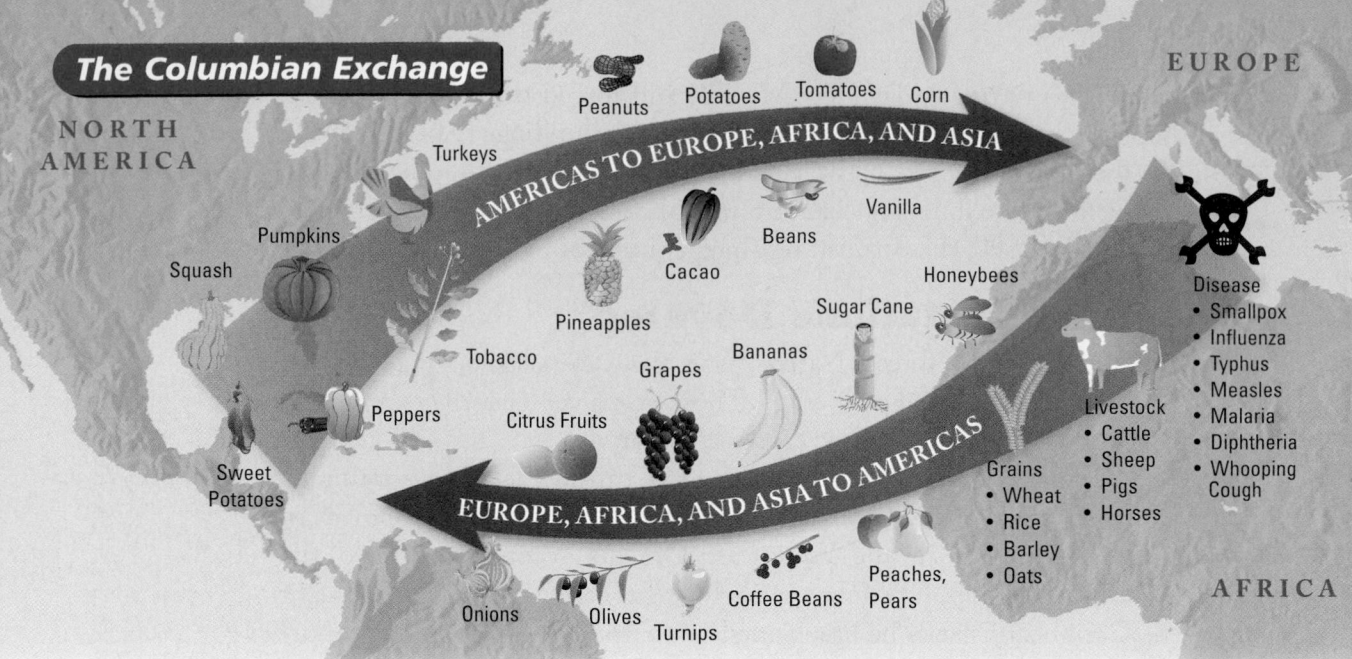

The Columbian Exchange

EUROPE

NORTH AMERICA

AMERICAS TO EUROPE, AFRICA, AND ASIA

Peanuts
Potatoes
Tomatoes
Corn
Turkeys
Vanilla
Pumpkins
Beans
Squash
Cacao
Honeybees
Pineapples
Sugar Cane
Tobacco
Bananas
Grapes
Peppers
Citrus Fruits
Sweet Potatoes

EUROPE, AFRICA, AND ASIA TO AMERICAS

Grains
• Wheat
• Rice
• Barley
• Oats

Livestock
• Cattle
• Sheep
• Pigs
• Horses

Disease
• Smallpox
• Influenza
• Typhus
• Measles
• Malaria
• Diphtheria
• Whooping Cough

Onions
Olives
Turnips
Coffee Beans
Peaches, Pears

AFRICA

Americans. His name was **Bartolomé de Las Casas**. Las Casas had come to Hispaniola in 1502 and taken part in the conquest of Cuba a decade later. For his part in the conquest, he received an *encomienda*. Las Casas was also a Catholic priest, however, and he soon faced a moral dilemma: How can a person serve God and enslave Native Americans at the same time?

In 1514, Las Casas gave up his claim to the Native Americans who worked for him. For the next 50 years, he fought against the abuse of Native Americans, earning the title "Protector of the Indians."

Because of his efforts, the Spanish king issued the New Laws in 1542. These laws ordered the gradual freeing of all enslaved Native Americans. Holders of *encomiendas* who were found guilty of mistreating Native Americans had their *encomiendas* taken away. However, Spanish colonists strongly protested against the New Laws, and the king eventually reversed many of them.

The Columbian Exchange

The arrival of the Spanish in the Americas brought more than a clash of peoples and cultures. It also brought a movement of plants, animals, and diseases between the Eastern and Western hemispheres. This movement of living things between hemispheres is called the **Columbian Exchange**.

One result of the Columbian Exchange was the transfer of germs from Europe to the Americas. When Europeans came to America, they brought with them germs that caused diseases such as smallpox, measles, and influenza. Native Americans had no immunity to them.

Although exact numbers are unknown, historians estimate that diseases brought by Europeans killed more than 20 million Native Americans in Mexico in the first century after conquest. Many scholars agree that the population of Native Americans in Central America decreased by 90 to 95 percent between the years 1519 and 1619. The

Reading **History**

B. Making Inferences What might have happened if Native Americans had been immune to European diseases?

result was similar in Peru and other parts of the Americas. A Spanish missionary in Mexico described the effects of smallpox on the Aztecs.

A VOICE FROM THE PAST

There was a great havoc. Very many died of it. They could not walk. . . . They could not move; they could not stir; they could not change position, nor lie on one side; nor face down, nor on their backs. And if they stirred, much did they cry out. Great was its destruction.

Bernardino de Sahagún, quoted in *Seeds of Change*

Other effects of the Columbian Exchange were more positive. The Spanish brought many plants and animals to the Americas. European livestock—cattle, pigs, and horses—all thrived in the Americas. Crops from the Eastern Hemisphere, such as grapes, onions, and wheat, also thrived in the Western Hemisphere.

The Columbian Exchange benefited Europe, too. Many American crops became part of the European diet. Two that had a huge impact were potatoes and corn, which are highly nutritious. They helped feed European populations that might otherwise have gone hungry. Potatoes, for example, became an important food in Ireland, Russia, and other parts of northern Europe. Without potatoes, Europe's population might not have grown as rapidly as it did.

By mixing the products of two hemispheres, the Columbian Exchange brought the world closer together. Of course, people were also moving from one hemisphere to the other, blending their cultures in the process. The next section focuses on one important aspect of the movement of peoples: the forced migration of enslaved Africans to the Americas.

Background
In Ireland, the population increased from 3.2 million in 1754 to more than 8 million in 1845, largely because of the high level of nutrients in potatoes.

Now and then

KILLER BEES
Even today, plant and animal species continue to move from one hemisphere to the other. A recent example of this is the killer bee (shown below).

Killer bees were first brought to Brazil from Africa to help make honey in the 1950s. Killer bees are aggressive, however, and can kill large animals when they swarm. After some of these bees escaped from a Brazilian laboratory in 1957, they began to migrate. In recent years, they have been responsible for the deaths of a number of pets in the American Southwest.

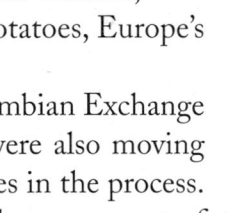

Section **3** *Assessment*

1. Terms & Names

Explain the significance of:
• viceroyalty
• *encomienda*
• *hacienda*
• mission
• Popé
• plantation
• Bartolomé de Las Casas
• Columbian Exchange

2. Using Graphics

Use a cluster diagram like the one below to show how Spain organized its colonies.

How did these actions help the Spanish control the Americas?

3. Main Ideas

a. What were the four levels of Spanish colonial society?

b. What was the main crop grown on colonial plantations?

c. How were Native Americans abused in the colonies?

4. Critical Thinking

Recognizing Effects
What were the positive and negative effects of the Columbian Exchange?

THINK ABOUT
• disease
• food
• livestock

ACTIVITY OPTIONS

ART

LANGUAGE ARTS

Make a **collage** that shows the plants and animals involved in the Columbian Exchange, or write a **story** that tells how Native Americans reacted to the animals.

4

Beginnings of Slavery in the Americas

MAIN IDEA	WHY IT MATTERS NOW	TERMS & NAMES
Slavery in the Americas began in order to provide cheap labor for the colonies.	The effects of slavery, including racism, helped shape attitudes and social conditions in the United States.	slavery slave codes African Diaspora racism middle passage

ONE AMERICAN'S STORY

In 1546, Diego de Campo was the leader of 7,000 maroons, or runaway slaves on the island of Hispaniola. There were only about 1,000 European men on the island.

The Spanish planters greatly feared de Campo. When the Spanish attacked the maroons, de Campo and his followers defeated the Spanish.

Eventually the Spaniards captured de Campo. He offered to lead the fight against the maroons. The Spanish accepted the offer. With de Campo's help, the Spanish defeated the maroons, and slavery in Hispaniola grew. In this section, you will read how slave labor expanded in the Americas.

Colonial troops searched for communities of maroons to destroy them.

Taking Notes

Use your chart to take notes about the origins of slavery.

Event/Idea	Notes
Exploration	
Establishing Colonies	
European Competition	
Columbian Exchange	
Origins of Slavery	

The Origins of American Slavery

By the 1600s, **slavery**, the practice of holding a person in bondage for labor, was firmly established in the Americas. But slavery was not new. Its roots went back to the world's ancient civilizations.

Slavery took many different forms throughout history. In some societies, slaves were mainly domestic servants in wealthy households. Some slaves also labored in mines and fields.

People were often enslaved when they were captured in battle or sold to pay off debts. Some slaves were treated with respect. Some were allowed to marry and own property. The children of many slaves were allowed to go free.

Slavery began to change, however, with the rise of sugar plantations. Europeans had used slaves to grow sugar in the eastern Mediterranean since the 1100s. Then, in the 1400s and 1500s, Portugal and Spain set up sugar plantations on islands in the eastern Atlantic. To work these plantations, they used African slaves bought from traders in Africa.

When the Spanish and Portuguese founded their colonies in the Americas, they brought the plantation system with them. At first they tried to enslave Native Americans to work in the fields and mines. But the Native Americans quickly died from overwork and disease. In some cases, they rebelled with the help of local allies.

The Spaniards then looked to other sources of slave labor, including Spanish slaves, black Christian slaves, and Asian slaves. But there was not enough of any of these groups to meet demand.

Finally, the Spanish and Portuguese enslaved Africans to provide labor. They enslaved Africans for four basic reasons. First, Africans were immune to most European diseases. Second, Africans had no friends or family in the Americas to help them resist or escape enslavement. Third, enslaved Africans provided a permanent source of cheap labor. Even their children could be held in bondage. Fourth, many Africans had worked on farms in their native lands.

*Reading*History
A. Drawing Conclusions Why did colonists decide that African slaves were more useful than Native American slaves?

The Slave Trade

The slave trade grew slowly at first. In 1509, the Spanish governor of Hispaniola, Diego Colón—Columbus's son—wrote to King Ferdinand to complain about a labor shortage on the island. In response, the king sent 50 African slaves to Hispaniola. The slave trade increased with the demand for slaves to work in the colonies. Eventually the colonies came to depend on slave labor. As one Spanish official in Peru wrote, "The black slave is the basis of the *hacienda* and the source of all wealth which this realm produces."

European slave traders carried out the shipment of Africans to the Americas. The rulers of West African kingdoms participated in the trade, too. On the coast of Africa, local kings gathered captives from inland. The local kings then traded these captives for European goods, such as textiles, ironware, wine, and guns.

This trade made the coastal kingdoms rich while weakening inland African societies. In 1526, King Afonso, a West African ruler, protested against the slave trade in a letter to Portugal's king. Afonso wrote, "Everyday these [slave] merchants take our people. . . . So great is this corruption and evil that our country is becoming completely depopulated."

Vocabulary
depopulated: to lose population

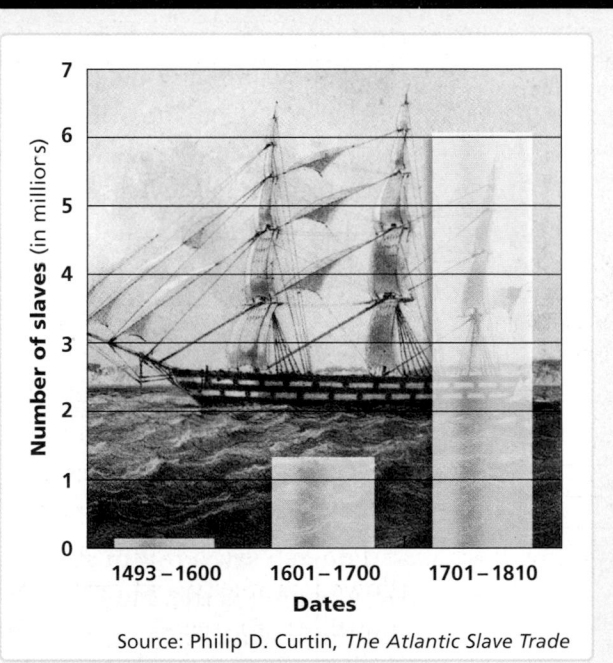

CONNECTIONS TO MATH

Slaves Imported to the Americas, *1493–1810*

Number of slaves (in millions) [y-axis: 0–7]

Dates [x-axis: 1493–1600, 1601–1700, 1701–1810]

Source: Philip D. Curtin, *The Atlantic Slave Trade*

SKILLBUILDER Interpreting Graphs
1. *About how many slaves were imported to the Americas between 1493 and 1810?*
2. *Why do you think the numbers increased?*

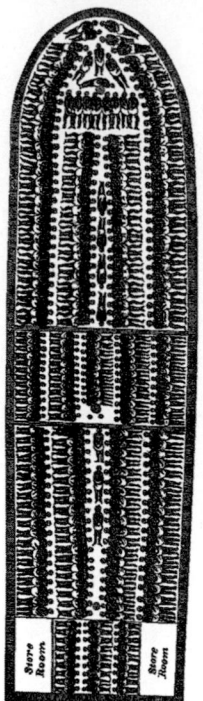

The diagram above shows how slave traders packed enslaved Africans onto slave ships for the middle passage. A British naval officer painted the picture on the right, which also shows the crowded conditions on slave ships.

The Middle Passage

Afonso's protest did not stop the forced removal of people from Africa. This removal has become known as the **African Diaspora**. Before the slave trade ended in the late 1800s, approximately 12 million Africans had been enslaved and shipped to the Western Hemisphere. Of these, perhaps two million died during the voyage.

The voyage from Africa to the Americas was called the **middle passage.** The voyage was given this name because it was the middle leg of the triangular trade. The triangular trade refers to the movement of trade ships between Europe, Africa, and the Americas. You will learn more about the triangular trade in Chapter 4.

Olaudah Equiano (oh•LOW•duh EHK•wee•AHN•oh) was one of these kidnapped Africans. He made this journey in the 1700s. He was about 11 years old when he was taken from his home and sold into slavery. Later, after he bought his freedom, he wrote his life story and told what the middle passage was like.

Vocabulary
diaspora: the scattering of people outside their homeland

> *A VOICE FROM THE PAST*
>
> The first object which saluted my eyes when I arrived on the coast, was the sea, and a slave ship . . . waiting for its cargo. These filled me with astonishment, which was soon converted into terror, when I was carried on board.
>
> **Olaudah Equiano,** quoted in *Great Slave Narratives*

Equiano saw a row of men shackled together in chains. He also saw a large boiling kettle. He feared that he was going to be cooked and eaten "by those white men with horrible looks, red faces, and long hair."

The scene on the slave deck below was even worse. Several hundred slaves were crammed into a space so small that there was not even enough room to stand up. Foul smells and disease, along with the shrieks and groans of the dying, made the middle passage a terrifying experience. The captives who did not die faced new horrors in the Americas.

Reading **History**
B. Making Inferences Why would slave traders pack so many captives onto slave ships?

Slavery in the Americas

Once the enslaved Africans arrived in the colonies, they were sold at auction. Some were taken to large homes where they worked as servants. Most were forced to do hard labor in *haciendas* or mines. They were also fed and housed poorly.

Many slaves resisted slavery by running away. Across Peru and New Spain, maroons formed communities, often with Native Americans. Sometimes enslaved Africans rebelled. To prevent rebellion, the Spanish government passed **slave codes,** laws to regulate the treatment of slaves. Some of these laws tried to soften the harsh conditions of slavery, but most were designed to punish slaves and keep them in bondage.

Over time, Europeans came to associate slavery with black Africans. To many Europeans, dark skin color became a sign of inferiority. Slavery, which developed to provide a labor force, led to racism. **Racism** is the belief that some people are inferior because of their race.

The slave trade lasted for nearly 400 years, from the early 1500s to the mid-1800s. This contact between Africa and the Americas also formed part of the Columbian Exchange that you read about in Section 3. Africans brought to the Americas a vast knowledge about farming and animals. At the same time, American crops such as sweet potatoes, peanuts, and chilies made their way to Africa.

Enslaved Africans also brought with them a strong artistic heritage of dance, music, and storytelling. The slave trade brought together people from different parts of Africa with different cultural traditions. The experience of slavery helped create a common African-based culture in the Americas. By the 1700s, all the American colonies of European countries had African slaves. As you will read in the next chapter, African culture would be one of the forces that shaped life in the American colonies.

Reading **History**

C. Analyzing Causes What could have caused slave traders to treat other humans with such cruelty?

Section 4 Assessment

1. Terms & Names

Explain the significance of:
- slavery
- African Diaspora
- middle passage
- slave codes
- racism

2. Using Graphics

Use a diagram like the one below to compare the experience of Native Americans and Africans under slavery.

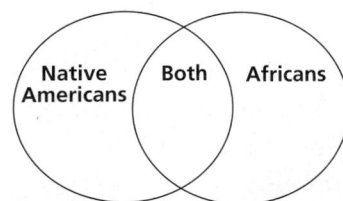

3. Main Ideas

a. When did slavery begin?

b. Why did Europeans bring Africans to the Americas?

c. What are three examples of bad conditions faced by enslaved Africans?

4. Critical Thinking

Recognizing Effects What were the long-term effects of slavery in the Americas?

THINK ABOUT
- the economy in the Americas
- the African Diaspora
- cultural diversity in the Americas

ACTIVITY OPTIONS

ART

MATH

Research some aspect of the slave trade, such as the middle passage or the number of people enslaved. Paint a **picture** or draw a **graph** to show what you learned.

TERMS & NAMES

Briefly explain the significance of each of the following.

1. mercantilism
2. Hernando Cortés
3. Montezuma
4. Spanish Armada
5. New France
6. *encomienda*
7. Columbian Exchange
8. slavery
9. African Diaspora
10. middle passage

REVIEW QUESTIONS

Spain Claims an Empire (pages 61–66)

1. What were three reasons for the European voyages of exploration in the 1400s and 1500s?
2. Who conquered the Aztecs and Incas?
3. What three reasons explain Spain's success in building an empire in the Americas?

European Competition in North America (pages 67–70)

4. What was the Northwest Passage?
5. Why did the Spanish Armada attack England?
6. What did the French and Dutch colonists trade?

The Spanish and Native Americans (pages 71–75)

7. How did Spanish rule affect Native Americans?
8. How did the Columbian Exchange affect Europe?

Beginnings of Slavery in the Americas (pages 76–79)

9. Why did the Spanish and Portuguese use slave labor in their colonies?
10. How did the slave trade work?

CRITICAL THINKING

1. USING YOUR NOTES: FINDING MAIN IDEAS

Event/Idea	Notes
Exploration	
Establishing Colonies	
European Competition	
Columbian Exchange	
Origins of Slavery	

Using your completed chart, answer the questions below.

a. What causes did European competition and exploration have in common?

b. How did the establishment of colonies in the Americas lead to slavery?

c. Which concept in the chart contributed most to the Columbian Exchange?

2. ANALYZING LEADERSHIP

Think about the explorers and *conquistadors* discussed in this chapter. What qualities did they possess that made them successful in their efforts?

3. THEME: IMMIGRATION AND MIGRATION

What were the causes and effects of the migration of Europeans and Africans to the Americas?

4. APPLYING CITIZENSHIP SKILLS

What kind of values did Bartolomé de Las Casas demonstrate in his actions? How effective was he in improving his society?

Interact *with* History

Have your answers about whether or not you would join a voyage of exploration changed after reading the chapter? Explain.

VISUAL SUMMARY

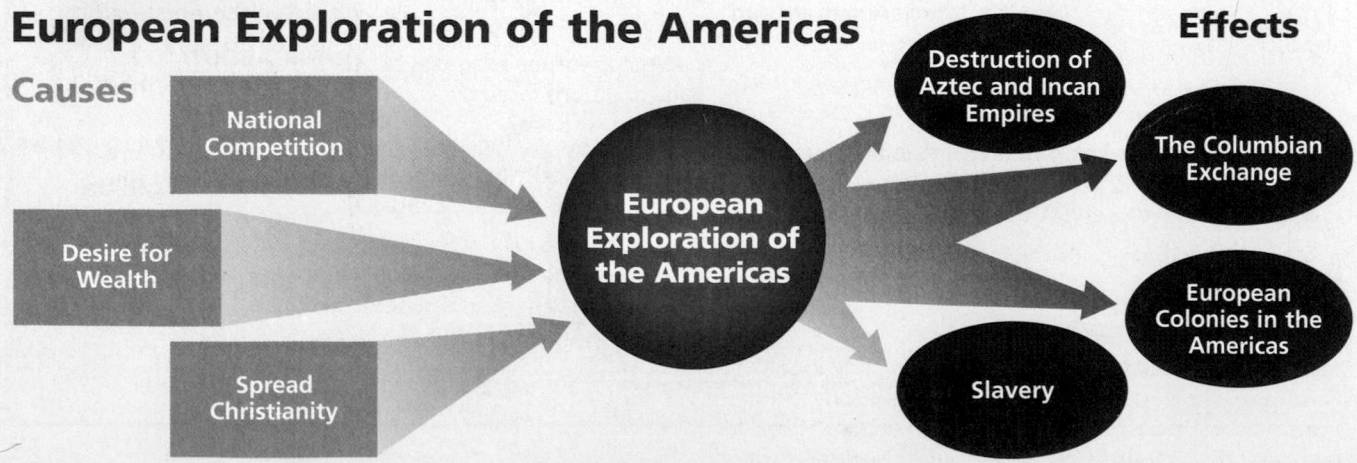

European Exploration of the Americas

Causes

National Competition

Desire for Wealth

Spread Christianity

European Exploration of the Americas

Effects

Destruction of Aztec and Incan Empires

The Columbian Exchange

Slavery

European Colonies in the Americas

Use the chart and your knowledge of U.S. history to answer questions 1 and 2.

Additional Test Practice, pp. S1–S33.

Slaves Imported to the Americas (in thousands)	1601–1810	
REGION/COUNTRY	1601–1700	1701–1810
British N. America	*	348
British Caribbean	263.7	1,401.3
French Caribbean	155.8	1,348.4
Spanish America	292.5	578.6
Dutch Caribbean	40	460
Danish Caribbean	4	24
Brazil (Portugal)	560	1,891.4

*=less than 1,000

Source: Philip D. Curtin, *The Atlantic Slave Trade*

1. Which region or country imported the most slaves to the Americas?
   A. British Caribbean
   B. French Caribbean
   C. Brazil (Portugal)
   D. Spanish Caribbean

2. Which region imported less than 1,000 slaves before 1700?
   A. Brazil (Portugal)
   B. British North America
   C. Danish Caribbean
   D. Dutch Caribbean

This quotation is from Olaudah Equiano, an African slave. Use the quotation and your knowledge of U.S. history to answer question 3.

PRIMARY SOURCE

The first object which saluted my eyes when I arrived on the coast, was the sea, and a slave ship . . . waiting for its cargo. These filled me with astonishment, which was soon converted into terror, when I was carried on board.

Olaudah Equiano, *Great Slave Narratives*

3. The passage supports which of the following conclusions?
   A. Equiano and the others on board felt safe.
   B. The conditions on the ship were horrifying.
   C. Because he protested, Equiano was allowed to return home.
   D. Equiano's circumstances improved after he arrived in the colonies.

TEST PRACTICE
CLASSZONE.COM

ALTERNATIVE ASSESSMENT

1. WRITING ABOUT HISTORY

Write a **newspaper article** about one of these events: *La Noche Triste* in Mexico or the murder of the Incan emperor Atahualpa.

- Use library resources to research Mexican or Incan history.
- Your article should explain what happened and who was involved. Add details that explain when, where, why, and how the event occurred.
- Give your article an interesting headline.

2. COOPERATIVE LEARNING

With a group, create a diorama to depict one of the communities of Spanish America in the 1600s. Your diorama should include features such as a mission, a *hacienda*, roads, mines or sugar mills. Use drawings, maps, and written descriptions that depict daily life.

INTEGRATED TECHNOLOGY

DOING INTERNET RESEARCH

The Columbian Exchange is the movement of plants and animals around the world as a result of exploration. Use the Internet and other library resources to research the movement of a plant or animal around the world.

- Choose a specific plant or animal. You might choose corn, potatoes, chocolate, tea, coffee, sugar, or horses, cattle, or pigs.
- Use your plant or animal as a keyword. Search the Internet to find where the plant or animal first existed and where it moved.

For more about the Columbian Exchange . . .

INTERNET ACTIVITY
CLASSZONE.COM

CHAPTER 3

The English Establish 13 Colonies 1585–1732

Section 1
Early Colonies Have Mixed Success

Section 2
New England Colonies

Section 3
Founding the Middle and Southern Colonies

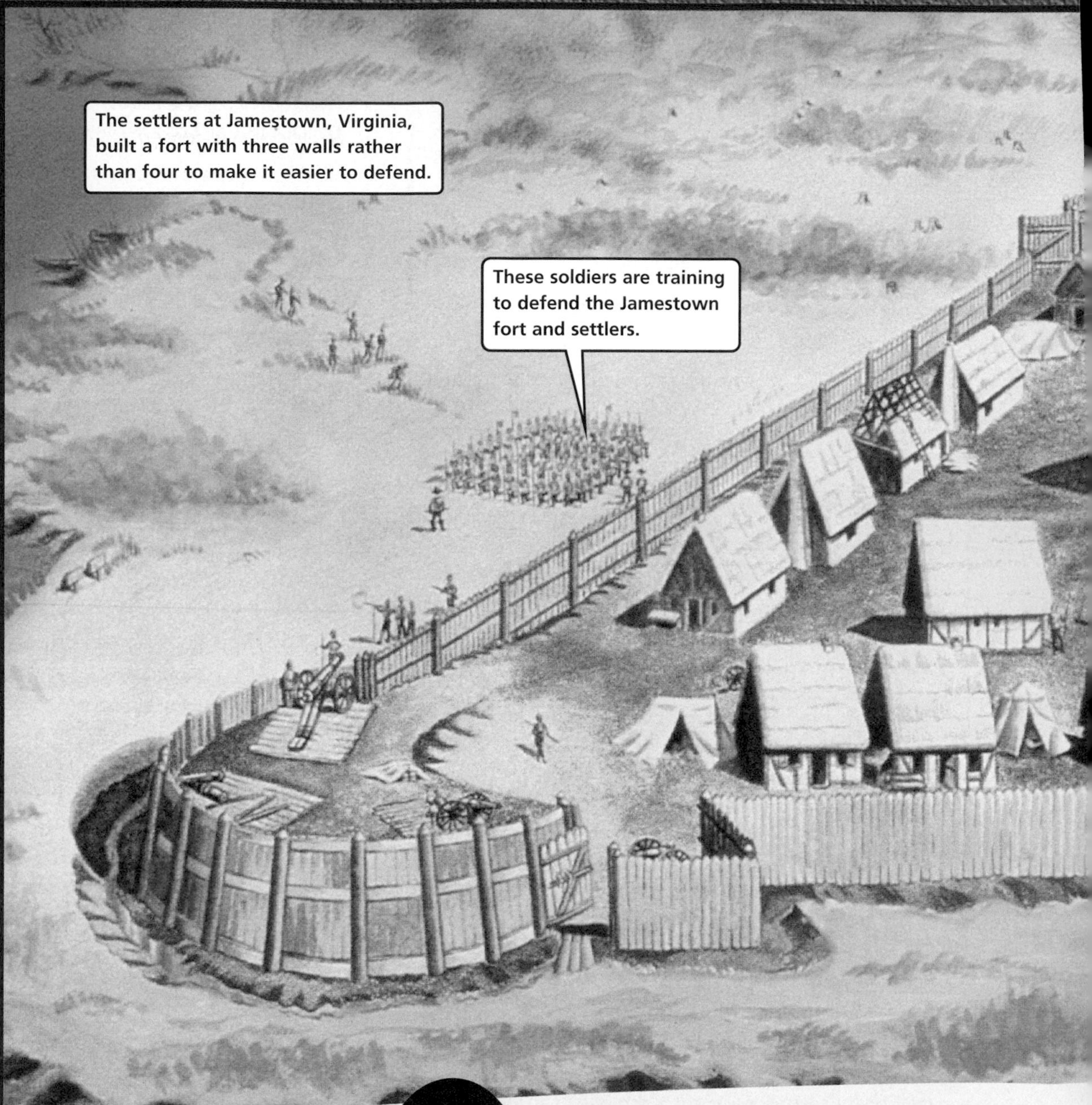

The settlers at Jamestown, Virginia, built a fort with three walls rather than four to make it easier to defend.
These soldiers are training to defend the Jamestown fort and settlers.

N. America
World

1585

1585 First English colony established at Roanoke.

1607 John Smith and other English settlers establish Jamestown.

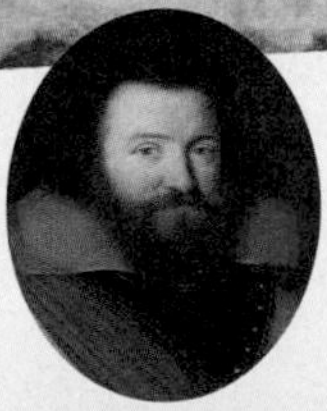

1620 Pilgrims land at Plymouth.

1630 Puritans found Massachusetts Bay Colony.

1587 Foreign missionaries are banished from Japan.

1588 England defeats Spanish Armada.

1605 Akbar, Mughal emperor of India, dies.

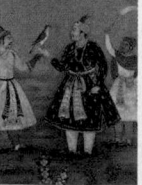

1649 Charles I of England is beheaded.

The year is 1607. You have just sailed across the ocean and arrived in a strange land. Your family has traveled to the eastern coast of North America in search of freedom and prosperity. Your first task in the new land is to decide what you need to do to survive.

What dangers would you face as a settler?

What Do You Think?

- What do you need to survive in the wilderness?
- This settlement is actually a fort, with an armed force and high fences. What reasons might there be for building a fort?
- What kind of settlement would you build?

RESEARCH LINKS
CLASSZONE.COM
Visit the Chapter 3 links for more information about the English colonies.

The settlers' houses were built inside the fort walls for protection.

1664
England takes New Amsterdam from Dutch.

1675
King Philip's War erupts.

1681
William Penn receives charter for Pennsylvania.

1692
Salem witchcraft trials are held.

1732
Colony of Georgia is founded by James Oglethorpe.

1732

1660
English monarchy is restored when Charles II returns from exile.

1688
William and Mary take power in Britain's Glorious Revolution.

Reading Strategy: Sequencing Events

What Do You Know?

What do you already know about the American colonies? What sort of person might choose to leave his or her native country and cross the ocean to settle in a new land?

Think About

- what you've learned about American settlers from movies, television, historical fiction, or science fiction about space travel
- opportunities and challenges offered in a new land
- your responses to the Interact with History about facing dangers as a settler (see page 83)

What Do You Want to Know?

What questions do you have about the Europeans who settled in North America? about those who were already here? Record your questions in your notebook before you read this chapter.

Sequencing Events

Sequencing means putting events in order. In learning about the early colonies, for example, it will be useful to you to list the 13 original colonies and an important early date mentioned for each in the chapter. You might record the name and a date for each colony in a graphic organizer such as the one below. Copy this organizer in your notebook. Fill it in as you read the chapter.

 See Skillbuilder Handbook, page R4.

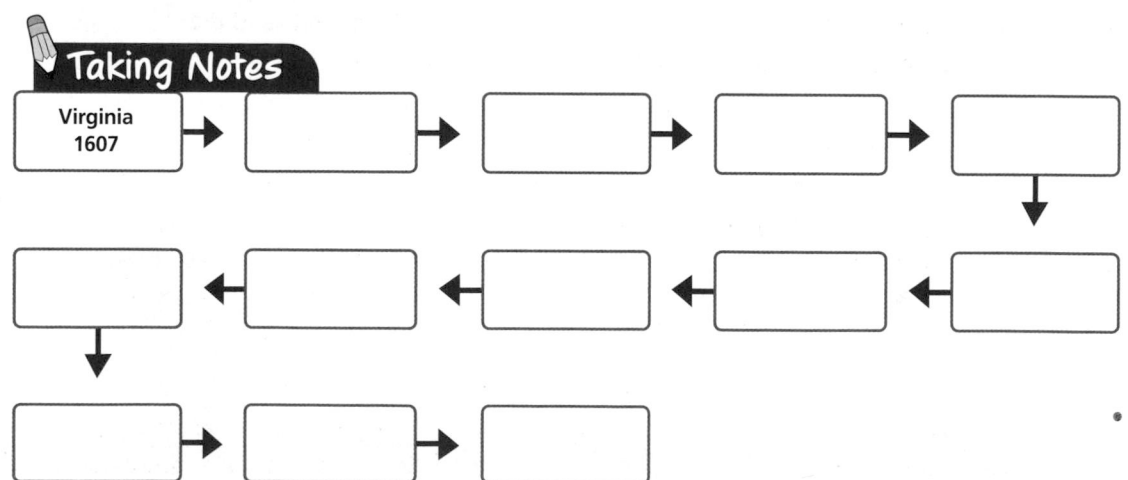

Taking Notes

Virginia 1607

Early Colonies Have Mixed Success

MAIN IDEA	WHY IT MATTERS NOW	TERMS & NAMES
Two early English colonies failed, but Jamestown survived—partly through individual effort and hard work.	Jamestown's survival led to more English colonies and a lasting English influence in the United States.	joint-stock company indentured servant charter House of Burgesses Jamestown Bacon's Rebellion John Smith

ONE AMERICAN'S STORY

In 1585, John White traveled with the first English expedition to Roanoke, an island off North Carolina. White sailed back to England in 1586 and then returned to Roanoke as governor the next year, bringing with him more than 100 settlers. Soon White's daughter Elinor gave birth to a baby girl. John White described the event.

A VOICE FROM THE PAST

On August 18 a daughter was born to Elinor, . . . wife of Ananias Dare. . . . The child was christened on the following Sunday and was named Virginia because she was the first Christian born in Virginia.

John White, *The New World*

In 1587, White was forced to sail back to England a second time to get needed supplies. He left the colonists, including his granddaughter, Virginia, in Roanoke. White was delayed and did not return to Roanoke until 1590.

To his shock and grief, he found no trace of the colonists or his granddaughter, all of whom had disappeared. The only clues to their whereabouts were the letters *CRO* carved in a tree and the word *Croatoan* carved in a doorpost. White never discovered the fate of his family and the other colonists. In this section, you will learn why English settlers such as White came to America despite such hardships.

Drawing by John White of an old man of the Pomeiock tribe.

The English Plan Colonies

As you read in Chapter 2, religious and political rivalries increased between England and Spain in the late 1500s. Spain had many colonies in the Americas, but England had none. England began directing its resources toward establishing colonies after its defeat of the Spanish Armada in 1588.

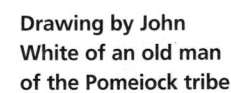

Use your chart to take notes about the early colonies.

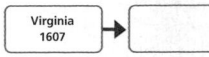

Virginia 1607 →

Richard Hakluyt (HAK•LOOT), an English geographer, urged England to start a colony. Hakluyt thought that colonies would provide a market for English exports. They also would serve as a source of raw materials. By having colonies, England hoped to increase its trade and build up its gold supply. This is the economic theory of mercantilism (see page 62). In mercantilism, the state controls trade and attempts to transfer wealth from colonies to the parent country. Hakluyt also thought that English colonies would help to plant the Protestant faith in the Americas.

The earliest English colonists had many reasons for going to America. The lack of economic opportunity in England forced many to seek their fortunes abroad. Stories of gold mines lured some to leave England. Others left to escape religious persecution.

Reading **History**
A. Summarizing
Why did English colonists settle in America?

Two Early Colonies Fail

Sir Walter Raleigh was a soldier, statesman, and adventurer who served under Queen Elizabeth I of England. She gave him permission to sponsor the colony at Roanoke. He named England's first colony Virginia after the unmarried, or virgin, queen. Financed by Raleigh, the colony began in 1585 on Roanoke Island. The colonists relied on the Native Americans for food. But when the Native Americans realized that the settlers wanted their land, they cut off the colonists' food supply. Those who survived returned to England in 1586.

Vocabulary
financed: paid for; raised funds for

In 1587, artist John White convinced Raleigh to try again to establish the Roanoke colony, with the disastrous results described in One American's Story (page 85). To this day, no one knows for sure what happened. Some historians think that the colonists mingled with the neighboring Native Americans. Others believe that they moved to Chesapeake Bay and were killed by Native Americans defending their land.

In 1607, the Plymouth Company sponsored the Sagadahoc colony at the mouth of the Kennebec River in Maine. Some of the settlers were English convicts. One colonist wrote of George Popham, the governor, "He stocked or planted [the colony] out of all the jails of England." Within the first year, arguments among colonists, a harsh winter, fights with Native Americans, and food shortages forced most of the colonists to return to England.

Now and then

THE LUMBEE AND THE LOST COLONISTS

The Lumbee tribe lives mainly in North Carolina. Some of the Lumbee believe they are descendants of the lost colonists of Roanoke. Among the evidence cited is the fact that 41 of the 95 last names of the Lumbee were last names of the colonists.

Other Lumbee don't believe that they are descended from English ancestors. The Lumbee are trying to win federal recognition as a Native American tribe. English ancestry might weaken their claim for federal financial support.

Financing a Colony

Raleigh had financed the colony at Roanoke. When the colony failed, he lost his investment. The English learned from Raleigh's financial loss at Roanoke that one person could not finance a colony. To raise money, they turned to the **joint-stock company**. Joint-stock companies were backed by investors, people who put money into a project to earn profits. Each investor received pieces of ownership of the company called

shares of stock. In this way, the investors split any profits and divided any losses.

Merchants organized the Virginia Company of London and the Virginia Company of Plymouth. King James I of England granted charters to both companies in 1606. A **charter** was a written contract, issued by a government, giving the holder the right to establish a colony.

Jamestown Is Founded in 1607

In 1607, the Virginia Company of London financed an expedition to Chesapeake Bay that included more than 100 colonists. They sailed up the James River until they found a spot to settle. They named the first permanent English settlement **Jamestown** in honor of King James.

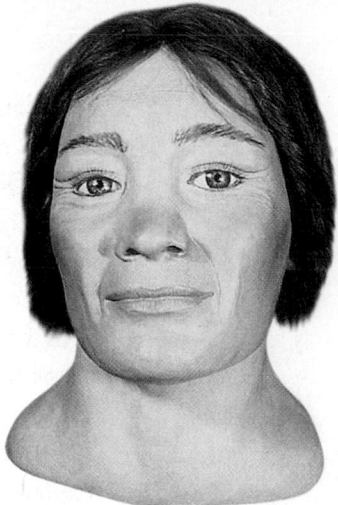

This is a computer reconstruction of the face of Mistress Forrest, believed to be the first English woman to come to Jamestown.

Background
Historians used to believe that the colony's original site had been flooded by the James River. Recent archaeological digs, however, have discovered the site on higher ground.

From the start, the Jamestown colonists endured terrible hardships. The site of the colony was swampy and full of malaria-carrying mosquitoes. This disease made the colonists sick with fever. Many also became ill from drinking the river water. To make matters worse, the London Company had incorrectly told the settlers that the colony would be rich in gold. They spent their days searching for gold rather than building houses and growing food.

The climate was also a hardship. The colonists soon learned that the summers were hot and humid and the winters bitter cold. As one colonist recalled, "There were never Englishmen left in a foreign country in such misery as we were in this newly discovered Virginia."

Jamestown Grows

By January 1608, only 38 colonists remained alive. Later that year, **John Smith,** a soldier and adventurer, took control. To make sure the colonists worked, Smith announced, "He that will not work shall not eat." Smith's methods worked. He ordered an existing wall extended around Jamestown. He also persuaded the Powhatan tribe to trade their corn to the colonists. In 1609, Smith was injured in a gunpowder explosion and returned to England. That same year, 800 more English settlers arrived in Jamestown.

Reading**History**
B. Solving Problems If you had been John Smith, how would you have forced the colonists to work?

Early English Settlements, 1585–1607

Sagadahoc R. (Kennebec)

Sagadahoc, 1607

Massachusetts Bay

Hudson R.

ATLANTIC OCEAN

0   100 Miles

0   200 Kilometers

Potomac R.

Chesapeake Bay

James R.

Jamestown, 1607

Roanoke R.

Roanoke I., 1585, 1587

45°N

40°N

35°N

30°N

GEOGRAPHY SKILLBUILDER Interpreting Maps
1. **Location** Which colony was located northeast of Jamestown? How many miles northeast was it?
2. **Human-Environment Interaction** Why did the colonists settle near the coast?

Because of growing tensions between the settlers and Native Americans, the Powhatan stopped trading food and attacked the settlers. The settlers did not dare leave the fort. During the "starving time," the colonists ate rats, mice, and snakes. Only 60 of the colonists were still alive when two ships arrived in 1610. Lord De La Warr, the new governor, imposed discipline, and the "starving time" ended.

In 1612, John Rolfe developed a high-grade tobacco that the colonists learned to grow. It quickly became very popular in England. The success of tobacco growing changed Jamestown in many ways. The Virginia Company thought of the colonists as employees. The colonists, however, wanted a share of the profits.

The company responded by letting settlers own land. Settlers worked harder when the land was their own. The company offered a 50-acre land grant for each man, woman, or child who could pay his or her way to the colony. In 1619, the first African Americans arrived in Jamestown. The population of Virginia jumped from about 600 in 1619 to more than 2,000 in 1621.

Even more laborers were needed. Those who could not afford passage to America were encouraged to become **indentured servants.** These men and women sold their labor to the person who paid their passage to the colony. After working for a number of years, they were free to farm or take up a trade of their own.

The colonists soon became annoyed at the strict rule of the governor, who represented the Virginia Company's interests back in London. To provide for more local control, the company decided that burgesses, or elected representatives, of the colonists would meet once a year in an assembly. The **House of Burgesses,** created in 1619, became the first representative assembly in the American colonies.

Conflicts with the Powhatan

Cultural differences put the Powhatan and the English on a collision course. At first, the Powhatan traded food with the colonists. Then, as more colonists arrived and wanted land, relations grew worse. In an effort to improve relations between the English colonists and the Powhatan, John Rolfe married Chief Powhatan's daughter, Pocahontas, in 1614.

For a time, there was an uneasy peace. The colonists learned from the Powhatan how to grow corn, catch fish, and capture wild fowl. However, the expanding tobacco plantations took over more and more Powhatan land. In 1622, in response to land grabs by the colonists, the Powhatan killed hundreds of Jamestown's residents.

*Reading*History

C. Analyzing Causes What was the main reason for the various arrangements the Virginia Company came up with to bring people to America?

*Reading*History

D. Finding Main Ideas What was the central dispute between the Powhatan and the settlers?

AMERICA'S HISTORY MAKERS

POCAHONTAS

1595?–1617

Pocahontas met John Smith when she was about 12 years old. Smith taught her English and admired her spirit. She admired Smith's bravery and saved his life twice. After Smith returned to England, she married the colonist John Rolfe in 1614. Shown below is a portrait of Pocahontas, done in 1616.

Two years later, the Rolfes went to England to raise money for the Jamestown colony. While getting ready to sail home, Pocahontas died of smallpox.

How did Pocahontas show that Native Americans and white settlers might live in peace?

Bacon's Rebellion in 1676

As you have seen, many of the English colonists who came to Virginia during the 1600s fought with the Native Americans. They also battled one another. By the 1670s, one-fourth of the free white men were former indentured servants. These colonists, who did not own land, resented the wealthy eastern landowners. The poor settlers lived mostly on Virginia's western frontier, where they battled the Native Americans for land.

Nathaniel Bacon and a group of landless frontier settlers opposed Governor William Berkeley. They complained about high taxes and Governor Berkeley's favoritism toward large plantation owners. Bacon demanded that Berkeley approve a war against the Native Americans to seize their land for tobacco plantations. Governor Berkeley's refusal of Nathaniel Bacon's demand sparked **Bacon's Rebellion** in 1676.

Bacon marched into Jamestown, took control of the House of Burgesses, and burned Jamestown to the ground. Bacon's sudden illness and death ended the rebellion. Berkeley hanged Bacon's followers. Angered by Berkeley's actions, King Charles II recalled the governor to England. After that incident, the House of Burgesses passed laws to prevent a royal governor from assuming such power again. The burgesses had taken an important step against tyranny. In the next section, you will read about the New England colonies and their steps toward independence.

Vocabulary
tyranny: a government in which a single ruler has absolute power

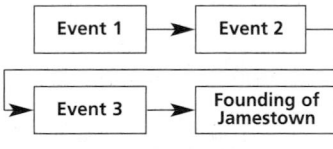

Nathaniel Bacon (right) confronts Virginia governor William Berkeley at Jamestown in 1676.

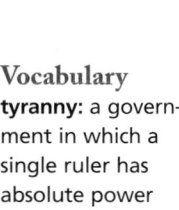
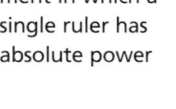

Section 1 Assessment

1. Terms & Names

Explain the significance of:
- joint-stock company
- charter
- Jamestown
- John Smith
- indentured servant
- House of Burgesses
- Bacon's Rebellion

2. Using Graphics

Use a series-of-events chain to review events that led to the founding of Jamestown.

Event 1 → Event 2 → Event 3 → Founding of Jamestown

What were reasons England wanted colonies in America?

3. Main Ideas

a. Why did the first English settlement at Roanoke fail?

b. How did the English finance their colonies after 1606?

c. What was the outcome of Bacon's Rebellion?

4. Critical Thinking

Drawing Conclusions
What were the main reasons that Jamestown survived and prospered?

THINK ABOUT
- how, after the "starving time," Lord De La Warr took control
- John Rolfe's development of a high-grade tobacco plant

ACTIVITY OPTIONS

ART
LANGUAGE ARTS

You need indentured servants to work on your plantation. Draw a **poster** or write an **advertisement** that will attract people to your plantation.

Report from the New World

You are a settler who has landed on the wild eastern shore of North America. You and your 93 fellow colonists survived a frightening nine-week Atlantic voyage. Now you are struggling to build a new home in the wilderness. There are no roads, inns, or towns in this land. The game, berries, and fish here taste strange, sometimes unpleasant. Your only neighbors are small groups of Native Americans.

COOPERATIVE LEARNING On these pages are challenges you face as you put down roots in America. Working with a small group, decide how to deal with each challenge. Choose an option, assign a task to each group member, and do the activity. You will find useful information in the Data File. Be prepared to present your solutions to the class as part of a report to your sponsors back in England.

CIVICS CHALLENGE

"They had little or no care of any other thing, but to pamper their bellies."

As your colony takes root, most members work hard to farm, cook, wash, mend, trade, and defend the colony. But a few colonists think only of their own comfort. You call a meeting to set some rules about work. Present your solution to this problem using one of these options:

• Make a poster for the meeting hall that states the new work rules and punishments.

• Write a report describing the problem and how the colony solved it.

ECONOMICS CHALLENGE

"A bright tin dish most pleased him."

By the time spring arrives, your stores of English foods are running low. You and your friends decide to try trading with the neighboring Native Americans. They could provide a steady supply of meat, fish, and vegetables until your harvest comes in. Develop a plan for opening trade. Present your plan using one of these options:

- As a group, role-play the meeting in which you create your trading plan.
- Write instructions for the team of colonists who will open trade with the Native Americans.

ACTIVITY WRAP-UP

Present to the class As a group, review your solution to each challenge. Consider the following:

- How well each solution meets its particular challenge
- Which solution shows the most creativity

Once you have made your decision, present your solutions to the class. Each group member should take part in the presentation.

The Journey

Distance: more than 5,000 nautical miles from Europe to the east coast of North America

Length: 6–14 weeks

Dangers: storms, scurvy, dysentery, malnutrition, seasickness, overcrowding

Food and Livestock Taken

barrels of salted beef, oatmeal, dried grains, cheese, oil, vinegar, and salt; seeds for peas, barley, herbs, and other crops; cows, horses, goats, pigs, sheep, and chickens

Equipment Taken

axes, hoes, nails, hooks for doors, hammers, chisels, hatchets, spades, pickaxes, iron pots, copper kettles, skillets, platters, dishes, wooden spoons, rugs

Weapons Taken

swords, muskets, daggers, gunpowder, light armor, cannon

Clothes Taken

shirts, several pairs of shoes, leather for mending, waistcoats, caps, skirts, jackets, trousers

Dangers in America

Biggest killers: typhoid, dysentery, famine

Other dangers: pneumonia, malaria, and other diseases; exposure to harsh weather; fire; wild animals; attacks by Native Americans

Benefits in America

religious and political freedom; opportunity to own land; abundant timber for shelters, forts, heat, ships, and trade; rich food resources

For more about the American colonies . . .

RESEARCH LINKS
CLASSZONE.COM

New England Colonies

MAIN IDEA	WHY IT MATTERS NOW	TERMS & NAMES
Religion influenced the settlement and government of the New England colonies.	The Puritan work ethic and religious beliefs influence American culture today.	Pilgrims Mayflower Compact Puritans Great Migration Fundamental Orders of Connecticut Roger Williams Anne Hutchinson King Philip's War

ONE AMERICAN'S STORY

In 1605, Englishmen captured and enslaved a Native American named Squanto and took him to England. Squanto returned to America in 1619. There he discovered that his Pawtuxet tribe had been killed by disease. In 1621, Squanto set about helping the English plant crops on tribal lands. Colonist William Bradford made the following comment.

A VOICE FROM THE PAST

Squanto . . . was a special instrument sent of God for their [the colonists'] good beyond their expectation. . . . He directed them how to set their corn, where to take fish, and to procure other commodities, and was also their pilot to bring them to unknown places.

William Bradford, quoted in *The Pilgrim Reader*

In this section, you will learn about the Pilgrims and Puritans, their relations with the Native Americans, and their settlement of the New England colonies.

Squanto teaches the Pilgrims how to grow corn.

The Voyage of the *Mayflower*

Taking Notes

Use your chart to take notes about the New England colonies.

Virginia 1607 → ▢

In the early 1500s, King Henry VIII of England broke that country's ties with the Catholic Church and established the Church of England, an official state church under his control. In the early 1600s, a religious group called the Separatists called for a total break with the Church of England. They thought it was too much like the Catholic Church.

The **Pilgrims** were a Separatist group. King James attacked them for rejecting England's official church. To escape this harsh treatment, the Pilgrims fled to Holland, a country known for its acceptance of different opinions. Eventually, the Pilgrims became dissatisfied with life in Holland. They approached the Virginia Company and asked if they could settle in America "as a distinct body by themselves." The Virginia

The *Mayflower* brings the Pilgrims to Plymouth in 1620.

Company arranged for them to settle on land within its boundaries on the eastern coast of North America.

On a cold, raw November day in 1620, a ship called the *Mayflower* arrived off Cape Cod on the Massachusetts coast. Blown north of its course, the *Mayflower* landed in an area that John Smith had mapped and called New England. They landed at a site that had been named Plymouth.

Because the Pilgrims landed outside the limits of the Virginia Company, their charter did not apply. For the sake of order, the men aboard the *Mayflower* signed an agreement called the **Mayflower Compact.** In it, they vowed to obey laws agreed upon for the good of the colony. The Mayflower Compact helped establish the idea of self-government and majority rule. (See Interactive Primary Sources, page 98.)

The Pilgrims Found Plymouth

Like the early settlers at Jamestown, the Pilgrims at Plymouth endured a starving time. That first winter, disease and death struck with such fury that "the living were scarce able to bury the dead." Half the group had died by spring.

However, energy, hope, and help returned. One day a Native American walked up to a group of colonists. To their astonishment, he called out, "Welcome, Englishmen." This was Samoset, a Pemaquid who had learned to speak English from European fishermen. Samoset introduced the settlers to another Native American named Squanto, a Pawtuxet, who also spoke English.

> "Welcome, Englishmen."
> Samoset

Reading History
A. Making Inferences
Why do you think Squanto was so helpful to the Pilgrims?

The Pilgrims had angered the Native Americans by taking their corn. Squanto acted as an interpreter between the Pilgrims and Chief Massasoit. He helped them to negotiate a peace treaty and showed them how to plant, hunt, and fish. While their crops grew, the colonists began trading with the Native Americans for furs and preparing lumber to ship back to England in order to make a profit.

Sometime in the fall—no one knows exactly when—the Plymouth settlement celebrated the blessings of a good harvest by holding a three-day feast. It was the first Thanksgiving. This Thanksgiving came to represent the peace that existed at that time between the Native Americans and Pilgrims.

America's
HERITAGE

THE FIRST THANKSGIVING
It is hard to believe, but turkey was not on the menu at the first Thanksgiving. The Pilgrims and Native Americans ate venison (deer), roast duck, roast goose, clams and other shellfish, and eel (shown below). Other treats were white bread and corn bread, leeks, watercress, and salad herbs. The guests topped off their meal with wild plums and dried berries for dessert.

Thanks to the help of Squanto and other Native Americans, the Pilgrims learned to survive in their new environment. Soon more people would sail to New England seeking religious freedom.

The Puritans Come to Massachusetts Bay

Between about 1630 and 1640, a religious group called the **Puritans** left England to escape bad treatment by King James I. Unlike the Separatists, who wanted to break away from the Church of England, the Puritans wanted to reform, or "purify," its practices. By the thousands, Puritan families left for the Americas. Their leaving is known as the **Great Migration**. Many thousands of Puritans left their homeland to found new settlements around the world. Of these settlers, about 20,000 crossed the Atlantic Ocean to New England.

Many Puritan merchants had invested in the Massachusetts Bay Company. In 1629, the company received a royal charter to settle land in New England. In 1630, 11 well-supplied ships carried about 1,000 passengers to the Massachusetts Bay Colony. Unlike earlier colonists, the Puritans were well prepared and did not suffer through a starving time. John Winthrop was the colony's Puritan governor. He stated that the new colony would be a commonwealth, a community in which people work together for the good of the whole.

Background
During the Great Migration, the Puritans also went to Ireland, the Netherlands, the Rhineland, and the West Indies.

> *A VOICE FROM THE PAST*
>
> So shall we keep the unity of the spirit, in the bond of peace. . . . Ten of us will be able to resist a thousand of our enemies. . . . For we must consider that we shall be as a City upon a Hill, the eyes of all people are on us.
>
> **John Winthrop,** *"Model of Christian Charity"*

Reading **History**
B. Making Inferences After Winthrop, politicians sometimes spoke of America as "a city upon a hill." What does this phrase suggest about America's role in the world?

The New England Way

The basic unit of the commonwealth was the congregation—a group of people who belong to the same church. Each Puritan congregation set up its own town. The meetinghouse was the most important building in each town. There people gathered for town meetings, a form of self-government in which people made laws and other decisions for the community. In the Massachusetts Bay Colony, only male church members could vote or hold office. They elected representatives to a lawmaking body called the General Court, which in turn chose the governor.

By law, everyone in town had to attend church services held in the meetinghouse. The sermon, the most important part of the church service, provided instruction in the "New England Way." This was a term

Vocabulary
godliness: piety, reverence

used by the Puritans to describe both their beliefs and their society, which emphasized duty, godliness, hard work, and honesty. The Puritans thought that amusements such as dancing and playing games would lead to laziness. They believed that God required them to work long and hard at their vocation.

Reading **History**
C. Summarizing
What were some important elements of the New England Way?

The Puritan work ethic helped contribute to the rapid growth and success of the New England colonies. The New England Way also depended on education. Because the Puritans wanted everyone to be able to read the Bible, laws required that all children learn to read.

Some Puritan congregations set up new colonies. In 1636, Thomas Hooker moved his congregation to the Connecticut Valley. There they wrote and adopted the **Fundamental Orders of Connecticut** in 1639 (see page 98). In effect, these laws were a constitution. The Fundamental Orders extended voting rights to non-church members and limited the power of the governor. They expanded the idea of representative government.

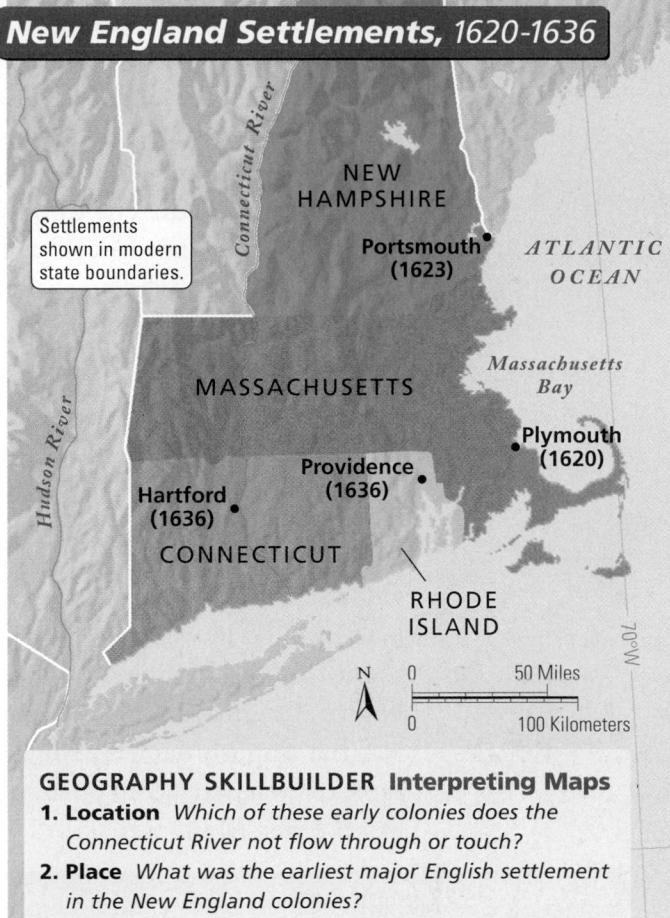

New England Settlements, 1620-1636

Settlements shown in modern state boundaries.

NEW HAMPSHIRE

Portsmouth (1623)

ATLANTIC OCEAN

MASSACHUSETTS

Massachusetts Bay

Plymouth (1620)

Providence (1636)

Hartford (1636)

CONNECTICUT

RHODE ISLAND

N

0   50 Miles

0   100 Kilometers

GEOGRAPHY SKILLBUILDER Interpreting Maps
1. **Location** Which of these early colonies does the Connecticut River not flow through or touch?
2. **Place** What was the earliest major English settlement in the New England colonies?

The first European settlement in New Hampshire was a village near Portsmouth in 1623. In 1638, John Wheelwright established the town of Exeter. The town's founders drew up the Exeter Compact, which was based on the Mayflower Compact.

Challenges to Puritan Leaders

Not everyone agreed with the New England Way. **Roger Williams** was a minister in Salem, Massachusetts, who founded the first Baptist church in America. He opposed forced attendance at church. He also opposed the English colonists' taking of Native American lands by force. Because of his beliefs, the General Court forced Williams to leave the colony. In 1636, he fled southward and founded the colony of Rhode Island, which guaranteed religious freedom and the separation of church and state.

Anne Hutchinson believed that a person could worship God without the help of a church, minister, or Bible. She conducted discussions in her home that challenged church authority. Hutchinson was brought to trial and forced to leave Massachusetts. In 1638, she fled to Rhode Island.

Anne Hutchinson preaches in her home in Boston.

Another religious group was the Quakers. Their name came from an early leader's statement that they should "tremble [quake] at the word of the Lord." Opponents coined the name as an insult. Quakers challenged the Massachusetts commonwealth. They believed that each person could know God directly through "an inner light." Neither ministers nor the Bible was needed. Quakers also believed in treating Native Americans fairly, which set them apart from other colonists. For such beliefs, Quakers were whipped, imprisoned, and hanged. Many left for Rhode Island.

Reading **History**
D. Forming Opinions Why is it odd that the Puritans persecuted certain individuals and groups for their religious beliefs?

King Philip's War

The growing population of colonists began to force the Native Americans from their land. Europeans and Native Americans defined land ownership differently. To Europeans, land could be owned by individuals. To Native Americans, land belonged to everyone. Conflict over land resulted in warfare.

In 1675–1676, the Puritan colonies fought a brutal war with the Native Americans. This was known as **King Philip's War.** "King Philip" was the English name of Metacom, leader of the Wampanoag. To help fight the war, Metacom organized an alliance of tribes. The Wampanoag lost the war. Many were killed, while others were sold into slavery in the West Indies. Those who remained lost their land and were forced to become laborers. English settlers expanded even farther into Native American land.

Background
Metacom was the son of Massasoit, friend of the Pilgrims.

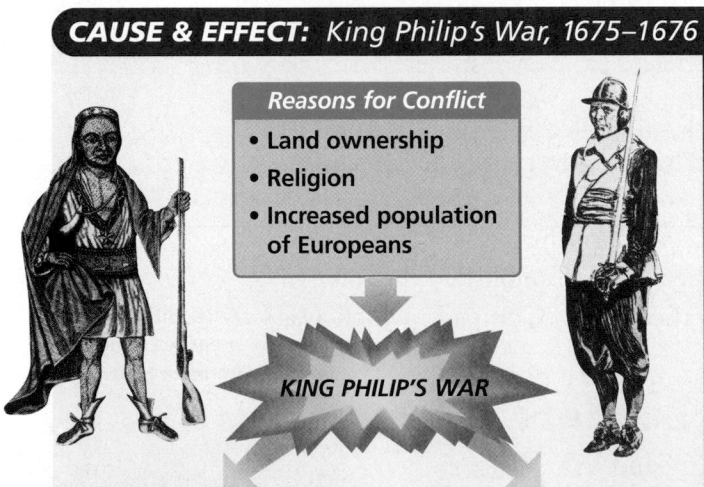

CAUSE & EFFECT: *King Philip's War, 1675–1676*

Reasons for Conflict
• Land ownership
• Religion
• Increased population of Europeans

KING PHILIP'S WAR

Native American Losses
• Approximately 3,000 killed
• King Philip (Metacom) killed
• About 500 Native Americans enslaved

European Losses
• About 600 settlers killed
• More than 45 villages attacked
• About 12 villages destroyed

Sources: *Encyclopedia Britannica, World Book Encyclopedia*

SKILLBUILDER Interpreting Charts

1. *Was there a greater loss of life among the settlers or the Native Americans?*
2. *How might the growing population of Europeans have created more conflict with the Native Americans?*

The Salem Witchcraft Trials

Puritan New England was originally a society centered on the church. By the late 1600s, however, this had begun to change. Societal changes in Puritan New England had led to an atmosphere of fear and suspicion. Then, several Salem village girls were told frightening stories about witches by Tituba, a slave from the West Indies. Pretending to be bewitched, the girls falsely accused others of witchcraft. The witch-hunts began in 1692. The clergy viewed the Salem witch-hunts and trials as a sign from God for the village to return to a strict Puritan lifestyle.

This mid-nineteenth-century oil painting, *The Trial of George Jacobs, August 5, 1692,* was painted by T. H. Matteson in 1855. It captures the horrors of the Salem witch trials. As the young women cry out, the accused tries to defend himself against charges that he bewitched them.

Jacobs's own granddaughter testified against him. He was tried and convicted on August 5, 1692, and executed two weeks later along with four neighbors.

How accurately do you think the painting shows the strong emotions in the courtroom?

Vocabulary
scapegoat: one that is made to bear the blame of others

Hysteria spread through Salem. Those accused were forced to name others as witches. More than 100 people were arrested and tried. Of those, 20 were found guilty and put to death. Nineteen persons were hanged, and another was pressed to death by heavy stones when he refused to enter a plea in response to the charge of witchcraft. The panic was short-lived, and Salem came to its senses. The experience showed, however, how a society can create scapegoats for its problems.

In the next section, you will read about the Middle and Southern colonies, how they were founded, and how they provided the new settlers with economic opportunities.

Section 2 Assessment

1. Terms & Names

Explain the significance of:
- Pilgrims
- Mayflower Compact
- Puritans
- Great Migration
- Fundamental Orders of Connecticut
- Roger Williams
- Anne Hutchinson
- King Philip's War

2. Using Graphics

Use a cluster diagram to review details about the New England Way.

New England Way

Which parts would you find easy to accept? Which difficult?

3. Main Ideas

a. What is the Mayflower Compact?

b. What is the meaning of the term the "Great Migration"?

c. What were some of the causes of King Philip's War?

4. Critical Thinking

Recognizing Effects What impact did the arrival of the English in New England have on the Native Americans?

THINK ABOUT
- Squanto
- Chief Massasoit
- King Philip's War

ACTIVITY OPTIONS

LANGUAGE ARTS
SPEECH

Choose one of the Puritan dissenters from this section and retell his or her story. Either write a **newspaper article** about the person or give an **oral history.**

The Mayflower Compact

Setting the Stage In 1620, 41 of the colonists aboard the *Mayflower* drew up the Mayflower Compact. This document refers to the area where they landed as "Virginia" because the land grants of the Virginia Company extended into New England. The colonists provided for self-government under majority rule of the male voters. **See Primary Source Explorer**

A CLOSER LOOK

REASONS FOR VOYAGE

The three reasons the colonists give for their voyage to the eastern seaboard of North America are the glory of God, the advancement of Christianity, and the honor of the king.

1. Why might sailing to new lands advance Christianity?

A CLOSER LOOK

GUIDING PURPOSE

The general good of the colony is the guiding purpose of the colonists in signing the compact.

2. What does this suggest about the relationship between the individual and the community?

We, whose names are underwritten, . . . having undertaken for the glory of God, and advancement of the Christian faith, and the honor of our King and country, a voyage to plant the first colony in the northern parts of Virginia, do by these presents, solemnly and mutually in the presence of God and one another **covenant**[1] and combine ourselves together into a civil **body politic**,[2] for our better ordering and preservation; and furtherance of the ends aforesaid . . . do enact, constitute, and frame such just and equal laws, ordinances, acts, constitutions, and offices from time to time as shall be thought most [proper] and convenient for the general good of the colony unto which we promise all due submission and obedience. In witness whereof we have hereunto subscribed our names at Cape Cod the eleventh of November, in the year of our **sovereign**[3] lord King James of England . . . Anno Domini 1620.

From B. P. Poore, ed., *The Federal and State Constitutions*, Part I, p. 931.

1. **covenant:** promise in a binding agreement.
2. **body politic:** the people of a politically organized group.
3. **sovereign:** supreme.

The Fundamental Orders of Connecticut

Setting the Stage In January 1639, male citizens of three townships in Connecticut (Hartford, Windsor, and Wethersfield) assembled and drew up the Fundamental Orders of Connecticut. This document is often called the first written constitution in America. It contains a preamble, or introduction, and a set of laws. **See Primary Source Explorer**

Preamble

Forasmuch as it has pleased the Almighty God by the wise disposition of His Divine Providence so to order and dispose of things that we, the inhabitants and residents of Windsor, Hartford, and Wethersfield are now cohabiting

and dwelling in and upon the river of Conectecotte [Connecticut] and the lands thereunto adjoining; and well knowing where a people are gathered together the Word of God requires that, to maintain the peace and union of such a people, there should be an orderly and decent government established according to God, to order and dispose of the affairs of the people at all seasons as occasion shall require; do therefore associate and **conjoin**[1] ourselves to be as one public state or commonwealth. . . . As also in our civil affairs to be guided and governed according to such laws, rules, orders, and decrees as shall be made, ordered and decreed, as follows:

Laws, Rules, and Orders

1. It is ordered, sentenced, and decreed that there shall be yearly two general assemblies or courts. . . . The first shall be called the Court of Election, wherein shall be yearly chosen . . . so many magistrates and other public officers as shall be found **requisite**.[2] . . .

4. It is ordered . . . that no person be chosen governor above once in two years, and that the governor be always a member of some approved congregation. . . .

5. It is ordered . . . that to the aforesaid Court of Election the several towns shall send their deputies. . . . Also, the other General Court in September shall be for making of laws, and any other public occasion which concerns the good of the Commonwealth. . . .

7. It is ordered . . . that after there are warrants given out for any of the said General Courts, the constable or constables of each town shall forthwith give notice distinctly to the inhabitants of the same . . . that at a place and time . . . they meet and assemble themselves together to elect and choose certain deputies to be at the General Court then following to [manage] the affairs of the Commonwealth. . . .

1. **conjoin:** unite.
2. **requisite:** required.

A CLOSER LOOK

GOOD GOVERNMENT

Good government is pleasing to God in the eyes of the colonists. An orderly and decent government helps to maintain peace and order within a community and between people.

3. How would you define good government today?

A CLOSER LOOK

THE GOVERNOR'S ROLE

The person serving as governor can serve only once every two years and must be a member of an approved congregation.

4. Why might the colonists have wished to limit the power of the chief executive?

A CLOSER LOOK

THE COURTS

The Court of Election chooses officials to serve; the General Court makes laws.

5. Why might it be a good idea to separate these two functions?

Interactive Primary Sources Assessment

1. Main Ideas

a. Whose rights did the Mayflower Compact protect?

b. Why are written documents useful in setting up a government?

c. How were the Fundamental Orders based on religion?

2. Critical Thinking

Supporting Opinions
How do you think these documents reflect the English contribution to American democracy?

THINK ABOUT
• self-government
• majority rule

Founding the Middle and Southern Colonies

MAIN IDEA	WHY IT MATTERS NOW	TERMS & NAMES
The founding of the Middle and Southern colonies provided settlers with many economic opportunities.	America is still a place where immigrants seek freedom and economic opportunity.	Peter Stuyvesant William Penn patroon Quaker Duke of York royal colony proprietary colony James Oglethorpe

ONE AMERICAN'S STORY

In 1624, the Dutch founded the colony of New Netherland (later New York) on the eastern coast of North America. **Peter Stuyvesant**, the new governor, arrived in the city of New Amsterdam in May 1647. Because of his rough manner, he lost the support of the Dutch colonists. In 1664, a British fleet ordered the city of New Amsterdam to surrender itself to British control. Unable to gain the support of the Dutch colonists, Stuyvesant surrendered. He then defended his decision to his superiors back in the Netherlands.

A VOICE FROM THE PAST

Powder and provisions failing, and no relief or reinforcements being expected, we were necessitated [forced] to come to terms with the enemy, not through neglect of duty or cowardice . . . but in consequence of an absolute impossibility to defend the fort.

Peter Stuyvesant, quoted in *Peter Stuyvesant and His New York*

In this section, you will read about the founding of the Middle Colonies (such as New York) and the Southern Colonies.

Peter Stuyvesant, governor of the Dutch colony of New Netherland, lost his leg in 1644 during a military action against the island of St. Martin in the Caribbean.

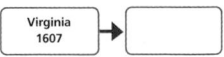

Taking Notes

Use your chart to take notes about the middle and southern colonies.

Virginia 1607 → [ ]

The Middle Colonies

The Middle Colonies were New York, New Jersey, Pennsylvania, and Delaware. They were located between New England to the north and the Chesapeake region to the south. (See the map on page 102.) Swedes, Dutch, English, Germans, and Africans were among the groups who came to these colonies.

Religious freedom attracted many groups, including Protestants, Catholics, Quakers, and Jews. The Hudson and Delaware rivers supported shipping and commerce. The river valleys had rich soil and mild winters. These conditions were favorable for farming and raising livestock.

New Netherland Becomes New York

In 1624, Dutch settlers financed by the Dutch West India Company founded the colony of New Netherland. New Netherland included the Hudson River valley, Long Island, and the land along the Delaware River.

To attract more settlers, the Dutch West India Company employed the patroon system. A **patroon** was a person who brought 50 settlers to New Netherland. As a reward, a patroon received a large land grant. He also received special privileges in hunting, fishing, and fur trading on his land.

In the early years, many different kinds of people settled in New Netherland. Twenty-three Jewish settlers arrived in 1654, and others soon followed. Later, Africans were brought to the colony as slaves and indentured servants. Many Puritans also came.

Peter Stuyvesant, the colony's governor, wanted to add land to New Netherland. He attacked the nearby charter colony of New Sweden in 1655. This colony was located along the Delaware River. The main settlement was Fort Christina (later named Wilmington, Delaware). It had been settled by Swedes in 1638. After an attack by the Dutch, the Swedes surrendered Fort Christina.

Background
The Duke of York became King James II in 1685.

England's King Charles II decided that his brother, the **Duke of York,** should drive the Dutch out of New Netherland. The Dutch colony was a threat to England because of its trade. It was also a threat because of its expanding settlements and its location. There were English colonies in New England to the north and Virginia to the south. As you have seen, when the duke's ships appeared off New Amsterdam in August 1664, the colony surrendered. New Netherland became the **proprietary colony** of New York. The Duke of York was now the proprietor, or owner, of the colony.

New Jersey, Pennsylvania, and Delaware

The Duke of York had become the largest single landowner in America. He gave part of his claim, the province of New Jersey, to his friends Sir George Carteret and Lord John Berkeley in 1664. They encouraged settlers to come by promising freedom of religion. They also promised large grants of land and a representative assembly.

Reading **History**
A. Forming Opinions Why might the promise of religious freedom encourage a diverse population in a colony?

William Penn became another large landowner in America. Born into a wealthy English family, Penn joined the **Quakers,** to his father's disapproval. The young Penn was attacked for his Quaker beliefs. King Charles II owed the Penn family money. In repayment, in 1681 he gave Penn a large piece of land in America that came to be called Pennsylvania. The name means "Penn's woods."

America's HERITAGE

THE LOG CABIN

Swedish colonists living in Delaware built the first log cabin in America in 1638. The log cabin was the perfect house to build where there were many trees. Settlers needed few tools to build such cabins, which were made of round logs with curved notches at the ends. After the ends were placed in the notches, the logs were secured. After 1780, the log cabin became the typical frontier home.

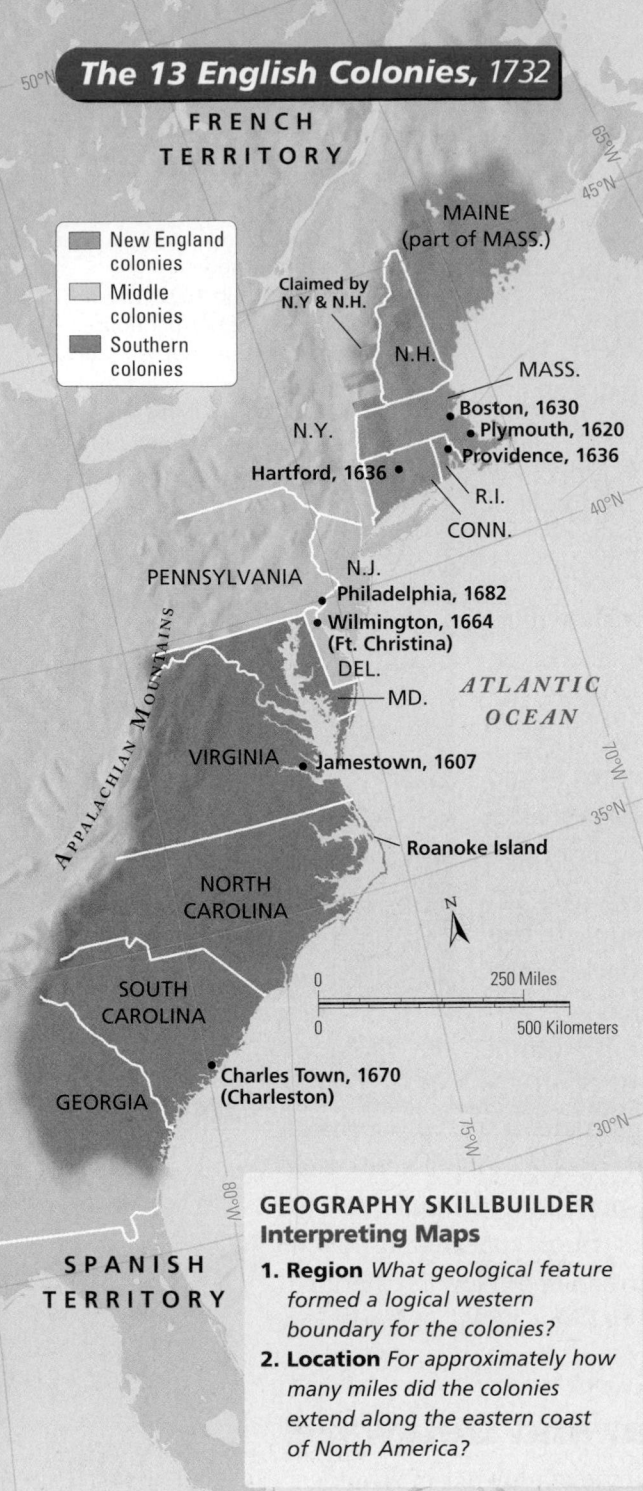

The 13 English Colonies, 1732

FRENCH TERRITORY

- New England colonies
- Middle colonies
- Southern colonies

MAINE (part of MASS.)

Claimed by N.Y & N.H.

N.H.

MASS.
Boston, 1630
Plymouth, 1620
Providence, 1636

N.Y.

Hartford, 1636

R.I.

CONN.

PENNSYLVANIA

N.J.

Philadelphia, 1682
Wilmington, 1664 (Ft. Christina)
DEL.
MD.

ATLANTIC OCEAN

VIRGINIA   Jamestown, 1607

Roanoke Island

NORTH CAROLINA

SOUTH CAROLINA

GEORGIA

Charles Town, 1670 (Charleston)

APPALACHIAN MOUNTAINS

0   250 Miles
0   500 Kilometers

SPANISH TERRITORY

GEOGRAPHY SKILLBUILDER
Interpreting Maps
1. **Region** What geological feature formed a logical western boundary for the colonies?
2. **Location** For approximately how many miles did the colonies extend along the eastern coast of North America?

Penn used this land to create a colony where Quakers could live according to their beliefs. Among other things, the Quakers believed that all people should live in peace and harmony. They welcomed different religions and ethnic groups. In Pennsylvania, Penn extended religious freedom and equality to all. He especially wanted the Native Americans to be treated fairly. In a letter to them in 1681, Penn said, "May [we] always live together as neighbors and friends."

Penn's policies helped make Pennsylvania one of the wealthiest of the American colonies. Many settlers came to Pennsylvania seeking religious freedom and a better life. In 1704, Penn granted the three lower counties of Delaware their own assembly. The counties later broke away to form the colony of Delaware.

Reading **History**
B. Comparing and Contrasting How did Penn's policies toward Native Americans compare with those of other colonies you have read about?

The Southern Colonies

The new Southern Colonies were Maryland, the Carolinas, and Georgia. The Appalachian Mountains bordered parts of these colonies in the west. In the east, the colonies bordered the Atlantic Ocean. The soil and climate of this region were suitable for warm-weather crops such as tobacco, rice, and indigo.

Maryland and the Carolinas

Lord Baltimore established Maryland in 1632 for Roman Catholics fleeing persecution in England. To attract other settlers besides Catholics, Lord Baltimore promised religious freedom. In 1649, Maryland passed the Toleration Act.

Maryland based its economy on tobacco, which required backbreaking work. Every three or four years, the tobacco crop used up the soil, and workers had to clear new land. Most laborers came as either servants or slaves. Maryland attracted few women as settlers.

In 1663, Carolina was founded as a colony. English settlers from Barbados built Charles Town, later called Charleston, in 1670. They

busied themselves cutting timber, raising cattle, and trading with the Native Americans. After 1685, Charleston became a refuge for Huguenots, French Protestants seeking religious freedom.

Carolina's colonists needed laborers to grow rice and indigo. The English settlers encouraged the use of enslaved Africans. They also sold local Native Americans into slavery. As a result, wars broke out between the settlers and the Tuscarora and Yamasee tribes. The settlers' taking of tribal lands also fueled the wars.

Carolina's proprietors, or owners, refused to send help to stop a threatened Spanish attack on Charleston. Because of this, the colonists overthrew the colony's proprietary rule in 1719. In 1729, Carolina became a **royal colony**. Then it was ruled by governors appointed by the king. The colony was divided into North Carolina and South Carolina.

Georgia

James Oglethorpe was the founder of Georgia.

In 1732, **James Oglethorpe** founded Georgia as a refuge for debtors. The English government wanted to use the colony as a military outpost against Spanish Florida to the south and French Louisiana to the west. In 1739, during a war between England and Spain, the Spanish tried to force the English colonists out of Georgia but were unsuccessful. English, German, Swiss, and Scottish colonists settled in Georgia. All religions were welcome. As the colony's leader, Oglethorpe set strict rules that upset the colonists. The king, in response to unrest, made Georgia a royal colony in 1752.

By the early 1700s, there were 13 English colonies along the eastern coast of North America. In the next chapter, you will read about how these colonies developed.

Reading **History**
C. Reading a Map Use the map on page 102 to check the location of Georgia in relation to the Spanish territory of Florida.

Section 3 Assessment

1. Terms & Names

Explain the significance of:

- Peter Stuyvesant
- patroon
- Duke of York
- proprietary colony
- William Penn
- Quaker
- royal colony
- James Oglethorpe

2. Using Graphics

Identify an effect for each cause listed in the chart below.

Cause	Effect
New Netherland threat to English	
English attacked Quakers	
Laborers needed in Carolinas	
Oglethorpe too strict in Georgia	

3. Main Ideas

a. What were the goals of the patroon system?

b. What three Middle Colonies offered religious freedom?

c. What were three crops grown in the Southern Colonies?

4. Critical Thinking

Analyzing Causes Why did colonists in Maryland and the Carolinas enslave Native Americans and use African slaves?

THINK ABOUT
- the crops being grown
- the nature of farm work

ACTIVITY OPTIONS

LANGUAGE ARTS
SCIENCE

What are the health effects of tobacco? Write a **news article** or give a **television report** for a science show about the effects of tobacco on the body.

TERMS & NAMES

Briefly explain the significance of each of the following.

1. joint-stock company
2. Jamestown
3. John Smith
4. House of Burgesses
5. Pilgrims
6. Mayflower Compact
7. Great Migration
8. Fundamental Orders of Connecticut
9. proprietary colony
10. William Penn

REVIEW QUESTIONS

Early Colonies Have Mixed Success (pages 85–91)

1. What were the reasons given by Richard Hakluyt that England should start a colony?
2. Why were Jamestown and Plymouth financed by joint-stock companies?
3. How did John Rolfe change the Virginia colony?

New England Colonies (pages 92–99)

4. What was John Winthrop's vision for Massachusetts Bay?
5. What was the system of government in the Massachusetts Bay Colony?
6. What were some of the effects of King Philip's War?

Founding the Middle and Southern Colonies (pages 100–103)

7. Why did Charles II want New Netherland?
8. What were relations like between Native Americans and settlers in Pennsylvania?
9. What was the Toleration Act of 1649?
10. What ethnic and racial groups settled in the Middle Colonies and why did they do so?

CRITICAL THINKING

1. USING YOUR NOTES: SEQUENCING EVENTS

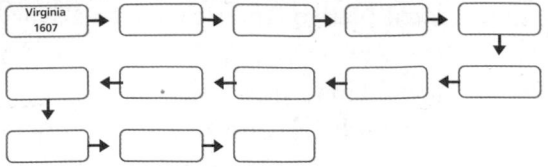

Using your completed chart, answer these questions:

a. Which was the earliest successful settlement in Virginia?
b. Which colony was founded last?

2. ANALYZING LEADERSHIP

Why do you think William Penn was a more successful leader than Peter Stuyvesant?

3. APPLYING CITIZENSHIP SKILLS

What were some of the common ideals that link the Mayflower Compact, the establishment of the House of Burgesses, and town meetings?

4. THEME: IMPACT OF THE INDIVIDUAL

How did individual effort help ensure the success of England's colonies in America?

5. ANALYZING CAUSES

What were the political, economic, and social causes for the founding of the different British colonies in North America?

Interact *with* History

How do the dangers you discussed before you read this chapter compare with the dangers people actually faced?

VISUAL SUMMARY

The 13 Colonies

		Important Early Dates	Founder(s)
New England Colonies	Massachusetts	Plymouth, 1620; Mass. Bay, 1630	Pilgrims; Puritans
	New Hampshire	Portsmouth, 1623	Proprietors
	Rhode Island	Providence, 1636	Roger Williams
	Connecticut	Hartford, 1636	Thomas Hooker
Middle Colonies	New York (New Netherland)	Dutch settlers arrive, 1624	Dutch West India Company
	Delaware	Fort Christina, 1638	Swedes
	New Jersey	Duke of York establishes, 1664	George Carteret, John Berkeley
	Pennsylvania	Charles II bestows land, 1681	William Penn
Southern Colonies	Virginia	Jamestown, 1607	Virginia Company of London
	Maryland	Founded as religious haven, 1632	Lord Baltimore
	North Carolina	Founded, 1663	Proprietors
	South Carolina	Founded, 1663	Proprietors
	Georgia	Founded as debtors' refuge, 1732	James Oglethorpe

Use the graph and your knowledge of U.S. history to answer questions 1 and 2.

Additional Test Practice, pp. S1–S33.

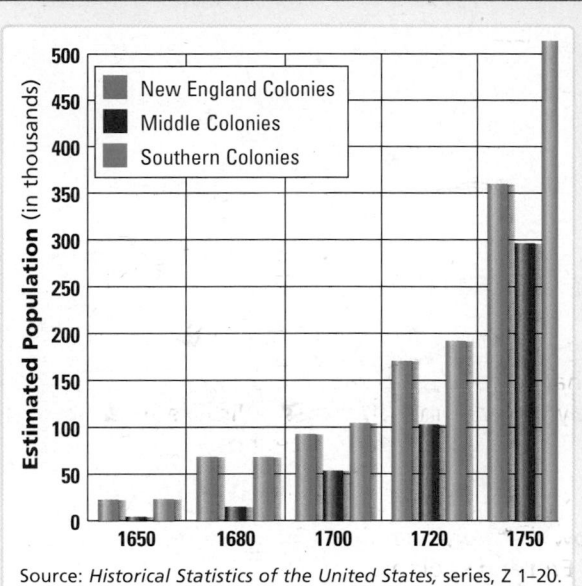

Population of the Colonies

Source: *Historical Statistics of the United States*, series, Z 1–20.

1. About how much did the population of the Southern colonies increase between 1720 and 1750?
   A. 100,000
   B. 200,000
   C. 300,000
   D. 500,000

2. Between what time periods was the increase in the population of the New England colonies greatest?
   A. between 1650 and 1680
   B. between 1680 and 1700
   C. between 1700 and 1720
   D. between 1720 and 1750

This quotation is from Peter Stuyvesant, Dutch governor of New Amsterdam, about his encounter with British forces. Use the quotation and your knowledge of U.S. history to answer question 3.

PRIMARY SOURCE

Powder and provisions failing, and no relief or reinforcements being expected, we were necessitated [forced] to come to terms with the enemy, not through neglect of duty or cowardice . . . but in consequence of an absolute impossibility to defend the fort.

Peter Stuyvesant, *Peter Stuyvesant and His New York*

3. The passage best supports which conclusion?
   A. Stuyvesant surrendered to the British.
   B. The citizens of New Amsterdam did not want to use their supplies.
   C. Stuyvesant feared the British forces.
   D. The people of New Amsterdam refused to surrender to the British.

TEST PRACTICE
CLASSZONE.COM

ALTERNATIVE ASSESSMENT

1. ✍ WRITING ABOUT HISTORY

How would an attorney have defended an accused woman during the Salem witchcraft trials? Write a **statement** to the court defending the woman.

- You can do research for your statement in books about the Salem witchcraft trials.
- Other sources of information include historical societies, archives, and museums.
- Your statement should persuade a jury of the time.

2. COOPERATIVE LEARNING

With a few of your classmates, write and perform a play about the "lost colonists" of Roanoke. Depict colonists dealing with food shortages, illness, and relations with Native Americans.

INTEGRATED TECHNOLOGY

DOING INTERNET RESEARCH

The Mayflower Compact was devised in response to the need for some sort of government. Use it as a model for planning a government for your class.

- Use the Internet or other library resources to learn more about the Mayflower Compact.
- Adapt ideas from the Mayflower Compact that might work for your class.
- Make decisions about what rules are needed, who will hold office, how they will be selected and how long they will serve, and whether or not there should be limits on majority rule.

For more about the Mayflower Compact . . .

INTERNET ACTIVITY
CLASSZONE.COM

The Colonies Develop 1700–1753

In 1702, a vast countryside surrounded Philadelphia. Most colonists earned their living in the country. Fewer than one in ten lived in cities.

Some Native Americans lived close to the American cities.

c. 1700
Colonial population reaches 257,000.

1712
Slave uprising occurs in New York City.

1718
French found city of New Orleans at mouth of Mississippi River.

Spanish priests build Alamo in Texas.

USA
World 1700

1701
War of the Spanish Succession begins in Europe.

1707
Act of Union unites England with Scotland and creates Great Britain.

Philadelphia was a major center of commerce.

It is the early 1700s when you arrive in one of America's larger port cities. After nearly a month of ocean travel, you are thrilled to see land. As you leave the ship, you wonder where you will live and how you will earn a living.

Would you settle on a farm or in a town?

What Do You Think?

- Will you choose to live where other people from your homeland live? Or will you try somewhere new?

- How did you make a living in your old country? Will this influence your choice?

RESEARCH LINKS
CLASSZONE.COM

Visit the Chapter 4 links for more information about the development of the colonies.

1733
Benjamin Franklin publishes *Poor Richard's Almanac.*

1739
Enslaved Africans revolt in Stono Rebellion.

1742
First European settlement west of Allegheny Mountains is established.

c. 1750 Population of the English colonies passes the one million mark.

1727
George II becomes King of Great Britain.

1739
Nadir Shah of Persia conquers Delhi, India.

1752
China suppresses Tibetan rebellion and forces Dalai Lama to accept its authority.

1753

Reading Strategy: Analyzing Causes and Effects

What Do You Know?

What ideas and pictures come to mind when you hear people talk about "the South" or "the North"? Why do you think these distinct regions developed?

Think About
- what you have learned about these regions from books or movies
- the way geography affects people's choices
- your responses to the Interact with History about settling on a farm or in a town (see page 107)

What Do You Want to Know?

What questions do you have about how the four colonial regions developed? Record these questions in your notebook before you read the chapter.

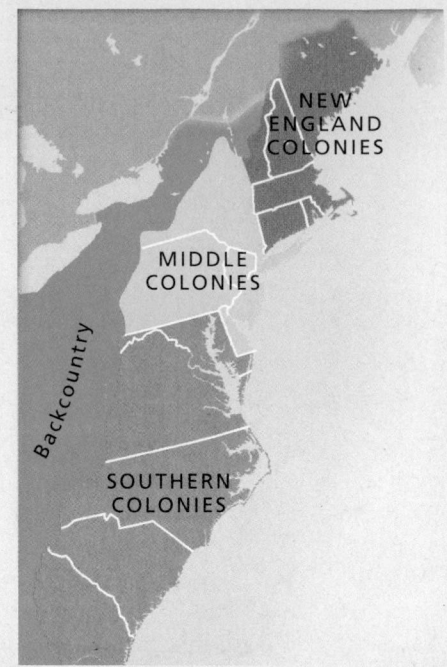

NEW ENGLAND COLONIES

MIDDLE COLONIES

Backcountry

SOUTHERN COLONIES

Analyzing Causes and Effects

As you read about history, it is important to understand not only what happened in the past, but also the reasons why it happened. Clue words that indicate cause—such as *because* and *since*—can help you look for causes of historical events. Use the chart below to list causes that contributed to the different economic developments in each of the colonial regions.

S See Skillbuilder Handbook, page R11.

Taking Notes

		NEW ENGLAND COLONIES	MIDDLE COLONIES	SOUTHERN COLONIES	BACKCOUNTRY
CAUSES	Climate				
	Resources				
	People				
EFFECT	Economic Development				

New England: Commerce and Religion

MAIN IDEA	WHY IT MATTERS NOW	TERMS & NAMES
Fishing and trade contributed to the growth and prosperity of the New England Colonies.	Coastal cities in New England continue to engage in trade.	Backcountry triangular trade subsistence Navigation Acts farming smuggling

ONE AMERICAN'S STORY

Peleg Folger, a New England sailor, kept a journal that describes what whaling was like in the 1750s. In one entry, he explained what happened after whales were sighted and small boats were launched to pursue them.

A VOICE FROM THE PAST

So we row'd about a mile and a Half from the [ship], and then a whale come up under us, & [smashed in] our boat . . . and threw us every man overboard [except] one. And we all came up and Got Hold of the Boat & Held to her until the other boat (which was a mile and half off) came up and took us in, all Safe, and not one man Hurt.

Peleg Folger, quoted in *The Sea-Hunters*

Whales hunted by New Englanders, such as Peleg Folger, might weigh as much as 50 tons and be over 60 feet in length.

When Folger and his mates killed a whale, they cut a hole in its head, and removed large amounts of oil from the animal. When the ship returned to port, this oil was sold to colonists, who used it as fuel in their lamps.

Many settlers in the New England Colonies—Massachusetts, New Hampshire, Connecticut, and Rhode Island—made a living from the sea. The majority of New Englanders, however, were farmers.

Distinct Colonial Regions Develop

Between 1700 and 1750, the population of England's colonies in North America doubled and then doubled again. At the start of the century, the colonial population stood at about 257,000. By 1750, more than 1,170,000 settlers called the English colonies home.

By the 1700s, the colonies formed three distinct regions: the New England Colonies, the Middle Colonies, and the Southern Colonies. Another area was the **Backcountry.** It ran along the Appalachian Mountains through the far western part of the other regions.

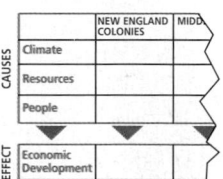

Taking Notes

Use your chart to take notes about the New England colonies.

Several factors made each colonial region distinct. Some of the most important were each region's climate, resources, and people.

1. New England had long winters and rocky soil. English settlers made up the largest group in the region's population.
2. The Middle Colonies had shorter winters and fertile soil. The region attracted immigrants from all over Europe.
3. The Southern Colonies had a warm climate and good soil. There, some settlers used enslaved Africans to work their plantations.
4. The Backcountry's climate and resources varied, depending on the latitude. Many Scots-Irish immigrants settled there.

During the colonial era, the majority of people made their living by farming. However, the type of agriculture they practiced depended on the climate and resources in the region where they settled.

Vocabulary
latitude: the distance north or south of the equator, measured in degrees

The Farms and Towns of New England

Life in New England was not easy. The growing season was short, and the soil was rocky. Most farmers practiced **subsistence farming**. That is, they produced just enough food for themselves and sometimes a little extra to trade in town.

Most New England farmers lived near a town. This was because colonial officials usually did not sell scattered plots of land to individual

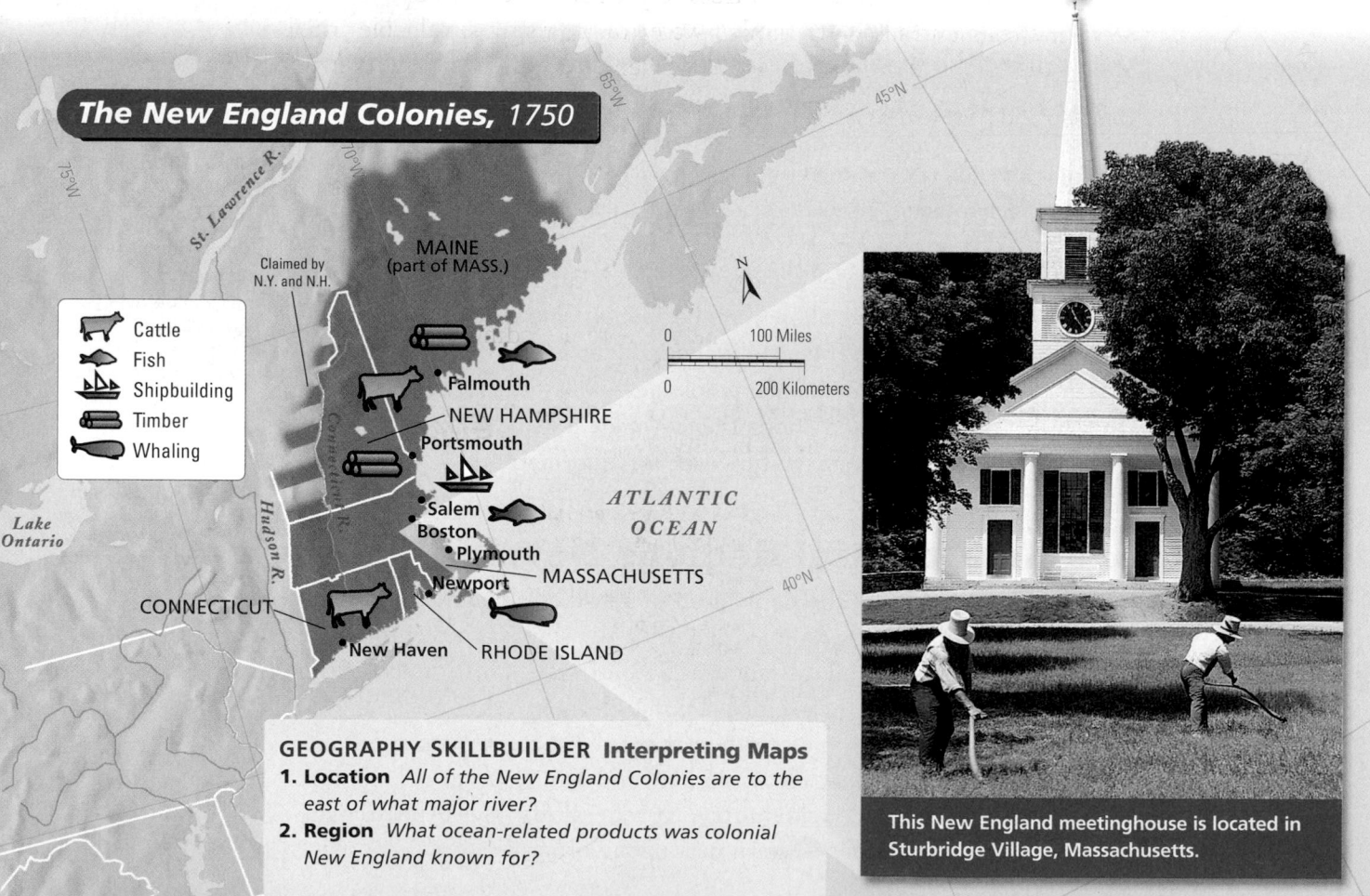

The New England Colonies, 1750

Cattle
Fish
Shipbuilding
Timber
Whaling

St. Lawrence R.

Lake Ontario

Claimed by N.Y. and N.H.

MAINE (part of MASS.)

NEW HAMPSHIRE

Portsmouth

Falmouth

Salem
Boston
Plymouth
Newport

MASSACHUSETTS

CONNECTICUT

New Haven

RHODE ISLAND

Hudson R.

Connecticut R.

ATLANTIC OCEAN

45°N

40°N

75°W

70°W

65°W

N

0   100 Miles

0   200 Kilometers

GEOGRAPHY SKILLBUILDER Interpreting Maps
1. **Location** All of the New England Colonies are to the east of what major river?
2. **Region** What ocean-related products was colonial New England known for?

This New England meetinghouse is located in Sturbridge Village, Massachusetts.

farmers. Instead, they sold larger plots of land to groups of people—often to the congregation of a Puritan church. A congregation then settled the town and divided the land among the members of its church.

This pattern of settlement led New England towns to develop in a unique way. Usually, a cluster of farmhouses surrounded a green—a central square where a meetinghouse was located and where public activities took place. Because people lived together in small towns, shopkeepers had enough customers to make a living. Also, if the townspeople needed a blacksmith or a carpenter, they could pool their money and hire one.

*Reading*History
A. Recognizing Effects How did the way land was sold in New England affect the way people lived?

Harvesting the Sea

New England's rocky soil made farming difficult. In contrast, the Atlantic Ocean offered many economic opportunities. In one story, a group of settlers was standing on a hill overlooking the Atlantic. One of them pointed out to sea and exclaimed, "There is a great pasture where our children's grandchildren will go for bread!"

The settler's prediction came true. Not far off New England's coast were some of the world's best fishing grounds. The Atlantic was filled with mackerel, halibut, cod, and many other types of fish.

New England's forests provided everything needed to harvest these great "pastures" of fish. The wood cut from iron-hard oak trees made excellent ship hulls. Hundred-foot-tall white pines were ideal for masts. Shipbuilders used about 2,500 trees to produce just one ship!

New England's fish and timber were among its most valuable articles of trade. Coastal cities like Boston, Salem, New Haven, and Newport grew rich as a result of shipbuilding, fishing, and trade.

Background
In 1742, over 16,000 people lived in Boston.

Atlantic Trade

New England settlers engaged in three types of trade. First was the trade with other colonies. Second was the direct exchange of goods with Europe. The third type was the triangular trade.

Triangular trade was the name given to a trading route with three stops. For example, a ship might leave New England with a cargo of rum

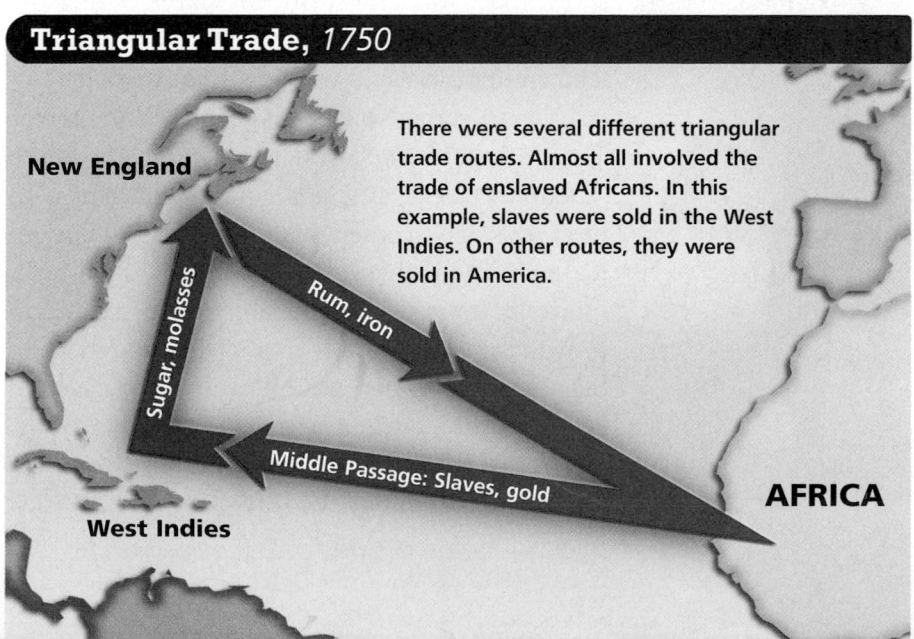

Triangular Trade, *1750*

There were several different triangular trade routes. Almost all involved the trade of enslaved Africans. In this example, slaves were sold in the West Indies. On other routes, they were sold in America.

New England

Sugar, molasses

Rum, iron

Middle Passage: Slaves, gold

AFRICA

West Indies

and iron. In Africa, the captain would trade his cargo for slaves. Slaves then endured the horrible Middle Passage to the West Indies, where they were exchanged for sugar and molasses. Traders then took the sugar and molasses back to New England. There, colonists used the molasses to make rum, and the pattern started over.

Background
See Olaudah Equiano's descriptions of the Middle Passage on page 78.

New England won enormous profits from trade. England wanted to make sure that it received part of those profits. So the English government began to pass the **Navigation Acts** in 1651. The Navigation Acts had four major provisions designed to ensure that England made money from its colonies' trade.

1. All shipping had to be done in English ships or ships made in the English colonies.
2. Products such as tobacco, wood, and sugar could be sold only to England or its colonies.
3. European imports to the colonies had to pass through English ports.
4. English officials were to tax any colonial goods not shipped to England.

But even after the passage of the Navigation Acts, England had trouble controlling colonial shipping. Merchants ignored the acts whenever possible. **Smuggling**—importing or exporting goods illegally—was common. England also had great difficulty preventing pirates—like the legendary Blackbeard—from interfering with colonial shipping.

STRANGE *but* True

BLACKBEARD THE PIRATE

Of all the pirates who attacked colonial ships, Blackbeard (shown below) was the most famous. He was a fearsome man known to stick matches in his hair to light up his face during battle.

Blackbeard's pirate career finally came to an end in 1718, when Virginia's governor sent an expedition against him. Nearly half the expedition's men died in the key battle. Blackbeard himself did not fall until he had suffered nearly 25 wounds. Before sailing back to port, sailors cut off his head and put it on the front of their ship.

African Americans in New England

There were few slaves in New England. Slavery simply was not economical in this region of small farms. Also, because the growing season was short, there was little work for slaves during the long winter months. Farmers could not afford to feed and house slaves who were not working.

Even so, some New Englanders in larger towns and cities did own slaves. They worked as house servants, cooks, gardeners, and stable-hands. In the 1700s, slave owners seldom had enough room to house more than one or two slaves. Instead, more and more slave owners hired out their slaves to work on the docks or in shops or warehouses. Slave owners sometimes allowed their slaves to keep a portion of their wages.

Occasionally, some enslaved persons were able to save enough to buy their freedom. In fact, New

Reading **History**
B. Analyzing Causes Why were there relatively few enslaved workers in New England?

England was home to more free blacks than any other region. A free black man might become a merchant, sailor, printer, carpenter, or landowner. Still, white colonists did not treat free blacks as equals.

Changes in Puritan Society

The early 1700s saw many changes in New England society. One of the most important was the gradual decline of the Puritan religion. There were a number of reasons for this decline.

One reason was that the drive for economic success competed with Puritan ideas. Many colonists, especially those who lived along the coast, seemed to care as much about business and material things as they did about religion. One observer had this complaint.

*Reading*History
C. Making Inferences Why might an interest in material things compete with the Puritan religion?

> *"[Boston] is so conveniently Situated for Trade."*
>
> **An observer in 1713**

A VOICE FROM THE PAST

[Boston] is so conveniently Situated for Trade and the Genius of the people are so inclined to merchandise, that they seek no other Education for their children than writing and Arithmetick.

An observer in 1713, quoted in *A History of American Life*

Another reason for the decline of the Puritan religion was the increasing competition from other religious groups. Baptists and Anglicans established churches in Massachusetts and Connecticut, where Puritans had once been the most powerful group.

Political changes also weakened the Puritan community. In 1691, a new royal charter for Massachusetts guaranteed religious freedom for all Protestants, not just Puritans. The new charter also granted the vote based on property ownership instead of church membership. This change put an end to the Puritan churches' ability to control elections.

To the south of New England were the Middle Colonies, which developed in quite different ways—as the next section shows.

Section 1 Assessment

1. Terms & Names

Explain the significance of:
• Backcountry
• subsistence farming
• triangular trade
• Navigation Acts
• smuggling

2. Using Graphics

Use a chart like the one shown to record how New Englanders prospered from the Atlantic Ocean.

Economic Activity	Benefits to Colonists

How did some profit illegally from the ocean?

3. Main Ideas

a. How did most people in New England earn a living?

b. Why did England pass the Navigation Acts?

c. What factors led to the decline of the Puritan religion in New England?

4. Critical Thinking

Making Inferences What advantages might there be in living near other people in small towns, such as those in New England?

THINK ABOUT
• the transportation options available to colonists
• why shopkeepers chose to open businesses in towns

ACTIVITY OPTIONS

ART
TECHNOLOGY

Read more about whaling. Make a **mobile** that shows different kinds of whales or plan a **multimedia presentation** on whaling today.

The Middle Colonies: Farms and Cities

MAIN IDEA	WHY IT MATTERS NOW	TERMS & NAMES
The people who settled in the Middle Colonies made a society of great diversity.	States in this region still boast some of the most diverse communities in the world.	cash crop artisan gristmill Conestoga wagon diversity

ONE AMERICAN'S STORY

Elizabeth Ashbridge was only 19 years old when she arrived in America from England in the 1730s. Although she was an indentured servant, she hoped to earn her freedom and find a way to express her strong religious feelings.

After several years, Elizabeth did gain freedom. In Pennsylvania, she joined a religious group called the Society of Friends, or Quakers. The new Quaker longed to share her beliefs openly.

> *A VOICE FROM THE PAST*
>
> I was permitted to see that all I had gone through was to prepare me for this day; and that the time was near, when it would be required of me, to go and declare to others what the God of mercy had done for my soul.
>
> **Elizabeth Ashbridge,** *Some Account . . . of the Life of Elizabeth Ashbridge*

The Quakers believed that people of different beliefs could live together in harmony. They helped to create a climate of tolerance and acceptance in the Middle Colonies of New York, New Jersey, Pennsylvania, and Delaware, as you will read in this section.

A woman speaks out at a Quaker meeting. The Society of Friends allowed women a more active role than other religions.

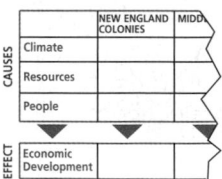

Taking Notes

Use your chart to take notes about the middle colonies.

	NEW ENGLAND COLONIES	MIDD...
CAUSES — Climate		
Resources		
People		
EFFECT — Economic Development		

A Wealth of Resources

The Middle Colonies had much to offer in addition to a climate of tolerance. A Frenchman named Michel Guillaume Jean de Crèvecoeur (krehv•KUR) praised the region's "fair cities, substantial villages, extensive fields . . . decent houses, good roads, orchards, meadows, and bridges, where an hundred years ago all was wild, woody, and uncultivated."

The prosperity that Crèvecoeur described was typical of the Middle Colonies. Immigrants from all over Europe came to take advantage of this region's productive land. Their settlements soon crowded out Native Americans, who had lived in the region for thousands of years.

Among the immigrants who came to the Middle Colonies were Dutch and German farmers. They brought the advanced agricultural methods of their countries with them. Their skills, knowledge, and hard work would soon result in an abundance of foods.

The Middle Colonies boasted a longer growing season than New England and a soil rich enough to grow **cash crops**. These were crops raised to be sold for money. Common cash crops included fruits, vegetables, and, above all, grain. The Middle Colonies produced so much grain that people began calling them the "breadbasket" colonies.

The Importance of Mills

Vocabulary
grist: another name for grain, the one-seeded fruit of cereal grasses like wheat and rye

After harvesting their crops of corn, wheat, rye, or other grains, farmers took them to a **gristmill**. There, millers crushed the grain between heavy stones to produce flour or meal. Human or animal power fueled some of these mills. But water wheels built along the region's plentiful rivers powered most of the mills.

The bread that colonists baked with these products was crucial to their diet. Colonists ate about a pound of grain in some form each day—nearly three times more than Americans eat today. Even though colonists ate a great deal of grain, they had plenty left over to send to the region's coastal markets for sale.

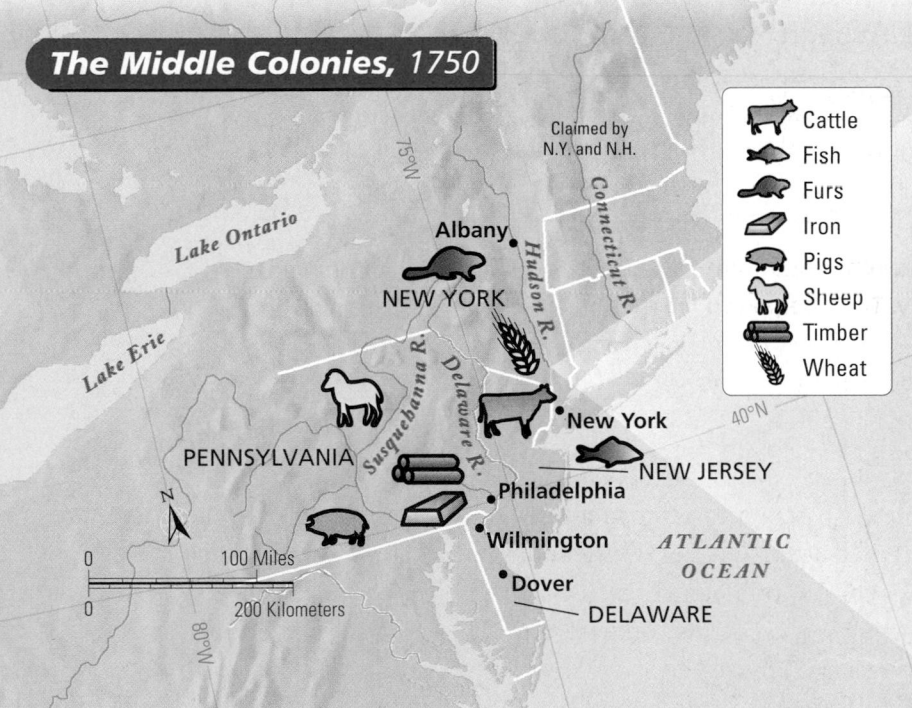

The Middle Colonies, 1750

Claimed by N.Y. and N.H.

Cattle
Fish
Furs
Iron
Pigs
Sheep
Timber
Wheat

Lake Ontario
Lake Erie
Albany
NEW YORK
Hudson R.
Connecticut R.
Susquehanna R.
Delaware R.
PENNSYLVANIA
New York
NEW JERSEY
Philadelphia
Wilmington
ATLANTIC OCEAN
Dover
DELAWARE

0   100 Miles
0   200 Kilometers

75°W
80°W
40°N
35°N

Philipsburg Manor, in Sleepy Hollow, New York, has a working 18th-century farm and a water-powered gristmill.

GEOGRAPHY SKILLBUILDER Interpreting Maps
1. **Place** What are the three major rivers in the Middle Colonies?
2. **Movement** Why might the Middle Colonies' rivers that empty into the ocean be important for farmers?

The Cities Prosper

The excellent harbors along the coasts of the Middle Colonies were ideal sites for cities. New York City grew up at the mouth of the Hudson River, and Philadelphia was founded on the Delaware River. The merchants who lived in these growing port cities exported cash crops, especially grain, and imported manufactured goods.

Because of its enormous trade, Philadelphia was the fastest growing city in the colonies. The city owed its expansion to a thriving trade in wheat and other cash crops. By 1720, it was home to a dozen large shipyards—places where ships are built or repaired.

The city's wealth also brought many public improvements. Large and graceful buildings, such as Philadelphia's statehouse—which was later renamed Independence Hall—graced the city's streets. Streetlights showed the way along paved roads. In 1748, a Swedish visitor named Peter Kalm exclaimed that Philadelphia had grown up overnight.

Reading **History**
A. Reading a Map Locate New York and Philadelphia on the map on page 115. Note the rivers next to which they were built.

daily *life*

NAMES AND OCCUPATIONS

Many English colonists had names like Miller and Smith—names that reflected how their families had made a living in England. For example, a colonist named Miller probably had an ancestor who had operated a mill. Similarly, Smith probably had an ancestor who had been a blacksmith.

Sometimes colonists continued in the same occupations as their ancestors. But as time went on, colonists turned to other occupations, and their names no longer reflected how they earned a living. Yet names like Smith and Miller remain common in the United States, reflecting the country's past as English colonies.

A VOICE FROM THE PAST

And yet its natural advantages, trade, riches and power, are by no means inferior to any, even of the most ancient towns in Europe.

Peter Kalm, quoted in *America at 1750*

New York could also thank trade for its rapid growth. This bustling port handled flour, bread, furs, and whale oil. At midcentury, an English naval officer admired the city's elegant brick houses, paved streets, and roomy warehouses. "Such is this city," he said, "that very few in England can rival it in its show."

Background
In 1742, New York City's population was about 11,000, and nearly 13,000 people lived in Philadelphia.

A Diverse Region

Many different immigrant groups arrived in the port cities of the Middle Colonies. Soon, the region's population showed a remarkable

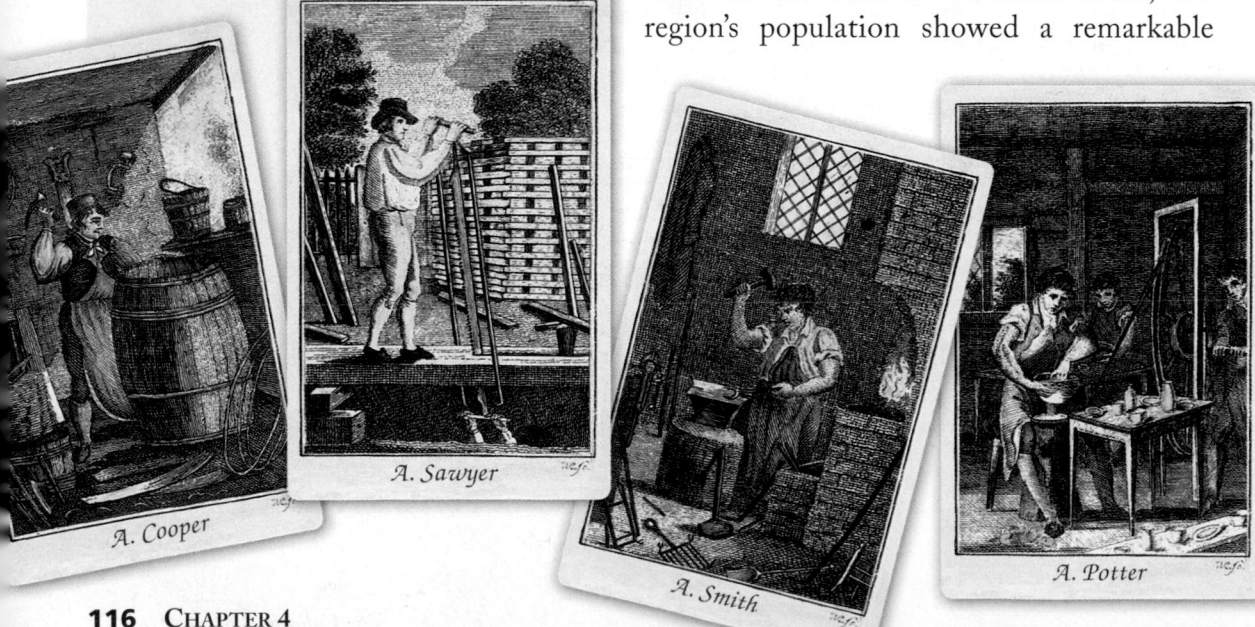

A. Cooper

A. Sawyer

A. Smith

A. Potter

diversity, or variety, in its people. One of the largest immigrant groups in the region, after the English, was the Germans.

Many of the Germans arrived between 1710 and 1740. Most came as indentured servants fleeing religious intolerance. Known for their skillful farming, these immigrants soon made a mark on the Middle Colonies. "German communities," wrote one historian, "could be identified by the huge barns, the sleek cattle, and the stout workhorses."

Germans also brought a strong tradition of craftsmanship to the Middle Colonies. For example, German gunsmiths first developed the long rifle. Other German **artisans,** or craftspeople, became ironworkers and makers of glass, furniture, and kitchenware.

Germans built **Conestoga wagons** to carry their produce to town. These wagons used wide wheels suitable for dirt roads, and the wagons' curved beds prevented spilling when climbing up and down hills. The wagons' canvas covers offered protection from rain. Conestoga wagons would later be important in settling the West.

The Middle Colonies became home to many people besides the Germans. There were also the English, Dutch, Scots-Irish, African, Irish, Scottish, Welsh, Swedish, and French. Because of the diversity in the Middle Colonies, different groups had to learn to accept, or at least tolerate, one another.

Background
By the second half of the 1700s, more than one in three colonists in Pennsylvania claimed German ancestry.

Reading **History**
B. Summarizing How would you describe the population of the Middle Colonies?

The Middle Colonies, *1750*
Population Diversity

French 2%
Swedish 3%
Welsh 3%
Scottish 4%
Irish 5%
African 7%
Scots-Irish 9%
Dutch 10%
German 18%
English 39%

Source: *Population of the British Colonies in America Before 1776,* 1975

SKILLBUILDER Interpreting Graphs
1. *What group made up nearly one-fifth of the population in the Middle Colonies?*
2. *What were the two main languages spoken in the Middle Colonies?*

A Climate of Tolerance

While the English Puritans shaped life in the New England Colonies, many different groups contributed to the culture of the Middle Colonies. Because of the greater number of different groups, it was difficult for any single group to dominate the others. Thus, the region's diversity helped to create a climate of tolerance. Some of the region's religious groups also helped to promote tolerance.

The Middle Colonies' earliest settlers, the Dutch in New York and the Quakers in Pennsylvania, both practiced religious tolerance. That is, they honored the right of religious groups to follow their own beliefs without interference. Quakers also insisted on the equality of men and women. As a result, Quaker women served as preachers, and female missionaries traveled the world spreading the Quaker message.

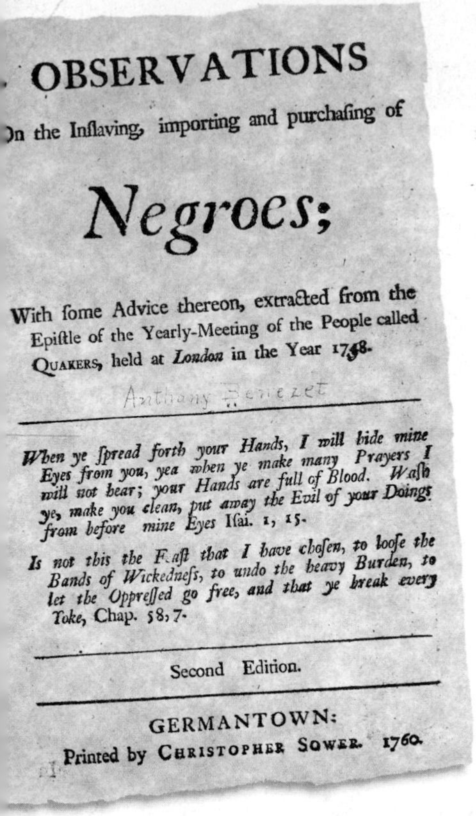

OBSERVATIONS

On the Inflaving, importing and purchafing of

Negroes;

With fome Advice thereon, extracted from the Epiftle of the Yearly-Meeting of the People called Quakers, held at *London* in the Year 1758.

Anthony Benezet

When ye fpread forth your Hands, I will hide mine Eyes from you, yea when ye make many Prayers I will not bear; your Hands are full of Blood. Wafh ye, make you clean, put away the Evil of your Doings from before mine Eyes Ifai. 1, 15.

Is not this the Faft that I have chofen, to loofe the Bands of Wickednefs, to undo the heavy Burden, to let the Oppreffed go free, and that ye break every Yoke, Chap. 58, 7.

Second Edition.

GERMANTOWN:
Printed by CHRISTOPHER SOWER. 1760.

Most Quakers were opposed to slavery. Shown here is a Quaker antislavery pamphlet printed in the Middle Colonies.

Quakers were also the first to raise their voices against slavery. Quaker ideals influenced immigrants in the Middle Colonies—and eventually the whole nation.

African Americans in the Middle Colonies

The tolerant attitude of many settlers in the Middle Colonies did not prevent slavery in the region. In 1750, about 7 percent of the Middle Colonies' population was enslaved. As in New England, many people of African descent lived and worked in cities.

New York City had a larger number of people of African descent than any other city in the Northern colonies. In New York City, enslaved persons worked as manual laborers, servants, drivers, and as assistants to artisans and craftspeople. Free African-American men and women also made their way to the city, where they worked as laborers, servants, or sailors.

Tensions existed between the races in New York City, sometimes leading to violence. In 1712, for example, about 24 rebellious slaves set fire to a building. They then killed nine whites and wounded several others who came to put out the fire. Armed colonists caught the suspects, who were punished horribly. Such punishments showed that whites would resort to force and violence to control slaves. Even so, the use of violence did little to prevent the outbreak of other slave rebellions.

Force would also be used in the South, which had far more enslaved Africans than the North. In the next section, you will learn how the South's plantation economy came to depend on the labor of enslaved Africans.

*Reading*History
C. Forming Opinions Why do you think that force was needed to keep Africans enslaved?

Section **2** Assessment

1. Terms & Names

Explain the significance of:
- cash crop
- gristmill
- diversity
- artisan
- Conestoga wagon

2. Using Graphics

Use a cluster diagram like the one shown to indicate where different immigrants in the Middle Colonies came from.

Middle Colonies' Population

What was the third largest group in the region?

3. Main Ideas

a. What attracted settlers to the Middle Colonies?

b. What service was performed at gristmills?

c. Why might enslaved Africans be able to join in rebellion more easily in the city than the country?

4. Critical Thinking

Analyzing Causes What factors allowed large coastal cities to develop in the Middle Colonies?

THINK ABOUT
- geography
- people
- trade

ACTIVITY OPTIONS

MATH

GEOGRAPHY

Read more about Philadelphia. Create a **database** of the city's population growth in the 1700s or draw a **map** that shows its physical growth.

The Southern Colonies: Plantations and Slavery

MAIN IDEA	WHY IT MATTERS NOW	TERMS & NAMES
The economy of the Southern Colonies relied heavily on slave labor.	The existence of slavery deeply affected the South and the nation.	indigo overseer Eliza Lucas Stono Rebellion William Byrd II

ONE AMERICAN'S STORY

George Mason was born to a wealthy Virginia family in 1725. Mason—who later described the slave trade as "disgraceful to mankind"—wrote about the contributions of enslaved persons on his family's plantation.

A VOICE FROM THE PAST

My father had among his slaves carpenters, coopers [barrel makers], sawyers, blacksmiths, tanners, curriers, shoemakers, spinners, weavers and knitters, and even a distiller.

George Mason, quoted in *Common Landscape of America*

Because the Masons and other wealthy landowners produced all that they needed on their own plantations, they appeared to be independent. But their independence usually depended on the labor of enslaved Africans. Although planters were only a small part of the Southern population, the plantation economy and slavery shaped life in the Southern Colonies: Maryland, Virginia, the Carolinas, and Georgia.

George Mason was active in local affairs in Virginia. He would later play a role in the drafting of the United States Constitution.

The Plantation Economy

The South's soil and almost year-round growing season were ideal for plantation crops like rice and tobacco. These valuable plants required much labor to produce, but with enough workers they could be grown as cash crops. Planters had no trouble transporting their crops because the region's many waterways made it easy for oceangoing ships to tie up at plantation docks.

Like George Mason's boyhood home, most plantations were largely self-sufficient. That is, nearly everything that planters, their families, and their workers needed was produced on the plantation. Because plantations were so self-sufficient, large cities like those in the North were rare

Taking Notes

Use your chart to take notes about the Southern colonies.

CAUSES		NEW ENGLAND COLONIES	MIDD
	Climate		
	Resources		
	People		
EFFECT	Economic Development		

The Southern Colonies, 1750

Legend:
- Corn
- Indigo
- Naval stores
- Pigs
- Rice
- Tobacco

MARYLAND
Baltimore
Potomac R.
Chesapeake Bay
VIRGINIA
Richmond
James R. Jamestown
Roanoke R.
NORTH CAROLINA
Wilmington
SOUTH CAROLINA
ATLANTIC OCEAN
Savannah R.
Charles Town (Charleston)
GEORGIA
Savannah
Altamaha R.
APPALACHIAN MOUNTAINS
40°N
35°N
85°W
75°W
0 100 Miles
0 200 Kilometers

The Orton plantation, south of Wilmington, North Carolina, was founded around 1725. Such plantations were representative of the economic and political power held by Southern planters.

GEOGRAPHY SKILLBUILDER Interpreting Maps
1. **Location** *The Southern Colonies were south of what latitude?*
2. **Place** *Which Southern Colonies grew crops of both rice and indigo?*

in the Southern Colonies. The port city of Charles Town (later called Charleston) in South Carolina was an early exception.

As the plantation economy continued to grow, planters began to have difficulty finding enough laborers to work their plantations. Toward the end of the 1600s, the planters began to turn to enslaved Africans for labor.

The Turn to Slavery

For the first half of the 1600s, there were few Africans in Virginia, whether enslaved or free. In 1665, fewer than 500 Africans had been brought into the colony. At that time, African and European indentured servants worked in the fields together.

Starting in the 1660s, the labor system began to change as indentured white servants started to leave the plantations. One reason they left was the large amount of land available in the Americas. It was fairly easy for white men to save enough money to buy land and start their own farms. White servants could not be kept on the plantations permanently. As Bacon's Rebellion showed, it was also politically dangerous for planters to try to keep them there (see page 89). As a result, the landowners had to find another source of labor.

Background
In 1742, Charles Town's population was 6,800.

U.S. Slave Population

Percentage of Population
40
30
20
10
0
1650 1670 1690 1710 1730 1750
■ North   ■ South
Source: Fogel and Engerman, *Time on the Cross*, 1974

Reading **History**
A. Reading a Graph Ask and answer a question about the geopgraphic pattern of changes in the slave population.

Planters tried to force Native Americans to work for them. But European diseases caused many Native Americans to die. Those who survived usually knew the country well enough to run away.

Reading**History**
B. Analyzing Causes What factors led to the importation of enslaved Africans into the South?

To meet their labor needs, the planters turned to enslaved Africans. As a result, the population of people of African descent began to grow rapidly. By 1750, there were over 235,000 enslaved Africans in America. About 85 percent lived in the Southern Colonies. Enslaved Africans made up about 40 percent of the South's population.

Plantations Expand

The growth of slavery allowed plantation farming to expand in South Carolina and Georgia. Without slave labor, there probably would have been no rice plantations in the region's swampy lowlands.

Enslaved workers drained swamps, raked fields, burned stubble, and broke ground before planting. They also had to flood, drain, dry, hoe, and weed the same fields several times before the harvest.

The cultivation of rice required not only back-breaking labor but also considerable skill. Because West Africans had these skills, planters sought out slaves who came from Africa's rice-growing regions.

On higher ground, planters grew **indigo,** a plant that yields a deep blue dye. A young woman named **Eliza Lucas** had introduced indigo as a successful plantation crop after her father sent her to supervise his South Carolina plantations when she was 17.

The Planter Class

Slave labor allowed planters, such as the Byrd family of Virginia, to become even wealthier. These families formed an elite planter class. They had money or credit to buy the most slaves. And because they had more slaves, they could grow more tobacco, rice, or indigo to sell.

Small landowners with just one or two slaves simply could not compete. Many gave up their land and moved westward. As a result, the powerful planter class gained control of the rich land along the coast. The planter class was relatively small compared to the rest of the population. However, this upper class soon took control of political and economic power in the South. A foreign traveler in the South commented that the planters "think and act precisely as do the nobility in other countries."

Some planters, following the traditions of nobility, did feel responsible for the welfare of their enslaved

Reading**History**
C. Recognizing Effects How did the growth of slavery affect political power in the South?

AMERICA'S HISTORY MAKERS

WILLIAM BYRD II
1674–1744

William Byrd II was one of the best known of the Southern planters. His family owned a large estate in Virginia. After his father died, Byrd took on his father's responsibilities, including membership in the House of Burgesses.

But Byrd is best remembered for his writing. His most famous work is *History of the Dividing Line betwixt Virginia and North Carolina.* In it, Byrd celebrates the land and climate of the South. At times, however, he is critical of its people. Even today, the book creates a vivid picture of life in the Southern Colonies.

How did William Byrd II demonstrate his leadership abilities?

HISTORY *through*ART

Benjamin Henry Latrobe's watercolor sketch, *An Overseer Doing His Duty,* shows enslaved African women on a Virginia plantation. An overseer looks on as the two women work to remove tree stumps.

What opinion do you think Latrobe had of the conditions on plantations?

workers. Power, they believed, brought with it the responsibility to do good. Many planters, though, were tyrants. They held complete authority over everyone in their households. Planters frequently used violence against slaves to enforce their will.

Vocabulary
tyrant: harsh ruler

Life Under Slavery

On large Southern plantations, slaves toiled in groups of about 20 to 25 under the supervision of **overseers**. Overseers were men hired by planters to watch over and direct the work of slaves. Enslaved persons performed strenuous and exhausting work, often for 15 hours a day at the peak of the harvest season. If slaves did not appear to be doing their full share of work, they were often whipped by the overseer.

Enslaved people usually lived in small, one-room cabins that were furnished only with sleeping cots. For a week's food, a slave might receive only around a quarter bushel of corn and a pound of pork. Some planters allowed their slaves to add to this meager ration by letting them raise their own potatoes, greens, fruit, or chicken.

In spite of the brutal living conditions, Africans preserved many customs and beliefs from their homelands. These included music, dances, stories, and, for a time, African religions—including Islam. African kinship customs became the basis of African-American family culture. A network of kin was a source of strength even when families were separated.

*Reading*History

D. Finding Main Ideas What customs and beliefs from their homelands provided strength for enslaved Africans?

Resistance to Slavery

At the same time that enslaved Africans struggled to maintain their own culture, they fought against their enslavement. They sometimes worked

slowly, damaged goods, or purposely carried out orders the wrong way. A British traveler in 1746 noted that many slaves pretended not to understand tasks they often had performed as farmers in West Africa.

A VOICE FROM THE PAST

You would really be surpriz'd at their Perseverance; let an hundred Men shew him how to hoe, or drive a wheelbarrow, he'll still take the one by the Bottom, and the other by the Wheel; and they often die before they can be conquer'd.

Edward Kimber, quoted in *White over Black*

At times, slaves became so angry and frustrated by their loss of freedom that they rose up in rebellion. One of the most famous incidents was the **Stono Rebellion.** In September 1739, about 20 slaves gathered at the Stono River just south of Charles Town. Wielding guns and other weapons, they killed several planter families and marched south, beating drums and loudly inviting other slaves to join them in their plan to seek freedom in Spanish-held Florida. By late that afternoon, however, a white militia had surrounded the group of escaping slaves. The two sides clashed, and many slaves died in the fighting. Those captured were executed.

Background
Slave codes were laws designed to control slaves and keep them in bondage.

Stono and similar revolts led planters to make slave codes even stricter. Slaves were now forbidden from leaving plantations without permission. The laws also made it illegal for slaves to meet with free blacks. Such laws made the conditions of slavery even more inhumane.

The Southern Colonies' plantation economy and widespread use of slaves set the region on a very different path from that of the New England and Middle Colonies. In the next section, you will learn how settlers used the unique resources of the Backcountry to create settlements there.

Section 3 Assessment

1. Terms & Names

Explain the significance of:
- indigo
- Eliza Lucas
- William Byrd II
- overseer
- Stono Rebellion

2. Using Graphics

Use a diagram like the one shown to review the factors that led to the use of slaves in the South.

Causes		Effect

Why didn't planters use Native American workers?

3. Main Ideas

a. What percentage of the South's population was enslaved in 1750?

b. What crops did plantations in Georgia and South Carolina grow?

c. How did enslaved persons resist their slavery?

4. Critical Thinking

Contrasting How did geographic differences between the Southern Colonies and the New England Colonies affect their labor systems?

THINK ABOUT
- the climate of the regions
- the nature of the soil

ACTIVITY OPTIONS

ART

SCIENCE

Do more research on rice plantations. Draw a **diagram** of a typical plantation or write a **report** on how rice is cultivated today.

REGION AND HUMAN-ENVIRONMENT INTERACTION

Differences Among the Colonies

Many factors shape a region's economy and the way its settlers make a living. One of the most important is its physical geography—the climate, soil, and natural resources of the region. The geography of the American colonies varied from one colony to another. For example, in some areas, farmers could dig into rich, fertile soil. In others, they could not stick their shovels in the ground without hitting rocks.

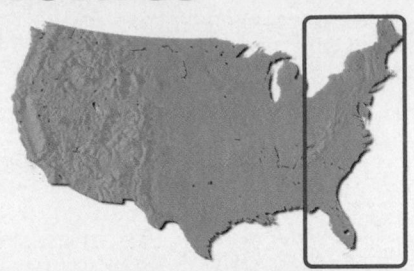

Major Regional Exports (by export value*)

NEW ENGLAND COLONIES

New England had a short growing season and rocky soil. Colonists took advantage of other opportunities in the region, especially fishing and whaling.

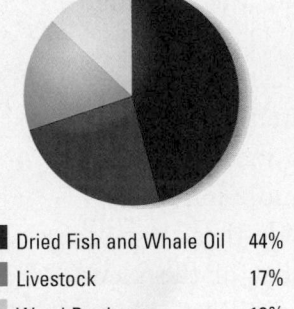

■ Dried Fish and Whale Oil	44%
■ Livestock	17%
■ Wood Products	13%
■ Other	26%

MIDDLE COLONIES

The longer growing season of the Middle Colonies—the "breadbasket colonies"—allowed farmers to grow cash crops of grain.

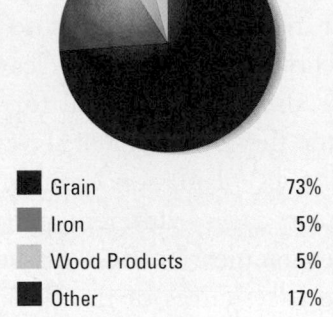

■ Grain	73%
■ Iron	5%
■ Wood Products	5%
■ Other	17%

SOUTHERN COLONIES

The South had a nearly year-round growing season. The use of enslaved Africans allowed Southern planters to produce cash crops of tobacco and rice.

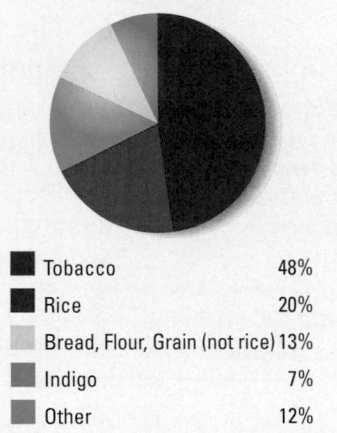

■ Tobacco	48%
■ Rice	20%
■ Bread, Flour, Grain (not rice)	13%
■ Indigo	7%
■ Other	12%

*Export Value in Pounds Sterling (Five-Year Average, 1768–1772)

Source: James F. Shepherd and Gary M. Walton, *Shipping, Maritime Trade, and the Economic Development of Colonial North America* (Cambridge: Cambridge University Press, 1972.)

ARTIFACT FILE

Farmer's Plow Middle colonists relied on the heavy blades of plows to cut seed rows into the region's fertile soil.

Indigo On some plantations in the South, planters grew crops of indigo plants—like the one pictured here—to produce the rich blue dyes used to color this yarn.

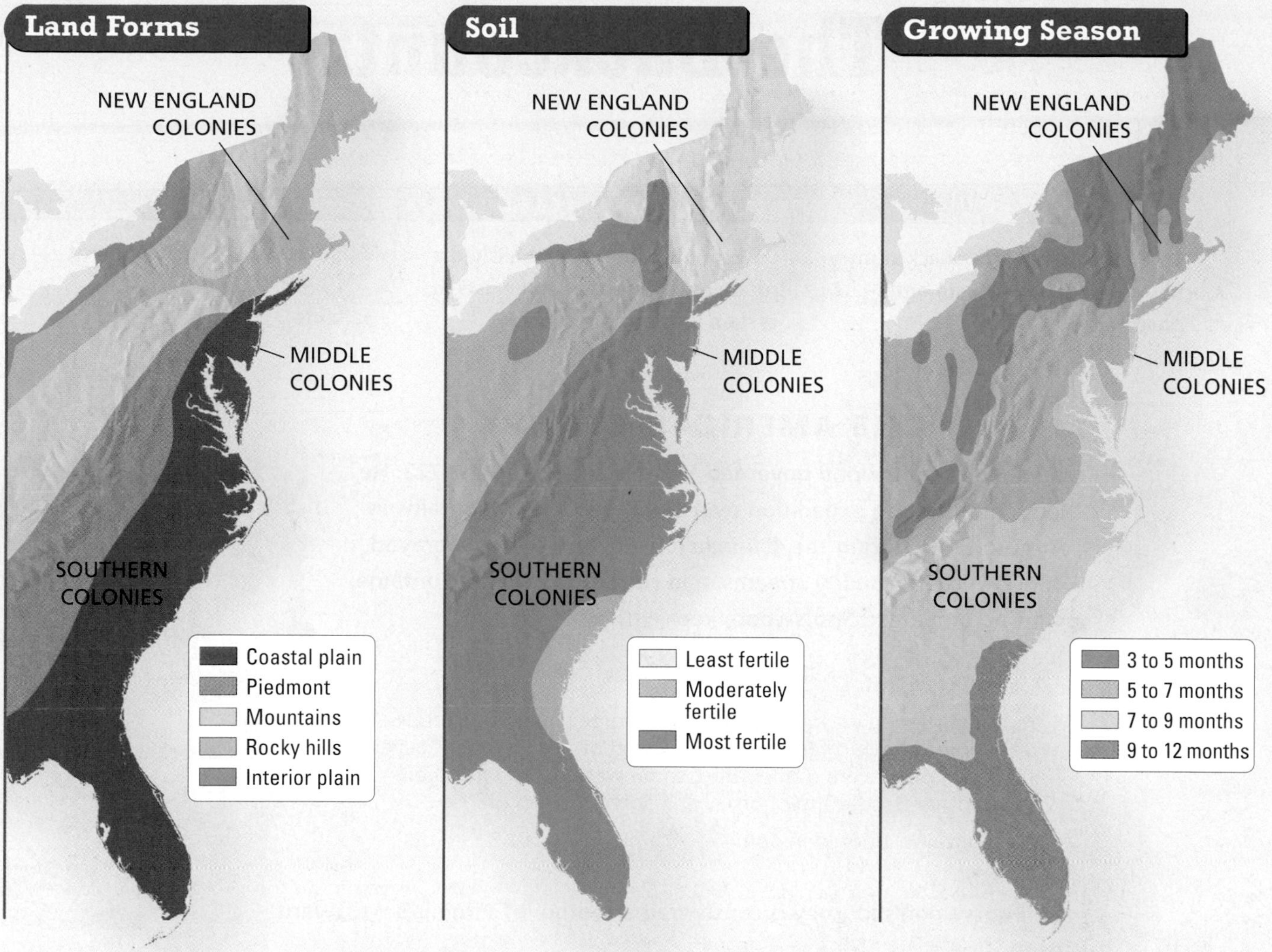

Land Forms

NEW ENGLAND
COLONIES

MIDDLE
COLONIES

SOUTHERN
COLONIES

■	Coastal plain
■	Piedmont
■	Mountains
■	Rocky hills
■	Interior plain

Soil

NEW ENGLAND
COLONIES

MIDDLE
COLONIES

SOUTHERN
COLONIES

□	Least fertile
■	Moderately fertile
■	Most fertile

Growing Season

NEW ENGLAND
COLONIES

MIDDLE
COLONIES

SOUTHERN
COLONIES

■	3 to 5 months
■	5 to 7 months
■	7 to 9 months
■	9 to 12 months

Physical Geography The maps above show the different types of land forms, soil, and growing seasons that were found in the different colonial regions. These factors helped to shape the economies of each of the regions, which were quite different, as the pie graphs show on the previous page.

On-Line Field Trip

The New Bedford Whaling Museum in Massachusetts has many objects related to whaling, including bone or ivory objects called scrimshaws. A sailor carved this whale's tooth with a jackknife or sail needle and colored the design with ink.

For more about whaling . . .

RESEARCH LINKS
CLASSZONE.COM

CONNECT TO GEOGRAPHY

1. **Region** How long was the growing season in most of the Southern Colonies?

2. **Human-Environment Interaction** How might the soil quality in the Middle Colonies have influenced the region's population?

 See Geography Handbook, pages 10–13.

CONNECT TO HISTORY

3. **Analyzing Causes** Why did the land forms and soil of New England cause many to turn to the Atlantic Ocean for a living?

The Backcountry

	MAIN IDEA		WHY IT MATTERS NOW		TERMS & NAMES

MAIN IDEA

Settlers moved to the Backcountry because land was cheap and plentiful.

WHY IT MATTERS NOW

Backcountry settlers established a rural way of life that still exists in certain parts of the country.

TERMS & NAMES

Appalachian Mountains

fall line

piedmont

clan

ONE AMERICAN'S STORY

Alexander Spotswood governed Virginia from 1710 to 1722. He led a month-long expedition over the Blue Ridge Mountains in August 1716. During the 400-mile journey, adventurers braved dense thickets, muddy streams, and rattlesnakes. John Fontaine, who accompanied Spotswood, kept a diary of the trip.

A VOICE FROM THE PAST

We had a rugged way; we passed over a great many small runs of water, some of which were very deep, and others very miry. Several of our company were dismounted, some were down with their horses, others under their horses, and some thrown off.

John Fontaine, quoted in *Colonial Virginia*

Spotswood's journey is considered a symbol of Virginia's westward expansion.

Alexander Spotswood meets Native Americans in the Blue Ridge Mountains—a segment of the Appalachians Mountains.

Geography of the Backcountry

Just as Spotswood predicted, settlers soon began to move into the Backcountry. This was a region of dense forests and rushing streams in or near the **Appalachian Mountains.** The Appalachians stretch from eastern Canada south to Alabama.

In the South, the Backcountry began at the **fall line.** The fall line is where waterfalls prevent large boats from moving farther upriver. Beyond the fall line is the **piedmont.** Piedmont means "foot of the mountains." It is the broad plateau that leads to the Blue Ridge Mountains of the Appalachian range.

The Backcountry's resources made it relatively easy for a family to start a small farm. The region's many springs and streams provided water, and forests furnished wood that settlers could use for log cabins and fences.

Taking Notes

Use your chart to take notes about the backcountry.

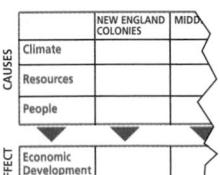

Backcountry Settlers

The first Europeans in the Backcountry made a living by trading with the Native Americans. Backcountry settlers paid for goods with deerskins. A unit of value was one buckskin or, for short, a "buck."

Vocabulary
buck: an adult male deer; the adult female is called a *doe*

Farmers soon followed the traders into the region, but they had to be cautious. As the number of settlements grew, the farmers often clashed with the Native Americans whose land they were taking.

Farmers sheltered their families in log cabins. They filled holes between the logs with mud, moss, and clay. Then they sawed out doors and windows. Lacking glass, settlers used paper smeared with animal fat to cover their windows.

Reading **History**
A. Analyzing Points of View
What was William Byrd's attitude toward Backcountry settlers?

William Byrd—on his expedition to establish the southern border of Virginia—described a long night that he spent in one such cabin. He complained that he and at least ten other people were "forct to pig together in a Room . . . troubled with the Squalling of peevish, dirty children into the Bargain."

Backcountry life may have been harsh, but by the late 1600s many families had chosen to move there. Some of them went to escape the plantation system, which had crowded out many small farmers closer to the seacoast. Then, in the 1700s, a new group of emigrants—the Scots-Irish—began to move into the Backcountry.

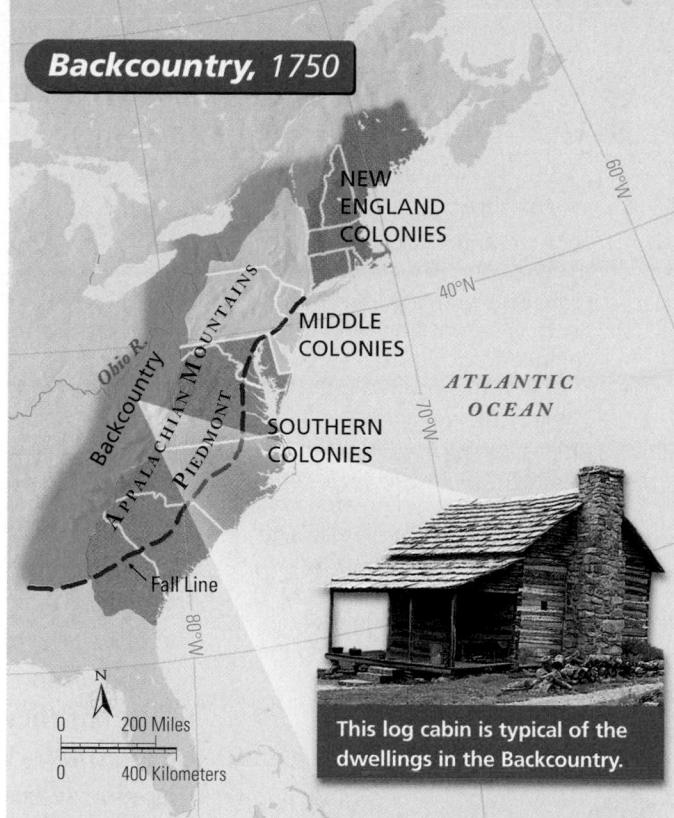

Backcountry, 1750

This log cabin is typical of the dwellings in the Backcountry.

GEOGRAPHY SKILLBUILDER Interpreting Maps
Region *What geographical feature did the northern and southern areas of the Backcountry have in common?*

The Scots-Irish

The Scots-Irish came from the borderland between Scotland and England. Most of them had lived for a time in northern Ireland. In 1707, England and Scotland merged and formed Great Britain. The merger caused many hardships for the Scots-Irish. Poverty and crop failures made this bad situation even worse.

Vocabulary
clan: comes from an Old Irish word that means offspring, or descendants

As a result, Scots-Irish headed to America by the thousands. After they arrived, they quickly moved into the Backcountry. The Scots-Irish brought their clan system with them to the Backcountry. **Clans** are large groups of families—sometimes in the thousands—that claim a common ancestor. Clan members were suspicious of outsiders and banded together when danger threatened. These clans helped families to deal with the dangers and problems of the Backcountry.

BACKCOUNTRY SPORTS TODAY

Three centuries ago, crowds in the Backcountry were thrilled by some of the same games that are now part of track and field competitions.

One of these games is the hammer throw. In this event, an athlete swings around a 16-pound metal ball on a wire-rope handle. After whirling around several times, the athlete lets go of the hammer, hoping it will travel the farthest distance.

The Scots-Irish brought other games to America, including the shotput, high jump, and long jump.

Backcountry Life

Life in the Backcountry was very different from life along the seaboard. Settlers along the coast carried on a lively trade with England. But in the Backcountry, rough roads and rivers made it almost impossible to move goods.

As a result, Backcountry farmers learned quickly to depend on themselves. They built log cabins and furnished them with cornhusk mattresses and homemade benches and tables. They fed their families with the hogs and cattle they raised and with the fish and game they killed. They grew yellow corn to feed their livestock and white corn to eat. Popcorn was probably their only snack food. To protect their precious corn from pests, daytime patrols of women, children, and the elderly served as human scarecrows.

Women in the Backcountry worked in the cabin and fields, but they also learned to use guns and axes. An explorer who traveled in the region described one of these hardy Backcountry women.

Reading **History**
B. Making Inferences How would you describe the way people in the Backcountry lived?

> **A VOICE FROM THE PAST**
>
> She is a very civil woman and shows nothing of ruggedness or Immodesty in her carriage, yett she will carry a gunn in the woods and kill deer, turkeys, etc., shoot doun wild cattle, catch and tye hoggs, knock down [cattle] with an ax and perform the most manfull Exercises.
>
> **A visitor to the Backcountry,** quoted in *A History of American Life*

Settlers in the Backcountry often acted as if there were no other people in the region, but this was not so. In the woods and meadows that surrounded their cabins, settlers often encountered Native Americans and other groups that had made America their home.

Other Peoples in North America

The Backcountry settlers started a westward movement that would play a critical role in American history. Most settlers' motivation to move west was simple—the desire for land.

Yet the push to the west brought settlers into contact with other peoples of North America. Native Americans had made their homes there for thousands of years. In addition, France and Spain claimed considerable territory in North America.

Sometimes this contact led to changes in people's cultures. For instance, North America had no horses until the Spanish colonists brought them into Mexico in the 1500s. Horses migrated north, and Native Americans caught them and made them an important part of their culture.

Reading **History**
C. Summarizing As England's colonies expanded westward, what groups did they encounter?

Contact also led to conflict. As English settlers pushed into the Backcountry, they put pressure on Native American tribes. Some tribes reacted by raiding isolated homesteads and small settlements. White settlers struck back, leading to more bloodshed.

Vocabulary
shears: scissors

The English colonists also came into conflict with the French. The French had colonized eastern Canada and had moved into the territories, rich with fur, along the Mississippi River. French fur traders wanted to prevent English settlers from moving west and taking away part of the trade. One Native American told an Englishman, "You and the French are like two edges of a pair of shears, and we are the cloth that is cut to pieces between them."

This painting shows Native Americans catching wild horses. Many would later use the horses to hunt buffalo on the Great Plains.

Spain also controlled large areas of North America—including territories that today form part or all of the states of Arizona, California, Colorado, Florida, Nevada, New Mexico, Texas, Utah, and Wyoming. Spanish settlers were farmers, ranchers, and priests. Priests, who established missions to convert Native Americans, built forts near the missions for protection. In 1718, Spaniards built Fort San Antonio de Bexar to guard the mission of San Antonio de Valero, later renamed the Alamo.

These different groups continued to compete—and sometimes fight—with one another. Frequently, England's colonies had to unite against these other groups. As a result, a common American identity began to take shape, as you will read in Chapter 5.

Section 4 Assessment

1. Terms & Names

Explain the significance of:
- Appalachian Mountains
- fall line
- piedmont
- clan

2. Using Graphics

Use a chart like the one shown to list some of the geographic characteristics of the Backcountry.

Backcountry Geography
1.
2.
3.
4.

3. Main Ideas

a. Which settlers migrated to the Backcountry?

b. How did clans help the Scots-Irish survive?

c. What economic activities did women carry out in the region?

4. Critical Thinking

Identifying Problems As England's colonies expanded farther west, what problems would they face?

THINK ABOUT
- other inhabitants of the Americas
- the resources desired by the colonists

ACTIVITY OPTIONS

LANGUAGE ARTS
ART

Read an account of the Backcountry written in the 1700s. Write a **newspaper article** or draw a series of **cartoons** that describe what you have read.

The Colonies Develop

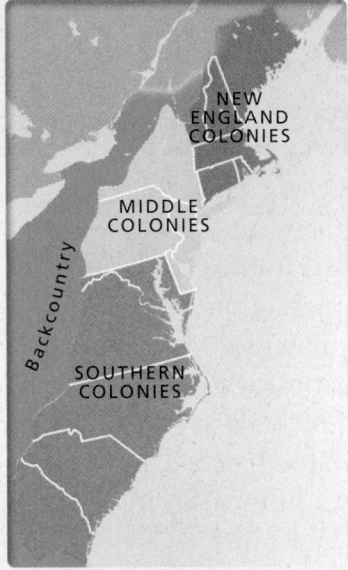

NEW
ENGLAND
COLONIES

MIDDLE
COLONIES

Backcountry

SOUTHERN
COLONIES

New England: Commerce and Religion

New England was distinguished by its small farming towns and profitable fishing and trade.

The Middle Colonies: Farms and Cities

The Middle Colonies' farms produced large cash crops that fueled trade in its coastal cities.

The Southern Colonies: Plantations and Slavery

The South's plantation economy and large number of enslaved Africans made it different from the other regions.

The Backcountry

The Backcountry was distant from the denser coastal populations, so settlers there developed an independent and rugged way of life.

TERMS & NAMES

Briefly explain the significance of the following.

1. Backcountry
2. subsistence farming
3. triangular trade
4. Navigation Acts
5. cash crop
6. gristmill
7. Conestoga wagon
8. overseer
9. Stono Rebellion
10. Appalachian Mountains

REVIEW QUESTIONS

New England: Commerce and Religion (pages 109–113)

1. How would you describe the life of a New England farmer?
2. In what ways did settlers in the region take advantage of the Atlantic Ocean?
3. How were New England towns settled?

The Middle Colonies: Farms and Cities (pages 114–118)

4. How were farms in the Middle Colonies different from those in New England?
5. What characterized the population of the Middle Colonies?

The Southern Colonies: Plantations and Slavery (pages 119–125)

6. Why did Southern planters infrequently travel to towns to sell their crops or to buy food and supplies?
7. Why did planters turn to enslaved Africans for labor?
8. In what ways did slaves resist?

The Backcountry (pages 126–129)

9. Where was the Backcountry located in the 1700s?
10. How was life in the Backcountry different from that along the coast?

CRITICAL THINKING

1. USING YOUR NOTES: ANALYZING CAUSES AND EFFECTS

Using your completed chart, answer the questions below.

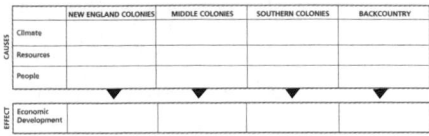

a. How was the Middle Colonies' climate different from the Backcountry's?
b. How did the South's labor system differ from the North's?
c. How did the resources of New England affect its economy?

2. ANALYZING LEADERSHIP

How did the South's plantation economy influence who became leaders in the region?

3. THEME: ECONOMICS IN HISTORY

What factors influenced the economic development of each of the four colonial regions?

4. APPLYING CITIZENSHIP SKILLS

How did the Quaker influence in the Middle Colonies contribute to the behavior of citizens of the region?

5. SEQUENCING EVENTS

What changes took place in the population and treatment of African Americans between 1650 and 1750?

Interact *with* History

How would the choice that you made at the beginning of the chapter have varied according to the region in which you lived? Would you still make the same choice?

Use the map and your knowledge of U.S. history to answer questions 1 and 2.

Additional Test Practice, pp. S1–S33.

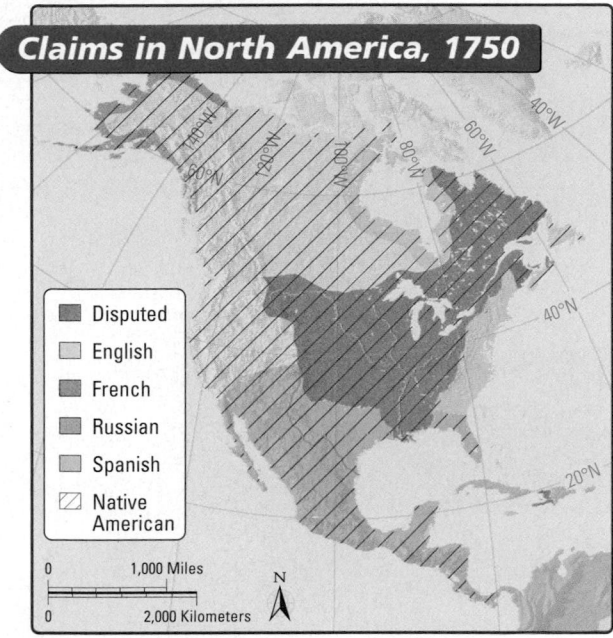

Claims in North America, 1750

Legend:
- ■ Disputed
- □ English
- ■ French
- ■ Russian
- □ Spanish
- ▨ Native American

0 — 1,000 Miles
0 — 2,000 Kilometers
N

1. Which of the groups shown inhabited the largest area of North America?
- **A.** English
- **B.** Native American
- **C.** Russian
- **D.** Spanish

2. Which European group claimed the northernmost territory?
- **A.** English
- **B.** French
- **C.** Russian
- **D.** Spanish

This quotation from Edward Kimber is about slaves in the United States. Use the quotation and your knowledge of U.S. history to answer question 3.

PRIMARY SOURCE

You would really be surpriz'd at their Perseverance; let an hundred Men shew him how to hoe, or drive a wheelbarrow, he'll still take the one by the Bottom, and the other by the Wheel; and they often die before they can be conquer'd.

Edward Kimber, quoted in *White over Black*

3. The speaker uses the word *Perseverance* to emphasize which of the following?
- **A.** the slave's belief in working hard at his or her tasks
- **B.** the slave's determination to resist enslavement
- **C.** the slave's confusion about what is expected of him or her
- **D.** the slave's submission to the condition of slavery

TEST PRACTICE
CLASSZONE.COM

ALTERNATIVE ASSESSMENT

1. ✎ WRITING ABOUT HISTORY

Imagine that you are a Quaker living in colonial America. Write a **diary** entry about your typical day.

- You can learn more about Quaker life in colonial times by reading primary sources found in the library.
- Before you begin to write, make a list of the ways in which you might spend a typical day as a Quaker. Use your notes to write your diary entry.

2. COOPERATIVE LEARNING

Work with a few of your classmates to design and construct a model of a log cabin. Group members can share the responsibilities for researching the history of log cabins, recording details about the location of your log cabin, and designing and building the cabin.

INTEGRATED TECHNOLOGY

DOING INTERNET RESEARCH

You can learn about different aspects of colonial farm life from primary sources. Use the Internet or library resources to begin your research.

- Use the Internet to find primary sources such as diaries, journal entries, or letters.
- Another source of information might be historical or living history museums.
- Use your research to create a chart listing the differences between your family's lifestyle and a colonial family's.

For more about colonial farming . . .

INTERNET ACTIVITY
CLASSZONE.COM

CHAPTER 5

Beginnings of an American Identity 1689–1763

Section 1 **Early American Culture**

Section 2 **Roots of Representative Government**

Section 3 **The French and Indian War**

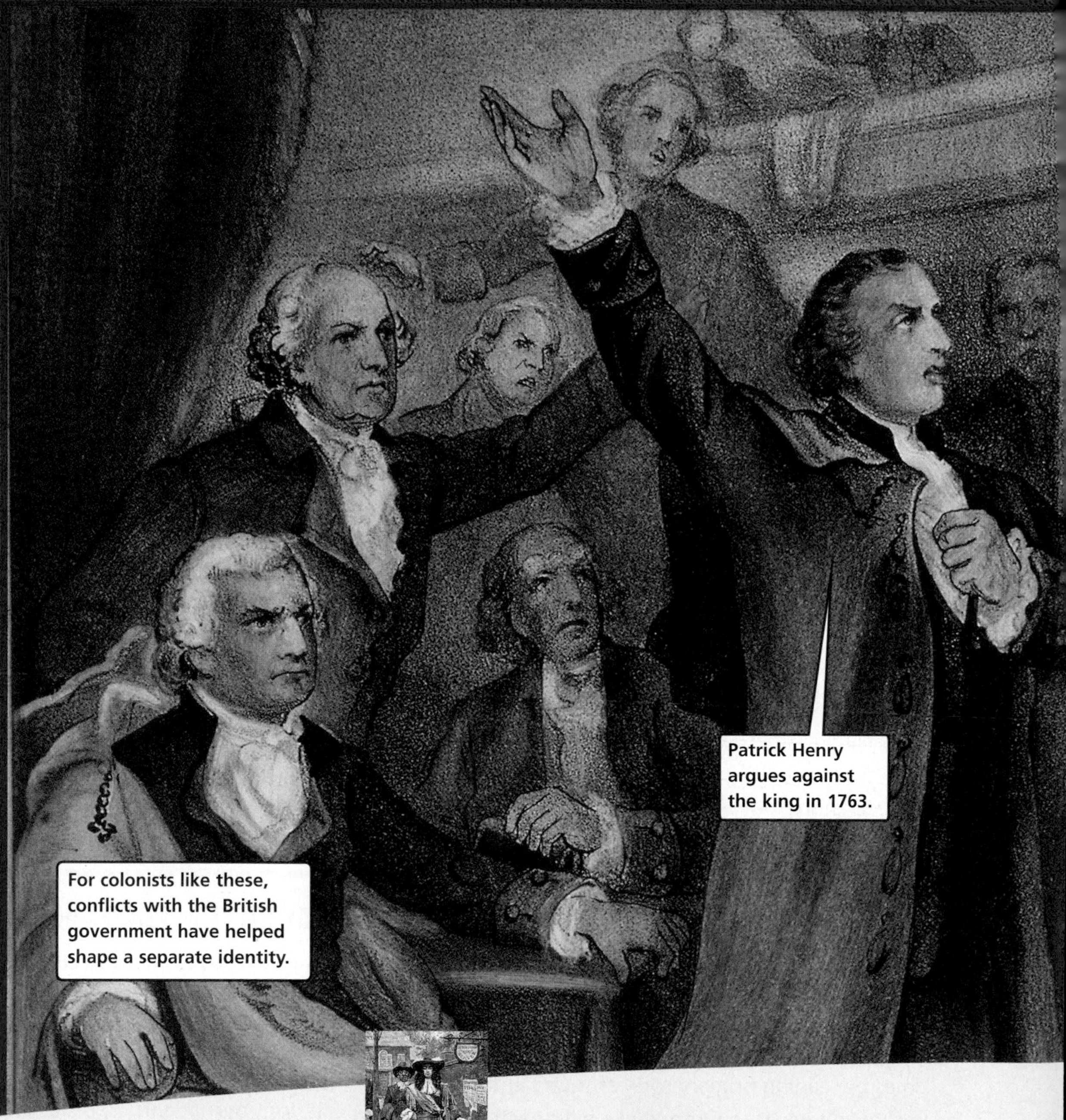

Patrick Henry argues against the king in 1763.

For colonists like these, conflicts with the British government have helped shape a separate identity.

USA / World 1680

1689 Massachusetts colonists overthrow royal governor Andros.

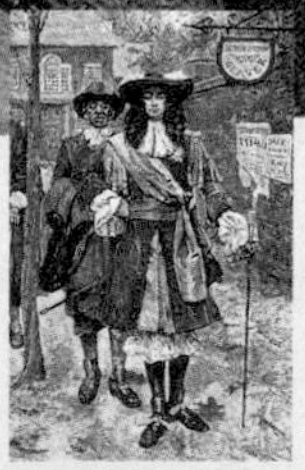

1704 *Boston Newsletter* is founded.

1689 William and Mary replace James II as rulers of England.

1707 England and Scotland join to form Great Britain.

1709 About 13,500 people leave the German states and emigrate to England.

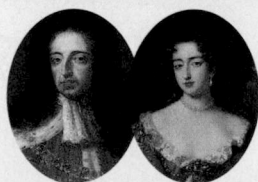

You are outraged by the attacks on British traders and settlers. You wonder whether it is wise to join with other colonies, though. Will it mean that Virginians or New Englanders will be able to make laws for Pennsylvania?

What do you have in common with other British colonists?

What Do You Think?

- What are some good reasons to join with the other British colonies?
- How great are the differences between the British colonies?
- What separates British and French colonists?

RESEARCH LINKS
CLASSZONE.COM
Visit the Chapter 5 links for more information about early-American identity.

1727
George II becomes king of Great Britain.

1735
Decision in the Zenger trial supports freedom of the press.

1738
Minister George Whitefield arrives in Georgia.

1754
French and Indian War begins.

1756
Seven Years' War between France and Britain is declared.

1759
Quebec falls to the British.

1763
French and Indian War ends.

1763

Reading Strategy: Finding Main Ideas

What Do You know?

What beliefs do you consider American? How do you think people in Britain's American colonies saw themselves?

Think About

- your own beliefs as an American
- what you know about the regions where the colonies were established
- what you know about the backgrounds and beliefs of colonists in different regions
- your responses to the Interact with History about what you have in common with other British colonists (see page 133)

JOIN, or DIE.

This cartoon was published by Benjamin Franklin in 1754. It urged the colonies to unite.

What Do You Want to Know?

 What questions do you have about colonial America in the early and middle 1700s? Write them down in your notebook before you read this chapter.

Finding Main Ideas

To recognize a main idea, you must notice how smaller details are connected. In your notebook, copy a web like the one shown here. Write brief notes about the main things people in the British colonies had in common—the beliefs and experiences that formed an American identity.

- Read and remember the Main Idea at the beginning of each section.
- At the end of each group of paragraphs under a heading, ask yourself, "Have I learned about something that united the colonists?"

S See Skillbuilder Handbook, page R5.

 Taking Notes

Economy

Education

Religion

American Identity

Publishing

Political Ideas

War

Early American Culture

MAIN IDEA	WHY IT MATTERS NOW	TERMS & NAMES
The British colonies were shaped by prosperity, literacy, and new movements in religion and thought.	These forces began to create an American identity that is still developing today.	apprentice Enlightenment Great Awakening Benjamin Franklin Jonathan Edwards John Locke George Whitefield

ONE AMERICAN'S STORY

In 1704, Sarah Kemble Knight traveled on horseback from her home in Boston to New Haven, Connecticut. The journey took five days.

In her journal, Madam Knight described her travel hardships and commented on people she met.

A VOICE FROM THE PAST

We hoped to reach the french town and Lodg there that night, but unhapily lost our way about four miles short. . . . A surly old shee Creature, not worthy the name of woman, . . . would hardly let us go into her Door, though the weather was so stormy.

Sarah Kemble Knight, *The Journal of Madam Knight*

This reprint of *The Journal of Madam Knight* is a 1920 edition.

Knight's attitude toward people from other colonies was typical. In the early 1700s, people of the different British colonies did not think of themselves as living in one country. In this section, you will learn what began to draw the colonies together.

Land, Rights, and Wealth

At the time of Madam Knight's journey, the colonies were thriving. Cheap farmland and plentiful natural resources gave colonists a chance to prosper. They would have had less opportunity in Europe. In England, fewer than 5 percent of the people owned land. In fact, land rarely went up for sale. By contrast, in the colonies, land was plentiful—once Native American groups were forced to give up their claims. Colonists who owned land were free to use or sell whatever it produced.

Land ownership gave colonists political rights as well as prosperity. Generally, only white male landowners or property owners could vote. There were some exceptions. City dwellers could vote by paying a fee.

Taking Notes

Use your chart to take notes about early American culture.

American Identity

Colonial Social Ranks

HIGH
- large landowners
- church officials
- government officials
- wealthy merchants

UPPER MIDDLE
- small farmers
- tradespeople

LOWER MIDDLE
- renters
- unskilled workers

LOW
- indentured servants
- slaves

Land ownership also helped determine colonists' social position. Unlike England, America had no class of nobles whose titles passed from parent to child. But people were still divided into high, middle, and low ranks, as they were in England. Large landholders were high in rank. Small farmers who owned their land were in the middle rank. Most colonists fit this category. People who did not own land, such as servants, slaves, or hired workers, were low in rank. Colonial women held the same rank as their husbands or fathers.

Colonists showed respect to their "betters" by curtsying or tipping a hat, for example. Seats in church were assigned by rank, with wealthy families in the front pews and poor people in the back. Despite such divisions, the wealthy were expected to aid the poor.

Reading **History**
A. Finding Main Ideas What did colonists gain by owning land?

Women and the Economy

Although women were not landholders, their work was essential to the colonial economy. As you learned in Chapter 4, enslaved African women helped raise cash crops such as tobacco and indigo. Most white women were farm wives who performed tasks and made products their families needed. They cooked, churned butter, made soap and candles, spun fibers, wove cloth, sewed and knitted clothes, and did many other chores. They usually tended a garden and looked after farm animals. At harvest time, they often worked in the fields alongside men and older children.

Because cash was scarce, farm wives bartered, or traded, with their neighbors for goods and services. For example, a woman who nursed a sick neighbor or helped deliver a baby might be paid in sugar or cloth.

Women in towns and cities usually did the same types of housework that rural women did. In addition, some urban women ran inns or other businesses. Madam Knight, whose journey was described in One American's Story on page 135, sold writing paper, taught handwriting, and rented rooms to guests. A few women, usually the wives or widows of tradesmen, practiced trades themselves.

Reading **History**
B. Finding Main Ideas In what ways was women's work essential to the economy?

Although women contributed to the colonial economy, they did not have many rights. Women could not vote. In most churches, they could not preach or hold office. (Quaker meetings were an exception.) A married woman could not own property without her husband's permission. By law, even the money a woman earned belonged to her husband.

Young People at Work

Children's work also supported the colonial economy. Families were large. New England families, for example, had an average of six to eight children. More children meant more workers. Children as young as three or four were expected to be useful. They might help look after farm animals, gather berries, and watch younger children.

Around age six, boys were "breeched." This meant that they no longer wore the skirts or smocks of all young children but were given a pair of pants. They then began to help their fathers at work. Sons of farmers worked all day clearing land and learning to farm. Sons of craftsmen tended their fathers' shops and learned their fathers' trades.

Around age 11, many boys left their fathers to become apprentices. An **apprentice** learned a trade from an experienced craftsman. The apprentice received food, clothing, lodging, and a general education, as well as training in the specific craft or business. He worked for free, usually for four to seven years, until his contract was fulfilled. Then he could work for wages or start his own business.

*Reading*History
C. Contrasting
How did the training of boys and girls differ?

Girls rarely were apprenticed. They learned sewing and other household skills from their mothers. In New England, girls of 13 or 14 often were sent away to other households to learn specialized skills such as weaving or cheese making. Orphaned girls and boys worked as servants for families who housed and fed them until adulthood.

Colonial Schooling

If land, wealth, and hard work were valued across the colonies, so was education. Most children were taught to read so that they could understand the Bible. Only children from wealthy families went beyond reading to learn writing and arithmetic. These children learned either from private tutors or in private schools. Poorer children sometimes learned to read from their mothers.

HISTORY through ART

This drawing shows the inside of an 18th-century one-room schoolhouse.

What does the picture suggest to you about colonial schooling?

Colonial children learned proper behavior from *The School of Manners,* a book published in 1701. Here are examples of rules and an illustration from the book.

"Spit not in the Room, but in a corner, and rub it out with thy Foot, or rather go out and do it abroad."

"If thou meetest the scholars of any other School jeer not nor affront them, but show them love and respect and quietly let them pass along."

Or they attended "dame schools," where women taught the alphabet and used the Bible to teach reading. Most children finished their formal education at age seven.

Children's textbooks emphasized religion. The widely used *New England Primer* paired the letter *A* with the verse "In *Adam's* fall / We Sinned all." Beside the letter *B* was a picture of the Bible. The primer contained the Lord's Prayer and *The Shorter Catechism,* more than 100 questions and answers about religion.

Colonial America had a high literacy rate, as measured by the number of people who could sign their names. In New England, 85 percent of white men were literate, compared with 60 percent of men in England. In the Middle Colonies, 65 percent of white men were literate, and in the South, about 50 percent were. In each region of the colonies, roughly half as many white women as men were literate. Most colonists thought schooling was more important for males. Educated African Americans were rare. If they were enslaved, teaching them to read was illegal. If they were free, they were often kept out of schools.

*Reading*History
D. Contrasting
How was colonial education different from education today?

Newspapers and Books

Colonial readers supported a publishing industry that also drew the colonies together. In the early 1700s, the colonies had only one local newspaper, the *Boston News-letter.* But over the next 70 years, almost 80 different newspapers appeared in America. Many were published for decades.

Most books in the colonies were imported from England, but colonists slowly began to publish their own books. Almanacs were very popular. A typical almanac included a calendar, weather predictions, star charts, farming advice, home remedies, recipes, jokes, and proverbs. In 1732, Benjamin Franklin began to publish *Poor Richard's Almanack.* It contained sayings that are still repeated today, such as "Haste makes waste."

Colonists also published poetry, regional histories, and autobiographies. Most personal stories told of struggles to maintain religious faith during hard times. A form of literature unique to the Americas was the captivity narrative. In it, a colonist captured by Native Americans described living among them.

Mary Rowlandson's 1682 captivity narrative, *The Sovereignty and Goodness of God,* was one of the first colonial bestsellers. Native Americans attacked Rowlandson's Massachusetts village in 1676, during King Philip's War. They held her hostage for 11 weeks. During that time, she was a servant to a Narragansett chieftain, knitting stockings and making shirts for his family and others. "I told them it was Sabbath day," she recalled, "and desired them to let me rest, and told them I

*Reading*History
E. Categorizing
What were some types of colonial literature?

Vocabulary
ransom: to pay for a captive's release

would do as much more tomorrow. To which they answered me, they would break my face." After townspeople raised money to ransom Rowlandson, she was released. Although she mourned a young daughter who had died in captivity, she praised God for returning her safely.

The Great Awakening

Mary Rowlandson's religious faith was central to her life. But in the early 1700s, many colonists feared they had lost the religious passion that had driven their ancestors to found the colonies. Religion seemed distant, even to regular churchgoers.

In the 1730s and 1740s, a religious movement called the **Great Awakening** swept through the colonies. The traveling ministers of this movement preached that inner religious emotion was more important than outward religious behavior. Their sermons appealed to the heart and drew large crowds. **Jonathan Edwards,** one of the best-known preachers, terrified listeners with images of God's anger but promised they could be saved.

Background
Religious meetings with large, intensely emotional crowds remain part of American religious tradition.

A VOICE FROM THE PAST

And now you have an extraordinary opportunity, a day wherein Christ has thrown the door of mercy wide open, and stands in calling and crying with a loud voice to poor sinners. . . . How awful it is to be left behind at such a day!

Jonathan Edwards, "Sinners in the Hands of an Angry God"

The Great Awakening lasted for years and changed colonial culture. Congregations argued over religious practices and often split apart. People left their old churches and joined other Protestant groups such as Baptists. Some of these groups welcomed women, African Americans, and Native Americans. Overall, churches gained 20,000 to 50,000 new members. To train ministers, religious groups founded colleges such as Princeton and Brown.

The Great Awakening inspired colonists to help others. **George Whitefield** (HWIT•feeld) drew thousands of people with his sermons and raised funds to start a home for orphans. Other ministers taught Christianity and reading to Native Americans and African Americans. The

George Whitefield preaching to a crowd

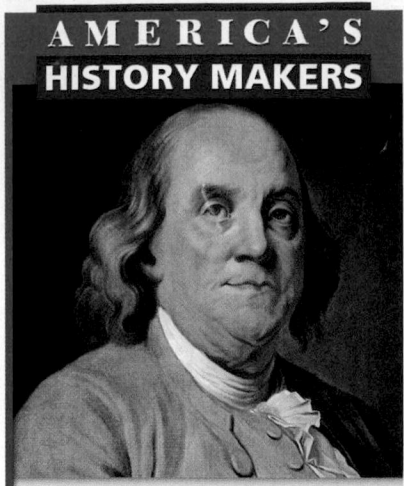

BENJAMIN FRANKLIN

1706–1790

As an Enlightenment thinker, Benjamin Franklin used reason to improve society. At 42, he retired from business to devote his life to science and public service. He proved that lightning was a form of electricity. Then he invented the lightning rod to protect buildings. The Franklin stove and bifocal eyeglasses were also his inventions. He organized a fire department, a lending library, and a society to discuss philosophy. Later he helped draft the Declaration of Independence.

How did Franklin help improve colonial society?

Great Awakening encouraged ideas of equality and the right to challenge authority. In this way, the movement contributed to the revolutionary fervor of the colonists when they declared independence from England years later.

The Enlightenment

Unlike the Great Awakening, which stressed religious emotion, the **Enlightenment** emphasized reason and science as the paths to knowledge. **Benjamin Franklin** was a famous American Enlightenment figure. This intellectual movement appealed mostly to wealthy, educated men. But it, too, had far-reaching effects on the colonies.

The Enlightenment began in Europe, as scientists discovered natural laws governing the universe. Isaac Newton, for example, explained the law of gravity.

Other Enlightenment thinkers applied the idea of natural law to human societies. The English philosopher **John Locke** argued that people have natural rights. These are rights to life, liberty, and property. People create governments to protect their natural rights, he claimed. If a government fails in this duty, people have the right to change it. Locke challenged the belief that kings had a God-given right to rule.

Enlightenment ideas of natural rights and government by agreement influenced leaders across Europe and the colonies. As you will see in Section 2, colonists began to wonder whether the British government protected their rights and freedoms. Eventually, they would rebel and form a new government.

*Reading*History

F. Recognizing Effects What were five effects of the Great Awakening?

Background
Locke argued against the idea that the kings had a God-given right to rule. But he still believed that the natural rights of individuals came from God.

Section **1** *Assessment*

1. Terms & Names

Explain the significance of:

- apprentice
- Great Awakening
- Jonathan Edwards
- George Whitefield
- Enlightenment
- Benjamin Franklin
- John Locke

2. Using Graphics

Describe the parts of colonial culture in a chart.

Economy	
Education	
Publishing	
Religion	

Why was each important in colonial culture?

3. Main Ideas

a. Why was land ownership so important to the colonists?

b. How did women and young people contribute to the colonial economy?

c. How did the Great Awakening affect the colonies?

4. Critical Thinking

Contrasting How were the Great Awakening and the Enlightenment different?

THINK ABOUT

- the ideas each movement promoted
- the people to whom each movement appealed

ACTIVITY OPTIONS

LANGUAGE ARTS

ART

Make up a **saying** that reflects some part of colonial culture, or draw an **illustration** of a saying from colonial times.

Roots of Representative Government

MAIN IDEA	WHY IT MATTERS NOW	TERMS & NAMES
Colonists expected their government to preserve their basic rights as English subjects.	U.S. citizens expect these same rights, such as the right to a trial by jury.	Magna Carta English Bill of Rights Parliament salutary neglect Edmund Andros John Peter Zenger Glorious Revolution

ONE AMERICAN'S STORY

In 1688, the Puritan minister Increase Mather sailed to England to get relief for Massachusetts. The English government had canceled the charter of Massachusetts and sent a royal governor to rule.

The colonists thought the governor trampled their rights as English subjects. After four years in England, Mather came home with a new charter that he hoped would satisfy the colonists.

> **A VOICE FROM THE PAST**
>
> For all English liberties are restored to them: No Persons shall have a Penny of their Estates taken from them; nor any Laws imposed on them, without their own Consent by Representatives chosen by themselves.
>
> **Increase Mather,** quoted in *The Last American Puritan*

This is a detail of *Increase Mather* by Jan van der Spriett.

Mather called the new charter "a Magna Carta for New England." In this section, you will learn about the rights of English people set forth in the Magna Carta and later documents. These rights are the basis for the rights Americans enjoy today.

The Rights of Englishmen

English colonists expected certain rights that came from living under an English government. These "rights of Englishmen" had developed over centuries.

The first step toward guaranteeing these rights came in 1215. That year, a group of English noblemen forced King John to accept the **Magna Carta** (Great Charter). The king needed the nobles' money to finance a war. This document guaranteed important rights to noblemen and freemen—those not bound to a master. They could not have their property seized by the king or his officials. They could not be taxed, in most

Taking Notes

Use your chart to take notes about the roots of representative government in the American colonies.

American Identity

cases, unless a council of prominent men agreed. They could not be put to trial based only on an official's word, without witnesses. They could be punished only by a jury of their peers, people of the same social rank.

> ### A VOICE FROM THE PAST
>
> No freeman shall be seized, imprisoned, dispossessed, outlawed, or exiled, . . . nor will we proceed against or prosecute him except by the lawful judgment of his peers, or by the law of the land.
>
> **Magna Carta**, translated in *A Documentary History of England*

Reading **History**

A. Comparing
What rights from the Magna Carta remain rights in America today?

The Magna Carta limited the powers of the king. Over time, the rights it listed were granted to all English people, not just noblemen and freemen.

Parliament and Colonial Government

One of the most important English rights was the right to elect representatives to government. **Parliament**, England's chief lawmaking body, was the colonists' model for representative government. Parliament was made up of two houses. Members of the House of Commons were elected by the people. Members of the House of Lords were nonelected nobles, judges, and church officials.

The king and Parliament were too far away to manage every detail of the colonies. Also, like the citizens of England, English colonists in America wanted to have a say in the laws governing them. So they formed

CITIZENSHIP TODAY

The Importance of Juries

The right to a trial by jury, established in the Magna Carta, is an important legal right. When you become an adult, you will likely be asked to serve on a jury.

Many young people in Knox County, Illinois, have already served as jurors on a teen court (shown below, with an advisor). They decide the best punishment for other teenagers who have admitted breaking a law. For example, shoplifters might be sentenced to write an apology to the store. Knox County is one of more than 500 U.S. communities that have teen courts.

How Can You Serve on a Teen Court?

1. Search the library or Internet to learn more about teen courts.

2. Ask the police department whether your town has a teen court. If it does, volunteer.

3. If you want to start a teen court, seek advice from a community that has one.

4. Invite a lawyer to your class to talk about a juror's role.

5. Find a group to sponsor your court, and get support from youth officers and judges.

 See the Citizenship Handbook, page 280.

For more about courts and juries . . .

 **RESEARCH LINKS** CLASSZONE.COM

Knox County Teen Court volunteers

their own elected assemblies, similar to the House of Commons. Virginia's House of Burgesses was the first of these. In Pennsylvania, William Penn allowed colonists to have their own General Assembly. These Virginia and Pennsylvania assemblies imposed taxes and managed the colonies.

Although the colonists governed themselves in some ways, England still had authority over them. The king appointed royal governors to rule some colonies on his behalf. Parliament had no representatives from the colonies. Even so, it passed laws that affected the colonies. The colonists disliked these laws, and they began to clash with royal governors over how much power England should have in America. These conflicts became more intense in the late 1600s.

Reading **History**
B. Making Inferences Why did the colonists dislike laws passed by Parliament?

A Royal Governor's Rule

The reign of James II threatened the colonies' tradition of self-government. James became king in 1685. He wanted to rule England and its colonies with total authority. One of his first orders changed the way the Northern colonies were governed. These colonies, especially Massachusetts, had been smuggling goods and ignoring the Navigation Acts (see Chapter 4). When challenged, the people of Massachusetts had claimed that England had no right to make laws for them. The previous king, Charles II, had then canceled their charter.

Reading **History**
C. Recognizing Effects How did James II weaken self-government in the colonies?

King James combined Massachusetts and the other Northern colonies into one Dominion of New England, ruled by royal governor **Edmund Andros.** Andros angered the colonists by ending their representative assemblies and allowing town meetings to be held only once a year.

With their assemblies outlawed, some colonists refused to pay taxes. They said that being taxed without having a voice in government violated their rights. Andros jailed the loudest complainers. At their trial, they were told, "You have no more privileges left you than not to be Sould [sold] for Slaves."

The colonists sent Increase Mather to England to plead with King James (see One American's Story on page 141). However, a revolution in England swept King James and Governor Andros from power.

"You have no more privileges left you."
a Boston court official

The colonists hated Governor Andros.

England's Glorious Revolution

Background
England had become Protestant in the 16th century. Catholics were kept out of high office.

The English Parliament had decided to overthrow King James for not respecting its rights. Events came to a head in 1688. King James, a Catholic, had been trying to pack his next Parliament with officials who would overturn anti-Catholic laws. He had dismissed the last Parliament in 1685. The Protestant leaders of Parliament were outraged. They offered

the throne to James's Protestant daughter, Mary, and her husband, William of Orange. William was the ruler of the Netherlands. Having little support from the people, James fled the country at the end of 1688. Parliament named William and Mary the new monarchs of England. This change in leadership was called England's **Glorious Revolution.**

After accepting the throne, William and Mary agreed in 1689 to uphold the **English Bill of Rights.** This was an agreement to respect the rights of English citizens and of Parliament. Under it, the king or queen could not cancel laws or impose taxes unless Parliament agreed. Free elections and frequent meetings of Parliament must be held. Excessive fines and cruel punishments were forbidden. People had the right to complain to the king or queen in Parliament without being arrested.

Background
The English Bill of Rights was the model for the Bill of Rights in the U.S. Constitution.

The English Bill of Rights established an important principle: the government was to be based on laws made by Parliament, not on the desires of a ruler. The rights of English people were strengthened.

The American colonists were quick to claim these rights. When the people of Boston heard of King James's fall, they jailed Governor Andros and asked Parliament to restore their old government.

Shared Power in the Colonies

After the Glorious Revolution, the Massachusetts colonists regained some self-government. They could again elect representatives to an assembly. However, they still had a governor appointed by the crown.

Background
Massachusetts colonists also gained more religious freedom. They no longer had to be church members to vote.

The diagram on this page shows how most colonial governments were organized by 1700. Note how the royal governor, his council, and the colonial assembly shared power. The governor could strike down laws passed by the assembly, but the assembly was responsible for the governor's salary. If he blocked the assembly, the assembly might refuse to pay him.

During the first half of the 1700s, England interfered very little in colonial affairs. This hands-off policy was called **salutary neglect.** Parliament passed many laws regulating trade, the use of money, and even apprenticeships in the colonies. But governors rarely enforced these laws. The colonists got used to acting on their own.

Vocabulary
salutary: healthful or beneficial

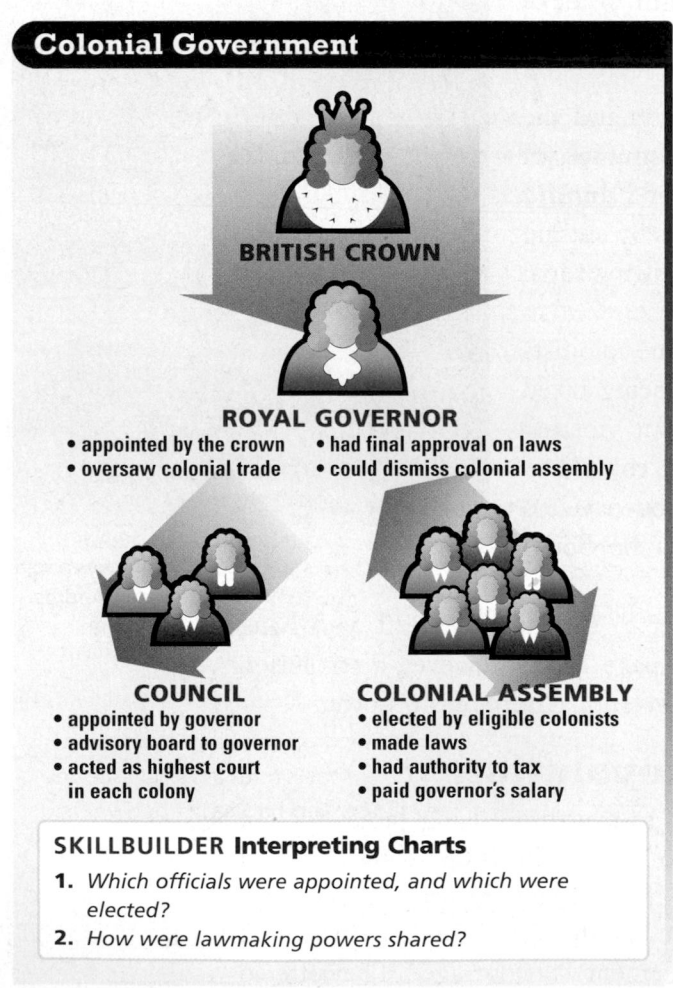

Colonial Government

BRITISH CROWN

ROYAL GOVERNOR
- appointed by the crown
- oversaw colonial trade
- had final approval on laws
- could dismiss colonial assembly

COUNCIL
- appointed by governor
- advisory board to governor
- acted as highest court in each colony

COLONIAL ASSEMBLY
- elected by eligible colonists
- made laws
- had authority to tax
- paid governor's salary

SKILLBUILDER Interpreting Charts
1. *Which officials were appointed, and which were elected?*
2. *How were lawmaking powers shared?*

Government officials burn the *New-York Weekly Journal.*

The Zenger Trial

Colonists moved toward gaining a new right, freedom of the press, in 1735. That year, **John Peter Zenger,** publisher of the *New-York Weekly Journal,* stood trial for printing criticism of New York's governor. The governor had removed a judge and tried to fix an election.

A VOICE FROM THE PAST

A Governor turns rogue [criminal], does a thousand things for which a small rogue would have deserved a halter [hanging], and because it is difficult . . . to obtain relief against him, . . . it is prudent [wise] to . . . join in the roguery.

New-York Weekly Journal, quoted in *Colonial America, 1607–1763*

*Reading*History
D. Drawing Conclusions Why was the Zenger trial a step toward freedom of the press?

At that time, it was illegal to criticize the government in print. Andrew Hamilton defended Zenger at his trial, claiming that people had the right to speak the truth. The jury agreed, and Zenger was released.

English rights were part of the heritage uniting people in the British colonies. In the next section, you will read about another unifying force—a war against the French and their Indian allies.

Section 2 Assessment

1. Terms & Names

Explain the significance of:
- Magna Carta
- Parliament
- Edmund Andros
- Glorious Revolution
- English Bill of Rights
- salutary neglect
- John Peter Zenger

2. Using Graphics

In the boxes, show how the rights of English people developed in the three years mentioned.

English Rights

1215   1689   1735

Which right is most important to you?

3. Main Ideas

a. What were three of the traditional rights expected by English colonists?

b. In what ways did the English government anger the colonists in the late 1600s?

c. How did England's policies toward the colonies change after the Glorious Revolution?

4. Critical Thinking

Supporting Opinions
In your opinion, who had the most power—the royal governor, the council, or the assemblies? Defend your opinion.

THINK ABOUT
- their roles in making laws
- their roles in raising money
- who had final approval in matters

ACTIVITY OPTIONS

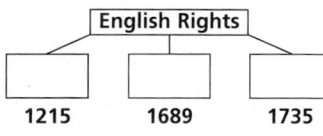

Deliver **closing arguments** or create a **leaflet** defending John Peter Zenger and freedom of the press.

The French and Indian War

MAIN IDEA	WHY IT MATTERS NOW	TERMS & NAMES
Britain's victory in the French and Indian War forced France to give up its North American colonies.	British influence spread over North America, though French populations and place names still exist here.	French and Indian War Albany Plan of Union Battle of Quebec Treaty of Paris Pontiac's Rebellion Proclamation of 1763

ONE AMERICAN'S STORY

The Frenchman, Charles de Langlade, and his family controlled the fur trade around what is now Green Bay, Wisconsin.

In 1752, Charles commanded 250 Ottawa and Chippewa warriors in an attack on a village in present-day Ohio. His reason: the Miami people there had stopped trading with the French and were now trading with the British. Charles and his men destroyed the village's British trading post. This attack helped lead to the French and Indian War.

This section describes the war, in which French forces fought British forces in North America. Each side had Native American allies.

Taking Notes

Use your chart to take notes about the French and Indian War.

American Identity

France Claims Western Lands

As you learned in Chapters 2 and 4, the French were exploring the North American interior while English colonists were settling the eastern coast. By the late 1600s, French explorers had claimed the Ohio River valley, the Mississippi River valley, and the entire Great Lakes region. The French territory of Louisiana, claimed by the explorer La Salle in 1682, stretched from the Appalachian Mountains to the Rocky Mountains.

The French built their main settlements, Quebec and Montreal, along the St. Lawrence River in Canada. (See the map on page 148.) They also built forts along the Great Lakes and along rivers draining into the Mississippi. By 1760, the French colony, New France, had a European population of about 80,000. By contrast, the British colonies had more than a million settlers.

Some Europeans in New France were Jesuit priests. They wanted to convert Native Americans to Christianity. Other Europeans in New France worked as fur traders. Native Americans brought furs to French forts and

This 1903 painting by Edward Deming shows Charles de Langlade attacking British forces in 1755.

Background
Often French traders lived among and married Native Americans.

exchanged them for goods such as iron pots and steel knives. Many French traders carried goods by canoe into remote parts of New France.

Native American Alliances

The English competed with the French for furs. Also, different Native American groups competed to supply furs to the Europeans. The fur trade created economic and military alliances between the Europeans and their Native American trading partners. The Huron and Algonquin peoples of the Great Lakes region were allied with the French. The Iroquois of upper New York often were allied with the Dutch and, later, the English.

Background
The Iroquois were a union of six nations.

Alliances between Europeans and Native Americans led to their involvement in each other's wars. For example, by the mid-1600s, the Iroquois had trapped all the beavers in their own lands. To get more furs, they made war on their Huron and Algonquin neighbors, driving them west. Eventually the Iroquois controlled an area ranging from Maine west to the Ohio Valley and north to Lake Michigan. Iroquois expansion threatened the French fur trade. In response, the French armed the Huron and Algonquin peoples to fight the Iroquois. The Iroquois were armed by the English.

Reading History
A. Recognizing Effects How did the fur trade lead to wars?

When France and England declared war on each other in Europe in 1689, French and English colonists in America also began to fight. With their Native American allies, they attacked each other's settlements and forts. During the 1700s, two more wars between France and England fueled wars in their colonies. Neither side won a clear victory in these wars. A final war, the **French and Indian War** (1754–1763), decided which nation would control the northern and eastern parts of North America.

A French trader visits a Native American family.

Conflict in the Ohio River Valley

The seeds for the French and Indian War were planted when British fur traders began moving into the Ohio River valley in the 1750s. British land companies were also planning to settle colonists there. The French and their Native American allies became alarmed. To keep the British out of the valley, Charles de Langlade destroyed the village of Pickawillany and its British trading post (see One American's Story on page 146).

Reading History
B. Making Inferences Why was the Ohio River Valley important to the French and British governments?

The British traders left, and the French built forts to protect the region linking their Canadian and Louisiana settlements. This upset the Virginia colony, which claimed title to the land. In 1753, the lieutenant governor of Virginia sent a small group of soldiers to tell the French to

leave. Their leader was a 21-year-old major named George Washington. Washington reported the French commander's reply.

A VOICE FROM THE PAST

He told me the Country belong'd to them, that no English Man had a right to trade upon them Waters; & that he had Orders to make every Person Prisoner that attempted it on the Ohio or the Waters of it.

George Washington, *"Journey to the French Commandant"*

Virginia's lieutenant governor sent about 40 men to build a fort at the head of the Ohio River, where Pittsburgh stands today. French and Native American troops seized the partially built fort in April 1754 and completed it themselves. The French named it Fort Duquesne (du•KAYN).

War Begins and Spreads

George Washington was on his way to defend Fort Duquesne when he learned of its surrender. He and his men pushed on and built another small fort, Fort Necessity. Following Washington's surprise attack on a French force, the French and their allies attacked Fort Necessity on July 3, 1754. After Washington surrendered, the French let him march back to Virginia. The French and Indian War had begun. This war became part of the Seven Years' War (1756–1763), a worldwide struggle for empire between France and Great Britain.

Background
The Seven Years' War was fought not only in North America but also in the Caribbean, throughout Europe, and in India and Africa.

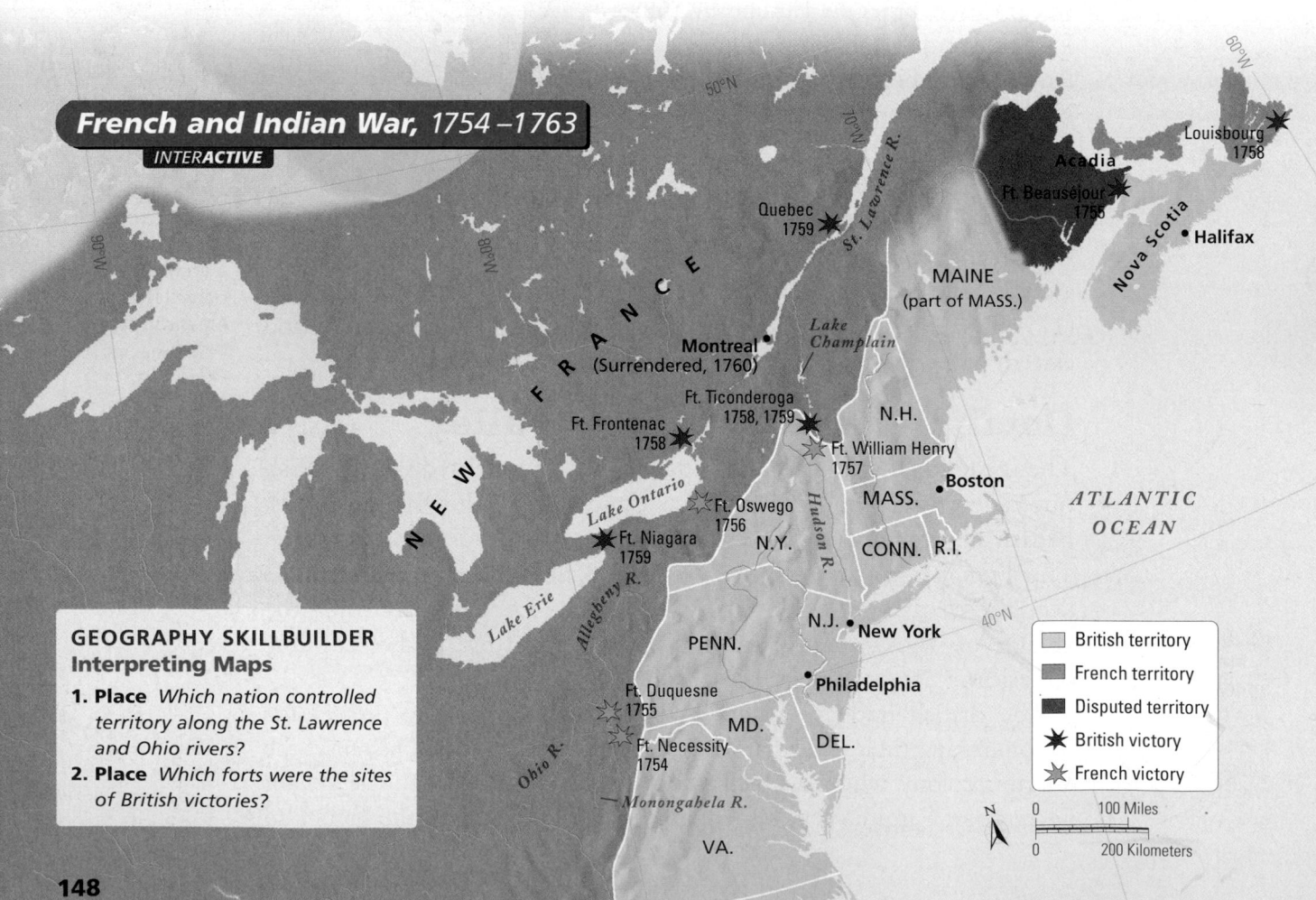

French and Indian War, 1754–1763
INTERACTIVE

Louisbourg 1758
Acadia
Ft. Beauséjour 1755
Nova Scotia
• Halifax
Quebec 1759
St. Lawrence R.
MAINE (part of MASS.)
NEW FRANCE
Montreal (Surrendered, 1760)
Lake Champlain
Ft. Ticonderoga 1758, 1759
N.H.
Ft. Frontenac 1758
Ft. William Henry 1757
MASS. • Boston
Lake Ontario
Ft. Oswego 1756
Hudson R.
ATLANTIC OCEAN
Ft. Niagara 1759
N.Y.
CONN. R.I.
Lake Erie
Allegheny R.
N.J. • New York
GEOGRAPHY SKILLBUILDER
Interpreting Maps
PENN.
1. **Place** *Which nation controlled territory along the St. Lawrence and Ohio rivers?*
Ft. Duquesne 1755
• Philadelphia
MD. DEL.
2. **Place** *Which forts were the sites of British victories?*
Ft. Necessity 1754
Ohio R.
Monongahela R.
VA.

British territory
French territory
Disputed territory
British victory
French victory

0   100 Miles
0   200 Kilometers

148

While Washington was surrendering Fort Necessity, representatives from the British colonies and the Iroquois nations were meeting at Albany, New York. The colonists wanted the Iroquois to fight with them against the French. The Iroquois would not commit to this alliance.

Benjamin Franklin, who admired the union of the six Iroquois nations, suggested that the colonies band together for defense. His **Albany Plan of Union** was the first formal proposal to unite the colonies. The plan called for each colony to send representatives to a Grand Council. This council would be able to collect taxes, raise armies, make treaties, and start new settlements. The leaders in Albany supported Franklin's plan, but the colonial legislatures later defeated it because they did not want to give up control of their own affairs.

Braddock's Defeat

Britain realized that to win the war, it could not rely solely on the colonists for funding or for troops. Therefore, the British sent General Edward Braddock and two regiments to Virginia. In 1755, Braddock marched toward the French at Fort Duquesne. George Washington was at his side. Their red-coated army of 2,100 moved slowly over the mountains, weighed down by a huge cannon.

On July 9, on a narrow trail eight miles from Fort Duquesne, fewer than 900 French and Indian troops surprised Braddock's forces. Washington suggested that his men break formation and fight from behind the trees, but Braddock would not listen. The general held his position and had four horses shot out from under him. Washington lost two horses. Four bullets went through Washington's coat, but, miraculously, none hit him. In the end, nearly 1,000 men were killed or wounded. General Braddock died from his wounds. American colonists were stunned by Braddock's defeat and by many other British losses over the next two years.

The British Take Quebec

In 1757, Britain had a new secretary of state, William Pitt, who was determined to win the war in the colonies. He sent the nation's best generals to America and borrowed money to pay colonial troops for fighting. The British controlled six French forts by August 1759, including Fort Duquesne (rebuilt as Fort Pitt). In late summer, the British began to attack New France at its capital, Quebec.

*Reading***History**
C. Drawing Conclusions Why was Braddock defeated by a smaller enemy force?

Background
Because the British seemed likely to win the war, some Iroquois had joined them as allies.

America's
HERITAGE

ACADIANS TO CAJUNS
Braddock's defeat and other early losses in the war increased British concern about the loyalty of the French people in Acadia (now Nova Scotia). The British had won Acadia from France in 1713.

In 1755, British officers forced out 6,000 Acadians who would not take a loyalty oath. The British burned Acadian villages and spread the people to various British colonies, as shown. Eventually, some Acadians made their way to the French territory of Louisiana. There they became known as Cajuns.

149

Quebec sat on cliffs 300 feet above the St. Lawrence River. Cannon and thousands of soldiers guarded its thick walls. British general James Wolfe sailed around the fort for two months, unable to capture it. Then, in September, a scout found a steep, unguarded path up the cliffs to the plains just west of Quebec. At night, Wolfe and 4,000 of his men floated to the path and secretly climbed the cliffs.

When the French awoke, the British were lined up on the plains, ready to attack. In the short, fierce battle that followed, Wolfe was killed. The French commander, Montcalm, died of his wounds the next day. Quebec surrendered to the British. The **Battle of Quebec** was the turning point of the war. When Montreal fell the next year, all of Canada was in British hands.

Reading **History**
D. Finding Main Ideas How were the British able to capture Quebec?

The Treaty of Paris

Britain and France battled in other parts of the world for almost three more years. Spain made a pact in 1761 to aid France, but its help came too late. When the Seven Years' War ended in 1763, Britain had won.

By the **Treaty of Paris,** Britain claimed all of North America east of the Mississippi River. To reward Spain for its help, France gave it New Orleans and Louisiana, the French territory west of the Mississippi. Britain, which had seized Cuba and the Philippines from Spain, gave them back in exchange for Florida. The treaty ended French power in North America.

Background
France kept only a few islands near Newfoundland and in the West Indies.

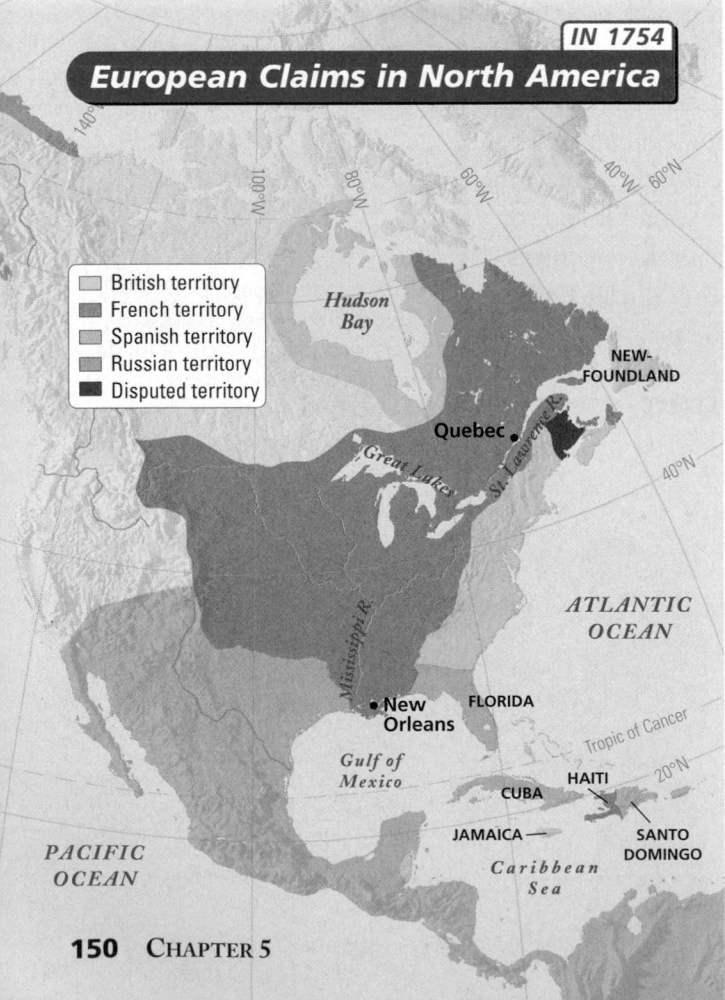

IN 1754
European Claims in North America

- British territory
- French territory
- Spanish territory
- Russian territory
- Disputed territory

Hudson Bay

NEWFOUNDLAND

Quebec

Great Lakes

St. Lawrence R.

ATLANTIC OCEAN

Mississippi R.

New Orleans

FLORIDA

Gulf of Mexico

Tropic of Cancer

CUBA

HAITI

JAMAICA

SANTO DOMINGO

Caribbean Sea

PACIFIC OCEAN

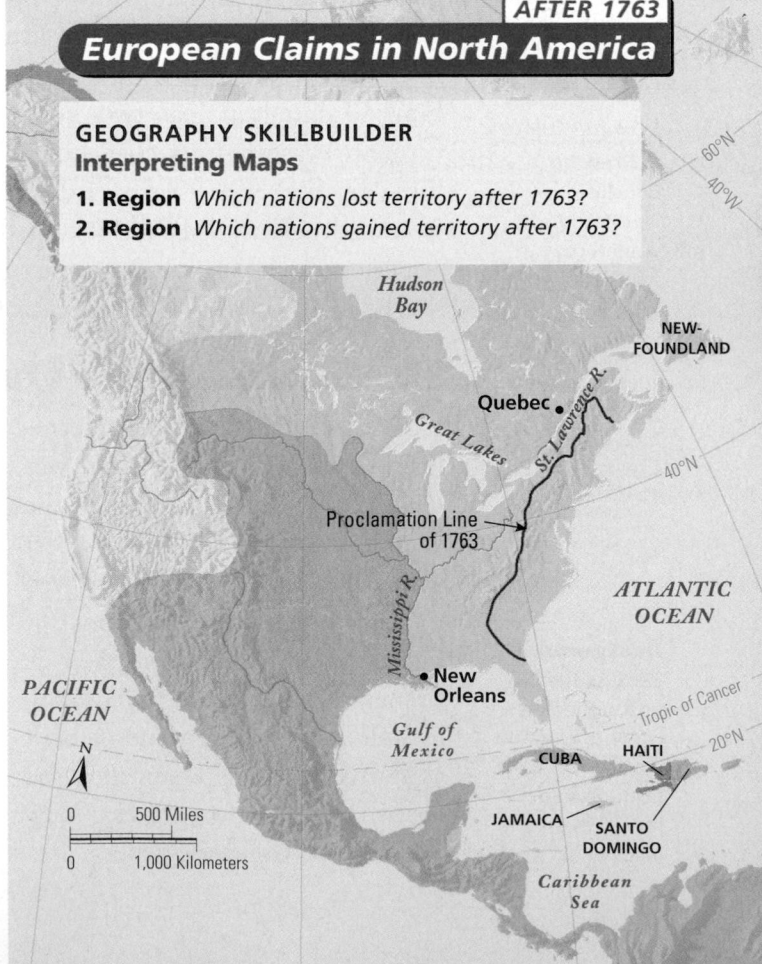

AFTER 1763
European Claims in North America

GEOGRAPHY SKILLBUILDER
Interpreting Maps
1. **Region** Which nations lost territory after 1763?
2. **Region** Which nations gained territory after 1763?

Hudson Bay

NEWFOUNDLAND

Quebec

Great Lakes

St. Lawrence R.

Proclamation Line of 1763

Mississippi R.

PACIFIC OCEAN

New Orleans

ATLANTIC OCEAN

Gulf of Mexico

Tropic of Cancer

CUBA

HAITI

JAMAICA

SANTO DOMINGO

Caribbean Sea

0   500 Miles
0   1,000 Kilometers

Pontiac's Rebellion

Pontiac

After French forces withdrew, the British took over their forts. They refused to give supplies to the Native Americans, as the French had. British settlers also moved across the mountains onto Native American land. In the spring and summer of 1763, Native American groups responded by attacking settlers and destroying almost every British fort west of the Appalachians. They surrounded the three remaining forts. This revolt was called **Pontiac's Rebellion,** although the Ottawa war leader Pontiac was only one of many organizers.

British settlers reacted with equal viciousness, killing even Indians who had not attacked them. British officers came up with a brutal plan to end the Delaware siege at Fort Pitt.

*Reading*History
E. Analyzing Points of View
Why did the Native Americans attack the British?

A VOICE FROM THE PAST

Could it not be contrived to send the Small Pox among those disaffected [angry] tribes of Indians? We must on this occasion use every stratagem in our power to reduce them.

Major General Jeffrey Amherst, quoted in *The Conspiracy of Pontiac*

*Reading*History
F. Reading a Map
Find the Proclamation Line of 1763 on the map on page 150.

The officers invited Delaware war leaders in to talk and then gave them smallpox-infected blankets as gifts. This started a deadly outbreak.

By the fall, the Native Americans had retreated. Even so, the uprising made the British government see that defending Western lands would be costly. Therefore, the British issued the **Proclamation of 1763,** which forbade colonists to settle west of the Appalachians.

The colonists were angry. They thought they had won the right to settle the Ohio River Valley. The British government was angry at the colonists, who did not want to pay for their own defense. This hostility helped cause the war for American independence, as you will read.

Section 3 Assessment

1. Terms & Names

Explain the significance of:
- French and Indian War
- Albany Plan of Union
- Battle of Quebec
- Treaty of Paris
- Pontiac's Rebellion
- Proclamation of 1763

2. Using Graphics

Write the month and year each battle occurred. Classify each as a French or British victory.

Date	Incident	Victor
	Seizure of Fort Duquesne	
	Surrender of Fort Necessity	
	Braddock's defeat	
	Battle of Quebec	

Which was most important?

3. Main Ideas

a. How did the fur trade contribute to the French and Indian War?

b. Why did the British begin to win the war after 1758?

c. What were some causes and effects of Pontiac's Rebellion?

4. Critical Thinking

Analyzing Points of View
Why did the French, British, and Native Americans fight over the Ohio River Valley?

THINK ABOUT
- how the British viewed the valley
- how the French viewed it
- how the Native Americans viewed it

ACTIVITY OPTIONS

GEOGRAPHY

MUSIC

Learn more about the Battle of Quebec and its setting. Make a three-dimensional **model** of the battle or write a **song** about it.

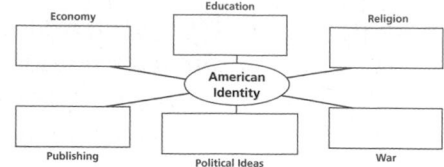
Beginnings of an American Identity

Separate Colonies

Early American Culture

English colonists shared certain values, such as land ownership and hard work. The Great Awakening and the Enlightenment also drew colonists together.

Roots of Representative Government

English colonists expected the right to elect representatives to government and other political rights that had developed in England over centuries.

The French and Indian War

English colonists were also drawn together as they fought against common enemies—the French and their Native American allies.

Common Identity

TERMS & NAMES

Briefly explain the significance of each of the following.

1. Great Awakening
2. Enlightenment
3. John Peter Zenger
4. Magna Carta
5. Parliament
6. Glorious Revolution
7. Edmund Andros
8. French and Indian War
9. Treaty of Paris
10. Proclamation of 1763

REVIEW QUESTIONS

Early American Culture (pages 135–140)

1. Why did colonists want to own land?
2. What was women's role in the colonial economy?
3. What were the effects of the Great Awakening on colonial culture and politics?

Roots of Representative Government (pages 141–145)

4. Why did colonies have representative assemblies?
5. What was one important right granted in the Magna Carta?
6. How did the Zenger trial help lead to freedom of the press?
7. How was the English Bill of Rights related to the Glorious Revolution?

The French and Indian War (pages 146–151)

8. What was George Washington's role in the French and Indian War?
9. What did England gain as a result of the French and Indian War?
10. What was one reason for Pontiac's Rebellion?

CRITICAL THINKING

1. USING YOUR NOTES: FINDING MAIN IDEAS

Using your completed chart, answer the questions below.

```
  Economy          Education          Religion
  [      ]         [      ]          [      ]
           \          |          /
              ( American
                Identity )
           /          |          \
  [      ]         [      ]          [      ]
  Publishing     Political Ideas       War
```

a. What were some political ideas shared by people in the American colonies?
b. How was religion important to American identity?
c. How did publishing help build an American identity?

2. THEME: DEMOCRATIC IDEALS

What democratic ideals did Americans inherit from England?

3. APPLYING CITIZENSHIP SKILLS

Why is jury duty an example of responsible citizenship?

4. CONTRASTING

How did colonial government differ from present-day government in the United States?

5. ANALYZING CAUSES

What do you think was the most important cause of the French and Indian War?

6. ANALYZING LEADERSHIP

Give an example of bad military or political leadership from the chapter. What mistake was made?

Interact with History

Now that you have read the chapter, what would you say British colonists in America had in common?

STANDARDS-BASED ASSESSMENT

Use the map and your knowledge of U.S. history to answer questions 1 and 2.

Additional Test Practice, pp. S1–S33.

French Explorers on the Mississippi

Marquette and Joliet, 1673

La Salle 1679–1682

Present-day state boundary

1. Where did La Salle's journey begin?

A. Lake Erie

B. Lake Huron

C. Lake Michigan

D. Lake Ontario

2. Along which river did both teams of explorers travel?

A. Illinois River

B. Mississippi River

C. Ohio River

D. Wisconsin River

This is a quotation from Increase Mather about colonial government. Use the quotation and your knowledge of U.S. history to answer question 3.

PRIMARY SOURCE

For all English liberties are restored to them: No Persons shall have a Penny of their Estates taken from them; nor any Laws imposed on them, without their own Consent by Representatives chosen by themselves.

Increase Mather, quoted in *The Last American Puritan*

3. The passage best represents which point of view?

A. The colonists were entitled to the basic rights of English subjects.

B. The colonists' land belonged to the government.

C. Colonists did not have to pay taxes to the English government.

D. Colonists were not entitled to liberties granted to English subjects.

TEST PRACTICE
CLASSZONE.COM

ALTERNATIVE ASSESSMENT

1. WRITING ABOUT HISTORY

During colonial times, children often had to learn work skills. Imagine that you were a young person during this time. Write a **letter** to your family describing your life and the work you do.

- Use library resources to learn more about the roles of children during colonial times.

- Explain what you have learned about your work, and describe what you like or don't like about it.

2. COOPERATIVE LEARNING

Working in a group, hold a diplomatic council trying to prevent the French and Indian War. Group members can assume different roles: English and French officials, English settlers, French fur traders, English-allied Iroquois, French-allied Huron or Algonquin.

INTEGRATED TECHNOLOGY

DOING INTERNET RESEARCH

Colonial American culture was not like modern American culture. Use the Internet to do research about life in 18th century colonial America. Then prepare a dramatic presentation featuring one of the important figures from the time, such as Benjamin Franklin, Madam Sarah Knight, or Pontiac.

- On the Internet, find images, stories, poems, or novels, and articles about daily life, interests, or entertainment in the early and middle 1700s.

- Historical societies or living history museums in the original 13 states may also provide information about this period of time in American history.

For more about colonial American culture . . .

INTERNET ACTIVITY
CLASSZONE.COM

Creating a New Nation

"By the rude bridge . . . the embattled farmers stood and fired the shot heard round the world."

—Ralph Waldo Emerson, "Concord Hymn"

Americans battled British troops at Old North Bridge, Concord, Massachusetts, in April 1775.

The Road to Revolution 1763–1776

Angry confrontations between colonial protestors and British Red Coats became common as the colonies moved towards independence.

1763
Proclamation of 1763 becomes law.

1765
Stamp Act is passed.

1767
Townshend Acts are passed.

1769
Spanish begin to establish military posts and missions in California.

USA
World 1763

1763
Treaty of Paris ends Seven Years' War in Europe.

1765
Chinese forces invade Burma.

1769
Scotland's James Watt patents a steam engine capable of running other machines.

The bayonets, or blades, on the soldiers' gun were very dangerous in close combat.

The fife and drum corps played music to keep soldiers at a steady march. During battle, the drummers beat out orders and the fifers carried messages and stretchers.

The year is 1765. Your neighbors are enraged by Britain's demand that British troops be housed in American cities at American expense. Britain has never done this before. There are protests in many cities. You have to decide what you would do.

Would you join the protest?

What Do You Think?

- What is the best way to show opposition to policies you consider unjust?
- Is there anything to be gained by protesting? Anything to be lost?
- Does government have the right to make demands without consent of the people? Why or why not?

RESEARCH LINKS
CLASSZONE.COM

Visit the Chapter 6 links for more information about the American Revolution.

1770
Boston Massacre

1772
Captain Cook explores the South Pacific.

1773
Boston Tea Party

1774
Intolerable Acts are passed; First Continental Congress meets.

1774
Reign of Louis XVI begins in France.

1775
Battles of Lexington and Concord

1776
Declaration of Independence is signed.

1776

Reading Strategy: Sequencing Events

What Do You Know?

What do you already know about the time before the Revolution? What were the issues that caused the colonists to choose independence?

Think About

- what you have learned about this period from movies, television, or historical fiction
- reasons people in history have chosen to fight for freedom from oppression
- your responses to the Interact with History about joining the protest (see page 157)

What Do You Want to Know?

What questions do you have about the issues and events that pushed the American colonists toward rebellion? Record them in your notebook before you read the chapter.

Sequencing Events

Sequencing means putting events in the order in which they happen in time. In learning about how the American colonies moved toward independence, it would be helpful to list the important events. Place them in the order in which they occurred. You might record the event and its date in a graphic organizer such as the one below. Copy this organizer in your notebook. Fill it in as you read the chapter.

S See Skillbuilder Handbook, page R4.

Taking Notes

Proclamation of 1763 → ▢ → ▢ → ▢ ↓
▢ ← ▢ ← ▢ ← ▢ ↓
▢ → ▢ → ▢ → Declaration of Independence, 1776

Tighter British Control

MAIN IDEA	WHY IT MATTERS NOW	TERMS & NAMES
Americans saw British efforts to tax them and to increase control over the colonies as violations of their rights.	Colonial protests were the first steps on the road to American independence.	King George III Quartering Act revenue Sugar Act Stamp Act Patrick Henry boycott Sons of Liberty

ONE AMERICAN'S STORY

James Otis, Jr., a young Massachusetts lawyer, stormed through the streets of Boston one day in 1760. He was furious. His father had just been denied the post of chief justice of the Massachusetts colony by the royal governor. To Otis, this was one more example of Britain's lack of respect for colonial rights. Another example was its use of search warrants that allowed customs officers to enter any home or business to look for smuggled goods. Otis believed these searches were illegal.

In court in February 1761, Otis spoke with great emotion for five hours about the search warrant and its use.

> ### A VOICE FROM THE PAST
> It appears to me the worst instrument of arbitrary power, the most destructive of English liberty and the fundamental principles of law, that was ever found in an English law-book.
>
> **James Otis, Jr.,** quoted in *James Otis: The Pre-Revolutionist* by J. C. Ridpath

James Otis, Jr., argues in court against illegal search warrants in 1761.

In making the first public speech demanding English liberties for the colonists, James Otis planted a seed of freedom. In this section, you will read more about the early protests against Britain's policies in America.

The Colonies and Britain Grow Apart

During the French and Indian War, Britain and the colonies fought side by side. Americans took great pride in being partners in the victory over the French. However, when the war ended, problems arose. Britain wanted to govern its 13 original colonies and the territories gained in the war in a uniform way. So the British Parliament in London imposed new laws and restrictions. Previously, the colonies had been allowed to develop largely on their own. Now they felt that their freedom was being limited.

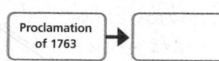

Taking Notes

Use your chart to take notes about the tightening of British control.

| Proclamation of 1763 | → | |

The first of Parliament's laws was the Proclamation of 1763. (See Chapter 5.) It said that colonists could not settle west of the Appalachian Mountains. Britain wanted this land to remain in the hands of its Native American allies to prevent another revolt like Pontiac's Rebellion.

The proclamation angered colonists who had hoped to move to the fertile Ohio Valley. Many of these colonists had no land of their own. It also upset colonists who had bought land as an investment. As a result, many ignored the law.

*Reading***History**
A. Summarizing Who was upset by the Proclamation of 1763?

British Troops and Taxes

King George III, the British monarch, wanted to enforce the proclamation and also keep peace with Britain's Native American allies. To do this, he decided to keep 10,000 soldiers in the colonies. In 1765, Parliament passed the **Quartering Act.** This was a cost-saving measure that required the colonies to quarter, or house, British soldiers and provide them with supplies. General Thomas Gage, commander of these forces, put most of the troops in New York.

Britain owed a large debt from the French and Indian War. Keeping troops in the colonies would raise that debt even higher. Britain needed more **revenue,** or income, to meet its expenses. So it attempted to have the colonies pay part of the war debt. It also wanted them to contribute toward the costs of frontier defense and colonial government.

In the past, the king had asked the colonial assemblies to pass taxes to support military actions that took place in the colonies. This time, however, Parliament voted to tax the Americans directly.

In 1764, Parliament passed the **Sugar Act.** This law placed a tax on sugar, molasses, and other products shipped to the colonies. It also called for strict enforcement of the act and harsh punishment of smugglers. Colonial merchants, who often traded in smuggled goods, reacted with anger.

Colonial leaders such as James Otis claimed that Parliament had no right to tax the colonies, since the colonists were not represented in Parliament. As Otis exclaimed, "Taxation without representation is tyranny!" British finance minister George Grenville disagreed. The colonists were subjects of Britain, he said, and enjoyed the protection of its laws. For that reason, they were subject to taxation.

Vocabulary
tyranny: absolute power in the hands of a single ruler

Britain Passes the Stamp Act

The Sugar Act was just the first in a series of acts that increased tension between the mother country and the colonies. In 1765, Parliament passed the **Stamp Act.** This law required all legal and commercial documents to carry an official stamp showing that a tax had been paid. All diplomas, contracts, and wills had to carry a stamp.

The colonial view of the hated stamp tax is shown by the skull and crossbones on this emblem (above); a royal stamp is pictured at right.

Even published materials such as newspapers had to be written on special stamped paper.

The Stamp Act was a new kind of tax for the colonies. The Sugar Act had been a tax on imported goods. It mainly affected merchants. In contrast, the Stamp Act was a tax applied within the colonies. It fell directly on all colonists. Even more, the colonists had to pay for stamps in silver coin—a scarce item in the colonies.

Colonial leaders vigorously protested. For them, the issue was clear. They were being taxed without their consent by a Parliament in which they had no voice. If Britain could pass the Stamp Act, what other taxes might it pass in the future? Samuel Adams, a leader in the Massachusetts legislature, asked, "Why not our lands? Why not the produce of our lands and, in short, everything we possess and make use of?" **Patrick Henry,** a member of Virginia's House of Burgesses, called for resistance to the tax. When another member shouted that resistance was treason, Henry reportedly replied, "If this be treason, make the most of it!"

The Colonies Protest the Stamp Act

Colonial assemblies and newspapers took up the cry—"No taxation without representation!" In October 1765, nine colonies sent delegates to the Stamp Act Congress in New York City. This was the first time the colonies met to consider acting together in protest. Delegates drew up a petition to the king protesting the Stamp Act. The petition declared that the right to tax the colonies belonged to the colonial assemblies, not to Parliament. Later, colonial merchants organized a **boycott** of British goods. A boycott is a refusal to buy.

Meanwhile, some colonists formed secret societies to oppose British policies. The most famous of these groups was the **Sons of Liberty.** Many Sons of Liberty were lawyers, merchants, and craftspeople—the colonists most affected by the Stamp Act. These groups staged protests against the act.

Not all of their protests were peaceful. The Sons of Liberty burned the stamped paper whenever they could find it. They also attacked customs officials, whom they covered with hot tar and feathers and paraded in public. Fearing for their safety, many customs officials quit their jobs.

The protests in the colonies had an effect in Britain. Merchants thought that their trade with America would be hurt. Some British political leaders, including

Reading **History**
B. Making Inferences Why did the colonists boycott goods?

Background
To voice their protests, the Sons of Liberty in Boston met under a huge, 120-year-old elm tree that they called the Liberty Tree.

Colonists protest the Stamp Act.

Bostonians Paying the Taxman
INTER*ACTIVE*

In this British political cartoon, Americans are depicted as barbarians who would tar and feather a customs official, or tax collector, and pour hot tea down his throat.

A Liberty Tree as a gallows

B Stamp Act posted upside down

C Protesters in Boston

D Customs official tarred and feathered

the popular parliamentary leader William Pitt, agreed with American thinking about taxing the colonies. Pitt spoke out against the Stamp Act.

A VOICE FROM THE PAST

The Americans have not acted in all things with prudence and [good] temper. They have been driven to madness by injustice. Will you punish them for the madness you have [caused]? . . . My opinion . . . is that the Stamp Act be repealed absolutely, totally and immediately.

William Pitt, quoted in *Patriots* by A. J. Langguth

Parliament finally saw that the Stamp Act was a mistake and repealed it in 1766. But at the same time, Parliament passed another law—the Declaratory Act. This law said that Parliament had supreme authority to govern the colonies. The Americans celebrated the repeal of the Stamp Act and tried to ignore the Declaratory Act. A great tug of war between Parliament and the colonies had begun. The central issue was control of the colonies, as you will learn in the next section.

Reading **History**

C. Drawing Conclusions Why was it important for Parliament to pass the Declaratory Act?

Section 1 Assessment

1. Terms & Names

Explain the significance of:

- King George III
- Quartering Act
- revenue
- Sugar Act
- Stamp Act
- Patrick Henry
- boycott
- Sons of Liberty

2. Using Graphics

Use a cluster diagram like the one below to review points of conflict between Britain and the colonies.

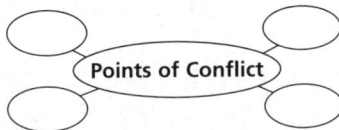

Points of Conflict

Which do you think was the most serious? Explain.

3. Main Ideas

a. Why did the Proclamation of 1763 anger colonists?

b. How did colonists react to the Stamp Act?

c. What was the goal of secret societies such as the Sons of Liberty?

4. Critical Thinking

Analyzing Points of View What were the two sides in the debate over British taxation of the colonies?

THINK ABOUT

- how Parliament viewed the colonies
- what concerned the colonists about taxes

ACTIVITY OPTIONS

ART

MUSIC

Imagine that you are a colonial leader who wants to get your fellow colonists to protest British policy. Design a **poster** or write a **song of protest**.

Colonial Resistance Grows

MAIN IDEA	WHY IT MATTERS NOW	TERMS & NAMES
Many Americans began to organize to oppose British policies.	Americans continue to protest what they view as wrongs and injustices.	Crispus Attucks Boston Massacre Townshend Acts John Adams writs of assistance committee of correspondence Samuel Adams Boston Tea Party

ONE AMERICAN'S STORY

<u>Crispus Attucks</u> knew about the struggle for freedom. The son of an African-American father and a Native American mother, Attucks was born into slavery in Framingham, Massachusetts, around 1723. As a young man, Attucks escaped by running away to sea.

In March 1770, Attucks found himself in Boston, where feelings against British rule were hot. One night Attucks took part in a disturbance between colonists and British troops. He was about to play a key role in U.S. history—losing his life to a British bullet in a protest that came to be called the Boston Massacre. In Section 2, you will read how tension between Britain and its colonies led to violence.

Crispus Attucks, a sailor of African-American and Native American ancestry, was an early hero of America's struggle for freedom.

The Townshend Acts Are Passed

After the uproar over the Stamp Act, Britain hoped to avoid further conflict. Even so, it still needed to raise money to pay for troops and other expenses in America. The Quartering Act was not working. Most of the British army was in New York, and New York saw that as an unfair burden. Its assembly refused to pay to house the troops.

The king's finance minister, Charles Townshend, told Parliament that he had a way to raise revenue in the colonies. So in 1767, Parliament passed his plan, known as the **Townshend Acts**.

The first of the Townshend Acts suspended New York's assembly until New Yorkers agreed to provide housing for the troops. The other acts placed duties, or import taxes, on various goods brought into the colonies, such as glass, paper, paint, lead, and tea. Townshend thought that duties, which were collected before the goods entered the colonies, would anger the colonists less than the direct taxes of the Stamp Act. The money raised would be used to pay the salaries of British governors and other officials in the colonies. To enforce the acts, British officers

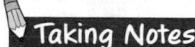

Taking Notes

Use your chart to take notes about colonial resistance.

Proclamation of 1763 → [ ]

The Road to Revolution **163**

would use **writs of assistance,** or search warrants, to enter homes or businesses to search for smuggled goods.

The Reasons for Protest

Protests immediately broke out at news of the Townshend Acts. New Yorkers were angry that their elected assembly had been suspended. People throughout the colonies were upset that Britain was placing new taxes on them. "The issue," said John Dickinson, an important Pennsylvania lawyer, was "whether Parliament can legally take money out of our pockets without our consent." He explained his opposition to the Townshend Acts in essays called *Letters from a Farmer in Pennsylvania*, published in 1767.

*Reading*History
A. Making Inferences Why does Dickinson believe that taxes interfere with happiness?

daily*life*

WOMEN AND PROTEST

Women were not allowed to participate in political life in the colonies. So their role in protesting British actions was not as prominent as that of men. However, women made their beliefs known by taking part in demonstrations.

Also, some women formed the Daughters of Liberty. This was a patriotic organization that joined in the boycott of British tea and other goods. The refusal of these colonial women to use British imports caused them personal hardship. They were forced to make many of the boycotted items, such as clothing, themselves.

A VOICE FROM THE PAST

Let these truths be . . . impressed on our minds—that we cannot be happy without being free—that we cannot be free without being secure in our property—that we cannot be secure in our property if without our consent others may . . . take it away—that taxes imposed on us by Parliament do thus take it away—that duties laid for the sole purpose of raising money are taxes—that attempts to lay such duties should be instantly and firmly opposed.

John Dickinson, quoted in *A New Age Now Begins* by Page Smith

The colonists were also angry about the writs of assistance. Many believed, as James Otis had argued (see page 159), that the writs went against their natural rights. These rights had been described by English philosopher John Locke during the Enlightenment. The law of nature, said Locke, teaches that "no one ought to harm another in his life, health, liberty, or possessions." The colonists felt that the Townshend Acts were a serious threat to their rights and freedoms.

Tools of Protest

To protest the Townshend Acts, colonists in Boston announced another boycott of British goods in October 1767. The driving force behind this protest was **Samuel Adams,** a leader of the Boston Sons of Liberty. Adams urged colonists to continue to resist British controls.

The boycott spread throughout the colonies. The Sons of Liberty pressured shopkeepers not to sell imported goods. The Daughters of Liberty called on colonists to weave their own cloth and use American products. As a result, trade with Britain fell sharply.

Colonial leaders asked for peaceful protests. Articles in the *Boston Gazette* asked the people to remain calm—

This engraving, *The Bloody Massacre Perpetrated in King Street* by Boston silversmith Paul Revere, appeared in the *Boston Gazette.*

"no mobs. . . . Constitutional methods are best." However, tempers were running high. When customs officers in Boston tried to seize the American merchant ship *Liberty*, which was carrying smuggled wine, a riot broke out. The rioters forced the customs officers to flee.

Fearing a loss of control, officials called for more British troops. A defiant Samuel Adams replied, "We will destroy every soldier that dares put his foot on shore. . . . I look upon them as foreign enemies."

For an activity about the Boston Massacre . . .

NET SIMULATION
CLASSZONE.COM

The Boston Massacre

In the fall of 1768, 1,000 British soldiers (known as redcoats for their bright red jackets) arrived in Boston under the command of General Thomas Gage. With their arrival, tension filled the streets of Boston.

Since the soldiers were poorly paid, they hired themselves out as workers, usually at rates lower than those of American workers. Resentment against the redcoats grew. Soldiers and street youths often yelled insults at each other. "Lobsters for sale!" the youths would yell, referring to the soldiers' red coats. "Yankees!" the soldiers jeered. *Yankee* was supposed to be an insult, but the colonists soon took pride in the name.

On March 5, 1770, tensions finally exploded into violence. A group of youths and dockworkers—among them Crispus Attucks—started trading insults in front of the Custom House. A fight broke out, and the soldiers began firing. Attucks and four laborers were killed.

The Sons of Liberty called the shooting the **Boston Massacre.** They said that Attucks and the four others had given their lives for freedom. The incident became a tool for anti-British propaganda in newspaper articles, pamphlets, and posters. The people of Boston were outraged.

Reading **History**
B. Recognizing Propaganda How did the use of the word *massacre* show an anti-British view?

Meanwhile, the redcoats who had fired the shots were arrested for murder. **John Adams,** a lawyer and cousin of Samuel Adams, defended them in court. Adams was criticized for taking the case. He replied that the law should be "deaf . . . to the clamors of the populace." He supported

SAMUEL ADAMS
1722–1803

Samuel Adams was a Harvard graduate. But unlike his cousin John, also a Harvard graduate, he showed little skill for the law. Later, when he took control of the family business, he lost his father's fortune. Yet he succeeded in one important undertaking—moving America toward independence.

Adams's true talent lay in rousing people to action in support of a cause. A fiery orator and a master of propaganda, he used words as a weapon. One British official said that "every dip of his pen stings."

JOHN ADAMS
1735–1826

John Adams, unlike Samuel, was considered a moderate in the struggle against Britain. He was an important voice of reason and at first opposed resisting by force.

Adams believed in the rule of law. He called his defense of the soldiers in the Boston Massacre "one of the best pieces of service I ever rendered my country."

Eventually, Adams became convinced that only outright resistance would gain liberty for America. He said, "Britain has at last driven America, to the last Step, a compleat Seperation from her."

How did the cousins John and Samuel Adams differ in the way they protested British actions?

the colonial cause but wanted to show that the colonists followed the rule of law. Adams argued that the soldiers had acted in self-defense. The jury agreed. To many colonists, however, the Boston Massacre would stand as a symbol of British tyranny.

The Tea Act

The colonists were unaware that on the day of the Boston Massacre, Parliament proposed the repeal of the Townshend Acts. One month later, all the acts except the tax on tea were repealed. The colonial boycott had been effective—British trade had been hurt. But Parliament kept the tea tax to show that it still had the right to tax the colonists. For most Americans, the crisis was over.

Samuel Adams, however, wanted to make sure people did not forget the cause of liberty. He started a drive to form **committees of correspondence** in various towns in Massachusetts. These groups exchanged letters on colonial affairs. Before long, committees throughout Massachusetts were corresponding with one another and with committees in other colonies.

Then, in 1773, Parliament opened up old wounds when it passed the Tea Act. Tea was very popular in the colonies, but much of it was smuggled in from Holland. The Tea Act gave the British East India Company control over the American tea trade. The tea would arrive in the colonies only in the trading company's ships and be sold there by its merchants. Colonists who had not been paying any tax on smuggled tea would now have to pay a tax on this regulated tea. This enraged colonial shippers and merchants. The colonists wondered what Parliament would do next.

*Reading*History

C. Drawing Conclusions Why did Samuel Adams think that the colonists might forget the cause of liberty?

The Boston Tea Party

Protests against the Tea Act took place all over the colonies. In Charleston, South Carolina, colonists unloaded tea and let it rot on the docks. In New York City and Philadelphia, colonists blocked tea ships from landing. In Boston, the Sons of Liberty organized what came to be known as the **Boston Tea Party**.

On the evening of December 16, 1773, a group of men disguised as Native Americans boarded three tea ships docked in Boston Harbor. One of the men, George Hewes, a Boston shoemaker, later recalled the events.

Reading **History**

D. Reading a Map Find Boston Harbor on the map on page 172.

Colonists dumped hundreds of chests of tea into Boston Harbor in 1773 to protest the Tea Act.

> ### A VOICE FROM THE PAST
>
> We then were ordered by our commander to open the hatches and take out all the chests of tea and throw them overboard. . . . In about three hours from the time we went on board, we had thus broken and thrown overboard every tea chest to be found on the ship, while those in the other ships were disposing of the tea in the same way, at the same time.
>
> **George Hewes,** quoted in *A Retrospect of the Boston Tea-Party*

That night, Hewes and the others destroyed 342 chests of tea. Many colonists rejoiced at the news. They believed that Britain would now see how strongly colonists opposed taxation without representation.

Others doubted that destroying property was the best way to settle the tax debate. Some colonial leaders offered to pay for the tea if Parliament would repeal the Tea Act. Britain rejected the offer. It not only wanted repayment, but it also wanted the men who destroyed the tea to be brought to trial. The British reaction to the Boston Tea Party would fan the flames of rebellion in the 13 colonies, as you will read in the next section.

Reading **History**

E. Recognizing Effects How did Britain react to the Tea Party?

Section 2 Assessment

1. Terms & Names

Explain the significance of:
- Crispus Attucks
- Townshend Acts
- writs of assistance
- Samuel Adams
- Boston Massacre
- John Adams
- committee of correspondence
- Boston Tea Party

2. Using Graphics

Create a time line like the one below to show the significant people and events described in this section.

1767   1773

Which event do you think was the most important? Explain.

3. Main Ideas

a. Why did colonists oppose the Townshend Acts?

b. Why were British troops sent to Boston?

c. What prompted the Boston Tea Party?

4. Critical Thinking

Drawing Conclusions Do you think colonial outrage over the Boston Massacre was justified? Explain.

THINK ABOUT
- how the British troops were taunted
- whether troops have the right to fire on citizens

ACTIVITY OPTIONS

SPEECH

TECHNOLOGY

Read more about the Boston Massacre or the Boston Tea Party. Present an **oral report** or plan a **multimedia presentation** about the event.

Fight for Representative Government!

You are a colonist living in Boston on the eve of the American Revolution. Nearly a decade of protest against British policies has failed to secure American rights. Redcoats continue to be quartered in the city. The Tea Act still stands. Now the dumping of tea in Boston Harbor by some Patriots has charged the atmosphere with tension. Trouble lies ahead, but you are determined to fight for a government that will protect your rights.

COOPERATIVE LEARNING On this page are two challenges that you face as the conflict with Britain unfolds. Working with a small group, decide how to deal with each challenge. Choose an option, assign a task to each group member, and do the activity. You will find useful information in the Data File. Present your solutions to the class.

ART CHALLENGE

"Do not . . . sip the accursed, dutied STUFF"

People all over Boston are worried about the Tea Act. It taxes tea, but it also lets the British East India Company sell tea through its own agents. In time, the plan could drive American tea sellers out of business. How can you protest these threats to American commerce and liberty? Present your viewpoint using one of these options:

• Design an anti–Tea Act poster.

• Draw a political cartoon showing the dangers of the Tea Act.

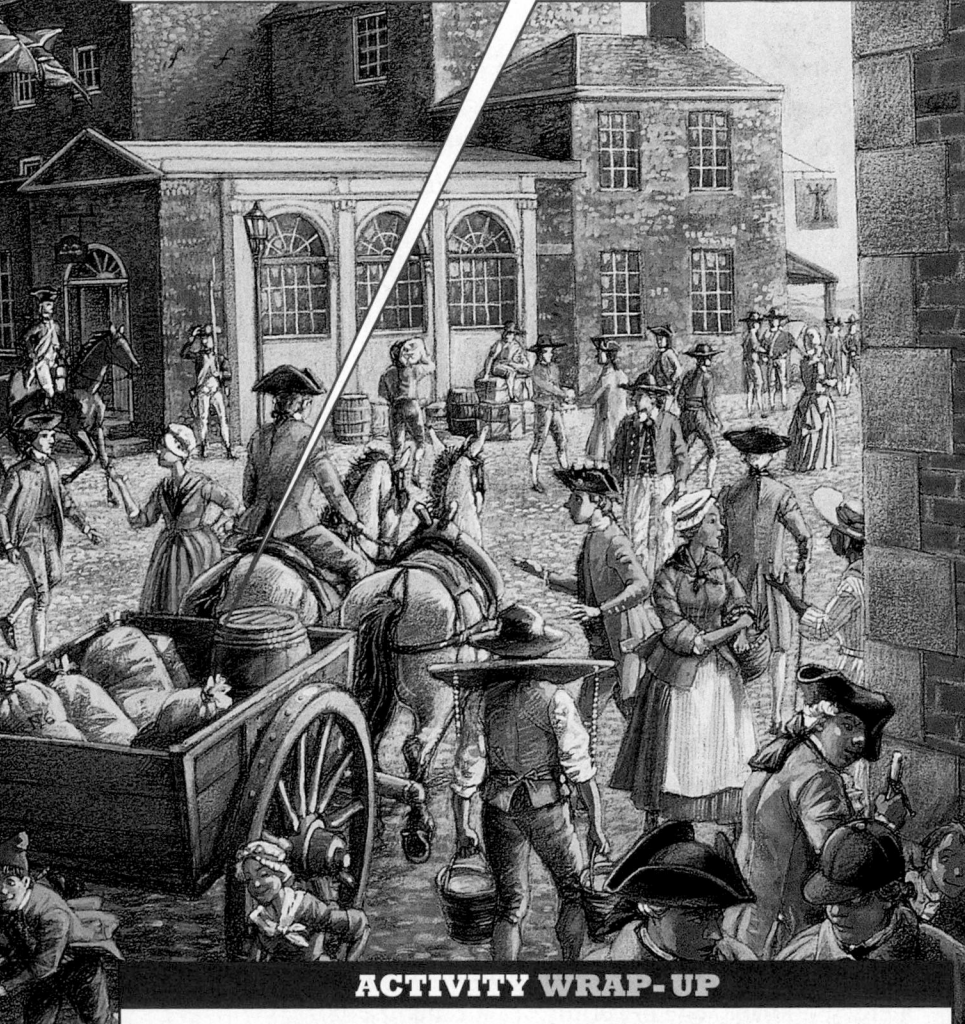

MATH CHALLENGE

"Wear none but your own country linen"

Years of struggle have taken their toll on Boston. People are tired of soldiers and of boycotting British goods, such as clothing. But the Tea Act presents a huge threat. The Boston Tea Party took care of only one shipment. How can you help encourage the boycott of other British goods, such as clothing? Look at the Data File for help. Present your appeal using one of these options:

• Make a graph showing the effect of colonial boycotts on imports of British goods to America.

• Write an editorial using statistics to show how American boycotts have hurt the British.

ACTIVITY WRAP-UP

Present to the Class Meet as a group to review your responses to British attacks on American liberty. Pick the most creative solution for each challenge and present these solutions to the class.

Population in 1774–1775

Britain: 7,860,000
  London: 700,000

The 13 colonies: 2,350,000
  Philadelphia: 33,000
  New York: 22,000
  Boston: 16,000

North American Imports from Britain

(in millions of pounds sterling)

1763	1.6	1770	1.9
1764	2.3	1771	4.2
1765	1.9	1772	3.0
1766	1.8	1773	2.1
1767	1.9	1774	2.6
1768	2.2	1775	0.2
1769	1.3	1776	0.1

North American Exports to Britain

(in millions of pounds sterling)

1763	1.1	1770	1.0
1764	1.1	1771	1.3
1765	1.2	1772	1.3
1766	1.0	1773	1.4
1767	1.1	1774	1.4
1768	1.3	1775	1.9
1769	1.1	1776	0.1

Key Boycott Dates

1764 Boycott after passage of Sugar Act
1765 Boycott after passage of Stamp Act
1766 Boycott relaxed after Stamp Act repealed
1767 Boycott after passage of Townshend Acts
1770 Townshend Acts repealed
1774 Boycott after passage of Intolerable Acts

Sales and Consumption of Tea at the Time of the Boston Tea Party

British sales: fourth most important product shipped to America
American consumption: 1.2 million pounds per year

For more on Revolutionary America . . .

 **RESEARCH LINKS** CLASSZONE.COM

3

The Road to Lexington and Concord

MAIN IDEA	WHY IT MATTERS NOW	TERMS & NAMES
The tensions between Britain and the colonies led to armed conflict in Massachusetts.	Americans at times still find themselves called upon to fight for their principles.	militia Minuteman Intolerable Acts First Continental Congress	Paul Revere Lexington and Concord Loyalist Patriot

ONE AMERICAN'S STORY

On April 19, 1775, some 70 militiamen led by Captin John Parker gathered in Lexington, Massachusetts, a town near Boston. A **militia** is a force of armed civilians pledged to defend their community. About one-third of the Lexington militia were **Minutemen**, trained to "act at a minute's warning." They had heard that the British were coming.

Parker's troops had never faced soldiers. Soon they would meet the British on Lexington Green in the first battle of the Revolutionary War. According to tradition, Parker told his men, "Stand your ground; don't fire unless fired upon, but if they mean to have war, let it begin here."

In this section, you will read how colonial protests led to revolution.

Taking Notes

Use your chart to take notes about the beginning of the American Revolution.

Proclamation of 1763 ➡ ☐

The Intolerable Acts

The Boston Tea Party had aroused fury in Britain. One British official said that the people of Boston "ought to be knocked about their ears." King George III declared, "We must master them or totally leave them to themselves and treat them as aliens." Britain chose to "master" the colonies.

In 1774, Parliament passed a series of laws to punish the Massachusetts colony and to serve as a warning to other colonies. The British called these laws the Coercive Acts, but they were so harsh that the colonists called them the **Intolerable Acts.**

One of the acts would close the port of Boston until colonists paid for the destroyed tea. Others banned committees of correspondence, allowed Britain to house troops wherever necessary, and let British officials accused of crimes in the colonies stand trial in Britain. To enforce the acts, Parliament appointed General Thomas Gage governor of Massachusetts.

In 1773, Sam Adams had written, "I wish we could arouse the continent." The Intolerable Acts answered his wish. Other colonies

This statue of Captain John Parker stands in Lexington, Massachusetts.

immediately offered Massachusetts their support. They sent food and money to Boston. The committees of correspondence also called for a meeting of colonial delegates to discuss what to do next.

The First Continental Congress Meets

In September 1774, delegates from all the colonies except Georgia met in Philadelphia. At this meeting, called the **First Continental Congress,** delegates voted to ban all trade with Britain until the Intolerable Acts were repealed. They also called on each colony to begin training troops. Georgia agreed to be a part of the actions of the Congress even though it had voted not to send delegates.

The First Continental Congress marked a key step in American history. Although most delegates were not ready to call for independence, they were determined to uphold colonial rights. This meeting planted the seeds of a future independent government. John Adams called it "a nursery of American statesmen." The delegates agreed to meet in seven months, if necessary. By that time, however, fighting with Britain had begun.

*Reading***History**
A. Evaluating
Why do you think the First Continental Congress was important?

Between War and Peace

The colonists hoped that the trade boycott would force a repeal of the Intolerable Acts. After all, past boycotts had led to the repeal of the Stamp Act and the Townshend Acts. This time, however, Parliament stood firm. It even increased restrictions on colonial trade and sent more troops.

By the end of 1774, some colonists were preparing to fight. In Massachusetts, John Hancock headed the Committee of Safety, which had the power to call out the militia. The colonial troops continued to train.

CAUSE AND EFFECT: *Growing Conflict Between Britain and America*

DATE	BRITISH ACTION		COLONIAL REACTION
1763	Proclamation of 1763 issued	▶	Proclamation leads to anger
1765	Stamp Act passed	▶	Boycott of British goods; Stamp Act Resolves passed
1766	Stamp Act repealed; Declaration Act passed	▶	Boycott ended
1767	Townshend Acts passed	▶	New boycotts; Boston Massacre (March 1770)
1770	Townshend Acts repealed (April)	▶	Tension between colonies and Britain reduced
1773	Tea Act passed	▶	Boston Tea Party
1774	Intolerable Acts passed	▶	First Continental Congress bans trade; militias organized
1775	Troops ordered to Lexington and Concord, Massachusetts	▶	Militia fights British troops; Second Continental Congress; Continental Army established

SKILLBUILDER Interpreting Charts
1. *What British action caused the first violence in the growing conflict between Britain and America?*
2. *How might the Intolerable Acts be seen as a reaction as well as an action?*

Most colonial leaders believed that any fight with Britain would be short. They thought that a show of force would make Britain change its policies. Few expected a war. One who did was Patrick Henry.

A VOICE FROM THE PAST

Gentlemen may cry peace, peace—but there is no peace. The war is actually begun! The next gale that sweeps from the north will bring to our ears the clash of resounding arms! Our brethren are already in the field! Why should we idle here? . . . I know not what course others may take. But as for me, give me liberty or give me death.

Patrick Henry, quoted in *Patriots* by A. J. Langguth

Henry delivered what became his most famous speech in the Virginia House of Burgesses in March 1775.

The Midnight Ride

Meanwhile, spies were busy on both sides. Sam Adams had built a spy network to keep watch over British activities. The British had their spies too. They were Americans who were loyal to Britain. From them, General Gage learned that the Massachusetts militia was storing arms and ammunition in Concord, about 20 miles northwest of Boston. He also heard that Sam Adams and John Hancock were in Lexington. On the night of April 18, 1775, Gage ordered his troops to arrest Adams and Hancock in Lexington and to destroy the supplies in Concord.

The Sons of Liberty had prepared for this moment. **Paul Revere,** a Boston silversmith, and a second messenger, William Dawes, were charged with spreading the news about British troop movements. Revere had arranged a system of signals to alert colonists in Charlestown, on the shore opposite Boston. If one lantern burned in the Old North Church steeple, the British troops were coming by land; if two, they were coming by water. Revere would go across the water from Boston to Charlestown and ride to Lexington and Concord from there. Dawes would take the land route.

Reading **History**
B. Recognizing Effects What effect might spying have had on the people of Boston?

Background
The signals were a backup system in case Revere was captured.

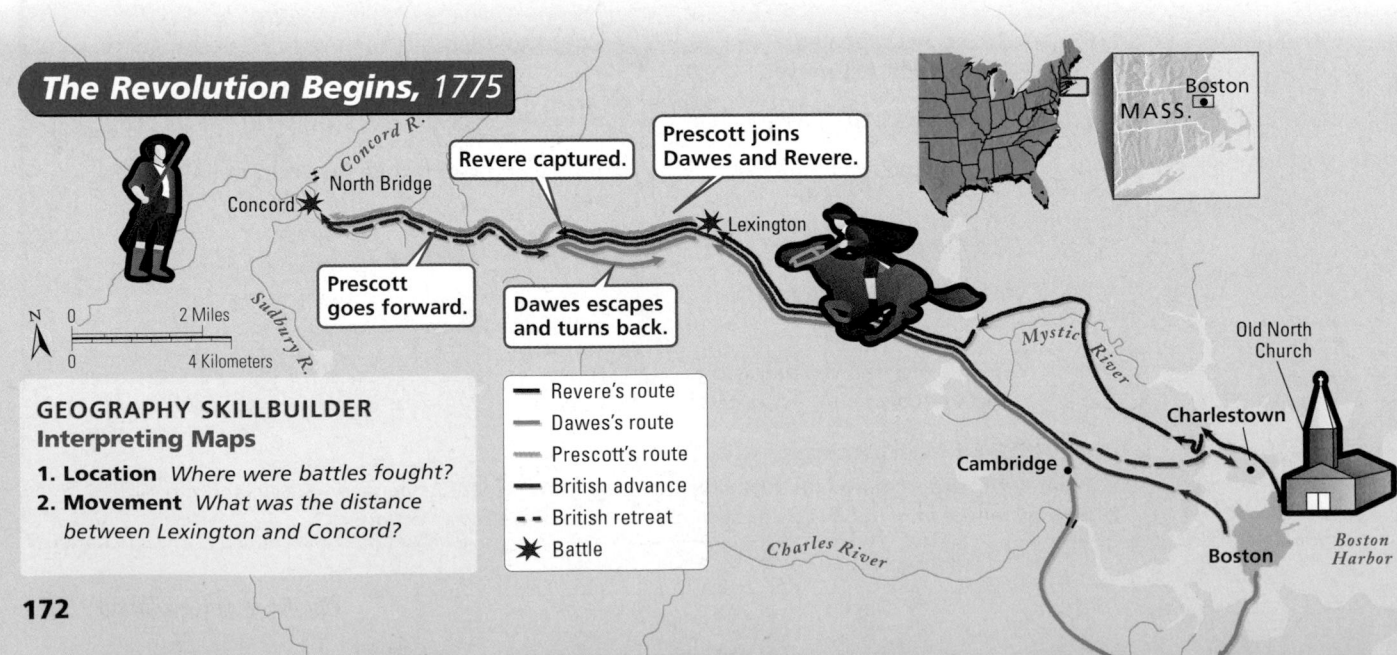

The Revolution Begins, *1775*

Concord R.
North Bridge
Concord
Revere captured.
Prescott joins Dawes and Revere.
Lexington
Prescott goes forward.
Dawes escapes and turns back.
Sudbury R.
Mystic River
Old North Church
Charlestown
Cambridge
Charles River
Boston
Boston Harbor
Boston
MASS.

N
0   2 Miles
0   4 Kilometers

GEOGRAPHY SKILLBUILDER
Interpreting Maps
1. **Location** *Where were battles fought?*
2. **Movement** *What was the distance between Lexington and Concord?*

— Revere's route
— Dawes's route
— Prescott's route
— British advance
- - British retreat
✳ Battle

When the British moved, so did Revere and Dawes. They galloped over the countryside on their "midnight ride," spreading the news. In Lexington, they were joined by Dr. Samuel Prescott. When Revere and Dawes were stopped by a British patrol, Prescott broke away and carried the message to Concord.

Lexington and Concord

At dawn on April 19, some 700 British troops reached Lexington. They found Captain John Parker and about 70 militiamen waiting. The British commander ordered the Americans to drop their muskets. They refused. No one knows who fired first, but within a few minutes eight militiamen lay dead. The British then marched to Concord, where they destroyed military supplies. A battle broke out at a bridge north of town, forcing the British to retreat.

Nearly 4,000 Minutemen and militiamen arrived in the area. They lined the road from Concord to Lexington and peppered the retreating redcoats with musket fire. "It seemed as if men came down from the clouds," one soldier said. Only the arrival of 1,000 more troops saved the British from destruction as they scrambled back to Boston.

Lexington and Concord were the first battles of the Revolutionary War. As Ralph Waldo Emerson later wrote, colonial troops had fired the "shot heard 'round the world." Americans would now have to choose sides and back up their political opinions by force of arms. Those who supported the British were called **Loyalists**. Those who sided with the rebels were **Patriots**. The conflict between the two sides divided communities, families, and friends. The war was on!

Background
British losses totaled 273 soldiers compared to 95 militiamen.

Reading **History**
C. Drawing Conclusions
Why did Emerson call it the "shot heard 'round the world"?

Now and then
PATRIOTS' DAY
The "shot heard 'round the world" is celebrated every year in Massachusetts and Maine. Patriots' Day, as it is called, is the third Monday of April. In Concord and nearby towns, modern-day Minutemen like those below reenact the battle that began the Revolution on April 19, 1775. The Boston Marathon is also run on Patriots' Day.

Section 3 Assessment

1. Terms & Names
Explain the significance of:
- militia
- Minuteman
- Intolerable Acts
- First Continental Congress
- Paul Revere
- Lexington and Concord
- Loyalist
- Patriot

2. Using Graphics
Use a diagram like the one below to show events that led to the Revolutionary War.

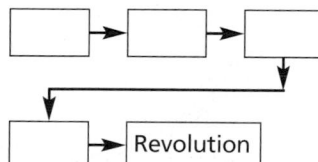

3. Main Ideas
a. Why did Britain pass the Intolerable Acts?

b. Who took part in the First Continental Congress?

c. What was the purpose of the "midnight ride"?

4. Critical Thinking
Supporting Opinions
Do you think the fighting between Britain and the colonies could have been avoided? Why or why not?

THINK ABOUT
- Britain's attitude toward the colonies
- colonial feelings about Britain

ACTIVITY OPTIONS
GEOGRAPHY
MATH
Research the Battles of Lexington and Concord. Draw a **map** of key events or create a **chart** showing statistics from the battles.

From

JOHNNY
TREMAIN

by Esther Forbes

In 1775, 16-year-old Johnny Tremain lives in Boston and works as a delivery boy for a newspaper. Because he travels so much around the city, he is able to help the Patriots gather information about what the British are doing.

On the night of April 18, Johnny learns that British troops will be leaving on an expedition to seize the gunpowder at Lexington and Concord. He rushes to tell this news to Dr. Joseph Warren, who is a Patriot. Then Johnny goes to bed, wondering if the war has started and worried about his friend Rab, who has gone to join the Minutemen at Lexington.

So Johnny slept. It was daylight when he woke with Warren's hand upon his shoulder. Outside on Tremont Street he could hear the clumping of army boots. A sergeant was swearing at his men. The soldiers were paraded so close to the house, which stood **flush**[1] with the sidewalk-less street, that Johnny at first thought they must be in the room.

Doctor Warren dared speak no louder than a whisper.

"I'm going now."

"Something's happened?"

"Yes." He motioned Johnny to follow him into the kitchen. This room was on the back of the house. They could talk without danger of being overheard by the troops in the street.

Doctor Warren had on the same clothes as the day before. He had not been to bed. But now his hat was on his head. His black bag of instruments and medicines was packed and on the table. Silently he put milk, bread, herrings beside it, and gestured to Johnny to join him.

"Where did it begin?" asked Johnny.

"Lexington."

"Who won?"

"They did. Seven hundred against seventy. It wasn't a battle. It was . . . just target practice . . . for them. Some of our men were killed and the British **huzzaed**[2] and took the road to Concord."

"And did they get our supplies there?"

"I don't know. Paul Revere sent for me just after the firing on Lexington Green."

The young man's usually fresh-colored face was **haggard**[3]. He knew the seriousness of this day for himself and for his country.

"But everywhere the alarm is spreading. Men are grabbing their guns—marching for Concord. Paul Revere did get through in time last night. Billy Dawes a little later. Hundreds—maybe thousands—of Minute Men are on the march. Before the day's over, there'll be real fighting—not target practice. But Gage doesn't know that it's begun. You see, long before Colonel Smith got to Lexington—just as soon as he heard that Revere had warned the country—he sent back for reinforcements. For Earl Percy. You and I, Johnny, are just about the only people in Boston who know that blood has already been shed."

"Were many killed—at Lexington?"

"No, not many. They stood up—just a handful. The British fired on them. It was dawn."

Johnny licked his lips. "Did they tell you the names of those killed?"

---

1. **flush:** in a line with.

2. **huzzaed:** cheered.

3. **haggard:** tired.

"No. Did Rab get out in time?"

"Yes. Last Sunday."

The Doctor's clear blue eyes darkened. He knew what was in Johnny's mind. He picked up his bag. "I've got to get to them. They'll need surgeons. Then, too, I'd rather die fighting than on a gallows. Gage won't be so **lenient**[4] now—soon as he learns war has begun."

"Wait until I get my shoes on."

"No, Johnny, you are to stay here today. Pick up for me any information. For instance, out of my bedroom window I can see soldiers standing the length of the street 'way over to the Common. You find out what regiments are being sent—and all that. And today go about and listen to what folk are saying. And the names of any the British arrest. We know Gage expects to move his men back here tonight. If so, there'll be a lot of confusion getting them into town. You watch your chance and slip out to me."

"Where'll I find you?"

" . . . Ask about."

"I will do so."

"They've begun it. We'll end it, but this war . . . it may last quite a long time."

They shook hands silently. Johnny knew that Warren was always conscious of the fact that he had a crippled hand. Everybody else had accepted and forgotten it. The back door closed softly. Warren was gone.

Johnny went to the **surgery**,[5] put on his boots and jacket. The wall clock said eight o'clock. It was time to be about. There was no leaving by the front door. The soldiers were leaning against it. Through the curtains of the windows he could see the muskets. He noticed the facings on their uniforms. The Twenty-Third Regiment. The narrow course of Tremont Street was filled to the brim and overflowing with the waiting scarlet-coated men. Like a river of blood. He left by the kitchen.

---

4. **lenient:** not strict.

5. **surgery:** operating room.

CONNECT TO HISTORY

1. **Recognizing Effects** What was Johnny's reaction to the news about Lexington? Discuss what roles Johnny and Dr. Warren were to play in the early days of the Revolutionary War.

   S See Skillbuilder Handbook, page R11.

CONNECT TO TODAY

2. **Researching** Where are there revolutions in the world today?

For more about revolutions . . .

RESEARCH LINKS
CLASSZONE.COM

British troops fire on the Lexington militia on April 19, 1775. The war begins here!

175

Declaring Independence

MAIN IDEA	WHY IT MATTERS NOW	TERMS & NAMES
Fighting between American and British troops led the colonies to declare their independence.	The United States of America was founded at this time.	Ethan Allen artillery Second Continental Congress Continental Army Benedict Arnold Declaration of Independence Thomas Jefferson

ONE AMERICAN'S STORY

Abigail Adams and her husband, John Adams, would spend most of the Revolutionary War apart. He was often away in Philadelphia meeting with other Patriot leaders. In his absence, she ran the household and farm in Braintree, Massachusetts, and raised their four children. During their separation, they exchanged many letters. Abigail was a very sharp observer of the political scene. In one letter, she shared her concerns about the future of the American government.

A VOICE FROM THE PAST

If we separate from Britain, what Code of Laws will be established? How shall we be governed so as to retain our Liberties? Can any government be free which is not administered by general stated Laws? Who shall frame these Laws? Who will give them force and energy?

Abigail Adams, quoted in *Abigail Adams: Witness to a Revolution* by Natalie S. Bober

Abigail Adams was an early advocate of women's rights and one of the great letter writers in history.

These questions would be answered later. First, a war had to be fought and won.

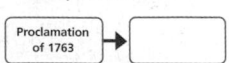

Taking Notes

Use your chart to take notes about the start of the Revolution and the Declaration of Independence.

Proclamation of 1763 ▸ ☐

The Continental Army Is Formed

After the fighting at Lexington and Concord, militiamen from Massachusetts and other colonies began gathering around Boston. Their numbers eventually reached some 20,000. General Gage decided to move his soldiers from the peninsula opposite Boston to the city itself. Boston was nearly surrounded by water. This fact, he thought, made a colonial attack by land almost impossible.

Not long after, on May 10, 1775, Americans attacked Britain's Fort Ticonderoga on the New York side of Lake Champlain. **Ethan Allen** led

this band of backwoodsmen known as the Green Mountain Boys. They captured the fort and its large supply of **artillery**—cannon and large guns. These guns would be used later to drive the British from Boston.

Also on May 10, the **Second Continental Congress** began meeting in Philadelphia. Delegates included John and Samuel Adams, John Hancock, Benjamin Franklin, George Washington, and Patrick Henry. They agreed to form the **Continental Army**. Washington, who was from Virginia, was chosen as its commanding general. He had served as a colonial officer with the British during the French and Indian War. Congress also authorized the printing of paper money to pay the troops. It was beginning to act as a government.

The Battle of Bunker Hill

Background
The battle was called Bunker Hill because the original plan was to fight the battle there.

Meanwhile, tensions were building in Boston in June 1775. Militiamen seized Bunker Hill and Breed's Hill behind Charlestown. They built fortifications on Breed's Hill. Alarmed, the British decided to attack.

General William Howe crossed the bay with 2,200 British soldiers. Forming in ranks, they marched up Breed's Hill. On the hilltop, the militia waited. According to the legend, Colonel William Prescott ordered, "Don't fire until you see the whites of their eyes!" When the British got close, the militia unleashed murderous fire. The British fell back and then charged again. Finally, they forced the militia off the hill.

The redcoats had won the Battle of Bunker Hill, but at tremendous cost. More than 1,000 were killed or wounded, compared with some 400 militia casualties. "The loss we have sustained is greater than we can bear," wrote General Gage. The inexperienced colonial militia had held its own against the world's most powerful army.

"Don't fire until you see the whites of their eyes!"
Colonel William Prescott

The bloody fighting between militiamen and British troops is shown in *The Death of General Warren at Bunker Hill* by John Trumbull (1786).

Phillis Wheatley was America's first important African-American poet. She was born in Africa about 1753 and sold into slavery as a child. She was a household servant for the Wheatley family of Boston but was raised and educated as a family member.

Some of Wheatley's poems were about the Patriot cause. Of George Washington, she wrote:

Proceed, great chief, with
    virtue on thy side,
Thy ev'ry action let the
    goddess guide.
A crown, a mansion, and
    a throne that shine,
With gold unfading,
    Washington! be thine.

In other poems, Wheatley connected America's fight against British oppression with the struggle for freedom for enslaved African Americans.

A Last Attempt at Peace

Despite this deepening conflict, most colonists still hoped for peace. Even some Patriot leaders considered themselves loyal subjects of the king. They blamed Parliament for the terrible events taking place.

In July 1775, moderates in Congress drafted the Olive Branch Petition and sent it to London. This document asked the king to restore harmony between Britain and the colonies. Some members opposed the petition but signed it anyway as a last hope.

The king rejected the petition, however, and announced new measures to punish the colonies. He would use the British navy to block American ships from leaving their ports. He also would send thousands of hired German soldiers, called Hessians, to fight in America. "When once these rebels have felt a smart blow, they will submit," he declared.

The colonial forces were not going to back down, though. They thought they were equal to the British troops. George Washington knew otherwise. The British soldiers were professionals, while the colonial troops had little training and were poorly equipped. The Massachusetts militia barely had enough gunpowder to fight one battle.

During the summer of 1775, Washington arrived at the militia camp near Boston. He immediately began to gather supplies and train the army. In the fall, Washington approved a bold plan. Continental Army troops would invade Quebec, in eastern Canada. They hoped to defeat British forces there and draw Canadians into the Patriot camp. One of the leaders of this expedition was **Benedict Arnold**. He was an officer who had played a role in the victory at Fort Ticonderoga.

After a grueling march across Maine, Arnold arrived at Quebec in November 1775. By that time, however, winter had set in. Under harsh conditions, the Americans launched their attack but failed. After several months, they limped home in defeat.

The British Retreat from Boston

In Massachusetts, the Continental Army had surrounded British forces in Boston. Neither side was able or willing to break the standoff. However, help for Washington was on the way. Cannons were being hauled from Fort Ticonderoga. This was a rough job, since there were no roads across the snow-covered mountains. It took soldiers two months to drag the 59 heavy weapons to Boston, where they arrived in January 1776.

Background
The olive branch is considered a symbol of peace.

Reading **History**
A. Analyzing Points of View
Why did King George reject the petition?

Armed with these cannons, Washington moved his troops to Dorchester Heights, overlooking Boston. The Americans threatened to bombard the city. General Howe, who was now in charge of the British forces, decided to withdraw his troops. On March 17, about 9,000 British soldiers departed Boston in more than 100 ships. Boston Patriots joyfully reclaimed their city. Although the British had damaged homes and destroyed possessions, Boston was still standing.

More than 1,000 Loyalist supporters left along with the British troops. Anti-British feeling in Boston was so strong that the Loyalists feared for their safety. Some Patriots even called for Loyalists to be hanged as traitors. This did not happen, but Loyalists' homes and property were seized.

*Reading*History
B. Forming Opinions Did the Loyalists deserve punishment? Explain.

Common Sense Is Published

In early 1776, most Americans still wanted to avoid a final break with Britain. However, the publication of a pamphlet titled *Common Sense* helped convince many Americans that a complete break with Britain was necessary. Written by Thomas Paine, a recent immigrant from England, this pamphlet made a strong case for American independence.

Paine ridiculed the idea that kings ruled by the will of God. Calling George III "the Royal Brute," Paine argued that all monarchies were corrupt. He also disagreed with the economic arguments for remaining with Britain. "Our corn," he said, "will fetch its price in any market in Europe." He believed that America should follow its own destiny.

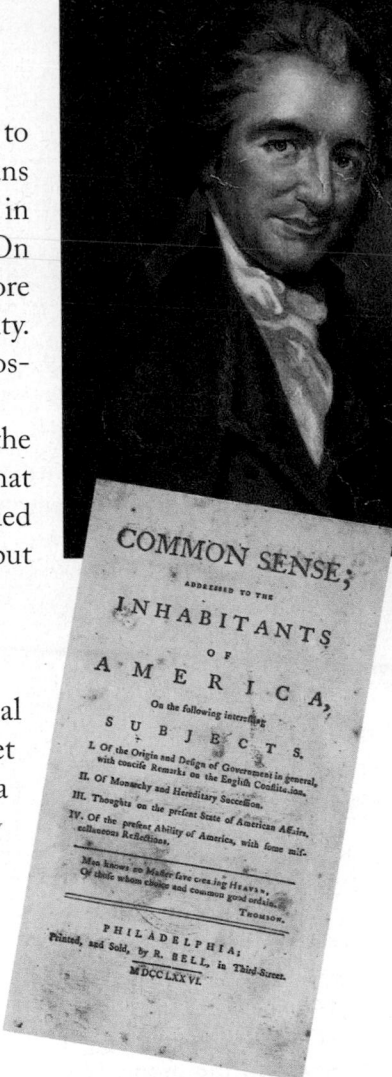

This is the front page of *Common Sense* by Thomas Paine (above). It was one of the most influential political documents in history.

A VOICE FROM THE PAST

Everything that is right or natural pleads for separation. The blood of the slain, the weeping voice of nature cries, "'Tis time to part." Even the distance at which the Almighty has placed England and America is a strong and natural proof that the authority of the one over the other was never the design of heaven.

Thomas Paine, *Common Sense*

Common Sense was an instant success. Published in January, it sold more than 100,000 copies in three months. The call for independence had become a roar.

A Time of Decision

The Continental Congress remained undecided. A majority of the delegates still did not support independence. Even so, in May 1776, Congress adopted a resolution authorizing each of the 13 colonies to establish its own government.

On June 7, Richard Henry Lee of Virginia introduced a key resolution. It called the colonies "free and independent states" and declared

HISTORY *through* ART

The Declaration of Independence is presented for adoption to the Continental Congress by John Adams, Roger Sherman, Robert Livingston, Thomas Jefferson, and Benjamin Franklin (left to right). John Trumbull painted this work many years after the adoption of the Declaration on July 4, 1776.

What is the artist trying to show about the mood of the American leaders as they declare independence?

that "all political connection between them and the state of Great Britain is . . . totally dissolved."

Congress debated the resolution, but not all the delegates were ready to vote on it. They did, however, appoint a committee to draft a **Declaration of Independence**. The committee included Benjamin Franklin, John Adams, Roger Sherman, Robert Livingston, and **Thomas Jefferson**.

The group chose Jefferson to compose the Declaration. Two reasons for selecting Jefferson were that he was an excellent writer and that he came from Virginia. The members knew that no independence movement could succeed without Virginia's support. Jefferson immediately went to work. In two weeks, he had prepared most of the Declaration. (See pages 182–185.) On July 2, 1776, Congress considered Lee's resolution again. Despite some strong opposition, the measure passed. From this point forward, the colonies considered themselves independent.

The Declaration Is Adopted

Two days later, on July 4, 1776, Congress adopted the document that proclaimed independence—the Declaration of Independence. John Hancock, the president of the Congress, was the first to sign the Declaration. According to tradition, he wrote in large letters and commented, "There, I guess King George will be able to read that." The core idea of the Declaration is based on the philosophy of John Locke. This idea is that people have unalienable rights, or rights that government

The Liberty Bell was rung to announce the first public reading of the Declaration of Independence, in Philadelphia on July 8, 1776.

cannot take away. Jefferson stated this belief in what was to become the Declaration's best-known passage.

A VOICE FROM THE PAST

We hold these truths to be self-evident, that all men are created equal, that they are endowed by their Creator with certain unalienable Rights, that among these are Life, Liberty and the pursuit of Happiness.

Thomas Jefferson, The Declaration of Independence

*Reading*History
C. Summarizing
When does the Declaration say it is right to overthrow an established government?

If a government disregards these rights, Jefferson explained, it loses its right to govern. The people then have the right to abolish that government, by force if necessary. They can form a new government that will protect their rights. When Jefferson spoke of "the people," however, he meant only free white men. Women and enslaved persons were left out of the Declaration.

The Declaration also explained the reasons for breaking with Britain. It then declared the colonies to be free and independent states. This was a very serious action—treason from the British point of view—and the delegates knew it. John Hancock urged the delegates to stand together in mutual defense. Each realized that if the war were to be lost, they would most likely be hanged.

The Declaration closed with this pledge: "And for the support of this Declaration, with a firm reliance on the protection of divine Providence, we mutually pledge to each other our Lives, our Fortunes, and our sacred Honor."

Americans had declared independence. Now they had to win their freedom on the battlefield.

AMERICA'S HISTORY MAKERS

THOMAS JEFFERSON
1743–1826

Jefferson was just 33 when chosen to write the Declaration of Independence. He was already a brilliant thinker and writer and a highly respected political leader. Jefferson came from a wealthy Virginia family. As a child, he was interested in everything, and he became an inventor, scientist, and architect, among other things. In 1769, he began his political career in the House of Burgesses.

Jefferson felt that writing the Declaration was a major achievement of his life. He had that fact carved on his tombstone.

Why do you think Jefferson felt the Declaration was one of his greatest achievements?

Section 4 Assessment

1. Terms & Names

Explain the significance of:
- Ethan Allen
- artillery
- Second Continental Congress
- Continental Army
- Benedict Arnold
- Declaration of Independence
- Thomas Jefferson

2. Using Graphics

Use the chart below to explain colonial views for and against independence.

Views About Independence

For	
Against	

What is the strongest reason for independence? against independence?

3. Main Ideas

a. What challenges did George Washington face in forming the army?

b. What forced the British to leave Boston?

c. What is *Common Sense*?

4. Critical Thinking

Drawing Conclusions
Why did it take colonists so long to declare independence?

THINK ABOUT
- the colonists' British traditions
- the risk of revolution

ACTIVITY OPTIONS

ART
LANGUAGE ARTS

Find out more about a person discussed in this section. Create a **trading card** or write a **biography** of that person.

The Declaration of Independence

Setting the Stage On July 4, 1776, the Second Continental Congress adopted what became one of America's most cherished documents. Written by Thomas Jefferson, the Declaration of Independence voiced the reasons for separating from Britain and provided the principles of government upon which the United States would be built. **See Primary Source Explorer** ⊙

[Preamble]

When in the Course of human events, it becomes necessary for one people to dissolve the political bands which have connected them with another, and to assume among the powers of the earth, the separate and equal station to which the Laws of Nature and of Nature's God entitle them, a decent respect to the opinions of mankind requires that they should declare the causes which impel them to the separation.

[The Right of the People to Control Their Government]

We hold these truths to be self-evident, that all men are created equal, that they are **endowed**[1] by their Creator with certain **unalienable**[2] Rights, that among these are Life, Liberty and the pursuit of Happiness; that, to secure these rights, Governments are instituted among Men, deriving their just powers from the consent of the governed; that whenever any Form of Government becomes destructive of these ends, it is the Right of the People to alter or to abolish it, and to institute new Government, laying its foundation on such principles and organizing its powers in such form, as to them shall seem most likely to effect their Safety and Happiness. Prudence, indeed, will dictate that Governments long established should not be changed for light and transient causes; and accordingly all experience hath shewn that mankind are more disposed to suffer, while evils are sufferable, than to right themselves by abolishing the forms to which they are accustomed. But when a long train of abuses and **usurpations,**[3] pursuing invariably the same Object, evinces a design to reduce them under absolute **Despotism,**[4] it is their right, it is their duty, to throw off such Government, and to provide new Guards for their future security.

Such has been the patient sufferance of these Colonies; and such is now the necessity which constrains them to alter their former Systems of Government. The history of the present King of Great Britain is a history of repeated injuries and usurpations, all having in direct object the establishment of an absolute Tyranny over these States. To prove this, let facts be submitted to a **candid**[5] world.

A CLOSER LOOK

RIGHTS OF THE PEOPLE

The ideas in this passage reflect the views of John Locke. Locke was an English philosopher who believed that the natural rights of individuals came from God, but that a government's power comes from the consent of the governed. This belief is the foundation of modern democracy.

1. In what way can American voters bring about changes in their government?

---

1. **endowed:** provided.
2. **unalienable:** unable to be taken away.
3. **usurpations:** unjust seizures of power.
4. **Despotism:** rule by a tyrant with absolute power.
5. **candid:** fair, impartial.

[Tyrannical Acts of the British King]

He has refused his Assent to Laws, the most wholesome and necessary for the public good.

He has forbidden his Governors to pass Laws of immediate and pressing importance, unless suspended in their operation till his assent should be obtained; and, when so suspended, he has utterly neglected to attend to them.

He has refused to pass other Laws for the accommodation of large districts of people, unless those people would **relinquish**[6] the right of Representation in the Legislature, a right inestimable to them, and formidable to tyrants only.

He has called together legislative bodies at places unusual, uncomfortable, and distant from the depository of their public Records, for the sole purpose of fatiguing them into compliance with his measures.

He has dissolved Representative Houses repeatedly, for opposing with manly firmness his invasions on the rights of the people.

He has refused for a long time, after such dissolutions, to cause others to be elected; whereby the Legislative powers, incapable of Annihilation, have returned to the people at large for their exercise; the State remaining in the mean time exposed to all the dangers of invasions from without, and **convulsions**[7] within.

He has endeavoured to prevent the population of these States; for that purpose obstructing the Laws for **Naturalization**[8] of Foreigners; refusing to pass others to encourage their migration hither, and raising the conditions of new Appropriations of Lands.

He has obstructed the Administration of Justice, by refusing his Assent to Laws for establishing Judiciary powers.

He has made Judges dependent on his Will alone, for the **tenure**[9] of their offices, and the amount and payment of their salaries.

He has erected a multitude of New Offices, and sent hither swarms of Officers to harass our people and **eat out their substance**.[10]

He has kept among us, in times of peace, Standing Armies, without the Consent of our legislatures.

He has affected to render the Military independent of and superior to the Civil power. He has combined with others to subject us to a jurisdiction foreign to our constitution and unacknowledged by our laws; giving his Assent to their Acts of pretended Legislation:

For **quartering**[11] large bodies of armed troops among us;

For protecting them, by a mock Trial, from punishment for any Murders which they should commit on the Inhabitants of these States;

For cutting off our Trade with all parts of the world;

A CLOSER LOOK

GRIEVANCES AGAINST BRITAIN

The list contains 27 offenses by the British king and others against the colonies. It helps explain why it became necessary to seek independence.

2. Which offense do you think was the worst? Why?

A CLOSER LOOK

LOSS OF REPRESENTATIVE GOVERNMENT

One of the Intolerable Acts of 1774 stripped the Massachusetts Legislature of many powers and gave them to the colony's British governor.

3. Why was this action so "intolerable"?

A CLOSER LOOK

QUARTERING TROOPS WITHOUT CONSENT

The Quartering Act of 1765 required colonists to provide housing and supplies for British troops in America.

4. Why did colonists object to this act?

---

6. **relinquish:** give up.
7. **convulsions:** violent disturbances.
8. **Naturalization:** process of becoming a citizen.
9. **tenure:** term.
10. **eat out their substance:** drain their resources.
11. **quartering:** housing or giving lodging to.

A CLOSER LOOK

TAXATION WITHOUT REPRESENTATION

The colonists believed in the long-standing British tradition that Parliament could tax only those citizens it represented—and the colonists claimed to have no representation in Parliament.

5. How do persons today give consent to taxation?

For imposing Taxes on us without our Consent;

For depriving us, in many cases, of the benefits of Trial by Jury;

For transporting us beyond Seas to be tried for pretended offenses;

For abolishing the free System of English Laws in a neighboring Province, establishing therein an **Arbitrary**[12] government, and enlarging its Boundaries so as to render it at once an example and fit instrument for introducing the same absolute rule into these Colonies;

For taking away our Charters, abolishing our most valuable laws, and altering fundamentally the Forms of our Governments;

For suspending our own Legislatures, and declaring themselves invested with power to legislate for us in all cases whatsoever.

He has **abdicated**[13] Government here, by declaring us out of his Protection and waging War against us.

He has plundered our seas, ravaged our Coasts, burnt our towns, and destroyed the lives of our people.

He is at this time transporting large Armies of **foreign Mercenaries**[14] to compleat the works of death, desolation, and tyranny, already begun with circumstances of Cruelty & **perfidy**[15] scarcely paralleled in the most barbarous ages, and totally unworthy the Head of a civilized nation.

He has constrained our fellow Citizens, taken Captive on the high Seas, to bear Arms against their Country, to become the executioners of their friends and Brethren, or to fall themselves by their Hands.

He has excited **domestic insurrections**[16] amongst us, and has endeavoured to bring on the inhabitants of our frontiers the merciless Indian Savages, whose known rule of warfare is an undistinguished destruction of all ages, sexes and conditions.

[Efforts of the Colonies to Avoid Separation]

In every stage of these Oppressions We have **Petitioned for Redress**[17] in the most humble terms; Our repeated Petitions have been answered only by repeated injury. A Prince, whose character is thus marked by every act which may define a Tyrant, is unfit to be the ruler of a free people.

Nor have We been wanting in attentions to our British brethren. We have warned them from time to time of attempts by their legislature to extend an unwarrantable jurisdiction over us. We have reminded them of the circumstances of our emigration and settlement here. We have appealed to their native justice and **magnanimity,**[18] and we have conjured them by the ties of our common kindred, to disavow these usurpations, which would inevitably interrupt our connections and correspondence. They too have been deaf to

A CLOSER LOOK

PETITIONING THE KING

The colonists sent many petitions to King George III. In the Olive Branch Petition of 1775, the colonists expressed their desire to achieve "a happy and permanent reconciliation." The king rejected the petition.

6. Why did the colonists at first attempt to solve the dispute and remain loyal?

12. **Arbitrary:** not limited by law.

13. **abdicated:** given up.

14. **foreign Mercenaries:** professional soldiers hired to serve in a foreign army.

15. **perfidy:** dishonesty, disloyalty.

16. **domestic insurrections:** rebellions at home.

17. **Petitioned for Redress:** asked for the correction of wrongs.

18. **magnanimity:** generosity, forgiveness.

the voice of justice and of **consanguinity**.[19] We must, therefore, **acquiesce**[20] in the necessity, which denounces our Separation, and hold them, as we hold the rest of mankind, Enemies in War, in Peace Friends.

[The Colonies Are Declared Free and Independent]

We, therefore, the Representatives of the United States of America, in General Congress, Assembled, appealing to the Supreme Judge of the world for the **rectitude**[21] of our intentions, do, in the name, and by the Authority of the good People of these Colonies solemnly publish and declare, That these United Colonies are, and of Right ought to be, Free and Independent States; that they are Absolved from all Allegiance to the British Crown, and that all political connection between them and the State of Great Britain is, and ought to be, totally dissolved; and that as Free and Independent States, they have full Power to levy War, conclude Peace, contract Alliances, establish Commerce, and do all other Acts and Things which Independent States may of right do.

And for the support of this Declaration, with a firm reliance on the protection of divine Providence, we mutually pledge to each other our Lives, our Fortunes, and our sacred Honor. [Signed by]

John Hancock *President, from Massachusetts*

[Georgia] Button Gwinnett; Lyman Hall; George Walton

[Rhode Island] Stephen Hopkins; William Ellery

[Connecticut] Roger Sherman; Samuel Huntington; William Williams; Oliver Wolcott

[North Carolina] William Hooper; Joseph Hewes; John Penn

[South Carolina] Edward Rutledge; Thomas Heyward, Jr.; Thomas Lynch, Jr.; Arthur Middleton

[Maryland] Samuel Chase; William Paca; Thomas Stone; Charles Carroll

[Virginia] George Wythe; Richard Henry Lee; Thomas Jefferson;

Benjamin Harrison; Thomas Nelson, Jr.; Francis Lightfoot Lee; Carter Braxton

[Pennsylvania] Robert Morris; Benjamin Rush; Benjamin Franklin; John Morton; George Clymer; James Smith; George Taylor; James Wilson; George Ross

[Delaware] Caesar Rodney; George Read; Thomas McKean

[New York] William Floyd; Philip Livingston; Francis Lewis; Lewis Morris

[New Jersey] Richard Stockton; John Witherspoon; Francis Hopkinson; John Hart; Abraham Clark

[New Hampshire] Josiah Bartlett; William Whipple; Matthew Thornton

[Massachusetts] Samuel Adams; John Adams; Robert Treat Paine; Elbridge Gerry

19. **consanguinity:** relationship by a common ancestor; close connection.

20. **acquiesce:** accept without protest.

21. **rectitude:** moral uprightness.

A CLOSER LOOK

POWERS OF AN INDEPENDENT GOVERNMENT

The colonists identified the ability to wage war and agree to peace; to make alliances with other nations; and to set up an economic system as powers of a free and independent government.

7. What other powers are held by an independent government?

A CLOSER LOOK

DECLARATION SIGNERS

The Declaration was signed by 56 representatives from the 13 original states.

8. Which signers do you recognize? Write one line about each of those signers.

Interactive Primary Source Assessment

1. Main Ideas

a. What is the purpose of the Declaration of Independence as stated in the Preamble?

b. What are the five main parts of the Declaration?

c. What are three rights that all people have?

2. Critical Thinking

Drawing Conclusions Why did the colonies feel that they had to declare their independence?

THINK ABOUT

• colonial grievances against Britain

• Britain's response to these grievances

Chapter 6 ASSESSMENT

The Road to Revolution

1763 —○
Proclamation of 1763

○— **1764**
Sugar Act

1765
Quartering Act; Stamp Act; Sons of Liberty; Stamp Act Congress

○— **1766**
Repeal of Stamp Act; Declaratory Act

1767
Townshend Acts; Suspension of New York Assembly

○— **1768**
Occupation of Boston by British troops

1769 —○
Daughters of Liberty

○— **1770**
Boston Massacre; Repeal of all Townshend Acts except tea tax

1772 —○
Committees of Correspondence

○— **1773**
Tea Act; Boston Tea Party

1774
Intolerable Acts; First Continental Congress; Boycott of British goods

1775
Battles of Lexington and Concord; Second Continental Congress; Appointment of Washington as commander of Continental Army; Battle of Bunker Hill; Olive Branch Petition

1776 —○
Common Sense; Declaration of Independence

TERMS & NAMES

Briefly explain the significance of each of the following.

1. Stamp Act
2. Sons of Liberty
3. writs of assistance
4. Samuel Adams
5. Boston Tea Party
6. militia
7. Lexington and Concord
8. Loyalist
9. Declaration of Independence
10. Thomas Jefferson

REVIEW QUESTIONS

Tighter British Control (pages 159–162)

1. How did relations between Britain and the colonies change after the Seven Years' War?
2. Why did Britain try to tax the colonies?
3. Why did the colonists cry, "No taxation without representation"?

Colonial Resistance Grows (pages 163–169)

4. How did the colonists protest the Townshend Acts?
5. How was the Boston Massacre used for propaganda purposes?
6. How did the committees of correspondence help keep people informed?

The Road to Lexington and Concord (pages 170–175)

7. Why was the First Continental Congress held?
8. What was the Midnight Ride?

Declaring Independence (pages 176–185)

9. What was the Battle of Bunker Hill?
10. What was the core idea of the Declaration of Independence?

CRITICAL THINKING

1. USING YOUR NOTES: SEQUENCING EVENTS

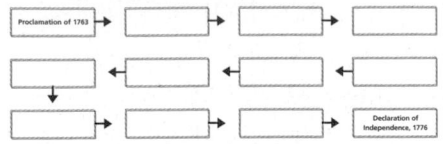

Using your completed chart, answer the questions below.

a. What city was the site of early protest activity?
b. What event happened after the Tea Act?

2. ANALYZING LEADERSHIP

How did colonial leaders differ in their methods of defending and securing basic rights for the colonies?

3. APPLYING CITIZENSHIP SKILLS

Did colonial leaders have a responsibility to include women, African Americans, and other groups in the Declaration of Independence? Explain.

4. THEME: IMPACT OF THE INDIVIDUAL

How did John Adams's role as lawyer for the British soldiers involved in the Boston Massacre help set a tone for the Revolutionary cause?

5. DRAWING CONCLUSIONS

What factors and events led the colonies to seek independence?

6. SUPPORTING OPINIONS

Do you think the American Revolution would have occurred if Britain had not taxed the colonies? Why or why not?

Interact *with* History

Now that you have read about the road to revolution, do you consider your decision made at the beginning of the chapter to join or not join the protest a wise choice or a poor choice? Explain.

STANDARDS-BASED ASSESSMENT

Use the map and your knowledge of U.S. history to answer questions 1 and 2.

Additional Test Practice, pp. S1–S33.

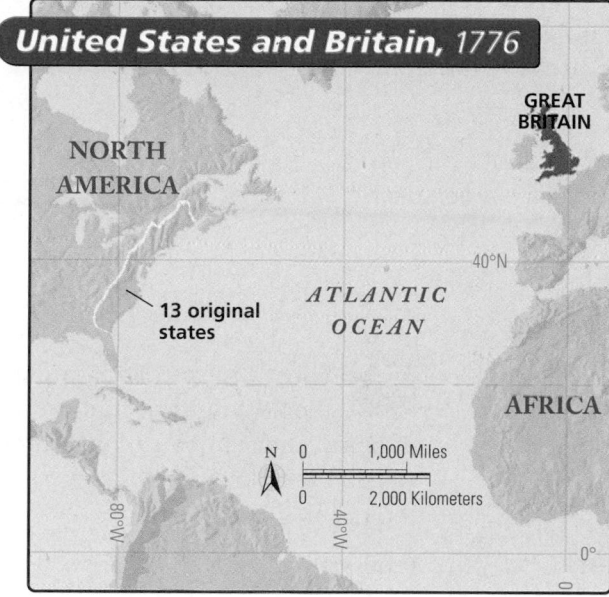

United States and Britain, 1776

GREAT BRITAIN

NORTH AMERICA

40°N

13 original states

ATLANTIC OCEAN

AFRICA

N 0 1,000 Miles

0 2,000 Kilometers

80°W

40°W

0°

1. What does the yellow shaded area on the map represent?

A. the original colonies

B. Great Britain

C. North America

D. the United States

2. What is the approximate distance between the northernmost colony and Great Britain?

A. 1,000 miles

B. 2,000 kilometers

C. 3,000 miles

D. 5,000 kilometers

This quotation from James Otis is about the use of search warrants by the British. Use the quotation and your knowledge of U.S. history to answer question 3.

PRIMARY SOURCE

It appears to me the worst instrument of arbitrary power, the most destructive of English liberty and the fundamental principles of law, that was ever found in an English law-book.

James Otis, Jr., quoted in *James Otis: The Pre-Revolutionist* by J. C. Ridpath

3. What conclusion can you draw about Otis's point of view?

A. Otis believed that the searches would benefit the colonists.

B. Otis realized that British searches were more important than colonial liberties.

C. Otis believed that colonists were entitled to certain liberties.

D. Otis thought the searches were right.

TEST PRACTICE
CLASSZONE.COM

ALTERNATIVE ASSESSMENT

1. 📝 WRITING ABOUT HISTORY

Colonists had divided opinions about the Boston Tea Party. Suppose you are a pollster, attempting to gather data about public opinion. Write **quotations** from five colonists who support the Tea Party and another five quotes from people who condemn the act.

• You can write your quotations based on information found in books or on the Internet.

• Using a word processor, you can use different type sizes and fonts to emphasize the question you pose and the two opposing responses.

2. COOPERATIVE LEARNING

Participate in a class debate modeled after the discussions held by members of the Continental Congress concerning independence and the slave trade.

INTEGRATED TECHNOLOGY ACTIVITY

PARTICIPATING IN A NET SIMULATION

Go to *NetSimulations: Boston Massacre* at **classzone.com** to participate in the jury trial of Captain Thomas Preston. He and the soldiers of the 29th British Regiment have been arrested for the murder of five citizens.

• Use the information in this chapter and the simulation to review the events surrounding the Boston Massacre. Use the Juror's Journal to take notes.

• Read Captain Preston's statement, then begin questioning the prosecution and defense witnesses. Answer the questions in the Juror's Journal to record the evidence you hear.

• Listen to each attorney's closing arguments, then enter your verdict.

NET SIMULATION
CLASSZONE.COM

Raise the Liberty Pole

In 1765, the Sons of Liberty gathered around a huge elm tree in Boston that they named the Liberty Tree. It became a meeting place where people voiced their protests against British policies. Replicas of the Liberty Tree—giant poles sometimes decorated with the flags of the colonies—were raised throughout the colonies. These liberty poles represented the unity of the American colonies as they struggled to break away from British rule.

ACTIVITY Like the American Patriots, each group of students will raise its own liberty pole. Each group also will write and deliver a persuasive speech supporting the cause of the American colonies.

TOOLBOX

Each group will need:

scissors

poster board

pencil

markers

masking tape

3 cardboard tubes from wrapping paper

construction paper

twine

stapler

STEP BY STEP

1 **Form groups.** Each group should consist of four or five students. The members of your group will do the following jobs:

- research each colony
- design and create flags
- construct a pole
- write and deliver a speech

2 **Do research on the 13 colonies.** For each colony, your group should find a person, place, or object that represents that colony. For example, a Pilgrim's hat might represent Massachusetts. The 13 colonies are listed below.

New England Colonies	Middle Colonies	Southern Colonies
Massachusetts (including Maine)	New York	North Carolina
New Hampshire	Delaware	Virginia
Connecticut	New Jersey	Maryland
Rhode Island	Pennsylvania	South Carolina
		Georgia

Members of the Sons of Liberty raise a liberty pole in July 1776 to celebrate America's independence.

3 **Design and create 13 flags for the colonies.** Decide what person, place, or object you will use on your flag for each colony. Cut each flag out of the poster board. Sketch your design on the flag with a pencil. Then use markers to decorate it. On the back of each flag, explain how your design portrays the characteristics of that colony.

4 **Construct the pole.** Using masking tape, fasten the three cardboard tubes together to form one long tube. Then reinforce the tube by taping construction paper around it.

5 **String the flags on the pole.** Feed a piece of twine through the open ends of the long tube. Tie the ends of the twine together to form a tight loop. Now staple all 13 flags to the twine.

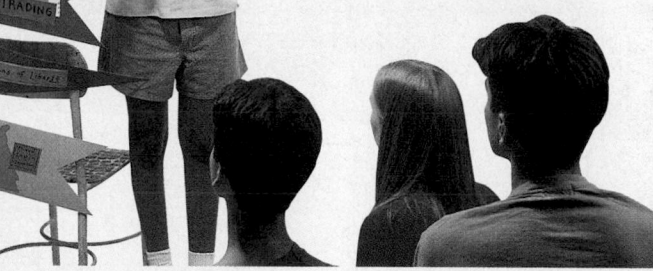

6 **Raise your liberty pole.** Lean your liberty pole next to a small table or desk. Take turns with members of your group and visit other liberty poles. As students visit your station, explain the significance of your flag designs.

WRITE AND SPEAK

Write a persuasive speech to recruit others to join the cause of liberty. In your speech, explain what is wrong with British policies. Give reasons why the colonies should become independent. Then read your speech to the other groups as part of the recruitment process.

HELP DESK

For related information on the Liberty Tree, see pages 161–162 in Chapter 6.

Researching Your Project
- *The Revolutionary War* by Bart McDowell
- *The American Revolutionaries* edited by Milton Meltzer

For more about the American Revolution . . .

RESEARCH LINKS
CLASSZONE.COM

Did You Know?
The numbers 45 and 92 played an important part in the history of these liberty poles. The 45th issue of a British newspaper openly criticized the king in 1763 and was reprinted in the colonies. In 1768, 92 members of the Massachusetts General Assembly voted against canceling a letter to the other 12 colonies that called for action against Britain. To represent the numbers, 92 members of the Sons of Liberty would often raise liberty poles to a height of about 45 feet.

REFLECT & ASSESS
- How well do your flags represent the colonies?
- How clearly does your speech explain grievances against the British?
- Why do you think the practice of raising liberty poles spread to many of the colonies?

CHAPTER 7

The American Revolution 1776–1783

Section 1
The Early Years of the War

Section 2
The War Expands

Section 3
The Path to Victory

Section 4
The Legacy of the War

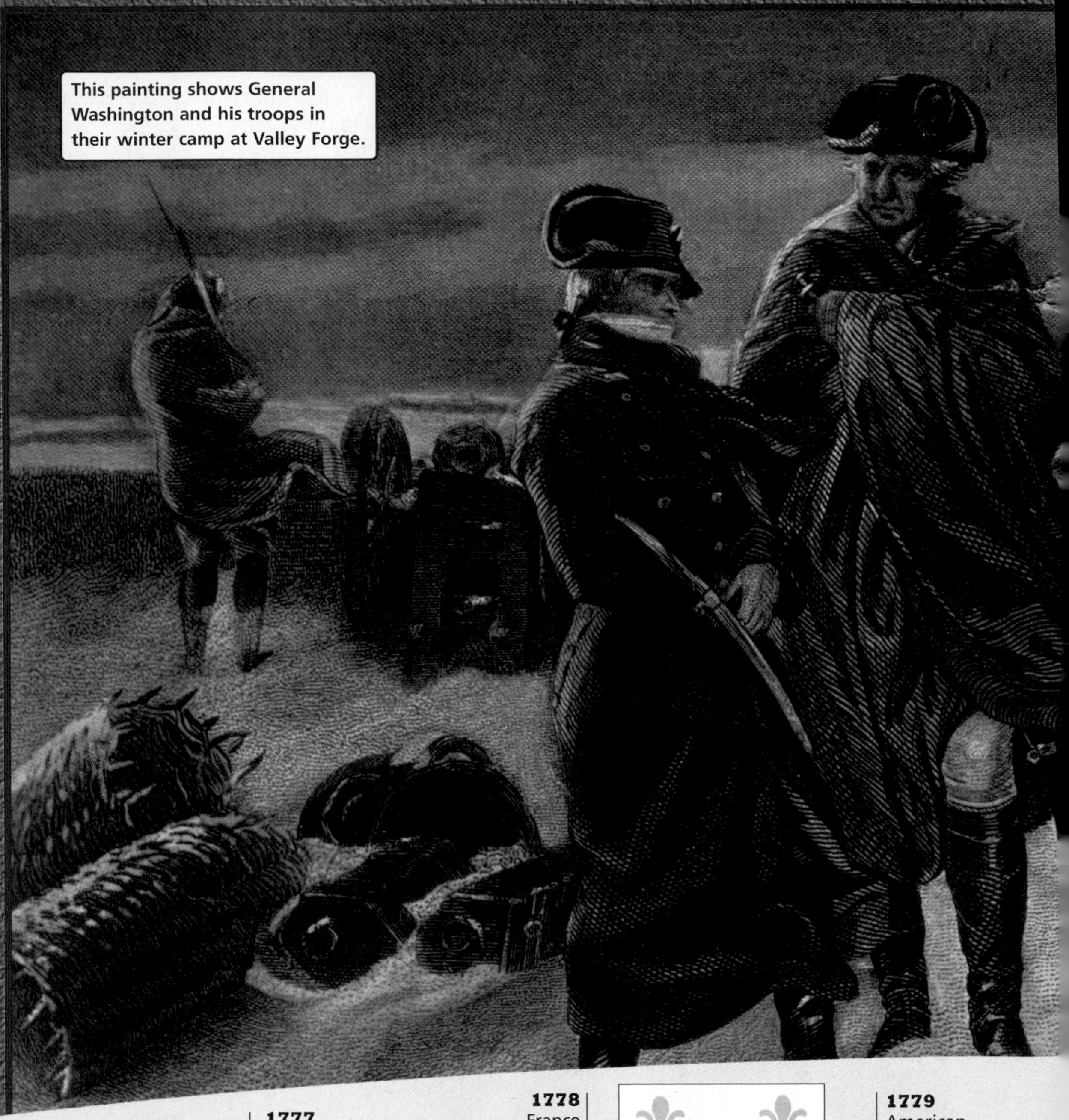

This painting shows General Washington and his troops in their winter camp at Valley Forge.

USA

1776
British capture New York, but Americans win a battle in New Jersey.

1777
Battles of Saratoga convince Europeans that America might win the war.

1778
France enters the war on the American side.

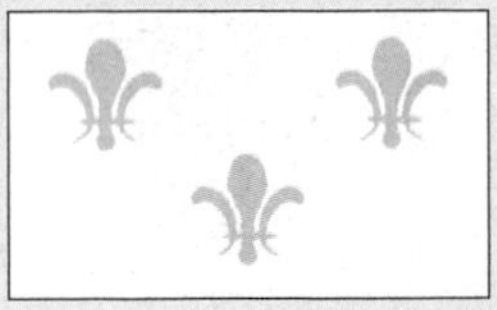

1779
American frontier soldiers take a British fort in what is now Indiana.

World

1776
Scotsman Adam Smith publishes a book saying that government shouldn't control the economy.

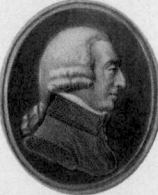

1778
Voltaire, who wrote about the rights of people, dies in Paris.

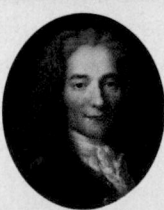

It is 1777. Your brother is an American soldier. In his last letter to you, he wrote that the army has no shoes or bullets and little food. But he plans to keep fighting.

Now, a British army is coming toward your farm. You hear that the soldiers are stealing crops to feed themselves and their horses.

What would you sacrifice to win freedom?

What Do You Think?

- What sacrifices do civilians make during wartime?
- What sacrifices do soldiers make?
- Is it worth such sacrifices to win independence for your country? Why or why not?

RESEARCH LINKS
CLASSZONE.COM

Visit the Chapter 7 links for more information about the American Revolution.

1780
Moving south, the British capture Charles Town (Charleston).

1781
In the war's last big battle, the Americans and French defeat the British at Yorktown.

1783
Treaty of Paris ends the war.

1783

1781
Emperor Joseph II of Austria ends serfdom, which forced peasants to farm someone else's land for life.

1783
Simón Bolívar, who will become a revolutionary leader in South America, is born in what is now Venezuela.

CHAPTER 7

Reading Strategy: Sequencing Events

What Do You Know?

What stories do you know about the people or events of the Revolution? How do people display courage and self-sacrifice during wartime?

Think About

- what you've learned about American settlers from movies, television, historical fiction, or science fiction about space travel
- opportunities and challenges offered in a new land
- your responses to the Interact with History about sacrificing to win freedom (see page 191)

Colonists burn the harvest to keep it from the British.

What Do You Want to Know?

 What would you like to learn about the steps that people took to win the American Revolution? In your notebook, record what you hope to learn from this chapter.

Sequencing Events

To sequence is to put events in the order in which they happened. You learned this skill in Chapter 6 by sequencing the events that led to the American Revolution. Now as you read Chapter 7, practice sequencing again. Put the major battles and events of the war in order by recording them on a time line. Copy the time line below in your notebook. You may want to make it bigger.

S See Skillbuilder Handbook, page R4.

 Taking Notes

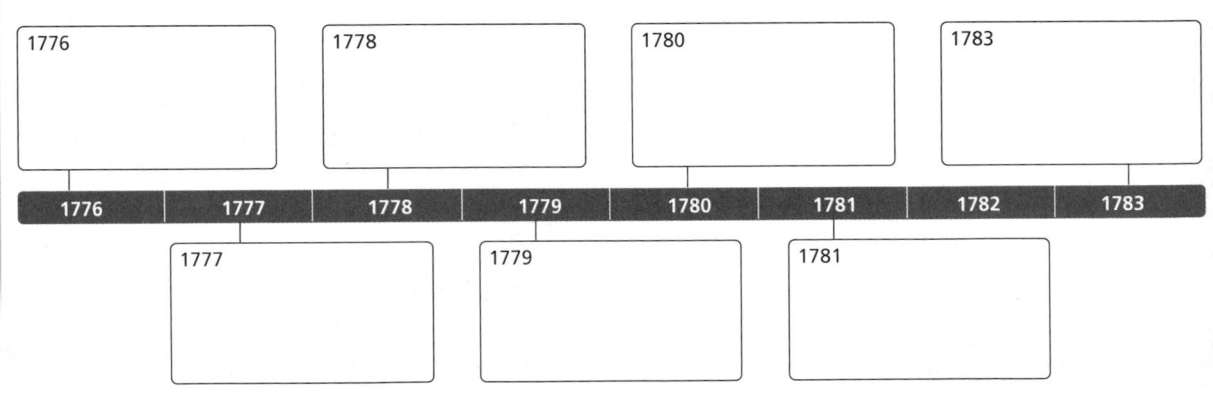

The Early Years of the War

MAIN IDEA	WHY IT MATTERS NOW	TERMS & NAMES
The American desire to gain rights and liberties led them to fight for independence from Britain.	Today those same rights and liberties are protected by the U.S. Constitution.	George Washington rendezvous mercenary Battles of strategy Saratoga

ONE AMERICAN'S STORY

In search of liberty, Haym Salomon moved from Europe to New York sometime between 1764 and 1775. He was a Jew from Poland. Salomon soon became a successful merchant and banker. During the war, Salomon supported the Patriot cause.

When the British captured New York in 1776, many Patriots fled but Salomon stayed. The British arrested him. Salomon spoke many languages. The British thought he could help them deal with foreign merchants, so they let him out of prison. Salomon used this opportunity to help other prisoners escape.

In 1778, the British wanted to arrest him again, so he fled to Philadelphia and continued to aid the Patriots. He loaned the new government more than $600,000, which was never repaid.

Like Salomon, many people made hard choices about which side to support during the Revolutionary War. This section discusses those choices and the obstacles Americans faced in the war's early years.

Haym Salomon sacrificed his health and his fortune to help his new country.

Americans Divided

The issue of separating from Great Britain divided American society. Opinion polls did not exist in the 1700s, so we don't know exactly how many people were on each side. But historians estimate that roughly 20 to 30 percent of Americans were Loyalists, roughly 40 to 45 percent were Patriots, and the rest remained neutral. Most Americans did not support the Revolution.

Both Patriots and Loyalists came from all walks of life and all parts of America. In general, New England and Virginia had high numbers of Patriots. Loyalists were numerous in cities, in New York State, and in the

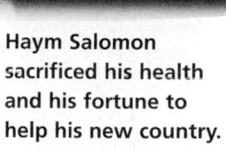

Taking Notes

Use your chart to take notes about the early years of the American Revolution.

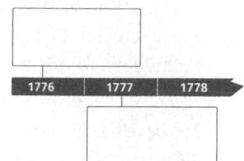

| 1776 | 1777 | 1778 |

South. Many Loyalists worked for the British government or were clergy in the Church of England. Some Quakers were Loyalists, although many wanted peace. (Their faith taught that war was wrong.)

The war divided Native Americans, too. For instance, some Iroquois nations fought with the British and others with the Americans. Those Native Americans who joined the British feared that if the Americans won, they would take Native American land. Some Native Americans who lived near colonists and interacted with them sided with the Americans.

African Americans also fought on both sides. At first, slave owners feared that African Americans who had guns might lead slave revolts. Therefore, few states allowed African Americans to enlist, or sign up with the army. Then a British governor offered freedom to any enslaved person who joined the British army. Many slaves ran away to fight for the British. In response, most states began to accept African-American soldiers. In all, about 5,000 African Americans served in the Continental Army. Many African Americans who did so hoped that American independence would bring greater equality.

Differences over the war split families, too. For example, Benjamin Franklin's son William took Britain's side. The father and son stopped speaking.

Background
The Iroquois League had generally kept peace among the Iroquois nations for about 200 years—until the American Revolution.

Creating an Army

Because not everyone supported the war, raising an army was difficult. The army also faced other problems. In June 1775, **George Washington** became the commander of the Continental Army. At first, this new national army was formed from state militias, made up of untrained and undisciplined volunteers.

After Congress created the Continental Army, men began to enlist, but most of them didn't stay long. At the start of the war, Congress asked men to enlist only for one year. Later Congress did lengthen the term of service. When the soldiers' time was up, they went home. As a result, Washington's army never numbered more than 17,000 men.

Congress's inability to supply the army also frustrated Washington. The soldiers needed everything— blankets, shoes, food, and even guns and ammunition. Angrily, Washington wrote, "Could I have foreseen what I have, and am likely to experience, no consideration upon earth should have induced [persuaded] me to accept this command."

Many women tried to help the army. Martha Washington and other wives followed their husbands to army camps. The women cooked, did laundry, and

*Reading*History
A. Analyzing Causes Why would the lack of agreement about the war make it hard to raise an army?

AMERICA'S HISTORY MAKERS

GEORGE WASHINGTON
1732–1799

At the age of 16, George Washington worked as a surveyor, setting land boundaries in the wilderness. He learned to handle hardship by hunting for food and sleeping outdoors.

In the French and Indian War, Washington had many brushes with death. Yet he wrote, "I heard the bullets whistle, and, believe me, there is something charming in the sound."

That war made him the most famous American officer. People loved him for his courage. As commander of the Continental Army, Washington's popularity helped unite Americans.

How did Washington's early life prepare him to lead the army?

nursed sick or wounded soldiers. A few women even helped fight. Mary Hays earned the nickname "Molly Pitcher" by carrying water to tired soldiers during a battle. Deborah Sampson dressed as a man, enlisted, and fought in several engagements.

Building an army was crucial to Washington's plan. To the British, the Americans were disorganized, inexperienced rebels. The British thought that if they won a decisive battle, the Americans would give up. By contrast, Washington's main goal was to survive. To do so, he needed to keep an army in the field, win some battles—no matter how small—and avoid a crushing defeat. He knew he could not hope to win a major battle until he had a large, well-equipped army.

*Reading*History
B. Solving Problems How did Washington try to solve the problem of leading a small, inexperienced force against a large professional army?

These Hessian boots weighed about 12 pounds a pair.

Struggle for the Middle States

As Chapter 6 explains, Washington had forced the British to retreat from Boston in March 1776. He then hurried his army to New York City, where he expected the British to go next. One British goal was to occupy coastal cities so that their navy could land troops and supplies in those cities. From there, they could launch their military campaigns.

Washington's hunch was correct. In July 1776, Britain's General William Howe arrived in New York with a large army. Then in August, more soldiers arrived, including about 9,000 Hessian mercenaries. A **mercenary** is a professional soldier hired to fight for a foreign country. British soldiers usually signed up for life—which discouraged enlistment. So Britain needed mercenaries, whom it hired from the German states.

Background
The British-hired mercenaries came from a part of Germany called Hesse, which is the origin of the term *Hessian.*

For several months, the British and American armies fought for New York State. Finally, the British forced Washington to retreat through New Jersey. By December, when the American army crossed the Delaware River into Pennsylvania, it was in terrible condition. Charles Willson Peale, a Philadelphia painter who watched the crossing, saw one muddy soldier who "had lost all his clothes. He was in an old, dirty blanket jacket, his beard long, and his face so full of sores he could not clean it." To Peale's shock, the soldier called his name. He was Peale's brother!

Political writer Thomas Paine also witnessed the hard conditions and the soldiers' low spirits on the retreat. To

War in the Middle States, 1776–1777
INTER*ACTIVE*

Map legend:
← American forces
← British forces
✳ American victory
✳ British victory

Labels on map: Lake Champlain, MAINE (part of Mass.), N.H., N.Y., MASS., Boston, CONN., R.I., Washington, Morristown, PENNSYLVANIA, New York, Germantown, Princeton, Brandywine, Trenton, MARYLAND, N.J., Philadelphia, Washington, DEL., ATLANTIC OCEAN, VIRGINIA, Howe, Chesapeake Bay, Hudson R., Delaware R., 45°N, 40°N, 75°W, 70°W, 80°W, 100 Miles, 200 Kilometers

GEOGRAPHY SKILLBUILDER Interpreting Maps
1. **Place** In what state did the American victories take place?
2. **Movement** How did the British general Howe travel from New York to Brandywine?

195

Thomas Sully's *Passage of the Delaware* shows Washington at the Delaware River, leading to the American attack on the British at Trenton, New Jersey.

urge them to keep fighting, Paine published the first in a series of pamphlets called *The American Crisis*.

> **A VOICE FROM THE PAST**
>
> These are the times that try men's souls. The summer soldier and the sunshine patriot will, in this crisis, shrink from the service of their country; but he that stands it *now*, deserves the love and thanks of man and woman.
>
> **Thomas Paine**, *The American Crisis*

Reading **History**
C. Recognizing Propaganda How does this passage promote the American cause?

Washington hoped a victory would encourage his weary men. He also knew that he must attack the British quickly because most of his soldiers would leave once their enlistments ended on December 31.

Late on December 25, 1776, Washington's troops rowed across the icy Delaware River to New Jersey. From there, they marched in bitter, early-morning cold to Trenton to surprise the Hessians, some of whom were sleeping after their Christmas celebration. The Americans captured or killed more than 900 Hessians and gained needed supplies. Washington's army won another victory at Princeton eight days later. These victories proved that the American general was better than the British had thought. The American army began to attract new recruits.

Britain's Strategy

Meanwhile, the British were pursuing a **strategy**—an overall plan of action—to seize the Hudson River Valley. If successful, they would cut off New England from the other states. The strategy called for three armies to meet at Albany, New York. General John Burgoyne would lead a force south from Canada. Lieutenant Colonel Barry St. Leger would lead his army from Lake Ontario down the Mohawk Valley. Burgoyne expected General Howe to follow the Hudson north from New York City.

Copyright © 2002 Museum of Fine Arts, Boston.

Burgoyne left Canada in June 1777 with an army that included British, Hessians, and Iroquois. In July, they captured Fort Ticonderoga.

Called "Gentleman Johnny" by his soldiers, Burgoyne enjoyed traveling slowly and throwing parties to celebrate victories. After Ticonderoga, his delays gave the Americans time to cut down trees to block his route. They also burned crops and drove off cattle, leaving the countryside bare of supplies for the British troops.

Things grew rougher during the last 25 miles of Burgoyne's march to Albany. On a map, the route looked easy, but it really crossed a swampy wilderness. The army had to build bridges and roads. Burgoyne took four weeks to reach the Hudson. Still confident, he looked forward to the **rendezvous,** or meeting, with St. Leger and Howe in Albany.

On August 4, Burgoyne received a message from Howe. He would not be coming north, Howe wrote, because he had decided to invade Pennsylvania to try to capture General Washington and Philadelphia—where the Continental Congress met. "Success be ever with you," wrote Howe. Yet Burgoyne needed Howe's soldiers, not his good wishes.

Howe did invade Pennsylvania. In September 1777, he defeated but did not capture Washington at the Battle of Brandywine. Howe then occupied Philadelphia. In October, Washington attacked Howe at Germantown. Washington lost the battle, however, and retreated.

War in the North, 1777
INTER**ACTIVE**

← American forces
← British forces
✳ American victory
✳ British victory

GEOGRAPHY SKILLBUILDER Interpreting Maps
1. **Place** *From which two cities did the British invade the United States?*
2. **Movement** *What did St. Leger want to capture by taking the longer route by way of Lake Ontario?*

Reading **History**
D. Evaluating
Review Howe's two goals for his invasion of Pennsylvania. Was he successful?

Battles Along the Mohawk

As Burgoyne received Howe's message, St. Leger faced his own obstacle in reaching Albany. In the summer of 1777, he was trying to defeat a small American force at Fort Stanwix in the Mohawk River valley of New York. St. Leger's forces included Iroquois led by Mohawk chief Joseph Brant, also called Thayendanegea (THĪ•ehn•DAHG•ee).

Vocabulary
convert: a person who changes religions

Brant and his sister, Molly, had strong ties to the British. Molly was a British official's wife, and Joseph was a convert to the Church of England. Both Joseph and Molly tried to convince the Iroquois to fight for the British, who upheld Iroquois rights to their land.

During August 1777, American general Benedict Arnold led a small army up the Mohawk River. He wanted to chase the British away from

The Iroquois chief Joseph Brant was a British ally.

Fort Stanwix. Arnold sent a captured Loyalist and some Iroquois who were American allies to spread the rumor that he had a large army.

The trick worked. St. Leger's troops were afraid they were about to be outnumbered. The army retreated so fast that it left behind tents, cannon, and supplies. Because of St. Leger's flight and Howe's refusal to follow the strategy, no one was left to rendezvous with Burgoyne.

Saratoga: A Turning Point

By this time, Burgoyne's army was running out of supplies, and it needed horses. The general sent a raiding party into Vermont to see what it could find. The raiding party encountered New England troops, who badly defeated it at the Battle of Bennington on August 16, 1777.

Despite this setback, Burgoyne's army headed slowly toward Albany. On the way, it met a powerful Continental Army force led by General Horatio Gates. Gates's soldiers were waiting on a ridge called Bemis Heights, near Saratoga, New York. There the Americans had created fortifications, or built-up earthen walls, behind which to fight. The Polish engineer Tadeusz Kosciuszko (TAH•deh•oosh KAWSH•choosh•kaw) had helped the Americans do this.

Burgoyne would have to break through the fortifications to proceed to Albany. On September 19, he attacked. While Gates commanded the Americans on the ridge, Benedict Arnold led an attack on nearby

Reading **History**
E. Reading a Map
Find Saratoga on the map on page 197. Notice how close it is to Burgoyne's goal of Albany.

CITIZENSHIP TODAY

Exercising Free Speech

The British could have charged Thomas Paine with a crime for writing *The American Crisis.* The crime was sedition, or stirring up rebellion. By saying what he thought, Paine risked going to prison. Today U.S. citizens have the right to speak freely without fear of jail.

Like Thomas Paine, some students have used free speech to urge people to take action. For example, the Sidney Lanier Middle School in Houston, Texas, has published its school newspaper on the Internet. In October 1996, one writer urged other students to get involved in that year's election, saying, "Even though you will not be able to vote yet, you can still influence your parents to do so."

These students are working together to produce a school newspaper.

How Do You Exercise Free Speech?

1. Working in a small group, choose an issue that you care about. Look through newsmagazines for ideas.

2. Use a cluster diagram to record your feelings and opinions about the issue.

3. As a group, decide what action you think people should take on the issue.

4. Write an article expressing the group's opinion. Each member should read the article and suggest changes. Revise the article.

5. Send the revised article to the editorial page of your school or local newspaper.

 See Citizenship Handbook, page 282.

For more about free speech . . .

 RESEARCH LINKS
CLASSZONE.COM

Freeman's Farm. His men repeatedly charged the British and inflicted heavy casualties. Still, the British held their position.

On October 7, another battle broke out. Again Arnold led daring charges against the British. Although hundreds of muskets were firing at him, he galloped through the battlefield "like a madman," a sergeant later said. Frightened, Burgoyne's Hessian mercenaries began to fall back. Eventually, a bullet tore into Arnold's leg and stopped him. Even so, the Americans forced Burgoyne to retreat.

Burgoyne's army moved slowly through heavy rain to a former army camp at Saratoga. By the time they arrived, the men were exhausted. Some fell in the mud and slept in their wet uniforms. The Continental Army then surrounded Burgoyne's army and fired on it day and night without stopping. Burgoyne decided to surrender. The series of conflicts that led to this surrender is known as the **Battles of Saratoga.**

The Battles of Saratoga had two very different consequences. As Benedict Arnold was recovering from his wound, he married a woman who was a Loyalist. Over time, Arnold came to feel that Congress had not rewarded him enough for his heroic actions at Saratoga and other battles. Influenced by his bitterness and his wife, he betrayed his army. In 1780, he agreed to turn over an American fort to the British. Although his plot was discovered before he could carry it out, he escaped. Even today, the name *Benedict Arnold* is used to mean traitor.

On the positive side, the victory at Saratoga was a turning point in the Revolution. It caused European nations to think that the Americans might win their war for independence. As you will read in Section 2, several European nations decided to help America in its struggle.

*Reading***History**
F. Forming and Supporting Opinions Which of the two consequences of the Battles of Saratoga was more significant? Why?

America's
HERITAGE

THE FIRST FLAG
June 14 is Flag Day in the United States. On June 14, 1777, the Continental Congress adopted the stars and stripes design for the U.S. flag. According to legend, a Philadelphia seamstress named Betsy Ross designed the first flag, illustrated below. Historians have found no evidence to support this legend. However, Ross did make flags for the Pennsylvania navy.

Section 1 Assessment

1. Terms & Names

Explain the significance of:
• George Washington
• mercenary
• strategy
• rendezvous
• Battles of Saratoga

2. Using Graphics

Use a cluster diagram like the one shown to list the difficulties Americans faced in the early years of the war.

American Difficulties

Which difficulty do you think was hardest to overcome?

3. Main Ideas

a. How were Americans divided over the issue of separating from Great Britain?

b. Why was it difficult for George Washington to form and keep a large army?

c. How did the Battles of Saratoga mark a turning point in the war?

4. Critical Thinking

Contrasting How did the British and American strategies differ during the early years of the war?

THINK ABOUT
• what the British expected from the Americans
• Washington's main goals for the American army
• why Burgoyne invaded from Canada

ACTIVITY OPTIONS

LANGUAGE ARTS

ART

Learn more about a Revolutionary War leader. Write a brief **biography** or create a **trading card** with a picture on one side and important facts on the other.

The War Expands

MAIN IDEA	WHY IT MATTERS NOW	TERMS & NAMES
Some Europeans decided to help America. As the war continued, it spread to the sea and the frontier.	This was the beginning of the United States' formal relationships with other nations.	ally Marquis de Lafayette bayonet desert privateer James Forten John Paul Jones

ONE AMERICAN'S STORY

To defeat the British Empire, the United States needed a foreign ally. An **ally** is a country that agrees to help another country achieve a common goal. The ideal ally would share America's goal of defeating Britain. So the United States turned to France—Britain's long-time enemy.

In 1776, Congress sent Benjamin Franklin to France to persuade it to be the ally of the United States. Famous for his experiments with electricity, Franklin became a celebrity in Paris. He wrote to his daughter, saying that medallions with his likeness were popular there.

A VOICE FROM THE PAST

These, with the pictures, busts [sculptures of the head and shoulders], and prints (of which copies upon copies are spread everywhere), have made your father's face as well known as that of the moon.

Benjamin Franklin, letter to his daughter Sally

After America's victory at Saratoga, the French agreed to an alliance. This section explains how the war expanded with foreign aid.

Franklin's simple Quaker coat and fur hat amused the French. The clothes fit the image they had of him—a wise, noble man from a wild country.

Taking Notes

Use your chart to take notes about the expansion of the American Revolution.

1776 1777 1778

Help from Abroad

France was still bitter over its defeat by Britain in the French and Indian War, in which France lost its North American colonies. The French hoped to take revenge on the British by helping Britain's American colonies break free. In 1776, France began to give secret aid to the Americans. However, the French didn't want to lose to Britain a second time. That is why they didn't publicly ally themselves with the United States until after the Americans had proved they could win battles.

After hearing of the American victory at Saratoga, King Louis XVI of France recognized U.S. independence. In 1778, France signed two treaties of alliance with the United States. By doing so, France went to

war with Britain. As part of its new alliance, France sent badly needed funds, supplies, and troops to America.

In 1779, France persuaded its ally Spain to help the Americans. Spain was also Britain's rival. The Spanish governor of Louisiana, General Bernardo de Gálvez, acted quickly. He captured the British strongholds of Natchez and Baton Rouge in the lower Mississippi Valley.

Background
Galveston, Texas, is named for Gálvez.

From there, his small army went on to take Mobile, and in 1781 Pensacola in West Florida. These victories prevented the British from attacking the United States from the southwest. In addition, Britain had to keep thousands of troops fighting Gálvez—instead of fighting the Americans. However, like France, Spain's motives were not simply to help the United States. Gálvez's victories helped extend Spain's empire in North America.

Reading**History**
A. **Recognizing Effects** How did America's allies prevent Britain from focusing all its might on the Americans?

By entering the war on America's side, France and Spain forced the British to fight a number of enemies on land and sea. The British had to spread their military resources over many fronts. For example, they were afraid they might have to fight the French in the West Indies, so they sent troops there. This prevented the British from concentrating their strength to defeat the inexperienced Americans.

Europeans Help Washington

The Americans gained some of the military experience they needed from Europe. Several European military officers came to Washington's aid, including men from France, Poland, and the German states.

Background
Many of these European officers were professional soldiers looking for an army that would hire them. Some, like Lafayette, also believed in the American cause.

The **Marquis de Lafayette** (LAF•ee•EHT) was a 19-year-old French nobleman who volunteered to serve in Washington's army. He wanted a military career, and he believed in the American cause. He quickly gained Washington's confidence and was given the command of an army division. Lafayette won respect and love from his men by sharing their hardships. Called "the soldier's friend," he used his own money to buy warm clothing for his ragged troops. Washington regarded him almost as a son.

Lafayette stands with the slave James Armistead, whose owner allowed him to spy for Lafayette. After the war, the state of Virginia set Armistead free. Armistead then took Lafayette's last name as his own.

Lafayette fought in many battles and also persuaded the French king to send a 6,000-man army to America. He became a hero in both France and the United States. Later he took part in France's own revolution.

Along with Lafayette came the Baron de Kalb, a German officer who had served in the French army. He became one of Washington's generals and earned a reputation for bravery. In 1780, he received 11 wounds in the Battle of Camden and died.

Another German, Baron von Steuben, helped turn the inexperienced Americans

into a skilled fighting force. Washington asked him to train the army. In 1778, Steuben began by forming a model company of 100 men. Then he taught them how to move in lines and columns and how to handle weapons properly. Under Steuben's direction, the soldiers practiced making charges with **bayonets**—long steel knives attached to the ends of guns. Within a month, the troops were executing drills with speed and precision. Once the model company succeeded, the rest of the army adopted Steuben's methods.

Winter at Valley Forge

Help from Europeans came at a time when the Americans desperately needed it. In late 1777, Britain's General Howe forced Washington to retreat from Philadelphia. Beginning in the winter of 1777–1778, Washington and his army camped at Valley Forge in southeast Pennsylvania.

On the march to Valley Forge, Washington's army was so short on supplies that many soldiers had only blankets to cover themselves. They also lacked shoes. The barefoot men left tracks of blood on the frozen ground as they marched. The soldiers' condition did not improve at camp. The Marquis de Lafayette described what he saw.

A VOICE FROM THE PAST

The unfortunate soldiers were in want of everything; they had neither coats, nor hats, nor shirts, nor shoes; their feet and their legs froze till they grew black and it was often necessary to amputate them. . . . The Army frequently passed whole days without food.

Marquis de Lafayette, quoted in *Valley Forge: Pinnacle of Courage*

Reading **History**

B. Identifying Facts and Opinions Is Lafayette mainly recounting facts or expressing opinions? Explain.

Because of this, the name *Valley Forge* came to stand for the great hardships that Americans endured in the Revolutionary War. Over the winter, the soldiers at Valley Forge grew weak from not having enough food or warm clothing. Roughly a quarter of them died from malnutrition, exposure to the cold, or diseases such as smallpox and typhoid fever.

daily *life*

CAMP LIFE IN WINTER

At Valley Forge, soldiers slept in small huts, 12 men to a hut. They slept in shifts so they could take turns using the scarce blankets. The men also shared clothing. If one went on guard duty, the others lent him their clothes and stayed by the fire in the hut until he came back. Guards had to stand in old hats to keep their shoeless feet warm.

The soldiers cooked on hot stones, in iron kettles, or on portable iron braziers. Often the only food they had was fire cakes—a bread made of flour and water paste.

These iron kettles were so heavy that soldiers often threw them away on a march.

This surgeon's kit includes a saw, used to perform amputations.

Soldiers would place burning coals in braziers like this. Braziers were used to cook food and heat huts.

Washington appealed to Congress to send the soldiers supplies, but it was slow in responding. Luckily, private citizens sometimes came to the soldiers' aid. According to one story, on New Year's Day 1778, a group of Philadelphia women drove ten teams of oxen into camp. The oxen were pulling wagons loaded with supplies and 2,000 shirts. The women had the oxen killed to provide food for the men.

Reading **History**

C. Analyzing Points of View What are two different explanations for why American soldiers did not desert?

Despite the hardships, Washington and his soldiers showed amazing endurance. Under such circumstances, soldiers often **desert,** or leave military duty without intending to return. Some soldiers did desert, but Lieutenant Colonel John Brooks wrote that the army stayed together because of "Love of our Country." The men also stayed because of Washington. Private Samuel Downing declared that the soldiers "loved him. They'd sell their lives for him."

War on the Frontier

Elsewhere, other Americans also took on difficult challenges. In 1777, a 24-year-old frontiersman named George Rogers Clark walked into the office of Virginia's governor, Patrick Henry. Clark said he had come to take part in defending the Western frontier. He lived in Kentucky, which was claimed by Virginia. Clark wanted Virginia to defend that region against British soldiers and their Native American allies in what is now Indiana and Illinois. "If a country is not worth protecting," he said, "it is not worth claiming."

"If a country is not worth protecting, it is not worth claiming."
George Rogers Clark

Background
In the late 1700s, the Western frontier was the region between the Appalachian Mountains and the Mississippi River.

Clark was difficult to ignore. He stood six feet tall, had red hair, and displayed a dramatic personality. He persuaded Governor Henry that he was right. The governor told Clark to raise an army to capture British posts on the Western frontier.

In May of 1778, Clark and a group of frontiersmen began to travel down the Ohio River. He recruited others on the way, until he had a force of 175 to 200. They went by boat and later on foot to Kaskaskia, a British post on the Mississippi River. They captured Kaskaskia without a fight.

Then they moved east to take Fort Sackville at Vincennes, in present-day Indiana. Earlier, a small force sent by Clark had taken Vincennes, but British forces under Henry Hamilton had recaptured it. Settlers called Hamilton the "Hair Buyer" because he supposedly paid rewards for American scalps.

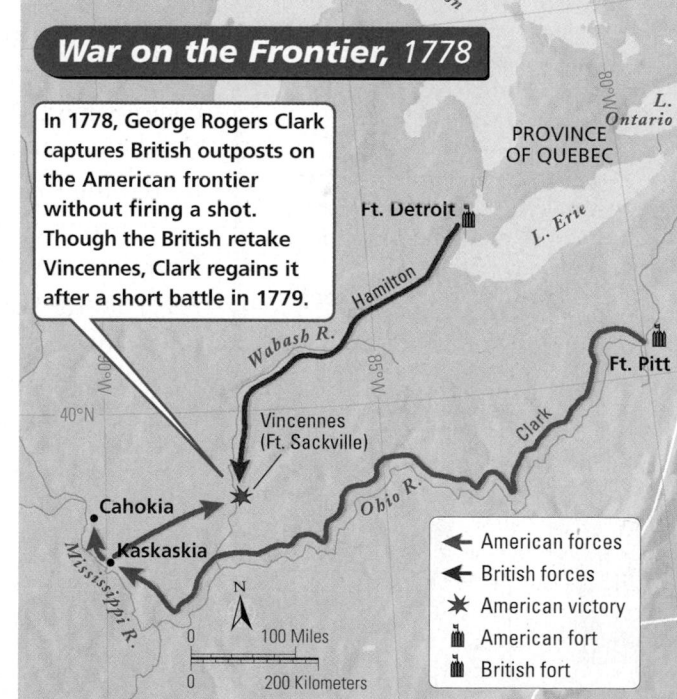

War on the Frontier, 1778

In 1778, George Rogers Clark captures British outposts on the American frontier without firing a shot. Though the British retake Vincennes, Clark regains it after a short battle in 1779.

American forces
British forces
American victory
American fort
British fort

GEOGRAPHY SKILLBUILDER Interpreting Maps
1. **Movement** From what fort did British general Hamilton travel to Vincennes?
2. **Region** What rivers form the boundaries of the region captured by Clark and his men?

203

Determined to retake Fort Sackville, Clark and his men set out for Vincennes from Kaskaskia in February 1779. Hamilton wasn't expecting an attack because the rivers were overflowing their banks and the woods were flooded. Clark's men slogged through miles of icy swamps and waded through chest-deep water. They caught the British at Vincennes by surprise.

When Hamilton and his troops tried to remain in the fort, Clark pretended to have a larger force than he really had. He also found a way to frighten the British into leaving. Clark and his men had captured several Native Americans, who were allies of the British and had American scalps on their belts. Clark executed some of them in plain view of the fort. He promised to do the same to Hamilton and his men if they didn't surrender immediately. The British gave up.

Reading **History**
D. Making Decisions What factors do you think influenced Clark's decision to execute his prisoners?

Clark's victory gave the Americans a hold on the vast region between the Great Lakes and the Ohio River. This area was more than half the total size of the original 13 states. However, Fort Detroit on Lake Erie remained in the hands of the British.

STRANGE *but* True

THE FIRST COMBAT SUBMARINE

During the Revolution, the Americans built the first combat submarine—the *Turtle,* shown below. It held only a pilot, who steered with one hand and cranked a propeller with the other. To submerge, the pilot used a foot pump to let in water.

In 1776, the *Turtle* failed on its mission to attach a bomb to a British warship in New York harbor. It reached the ship but couldn't drill through its copper-clad hull. The *Turtle* failed at later missions, too.

War at Sea

The war expanded not only to the frontier but also to the sea. By 1777, Britain had about 100 warships off the American coast. This allowed Britain to control the Atlantic trade routes. There was no way the Americans could defeat the powerful British navy.

But American privateers attacked British merchant ships. A **privateer** is a privately owned ship that a wartime government gives permission to attack an enemy's merchant ships. After capturing a British merchant ship, the crew of a privateer sold its cargo and shared the money. As a result, a desire for profit as well as patriotism motivated privateers. The states and Congress commissioned more than 1,000 privateers to prey on the British. During the war, they captured hundreds of British ships. This disrupted trade, causing British merchants to call for the war to end.

Many men answered the privateers' call for volunteers. Among them was 14-year-old **James Forten,** who was the son of a free African-American sail maker. In 1780, Forten signed up to sail on the *Royal Louis* to earn money for his family after his father died. When a British ship captured the *Royal Louis* in 1781, the British offered Forten a free trip to England. Reportedly, Forten refused, saying he would never betray his country. Released from a British prison after the war, Forten walked barefoot from New York to his home in Philadelphia. He later became famous for his efforts to end slavery.

Vocabulary
merchant ship: a ship used in trade

A Naval Hero

Though outnumbered, the Continental Navy scored several victories against the British. An officer named **John Paul Jones** won the most famous sea battle.

In 1779, Jones became the commander of a ship named *Bonhomme Richard*. With four other ships, he patrolled the English coast. In September, Jones's vessels approached a convoy in which two British warships were guarding a number of supply ships.

Vocabulary
convoy: a group of ships traveling together for safety

Jones closed in on the *Serapis*, the larger of the two warships. At one point, the *Bonhomme Richard* rammed the better-armed British vessel. As the two ships locked together, the confident British captain demanded that Jones surrender. In words that have become a famous U.S. Navy slogan, Jones replied, "I have not yet begun to fight!"

The two warships were so close together that the muzzles of their guns almost touched. They blasted away, each seriously damaging the other. On the shore, crowds of Britons gathered under a full moon to watch the fighting. After a fierce three-and-a-half-hour battle, the main mast of the *Serapis* cracked and fell. The ship's captain then surrendered. The *Bonhomme Richard* was so full of holes that it eventually sank, so Jones and his crew had to sail away in the *Serapis*!

Jones's success against the best navy in the world angered the British and inspired the Americans. Even so, the Americans knew that the war had to be won on land. The next section discusses the major land battles in the closing years of the war.

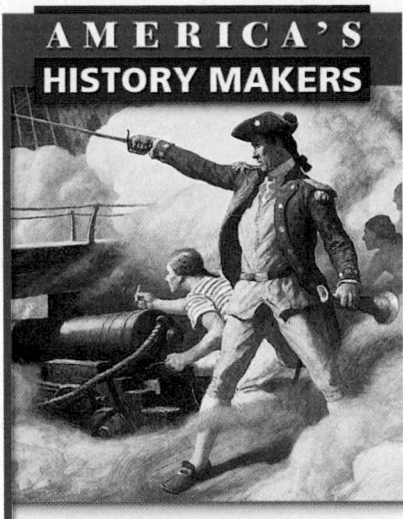

AMERICA'S HISTORY MAKERS

JOHN PAUL JONES
1747–1792

The most famous naval officer of the Revolution is known by a fake name. He was born John Paul in Scotland and first went to sea as a 12-year-old. By age 21, he had command of a merchant ship.

In 1773, Paul killed the leader of a mutiny on his ship. To avoid a murder trial, he fled to America and added Jones to his name.

Bold and daring, Jones scored many victories against the British. But his battle with the *Serapis* is what earned his place in history.

What are the two words that you think best describe Jones's character? Explain.

Section ② Assessment

1. Terms & Names

Explain the significance of:
- ally
- Marquis de Lafayette
- bayonet
- desert
- privateer
- James Forten
- John Paul Jones

2. Using Graphics

Use this diagram to list the effects of the entry of France and Spain into the war.

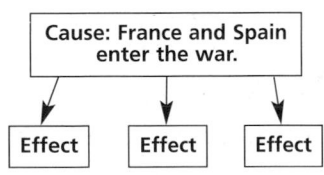

Cause: France and Spain enter the war.

Effect   Effect   Effect

3. Main Ideas

a. What role did Benjamin Franklin play in helping America win the Revolution?

b. How did European officers such as Lafayette aid America in the Revolutionary War?

c. What was John Paul Jones's major contribution during the war, and why was it important?

4. Critical Thinking

Analyzing Points of View
Why do you think George Rogers Clark thought the frontier was important to defend?

THINK ABOUT
- why General Hamilton was called "Hair Buyer"
- why America might have wanted the frontier region after the war

ACTIVITY OPTIONS

ART

SPEECH

Imagine yourself at Valley Forge in the winter of 1777–1778. Create a **comic strip** or give a **talk** describing your response to the harsh conditions.

The Path to Victory

MAIN IDEA	WHY IT MATTERS NOW	TERMS & NAMES
Seeking Loyalist support, the British invaded the South—but ultimately lost the war there.	For more than two centuries, the American Revolution has inspired other people to fight tyranny.	Lord Cornwallis pacifist guerrillas Battle of Yorktown

ONE AMERICAN'S STORY

Patriot Nancy Hart glared at the five armed Loyalists who burst into her Georgia cabin. Tradition says that the men had shot her last turkey and ordered her to cook it for them. Raids like this were common in the South, where feuding neighbors used the war as an excuse to fight each other. Both Patriots and Loyalists took part in the raids.

As Hart prepared the food, she planned her attack. When dinner was ready, the men sat down to eat. Seizing one of their muskets, Hart shot and killed one man and wounded another. She aimed the gun at the others as her daughter ran for help. A group of Patriots arrived and hanged the Loyalists.

As Nancy Hart's story demonstrates, the fighting between Patriots and Loyalists in the South was vicious. In this section, you will learn why the British war effort shifted to the South and why it failed.

The state of Georgia named a county after Nancy Hart, who is shown here holding Loyalists prisoner.

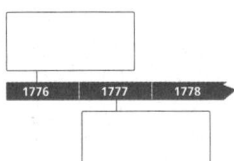

Taking Notes

Use your chart to take notes about the events that led to an American victory.

| 1776 | 1777 | 1778 |

Savannah and Charles Town

The British believed that most Southerners were Loyalists. Because of this, in 1778 the British decided to move the war to the South. After three years of fighting in the North, the British were no closer to victory. Although they had captured Northern cities, they couldn't control the countryside because they did not have enough troops to occupy it. The British believed that if they gained territory in the South, Southern Loyalists would hold it for them.

The British also expected large numbers of Southern slaves to join them because they had promised to grant the slaves freedom. Although thousands of African Americans did run away to join the British, not all of them were set free. Instead, some British officers sold African Americans into slavery in the West Indies.

Reading History
A. Drawing Conclusions Why was it an advantage to be able to move troops between the West Indies and the South?

Britain's West Indian colonies were a third reason the British invaded the South. Southern seaports were closer to the West Indies, where British troops were stationed. If the British captured Southern ports, they could move troops back and forth between the two regions.

In December 1778, the British captured the port of Savannah, Georgia. Using Savannah as a base, they then conquered most of Georgia. In 1780, a British army led by General Henry Clinton landed in South Carolina. They trapped American forces in Charles Town (now Charleston), which was the largest Southern city. When the city's 5,000 defenders surrendered, the Americans lost almost their entire Southern army. It was the worst American defeat of the war.

The Swamp Fox and Guerrilla Fighting

After that loss, Congress assigned General Horatio Gates—the victor at Saratoga—to form a new Southern army. Continental soldiers led by Baron de Kalb formed the army's core. Gates added about 2,000 new and untrained militia. He then headed for Camden, South Carolina, to challenge the army led by the British general **Lord Cornwallis.**

On the way, a band of Patriots from South Carolina approached Gates. "Their number did not exceed 20 men and boys, some white, some black, and all mounted, but most of them miserably equipped," wrote an officer. Their leader was Francis Marion, called the "Swamp Fox." He provided Gates with helpful knowledge of South Carolina's coastal swamplands. Gates sent Marion to destroy boats on the Santee River behind Camden. (See the map on page 209.) This would cut off British communications with Charles Town.

In August 1780, Gates's army ran into British troops outside Camden. The Americans were in no condition to fight. They were out of supplies and half-starved. Even worse, Gates put the inexperienced militia along part of the frontline instead of behind the veterans. When the British attacked, the militia panicked and ran. Gates also fled, but Kalb remained with his soldiers and received fatal wounds. This second defeat in the South ended Gates's term as head of an army and caused American spirits to fall to a new low.

Reading History
B. Evaluating What do you think was most responsible for the American loss at Camden?

After Camden, a small British force set out for Charles Town with a column of American prisoners. Marion's band overwhelmed the British and freed the prisoners. Fighting from a base in the swamps, Marion's men cut the British supply line that led inland and north from Charles Town. Marion used the methods of a guerrilla. **Guerrillas** are small bands of fighters who weaken the enemy with surprise raids and hit-and-run attacks. Both Patriots and Loyalists formed guerrilla bands in the South. They carried out vicious raids.

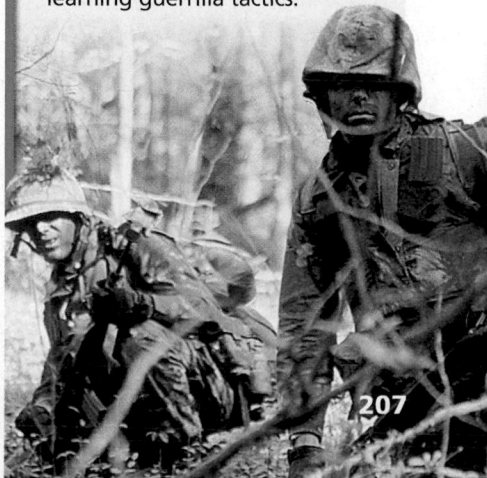

Now and then

BATTLE TACTICS

A difference in battle tactics affected future warfare. British soldiers marched shoulder to shoulder in three rows. When they neared the enemy, the first row knelt, the second crouched, and the third remained standing. They all fired without aiming.

The Americans were better shots. They often marched in rows, but sometimes they hid in woods or behind walls to take aim. Guerrillas attacked swiftly, then fled into the countryside. Those tactics succeeded and are still used today. This photograph shows modern U.S. soldiers learning guerrilla tactics.

Artillery of the Revolution

Artillery—large guns and cannon—played a key role in the American Revolution. The ability of these guns to kill and destroy from a distance made them essential in war. One witness of a battle described the destruction: "Many men were badly injured and mortally wounded by the fragments of bombs, . . . their arms and legs severed or themselves struck dead." Most cannon used in the Revolution were made of cast bronze. During the 1700s, artillery design did not change significantly. However, artillery became more mobile (more easily moved).

After each shot, a soldier sponged the inside of the barrel. This put out sparks and cleaned away any dirt left from the last shot.

A soldier loaded the cannon with gunpowder and a cannonball. He did so by ramming them down the barrel.

Soldiers aimed the gun by turning the entire carriage. An instrument called a quadrant told them how high to raise the barrel to reach their target.

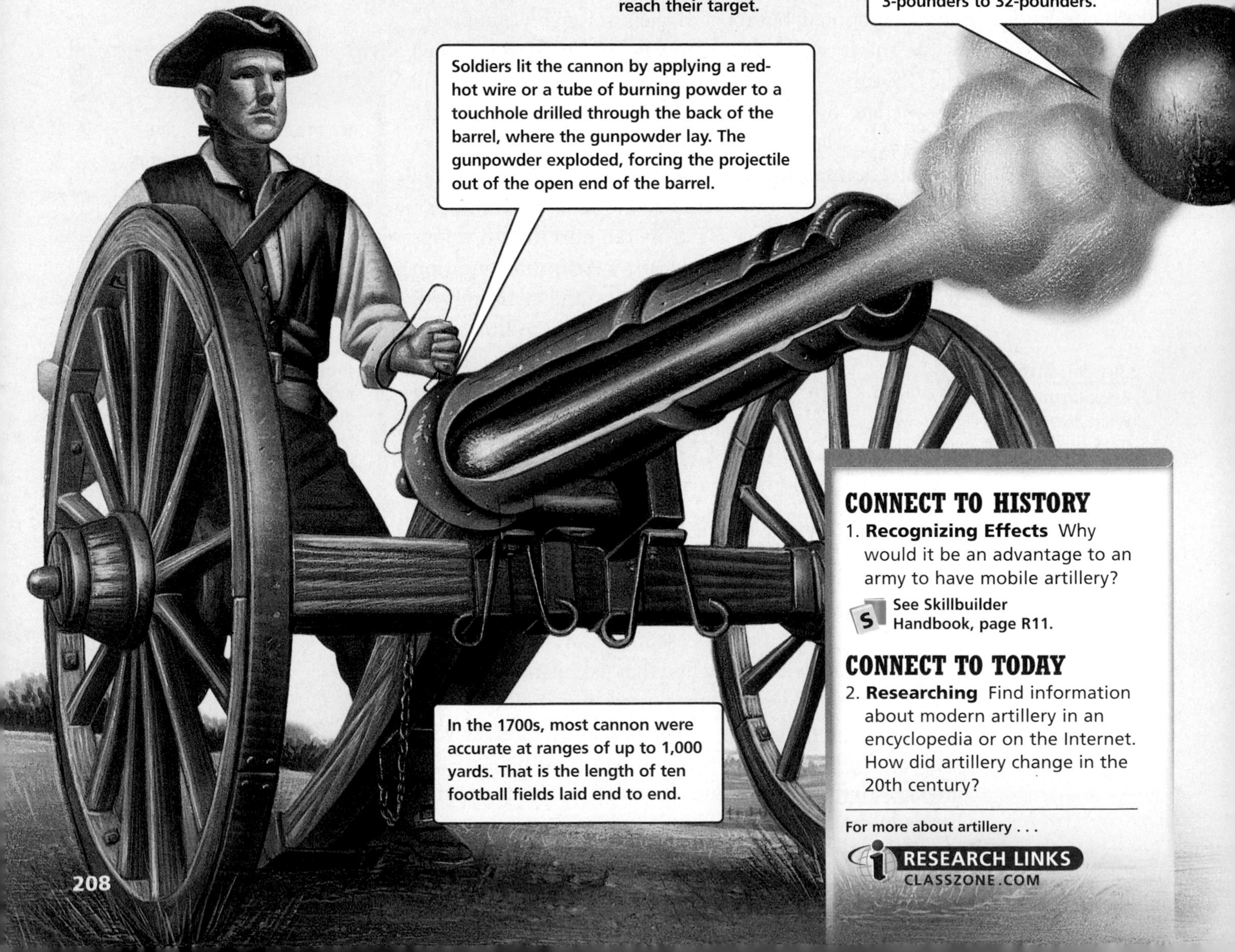

Cannon were classified by the weight of the iron ball they fired. American artillery ranged from 3-pounders to 32-pounders.

Soldiers lit the cannon by applying a red-hot wire or a tube of burning powder to a touchhole drilled through the back of the barrel, where the gunpowder lay. The gunpowder exploded, forcing the projectile out of the open end of the barrel.

In the 1700s, most cannon were accurate at ranges of up to 1,000 yards. That is the length of ten football fields laid end to end.

CONNECT TO HISTORY

1. **Recognizing Effects** Why would it be an advantage to an army to have mobile artillery?

   S See Skillbuilder Handbook, page R11.

CONNECT TO TODAY

2. **Researching** Find information about modern artillery in an encyclopedia or on the Internet. How did artillery change in the 20th century?

For more about artillery . . .

RESEARCH LINKS
CLASSZONE.COM

The Tide Turns

Even battles in the South sometimes turned vicious. One example was the Battle of Kings Mountain, fought on the border of North and South Carolina in October 1780. After surrounding a force of about 1,000 Loyalist militia and British soldiers, the Americans slaughtered most of them. James P. Collins, a 16-year-old American, described the scene.

A VOICE FROM THE PAST

The dead lay in heaps on all sides, while the groans of the wounded were heard in every direction. I could not help turning away from the scene before me with horror and, though exulting in victory, could not refrain from shedding tears.

James P. Collins, quoted in *The Spirit of Seventy-Six*

Many of the dead had been shot or hanged after they surrendered. The Americans killed them in revenge for Loyalist raids and an earlier incident in which the British had butchered Americans. Kings Mountain was one of Britain's first losses in the South. It soon suffered more.

After Gates's defeat at Camden, Washington put a new general, Nathanael Greene, in charge of the Southern army. Greene was one of Washington's most able officers. He had been a Quaker, but his church had cast him out because of his belief in the armed struggle against the British. Most Quakers are **pacifist,** or opposed to war.

Under Greene's command, the American army avoided full-scale battles, in which the British had the edge because of superior firepower. So the American forces let the British chase them around the countryside and wear themselves out. When the Americans did fight, they did their best to make sure the British suffered heavy losses.

Reading **History**

C. Contrasting How did Greene's strategy as a general differ from that of Gates at Camden?

As the fighting dragged on into its sixth year, opposition to the war grew in Britain. As a result, some British leaders began to think that American independence would not be so bad.

The End of the War

In 1781, most of the fighting took place in Virginia. In July of that year, the British general Cornwallis set up his base at Yorktown, located on a peninsula in Chesapeake Bay. From there, his army could receive supplies by ship from New York.

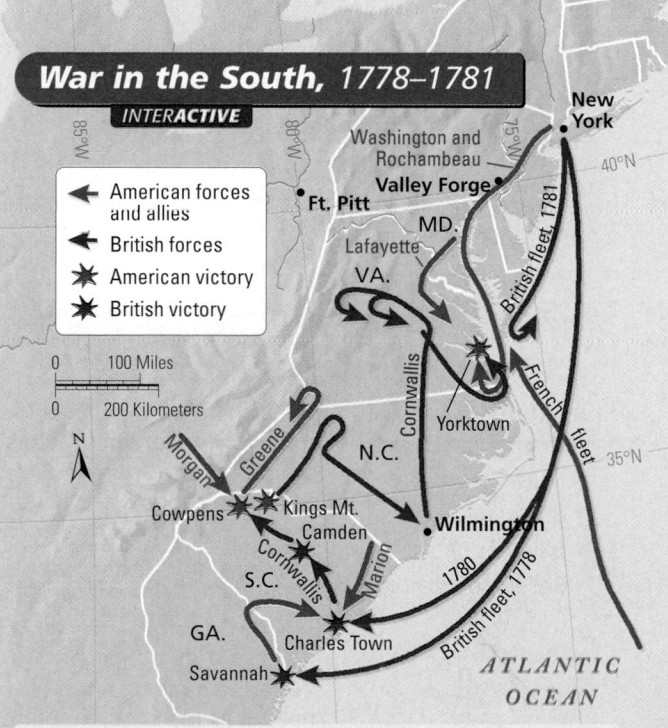

War in the South, *1778–1781*

INTER*ACTIVE*

← American forces and allies
← British forces
✱ American victory
✱ British victory

0   100 Miles
0   200 Kilometers

N

GEOGRAPHY SKILLBUILDER Interpreting Maps

1. Place *What ports did the British use to invade the South?*

2. Movement *Who traveled from Wilmington to Yorktown, and who traveled from New York?*

The victorious American forces accept the British surrender at Yorktown. George Washington is to the left of the American flag.

Washington saw Cornwallis's decision as a golden opportunity. In August 1781, a large French fleet arrived from the West Indies and blocked Chesapeake Bay. These ships prevented the British from receiving supplies—and from escaping. They also allowed Washington to come from the North and trap Cornwallis on the peninsula. Washington had enough men to do this because a large French force led by General Jean Rochambeau had joined his army.

Washington and Rochambeau moved south. When British ships tried to reach Cornwallis, French ships drove them back. In the **Battle of Yorktown,** the American and French troops bombarded Yorktown with cannon fire, turning its buildings to rubble. Cornwallis had no way out. On October 19, 1781, he surrendered his force of about 8,000.

Although some fighting continued, Yorktown was the last major battle of the war. When the British prime minister, Lord North, heard the news, he gasped, "It is all over!" Indeed, he and other British leaders were soon forced to resign. Britain's new leaders began to negotiate a peace treaty, which is discussed in the next section.

Vocabulary
bombard: to attack with artillery

Section 3 Assessment

1. Terms & Names
Explain the significance of:
- Lord Cornwallis
- guerrillas
- pacifist
- Battle of Yorktown

2. Using Graphics
Use a chart like the one below to list the geographic factors that made the British move their war effort to the South.

Physical factors, such as location	Human factors, such as who lived there

Were the human factors as helpful as the British hoped?

3. Main Ideas
a. Why did the fighting between Patriots and Loyalists in the South turn vicious?

b. What type of warfare did Francis Marion and his men employ?

c. How did Gates's errors in leadership contribute to the American loss at Camden?

4. Critical Thinking
Analyzing Causes How did each of the following help bring about the British defeat at Yorktown?

THINK ABOUT
- the location chosen by Cornwallis
- the French fleet
- the French troops under Rochambeau
- Washington's planning

ACTIVITY OPTIONS

TECHNOLOGY

MUSIC

Imagine that Congress has asked you to commemorate the Battle of Yorktown. Design a **Web page** or write a **song** celebrating the U.S. victory.

The Legacy of the War

MAIN IDEA	WHY IT MATTERS NOW	TERMS & NAMES
After the war, the new nation faced issues such as a high national debt and calls for equality.	To promote liberty, some states passed laws outlawing slavery and protecting religious freedom.	Treaty of Paris of 1783 Elizabeth Freeman republicanism Richard Allen

ONE AMERICAN'S STORY

In 1776, 15-year-old Joseph Plumb Martin of Connecticut signed up to fight for the Americans. He stayed with the army until the war ended. Many years later, Martin wrote about leaving the army.

> *A VOICE FROM THE PAST*
>
> There was as much sorrow as joy. . . . We had lived together as a family of brothers for several years, . . . had shared with each other the hardships, dangers, and sufferings incident to a soldier's life; had sympathized with each other in trouble and sickness; . . . And now we were to be . . . parted forever.
>
> **Joseph Plumb Martin,** quoted in *The Revolutionaries*

Although this painting is not of Joseph Plumb Martin himself, he may have dressed like this American soldier.

At war's end, Martin and his country faced an uncertain future. How would the United States recover from the war? What issues would confront the new nation? Section 4 discusses those questions.

Why the Americans Won

In November 1783, the last British ships and troops left New York City, and American troops marched in. As Washington said good-bye to his officers in a New York tavern, he hugged each one. Tears ran down his face. He became so upset that he had to leave the room.

Earlier in the fall, Washington had written a farewell letter to his armies. In it, he praised them by saying that their endurance "through almost every possible suffering and discouragement for the space of eight long years, was little short of a standing miracle."

By their persistence, the Americans won independence even though they faced many obstacles. As you have read, they lacked training and experience. They were often short of supplies and weapons. By contrast, the British forces ranked among the best trained in the world. They were

Taking Notes

Use your chart to take notes about the results of the American Revolution.

1776	1777	1778

experienced and well-supplied professional soldiers. Yet the Americans had certain advantages that enabled them to win.

*Reading*History

A. Evaluating
What do you think was Washington's best characteristic as a leader?

1. **Better leadership.** British generals were overconfident and made poor decisions. By contrast, Washington learned from his mistakes. After early defeats, he developed the strategy of dragging out the war to wear down the British. Despite difficulties, he never gave up.
2. **Foreign aid.** Britain's rivals, especially France, helped America. Foreign loans and military aid were essential to America's victory.
3. **Knowledge of the land.** The Americans knew the land where the war took place and used that knowledge well. The British could control coastal cities but could not extend their control to the interior.
4. **Motivation.** The Americans had more reason to fight. At stake were not only their lives but also their property and their dream of liberty.

The Treaty of Paris

As the winners, the Americans won favorable terms in the **Treaty of Paris of 1783,** which ended the Revolutionary War. The treaty included the following six conditions:

1. The United States was independent.
2. Its boundaries would be the Mississippi River on the west, Canada on the north, and Spanish Florida on the south.
3. The United States would receive the right to fish off Canada's Atlantic Coast, near Newfoundland and Nova Scotia.
4. Each side would repay debts it owed the other.
5. The British would return any enslaved persons they had captured.
6. Congress would recommend that the states return any property they had seized from Loyalists.

Neither Britain nor the United States fully lived up to the treaty's terms. Americans did not repay the prewar debts they owed British merchants or return Loyalist property. For their part, the British did not return

HISTORY *through*ART

The American painter Benjamin West began a portrait of the men who negotiated the Treaty of Paris. But the British officials refused to pose, so West never finished the painting. From left to right are the American officials John Jay, John Adams, Benjamin Franklin, and two others.

What does this painting reveal about the British response to losing the war?

212

runaway slaves. They also refused to give up military outposts in the Great Lakes area, such as Fort Detroit.

Background
Even after George Rogers Clark's Western victories, the British stayed at Fort Detroit.

Costs of the War

No one knows exactly how many people died in the war, but eight years of fighting took a terrible toll. An estimated 25,700 Americans died in the war, and 1,400 remained missing. About 8,200 Americans were wounded. Some were left with permanent disabilities, such as amputated limbs. The British suffered about 10,000 military deaths.

Many soldiers who survived the war left the army with no money. They had received little or no pay for their service. Instead of back pay, the government gave some soldiers certificates for land in the West. Many men sold that land to get money for food and other basic needs.

Both the Congress and the states had borrowed money to finance the conflict. The war left the nation with a debt of about $27 million—a debt that would prove difficult to pay off.

The losers of the war also suffered. Thousands of Loyalists lost their property. Between 60,000 and 100,000 Loyalists left the United States during and after the war. Among them were several thousand African Americans and Native Americans, including Joseph Brant. Most of the Loyalists went to Canada. There they settled new towns and provinces. They also brought English traditions to areas that the French had settled. Even today, Canada has both French and English as official languages.

*Reading*History
B. Analyzing Causes Why do you think the Loyalists left the United States?

Postwar Boundaries, 1783

RUSSIAN TERRITORY

BRITISH TERRITORY

QUEBEC

Hudson Bay

Claimed by Great Britain, Spain, and Russia

Claimed by U.S and Great Britain

Claimed by U.S and Great Britain

SPANISH TERRITORY

UNITED STATES

Claimed by U.S. and Spain

PACIFIC OCEAN

ATLANTIC OCEAN

MEXICO

Gulf of Mexico

FRENCH TERRITORY

N

0 500 Miles

0 1,000 Kilometers

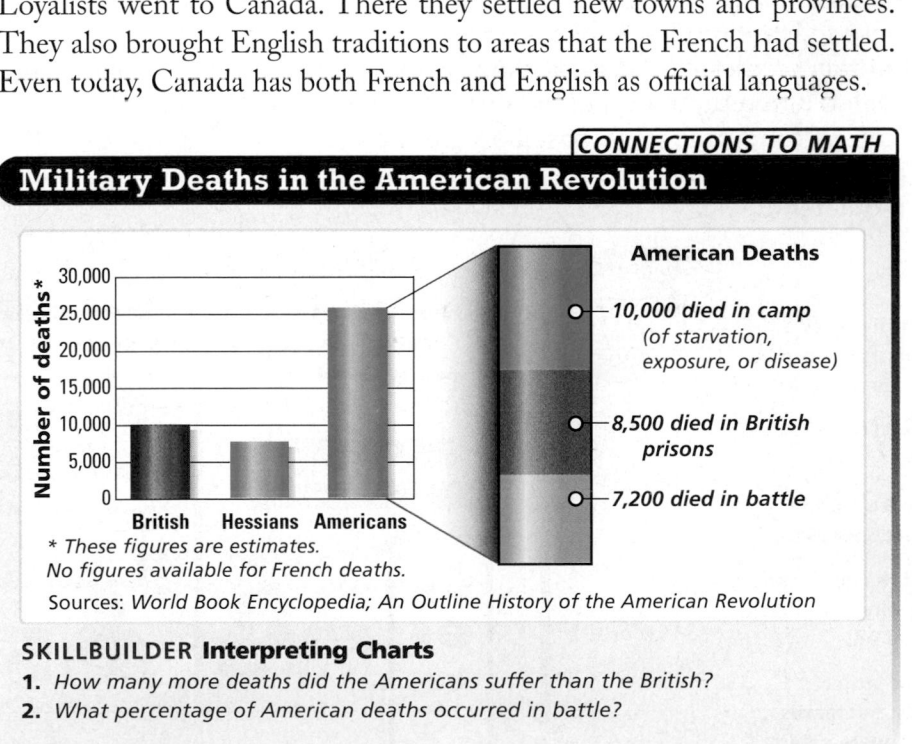

CONNECTIONS TO MATH

Military Deaths in the American Revolution

American Deaths

- 10,000 died in camp (of starvation, exposure, or disease)
- 8,500 died in British prisons
- 7,200 died in battle

Number of deaths*

30,000
25,000
20,000
15,000
10,000
5,000
0

British   Hessians   Americans

* These figures are estimates.
No figures available for French deaths.

Sources: *World Book Encyclopedia; An Outline History of the American Revolution*

SKILLBUILDER Interpreting Charts
1. How many more deaths did the Americans suffer than the British?
2. What percentage of American deaths occurred in battle?

Issues After the War

The American Revolution was not just a war, but a change in ideas about government. Before the war, Americans had demanded their rights as English citizens. But after declaring their independence, they replaced that goal with the idea of **republicanism**. This idea stated that instead of a king, the people would rule. The government would obtain its authority from the citizens and be responsible to them.

For this system to work, individuals would have to place the good of the country above their own interests. At first, only land-owning white males were allowed to take part in governing by voting or holding public office. However, women could help the nation by teaching their children the virtues that benefited public life. Such virtues included honesty, duty, and the willingness to make sacrifices.

Economics *in* History

Free Enterprise

One cause of the Revolution was the colonists' resentment of British mercantilism. Parliament passed laws to discourage the colonists from developing their own manufacturing and to force them to buy British goods. During the war, British economic control weakened. British exports of woolens to the colonies dropped from £645,900 in 1774 to only £2,540 in 1776. As a result, the colonists were able to make more economic choices—for example, they could choose to manufacture wool clothing.

The end of Britain's mercantilist control allowed free enterprise to begin to develop in the United States. In a free-enterprise system, business can be conducted freely based on the choices of individuals. The government does not control the system, but only protects and regulates it.

CONNECT TO HISTORY

1. **Analyzing Causes** Why do you think the colonists were able to manufacture their own wool clothing during the war?

S See Skillbuilder Handbook, page R11.

CONNECT TO TODAY

2. **Comparing** Think about a mall where you shop. Name examples of businesses that compete with each other. Compare the methods they use to attract customers.

For more about free enterprise . . .

 RESEARCH LINKS CLASSZONE.COM

A Competition encourages businesses to improve goods and services and to keep prices down.

B Property is owned by individuals and businesses.

C The desire to make a profit motivates businesspeople.

D Individuals, not the government, decide what to buy and what to manufacture and sell.

E The government protects private property and makes sure businesses operate fairly.

THE FREE ENTERPRISE MALL

THE BARGAIN STORE

PAY LESS GET MORE STORE

As part of their liberty, Americans called for more religious freedom. Before the war, some laws discriminated against certain religions. Some states had not allowed Jews or Catholics to hold public office. After the war, states began to abolish those laws. They also ended the practice of using tax money to support churches.

Many people began to see a conflict between slavery and the ideal of liberty. Vermont outlawed slavery, and Pennsylvania passed a law to free slaves gradually. Individual African Americans also tried to end slavery. For example, **Elizabeth Freeman** sued for her freedom in a Massachusetts court and won. Her victory in 1781 and other similar cases ended slavery in that state. Freeman later described her desire for freedom.

Background
Only Northern states ended slavery after the war. In the North, slavery was not as important a part of the economy as in the South.

A VOICE FROM THE PAST

Anytime while I was a slave, if one minute's freedom had been offered to me, and I had been told I must die at the end of that minute, I would have taken it—just to stand one minute on God's earth a free woman.

Elizabeth Freeman, quoted in *Notable Black American Women*

Reading **History**

C. Solving Problems How did free African Americans take on the responsibility of trying to improve their lives?

With freedom, African Americans began to form their own institutions. For example, the preacher **Richard Allen** helped start the Free African Society. That society encouraged African Americans to help each other. Allen also founded the African Methodist Episcopal Church, the first African-American church in the United States.

Elizabeth Freeman fought a court case that helped end slavery in Massachusetts.

Perhaps the main issue facing Americans after the war was how to shape their national government. American anger over British taxes, violation of rights, and control of trade had caused the war. Now the United States needed a government that would protect citizens' rights and economic freedom. In Chapter 8, you will read how U.S. leaders worked to create such a government.

Section 4 Assessment

1. Terms & Names

Explain the significance of:
- Treaty of Paris of 1783
- republicanism
- Elizabeth Freeman
- Richard Allen

2. Using Graphics

Use a chart like the one below to classify the terms of the Treaty of Paris according to which side they favored. (Do not list terms that don't favor either side.)

Terms of the Treaty of Paris	
Favorable to America	Favorable to Britain

3. Main Ideas

a. What advantages helped the Americans win the Revolutionary War?

b. How did the end of the war affect Loyalists?

c. What were the economic costs of the war to individuals and to the government?

4. Critical Thinking

Recognizing Effects How did republicanism shape the United States after the war?

THINK ABOUT
- American ideas about government
- the roles men and women could play in public life
- religious freedom
- the antislavery movement

ACTIVITY OPTIONS

SPEECH

MATH

Look up the U.S. population in 1780. Calculate what percentage of American people died in the war. Report your findings in a **speech** or a **pie graph**.

TERMS & NAMES

Briefly explain the significance of each of the following.

1. George Washington
2. mercenary
3. Battles of Saratoga
4. ally
5. Marquis de Lafayette
6. John Paul Jones
7. Lord Cornwallis
8. Battle of Yorktown
9. Treaty of Paris of 1783
10. republicanism

REVIEW QUESTIONS

The Early Years of the War (pages 193–199)

1. What motives led African Americans to fight for the British? The Americans?
2. How did women help the American war effort?
3. What events led to the British defeat at Saratoga?

The War Expands (pages 200–205)

4. What foreign countries helped America? How?
5. What were conditions like at Valley Forge?

The Path to Victory (pages 206–210)

6. What two Southern ports did the British capture?
7. How did America's ally France contribute to the victory at Yorktown?

The Legacy of the War (pages 211–215)

8. For what did Washington praise his army in his farewell letter?
9. What land did the United States acquire from Britain as a result of the Treaty of Paris?
10. What three states outlawed slavery after the war?

CRITICAL THINKING

1. USING YOUR NOTES: SEQUENCING EVENTS

Using your completed time line, answer the questions below.

| 1776 | 1777 | 1778 | 1779 | 1780 | 1781 | 1782 | 1783 |

a. What were the main events of 1776 and 1777?
b. While George Rogers Clark was capturing Kaskaskia, what was happening in the South?

2. ANALYZING LEADERSHIP

George Washington was the most beloved American leader of his time. What qualities do you think made him such a respected leader?

3. THEME: CITIZENSHIP

What Revolutionary leaders displayed civic virtue by putting the good of the nation ahead of their own interests? Explain your answer.

4. RECOGNIZING EFFECTS

How did Britain's loss in the war allow free enterprise to develop in the United States?

5. APPLYING CITIZENSHIP SKILLS

How was the writing of *The American Crisis* an example of good U.S. citizenship?

Interact *with* History

How did the sacrifices you discussed before you read the chapter compare with what Patriots really did?

VISUAL SUMMARY

The American Revolution

People and Events of the Revolution

Military		Civilian	
George Washington	commanded the Continental Army.	Haym Salomon	helped finance the war for America.
Marquis de Lafayette	fought for the Americans.	Molly Pitcher	aided soldiers by bringing them water in battle.
John Burgoyne	surrendered to the Americans at Saratoga.	Thomas Paine	wrote *The American Crisis* to inspire Americans.
John Paul Jones	won a major naval victory for America.	Benjamin Franklin	was a diplomat to France and Britain.
George Rogers Clark	helped hold the Western frontier for America.	James Forten	was captured by the British but would not betray America.
Lord Cornwallis	surrendered at Yorktown, ending the war.	Nancy Hart	defended her Georgia home against Loyalist raiders.

Use the map and your knowledge of U.S. history to answer questions 1 and 2.

Additional Test Practice, pp. S1–S33.

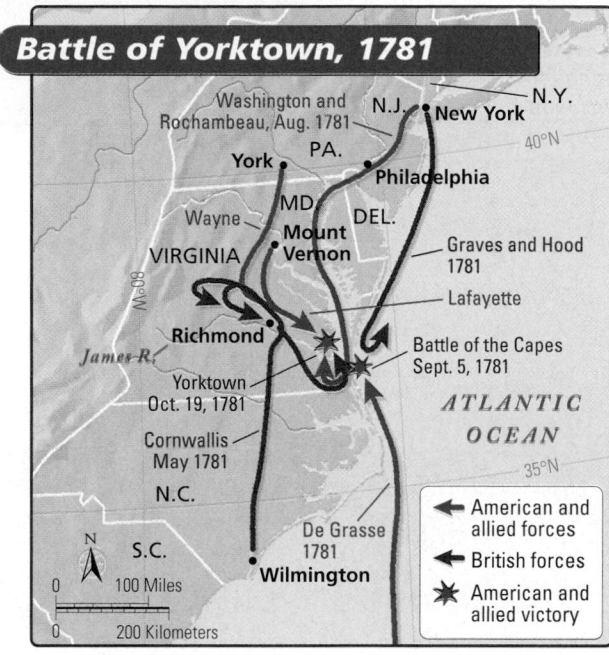

Battle of Yorktown, 1781

1. In what state was the Battle of Yorktown fought?
   A. North Carolina
   B. Pennsylvania
   C. South Carolina
   D. Virginia

2. Which of the following describes the route of the forces led by Cornwallis?
   A. south from York, PA to Yorktown, VA
   B. south from New York to Yorktown, VA
   C. north from Wilmington, NC to Richmond, VA
   D. north from Richmond, VA to Wilmington, NC

This quotation is from Thomas Paine discussing the Revolutionary War. Use the quotation and your knowledge of U.S. history to answer question 3.

PRIMARY SOURCE

These are the times that try men's souls. The summer soldier and the sunshine patriot will, in this crisis, shrink from the service of their country; but he that stands it now, deserves the love and thanks of man and woman.

Thomas Paine, *The American Crisis*

3. Who is Paine referring to as "the summer soldier and the sunshine patriot"?
   A. Americans who support the war only when it is going well
   B. Loyalists who never support the war efforts
   C. Americans who show continuous support for the war
   D. soldiers who perform best in good weather

TEST PRACTICE
CLASSZONE.COM

ALTERNATIVE ASSESSMENT

1. 📝 WRITING ABOUT HISTORY

Suppose you are a soldier at Valley Forge during the winter of 1777–1778. Write daily **journal** entries for one week, describing the harsh conditions of the camp and your physical and emotional state.

- Research Valley Forge in books or encyclopedias.
- Try to locate primary sources such as letters, diaries, and journals of soldiers at Valley Forge.

2. COOPERATIVE LEARNING

Working in groups, prepare a talk show in which guests discuss which side to take in the Revolutionary War. One group member should be the host. Other members should be guests. Consider some of the following guests: the wife of an American soldier, an enslaved African American, an Iroquois chief, a Quaker minister, and an employee of the British government.

INTEGRATED TECHNOLOGY

CREATING A MULTIMEDIA PRESENTATION

Choose a major battle of the Revolution. Then use the Internet and other library resources to research that battle. Gather information that represents the American and British points of view.

- Locate details about the battle, as well as primary sources, such as quotations from participants on both sides. Make copies of any images you find, being careful to credit your sources.
- Find music of the time period and sound effects.
- Once you have collected these audio and visual materials, combine them to create a multimedia presentation.

For more about the battles . . .

INTERNET ACTIVITY
CLASSZONE.COM

CHAPTER 8

Confederation to Constitution 1776–1791

Section 1
The Confederation Era

Section 2
Creating the Constitution

Section 3
Ratifying the Constitution

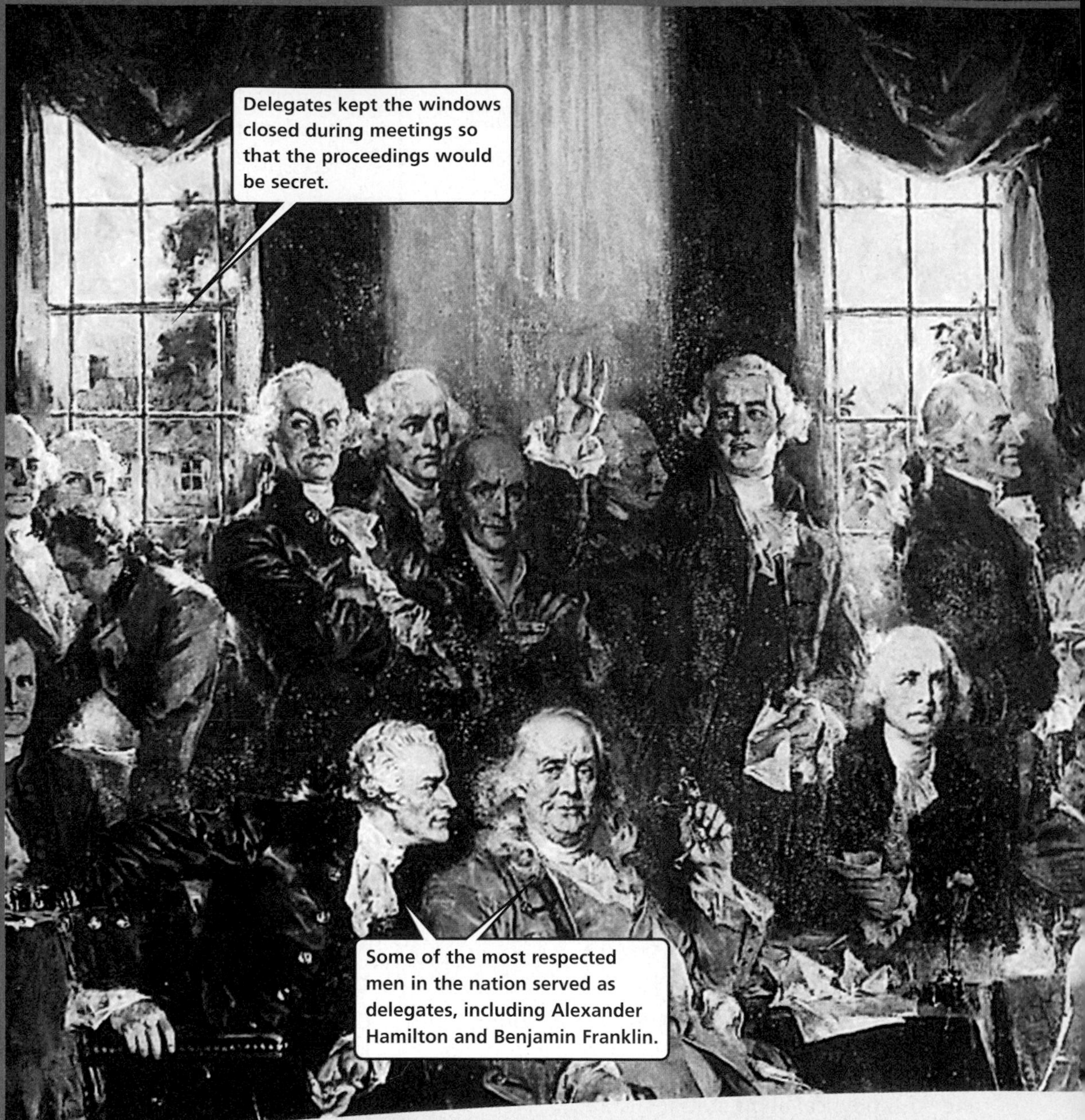
Delegates kept the windows closed during meetings so that the proceedings would be secret.
Some of the most respected men in the nation served as delegates, including Alexander Hamilton and Benjamin Franklin.

USA / World 1776

1777
Patriots win Battles of Saratoga.
Continental Congress passes the Articles of Confederation.

1779
Spain declares war on Britain.

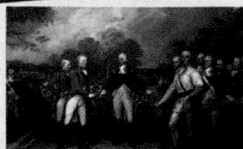

1781
Articles of Confederation go into effect.
British surrender at Yorktown.

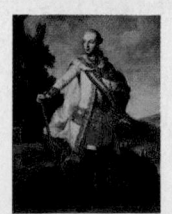

1781
Joseph II allows religious freedom for Christians in Austria.

1783
Treaty of Paris formally ends the Revolutionary War.

The delegates of the Constitutional Convention chose George Washington, hero of the Revolutionary War, to be president of the convention.

The year is 1787, and your young country needs to reform its government. Now everyone is wondering what the new government will be like. You have been called to a convention to decide how the new government should be organized.

How do you form a government?

What Do You Think?

- What will be your main goal in creating a new government?

- How will you get the people at the convention to agree on important issues?

RESEARCH LINKS
CLASSZONE.COM

Visit the Chapter 8 links for more information about America after the revolution.

1786–1787
Daniel Shays leads a rebellion of Massachusetts farmers.

1787
Constitutional Convention is held in Philadelphia.

1788
U.S. Constitution is ratified.

1789
George Washington becomes the first president of the United States.

1791
Bill of Rights is ratified.

1791

1785
Jean-Paul Blanchard and John Jefferies cross the English Channel in a balloon.

1787
Freetown, Sierra Leone, is made a home for freed slaves.

1789
French Revolution begins.

Reading Strategy: Solving Problems

What Do You Know?

What do you think of when people talk about the U.S. government? Why do nations have governments? What does the U.S. government do?

Think About

- what you've learned about the U.S. government from the news or your teachers
- what the purpose of a government is
- how the government affects your everyday life
- your responses to the Interact with History about forming a government (see page 219)

The Constitutional Convention met in what is now known as Independence Hall (shown above).

What Do You Want to Know?

 What questions do you have about how the four colonial regions developed? Record these questions in your notebook before you read the chapter.

Solving Problems

When you read history, look for how people solved problems they faced in the past. Copy the chart below in your notebook. Use it to identify the methods that Americans used to solve the problems faced by the nation after declaring its independence.

S See Skillbuilder Handbook, page R18.

Taking Notes

Problems	Solutions
Western lands	
Postwar depression	
Representation in the new government	
Slavery	

The Confederation Era

MAIN IDEA	WHY IT MATTERS NOW	TERMS & NAMES
The Articles of Confederation were too weak to govern the nation after the war ended.	The weakness of the Articles of Confederation led to the writing of the U.S. Constitution.	Wilderness Road Land Ordinance of 1785 republic Northwest Territory Articles of Northwest Ordinance Confederation Shays's Rebellion

ONE AMERICAN'S STORY

In 1775, Daniel Boone and 30 woodsmen cut a road over the Appalachian Mountains into Kentucky. After about 250 miles, they arrived in a meadow along the banks of the Kentucky River. Felix Walker, a member of Boone's party, described what they saw.

A VOICE FROM THE PAST

On entering the plain we were permitted to view a very interesting and romantic sight. A number of buffaloes . . . between two and three hundred, made off. . . . Such a sight some of us never saw before, nor perhaps ever may again.

Felix Walker, quoted in *The Life and Adventures of Daniel Boone*

Early travel to Kentucky is shown in this detail of *Daniel Boone Escorting Settlers Through the Cumberland Gap* (1851–1852) by George Caleb Bingham.

In the late 1700s, most Americans thought of Kentucky as the wild frontier. Some, like Boone, looked at the frontier and saw a world of opportunity. Exploring and governing these lands was one of the many challenges facing the new government of the United States.

Moving West

The trail into Kentucky that Daniel Boone helped build was called the **Wilderness Road**. This road was not easy to travel. It was too narrow for carts or wagons, but it became the main road into Kentucky. The settlers came on foot or on horseback. Settlers were drawn to Kentucky's rich river valleys, where few Native Americans lived. But some Native Americans, such as the Shawnee, did live, hunt, and fish in the area.

Tensions between Native Americans and settlers led to violent confrontations. But the settlers did not stop coming. By the early 1790s, about 100,000 Americans lived there. While settlers headed into the Western territories, the people in the East began to create new state governments.

Taking Notes

Use your chart to take notes about the western lands and postwar depression.

Problems	
Western lands	
Postwar depression	
Representation in the new government	
Slavery	

New State Governments

Once the American colonies declared independence, each of the states set out to create its own government. The framers, or creators, of the state constitutions did not want to destroy the political systems that they had had as colonies. They simply wanted to make those systems more democratic. Some states experimented with creating separate branches of government, giving different powers to different branches. By creating separate branches, Americans hoped to prevent the government from becoming too powerful.

Some states included a bill of rights in their constitutions as a way to keep the government under control. The idea of a bill of rights came from the English Bill of Rights of 1689. This was a list of rights that the government guaranteed to English citizens.

Although not all the states had a bill of rights, all of them did have a republican form of government. In a **republic,** the people choose representatives to govern them.

Background
Two states, Connecticut and Rhode Island, kept their old colonial charters as their constitutions. The other 11 states wrote new constitutions.

The Articles of Confederation

While the states were setting up their governments, Americans also discussed the form of their national government. During the Revolutionary War, Americans realized that they needed to unite to win the war against Britain. As Silas Deane, a diplomat from Connecticut, wrote, "United we stand, divided we fall."

In 1776, the Continental Congress began to develop a plan for a national government. Congress agreed that the government should be a republic. But the delegates disagreed about whether each state should have one vote or voting should be based on population. They also disagreed about whether the national government or the individual states should control the lands west of the Appalachians.

The Continental Congress eventually arrived at a final plan, called the **Articles of Confederation**. In the Articles, the national government had few powers, because many Americans were afraid that a strong government would lead to tyranny, or oppressive rule. The national government was run by a Confederation Congress. Each state had only one vote in the Congress. The national government had the power to wage war, make peace, sign treaties, and issue money.

But the Articles left most important powers to the states. These powers included the authority to set taxes and enforce national laws. The Articles proposed to leave the states in control of the lands west of the Appalachian Mountains.

"United we stand, divided we fall."

Silas Deane

*Reading*History

A. Reading a Map Look at the map on page 223 to see which states claimed territories in the West.

The Continental Congress passed the Articles of Confederation in November 1777. It then sent the Articles to the states for ratification, or approval. By July 1778, eight states had ratified the Articles. But some of the small states that did not have Western land claims refused to sign.

These states felt that unless the Western lands were placed under the control of the national government, they would be at a disadvantage. The states with Western lands could sell them to pay off debts left from the Revolution. But states without lands would have difficulty paying off the high war debts.

Over the next three years, all the states gave up their claims to Western lands. This led the small states to ratify the Articles. In 1781, Maryland became the 13th state to accept the Articles. As a result, the United States finally had an official government.

Reading **History**
B. Finding Main Ideas Why did the states without Western land claims want the other states to give up their claims?

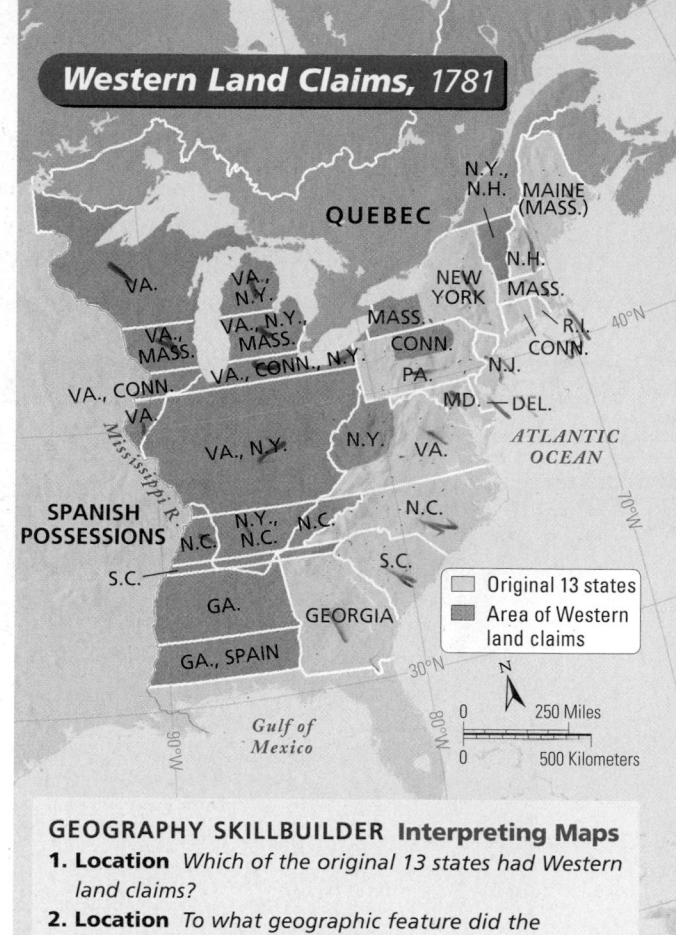

Western Land Claims, 1781

Original 13 states
Area of Western land claims

0   250 Miles
0   500 Kilometers

GEOGRAPHY SKILLBUILDER Interpreting Maps
1. **Location** *Which of the original 13 states had Western land claims?*
2. **Location** *To what geographic feature did the Western land claims extend?*

The Northwest Ordinance

One of the most important questions that the Confederation Congress faced was what to do with the Western lands that it now controlled. Congress passed important laws on how to divide and govern these lands—the Land Ordinance of 1785 and the Northwest Ordinance (1787). (See Geography in History on pages 226–227.)

The **Land Ordinance of 1785** called for surveyors to stake out six-mile-square plots, called townships, in the Western lands. These lands later became known as the **Northwest Territory**. The Northwest Territory included land that formed the states of Ohio, Indiana, Michigan, Illinois, and Wisconsin and part of Minnesota.

The **Northwest Ordinance** (1787) described how the Northwest Territory was to be governed. As the territory grew in population, it would gain rights to self-government. When there were 5,000 free males in an area, men who owned at least 50 acres of land could elect an assembly. When there were 60,000 people, they could apply to become a new state.

Background
According to the Northwest Ordinance, Native Americans were to be treated fairly, and their lands were not to be taken from them.

The Northwest Ordinance also set conditions for settlement in the Northwest Territory and outlined the settlers' rights. Slavery was outlawed, and the rivers were to be open to navigation by all. Freedom of religion and trial by jury were guaranteed.

The Northwest Ordinance was important because it set a pattern for the orderly growth of the United States. As the nation grew, it followed this pattern in territories added after the Northwest Territory.

Weaknesses of the Articles

Aside from its handling of land issues, however, the Confederation Congress had few successes. By the end of the Revolutionary War, the United States faced serious problems, and the Confederation Congress did not have enough power to solve them.

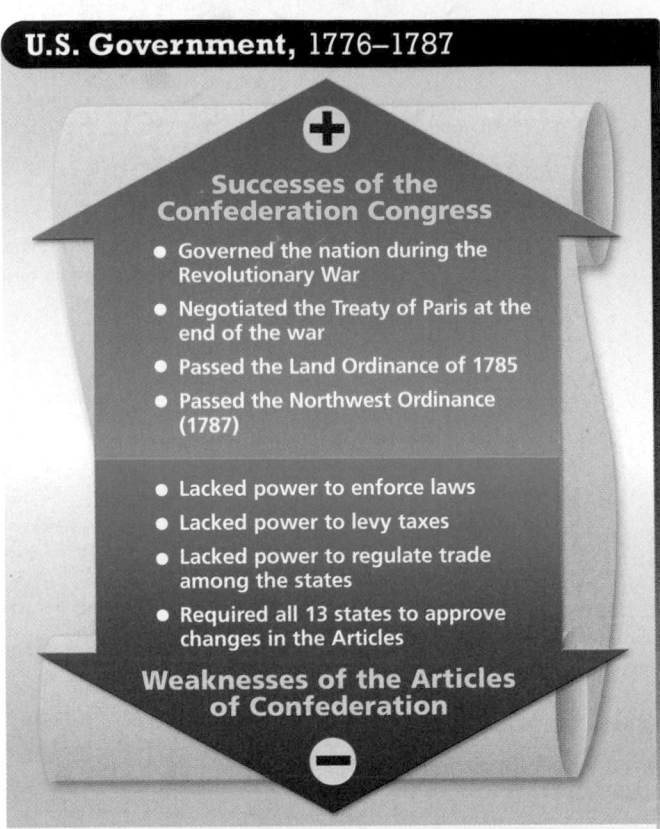

U.S. Government, 1776–1787

Successes of the Confederation Congress
- Governed the nation during the Revolutionary War
- Negotiated the Treaty of Paris at the end of the war
- Passed the Land Ordinance of 1785
- Passed the Northwest Ordinance (1787)

- Lacked power to enforce laws
- Lacked power to levy taxes
- Lacked power to regulate trade among the states
- Required all 13 states to approve changes in the Articles

Weaknesses of the Articles of Confederation

SKILLBUILDER Interpreting Charts
1. What do you think was the greatest success of the Confederation Congress?
2. What do you think was the greatest weakness of the Articles of Confederation?

Debt was a critical problem for the government. Congress had borrowed large sums to pay for the Revolutionary War. Much of that money was owed to soldiers of its own army. Upset at not being paid, several hundred soldiers surrounded the Pennsylvania State House where Congress was meeting in June 1783. The soldiers threatened the legislators, thrusting their bayonets through the windows. The delegates were forced to flee the city. The event was a clear sign of Congress's weakness.

Even if Congress wanted to pay the soldiers, it did not have the power to levy taxes. The national government depended on the states to send money to Congress. But the states sent very little money.

Congress was not alone in facing economic crises. People throughout the nation faced hard times. In Massachusetts, the economy was so bad that people rose up in arms against the government.

Reading **History**
C. Analyzing Causes How did debt cause problems for the U.S. government under the Articles of Confederation?

Shays's Rebellion

In the mid-1780s, Massachusetts faced economic problems, as did other states. People had little money, but the state continued to levy high taxes. The average family owed $200 in taxes per year—more money than most farmers made. Many Massachusetts farmers fell deeply into debt. Debt laws at the time were strict. Anyone who could not repay his debts would have his property auctioned off. If the auction didn't raise enough money to settle the debts, the debtor could be put in jail. In western Massachusetts, many jails were packed with debtors.

Farmers asked the Massachusetts legislature to provide debt relief. But the legislature refused—and the farmers rebelled. One of the leaders of the rebellion was a Revolutionary War veteran named Daniel Shays. He commanded a group of about 1,500 men.

In January 1787, Shays and his men marched on a federal arsenal, a place to store weapons. The arsenal was defended by 900 soldiers from the state militia. The militia quickly defeated Shays's men. But even though the militia put down **Shays's Rebellion,** as the uprising came to be known, the farmers won the sympathy of many people. America's leaders realized that an armed uprising of common farmers spelled danger for the nation.

Some leaders hoped that the nation's ills could be solved by strengthening the national government. In the next section, you'll read how Americans held a convention to change the Articles of Confederation.

Background
In 1788, Daniel Shays was pardoned for his actions.

Shays's rebels take over a Massachusetts courthouse. A stone marker rests on the spot of the rebellion.

Section 1 Assessment

1. Terms & Names

Explain the significance of:
- Wilderness Road
- republic
- Articles of Confederation
- Land Ordinance of 1785
- Northwest Territory
- Northwest Ordinance
- Shays's Rebellion

2. Using Graphics

Use a diagram like the one below to list some of the challenges Americans faced in shaping a new government.

Challenges

Which challenge do you think was the toughest? Why?

3. Main Ideas

a. What issues affected the Western territories between 1775 and 1787?

b. What were three successes of the Continental Congress?

c. What were the strengths and weaknesses of the Articles of Confederation?

4. Critical Thinking

Forming and Supporting Opinions Which side would you have supported during Shays's Rebellion—the farmers or the officials who called out the militia? Why?

THINK ABOUT
- the farmers' problems
- the farmers' march on the arsenal
- the job of the government

ACTIVITY OPTIONS

Write an **opinion article** about how the United States should govern the Western territories or draw a **map** showing how you would have divided the lands.

The Northwest Territory

The Northwest Territory was officially known as "the Territory Northwest of the River Ohio." In the mid-1780s, Congress decided to sell the land in the territory to settlers. The sale of land solved two problems. First, it provided cash for the government. Second, it increased American control over the land.

The Land Ordinance of 1785 outlined how the land in the Northwest Territory would be divided. Congress split the land into grids with clearly defined boundaries. It created townships that could be divided into sections, as shown on the map below. Each township was six miles by six miles. This was an improvement over earlier methods of setting boundaries. Previously, people had used rocks, trees, or other landmarks to set boundaries. There had been constant fights over disputed claims.

TOWNSHIP, 1785

36	30	24	18	12	6
35	29	23	17	11	5
34	28	22	16	10	4
33	27	21	15	9	3
32	26	20	14	8	2
31	25	19	13	7	1

Each township contained 36 sections. Each section was one square mile.

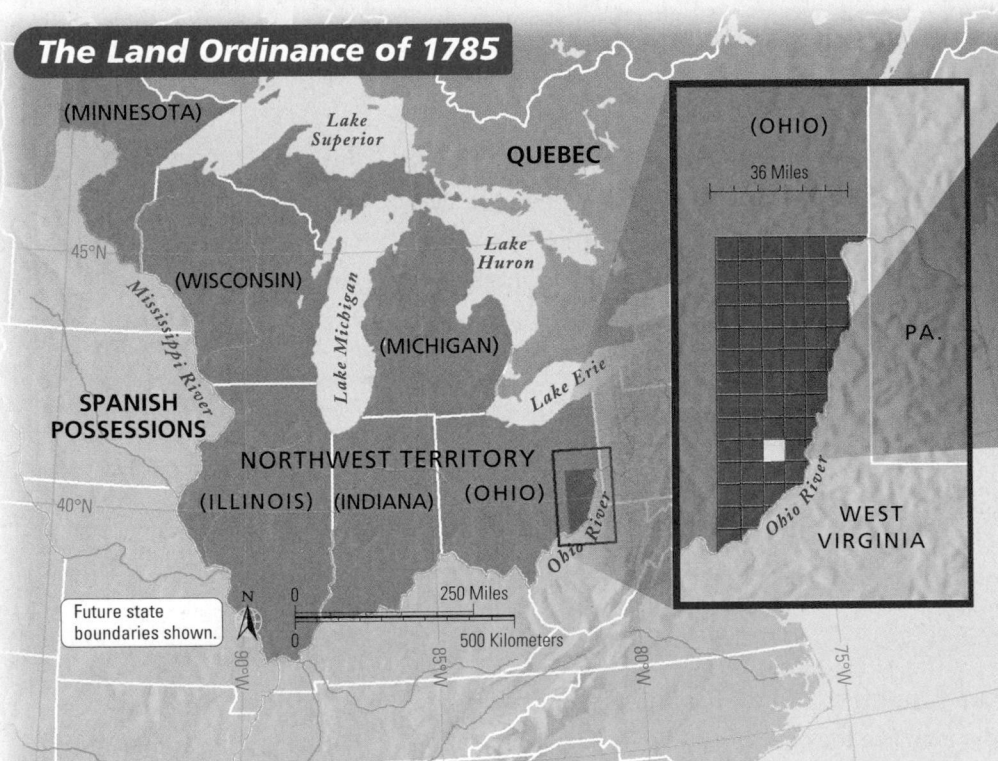

The Land Ordinance of 1785

(MINNESOTA)

Lake Superior

QUEBEC

45°N

Lake Huron

(WISCONSIN)

Lake Michigan

(MICHIGAN)

Lake Erie

Mississippi River

SPANISH POSSESSIONS

NORTHWEST TERRITORY

(ILLINOIS) (INDIANA) (OHIO)

40°N

Ohio River

(OHIO)

36 Miles

PA.

WEST VIRGINIA

Ohio River

Future state boundaries shown.

N

0   250 Miles

0   500 Kilometers

90°W   85°W   80°W   75°W

ARTIFACT FILE

The Theodolite The theodolite is a surveying tool. It consists of a telescope that can be moved from side to side and up and down. A theodolite measures angles and determines alignment. These functions are necessary for land surveyors to establish accurate boundaries for land claims.

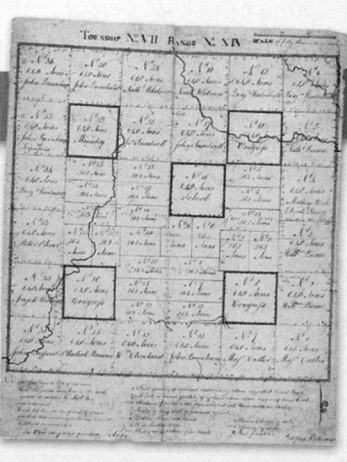

Township Map Congress reserved several plots (outlined on map) for special purposes. A few were set aside for later sale to raise money for the government. One plot was reserved to support a local school.

1 The first things settlers needed were food and shelter. Cutting trees provided fields for crops and wood for log cabins. The first crop most farmers planted was corn. Even if the land was not fully cleared of trees, farmers planted corn between the stumps.

2 A shortage of labor meant that a farmer working alone was doing well if he cleared several acres a year. As a result, few farms were completely fenced in, and forest covered most of the property. Hogs were allowed to find food in the woods. Farmers collected apples from trees and used sap to make syrup.

3 Over time, families planted fruits and vegetables. Cattle raising also became more common. Beef cattle supplied families with meat. Dairy cattle provided milk. Families could sell extra fruits, vegetables, and dairy products, such as butter and cheese.

CONNECT TO GEOGRAPHY

1. **Region** What was the land in the Northwest Territory like before Americans settled there?
2. **Human-Environment Interaction** How did American settlers affect the landscape in the territory?

   G See Geography Handbook, pages 4–5.

CONNECT TO HISTORY

3. **Making Inferences** Why did so many people buy land in the new territory?

On-Line Field Trip

The Ohio Historical Society is located in Columbus, Ohio. It maintains a Web site called Ohio History Central that includes information on the Ohio portion of the Northwest Territory.

For more about the Northwest Territory . . .

RESEARCH LINKS
CLASSZONE.COM

Creating the Constitution

2

MAIN IDEA	WHY IT MATTERS NOW	TERMS & NAMES
The states sent delegates to a convention to solve the problems of the Articles of Confederation.	The Constitutional Convention formed the plan of government that the United States still has today.	Constitutional Convention • James Madison • Virginia Plan • New Jersey Plan • Great Compromise • Three-Fifths Compromise

ONE AMERICAN'S STORY

On May 15, 1787, Virginia Governor Edmund Randolph arrived in Philadelphia. The young nation faced lawlessness, as Shays's Rebellion had shown. Now delegates from throughout the states were coming to Philadelphia to discuss reforming the government. Early in the convention Randolph rose to speak.

A VOICE FROM THE PAST

Let us not be afraid to view with a steady eye the [dangers] with which we are surrounded. . . . Are we not on the eve of [a civil] war, which is only to be prevented by the hopes from this convention?

Edmund Randolph, quoted in *Edmund Randolph: A Biography*

Edmund Randolph (left) and the other delegates gathered in the Pennsylvania State House (above).

Over the next four months, the delegates debated how best to keep the United States from falling apart. In this section, you will read about the Convention of 1787 and the creation of the U.S. Constitution.

Taking Notes

Use your chart to take notes about the new government and slavery.

Problems	
Western lands	
Postwar depression	
Representation in the new government	
Slavery	

A Constitutional Convention Is Called

In 1786, a series of events began that would eventually lead to a new form of government for the United States. In September of that year, delegates from five states met in Annapolis, Maryland, to discuss ways to promote trade among their states. At the time, most states placed high taxes on goods from other states. The delegates believed that creating national trade laws would help the economies of all the states.

Making such changes required amending the Articles of Confederation, because the national government had been granted no power to regulate trade among the states. The Annapolis delegates, led by Alexander Hamilton of New York, called for the states to send representatives to

Philadelphia the following May to discuss such changes.

At first, many Americans doubted that the national government needed strengthening. But news of Shays's Rebellion in late 1786 and early 1787 quickly changed many people's minds. Fearing that rebellion might spread, 12 states sent delegates to the meeting in Philadelphia in the summer of 1787. Only Rhode Island refused to participate.

Background
Rhode Island did not send delegates because it feared that a strong national government would force people to repay the war debts on difficult terms.

The Convention's Delegates

The 55 delegates to the **Constitutional Convention,** as the Philadelphia meeting became known, were a very impressive group. About half were lawyers. Others were planters, merchants, and doctors. Three-fourths of them had been representatives in the Continental Congress. Many had been members of their state legislatures and had helped write their state constitutions. Along with other leaders of the time, these delegates are called the Founders, or Founding Fathers, of the United States.

America's most famous men were at the Constitutional Convention. George Washington, the hero of the Revolution, came out of retirement for the meeting. Benjamin Franklin, the famous scientist and statesman, lent his wit and wisdom to the convention. One of the ablest delegates was **James Madison.** Madison had read more than a hundred books on government in preparation for the meeting. When Thomas Jefferson, serving as ambassador to France, read the list of delegates, he wrote, "It is really an assembly of demigods."

*Reading*History
A. Evaluating
How well do the characteristics of the Founders serve as models of civic virtue?

Not everyone was at the Constitutional Convention. Thomas Jefferson and John Adams were overseas at their diplomatic posts. But they wrote home to encourage the delegates. Others had a less positive outlook on the convention. For example, Patrick Henry, who had been elected as a delegate from Virginia, refused to attend. He said he "smelled a rat in Philadelphia, tending toward monarchy."

Also, the convention did not reflect the diverse U.S. population of the 1780s. There were no Native Americans, African Americans, or women among the delegates. The nation's early leaders did not consider these groups of people to be citizens and did not invite any of them to attend. However, the framework of government the Founders established is the very one that would eventually provide full rights and responsibilities to all Americans.

The Delegates Assemble

Most of the delegates arrived at the Constitutional Convention without a clear idea of what to expect. Some thought they would only draft

America's
HERITAGE

INDEPENDENCE HALL
The Pennsylvania State House, where the Constitutional Convention took place, is now called Independence Hall. It is protected as part of a national park in Philadelphia.

The State House itself was the site where George Washington received his commission to lead the Continental Army and where the Declaration of Independence was signed. The Liberty Bell is nearby. Many visitors come to Philadelphia to stand in the building where much of America's early history as a nation was made.

JAMES MADISON

1751–1836

James Madison was a short, soft-spoken man, but he may have made the greatest contribution of any of the Founders at the Constitutional Convention. He took thorough notes of the convention's proceedings. His notes are the most detailed picture we have of the debates and drama of the convention.

But Madison did not just observe the convention. He was perhaps the most important participant. One of the other delegates called him "the best informed Man of any point in debate." Madison was so important that he earned the title "Father of the Constitution."

How did Madison contribute to the Constitutional Convention?

amendments to the Articles of Confederation. Others thought they would design an entirely new plan for the government. But they all agreed that the government should protect people's rights.

Back in 1776, many Americans thought that government was the main threat to people's rights. But by 1787, many realized that the people often came into conflict and needed a government that could maintain order. As a result, the government had to be strong enough to protect people's rights but not too strong to be controlled. Madison later wrote about this problem.

A VOICE FROM THE PAST

If men were angels, no government would be necessary. If angels were to govern men, neither external nor internal controls on government would be necessary. In framing a government which is to be administered by men over men, the great difficulty lies in this: you must first enable the government to control the governed; and in the next place oblige it [the government] to control itself.

James Madison, *The Federalist* "Number 51"

*Reading*History

B. Using Primary Sources According to Madison, what is the central problem in framing a government?

This was the challenge that faced the delegates: how to set up a strong but limited federal government. By May 25, 1787, at least two delegates from each of seven states had arrived in Philadelphia. With 29 delegates in attendance, the convention was officially under way.

The Convention Begins

The first order of business was to elect a president for the convention. Robert Morris of Pennsylvania nominated George Washington. No American was more respected or admired than Washington. Every delegate voted for him. Washington's quiet and dignified leadership set a solemn and serious tone for the convention.

At their next meeting, the delegates decided on the rules for the convention. They wanted to be able to consider all ideas and to be able to change sides in any debate. They did not want to be pressured by the politics of the day. For these reasons, they decided that their discussions would remain secret. To ensure privacy, the windows in their meeting room were kept shut even though it was summer. Guards were posted outside the door. Whenever the door was opened, the delegates stopped talking. With the secrecy rule approved, they got down to business.

*Reading*History

C. Making Decisions Do you agree with the Founders' decision to keep the convention secret? Why or why not?

The Virginia Plan

On May 29, the delegates began the real work of designing a new national government. Presiding over the convention, George Washington

The delegates at the Constitutional Convention debated the Constitution intensely.

recognized Edmund Randolph as the first speaker. Randolph offered a plan for a whole new government. The plan became known as the **Virginia Plan.** Madison, Randolph, and the other Virginia delegates had drawn up the plan while they waited for the convention to open.

The Virginia Plan proposed a government that would have three branches. The first branch of government was the legislature, which made the laws. The second branch was the executive, which enforced the laws. The third branch was the judiciary, which interpreted the laws.

The Virginia Plan proposed a legislature with two houses. In both houses, the number of representatives from each state would be based on the state's population or its wealth. The legislature would have the power to levy taxes, regulate commerce, and make laws "in all cases where the separate states are incompetent [unable]."

The Virginia Plan led to weeks of debate. Because they had larger populations, larger states supported the plan. It would give them greater representation in the legislature. The smaller states opposed this plan. They worried that the larger states would end up ruling the others. Delaware delegate John Dickinson voiced the concerns of the small states.

*Reading***History**
D. Summarizing
What was the Virginia Plan?

> *"If men were angels, no government would be necessary."*
> James Madison

A VOICE FROM THE PAST

Some of the members from the small states wish for two branches in the general legislature and are friends to a good [strong] national government; but we would sooner submit [give in] to a foreign power than submit to be deprived, in both branches of the legislature, of an equal suffrage [vote], and thereby be thrown under the domination of the larger states.

John Dickinson, quoted in *Mr. Madison's Constitution*

The Great Compromise

In response to the Virginia Plan, New Jersey delegate William Paterson presented an alternative on June 15. The **New Jersey Plan** called for a legislature with only one house. In it, each state would have one vote. In providing equal representation to each state, the New Jersey Plan was similar to the Articles of Confederation.

Even though the New Jersey Plan gave the legislature the power to regulate trade and to raise money by taxing foreign goods, it did not offer the broad powers proposed by the Virginia Plan. The delegates

The Great Compromise

VIRGINIA PLAN

- The legislative branch would have two houses.

- Both houses in the legislature would assign representatives according to state population or wealth.

NEW JERSEY PLAN

- The legislature would have one house.

- Each state would have one vote in the legislature.

THE GREAT COMPROMISE

- The Senate would give each state equal representation.

- The legislature would have two houses.

- The House of Representatives would have representation according to state population.

SKILLBUILDER Interpreting Charts

1. Which plan appealed more to the small states?
2. Did the Great Compromise include more of what the large states wanted or more of what the small states wanted?

voted on these two plans on June 19. The Virginia Plan won and became the framework for drafting the Constitution.

During the rest of June, the delegates argued over representation in the legislature. Emotions ran high as the delegates struggled for a solution. In desperation, the delegates selected a committee to work out a compromise in early July. The committee offered the **Great Compromise**. (Some people also refer to it as the Connecticut Compromise.)

To satisfy the smaller states, each state would have an equal number of votes in the Senate. To satisfy the larger states, the committee set representation in the House of Representatives according to state populations. More than a week of arguing followed the introduction of the plan, but on July 16, 1787, the convention passed it.

Background
Roger Sherman of Connecticut is widely credited with proposing the Great Compromise.

Slavery and the Constitution

Because representation in the House of Representatives would be based on the population of each state, the delegates had to decide who would be counted in that population. The Southern states had many more slaves than the Northern states. Southerners wanted the slaves to be counted as part of the general population for representation but not for taxation. Northerners argued that slaves were not citizens and should not be counted for representation but should be counted for taxation.

On this issue, the delegates reached another compromise, known as the **Three-Fifths Compromise.** Under this compromise, three-fifths of the slave population would be counted when setting direct taxes on the states. This three-fifths ratio also would be used to determine representation in the legislature.

The delegates had another heated debate about the slave trade. Slavery had already been outlawed in several Northern states. All of the Northern states and several of the Southern states had banned the

*Reading*History
E. Forming and Supporting Opinions Did the delegates do the right thing in agreeing to the Three-Fifths Compromise? Explain.

importation of slaves. Many Northerners wanted to see this ban extended to the rest of the nation. But Southern slaveholders strongly disagreed. The delegates from South Carolina and Georgia stated that they would never accept any plan "unless their right to import slaves be untouched." Again, the delegates settled on a compromise. On August 29, they agreed that Congress could not ban the slave trade until 1808.

Regulating Trade

Aside from delaying any ban on the slave trade, the Constitution placed few limits on Congress's power "to regulate commerce with foreign nations, and among the several states, and with the Indian tribes." Most delegates were glad that Congress would regulate—and even promote—commerce. After all, commercial problems were the main cause of the Annapolis Convention in 1786. Southerners, however, succeeded in banning Congress from taxing exports because Southern economies depended on exports. The commerce clause also showed the shadowy status that Native Americans had under the Constitution. They were neither foreign nations nor part of the separate states.

The Constitutional Convention continued to meet into September. On Saturday, September 15, 1787, the delegates voted their support for the Constitution in its final form. On Sunday, it was written out on four sheets of thick parchment. On Monday, all but three delegates signed the Constitution. It was then sent, with a letter signed by George Washington, to the Confederation Congress, which sent it to the states for ratification, or approval. In the next section, you will read about the debate over ratification.

Now and then

PRESERVING THE CONSTITUTION

The National Archives is responsible for preserving the 200-year-old sheets of parchment on which the original Constitution was first written.

The Archives stores the document in an airtight glass case enclosed in a 55-ton vault of steel and concrete. Every few years, scientists examine the pages with the latest technology. For the last examination in 1995, they used fiber-optic light sources and computer-guided electronic cameras designed for space exploration.

Section **2** *Assessment*

1. Terms & Names

Explain the significance of:

• Constitutional Convention
• James Madison
• Virginia Plan
• New Jersey Plan
• Great Compromise
• Three-Fifths Compromise

2. Using Graphics

Use a chart like the one below to take notes on the contributions made by the leading delegates at the Constitutional Convention.

Delegate	Contribution

3. Main Ideas

a. What was the relationship between the Annapolis Convention and the Constitutional Convention?

b. What is the significance of the date 1787?

c. How did the Constitutional Convention reach a compromise on the issue of slavery?

4. Critical Thinking

Analyzing Points of View How did the delegates at the convention differ on the issue of representation in the new government?

THINK ABOUT

• the large states and the small states
• the Virginia Plan
• the New Jersey Plan
• the Great Compromise

ACTIVITY OPTIONS

TECHNOLOGY

ART

Think about the Three-Fifths Compromise. Make an **audio recording** of a speech or draw a **political cartoon** that expresses your views on the issue.

3

Ratifying the Constitution

MAIN IDEA	WHY IT MATTERS NOW	TERMS & NAMES
Americans across the nation debated whether the Constitution would produce the best government.	American liberties today are protected by the U.S. Constitution, including the Bill of Rights.	federalism *The Federalist* papers Federalists George Mason Antifederalists Bill of Rights

ONE AMERICAN'S STORY

In 1788, in Hartford, Connecticut, 168 delegates met to decide whether their state should ratify the U.S. Constitution. Samuel Huntington, Connecticut's governor, addressed the assembly.

A VOICE FROM THE PAST

This is a new event in the history of mankind. Heretofore, most governments have been formed by tyrants and imposed on mankind by force. Never before did a people, . . . meet together by their representatives and . . . frame for themselves a system of government.

Samuel Huntington, quoted in *Original Meanings*

Samuel Huntington

In this section, you will learn about the ratification of the Constitution.

Taking Notes

Use your chart to take notes about the new government.

Problems	
Western lands	
Postwar depression	
Representation in the new government	
Slavery	

Federalists and Antifederalists

By the time the convention in Connecticut opened, Americans had already been debating the new Constitution for months. The document had been printed in newspapers and handed out in pamphlets across the United States. The framers of the Constitution knew that the document would cause controversy. They immediately began to campaign for ratification, or approval, of the Constitution.

The framers suspected that people might be afraid the Constitution would take too much power away from the states. To address this fear, the framers explained that the Constitution was based on federalism. **Federalism** is a system of government in which power is shared between the central (or federal) government and the states. Linking themselves to the idea of federalism, the people who supported the Constitution took the name **Federalists.**

People who opposed the Constitution were called **Antifederalists.** They thought the Constitution took too much power away from the

Vocabulary
aristocracy:
a group or class
considered supe-
rior to others

states and did not guarantee rights for the people. Some were afraid that a strong president might be declared king. Others thought the Senate might turn into a powerful aristocracy. In either case, the liberties won at great cost during the Revolution might be lost.

Antifederalists published their views about the Constitution in newspapers and pamphlets. They used logical arguments to convince people to oppose the Constitution. But they also tried to stir people's emotions by charging that it would destroy American liberties. As one Antifederalist wrote, "After so recent a triumph over British despots [oppressive rulers], . . . it is truly astonishing that a set of men among ourselves should have had the effrontery [nerve] to attempt the destruction of our liberties."

The Federalist Papers

The Federalists did not sit still while the Antifederalists attacked the Constitution. They wrote essays to answer the Antifederalists' attacks. The best known of the Federalist essays are ***The Federalist* papers**. These essays first appeared as letters in New York newspapers. They were later published together in a book called *The Federalist*.

Three well-known politicians wrote *The Federalist* papers—James Madison, Alexander Hamilton, and John Jay, the secretary of foreign affairs for the Confederation Congress. Like the Antifederalists, the Federalists appealed to reason and emotion. In *The Federalist* papers, Hamilton described why people should support ratification.

*Reading***History**
**A. Making
Inferences** What
does Hamilton
think will happen
if the Constitution
is not ratified?

A VOICE FROM THE PAST

Yes, my countrymen, . . . I am clearly of opinion it is in your interest to adopt it [the Constitution]. I am convinced that this is the safest course for your liberty, your dignity, and your happiness.

Alexander Hamilton, *The Federalist* "Number 1"

Federalists and Antifederalists

FEDERALISTS	ANTIFEDERALISTS
• Supported removing some powers from the states and giving more powers to the national government	• Wanted important political powers to remain with the states
• Favored dividing powers among different branches of government	• Wanted the legislative branch to have more power than the executive
• Proposed a single person to lead the executive branch	• Feared that a strong executive might become a king or tyrant
	• Believed a bill of rights needed to be added to the Constitution to protect people's rights

SKILLBUILDER Interpreting Charts
1. *Which group wanted a stronger central government?*
2. *If you had been alive in 1787, would you have been a Federalist or an Antifederalist?*

John Jay

George Mason

HISTORY *through***ART**

Supporters of the Constitution turned out in parades like this one in New York in 1788. The "Ship of State" float has Alexander Hamilton's name on it to celebrate his role in creating the Constitution.

What does the picture indicate about the importance of the Constitution in people's lives?

The Federalists had an important advantage over the Antifederalists. Most of the newspapers supported the Constitution, giving the Federalists more publicity than the Antifederalists. Even so, there was strong opposition to ratification in Massachusetts, North Carolina, Rhode Island, New York, and Virginia. If some of these states failed to ratify the Constitution, the United States might not survive.

The Battle for Ratification

The first four state conventions to ratify the Constitution were held in December 1787. It was a good month for the Federalists. Delaware, New Jersey, and Pennsylvania voted for ratification. In January 1788, Georgia and Connecticut ratified the Constitution. Massachusetts joined these states in early February.

By late June, nine states had voted to ratify the Constitution. That meant that the document was now officially ratified. But New York and Virginia had not yet cast their votes. There were many powerful Antifederalists in both of those states. Without Virginia, the new government would lack the support of the largest state. Without New York, the nation would be separated into two parts geographically.

Virginia's convention opened the first week in June. The patriot Patrick Henry fought against ratification. **George Mason,** perhaps the most influential Virginian aside from Washington, also was opposed to it. Mason had been a delegate to the Constitutional Convention in Philadelphia, but he had refused to sign the final document. Both Henry and Mason would not consider voting for the Constitution until a bill of rights was added. A bill of rights is a set of rules that defines people's rights.

James Madison was also at Virginia's convention. He suggested that Virginia follow Massachusetts's lead and ratify the Constitution, and he recommended the addition of a bill of rights. With the addition of a bill of rights likely, Virginia ratified the Constitution at the end of June.

*Reading***History**
B. Drawing Conclusions How did the lack of a bill of rights endanger the Constitution?

The news of Virginia's vote arrived while the New York convention was in debate. The Antifederalists had outnumbered the Federalists when the convention had begun. But with the news of Virginia's ratification, New Yorkers decided to join the Union. New York also called for a bill of rights.

It was another year before North Carolina ratified the Constitution. In 1790, Rhode Island became the last state to ratify it. By then, the new Congress had already written a bill of rights and submitted it to the states for approval.

The Bill of Rights

Background
The seven states that asked for a bill of rights were Massachusetts, South Carolina, New Hampshire, Virginia, New York, North Carolina, and Rhode Island.

At the same time that seven of the states ratified the Constitution, they asked that it be amended to include a bill of rights. Supporters of a bill of rights hoped that it would set forth the rights of all Americans. They believed it was needed to protect people against the power of the national government.

Madison, who was elected to the new Congress in the winter of 1789, took up the cause. He proposed a set of changes to the Constitution. Congress edited Madison's list and proposed placing the amendments at the end of the Constitution in a separate section.

The amendments went to the states for ratification. As with the Constitution, three-quarters of the states had to ratify the amendments for them to take effect. With Virginia's vote in 1791, ten of the amendments were ratified and became law. These ten amendments to the U.S. Constitution became known as the **Bill of Rights**. (See the Constitution Handbook, pages 266-268.)

The passage of the Bill of Rights was one of the first acts of the new government. In the next chapter, you will read about other issues that faced the new government.

America's HERITAGE

RELIGIOUS FREEDOM

Freedom of religion was an important part of the First Amendment. Jefferson and Madison believed that government enforcement of religious laws was the source of much social conflict. They supported freedom of religion as a way to prevent such conflict.

Even before Madison wrote the Bill of Rights, he worked to ensure religious liberty in Virginia. In 1786, he helped pass the Virginia Statute for Religious Freedom, originally written by Jefferson in 1777.

Section 3 Assessment

1. Terms & Names

Explain the significance of:
• federalism
• Federalists
• Antifederalists
• *The Federalist* papers
• George Mason
• Bill of Rights

2. Using Graphics

Use a diagram like the one below to compare and contrast the Federalists and the Antifederalists.

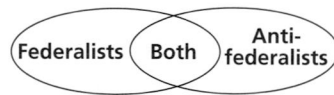

Which group do you think made the stronger argument about ratification? Why?

3. Main Ideas

a. What were Patrick Henry's and George Mason's views on ratification?

b. How did the Federalists and the Antifederalists try to convince people to take their sides in the debate over the Constitution?

c. What was the significance of the Bill of Rights?

4. Critical Thinking

Recognizing Propaganda
Reread the quotation by Hamilton on page 235. Is it an example of propaganda? Why or why not?

THINK ABOUT
• Hamilton's use of the word *countrymen*
• Hamilton's reference to liberty, dignity, and happiness

ACTIVITY OPTIONS

SPEECH
LANGUAGE ARTS

Review the major arguments for and against ratification of the Constitution.
Hold a **press conference** or write a **news report** on the ratification debate.

The Federalist "Number 51"

Setting the Stage James Madison wrote 29 essays in *The Federalist* papers to argue in favor of ratifying the Constitution. In *The Federalist* "Number 51," Madison explains how the government set up by the Constitution will protect the rights of the people by weakening the power of any interest, or group, to dominate the government. **See Primary Source Explorer** ⊚

A CLOSER LOOK

MINORITY RIGHTS

In the 1700s, people feared that democratic majorities could turn into mobs that would violate other people's rights. Madison had to explain how the Constitution would prevent this.

1. What two methods does Madison suggest a society can use to protect minority rights?

A CLOSER LOOK

REPUBLICS IN LARGE SOCIETIES

For centuries, people believed that only small societies could be republics. But Madison argues that large societies are more likely to remain republics.

2. Why does Madison believe that a large republic is likely to protect justice?

It is of great importance in a republic not only to guard the society against the oppression of its rulers, but to guard one part of the society against the injustice of the other part. Different interests necessarily exist in different classes of citizens. If a majority be united by a common interest, the rights of the minority will be insecure. There are but two methods of providing against this evil: the one by creating a will in the community independent of the majority—that is, of the society itself; the other, by **comprehending**[1] in the society so many separate descriptions of citizens as will render an unjust combination of a majority of the whole very improbable, if not **impracticable**.[2] . . .

Whilst[3] all authority in it will be derived from and dependent on the society, the society itself will be broken into so many parts, interests and classes of citizens, that the rights of individuals, or of the minority, will be in little danger from interested combinations of the majority. In a free government the security for civil rights must be the same as that for religious rights. It consists in the one case in the multiplicity of interests, and in the other in the **multiplicity of sects**.[4] . . .

In the extended republic of the United States, and among the great variety of interests, parties, and sects which it embraces, a **coalition**[5] of a majority of the whole society could seldom take place on any other principles than those of justice and the general good. . . .

It is no less certain than it is important . . . that the larger the society, provided it lie within a practicable sphere, the more duly capable it will be of self-government. And happily for the republican cause, the practicable sphere may be carried to a very great extent by a **judicious modification**[6] and mixture of the *federal principle*.

—James Madison

---

1. **comprehending:** understanding.
2. **impracticable:** not practical or realistic.
3. **whilst:** while.
4. **multiplicity of sects:** large number of groups.
5. **coalition:** alliance of groups.
6. **judicious modification:** careful change.

Objections to the Constitution

Setting the Stage George Mason was one of the leading Antifederalists. In "Objections to the Constitution of Government Formed by the Convention," he listed his reasons for opposing ratification. Above all, he feared that the Constitution created a government that would destroy democracy in the young nation. **See Primary Source Explorer** 💿

There is no Declaration of Rights; and the Laws of the general Government being **paramount**[1] to the Laws and Constitutions of the several States, the Declaration of Rights in the separate States are no Security. Nor are the people secured even in the Enjoyment of the Benefits of the common-Law. . . .

In the House of Representatives, there is not the Substance, but the Shadow only of Representation; which can never produce proper Information in the Legislature, or inspire Confidence in the People; the Laws will therefore be generally made by Men little concern'd in, and **unacquainted**[2] with their Effects and Consequences.

The Senate have the Power of altering all Money-Bills, and of originating Appropriations of Money and the **Sallerys**[3] of the Officers of their own Appointment in **Conjunction**[4] with the President of the United States; altho' they are not the Representatives of the People, or **amenable**[5] to them. . . .

The President of the United States has the unrestrained Power of granting Pardon for Treason; which may be sometimes exercised to screen from Punishment those whom he had secretly **instigated**[6] to commit the Crime, and thereby prevent a Discovery of his own Guilt.

This Government will **commence**[7] in a moderate **Aristocracy**;[8] it is at present impossible to foresee whether it will, in [its] Operation, produce a **Monarchy**,[9] or a corrupt oppressive Aristocracy; it will most probably vibrate some Years between the two, and then terminate in the one or the other.

—George Mason

A CLOSER LOOK

DECLARATION OF RIGHTS

At the time of the ratification debate, Americans across the nation complained that the Constitution did not include a bill of rights.

3. What arguments does Mason make about the lack of a Declaration of Rights?

A CLOSER LOOK

ABUSE OF POWER

Mason believed that presidents might abuse the power to grant pardons for treason in order to protect the guilty.

4. Can you think of any presidents who have granted pardons?

1. **paramount:** most important.
2. **unacquainted:** unfamiliar.
3. **sallerys:** salaries.
4. **conjunction:** joining.
5. **amenable:** agreeable.
6. **instigated:** caused.
7. **commence:** begin.
8. **aristocracy:** rule by a few, usually nobles.
9. **monarchy:** rule by one, usually a king.

Interactive Primary Sources Assessment

1. Main Ideas

a. Why does Madison believe that a society broken into many parts will not endanger minority rights?

b. What does Mason argue might happen if the president had the power to pardon people?

c. For each writer, what is one example of a fact and one example of an opinion?

2. Critical Thinking

Drawing Conclusions Who do you think makes the stronger argument? Explain your reasons.

THINK ABOUT
- what you know about the history of the United States
- the evidence used by each writer

Chapter ❽ ASSESSMENT

Confederation to Constitution

Articles of Confederation

1777
Continental Congress passes the Articles of Confederation.

1777–1781
States debate ratification of the Articles of Confederation.

1781
Articles of Confederation go into effect.

1786
Annapolis Convention is held.

1786–1787
Shays's Rebellion occurs.

1787
Constitutional Convention is held in Philadelphia.

1788
U.S. Constitution is ratified.

1789
Government created by the new Constitution takes power.

★

1791
Bill of Rights is added to the Constitution.

Constitution
Bill of Rights

TERMS & NAMES

Briefly explain the significance of each of the following.

1. republic
2. Articles of Confederation
3. Northwest Ordinance
4. Shays's Rebellion
5. Constitutional Convention
6. James Madison
7. Great Compromise
8. Federalists
9. George Mason
10. Bill of Rights

REVIEW QUESTIONS

The Confederation Era (pages 221–227)

1. What is the Wilderness Road, and where did it lead?
2. What problems did the Confederation Congress successfully address?
3. What powers did the government have under the Articles of Confederation?
4. How did Shays's Rebellion affect people's views on the Articles of Confederation?

Creating the Constitution (pages 228–233)

5. What groups of people were not represented at the Constitutional Convention?
6. What were some things the delegates agreed on at the convention?
7. What compromises did the delegates make during the convention?

Ratifying the Constitution (pages 234–239)

8. What is federalism?
9. Why were Virginia and New York important in the battle for ratification of the Constitution?
10. Why did some states think that it was necessary to add a bill of rights to the Constitution?

CRITICAL THINKING

1. USING YOUR NOTES: SOLVING PROBLEMS

Problems	Solutions
Western lands	
Postwar depression	
Representation in the new government	
Slavery	

Using your completed chart, answer the questions below.

a. What were the major problems facing the nation during the Confederation Era?
b. How well did the nation solve these problems? Explain.

2. ANALYZING LEADERSHIP

Think about the leaders discussed in this chapter. Based on their actions, which leader do you think made the greatest contribution to the Constitutional Convention? Why?

3. THEME: DEMOCRATIC IDEALS

How do the Articles of Confederation and the Constitution each carry out democratic ideals?

4. APPLYING CITIZENSHIP SKILLS

Do you think the Founders were right to make the compromises they did in the Constitution on the issues of representation and slavery? What might have happened if they had not compromised?

5. RECOGNIZING EFFECTS

How might U.S. history be different if Virginia had refused to ratify the Constitution? If New York had refused? If both had refused?

Interact *with* History

How did your ideas about how you would form a government change after reading this chapter?

STANDARDS-BASED ASSESSMENT

Use the map and your knowledge of U.S. history to answer questions 1 and 2.

Additional Test Practice, pp. S1–S33.

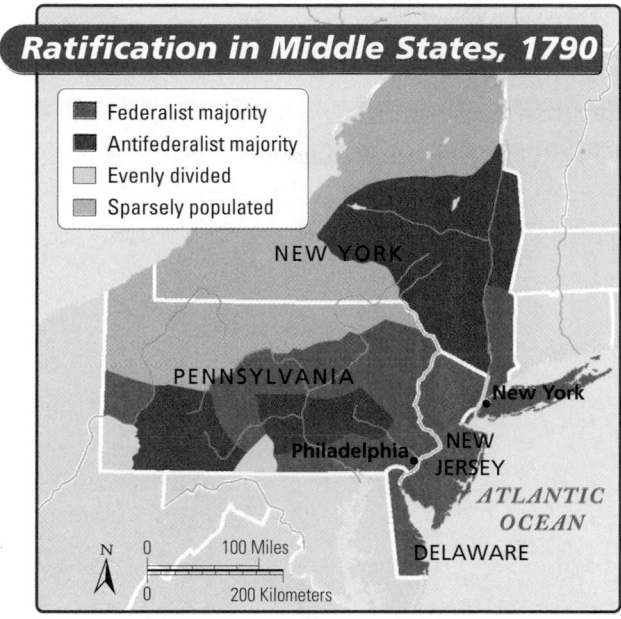

Ratification in Middle States, 1790

- Federalist majority
- Antifederalist majority
- Evenly divided
- Sparsely populated

NEW YORK

PENNSYLVANIA

New York

Philadelphia

NEW JERSEY

ATLANTIC OCEAN

DELAWARE

N

0   100 Miles

0   200 Kilometers

Source: *American Heritage Pictorial Atlas of United States History*

1. In which two states did the Federalists have statewide majorities?

A. Delaware and New Jersey

B. Delaware and New York

C. New Jersey and Pennsylvania

D. New York and Pennsylvania

2. Which of the following is true?

A. Most of New York supported the Federalists.

B. Most of Pennsylvania supported the Antifederalists.

C. Philadelphia supported the Federalists.

D. New Jersey supported both positions equally.

This quotation from John Dickinson describes his view of the Virginia Plan. Use the quotation and your knowledge of U.S. history to answer question 3.

PRIMARY SOURCE

Some of the members from the small states wish for two branches in the general legislature and are friends to a good [strong] national government; but we would sooner submit [give in] to a foreign power than submit to be deprived, in both branches of the legislature, of an equal suffrage [vote], and thereby be thrown under the domination of the larger states.

John Dickinson, quoted in *Mr. Madison's Constitution*

3. Which statement best summarizes his concern?

A. Large states should have more votes.

B. Small states should have more votes.

C. All states should have equal votes.

D. The states should not have any votes.

TEST PRACTICE
CLASSZONE.COM

ALTERNATIVE ASSESSMENT

1. 📝 WRITING ABOUT HISTORY

Suppose you are a reporter covering the Constitutional Convention. Write an **article** to inform readers about the Virginia Plan and the New Jersey Plan.

- Conduct research about both plans in the library.
- Quote delegates in your article.
- Make your article objective.

2. COOPERATIVE LEARNING

Work with a group to stage a debate between a Federalist and an Antifederalist. In preparation, research arguments on each side of these issues:

- the representation of people in Congress
- the strength of the president and Senate
- the need for a bill of rights

INTEGRATED TECHNOLOGY

DOING INTERNET RESEARCH

Conduct research to acquire biographical information about one of the following people highlighted in this chapter: Daniel Boone, John Jay, William Paterson, or George Mason.

- On the Internet, locate Web sites that include details about the person's early life, family life, education, accomplishments, and historical significance.
- Take notes from your Internet sources, keeping track of the addresses of Web sites you find to be most informative. Then write a short biography about the person you chose.

For more about these individuals . . .

INTERNET ACTIVITY
CLASSZONE.COM

The Living Constitution

The Framers of the Constitution created a flexible plan for governing the United States far into the future. They also described ways to allow changes in the Constitution. For over 200 years, the Constitution has guided the American people. It remains a "living document." The Constitution still thrives, in part, because it echoes the principles the delegates valued. Each generation of Americans renews the meaning of the Constitution's timeless ideas. These two pages show you some ways in which the Constitution has shaped events in American history. **See Primary Source Explorer** 💿

> *"In framing a system which we wish to last for ages, we should not lose sight of the changes which ages will produce."*
>
> —JAMES MADISON, CONSTITUTIONAL CONVENTION

1787

Delegates in Philadelphia sign the Constitution.

1965

Civil rights leaders protest to end the violation of their constitutional rights. Dr. Martin Luther King, Jr., Coretta Scott King, and others march from Selma toward Montgomery, Alabama, to gain voting rights.

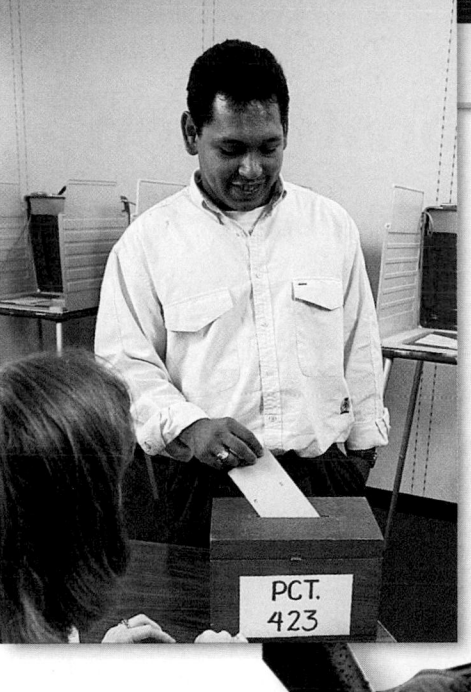

1971

The 26th Amendment to the Constitution gives young people "18 years of age or older" the right to vote.

1981

A Supreme Court decision rules that Congress can exclude women from the draft. Still, many women who have joined the armed forces have served in combat.

HOW TO READ THE CONSTITUTION

The complete text of the Constitution of the United States begins on page 248. The main column has the actual text. Some of the spellings and punctuation have been updated for easier reading. Headings and subheadings have been added to the Constitution to help you find specific topics. Those parts of the Constitution that are no longer in use have been crossed out. "A Closer Look" notes and charts will help you understand issues related to the Constitution.

National Edition

Midwest: Mostly sunny, breezy and seasonable in the Great Lakes area and Ohio Valley. Becoming very warm after a cold start in the western Plains. Weather map is on page A6.

The New York Times

"All the News That's Fit to Print"

SATURDAY, FEBRUARY 13, 1999

Printed in Chicago — **ONE DOLLAR**

VOL. CXLVIII .... No. 51,432 Copyright © 1999 The New York Times

CLINTON ACQUITTED DECISIVELY: NO MAJORITY FOR EITHER CHARGE

CENSURE IS BARRED

President Says He Is Sorry And Seeks Reconciliation

But Rebuke From Both Sides of Aisle Dilutes President's Victory

By JAMES BENNET and JOHN M. BRODER

WASHINGTON, Feb. 12 — Teetering between remorse and anticipation, President Clinton said today that he felt humbled and "profoundly sorry," as he pledged to make the most of his latest second chance.

Bill Clinton has survived. Again. After the Senate found him not guilty on two articles of impeachment, he tried today to contend with two inescapable questions: At what cost, and for what purpose?

"I want to say again to the American people how profoundly sorry I am for what I said and did to trigger these events and the great burden they have imposed on the Congress and on the American people," Mr. Clinton said. But, he said, the outcome of his trial presented an opportunity. "This can be and this must be a time of reconciliation and renewal for America."

Hoping to betray no hint of smugness, the President spent part of Thursday evening in the White...

House residence working on his five-sentence statement, barely longer than a sound bite, his aides said. Presumably...

By ALISON MITCHELL

WASHINGTON, Feb. 12 — The Senate today acquitted President Clinton on two articles of impeachment, falling short of even a majority vote on either of the charges against him: perjury and obstruction of justice.

After a harrowing year of scandal and investigation, the five-week-long Senate trial of the President — only the second in the 210-year history of the Republic — culminated shortly after noon when the roll calls began that would determine Mr. Clinton's fate.

"Is responded William Jefferson Clinton guilty or not guilty?" asked Chief Justice William H. Rehnquist, in his gold-striped black robe. In a hushed chamber, with senators standing one by one to pronounce Mr. Clinton "guilty" or "not guilty," the Senate rejected the charge of perjury, 55 to 45, with 10 Republicans voting against conviction.

It then split 50–50 on a second article accusing Mr. Clinton of obstruction of justice in concealing his affair with Monica S. Lewinsky. Five Republicans broke ranks on the obstruction-of-justice charge, too. Democrats voted to convict on neither charge, and it would have taken a dozen of them, and all 55 Republicans, to reach the two-thirds majority of 67 senators required for conviction.

Chief Justice Rehnquist announced the acquittal of the nation's 42d President at 12:39 P.M. "It is therefore ordered and adjudged that the said William Jefferson Clinton be, and he is hereby is, acquitted of the...

The Fallout Of the Trial

Effects on the Office Are Far From Certain

By R. W. APPLE Jr.
WASHINGTON, Feb. 12 — There...

'Senators, How Say You?'

	GUILTY	NOT GUILTY		GUILTY	NOT GUILTY
Article 1			**Article 2**		
Republicans	45	10	OBSTRUCTION OF JUSTICE Republicans	50	5
			Democrats	0	45

1999

The Senate tries President Bill Clinton for the impeachment charges brought against him by the House of Representatives. As required by the Constitution, the Senate needs a two-thirds majority vote to convict him. This rule saves his presidency.

Seven Principles of the Constitution

The Framers of the Constitution constructed a new system of government. Seven principles supported their efforts. To picture how these principles work, imagine seven building blocks. Together they form the foundation of the United States Constitution. In the pages that follow, you will find the definitions and main ideas of the principles shown in the graphic below.

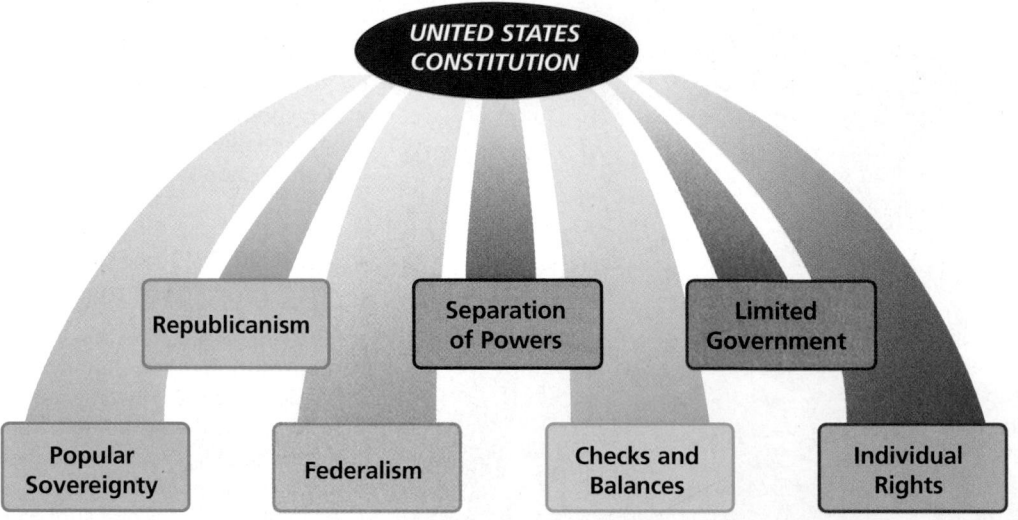

UNITED STATES CONSTITUTION

Republicanism

Separation of Powers

Limited Government

Popular Sovereignty

Federalism

Checks and Balances

Individual Rights

1 Popular Sovereignty
Who Gives the Government Its Power?

"We the people of the United States . . . establish this Constitution for the United States of America." These words from the Preamble, or introduction, to the Constitution clearly spell out the source of the government's power. The Constitution rests on the idea of **popular sovereignty**—a government in which the people rule. As the nation changed and grew, popular sovereignty took on new meaning. A broader range of Americans shared in the power to govern themselves.

In 1987, Americans gathered in Washington, D.C., to celebrate the 200th anniversary of the Constitution. The banner proudly displays that the power to govern belongs to the people.

In a republican government, voting citizens make their voices heard at the polls. The power of the ballot prompts candidates to listen to people's concerns.

2 Republicanism
How Are People's Views Represented in Government?

The Framers of the Constitution wanted the people to have a voice in government. Yet the Framers also feared that public opinion might stand in the way of sound decision making. To solve this problem, they looked to republicanism as a model of government.

Republicanism is based on this belief: The people exercise their power by voting for their political representatives. According to the Framers, these lawmakers played the key role in making a republican government work. Article 4, Section 4, of the Constitution also calls for every state to have a "republican form of government."

3 Federalism
How Is Power Shared?

The Framers wanted the states and the nation to become partners in governing. To build cooperation, the Framers turned to federalism. **Federalism** is a system of government in which power is divided between a central government and smaller political units, such as states. Before the Civil War, federalism in the United States was closely related to dual sovereignty, the idea that the federal government and the states each had exclusive power over their own spheres.

The Framers used federalism to structure the Constitution. The Constitution assigns certain powers to the national government. These are *delegated powers*. Powers kept by the states are *reserved powers*. Powers shared or exercised by national and state governments are known as *concurrent powers*.

Federalism

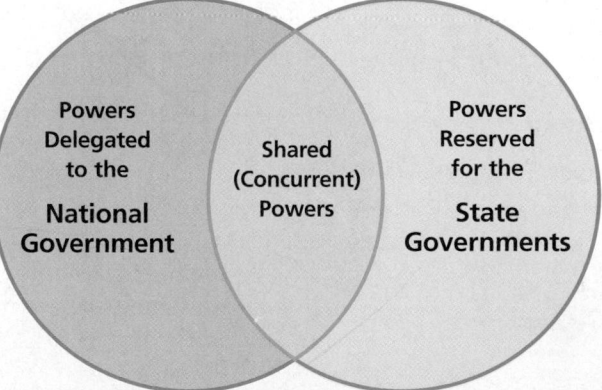

Powers Delegated to the **National Government**

Shared (Concurrent) Powers

Powers Reserved for the **State Governments**

The overlapping spheres of power bind the American people together.

4 Separation of Powers
How Is Power Divided?

The Framers were concerned that too much power might fall into the hands of a single group. To avoid this problem, they built the idea of **separation of powers** into the Constitution. This principle means the division of basic government roles into branches. No one branch is given all the power. Articles 1, 2, and 3 of the Constitution detail how powers are split among the three branches.

Separation of Powers

```
                    UNITED STATES
                    CONSTITUTION
```

Article 1	Article 2	Article 3
Legislative Branch	**Executive Branch**	**Judicial Branch**
Congress makes the laws.	President enforces the laws.	Supreme Court interprets the law.

5 Checks and Balances
How Is Power Evenly Distributed?

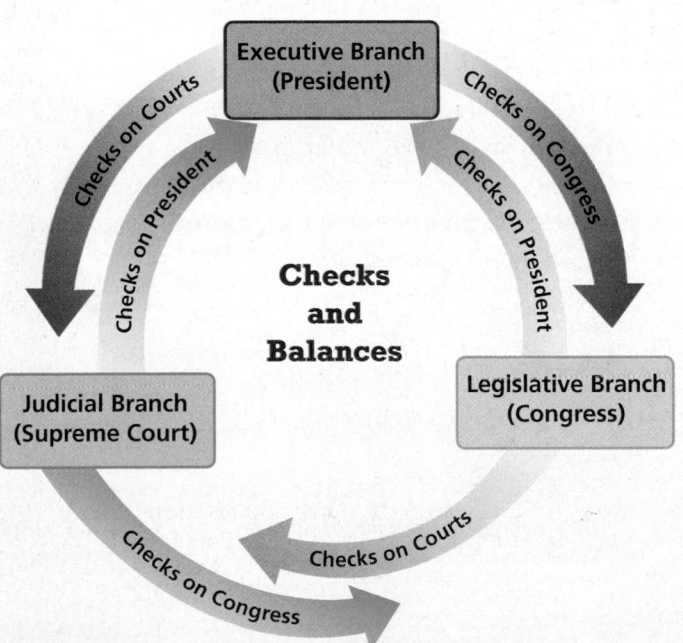

Baron de Montesquieu, an 18th-century French thinker, wrote, "Power should be a check to power." His comment refers to the principle of **checks and balances.** Each branch of government can exercise checks, or controls, over the other branches. Though the branches of government are separate, they rely on one another to perform the work of government.

The Framers included a system of checks and balances in the Constitution to help make sure that the branches work together fairly. For example, only Congress can pass laws. Yet the president can check this power by refusing to sign a law into action. In turn, the Supreme Court can declare that a law, passed by Congress and signed by the president, violates the Constitution.

6 Limited Government
How Is Abuse of Power Prevented?

The Framers restricted the power of government. Article 1, Section 9, of the Constitution lists the powers denied to the Congress. Article 1, Section 10, forbids the states to take certain actions.

The principle of **limited government** is also closely related to the "rule of law": In the American government everyone, citizens and powerful leaders alike, must obey the law. Individuals or groups cannot twist or bypass the law to serve their own interests.

'I AM THE LAW!'

In this political cartoon, President Richard Nixon shakes his fist as he defies the "rule of law." Faced with charges of violating the Constitution, Nixon resigned as president in 1974.

Students exercise their right to protest. They urge the community to protect the environment.

7 Individual Rights
How Are Personal Freedoms Protected?

The first ten amendments to the Constitution shield people from an overly powerful government. These amendments are called the Bill of Rights. The Bill of Rights guarantees certain **individual rights,** or personal liberties and privileges. For example, government cannot control what people write or say. People also have the right to meet peacefully and to ask the government to correct a problem. Later amendments to the Constitution also advanced the cause of individual rights.

Assessment: Principles of the Constitution

1. Main Ideas

a. What are the seven principles of government?

b. How does the Constitution reflect the principle of separation of powers?

c. Why did the Framers include a system of checks and balances in the Constitution?

2. Critical Thinking

Forming Opinions How do the rights and responsibilities of U.S. citizenship reflect American national identity?

THINK ABOUT

• what it means to be an American

• the rights and responsibilities of U.S. citizens

The Constitution of the United States

See Primary
Source Explorer ⊚

" *In 1787, I was not included in that 'We the people.' . . . But through the process of amendment, interpretation, and court decision, I have finally been included in 'We the people.' "*

—BARBARA JORDAN, 1974
The first African-American congresswoman from the South (Texas)

Preamble. *Purpose of the Constitution*

We the people of the United States, in order to form a more perfect Union, establish justice, insure domestic tranquility, provide for the common defense, promote the general welfare, and secure the blessings of liberty to ourselves and our posterity, do ordain and establish this Constitution for the United States of America.

A CLOSER LOOK Goals of the Preamble

PREAMBLE	EXPLANATION	EXAMPLES
"Form a more perfect Union"	Create a nation in which states work together	• U.S. Postal System • U.S. coins, paper money
"Establish justice"	Make laws and set up courts that are fair	• Court system • Jury system
"Insure domestic tranquility"	Keep peace within the country	• National Guard • Federal marshals
"Provide for the common defense"	Safeguard the country against attack	• Army • Navy
"Promote the general welfare"	Contribute to the happiness and well-being of all the people	• Social Security • Food and drug laws
"Secure the blessings of liberty to ourselves and our posterity"	Make sure future citizens remain free	• Commission on Civil Rights • National Council on Disability

SKILLBUILDER Interpreting Charts

1. *Which goal of the Preamble do you think is most important? Why?*
2. *How does the Preamble reflect the principle of popular sovereignty?*

Article 1. *The Legislature*

MAIN IDEA The main role of Congress, the legislative branch, is to make laws. Congress is made up of two houses—the Senate and the House of Representatives. Candidates for each house must meet certain requirements. Congress performs specific duties, also called delegated powers.

WHY IT MATTERS NOW Representatives in Congress still voice the views and concerns of the people.

Section 1. Congress All legislative powers herein granted shall be vested in a Congress of the United States, which shall consist of a Senate and House of Representatives.

Section 2. The House of Representatives

1. Elections The House of Representatives shall be composed of members chosen every second year by the people of the several states, and the **electors** in each state shall have the qualifications requisite for electors of the most numerous branch of the state legislature.

2. Qualifications No person shall be a Representative who shall not have attained to the age of twenty-five years, and been seven years a citizen of the United States, and who shall not, when elected, be an inhabitant of that state in which he shall be chosen.

3. Number of Representatives Representatives and direct taxes shall be apportioned among the several states which may be included within this Union, according to their respective numbers, which shall be determined by adding to the whole number of free persons, including those bound to service for a term of years, and excluding Indians not taxed, three-fifths of all other Persons. The actual **enumeration** shall be made within three years after the first meeting of the Congress of the United States, and within every subsequent term of ten years, in such manner as they shall by law direct. The number of Representatives shall not exceed one for every thirty thousand, but each state shall have at least one Representative; and until such enumeration shall be made, the state of New Hampshire shall be entitled to choose three, Massachusetts eight, Rhode Island and Providence Plantations one, Connecticut five, New York six, New Jersey four, Pennsylvania eight, Delaware one, Maryland six, Virginia ten, North Carolina five, South Carolina five, and Georgia three.

4. Vacancies When vacancies happen in the representation from any state, the executive authority thereof shall issue writs of election to fill such vacancies.

5. Officers and Impeachment The House of Representatives shall choose their Speaker and other officers; and shall have the sole power of **impeachment.**

VOCABULARY

electors voters

enumeration an official count, such as a census

impeachment the process of accusing a public official of wrongdoing

A CLOSER LOOK

ELECTIONS

Representatives are elected every two years. There are no limits on the number of terms a person can serve.

1. What do you think are the advantages of holding frequent elections of representatives?

A CLOSER LOOK

REPRESENTATION

Some delegates, such as Gouverneur Morris, thought that representation should be based on wealth as well as population. Others, such as James Wilson, thought representation should be based on population only. Ultimately, the delegates voted against including wealth as a basis for apportioning representatives.

2. How do you think the United States would be different today if representation were based on wealth?

VOCABULARY

pro tempore for the time being

indictment a written statement issued by a grand jury charging a person with a crime

quorum the minimum number of members that must be present for official business to take place

Section 3. The Senate

1. Numbers The Senate of the United States shall be composed of two Senators from each state, ~~chosen by the legislature thereof~~, for six years; and each Senator shall have one vote.

2. Classifying Terms Immediately after they shall be assembled in consequence of the first election, they shall be divided as equally as may be into three classes. The seats of the Senators of the first class shall be vacated at the expiration of the second year, of the second class at the expiration of the fourth year, and of the third class at the expiration of the sixth year, so that one-third may be chosen every second year; ~~and if vacancies happen by resignation, or otherwise, during the recess of the legislature of any state, the executive thereof may make temporary appointments until the next meeting of the legislature, which shall then fill such vacancies.~~

3. Qualifications No person shall be a Senator who shall not have attained to the age of thirty years, and been nine years a citizen of the United States, and who shall not, when elected, be an inhabitant of that state for which he shall be chosen.

A CLOSER LOOK Federal Office Terms and Requirements

POSITION	TERM	MINIMUM AGE	RESIDENCY	CITIZENSHIP
Representative	2 years	25	state in which elected	7 years
Senator	6 years	30	state in which elected	9 years
President	4 years	35	14 years in the U.S.	natural-born
Supreme Court Justice	unlimited	none	none	none

SKILLBUILDER Interpreting Charts

Why do you think the term and qualifications for a senator are more demanding than for a representative?

4. Role of Vice-President The Vice-President of the United States shall be President of the Senate, but shall have no vote, unless they be equally divided.

5. Officers The Senate shall choose their other officers, and also a President **pro tempore**, in the absence of the Vice-President, or when he shall exercise the office of President of the United States.

6. Impeachment Trials The Senate shall have the sole power to try all impeachments. When sitting for that purpose, they shall be on oath or affirmation. When the President of the United States is tried, the Chief Justice shall preside: and no person shall be convicted without the concurrence of two-thirds of the members present.

7. Punishment for Impeachment Judgment in cases of impeachment shall not extend further than to removal from office, and disqualification to hold and enjoy any office of honor, trust or profit under the United States; but the party convicted shall nevertheless be liable and subject to **indictment**, trial, judgment and punishment, according to law.

A CLOSER LOOK

IMPEACHMENT

The House brings charges against the president. The Senate acts as the jury. The Chief Justice of the Supreme Court presides over the hearings.

3. How many presidents have been impeached?

Section 4. Congressional Elections

1. Regulations The times, places and manner of holding elections for Senators and Representatives shall be prescribed in each state by the legislature thereof; but the Congress may at any time by law make or alter such regulations, except as to the places of choosing Senators.

2. Sessions The Congress shall assemble at least once in every year, ~~and such meeting shall be on the first Monday in December, unless they shall by law appoint a different day.~~

Section 5. Rules and Procedures

1. Quorum Each house shall be the judge of the elections, returns and qualifications of its own members, and a majority of each shall constitute a **quorum** to do business; but a smaller number may adjourn from day to day, and may be authorized to compel the attendance of absent members, in such manner, and under such penalties as each house may provide.

2. Rules and Conduct Each house may determine the rules of its proceedings, punish its members for disorderly behavior, and, with the concurrence of two-thirds, expel a member.

3. Congressional Records Each house shall keep a journal of its proceedings, and from time to time publish the same, excepting such parts as may in their judgment require secrecy; and the yeas and nays of the members of either house on any question shall, at the desire of one-fifth of those present, be entered on the journal.

4. Adjournment Neither house, during the session of Congress, shall, without the consent of the other, adjourn for more than three days, nor to any other place than that in which the two houses shall be sitting.

Section 6. Payment and Privileges

1. Salary The Senators and Representatives shall receive a compensation for their services, to be ascertained by law, and paid out of the treasury of the United States. They shall in all cases, except treason, felony and breach of the peace, be privileged from arrest during their attendance at the session of their respective houses, and in going to and returning from the same; and for any speech or debate in either house, they shall not be questioned in any other place.

2. Restrictions No Senator or Representative shall, during the time for which he was elected, be appointed to any civil office under the authority of the United States, which shall have been created, or the emoluments whereof shall have been increased during such time; and no person holding any office under the United States, shall be a member of either house during his continuance in office.

A CLOSER LOOK

SENATE RULES

Senate rules allow for debate on the floor. Using a tactic called filibustering, senators give long speeches to block the passage of a bill. Senator Strom Thurmond holds the filibustering record—24 hours, 18 minutes.

4. Why might a senator choose filibustering as a tactic to block a bill?

A CLOSER LOOK

SALARIES

Senators and representatives are paid $136,700 a year. The Speaker of the House is paid $175,400—the same as the vice-president.

5. How do the salaries of members of Congress compare to those of adults you know?

INTERACTIVE

VOCABULARY

revenue income a government collects to cover expenses

naturalization a way to give full citizenship to a person of foreign birth

tribunals courts

felonies serious crimes

appropriation public funds set aside for a specific purpose

Section 7. How a Bill Becomes a Law

1. Tax Bills All bills for raising **revenue** shall originate in the House of Representatives; but the Senate may propose or concur with amendments as on other Bills.

2. Lawmaking Process Every bill which shall have passed the House of Representatives and the Senate, shall, before it become a law, be presented to the President of the United States; if he approves he shall sign it, but if not he shall return it, with his objections to that house in which it shall have originated, who shall enter the objections at large on their journal, and proceed to reconsider it. If after such reconsideration two-thirds of that house shall agree to pass the bill, it shall be sent, together with the objections, to the other house, by which it shall likewise be reconsidered, and if approved by two-thirds of that house, it shall become a law. But in all such cases the votes of both houses shall be determined by yeas and nays, and the names of the persons voting for and against the bill shall be entered on the journal of each house respectively. If any bill shall not be returned by the President within ten days (Sundays excepted) after it shall have been presented to him, the same shall be a law, in like manner as if he had signed it, unless the Congress by their adjournment prevent its return, in which case it shall not be a law.

3. Role of the President Every order, resolution, or vote to which the concurrence of the Senate and House of Representatives may be necessary (except on a question of adjournment) shall be presented to the President of the United States; and before the same shall take effect, shall be approved by him, or being disapproved by him, shall be repassed by two-thirds of the Senate and House of Representatives, according to the rules and limitations prescribed in the case of a bill.

A CLOSER LOOK How a Bill Becomes a Law

Introduction

The House introduces a bill and refers it to a committee.

The Senate introduces a bill and refers it to a committee.

Committee Action

The House committee may approve, rewrite, or kill the bill.

The Senate committee may approve, rewrite, or kill the bill.

Floor Action

The House debates and votes on its version of the bill.

The Senate debates and votes on its version of the bill.

House and Senate committee members work out the differences between the two versions.

Section 8. Powers Granted to Congress

1. Taxation The Congress shall have power to lay and collect taxes, duties, imposts and excises, to pay the debts and provide for the common defense and general welfare of the United States; but all duties, imposts and excises shall be uniform throughout the United States;

2. Credit To borrow money on the credit of the United States;

3. Commerce To regulate commerce with foreign nations, and among the several states, and with the Indian tribes;

4. Naturalization, Bankruptcy To establish a uniform rule of __naturalization,__ and uniform laws on the subject of bankruptcies throughout the United States;

5. Money To coin money, regulate the value thereof, and of foreign coin, and fix the standard of weights and measures;

6. Counterfeiting To provide for the punishment of counterfeiting the securities and current coin of the United States;

7. Post Office To establish post offices and post roads;

8. Patents, Copyrights To promote the progress of science and useful arts, by securing for limited times to authors and inventors the exclusive right to their respective writings and discoveries;

9. Federal Courts To constitute __tribunals__ inferior to the Supreme Court;

10. International Law To define and punish piracies and __felonies__ committed on the high seas, and offenses against the law of nations;

11. War To declare war, grant letters of marque and reprisal, and make rules concerning captures on land and water;

12. Army To raise and support armies, but no __appropriation__ of money to that use shall be for a longer term than two years;

13. Navy To provide and maintain a navy;

A CLOSER LOOK

REGULATING COMMERCE

Commerce can also apply to travelers crossing state lines. Congress's power to regulate the movement of people from state to state paved the way for the Civil Rights Act of 1964. This act included fair treatment of interstate travelers. People of all races can use public places, such as hotels and bus stations.

6. To what other areas might the commerce clause apply?

A CLOSER LOOK

DECLARING WAR

Only Congress can declare war. Yet in the following "undeclared" wars, Congress bowed to the president's power to take military action and send troops overseas: Korean War (1950–1953), Vietnam War (1957–1975), Persian Gulf War (1991), and Kosovo crisis (1999).

7. Why do you think the Constitution sets limits on the president's war-making powers?

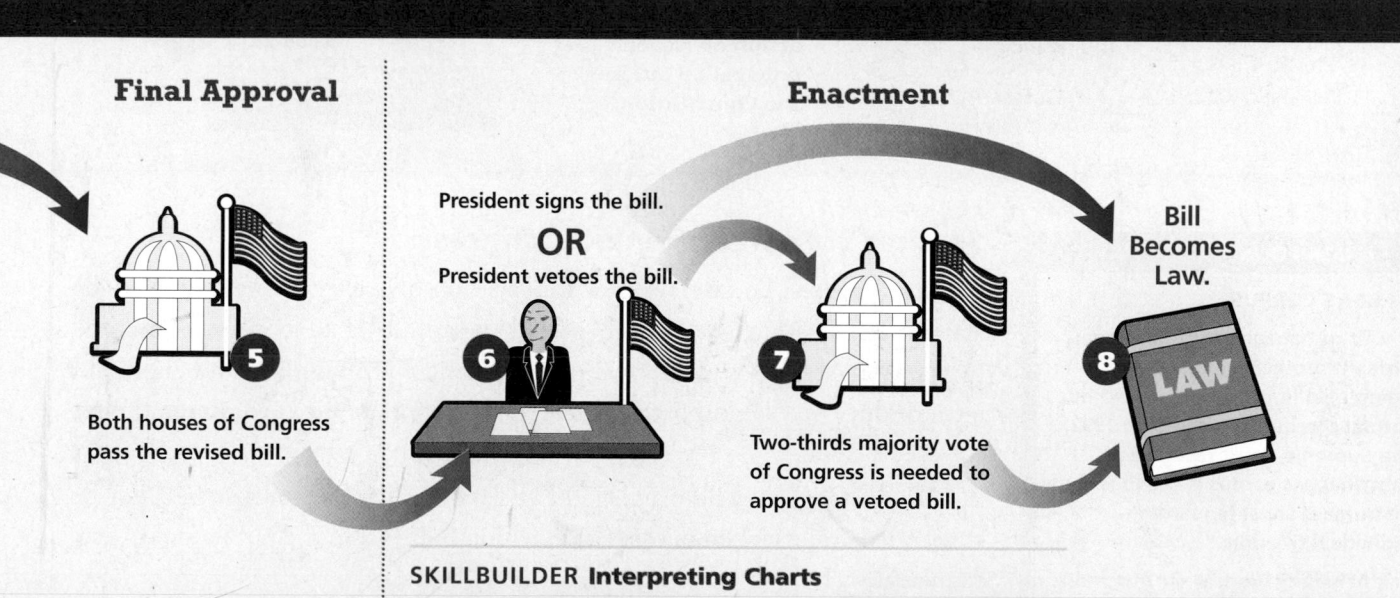

Final Approval

Enactment

Both houses of Congress pass the revised bill. **5**

President signs the bill.
OR
President vetoes the bill. **6**

Two-thirds majority vote of Congress is needed to approve a vetoed bill. **7**

Bill Becomes Law. **8**

LAW

SKILLBUILDER Interpreting Charts

1. *How can a president block a bill?*
2. *What examples of checks and balances are shown in the chart?*

14. Regulation of Armed Forces To make rules for the government and regulation of the land and naval forces;

15. Militia To provide for calling forth the **militia** to execute the laws of the Union, suppress insurrections and repel invasions;

16. Regulations for Militia To provide for organizing, arming, and disciplining the militia, and for governing such part of them as may be employed in the service of the United States, reserving to the states respectively the appointment of the officers, and the authority of training the militia according to the discipline prescribed by Congress;

17. District of Columbia To exercise exclusive legislation in all cases whatsoever, over such district (not exceeding ten miles square) as may, by cession of particular states, and the acceptance of Congress, become the seat of the government of the United States, and to exercise like authority over all places purchased by the consent of the legislature of the state in which the same shall be, for the erection of forts, magazines, arsenals, dockyards, and other needful buildings;—and

18. Elastic Clause To make all laws which shall be necessary and proper for carrying into execution the foregoing powers, and all other powers vested by this Constitution in the government of the United States, or in any department or officer thereof.

A CLOSER LOOK The Elastic Clause

ELASTIC CLAUSE

1787 13 states • agricultural • rural about 4 million people POP.

The elastic clause allows future generations to expand the meaning of the Constitution. Congress can take action on issues not spelled out in the Constitution.

TODAY 50 states • industrial • high-tech • urban POP. about 250 million people

A CLOSER LOOK

HABEAS CORPUS

A writ of habeas corpus is a legal order. It protects people from being held in prison or jail without formal charges of a crime. In 1992, the Supreme Court recognized that "habeas corpus is the [basic] instrument for safeguarding individual freedom."

8. How does habeas corpus help ensure fairness and justice?

Section 9. Powers Denied Congress

1. Slave Trade ~~The migration or importation of such persons as any of the states now existing shall think proper to admit, shall not be prohibited by the Congress prior to the year one thousand eight hundred and eight, but a tax or duty may be imposed on such importation, not exceeding ten dollars for each person.~~

2. Habeas Corpus The privilege of the writ of habeas corpus shall not be suspended, unless when in cases of rebellion or invasion the public safety may require it.

3. Illegal Punishment No **bill of attainder** or **ex post facto law** shall be passed.

4. Direct Taxes No capitation, ~~or other direct,~~ tax shall be laid, ~~unless in proportion to the census or enumeration herein before directed to be taken.~~

5. Export Taxes No tax or duty shall be laid on articles exported from any state.

6. No Favorites No preference shall be given by any regulation of commerce or revenue to the ports of one state over those of another: nor shall vessels bound to, or from, one state be obliged to enter, clear, or pay duties in another.

7. Public Money No money shall be drawn from the treasury, but in consequence of appropriations made by law; and a regular statement and account of the receipts and expenditures of all public money shall be published from time to time.

8. Titles of Nobility No title of nobility shall be granted by the United States: and no person holding any office of profit or trust under them shall, without the consent of the Congress, accept of any present, emolument, office, or title, of any kind whatever, from any king, prince, or foreign state.

Section 10. Powers Denied the States

1. Restrictions No state shall enter into any treaty, alliance, or confederation; grant letters of marque and reprisal; coin money; emit bills of credit; make anything but gold and silver coin a **tender** in payment of debts; pass any bill of attainder, ex post facto law, or law impairing the obligation of contracts, or grant any title of nobility.

2. Import and Export Taxes No state shall, without the consent of the Congress, lay any imposts or duties on imports or exports, except what may be absolutely necessary for executing its inspection laws; and the net produce of all duties and imposts, laid by any state on imports or exports, shall be for the use of the treasury of the United States; and all such laws shall be subject to the revision and control of the Congress.

3. Peacetime and War Restraints No state shall, without the consent of Congress, lay any duty of tonnage, keep troops or ships of war in time of peace, enter into any agreement or compact with another state, or with a foreign power, or engage in war, unless actually invaded, or in such imminent danger as will not admit of delay.

A CLOSER LOOK

DIRECT TAX

In 1913, the 16th Amendment allowed Congress to collect an income tax—a direct tax on the amount of money a person earns. Americans today pay much more in taxes than their ancestors would have imagined.

9. Why do you think the issue of taxes is so important to people?

A CLOSER LOOK

TITLES OF NOBILITY

The Framers disapproved of titles of nobility. The list of grievances in the Declaration of Independence included numerous examples of King George III's abuses of power. Symbols of these abuses included English titles of nobility, such as "king," "queen," and "duke." The Framers said clearly that there would be no such titles in the new republic.

10. How do TV news reporters address members of Congress and the president?

Article 1 Assessment

1. Main Ideas

a. What is the main job of the legislative branch?

b. What role does the vice-president of the United States play in the Senate?

c. Why are there more members in the House of Representatives than the Senate?

d. What is one of the powers denied to Congress?

2. Critical Thinking

Drawing Conclusions How does Article 1 show that the Constitution is a clearly defined yet flexible document?

THINK ABOUT
• the powers of Congress
• the "elastic clause"

VOCABULARY

natural-born citizen a citizen born in the United States or a U.S. commonwealth, or to parents who are U.S. citizens living outside the country

affirmation a statement declaring that something is true

Article 2. *The Executive*

> **MAIN IDEA** The president and vice-president are the leaders of the executive branch. Their main role is to enforce the laws. The president commands the military and makes foreign treaties with the Senate's approval.
>
> **WHY IT MATTERS NOW** As the United States has become a world power, the authority of the president has also expanded.

Section 1. The Presidency

1. Terms of Office The executive power shall be vested in a President of the United States of America. He shall hold his office during the term of four years, and, together with the Vice-President, chosen for the same term, be elected, as follows:

2. Electoral College Each state shall appoint, in such manner as the Legislature thereof may direct, a number of electors, equal to the whole number of Senators and Representatives to which the State may be entitled in the Congress; but no Senator or Representative, or person holding an office of trust or profit under the United States, shall be appointed an elector.

A CLOSER LOOK Electoral College *(based on 2000 Census)*

American voters do not choose their president directly. Members of a group called the electoral college actually elect the president. Each state has electors. Together they form the electoral college. In most states, the winner takes all. Except for Maine and Nebraska, all the electoral votes of a state go to one set of candidates.

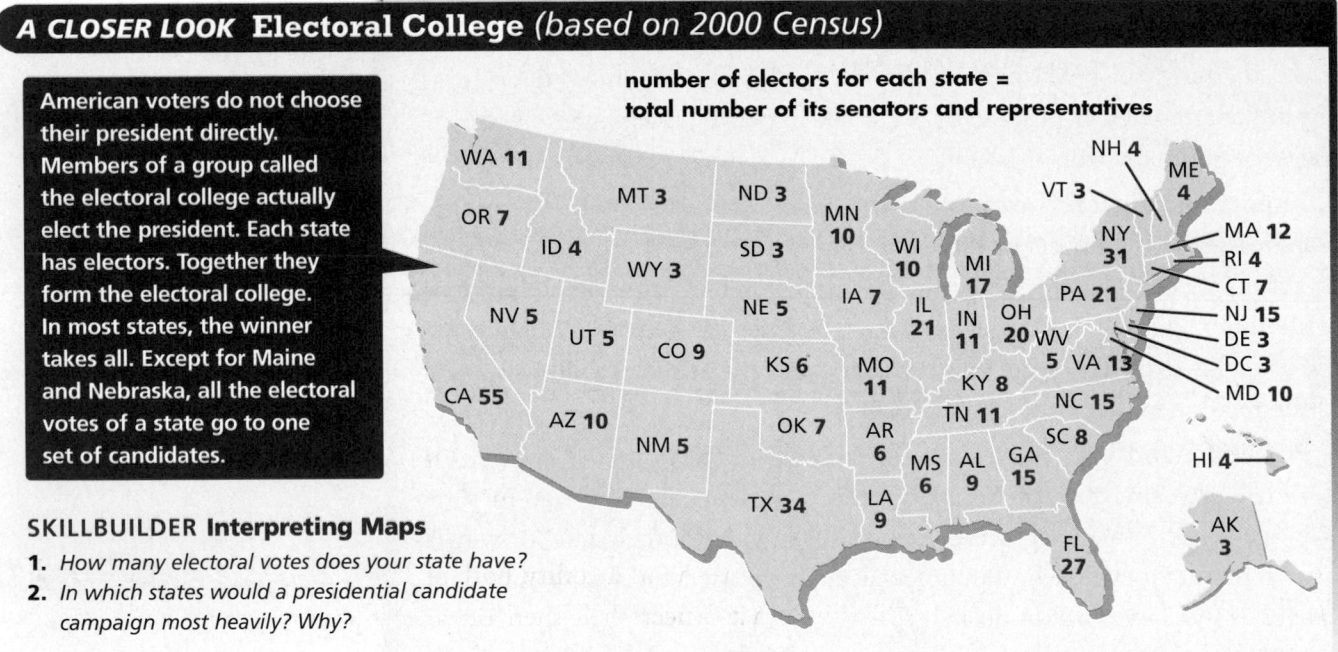

number of electors for each state = total number of its senators and representatives

WA 11
OR 7
MT 3
ND 3
MN 10
NH 4
VT 3
ME 4
ID 4
WY 3
SD 3
WI 10
NY 31
MA 12
RI 4
NV 5
UT 5
CO 9
NE 5
IA 7
MI 17
PA 21
CT 7
NJ 15
CA 55
AZ 10
NM 5
KS 6
IL 21
IN 11
OH 20
WV 5
VA 13
DE 3
DC 3
MD 10
OK 7
MO 11
KY 8
TN 11
NC 15
SC 8
HI 4
TX 34
AR 6
MS 6
AL 9
LA 9
GA 15
FL 27
AK 3

SKILLBUILDER Interpreting Maps
1. *How many electoral votes does your state have?*
2. *In which states would a presidential candidate campaign most heavily? Why?*

3. Former Method of Electing President ~~The electors shall meet in their respective states, and vote by ballot for two persons, of whom one at least shall not be an inhabitant of the same state with themselves. And they shall make a list of all the persons voted for, and of the number of votes for each; which list they shall sign and certify, and transmit sealed to the seat of the government of the United States, directed to the President of the Senate. The President of the Senate shall, in the presence of the Senate and House of Representatives, open all the certificates, and the votes shall then be counted. The person having the greatest number of votes shall be the~~

President, if such number be a majority of the whole number of electors appointed; and if there be more than one who have such majority, and have an equal number of votes, then the House of Representatives shall immediately choose by ballot one of them for President; and if no person have a majority, then from the five highest on the list the said House shall in like manner choose the President. But in choosing the President, the votes shall be taken by States, the representation from each state having one vote; a quorum for this purpose shall consist of a member or members from two-thirds of the states, and a majority of all the states shall be necessary to a choice. In every case, after the choice of the President, the person having the greatest number of votes of the electors shall be the Vice-President. But if there should remain two or more who have equal votes, the Senate shall choose from them by ballot the Vice-President.

4. Election Day The Congress may determine the time of choosing the electors, and the day on which they shall give their votes, which day shall be the same throughout the United States.

5. Qualifications No person except a **natural-born citizen,** or a citizen of the United States at the time of the adoption of this Constitution, shall be eligible to the office of President; neither shall any person be eligible to that office who shall not have attained to the age of thirty-five years, and been fourteen years a resident within the United States.

6. Succession In case of the removal of the President from office, or of his death, resignation, or inability to discharge the powers and duties of the said office, the same shall devolve on the Vice-President, and the Congress may by law provide for the case of removal, death, resignation or inability, both of the President and Vice-President, declaring what officer shall then act as President, and such officer shall act accordingly, until the disability be removed, or a President shall be elected.

7. Salary The President shall, at stated times, receive for his services, a compensation, which shall neither be increased nor diminished during the period for which he shall have been elected, and he shall not receive within that period any other emolument from the United States, or any of them.

8. Oath of Office Before he enter on the execution of his office, he shall take the following oath or **affirmation:**—"I do solemnly swear (or affirm) that I will faithfully execute the office of President of the United States, and will to the best of my ability, preserve, protect and defend the Constitution of the United States."

A CLOSER LOOK

Vice-President Lyndon Johnson, next in line of succession, takes the oath of office after the assassination of President John F. Kennedy in 1963. Johnson, like every U.S. president, promises to uphold the Constitution. The 25th Amendment sets up clearer procedures for presidential succession.

A CLOSER LOOK

PRESIDENT'S SALARY

The president's yearly salary is $400,000. The president also gets special allowances, such as funds for travel expenses. Here are some other benefits:

- living in a mansion, the White House
- vacationing at Camp David, an estate in Maryland
- using *Air Force One*, a personal jet plane

11. Why do you think the president needs to have a plane and a vacation spot?

Commander in Chief

As a military leader, President Abraham Lincoln meets with his generals during the Civil War.

Chief Executive

Like a business executive, the president solves problems and makes key decisions. President John F. Kennedy is shown in the oval office in 1962.

Chief Diplomat and Chief of State

As a foreign policy maker, President Richard M. Nixon visits the People's Republic of China in 1972.

Legislative Leader

President Lyndon Johnson signs the Civil Rights Act of 1964. All modern presidents have legislative programs they want Congress to pass.

Head of a Political Party

President Ronald Reagan rallies support at the 1984 Republican Convention. By this time, Reagan had put together a strong bloc of voters who supported the Republican Party's policies. During his presidency (1981–1989), Reagan helped build new unity among party members.

Section 2. Powers of the President

1. Military Powers The President shall be commander in chief of the Army and Navy of the United States, and of the militia of the several states, when called into the actual service of the United States; he may require the opinion, in writing, of the principal officer in each of the executive departments, upon any subject relating to the duties of their respective offices, and he shall have power to grant <u>reprieves</u> and pardons for offenses against the United States, except in cases of impeachment.

2. Treaties, Appointments He shall have power, by and with the advice and consent of the Senate, to make treaties, provided two-thirds of the Senators present concur; and he shall nominate, and by and with the advice and consent of the Senate, shall appoint ambassadors, other public ministers and consuls, judges of the Supreme Court, and all other officers of the United States, whose appointments are not herein otherwise provided for, and which shall be established by law; but the Congress may by law vest the appointment of such inferior officers, as they think proper, in the President alone, in the courts of law, or in the heads of departments.

3. Vacancies The President shall have power to fill up all vacancies that may happen during the recess of the Senate, by granting commissions which shall expire at the end of their next session.

Section 3. Presidential Duties
He shall from time to time give to the Congress information of the State of the Union, and recommend to their consideration such measures as he shall judge necessary and expedient; he may, on extraordinary occasions, <u>convene</u> both houses, or either of them, and in case of disagreement between them, with respect to the time of adjournment, he may adjourn them to such time as he shall think proper; he shall receive ambassadors and other public ministers; he shall take care that the laws be faithfully executed, and shall commission all the officers of the United States.

Section 4. Impeachment
The President, Vice-President and all civil officers of the United States shall be removed from office on impeachment for, and conviction of, treason, bribery, or other high crimes and <u>misdemeanors</u>.

VOCABULARY

reprieves delays or cancellations of punishment

convene call together

misdemeanors violations of the law

A CLOSER LOOK

SUPREME COURT APPOINTMENTS

Recent presidents have used their power of appointment to add minorities and women to the Supreme Court. In 1967, President Lyndon Johnson appointed the first African-American justice, Thurgood Marshall. In 1981, President Ronald Reagan appointed the first woman, Sandra Day O'Connor.

12. What do you think influences a president's choice for a Supreme Court justice?

A CLOSER LOOK

STATE OF THE UNION

Major TV networks broadcast the State of the Union address to the whole nation. In this yearly message, the president urges Congress to achieve certain lawmaking goals. The president's speech also must gain the attention of TV viewers.

13. Why is the president's power to persuade an important political skill?

Article 2 Assessment

1. Main Ideas

a. What is the chief purpose of the executive branch?

b. What are the requirements for becoming president?

c. How does the Constitution limit the president's power to make appointments and treaties?

2. Critical Thinking

Analyzing Issues Why do you think the Constitution states that the president must seek approval from the Senate for most political appointments and treaties?

THINK ABOUT
- the abuse of power
- the will of the voters

A CLOSER LOOK

ORGANIZING FEDERAL COURTS

The Judiciary Act of 1789, passed by the First Congress, included establishing a Supreme Court with a chief justice and five associate justices and other lower federal courts.

14. How many Supreme Court justices are there today?

A CLOSER LOOK

JUDICIAL POWER

Judicial power gives the Supreme Court and other federal courts the authority to hear certain kinds of cases. These courts have the power to rule in cases involving the Constitution, national laws, treaties, and states' conflicts.

15. What federal cases have you seen reported on TV?

Article 3. *The Judiciary*

> **MAIN IDEA** The judicial branch interprets the laws. This branch includes the Supreme Court, the highest court in the nation, and other federal courts.
>
> **WHY IT MATTERS NOW** Supreme Court rulings can shape government policies on hotly debated issues.

Section 1. Federal Courts and Judges The judicial power of the United States shall be vested in one Supreme Court, and in such **inferior courts** as the Congress may from time to time ordain and establish. The judges, both of the Supreme and inferior courts, shall hold their offices during good behavior, and shall, at stated times, receive for their services a compensation, which shall not be diminished during their continuance in office.

Section 2. The Courts' Authority

1. General Authority The judicial power shall extend to all cases, in law and equity, arising under this Constitution, the laws of the United States, and treaties made, or which shall be made, under their authority;—to all cases affecting ambassadors, other public ministers and consuls;—to all cases of admiralty and maritime jurisdiction;—to controversies to which the United States shall be a party;—to controversies between two or more states;—between a state and citizens of another state;—between citizens of different states;—between citizens of the same state claiming lands under grants of different states, and between a state, or the citizens thereof, and foreign states, citizens or subjects.

A CLOSER LOOK Judicial Review

Judicial review allows the Supreme Court and other federal courts to play a key role in lawmaking. The judges examine a law or government activity. They then decide whether it violates the Constitution. The Supreme Court established this important right in the case of *Marbury* v. *Madison* (1803). (See Chapter 10.)

2. Supreme Court In all cases affecting ambassadors, other public ministers and consuls, and those in which a state shall be party, the Supreme Court shall have original jurisdiction. In all the other cases before mentioned, the Supreme Court shall have **appellate** jurisdiction, both as to law and fact, with such exceptions, and under such regulations, as the Congress shall make.

CHECKS ON COURTS

- Appoints federal judges
- Can grant reprieves and pardons for federal crimes

Executive Branch
(President)

CHECKS ON CONGRESS

- Can veto acts of Congress
- Can call special sessions of Congress
- Can suggest laws and send messages to Congress

CHECKS ON PRESIDENT

- Can impeach and remove the president
- Can override veto
- Controls spending of money
- Senate can refuse to confirm presidential appointments and to ratify treaties

Legislative Branch
(Congress)

CHECKS ON COURT

- Can impeach and remove federal judges
- Establishes lower federal courts
- Can refuse to confirm judicial appointments

CHECKS ON PRESIDENT

- Can declare executive acts unconstitutional
- Judges, appointed for life, are free from executive control

Judicial Branch
(Supreme Court)

CHECKS ON CONGRESS

- Judicial review—Can declare acts of Congress unconstitutional

SKILLBUILDER Interpreting Charts

1. *Why is judicial review an important action of the Supreme Court?*
2. *Which check do you think is most powerful? Why?*

3. Trial by Jury The trial of all crimes, except in cases of impeachment, shall be by jury; and such trial shall be held in the state where the said crimes shall have been committed; but when not committed within any state, the trial shall be at such place or places as the Congress may by law have directed.

Section 3. Treason

1. Definition Treason against the United States shall consist only in levying war against them, or in adhering to their enemies, giving them aid and comfort. No person shall be convicted of treason unless on the testimony of two witnesses to the same overt act, or on confession in open court.

2. Punishment The Congress shall have power to declare the punishment of treason, but no attainder of treason shall work corruption of blood, or forfeiture except during the life of the person attained.

Article 3 Assessment

1. Main Ideas

a. What is the main purpose of the judicial branch?

b. What is judicial review?

c. What are two kinds of cases that can begin in the Supreme Court?

2. Critical Thinking

Drawing Conclusions Why might the Supreme Court feel less political pressure than Congress in making judgments about the Constitution?

THINK ABOUT

- the appointment of Supreme Court justices
- Congress members' obligation to voters

A CLOSER LOOK Federalism

Americans live under both national and state governments.

NATIONAL POWERS
- Maintain military
- Declare war
- Establish postal system
- Set standards for weights and measures
- Protect copyrights and patents

SHARED POWERS
- Collect taxes
- Establish courts
- Regulate interstate commerce
- Regulate banks
- Borrow money
- Provide for the general welfare
- Punish criminals

STATE POWERS
- Establish local governments
- Set up schools
- Regulate state commerce
- Make regulations for marriage
- Establish and regulate corporations

SKILLBUILDER Interpreting Charts
What do you think is the purpose of dividing the powers between national and state governments?

Article 4. *Relations Among States*

MAIN IDEA States must honor one another's laws, records, and court rulings.

WHY IT MATTERS NOW Article 4 promotes cooperation, equality, and fair treatment of citizens from all the states.

Section 1. State Acts and Records Full faith and credit shall be given in each state to the public acts, records, and judicial proceedings of every other state. And the Congress may by general laws prescribe the manner in which such acts, records and proceedings shall be proved, and the effect thereof.

Section 2. Rights of Citizens

1. Citizenship The citizens of each state shall be entitled to all privileges and **immunities** of citizens in the several states.

2. Extradition A person charged in any state with treason, felony, or other crime, who shall flee from justice, and be found in another state, shall on demand of the executive authority of the state from which he fled, be delivered up, to be removed to the state having jurisdiction of the crime.
3. Fugitive Slaves No person held to service or labor in one state, under the laws thereof, escaping into another, shall, in consequence of any law or regulation therein, be discharged from such service or labor, but shall be delivered up on claim of the party to whom such service or labor may be due.

A CLOSER LOOK

EXTRADITION

Persons charged with serious crimes cannot escape punishment by fleeing to another state. They must be returned to the first state and stand trial there.

16. Why do you think the Framers included the power of extradition?

Section 3. New States

1. Admission New states may be admitted by the Congress into this Union; but no new state shall be formed or erected within the jurisdiction of any other state; nor any state be formed by the junction of two or more states, or parts of states, without the consent of the legislatures of the states concerned as well as of the Congress.

2. Congressional Authority The Congress shall have power to dispose of and make all needful rules and regulations respecting the territory or other property belonging to the United States; and nothing in this Constitution shall be so construed as to prejudice any claims of the United States, or of any particular state.

Section 4. Guarantees to the States

The United States shall guarantee to every state in this Union a republican form of government, and shall protect each of them against invasion; and on application of the legislature, or of the executive (when the legislature cannot be convened) against domestic violence.

A CLOSER LOOK

ADMISSION TO STATEHOOD

In 1998, Puerto Ricans voted against their island becoming the 51st state. A lawyer in Puerto Rico summed up a main reason: "Puerto Ricans want to have ties to the U. S., but they want to protect their language and culture." Also, as a U.S. commonwealth, Puerto Rico makes its own laws and handles its own finances.

17. Do you think Puerto Rico should become a state? Why or why not?

Article 5. *Amending the Constitution*

> **MAIN IDEA** The Constitution can be amended, or formally changed.
>
> **WHY IT MATTERS NOW** The amendment process allows the Constitution to adapt to modern times.

The Congress, whenever two-thirds of both houses shall deem it necessary, shall propose amendments to this Constitution, or, on the application of the legislatures of two-thirds of the several states, shall call a convention for proposing amendments, which, in either case, shall be valid to all intents and purposes, as part of this Constitution, when ratified by the legislatures of three-fourths of the several states, or by conventions in three-fourths thereof, as the one or the other mode of ratification may be proposed by the Congress; provided that no amendment which may be made prior to the year one thousand eight hundred and eight shall in any manner affect the first and fourth clauses in the ninth section of the first article; and that no state, without its consent, shall be deprived of its equal **suffrage** in the Senate.

A CLOSER LOOK Process for Amending the Constitution

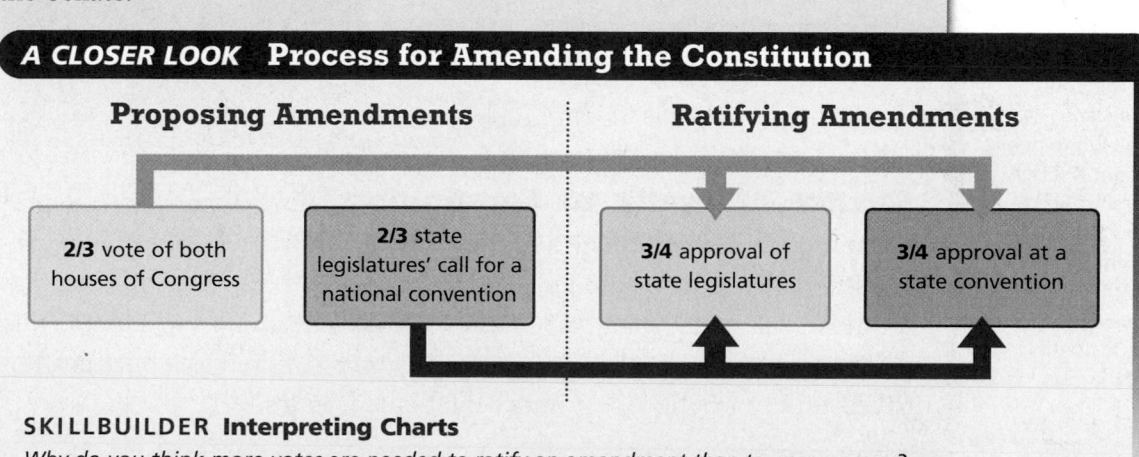

Proposing Amendments		Ratifying Amendments	
2/3 vote of both houses of Congress	2/3 state legislatures' call for a national convention	3/4 approval of state legislatures	3/4 approval at a state convention

SKILLBUILDER Interpreting Charts
Why do you think more votes are needed to ratify an amendment than to propose one?

A CLOSER LOOK

PAYING DEBTS

The U.S. government agreed to pay all debts held under the Articles of Confederation. For example, the United States still owed money from the costs of the Revolutionary War.

18. What problems might arise in a country that has a huge national debt?

Article 6. *Supremacy of the National Government*

> **MAIN IDEA** The Constitution, national laws, and treaties are the supreme, or highest, law of the land. All government officials must promise to support the Constitution.
>
> **WHY IT MATTERS NOW** The authority of federal laws over state laws helps keep the nation unified.

Section 1. Valid Debts All debts contracted and engagements entered into, before the adoption of this Constitution, shall be as valid against the United States under this Constitution, as under the Confederation.

Section 2. Supreme Law This Constitution, and the laws of the United States which shall be made in pursuance thereof; and all treaties made, or which shall be made, under the authority of the United States, shall be the supreme law of the land; and the judges in every state shall be bound thereby, anything in the constitution or laws of any state to the contrary notwithstanding.

A CLOSER LOOK

In 1957, the "supreme law of the land" was put to a test. The governor of Arkansas defied a Supreme Court order. The Court ruled that African-American students could go to all-white public schools. President Dwight D. Eisenhower then sent federal troops to protect the first African-American students to enroll in Central High School in Little Rock, Arkansas.

Section 3. Loyalty to Constitution The Senators and Representatives before mentioned, and the members of the several state legislatures, and all executive and judicial officers, both of the United States and of the several states, shall be bound by oath or affirmation to support this Constitution; but no religious test shall ever be required as a qualification to any office or public trust under the United States.

The CENTINEL. VOL IX

REDEUNT SATURNIA REGNA.

On the erection of the Eleventh PILLAR of the great National DOME, we beg leave most sincerely to felicitate "OUR DEAR COUNTRY."

Rise it will.

The foundation good—it may yet be SAVED.

The FEDERAL EDIFICE.

A CLOSER LOOK

This political cartoon shows that New York was the 11th state to ratify the Constitution. Each of the 13 states is represented by a pillar.

Article 7. Ratification

> **MAIN IDEA** Nine of the 13 states had to ratify, or approve, the Constitution before it could go into effect.
>
> **WHY IT MATTERS NOW** The approval of the Constitution launched a new plan of government still followed today.

The **ratification** of the conventions of nine states shall be sufficient for the establishment of this Constitution between the states so ratifying the same. Done in convention by the **unanimous consent** of the states present, the seventeenth day of September in the year of our Lord one thousand seven hundred and eighty-seven and of the independence of the United States of America the twelfth. In witness whereof we have hereunto subscribed our names.

George Washington—President and deputy from Virginia

New Hampshire: *John Langdon, Nicholas Gilman*

Massachusetts: *Nathaniel Gorham, Rufus King*

Connecticut: *William Samuel Johnson, Roger Sherman*

New York: *Alexander Hamilton*

New Jersey: *William Livingston, David Brearley, William Paterson, Jonathan Dayton*

Pennsylvania: *Benjamin Franklin, Thomas Mifflin, Robert Morris, George Clymer, Thomas FitzSimons, Jared Ingersoll, James Wilson, Gouverneur Morris*

Delaware: *George Read, Gunning Bedford, Jr., John Dickinson, Richard Bassett, Jacob Broom*

Maryland: *James McHenry, Dan of St. Thomas Jenifer, Daniel Carroll*

Virginia: *John Blair, James Madison, Jr.*

North Carolina: *William Blount, Richard Dobbs Spaight, Hugh Williamson*

South Carolina: *John Rutledge, Charles Cotesworth Pinckney, Charles Pinckney, Pierce Butler*

Georgia: *William Few, Abraham Baldwin*

A CLOSER LOOK

THE SIGNERS

The 39 men who signed the Constitution were wealthy and well-educated. About half of them were trained in law. Others were doctors, merchants, bankers, and slaveholding planters. Missing from the list of signatures are the names of African Americans, Native Americans, and women. These groups reflected the varied population of the United States in the 1780s.

19. How do you think the absence of these groups affected the decisions made in creating the Constitution?

Articles 4–7 Assessment

1. Main Ideas

a. What rights does Article 4 guarantee to citizens if they go to other states in the nation?

b. What are two ways of proposing an amendment to the Constitution?

c. What makes up "the supreme law of the land"?

2. Critical Thinking

Forming and Supporting Opinions Should the Framers of the Constitution have allowed the people to vote directly for ratification of the Constitution? Why or why not?

THINK ABOUT

• the idea that the government belongs to the people
• the general public's ability to make sound political decisions

The Bill of Rights and Amendments 11–27

In 1787, Thomas Jefferson sent James Madison a letter about the Constitution. Jefferson wrote, "I will now add what I do not like . . . [there is no] bill of rights." He explained his reasons: "A bill of rights is what the people are entitled to against every government on earth . . . and what no just government should refuse." Jefferson's disapproval is not surprising. In writing the Declaration of Independence, he spelled out basic individual rights that cannot be taken way. These are "life, liberty, and the pursuit of happiness." The Declaration states that governments are formed to protect these rights.

Several states approved the Constitution only if a list of guaranteed freedoms was added. While serving in the nation's first Congress, James Madison helped draft the Bill of Rights. In 1791, these first ten amendments became part of the Constitution.

AMENDMENTS 1–10. *The Bill of Rights*

MAIN IDEA The Bill of Rights protects citizens from government interference.

WHY IT MATTERS NOW Issues related to the Bill of Rights are still being applied, tested, and interpreted.

AMENDMENT 1. Religious and Political Freedom (1791)

Congress shall make no law respecting an establishment of religion, or prohibiting the free exercise thereof; or **abridging** the freedom of speech, or of the press; or the right of the people peaceably to assemble, and to petition the Government for a redress of grievances.

A CLOSER LOOK The Five Freedoms

Freedom of Religion
Right to worship

Freedom of Speech
Right to state ideas

Freedom of the Press
Right to publish ideas

Freedom of Assembly
Right to meet peacefully in groups

Freedom to Petition
Right to protest the government

SKILLBUILDER Interpreting Charts
1. *Why is freedom of speech and the press important in a democratic society?*
2. *What impact has religious freedom had on the American way of life?*

AMENDMENT 2. Right to Bear Arms (1791) A well-regulated militia, being necessary to the security of a free state, the right of the people to keep and bear arms, shall not be infringed.

AMENDMENT 3. Quartering Troops (1791) No soldier shall, in time of peace be **quartered** in any house, without the consent of the owner, nor in time of war, but in a manner to be prescribed by law.

AMENDMENT 4. Search and Seizure (1791) The right of the people to be secure in their persons, houses, papers, and effects, against unreasonable searches and seizures, shall not be violated, and no warrants shall issue, but upon probable cause, supported by oath or affirmation, and particularly describing the place to be searched, and the persons or things to be seized.

AMENDMENT 5. Rights of Accused Persons (1791) No person shall be held to answer for a capital, or otherwise infamous crime, unless on a presentment or indictment of a Grand Jury, except in cases arising in the land or naval forces, or in the militia, when in actual service in time of war or public danger; nor shall any person be subject for the same offense to be twice put in jeopardy of life or limb; nor shall be compelled in any criminal case to be a witness against himself, nor be deprived of life, liberty, or property, without **due process of law**; nor shall private property be taken for public use, without just compensation.

AMENDMENT 6. Right to a Speedy, Public Trial (1791) In all criminal prosecutions, the accused shall enjoy the right to a speedy and public trial, by an impartial jury of the State and district wherein the crime shall have been committed, which district shall have been previously ascertained by law, and to be informed of the nature and cause of the accusation; to be confronted with the witnesses against him; to have **compulsory process** for obtaining witnesses in his favor, and to have the assistance of **counsel** for his defense.

VOCABULARY

abridging reducing

quartered given a place to stay

due process of law fair treatment under the law

compulsory process required procedure

counsel a lawyer

A CLOSER LOOK

SEARCHES

Metal detectors at airports search passengers. Airline workers search all carry-on luggage. Do these actions violate the 4th Amendment? The courts say no. They have cited many situations that allow for searches without a warrant, or written order. A person's right to privacy is balanced against the government's need to prevent crime.

20. What does the right to privacy mean to you at home and at school?

A CLOSER LOOK

In 1966, the Supreme Court made a decision based on the 5th and 6th Amendments. The warnings outlined in this ruling are often called "Miranda rights." Miranda rights protect suspects from giving forced confessions. Police must read these rights to a suspect they are questioning. For example:

• "You have the right to remain silent."
• "Anything that you say can and will be used against you in a court of law."
• "You have the right to an attorney."

A CLOSER LOOK

Protesters such as the young woman at left claim that the death penalty violates the 8th Amendment, which protects people against "cruel and unusual punishment." Supporters (above) believe that the death penalty is a justly deserved punishment.

A CLOSER LOOK

STATES' POWERS

The 10th Amendment gives the states reserved powers. Any powers not clearly given to the national government by the U.S. Constitution or denied to the states in Article I, Section 10, belong to the states. State constitutions sometimes assume authority in unexpected areas. For example, California's constitution sets rules for governing the use of fishing nets.

21. What are some common areas in which states have authority?

AMENDMENT 7. Trial by Jury in Civil Cases (1791) In suits at __common law,__ where the value in controversy shall exceed twenty dollars, the right of trial by jury shall be preserved, and no fact tried by a jury, shall be otherwise reexamined in any court of the United States, than according to the rules of the common law.

AMENDMENT 8. Limits of Fines and Punishments (1791) Excessive __bail__ shall not be required, nor excessive fines imposed, nor cruel and unusual punishments inflicted.

AMENDMENT 9. Rights of People (1791) The enumeration in the Constitution of certain rights shall not be construed to deny or disparage others retained by the people.

AMENDMENT 10. Powers of States and People (1791) The powers not delegated to the United States by the Constitution, nor prohibited by it to the States, are reserved to the States respectively, or to the people.

Bill of Rights Assessment

1. Main Ideas

a. Which amendment protects your privacy?

b. Which amendments guarantee fair legal treatment?

c. Which amendment prevents the federal government from taking powers away from the states and the people?

2. Critical Thinking

Forming and Supporting Opinions The 4th, 5th, 6th, 7th, and 8th Amendments protect innocent people accused of crimes. Do you think these five amendments also favor the rights of actual criminals? Explain.

THINK ABOUT

- criminals who go free if valuable evidence is found after their trials
- criminals released on bail

Amendments 11–27

> **MAIN IDEA** The Constitution has adapted to social changes and historical trends.
> **WHY IT MATTERS NOW** Amendments 11–27 show that the Constitution is a living document.

AMENDMENT 11. Lawsuits Against States (1798)

Passed by Congress March 4, 1794. Ratified February 7, 1795. Proclaimed 1798.
Note: Article 3, Section 2, of the Constitution was modified by Amendment 11.

The Judicial power of the United States shall not be construed to extend to any suit in law or **equity**, commenced or prosecuted against one of the United States by citizens of another state, or by citizens or subjects of any foreign state.

AMENDMENT 12. Election of Executives (1804)

Passed by Congress December 9, 1803. Ratified June 15, 1804.
Note: Part of Article 2, Section 1, of the Constitution was replaced by the 12th Amendment.

The electors shall meet in their respective states and vote by ballot for President and Vice-President, one of whom, at least, shall not be an inhabitant of the same state with themselves; they shall name in their ballots the person voted for as President, and in distinct ballots the person voted for as Vice-President, and they shall make distinct lists of all persons voted for as President, and of all persons voted for as Vice-President, and of the number of votes for each, which lists they shall sign and certify, and transmit sealed to the seat of the government of the United States, directed to the President of the Senate;—the President of the Senate shall, in the presence of the Senate and House of Representatives, open all the certificates and the votes shall then be counted;—the person having the greatest number of votes for President, shall be the President, if such number be a majority of the whole number of electors appointed; and if no person have such majority, then from the persons having the highest numbers not exceeding three on the list of those voted for as President, the House of Representatives shall choose immediately, by ballot, the President. But in choosing the President, the votes shall be taken by states, the representation from each state having one vote; a quorum for this purpose shall consist of a member or members from two-thirds of the states, and a majority of all the states shall be necessary to a choice. And if the House of Representatives shall not choose a President whenever the right of choice shall devolve upon them, before the fourth day of March next following, then the Vice-President shall act as President, as in the case of the death or other constitutional disability of the President. The person having the greatest number of votes as Vice-President, shall be the Vice-President, if such number be a majority of the whole number of Electors appointed, and if no person have a majority, then from the two highest numbers on the list, the Senate shall choose the Vice-President; a quorum for the purpose shall consist of two-thirds of the whole number of Senators, and a majority of the whole number shall be necessary to a choice. But no person constitutionally ineligible to the office of President shall be eligible to that of Vice-President of the United States.

VOCABULARY

common law a system of law developed in England, based on customs and previous court decisions

bail money paid by arrested persons to guarantee they will return for trial

equity a system of justice not covered under common law

A CLOSER LOOK

SEPARATE BALLOTS

The presidential election of 1800 ended in a tie between Thomas Jefferson and Aaron Burr. At this time, the candidate with the most votes became president. The runner-up became vice-president. The 12th Amendment calls for separate ballots for the president and vice-president. The vice-president is specifically elected to the office, rather than being the presidential candidate with the second-most votes.

22. Why do you think it's important for a presidential election to result in a clear-cut winner?

VOCABULARY

servitude being under the authority of an owner or master

naturalized granted nationality

insurrection revolt against authority

bounties rewards

AMENDMENT 13. Slavery Abolished (1865)

Passed by Congress January 31, 1865. Ratified December 6, 1865.

Note: A portion of Article 4, Section 2, of the Constitution was superseded by the 13th Amendment.

Section 1. Neither slavery nor involuntary **servitude,** except as a punishment for crime whereof the party shall have been duly convicted, shall exist within the United States, or any place subject to their jurisdiction.

Section 2. Congress shall have power to enforce this article by appropriate legislation.

AMENDMENT 14. Civil Rights (1868)

Passed by Congress June 13, 1866. Ratified July 9, 1868.

Note: Article 1, Section 2, of the Constitution was modified by Section 2 of the 14th Amendment.

Section 1. All persons born or **naturalized** in the United States, and subject to the jurisdiction thereof, are citizens of the United States and of the state wherein they reside. No state shall make or enforce any law which shall abridge the privileges or immunities of citizens of the United States; nor shall any state deprive any person of life, liberty, or property, without due process of law; nor deny to any person within its jurisdiction the equal protection of the laws.

Section 2. Representatives shall be apportioned among the several states according to their respective numbers, counting the whole number of persons in each state, excluding Indians not taxed. But when the right to vote at any election for the choice of electors for President and Vice-President of the United States, Representatives in Congress, the executive and judicial officers of a state, or the members of the legislature thereof, is denied to any of the male inhabitants of such state, being twenty-one years of age, and citizens of the United States, or in any way abridged, except for participation in rebellion, or other crime, the basis of representation therein shall be reduced in the proportion which the number of such male citizens shall bear to the whole number of male citizens twenty-one years of age in such state.

A CLOSER LOOK

The 14th Amendment laid the groundwork for many civil rights laws, such as the Americans with Disabilities Act (1990). This act gave people with mental or physical disabilities "equal protection of the laws." For example, public places had to be designed for wheelchair use. Wider doors and ramps allow disabled people to go in and out of buildings.

Section 3. No person shall be a Senator or Representative in Congress, or elector of President and Vice-President, or hold any office, civil or military, under the United States, or under any state, who, having previously taken an oath, as a member of Congress, or as an officer of the United States, or as a member of any state legislature, or as an executive or judicial officer of any state, to support the Constitution of the United States, shall have engaged in **insurrection** or rebellion against the same, or given aid or comfort to the enemies thereof. But Congress may, by a vote of two-thirds of each house, remove such disability.

Section 4. The validity of the public debt of the United States, authorized by law, including debts incurred for payment of pensions and **bounties** for services in suppressing insurrection or rebellion, shall not be questioned. But neither the United States nor any state shall assume or pay any debt or obligation incurred in aid of insurrection or rebellion against the United States, or any claim for the loss or emancipation of any slave; but all such debts, obligations and claims shall be held illegal and void.

Section 5. The Congress shall have power to enforce, by appropriate legislation, the provisions of this article.

AMENDMENT 15. Right to Vote (1870)

Passed by Congress February 26, 1869. Ratified February 3, 1870.

Section 1. The right of citizens of the United States to vote shall not be denied or abridged by the United States or by any state on account of race, color, or previous condition of servitude.

Section 2. The Congress shall have power to enforce this article by appropriate legislation.

A CLOSER LOOK Reconstruction Amendments

The 13th, 14th, and 15th Amendments are often called the Reconstruction Amendments. They were passed after the Civil War during the government's attempt to rebuild the Union and to grant rights to recently freed African Americans.

Amendment 13	Amendment 14	Amendment 15

1865	1868	1870
• Ended slavery in the United States	• Defined national and state citizenship • Protected citizens' rights • Promised "equal protection of the laws"	• Designed to protect African Americans' voting rights

SKILLBUILDER Interpreting Charts
What problems did these amendments try to solve?

A CLOSER LOOK

VOTING RIGHTS

The Voting Rights Act of 1965 extended the 15th Amendment. To qualify as voters, African Americans were no longer required to take tests proving that they could read and write. Also, federal examiners could help register voters. As a result, the number of African-American voters rose sharply.

23. What effect do you think the Voting Rights Act had on candidates running for office?

INCOME TAX

People below the poverty level, as defined by the federal government, do not have to pay income tax. In 1997, the poverty level for a family of four was $16,400 per year. About 13.3 percent of all Americans were considered poor in 1997.

24. Why do you think people below the poverty level do not pay any income tax?

Under Prohibition, people broke the law if they made, sold, or shipped alcoholic beverages. Powerful crime gangs turned selling illegal liquor into a big business. This photo shows federal agents getting ready to smash containers of illegal whiskey. The 21st Amendment ended Prohibition.

AMENDMENT 16. Income Tax (1913)

Passed by Congress July 12, 1909. Ratified February 3, 1913.

Note: Article 1, Section 9, of the Constitution was modified by the 16th Amendment.

The Congress shall have power to lay and collect taxes on incomes, from whatever source derived, without apportionment among the several states, and without regard to any census or enumeration.

AMENDMENT 17. Direct Election of Senators (1913)

Passed by Congress May 13, 1912. Ratified April 8, 1913.

Note: Article 1, Section 3, of the Constitution was modified by the 17th Amendment.

Section 1. The Senate of the United States shall be composed of two Senators from each state, elected by the people thereof, for six years; and each Senator shall have one vote. The electors in each state shall have the qualifications requisite for electors of the most numerous branch of the state legislatures.

Section 2. When vacancies happen in the representation of any state in the Senate, the executive authority of such state shall issue writs of election to fill such vacancies: Provided, that the legislature of any state may empower the executive thereof to make temporary appointments until the people fill the vacancies by election as the legislature may direct.

Section 3. This amendment shall not be so construed as to affect the election or term of any Senator chosen before it becomes valid as part of the Constitution.

AMENDMENT 18. Prohibition (1919)

Passed by Congress December 18, 1917. Ratified January 16, 1919. Repealed by the 21st Amendment.

Section 1. After one year from the ratification of this article the manufacture, sale, or transportation of intoxicating liquors within, the importation thereof into, or the exportation thereof from the United States and all territory subject to the jurisdiction thereof for beverage purposes is hereby prohibited.

Section 2. The Congress and the several states shall have concurrent power to enforce this article by appropriate legislation.

Section 3. This article shall be inoperative unless it shall have been ratified as an amendment to the Constitution by the legislatures of the several states, as provided in the Constitution, within seven years from the date of the submission hereof to the states by the Congress.

A CLOSER LOOK

At left, marchers campaign for the 19th Amendment—woman suffrage. Since winning the right to vote in 1920, women have slowly gained political power. Pictured below are Congress members who belong to the Congressional Caucus for Women's Issues.

AMENDMENT 19. Woman Suffrage (1920)

Passed by Congress June 4, 1919. Ratified August 18, 1920.

Section 1. The right of citizens of the United States to vote shall not be denied or abridged by the United States or by any state on account of sex.

Section 2. Congress shall have power to enforce this article by appropriate legislation.

AMENDMENT 20. "Lame Duck" Sessions (1933)

Passed by Congress March 2, 1932. Ratified January 23, 1933.

Note: Article 1, Section 4, of the Constitution was modified by Section 2 of this amendment. In addition, a portion of the 12th Amendment was superseded by Section 3.

Section 1. The terms of the President and Vice-President shall end at noon on the 20th day of January, and the terms of Senators and Representatives at noon on the 3rd day of January, of the years in which such terms would have ended if this article had not been ratified; and the terms of their successors shall then begin.

Section 2. The Congress shall assemble at least once in every year, and such meeting shall begin at noon on the 3rd day of January, unless they shall by law appoint a different day.

Section 3. If, at the time fixed for the beginning of the term of the President, the President elect shall have died, the Vice-President elect shall become President. If a President shall not have been chosen before the time fixed for the beginning of his term, or if the President elect shall have failed to qualify, then the Vice-President elect shall act as President until a President shall have qualified; and the Congress may by law provide for the case wherein neither a President elect nor a Vice-President elect shall have

A CLOSER LOOK

THE EQUAL RIGHTS AMENDMENT

In 1920, the 19th Amendment took effect, guaranteeing women the right to vote. Nevertheless, many women have continued to face discrimination in the United States. In 1923, the National Women's Party supported the passage of an equal rights amendment to protect women. Congress did not pass such an amendment until 1972. In 1982, however, the amendment died after it failed to be ratified by enough states to be added to the Constitution.

25. Why do you think the 19th Amendment failed to create equality for women?

VOCABULARY

inoperative no longer in force

primary an election in which registered members of a political party nominate candidates for office

qualified, declaring who shall then act as President, or the manner in which one who is to act shall be selected, and such person shall act accordingly until a President or Vice-President shall have qualified.

Section 4. The Congress may by law provide for the case of the death of any of the persons from whom the House of Representatives may choose a President whenever the right of choice shall have devolved upon them, and for the case of the death of any of the persons from whom the Senate may choose a Vice-President whenever the right of choice shall have devolved upon them.

Section 5. Sections 1 and 2 shall take effect on the 15th day of October following the ratification of this article.

Section 6. This article shall be **inoperative** unless it shall have been ratified as an amendment to the Constitution by the legislatures of three-fourths of the several states within seven years from the date of its submission.

AMENDMENT 21. Repeal of Prohibition (1933)

Passed by Congress February 20, 1933. Ratified December 5, 1933.

Section 1. The eighteenth article of amendment to the Constitution of the United States is hereby repealed.

Section 2. The transportation or importation into any state, territory, or possession of the United States for delivery or use therein of intoxicating liquors, in violation of the laws thereof, is hereby prohibited.

Section 3. This article shall be inoperative unless it shall have been ratified as an amendment to the Constitution by conventions in the several states, as provided in the Constitution, within seven years from the date of the submission hereof to the states by the Congress.

AMENDMENT 22. Limit on Presidential Terms (1951)

Passed by Congress March 21, 1947. Ratified February 27, 1951.

Section 1. No person shall be elected to the office of the President more than twice, and no person who has held the office of President, or acted as President, for more than two years of a term to which some other person was elected President shall be elected to the office of the President more than once. But this article shall not apply to any person holding the office of President when this article was proposed by the Congress, and shall not prevent any person who may be holding the office of President, or acting as President, during the term within which this article becomes operative from holding the office of President or acting as President during the remainder of such term.

Section 2. This article shall be inoperative unless it shall have been ratified as an amendment to the Constitution by the legislatures of three-fourths of the several states within seven years from the date of its submission to the states by the Congress.

A CLOSER LOOK

George Washington set the tradition of limiting the presidency to two terms. Franklin Roosevelt broke this custom when he was elected president four terms in a row—1932, 1936, 1940, and 1944. His record-long presidency led to the 22nd Amendment. A two-term limit, written into the Constitution, checks the president's power.

AMENDMENT 23. Voting in District of Columbia (1961)

Passed by Congress June 17, 1960. Ratified March 29, 1961.

Section 1. The district constituting the seat of government of the United States shall appoint in such manner as Congress may direct: a number of electors of President and Vice-President equal to the whole number of Senators and Representatives in Congress to which the district would be entitled if it were a state, but in no event more than the least populous state; they shall be in addition to those appointed by the states, but they shall be considered, for the purposes of the election of President and Vice-President, to be electors appointed by a state; and they shall meet in the district and perform such duties as provided by the twelfth article of amendment.

Section 2. The Congress shall have power to enforce this article by appropriate legislation.

AMENDMENT 24. Abolition of Poll Taxes (1964)

Passed by Congress August 27, 1962. Ratified January 23, 1964.

Section 1. The right of citizens of the United States to vote in any **primary** or other election for President or Vice-President, for electors for President or Vice-President, or for Senator or Representative in Congress, shall not be denied or abridged by the United States or any state by reason of failure to pay any poll tax or other tax.

Section 2. The Congress shall have power to enforce this article by appropriate legislation.

AMENDMENT 25. Presidential Disability, Succession (1967)

Passed by Congress July 6, 1965. Ratified February 10, 1967.

Note: Article 2, Section 1, of the Constitution was affected by the 25th Amendment.

Section 1. In case of the removal of the President from office or of his death or resignation, the Vice-President shall become President.

Section 2. Whenever there is a vacancy in the office of the Vice-President, the President shall nominate a Vice-President who shall take office upon confirmation by a majority vote of both houses of Congress.

Section 3. Whenever the President transmits to the President pro tempore of the Senate and the Speaker of the House of Representatives his written declaration that he is unable to discharge the powers and duties of his office, and until he transmits to them a written declaration to the contrary, such powers and duties shall be discharged by the Vice-President as Acting President.

A CLOSER LOOK

POLL TAX

The poll tax was aimed at preventing African Americans from exercising their rights. Many could not afford to pay this fee required for voting.

26. How do you think the 24th Amendment affected elections?

A CLOSER LOOK

PRESIDENTIAL DISABILITY

President John F. Kennedy's death in 1963 signaled the need for the 25th Amendment. The Constitution did not explain what to do in the case of a disabled president. James Reston, a writer for *The New York Times,* summed up the problem: Suppose Kennedy was "strong enough to survive [the bullet wounds], but too weak to govern." The 25th Amendment provides for an orderly transfer of power.

27. What do you think can happen in a country where the rules for succession are not clear?

SUCCESSION

Who takes over if a president dies in office or is unable to serve? The top five in the line of succession follow:

- vice-president
- speaker of the house
- president pro tempore of the Senate
- secretary of state
- secretary of the treasury

28. Why should voters know the views of the vice-president?

Section 4. Whenever the Vice-President and a majority of either the principal officers of the executive departments or of such other body as Congress may by law provide, transmit to the President pro tempore of the Senate and the Speaker of the House of Representatives their written declaration that the President is unable to discharge the powers and duties of his office, the Vice-President shall immediately assume the powers and duties of the office as Acting President. Thereafter, when the President transmits to the President pro tempore of the Senate and the Speaker of the House of Representatives his written declaration that no inability exists, he shall resume the powers and duties of his office unless the Vice-President and a majority of either the principal officers of the executive department[s] or of such other body as Congress may by law provide, transmit within four days to the President pro tempore of the Senate and the Speaker of the House of Representatives their written declaration that the President is unable to discharge the powers and duties of his office. Thereupon Congress shall decide the issue, assembling within forty-eight hours for that purpose if not in session. If the Congress, within twenty-one days after receipt of the latter written declaration, or, if Congress is not in session, within twenty-one days after Congress is required to assemble, determines by two thirds vote of both houses that the President is unable to discharge the powers and duties of his office, the Vice-President shall continue to discharge the same as Acting President; otherwise, the President shall resume the powers and duties of his office.

A CLOSER LOOK Amendments Time Line *1791–1992*

Use the key below to help you categorize the amendments.

- ■ **Voting Rights**
- ■ **Social Changes**
- ■ **Overturned Supreme Court Decisions**
- ■ **Election Procedures and Conditions of Office**

Amendment 15
1870
Stops national and state governments from denying the vote based on race.

Bill of Rights
Amendments 1–10
1791

Amendment 13
1865
Bans slavery.

1790

Amendment 11
1798
Protects state from lawsuits filed by citizens of other states or countries.

Amendment 12
1804
Requires separate electoral ballots for president and vice-president.

Amendment 14
1868
Defines American citizenship and citizens' rights.

AMENDMENT 26. 18-year-old Vote (1971)

Passed by Congress March 23, 1971. Ratified July 1, 1971.

Note: Amendment 14, Section 2, of the Constitution was modified by Section 1 of the 26th Amendment.

Section 1. The right of citizens of the United States, who are eighteen years of age or older, to vote shall not be denied or abridged by the United States or by any state on account of age.

Section 2. The Congress shall have power to enforce this article by appropriate legislation.

AMENDMENT 27. Congressional Pay (1992)

Passed by Congress September 25, 1789. Ratified May 7, 1992.

No law, varying the compensation for the services of the Senators and Representatives, shall take effect, until an election of Representatives shall have intervened.

A CLOSER LOOK

Members of the recording industry founded Rock the Vote. They urge young people to vote in elections.

Amendments 11–27 Assessment

1. Main Ideas

a. Which amendments affected the office of president?

b. Which pair of amendments shows the failure of laws to solve a social problem?

c. Which amendments corrected unfair treatment toward African Americans and women?

2. Critical Thinking

Summarizing What is the purpose of amending the Constitution?

THINK ABOUT

• the purpose of the Constitution

• problems and issues that Americans have faced throughout U.S. history

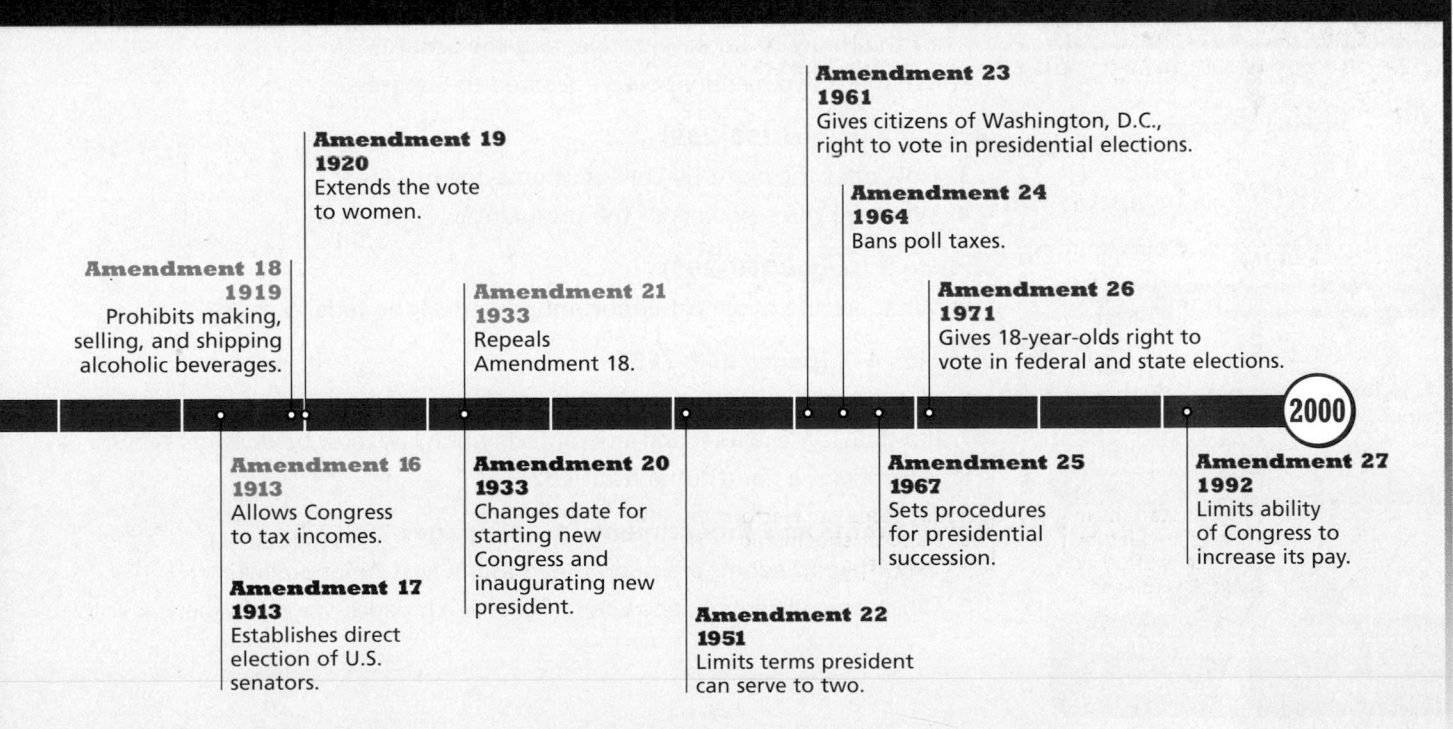

Amendment 18
1919
Prohibits making, selling, and shipping alcoholic beverages.

Amendment 19
1920
Extends the vote to women.

Amendment 23
1961
Gives citizens of Washington, D.C., right to vote in presidential elections.

Amendment 24
1964
Bans poll taxes.

Amendment 21
1933
Repeals Amendment 18.

Amendment 26
1971
Gives 18-year-olds right to vote in federal and state elections.

2000

Amendment 16
1913
Allows Congress to tax incomes.

Amendment 17
1913
Establishes direct election of U.S. senators.

Amendment 20
1933
Changes date for starting new Congress and inaugurating new president.

Amendment 22
1951
Limits terms president can serve to two.

Amendment 25
1967
Sets procedures for presidential succession.

Amendment 27
1992
Limits ability of Congress to increase its pay.

VISUAL SUMMARY

The Constitution of the United States

Preamble

WE THE PEOPLE

Article 1   Article 2   Article 3

The Branches of Government

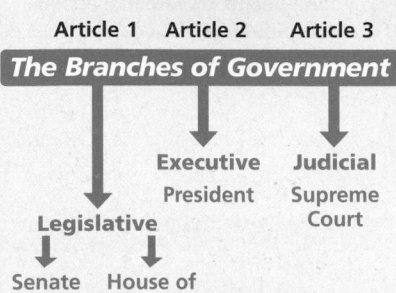

Executive
President

Judicial
Supreme Court

Legislative

Senate   House of Representatives

Article 4   Article 6

The Federal System

Powers of the State

Powers of the National Government

"Supreme law of the land"

Article 5

Amending the Constitution

Making Changes

Bill of Rights

Amendments 1–10

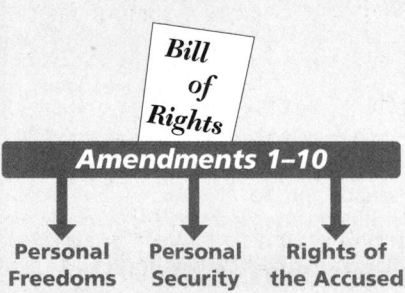

Personal Freedoms

Personal Security

Rights of the Accused

Amendments 11–27

The living Constitution changes with the times.

278 THE LIVING CONSTITUTION

VOCABULARY

Briefly explain the significance of each of the following.

1. electors
2. impeachment
3. naturalization
4. felonies
5. bill of attainder
6. ex post facto law
7. suffrage
8. due process of law
9. servitude
10. primary

SEVEN PRINCIPLES OF THE CONSTITUTION

Make a chart like the one shown. Then fill it in with a definition of each principle and an example from the Constitution.

Principle	Definition	Example
1. popular sovereignty		
2. republicanism		
3. federalism		
4. separation of powers		
5. checks and balances		
6. limited government		
7. individual rights		

REVIEW QUESTIONS

Article 1 (pages 249–255)

1. What are the requirements for becoming a member of the House of Representatives and the Senate?
2. What are two military powers granted to Congress?

Article 2 (pages 256–259)

3. How does the electoral college choose the president?
4. What are three powers of the president?

Article 3 (pages 260–261)

5. What are the two most important powers of the federal courts?

Articles 4–7 (pages 262–265)

6. How can the Constitution be changed?
7. If a state law and a federal law conflict, which law must be obeyed? Why?
8. How was the Constitution ratified?

Bill of Rights and Amendments 11–27 (pages 266–277)

9. What five freedoms are guaranteed in the First Amendment?
10. Which amendments extend voting rights to a broader range of Americans?

CRITICAL THINKING

1. DRAWING CONCLUSIONS

In a two-column chart, summarize the processes for changing the Constitution. Then use your completed chart to answer the questions below.

Proposing Amendments	Ratifying Amendments
1.	1.
2.	2.

a. What role can citizens play in proposing amendments?

b. What do you think are the main reasons for changing the Constitution?

2. MAKING INFERENCES

Explain how the "elastic clause" in Article 1 gives Congress the authority to take action on other issues unknown to the Framers of the Constitution.

3. ANALYZING LEADERSHIP

Think about the president's roles described in the Constitution. What qualities does a president need to succeed as a leader in so many different areas?

4. RECOGNIZING EFFECTS

How would you describe the impact of the 14th, 15th, and 16th Amendments on life in the United States?

5. APPLYING CITIZENSHIP

Suppose you and your family go on a road trip across several states. According to Article 4 of the Constitution, what citizens' rights do you have in the states you are visiting?

HISTORY SKILLS

INTERPRETING PRIMARY SOURCES

In 1937, President Franklin D. Roosevelt gave a speech over the radio. He used interesting comparisons to explain how the government works.

> I described the American form of government as a three-horse team provided by the Constitution to the American people so that their field might be plowed. The three horses are, of course, the three branches of government—the Congress, the Executive, and the Courts. . . . It is the American people themselves who are in the driver's seat. It is the American people themselves who want the furrow plowed.
>
> **Franklin D. Roosevelt,** Radio Address

- How does Roosevelt describe the separation of powers?
- How does Roosevelt explain popular sovereignty?

ALTERNATIVE ASSESSMENT

1. INTERDISCIPLINARY ACTIVITY: Government

Creating a Database Review the grievances against King George III listed in the Declaration of Independence. Then create a database that shows how specific sections of the U.S. Constitution addressed those grievances. Write a brief summary stating how well the Constitution addressed the grievances.

2. COOPERATIVE LEARNING ACTIVITY

Drafting a Constitution Imagine you are asked to write a constitution for a newly formed country. Working with a group, use the outline below to organize and write your constitution.

I. Purpose of the Constitution (Preamble)

II. Making Laws (Legislative Branch)

III. Carrying Out the Laws (Executive Branch)

IV. Making Laws Fair (Judicial Branch)

V. Choosing Leaders

VI. Citizens' Rights (Bill of Rights)

3. PRIMARY SOURCE EXPLORER

Making a Learning Center Creating the U.S. Constitution was one of the most important events in the nation's history. Use the CD-ROM and the library to collect information on different topics related to the Constitution.

Create a learning center featuring the suggestions below.

- Find biographies and portraits of the Framers.
- Collect important primary sources such as James Madison's notes and *The Federalist* papers.
- Gather recent pictures and news articles about the Congress, the president, the Supreme Court, and the Bill of Rights.

4. HISTORY PORTFOLIO

Review your draft of the constitution you wrote for the assessment activity. Choose one of these options below.

 Option 1 Use comments made by your teacher or classmates to improve your work.

Option 2 Illustrate your constitution. Add your work to your history portfolio.

Additional Test Practice, pp. S1–S33

 **TEST PRACTICE** CLASSZONE.COM

The Role of the Citizen

Citizens of the United States enjoy many basic rights and freedoms. Freedom of speech and religion are examples. These rights are guaranteed by the Constitution, the Bill of Rights, and other amendments to the Constitution. Along with these rights, however, come responsibilities. Obeying rules and laws, voting, and serving on juries are some examples.

Active citizenship is not limited to adults. Younger citizens can help their communities become better places. The following pages will help you to learn about your rights and responsibilities. Knowing them will help you to become an active and involved citizen of your community, state, and nation.

In this book you will find examples of active citizenship by young people like yourself. **Look for the Citizenship Today features.**

Citizen ▸ **KNOW YOUR RIGHTS** ▸ **BE RESPONSIBLE** ▸ **STAY INFORMED** ▸ **MAKE GOOD DECISIONS** ▸ **PARTICIPATE IN YOUR COMMUNITY** ▸ **Model Citizen**

President John F. Kennedy urged all Americans to become active citizens and work to improve their communities.

The weather was sunny but cold on January 20, 1961—the day that John F. Kennedy became the 35th president of the United States. In his first speech as president, he urged all Americans to serve their country. Since then, Kennedy's words have inspired millions of Americans to become more active citizens.

"Ask not what your country can do for you—ask what you can do for your country!"

—JOHN F. KENNEDY

What Is a Citizen?

A citizen is a legal member of a nation and pledges loyalty to that nation. A citizen has certain guaranteed rights, protections, and responsibilities. A citizen is a member of a community and wants to make it a good place to live.

Today in the United States there are a number of ways to become a citizen. The most familiar are citizenship by birth and citizenship by naturalization. All citizens have the right to equal protection under the law.

CITIZENSHIP BY BIRTH A child born in the United States is a citizen by birth. Children born to U.S. citizens traveling or living outside the country, such as military personnel, are citizens. Even children born in the United States to parents who are not citizens of the United States are considered U.S. citizens. These children have dual citizenship. This means they are citizens of two countries—both the United States and the country of their parents' citizenship. At the age of 18, the child may choose one of the countries for permanent citizenship.

CITIZENSHIP BY NATURALIZATION A person who is not a citizen of the United States may become one through a process called naturalization. The steps in this process are shown below. To become a naturalized citizen, a person must meet certain requirements.

- Be at least 18 years old. Children under the age of 18 automatically become naturalized citizens when their parents do.
- Enter the United States legally.
- Live in the United States for at least five years immediately prior to application.
- Read, write, and speak English.
- Show knowledge of American history and government.

See Citizenship Today: Becoming a Citizen, p. 427

Steps in the Naturalization Process

1. File an application.
2. Take an examination.
3. File a legal petition for naturalization.
4. Appear at a court hearing.
5. Take an oath of allegiance.

Hundreds of people become new citizens at a single ceremony in San Antonio, Texas.

What Are Your Rights?

Citizens of the United States are guaranteed rights by the U.S. Constitution, state constitutions, and state and federal laws. All citizens have three kinds of rights: basic freedoms, protection from unfair government actions, and equal treatment under the law.

Citizens' basic rights and freedoms are sometimes called **civil rights**. Some of these rights are personal, and others are political.

The U.S. Constitution grants these five basic freedoms.

BASIC FREEDOMS

- Freedom of religion
- Freedom of speech
- Freedom of the press
- Freedom of peaceful assembly
- Freedom to petition the government for change

The second category of rights is intended to protect citizens from unfair government actions.

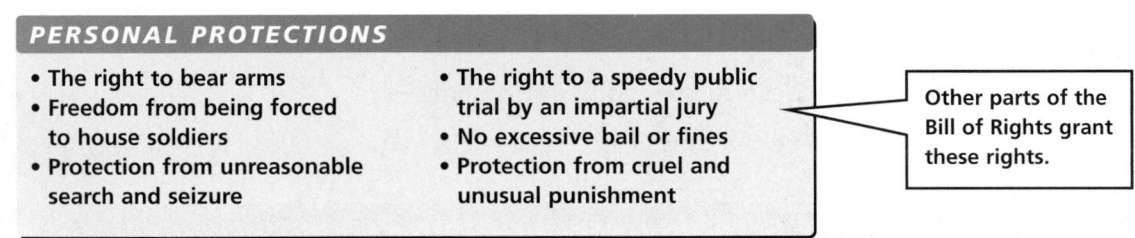

PERSONAL PROTECTIONS

- The right to bear arms
- Freedom from being forced to house soldiers
- Protection from unreasonable search and seizure
- The right to a speedy public trial by an impartial jury
- No excessive bail or fines
- Protection from cruel and unusual punishment

Other parts of the Bill of Rights grant these rights.

The third category is the right to equal treatment under the law. The government cannot treat one individual or group differently from another.

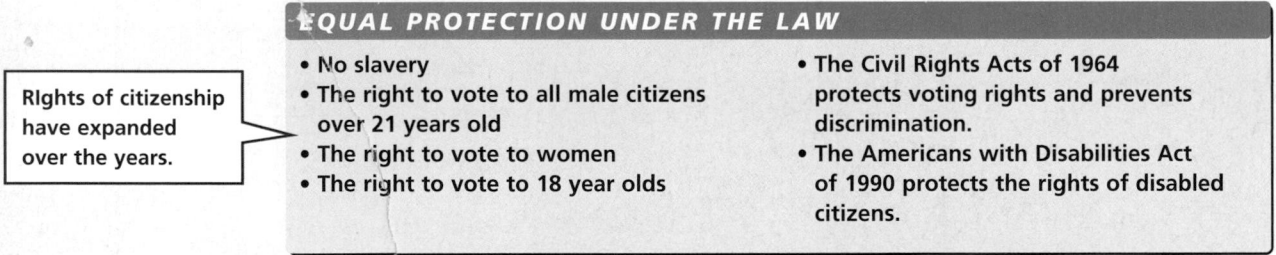

Rights of citizenship have expanded over the years.

EQUAL PROTECTION UNDER THE LAW

- No slavery
- The right to vote to all male citizens over 21 years old
- The right to vote to women
- The right to vote to 18 year olds
- The Civil Rights Acts of 1964 protects voting rights and prevents discrimination.
- The Americans with Disabilities Act of 1990 protects the rights of disabled citizens.

LIMITS TO RIGHTS The rights guaranteed to citizens have sensible limits. For example, the right to free speech does not allow a person to falsely shout, "Fire!" at a crowded concert. The government may place limits on certain rights to protect national security or to provide equal opportunities for all citizens. And rights come with responsibilities.

What Are Your Responsibilities?

For American democracy to work, citizens must carry out important responsibilities. There are two kinds of responsibilities—personal and civic. Personal responsibilities include taking care of yourself, helping your family, knowing right from wrong, and behaving in a respectful way.

Civic responsibilities are those that involve your government and community. They include obeying rules and laws, serving on juries, paying taxes, and defending your country when called upon. One of the most important responsibilities is voting. When you turn 18, you will have that right.

As a young person, you can be a good citizen in a number of ways. You might work with other people in your community to make it a fair and just place to live. Working for a political party or writing to your elected officials about issues that concern you are some other examples.

The chart below shows how responsibilities change with a citizen's age. Notice that all citizens share the responsibility to obey the laws of their communities.

See Citizenship Today: Obeying Rules and Laws, p. 300

Responsibilities of a Citizen

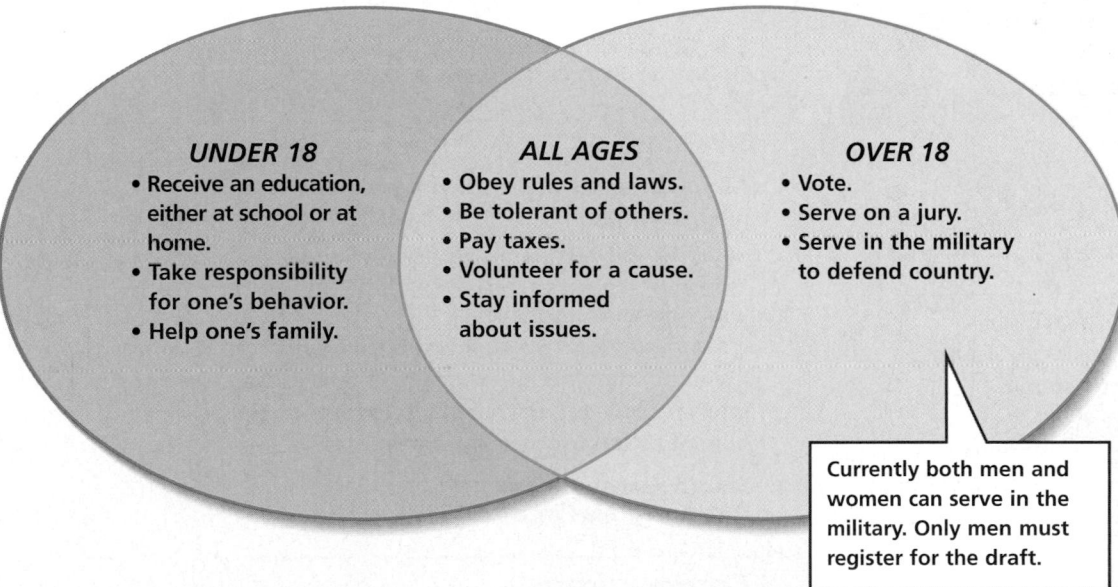

UNDER 18
- Receive an education, either at school or at home.
- Take responsibility for one's behavior.
- Help one's family.

ALL AGES
- Obey rules and laws.
- Be tolerant of others.
- Pay taxes.
- Volunteer for a cause.
- Stay informed about issues.

OVER 18
- Vote.
- Serve on a jury.
- Serve in the military to defend country.

Currently both men and women can serve in the military. Only men must register for the draft.

CITIZENSHIP ACTIVITIES

1. Interview a recently naturalized citizen. Ask about the test he or she took to become a U.S. citizen. Write a report of your findings.

2. Using newspapers or magazines, find examples of citizens using their unalienable rights or practicing responsible citizenship. Cut out five articles to illustrate the points. Mount them and write a one-sentence explanation of each article.

Building Citizenship Skills

Good citizenship skills include **staying informed, solving problems** or **making decisions,** and **taking action.** Every citizen can find ways to build citizenship skills. By showing respect for the law and for the rights of others in your daily life, you promote democracy. You can also work to change conditions in your community to make sure all citizens experience freedom and justice.

How Do You Stay Informed?

Americans can sometimes feel that they have access to too much information. It may seem overwhelming. Even so, you should stay informed on issues that affect your life. Staying informed gives you the information you need to make wise decisions and helps you find ways to solve problems.

These Texas middle school students are staying informed by talking to their Texas state representative. Many public officials enjoy having students visit and ask them questions about their jobs, and about issues students think are important.

Watch, Listen, and Read

The first step in practicing good citizenship is to know how to find information that you need.

Sources of information include broadcast and print media and the Internet. Public officials and civic organizations are also good sources for additional information. Remember as you are reading to evaluate your sources.

See Citizenship Today:
Debating Points of View, p. 469

Evaluate

As you become informed, you will need to make judgments about the accuracy of your news sources. You must also be aware of those sources' points of view and biases. (A bias is a judgment formed without knowing all of the facts.)

You should determine if you need more information. If you do, then decide where to find it. After gathering information, you may be ready to form an opinion or a plan of action to solve a problem.

See Citizenship Today:
Detecting Bias in the Media, p. 664

Communicate

To bring about change in their communities, active citizens may need to contact public officials. In today's world, making contact is easy.

You can reach most public officials by telephone, voice mail, fax, or letter. Many public officials also have Internet pages or e-mail that encourages input from the public.

How Do You Make Wise Decisions?

Civic life involves making important decisions. As a voter, whom should you vote for? As a juror, should you find the defendant guilty or not guilty? As an informed citizen, should you support or oppose a proposed government action? Unlike decisions about which video to rent, civic decisions cannot be made by a process as easy as tossing a coin. Instead, you should use a problem-solving approach like the one shown in the chart below. Decision making won't always proceed directly from step to step. Sometimes it's necessary to backtrack a little. For example, you may get to the "Analyze the Information" step and realize that you don't have enough information to analyze. Then you can go back a step and gather more information.

Problem-Solving and Decision-Making Process

Problem-solving and decision-making involves many steps. This diagram shows you how to take those steps. Notice that you may have to repeat some steps depending on the information you gather.

EVALUATE THE SOLUTION
Review the results of putting your solution into action. Did the solution work? Do you need to adjust the solution in some way?

IMPLEMENT THE SOLUTION
Take action or plan to take action on a chosen solution.

CHOOSE A SOLUTION
Choose the solution you believe will best solve the problem and help you reach your goal.

CONSIDER OPTIONS
Think of as many ways as possible to solve the problem. Don't be afraid to include ideas that others might think are unacceptable.

ANALYZE THE INFORMATION
Look at the information and determine what it reveals about solving the problem.

GATHER INFORMATION
Get to know the basics of the problem. Find out as much as possible about the issues.

IDENTIFY THE PROBLEM
Decide what the main issues are and what your goal is.

Students working on an environmental project are gathering and analyzing information to help them make decisions.

How Do You Participate in Your Community?

Across the country many young people have come up with ways to make their communities better places to live. Thirteen-year-old Aubyn Burnside of Hickory, North Carolina, is just one example. Aubyn felt sorry for foster children she saw moving their belongings in plastic trash bags. She founded Suitcases for Kids. This program provides used luggage for foster children who are moving from one home to another. Her program has been adopted by other young people in several states. Below are some ways in which you can participate in your community.

See Citizenship Today: Community Service, p. 612

Students participate in a rally to promote safety in their school.

Find a Cause

How can you become involved in your community? First, select a community problem or issue that interests you. Some ideas from other young people include starting a support group for children with cancer, publishing a neighborhood newspaper with children's stories and art, and putting on performances to entertain people in shelters and hospitals.

Develop Solutions

Once you have found a cause on which you want to work, develop a plan for solving the problem. Use the decision-making or problem-solving skills you have learned to find ways to approach the problem. You may want to involve other people in your activities.

Follow Through

Solving problems takes time. You'll need to be patient in developing a plan. You can show leadership in working with your group by following through on meetings you set up and plans you make. When you finally solve the problem, you will feel proud of your accomplishments.

CITIZENSHIP ACTIVITIES

1. Use the telephone directory to make a list of names, addresses, and phone numbers of public officials or organizations that could provide information about solving problems in your community.

2. Copy the steps in the problem-solving and decision-making diagram and show how you followed them to solve a problem or make a decision. Be sure to clearly state the problem and the final decision.

Practicing Citizenship Skills

You have learned that good citizenship involves three skills: staying informed, solving problems, and taking action. Below are some activities to help you improve your citizenship skills. By practicing these skills you can work to make a difference in your own life and in the lives of those in your community.

Citizen ▶ KNOW YOUR RIGHTS ▶ BE RESPONSIBLE ▶ STAY INFORMED ▶ MAKE GOOD DECISIONS ▶ PARTICIPATE IN YOUR COMMUNITY ▶ Model Citizen

CITIZENSHIP ACTIVITIES

Stay Informed

CREATE A PAMPHLET OR RECRUITING COMMERCIAL

Ask your school counselors or write to your state department of education to get information on state-run colleges, universities, or technical schools. Use this information to create a brochure or recruiting commercial showing these schools and the different programs and degrees they offer.

KEEP IN MIND

What's there for me? It may help you think about what areas students are interested in and may want to pursue in later life.

Where is it? You may want to have a map showing where the schools are located in your state.

How can I afford it? Students might want to know if financial aid is available to attend the schools you have featured.

Make Wise Decisions

CREATE A GAME BOARD OR SKIT

Study the decision-making diagram on page 285. With a small group, develop a skit that explains the steps in problem solving. Present your skit to younger students in your school. As an alternative, create a game board that would help younger students understand the steps in making a decision.

KEEP IN MIND

What do children this age understand? Be sure to create a skit or game at an age-appropriate level.

What kinds of decisions do younger students make? Think about the kinds of decisions that the viewers of your skit or players of the game might make.

How can I make it interesting? Use visual aids to help students understand the steps in decision making.

Take Action

CREATE A BULLETIN BOARD FOR YOUR CLASS

Do some research on the Internet or consult the yellow pages under "Social Services" to find the names of organizations that have volunteer opportunities for young people. Call or write for more information. Then create a bulletin board for your class showing groups that would like volunteer help.

KEEP IN MIND

What kinds of jobs are they? You may want to list the types of skills or jobs volunteer groups are looking for.

How old do I have to be? Some groups may be looking for younger volunteers; others may need older persons.

How do I get there? How easy is it to get to the volunteer group's location?

The Early Republic

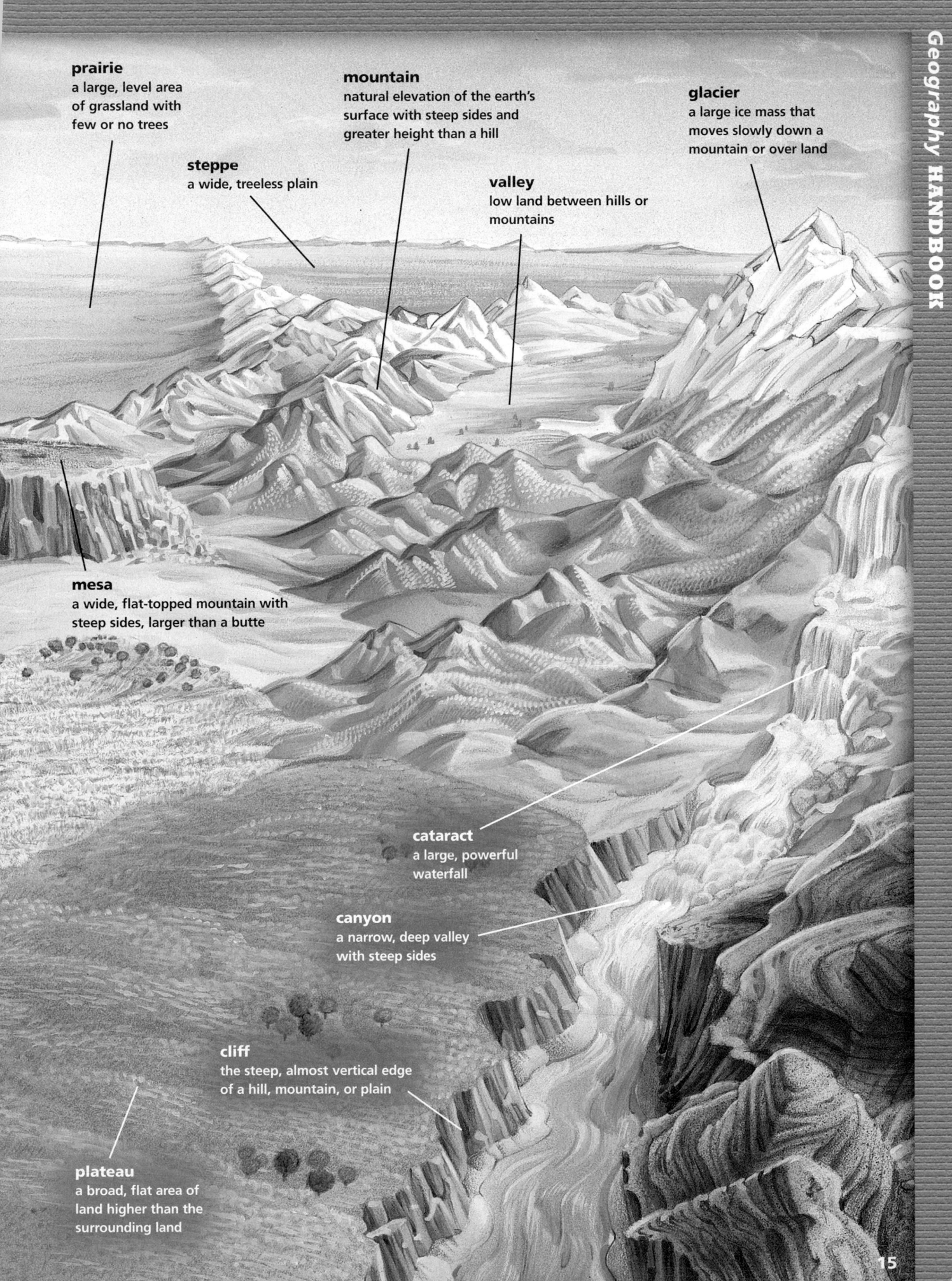

prairie
a large, level area of grassland with few or no trees

steppe
a wide, treeless plain

mountain
natural elevation of the earth's surface with steep sides and greater height than a hill

valley
low land between hills or mountains

glacier
a large ice mass that moves slowly down a mountain or over land

mesa
a wide, flat-topped mountain with steep sides, larger than a butte

cataract
a large, powerful waterfall

canyon
a narrow, deep valley with steep sides

cliff
the steep, almost vertical edge of a hill, mountain, or plain

plateau
a broad, flat area of land higher than the surrounding land

15

Human Geography of the United States

Human geography focuses on people's relationships with each other and the surrounding environment. It includes two main themes of geography: human-environment interaction and movement. The following pages will help you to better understand the link between people and geography.

Humans Adapt to Their Surroundings

Humans have always adapted to their environment. For example, in North America, many Native American tribes burned forest patches to create grazing area to attract animals and to clear area for farmland. In addition, Americans have adapted to their environment by building numerous dams, bridges, and tunnels. More recently, scientists and engineers have been developing building materials that will better withstand the earthquakes that occasionally strike California.

THINKING ABOUT GEOGRAPHY What are some of the ways in which you interact with your environment on a daily basis?

Early Americans of the Southwest protected themselves from the weather by building cliff dwellings.

The Hoover Dam, located on the Colorado River between Arizona and Nevada, provides electricity for Arizona, Nevada, and Southern California.

An oil spill from the ship *Exxon Valdez* harmed wildlife, such as this bird, in Prince William Sound, Alaska, in 1989.

Humans Affect the Environment

When humans interact with the environment, sometimes nature suffers. In the United States, for example, major oil leaks or spills occur each year—fouling shorelines and harming wildlife. Building suburbs and strip malls has also destroyed forests, farmland, and valuable wetlands.

THINKING ABOUT GEOGRAPHY What are some of the environmental problems in your city or town?

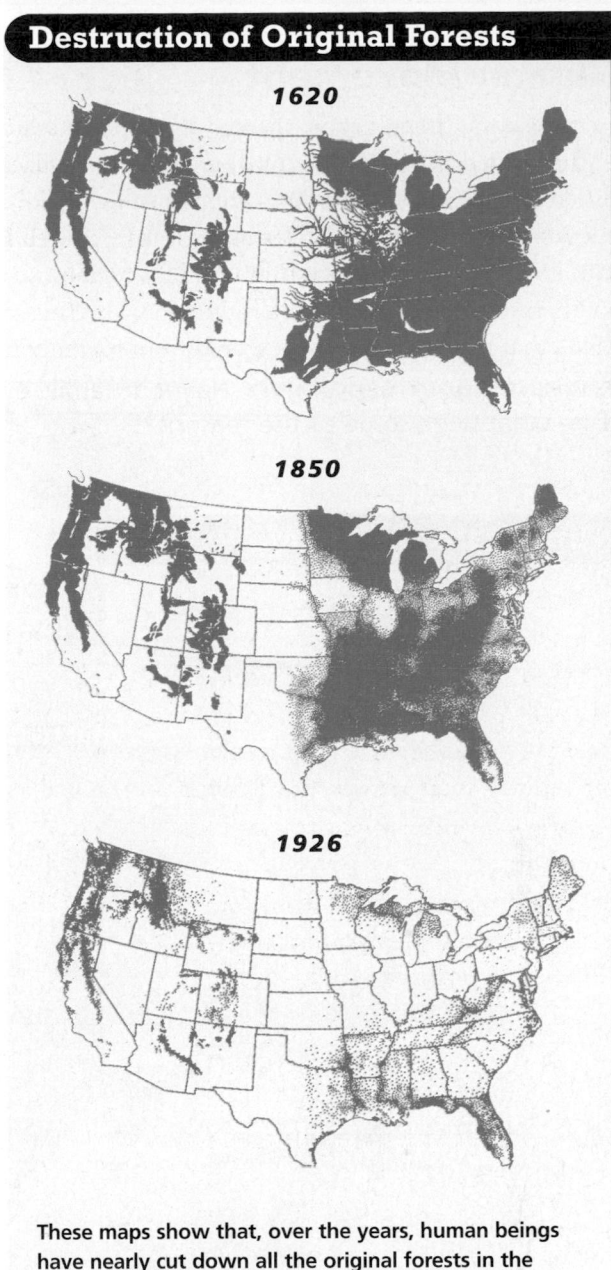

Destruction of Original Forests

1620

1850

1926

These maps show that, over the years, human beings have nearly cut down all the original forests in the United States. Each dot represents 25,000 acres.

Children plant trees along a Chicago expressway.

Preserving and Restoring

Americans—as well as people all over the world—have been working hard to balance economic progress with conservation. For example, car companies in the United States and around the world are working to develop pollution-free vehicles. In 1994, the average American family of four recycled around 1,100 pounds of waste. And, in the 1990s, Americans have planted more than two million acres of new trees each year.

THINKING ABOUT GEOGRAPHY What are some of the ways in which you help the environment?

Human Movement

In prehistoric times, people roamed the earth in search of food. Today in the United States, people move from place to place for many different reasons. Among them are cost of living, job availability, and climate. Since the 1970s, many Americans—as well as many new immigrants—moved to the Sunbelt. This region runs through the southern United States from Virginia to California. Between 1950 and 1990, that region's population soared from 52 million to 118 million.

THINKING ABOUT GEOGRAPHY Has your family ever moved? If so, what were some of the reasons?

This map shows human movement in the 1970s. The information below explains some of the results of this movement in the 1990s.

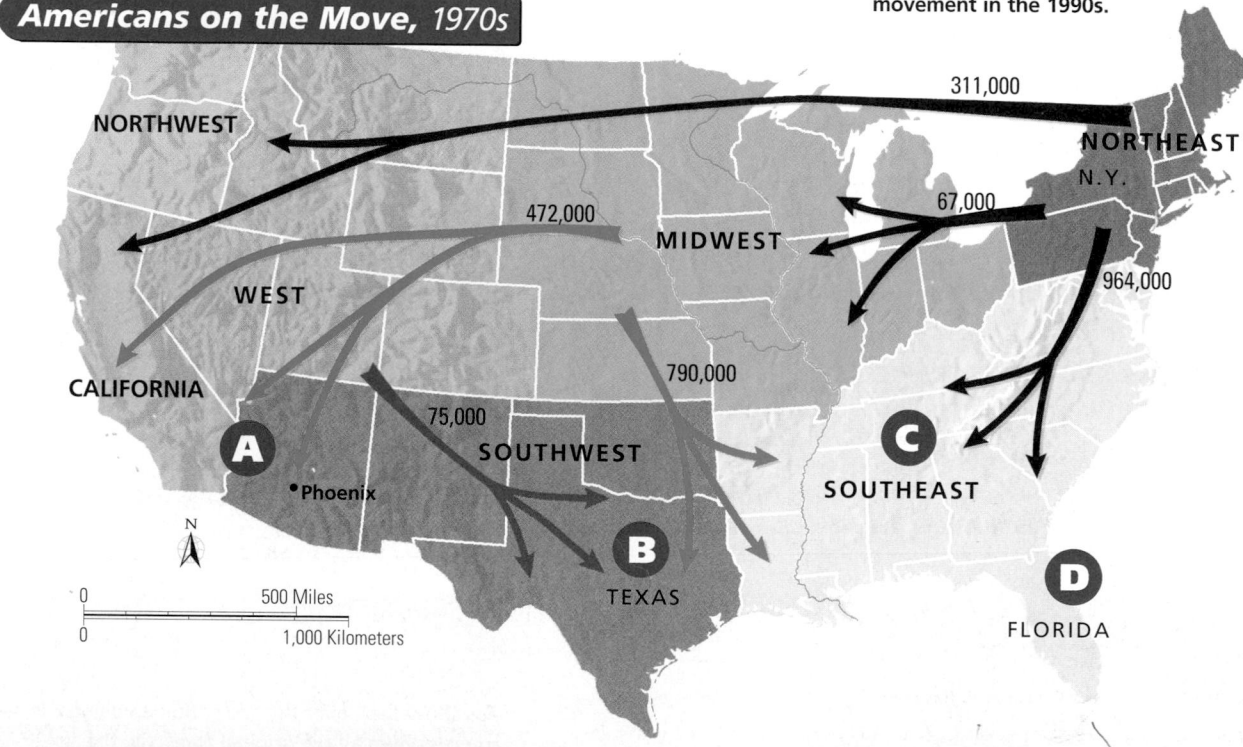

Americans on the Move, 1970s

NORTHWEST

NORTHEAST
N.Y.

311,000

67,000

472,000

MIDWEST

964,000

WEST

790,000

CALIFORNIA

75,000

A

SOUTHWEST

C

SOUTHEAST

•Phoenix

N

B

D

0   500 Miles

TEXAS

FLORIDA

0   1,000 Kilometers

New home developments cover the desert in Las Vegas, Nevada.

A By 1996, the Phoenix-Mesa metropolitan area reached a population of 2.75 million, more than the number of people living in the entire state in 1980.

B Between 1990 and 1994, Texas overtook New York as the nation's second most populous state, behind California.

C One of the nation's fastest growing areas was the Southeast, where population growth ranged from six to nine percent between 1990 and 1994. Jobs grew in the area by 14 percent.

D Florida's population is growing so much that it could become as populous as New York state by around 2020.

In the late 19th century, millions of immigrants arrived on the shores of the United States.

The Sears Tower overlooks Chinatown in Chicago.

Humans Spread Ideas and Information

Throughout U.S. history, people from all over the world have come to the United States. They have brought with them food, music, language, technology, and other aspects of their culture. As a result, the United States is one of the most culturally rich and diverse nations in the world. Look around your town or city. You'll probably notice different people, languages, and foods.

Today, the spreading of ideas and customs does not rely solely on human movement. Technology—from the Internet to television to satellites—spreads ideas and information throughout the world faster than ever. This has created an ever-growing, interconnected world. As the 21st century opens, human geography will continue to play a key role in shaping the United States and the world.

THINKING ABOUT GEOGRAPHY How have computers and the Internet affected your life?

Human Geography Assessment

1. Main Ideas

a. What are some of the ways that people have helped to restore the environment?

b. What are some of the ways that residents of your region have successfully modified their landscape?

c. What are some of the reasons that people move from place to place?

2. Critical Thinking

Recognizing Effects In what ways has technology helped bring people in the world together?

THINK ABOUT

• the different ways in which people communicate today

• the speed in which people today can communicate over long distances

TERMS

Briefly explain the significance of each of the following.

1. physical map
2. political map
3. longitude
4. latitude
5. hemisphere
6. projection
7. flood plain
8. sea level
9. human geography
10. human movement

REVIEW QUESTIONS

Themes of Geography (pages 4–5)

1. What is the difference between *absolute* location and *relative* location?
2. What is meant by the theme of place?
3. What are the themes of movement and human-environment interaction?

Map Basics (pages 6–9)

4. What do you think are some of the benefits of using technology to study geography?
5. What are the three major kinds of maps?
6. What are latitude and longitude lines?

Physical Geography (pages 10–13)

7. How have the natural resources in the United States helped its economic development?
8. What are the different climates within the United States?

Human Geography (pages 16–19)

9. How is human geography different from physical geography?
10. What aspects of human geography might cause people to move?

CRITICAL THINKING

1. **Forming and Supporting Opinions** Which of the five themes of geography do you think has had the most impact on history? Why?
2. **Analyzing Causes** How do the climate and natural resources of an area affect its economy?
3. **Drawing Conclusions** How have computers helped geographers make more accurate maps?
4. **Making Inferences** Why do you think the Mercator projection is used for all types of navigation?
5. **Recognizing Effects** How does a diverse land-scape help or hurt the economy of an area?

GEOGRAPHY SKILLS

1. INTERPRETING MAPS: Movement

Basic Map Elements

a. What region of the United States is shown?
b. Compare the number of teams on the 1987 map and the 2000 map. How many more teams are on the 2000 map?

Interpreting the Map

c. What geographic theme(s) is most responsible for the increase in sports teams in this region?
d. According to the map, which sport enjoyed the biggest surge in popularity in this region?

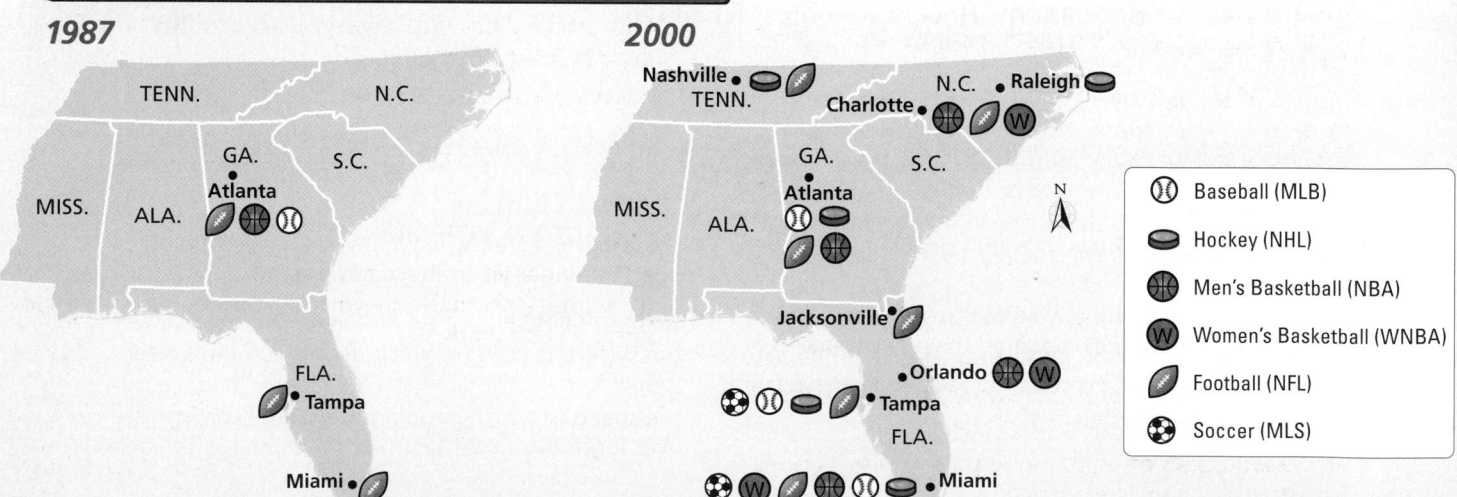

Major League Sports in Southeast Cities

1987

2000

Baseball (MLB)
Hockey (NHL)
Men's Basketball (NBA)
Women's Basketball (WNBA)
Football (NFL)
Soccer (MLS)

GEOGRAPHY SKILLS

2. INTERPRETING MAPS: Region

Study the map and then answer the questions.

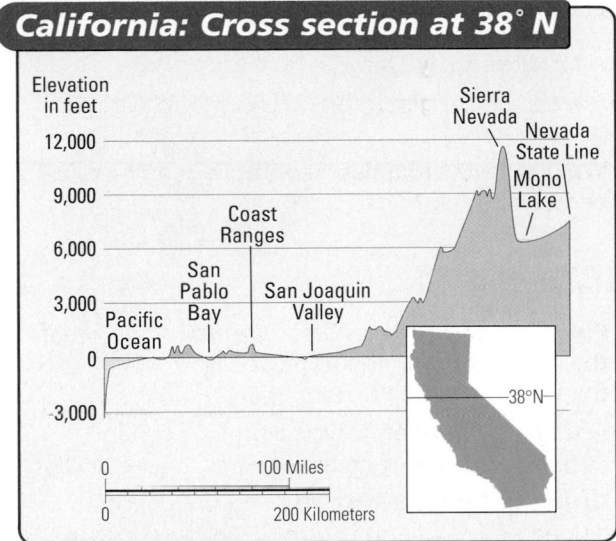

California: Cross section at 38° N

Basic Map Elements

a. What are the different landforms on the map?

Interpreting the Map

b. What is the level of the San Joaquin Valley? How many miles does it take to get from there to the highest point in California at the 38th parallel?

3. INTERPRETING PRIMARY SOURCES

In 1803, President Thomas Jefferson appointed Meriwether Lewis to explore the lands of the Louisiana Purchase. Jefferson gave him these instructions:

> The object of your mission is to explore the Missouri river . . . by its course & communication with the waters of the Pacific Ocean, may offer the most direct & practicable water communication across this continent, for the purposes of commerce. . . .
>
> Other objects worthy of notice will be the soil & face of the country, its growth & vegetable productions . . . the mineral productions of every kind. . . . climate as characterized by the thermometer . . . the dates at which particular plants put forth or lose their flowers, or leaf, times of appearance of particular birds, reptiles, or insects.
>
> **Thomas Jefferson**, quoted in *The Journals of Lewis and Clark*

a. What was Jefferson expecting to find in the West?

b. Why might the president want to know about the land's soil and vegetable production?

c. What aspect of human geography might be of interest to the president?

ALTERNATIVE ASSESSMENT

1. INTERDISCIPLINARY ACTIVITY: Math

Plotting Latitude and Longitude On a piece of graph paper, sketch a map of the United States. Be sure to draw in state boundaries, too. Then, using an atlas as a reference, draw and mark the latitude and longitude lines that cross the nation at five degree intervals. Plot the estimated longitude and latitude location of your city or town. Determine at which degrees the lines intersect where you live. Repeat this exercise for at least five different places you have visited or would like to visit within the United States.

2. COOPERATIVE LEARNING ACTIVITY

Making a Map How well do you know the neighborhood around your school? Form groups of three to four students. Then work together to draw a map of the neighborhood around your school. Include:

- streets
- residences
- stores
- geographic features
- important landmarks

The map should be accurate but not too cluttered with unnecessary details. Compare your group's map with those of the other groups in the class.

3. TECHNOLOGY ACTIVITY

Writing Directions Several Internet sites provide detailed maps of the United States. They also provide driving directions to most places in the country.

- Locate one of these map sites on the Internet.
- Think of a place in the United States that you would like to visit.
- Work with the computer to find the best route for reaching it.

Write out clear directions as well as the total mileage of your trip. Also, note the type of map it is and the features it highlights.

For more important geography sites . . .

INTERNET ACTIVITY
CLASSZONE.COM

4. HISTORY PORTFOLIO

Review your alternative assessment activities. Use comments made by your teacher or classmates to improve your work.

Additional Test Practice, pp. S1–S33

TEST PRACTICE
CLASSZONE.COM

Three Worlds Meet

The ruins of the Anasazi Cliff Palace, in modern-day Colorado, stand as a reminder of the Native American societies that existed before the arrival of Europeans.

> *"Our country! May she always be in the right; but our country, right or wrong."*
>
> —Stephen Decatur

Known as "Old Ironsides," the U.S.S. *Constitution* won more battles than any other early American warship. Today it rests in Boston Harbor.

Launching a New Republic 1789–1800

George Washington's first cabinet. Left to right: Secretary of War Henry Knox, Secretary of State Thomas Jefferson, Attorney General Edmund Randolph, Secretary of the Treasury Alexander Hamilton, and President George Washington.

1789
George Washington inaugurated as president.

1791
The first Bank of the United States is established.

1792
Washington reelected president.

1794
Whiskey Rebellion occurs.

USA
World 1789

1789
French Revolution begins.

1791
Slaves revolt in Santo Domingo.

1793
French king Louis XVI executed; Reign of Terror begins in France

The year is 1789, and George Washington has been inaugurated as the first president of the United States. It quickly becomes obvious to you and to others that the president will need help. He chooses people with different talents and experience to help him govern.

What kind of person would you choose to help you govern?

What Do You Think?

- Why might you want people with different viewpoints in your government?

- What do you think your biggest challenges would be?

 **RESEARCH LINKS**
CLASSZONE.COM

Visit the Chapter 9 links for more information about the new republic.

1796
John Adams elected president.

1797
Britain appoints Richard Wellesley Governor-General of India.

1798
Alien and Sedition Acts

1798
French Expedition to Egypt

1800
Thomas Jefferson elected president.

1800

1800
Napoleon becomes First Consul of France.

Reading Strategy: Identifying and Solving Problems

What Do You Know?

What do you think of when you hear the words *democracy* and *republic*? Why do you think the citizens and leaders of the new country wanted to establish a republic governed by laws?

Think About

- the experience of the colonists under British rule
- the effect of the Revolutionary War and the period immediately after the war
- your responses to the Interact with History about choosing people to govern (see page 291)

This early American flag has 13 stars representing the original 13 colonies.

What Do You Want to Know?

What questions do you have about the people who created the U.S. government? Record your questions in your notebook before you read the chapter.

Identifying and Solving Problems

As you read history, try to identify problems in past times and the solutions that people came up with to solve their problems. A graphic organizer such as the chart below can help you to keep track of problems and their solutions. In the middle of the chart, four headings categorize the major issues faced by the young nation. Copy the chart into your notebook and then record problems and the proposed solutions in each category.

S See Skillbuilder Handbook, page R18.

 Taking Notes

PROBLEMS		SOLUTIONS
	Economics	
	Politics	
	Foreign Affairs	
	Relations with Native Americans	

Washington's Presidency

MAIN IDEA	WHY IT MATTERS NOW	TERMS & NAMES
The president and the Congress began to set up the new government.	The strength of the U.S. today is due to the decisions of the Founders about how to organize the government.	inaugurate cabinet Federal Judiciary tariff Act

ONE AMERICAN'S STORY

Charles Thomson had served as secretary of the Continental Congress in 1774. Now, on April 14, 1789, he came to Mount Vernon in Virginia with a letter for George Washington. Washington knew the reason for the visit. Thomson's letter was to tell him that he had been elected the nation's first president. Before giving Washington the letter, Thomson made a short speech.

A VOICE FROM THE PAST

I have now Sir to inform you that . . . your patriotism and your readiness to sacrifice . . . private enjoyments to preserve the liberty and promote the happiness of your Country [convinced the Congress that you would accept] this important Office to which you are called not only by the unanimous votes of the Electors but by the voice of America.

Charles Thomson, quoted in Washington's Papers, Library of Congress

Charles Thomson delivers the letter to Washington announcing his election as president.

As you will read in this section, Washington accepted the honor and the burden of his new office. He guided the nation through its early years.

Washington Takes Office

Washington had been elected only a few months before. Each member of the electoral college had written down two names. The top vote-getter, Washington, became president. The runner-up, John Adams, became vice-president. Washington left Mount Vernon on April 16, 1789. He traveled north through Baltimore and Philadelphia to New York City, the nation's capital. On April 30 at Federal Hall, Washington was **inaugurated,** or sworn in, as president. John Adams of Massachusetts was his vice-president.

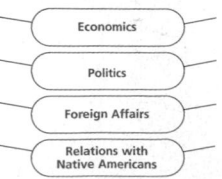

Taking Notes

Use your chart to take notes about Washington's presidency.

- Economics
- Politics
- Foreign Affairs
- Relations with Native Americans

As the nation's first president, Washington faced a difficult task. He knew that all eyes would be on him. His every action as president would set a precedent—an example that would become standard practice. People argued over what to call him. Some, including John Adams, suggested "His Excellency" or "His Highness." Others argued that such titles would suggest that he was a king. The debate tied up Congress for a month. Finally, "Mr. President" was agreed upon. Congress had to settle other differences about how the new government should be run.

*Reading*History

A. Making Inferences Why were people so concerned about how to address the president?

Setting Up the Courts

The writers of the Constitution had left many matters to be decided by Congress. For example, the Constitution created a Supreme Court but left it to Congress to decide the number of justices. Leaders also argued about how much power the Supreme Court should have. One reason for disagreement was that the states already had their own courts. How would authority be divided between the state and federal courts?

To create a court system, Congress passed the **Federal Judiciary Act** of 1789. This act gave the Supreme Court six members: a chief justice, or judge, and five associate justices. Over time, that number has grown to nine. The act also provided for other lower, less powerful federal courts. Washington appointed John Jay, the prominent New York lawyer and diplomat, as chief justice.

Vocabulary
judiciary: system of courts and judges

Now and **then**

THE PRESIDENT'S CABINET

The president's cabinet has more than tripled in size since it began with the secretaries of state, war, and treasury, and the attorney general. As the nation has faced new challenges, the government has added new departments. In 1977, concerns about oil shortages led to the creation of the Department of Energy. The Department of Veterans' Affairs was added in 1989. Today the cabinet (shown below) includes the heads of 14 departments.

Washington's Cabinet

The Constitution also gave Congress the task of creating departments to help the president lead the nation. The president had the power to appoint the heads of these departments, who were to assist the president with the many issues and problems he had to face. These heads of departments became his **cabinet**.

The Congress created three departments. In his first major task as president, Washington chose talented people to run them. For secretary of war, he picked Henry Knox, a trusted general during the Revolution. It was Knox's job to oversee the nation's defenses. For secretary of state, Washington chose Thomas Jefferson. He had been serving as U.S. minister to France. The State Department oversaw relations between the United States and other countries. Washington turned to the brilliant Alexander Hamilton to be the secretary of the treasury. Hamilton had to manage the government's money. The secretary's ties to the president began during the war when he had served as one of Washington's aides. To advise the

government on legal matters, Washington picked Edmund Randolph as attorney general.

These department heads and the attorney general made up Washington's cabinet. The Constitution made no mention of a cabinet. However, Washington began the practice of calling his department heads together to advise him.

Economic Problems

As secretary of the treasury, Alexander Hamilton faced the task of straightening out the nation's finances. First of all, the new government needed to pay its war debts. During the Revolution, the United States had borrowed millions of dollars from France, the Netherlands, and Spain. Within the United States, merchants and other private citizens had loaned money to the government. State governments also had wartime debts to pay back. By 1789, the national debt totaled more than $52 million.

Most government leaders agreed that the nation must repay its debts to win the respect of both foreign nations and its own citizens. Hamilton saw that the new nation must assure other countries that it was responsible about money. These nations would do business with the United States if they saw that the country would pay its debts. If the nation failed to do so, no country would lend it money in the future.

Hamilton came up with a financial plan that reflected his belief in a strong central government. He thought the power of the national government should be stronger than that of the state governments. Hamilton also believed that government should encourage business and industry. He sought the support of the nation's wealthy merchants and manufacturers. He thought that the nation's prosperity depended on them. The government owed money to many of these rich men. By paying them back, Hamilton hoped to win their support for the new government.

ALEXANDER HAMILTON
1755?–1804

Alexander Hamilton was born into poverty in the British West Indies. When he was ten years old, the young Alexander went to work as a clerk. He so impressed his employers that they helped to send him to school at King's College (now Columbia University) in New York.

During the Revolutionary War, he became an aide to General Washington. Hamilton moved up quickly in the army and later in political life. Although of humble origins, Hamilton had little faith in the common people and put his trust in the wealthy and educated to govern.

Why is it odd that Hamilton distrusted the common people to govern?

*Reading*History
B. Making Inferences Why might merchants and manufacturers support a strong central government?

Hamilton's Financial Plan

In 1790, Hamilton presented his plan to Congress. He proposed three steps to improve the nation's finances.

1. paying off all war debts
2. raising government revenues
3. creating a national bank

Hamilton wanted the federal government to pay off the war debts of the states. However, sectional differences arose over repayment of state debts. Virginia, Georgia, and many other Southern states had already repaid their debts and did not like being asked to help Northern states pay theirs.

Launching a New Republic **295**

Hamilton asked Thomas Jefferson of Virginia to help him gain Southern support. They reached a compromise. In exchange for Southern support of the plan, Northerners agreed to place the new nation's capital in the South. The location chosen was on the Potomac River between Virginia and Maryland.

The secretary of the treasury favored tariffs. A **tariff** is a tax on imported goods. It serves two purposes: raising money for the government and encouraging the growth of American industry. The government placed the highest tariffs on foreign goods—such as shoes and textiles—that Americans bought in great quantities. This ensured a steady flow of income to the government. In addition, since tariffs made foreign goods more expensive, they encouraged people to buy American goods.

Hamilton also called for the creation of a national bank. Such a bank would meet many needs. It would give the government a safe place to keep

Economics *in* History

How Banks Work

Why did Hamilton want to create a national bank? He believed that such a bank could help the economy of the new nation. It would create a partnership between the federal government and American business.

Let's say you deposited money into a bank account. Then you went back another day to withdraw some of the money. What happened in the meantime? Did the money just sit in the bank until you wanted it back? No—the bank used your money, and in doing so, helped fuel economic growth. In this way, money flows in a circular path from people like you into the general economy and back to you again. In the process, money can create goods and services, jobs, and profits, as the diagram explains.

CONNECT TO HISTORY
1. **Analyzing Points of View** Do you think that the people who feared a strong central government supported Hamilton's idea of a national bank? Why or why not?

S See Skillbuilder Handbook, page R9.

CONNECT TO TODAY
2. **Making Inferences** How do banks make money?

For more about banking . . .

RESEARCH LINKS
CLASSZONE.COM

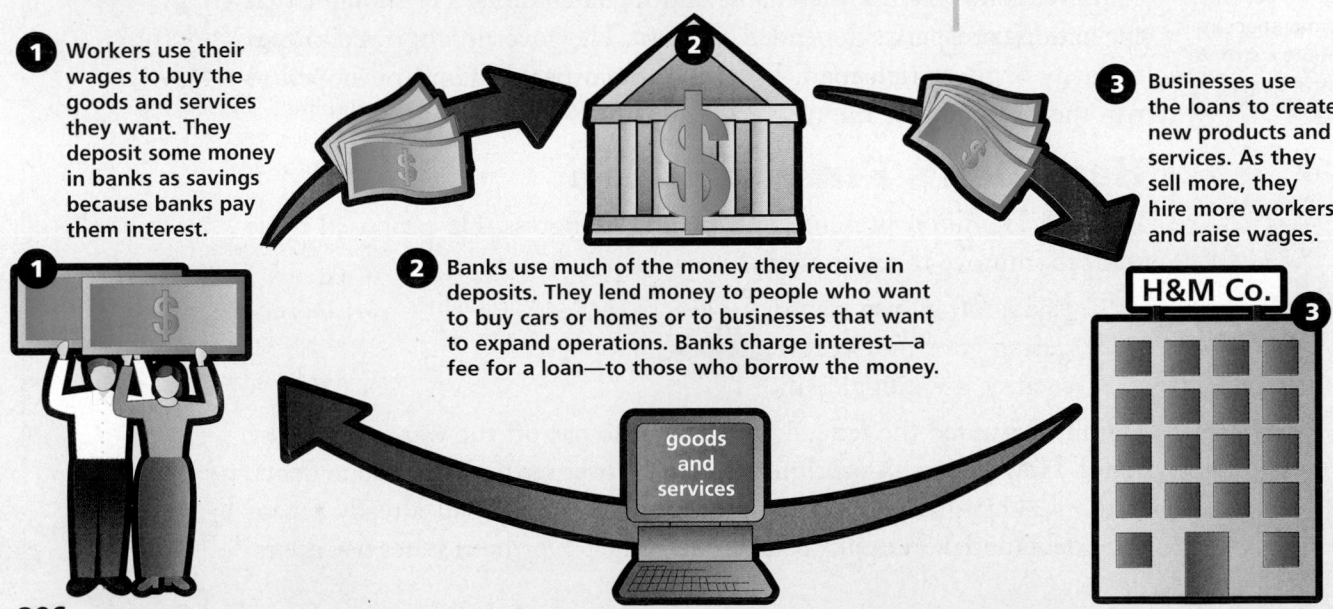

1. Workers use their wages to buy the goods and services they want. They deposit some money in banks as savings because banks pay them interest.

2. Banks use much of the money they receive in deposits. They lend money to people who want to buy cars or homes or to businesses that want to expand operations. Banks charge interest—a fee for a loan—to those who borrow the money.

3. Businesses use the loans to create new products and services. As they sell more, they hire more workers and raise wages.

H&M Co.

goods and services

Vocabulary
currency: money

money. It would also make loans to businesses and government. Most important, it would issue bank notes—paper money that could be used as currency. Overall, Hamilton's plan would strengthen the central government. However, this worried Jefferson and Madison.

Two of the first
U.S. coins, 1792

Interpreting the Constitution

Jefferson and Madison believed that the Constitution discouraged the concentration of power in the federal government. The Constitution's writers had tried to make the document general enough so that it would be flexible. As a result, disagreements sometimes arose over the document's meaning.

The debate over Hamilton's plan for a national bank exposed differences about how to interpret the Constitution. Madison and Jefferson argued that the Constitution did not give the government the power to set up a bank. They believed in the strict construction—narrow or strict interpretation—of the Constitution. They stated that the government has only those powers that the Constitution clearly says it has. Therefore, since the Constitution does not mention a national bank, the government cannot create one.

Hamilton disagreed. He favored a loose construction—broad or flexible interpretation—of the Constitution. Pointing to the elastic clause in the document, he argued that the bank was "necessary and proper" to carry out the government's duties. (See The Living Constitution, page 254.) According to this view, when the Constitution grants a power to Congress, it also grants Congress the "necessary and proper" means to carry out that power. Jefferson and Hamilton argued their positions to Washington. Hamilton won, and the Bank of the United States was set up in 1791. The president, meanwhile, was dealing with other challenges at home and abroad, which you will read about in Section 2.

Reading **History**
C. Contrasting
What is the main difference between strict and loose interpretations of the Constitution?

Section ❶ Assessment

1. Terms & Names

Explain the significance of:
- inaugurate
- Federal Judiciary Act
- cabinet
- tariff

2. Using Graphics

In a chart, list members of Washington's cabinet and their responsibilities.

Cabinet member	Responsibilities

Which cabinet member had the greatest responsibilities? Explain.

3. Main Ideas

a. What was the purpose of Washington's cabinet?

b. What economic problems did the new government face?

c. How did Hamilton's financial plan attempt to solve the nation's economic problems?

4. Critical Thinking

Contrasting How did Hamilton and Jefferson differ in their interpretation of the Constitution?

THINK ABOUT
- views on the national bank
- views on the role of government

ACTIVITY OPTIONS

LANGUAGE ARTS

ART

Imagine you oppose or support Hamilton's plan for the nation's finances. Write a **letter to the editor** or draw a **political cartoon** expressing your opinion.

Challenges to the New Government

MAIN IDEA	WHY IT MATTERS NOW	TERMS & NAMES
Washington established central authority at home and avoided war with European powers.	Washington's policies at home and abroad set an example for later presidents.	Battle of Fallen Timbers French Revolution Treaty of Greenville neutral Jay's Treaty Whiskey Rebellion Pinckney's Treaty

ONE AMERICAN'S STORY

In the West, American settlers met fierce resistance from Native Americans. Chief Little Turtle of the Miami tribe of Ohio had won decisive victories against U.S. troops.

In 1793, the Miami again faced attack by American forces. Little Turtle warned his people about the troops led by General Anthony Wayne.

A VOICE FROM THE PAST

We have beaten the enemy twice under different commanders. . . . The Americans are now led by a chief [Wayne] who never sleeps. . . . We have not been able to surprise him. Think well of it. . . . It would be prudent [wise] to listen to his offers of peace.

Little Turtle, quoted in *The Life and Times of Little Turtle*

General Anthony Wayne negotiates with a Miami war chief.

While the council members weighed Little Turtle's warning, President Washington was making plans to secure—guard or protect—the western borders of the new nation.

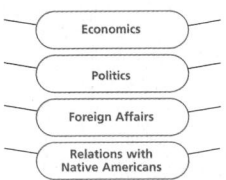

Taking Notes

Use your chart to take notes about challenges to the new government.

- Economics
- Politics
- Foreign Affairs
- Relations with Native Americans

Securing the Northwest Territory

As a general, Washington had skillfully waged war. As the nation's president, however, he saw that the country needed peace in order to prosper. But in spite of his desire for peace, he considered military action as trouble brewed in the Trans-Appalachian West, the land between the Appalachian Mountains and the Mississippi River. The 1783 Treaty of Paris had attempted to resolve the claims. The source of the trouble was competing claims for these lands. Some years later, however, Spain, Britain, the United States, and Native Americans claimed parts of the area as their own.

Spain held much of North America west of the Mississippi. It also claimed Florida and the port of New Orleans at the mouth of the

Mississippi. For American settlers in the West, this port was key to trade. They carried their goods to market by flatboat down the Mississippi to New Orleans. They took Spanish threats to close the port very seriously. The Spanish also stirred up trouble between the white settlers and the Creeks, Choctaws, and other Native American groups in the Southeast.

*Reading*History

A. Making Inferences What expectations might the Native Americans have had of the British as the tribes came into conflict with white settlers?

The strongest resistance to white settlement came from Native Americans in the Northwest Territory. This territory was bordered by the Ohio River to the south and Canada to the north. Native Americans in that territory hoped to join together to form an independent Native American nation. In violation of the Treaty of Paris, the British still held forts north of the Ohio River. The British supported Native Americans in order to maintain their access to fur in these territories. Eventually, Native Americans and white settlers clashed over the Northwest Territory.

Battle of Fallen Timbers

Believing the Northwest Territory was critical to the security and growth of the new nation, Washington sent troops to the Ohio Valley. As you read in One American's Story, this first federal army took a beating from warriors led by Little Turtle in 1790. The chief's force came from many tribes, including the Shawnee, Ottawa, and Chippewa, who joined in a confederation to defeat the federal army.

After a second defeat in 1791 of an army headed by General Arthur St. Clair, Washington ordered another army west. This time Anthony Wayne, known as "Mad Anthony" for his reckless courage, was at its head.

The other chiefs ignored Little Turtle's advice to negotiate. They replaced him with a less able leader. Expecting British help, Native American warriors gathered at British-held Fort Miami. On August 20, 1794, a fighting force of around 2,000 Native Americans clashed with Wayne's troops. The site was covered with trees that had been struck down by a storm. The Native Americans were defeated in what became known as the **Battle of Fallen Timbers**.

The Battle of Fallen Timbers memorial sculpture below shows two American soldiers and a Native American.

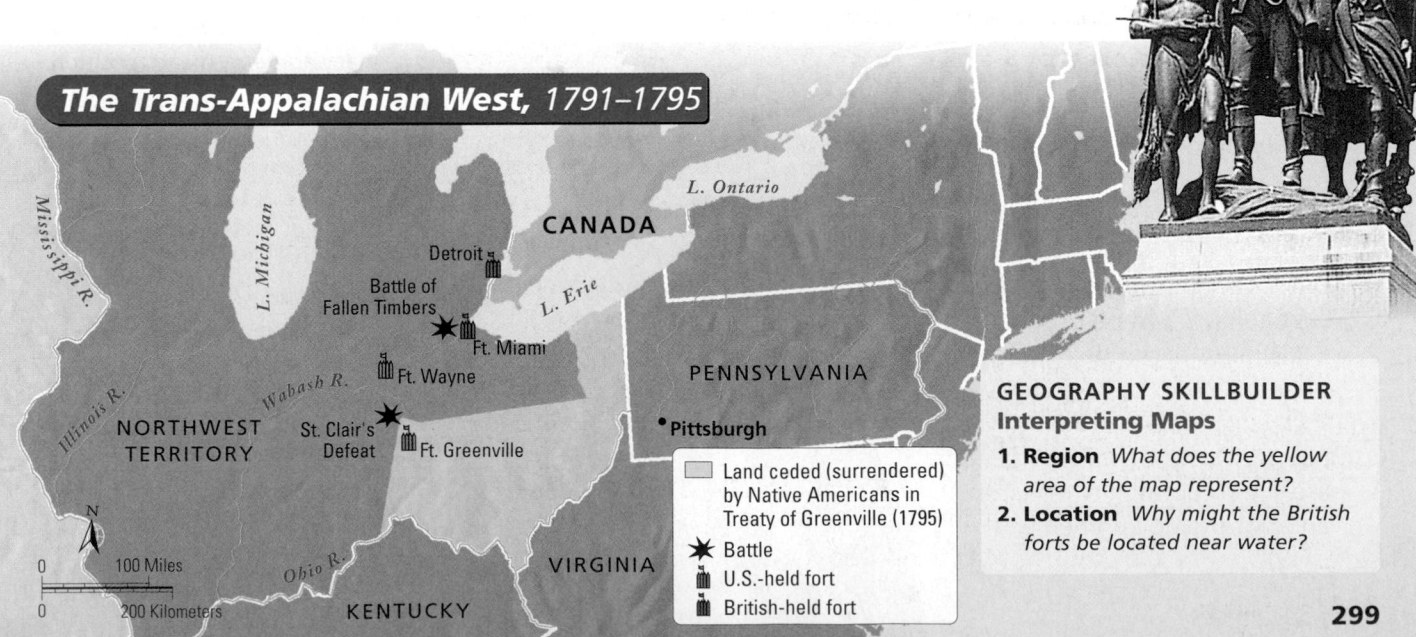

The Trans-Appalachian West, 1791–1795

Mississippi R.

L. Michigan

L. Ontario

CANADA

Detroit

Battle of Fallen Timbers

L. Erie

Ft. Miami

Ft. Wayne

PENNSYLVANIA

Wabash R.

•Pittsburgh

Illinois R.

NORTHWEST TERRITORY

St. Clair's Defeat

Ft. Greenville

N

0   100 Miles
0   200 Kilometers

Ohio R.

VIRGINIA

KENTUCKY

Land ceded (surrendered) by Native Americans in Treaty of Greenville (1795)

★ Battle

U.S.-held fort

British-held fort

GEOGRAPHY SKILLBUILDER
Interpreting Maps

1. **Region** *What does the yellow area of the map represent?*
2. **Location** *Why might the British forts be located near water?*

The Native Americans retreated to Fort Miami. The British, not wanting war with the United States, refused to help them. The Battle of Fallen Timbers crushed Native American hopes of keeping their land in the Northwest Territory. Twelve tribes signed the **Treaty of Greenville** in 1795. They agreed to cede, or surrender, much of present-day Ohio and Indiana to the U.S. government.

*Reading*History

B. Reading a Map
Use the map on page 299 to see which two states to the south bordered the land ceded by Native Americans.

The Whiskey Rebellion

Not long after the Battle of Fallen Timbers, Washington put another army into the field. The conflict arose over the government's tax on whiskey, part of Hamilton's financial plan. From Pennsylvania to Georgia, outraged farmers resisted the tax. For them, whiskey—and the grain it was made from—were important products.

Because of poor roads, backcountry farmers had trouble getting their grain to market. Crops such as wheat and rye were more easily carried to market in liquid form, so farmers made their grain into whiskey. A farmer's horse could haul only two bushels of rye but could carry two barrels of rye whiskey. This was an amount equal to 24 bushels of the grain. In addition, their customers paid more for whiskey than grain. With little cash to buy goods, let alone pay the tax, farmers often traded whiskey for salt, sugar, and other goods. The farmers used whiskey as money to get whatever supplies they needed.

CITIZENSHIP TODAY

Obeying Rules and Laws

As the Whiskey Rebellion shows, since the earliest days of the republic our government has made laws and punished those who broke them. These laws affect not only adult citizens, but young people as well.

Today, for example, communities across the country are trying to control the problem of juvenile crime by imposing curfews on young people. These laws require minors to be off the streets after a certain time, often ten or eleven at night. Penalties can be harsh. In certain communities, minors who break curfew laws can be detained, and their parents can be fined.

People who favor curfews believe such laws cut crime. Those who oppose curfews think such limits are the responsibility of parents and not the government.

Why Should You Obey Rules and Laws?

1. What are some arguments in favor of curfew laws? What are arguments against them? Make a list of each.

2. Poll your classmates to see how many agree with each position.

3. Write an essay expressing your opinion on this issue.

4. Brainstorm changes or adaptations to curfew laws that you think would make them more flexible.

 See Citizenship Handbook, page 283.

For more about young people and the law . . .

 RESEARCH LINKS
CLASSZONE.COM

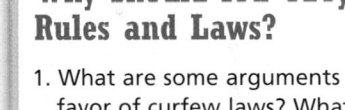

In the summer of 1794, a group of farmers in western Pennsylvania staged the **Whiskey Rebellion** against the tax. One armed group beat up a tax collector, coated him with tar and feathers, and stole his horse. Others threatened an armed attack on Pittsburgh.

Washington, urged on by Hamilton, was prepared to enforce the tax and crush the Whiskey Rebellion. They feared that not to act might undermine the new government and weaken its authority. Hamilton condemned the rebels for resisting the law.

"Such a resistance is treason."
Alexander Hamilton

A VOICE FROM THE PAST

Such a resistance is treason against society, against liberty, against everything that ought to be dear to a free, enlightened, and prudent people. To tolerate it were to abandon your most precious interests. Not to subdue it were to tolerate it.

Alexander Hamilton, *The Works of Alexander Hamilton*

In October 1794, General Henry Lee, with Hamilton at his side, led an army of 13,000 soldiers into western Pennsylvania to put down the uprising. As news of the army's approach spread, the rebels fled. After much effort, federal troops rounded up 20 barefoot, ragged prisoners. Washington had proved his point. He had shown that the government had the power and the will to enforce its laws. Meanwhile, events in Europe gave Washington a different kind of challenge.

The French Revolution

In 1789, a financial crisis led the French people to rebel against their government. Inspired by the American Revolution, the French revolutionaries demanded liberty and equality. At first, Americans supported the **French Revolution**. By 1792, however, the revolution had become very violent. Thousands of French citizens were massacred. Then, in 1793, Louis XVI, the king of France, was executed.

Other European monarchs believed the revolution threatened their own thrones. France soon declared war on Britain, Holland, and Spain. Britain led the fight against France.

The war between France and Britain put the United States in an awkward position. France had been America's ally in the Revolution against the British.

Connections TO
WORLD HISTORY

EYEWITNESS TO REVOLUTION

In 1789, an American citizen with a strange first name, Gouverneur Morris, went to Paris as a private business agent. Three years later, President Washington appointed him U.S. minister to France. An eyewitness to the French Revolution, Morris kept a detailed record of what he saw, including the execution of the king and queen by guillotine, as shown below.

Here is part of a letter he wrote on October 18, 1793:

"Terror is the order of the Day. . . . The Queen was executed the Day before yesterday. Insulted during her Trial and reviled in her last Moments, she behav'd with Dignity throughout."

A 1778 treaty still bound the two nations together. In addition, many saw France's revolution as proof that the American cause had been just. Jefferson felt that a move to crush the French Revolution was an attack on liberty everywhere. Hamilton, though, pointed out that Britain was the United States' most important trading partner, and British trade was too important to risk war.

In April 1793, Washington declared that the United States would remain **neutral,** not siding with one country or the other. He stated that the nation would be "friendly and impartial" to both sides. Congress then passed a law forbidding the United States to help either side.

*Reading*History
C. Drawing Conclusions
What sort of U.S. obligation to France did the wartime alliance and treaty of 1778 create?

Remaining Neutral

Britain made it hard for the United States to remain neutral. Late in 1792, the British began seizing the cargoes of American ships carrying goods from the French West Indies.

Washington sent Chief Justice John Jay to England for talks about the seizure of U.S. ships. Jay also hoped to persuade the British to give up their forts on the Northwest frontier. During the talks in 1794, news came of the U.S. victory at the Battle of Fallen Timbers. Fearing another entanglement, the British agreed to leave the Ohio Valley by 1796. In **Jay's Treaty,** the British also agreed to pay damages for U.S. vessels they had seized. Jay failed, however, to open up the profitable British West Indies trade to Americans. Because of this, Jay's Treaty was unpopular.

Like Jay, Thomas Pinckney helped the United States reduce tensions along the frontier. In 1795, **Pinckney's Treaty** with Spain gave Americans the right to travel freely on the Mississippi River. It also gave them the right to store goods at the port of New Orleans without paying customs duties. In addition, Spain accepted the 31st parallel as the northern boundary of Florida and the southern boundary of the United States.

Meanwhile, more American settlers moved west. As you will read in the next section, change was coming back east as Washington stepped down.

*Reading*History
D. Evaluating
What were some of the advantages to the new nation of remaining neutral?

Section 2 Assessment

1. Terms & Names

Explain the significance of:
- Battle of Fallen Timbers
- Treaty of Greenville
- Whiskey Rebellion
- French Revolution
- neutral
- Jay's Treaty
- Pinckney's Treaty

2. Using Graphics

Use a chart to record U.S. responses to various challenges.

Challenge	Response
From Spain	
From Britain	
From France	

Which challenge seemed greatest? Why?

3. Main Ideas

a. What military and other actions secured the West for the United States?

b. Why did Washington consider it important to put down the Whiskey Rebellion?

c. How did the French Revolution create problems for the United States?

4. Critical Thinking

Drawing Conclusions
Why was neutrality a difficult policy for the United States to maintain?

THINK ABOUT
- ties with France
- ties with Britain
- restrictions on trade

ACTIVITY OPTIONS

GEOGRAPHY
ART

Make a **map** that describes the Battle of Fallen Timbers, or draw a **scene** from that battle.

The Federalists in Charge

MAIN IDEA	WHY IT MATTERS NOW	TERMS & NAMES
The split between Hamilton and Jefferson led to the growth of political parties.	The two-party system is still a major feature of politics in the United States.	foreign policy · Alien and Sedition Acts political party · states' rights XYZ Affair

ONE AMERICAN'S STORY

In 1796, President George Washington decided that two terms in office was enough. But as he left office, he feared the growth of political parties would split the nation into enemy camps. In 1796, he wrote a final address to the nation.

This painting portrays Mount Vernon in 1792.

A VOICE FROM THE PAST

Let me now . . . warn you . . . against the [harmful] effects of the spirit of party. . . . This spirit, unfortunately . . . exists in different shapes in all governments . . . but in those of the popular form, it is seen in its greatest rankness and is truly their worst enemy.

George Washington, Farewell Address

In his address, Washington warned of the dangers of political division, or what he termed "the spirit of party." As you will see in this section, few people took his advice.

Washington Retires

Washington had come to the presidency greatly admired by the American people. Throughout his eight years in office (1789–1797), he had tried to serve as a symbol of national unity. In large part, he succeeded. During his second term, however, opponents of Jay's Treaty led attacks on the president. Thomas Paine called Washington "treacherous in private friendship . . . and a hypocrite in public life" because he failed to support the French Revolution.

Washington saw such attacks as the outcome of political disagreements. In his farewell address, he warned that such differences could weaken the nation. Despite his advice, political parties became a part of American politics.

> **Taking Notes**
>
> Use your chart to take notes about the Federalists and the establishment of a two-party system.
>
> - Economics
> - Politics
> - Foreign Affairs
> - Relations with Native Americans

Americans listened more closely to Washington's parting advice on **foreign policy**—relations with the governments of other countries. He urged the nation's leaders to remain neutral and "steer clear of permanent alliances with any portion of the foreign world." He warned that agreements with foreign nations might work against U.S. interests. His advice served to guide U.S. foreign policy into the twentieth century.

Growth of Political Parties

Despite Washington's warning against political parties, Americans were deeply divided over how the nation should be run. During Washington's first term (1789–1792), Hamilton and Jefferson had hotly debated the direction the new nation should take. Then Jefferson returned to Virginia in 1793. During Washington's second term, Madison took Jefferson's place in the debates with Hamilton.

Both sides disagreed on how to interpret the Constitution and on economic policy. Hamilton favored the British government and opposed the French Revolution. Jefferson and Madison were the opposite. Hamilton fought for a strong central government. Jefferson and Madison feared such a government might lead to tyranny. They had different visions of what the nation should become. Hamilton wanted a United States in which trade, manufacturing, and cities grew. Jefferson and Madison pictured a rural nation of planters and farmers.

These differences on foreign and domestic policy led to the nation's first political parties. A **political party** is a group of people that tries to promote its ideas and influence government. It also backs candidates for office. Together, Jefferson and Madison founded the Democratic-Republican Party. The party name reflected their strong belief in democracy and the republican system. Their ideas drew farmers and workers to the new party. Hamilton and his friends formed the Federalist Party. Many Northern merchants and manufacturers became Federalists.

*Reading*History
A. Summarizing
What were the major beliefs of each party?

The First Political Parties

FEDERALISTS	DEMOCRATIC-REPUBLICANS
Strong national government	Limited national government
Fear of mob rule	Fear of rule by one person or a powerful few
Loose construction (interpretation) of the Constitution	Strict construction (interpretation) of the Constitution
Favored national bank	Opposed national bank
Economy based on manufacturing and shipping	Economy based on farming
Supporters: lawyers, merchants, manufacturers, clergy	Supporters: farmers, tradespeople

SKILLBUILDER Interpreting Charts
1. *Which economic interests were served by the Federalists?*
2. *Which party favored a ruling elite? Which put more trust in the common people?*

WASHINGTON, D.C., AND BENJAMIN BANNEKER

Benjamin Banneker was a free African-American farmer. He was a self-taught mathematician and astronomer. He also wrote an almanac (see below). He was named to the survey commission appointed to lay out the boundaries of the nation's new capital. Working with chief planner Pierre L'Enfant, Banneker helped to decide where the White House and Capitol would be located. Their final design is shown at the left.

John Adams Takes Office

In 1796, the United States held its first elections in which political parties competed. The Federalists picked Washington's vice-president, John Adams, as their candidate for president. An experienced public servant, Adams had been a leader during the Revolution and at the Continental Congress. He had also been a diplomat in France, the Netherlands, and Britain before serving with Washington. The Democratic-Republicans chose Jefferson.

In the electoral college, Adams received 71 votes and Jefferson 68. The Constitution stated that the runner-up should become vice-president. Therefore, the country had a Federalist president and a Democratic-Republican vice-president. Adams became president in 1797. His chief rival, Jefferson, entered office as his vice-president. In 1800, Adams became the first president to govern from the nation's new capital city, Washington, D.C.

Problems with France

When Washington left office in 1797, relations between France and the United States were tense. With Britain and France still at war, the French began seizing U.S. ships to prevent them from trading with the British. Within the year, the French had looted more than 300 U.S. ships.

Although some Federalists called for war with France, Adams hoped talks would restore calm. To this end, he sent Charles Pinckney, Elbridge Gerry, and John Marshall to Paris. Arriving there, they requested a meeting with the French minister of foreign affairs. For weeks, they were

American newspapers fueled public anger over the XYZ Affair by publishing editorials and cartoons like this one. Here the five-man group ruling France demands money at dagger point from the three Americans. The American diplomats respond, "Cease bawling, monster! We will not give you sixpence!"

What attitude does the cartoonist have toward France's role in this affair? How can you tell?

ignored. Then three French agents—later referred to as X, Y, and Z—took the Americans aside to tell them the minister would hold talks. However, the talks would occur only if the Americans agreed to loan France $10 million and to pay the minister a bribe of $250,000. The Americans refused. "No, no, not a sixpence," Pinckney shot back.

Adams received a full report of what became known as the **XYZ Affair**. After Congress and an outraged public learned of it, the press turned Pinckney's words into a popular slogan: "Millions for defense, not one cent for tribute!" In 1798, Congress canceled its treaties with France and allowed U.S. ships to seize French vessels. Congress also set aside money to expand the navy and the army.

*Reading*History

B. Drawing Conclusions How did the XYZ Affair show the young nation's growing confidence?

The Alien and Sedition Acts

The conflict with France made Adams and the Federalists popular with the public. Many Democratic-Republicans, however, were sympathetic to France. One Democratic-Republican newspaper called Adams "the blasted tyrant of America." In turn, Federalists labeled Democratic-Republicans "democrats, mobcrats, and other kinds of rats."

Angered by criticism in a time of crisis, Adams blamed the Democratic-Republican newspapers and new immigrants. Many of the immigrants were Democratic-Republicans. To silence their critics, the Federalist Congress passed the **Alien and Sedition Acts** in 1798. These acts targeted aliens—immigrants who were not yet citizens. One act increased the waiting period for becoming a U.S. citizen from 5 to 14 years. Other acts gave the president the power to arrest disloyal aliens or order them out of the country during wartime. A fourth act outlawed sedition, saying or writing anything false or harmful about the government.

With these acts, the Federalists clamped down on freedom of speech and the press. About 25 Democratic-Republican newspaper editors were

charged under this act, and 10 were convicted of expressing opinions damaging to the government. A Vermont congressman, Matthew Lyon, was also locked up for saying that the president should be sent "to a mad house." The voters re-elected Lyon while he was in jail.

Reading **History**

C. Making Inferences How might the theory of states' rights undermine the federal government?

The Democratic-Republicans, led by Jefferson and Madison, searched for a way to fight the Alien and Sedition Acts. They found it in a theory called **states' rights**. According to this theory, states had rights that the federal government could not violate. Jefferson and Madison wrote resolutions (or statements) passed by the Kentucky and Virginia legislatures in 1798 and 1799. In the Kentucky Resolutions, Jefferson proposed nullification, the idea that a state could nullify a federal law within the state. In the Virginia Resolutions, Madison said a state could interpose, or place, itself between the federal government and its citizens. These resolutions declared that the Alien and Sedition Acts violated the Constitution. No other states supported Kentucky and Virginia. However, within two years the Democratic-Republicans won control of Congress, and they either repealed the Alien and Sedition Acts or let them expire between 1800 and 1802.

Peace with France

While Federalists and Democratic-Republicans battled at home, the United States made peace with France. Although war fever was high, Adams reopened talks with France. This time the two sides quickly signed the Convention of 1800, an agreement to stop all naval attacks. This treaty cleared the way for U.S. and French ships to sail the ocean in peace.

Adams's actions made him enemies among the Federalists. Despite this, he spoke proudly of having saved the nation from bloodshed. "I desire no other inscription over my gravestone than: 'Here lies John Adams, who took upon himself the responsibility of the peace with France in the year 1800.'" Adams lost the presidential election of 1800 to Thomas Jefferson. You will read more about Jefferson in the next chapter.

Section **3** *Assessment*

1. Terms & Names

Explain the significance of:
- foreign policy
- political party
- XYZ Affair
- Alien and Sedition Acts
- states' rights

2. Using Graphics

Use a cluster diagram to review details about the Alien and Sedition Acts.

Alien and Sedition Acts

What was the worst effect of the Alien and Sedition Acts? Why?

3. Main Ideas

a. What two pieces of advice did Washington give in his Farewell Address?

b. What led to the rise of political parties?

c. Why did Congress pass the Alien and Sedition Acts? How did Kentucky and Virginia respond?

4. Critical Thinking

Evaluating Do you think Washington's warning about political parties was good advice? Explain.

THINK ABOUT
- roles of political parties
- advantages of parties
- disadvantages of parties

ACTIVITY OPTIONS

TECHNOLOGY ——— **SPEECH**

Read more about Benjamin Banneker. Plan part of a **video presentation** on him or present **dramatic readings** of excerpts from the almanac he wrote.

TERMS & NAMES

Briefly explain the significance of each of the following.

1. inaugurate
2. cabinet
3. tariff
4. Battle of Fallen Timbers
5. Whiskey Rebellion
6. neutral
7. foreign policy
8. political party
9. Alien and Sedition Acts
10. states' rights

REVIEW QUESTIONS

Washington's Presidency (pages 293–297)

1. What questions about the judiciary were left open by the Constitution? How were they answered?
2. What financial problems did the new nation face?
3. How did Hamilton and Jefferson interpret the Constitution differently?

Challenges to the New Government (pages 298–302)

4. What did Washington do to secure the West?
5. What were the major arguments regarding taxation under the new government?
6. Why did Washington favor neutrality in the conflict between France and Britain?
7. What problems did the Jay and Pinckney treaties address?

The Federalists in Charge (pages 303–307)

8. Why did Washington oppose political parties?
9. What was the XYZ Affair?
10. Why did Federalists pass the Alien and Sedition Acts? How did Republicans respond?

CRITICAL THINKING

1. USING YOUR NOTES: IDENTIFYING AND SOLVING PROBLEMS

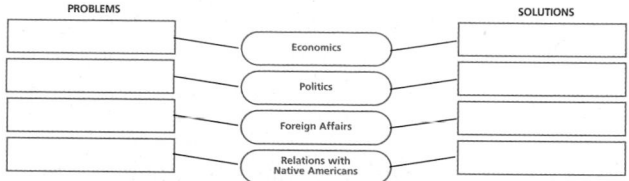

PROBLEMS | Economics | Politics | Foreign Affairs | Relations with Native Americans | SOLUTIONS

Using your completed chart, answer the questions.

a. What were the problems that characterized the Federalist era?

b. What do the solutions to these problems reveal about the characteristics of the era?

2. ANALYZING LEADERSHIP

How did Washington's efforts to serve as a symbol of national unity help the new nation?

3. APPLYING CITIZENSHIP SKILLS

How might the farmers in the Whiskey Rebellion have expressed their disapproval of the whiskey tax while staying within the law?

4. THEME: DEMOCRATIC IDEALS

Did the formation of political parties make the nation more or less democratic?

Interact *with* History

How did the challenges of setting up a government that you discussed before you read the chapter compare with the actual challenges you read about?

VISUAL SUMMARY

The First Presidents

WASHINGTON PRESIDENCY 1789–1797

Strong Government
- Cabinet
- Judiciary

Remaining Neutral
- Jay's Treaty
- Pinckney's Treaty

Secure the West
- Battle of Fallen Timbers
- Treaty of Greenville

ADAMS PRESIDENCY 1797–1801

Federalists vs. Democratic-Republicans
- Differed over Constitution
- Disagreed on national bank

Problems with France
- XYZ Affair
- Convention of 1800

STANDARDS-BASED ASSESSMENT

Use the chart and your knowledge of U.S. history to answer questions 1 and 2.

Additional Test Practice, pp. S1–S33.

Financial Problems, 1789–1791

DEBTS	EXPENSES	INCOME
$77,230,000 = total public debt	$4,270,000 budget to run government	$4,400,000 from duties or taxes imposed on imported and exported goods

Source: *Historical Statistics of the United States*

1. How much money did the government owe during the period shown on the chart?

  A. $4,270,000

  B. $4,400,000

  C. $77,000,000

  D. $77,230,000

2. What could the government do to increase income?

  A. decrease duties and taxes

  B. increase duties and taxes

  C. increase the national budget

  D. pay off the public debt

This quotation from George Washington's Farewell Address is a warning to future leaders. Use this quotation and your knowledge of U.S. history to answer question 3.

PRIMARY SOURCE

Let me now . . . warn you . . . against the [harmful] effects of the spirit of party. . . . This spirit, unfortunately . . . exists in different shapes in all governments . . . but in those of the popular form, it is seen in its greatest rankness and is truly their worst enemy.

George Washington, Farewell Address

3. What danger was Washington warning Americans about in his Farewell Address?

  A. foreign governments

  B. Antifederalists

  C. political parties

  D. taxation

TEST PRACTICE
CLASSZONE.COM

ALTERNATIVE ASSESSMENT

1. ✎ WRITING ABOUT HISTORY

Imagine that you are a U.S. citizen during the French Revolution. Write a **letter** to the secretary of state giving reasons why you think the United States should aid the French, aid the British, or remain neutral.

• Use library resources to research the different sides.

• Use your research to persuade the secretary of state to your point of view.

2. COOPERATIVE LEARNING

Work with other students to research the Alien and Sedition Acts and the positions taken by both political parties. Consider these questions: Were the acts constitutional or an abuse of basic rights? Should criticism of the government be allowed in a time of possible war? Choose two group members to debate the Federalist and Democratic-Republican positions.

INTEGRATED TECHNOLOGY

CREATING A CAMPAIGN COMMERCIAL

Create a 30-second television commercial for either John Adams, the Federalist party candidate, or Thomas Jefferson, the Democratic-Republican party candidate.

• On the Internet, find information about your candidate that shows why he is a good choice.

• Locate at least two pictures that reveal different images of the candidate. Also, use the Internet to find suitable background music for the commercial.

• Use your resource materials to create a 30-second campaign commercial.

For more about the 1796 election . . .

INTERNET ACTIVITY
CLASSZONE.COM

CHAPTER 10

The Jefferson Era 1800–1816

Section 1
Jefferson Takes Office

Section 2
The Louisiana Purchase and Exploration

Section 3
Problems with Foreign Powers

Section 4
The War of 1812

Adult grizzly bears might weigh as much as 900 pounds and run 30 miles per hour.

1801
Thomas Jefferson is elected president.

1803
Louisiana Purchase is made.

1804
Jefferson is reelected.
Lewis and Clark expedition begins.

1807
Embargo Act is passed.

USA
World | 1800

1801
Tripoli declares war on the United States.

1803
Europe's Napoleonic wars resume after brief peace.

1805
British win at Trafalgar.
French win at Austerlitz.

You have been chosen to participate in an expedition to the West in the early 1800s. You are excited and curious, but also a little scared. You know that you will see and experience many new things. But you know there are risks involved, too.

What dangers will you face on an expedition west?

In the early 1800s, it took about 20 seconds to load and fire a gun.

What Do You Think?

- Notice the land features in these scenes. What problems might they hold for an explorer?
- What other people might you meet on the expedition?

RESEARCH LINKS
CLASSZONE.COM

Visit the Chapter 10 links for more information about the Jefferson Era.

1808
James Madison is elected president.

1811
Battle of Tippecanoe is fought.

1812
War of 1812 begins.

1814
British attack Washington, D.C.

1815
Battle of New Orleans is fought.

1816

1810
Father Hidalgo calls for Mexican independence.

1814
Napoleon is defeated and exiled to Elba.

1815
Napoleon returns and is defeated at Waterloo.

Reading Strategy: Summarizing

What Do You Know?

What parts of the United States today were not part of the country in 1800? What should leaders consider before they buy land for their countries?

Think About
- where the money for the purchase will come from
- what should be done if people already live on the land
- your responses to the Interact with History about facing dangers on an expedition west (see page 311)

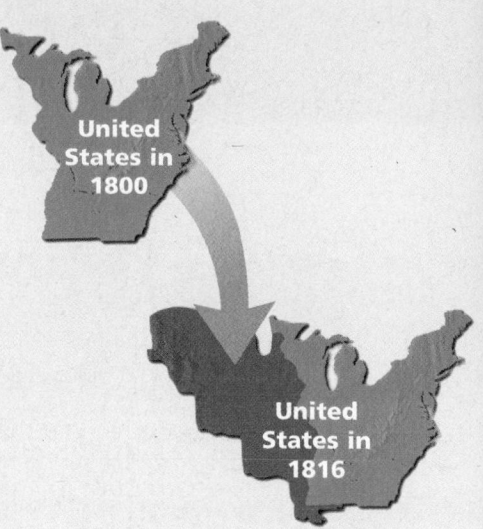

United States in 1800

United States in 1816

What Do You Want to Know?

 What details do you need to help you understand the nation's expansion in the early 1800s? Make a list of information you need in your notebook before you read the chapter.

Summarizing

When you study history, it is important to clearly understand what you read. One way to achieve a clear understanding is to summarize. When you summarize, you restate what you have read into fewer words, stating only the main ideas and essential details. It is important to use your own words in a summary. Use the chart below to record your summaries of the main ideas and essential details in Chapter 10.

S See Skillbuilder Handbook, page R2.

 Taking Notes

The Jefferson Era
Summaries
Main Idea: Thomas Jefferson is elected president.   **Details:** Jefferson replaces Federalist policies with his own but has problems with the judiciary.
Main Idea: **Details:**
Main Idea: **Details:**
Main Idea: **Details:**

Jefferson Takes Office

MAIN IDEA	WHY IT MATTERS NOW	TERMS & NAMES
When Jefferson became president in 1801, his party replaced Federalist programs with its own.	Today's Democratic Party traces its roots to the party of Jefferson, the Democratic-Republicans.	radical Judiciary Act of 1801 John Marshall *Marbury* v. *Madison* unconstitutional judicial review

ONE AMERICAN'S STORY

In the election of 1800, backers of John Adams and Thomas Jefferson fought for their candidates with nasty personal attacks. For instance, James Callender warned voters not to reelect President John Adams.

A VOICE FROM THE PAST

In the fall of 1796 . . . the country fell into a more dangerous juncture than almost any the old confederation ever endured. The tardiness and timidity of Mr. Washington were succeeded by the rancour [bitterness] and insolence [arrogance] of Mr. Adams. . . . Think what you have been, what you are, and what, under [Adams], you are likely to become.

James Callender, quoted in *American Aurora*

In the presidential election of 1800, Thomas Jefferson was the candidate of the Democratic-Republican Party. John Adams represented the Federalists.

Adams's defenders were just as vicious. Yet, in spite of the campaign's nastiness, the election ended with a peaceful transfer of power from one party to another. The 1800 election was a contest between two parties with different ideas about the role of government.

The Election of 1800

The two parties contesting the election of 1800 were the Federalists, led by President John Adams, and the Democratic-Republicans, represented by Thomas Jefferson. Each party believed that the other was endangering the Constitution and the American republic.

The Democratic-Republicans thought they were saving the nation from monarchy and oppression. They argued, again and again, that the Alien and Sedition Acts supported by the Federalists violated the Bill of Rights. (See pages 306–307.) The Federalists thought that the nation was about to be ruined by **radicals**—people who take extreme political positions. They remembered the violence of the French Revolution, in which radicals executed thousands in the name of liberty.

Taking Notes

Use your chart to take notes about Jefferson's presidency.

The Jefferson Era
Summaries
Main Idea: . Details:
Main Idea: Details:
Main Idea: Details:
Main Idea: Details:

When election day came, the Democratic-Republicans won the presidency. Jefferson received 73 votes in the electoral college, and Adams earned 65. But there was a problem. Aaron Burr, whom the Democratic-Republicans wanted as vice president, also received 73 votes.

Background
In 1804, the Twelfth Amendment solved this problem by creating separate ballots for president and vice president.

Breaking the Tie

According to the Constitution, the House of Representatives had to choose between Burr and Jefferson. The Democratic-Republicans clearly intended for Jefferson to be president. However, the new House of Representatives, dominated by Jefferson's party, would not take office for some months. Federalists still held a majority in the House, and their votes would decide the winner.

The Federalists were divided. Some feared Jefferson so much that they decided to back Burr. Others, such as Alexander Hamilton, considered Burr an unreliable man and urged the election of Jefferson. Hamilton did not like Jefferson, but he believed that Jefferson would do more for the good of the nation than Burr. "If there be a man in the world I ought to hate," he said, "it is Jefferson. . . . But the public good must be [more important than] every private consideration."

Over a period of seven days, the House voted 35 times without determining a winner. Finally, two weeks before the inauguration, Alexander Hamilton's friend James A. Bayard persuaded several Federalists not to vote for Burr. On the thirty-sixth ballot, Jefferson was elected president. Aaron Burr, who became vice president, would never forget Hamilton's insults.

People were overjoyed by Jefferson's election. A Philadelphia newspaper reported that bells rang, guns fired, dogs barked, cats meowed, and children cried over the news of Jefferson's victory.

Reading **History**
A. Analyzing Points of View
Why did Hamilton think that Jefferson was the better choice for president?

STRANGE *but* True

HAMILTON-BURR DUEL

In 1804, the Democratic-Republicans replaced Aaron Burr as their candidate for vice president. Burr then decided to run for governor of New York.

Alexander Hamilton questioned Burr's fitness for public office. He wrote that Burr was a "dangerous man . . . who ought not to be trusted with the reins of government."

Burr lost the election. Furious, he challenged Hamilton to a duel. Hamilton went to the duel but resolved not to fire. Burr, however, shot Hamilton, who died the next day.

The Talented Jefferson

In over 200 years, the United States has had more than 40 presidents. Many of them were great leaders. But no president has ever matched Thomas Jefferson in the variety of his achievements.

Jefferson's talents went beyond politics. He was still a young lawyer when he became interested in the architecture of classical Greece and Rome. The look of our nation's capital today reflects that interest. When Washington, D.C., was being built during the 1790s, Jefferson advised its architects and designers.

Jefferson's passion for classical styles can also be seen in his plan of Monticello, his Virginia home. For this elegant mansion, Jefferson designed storm windows, a seven-day clock, and a dumbwaiter—a small elevator that brought bottles of wine from the cellar.

Jefferson was a skilled violinist, horseman, amateur scientist, and a devoted reader, too. His book collection later became the core of the Library of Congress. After his election, Jefferson applied his many talents and ideas to the government of the United States.

Jefferson's Philosophy

The new president had strong opinions about what kind of country the United States ought to be. But his first order of business was to calm the nation's political quarrels.

A VOICE FROM THE PAST

Let us, then, fellow-citizens, unite with one heart and one mind. . . . Every difference of opinion is not a difference of principle. . . . We are all Republicans, we are all Federalists.

Thomas Jefferson, First Inaugural Address

Reading **History**

B. Summarizing How did Thomas Jefferson try to unite the nation after he was elected?

One way Jefferson tried to unite Americans was by promoting a common way of life. He wanted the United States to remain a nation of small independent farmers. Such a nation, he believed, would uphold the strong morals and democratic values that he associated with country living. He hoped that the enormous amount of available land would prevent Americans from crowding into cities, as people had in Europe.

As president, Jefferson behaved more like a gentleman farmer than a privileged politician. Instead of riding in a fancy carriage to his inauguration, Jefferson walked the two blocks from his boarding house to the Capitol. Though his chef served elegant meals, the president's guests ate at round tables so that no one could sit at the head of the table.

To the end, Jefferson refused to elevate himself because of his office. For his tombstone, he chose this simple epitaph: "Here was buried

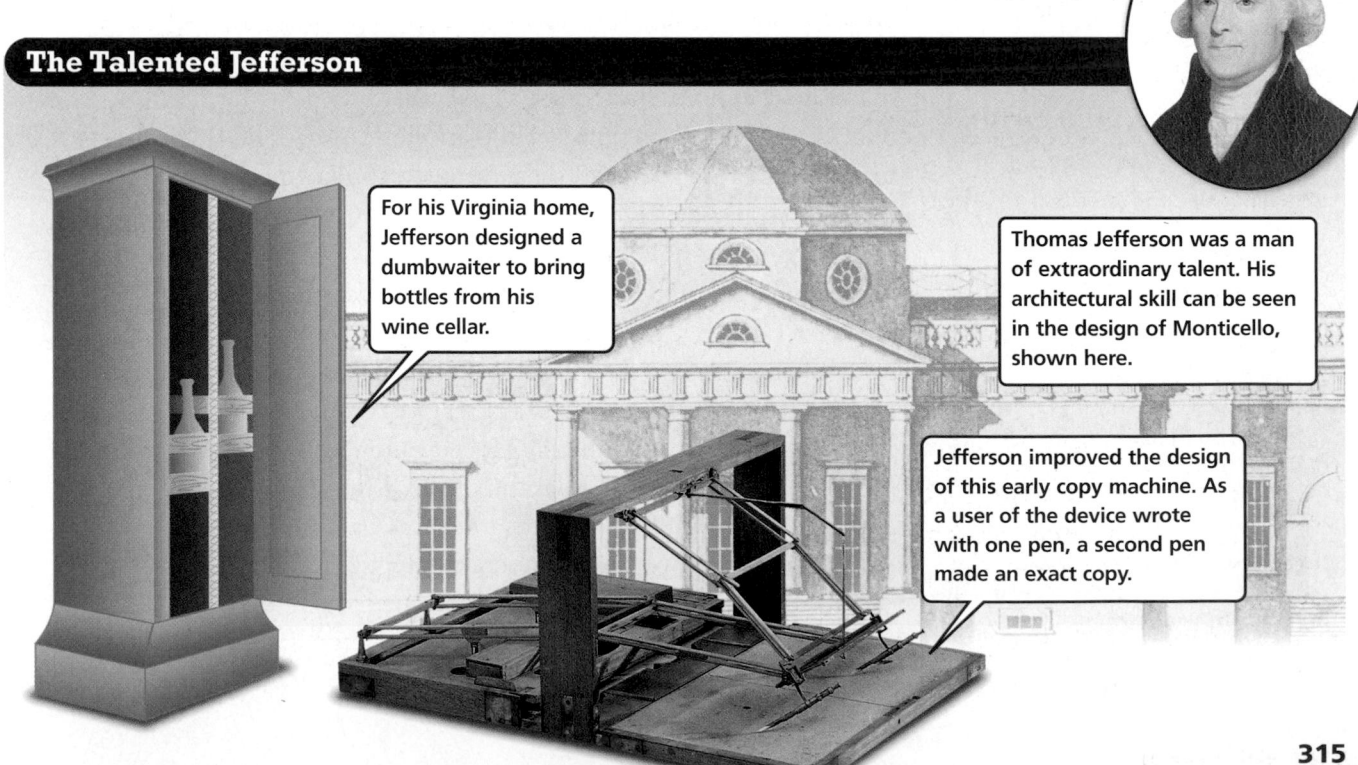

The Talented Jefferson

For his Virginia home, Jefferson designed a dumbwaiter to bring bottles from his wine cellar.

Thomas Jefferson was a man of extraordinary talent. His architectural skill can be seen in the design of Monticello, shown here.

Jefferson improved the design of this early copy machine. As a user of the device wrote with one pen, a second pen made an exact copy.

Thomas Jefferson, author of the Declaration of American Independence, of the statute of Virginia for religious freedom, and father of the University of Virginia." Jefferson chose not to list his presidency. His belief in a modest role for the central government is reflected in the changes he made during his presidency.

Background
In addition to founding the University of Virginia in 1819, Jefferson designed its buildings and supervised their construction.

Undoing Federalist Programs

Jefferson believed that the federal government should have less power than it had had under the Federalists. During his term of office, he sought to end many Federalist programs.

At the president's urging, Congress—now controlled by Democratic-Republicans—allowed the Alien and Sedition Acts to end. Jefferson then released prisoners convicted under the acts—among them, James Callender. Congress also ended many taxes, including the unpopular whiskey tax. Because the loss of tax revenue lowered the government's income, Jefferson reduced the number of federal employees to cut costs. He also reduced the size of the military.

Jefferson next made changes to the Federalists' financial policies. Alexander Hamilton had created a system that depended on a certain amount of public debt. He believed that people who were owed money by their government would make sure the government was run properly. But Jefferson opposed public debt. He used revenues from tariffs and land sales to reduce the amount of money owed by the government.

Marshall and the Judiciary

Though Jefferson ended many Federalist programs, he had little power over the courts. John Adams had seen to that with the **Judiciary Act of 1801**. Under this act, Adams had appointed as many Federalist judges as he could between the election of 1800 and Jefferson's inauguration in 1801. These last-minute appointments meant that the new Democratic-Republican president would face a firmly Federalist judiciary.

Jefferson often felt frustrated by Federalist control of the courts. Yet because judges received their appointments for life, the president could do little.

Before he left office in 1801, President Adams also appointed a new Chief Justice of the Supreme Court. He chose a 45-year-old Federalist, **John Marshall**. He guessed that Marshall would be around for a long time to check the power of the Democratic-Republicans. He was right. Marshall served as Chief Justice for over three decades. Under Marshall, the Supreme Court upheld federal authority and strengthened federal

AMERICA'S HISTORY MAKERS

JOHN MARSHALL
1755–1835
John Marshall was born, the first of 15 children, in Virginia's back-country. He had little formal schooling. He received most of his education from his parents and a minister who lived with the family one year.

Even so, the lasting strength of the U.S. Constitution is partly due to Marshall's brilliant legal mind. In his long tenure as Chief Justice, John Marshall participated in more than 1,000 decisions and wrote 519 of them himself.

How does Marshall's record as Chief Justice demonstrate his decision-making abilities?

*Reading*History
C. Analyzing Causes Why did the Federalists retain a great deal of power even after they were defeated by the Democratic-Republicans?

courts. One of the most important decisions of the Marshall Court was ***Marbury v. Madison*** (1803).

Marbury v. Madison

Vocabulary
justice of the peace: a low-level official with limited authority, including the power to perform marriages

William Marbury was one of Adams's last-minute appointments. Adams had named him as a justice of the peace for the District of Columbia.

Marbury was supposed to be installed in his position by Secretary of State James Madison. When Madison refused to give him the job, Marbury sued. The case went to the Supreme Court, which ruled that the law under which Marbury sued was **unconstitutional**—that is, it contradicted the law of the Constitution.

Although the Court denied Marbury's claim, it did establish the principle of **judicial review**. This principle states that the Supreme Court has the final say in interpreting the Constitution. In his decision, Marshall declared, "It is emphatically the province and duty of the Judicial Department to say what the law is." If the Supreme Court decides that a law violates the Constitution, then that law cannot be put into effect.

Jefferson and Madison were angry when Marshall seized this new power for the Supreme Court, but they could hardly fight his decision. After all, he had decided *Marbury* v. *Madison* in their favor.

By establishing judicial review, Marshall helped to create a lasting balance among the three branches of government. The strength of this balance would be tested as the United States grew. In the next section, you will read about a period of great national growth.

Now and then

THE SUPREME COURT TODAY

The principle of judicial review is still a major force in American society. In June 1999, the Supreme Court used this power to restrict the ability of the federal government to enforce its laws in the 50 states.

In one case, *Alden v. Maine*, the Court ruled that employees of a state government cannot sue their state even when the state violates federal labor laws—such as those that set guidelines for overtime wages.

Section 1 Assessment

1. Terms & Names

Explain the significance of:
- radical
- Judiciary Act of 1801
- John Marshall
- *Marbury* v. *Madison*
- unconstitutional
- judicial review

2. Using Graphics

Use a chart like the one below to list some of the changes made by Jefferson and his party.

Changes made by Democratic-Republicans
1.

What branch of government gave Jefferson trouble?

3. Main Ideas

a. How was the tie between Jefferson and Burr settled after the election of 1800?

b. In what ways did Jefferson's talents reach beyond politics?

c. How did the opinions of Jefferson and Hamilton regarding the public debt differ?

4. Critical Thinking

Making Generalizations
How was Thomas Jefferson's philosophy reflected in his personal life?

THINK ABOUT
- how he behaved after being elected
- how he felt about his presidency later in life

ACTIVITY OPTIONS

TECHNOLOGY
ART

Read more about Thomas Jefferson. Design Jefferson's **Internet home page** showing his inventions or create a **model** of a building he designed.

The Louisiana Purchase and Exploration

MAIN IDEA	WHY IT MATTERS NOW	TERMS & NAMES
Jefferson purchased the Louisiana Territory in 1803 and doubled the size of the United States.	Thirteen more states were eventually organized on the land acquired by the Louisiana Purchase.	Louisiana Purchase — Lewis and Clark expedition Meriwether Lewis — Sacagawea William Clark — Zebulon Pike

ONE AMERICAN'S STORY

In 1790, Captain Robert Gray became the first American to sail around the world. Two years later, Gray explored a harbor in what is now Washington state. New England merchants like Captain Gray had to sail all the way around South America to reach the profitable trading regions of the Oregon Country. (See the map on page 320.) In spite of the long trip, merchants from Boston soon began to appear there frequently.

Gray's explorations helped to establish U.S. claims to the Pacific Northwest. In this section, you will learn how a lucky land purchase and a daring expedition further hastened westward expansion.

The West in 1800

Taking Notes

Use your chart to take notes about the exploration of the West.

The Jefferson Era		
Summaries		
Main Idea: . Details:		
Main Idea: Details:		
Main Idea: Details:		
Main Idea: Details:		

In 1800, when Americans talked about the "West," they meant the area between the Appalachian Mountains and the Mississippi River. Thousands of settlers were moving westward across the Appalachians to settle in this region. Many moved onto land long inhabited by Native Americans. Even so, several U.S. territories soon declared statehood. Kentucky and Tennessee had become states by 1800, and Ohio entered the union in 1803.

Although the Mississippi River was the western border of the United States, there was a great deal of activity further west. In 1800, France and Spain were negotiating for ownership of the Louisiana Territory—the vast region between the Mississippi River and the Rocky Mountains.

The Pacific coast region and the Oregon Country, as you read in One American's Story, also attracted increasing attention. In California, Spain had a chain of 21 missions stretching from San Diego to San Francisco. Starting just north of San Francisco, Russian settlements dotted the Pacific coast all the way to Alaska. Great Britain also claimed land in the region.

Robert Gray sailed his ship *Columbia* on trading voyages to the Northwest and China.

*Reading*History
A. Reading a Map Use the map on page 320 to find the location of New Orleans.

As the number of Westerners grew, so did their political influence. A vital issue for many settlers was the use of the Mississippi River. Farmers and merchants used the river to move their products to the port of New Orleans, and from there to east coast markets. Threats to the free navigation of the Mississippi and the use of the port at New Orleans brought America to the brink of war.

Napoleon and New Orleans

"There is on the globe one single spot the possessor of which is our natural and habitual enemy," President Jefferson wrote. That spot was New Orleans. This strategic port was originally claimed by France. After losing the French and Indian War, France turned over the Louisiana Territory—including New Orleans—to Spain. But in a secret treaty in 1800, Spain returned Louisiana and the port to France's powerful leader, Napoleon. Now Napoleon planned to colonize the American territory.

Background
In 1799, Napoleon was made the top official of the French Republic. In 1804, he became emperor.

In 1802, these developments nearly resulted in war. Just before turning Louisiana over to France, Spain closed New Orleans to American shipping. Angry Westerners called for war against both Spain and France. To avoid hostilities, Jefferson offered to buy New Orleans from France. He received a surprising offer back. The French asked if the United States wanted to buy all of the Louisiana Territory—a tract of land even larger than the United States at that time.

The Louisiana Purchase

A number of factors may have led Napoleon to make his surprising offer. He was probably alarmed by America's fierce determination to keep the port of New Orleans open. Also, his enthusiasm for a colony in America may have been lessened by events in a French colony in the West Indies. There, a revolt led by Toussaint L'Ouverture (too•SAN loo•vehr•TOOR) had resulted in disastrous losses for the French. Another factor was France's costly war against Britain. America's money may have been more valuable to Napoleon than its land.

*Reading*History
B. Making Inferences Why did Jefferson purchase Louisiana even though the Constitution said nothing about the president's right to buy land?

Jefferson was thrilled by Napoleon's offer. However, the Constitution said nothing about the president's right to buy land. This troubled Jefferson, who believed in the strict interpretation of the Constitution. But he also believed in a republic of small farmers, and that required land. So, on April 30, 1803, the **Louisiana Purchase** was approved for $15 million—about three cents per acre. The purchase doubled the size of the United States. At the time, Americans knew little about the territory. But that would soon change.

Connections TO WORLD HISTORY

TOUSSAINT L'OUVERTURE

Toussaint L'Ouverture was born in Hispaniola, an island in the West Indies once colonized by both France and Spain. In 1791, L'Ouverture helped to lead a slave revolt against the French-controlled part of Hispaniola. A natural leader, L'Ouverture won admiration when he preached harmony between former slaves and planters.

In 1801, L'Ouverture overran the Spanish part of the island. He then freed all the slaves and put himself in charge of the entire island.

Hoping to regain their territory, the French invaded in 1802. They arrested L'Ouverture but failed to end the rebellion.

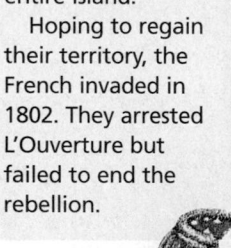

Lewis and Clark Explore

Since 1802, Thomas Jefferson had planned an expedition to explore the Louisiana country. Now that the Louisiana Purchase had been made, learning about the territory became even more important.

Jefferson chose a young officer, Captain **Meriwether Lewis,** to lead the expedition. In Jefferson's map-lined study, the two men eagerly planned the trip. Lewis turned to his old friend, Lieutenant **William Clark,** to select and oversee a volunteer force, which they called the Corps of Discovery. Clark was a skilled mapmaker and outdoorsman and proved to be a natural leader. The Corps of Discovery soon became known as the **Lewis and Clark expedition.**

Clark was accompanied by York, his African-American slave. York's hunting skills won him many admirers among the Native Americans met by the explorers. The first black man that many Indians had ever seen, York became something of a celebrity among them.

Lewis and Clark set out in the summer of 1803. By winter, they reached St. Louis. Located on the western bank of the Mississippi River, St. Louis would soon become the gateway to the West. But in 1803, the city was a sleepy town with just 180 houses. Lewis and Clark spent the winter at St. Louis and waited for the ceremony that would mark the transfer of Louisiana to the United States. In March 1804, the American flag flew over St. Louis for the first time.

Vocabulary
corps (kor): a number of people acting together for a similar purpose

The Louisiana Purchase and Explorations, *1804–1807*

The Rocky Mountain summit of Pikes Peak is 14,110 feet high.

GEOGRAPHY SKILLBUILDER Interpreting Maps
1. **Location** *What two rivers met at the starting point of the Lewis and Clark expedition?*
2. **Movement** *How were Lewis and Clark's return routes different from each other?*

MERIWETHER LEWIS
1774–1809

Meriwether Lewis was well qualified for the first overland expedition to the Pacific Northwest. In Virginia, he had become an expert hunter. From 1801 to 1803, he worked for President Jefferson, who had him trained in geography, mineralogy, and astronomy.

The journals Lewis kept tell what the West was like in the early 1800s and are still exciting to read. In one entry, dated September 17, 1804, Lewis describes the "immense herds of Buffaloe, deer Elk and Antelopes which we saw in every direction feeding on the hills and plains."

WILLIAM CLARK
1770–1838

William Clark was an army friend of Meriwether Lewis. Lewis personally chose him to be co-captain of the Corps of Discovery.

Clark's experience in his state militia and the U.S. Army had taught him how to build forts, draw maps, and lead expeditions through enemy territory.

He had less formal training than Lewis, but with his six feet of height and muscular build, he was a more rugged explorer.

Clark's leadership skills smoothed disputes. Also, his artistic skills made the expedition's maps and drawings both accurate and beautiful.

What were the different skills of Lewis and Clark that qualified them as co-leaders of the expedition?

Up the Missouri River

Reading **History**

C. Making Inferences Why did Lewis and Clark travel on the Missouri River?

The explorers, who numbered about 40, set out from St. Louis in May of 1804. They headed up the Missouri River in one shallow-bottomed river-boat and two pirogues—canoes made from hollowed-out tree trunks. They had instructions from President Jefferson to explore the river and hoped to find a water route across the continent. Lewis and Clark were also told to establish good relations with Native Americans and describe the landscape, plants, and animals they saw.

The explorers inched up the Missouri. The first afternoon, they traveled only about three miles. Sometimes the men had to pull, rather than row or sail, their boats against the current. In late October, they reached the Mandan Indian villages in what is now North Dakota.

The explorers built a small fort and spent the winter with the friendly Mandan. There, they also met British and French-Canadian trappers and traders. They were not happy to see the Americans. They suspected that the Americans would soon compete with them for the rich trade in beaver furs—and they were right.

In the spring of 1805, the expedition set out again. A French trapper, his 17-year-old-wife, **Sacagawea** (SAK•uh•juh•WEE•uh), and their baby went with them. Sacagawea was a Shoshone woman whose language skills and knowledge of geography would be of great value to Lewis and Clark—especially when they reached the area where she was born.

On to the Pacific Ocean

On their way west, the expedition had to stop at the Great Falls of the Missouri. Lewis called this ten-mile-long series of waterfalls "the grandest sight I ever beheld." He described his approach to the falls.

A VOICE FROM THE PAST

I had proceeded on this course about two miles . . . whin my ears were saluted with the agreeable sound of a fall of water and advancing a little further I saw the spray arrise above the plain like a collumn of smoke. . . . (It) soon began to make a roaring too tremendous to be mistaken for any cause short of the great falls of the Missouri.

Meriwether Lewis, quoted in *Undaunted Courage*

Lewis and Clark kept beautiful journals that provided priceless information about the West.

To get around the Great Falls, the explorers had to carry their boats and heavy supplies for 18 miles. They built wheels from cottonwood trees to move the boats. Even with wheels, the trek took nearly two weeks. Rattlesnakes, bears, and even a hailstorm slowed their steps.

As they approached the Rocky Mountains, Sacagawea excitedly pointed out Shoshone lands. Eager to make contact with the tribe, Lewis and a small party made their way overland. Lewis soon found the Shoshone, whose chief recognized Sacagawea as his sister. The chief traded horses to Lewis and Clark, and the Shoshone helped them cross the Rocky Mountains.

The explorers then journeyed to the mighty Columbia River, which leads to the Pacific Ocean. In November 1805, Clark wrote in his journal, "Ocian in view! O! The joy." They soon arrived at the Pacific Coast. There, they spent a rain-soaked winter before returning to St. Louis the following year.

The Lewis and Clark expedition brought back a wealth of scientific and geographic information. Though they learned that an all-water route across the continent did not exist, Americans received an exciting report of what lay to the west.

Reading **History**

D. Finding Main Ideas Why was the Lewis and Clark expedition valuable?

Pike's Expedition

Lewis and Clark explored the northern part of the Louisiana Purchase. In 1806, an expedition led by **Zebulon Pike** left St. Louis on a southerly route. (Refer to the map on page 320.) Pike's mission was to find the sources of the Arkansas and Red rivers. The Red River formed a boundary between Spanish territory and Louisiana.

Pike's party of two dozen men headed westward across the Great Plains. When they reached the Arkansas River, they followed it toward the Rocky Mountains. From 150 miles away, Pike spied the Rocky Mountain peak that would later bear his name—Pikes Peak. However, he failed in his attempt to climb it. Then they turned south, hoping that they would eventually run into the Red River. Instead, they ran into the

Background
The previous year, Pike had led a 5,000-mile expedition to search for the source of the Mississippi River.

EFFECTS: Exploration of the West, 1804–1807

▶ **1. Accurate maps**
Lewis and Clark and Pike produced the first good maps of the Louisiana Territory. Later travelers would use these maps to make their way west.

▶ **2. Growth of fur trade**
Exploration boosted interest in the fur trade. Hunters and trappers would add to the knowledge of the West.

▶ **3. Mistaken view of Great Plains**
Pike inaccurately described the treeless Great Plains as a desert. This led many Americans to believe that the Plains were useless for farming.

SKILLBUILDER Interpreting Charts
Why might Pike's description of the Great Plains have led to the idea that Native Americans east of the Mississippi should be moved there?

Compass used by Lewis and Clark

Vocabulary
Rio Grande: Spanish for *big river*

Rio Grande, which was in Spanish territory. There, they were arrested by Spanish troops.

The explorers returned to the United States after being released by Spanish officials in 1807. Though Pike and his men never explored the Red River, they did bring back valuable descriptions of the Great Plains and the Rio Grande River Valley.

The Effects of Exploration

The first American explorers of the West brought back tales of adventure as well as scientific and geographical information. As the chart above shows, this information would have long-lasting effects.

Early in Jefferson's presidency, events at home occupied much of the new president's time. In the next section, you will learn about foreign affairs during the same time period.

Section 2 Assessment

1. Terms & Names

Explain the significance of:
- Louisiana Purchase
- Meriwether Lewis
- William Clark
- Lewis and Clark expedition
- Sacagawea
- Zebulon Pike

2. Using Graphics

Use a chart like the one below to record the factors that might have led Napoleon to sell the Louisiana Territory.

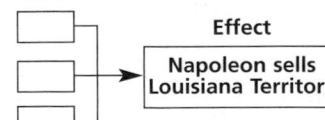

3. Main Ideas

a. What groups might dispute European land claims in the West?

b. Why was New Orleans important to Americans?

c. How did Sacagawea help Lewis and Clark?

4. Critical Thinking

Recognizing Effects What were some of the effects of the explorations of the West in the 1800s?

THINK ABOUT
- how other people might use the information brought back by the explorers
- the economic effects of the expedition

ACTIVITY OPTIONS

WORLD HISTORY
GEOGRAPHY

Read more about New Orleans. Make an illustrated **time line** of the French, Spanish, and U.S. ownership of the city or create a **map** of its port.

Native Americans on the Explorers' Route

When Thomas Jefferson bought the Louisiana Territory, Native Americans had already been living in that area for thousands of years. Before Lewis and Clark began their trip, Jefferson instructed them to deal with Native Americans in a peaceful manner and to make it clear that the United States wished to be "friendly and useful to them." On their journey, Lewis and Clark met almost 50 different tribes.

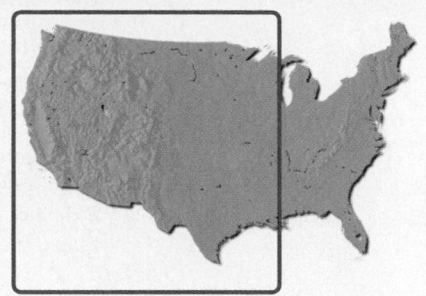

Sacagawea
In 1805, the explorers arrived in Shoshone territory near the Rocky Mountains. A Shoshone chief, Cameahwait, confirmed that there was no all-water route to the Pacific. Later, when Cameahwait recognized Sacagawea as his sister, he agreed to sell the explorers the horses they needed to cross the mountains.

1 Oto
In 1804, Lewis and Clark met the Oto, a buffalo-hunting people. This was the first formal meeting of U.S. representatives with western Native Americans. Lewis told the Oto that they were "children" of a new great "father"—President Thomas Jefferson.

ARTIFACT FILE

Buffalo Robe Pictured to the right is a section of a Mandan buffalo robe. On it, a Mandan painted a battle scene between the Mandan and the Sioux.

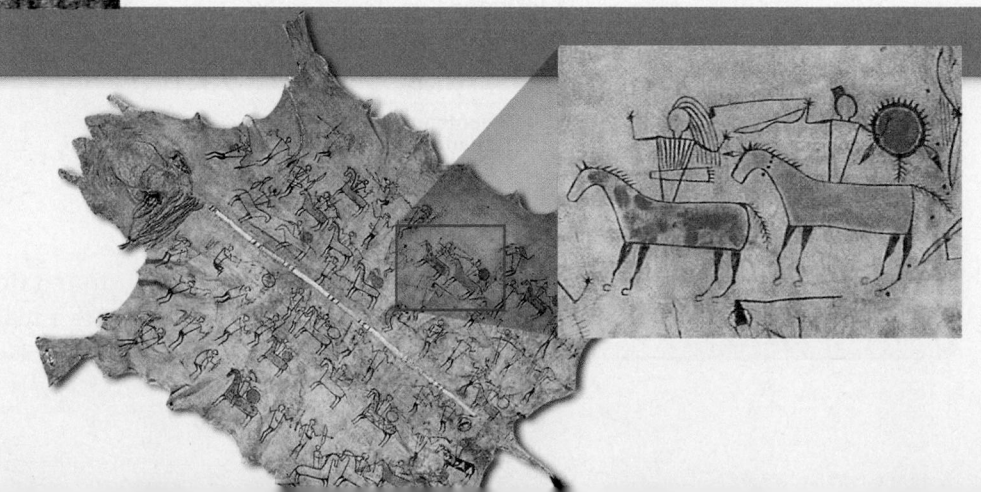

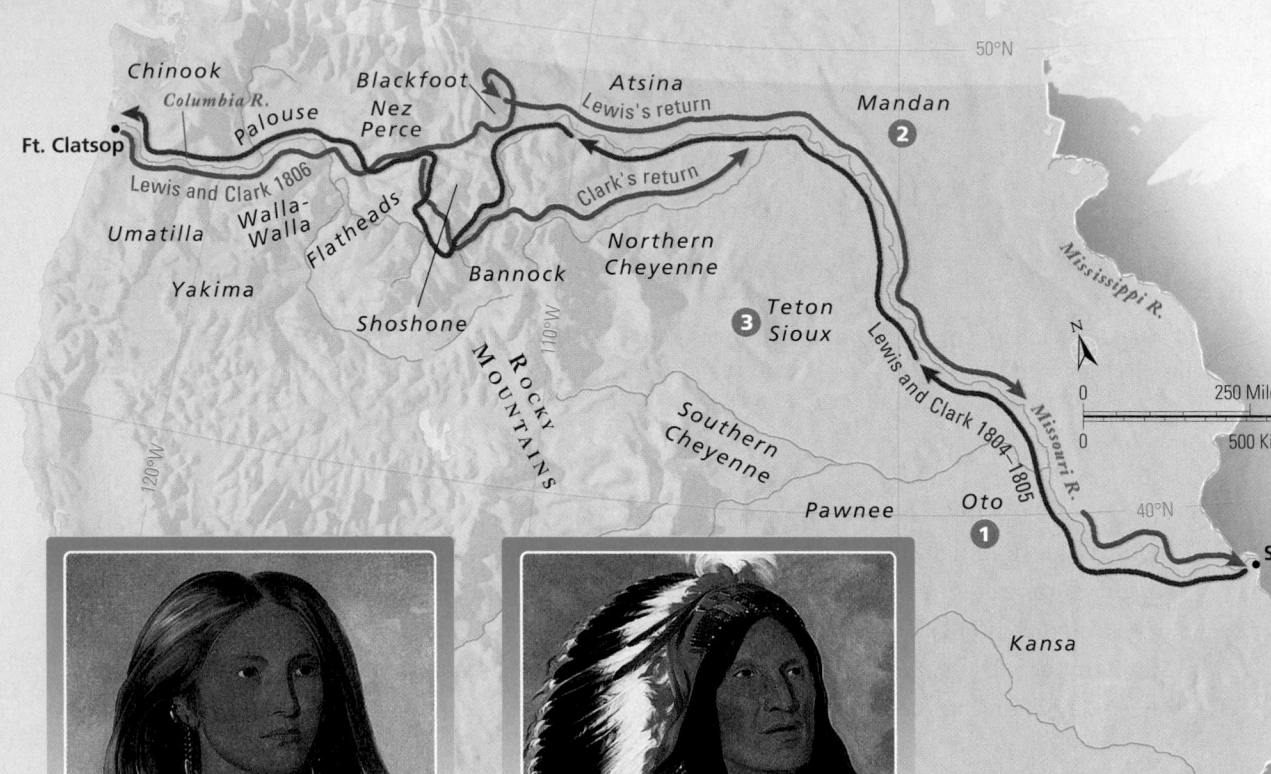

Chinook
Columbia R.
Palouse
Ft. Clatsop
Lewis and Clark 1806
Umatilla
Walla-Walla
Yakima
Flatheads
Bannock
Shoshone
Blackfoot
Nez Perce
Atsina
Lewis's return
Clark's return
Northern Cheyenne
ROCKY MOUNTAINS
Southern Cheyenne
Mandan ②
③ Teton Sioux
Lewis and Clark 1804–1805
Pawnee
Oto ①
Kansa
Mississippi R.
Missouri R.
St. Louis
PACIFIC OCEAN
50°N
40°N
30°N
120°W
110°W
Gulf of Mexico

0   250 Miles
0   500 Kilometers

② **Mandan**
Neighboring tribes as well as exploring Europeans relied on the mainstay of Mandan culture—corn. The Mandan also crafted beautiful leatherwork and pottery. Lewis and Clark spent an entire winter with the Mandan.

③ **Teton Sioux**
Upon meeting the Teton Sioux, Lewis and Clark showed off an air gun. Known for their aggressiveness, the Teton already viewed the Americans as competitors for trade in this region. As a result, confrontation marked Lewis and Clark's visit.

CONNECT TO GEOGRAPHY
1. **Place** What fort was built where the Columbia River empties into the Pacific Ocean?
2. **Location** In what mountain range did the Shoshone tribe live?

 See Geography Handbook, page 4.

CONNECT TO HISTORY
3. **Forming Opinions** What do you think the Native Americans that Lewis and Clark met thought about the explorers?

On-Line Field Trip

The Peabody Museum in Cambridge, Massachusetts, holds an important collection of Native American artifacts. This rain hat was worn by Chinook whalers of the Northwest. The Chinook made these water-repellent hats out of cedar bark and bear grass.

For more about Native American artifacts . . .

 **RESEARCH LINKS**
CLASSZONE.COM

Problems with Foreign Powers

MAIN IDEA	WHY IT MATTERS NOW	TERMS & NAMES
Jefferson tried to avoid involvement in the problems of other nations.	British interference with the affairs of the United States led to the War of 1812.	impressment Tecumseh Embargo Act War Hawk of 1807

ONE AMERICAN'S STORY

In 1804, the United States was at war with Tripoli, a state on the North African coast. The war was the result of repeated attacks on American merchant ships by African pirates. U.S. Navy Lieutenant Stephen Decatur was sent to destroy the U.S. warship *Philadelphia*—which had been captured by Tripoli—so that it could not be used by the enemy.

Decatur set fire to the *Philadelphia* and then escaped under enemy fire with only one man wounded. Decatur later issued this rallying cry for all Americans.

> *A VOICE FROM THE PAST*
>
> Our country! In her [relationships] with foreign nations may she always be in the right; but our country, right or wrong.
>
> **Stephen Decatur,** 1816

The conflict with Tripoli showed how hard it was for the United States to stay out of foreign affairs while its citizens participated so heavily in overseas trade. In this section, you will learn how President Jefferson handled problems with other nations.

Stephen Decatur struggles in hand-to-hand combat with African pirates.

Taking Notes

Use your chart to take notes about problems with foreign powers.

The Jefferson Era
Summaries
Main Idea: Details:
Main Idea: Details:
Main Idea: Details:
Main Idea: Details:

Jefferson's Foreign Policy

When Thomas Jefferson took office in 1801, he wanted to focus on domestic concerns. In his inaugural address, he noted that America was "kindly separated by nature and a wide ocean from the exterminating havoc [wars] of one quarter of the globe." He advised the United States to seek the friendship of all nations, but to enter into "entangling alliances with none."

However, the president's desire to keep the United States separated from other nations and their problems was doomed to fail. For one thing, American merchants were busily engaged in trade all over the world. For

another, the Louisiana Purchase and the Lewis and Clark expedition were about to open the country to westward expansion. Expansion would bring Americans into closer contact with people from other nations who had already established settlements in the West.

Finally, the United States had little control over the actions of foreign nations—as North African interference with U.S. shipping had shown. Staying out of the ongoing conflict between France and England would be just as difficult.

*Reading***History**
A. Analyzing Causes Why was it hard for the United States to avoid other nations' problems?

Problems with France and England

For a long time, the United States managed not to get involved in the European wars that followed the French Revolution. At times, the nation even benefited from the conflict. Busy with affairs in Europe, France sold the Louisiana Territory to the United States. And American shippers eagerly took over the trade interrupted by the war.

By 1805, however, the British began to clamp down on U.S. shipping. They did not want Americans to provide their enemies with food and supplies. After the United States threatened to take action, the British decided to set up a partial blockade. This would only allow some American ships to bring provisions to Europe.

This partial blockade angered France, which enacted its own laws to control foreign shipping. These changes put American merchants in a difficult position. If they obeyed the British rules, their ships could be seized by the French. If they obeyed the French rules, their ships could be seized by the British.

British officers seize an American sailor at gunpoint.

Britain also interfered with U.S. trade by the **impressment,** or kidnapping, of American sailors to work on British ships. Between 1803 and 1812, the British impressed about 6,000 American sailors.

One of the most famous incidents occurred in 1807. The British ship *Leopard* attacked an American naval ship, the *Chesapeake,* off the coast of Virginia. Three Americans lost their lives in the battle. The attack aroused widespread anger. Had Congress been in session, America might have declared war. But Jefferson, who had been re-elected in 1804, decided against it. One critic, furious at the president's caution, called Jefferson a "dish of skim milk curdling at the head of our nation."

Trade as a Weapon

Vocabulary
coercion: the practice of forcing someone to act in a certain way by use of pressure or threats

Instead of declaring war, Jefferson asked Congress to pass legislation that would stop all foreign trade. "Peaceable coercion," as the president described his policy, would prevent further bloodshed.

In December, Congress passed the **Embargo Act of 1807**. Now American ships were no longer allowed to sail to foreign ports. The act also closed American ports to British ships.

Jefferson's policy was a disaster. It was more harmful to the United States than to the British and French. American farmers and merchants were especially hard hit. Southern and Western farmers, for example, lost important markets for their grain, cotton, and tobacco. Shippers lost income, and many chose to violate the embargo by making false claims about where they were going. One New Englander said the embargo was like "cutting one's throat to cure the nosebleed."

The embargo became a major issue in the election of 1808. Jefferson's old friend James Madison won the election. By the time he took office, Congress had already repealed the embargo.

Madison's solution to the problem was a law that allowed merchants to trade with any country except France and Britain. Trade with these countries would start again when they agreed to respect U.S. ships. But this law proved no more effective than the embargo.

Reading History
B. Recognizing Effects What were the results of the Embargo Act?

Tecumseh and Native American Unity

The Shawnee chief Tecumseh led Native American resistance to white rule in the Ohio River Valley.

British interference with American shipping and impressment of U.S. citizens made Americans furious. They also were angered by Britain's actions in the Northwest. Many settlers believed that the British were stirring up Native American resistance to frontier settlements.

Since the Battle of Fallen Timbers in 1794 (see page 299), Native Americans continued to lose their land. Thousands of white settlers had swarmed into Ohio and then into Indiana.

Tecumseh, a Shawnee chief, vowed to stop the loss of Native American land. He believed that the reason Native Americans continued to lose their land was because they were separated into many different tribes. He concluded that Native Americans had to do what white Americans had done: unite. Events in 1809 proved him right.

That September, William Henry Harrison, governor of the Indiana Territory, signed the Treaty of Fort Wayne with chiefs of the Miami, Delaware, and Potawatomi tribes. They agreed to sell over three million acres of land. But Tecumseh declared the treaty meaningless.

A VOICE FROM THE PAST

[Whites] have taken upon themselves to say this [land] belongs to the Miamis, this to the Delawares and so on. But the Great Spirit intended [Native American land] to be the common property of all the tribes, [and it cannot] be sold without the consent of all.

Tecumseh, quoted in *Tecumseh and the Quest for Indian Leadership*

Reading History
C. Forming Opinions Why did Tecumseh declare the Treaty of Fort Wayne meaningless?

After the Treaty of Fort Wayne, many Native Americans began to answer Tecumseh's call for unity. But his efforts ultimately failed. In November 1811, while Tecumseh was away recruiting tribes for his alliance, the Shawnee were defeated by Harrison's forces at the Battle of

Tippecanoe. It was a severe setback for Tecumseh's movement.

War Hawks

After the battle of Tippecanoe, Tecumseh and his warriors found a warm welcome with the British in Canada. At that point, the Native Americans and the British became allies. Tecumseh's welcome in Canada raised even higher the anti-British feelings in the West.

Leaders such as Congressman Henry Clay of Kentucky angrily demanded war against Britain. Westerners who called for war were known as **War Hawks.** They wanted British aid to Native Americans stopped, and they wanted the British out of Canada. Conquering Canada would open up a vast new empire for Americans.

Vocabulary
hawk: a person who favors the use of military force to carry out foreign policy

Other Americans sought war because of the British violations of American rights at sea. Future president Andrew Jackson said hostilities were necessary "for the protection of our maritime citizens impressed on board British ships of war," and to "open a market for the productions of our soil."

Urged on by Jackson and the War Hawks, Congress declared war on Britain on June 18, 1812. In the next section, you will read about the second—and final—war between the United States and Great Britain.

Causes of the War of 1812

| Impressment of U.S. Citizens | Interference with American shipping | British support of Native-American resistance |

WAR

SKILLBUILDER Interpreting Charts
Which cause of the War of 1812 was not related to activities on the sea?

Section 3 Assessment

1. Terms & Names
Explain the significance of:
• impressment
• Embargo Act of 1807
• Tecumseh
• War Hawk

2. Using Graphics
Use a chart like the one below to record the effects of Jefferson's Embargo Act.

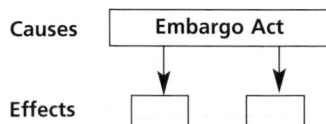

Causes

Embargo Act

Effects

Why didn't the act work?

3. Main Ideas
a. How did the British and French interfere with American shipping?

b. How did Jefferson respond to the interference?

c. Why did the War Hawks favor war?

4. Critical Thinking
Analyzing Points of View
Why did Tecumseh think it was important for Native Americans to unite?

THINK ABOUT
• what he learned about white men
• what Native Americans would lose if they did not act together

---

ACTIVITY OPTIONS

ART

SPEECH

Do research on the Battle of Tippecanoe. Draw a **comic strip story** of the battle or hold a **press conference** to describe the battle's outcome.

4

The War of 1812

MAIN IDEA	WHY IT MATTERS NOW	TERMS & NAMES
Angered by Britain's interference in the nation's affairs, the United States went to war.	The War of 1812 showed that the United States was willing and able to protect its national interests.	Oliver Hazard Perry Battle of the Thames Francis Scott Key Treaty of Ghent

ONE AMERICAN'S STORY

The war between the United States and Britain had begun in 1812. Two years later, British troops were marching toward Washington, D.C. Dolley Madison, the president's wife, stayed behind until the last minute to save important historical objects from the White House.

A VOICE FROM THE PAST

I have had [a wagon] filled with . . . the most valuable portable articles belonging to the house. . . . I insist on waiting until the large picture of General Washington is secured.

Dolley Madison, from a letter sent to her sister

When the British troops arrived in the city, they set fire to many public buildings, including the White House and the Capitol. You will learn about other events of the War of 1812 in this section.

Before British troops set fire to the president's mansion, Dolley Madison saved priceless historical objects.

Taking Notes

Use your chart to take notes about the War of 1812.

The Jefferson Era
Summaries
Main Idea: . Details:
Main Idea: Details:
Main Idea: Details:
Main Idea: Details:

The War Begins

Britain did not really want a war with the United States because it was already involved in another war with France. To try to avoid war, the British announced that they would no longer interfere with American shipping. But the slow mails of the day prevented this news from reaching the United States until weeks after June 18th, when Congress approved Madison's request for a declaration of war.

The War of 1812 had two main phases. From 1812 to 1814, Britain concentrated on its war against France. It devoted little energy to the conflict in North America, although it did send ships to blockade the American coast. The second phase of the war began after the British defeated France in April 1814. With their European war nearly at an end, the British could turn their complete attention to the United States.

The United States military was weak when the war was declared. Democratic-Republicans had reduced the size of the armed forces. When the war began, the Navy had only about 16 ships. The army had fewer than 7,000 men. These men were poorly trained and equipped, and were often led by inexperienced officers. A young Virginia army officer complained that the older officers were victims of "sloth, ignorance, or habits of [excessive] drinking."

The First Phase of the War

In spite of its small size, the United States Navy rose to the challenge. Its warships were the fastest afloat. American naval officers had gained valuable experience fighting pirates in the Mediterranean Sea. Early in the war, before the British blockaded the coast, ships such as the *Constitution* and the *United States* won stirring victories. These victories on the high seas boosted American confidence.

The most important U.S. naval victory took place on Lake Erie. In the winter of 1812-1813, the Americans had begun to build a fleet on the shores of Lake Erie. **Oliver Hazard Perry,** an experienced officer, took charge of this infant fleet. In September 1813, the small British force on the lake set out to attack the American ships. Commodore Perry, who had predicted that this would be "the most important day of my life," sailed out to meet the enemy. Perry's ship, the *Lawrence,* flew a banner declaring, "Don't give up the ship."

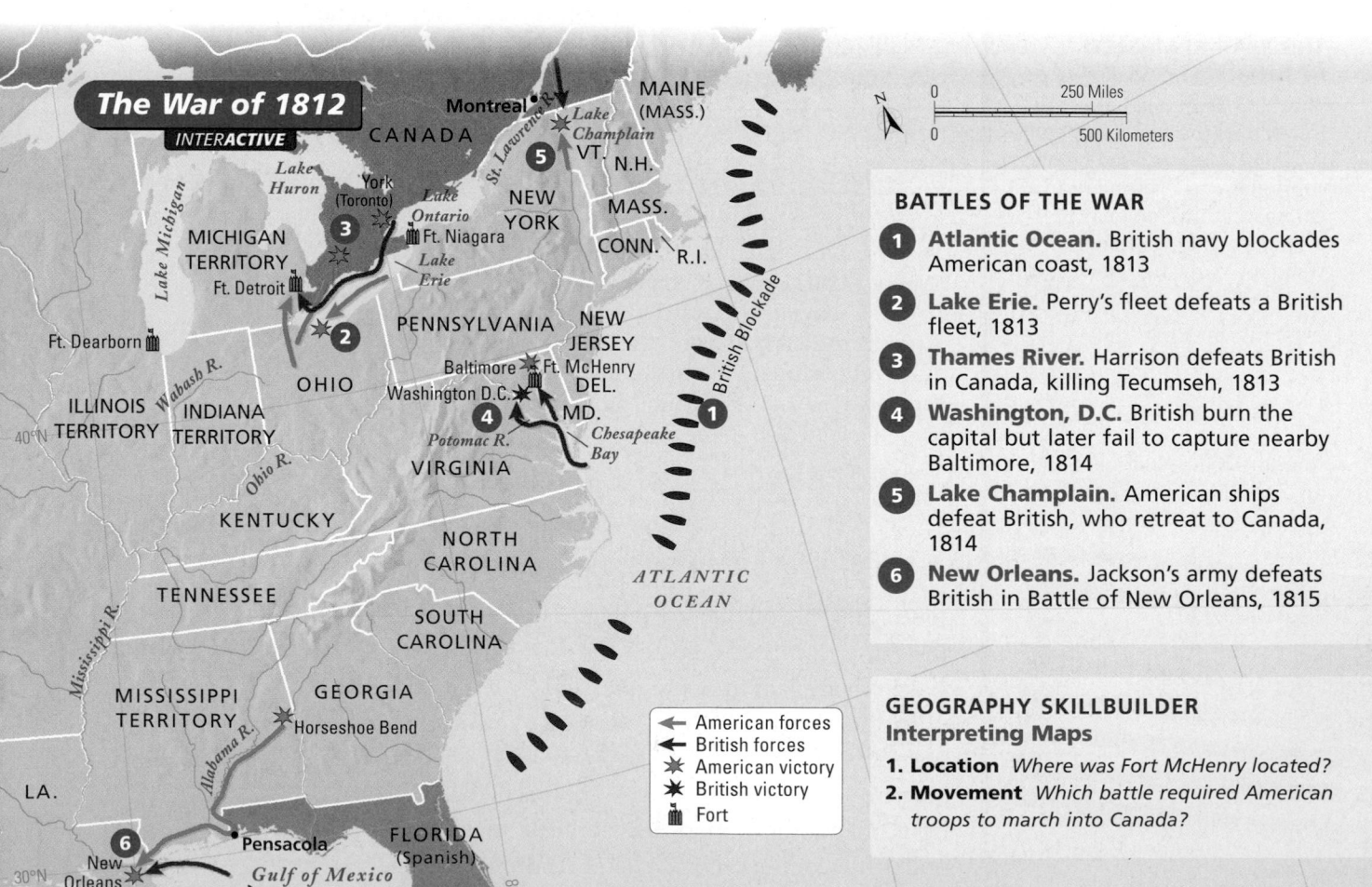

The War of 1812
INTERACTIVE

BATTLES OF THE WAR

1. **Atlantic Ocean.** British navy blockades American coast, 1813
2. **Lake Erie.** Perry's fleet defeats a British fleet, 1813
3. **Thames River.** Harrison defeats British in Canada, killing Tecumseh, 1813
4. **Washington, D.C.** British burn the capital but later fail to capture nearby Baltimore, 1814
5. **Lake Champlain.** American ships defeat British, who retreat to Canada, 1814
6. **New Orleans.** Jackson's army defeats British in Battle of New Orleans, 1815

← American forces
← British forces
✳ American victory
✸ British victory
🏛 Fort

GEOGRAPHY SKILLBUILDER
Interpreting Maps

1. **Location** Where was Fort McHenry located?
2. **Movement** Which battle required American troops to march into Canada?

For two hours, the British and Americans exchanged cannon shots. Perry's ship was demolished and the guns put out of action. He grabbed his ship's banner and leaped into a rowboat. Under British fire, he and four companions rowed to another ship. In command of the second ship, Perry destroyed two of the enemy's ships and soon forced the British to surrender. After the battle, Perry sent a message to General Harrison: "We have met the enemy and they are ours."

When General Harrison received Perry's note, he set out to attack the British. But when Harrison transported his army across Lake Erie to Detroit, he discovered that the British had retreated into Canada. Harrison pursued the British forces and defeated them at the **Battle of the Thames** in October. This victory put an end to the British threat to the Northwest—and also claimed the life of Tecumseh, who died in the battle fighting for the British.

> ## "Don't give up the ship."
> **Banner on Perry's ship, the *Lawrence***

*Reading*History

A. Drawing Conclusions What was the overall result of the Battle of the Thames?

The Second Phase of the War

After defeating Napoleon in April 1814, Britain turned its full attention to the United States. As you read in One American's Story, British forces burned the Capitol building and the president's mansion in August. The British then attacked Fort McHenry at Baltimore.

The commander of Fort McHenry had earlier requested a flag "so large that the British will have no difficulty in seeing it." Detained on a British ship, a Washington lawyer named **Francis Scott Key** watched the all-night battle. At dawn, Key discovered that the flag was still flying. He expressed his pride in what became the U.S. national anthem.

America's HERITAGE

THE STAR-SPANGLED BANNER

The "Star-Spangled Banner," inspired by the flag that flew over Fort McHenry (see below), continues to move Americans. On hearing this national anthem, patriotic listeners stand, take off their hats, and put their hands over their hearts. These actions pay respect to the American flag and the song that celebrates it.

Francis Scott Key's song enjoyed widespread popularity for more than 100 years before an act of Congress made it the national anthem in 1931.

A VOICE FROM THE PAST

Oh say can you see by the dawn's early light
What so proudly we hail'd at the twilight's last gleaming,
Whose broad stripes and bright stars through the perilous fight
O'er the ramparts we watch'd were so gallantly streaming?
And the rockets' red glare, the bombs bursting in air,
Gave proof through the night that our flag was still there.
Oh, say does that star-spangled banner yet wave
O'er the land of the free and the home of the brave?

Francis Scott Key, *Star-Spangled Banner*

Meanwhile, in the north, the British sent a force from Canada across Lake Champlain. Its goal was to push south and cut off New England. The plan failed when the American fleet defeated the British in the Battle of Lake Champlain in September 1814.

In the south, the British moved against the strategic port of New Orleans. In December 1814, dozens of ships carrying 7,500 British troops approached Louisiana. To fight them, the Americans patched together an army under the command of General Andrew Jackson.

*Reading*History

B. Reading a Map Locate the battles of the second phase of the war on the map on page 331. Note how far apart the sites were.

*Reading*History

C. Making Inferences Why did Jackson fight the British at New Orleans after a peace treaty was signed?

The British attacked Jackson's forces on January 8, 1815. Protected by earthworks, American riflemen mowed down the advancing redcoats. It was a great victory for Jackson. American casualties totaled 71, compared to Britain's 2,000. Though the Battle of New Orleans made Jackson a hero, it was unnecessary. Slow mails from Europe had delayed news of the **Treaty of Ghent,** which ended the War of 1812. It had been signed two weeks earlier, on December 24, 1814.

The Legacy of the War

The treaty showed that the war had no clear winner. No territory changed hands, and trade disputes were left unresolved. Still, the war had important consequences. First, the heroic exploits of men such as Andrew Jackson and Oliver Perry increased American patriotism. Second, the war broke the strength of Native Americans, who had sided with the British. Finally, when war interrupted trade, the Americans were forced to make many of the goods they had previously imported. This encouraged the growth of U.S. manufactures.

The United States had also proved that it could defend itself against the mightiest military power of the era. For perhaps the first time, Americans believed that the young nation would survive and prosper. You will learn about the country's growing prosperity in Chapter 11.

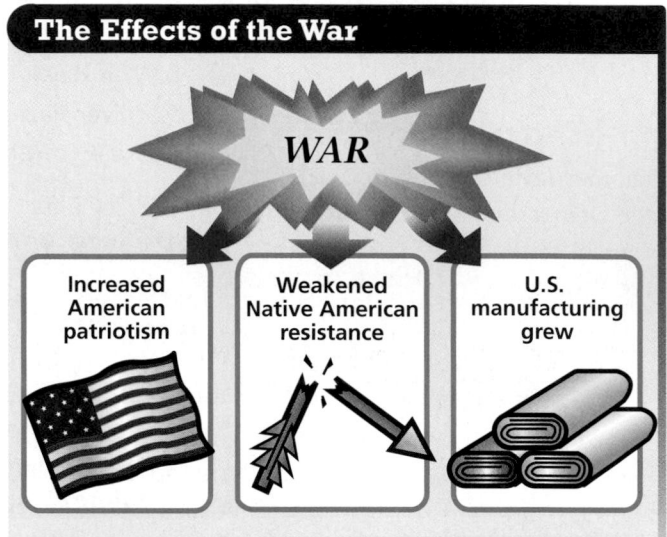

The Effects of the War

WAR

| Increased American patriotism | Weakened Native American resistance | U.S. manufacturing grew |

SKILLBUILDER Interpreting Charts
Which effect do you think resulted from the war's interruption of U.S. trade?

Section **4** *Assessment*

1. Terms & Names

Explain the significance of:
- Oliver Hazard Perry
- Battle of the Thames
- Francis Scott Key
- Treaty of Ghent

2. Using Graphics

Use a chart like the one shown to record military events of the War of 1812.

First Phase of War	Second Phase of War
1.	2.

Why was the war divided into two phases?

3. Main Ideas

a. What was the state of the U.S. military when the war began?

b. What were the results of General Harrison's victory at the Battle of the Thames?

c. Where did the British focus their attacks during the second phase of the war?

4. Critical Thinking

Recognizing Effects What was the legacy of the War of 1812?

THINK ABOUT
- Americans' feelings toward their country
- U.S. relations with Native Americans
- possible economic effects

ACTIVITY OPTIONS

LANGUAGE ARTS

ART

Research the U.S.S. *Constitution.* Write a **poem** to commemorate one of its victories or design a **model** to show its parts.

The Jefferson Era

Jefferson Takes Office

Thomas Jefferson and his party, the Democratic-Republicans, win control of the government from the Federalists.

The Louisiana Purchase and Exploration

After Jefferson purchases Louisiana from France, Lewis and Clark are sent to explore the new American territory.

Problems with Foreign Powers

Other countries' interference makes it difficult for Jefferson to stay out of foreign affairs.

The War of 1812

When Britain continues to interfere in American affairs, the two nations battle in the War of 1812.

TERMS & NAMES

Briefly explain the significance of each of the following:

1. *Marbury* v. *Madison*
2. judicial review
3. Louisiana Purchase
4. Lewis and Clark expedition
5. impressment
6. Embargo Act of 1807
7. Tecumseh
8. War Hawk
9. Oliver Hazard Perry
10. Treaty of Ghent

REVIEW QUESTIONS

Jefferson Takes Office (pages 313–317)

1. What were the main parties in the election of 1800, and how did their views differ?
2. How did Jefferson envision the future of America?

The Louisiana Purchase and Exploration (pages 318–325)

3. What was the extent of U.S. territory after the Louisiana Purchase?
4. What difficulties did Lewis and Clark face on their expedition?
5. What troubles did Zebulon Pike have on his 1806-1807 trip?

Problems with Foreign Powers (pages 326–329)

6. Why did Jefferson have difficulty staying out of foreign affairs?
7. How did Tecumseh intend to prevent the loss of Native American land?
8. What were some of the causes of the War of 1812?

The War of 1812 (pages 330–333)

9. Which battle ended the British threat to the U.S. Northwest?
10. What event preceded the second phase of the war?

CRITICAL THINKING

1. USING YOUR NOTES: SUMMARIZING

Using your completed chart, answer the questions below.

The Jefferson Era		
Summaries		
Main Idea: Thomas Jefferson is elected president. **Details:** Jefferson replaces Federalist policies with his own but has problems with the judiciary.		
Main Idea: **Details:**		
Main Idea: **Details:**		
Main Idea: **Details:**		

a. What were the major events of the Jefferson era?

b. Based on these events, how would you describe the characteristics of the era?

2. ANALYZING LEADERSHIP

How do you think Thomas Jefferson's behavior as president might have affected the way future presidents viewed the office?

3. THEME: EXPANSION

How did the expansion of the United States affect its foreign policy?

4. RECOGNIZING PROPAGANDA

Before elections, supporters of different candidates sometimes make outrageous claims. How was the election of 1800 an example of this?

5. APPLYING CITIZENSHIP SKILLS

In what ways did Jefferson's behavior as president reflect his idea of good citizenship?

Interact *with* History

How did the dangers you predicted before you read the chapter compare to those experienced by people on expeditions west?

Use the graph and your knowledge of U.S. history to answer questions 1 and 2.

Additional Test Practice, pp. S1–S33.

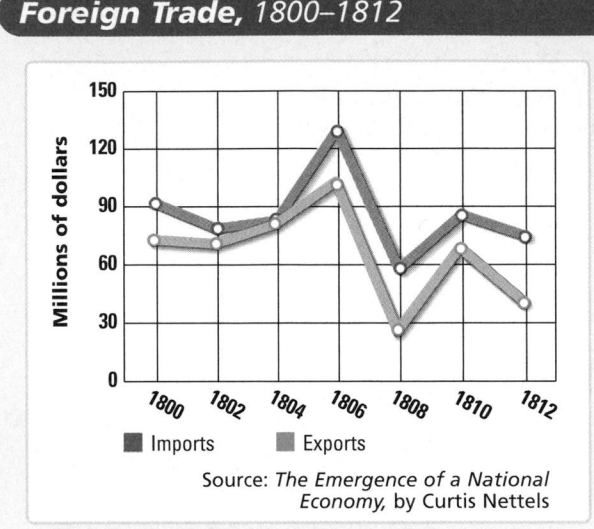

Foreign Trade, *1800–1812*

Millions of dollars

150
120
90
60
30
0

1800 1802 1804 1806 1808 1810 1812

■ Imports ■ Exports

Source: *The Emergence of a National Economy,* by Curtis Nettels

1. What was the value of imports in 1812?
   A. about 30 million dollars
   B. about 40 million dollars
   C. about 60 million dollars
   D. about 70 million dollars

2. Between which years did the value of U.S. trade decrease dramatically?
   A. 1800–1802
   B. 1804–1806
   C. 1806–1808
   D. 1810–1812

This quotation from Thomas Jefferson is about political parties. Use the quotation and your knowledge of U.S. history to answer question 3.

PRIMARY SOURCE

Let us, then, fellow-citizens, unite with one heart and one mind. . . . Every difference of opinion is a difference of principle. . . . We are all Republicans, we are all Federalists.

Thomas Jefferson, First Inaugural Address

3. Which of the following statements best summarizes Jefferson's point of view?
   A. Political parties are divisive and should be dissolved.
   B. A new party, the Republican-Federalist party, should be formed.
   C. Political parties should cooperate on issues of government.
   D. The Republican party should be dissolved.

TEST PRACTICE
CLASSZONE.COM

ALTERNATIVE ASSESSMENT

1. WRITING ABOUT HISTORY

Suppose you are John Adams and the year is 1800. Thomas Jefferson is ending many of the Federalist programs that you initiated while president. Write a **letter** to a friend that describes your distress.

- Use library resources to find the programs that Jefferson eliminated and write about them.
- Find quotations that convey Adams's emotions.

2. COOPERATIVE LEARNING

Work with two other students to develop a plan to end British interference with U.S. shipping. Have one student represent shippers, another represent farmers, and the third represent citizens who are demanding war. Discuss the interests of these groups and possible compromises. Then write a policy statement.

INTEGRATED TECHNOLOGY

CREATING A MULTIMEDIA PRESENTATION

Use the Internet, books, and other reference materials to create a multimedia presentation about one of the major battles of the War of 1812.

- Using the Internet and resources in the library, find written descriptions of the battle, paintings of the battle, pictures of weaponry, battle statistics, and music from the time period.
- Present your findings to the class in a multimedia presentation. Consider adding sound effects to enhance the presentation.

For more about the War of 1812 . . .

INTERNET ACTIVITY
CLASSZONE.COM

Making Explorers' Field Notes

On their expedition in the early 1800s, Lewis and Clark filled their journals with field notes—detailed observations and scientific illustrations of the land, plants, and wildlife they saw. Lewis made drawings of plants and animals. Clark drew detailed maps. For many years, their journals were the main source of information about the West.

ACTIVITY Create a journal of field notes that includes illustrations of plants, animals, and terrain found in your neighborhood. Then write a comparison article between your field notes and those of Lewis and Clark.

TOOLBOX

Each group will need:

drawing paper	ruler
poster board for covers	string
pencil and pen	hole punch and hole reinforcers
scissors	

STEP BY STEP

1 **Form groups.** Each group should consist of 3 to 4 students. The members of your group will do the following tasks:

- design and create a handmade journal
- take a walk in your neighborhood and record observations as field notes
- compare the field notes you have created with those of Lewis and Clark

2 **Make your journal.** Your group will need a journal to make field notes on the nature walk. Each page of the journal should be six inches wide and roughly eight inches long, approximately the size of the one used by Lewis and Clark. Cut 10–15 sheets of that size out of the drawing paper. Create a front and back cover for the journal using the poster board.

The scientific and artistic skills of Lewis and Clark made their journals both accurate and beautiful.

3 Put your journal together. Punch three holes in the left side of the pages, including the covers. Place hole reinforcers around the holes to ensure that the pages won't tear. Bind the pages and the covers together with string.

4 Explore your neighborhood. Take a walk in your neighborhood, in the area around your school, or in a nearby woods. You might want to divide the tasks of observing, drawing, describing, and mapping among the members of the group.

5 Model your field notes on those of Lewis and Clark. In their journals, Lewis and Clark included drawings of animals and plants, as well as detailed observations about them. Remember to draw the plants, insects, and animals as if you have never seen them before.

6 Make a map of your route. In addition to the drawings, create a map of your walk. Include any interesting landmarks as well as a detailed description of the terrain. Remember to sketch the route as if it's unexplored territory.

WRITE AND SPEAK

Write and present a paper that compares and contrasts Lewis and Clark's journal with the one your group has completed. Also, explain how your journal might help someone who has just moved to your school or neighborhood.

HELP DESK

For related information, see pages 320–325 in Chapter 10.

Researching Your Project

• You can find copies of Lewis and Clark's journals in many libraries.

• *Undaunted Courage* by Stephen Ambrose gives a fascinating account of the expedition.

For more about Lewis and Clark . . .

RESEARCH LINKS
CLASSZONE.COM

Did You Know?

• The Corps of Discovery sent Jefferson six live specimens of animals, including a prairie dog.

• At one point, the men on the expedition consumed nine pounds of buffalo meat a day.

• Swarms of mosquitoes plagued the expedition. The explorers often found it impossible to eat without inhaling some of the pesky insects.

• Clark estimated that the expedition traveled 4,162 miles. His guess was only 40 miles off the actual distance.

REFLECT & ASSESS

• What process did your group use to observe, draw, and describe your route?

• How did you decide what information to include in your journal?

• How important are the illustrations to understanding the area in which your group took its walk?

CHAPTER 11

National and Regional Growth 1800–1844

Section 1
Early Industry and Inventions

Section 2
Plantations and Slavery Spread

Section 3
Nationalism and Sectionalism

Robert Fulton made the steamboat a commercial success.

The steam locomotive helped build U.S. industry.

The telegraph could quickly send messeges over great distances.

This Currier and Ives print, *Progress of the Century*, shows some inventions of the 1800s.

1807
Robert Fulton launches a steamboat on the Hudson River.

1808
Congress bans the African slave trade.

1812
War of 1812 disrupts U.S. shipping.

1816
James Monroe is elected President.

1820
Missouri Compromise balances number of slave and free states.

USA
World 1800

1804
Haiti wins independence from France.

1815
Napoleon defeated at Waterloo.

1821
Peru and Mexico gain independence from Spain.

The rotery printing press was made for high volume printing.

From 1790 to 1840, you have seen an explosion of new inventions. These include the cotton gin, the steamboat, the steel plow, and the telegraph. You have also seen neighbors leave their farms to run machines in new factories. You sense that the country is changing.

How will new inventions change your country?

What Do You Think?

- What would it mean to be able to grow more grain and cotton?
- What would it mean to communicate and travel more quickly?
- How might it feel to do factory work instead of farm work?

RESEARCH LINKS
CLASSZONE.COM

Visit the Chapter 11 links for more information about the growing nation.

1823
Monroe Doctrine issued.

1825
Erie Canal completed.

1831
Nat Turner leads slave rebellion in Virginia.

1838
Frederick Douglass flees to New York City to escape slavery.

1844
Telegraph line connects Washington, D.C., and Baltimore.

1844

1825
First public railroad operates in England.

1833
Slavery is abolished in British Empire.

1839
Louis Daguerre is recognized for his photographic process.

CHAPTER 11

Reading Strategy: Analyzing Causes and Effects

What Do You Know?

What connects you to someone who lives in the same region? When have you felt a bond with someone from a different region?

Think About

- the activities of people in different regions
- the things that unite people as a nation
- your responses to the Interact with History about how inventions change your country (see page 339)

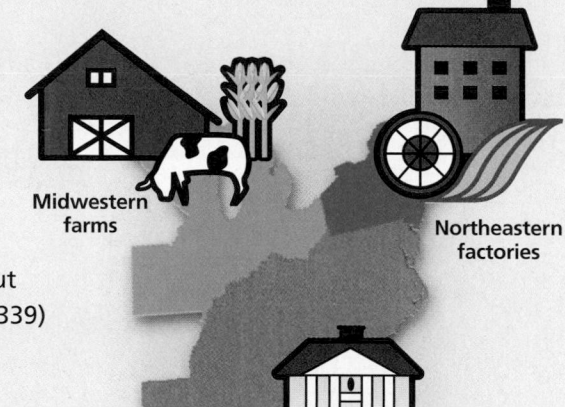

Midwestern farms

Northeastern factories

Southern cotton plantations

What Do You Want to Know?

What would you ask people from different regions—a factory worker, wheat farmer, plantation owner, or field slave—about their lives in the 1800s? Write these questions in your notebook. Read to see if they are answered in Chapter 11.

Analyzing Causes and Effects

To help you understand the development of regional growth, sectional tensions, and national unity in Chapter 11, pay attention to causes and effects. Growth, tensions, and unity each had more than one cause. As you read, identify different causes and note them on the chart below. Often a topic sentence at the beginning of a paragraph will state a cause and effect. Be alert for such clue words as "led to," "as a result," and "changed."

 See Skillbuilder Handbook, page R10.

Taking Notes

Causes		Effects
	→	REGIONAL GROWTH
	→	SECTIONAL TENSIONS
	→	NATIONAL UNITY

Early Industry and Inventions

MAIN IDEA	WHY IT MATTERS NOW	TERMS & NAMES
New machines and factories changed the way people lived and worked in the late 1700s and early 1800s.	The industrial development that began more than 200 years ago continues today.	Samuel Slater Industrial Revolution factory system Lowell mills interchangeable parts Robert Fulton Samuel F. B. Morse

ONE AMERICAN'S STORY

In 1789, the Englishman **Samuel Slater** sailed to the United States under a false name. It was illegal for textile workers like him to leave the country. Britain wanted no other nation to copy its new machines for making thread and cloth. But Slater was going to bring the secret to America.

With the backing of investor Moses Brown, Slater built the first successful water-powered textile mill in America. You will learn in Section 1 how the development of industries changed the ways Americans lived and worked.

Samuel Slater's mill was located in Pawtucket, Rhode Island.

Free Enterprise and Factories

The War of 1812 brought great economic changes to the United States. It sowed the seeds for an Industrial Revolution like the one begun in Britain during the late 18th century. During the **Industrial Revolution,** factory machines replaced hand tools, and large-scale manufacturing replaced farming as the main form of work. For example, before the Industrial Revolution, women spun thread and wove cloth at home using spinning wheels and hand looms. The invention of such machines as the spinning jenny and the power loom made it possible for unskilled workers to produce cloth. These workers, who were often children, could produce more cloth, more quickly.

The **factory system** brought many workers and machines together under one roof. Most factories were built near a source of water to power the machines. People left their farms and crowded into cities where the

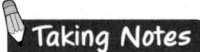

Taking Notes

Use your chart to take notes about early industry and inventions.

Causes

factories were. They worked for wages, on a set schedule. Their way of life changed, and not always for the better.

Many Americans did not want the United States to industrialize. But the War of 1812 led the country in that direction. Because the British naval blockade kept imported goods from reaching U.S. shores, Americans had to start manufacturing their own goods. The blockade also stopped investors from spending money on shipping and trade. Instead, they invested in new American industries. Taking advantage of the country's free enterprise system, American businessmen built their own factories, starting in New England. These businessmen and their region grew wealthier.

Vocabulary
industrialize: to develop factories

Reading **History**
A. Recognizing Effects How did the War of 1812 cause economic changes in America?

Factories Come to New England

New England was a good place to set up factories for several reasons. Factories needed water power, and New England had many fast-moving rivers. For transportation, it also had ships and access to the ocean. In addition, New England had a willing labor force. The area's first factory workers were families who were tired of scraping a living from their stony fields.

Samuel Slater built his first spinning mill in Pawtucket, Rhode Island, in 1790. He hired eight children between the ages of 7 and 12, paying them a low wage. Later, he built a larger mill and employed whole families. As Slater influenced others to start mills, his family system of employment spread through Rhode Island, Connecticut, and southern Massachusetts.

The Lowell Mills Hire Women

Lowell girls published a literary magazine.

In 1813, the American textile industry leaped forward when Francis Cabot Lowell built a factory in Waltham, in eastern Massachusetts. This factory not only spun raw cotton into yarn, but wove it into cloth on power looms. Lowell had seen power looms in English mills and had figured out how to build them. Like Samuel Slater, he had brought secrets to America.

The Waltham factory was so successful that Lowell and his partners built a new factory town, Lowell, near the Merrimack and Concord rivers. The **Lowell mills,** textile mills in the village, employed farm girls who lived in company-owned boardinghouses. "Lowell girls" worked 12½-hour days in deafening noise.

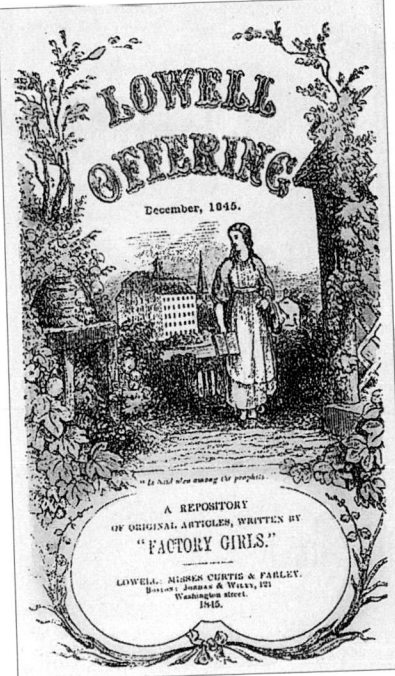

Background Founded in 1826, the town was named for Lowell, who died in 1817.

A VOICE FROM THE PAST

At first the hours seemed very long . . . and when I went out at night the sound of the mill was in my ears . . . . You know that people learn to sleep with the thunder of Niagara [falls] in their ears, and a cotton mill is no worse, though you wonder that we do not have to hold our breath in such a noise.

"Letters from Susan," quoted in the *Lowell Offering*

New England Textile Mill

1. Moving water turns a wheel, which powers the machines through a system of gears and belts.

2. Carding and drawing machines straighten raw cotton fibers and twist them loosely.

3. Spinning machines spin the fibers into yarn, or thread.

4. Power looms weave yarn into cloth.

In 1835, Lowell had 22 mills. In 1855, it had 52 mills employing more than 13,000 workers and producing 2.25 million yards of cotton cloth a week.

Young women came to Lowell in spite of the noise. In the early years, wages were high—between two and four dollars a week. Older women supervised the girls, making them follow strict rules and attend church. Girls read books, went to lectures, and even published a literary magazine—the *Lowell Offering*. Usually they worked for only a few years, until they married. By the 1830s, however, falling profits meant that wages dropped and working conditions worsened for the Lowell girls.

Reading **History**
B. Contrasting
How did the Lowell mills differ from Slater's mill?

The Lowell mills and other early factories ran on water power. Factories built after the 1830s were run by more powerful steam engines. Because steam engines used coal and wood, not fast-moving water, factories could be built away from rivers and beyond New England.

A New Way to Manufacture

New manufacturing methods changed the style of work in other industries besides the textile industry. In 1797, the U.S. government hired the inventor Eli Whitney to make 10,000 muskets for the army. He was to have the guns ready in two years. Before this time, guns were made one at a time by gunsmiths, from start to finish. Each gun differed slightly. If a part broke, a new part had to be created to match the broken one.

Whitney sought a better way to make guns. In 1801, he went to Washington with a box containing piles of musket parts. He took a part from each pile and assembled a musket in seconds. He had just demonstrated the use of **interchangeable parts,** parts that are exactly alike.

Robert Fulton invented the *Clermont*, a steamboat.

Machines that produced exactly matching parts soon became standard in industries. Interchangeable parts speeded up production, made repairs easy, and allowed the use of lower-paid, less-skilled workers. But the new system also required a new style of management, with inspectors to make sure each piece was uniform. Workers who were used to more independence disliked such close supervision.

Reading **History**

C. Recognizing Effects What were the effects of using interchangeable parts?

Moving People, Goods, and Messages

New inventions increased factory production. They also improved transportation and communication. Steamboats carried people and goods farther and faster and led to the growth of cities like New Orleans and St. Louis. **Robert Fulton** invented a steamboat that could move against the current or a strong wind. He launched the *Clermont* on the Hudson River in 1807. Its steam engine turned two side paddle wheels, which pulled the boat through the water.

The *Clermont* was dubbed "Fulton's Folly" and described as "looking precisely like a backwoods saw-mill mounted on a scow [boat] and set on fire." But it made the 300-mile trip from New York to Albany and back in a record 62 hours. Even Fulton had not expected to travel so quickly.

A VOICE FROM THE PAST

I overtook many sloops and schooners, beating to the windward, and parted with them as if they had been at anchor. The power of propelling boats by steam is now fully proved.

Robert Fulton, quoted in *Robert Fulton and the "Clermont"*

In 1811, the first steamship traveled down the Mississippi and Ohio rivers. But its engine was not powerful enough to return upriver, against the current. Henry Miller Shreve, a trader on the Mississippi, designed

a more powerful engine. He installed it on a double-decker boat with a paddle wheel in the back. In 1816, he sailed this boat up the Mississippi and launched a new era of trade and transportation on the river.

In 1837, **Samuel F. B. Morse** first demonstrated his telegraph. This machine sent long and short pulses of electricity along a wire. These pulses could be translated into letters of a message. With the telegraph, it took only seconds to communicate with someone in another city. In 1844, the first long-distance telegraph line carried news from Baltimore to Washington, D.C., about who had been nominated for president. Telegraph lines spanned the country by 1861, bringing people closer as a nation. Both the telegraph and the steamboat brought more national unity.

*Reading*History
D. Recognizing Effects What made the steamboat and telegraph such important inventions?

Technology Improves Farming

Other new inventions increased farm production. In 1836, the blacksmith John Deere invented a lightweight plow with a steel cutting edge. Older cast-iron plows were designed for the light, sandy soil of New England. But rich, heavy Midwestern soil clung to the bottom of these plows and slowed farmers down. Deere's new plow made preparing ground much less work. As a result, more farmers began to move to the Midwest.

The mechanical reaper and the threshing machine were other inventions that improved agriculture. Cyrus McCormick's reaper, patented in 1834, cut ripe grain. The threshing machine separated kernels of wheat from husks.

Vocabulary
patented: protected by a patent, which gives an inventor the sole right to make, use, or sell an invention

John Deere invented the steel plow.

New technologies linked regions and contributed to national unity. With new farm equipment, Midwestern farmers grew food to feed Northeastern factory workers. In turn, Midwestern farmers became a market for Northeastern manufactured goods. The growth of Northeastern textile mills increased demand for Southern cotton. This led to the expansion of slavery in the South, as you will learn in Section 2.

Section 1 Assessment

1. Terms & Names

Explain the significance of:
• Samuel Slater
• Industrial Revolution
• factory system
• Lowell mills
• interchangeable parts
• Robert Fulton
• Samuel F. B. Morse

2. Using Graphics

On a chart like the one below, note new inventions, their dates, and their effects on the United States.

Invention	Date	Effects

Which inventions did most to link the nation? Explain.

3. Main Ideas

a. Why was New England a good place to build early factories?

b. What were working conditions like in Lowell mills?

c. How were different U.S. regions linked economically?

4. Critical Thinking

Evaluating How would you judge Samuel Slater and Francis Lowell, who brought secrets to the United States illegally?

THINK ABOUT
• what they gained
• how they affected the United States and England
• what you believe about keeping technology secret

ACTIVITY OPTIONS

SCIENCE

SPEECH

Explain how an invention from this chapter works, either in an **oral report** or a **labeled diagram**.

Run a Mill Town

You are the owner of a new water-powered textile mill that will soon open in New England. Mills have been around for more than 20 years, and you have studied their operations closely. Even so, you face many problems as you start your business. Machinery failures, labor problems, demanding investors—all will be part of your life from now on.

COOPERATIVE LEARNING On this page are two challenges you face as the owner of a textile mill. Working with a small group, decide how to deal with each challenge. Choose an option, assign a task to each group member, and do the activity. You will find useful information in the Data File. Be prepared to present your solutions to the class.

HEALTH CHALLENGE

"Anna Tripp lost three fingers today."

A neighboring mill owner has just left after sharing some bad news. Today 12-year-old Anna Tripp lost three fingers in one of his machines. Last week, one of his workers was hit and nearly killed by the flying end of a broken belt. Several girls went home because they had trouble breathing. They blamed the closed, damp machine rooms with lint-filled air. How will you reduce the number of costly health problems like these in your mill? Present your plan using one of these options:

• Write a speech to workers outlining the company's safety measures.

• Design a sign for each floor of the mill stating the company's safety rules.

MATH CHALLENGE

"So many applicants for employment"

To make a profit, you must operate at top capacity for the lowest cost. Your mill generates 2 mill power. This dictates how many spinners you can hire. You need about two-and-a-half times that many weavers. What will be your weekly payroll for spinners and weavers? How many men will you hire? Women? Look at the Data File for help. Present your hiring plan for spinners and weavers using one of these options:

• Write a report telling investors whom you plan to hire.

• Design want-ad posters aimed at the workers you are looking for.

ACTIVITY WRAP-UP

Present to the Class Meet as a group to review your responses to running a mill town. Pick the most creative solution for each challenge and present these solutions to the class.

DATA FILE

Water Power

Potential energy: energy released when water falls from a height.

Kinetic energy: energy provided by fast-moving water.

1 mill power: power produced by 25 cubic feet of water per second dropping over a 30-foot fall; about 60 horsepower.

1 mill power: runs 3,584 spindles.

Waterwheels

Overshot

Undershot

Mid-wheel

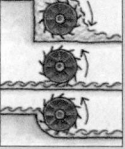

Wage Rates

Men: $.85–$2.09 per day, depending on skill

Women: $.52–$.78 per day, depending on skill

Positions

Pickers: clean raw cotton.

Carders: feed cotton into machine that makes a thick strand of fibers.

Spinners: operate a machine that twists thick fibers into yarn and winds it on bobbins fastened to moving spindles. One worker operates 128 spindles.

Dressers: treat finished yarn with a starch paste.

Drawing-in hands: attach dressed yarn to the mechanical loom for weavers.

Weavers: weave dressed yarn into finished cloth. One worker operates two looms.

Work Hours

12 hours per day, 6 days per week, 309 days per year with holidays on Fast Day (spring), the Fourth of July, and Thanksgiving

For more about textile mills . . .

RESEARCH LINKS
CLASSZONE.COM

Plantations and Slavery Spread

2

MAIN IDEA	WHY IT MATTERS NOW	TERMS & NAMES
The invention of the cotton gin and the demand for cotton caused slavery to spread in the South.	The spread of slavery created lasting racial and sectional tensions.	Eli Whitney spirituals cotton gin Nat Turner

ONE AMERICAN'S STORY

Catherine Beale was born into slavery in 1838. In 1929, she recalled her childhood on a plantation.

> *A VOICE FROM THE PAST*
>
> We had to work in the field in the day and at night we had to pick out the seed before we went to bed. And we had to clean the wool, we had to pick the burrs and sticks out so it would be clean and could be carded and spun and wove.
>
> **Catherine Beale,** quoted in *Slave Testimony*

Enslaved workers labor in the cotton fields.

Catherine had to clean cotton by hand because the plantation didn't have a cotton gin. This machine made it easier for enslaved workers to clean cotton. But it also made cotton growing and slave owning more profitable. In this section, you will learn how slavery expanded in the South and how it affected the lives of people living under it.

The Cotton Boom

Taking Notes

Use your chart to take notes about plantations and the spread of slavery.

Causes

<u>Eli Whitney</u> invented a machine for cleaning cotton in 1793, after visiting the Georgia plantation of Catherine Greene, the widow of a Revolutionary War general. Mrs. Greene was struggling to make her plantation profitable. English textile mills had created a huge demand for cotton, but the short-fibered cotton that grew in most parts of the South was hard to clean by hand. A worker could clean just one pound of this cotton in a day.

Whitney's **cotton gin** (short for "engine") made the cotton-cleaning process far more efficient. With the new machine, one worker could now clean as much as 50 pounds of cotton a day. The cotton gin helped set the South on a different course of development from the North. It made

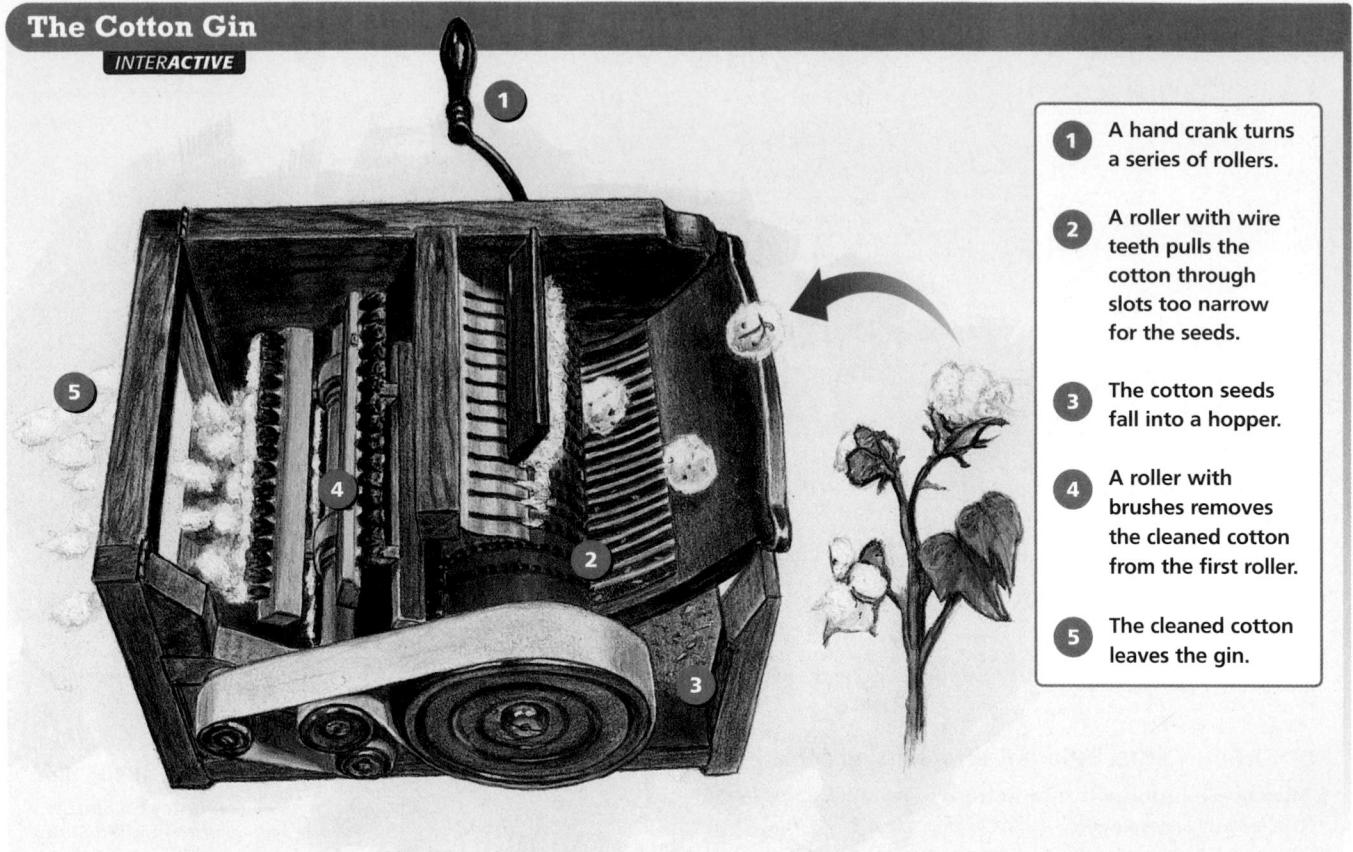

1. A hand crank turns a series of rollers.

2. A roller with wire teeth pulls the cotton through slots too narrow for the seeds.

3. The cotton seeds fall into a hopper.

4. A roller with brushes removes the cleaned cotton from the first roller.

5. The cleaned cotton leaves the gin.

short-fibered cotton a commercial product and changed Southern life in four important ways.

1. It triggered a vast move westward. Cotton farming moved beyond the Atlantic coastal states, where long-fibered, easy-to-clean cotton grew. Cotton plantations began to spread into northern Florida, Alabama, and Mississippi. Then they crossed into Louisiana and Arkansas. After 1840, they reached Texas.
2. Because cotton was valuable, planters grew more cotton rather than other goods, and cotton exports increased.
3. More Native American groups were driven off Southern land as it was taken over for cotton plantations.
4. Growing cotton required a large work force, and slavery continued to be important as a source of labor. Many slaves from the east were sold south and west to new cotton plantations.

*Reading*History
A. Reading a Map Use the map on page 350 to find cotton-growing areas in 1840.

*Reading*History
B. Recognizing Effects What impact did the cotton gin have on the South?

Slavery Expands

From 1790 to 1860, cotton production rose greatly. So did the number of enslaved people in the South. Using slave labor, the South raised millions of bales of cotton each year for the textile mills of England and the American Northeast. (See the graph on page 350.) In 1820, the South earned $22 million from cotton exports. By the late 1830s, earnings from cotton exports were nearly ten times greater, close to $200 million.

As cotton earnings rose, so did the price of slaves. A male field hand sold for $300 in the 1790s. By the late 1830s, the price had jumped to

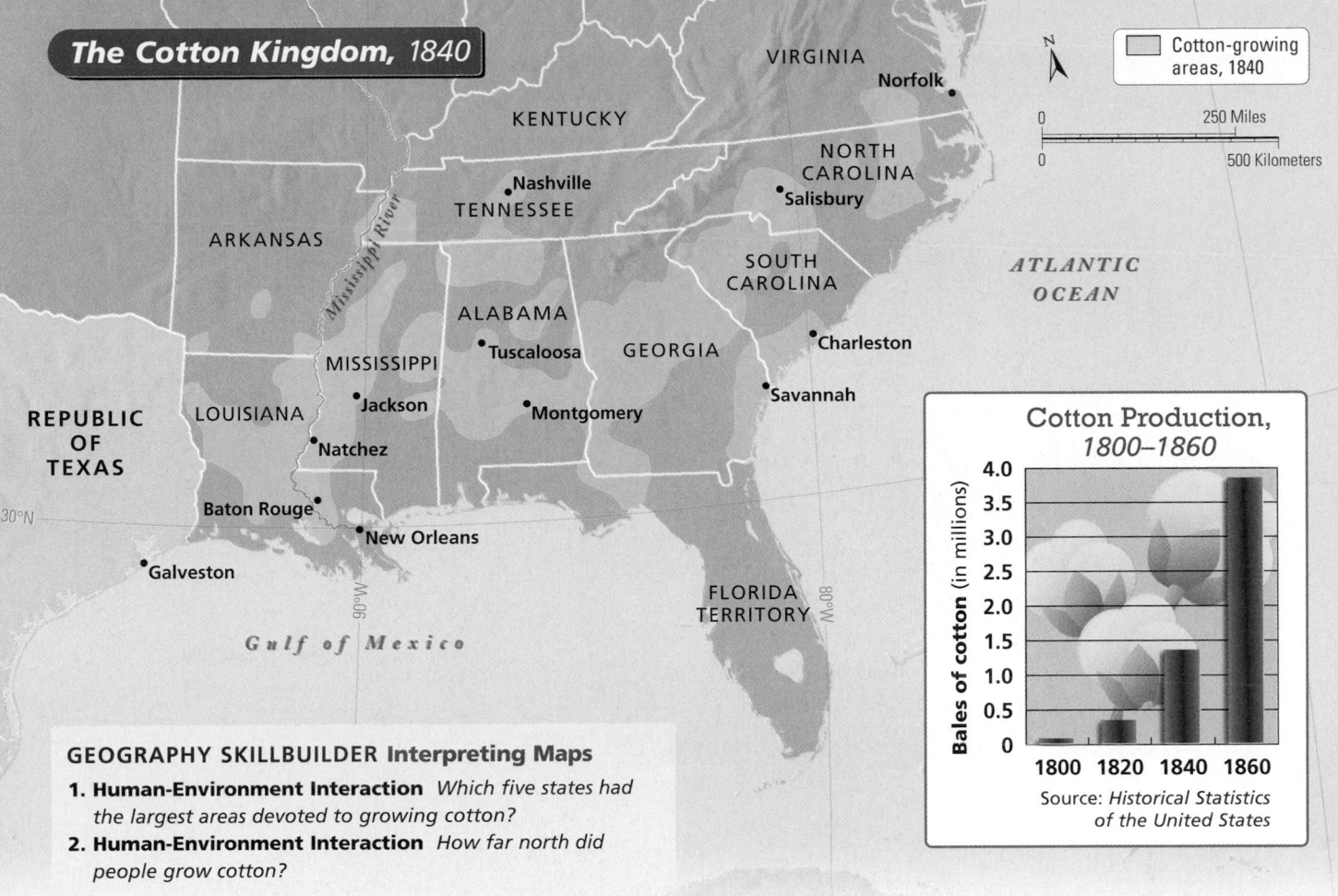

The Cotton Kingdom, 1840

VIRGINIA
Norfolk

KENTUCKY

NORTH CAROLINA

Nashville
TENNESSEE
Salisbury

ARKANSAS

Mississippi River

SOUTH CAROLINA

ATLANTIC OCEAN

ALABAMA
Tuscaloosa   GEORGIA
Charleston

MISSISSIPPI
Jackson   Montgomery   Savannah

REPUBLIC OF TEXAS   LOUISIANA
Natchez

30°N   Baton Rouge
New Orleans

Galveston

90°W

FLORIDA TERRITORY

80°W

Gulf of Mexico

Cotton-growing areas, 1840

N

0   250 Miles
0   500 Kilometers

Cotton Production, 1800–1860

Bales of cotton (in millions): 4.0, 3.5, 3.0, 2.5, 2.0, 1.5, 1.0, 0.5, 0

1800 1820 1840 1860

Source: *Historical Statistics of the United States*

GEOGRAPHY SKILLBUILDER Interpreting Maps

1. **Human-Environment Interaction** *Which five states had the largest areas devoted to growing cotton?*
2. **Human-Environment Interaction** *How far north did people grow cotton?*

$1,000. After 1808, when it became illegal to import Africans for use as slaves, the trading of slaves already in the country increased.

The expansion of slavery had a major impact on the South's economy. But its effect on the people living there was even greater.

Slavery Divides the South

Slavery divided white Southerners into those who held slaves and those who did not. Slaveholders with large plantations were the wealthiest and most powerful people in the South, but they were relatively few in number. Only about one-third of white families owned slaves in 1840. Of these slave-owning families, only about one-tenth had large plantations with 20 or more slaves.

Most white Southern farmers owned few or no slaves. Still, many supported slavery anyway. They worked their small farms themselves and hoped to buy slaves someday, which would allow them to raise more cotton and earn more money. For both small farmers and large planters, slavery had become necessary for increasing profits.

Reading **History**

C. Analyzing Points of View
Why did many white farmers without slaves still support slavery?

African Americans in the South

Slavery also divided black Southerners into those who were enslaved and those who were free. Enslaved African Americans formed about one-third of the South's population in 1840. About half of them

worked on large plantations with white overseers. Decades later, a former slave described the routine in an interview.

A VOICE FROM THE PAST

The overseer was 'straddle his big horse at three o'clock in the mornin', roustin' the hands off to the field. . . . The rows was a mile long and no matter how much grass [weeds] was in them, if you [left] one sprig on your row they [beat] you nearly to death.

Wes Brady, quoted in *Remembering Slavery*

Reading **History**

D. Contrasting How was plantation slavery different from slavery in cities?

Not all slaves faced the back-breaking conditions of plantations. In cities, enslaved persons worked as domestic servants, skilled craftsmen, factory hands, and day laborers. Sometimes they were hired out and allowed to keep part of their earnings. Frederick Douglass, an African-American speaker and publisher, once commented, "A city slave is almost a freeman, compared with a slave on the plantation." But they were still enslaved.

In 1840, about 8 percent of African Americans in the South were free. They had either been born free, been freed by an owner, or bought their own freedom. Many free African Americans in the South lived in cities such as Baltimore and Washington, D.C.

Though not enslaved, free blacks faced many problems. Some states made them leave once they gained their freedom. Most states did not permit them to vote or receive an education. Many employers refused to hire them. But their biggest threat was the possibility of being captured and sold into slavery.

Finding Strength in Religion

An African-American culture had emerged on plantations by the early 1800s. Slaves relied on that culture—with its strong religious convictions, close personal bonds, and abundance of music—to help them endure the brutal conditions of plantation life.

Reading **History**

E. Making Inferences Why would enslaved African Americans be inspired by the biblical story of Moses?

Some slaveholders tried to use religion to make slaves accept their treatment. White ministers stressed such Bible passages as "Servants, obey your masters." But enslaved people took their own messages from the Bible. They were particularly inspired by the story of Moses leading the Hebrews out of bondage in Egypt.

Enslaved people expressed their religious beliefs in **spirituals,** religious folk songs. Spirituals often contained coded messages about a planned escape or an owner's unexpected return. African-American spirituals later influenced blues, jazz, and other forms of American music.

daily *life*

SPIRITUALS

Singing spirituals offered comfort for pain, bound people together at religious meetings, and eased the boredom of daily tasks. This verse came from a spiritual sung by slaves in Missouri.

Dear Lord, dear lord,
  when slavery'll cease
Then we poor souls
  will have our peace;—
There's a better day a coming,
Will you go along with me?
There's a better day a coming,
Go sound the jubilee!

Detail of *Plantation Burial*, (1860), John Antrobus.

Families Under Slavery

Perhaps the cruelest part of slavery was the sale of family members away from one another. Although some slaveholders would not part mothers from children, many did, causing unforgettable grief. When enslaved people ran away, it was often to escape separation or to see family again.

When slave families could manage to be together, they took comfort in their family life. They married, though their marriages were not legally recognized. They tried to raise children, despite interference from owners. Most slave children lived with their mothers, who tried to protect them from punishment. Parents who lived on other plantations often stole away to visit their children, even at the cost of a whipping. Frederick Douglass recalled visits from his mother, who lived 12 miles away.

Reading **History**
F. Recognizing
Effects How did slavery harm family life?

A VOICE FROM THE PAST

I do not recollect of [remember] ever seeing my mother by the light of day. She was with me in the night. She would lie down with me, and get me to sleep, but long before I waked she was gone.

Frederick Douglass, *Narrative of the Life of Frederick Douglass*

Douglass's mother resisted slavery by the simple act of visiting her child. Douglass later rebelled by escaping to the North. Other enslaved people rebelled in more violent ways.

A slave auction threatens to split a family apart.

Slave Rebellions

Armed rebellion was an extreme form of resistance to slavery. Gabriel Prosser planned an attack on Richmond, Virginia, in 1800. In 1822, Denmark Vesey planned a revolt in Charleston, South Carolina. Both plots were betrayed, and the leaders were hanged.

The most famous rebellion was led by **Nat Turner** in Virginia in 1831. On August 21, Turner and 70 followers killed 55 white men, women, and children. Later, witnesses claimed that he spoke these words.

> ### A VOICE FROM THE PAST
>
> We do not go forth for the sake of blood and carnage; . . . Remember that ours is not a war for robbery, . . . it is a struggle for freedom.
>
> **Nat Turner,** quoted in *Nat Turner,* by Terry Bisson

Most of Turner's men were captured when their ammunition ran out, and 16 were killed. When Turner was caught, he was tried and hanged.

Turner's rebellion spread fear in the South. Whites killed more than 200 African Americans in revenge. State legislatures passed harsh laws that kept free blacks and slaves from having weapons or buying liquor. Slaves could not hold religious services unless whites were present. Postmasters stopped delivering antislavery publications.

After Turner's rebellion, the grip of slavery grew even tighter in the South. Tension over slavery increased between the South and the North, as you will see in the next section.

Reading **History**

G. Recognizing Effects How did Nat Turner's rebellion affect white Southerners?

AMERICA'S HISTORY MAKERS

NAT TURNER
1800–1831

Nat Turner was born on a plantation in Virginia. As a child, Turner learned to read and write. He became an enthusiastic reader of the Bible. Slaves gathered in forest clearings to listen to his powerful sermons. Turner believed that God wanted him to free the slaves, even if by armed rebellion. He defended the justice of his cause in what came to be known as *Confessions of Nat Turner,* which he dictated to a white lawyer before his execution.

How did Turner justify his rebellion?

Section 2 Assessment

1. Terms & Names

Explain the significance of:
• Eli Whitney
• cotton gin
• spirituals
• Nat Turner

2. Using Graphics

In a chart like the one below, note facts about each group of Southerners.

Group	Facts
slaveholding whites	
nonslaveholding whites	
enslaved blacks	
free blacks	

Why do you think many free blacks lived in cities?

3. Main Ideas

a. How did the cotton gin lead to the spread of slavery?

b. How was life different for plantation slaves, city slaves, and free blacks in the South?

c. What were three ways that enslaved people resisted slavery?

4. Critical Thinking

Forming Opinions How do you think slave rebellions affected the institution of slavery?

THINK ABOUT

• Nat Turner's reasons for rebelling

• the reaction of white Southerners and slave owners to Turner's rebellion

---

ACTIVITY OPTIONS

LANGUAGE ARTS

SPEECH

Write a **book report** on a slave narrative, or perform an **oral interpretation** of a passage from one.

3

Nationalism and Sectionalism

MAIN IDEA	WHY IT MATTERS NOW	TERMS & NAMES
Patriotic pride united the states, but tension between the North and South emerged.	The tension led to the Civil War, and regional differences can still be found in the United States today.	nationalism James Monroe Henry Clay sectionalism American System Missouri Compromise Erie Canal Monroe Doctrine

ONE AMERICAN'S STORY

The War of 1812 sent a wave of nationalist feeling through the United States. **Nationalism** is a feeling of pride, loyalty, and protectiveness toward your country. Representative **Henry Clay**, from Kentucky, was a strong nationalist. After the war, President James Madison supported Clay's plan to strengthen the country and unify its regions.

Henry Clay

> *A VOICE FROM THE PAST*
>
> Every nation should anxiously endeavor to establish its absolute independence, and consequently be able to feed and clothe and defend itself. If it rely upon a foreign supply that may be cut off . . . it cannot be independent.
>
> **Henry Clay,** quoted in *The Annals of America*

In this section, you will learn how nationalism affected U.S. economic growth and foreign policy. You'll also see how Americans were beginning to be torn between the interests of their own regions and those of the country as a whole.

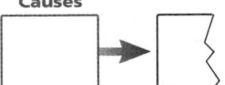

Taking Notes

Use your chart to take notes about nationalism and sectionalism.

Causes

Nationalism Unites the Country

In 1815, President Madison presented a plan to Congress for making the United States economically self-sufficient. In other words, the country would prosper and grow by itself, without foreign products or foreign markets.

The plan—which Henry Clay promoted as the **American System**—included three main actions.

1. **Establish a protective tariff,** a tax on imported goods that protects a nation's businesses from foreign competition. Congress passed a tariff in 1816. It made European goods more expensive and encouraged Americans to buy cheaper American-made products.

*Reading*History

A. Recognizing
Effects How
would the three
parts of the
American System
help to make
the country self-
sufficient?

2. **Establish a national bank** that would promote a single currency, making trade easier. (Most regional banks issued their own money.) In 1816, Congress set up the second Bank of the United States.

3. **Improve the country's transportation systems,** which were important for a strong economy. Poor roads made transportation slow and costly.

Roads and Canals Link Cities

Representative John C. Calhoun of South Carolina also called for better transportation systems. "Let us bind the Republic together with a perfect system of roads and canals," he declared in 1817. Earlier, in 1806, Congress had funded a road from Cumberland, Maryland, to Wheeling, Virginia. By 1841, the National Road, designed as the country's main east-west route, had been extended to Vandalia, Illinois.

Water transportation improved, too, with the building of canals. In fact, the period from 1825 to 1850 is often called the Age of Canals. Completed in 1825, the massive **Erie Canal** created a water route between New York City and Buffalo, New York. The canal opened the upper Ohio Valley and the Great Lakes region to settlement and trade. It also fueled nationalism by unifying these two sections of the country.

The Erie Canal allowed farm products from the Great Lakes region to flow east and people and manufactured goods from the East to flow

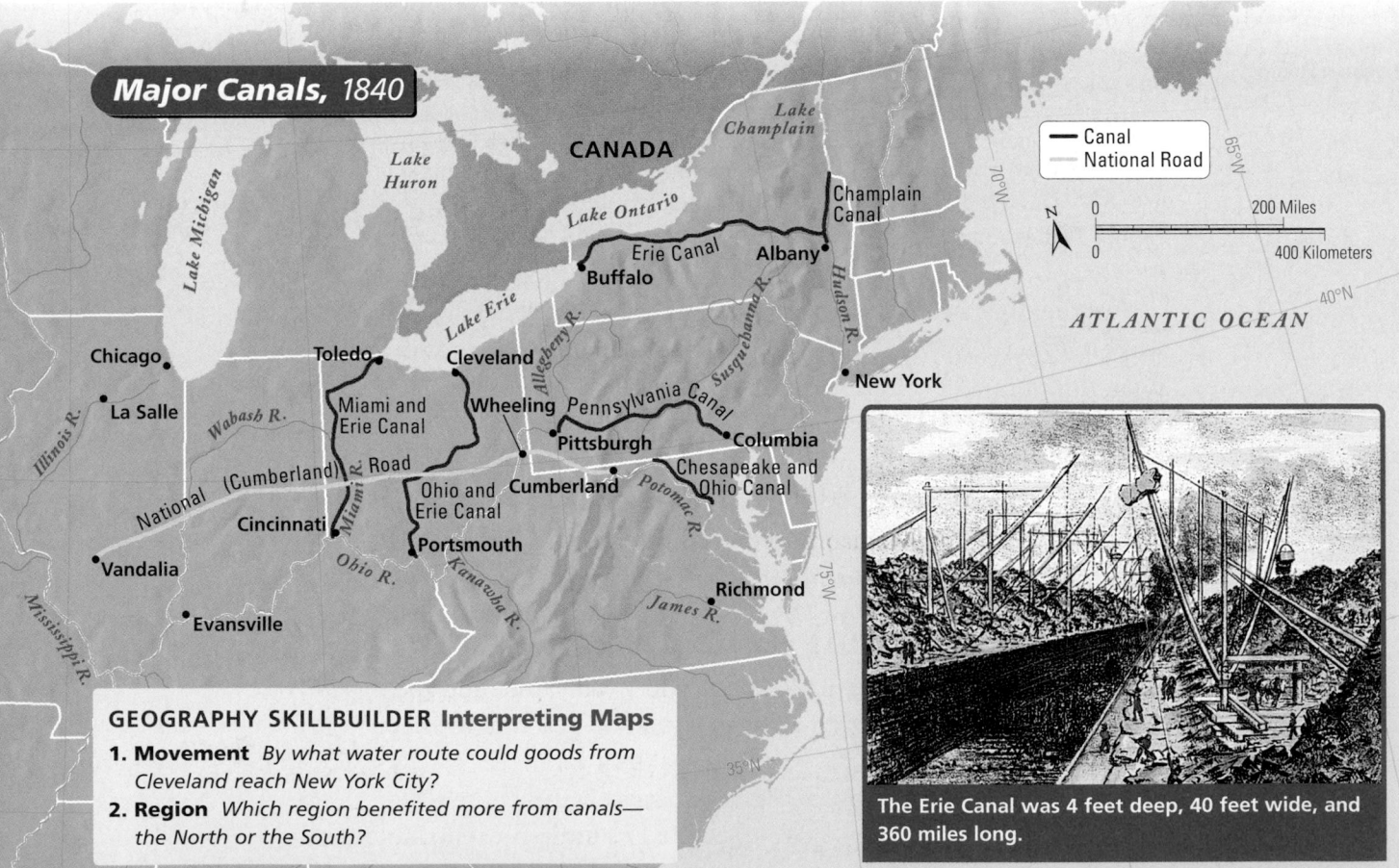

Major Canals, 1840

CANADA

Lake Superior — Lake Michigan — Lake Huron — Lake Ontario — Lake Erie — Lake Champlain

Canal
National Road

0   200 Miles
0   400 Kilometers

ATLANTIC OCEAN

Chicago
La Salle
Toledo
Cleveland
Champlain Canal
Erie Canal
Buffalo
Albany
New York
Miami and Erie Canal
Wheeling
Pennsylvania Canal
Pittsburgh
Columbia
Chesapeake and Ohio Canal
National (Cumberland) Road
Ohio and Erie Canal
Cumberland
Cincinnati
Portsmouth
Vandalia
Richmond
Evansville

Illinois R., Wabash R., Miami R., Ohio R., Kanawha R., Allegheny R., Susquehanna R., Hudson R., Potomac R., James R., Mississippi R.

GEOGRAPHY SKILLBUILDER Interpreting Maps

1. **Movement** By what water route could goods from Cleveland reach New York City?
2. **Region** Which region benefited more from canals—the North or the South?

The Erie Canal was 4 feet deep, 40 feet wide, and 360 miles long.

west. Trade stimulated by the canal helped New York City become the nation's largest city. Between 1820 and 1830, its population swelled from less than 125,000 to more than 200,000.

Around the 1830s, the nation began to use steam-powered trains for transportation. In 1830, only about 30 miles of track existed in the United States. But by 1850, the number had climbed to 9,000 miles. Improvements in rail travel led to a decline in the use of canals.

The Era of Good Feelings

As nationalist feelings spread, people slowly shifted their loyalty away from state governments and more toward the federal government. Democratic-Republican **James Monroe** won the presidency in 1816 with a large majority of electoral votes. The Federalist Party provided little opposition to Monroe and soon disappeared. Political differences gave way to what one Boston newspaper called the Era of Good Feelings.

During the Monroe administration, several landmark Supreme Court decisions promoted national unity by strengthening the federal government. For example, in *McCulloch* v. *Maryland* (1819), the state of Maryland wanted to tax its branch of the national bank. If this tax were allowed, the states could claim to have power over the federal government. The Court upheld federal authority by ruling that a state could not tax a national bank.

James Monroe

Background
Maryland also argued that Congress had no power to create the bank, but the Court ruled that it did have such power.

A VOICE FROM THE PAST

The States have no power, by taxation or otherwise, to retard, impede, burden, or in any manner control the operations of the constitutional laws enacted by Congress.

Chief Justice John Marshall, *McCulloch* v. *Maryland* (1819)

Another Court decision that strengthened the federal government was *Gibbons* v. *Ogden* (1824). Two steamship operators fought over shipping rights on the Hudson River in New York and New Jersey. The Court ruled that interstate commerce could be regulated only by the federal government, not the state governments.

The Supreme Court under John Marshall clearly stated important powers of the federal government. A stronger federal government reflected a growing nationalist spirit.

*Reading***History**
B. Finding Main Ideas How did the Supreme Court strengthen the federal government?

Settling National Boundaries

This nationalist spirit also made U.S. leaders want to define and expand the country's borders. To do this, they had to reach agreements with Britain and Spain.

Two agreements improved relations between the United States and Britain. The Rush-Bagot Agreement (1817) limited each side's naval

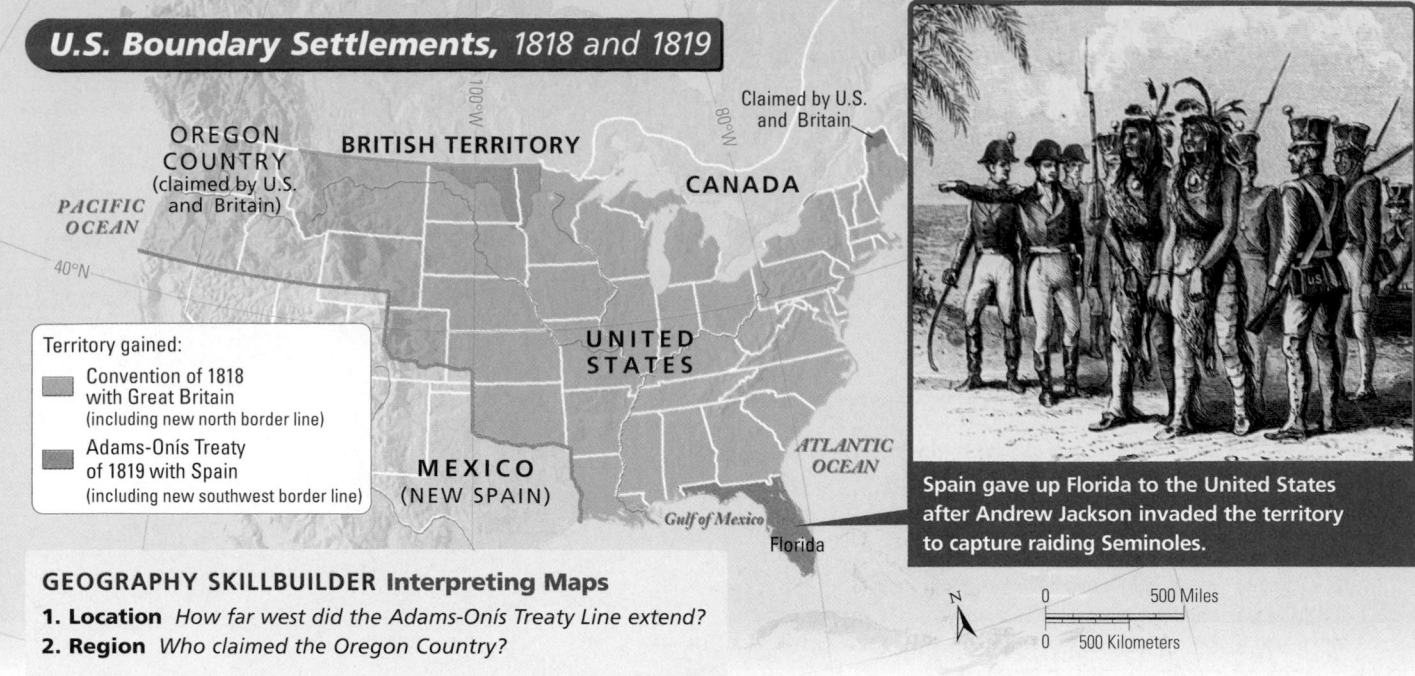

U.S. Boundary Settlements, 1818 and 1819

OREGON COUNTRY (claimed by U.S. and Britain)

PACIFIC OCEAN

40°N

BRITISH TERRITORY

Claimed by U.S. and Britain

CANADA

UNITED STATES

MEXICO (NEW SPAIN)

ATLANTIC OCEAN

Gulf of Mexico

Florida

Territory gained:
- Convention of 1818 with Great Britain (including new north border line)
- Adams-Onís Treaty of 1819 with Spain (including new southwest border line)

Spain gave up Florida to the United States after Andrew Jackson invaded the territory to capture raiding Seminoles.

0   500 Miles
0   500 Kilometers

GEOGRAPHY SKILLBUILDER Interpreting Maps
1. **Location** How far west did the Adams-Onís Treaty Line extend?
2. **Region** Who claimed the Oregon Country?

forces on the Great Lakes. In the Convention of 1818, the two countries set the 49th parallel as the U.S.-Canadian border as far west as the Rocky Mountains.

But U.S. relations with Spain were tense. The two nations disagreed on the boundaries of the Louisiana Purchase and the ownership of West Florida. Meanwhile, pirates and runaway slaves used Spanish-held East Florida as a refuge. In addition, the Seminoles of East Florida raided white settlements in Georgia to reclaim lost lands.

In 1817, President Monroe ordered General Andrew Jackson to stop the Seminole raids, but not to confront the Spanish. Jackson followed the Seminoles into Spanish territory and then claimed the Floridas for the United States.

Monroe ordered Jackson to withdraw but gave Spain a choice. It could either police the Floridas or turn them over to the United States. In the Adams-Onís Treaty of 1819, Spain handed Florida to the United States and gave up claims to the Oregon Country. The map above shows boundaries drawn and territories gained in 1818 and 1819.

Reading **History**
C. Analyzing Causes Why did Andrew Jackson invade East Florida?

Sectional Tensions Increase

At the same time nationalism was unifying the country, sectionalism was threatening to drive it apart. **Sectionalism** is loyalty to the interests of your own region or section of the country, rather than to the nation as a whole. Economic changes had created some divisions within the United States. As you have seen, white Southerners were relying more on cotton and slavery. In the Northeast, wealth was based on manufacturing and trade. In the West, settlers wanted cheap land and good transportation. The interests of these sections were often in conflict.

Sectionalism became a major issue when Missouri applied for statehood in 1817. People living in Missouri wanted to allow slavery in their state. At the time, the United States consisted of 11 slave states and 11

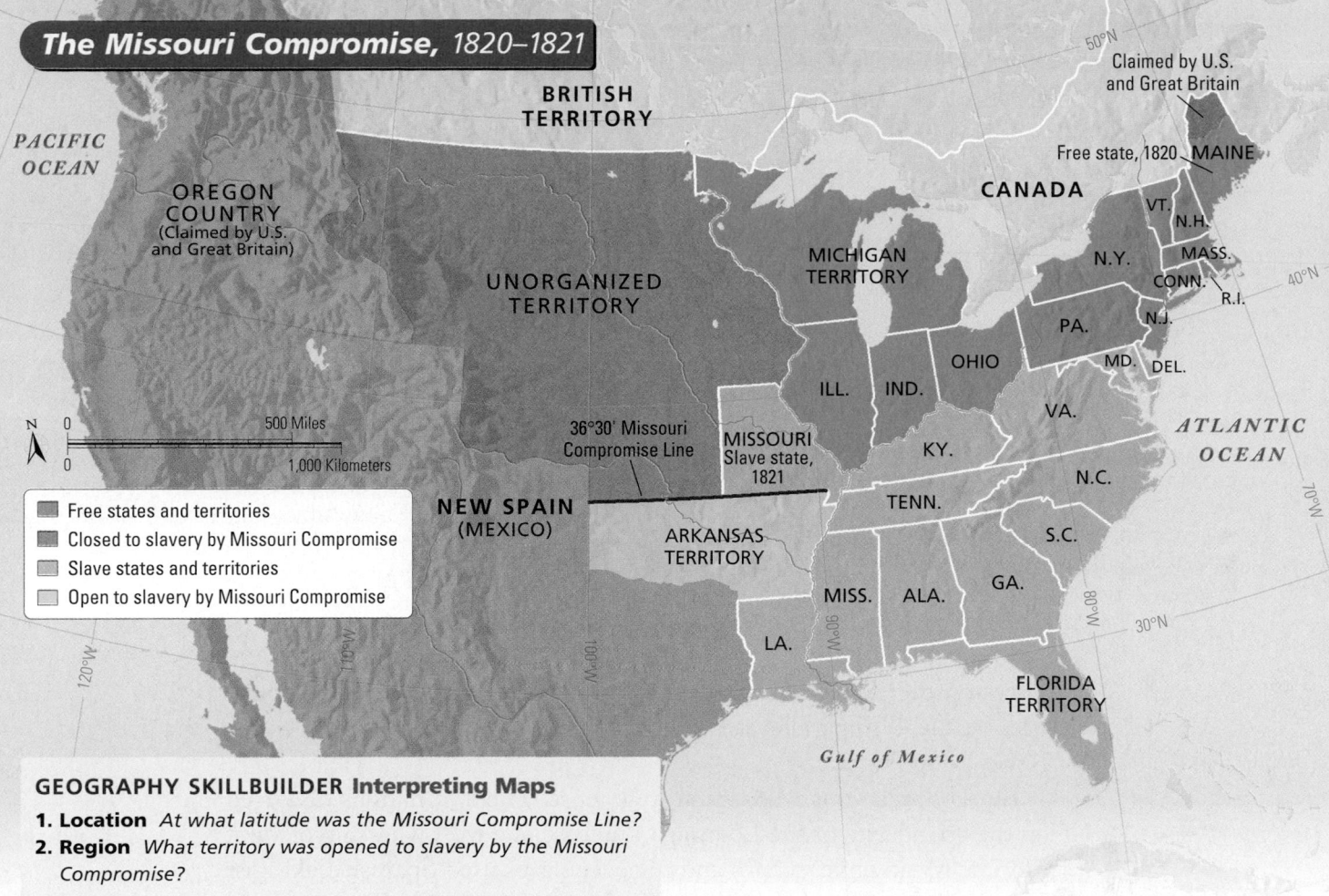

The Missouri Compromise, 1820–1821

PACIFIC
OCEAN

BRITISH
TERRITORY

Claimed by U.S.
and Great Britain

Free state, 1820 MAINE

OREGON
COUNTRY
(Claimed by U.S.
and Great Britain)

CANADA

VT.
N.H.

MICHIGAN
TERRITORY

N.Y.

MASS.

CONN.
R.I.

UNORGANIZED
TERRITORY

PA.

N.J.

OHIO

MD. DEL.

ILL. IND.

VA.

ATLANTIC
OCEAN

36°30' Missouri
Compromise Line

MISSOURI
Slave state,
1821

KY.

N.C.

NEW SPAIN
(MEXICO)

TENN.

S.C.

ARKANSAS
TERRITORY

GA.

MISS. ALA.

LA.

FLORIDA
TERRITORY

Gulf of Mexico

500 Miles
1,000 Kilometers

- Free states and territories
- Closed to slavery by Missouri Compromise
- Slave states and territories
- Open to slavery by Missouri Compromise

GEOGRAPHY SKILLBUILDER Interpreting Maps

1. **Location** At what latitude was the Missouri Compromise Line?
2. **Region** What territory was opened to slavery by the Missouri Compromise?

free states. Adding Missouri as a slave state would upset the balance of power in Congress. The question of Missouri soon divided the nation.

The Missouri Compromise

For months, the nation argued over admitting Missouri as a slave state or a free state. Debate raged in Congress over a proposal made by James Tallmadge of New York to ban slavery in Missouri. Angry Southerners claimed that the Constitution did not give Congress the power to ban slavery. They worried that free states could form a majority in Congress and ban slavery altogether. Representative Thomas Cobb of Georgia expressed the Southerners' point of view when he responded to Tallmadge.

Reading **History**

D. Analyzing Points of View Why was it so important to Southerners to admit Missouri as a slave state?

A VOICE FROM THE PAST

If you persist, the Union will be dissolved. You have kindled a fire which all the waters of the ocean cannot put out, which seas of blood can only extinguish.

Thomas Cobb, quoted in *Henry Clay: Statesman for the Union*

Meanwhile, Maine, which had been part of Massachusetts, also wanted statehood. Henry Clay, the Speaker of the House, saw a chance for compromise. He suggested that Missouri be admitted as a slave state and Maine as a free state. Congress passed Clay's plan, known as the **Missouri Compromise,** in 1820. It kept the balance of power in the Senate

between the slave states and free states. It also called for slavery to be banned from the Louisiana Territory north of the parallel 36° 30', Missouri's southern border.

Thomas Jefferson, nearing 80 years old and living quietly in Virginia, was troubled by the Missouri Compromise. Worried that sectionalism would destroy the country, Jefferson wrote: "In the gloomiest moment of the Revolutionary War I never had any apprehension equal to what I feel from this source."

"If you persist, the Union will be dissolved."
Thomas Cobb

The Monroe Doctrine

Background
Latin America refers to the Spanish- and Portugese-speaking nations of the Western Hemisphere south of the United States.

The nation felt threatened not only by sectionalism, but by events elsewhere in the Americas. In Latin America, several countries had successfully fought for their independence from Spain and Portugal. Some European monarchies planned to help Spain and Portugal regain their colonies, hoping to keep the urge to revolt from reaching Europe. U.S. leaders feared that if this happened, their own government would be in danger.

Russian colonies in the Pacific Northwest also concerned Americans. The Russians entered Alaska in 1784. By 1812, their trading posts reached almost to San Francisco.

Background
The ideas in the Monroe Doctrine came from John Quincy Adams, Monroe's secretary of state. Adams delivered a speech against colonization on July 4, 1821—two years before Monroe announced his doctrine.

In December 1823, President Monroe issued a statement that became known as the **Monroe Doctrine.** (See Interactive Primary Source, page 360.) Monroe said that the Americas were closed to further colonization. He also warned that European efforts to reestablish colonies would be considered "dangerous to our peace and safety." Finally, he promised that the United States would stay out of European affairs. The Monroe Doctrine showed that the United States saw itself as a world power and protector of Latin America.

In Chapter 12, you will learn how a new democratic spirit grew—and how Native Americans suffered—during Andrew Jackson's presidency.

Section 3 Assessment

1. Terms & Names

Explain the significance of:
- nationalism
- Henry Clay
- American System
- Erie Canal
- James Monroe
- sectionalism
- Missouri Compromise
- Monroe Doctrine

2. Using Graphics

On a diagram like the one below, name things that contributed to national unity in the early 1800s.

national unity

Which of these are still important for national unity?

3. Main Ideas

a. How did the Erie Canal help the nation grow?

b. How did the Missouri Compromise resolve a conflict between the North and South?

c. What was the main message of the Monroe Doctrine, and toward whom was it directed?

4. Critical Thinking

Recognizing Effects If the Supreme Court had decided differently in *Gibbons* v. *Ogden* or *McCulloch* v. *Maryland,* what might be one result today?

THINK ABOUT
- if states could interfere with federal laws
- if states controlled interstate commerce

ACTIVITY OPTIONS

LANGUAGE ARTS

ART

In an **editorial** or a **political cartoon,** give your opinion of either the Missouri Compromise or the Monroe Doctrine.

The Monroe Doctrine

Setting the Stage On December 6, 1823, President James Monroe gave a State of the Union address. Part of the speech became known as the Monroe Doctrine. The "allied powers" Monroe refers to are Russia, Prussia, Austria, and France. Earlier in the year, these European monarchies had crushed a revolution in Spain and restored the Spanish king to his throne. They were threatening to help Spain regain its Latin American colonies. See **Primary Source Explorer**

A CLOSER LOOK

NO FUTURE COLONIES

Monroe declares that European countries may not start any new colonies in the Americas.

1. Why might it threaten the United States to have new European colonies near them?

A CLOSER LOOK

NEUTRALITY TOWARD EUROPE

Monroe says that the United States will not take sides in European wars.

2. Why might the United States want to remain neutral toward conflicts in Europe?

[T]he occasion has been judged proper for asserting, as a principle in which the rights and interests of the United States are involved, that the American continents, by the free and independent condition which they have assumed and maintain, are henceforth not to be considered as subjects for future colonization by any European powers. . . .

It was stated at the commencement of the last session that great effort was then making in Spain and Portugal to improve the condition of the people of those countries and that it appeared to be conducted with extraordinary moderation. It need scarcely be remarked that the result has been so far very different from what was then anticipated. . . . The citizens of the United States cherish sentiments the most friendly in favor of the liberty and happiness of their fellowmen on that side of the Atlantic. In the wars of the European powers in matters relating to themselves we have never taken any part, nor does it **comport**[1] with our policy so to do. It is only when our rights are invaded or seriously **menaced**[2] that we resent injuries or make preparation for our defense.

With the movements in this hemisphere we are of necessity more immediately connected, and by causes which must be obvious to all enlightened and impartial observers. The political system of the allied powers is essentially different in this respect from that of America. This difference proceeds from that which exists in their respective governments; and to the defense of our own, which has been achieved by the loss of so much blood and treasure, and matured by the wisdom of their most enlightened citizens, and under which we have enjoyed **unexampled felicity,**[3] this whole nation is devoted. We owe it, therefore, to **candor**[4] and to the **amicable**[5] relations existing between the

---

1. **comport:** agree with.
2. **menaced:** threatened.
3. **unexampled felicity:** the greatest happiness.
4. **candor:** honesty.
5. **amicable:** friendly.

United States and those powers to declare that we should consider any attempt on their part to extend their system to any portion of this hemisphere as dangerous to our peace and safety.

With the existing colonies or dependencies of any European power we have not interfered and shall not interfere. But with the governments who have declared their independence and maintained it, and whose independence we have, on great consideration and on just principles, acknowledged, we could not view any **interposition**[6] for the purpose of oppressing them, or controlling in any other manner their destiny, by any European power in any other light than as the manifestation of an unfriendly disposition toward the United States. In the war between those new governments and Spain we declared our neutrality at the time of their recognition, and to this we have adhered and shall continue to adhere, provided no change shall occur which, in the judgment of the competent authorities of this government, shall make a corresponding change on the part of the United States indispensable to their security.

The late events in Spain and Portugal show that Europe is still unsettled. Of this important fact no stronger proof can be adduced than that the allied powers should have thought it proper, on any principle satisfactory to themselves, to have interposed by force in the internal concerns of Spain. To what extent such interposition may be carried, on the same principle, is a question in which all independent powers whose governments differ from theirs are interested, even those most remote, and surely none more so than the United States.

—*James Monroe*

6. **interposition:**
interference.

A CLOSER LOOK

A DIFFERENT SYSTEM

Monroe states that the United States will defend its republican form of government and would be threatened if Europeans set up monarchies in the Americas.

3. Why would U.S. citizens want their government to be a republic and not an absolute monarchy?

A CLOSER LOOK

NO INTERFERENCE

Monroe warns that if Europeans invade the newly independent republics in Latin America, this would be considered hostile to the United States as well.

4. What would the United States have to fear if these republics were overthrown?

Interactive Primary Source Assessment

1. Main Ideas

a. Why might the United States want no more European colonies in the Americas, particularly in Latin America?

b. How would staying neutral in European wars protect the United States?

c. How might the U.S. system of government be threatened if Europeans regained control of former colonies in the Americas?

2. Critical Thinking

Making Inferences For decades, the United States lacked the military power to enforce the Monroe Doctrine and depended on the British navy to keep other European powers out of Latin America. Why, then, did the United States proclaim the Monroe Doctrine?

THINK ABOUT

• what the doctrine shows about the values and wishes of the United States

• what it shows about how the country saw itself or wanted to be seen

Early Industry and Inventions

New machines allowed the Northeast to industrialize and the Midwest to increase farm production.

Plantations and Slavery Spread

The cotton gin led to the expansion of plantations and slavery in the South.

Nationalism and Sectionalism

Nationalism drew regions together. At the same time, economic differences created tension between regions.

TERMS & NAMES

Briefly explain the significance of each of the following.

1. Samuel Slater
2. Industrial Revolution
3. Robert Fulton
4. Eli Whitney
5. cotton gin
6. Nat Turner
7. nationalism
8. sectionalism
9. Missouri Compromise
10. Monroe Doctrine

REVIEW QUESTIONS

Early Industry and Inventions (pages 341–347)

1. How did the War of 1812 push the United States to build factories?
2. How did the War of 1812 and free enterprise affect the U.S. economy?
3. What was one effect of the steamboat?
4. How did interchangeable parts transform the manufacturing process?

Plantations and Slavery Spread (pages 348–353)

5. Why did slavery spread in the South?
6. What were three hardships faced by enslaved people on plantations?
7. How did religion help people endure or resist slavery?

Nationalism and Sectionalism (pages 354–361)

8. How did the Supreme Court's ruling in *McCulloch v. Maryland* strengthen the federal government?
9. How did the United States gain the territory of Florida?
10. What were the terms of the Missouri Compromise?

CRITICAL THINKING

1. USING YOUR NOTES: ANALYZING CAUSES AND EFFECTS

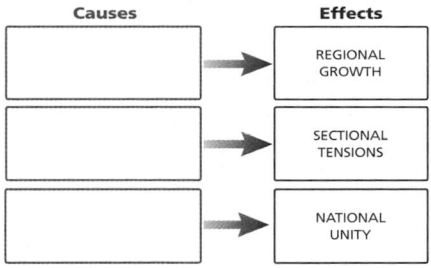

Using your completed chart, answer the questions.

a. What were three causes leading to national unity?
b. What was one cause of sectional tension?

2. THEME: SCIENCE AND TECHNOLOGY

Of all the new inventions mentioned in the chapter, which do you think was most important and why?

3. ANALYZING CAUSES

How did geographic differences between regions lead to economic differences between them?

4. APPLYING CITIZENSHIP SKILLS

Do you think the Missouri Compromise was a wise decision? Consider what might have happened without it, and also why it made Jefferson so uneasy.

5. ANALYZING LEADERSHIP

Think about the Monroe Doctrine and the boundary settlements achieved during the Monroe administration. How would you judge Monroe's foreign policy?

Interact *with* History

Did you predict the ways that new inventions would change the country? What surprised you?

Use the map and your knowledge of U.S. history to answer questions 1 and 2.

Additional Test Practice, pp. S1–S33.

Independence in Latin America, 1830

ATLANTIC OCEAN

HAITI 1804

MEXICO 1821 · Gulf of Mexico

SANTO DOMINGO 1821

Caribbean Sea

PACIFIC OCEAN

COLOMBIA 1830

VENEZUELA 1830

ECUADOR 1830

BRAZIL 1822

PERU 1821

PARAGUAY 1811

BOLIVIA 1825

☐ Independent republic
■ Under foreign control
1830 Date of independence

CHILE 1818

URUGUAY 1828

ARGENTINA 1816

N   0 ———— 2,000 Miles
    0 ———— 4,000 Kilometers

1. Which Latin American countries became independent the same year as Mexico?

A. Argentina and Brazil

B. Chile and Haiti

C. Peru and Santo Domingo

D. Peru and Uruguay

2. Which Latin American country was the first to gain independence?

A. Argentina

B. Haiti

C. Mexico

D. Paraguay

Henry Clay is talking about the United States in this quotation. Use the quotation and your knowledge of U.S. history to answer question 3.

> **PRIMARY SOURCE**
>
> Every nation should anxiously endeavor to establish its absolute independence, and consequently be able to feed and clothe and defend itself. If it rely upon a foreign supply that may be cut off . . . it cannot be independent.
>
> **Henry Clay,** quoted in *The Annals of America*

3. What idea was Henry Clay supporting in this speech?

A. separatism

B. nationalism

C. sectionalism

D. patriotism

TEST PRACTICE
CLASSZONE.COM

ALTERNATIVE ASSESSMENT

1. ✍ **WRITING ABOUT HISTORY**

Write the dialogue for a one-act **play** about the slave rebellion led by Nat Turner.

• Use library resources to learn about Nat Turner.

• Include the events that led up to the rebellion.

• Explain the lasting effects of the rebellion.

2. COOPERATIVE LEARNING

Participate in a class project to plan an exhibit depicting what slavery was like on cotton plantations. Choose one of the following topics: what enslaved people wore; what their living conditions were like; what rules they lived under; or what stories they told. Work with other students to research that subject. Discuss how to exhibit your findings.

INTEGRATED TECHNOLOGY

FINDING PRIMARY SOURCES ON THE INTERNET

There are many first-hand accounts of factory life at the Lowell mills. Use the Internet to find at least two of the following on-line primary sources. Read the excerpts and articles, write five interesting facts that you learned from these sources, and then share them with the class.

• "Tales of Factory Life" an excerpt from *Lowell Offering*

• "The Spirit of Discontent" an excerpt from *Lowell Offering*

• "Harriet Robinson: Lowell Mill Girls"

• Factory Rules from the *Handbook to Lowell*, 1848

For more about the Lowell mills . . .

INTERNET ACTIVITY
CLASSZONE.COM

A Changing Nation

Scotts Bluff in Nebraska became a landmark for settlers migrating west on the Oregon Trail.

"Our manifest destiny is to overspread the continent."

—John L. O'Sullivan

CHAPTER 12

The Age of Jackson 1824–1840

Section 1
Politics of the People

Section 2
Jackson's Policy Toward Native Americans

Section 3
Conflicts over States' Rights

Section 4
Prosperity and Panic

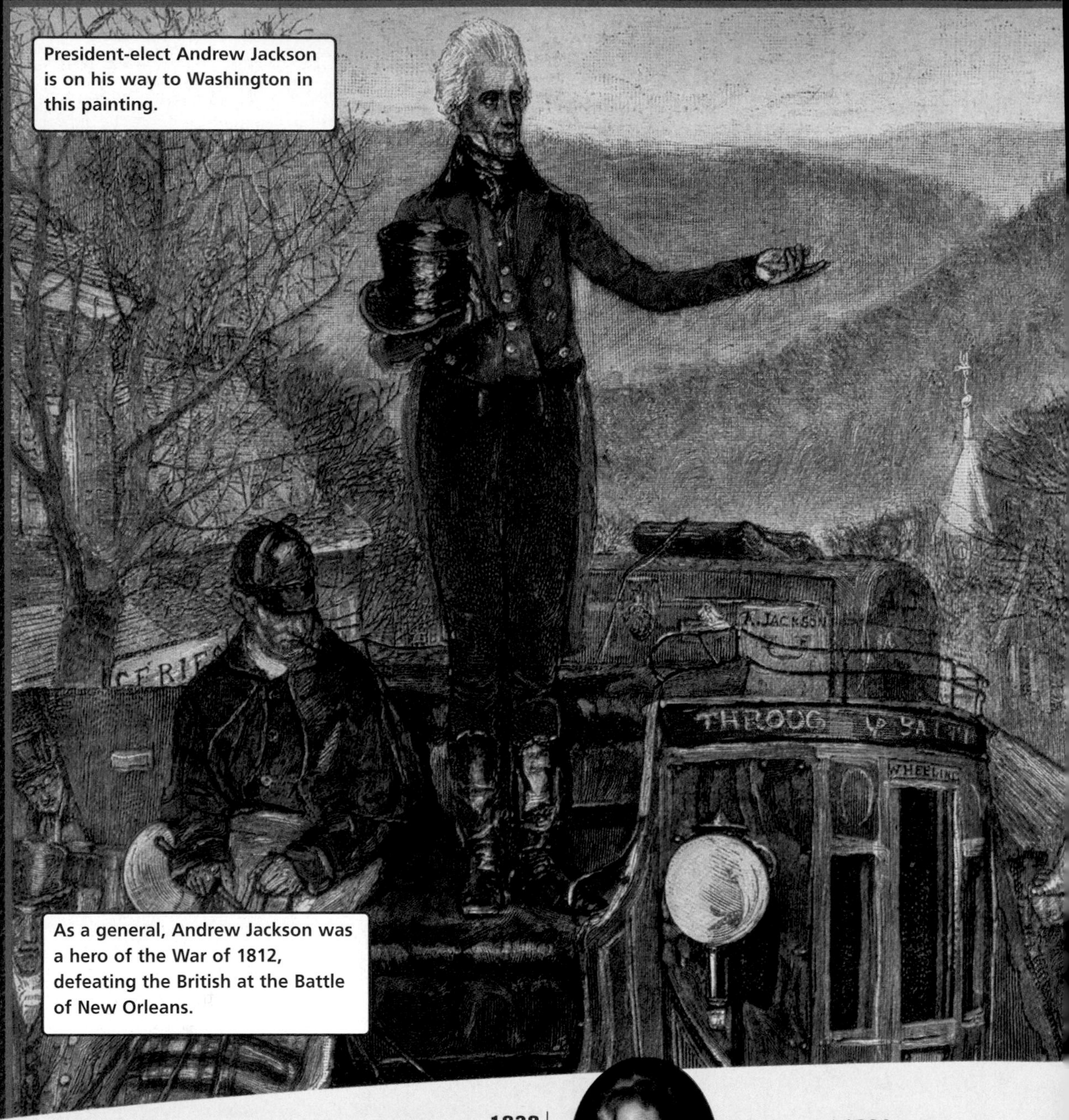

President-elect Andrew Jackson is on his way to Washington in this painting.

As a general, Andrew Jackson was a hero of the War of 1812, defeating the British at the Battle of New Orleans.

USA
World
1824

1824
John Quincy Adams is elected president.

1824
Simón Bolívar becomes president of Peru.

1828
Tariff of Abominations signed into law.
Andrew Jackson is elected president.

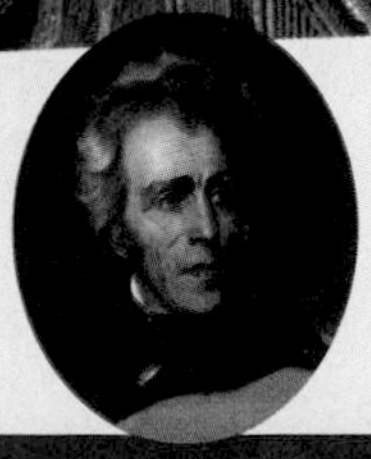

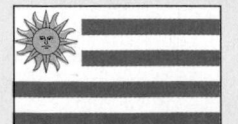

1828
Uruguay gains independence.

1830
Indian Removal Act is passed.

1830
Revolutions occur in Belgium, France, and Poland.

The year is 1828. You will vote for president for the first time. Important economic, social, and political issues face the country. The favored candidate is Andrew Jackson, a military hero. Before you vote, you should decide what you are looking for in a leader.

What qualities do you think make a strong leader?

What Do You Think?

- Which earlier presidents would you consider strong leaders and which not?

- Would qualities that make a military leader also make a good president? Why or why not?

RESEARCH LINKS
CLASSZONE.COM
Visit the Chapter 12 links for more information about the Age of Jackson.

1832
Jackson vetoes charter of Bank of the United States.
South Carolina nullifies tariffs.
Jackson is reelected.

1836
Martin Van Buren is elected president.

1838
Cherokees begin to travel the Trail of Tears.

1840
William Henry Harrison is elected president.

1840

1832
Reform Act increases number of voters in Britain.

1837
Victoria becomes queen of Great Britain.

1838
Zulu clash with Boer settlers in South Africa.

Reading Strategy: Finding Main Ideas

What Do You Know?

What do you already know about the issues that faced the nation in the first half of the 19th century? How did presidents before Jackson deal with problems?

Think About

- what you have learned about Andrew Jackson from books and movies
- how American life is affected by the actions of a president, by conflicts among different parts of the country, and by the will of the people
- your responses to the Interact with History about qualities that make a strong leader (see page 367)

President Andrew Jackson's time in office was so influential, it has been called the Age of Jackson.

What Do You Want to Know?

 What questions do you have about Jackson and his presidency? Record them in your notebook before reading the chapter.

Finding Main Ideas

To make it easier for you to understand what you read, learn to find the main idea of each paragraph, topic heading, and section. Remember that the supporting details help explain the main ideas. On the chart below, write down the main ideas about the political, economic, and social changes during Jackson's presidency.

S See Skillbuilder Handbook, page R5.

 Taking Notes

```
              ┌─────────────────────────┐
              │   CHANGES DURING         │
              │   JACKSON'S PRESIDENCY   │
              └─────────────────────────┘
        ┌──────────────┬───────────────┬──────────────┐
   ┌─────────┐    ┌──────────┐    ┌──────────┐
   │Political│    │ Economic │    │  Social  │
   └─────────┘    └──────────┘    └──────────┘
   ┌─────────┐    ┌──────────┐    ┌──────────┐
   │Main      │    │Main      │    │Main      │
   │Ideas:    │    │Ideas:    │    │Ideas:    │
   │          │    │          │    │          │
   └─────────┘    └──────────┘    └──────────┘
```

Politics of the People

MAIN IDEA	WHY IT MATTERS NOW	TERMS & NAMES
Andrew Jackson's election to the presidency in 1828 brought a new era of popular democracy.	Jackson's use of presidential powers laid the foundation of the modern presidency.	John Quincy Adams Jacksonian democracy
		Andrew Jackson spoils system

ONE AMERICAN'S STORY

For 40 years, Margaret Bayard Smith and her husband, a government official, were central figures in the political and social life of Washington. In 1824, Smith described how John Quincy Adams reacted to his election as president.

A VOICE FROM THE PAST

When the news of his election was communicated to Mr. Adams by the Committee . . . the sweat rolled down his face—he shook from head to foot and was so agitated that he could scarcely stand or speak.

Margaret Bayard Smith, *The First Forty Years of Washington Society*

Margaret Bayard Smith wrote about life in the nation's capital in the first half of the 19th century.

Adams had reason to be shaken by his election. It had been hotly contested, and he knew that he would face much opposition as he tried to govern. In this section, you will learn how Adams defeated Andrew Jackson in 1824, only to lose to him four years later.

The Election of 1824

In 1824, regional differences led to a fierce fight over the presidency. The Democratic-Republican Party split apart, with four men hoping to replace James Monroe as president. **John Quincy Adams,** Monroe's secretary of state, was New England's choice. The South backed William Crawford of Georgia. Westerners supported Henry Clay, the "Great Compromiser," and **Andrew Jackson,** a former military hero from Tennessee.

Jackson won the most popular votes. But he did not receive a majority of electoral votes. According to the Constitution, if no person wins a majority of electoral votes, the House of Representatives must choose the president. The selection was made from the top three vote getters.

Clay had come in fourth and was out of the running. In the House vote, he threw his support to Adams, who then won. Because Adams

Taking Notes

Use your chart to take notes about political changes.

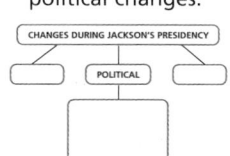

JOHN QUINCY ADAMS
1767–1848

John Quincy Adams was born into wealth and social position. He was the son of President John Adams. Like his father, he had a sharp mind, spoke eloquently, worked tirelessly in public service, and had high principles. But he was sometimes vain, and unwilling to compromise. This made him unpopular with many people and often ineffective. After his presidency, he served with distinction in Congress.

ANDREW JACKSON
1767–1845

Andrew Jackson was the son of a poor farm couple from South Carolina. Orphaned by age 14, he was a wild and reckless youth.

Jackson moved on to become a successful lawyer and plantation owner in Tennessee. But his quick temper still got him into brawls and duels. Bullets in his body from two duels frequently caused him pain.

Jackson's humble background and reputation for toughness endeared him to voters. They considered him one of their own.

Why do you think Jackson was popular but Adams was not?

later named Clay as his secretary of state, Jackson's supporters claimed that Adams gained the presidency by making a deal with Clay. Charges of a "corrupt bargain" followed Adams throughout his term.

Adams had many plans for his presidency. He wanted to build roads and canals, aid education and science, and regulate the use of natural resources. But Congress, led by Jackson supporters, defeated his proposals.

*Reading*History
A. Analyzing Causes What was the main reason John Quincy Adams was not effective as president?

Jacksonian Democracy

Jackson felt that the 1824 election had been stolen from him—that the will of the people had been ignored. Jackson and his supporters were outraged. He immediately set to work to gain the presidency in 1828.

For the next four years, the split in the Democratic-Republican Party between the supporters of Jackson and of Adams grew wider. Jackson claimed to represent the "common man." He said Adams represented a group of privileged, wealthy Easterners. This division eventually created two parties. The Democrats came from among the Jackson supporters, while the National Republicans grew out of the Adams camp.

The election of 1828 again matched Jackson against Adams. It was a bitter campaign—both sides made vicious personal attacks. Even Jackson's wife, Rachel, became a target. During the campaign, Jackson crusaded against control of the government by the wealthy. He promised to look out for the interests of common people. He also promoted the concept of majority rule. The idea of spreading political power to all the people and ensuring majority rule became known as **Jacksonian democracy.**

Actually, the process of spreading political power had begun before Jackson ran for office. When Jefferson was president in the early 1800s,

additional people had gained the right to vote as states reduced restrictions on who could vote. Before, for example, only those who owned property or paid taxes could vote in many states. This easing of voting restrictions increased the number of voters. But voting was still limited to adult white males.

The expansion of voting rights helped Jackson achieve an overwhelming win in the 1828 presidential election. Jackson's triumph was hailed as a victory for common people. Large numbers of Western farmers as well as workers in the nation's cities supported him. Their vote put an end to the idea that the government should be controlled by an educated elite. Now, the common people would be governed by one of their own. (See chart "Changes in Ideas About Democracy," page 373.)

Reading **History**
B. Recognizing Effects What factor made Jackson's appeal to the "common man" especially important in the election of 1828?

The People's President

Jackson's humble background, and his reputation as a war hero, helped make him president. Many saw his rise above hardship as a real American success story. He was the first president not from an aristocratic Massachusetts or Virginia family, and the first from the West.

Jackson indeed had had a hard life. His father died shortly before his birth, and Jackson grew up on a frontier farm in South Carolina. At 13, he joined the militia with his older brother to fight in the Revolutionary War. In 1781, they were taken prisoner by the British. While captive, he allegedly refused when commanded to shine an officer's boots. The officer struck Jackson with a sword, leaving scars on his hand and head. Later, Jackson's mother obtained her sons' release from a military prison, where they had become ill with smallpox. Jackson's brother died, but his mother nursed Jackson back to health. A short time later, she also died. Jackson's experiences during the Revolution left him with a lifelong hatred of the British.

After the war, Jackson moved to the Tennessee frontier. In 1784, he began to study law. He built a successful legal practice and also bought and sold land. Jackson then purchased a plantation near Nashville and ran successfully for Congress. After the War of 1812 broke out, he was appointed a general in the army. At the Battle of New Orleans in 1815, Jackson soundly defeated the British even though his troops were greatly outnumbered. He became a national war hero. He earned the nickname "Old Hickory," after a soldier claimed that he was "tough as hickory."

Jackson Takes Office

Jackson's success in the presidential election of 1828 came at a high price. Shortly after he won, his wife, Rachel, died of a heart attack. Jackson believed that the campaign attacks on her reputation had killed her. She was a private woman who preferred a quiet life. In fact, she had

STRANGE *but* True

ADAMS AND JEFFERSON
John Adams and Thomas Jefferson died on the same day—the Fourth of July, 1826, the 50th anniversary of the adoption of the Declaration of Independence.

Both Adams and Jefferson were founders of the nation, signers of the Declaration, and presidents. They were also political enemies who had become friends late in life.

Adams was 90; Jefferson, 83. Adams's last words were "Jefferson still survives." He was unaware that Jefferson had died hours earlier.

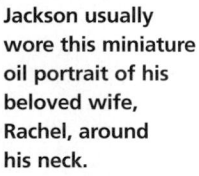

Jackson usually wore this miniature oil portrait of his beloved wife, Rachel, around his neck.

said that she would "rather be a doorkeeper in the house of God than . . . live in that palace at Washington." Margaret Bayard Smith described Rachel's importance to Jackson, saying she "not only made him a happier, but a better man."

Jackson looked thin, pale, and sad at his inauguration on March 4, 1829. But the capital was full of joy and excitement. Thousands of people were there. Senator Daniel Webster wrote about the inauguration.

> ### A VOICE FROM THE PAST
> I have never seen such a crowd before. Persons have come five hundred miles to see General Jackson, and they really seem to think that the country has been rescued from some dreadful danger.
>
> **Daniel Webster,** *Correspondence*

*Reading*History
C. Drawing Conclusions Why did Jackson's supporters react with such enthusiasm at his inauguration?

At the inauguration ceremony, the crowd shouted, waved, applauded, and saluted its hero. He bowed low to the people in turn. A throng followed Jackson to the White House reception. One person described the crowd as containing "all sorts of people, from the highest and most polished, down to the most vulgar and gross in the nation."

The crowd grew rowdy. People broke china and glasses as they grabbed for the food and drinks. The pushing and shoving finally drove the new president to flee the White House. As Supreme Court Justice Joseph Story observed, "The reign of King Mob seemed triumphant."

CITIZENSHIP TODAY

Exercising the Vote

During the Age of Jackson, rules on who could vote were eased. This increased the number of voters. But voting was still limited to adult white males. Over the years, other groups gained the right to vote, including African Americans, women, and Native Americans. Today's elections are open to all citizens aged 18 and over.

Future voters can practice casting their votes in mock, or pretend, elections. The National Student/Parent Mock Election teaches students to be informed voters. Mock presidential elections attract coverage by the media. Television stations may even broadcast live from schools, interviewing student voters.

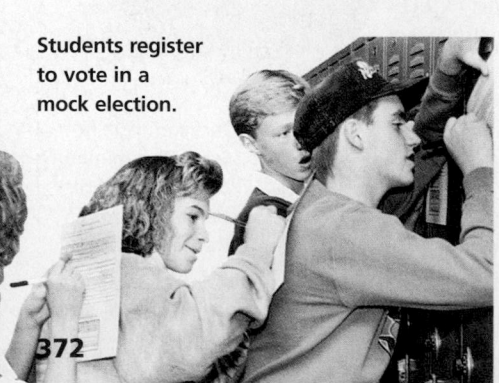
Students register to vote in a mock election.

One high school student, Charlie Tran from San Jose, California, said, "Students seem to catch the important political events surrounding them. Some students are taking their views . . . to a new level by campaigning for the candidate they support."

How Do You Set Up a Mock Election?

1. Choose issues and candidates and then set up a mock election in your classroom. (You could focus on the national, state, or local level.)

2. Create the materials of an election, such as the polling place, ballots, and posters.

3. Campaign for the candidates or the issues you support.

4. Conduct the voting.

5. Prepare mock media reports on the election's outcome. You may want to interview voters.

 See Citizenship Handbook, page 283.

For more about citizenship and voting . . .

 RESEARCH LINKS
CLASSZONE.COM

Changes in Ideas About Democracy

JEFFERSONIAN DEMOCRACY	JACKSONIAN DEMOCRACY
government for the people by capable, well-educated leaders	government by the people
democracy in political life	democracy in social, economic, and political life
championed the cause of the farmer in a mainly agricultural society	championed the cause of the farmer and the laborer in an agricultural and industrial society
limited government	limited government, but with a strong president

SKILLBUILDER Interpreting Charts

1. *What do you think was the most important change in democracy?*
2. *Did Jefferson or Jackson exercise more power?*

A New Political Era Begins

Jackson's inauguration began a new political era. In his campaign, he had promised to reform government. He started by replacing many government officials with his supporters. This practice of giving government jobs to political backers became known as the **spoils system**. The name comes from a statement that "to the victor belong the spoils [possessions] of the enemy." Jackson's opponents charged that the practice was corrupt. But he defended it, noting that it broke up one group's hold on government.

As president, Jackson would face three major issues—the status of Native Americans, the rights of the states, and the role of the Bank of the United States. In the next section, you will learn how Jackson's policies affected Native Americans.

Section 1 Assessment

1. Terms & Names

Explain the significance of:
- John Quincy Adams
- Andrew Jackson
- Jacksonian democracy
- spoils system

2. Using Graphics

Use a chart to identify important biographical information about Andrew Jackson.

Life of Andrew Jackson	
Youthful life	
Road to Congress	
War hero	
Appeal to voters	

3. Main Ideas

a. How did Andrew Jackson react to the election of 1824? Why?

b. What factors helped Jackson win the presidency in 1828?

c. What was the effect of expanding voting rights?

4. Critical Thinking

Analyzing Points of View
What are reasons for and against the spoils system?

THINK ABOUT
- the effects of giving government workers lifetime jobs
- the effects of rewarding political supporters

ACTIVITY OPTIONS

GEOGRAPHY

MATH

Find out which states Jackson and Adams won in the 1828 election. Show the results on a **map** or **chart** that includes vote totals and percentages.

Jackson's Policy Toward Native Americans

MAIN IDEA	WHY IT MATTERS NOW	TERMS & NAMES
During Jackson's presidency, Native Americans were forced to move west of the Mississippi River.	This forced removal forever changed the lives of Native Americans in the United States.	Sequoya Indian Removal Act	Indian Territory Trail of Tears Osceola

ONE AMERICAN'S STORY

In 1821, a brilliant Cherokee named **Sequoya** (sih KWOY uh) invented a writing system for the Cherokee language. Using this simple system, the Cherokees soon learned to read and write. A traveler in 1828 marveled at how many Cherokees had learned to read and write without schools or even paper and pens.

A VOICE FROM THE PAST

I frequently saw as I rode from place to place, Cherokee letters painted or cut on the trees by the roadside, on fences, houses, and often on pieces of bark or board, lying about the houses.

Anonymous traveler, quoted in the *Advocate*

Sequoya hoped that by gaining literacy—the ability to read and write—his people could share the power of whites and keep their independence. But even Sequoya's invention could not save the Cherokees from the upheaval to come. In this section, you will learn about President Jackson's policy toward Native Americans and its effects.

Sequoya invented a writing system of 86 characters, shown here, for the Cherokee language.

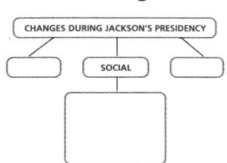

Taking Notes

Use your chart to take notes about social changes.

CHANGES DURING JACKSON'S PRESIDENCY

SOCIAL

Native Americans in the Southeast

Since the 1600s, white settlers had pushed Native Americans westward as they took more and more of their land. However, there were still many Native Americans in the East in the early 1800s. Some whites hoped that the Native Americans could adapt to the white people's way of life. Others wanted the Native Americans to move. They believed this was the only way to avoid conflict over land. Also, many whites felt that Native Americans were "uncivilized" and did not want to live near them.

By the 1820s, about 100,000 Native Americans remained east of the Mississippi River. The majority were in the Southeast. The major tribes

Reading **History**

A. Reading a Map Use the map on page 376 to locate Native American lands in the Southeast.

were the Cherokee, Chickasaw, Choctaw, Creek, and Seminole. Whites called them the Five Civilized Tribes because they had adopted many aspects of white culture. They held large areas of land in Georgia, the Carolinas, Alabama, Mississippi, and Tennessee.

The Cherokee Nation

More than any other Southeastern tribe, the Cherokee had adopted white customs, including their way of dressing. Cherokees owned prosperous farms and cattle ranches. Some even had slaves. From Sequoya, they acquired a written language, and they published their own newspaper, the *Cherokee Phoenix*. Some of their children attended missionary schools. In 1827, the Cherokees drew up a constitution based on the U.S. Constitution and founded the Cherokee Nation.

A year after the Cherokees adopted their constitution, gold was discovered on their land in Georgia. Now, not only settlers but also miners wanted these lands. The discovery of gold increased demands by whites to move the Cherokees. The federal government responded with a plan to remove all Native Americans from the Southeast.

Jackson's Removal Policy

Andrew Jackson had long supported a policy of moving Native Americans west of the Mississippi. He first dealt with the Southeastern tribes after the War of 1812. The federal government ordered Jackson, then acting as Indian treaty commissioner, to make treaties with the Native Americans of the region. Through these treaties forced on the tribes, the government gained large tracts of land.

Jackson believed that the government had the right to regulate where Native Americans could live. He viewed them as conquered subjects who lived within the borders of the United States. He thought that Native Americans had one of two choices. They could adopt white culture and become citizens of the United States. Or they could move into the Western territories. They could not, however, have their own governments within the nation's borders.

After the discovery of gold, whites began to move onto Cherokee land. Georgia and other Southern states passed laws that gave them the right to take over Native American lands. When the Cherokee and other tribes protested, Jackson supported the states.

To solve the problem, Jackson asked Congress to pass a law that would require Native Americans to either move west or submit to state laws. Many Americans objected to Jackson's proposal. Massachusetts congressman Edward Everett opposed removing Native Americans against their will to a distant land. There, he said, they would face "the

Now and then

CHEROKEE PEOPLE TODAY

Today, there are more than 300,000 Cherokees. They are part of three main groups—the Cherokee Nation of Oklahoma, the United Keetoowah Band in Oklahoma, and the Eastern Band of Cherokee Indians of North Carolina.

Wilma Mankiller, shown below, was the first woman elected principal chief of the Cherokee Nation of Oklahoma. She has said that the "Cherokee people possess an extraordinary ability to face down adversity and continue moving forward. We are able to do that because our culture, though certainly diminished, has sustained us since time immemorial."

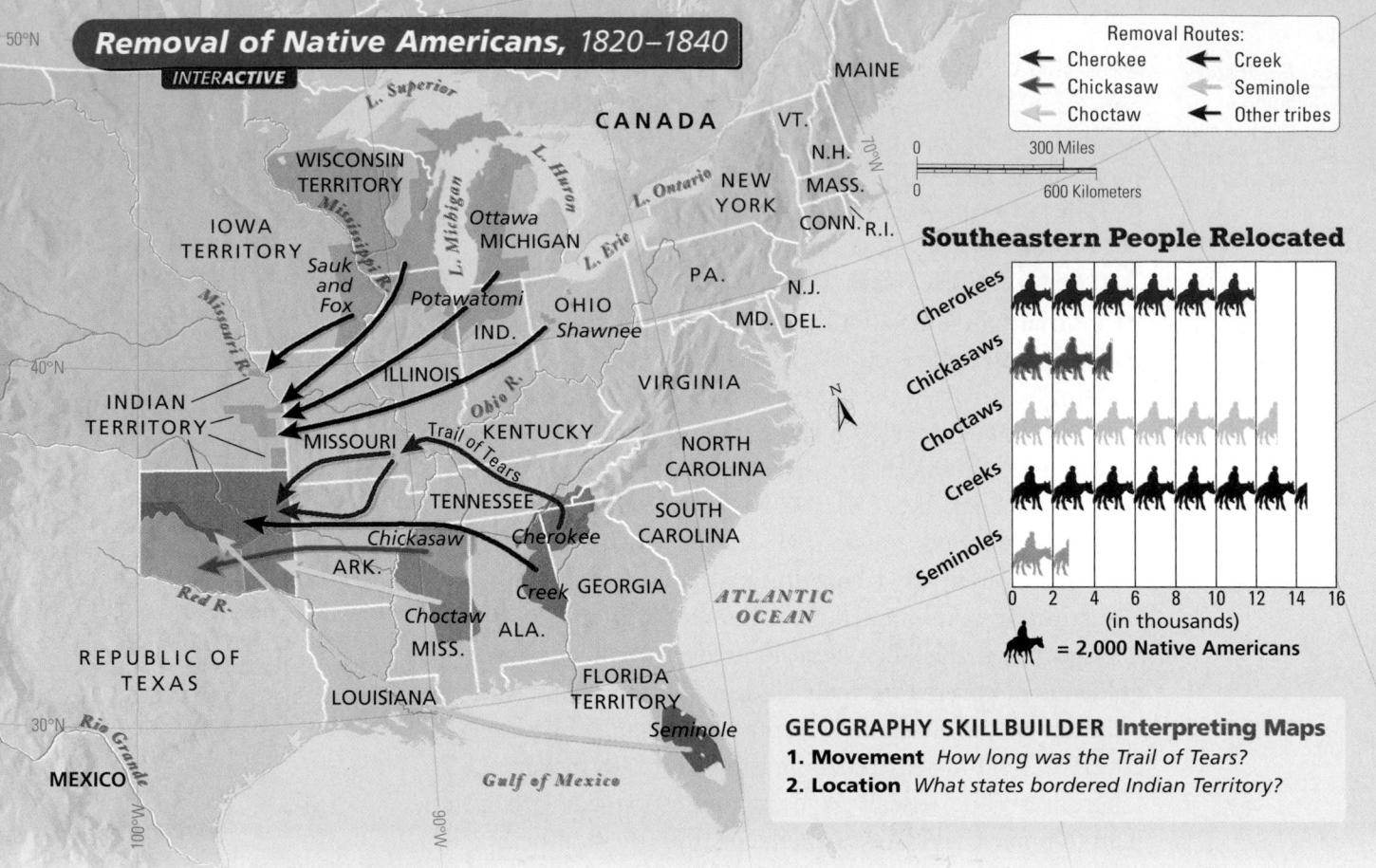

Removal of Native Americans, 1820–1840
INTERACTIVE

Removal Routes:
← Cherokee ← Creek
← Chickasaw ← Seminole
← Choctaw ← Other tribes

Southeastern People Relocated

= 2,000 Native Americans

Cherokees
Chickasaws
Choctaws
Creeks
Seminoles

0 2 4 6 8 10 12 14 16
(in thousands)

GEOGRAPHY SKILLBUILDER Interpreting Maps
1. **Movement** *How long was the Trail of Tears?*
2. **Location** *What states bordered Indian Territory?*

perils and hardships of a wilderness." Religious groups such as the Quakers also opposed forced removal of Native Americans. After heated debate, Congress passed the **Indian Removal Act** in 1830. The act called for the government to negotiate treaties that would require Native Americans to relocate west.

Jackson immediately set out to enforce the law. He thought his policy was "just and liberal" and would allow Native Americans to keep their way of life. Instead, his policy caused much hardship and forever changed relations between whites and Native Americans.

*Reading***History**

B. Drawing Conclusions
What were reasons for and against the Indian Removal Act?

The Trail of Tears

As whites invaded their homelands, many Native Americans saw no other choice but to sign treaties exchanging their land for land in the West. Under the treaties, Native Americans would be moved to an area that covered what is now Oklahoma and parts of Kansas and Nebraska. This area came to be called **Indian Territory**.

Beginning in the fall of 1831, the Choctaw and other Southeast tribes were removed from their lands and relocated to Indian Territory. The Cherokees, however, first appealed to the U.S. Supreme Court to protect their land from being seized by Georgia. In 1832, the Court, led by Chief Justice John Marshall, ruled that only the federal government, not the states, could make laws governing the Cherokees. This ruling meant that

the Georgia laws did not apply to the Cherokee Nation. However, both Georgia and President Jackson ignored the Supreme Court. Jackson said, "John Marshall has made his decision. . . . Now let him enforce it."

A small group of Cherokees gave up and signed a treaty to move west. But the majority of the Cherokees, led by John Ross, opposed the treaty. Jackson refused to negotiate with these Cherokees.

In 1838, federal troops commanded by General Winfield Scott rounded up about 16,000 Cherokees and forced them into camps. Soldiers took people from their homes with nothing but the clothes on their backs. Over the fall and winter of 1838–1839, these Cherokees set out on the long journey west. Forced to march in the cold, rain, and snow without adequate clothing, many grew weak and ill. One-fourth died. The dead included John Ross's wife. One soldier never forgot what he witnessed on the trail.

*Reading***History**

C. Recognizing Effects What happened to the Cherokees as a result of the Indian Removal Act?

A VOICE FROM THE PAST

Murder is murder and somebody must answer, somebody must explain the streams of blood that flowed in the Indian country in . . . 1838. Somebody must explain the four-thousand silent graves that mark the trail of the Cherokees to their exile. I wish I could forget it all, but the picture of six-hundred and forty-five wagons lumbering over the frozen ground with their Cargo of suffering humanity still lingers in my memory.

John G. Burnett, quoted in *The Native Americans,* edited by Betty and Ian Ballantine

This harsh journey of the Cherokee from their homeland to Indian Territory became known as the **Trail of Tears.**

HISTORY *through*ART

In 1838, the Cherokees left their homeland by wagon, horse, donkey, and foot, forced to travel hundreds of miles along the Trail of Tears. This painting is by Robert Lindneux, a 20th-century artist.

How does this portrayal of the Trail of Tears reflect continuity and change in 19th-century American life?

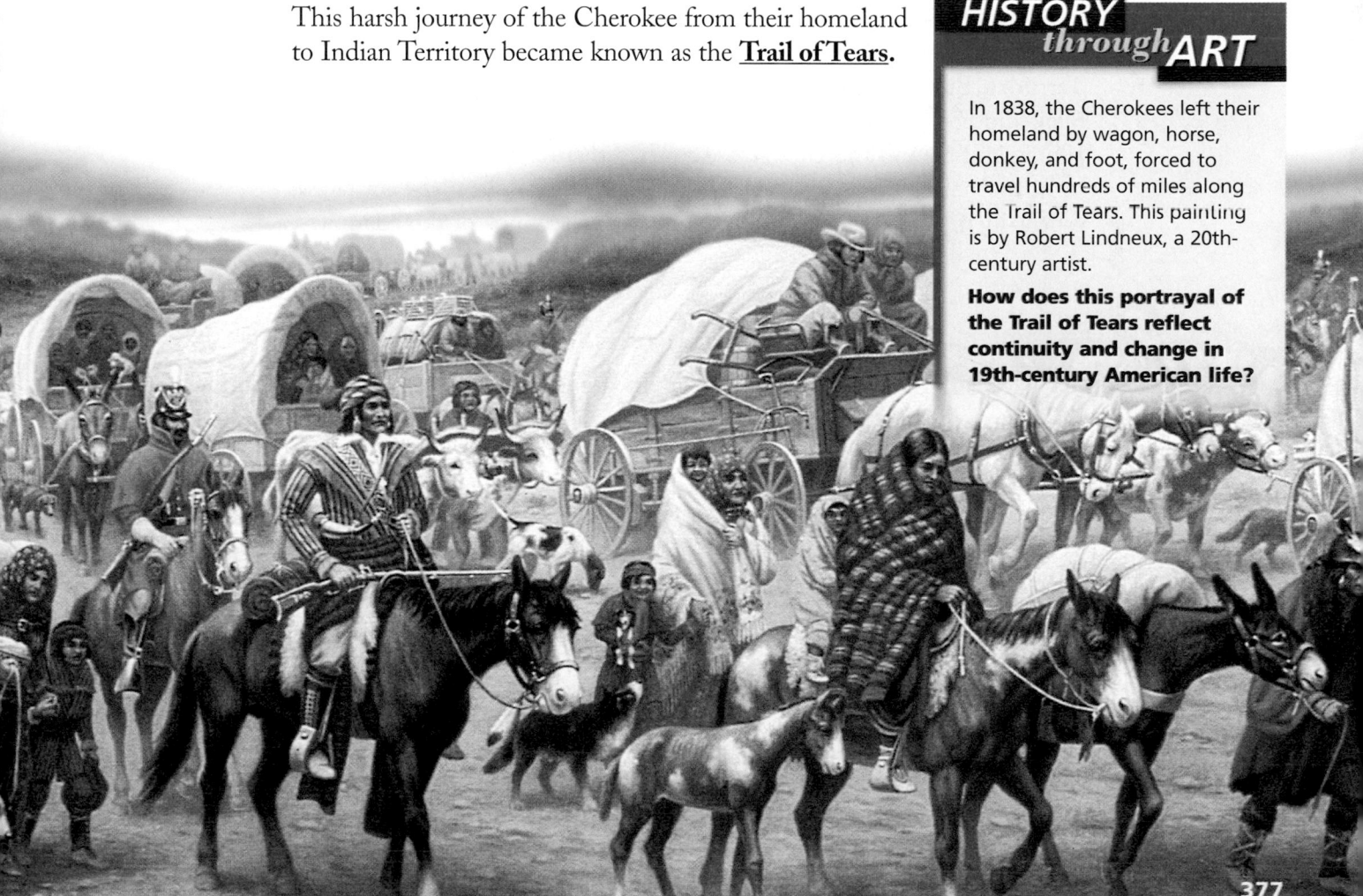

Osceola led the Seminoles in their fight against removal.

Native American Resistance

Not all the Cherokees moved west in 1838. That fall, soldiers had rounded up an old Cherokee farmer named Tsali and his family, including his grown sons. On the way to the stockade, they fought the soldiers. A soldier was killed before Tsali fled with his family to the Great Smoky Mountains in North Carolina. There they found other Cherokees. The U.S. Army sent a message to Tsali. If he and his sons would give themselves up, the others could remain. They surrendered, and all except the youngest son were shot. Their sacrifice allowed some Cherokees to stay in their homeland.

Other Southeast tribes also resisted relocation. In 1835, the Seminoles refused to leave Florida. This refusal led to the Second Seminole War. One elderly Seminole explained why he could not leave: "If suddenly we tear our hearts from the homes around which they are twined [wrapped around], our heart strings will snap."

One of the most important leaders in the war was **Osceola** (AHS ee OH luh). Hiding in the Everglades, Osceola and his band used surprise attacks to defeat the U.S. Army in many battles. In 1837, Osceola was tricked into capture when he came to peace talks during a truce. He later died in prison. But the Seminoles continued to fight. Some went deeper into the Everglades, where their descendants live today. Others moved west. The Second Seminole War ended in 1842.

Some tribes north of the Ohio River also resisted relocation. The Shawnee, Ottawa, Potawatomi, Sauk, and Fox were removed to Indian Territory. But in 1832, a Sauk chief named Black Hawk led a band of Sauk and Fox back to their lands in Illinois. In the Black Hawk War, the Illinois militia and the U.S. Army crushed the uprising.

In the next section, you will learn about other issues Jackson faced, especially increasing tensions between various sections of the country.

Background
The Seminoles fought three wars against the U.S. government between 1817 and 1858, when their resistance ended.

Section 2 Assessment

1. Terms & Names

Explain the significance of:
- Sequoya
- Indian Removal Act
- Indian Territory
- Trail of Tears
- Osceola

2. Using Graphics

Use a chart to list the reasons for Jackson's Native American removal policy.

Reasons Native Americans Were Forced West		
Economic	Political	Social

What do you think was the main reason?

3. Main Ideas

a. How did President Jackson justify the Indian Removal Act?

b. In what ways did Native Americans resist the Indian Removal Act?

c. What were the consequences of the Indian Removal Act?

4. Critical Thinking

Recognizing Effects
What were some economic effects of the Indian Removal Act on Native Americans? On whites?

THINK ABOUT
- what the Native Americans lost
- what the white settlers gained

ACTIVITY OPTIONS

GEOGRAPHY

MATH

Use the map on page 376 to estimate the distance traveled by each of the five Southeastern tribes. Show your calculation on a **map** or **chart**.

Conflicts Over States' Rights

MAIN IDEA	WHY IT MATTERS NOW	TERMS & NAMES
Jackson struggled to keep Southern states from breaking away from the Union over the issue of tariffs.	Disputes about states' rights and federal power remain important in national politics.	John C. Calhoun Webster-Hayne debate Tariff of Abominations Daniel Webster doctrine of nullification secession

ONE AMERICAN'S STORY

Raised in South Carolina, **John C. Calhoun** was elected to the U.S. Congress at the age of 28. He soon became one of its leaders. Calhoun supported the need for a strong central government and also spoke out against sectionalism.

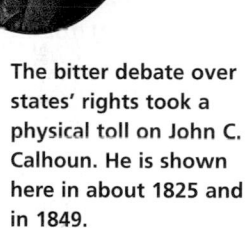

A VOICE FROM THE PAST

What is necessary for the common good may apparently be opposed to the interest of particular sections. It must be submitted to [accepted] as the condition of our [nation's] greatness.

John C. Calhoun, quoted in *John C. Calhoun: American Portrait* by Margaret L. Coit

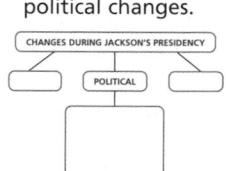

But Calhoun's concern for the economic and political well-being of his home state of South Carolina, and the South in general, later caused him to change his beliefs. He became a champion of states' rights.

In this section, you will learn how two strong-willed men—Calhoun and Jackson—came in conflict over the issue of states' rights.

The bitter debate over states' rights took a physical toll on John C. Calhoun. He is shown here in about 1825 and in 1849.

Rising Sectional Differences

Andrew Jackson had taken office in 1829. At the time, the country was being pulled apart by conflicts among its three main sections—the Northeast, the South, and the West. Legislators from these regions were arguing over three major economic issues: the sale of public lands, internal improvements, and tariffs.

The federal government had acquired vast areas of land through conquests, treaties, and purchases. It raised money partly by selling these public lands. However, Northeasterners did not want public lands in the West to be sold at low prices. The cheap land would attract workers who were needed in the factories of the Northeast. But Westerners wanted

Taking Notes

Use your chart to take notes about political changes.

CHANGES DURING JACKSON'S PRESIDENCY

POLITICAL

low land prices to encourage settlement. The more people who moved West, the more political power the section would have.

The issue of internal improvements also pulled the sections apart. Business leaders in the Northeast and West backed government spending on internal improvements, such as new roads and canals. Good transportation would help bring food and raw materials to the Northeast and take manufactured goods to Western markets. Southerners opposed more federal spending on internal improvements because the government financed these projects through tariffs, which were taxes on imported goods. The South did not want any increase in tariffs.

Since 1816, tariffs had risen steadily. They had become the government's main source of income. Northerners supported high tariffs because they made imported goods more expensive than American-made goods. The Northeast had most of the nation's manufacturing. Tariffs helped

Background During the Jackson era, the West included states that are now considered part of the Midwest.

Economics *in* History

How Tariffs Work

Tariffs are taxes added to the cost of goods imported from another country. There are two kinds of tariffs—revenue tariffs and protective tariffs. **Revenue tariffs** are used to raise money, like the sales taxes that states add to purchases today. These tariffs tend to be fairly low. **Protective tariffs** usually are much higher. They have another goal: to persuade consumers to buy goods made in their own country instead of purchasing foreign-made products. Congress passed a protective tariff in 1828 to help American companies.

The illustration shows how a protective tariff works. A British-made teapot sells for $3.50, and a similar teapot made in the United States sells for $4.00. Most shoppers will buy the British teapot and save 50 cents. But when the government adds a 40 percent tariff to British goods, the price of the British teapot soars to $4.90. The result: consumers buy the now-cheaper American teapots.

CONNECT TO HISTORY

1. **Recognizing Effects** Do consumers benefit from high tariffs? Why or why not?

   S See Skillbuilder Handbook, page R11.

CONNECT TO TODAY

2. **Making Inferences** Today, many leaders around the world promote the idea of "free trade." What do you think "free trade" means?

For more about tariffs . . .

RESEARCH LINKS
CLASSZONE.COM

$2.50 to produce in Britain $1.00 profit   = $3.50   + TARIFF 40%   + tariff $4.90

$3.00 to produce in the U.S. $1.00 profit   = $4.00 $4.00

American manufacturers sell their products at a lower price than imported goods.

The South opposed rising tariffs because its economy depended on foreign trade. Southern planters sold most of their cotton to foreign buyers. They were not paid in money but were given credit. They then used the credit to buy foreign manufactured goods. Because of higher tariffs, these foreign goods cost more. Eventually, the tariff issue would lead to conflict between North and South.

*Reading*History
A. Analyzing Causes Why did the three sections of the country differ on the sale of public lands, internal improvements, and tariffs?

Tariff of Abominations

In 1828, in the last months of John Quincy Adams's presidency, Congress passed a bill that significantly raised the tariffs on raw materials and manufactured goods. Southerners were outraged. They had to sell their cotton at low prices to be competitive. Yet tariffs forced them to pay high prices for manufactured goods. Southerners felt that the economic interests of the Northeast were determining national policy. They hated the tariff and called it the **Tariff of Abominations** (an abomination is a hateful thing).

Differences over the tariff helped Jackson win the election of 1828. Southerners blamed Adams for the tariff, since it was passed during his administration. So they voted against him.

Crisis over Nullification

The Tariff of Abominations hit South Carolinians especially hard because their economy was in a slump. Some leaders in the state even spoke of leaving the Union over the issue of tariffs. John C. Calhoun, then Jackson's vice-president, understood the problems of South Carolina's farmers because he was one himself. But he wanted to find a way to keep South Carolina from leaving the Union. The answer he arrived at was the **doctrine of nullification.** A state, Calhoun said, had the right to nullify, or reject, a federal law that it considers unconstitutional.

*Reading*History
B. Summarizing How did the issue of tariffs threaten to tear the Union apart?

Calhoun was not the first person to propose the doctrine of nullification. Thomas Jefferson developed it in 1799 in the Kentucky Resolutions. He argued that the Union was a league of sovereign, or self-governing, states that had the right to limit the federal government. Calhoun extended the doctrine. He said that any state could nullify, or make void, a federal law within its borders. He believed that Congress had no right to impose a tariff that favored one section of the country. Therefore, South Carolina had the right to nullify the tariff. Calhoun's doctrine was an extreme form of states' rights—the theory that states have the right to judge whether a law of Congress is unconstitutional.

In the summer of 1828, Calhoun wrote a document called the "South Carolina Exposition and Protest." It stated his theory. Calhoun allowed the document to be published, but he did not sign his name. He knew his ideas would cause controversy.

A South Carolina woman sews a palmetto emblem (inset) to her hat to show her support for nullification. The palmetto is a South Carolina symbol.

Vocabulary
controversy: a public dispute

"Liberty and Union, now and forever, one and inseparable!"
Daniel Webster of Massachusetts

"The measures of the federal government . . . will soon involve the whole South in . . . ruin."
Robert Y. Hayne of South Carolina

Daniel Webster (standing) and Robert Y. Hayne (seated, with hands extended) debated nullification in the U.S. Senate in 1830.

The States' Rights Debate

Calhoun was right. His ideas added fuel to the debate over the nature of the federal union. This debate had been going on since independence from Britain. More and more people took sides. Some supported a strong federal government. Others defended the rights of the states. This question would be a major political issue from this time until the Civil War was fought to resolve it some 30 years later.

One of the great debates in American history took place in the U.S. Senate over the doctrine of nullification—the **Webster-Hayne debate** of 1830. On one side was **Daniel Webster,** a senator from Massachusetts and the most powerful speaker of his time. On the other was Robert Y. Hayne, a senator from South Carolina. Hayne defended nullification. He argued that it gave the states a lawful way to protest and to maintain their freedom. He also said that the real enemies of the Union were those "who are constantly stealing power from the States, and adding strength to the Federal Government."

Webster argued that it was the people and not the states that made the Union. In words that were printed and spread across the country, Webster declared that freedom and the Union go together.

A VOICE FROM THE PAST

When my eyes shall be turned to behold for the last time the sun in heaven, may I not see him shining on the broken and dishonored fragments of a once glorious Union. . . . Liberty and Union, now and forever, one and inseparable!

Daniel Webster, a speech in the U.S. Senate, January 26, 1830

Jackson had not yet stated his position on the issue of states' rights, even though Calhoun was his vice-president. He got his chance in April at a dinner in honor of the birthday of Thomas Jefferson. Calhoun and other

Reading **History**

C. Analyzing Points of View
What do you think Calhoun meant by "the benefits and burdens of the Union" should be equally distributed?

supporters of nullification planned to use the event to win support for their position. Jackson learned of their plans and went to the dinner prepared.

After dinner, Jackson was invited to make a toast. He stood up, looked directly at Calhoun, and stated bluntly, "Our Federal Union—it must be preserved." As Calhoun raised his glass, his hand trembled. Called on to make the next toast, Calhoun stood slowly and said, "The Union—next to our liberty, the most dear; may we all remember that it can only be preserved by respecting the rights of the states and distributing equally the benefits and burdens of the Union." From that time, the two men were political enemies.

South Carolina Threatens to Secede

Even though Jackson made it clear that he opposed the doctrine of nullification, he did not want to drive the South out of the Union. He asked Congress to reduce the tariff, and Congress did so in 1832. But Southerners thought the reduced rates were still too high. South Carolina nullified the tariff acts of 1828 and 1832 and voted to build its own army. South Carolina's leaders threatened **secession,** or withdrawal from the Union, if the federal government tried to collect tariffs.

Jackson was enraged. He told a South Carolina congressman that if the state's leaders defied federal laws, he would "hang the first man of them I can get my hands on." Jackson ran for reelection in 1832, this time without Calhoun as his running mate. After he won, he made it clear that he would use force to see that federal laws were obeyed and the Union preserved.

In the Senate, Henry Clay came forward with a compromise tariff in 1833. He hoped that it would settle the issue and prevent bloodshed. Congress quickly passed the bill, and the crisis ended. South Carolina stayed in the Union. In the next section, you will read about another issue of Jackson's presidency—his war on the national bank.

Section Assessment

1. Terms & Names
Explain the significance of:
- John C. Calhoun
- Tariff of Abominations
- doctrine of nullification
- Webster-Hayne debate
- Daniel Webster
- secession

2. Using Graphics
Use a chart to indicate how each section stood on these issues.

	North-east	West	South
Sale of public lands			
Internal improvements			
High tariffs			

3. Main Ideas
a. Why did the South oppose high tariffs?

b. What were Calhoun's reasons for proposing the doctrine of nullification?

c. Why did South Carolina threaten secession, and how was the crisis resolved?

4. Critical Thinking
Recognizing Effects In what ways would the doctrine of nullification have made it difficult for the federal government to operate?

THINK ABOUT
- its effect on the enforcement of laws
- its effect on the power of the federal government

ACTIVITY OPTIONS

SPEECH

TECHNOLOGY

Research Daniel Webster's speech; a part of it appears on page 382. Deliver a **speech** for or against nullification to the class, or record it on an **audiocassette**.

Prosperity and Panic

MAIN IDEA	WHY IT MATTERS NOW	TERMS & NAMES
Jackson's policies caused the economy to collapse after he left office and affected the next election.	The condition of the economy continues to affect the outcomes of presidential elections.	inflation depression Martin Van Buren Whig Party Panic of 1837 William Henry Harrison John Tyler

ONE AMERICAN'S STORY

Nicholas Biddle was the president of the powerful Second Bank of the United States—the bank that Andrew Jackson believed to be corrupt. Jackson declared war on Biddle and the bank. But Biddle felt sure of his political power.

A VOICE FROM THE PAST

I have always deplored making the Bank a [political] question, but since the President will have it so, he must pay the penalty of his own rashness. . . . [M]y hope is that it will contribute to relieve the country of the domination of these miserable [Jackson] people.

Nicholas Biddle, from a letter to Henry Clay dated August 1, 1832

In this section, you will read about Jackson's war on the bank.

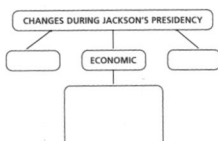

Taking Notes

Use your chart to take notes about economic changes.

CHANGES DURING JACKSON'S PRESIDENCY

ECONOMIC

Mr. Biddle's Bank

The Second Bank of the United States was the most powerful bank in the country. It held government funds and issued money. As its president, Nicholas Biddle set policies that controlled the nation's money supply.

Although the bank was run efficiently, Jackson had many reasons to dislike it. For one thing, he had come to distrust banks after losing money in financial deals early in his career. He also thought the bank had too much power. The bank made loans to members of Congress, and Biddle openly boasted that he could influence Congress. In addition, Jackson felt the bank's lending policies favored wealthy clients and hurt the average person.

To operate, the bank had to have a charter, or a written grant, from the federal government. In 1832, Biddle asked Congress to renew the bank's charter, even though it would not expire until 1836. Because 1832 was an election year, he thought Jackson would agree to renewal rather than risk angering its supporters. But Jackson took the risk.

Nicholas Biddle was the president of the powerful Second Bank of the United States, located in Philadelphia.

Jackson's War on the Bank

Vocabulary
monopoly: a company or group with complete control over a product or service

When Congress voted to renew the bank's charter, Jackson vetoed the renewal. In a strongly worded message to Congress, Jackson claimed the bank was unconstitutional. He said the bank was a monopoly that favored the few at the expense of the many. The Supreme Court earlier had ruled that the bank was constitutional. But Jackson claimed elected officials had to judge the constitutionality of a law for themselves. They did not need to rely on the Supreme Court. His veto message also contained this attack on the bank.

A VOICE FROM THE PAST

It is to be regretted that the rich and powerful too often bend the acts of government to their selfish purposes. . . . Distinctions in society will always exist under every just government. . . . [B]ut when the laws undertake to . . . make the rich richer and the potent more powerful, the humble members of society . . . have a right to complain of the injustice of their Government.

Andrew Jackson, veto message, July 10, 1832

Reading **History**
A. Analyzing Points of View
What reasons did Jackson have for wanting to destroy the Second Bank of the United States?

Jackson's war on the bank became the main issue in the presidential campaign of 1832. The National Republican Party and its candidate, Henry Clay, called Jackson a tyrant. They said he wanted too much power as president. The Democrats portrayed Jackson as a defender of the people. When he won reelection, Jackson took it as a sign that the public approved his war on the bank.

In his second term, Jackson set out to destroy the bank before its charter ended in 1836. He had government funds deposited in state banks, which opponents called Jackson's "pet banks." Biddle fought back by making it harder for people to borrow money. He hoped the resulting economic troubles would force Jackson to return government deposits to the bank. Instead, the people rallied to Jackson's position. Eventually, the bank went out of business. Jackson had won the war, but the economy would be a victim.

Jackson Fights the Second Bank

In this political cartoon, Jackson fights the many-headed monster—the Second Bank of the United States and its branches—with a cane labeled "VETO."

A President Jackson

B Cane labeled "VETO"

C Nicholas Biddle

D Vice-President Van Buren

Prosperity Becomes Panic

Most of the nation prospered during Jackson's last years in office. Because it was easier to borrow money, people took out loans to buy public lands, and the economy boomed. But the "pet banks" issued too much paper money. The rise in the money supply made each dollar worth less. As a result, prices rose. **Inflation,** which is an increase in prices and decrease in the value of money, was the outcome. To fight inflation, Jackson issued an order that required people to pay in gold or silver for public lands.

Jackson left office proud of the nation's prosperity. But it was a puffed-up prosperity. Like a balloon, it had little substance. Because of Jackson's popularity, his vice-president, **Martin Van Buren,** was elected president in 1836. Within a few months after Van Buren took office, a panic—a widespread fear about the state of the economy—spread throughout the country. It became known as the **Panic of 1837.**

People took their paper money to the banks and demanded gold or silver in exchange. The banks quickly ran out of gold and silver. When the government tried to get its money from the state banks, the banks could not pay. The banks defaulted, or went out of business. A **depression,** or severe economic slump, followed.

The depression caused much hardship. Because people had little money, manufacturers no longer had customers for their goods. Almost 90 percent of factories in the East closed in 1837. Jobless workers had no way of buying food or paying rent. People went hungry. They lived in shelters or on the streets, where many froze in the winter. Every section of the country suffered, but the depression hit hardest in the cities. Farmers were hurt less because they could at least grow their own food. The depression affected politics, too.

The Rise of the Whig Party

In the depths of the depression, Senators Henry Clay and Daniel Webster argued that the government needed to help the economy. Van Buren disagreed. He believed that the economy would improve if left alone. He argued that "the less government interferes with private pursuits the better for the general prosperity." Many Americans blamed Van Buren for the Panic, though he had taken office only weeks before it started. The continuing depression made it almost impossible for him to win reelection in 1840.

America's HERITAGE

POLITICAL PARTIES

Today's Democratic and Republican parties were born more than a century ago. Andrew Jackson's supporters first called themselves Democratic-Republicans. But in the 1830s, they became known simply as Democrats. They stood for states' rights and saw themselves as defenders of the common people. The modern Republican Party was formed in 1854 as the successor to the Whig Party, founded in 1834.

In the Jackson era, political parties campaigned for their candidates by staging parades and rallies. Participants often carried banners like the one below with a log cabin, the symbol for the campaign of William H. Harrison in 1840.

WM. H. HARRISON
THE OHIO FARMER

Reading **History**
B. Recognizing Effects What were the short-term and long-term effects of Jackson's war on the bank?

Van Buren faced a new political party in that election. During Jackson's war on the national bank, Clay, Webster, and other Jackson opponents had formed the **Whig Party**. It was named after a British party that opposed royal power. The Whigs opposed the concentration of power in the chief executive—whom they mockingly called "King Andrew" Jackson. In 1840, the Whigs chose **William Henry Harrison** of Ohio to run for president and **John Tyler** of Virginia to run for vice-president.

*Reading*History

C. Making Inferences Why did the Whigs want to nominate a candidate like Harrison, who did not have strong political views?

The Whigs nominated Harrison largely because of his military record and his lack of strong political views. Harrison had led the army that defeated the Shawnees in 1811 at the Battle of Tippecanoe. He also had been a hero during the War of 1812. The Whigs made the most of Harrison's military record and his nickname, "Old Tippecanoe." The phrase "Tippecanoe and Tyler too" became the Whig election slogan.

The Election of 1840

During the 1840 election campaign, the Whigs emphasized personalities more than issues. They tried to appeal to the common people, as Andrew Jackson had done. Harrison was the son of a Virginia plantation owner. However, because he had settled on a farm in Ohio, the Whigs said Harrison was a true Westerner. They used symbols of the frontier, such as a log cabin, to represent Harrison. The Whigs contrasted Harrison with the wealthy Van Buren. Harrison won in a close election.

At his inauguration, the 68-year-old president spoke for nearly two hours in cold March weather with no hat or coat. Later, he was caught in the rain. He came down with a cold that developed into pneumonia. On April 4, 1841, one month after being inaugurated, Harrison died—the first president to die in office. Vice-President Tyler became president.

The election of 1840 showed the importance of the West in American politics. In the next chapter, you'll learn more about the lure of the West and the westward expansion of the United States.

Section 4 Assessment

1. Terms & Names

Explain the significance of:

- inflation
- Martin Van Buren
- Panic of 1837
- depression
- Whig Party
- William Henry Harrison
- John Tyler

2. Using Graphics

Use a diagram to list the events that led to the closing of the Second Bank of the United States.

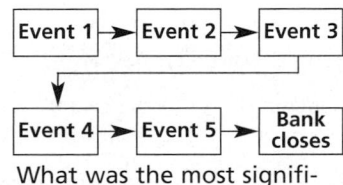

What was the most significant event?

3. Main Ideas

a. Why did Jackson declare war on the Second Bank of the United States?

b. How did Jackson kill the bank?

c. What role did Jackson's popularity play in the elections of 1836 and 1840?

4. Critical Thinking

Comparing What strategy did the Whig Party use in the 1840 election?

THINK ABOUT

- how Harrison was portrayed
- what group of voters it was trying to attract

ACTIVITY OPTIONS

LANGUAGE ARTS

ART

Imagine yourself as a presidential candidate in 1840. Focusing on the economy as an issue, write a campaign **slogan** or create a **banner** to rally support.

TERMS & NAMES

Briefly explain the significance of each of the following.

1. John Quincy Adams
2. Jacksonian democracy
3. spoils system
4. Sequoya
5. Indian Removal Act
6. Trail of Tears
7. secession
8. inflation
9. depression
10. Whig Party

REVIEW QUESTIONS

Politics of the People (pages 369–373)

1. How was Jackson different from earlier presidents?
2. How did Jackson appeal to voters in his election campaign of 1828?

Jackson's Policy Toward Native Americans (pages 374–378)

3. What were Georgia's policies toward Native Americans?
4. What was Jackson's position on Native Americans in the United States?
5. How did the Indian Removal Act affect Native Americans?

Conflicts over States' Rights (pages 379–383)

6. How did the issue of tariffs divide the country?
7. Why did nullification threaten the nation?
8. How was the nullification crisis resolved?

Prosperity and Panic (pages 384–387)

9. Why did Jackson oppose the Second Bank of the United States?
10. What were the effects of Jackson's war on the bank?

CRITICAL THINKING

1. USING YOUR NOTES: FINDING MAIN IDEAS

Use your completed chart to answer the questions.

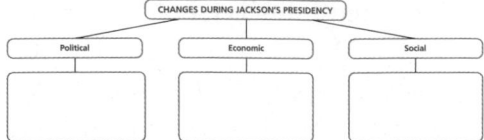

a. What do you think was the most positive change of the Jackson era? Explain.
b. What was the most negative change? Explain.
c. Based on these changes, how would you describe the characteristics of the Jackson era?

2. ANALYZING LEADERSHIP

What was the basis of Andrew Jackson's power as president?

3. APPLYING CITIZENSHIP SKILLS

How did the majority of voters in the presidential elections of 1828 and 1840 exercise their vote in a similar way?

4. THEME: ECONOMICS IN HISTORY

Based on its economic effects, was Jackson's decision to end the national bank a good one? Explain.

5. MAKING INFERENCES

In what ways did Andrew Jackson's policy toward Native Americans reflect bias?

Interact with History

Now that you have read the chapter, do you think the qualities that made Jackson a strong military leader made him a good president? Explain your answer.

VISUAL SUMMARY

Major Issues of Jackson's Presidency

POLICY TOWARD NATIVE AMERICANS	CONFLICT OVER STATES' RIGHTS	WAR ON BANK OF THE UNITED STATES
White settlers wanted Native American lands.	Sectional differences developed.	Second Bank of the United States had economic and political power.
Jackson proposed Indian Removal Act of 1830.	Jackson supported strong central government.	Jackson opposed bank and vetoed renewal of its charter.
Thousands of Native Americans removed to Indian Territory.	South Carolina threatened to secede over tariff issue, but compromise reached.	Bank driven out of business, but Jackson's policies eventually led to inflation and depression.

Use the graph and your knowledge of U.S. history to answer questions 1 and 2.

Additional Test Practice, pp. S1–S33.

Voter Participation, 1824 & 1828 Elections

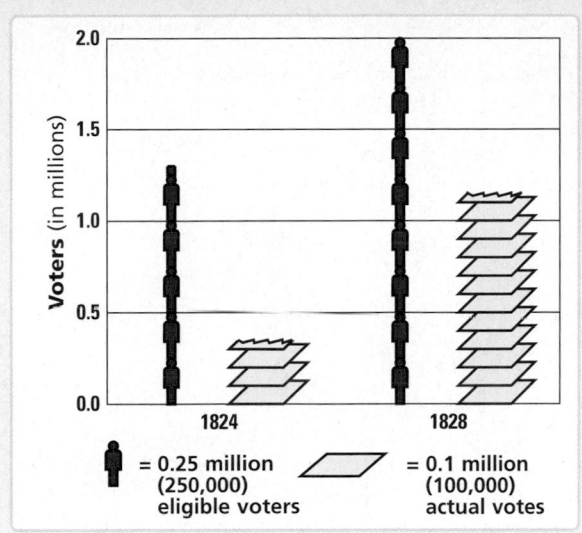

Source: *Historical Statistics of the United States*

Key:
👤 = 0.25 million (250,000) eligible voters

▱ = 0.1 million (100,000) actual votes

1. What does the red body figure represent on the graph?
   A. .01 million eligible voters
   B. .25 million eligible voters
   C. .01 million actual voters
   D. .25 million actual voters

2. Approximately what percentage of eligible voters cast their ballots in 1828?
   A. 15 percent
   B. 30 percent
   C. 60 percent
   D. 90 percent

In this speech Daniel Webster is speaking out against nullification. Use the quotation and your knowledge of U.S. history to answer question 3.

PRIMARY SOURCE

When my eyes shall be turned to behold for the last time the sun in heaven, may I not see him shining on the broken and dishonored fragments of a once glorious Union. . . . Liberty and Union, now and forever, one and inseparable!

Daniel Webster, a speech in the U.S. Senate, January 26, 1830

3. Which sentence sums up Webster's point of view?
   A. A divided Union would be an impressive sight.
   B. Webster has much to do before he dies.
   C. Environmental protection laws are important.
   D. A strong federal government is best for all states.

ⓘ **TEST PRACTICE**
CLASSZONE.COM

ALTERNATIVE ASSESSMENT

1. 📝 WRITING ABOUT HISTORY

Write an **editorial** to convince voters to select the Whig candidate in 1840, William Henry Harrison. Focus on the beliefs and image of the Whig party as well as on personal characteristics of Harrison.

- A good editorial supports an opinion with facts.
- Read editorials from a local newspaper to become familiar with the persuasive language.

2. COOPERATIVE LEARNING

Working in a small group, help plan and write a proposal outlining a solution to the problems between white settlers and Native Americans in the southeast in the early 1800s. List ideas and identify their positives and negatives. Divide the tasks of outlining, writing, revising, and presenting your plan to the class.

INTEGRATED TECHNOLOGY

DESIGNING A POLITICAL CAMPAIGN WEB SITE

Plan a Web site for candidate Andrew Jackson for the 1828 presidential campaign. Use the Internet and library resources to locate information about Jackson's personal and political life.

- Design the Web site to include biographical facts and photographs.
- Locate quotations from speeches and other primary sources. Include them to present Jackson's views on the major issues surrounding the campaign.
- Locate appropriate links for visitors to the Web site.

For more about Andrew Jackson . . .

ⓘ **INTERNET ACTIVITY**
CLASSZONE.COM

CHAPTER 13

Manifest Destiny 1810–1853

Section 1
Trails West

Section 2
The Texas Revolution

Section 3
The War with Mexico

Section 4
The California Gold Rush

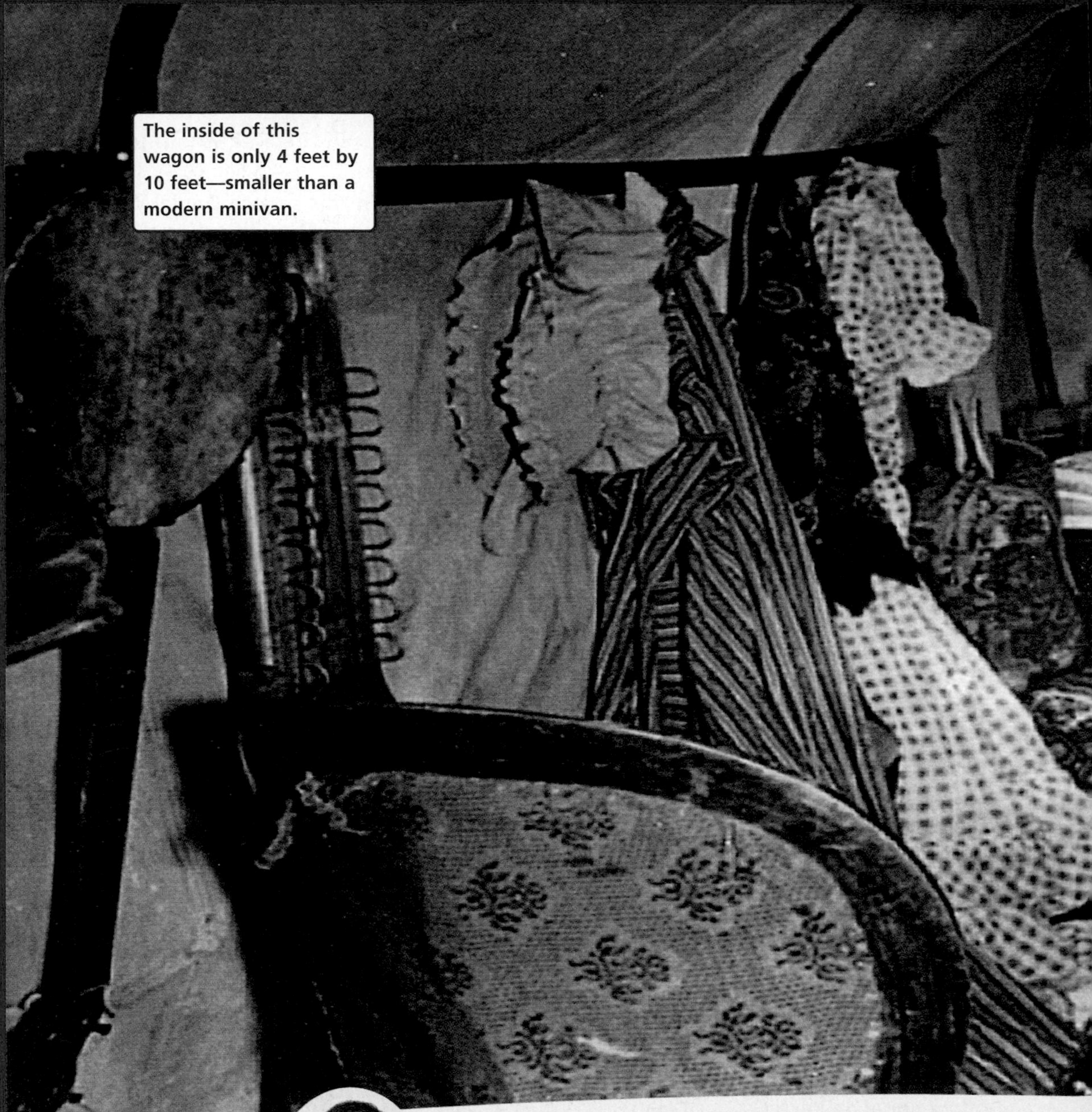

The inside of this wagon is only 4 feet by 10 feet—smaller than a modern minivan.

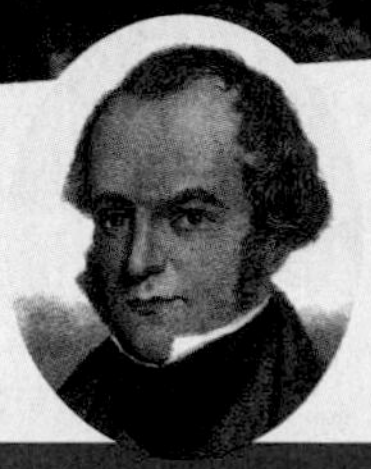

USA
World
1810

1815
Napoleon defeated at Waterloo.

1821
Stephen Austin settles in Texas.

1821
Mexico gains independence from Spain.

1824
Jedediah Smith finds South Pass.

1828
Andrew Jackson is elected president.

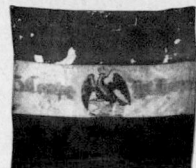

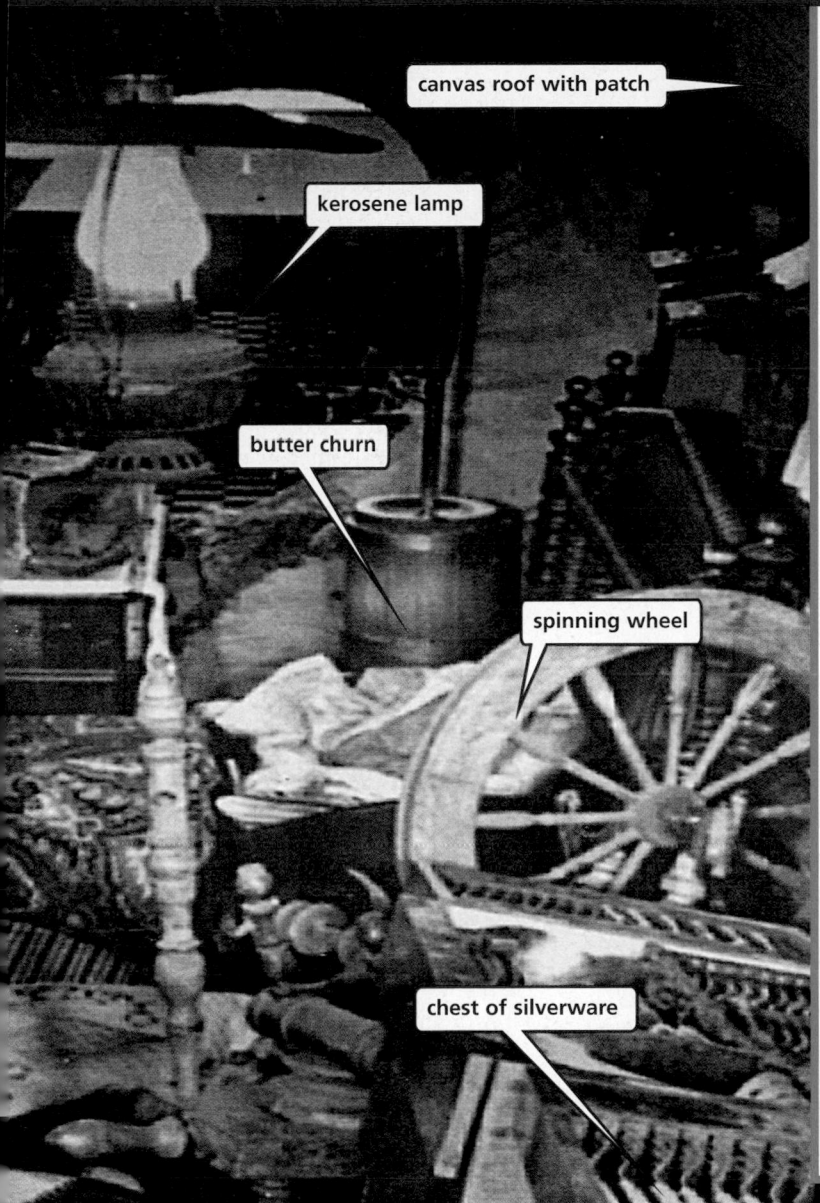

canvas roof with patch

kerosene lamp

butter churn

spinning wheel

chest of silverware

The year is 1844, and you live on a small rocky farm in Massachusetts. Your family has decided to move to Oregon to gain cheap, fertile land. Your father says this move will make your family better off—and give you a better future.

What might you gain or lose by going west?

What Do You Think?

- What do you think daily life on the trail west might be like?
- What might be the greatest obstacles that you face?
- Notice the necessities packed in this crowded wagon. What might have been left behind?

RESEARCH LINKS
CLASSZONE.COM
Visit the Chapter 13 links for more information about the westward movement.

1832
Chief Black Hawk leads Sauk rebellion. Andrew Jackson is reelected.

1836
Martin Van Buren is elected president.

1839
Opium War fought in China.

1840
Benito Juárez leads reform movement in Mexico.

1841
John Tyler becomes president.

1844
James Polk is elected president.

1847
Mormons migrate to Utah.

1847
Liberia, established by a former American slave, proclaimed an independent nation.

1848
Zachary Taylor is elected president.

1853
United States makes Gadsden Purchase.

1853

Reading Strategy: Categorizing Information

What Do You Know?

What do you think of when you hear the phrase "the West"?
Who do you think moved west in the early 1800s?
What do you think drew them to the West?

Think About
- what you've learned about the West from movies or travel
- reasons that people move to new places today
- your responses to the Interact with History about going West (see page 391)

What Do You Want to Know?

What questions do you have about the westword movement of the 1800s? Write those questions in your notebook before you read the chapter.

Wagons, like the one in this modern photograph, carried many settlers west.

Categorizing Information

To help you understand and remember historical information, learn to categorize. Categorizing means organizing information into groups. The chart below will help you categorize the information in this chapter about the westward movement. Use the chart to categorize information about what groups went west, why they went, and what events brought each territory into the United States.

S See Skillbuilder Handbook, page R6.

 Taking Notes

	Types of people who traveled there	Why they went there	Key events that brought the territory into the United States
New Mexico			
Utah			
Oregon			
Texas			
California			

Trails West

MAIN IDEA	WHY IT MATTERS NOW	TERMS & NAMES
Thousands of settlers followed trails through the West to gain land and a chance to make a fortune.	This migration brought Americans to the territories that became New Mexico, Oregon, and Utah.	Jedediah Smith Santa Fe Trail mountain man Oregon Trail Jim Beckwourth Mormon land speculator Brigham Young

ONE AMERICAN'S STORY

The mountain man **Jedediah Smith** was leading an expedition to find a route through the Rocky Mountains when a grizzly bear attacked. The bear seized Smith's head in its mouth, shredded his face, and partially tore off one ear. Smith's men chased the bear away. Jim Clyman recalled the scene.

Jedediah Smith

A VOICE FROM THE PAST

I asked [Smith] what was best. He said, "One or two go for water and if you have a needle and thread get it out and sew up my wounds around my head." . . . I told him I could do nothing for his ear. "Oh, you must try to stitch it up some way or other," said he. Then I put in my needle and stitched it through and through.

Jim Clyman, quoted in *The West,* by Geoffrey C. Ward

Ten days after this attack, Jedediah Smith was ready to continue exploring. Smith was one of the daring fur trappers and explorers known as **mountain men**. The mountain men opened up the West by discovering the best trails through the Rockies. In this section, you will learn about the trails—and why pioneers followed them west.

Mountain Men and the Rendezvous

Mountain men spent most of the year alone, trapping small animals such as beavers. Easterners wanted beaver furs to make the men's hats that were in fashion at the time. To obtain furs, mountain men roamed the Great Plains and the Far West, the regions between the Mississippi River and the Pacific Ocean, and set traps in icy mountain streams.

Because of their adventures, mountain men such as Jedediah Smith and **Jim Beckwourth** became famous as rugged loners. However, they were not as independent as the legends have portrayed them. Instead, they were connected economically to the businessmen who bought their furs.

Taking Notes

Use your chart to take notes about New Mexico, Oregon, and Utah.

	Types of people who traveled there
New Mexico	
Utah	
Oregon	
Texas	
California	

Jim Beckwourth was born in slavery and set free by his owner. At the age of 25, Beckwourth joined a group of fur traders going west and in time became a daring mountain man.

For several years, Beckwourth lived with a Crow tribe. Later, he worked as an army scout and gold prospector. In 1850, he discovered a mountain pass that became the route into present-day northern California. This pass is still called Beckwourth Pass.

What was Beckwourth's most important contribution to the westward movement?

One businessman, William Henry Ashley, created a trading arrangement called the rendezvous system. Under this system, individual trappers came to a pre-arranged site for a rendezvous with traders from the east. The trappers bought supplies from those traders and paid them in furs. The rendezvous took place every summer from 1825 to 1840. In that year, silk hats replaced beaver hats as the fashion, and the fur trade died out.

Mountain Men Open the West

During the height of the fur trade, mountain men worked some streams so heavily that they killed off the animals. This forced the trappers to search for new streams where beaver lived. The mountain men's explorations provided Americans with some of the earliest firsthand knowledge of the Far West. This knowledge, and the trails the mountain men blazed, made it possible for later pioneers to move west.

For example, thousands of pioneers used South Pass, the wide valley through the Rockies that Jedediah Smith had publicized. Smith learned of this pass, in present-day Wyoming, from Native Americans. Unlike the high northern passes used by Lewis and Clark, South Pass was low, so snow did not block it as often as it blocked higher passes. Also, because South Pass was wide and less steep, wagon trails could run through it.

Smith wrote to his brother that he wanted to help people in need: "It is for this that I go for days without eating, and am pretty well satisfied if I can gather a few roots, a few snails, . . . a piece of horseflesh, or a fine roasted dog."

Vocabulary
rendezvous
(RAHN•day•voo):
meeting; from
a French word
meaning "present
yourselves"

Reading **History**
A. Reading a Map Find South Pass on the map on page 395. Notice which two trails used that pass.

The Lure of the West

Few of the people who went west shared Smith's noble motive. To many, the West with its vast stretches of land offered a golden chance to make money. The Louisiana Purchase had doubled the size of the United States, and some Americans wanted to take the land away from Native Americans who inhabited this territory.

People called **land speculators** bought huge areas of land. To speculate means to buy something in the hope that it will increase in value. If land value did go up, speculators divided their land holdings into smaller sections. They made great profits by selling those sections to the thousands of settlers who dreamed of owning their own farms.

Manufacturers and merchants soon followed the settlers west. They hoped to earn money by making and selling items that farmers needed. Other people made the trip to find jobs or to escape people to whom they owed money.

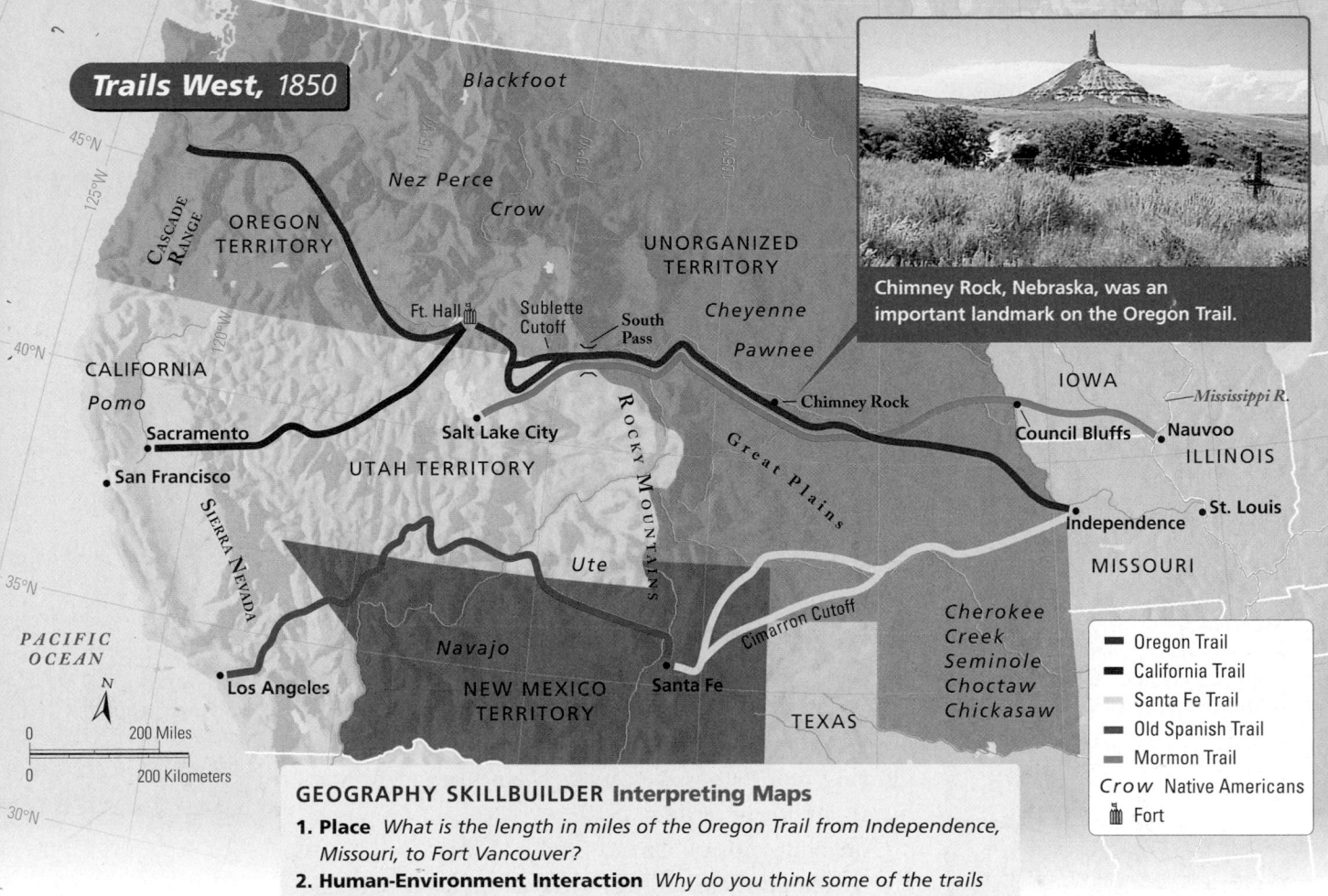

Trails West, 1850

Blackfoot

Nez Perce
Crow

OREGON TERRITORY

CASCADE RANGE

Ft. Hall · Sublette Cutoff · South Pass

UNORGANIZED TERRITORY

Cheyenne

Pawnee

CALIFORNIA

Pomo

Sacramento

San Francisco

SIERRA NEVADA

Salt Lake City

UTAH TERRITORY

ROCKY MOUNTAINS

Great Plains

Chimney Rock

IOWA

Mississippi R.

Council Bluffs · Nauvoo

ILLINOIS

Independence · St. Louis

MISSOURI

Ute

PACIFIC OCEAN

N

Navajo

Los Angeles

NEW MEXICO TERRITORY

Santa Fe

Cimarron Cutoff

TEXAS

Cherokee
Creek
Seminole
Choctaw
Chickasaw

0 ————— 200 Miles
0 ————— 200 Kilometers

Chimney Rock, Nebraska, was an important landmark on the Oregon Trail.

Legend
- ■ Oregon Trail
- ■ California Trail
- Santa Fe Trail
- ■ Old Spanish Trail
- ■ Mormon Trail
- *Crow* Native Americans
- 🏭 Fort

GEOGRAPHY SKILLBUILDER Interpreting Maps

1. **Place** What is the length in miles of the Oregon Trail from Independence, Missouri, to Fort Vancouver?
2. **Human-Environment Interaction** Why do you think some of the trails ran along rivers?

The Trail to Santa Fe

Traders also traveled west in search of markets. After Mexico gained independence from Spain in 1821, it opened its borders to American traders, whom Spain had kept out. In response, the Missouri trader William Becknell set out with hardware, cloth, and china for Santa Fe, capital of the Mexican province of New Mexico. By doing so, he opened the **Santa Fe Trail**, which led from Missouri to Santa Fe. Once in Santa Fe, he made a large profit because the New Mexicans were eager for new merchandise.

When Becknell returned to Missouri weeks later, a curious crowd met him. One man picked up one of Becknell's bags and slit it open with a knife. As gold and silver coins spilled onto the street, the onlookers gasped. The news spread that New Mexico was a place where traders could become rich.

The following spring, Becknell headed to Santa Fe again. This time he loaded his trade goods into covered wagons, which Westerners called prairie schooners. Their billowing white canvas tops made them look like schooners, or sailing ships.

Becknell could not haul wagons over the mountain pass he had used on his first trip to Santa Fe. Instead, he found a cutoff, a shortcut that avoided steep slopes but passed through a deadly desert to the south. As his traders crossed the burning sands, they ran out of water. Crazed by

Reading **History**

B. Making Inferences What do you think other Missourians might decide to do after seeing Becknell's wealth?

daily *life*

DINNER ON THE TRAIL

To add to their limited supplies, pioneers on the trail gathered berries and wild onions. They also hunted buffalo and small game. Below is a recipe that many might have used.

Fricasseed Squirrel
1 squirrel, skinned
3 slices of bacon, chopped
1 tablespoon chopped onions
2 teaspoons lemon juice
⅓ cup water
salt, pepper, & flour
Cut squirrel in pieces. Rub pieces with salt, pepper, and flour. Fry with bacon for 30 minutes. Add onion, lemon juice, and water. Cover tightly. Cook for 1½ hours.

Nebraska Centennial First Ladies Cookbook

thirst, they lopped off mules' ears and killed their dogs to drink the animals' blood. Finally, the men found a stream. The water saved them from death, and they reached Santa Fe.

Becknell returned home with another huge profit. Before long, hundreds of traders and prairie schooners braved the cutoff to make the 800-mile journey from Missouri to New Mexico each year.

Oregon Fever

Hundreds of settlers also began migrating west on the **Oregon Trail,** which ran from Independence, Missouri, to the Oregon Territory. The first whites to cross the continent to Oregon were missionaries, such as Marcus and Narcissa Whitman in 1836. At that time, the United States and Britain were locked in an argument about which country owned Oregon. To the Whitmans' great disappointment, they made few converts among the Native Americans. However, their glowing reports of Oregon's rich land began to attract other American settlers.

Amazing stories spread about Oregon. The sun always shone there. Wheat grew as tall as a man. One tale claimed that pigs were "running about, . . . round and fat, and already cooked, with knives and forks sticking in them so you can cut off a slice whenever you are hungry."

Such stories tempted many people to make the 2,000-mile journey to Oregon. In 1843, nearly 1,000 people traveled from Missouri to Oregon. The next year, twice as many came. "The Oregon Fever has broken out," observed a Boston newspaper, "and is now raging."

Vocabulary
converts: people who accept a new religious belief

One Family Heads West

The experiences of the Sager family show how difficult the trail could be. In 1844, Henry Sager, his wife, and six children left Missouri to find cheap, fertile land in Oregon. They had already moved four times in the past four years. Henry's daughter Catherine explained her family's moves.

A VOICE FROM THE PAST

Father was one of those restless men who are not content to remain in one place long at a time. . . . [He] had been talking of going to Texas. But mother, hearing much said about the healthfulness of Oregon, preferred to go there.

Catherine Sager, quoted in *The West,* by Geoffrey C. Ward

The Oregon Trail was dangerous, so pioneers joined wagon trains. They knew their survival would depend on cooperation. Before setting out, the wagon train members agreed on rules and elected leaders to enforce them.

Even so, life on the trail was full of hardship. The Sagers had barely begun the trip when Mrs. Sager gave birth to her seventh child. Two

months later, nine-year-old Catherine fell under a moving wagon, which crushed her left leg. Later, "camp fever" killed both of the Sager parents.

Even though the Sager parents had died, the other families in the train cooperated to help the Sager orphans make it to Oregon. There, the Whitmans agreed to adopt them. When Narcissa met them, Catherine recalled, "We thought as we shyly looked at her that she was the prettiest woman we had ever seen."

*Reading*History
C. Finding Main Ideas What difficulties did families like the Sagers face?

The Mormon Trail

While most pioneers went west in search of wealth, one group migrated for religious reasons. The **Mormons,** who settled Utah, were members of the Church of Jesus Christ of Latter-Day Saints. Joseph Smith had founded this church in upstate New York in 1830. The Mormons lived in close communities, worked hard, shared their goods, and prospered.

The Mormons, though, also made enemies. Some people reacted angrily to the Mormons' teachings. They saw the Mormon practice of polygamy—allowing a man to have more than one wife at a time—as immoral. Others objected to their holding property in common.

*Reading*History
D. Analyzing Causes Why did Brigham Young lead the Mormons to Utah?

In 1844, an anti-Mormon mob in Illinois killed Smith. **Brigham Young,** the next Mormon leader, moved his people out of the United States. His destination was Utah, then part of Mexico. In this desolate region, he hoped his people would be left to follow their faith in peace.

In 1847, about 1,600 Mormons followed part of the Oregon Trail to Utah. There they built a new settlement by the Great Salt Lake. Because Utah has little rainfall, the Mormons had to work together to build dams and canals. These structures captured water in the hills and carried it to the farms in the valleys below. Through teamwork, they made their desert homeland bloom.

In the meantime, changes were taking place in Texas. As you will read in Section 2, Americans had been moving into that Mexican territory, too.

Section 1 Assessment

1. Terms & Names

Explain the significance of:
- Jedediah Smith
- mountain man
- Jim Beckwourth
- land speculator
- Santa Fe Trail
- Oregon Trail
- Mormon
- Brigham Young

2. Using Graphics

Use a cluster diagram like the one shown to review details about the trails west.

Which trail would you have wanted to travel? Why?

3. Main Ideas

a. How did the mountain men open up the West for later settlement?

b. What are two examples of pioneer groups who used cooperation to overcome hardship?

c. What economic and social forces drew people to the West?

4. Critical Thinking

Drawing Conclusions Of all the hardships faced by people who went west, what do you think was the worst? Explain.

THINK ABOUT
- the mountain men
- William Becknell
- the Sagers
- the Mormons

ACTIVITY OPTIONS

LANGUAGE ARTS

ART

Research a pioneer from this section and either write a **letter** from his or her point of view to a friend or illustrate a **journal entry** with sights from your journey.

Survive the Oregon Trail!

You are part of a wagon train heading west on the Oregon Trail. During your journey, you will cross endless flat prairies and mountains that climb more steeply than a staircase. You will suffer through blazing heat and icy snowstorms. Food is scarce in the land you travel through—and human settlements are even more scarce.

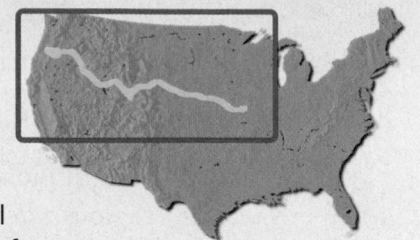

COOPERATIVE LEARNING On this page are three challenges you will face on your journey. Working with a small group, create a solution for each challenge. To help your group work together, assign a task to each group member. You will find helpful information in the Data File. Be prepared to present your solutions to the class.

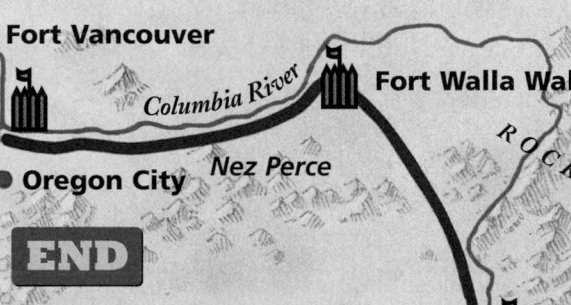

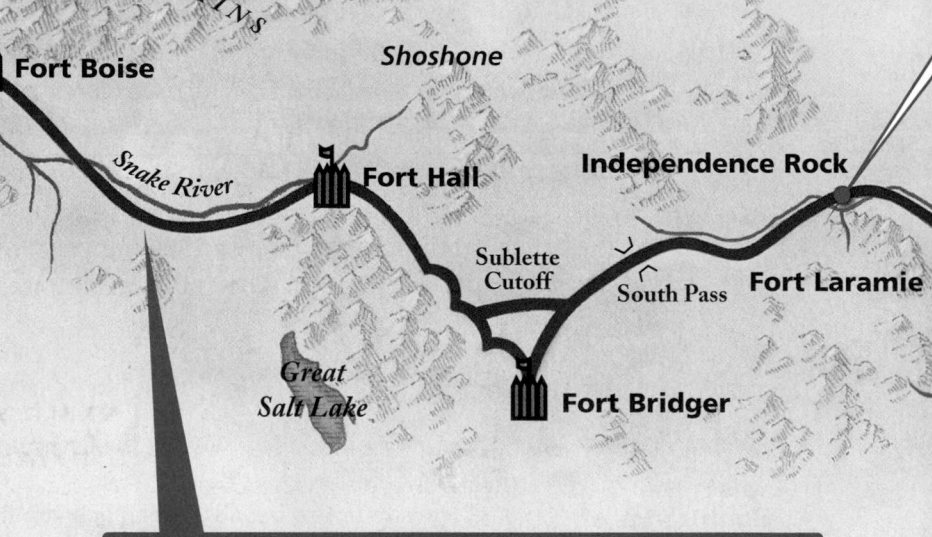

Fort Vancouver

Columbia River

Fort Walla Walla

Nez Perce

● **Oregon City**

END

ROCKY MOUNTAINS

Fort Boise

Shoshone

Snake River

Fort Hall

Independence Rock

Sublette Cutoff

South Pass

Fort Laramie

Great Salt Lake

Fort Bridger

SCIENCE CHALLENGE

"The most terrible mountains"

One pioneer called the Rockies "the most terrible mountains for steepness." Your oxen have struggled for hours to pull your wagon up a steep slope. Now you have to go down the other side without crashing—and wagon wheels have no brakes. How will you slow your descent? Use the Data File for help. Present your ideas using one of these options:

• Write instructions for climbing and descending the mountain.

• Illustrate your solution in a how-to diagram.

CIVICS CHALLENGE

"A thieving scoundrel"

You wake one morning to the sound of shouting. One of the men in the wagon train has been caught stealing another family's ox—to replace an ox that died from drinking bad water. The wagon train leader asks you to help decide how to punish the thief. Present your decision using one of these options:

• As a group, role-play a discussion of what the punishment should be.

• Write an explanation of a punishment to the wagon train leader.

HEALTH CHALLENGE

"A grand blow-out"

On July 4, your wagon train stops near Independence Rock for "a grand blow-out" to celebrate your progress. Each family will bring a dish to the party. What will you cook that is tasty and nutritious? You might use supplies from your wagon and berries or animals from the area. Look at the Data File for help. Present your choice using one of these options:

- Draw a picture of your dish and describe it.
- Write an original recipe.

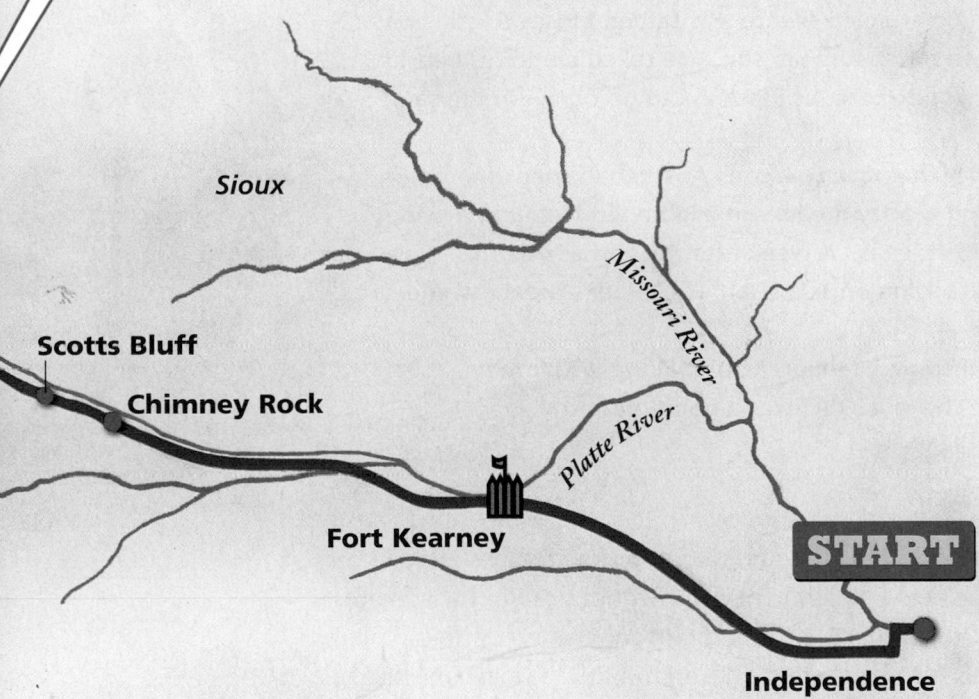

Sioux

Scotts Bluff

Chimney Rock

Fort Kearney

Missouri River

Platte River

START

Independence

ACTIVITY WRAP-UP

Present to the class Using the model shown here, ask and answer questions about geographic patterns in the West. Choose the best questions to present to the class.

The Journey

Distance: 2,000 miles

Length: 4–6 months

Average daily distance: 12–15 miles

Best time to travel: April–September

The Wagon

Size of box: 4 x 10 feet

Load: 1,600–2,500 pounds

Oxen needed per wagon: 4–8

Animals Taken

oxen, horses, dairy cows, cattle, chickens, mules, pigs, dogs, cats

Food Supplies

flour, corn meal, salt, baking soda, sugar, crackers, dried beans, rice, dried fruit, bacon, coffee, vinegar

Cooking Equipment

Dutch oven, large kettle, frying pan, bread pan, coffee grinder, rolling pin, tin cups and plates, water kegs, knives, spoons

Other Equipment

bedding, spare wagon parts, tar, rope, chains, pulleys, tools, fishing poles, guns, ammunition, matches, soap, medicines

Trail Hazards

Worst discomforts: heat, cold, wind, rain, dust, mud, mosquitoes, hunger, thirst

Biggest killer: disease

Most common accidents: shooting, drowning, crushing by wagon wheels, injuries from animals

For more about the Oregon Trail . . .

 **RESEARCH LINKS** CLASSZONE.COM

The Texas Revolution

MAIN IDEA	WHY IT MATTERS NOW	TERMS & NAMES
American and Tejano citizens led Texas to independence from Mexico.	The diverse culture of Texas has developed from the contributions of many different groups.	Stephen Austin / William Travis Tejano / Juan Seguín Antonio López de Santa Anna / Battle of the Alamo Lone Star Republic Sam Houston

ONE AMERICAN'S STORY

Son of a bankrupt Missouri mine owner, **Stephen Austin** read his mother's letter, written in 1821, in stunned silence. His father, Moses Austin, was dead. In his last moments, she told her son, "He called me to his bedside, . . . he begged me to tell you to take his place . . . to go on . . . in the same way he would have done."

Stephen knew what that meant. Moses Austin had spent the last years of his life chasing a crazy dream. He had hoped to found a colony for Americans in Spanish Texas. A week after his father's death, Stephen Austin was standing on Texas soil. His father's dream would become his destiny.

This section explains how Stephen Austin, along with others, worked hard to make the lands of Texas a good place to live.

Stephen Austin

Taking Notes

Use your chart to take notes about Texas.

	Types of people who traveled there
New Mexico	
Utah	
Oregon	
Texas	
California	

Spanish Texas

The Spanish land called *Tejas* (Tay•HAHS) bordered the United States territory called Louisiana. The land was rich and desirable. It had forests in the east, rich soil for growing corn and cotton, and great grassy plains for grazing animals. It also had rivers leading to natural ports on the Gulf of Mexico. It was home to Plains and Pueblo Native Americans. Even though *Tejas* was a state in the Spanish colony of New Spain, it had few Spanish settlers. Around 1819, Spanish soldiers drove off Americans trying to claim those lands as a part of the Louisiana Purchase.

In 1821, only about 4,000 *Tejanos* (Tay•HAH•nohs) lived in Texas. *Tejanos* are people of Spanish heritage who consider Texas their home. The Comanche, Apache, and other tribes fought fiercely against Spanish settlement of Texas. The Spanish officials wanted many more settlers to move to Texas. They hoped that new colonists would help to defend against Native Americans and Americans who illegally sneaked into Texas.

Vocabulary
empresarios:
individuals who
agreed to recruit
settlers for the
land

To attract more people to Texas, the Spanish government offered huge tracts of land to *empresarios*. But they were unable to attract Spanish settlers. So, when Moses Austin asked for permission to start a colony in Texas, Spain agreed. Austin was promised a large section of land. He had to agree that settlers on his land had to follow Spanish laws.

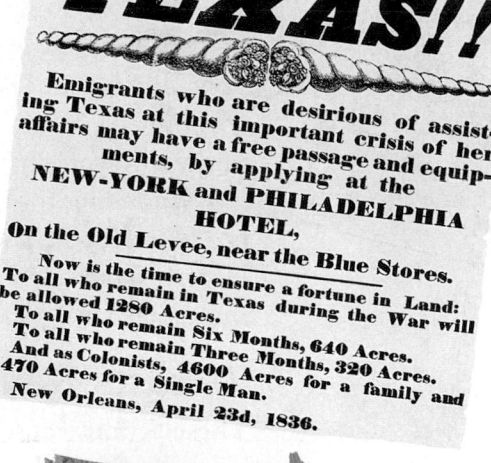

Mexican Independence Changes Texas

Shortly after Stephen Austin arrived in Texas in 1821, Mexico successfully gained its independence from Spain. *Tejas* was now a part of Mexico. With the change in government, the Spanish land grant given to Austin's father was worthless. Stephen Austin traveled to Mexico City to persuade the new Mexican government to let him start his colony. It took him almost a year to get permission. And the Mexican government would consent only if the new settlers agreed to become Mexican citizens and members of the Roman Catholic Church.

Between 1821 and 1827, Austin attracted 297 families to his new settlement. These original Texas settler families are known as the "Old Three Hundred." He demanded evidence that each family head was moral, worked hard, and did not drink. So law-abiding were his colonists that Austin could write to a new settler, "You will be astonished to see all our houses with no other fastening than a wooden pin or door latch."

The success of Austin's colony attracted more land speculators and settlers to Texas from the United States. Some were looking for a new life, some were escaping from the law, and others were looking for a chance to grow rich. By 1830, the population had swelled to about 30,000, with Americans outnumbering the *Tejanos* six to one.

Posters such as the one above encouraged Americans from the East to settle in Texas. Some people scrawled G.T.T. on their doors to indicate they had "gone to Texas."

Rising Tensions in Texas

Reading **History**
A. Analyzing
Causes Why was
there growing
tension between
Americans and
Tejanos?

As more and more Americans settled in Texas, tensions between them and the *Tejanos* increased. Used to governing themselves, Americans resented following Mexican laws. Since few Americans spoke Spanish, they were unhappy that all official documents had to be in that language. Slave owners were especially upset when Mexico outlawed slavery in 1829. They wanted to maintain slavery so they could grow cotton. Austin persuaded the government to allow slave owners to keep their slaves.

On the other hand, the *Tejanos* found the Americans difficult to live with, too. *Tejanos* thought that the Americans believed they were superior and deserved special privileges. The Americans seemed unwilling to adapt to Mexican laws.

The Mexican government sent an official to Texas to investigate the tensions. He was not happy with what he found. In 1829, he reported to his government, "I am warning you to take timely measures . . . Texas could throw this whole nation into revolution." His advice turned out to be right.

Responding to the warnings, the Mexican government cracked down on Texas. First, it closed the state to further American immigration. Next, it required Texans to pay taxes for the first time. Finally, to enforce these new laws, the government sent more Mexican troops to Texas.

Texans Revolt Against Mexico

These actions caused angry protests. Some Texans even talked of breaking away from Mexico. Most, however, listened to Austin, who remained loyal to Mexico. In 1833, Austin set off for Mexico City with a petition. This document listed reforms supported by both Americans and *Tejanos*. The most important request was that Texas become a self-governing state within Mexico.

In Mexico City, Austin met General **Antonio López de Santa Anna,** the Mexican president. At first, the general agreed to most of the reforms in Austin's petition. But then Santa Anna learned of a letter Austin had written. The letter said that if the changes weren't approved Austin would support breaking away from Mexican rule. This was rebellion! The general had Austin jailed for an entire year. The Texans were furious and ready to rebel.

Santa Anna's answer to talk of rebellion was to send more troops to Texas. In late September 1835, Mexican soldiers marched to the town of Gonzales. They had orders to seize a cannon used by the Texans for protection against Native Americans. Texas volunteers had hung a flag on the big gun that said, "Come and Take It."

The Mexican troops failed to capture the cannon. Two months later, Texans drove Mexican troops out of an old mission in San Antonio that was used as a fortress. It was called the Alamo. Among the Texas volunteers were free African Americans such as Hendrick Arnold and Greenbury Logan. Angered by these insults, Santa Anna and 6,000 troops headed for Texas.

The Fight for the Alamo

On March 1–2, 1836, Texans met at a settlement called Washington-on-the-Brazos to decide what to do about Santa Anna's troops. They believed they could do only one thing: to declare Texas a free and independent republic. **Sam Houston,** the only man at the meeting with military experience, was placed in command of the Texas army.

America's HERITAGE

REMEMBER THE ALAMO!

Today the Alamo, shown below, is again under siege. Moisture seeps into the limestone walls and causes them to crumble. Many people view the mission as a memorial to Americans' willingness to fight for freedom, so a Texas group has begun attempts to preserve the Alamo from further damage. The Alamo looks quite different from the battle site of 1836. The famous bell-shaped front was added in the 1850s.

*Reading*History
B. Summarizing
What three actions did the Mexican government take to control Texas?

*Reading*History
C. Analyzing Causes What Texan actions moved Santa Anna to head toward Texas?

The Texas army hardly existed. At that moment, there were two small forces ready to stand up to Santa Anna's army. One was a company of 420 men, led by James Fannin, stationed at Goliad, a fort in southeast Texas. The second was a company of 183 volunteers at the Alamo. Headed by **William Travis,** this small force included such famous frontiersmen as Davy Crockett and Jim Bowie. In addition, **Juan Seguín** (wahn seh•GEEN) led a band of 25 *Tejanos* in support of revolt.

On February 23, 1836, Santa Anna's troops surrounded San Antonio. The next day, Mexicans began their siege of the Alamo. Two nights later, Travis scrawled a message to the world.

Reading **History**
D. Making Inferences Why would William Travis address his message to all Americans?

"Remember the Alamo!"
a Texan soldier

> *A VOICE FROM THE PAST*
>
> The enemy has demanded a surrender. . . . I have answered the demand with a cannon shot, and our flag still waves proudly from the walls. I shall never surrender or retreat.
>
> **William Travis,** "To the People of Texas and all the Americans in the World"

Because Juan Seguín spoke Spanish, he was chosen to carry the plea through enemy lines. Seguín got the message through to other Texas defenders. But when he returned, he saw the Alamo in flames.

The Alamo's defenders held off the Mexican attack for 12 violent days. Travis and the defenders stubbornly refused to surrender. On the 13th day, Santa Anna ordered more than 1,800 men to storm the fortress. The Texans met the attackers with a hailstorm of cannon and gun fire. Then suddenly it became strangely quiet. The Texans had run out of ammunition. At day's end, all but five Texans were dead. The **Battle of the Alamo** was over.

HISTORY *through* **ART**

The Battle of the Alamo was so intense that Davy Crockett did not have time to reload his gun, which he called "Betsy." He used it as a club. This print is by a 20th-century illustrator, Frederick Yohn.

What does the print reveal about the battle?

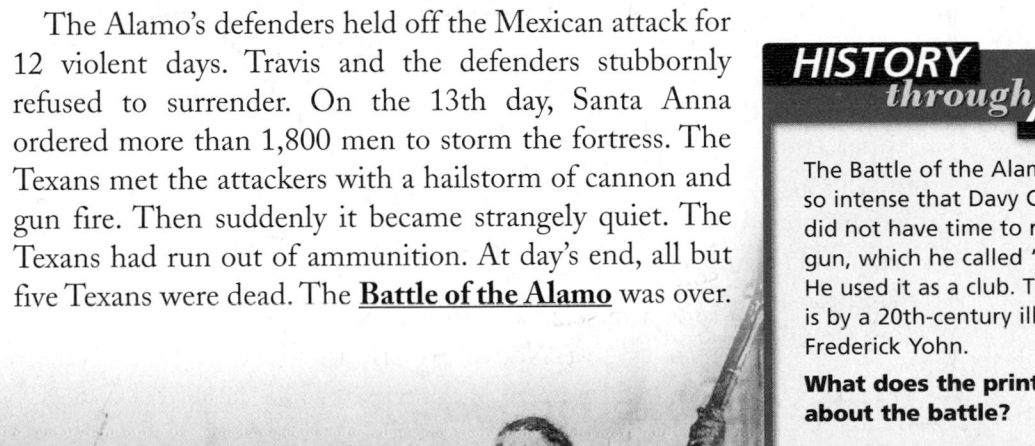

JUAN SEGUÍN
1806–1890

Juan Seguín was a *Tejano* hero of the Texas Revolution. It was Seguín who dashed through enemy lines at the Alamo with a last desperate attempt for aid.

And after the war, it was Seguín who arranged for the remains of the Alamo defenders to be buried with full military honors.

Newcomers to Texas who disliked all *Tejanos* falsely accused Seguín of planning rebellion. Fearing for his life, he fled to Mexico in 1842, there "to seek a refuge amongst my enemies."

SAM HOUSTON
1793–1863

Raised by a widowed mother, Sam Houston grew up in Tennessee. He lived with the Cherokee for about three years. Later, he served in the U.S. Army, in Congress, and as the governor of Tennessee.

"I was a General without an army," wrote Houston, after taking command of the Texas forces in 1836. Yet by the time the war was over, he and his troops had defeated Santa Anna's larger army.

Houston was elected the first president of the Republic of Texas. When Texas became a state, he served as a U.S. senator.

In what ways did the experiences of Seguín and Houston differ?

Those men who had not died in the fighting were executed at Santa Anna's command. A total of 183 Alamo defenders died. A few women and children were not killed. Susanna Dickinson, one of the survivors, was ordered by Santa Anna to tell the story of the Alamo to other Texans. He hoped the story would discourage more rebellion. The slaughter at the Alamo shocked Texans—and showed them how hard they would have to fight for their freedom from Mexico.

Victory at San Jacinto

With Santa Anna on the attack, Texans—both soldiers and settlers—fled eastward. Houston sent a message to the men at Goliad, ordering them to retreat. They were captured by Mexican forces, who executed more than 300. The Texans would not soon forget the massacre at Goliad. But even in retreat and defeat, Houston's army doubled. Now it was a fighting force of 800 angry men. It included *Tejanos,* American settlers, volunteers from the United States, and many free and enslaved African Americans.

In late April, Santa Anna caught up with Houston near the San Jacinto (san juh•SIN•toh) River. Late in the afternoon of April 21, 1836, the Texans advanced on the Mexican army "with the stillness of death." When close to Santa Anna's camp, they raced forward, rifles ready, screaming "Remember the Alamo!" "Remember Goliad!"

In just 18 minutes, the Texans killed more than half of the Mexican army. Santa Anna was forced to sign a treaty giving Texas its freedom. With the Battle of San Jacinto, Texas was now independent.

Reading **History**
E. Reading a Map Use the map on page 405 to see where battles were taking place.

Lone Star Republic

In September 1836, Texans raised a flag with a single star. They adopted a nickname—**Lone Star Republic**—and proclaimed Texas an independent nation. The new nation set up its own army and navy. Sam Houston was elected president of the Lone Star Republic by a landslide.

Many Texans did not want Texas to remain independent for long. They considered themselves Americans and wanted to be a part of the United States. In 1836, the Texas government asked Congress to annex Texas to the Union.

Vocabulary
annex: to join territory to an existing country

Many Northerners objected. They argued that Texas would become a slave state, and they opposed any expansion of slavery. If Texas joined the Union, slave states would outnumber free states and have a voting advantage in Congress. Other people feared that annexing Texas would lead to war with Mexico.

Reading**History**
F. Analyzing Causes Why didn't Congress annex Texas?

In response, Congress voted against annexation. Texas remained an independent republic for almost ten years. In the next section, you will learn that the question of annexing Texas did lead to a war between the United States and Mexico.

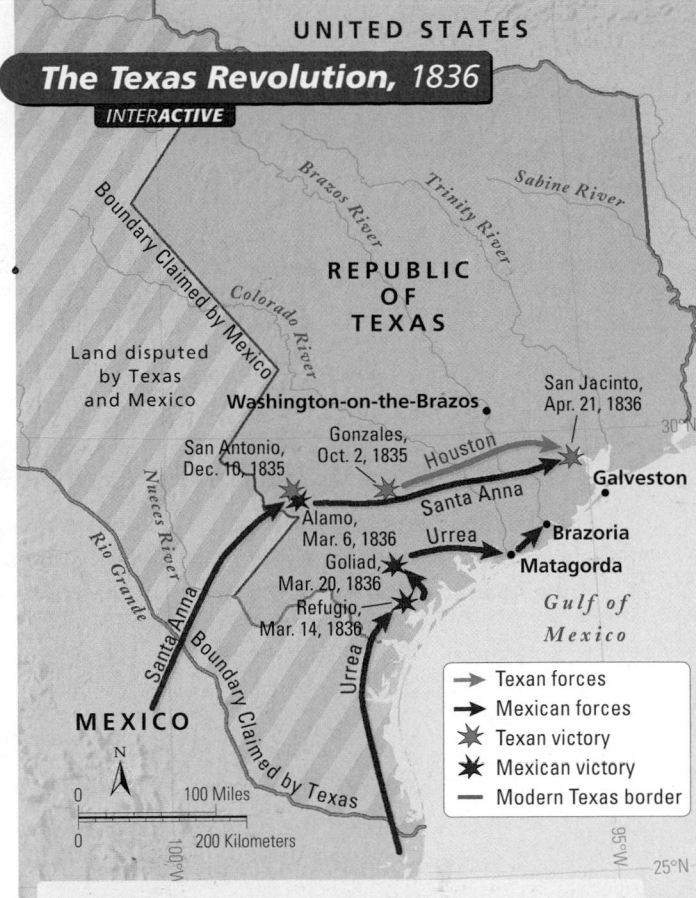

The Texas Revolution, 1836
INTERACTIVE

UNITED STATES

REPUBLIC OF TEXAS

Boundary Claimed by Mexico
Brazos River
Trinity River
Sabine River
Colorado River

Land disputed by Texas and Mexico

Washington-on-the-Brazos

San Jacinto, Apr. 21, 1836

San Antonio, Dec. 10, 1835
Gonzales, Oct. 2, 1835
Houston

Galveston

Alamo, Mar. 6, 1836
Santa Anna
Urrea
Brazoria
Goliad, Mar. 20, 1836
Matagorda
Refugio, Mar. 14, 1836

Gulf of Mexico

Nueces River
Rio Grande

Santa Anna

MEXICO

N

0   100 Miles
0   200 Kilometers

Boundary Claimed by Texas

Urrea

→ Texan forces
→ Mexican forces
✴ Texan victory
✴ Mexican victory
— Modern Texas border

GEOGRAPHY SKILLBUILDER Interpreting Maps
1. **Movement** About how many total miles did Santa Anna travel from Mexico to San Jacinto?
2. **Movement** Look at the distances traveled by Mexican forces and those traveled by the Texans. Which side do you think had an advantage? Explain.

Section 2 Assessment

1. Terms & Names

Explain the significance of:
- Stephen Austin
- *Tejano*
- Antonio López de Santa Anna
- Sam Houston
- William Travis
- Juan Seguín
- Battle of the Alamo
- Lone Star Republic

2. Using Graphics

Use a diagram like the one shown to review events that led to Texan independence and put them in order.

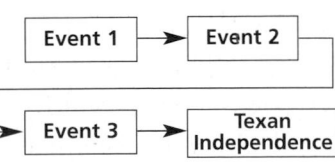

Event 1 → Event 2

Event 3 → Texan Independence

3. Main Ideas

a. Why did Americans want to move to Texas?

b. How did the Mexican government respond to the Texas rebellion?

c. Why did Congress refuse to annex Texas?

4. Critical Thinking

Recognizing Effects How did losing the Battle of the Alamo help the Texans win their independence?

THINK ABOUT
- the Texans' and Americans' shock over the loss of the battle to the Mexicans
- the need to recruit more forces to fight with the Texas army

ACTIVITY OPTIONS

ART
TECHNOLOGY

Research a figure from the Texas Revolution. Create a **trading card** or design that person's **Web page** for the Internet.

The War with Mexico

	MAIN IDEA	WHY IT MATTERS NOW	TERMS & NAMES

MAIN IDEA

The United States expanded its territory westward to stretch from the Atlantic to the Pacific coast.

WHY IT MATTERS NOW

Today, one-third of all Americans live in the areas added to the United States in 1848.

TERMS & NAMES

James K. Polk
manifest destiny
Zachary Taylor
Bear Flag Revolt

Winfield Scott
Treaty of Guadalupe Hidalgo
Mexican Cession

ONE AMERICAN'S STORY

Henry Clay sneered, "Who is **James K. Polk**?" Clay had just learned the name of the man nominated by Democrats to run against him for president in 1844. "A mistake!" answered Washington insiders.

News of Polk's nomination was flashed to the capital by the newly invented telegraph machine. People were convinced that the machine didn't work. How could the Democrats choose Polk? A joke!

Polk was America's first "dark horse," a candidate who received unexpected support. The Democrats had nominated this little-known man only when they could not agree on anyone else.

Still, Polk wasn't a complete nobody. He had been governor of Tennessee and served seven terms in Congress. Polk was committed to national expansion. He vowed to annex Texas and take over Oregon.

When the votes were counted, James Knox Polk became the 11th president of the United States. As you will read in this section, after his election Polk looked for ways to expand the nation.

James Polk

Taking Notes

Use your chart to take notes about Oregon, New Mexico, and California.

	Types of people who traveled there
New Mexico	
Utah	
Oregon	
Texas	
California	

Americans Support Manifest Destiny

The abundance of land in the West seemed to hold great promise for Americans. Although populated with Native Americans and Mexicans, those lands were viewed by white settlers as unoccupied. Many Americans wanted to settle those lands themselves, and they worried about competition from other nations. Mexico occupied the southwest lands, and Britain shared the northwest Oregon Territory with the United States. Many Americans believed that the United States was

destined to stretch across the continent from the Atlantic Ocean to the Pacific Ocean. In 1845, a newspaper editor named John O'Sullivan gave a name to that belief.

A VOICE FROM THE PAST

Our manifest destiny [is] to overspread and possess the whole of the continent which Providence [God] has given us for the development of the great experiment of liberty and . . . self-government.

John O'Sullivan, *United States Magazine and Democratic Review*

*Reading***History**

A. Drawing Conclusions
What were the positives and negatives of the idea of manifest destiny?

John O'Sullivan used the word *manifest* to mean clear or obvious. The word *destiny* means events sure to happen. Therefore, **manifest destiny** suggested that expansion was not only good but bound to happen—even if it meant pushing Mexicans and Native Americans out of the way. After Polk's election in 1844, manifest destiny became government policy.

The term "manifest destiny" was new, but the idea was not. By the 1840s, thousands of Americans had moved into the Oregon Territory. Since 1818, Oregon had been occupied jointly by the United States and Britain. In his campaign, Polk had talked of taking over all of Oregon. "Fifty-four forty or fight!" screamed one of his slogans. The parallel of 54° 40' N latitude was the northern boundary of the shared Oregon Territory.

Oregon, 1846
- British territory under 1846 treaty
- U. S. territory under 1846 treaty

Rather than fight for all of Oregon, however, Polk settled for half. In 1846, the United States and Great Britain agreed to divide Oregon at the 49th parallel. This agreement extended the boundary line already drawn between Canada and the United States. Today this line still serves as the border between much of the United States and Canada.

"Our manifest destiny [is] to . . . possess the whole of the continent."
John O'Sullivan

Troubles with Mexico

Polk had good reason for avoiding war with Britain over Oregon. By 1846, he had much bigger troubles brewing with Mexico over Texas.

In 1845, Congress admitted Texas as a slave state, in spite of Northern objections to the spread of slavery. However, Mexico still claimed Texas as its own. Mexico angrily viewed this annexation as an act of war. To make matters worse, Texas and Mexico could not agree on the official border between them. Texas claimed the Rio Grande, a river south of San Antonio, as its southern boundary. Mexico insisted on the Nueces (noo•AY•sis) River as the border of Texas. The difference in the distance between the two rivers was more than 100 miles at some points. Many thousands of miles of territory were at stake.

*Reading***History**

B. Reading a Map
Use the map on page 408 to find the locations of the disputed border between Texas and Mexico.

Mexico said it would fight to defend its claim. Hoping to settle the dispute peacefully, Polk sent John Slidell, a Spanish-speaking

ambassador, to offer Mexico $25 million for Texas, California, and New Mexico. But Slidell's diplomacy failed.

Believing that the American people supported his expansion plans, Polk wanted to force the issue with Mexico. He purposely ordered General **Zachary Taylor** to station troops on the northern bank of the Rio Grande. This river bank was part of the disputed territory. Viewing this as an act of war, Mexico moved an army into place on the southern bank. On April 25, 1846, a Mexican cavalry unit crossed the Rio Grande. They ambushed an American patrol and killed or wounded 16 American soldiers.

When news of the attack reached Washington, Polk sent a rousing war message to Congress, saying, "Mexico has invaded our territory and shed American blood upon American soil." Two days later, Congress declared war. The War with Mexico had begun. Thousands of volunteers, mostly from western states, rushed to enlist in the army. Santa Anna, who was president of Mexico, built up the Mexican army.

However, Americans had mixed reactions to Polk's call for war. Illinois representative Abraham Lincoln questioned the truthfulness of the president's message and the need to declare war. Northeasterners questioned the justice of men dying in such a war. Slavery became an issue in the debates over the war. Southerners saw expansion into Texas as an opportunity to extend slavery and to increase their power in Congress. To

Reading **History**
C. Analyzing Causes How did the War with Mexico start?

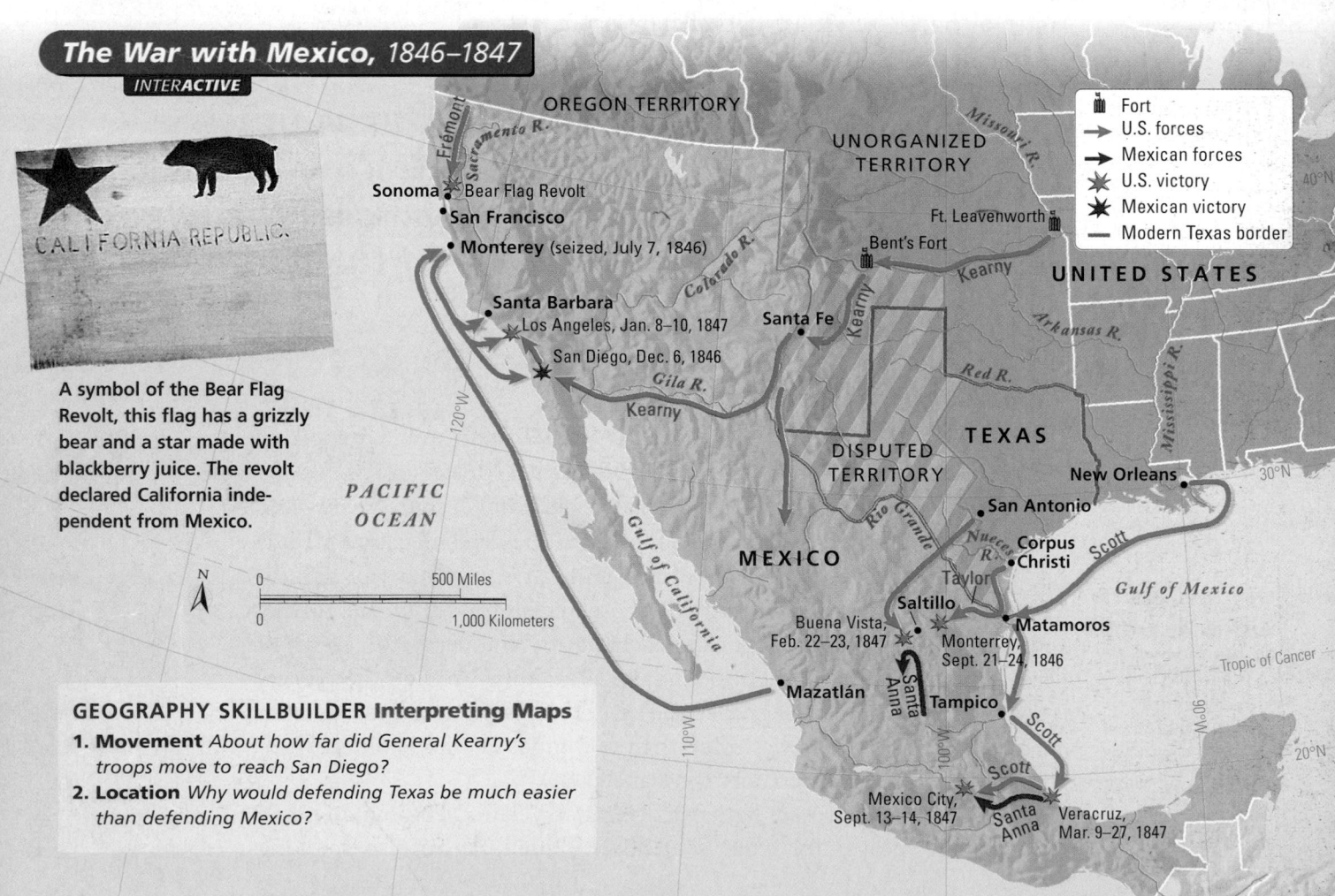

The War with Mexico, 1846–1847
INTERACTIVE

A symbol of the Bear Flag Revolt, this flag has a grizzly bear and a star made with blackberry juice. The revolt declared California independent from Mexico.

GEOGRAPHY SKILLBUILDER Interpreting Maps
1. **Movement** *About how far did General Kearny's troops move to reach San Diego?*
2. **Location** *Why would defending Texas be much easier than defending Mexico?*

prevent this from happening, antislavery representatives introduced a bill to prohibit slavery in any lands taken from Mexico. Frederick Douglass, the abolitionist, summarized the arguments.

A VOICE FROM THE PAST

The determination of our slaveholding President to prosecute the war, and the probability of his success in wringing from the people men and money to carry it on, is made evident, . . . None seem willing to take their stand for peace at all risks; and all seem willing that the war should be carried on in some form or other.

Frederick Douglass in *The North Star,* January 21, 1848

Despite opposition, the United States plunged into war. In May 1846, General Taylor led troops into Mexico. Many Americans thought it would be easy to defeat the Mexicans, and the war would end quickly.

Capturing New Mexico and California

Not long after the war began, General Stephen Kearny (KAHR•nee)— a U.S. Army officer—and his men left Fort Leavenworth, Kansas, with orders to occupy New Mexico. Then they were to continue west to California. As his troops marched along the Santa Fe Trail, they sang songs like this one.

Reading **History**

D. Making Inferences
How does this song support the idea of manifest destiny?

A VOICE FROM THE PAST

Old Colonel Kearny, you can bet,
Will keep the boys in motion,
Till Yankee Land includes the sand
On the Pacific Ocean.

Six weeks and 650 hot and rugged miles later, Kearny's army entered New Mexico. Using persuasion instead of force, he convinced the Mexican troops that he meant to withdraw. This allowed him to take New Mexico without firing a shot. Then Kearny and a small force of soldiers marched on toward California, which had only 8,000 to 12,000 Mexican residents. The remaining force moved south toward Mexico.

In California, Americans led by the explorer John C. Frémont rebelled against Mexican rule in the **Bear Flag Revolt.** They arrested the Mexican commander of Northern California and raised a crude flag showing a grizzly bear sketched in blackberry juice. The rebels declared California independent of Mexico and named it the Republic of California. In the fall, U.S. troops reached California and joined forces with the rebels. Within weeks, Americans controlled all of California.

The Invasion of Mexico

The defeat of Mexico proved far more difficult. The Mexican army was much larger, but the U.S. troops

STRANGE *but* True

SANTA ANNA'S LOST LEG
Santa Anna lost his left leg in a battle with the French. In 1842, he held a funeral for his severed limb. On that day, church and political officials followed the dictator's leg through the streets of Mexico City to its final resting place—an urn placed on a column.

Two years later, an angry mob broke the urn and threw the leg away. The leg was rescued by a loyal soldier who took it home and hid it.

Thirty years later, that soldier visited Santa Anna and returned the bones of his long-lost leg.

Mexican army was much larger, but the U.S. troops were led by well-trained officers. American forces invaded Mexico from two directions.

General Taylor battled his way south from Texas toward the city of Monterrey in northern Mexico. On February 22, 1847, his 4,800 troops met General Santa Anna's 15,000 Mexican soldiers near a ranch called Buena Vista. After the first day of fighting, Santa Anna sent Taylor a note offering him a chance to surrender. Taylor declined. At the end of the second bloody day of fighting, Santa Anna reported that "both armies have been cut to pieces." However, it was Santa Anna who retreated after the Battle of Buena Vista. The war in the north of Mexico was over.

In southern Mexico, fighting continued. A second force led by General **Winfield Scott** landed at Veracruz on the Gulf of Mexico and battled inland toward Mexico City. Outside the capital, Scott met fierce resistance at the castle of Chapultepec (chuh•POOL•tuh•pek). About 1,000 soldiers and 100 young military cadets bravely defended the fortress. Despite their determined resistance, Mexico City fell to Scott in September 1847. As he watched, a Mexican officer sighed and said, "God is a Yankee."

Background
General Winfield Scott had become a national hero during the War of 1812.

The Mexican Cession

On February 2, 1848, the war officially ended with the **Treaty of Guadalupe Hidalgo** (gwah•duh•LOOP•ay hih•DAHL•go). In this treaty, Mexico recognized that Texas was part of the United States, and the

Growth of the United States, 1783–1853

Ceded to Great Britain, 1818

Ceded by Great Britain, 1818

Ceded by Great Britain, Webster-Ashburton Treaty, 1842

CANADA

OREGON TERRITORY
From Great Britain, 1846

LOUISIANA PURCHASE
Bought from France, 1803

MEXICAN CESSION
From Mexico by Treaty of Guadalupe Hidalgo, 1848

From Great Britain by Treaty of Paris, 1783

Original 13 Colonies

PACIFIC OCEAN

ATLANTIC OCEAN

GADSDEN PURCHASE
Bought from Mexico, 1853

TEXAS ANNEXATION
Annexed Independent Republic, 1845

FLORIDA CESSION
From Spain, 1819

Modern U.S. boundaries shown.

Ceded by Spain, 1818

1810 1813 Annexed by United States

Gulf of Mexico

GEOGRAPHY SKILLBUILDER Interpreting Maps

1. **Region** How many states or parts of states were created by all the lands added after Polk's election in 1844?
2. **Region** Which addition to the United States after 1783 added the greatest area of land?

N

0   300 Miles
0   600 Kilometers

*Reading***History**

E. Finding Main Ideas What were the three main parts of the Treaty of Guadalupe Hidalgo?

Rio Grande was the border between the nations. Mexico also ceded, or gave up, a vast region known as the **Mexican Cession.** This area included the present-day states of California, Nevada, Utah, most of Arizona, and parts of New Mexico, Colorado, and Wyoming. Together with Texas, this land amounted to almost one-half of Mexico. The loss was a bitter defeat for Mexico, particularly because many Mexicans felt that the United States had provoked the war in the hope of gaining Mexican territory.

In return, the United States agreed to pay Mexico $15 million. The United States would also pay the $3.25 million of claims U.S. citizens had against Mexico. Finally, it also promised to protect the approximately 80,000 Mexicans living in Texas and the Mexican Cession.

Mexicans living in the United States saw the conquest of their land differently. Suddenly they were a minority in a nation with a strange language, culture, and legal system. At the same time, they would make important contributions to their new country. They taught new settlers how to develop the land for farming, ranching, and mining. A rich new culture resulted from the blend of many cultures in the Mexican Cession.

*Reading***History**

F. Making Inferences Why did the United States pay a large price for the Gadsden Purchase?

"From Sea to Shining Sea"

The last bit of territory added to the continental United States was a strip of land across what is now southern New Mexico and Arizona. The government wanted the land as a location for a southern transcontinental railroad. In 1853, Mexico sold the land—called the Gadsden Purchase—to the United States for $10 million.

On July 4, 1848, in Washington, President Polk laid the cornerstone of a monument to honor George Washington. In Washington's day, the western border of the United States was the Mississippi River. The United States in 1848 now stretched "from sea to shining sea." In August, Polk learned that gold had been found in California. In the next section, you will read about the California gold rush.

Section **3** *Assessment*

1. Terms & Names

Explain the significance of:
- James K. Polk
- manifest destiny
- Zachary Taylor
- Bear Flag Revolt
- Winfield Scott
- Treaty of Guadalupe Hidalgo
- Mexican Cession

2. Using Graphics

Review the chapter and find five key events to place on a time line as shown.

War with Mexico

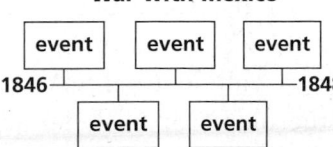

3. Main Ideas

a. How did the acquisitions of Oregon and the Mexican Cession relate to the idea of manifest destiny?

b. Why were some people opposed to the War with Mexico?

c. What does the phrase "sea to shining sea" mean?

4. Critical Thinking

Comparing Compare the different ways land was acquired by the United States in the period of manifest destiny from 1844 to 1853.

THINK ABOUT
- the acquisition of the Oregon Territory
- lands in the Southwest

ACTIVITY OPTIONS

MATH

GEOGRAPHY

In an almanac, find the current population of the states formed from the Mexican Cession. Create a **graph** or a **map** to display the information.

The California Gold Rush

MAIN IDEA	WHY IT MATTERS NOW	TERMS & NAMES
Gold was found in California, and thousands rushed to that territory. California quickly became a state.	The gold rush made California grow rapidly and helped bring about California's cultural diversity.	forty-niner John Sutter *Californio* James Marshall Mariano Vallejo California gold rush

ONE AMERICAN'S STORY

Luzena Wilson said of the year 1849, "The gold excitement spread like wildfire." The year before, James Marshall had discovered gold in California. Luzena's husband decided to become a **forty-niner**— someone who went to California to find gold, starting in 1849.

Most forty-niners left their families behind, but Luzena traveled to California with her husband. She soon discovered that women— and their homemaking skills—were rare in California. Shortly after she arrived, a miner offered her five dollars for the biscuits she was baking. Shocked, she just stared at him. He quickly doubled his offer and paid in gold. Luzena realized she could make money by feeding miners, so she opened a hotel.

In this section, you will read about the forty-niners like the Wilsons and what their mining experiences were like. You will also discover how the gold rush boosted California's economy and changed the nation's history.

This woman is carrying food to miners, just as Luzena Wilson did.

Taking Notes

Use your chart to take notes about California.

	Types of people who traveled there
New Mexico	
Utah	
Oregon	
Texas	
California	

California Before the Rush

Before the forty-niners came, California was populated by as many as 150,000 Native Americans and 8,000 to 12,000 *Californios*—settlers of Spanish or Mexican descent. Most *Californios* lived on huge cattle ranches. They had acquired their estates when the Mexican government took away the land that once belonged to the California missions.

One important *Californio* was **Mariano Vallejo** (mah•RYAH•noh vah•YEH•hoh). A member of one of the oldest Spanish families in America, he owned 250,000 acres of land. Proudly describing the accomplishments of the *Californios*, Vallejo wrote, "We were the pioneers of the Pacific coast . . . while General Washington was carrying on the war of the Revolution." Vallejo himself had been the commander of Northern California when it belonged to Mexico.

Vocabulary
immigration:
the movement
of people into a
country or region
where they were
not born

When Mexico owned California, its government feared American immigration and rarely gave land to foreigners. But <u>**John Sutter,**</u> a Swiss immigrant, was one exception. Dressed in a secondhand French army uniform, Sutter had visited the Mexican governor in 1839. A charming man, Sutter persuaded the governor to grant him 50,000 acres in the unsettled Sacramento Valley. Sutter built a fort on his land and dreamed of creating his own personal empire based on agriculture.

In 1848, Sutter sent a carpenter named <u>**James Marshall**</u> to build a sawmill on the nearby American River. One day Marshall inspected the canal that brought water to Sutter's Mill. He later said, "My eye was caught by a glimpse of something shining. . . . I reached my hand down and picked it up; it made my heart thump for I felt certain it was gold."

Rush for Gold

News of Marshall's thrilling discovery spread rapidly. From all over California, people raced to the American River—starting the <u>**California gold rush.**</u> A gold rush occurs when large numbers of people move to a site where gold has been found. Throughout history, people have valued gold because it is scarce, beautiful, easy to shape, and resistant to tarnish.

Miners soon found gold in other streams flowing out of the Sierra Nevada Mountains. Colonel R. B. Mason, the military governor of California, estimated that the region held enough gold to "pay the cost of the present war with Mexico a hundred times over." He sent this news to Washington with a box of gold dust as proof.

The following year thousands of gold seekers set out to make their fortunes. A forty-niner who wished to reach California from the East had a choice of three routes, all of them dangerous:

1. Sail 18,000 miles around South America and up the Pacific coast—suffering from storms, seasickness, and spoiled food.
2. Sail to the narrow Isthmus of Panama, cross overland (and risk catching a deadly tropical disease), and then sail to California.
3. Travel the trails across North America— braving rivers, prairies, mountains, and all the hardships of the trail.

*Reading*History

A. Categorizing
What were the three different types of transportation that people took to get to California?

Because the adventure was so difficult, most gold seekers were young men. "A gray beard is almost as rare as a petticoat," observed one miner. Luzena Wilson said that during the six months she lived in the mining city of Sacramento, she saw only two other women.

HISTORY *through*ART

Clipper ship companies used advertising cards such as this one to convince Easterners that their line provided the fastest, most pleasant voyages.

How has the artist tried to project a positive image for sailing west?

112 DAYS TO
SAN FRANCISCO.
MERCHANTS' EXPRESS LINE OF CLIPPER SHIPS.
Dispatching the Greatest Number of Vessels:
SMALLEST, CHEAPEST AND FASTEST VESSEL NOW UP !

THE MAGNIFICENT OUT-AND-OUT CLIPPER SHIP
WHITE SWALLOW
BUNKER, Commander, is now rapidly loading at PIER 16 E. R.
This splendid vessel, having made very short passages, and delivered her cargo in unexceptionable order, has established a reputation that will ensure immediate dispatch.
RANDOLPH M. COOLEY, 88 Wall Street,
Agents in San Francisco, Messrs. De Witt, Kittle & Co.
(POSTINE BUILDING.)
NESBITT & CO., PRINTERS.

Now and then

LEVI'S BLUE JEANS

Nearly everyone in the United States owns at least one pair of faded, comfortable blue jeans. The first jeans were invented for California miners.

In 1873, a man named Levi Strauss wanted to sell sturdy pants to miners. Strauss made his pants out of the strongest fabric he could buy—cotton denim. He reinforced the pockets with copper rivets so that they could hold heavy tools without ripping.

For more than 125 years, jeans have remained popular. Levi Strauss's pants have proved to be durable in more ways than one.

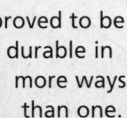

Life in the Mining Camps

The mining camps had colorful names like Mad Mule Gulch, Hangtown, and Coyote Diggings. They began as rows of tents along the streams flowing out of the Sierra Nevada. Gradually, the tents gave way to rough wooden buildings that housed stores and saloons.

Mining camps could be dangerous. One woman who lived in the region wrote about camp violence.

A VOICE FROM THE PAST

In the short space of twenty-four days, we have had murders, fearful accidents, bloody deaths, a mob, whippings, a hanging, . . . and a fatal duel.

Louise Clappe, quoted in *Frontier Women*

The mining life was hard for other reasons. Camp gossip told of miners who grew rich overnight by finding eight-pound nuggets, but in reality, such easy pickings were rare. Miners spent their days standing knee-deep in icy streams, where they sifted through tons of mud and sand to find small amounts of gold. Exhaustion, poor food, and disease all damaged the miners' health.

Not only was acquiring gold brutally difficult, but the miners had to pay outrageously high prices for basic supplies. In addition, gamblers and con artists swarmed into the camps to swindle the miners of their money. As a result, few miners grew rich.

*Reading*History

B. Making Inferences Why do you think life in the mining camps was so rough?

Miners from Around the World

About two-thirds of the forty-niners were Americans. Most of these were white men—many from New England. However, Native Americans, free blacks, and enslaved African Americans also worked the mines.

Thousands of experienced miners came from Sonora in Mexico. Other foreign miners came from Europe, South America, Australia, and China. Most of the Chinese miners were peasant farmers who fled from a region that had suffered several crop failures. By the end of 1851, one of every ten immigrants was Chinese.

Used to backbreaking labor in their homeland, the Chinese proved to be patient miners. They would take over sites that American miners had abandoned because the easy gold was gone. Through steady, hard work, the Chinese made these "played-out" sites yield profits. American miners resented the success of the Chinese and were suspicious of their different foods, dress, and customs. As the numbers of Chinese miners grew, American anger toward them also increased.

*Reading*History

C. Analyzing Causes Why did some Americans resent Chinese miners?

Surface Mining

Gold is found in cracks, called veins, in the earth's rocky crust. As mountains and other outcrops of rock erode, the gold veins come to the surface. The gold breaks apart into nuggets, flakes, and dust. Flood waters then wash it downhill into stream beds. To mine this surface gold, forty-niners had to use tools designed to separate it from the mud and sand around it. American miners learned some technology from Mexicans who came from the mining region of Sonora.

Miners shoveled dirt into the sluice. The rushing water carried lightweight materials along with it. Heavy gold sank to the bottom and was trapped between the ridges.

A sluice was a series of long boxes with ridges on the bottom. Water ran through the sluice, which angled downward.

Although this photograph shows American and Chinese miners working together, in many places Americans chased the Chinese away.

Mexican miners introduced the use of the pan. A miner would fill a pan with dirt and water. Then he would swirl the pan. Water sloshed over the sides, carrying lightweight minerals with it. Gold settled in the bottom.

CONNECT TO HISTORY

1. **Drawing Conclusions** Which mining method could be used by an individual miner and which needed a group of miners? Explain your answer.

S See Skillbuilder Handbook, page R13.

CONNECT TO TODAY

2. **Researching** How is gold mined today?

For more about the California gold rush . . .

RESEARCH LINKS
CLASSZONE.COM

Conflicts Among Miners

A mixture of greed, anger, and prejudice caused some miners to cheat others. For example, I. B. Gilman promised to free an enslaved African American named Tom if he saved enough gold. For more than a year, Tom mined for himself after each day's work was done. When he finally had $1,000, Gilman gave him a paper saying he was free. The next day, the paper suspiciously disappeared. Even though Tom was certain he had been robbed, he couldn't prove it. He had to work for another year before Gilman would free him.

Once the easy-to-find gold was gone, American miners began to force Native Americans and foreigners such as Mexicans and Chinese out of the gold fields to reduce competition. This practice increased after California became a state in 1850. One of the first acts of the California state legislature was to pass the Foreign Miners Tax, which imposed a tax of $20 a month on miners from other countries. That was more than most could afford to pay. As the tax collectors arrived in the camps, most foreigners left.

Reading **History**

D. Analyzing Causes How did the state government make mining harder for foreigners?

Driven from the mines, the Chinese opened shops, restaurants, and laundries. So many Chinese owned businesses in San Francisco that their neighborhood was called Chinatown, a name it still goes by today.

The Impact of the Gold Rush

By 1852, the gold rush was over. While it lasted, about 250,000 people flooded into California. This huge migration caused economic growth that changed California permanently. The port city of San Francisco grew to become a center of banking, manufacturing, shipping, and trade. Its population exploded from around 400 in 1845 to 35,000 in 1850. Sacramento became the center of a productive farming region.

However, the gold rush ruined many *Californios*. The newcomers did not respect *Californios*, their customs, or their legal rights. In many cases,

CAUSE AND EFFECT: U.S. Expansion, 1846–1853

CAUSE	EFFECT
Westward trails move thousands to new territories.	▶ Oregon Territory acquired by the United States.
Austin and others colonize Texas.	▶ Texas Revolution
United States annexes Texas.	▶ War with Mexico
Mexican Cession acquired by the United States.	▶ United States expands "sea to sea."
Transcontinental railroad route needed.	▶ Gadsden Purchase
Thousands of gold seekers rush to California.	▶ California becomes a state.

SKILLBUILDER Interpreting Charts

1. Which two causes are related to transportation?
2. Which cause fulfilled the nation's "manifest destiny"?

Reading History

E. Recognizing Effects What impact did the gold rush have on the people who lived in California before the forty-niners came?

Americans seized their property. For example, Mariano Vallejo lost all but 300 acres of his huge estate. Even so, their Spanish heritage became an important part of California culture.

Native Americans suffered even more. Thousands of them died from diseases brought by the newcomers. The miners hunted down and killed thousands more. The reason was the Anglo-American belief that Native Americans stood in the way of progress. By 1870, California's Native American population had fallen from 150,000 to only about 58,000.

A final effect of the gold rush was that by 1849 California had enough people to apply for statehood. Skipping the territorial stage, California applied to Congress for admission to the Union and was admitted as a free state in 1850. Although its constitution outlawed slavery, it did not grant African Americans the vote.

For some people, California's statehood proved to be the opportunity of a lifetime. The enslaved woman Nancy Gooch gained her freedom because of the law against slavery. She then worked as a cook and washerwoman until she saved enough money to buy the freedom of her son and daughter-in-law in Missouri. Nancy Gooch's family moved to California to join her. Eventually, they became so prosperous that they bought Sutter's sawmill, where the gold rush first started.

On a national level, California's statehood created turmoil. Before 1850, there was an equal number of free states and slave states. Southerners feared that because the statehood of California made free states outnumber slave states, Northerners might use their majority to abolish slavery. As Chapter 18 explains, conflict over this issue threatened the survival of the Union.

Mariano Vallejo, unhappy that *Californio* culture was ignored in the new American California, named his home "Tear of the Mountain."

Section 4 Assessment

1. Terms & Names

Explain the significance of:
- forty-niner
- *Californio*
- Mariano Vallejo
- John Sutter
- James Marshall
- California gold rush

2. Using Graphics

Use a chart like the one shown to review and record hardships faced by the forty-niners.

HARDSHIPS	
In the camps	
At work mining	

Which hardships would you have found most difficult?

3. Main Ideas

a. How did the California gold rush get started?

b. Why didn't many forty-niners become rich?

c. How did women and people of different racial, ethnic, or national groups contribute to the California gold rush?

4. Critical Thinking

Recognizing Effects
What were some of the effects of the California gold rush?

THINK ABOUT
- changes in San Francisco
- California's bid for statehood

ACTIVITY OPTIONS

SCIENCE
TECHNOLOGY

Research the hazards of mining gold and either plan a **science exhibit** or give an **electronic presentation**.

VISUAL SUMMARY

Manifest Destiny

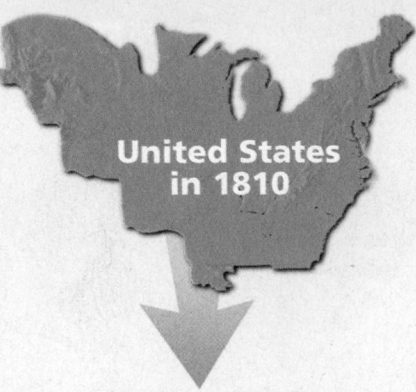

United States in 1810

Trails West

Mountain men and traders opened trails in the Far West. Pioneers then went west to gain land, wealth, or religious freedom.

The Texas Revolution

Americans moved into the Mexican territory of Texas. Conflicts led those Americans to revolt, and Texas gained independence.

The War with Mexico

President Polk wanted to expand the nation. He negotiated to gain Oregon. The United States fought Mexico to gain much of the Southwest.

The California Gold Rush

The discovery of gold lured thousands of people to California. California's economy and population grew, resulting in statehood.

United States in 1853

TERMS & NAMES

Briefly explain the significance of each of the following.

1. mountain man
2. Oregon Trail
3. Stephen Austin
4. *Tejano*
5. Antonio López de Santa Anna
6. manifest destiny
7. Bear Flag Revolt
8. Mexican Cession
9. forty-niner
10. California gold rush

REVIEW QUESTIONS

Trails West (pages 393–399)

1. What were three reasons why people moved west?
2. What were the three main trails that led to the West?
3. How did the Mormons make the land in Utah productive?

The Texas Revolution (pages 400–405)

4. Why were Texans unhappy with Mexican rule?
5. Why were the battles of the Alamo and San Jacinto important to the Texas Revolution?

The War with Mexico (pages 406–411)

6. What areas did the United States gain as a result of Americans' belief in manifest destiny?
7. How is the Bear Flag Revolt related to the War with Mexico?
8. What lands did the United States acquire as a result of the Treaty of Guadalupe Hidalgo?

The California Gold Rush (pages 412–417)

9. Who were four groups of people who became forty-niners?
10. What were three ways California changed because of the gold rush?

CRITICAL THINKING

1. USING YOUR NOTES: CATEGORIZING INFORMATION

	Types of people who traveled there	Why they went there	Key events that allowed the U.S. to take ownership of the territory
New Mexico			
Utah			
Oregon			
Texas			
California			

Using your completed chart, answer the questions below.

a. In what ways were the reasons people went west similar?
b. Which of the five regions listed on your chart entered the United States peacefully?
c. Which event added the most territory to the United States?

2. ANALYZING LEADERSHIP

Think about the leaders discussed in this chapter. What characteristics did they have that made them good leaders?

3. THEME: EXPANSION

How did the idea of manifest destiny help bring about the expansion of the United States?

4. DRAWING CONCLUSIONS

How did the War with Mexico and the California gold rush contribute to the cultural diversity of the United States?

5. APPLYING CITIZENSHIP SKILLS

What were the different viewpoints that people held about the War with Mexico?

Interact *with* History

Based on this chapter, what do you think you would have gained or lost by going west?

Use the map and your knowledge of U.S. history to answer questions 1 and 2.

Additional Test Practice, pp. S1-S33.

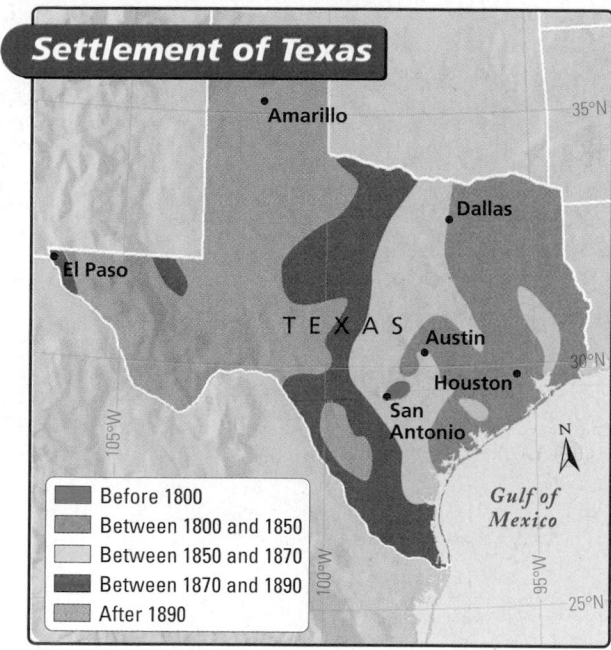

Settlement of Texas

Amarillo

Dallas

El Paso

TEXAS

Austin

Houston

San Antonio

N

Gulf of Mexico

35°N
30°N
25°N
105°W
100°W
95°W

- Before 1800
- Between 1800 and 1850
- Between 1850 and 1870
- Between 1870 and 1890
- After 1890

1. The area around which city in Texas was settled first?

   A. Houston

   B. Dallas

   C. San Antonio

   D. El Paso

2. In what general direction was Texas settled?

   A. north to south

   B. east to west

   C. west to east

   D. south to north

John O'Sullivan describes settling the United States in this quotation. Use the quotation and your knowledge of U.S. history to answer question 3.

PRIMARY SOURCE

Our manifest destiny[is] to overspread and possess the whole of the continent which Providence has given us for the development of the great experiment of liberty and . . . self-government.

John O'Sullivan, *United States Magazine and Democratic Review*

3. The passage supports which of the following points of view?

   A. Continental expansion by the United States is bound to happen.

   B. Continental expansion is limited by self-government.

   C. The claims of other countries to the same territory must be respected.

   D. Expansion across the entire continent will require some limits on liberty.

TEST PRACTICE
CLASSZONE.COM

ALTERNATIVE ASSESSMENT

1. ✍ WRITING ABOUT HISTORY

Suppose that you are a reporter for a newspaper in northern California in 1849. Write a **news article** about the discovery of gold. The article should follow the basic organization of a news article by answering the questions *Who? What? Where? When? And How?*

- You can research your article by looking in books about the California gold rush, in general histories of California, and on the Internet.

2. COOPERATIVE LEARNING

Work with a group of three or four other students to create a panel discussion that explores the different viewpoints surrounding the Mexican War. Research attitudes toward the war. Then outline and participate in the panel discussion for the class.

INTEGRATED TECHNOLOGY ACTIVITY

DOING INTERNET RESEARCH

Life on the wagon trains was not like life "back east."

- On the Internet or in other sources, find primary sources about life on the wagon trains, such as letters, diaries, journals, newspaper articles, and books.

- Once you have collected a number of primary sources, present your findings to your class.

INTERNET ACTIVITY
CLASSZONE.COM

CHAPTER 14

A New Spirit of Change 1820–1860

Section 1
The Hopes of Immigrants

Section 2
American Literature and Art

Section 3
Reforming American Society

Section 4
Abolition and Women's Rights

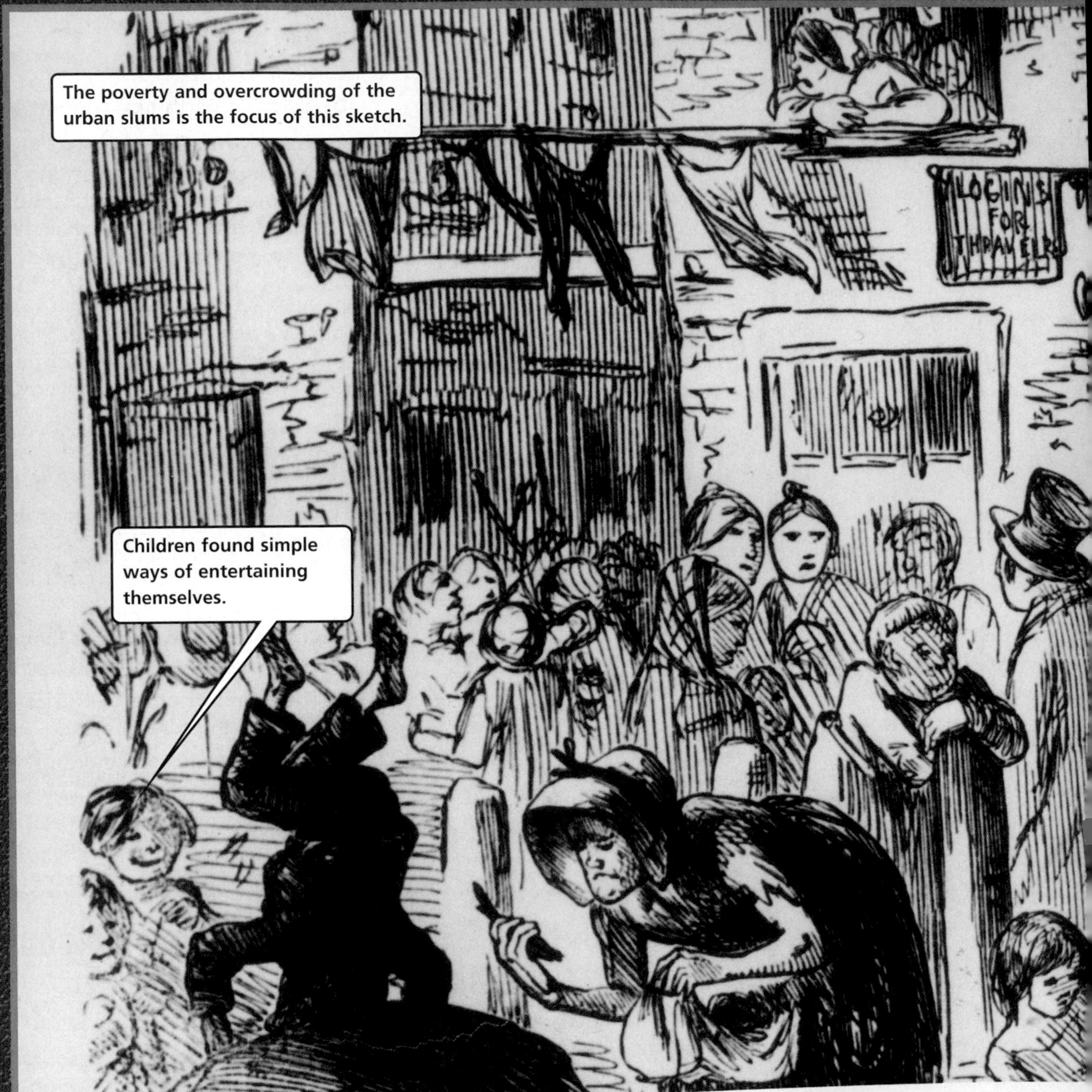
The poverty and overcrowding of the urban slums is the focus of this sketch.
Children found simple ways of entertaining themselves.

USA
World
1820

1824
The British Parliament makes trade unions illegal.

1827
Ludwig van Beethoven dies.

1828
Noah Webster publishes the *American Dictionary of the English Language*.

1829
David Walker prints *Appeal*, a pamphlet urging slaves to revolt.

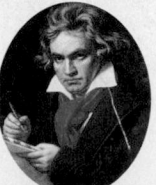

1829
Louis Braille invents a raised type that allows blind people to read.

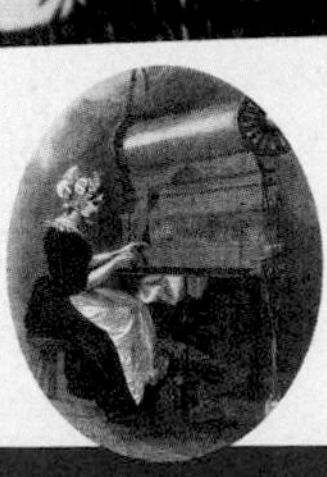

1836
The Lowell mill girls go on strike to demand better conditions.

You are a writer who moves to New York in the mid-1800s. A newspaper hires you to write about reform. One day, you hear a speaker call for the end of slavery. Another day you talk to a factory worker whose pay has been cut. In the city, you see great poverty and suffering.

What reforms do you think will most benefit American society?

What Do You Think?

- How might you persuade Americans to change life in the city?

- Should reform come about through new laws or through individual actions?

RESEARCH LINKS
CLASSZONE.COM

Visit the Chapter 14 links for more information about the changing nation.

1843
Dorothea Dix asks the Massachusetts legislature to improve the care of the mentally ill.

1848
The Seneca Falls Convention demands women's rights.

1851
Maine passes a law banning the sale of alcohol.

1860

1845
Ireland's potato crop fails, causing famine. Thousands flee to America.

1848
A revolution in Germany fails. Some Germans move to America.

1854
Brazil's first railway opens.

Reading Strategy: Comparing

What Do You Know?

What do you think were the worst problems in the United States in the mid-1800s? How do you think people tried to solve them?

Think About

- stories or films that are set in this period
- problems that exist now
- the actions people take to solve today's problems
- your responses to the Interact with History about reforms that will benefit American society (see page 421)

A young Frederick Douglass learns to read.

What Do You Want to Know?

What would you like to learn about the way individuals changed the United States in the mid-1800s? Record your questions in your notebook before you read the chapter.

Comparing

To understand the many influences on U.S. culture, learn to compare. Comparing means examining the similarities between people, actions, or ideas. The chart below will help you compare the influences that various people had upon America in the middle of the 19th century. Use the chart to take notes about how people changed America. Also take notes about people who tried to have an influence but failed.

 See Skillbuilder Handbook, page R10.

 Taking Notes

	How People Influenced America in the Mid-1800s
Immigrants	
Writers	
Reformers	
Abolitionists	
Women	

The Hopes of Immigrants

MAIN IDEA	WHY IT MATTERS NOW	TERMS & NAMES
In the mid-1800s, millions of Europeans came to the United States hoping to build a better life.	These Germans, Irish, and Scandinavians had a strong influence on American culture.	emigrant famine immigrant prejudice steerage nativist push-pull factor

ONE AMERICAN'S STORY

In June 1831, Gjert Hovland (YEHRT HAHV•LIHND) and his family left Norway for America. After a few years, Hovland wrote to a friend in Norway.

A VOICE FROM THE PAST

It would greatly please me to learn that all of you who are in need and have little chance of supporting yourselves and your families have decided to leave Norway and come to America; for, even if many more come, there will still be room here for all. Those who are willing to work will not lack employment or business here.

Gjert Hovland, letter to Torjuls Maeland, April 22, 1835

Advertisements for land attracted immigrants, who came to the United States with only what could fit in trunks like the one shown above.

Millions of people like Hovland decided to become **emigrants**, or people who leave a country. Arriving in the United States, they became **immigrants**, or people who settle in a new country. This section explains how immigrants enriched the United States with their work and their cultures.

Why People Migrated

Most immigrants endured hardships to come to America. Although some, like Hovland, brought their families, many immigrant men came alone and suffered loneliness. Nearly all immigrants made the ocean voyage in **steerage,** the cheapest deck on a ship. In steerage, hundreds of people lived jammed together for ten days to a month. Conditions were filthy. Many passengers became ill or died on the journey.

Despite the hard passage, immigrants flocked to the United States during the mid-1800s. They came from Britain, Ireland, Germany, Scandinavia (Sweden, Denmark, and Norway), and China. Most came from Europe. What made them come to America? Historians talk about

Taking Notes

Use your chart to take notes about the influence of immigrants.

	How People
Immigrants	
Writers	
Reformers	
Abolitionists	
Women	

Push–Pull Factors of Immigration

PULL

1. Freedom
2. Economic opportunity
3. Abundant land

1. Population growth
2. Agricultural changes
3. Crop failures
4. Industrial Revolution
5. Religious and political turmoil

PUSH

__push-pull factors__. These forces push people out of their native lands and pull them toward a new place. **Push factors** included the following:

1. **Population growth.** Better food and sanitation caused Europe's population to boom after 1750, and the land became overcrowded.
2. **Agricultural changes.** As Europe's population grew, so did cities. Landowners wanted to make money selling food to those cities. New methods made it more efficient to farm large areas of land than to rent small plots to tenants. So landlords forced tenants off the land.
3. **Crop failures.** Poor harvests made it difficult for small farmers to pay their debts. Some of these farmers chose to start over in America. Crop failures also led to hunger, causing people to emigrate.
4. **Industrial Revolution.** Goods produced in factories became cheaper than goods produced by artisans. Suddenly out of work, some artisans took factory jobs. Others emigrated.
5. **Religious and political turmoil.** To escape religious persecution, Quakers fled Norway and Jews left Germany. Also, many Germans came to America after a revolution in Germany failed in 1848.

Vocabulary
tenant: renter

Vocabulary
artisan: skilled worker

Immigrants chose the United States because of three main **pull factors**:

1. **Freedom.** As Gjert Hovland wrote, "Everyone has the freedom to practice the teaching and religion he prefers."
2. **Economic opportunity.** Immigrants sought a land where they could support their families and have a better future. Immigration often rose during times of U.S. prosperity and fell during hard times.
3. **Abundant land.** The acquisition of the Louisiana Purchase and the Mexican Cession gave the United States millions more acres of land. To land-starved Europeans, America was a land of opportunity.

Reading **History**
A. Solving Problems Many of the push factors were problems. Which pull factors were solutions to which problems?

Scandinavians Seek Land

Public land in America was sold for $1.25 an acre, which lured thousands of Scandinavians. At first, their governments tried to keep them at home. A Swedish law of 1768 restricted the right to emigrate. But growing poverty in Scandinavia caused officials to cancel this law in 1840.

Scandinavian clergymen also tried to halt the emigration. At first, they warned their church members against leaving the homeland. Eventually, though, the preachers realized their words had little effect. Some of them even went to America themselves.

Reading History

B. Making Inferences Why do you think Scandinavians moved to places that felt familiar?

In the United States, Scandinavians chose regions that felt familiar. Many settled in the Midwest, especially Minnesota and Wisconsin. These states had lakes, forests, and cold winters like their homelands. A high proportion of Scandinavian immigrants became farmers.

Germans Pursue Economic Opportunity

Like the Scandinavians, many Germans moved to the Midwest. Germans especially liked Wisconsin because the climate allowed them to grow their traditional crop of oats. Some moved to Milwaukee, Wisconsin, because the Catholic bishop there was German. (In the 1800s, German Christian immigrants included both Catholics and Protestants.)

Germans also settled in Texas. In New Braunfels, a group of German nobles bought land and sold it in parcels to German immigrants. The town had to survive poor harvests and conflicts with Native Americans, but it eventually prospered. Germans also founded Fredericksburg, Texas, which still retains its German culture today.

Immigrants from Germany settled in cities as well as on farms or the frontier. German artisans opened businesses as bakers, butchers, carpenters, printers, shoemakers, and tailors. Many German immigrants achieved great success. For instance, in 1853 John Jacob Bausch and Henry Lomb started a firm to make eyeglasses and other lenses. Their company became the world's largest lens maker.

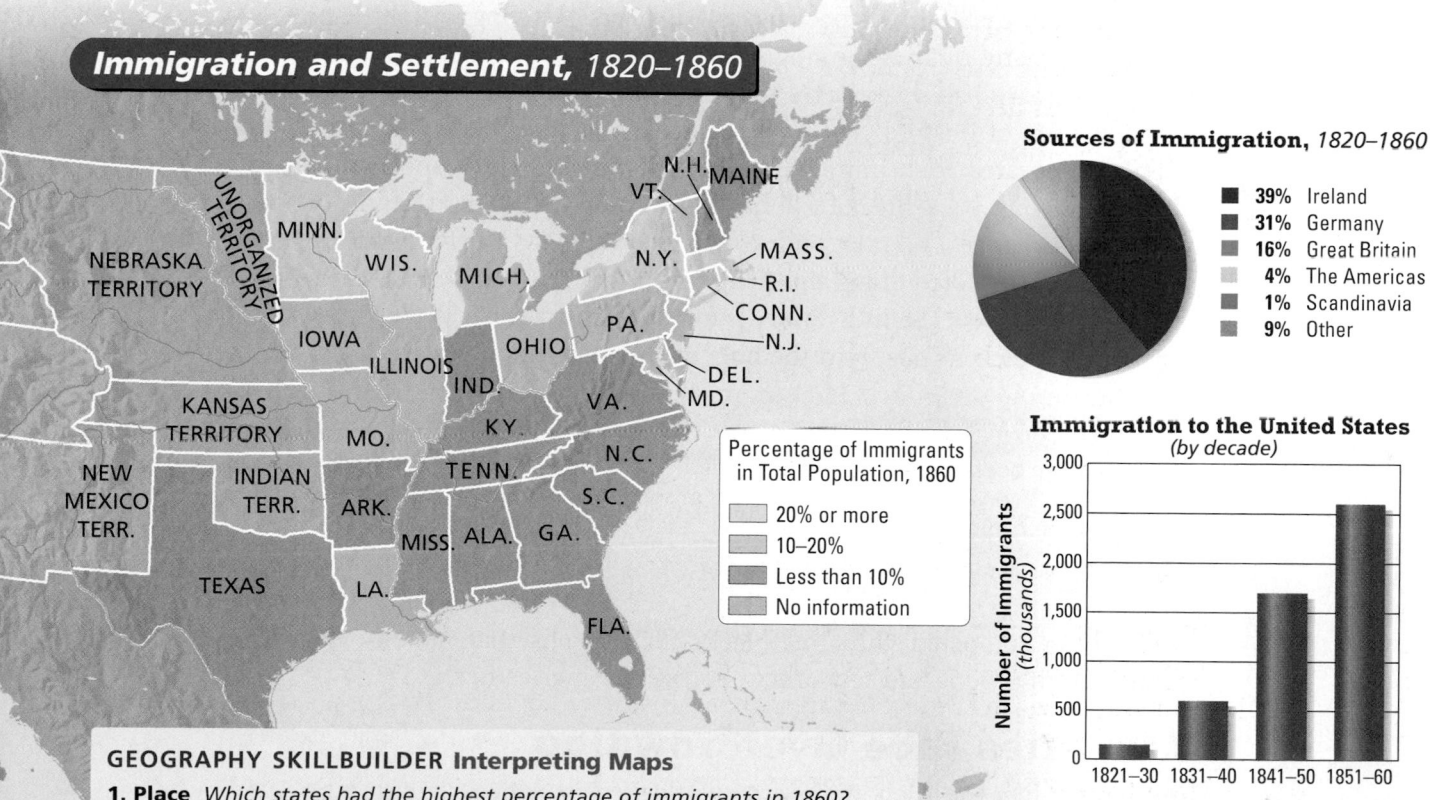

Immigration and Settlement, *1820–1860*

Sources of Immigration, *1820–1860*

- **39%** Ireland
- **31%** Germany
- **16%** Great Britain
- **4%** The Americas
- **1%** Scandinavia
- **9%** Other

Percentage of Immigrants in Total Population, 1860

- 20% or more
- 10–20%
- Less than 10%
- No information

Immigration to the United States *(by decade)*

Number of Immigrants *(thousands)*

1821–30 1831–40 1841–50 1851–60

GEOGRAPHY SKILLBUILDER Interpreting Maps

1. **Place** *Which states had the highest percentage of immigrants in 1860?*
2. **Region** *Compare the settlement of immigrants in the North and the South. What do you know about the South that might account for this difference?*

Source: *Historical Statistics of the United States*

A New Spirit of Change **425**

Some German immigrants were Jews. Many of them worked as traveling salespeople. They brought pins, needles, pots—and news—to frontier homes and mining camps. In time, some opened their own general stores. Other Jews settled in cities, where many found success. For example, Alexander Rothschild worked as a grocer upon arriving in Hartford, Connecticut, in the 1840s. By 1851, he ran a popular hotel.

The Germans were the largest immigrant group of the 1800s and strongly influenced American culture. Many things we think of as originating in America came from Germany—the Christmas tree, gymnasiums, kindergartens, and the hamburger and frankfurter.

daily *life*

IMMIGRANT CULTURE

To maintain their culture, immigrants continued many of their traditional activities in the United States. For example, German culture is rich in music. German immigrants put together marching bands, symphony orchestras, and choruses.

In Ireland, many of the Irish had poured their energy into defying the British. This gave them experience with political organization. As a result, Irish immigrants became active in U.S. politics, especially in the cities.

Background
The hamburger and frankfurter are named after the German cities Hamburg and Frankfurt am Main.

The Irish Flee Hunger

Most Irish immigrants were Catholic. Protestant Britain had ruled Ireland for centuries—and controlled the Catholic majority by denying them rights. Irish Catholics could not vote, hold office, own land, or go to school. Because of the poverty produced by Britain's rule, some Irish came to America in the early 1800s.

Then, in 1845, a disease attacked Ireland's main food crop, the potato, causing a severe food shortage called a **famine**. The Irish Potato Famine killed 1 million people and forced many to emigrate. By 1854, between 1.5 and 2 million Irish had fled their homeland.

In America, Irish farmers became city-dwellers. Arriving with little or no savings, many of these immigrants had to settle in the port cities where their ships had docked. By 1850, the Irish made up one-fourth of the population of Boston, New York, Philadelphia, and Baltimore.

The uneducated Irish immigrants arrived with few skills and had to take low-paying, back-breaking jobs. Irish women took in washing or worked as servants. The men built canals and railroads across America. So many Irishmen died doing this dangerous work that people said there was "an Irishman buried under every [railroad] tie." In 1841, British novelist Charles Dickens observed the huts in which railroad workers lived.

Reading **History**

C. Drawing Conclusions How did the effects of British rule make it hard for Irish immigrants to America to find good jobs?

A VOICE FROM THE PAST

The best were poor protection from the weather; the worst let in the wind and rain through the wide breaches in the roofs of sodden grass and in the walls of mud; some had neither door nor window; some had nearly fallen down.

Charles Dickens, quoted in *To Seek America*

The Irish competed with free blacks for the jobs that nobody else wanted. Both groups had few other choices in America in the 1800s.

U.S. Cities Face Overcrowding

Immigrants like the Irish and Germans flocked to American cities. So did native-born Americans, who hoped for the chance to make a better

living. Between 1800 and 1830, New York's population jumped from 60,489 to 202,589. St. Louis doubled its population every nine years. Cincinnati grew even faster, doubling every seven years.

Rapid urban growth brought problems. Not enough housing existed for all the newcomers. Greedy landlords profited from the housing shortage by squeezing large apartment buildings onto small lots. Using every inch of space for rooms, these cramped living quarters lacked sunlight and fresh air. Their outdoor toilets overflowed, spreading disease. In such depressing urban neighborhoods, crime flourished.

Reading **History**
D. Identifying Problems What problems were politicians trying to solve by offering to help new immigrants?

American cities were unprepared to tackle these problems. In fact, before 1845, New York City had no public police force. Until the 1860s, it had only a volunteer fire department. And in 1857, the rapidly growing city had only 138 miles of sewers for 500 miles of streets.

Most immigrant groups set up aid societies to help newcomers from their country. Many city politicians also offered to assist immigrants in exchange for votes. The politicians set up organizations to help new arrivals find housing and work.

Some Americans Oppose Immigration

Some native-born Americans feared that immigrants were too foreign to learn American ways. Others feared that immigrants might come to outnumber natives. As a result, immigrants faced anger and prejudice. **Prejudice** is a negative opinion that is not based on facts. For example,

CITIZENSHIP TODAY

Becoming a Citizen

Most immigrants who came to America in the 1800s shared one thing: an appreciation for the nation's values and laws. As a result, many chose to become U.S. citizens.

This trend continues today. In recent decades, more than half a million Vietnamese have immigrated to the United States. Many became citizens of their new country. One of them was Lam Ton, who is a successful restaurant owner in Chicago. Ton viewed U.S. citizenship as both a privilege and a duty. "We have to stick to this country and help it do better," he said.

Each year, immigrants from around the world are sworn in as U.S. citizens on Citizenship Day, September 17. But first they must pass a test on English, the U.S. political system, and the rights and duties of citizenship.

This young immigrant proudly holds up his certificate of citizenship.

How Does Someone Become a Citizen?

1. In a small group, discuss what questions you would ask those seeking to become U.S. citizens.

2. Create a citizenship test using your questions.

3. Have another group take the test and record their scores.

4. Use the McDougal Littell Internet site to link to the actual U.S. citizenship test. Compare it to your test.

See Citizenship Handbook, page 281.

For more about becoming a U.S. citizen . . .

 RESEARCH LINKS
CLASSZONE.COM

In 1844, a riot took place between Catholics and non-Catholics in Philadelphia. Several people were killed.

some Protestants in the 1800s believed that Catholics threatened democracy. Those Protestants feared that the Pope, the head of the Roman Catholic Church, was plotting to overthrow democracy in America.

Native-born Americans who wanted to eliminate foreign influence called themselves **nativists.** Some nativists refused to hire immigrants and put up signs like "No Irish need apply." In cities like New York and Boston, nativists formed a secret society. Members promised not to vote for any Catholics or immigrants running for political office. If asked about their secret group, they said, "I know nothing about it."

In the 1850s, nativists started a political party. Because of the members' answers to questions about their party, it was called the Know-Nothing Party. It wanted to ban Catholics and the foreign-born from holding office. It also called for a cut in immigration and a 21-year wait to become an American citizen. The Know-Nothings did elect six governors. But they disappeared quickly as a national party. Their northern and southern branches couldn't agree on the issue of slavery.

In spite of such barriers as prejudice, the immigrants of the 1800s had a strong impact on American culture. Writers and artists of the 1800s also shaped American culture. Section 2 discusses their influence.

Background
Protestants feared the Pope because in many European countries, the Catholic Church worked closely with the ruling monarchs.

Section 1 Assessment

1. Terms & Names

Explain the significance of:
• emigrant
• immigrant
• steerage
• push-pull factor
• famine
• prejudice
• nativist

2. Using Graphics

Use a cluster diagram like the one below to record details about immigration, such as which groups came, where they settled, and how they influenced America.

Immigration

3. Main Ideas

a. What were the push-pull factors that led to immigration?

b. How did the arrival of so many immigrants affect U.S. cities?

c. What was the Know-Nothing Party, and what was its point of view about immigration?

4. Critical Thinking

Analyzing Causes How did the rapid increase in immigration cause conflict?

THINK ABOUT
• why Irish immigrants and free blacks competed for jobs
• the growth of cities and the problems it created
• the prejudices of nativists
• religious differences

ACTIVITY OPTIONS

TECHNOLOGY

ART

Plan a **multimedia presentation** or design a **Web page** that shows immigrants the advantages of settling in the United States.

American Literature and Art

MAIN IDEA	WHY IT MATTERS NOW	TERMS & NAMES
Inspired by nature and democratic ideals, writers and artists produced some of America's greatest works.	Nineteenth-century writers such as Hawthorne and Thoreau laid the foundation for American literature.	romanticism Hudson River school transcendentalism civil disobedience

ONE AMERICAN'S STORY

Washington Irving wrote some of the first stories to describe America. For example, "Rip Van Winkle" tells of a man in New York State. Rip wakes up after a 20-year nap to find many changes. He goes to the inn, which once had a picture of King George on its sign.

> ### A VOICE FROM THE PAST
>
> The red coat was changed for one of blue and buff, a sword was held in the hand instead of a sceptre [staff of authority], the head was decorated with a cocked hat, and underneath was painted in large characters, GENERAL WASHINGTON.
>
> **Washington Irving,** "Rip Van Winkle"

While Rip slept, the Americans had fought and won their revolution!

Irving's work helped to win European respect for American writing for the first time. This section discusses other individuals of the 1800s who created uniquely American literature and art.

In another Irving tale, "The Legend of Sleepy Hollow," a spooky creature chases a teacher.

Writing About America

Irving and other writers were influenced by a style of European art called **romanticism.** It stressed the individual, imagination, creativity, and emotion. It drew inspiration from nature. American writers turned their interest in nature into a celebration of the American wilderness.

Many books featured the wilderness. James Fenimore Cooper wrote five novels about the dramatic adventures of wilderness scout Natty Bumppo. One that remains popular is *The Last of the Mohicans.* Francis Parkman wrote a travel book, *The Oregon Trail,* about the frontier trail.

Taking Notes

Use your chart to take notes about the influence of writers.

	How People
Immigrants	
Writers	
Reformers	
Abolitionists	
Women	

HISTORY *through*ART

Asher Durand was a founder of the Hudson River school of painting. His best-known work, *Kindred Spirits,* was painted in 1849. This romantic work shows two artists inspired by a beautiful landscape. The figures in the painting are Durand's friends, the poet William Cullen Bryant and the painter Thomas Cole.

Compare this painting to the one on page 180. Is the style different? If so, how?

In addition, writers began to use a more American style. A teacher and lawyer named Noah Webster gave guidelines to that style in his *American Dictionary of the English Language.* Webster first published his dictionary in 1828. He later revised it in 1840. The dictionary gave American, not British, spellings and included American slang.

Other writers besides Irving celebrated America's past. Henry Wadsworth Longfellow wrote many poems that retold stories from history. For example, "Paul Revere's Ride" depicted the Revolutionary hero's ride to warn of a British attack. Generations of students memorized lines from the poem, such as, "One if by land, and two if by sea; / And I on the opposite shore will be."

Creating American Art

European styles continued to influence American artists, but some took these styles in new directions. One group of painters influenced by romanticism worked near the Hudson River in New York State. **Hudson River school** artists painted lush natural landscapes. Several members of this school went west for a change of scenery. For example, Albert Bierstadt took several trips to America's mountainous West. He produced huge paintings that convey the majesty of the American landscape. (See page 310.)

Background
The National
Audubon Society,
whose goal is the
protection of
wildlife today, is
named for John
James Audubon.

Other artists also went west. John James Audubon came to the United States from France at age 18. Traveling across the continent, Audubon sketched the birds and animals of his adopted country.

Enslaved African Americans also contributed to American art. They made beautiful baskets, quilts, and pottery. Most of these slaves remained anonymous, but one did not. David Drake worked in a South Carolina pottery factory and signed the pottery he created. He was the only factory worker to do so.

Following One's Conscience

By the 1840s, Americans took new pride in their emerging culture. Ralph Waldo Emerson, a New England writer, encouraged this pride. He urged Americans to cast off European influence and develop their own beliefs. His advice was to learn about life from self-examination and from nature as well as books.

"No law can be sacred to me but that of my nature."
Ralph Waldo Emerson

Emerson's student, Henry David Thoreau, followed that advice. In 1845, Thoreau moved to a simple cabin he had built by Walden Pond near the town of Concord, Massachusetts. Thoreau furnished it with only a bed, a table, a desk, and three chairs. He wrote about his life in the woods in *Walden*. Thoreau said that people should live by their own individual standards.

*Reading*History
**A. Making
Inferences** What
do you think it
means to "hear
a different
drummer"?

A VOICE FROM THE PAST

If a man does not keep pace with his companions, perhaps it is because he hears a different drummer. Let him step to the music which he hears, however measured or far away.

Henry David Thoreau, *Walden*

Emerson and Thoreau belonged to a group of thinkers with a new philosophy called **transcendentalism**. It taught that the spiritual world is more important than the physical world. It also taught that people can find the truth within themselves—through feeling and intuition.

Because Thoreau believed in the importance of individual conscience, he urged people not to obey laws they considered unjust. Instead of protesting with violence, they should peacefully refuse to obey those laws. This form of protest is called **civil disobedience**. For example, Thoreau did not want to support the U.S. government, which allowed slavery and fought the War with Mexico. Instead of paying taxes that helped to finance the war, Thoreau went to jail.

Another New England transcendentalist, Margaret Fuller, also called for change. In her magazine, *The Dial*, and in her book, *Woman in the Nineteenth Century*, Fuller argued for women's rights.

Connections TO LITERATURE

"CIVIL DISOBEDIENCE"
In his essay "Civil Disobedience," Thoreau wrote that "Under a government which imprisons any unjustly the true place for a just man is also a prison."

Thoreau did land in prison when he refused to pay his taxes. According to legend, Emerson visited Thoreau in jail and asked, "Why are you here?" Thoreau replied, "Why are you not here?"

In the 20th century, Mohandas K. Gandhi of India and Martin Luther King, Jr., of the United States both used civil disobedience to fight injustice.

GIFTS ON POE'S GRAVE

Every year a mysterious figure dressed in black celebrates Edgar Allan Poe's birthday. He leaves three roses on the author's Baltimore grave at 3:00 A.M.

The puzzling tradition began in 1949, exactly 100 years after Poe's death. In 1993, a new black-coated visitor took over the tradition. The person who began the ritual was ill—and later died in 1999.

Although many witnesses watch the ritual each year, none ask the visitor his name. Poe's fans have always liked mysteries.

Exploring the Human Heart

Like Thoreau, other writers broke with tradition. In 1855, poet Walt Whitman published *Leaves of Grass,* a book that changed American poetry. His bold, unrhymed poems praised ordinary people. Emily Dickinson lived in her family's home almost her entire life. She wrote poems on small pieces of paper that she sewed into booklets. Her subjects include God, nature, love, and death. Most of her 1,775 poems were published only after her death. Both Whitman and Dickinson shaped modern poetry by experimenting with language.

Fiction writers of the 1800s also shaped American literature. Edgar Allan Poe wrote terrifying tales that influence today's horror story writers. He also wrote the first detective story, "The Murders in the Rue Morgue."

Nathaniel Hawthorne depicted love, guilt, and revenge during Puritan times in *The Scarlet Letter.* The novel shows that harsh judgment without mercy can lead to tragedy. Hawthorne may have learned that lesson from his family history. One of his ancestors condemned people at the Salem witchcraft trials.

Herman Melville won fame by writing thrilling novels about his experiences as a sailor. In 1851, Melville published his masterpiece, *Moby Dick.* This novel tells about a man's destructive desire to kill a white whale. Although the novel was not popular when it was published, it is widely read now. Several movie versions exist.

These fiction writers portrayed the harmful effects of cruel actions. Other people thought that individuals could alter society for good. Section 3 describes those reformers.

*Reading*History

B. Recognizing Effects How did Poe influence the fiction that people read today?

Section 2 Assessment

1. Terms & Names

Explain the significance of:
- romanticism
- Hudson River school
- transcendentalism
- civil disobedience

2. Using Graphics

Use a chart like the one below to list important individual writers and artists. For each one, name or describe one of his or her works.

Writer or artist	His or her work

Which one would you like to learn more about? Why?

3. Main Ideas

a. What was romanticism and how did Americans adapt it?

b. What is civil disobedience and what did Thoreau do that is an example of it?

c. How did the writers of the mid-1800s shape modern literature?

4. Critical Thinking

Evaluating Why do you think the literature and art of the mid-1800s are still valued?

THINK ABOUT
- the way they feature U.S. history and culture
- their universal themes—themes that relate to all people in all time periods
- the way they reflect changes happening at that time

ACTIVITY OPTIONS

ART

TECHNOLOGY

Choose an American painting, sketch it, and make it into a **jigsaw puzzle;** or make an **audio recording** of a museum guide's description of it.

Reforming American Society

MAIN IDEA	WHY IT MATTERS NOW	TERMS & NAMES
In the mid-1800s, several reform movements worked to improve American education and society.	Several laws and institutions, such as public schools, date back to this period.	revival Second Great Awakening temperance movement labor union strike Horace Mann Dorothea Dix

ONE AMERICAN'S STORY

Anne Newport Royall wrote about America's growing interest in religion. She also described a preacher at a Tennessee **revival**, or meeting to reawaken religious faith.

A VOICE FROM THE PAST

His text was, "He that hath ears to hear, let him hear." The people must have been deaf indeed that could not have heard him. . . . He began low but soon bawled to deafening. He spit in his hands, rubbed them against each other, and then would smite them together, till he made the woods ring.

Anne Newport Royall, *Letters from Alabama*

This revival meeting took place during the Second Great Awakening.

Section 3 explains how, in the mid-1800s, many individuals called on Americans to reform, or to improve themselves and their society.

A Spirit of Revival

The renewal of religious faith in the 1790s and early 1800s is called the **Second Great Awakening**. Revivalist preachers said that anyone could choose salvation. This appealed to equality-loving Americans. Revivals spread quickly across the frontier. Settlers eagerly awaited the visits of preachers like Peter Cartwright. At the age of 16, Cartwright had given up a life of gambling and joined a Methodist Church. He became a minister and spent more than 60 years preaching on the frontier.

The revival also traveled to Eastern cities. There, former lawyer Charles Grandison Finney held large revival meetings. He preached that "all sin consists in selfishness" and that religious faith led people to help others. Such teaching helped awaken a spirit of reform. Americans began to believe that they could act to make things better.

Taking Notes

Use your chart to take notes about the influence of reformers.

	How People
Immigrants	
Writers	
Reformers	
Abolitionists	
Women	

Temperance pledges often displayed inspiring pictures and mottoes.

Temperance Societies

Led by churches, some Americans began the **temperance movement,** which is a campaign to stop the drinking of alcohol. Heavy drinking was common in the early 1800s. Some workers spent most of their wages on alcohol—leaving their families without enough money to live on. As a result, many women joined the temperance movement. "There is no reform in which women can act better or more appropriately than temperance," said Mary C. Vaughan.

Some temperance workers handed out pamphlets urging people to stop drinking. Others produced dramas, such as one entitled *The Drunkard,* to dramatize the evils of alcohol. In addition, temperance speakers traveled widely, asking people to sign a pledge to give up alcohol. By 1838, a million people had signed.

Temperance also won the support of business owners. Industry needed workers who could keep schedules and run machines. Alcohol made it hard for workers to do either. New England businessman Neal Dow led the fight to make it illegal to sell alcohol. In 1851, Maine banned the sale of liquor. By 1855, 13 other states passed similar laws. But many people opposed these laws, and most were repealed. Still, the movement to ban alcohol remained strong, even into the 20th century.

Reading **History**

A. Evaluating
How did the temperance movement affect the development of drama?

Vocabulary
repeal: to cancel

Fighting for Workers' Rights

As business owners tried to improve workers' habits, workers called for improvements in working conditions. Factory work was noisy, boring, and unsafe. In the 1830s, American workers began to organize.

The young women mill workers in Lowell, Massachusetts, started a labor union. A **labor union** is a group of workers who band together to seek better working conditions. In 1836, the mill owners raised the rent of the company-owned boarding houses where the women lived. About 1,500 women went on **strike,** stopping work to demand better conditions. Eleven-year-old Harriet Hanson helped lead the strikers.

A VOICE FROM THE PAST

I . . . started on ahead, saying, . . . "I don't care what you do, I am going to turn out, whether anyone else does or not," and I marched out, and was followed by the others. As I looked back at the long line that followed me, I was more proud than I have ever been since.

Harriet Hanson, quoted in *A People's History of the United States*

Other workers called for shorter hours and higher wages. In 1835 and 1836, 140 strikes took place in the eastern United States. Then the Panic

Background
President Van
Buren's order
reduced the
workweek from
70 to 60 hours.

of 1837 brought hard times. Jobs were scarce, and workers were afraid to cause trouble. The young labor movement fell apart. Even so, workers achieved a few goals. For example, in 1840 President Martin Van Buren ordered a ten-hour workday for government workers.

Improving Education

In the 1830s, Americans also began to demand better schools. In 1837, Massachusetts set up the first state board of education in the United States. Its head was **Horace Mann**. Mann called public education "the great equalizer." He also argued that "education creates or develops new treasures—treasures never before possessed or dreamed of by any one." By 1850, many Northern states had opened public elementary schools.

Boston opened the first public high school in 1821. A few other Northern cities followed suit. In addition, churches and other groups founded hundreds of private colleges in the following decades. Many were located in states carved from the Northwest Territory. These included Antioch and Oberlin Colleges in Ohio, the University of Notre Dame in Indiana, and Northwestern University in Illinois.

Women could not attend most colleges. One exception was Oberlin. It was the first college to accept women as well as men. In 1849, English immigrant Elizabeth Blackwell became the first woman to earn a medical degree in the United States. Despite such individual efforts, it was rare for a woman to attend college until the late 1800s.

African Americans also faced obstacles to getting an education. This was especially true in the South. There, teaching an enslaved person to read had been illegal since the Nat Turner Rebellion in 1831. Enslaved African Americans who tried to learn were brutally punished. Even in the North, most public schools barred African-American children.

Reading History
B. Making
Inferences
Why do you
think women
and African
Americans had a
hard time getting
an education?

Few colleges accepted African Americans. Those that did often took only one or two blacks at a time. The first African American to receive a college degree was Alexander Twilight in 1823. John Russwurm received one in 1826 and later began the first African-American newspaper.

Caring for the Needy

As some people promoted education, others tried to improve society's care for its weakest members. In 1841, **Dorothea Dix**, a reformer from Boston, was teaching Sunday school at a women's jail. She discovered some women who were locked in cold, filthy cells

Mary Jane Patterson was the first African-American woman to earn a college degree. She graduated from Oberlin in 1862 and went on to work as a teacher.

AMERICA'S HISTORY MAKERS

HORACE MANN
1796–1859

Horace Mann once said in a speech to students, "Be ashamed to die until you have won some victory for humanity." Mann had no reason to be ashamed. As a child, he knew poverty and hardship. He educated himself and later fought for public education for other people.

Toward the end of his life, Mann became president of Antioch College. It committed itself to education for both men and women and equal rights for African Americans.

DOROTHEA DIX
1802–1887

At the age of 12, Dorothea Dix left an unhappy home to go live with her grandparents in Boston. Just two years later, she began teaching little children.

In 1841, Dix saw the harsh treatment of mentally ill women. Society frowned upon women traveling alone, but Dix defied custom. She went by train to several places where the mentally ill were housed.

Dix wrote a report about her research. (See page 438.) That report changed the care of the mentally ill.

How might their backgrounds have motivated Dorothea Dix and Horace Mann to become leaders in reform movements?

simply because they were mentally ill. Visiting other jails, Dix learned that the mentally ill often received no treatment. Instead, they were chained and beaten. Dix pleaded with the Massachusetts Legislature to improve the care of the mentally ill. Later, she traveled all over the United States on behalf of the mentally ill. Her efforts led to the building of 32 new hospitals.

Some reformers worked to improve life for people with other disabilities. Thomas H. Gallaudet started the first American school for deaf children in 1817. Samuel G. Howe founded the Perkins School for the Blind in Boston in the 1830s.

Reformers also tried to improve prisons. In the early 1800s, debtors, lifelong criminals, and child offenders were put in the same cells. Reformers demanded that children go to special jails. They also called for the rehabilitation of adult prisoners. Rehabilitation means preparing people to live useful lives after their release from prison.

*Reading*History
C. Recognizing Effects How did reformers change the treatment of the mentally ill, the disabled, and prisoners?

Spreading Ideas Through Print

During this period of reform, Americans began to receive more information about how they should lead their lives. In the 1830s, cheaper newsprint and the invention of the steam-driven press lowered the price of a newspaper to a penny. Average Americans could afford to buy the "penny papers." Penny papers were also popular because, in addition to serious news, they published gripping stories of fires and crimes.

Hundreds of new magazines also appeared. One was the *Ladies' Magazine*. Its editor was Sarah Hale, a widow who used writing to support her family. The magazine advocated education for women. It also

suggested that men and women were responsible for different, but equally important, areas of life. The magazine taught that a woman's area was the home and the world of "human ties." A man's area was politics and the business of earning a living for his family. Later, Hale edited *Godey's Lady's Book*, which published poems and stories as well as articles.

Creating Ideal Communities

While magazines sought to tell people how to live and reform movements tried to change society, some individuals decided to start over. They aimed to build an ideal society, called a utopia.

Two attempts at utopias were New Harmony, Indiana, and Brook Farm, Massachusetts. In both, residents received food and other necessities of life in exchange for work. However, both utopias experienced conflicts and financial difficulties. They ended after only a few years.

*Reading*History
D. Forming and Supporting Opinions Why do you think it was hard for utopias to succeed? Give reasons.

Religious belief led to some utopias. For example, the Shakers followed the beliefs of Ann Lee. She preached that people should lead holy lives in communities that demonstrate God's love to the world. When a person became a Shaker, he or she vowed not to marry or have children. Shakers shared their goods with each other, believed that men and women are equal, and refused to fight for any reason. Shakers set up communities in New York, New England, and on the frontier.

People called them *Shakers* because they shook with emotion during church services. Otherwise, Shaker life was calm. Shakers farmed and built simple furniture in styles that remain popular today. The childless Shakers depended on converts and adopting children to keep their communities going. In the 1840s, the Shakers had 6,000 members—their highest number. In 1999, only seven Shakers remained.

In the 1840s and 1850s, reform found a new direction. Many individuals began to try to win rights for two oppressed groups—women and enslaved persons. Section 4 discusses these efforts.

Section 3 Assessment

1. Terms & Names

Explain the significance of:
- revival
- Second Great Awakening
- temperance movement
- labor union
- strike
- Horace Mann
- Dorothea Dix

2. Using Graphics

Create a chart like the one below. Use it to list problems identified by reformers and their solutions to them.

Problem	Reformer's Solution

3. Main Ideas

a. How did the Second Great Awakening influence the reform movement?

b. How did labor unions try to force business owners to improve working conditions?

c. What were women's contributions to the reform movement?

4. Critical Thinking

Recognizing Effects What was the long-term impact of the reform movement that took place in the mid-1800s?

THINK ABOUT
- the changes reformers made in education, temperance, prisons, and the care of the disabled
- which of those changes are still in effect today

ACTIVITY OPTIONS

SPEECH

CIVICS

Think of a modern problem that is similar to an issue discussed in this section. Give a **speech** or write a **letter** to a government official suggesting a reform.

Report to the Massachusetts Legislature

Setting the Stage After traveling to several places where the mentally ill were kept, Dorothea Dix wrote a report describing the conditions she had discovered. In 1843, she presented her report to lawmakers to alert them to the horrible treatment of the mentally ill. This report has been called the "first piece of social research ever conducted in America." An excerpt from Dorothea Dix's report follows. **See Primary Source Explorer** ◉

Report to the Massachusetts Legislature

Gentlemen: . . . I come to present the strong claims of suffering humanity. I come to place before the Legislature of Massachusetts the condition of the miserable, the desolate, the outcast. I come as the **advocate**[1] of helpless, forgotten, insane, and idiotic men and women; of beings sunk to a condition from which the most unconcerned would start with real horror; of beings wretched in our prisons, and more wretched in our **almshouses.**[2]

I must confine myself to a few examples, but am ready to furnish other and more complete details, if required.

I proceed, gentlemen, briefly to call your attention to the *present* state of insane persons confined within this **Commonwealth,**[3] in *cages, closets, cellars, stalls, pens! Chained, naked, beaten with rods,* and *lashed* into obedience.

I offer the following extracts from my notebook and journal.

Springfield: In the jail, one lunatic woman, furiously mad, a state **pauper,**[4] improperly situated, both in regard to the prisoners, the keepers, and herself. It is a case of extreme self-forgetfulness and oblivion to all the decencies of life, to describe which would be to repeat only the grossest scenes. She is much worse since leaving Worcester. In the almshouse of the same town is a woman apparently only needing **judicious**[5] care and some well-chosen employment to make it unnecessary to confine her in solitude in a dreary unfurnished room. Her appeals for employment and companionship are most touching, but the mistress replied "she had no time to attend to her."

Lincoln: A woman in a cage. *Medford:* One idiotic subject chained, and one in a close stall for seventeen years. *Pepperell:* One often doubly chained, hand and foot; another violent; several peaceable now. *Brookfield:* One man caged, comfortable. *Granville:* One often closely confined, now losing the use of his

A CLOSER LOOK

ADVOCATE OF THE HELPLESS

In earlier times, the term *idiotic* did not mean stupid. It was used to describe someone who was mentally retarded.

1. For what groups of people is Dix pleading for help?

A CLOSER LOOK

JUDICIOUS CARE

Dix describes a woman who needs only some care and a useful task to do.

2. What did the woman's keeper say when Dix pointed that out?

1. **advocate:** a person who pleads another person's cause.
2. **almshouses:** homes for poor people.
3. **Commonwealth:** one of four U.S. states whose constitution uses this term to describe their form of self-government; in this case, Massachusetts.
4. **pauper:** a person who lives on the state's charity.
5. **judicious:** wise and careful.

limbs from want of exercise. *Charlemont:* One man caged. *Savoy:* One man caged. *Lenox:* Two in the jail, against whose unfit condition there the jailer protests.

Dedham: The insane **disadvantageously**[6] placed in the jail. In the almshouse, two females in stalls, situated in the main building, lie in wooden bunks filled with straw; always shut up. One of these subjects is supposed curable. The overseers of the poor have declined giving her a trial at the hospital, as I was informed, on account of expense.

Besides the above, I have seen many who, part of the year, are chained or caged. The use of cages is all but universal. Hardly a town but can refer to some not distant period of using them; chains are less common; **negligences**[7] frequent; willful abuse less frequent than sufferings proceeding from ignorance, or want of consideration. I encountered during the last three months many poor creatures wandering reckless and unprotected through the country. . . . But I cannot **particularize.**[8] In traversing the state, I have found hundreds of insane persons in every variety of circumstance and condition, many whose situation could not and need not be improved; a less number, but that very large, whose lives are the saddest pictures of human suffering and degradation.

I give a few illustrations; but description fades before reality. . . .

Men of Massachusetts, I beg, I implore, I demand pity and protection for these of my suffering, outraged sex. . . . Become the benefactors of your race, the just guardians of the solemn rights you hold in trust. Raise up the fallen, **succor**[9] the desolate, restore the outcast, defend the helpless, and for your eternal and great reward receive the benediction, "Well done, good and faithful servants, become rulers over many things!"

A CLOSER LOOK

I HAVE SEEN MANY

Notice that Dix cites evidence from many different towns.

3. Why do you think she includes so many specific details in her report?

A CLOSER LOOK

MEN OF MASSACHUSETTS

When Dix says "Men of Massachusetts," she is still speaking to the members of the state legislature.

4. What does Dix want the Massachusetts Legislature to do?

6. **disadvantageously:** harmfully.

7. **negligences:** careless actions.

8. **particularize:** to name in detail.

9. **succor:** to give help during a time of need.

Interactive Primary Source Assessment

1. Main Ideas

a. On what evidence did Dorothea Dix base her report about "suffering humanity"?

b. How were the mentally ill treated in Massachusetts?

c. Who did Dorothea Dix ask to help to improve the care of the mentally ill?

2. Critical Thinking

Evaluating Dix succeeded in convincing the legislature to provide funds for new hospitals. What do you think made her report so persuasive?

THINK ABOUT
• the details included in the report
• how Dix got the information to write her report
• the techniques you would use to persuade someone

Abolition and Women's Rights

MAIN IDEA	WHY IT MATTERS NOW	TERMS & NAMES
The spread of democracy led to calls for freedom for slaves and more rights for women.	The abolitionists and women reformers of this time inspired 20th–century reformers.	abolition Harriet Tubman Frederick Douglass Elizabeth Cady Stanton Sojourner Truth Seneca Falls Underground Convention Railroad suffrage

ONE AMERICAN'S STORY

African-American poet Frances Ellen Watkins Harper often wrote about the suffering of enslaved persons, such as enslaved mothers.

A VOICE FROM THE PAST

They tear him from her circling arms,
Her last and fond embrace.
Oh! never more may her sad eyes
Gaze on his mournful face.

No marvel, then, these bitter shrieks
Disturb the listening air:
She is a mother, and her heart
Is breaking in despair.

Frances Ellen Watkins Harper, "The Slave Mother"

As this section explains, many individuals in the mid-1800s demanded equal rights for African Americans and women.

Frances Ellen Watkins Harper impressed audiences with her speaking ability as she called for reform.

Taking Notes

Use your chart to take notes about the influence of abolitionists and women.

	How People
Immigrants	
Writers	
Reformers	
Abolitionists	
Women	

Abolitionists Call for Ending Slavery

Abolition, the movement to end slavery, began in the late 1700s. By 1804, most Northern states had outlawed slavery. In 1807, Congress banned the importation of African slaves into the United States. Abolitionists then began to demand a law ending slavery in the South.

David Walker, a free African American in Boston, printed a pamphlet in 1829 urging slaves to revolt. Copies of the pamphlet appeared in the South. This angered slaveholders. Shortly afterward, Walker died mysteriously.

A few Northern whites also fought slavery. In 1831, William Lloyd Garrison began to publish an abolitionist newspaper, *The Liberator,* in

Boston. Of his antislavery stand, he wrote, "I will not retreat a single inch—AND I WILL BE HEARD." Many people hated his views. In 1834, a furious mob in Boston grabbed Garrison and dragged him toward a park to hang him. The mayor stepped in and saved his life.

Two famous abolitionists were Southerners who had grown up on a plantation. Sisters Sarah and Angelina Grimké believed that slavery was morally wrong. They moved north and joined an antislavery society. At the time, women were not supposed to lecture in public. But the Grimkés lectured against slavery anyway. Theodore Weld, Angelina's husband, was also an abolitionist. He led a campaign to send antislavery petitions to Congress. Proslavery congressmen passed gag rules to prevent the reading of those petitions in Congress.

John Quincy Adams ignored the gag rules and read the petitions. He also introduced an amendment to abolish slavery. Proslavery congressmen tried to stop him. Such efforts, however, only weakened the proslavery cause by showing them to be opponents of free speech. Adams also defended a group of Africans who had rebelled on the slave ship *Amistad.* He successfully argued their case before the U.S. Supreme Court in 1841, and in 1842, the Africans returned home.

Eyewitnesses to Slavery

Two moving abolitionist speakers, **Frederick Douglass** and **Sojourner Truth,** spoke from their own experience of slavery. Douglass's courage and talent at public speaking won him a career as a lecturer for the Massachusetts Anti-Slavery Society. Poet James Russell Lowell said of him, "The very look and bearing of Douglass are an irresistible logic against the oppression of his race."

People who opposed abolition spread rumors that the brilliant speaker could never have been a slave. To prove them wrong, in 1845 Douglass published an autobiography that vividly narrated his slave experiences. Afterwards, he feared recapture by his owner, so he left America for a two-year speaking tour of Great Britain and Ireland. When Douglass returned, he bought his freedom. He began to publish an antislavery newspaper.

Sojourner Truth also began life enslaved. Originally named Isabella, Sojourner Truth was born in New York State. In 1827, she fled her owners and went to live with Quakers, who set her free. They also helped her win a court battle to recover her young son. He had been sold illegally into slavery in the South. A devout Christian, Truth changed her name in 1843 to reflect her life's work: to sojourn (or stay temporarily in a place) and "declare the truth to the people." Speaking for abolition, she drew huge crowds throughout the North.

Reading **History**
A. Drawing Conclusions How would the Grimké sisters' background help them as abolitionist speakers?

Reading **History**
B. Comparing How were Frederick Douglass and Sojourner Truth similar as abolitionists?

AMERICA'S HISTORY MAKERS

FREDERICK DOUGLASS
1817–1895
Douglass, born Frederick Bailey, was the son of a black mother and a white father. When he was eight, his owner sent him to be a servant for the Auld family. Mrs. Auld defied state law and taught young Frederick to read.

At the age of 16, Douglass returned to the plantation as a field hand. He endured so many whippings he later wrote, "I was seldom free from a sore back."

In 1838, he escaped to the North by hopping a train with a borrowed pass. To avoid recapture, he changed his last name.

How did Mrs. Auld unknowingly help Douglass become an abolitionist leader? Explain.

The Underground Railroad

Some abolitionists wanted to do more than campaign for laws ending slavery. Some brave people helped slaves escape to freedom along the Underground Railroad. Neither underground nor a railroad, the **Underground Railroad** was actually an aboveground series of escape routes from the South to the North. On these routes, runaway slaves traveled on foot. They also took wagons, boats, and trains.

Some enslaved persons found more unusual routes to freedom. For example, Henry Brown persuaded a white carpenter named Samuel A. Smith to pack him in a wooden box and ship him to Philadelphia. The box was only two and one half feet deep, two feet wide, and three feet long. It bore the label "This side up with care." Despite the label, Brown spent several miserable hours traveling head down. At the end of about 24 hours, Henry "Box" Brown climbed out of his box a free man in Philadelphia. Brown eventually made his way to Boston and worked on the Underground Railroad.

On the Underground Railroad, the runaways usually traveled by night and hid by day in places called stations. Stables, attics, and cellars all served as stations. At his home in Rochester, New York, Frederick Douglass hid up to 11 runaways at a time.

Harriet Tubman

The people who led the runaways to freedom were called conductors. One of the most famous conductors was **Harriet Tubman.** Born into slavery in Maryland, the 13-year-old Tubman once tried to save another slave from punishment. The angry overseer fractured Tubman's skull with a two-pound weight. She suffered fainting spells for the rest of her life but did not let that stop her from working for freedom. In 1849, Tubman learned that her owner was about to sell her. Instead, she escaped. She later described her feelings as she crossed into the free state of Pennsylvania: "I looked at my hands to see if I was the same person now that I was free. There was such a glory over everything."

After her escape, Harriet Tubman made 19 dangerous journeys to free enslaved persons. The tiny woman carried a pistol to frighten off slave hunters and medicine to quiet crying babies. Her enemies offered $40,000 for her capture, but no one caught her. "I never run my train off the track and I never lost a passenger," she proudly declared. Among the people she saved were her parents.

Now and then

THE UNDERGROUND RAILROAD

In 1996, historian Anthony Cohen took six weeks to travel from Maryland to Canada. Cohen followed the paths runaway slaves had taken 150 years earlier. He is shown below arriving in Canada.

Cohen walked, sometimes as much as 37 miles in a day. He also hitched rides on trains and canal boats.

About those long-ago slaves fleeing toward the hope of freedom, Cohen said, "They had no choice. . . . Nobody would do this if they didn't have to."

Reading **History**
C. Reading a Map The map on page 447 shows the routes of the Underground Railroad. Notice that most of these routes led to Canada.

Reading **History**
D. Forming and Supporting Opinions Why do you think escaped slaves such as Brown, Douglass, and Tubman risked their lives to help free others?

William Lloyd Garrison

Even after being threatened with hanging, Garrison continued to publish his antislavery newspaper, *The Liberator.*

Sojourner Truth and Harriet Tubman

Truth spoke out for both abolition and women's rights. Tubman risked her life leading people to freedom on the Underground Railroad.

Lucretia Mott and Susan B. Anthony

An abolitionist, Mott also helped lead the movement for women's rights. Anthony fought for women's suffrage into the 20th century.

Women Reformers Face Barriers

Other women besides the Grimké sisters and Sojourner Truth were abolitionists. Two of these were Lucretia Mott and **Elizabeth Cady Stanton**. Mott and Stanton were part of an American delegation that attended the World Anti-Slavery Convention in London in 1840. These women had much to say about their work. Yet when they tried to enter the convention, they were not allowed to do so. Men angrily claimed that it was not a woman's place to speak in public. Instead, the women had to sit silent behind a heavy curtain.

To show his support, William Lloyd Garrison joined them. He said, "After battling so many long years for the liberties of African slaves, I can take no part in a convention that strikes down the most sacred rights of all women."

Stanton applauded Garrison for giving up his chance to speak on abolition, the cause for which he had fought so long. "It was a great act of self-sacrifice that should never be forgotten by women."

However, most people agreed with the men who said that women should stay out of public life. Women in the 1800s enjoyed few legal or political rights. They could not vote, sit on juries, or hold public office. Many laws treated women—especially married women—as children. Single women enjoyed some freedoms, such as being able to manage their own property. But in most states, a husband controlled any property his wife inherited and any wages she might earn.

As the convention ended, Stanton and Mott decided it was time to demand equality for women. They made up their minds to hold a convention for women's rights when they returned home.

Vocabulary

delegation: a group that represents a larger group

ELIZABETH CADY STANTON
1815–1902

Elizabeth Cady Stanton's first memory was the birth of a sister when she was four. So many people said, "What a pity it is she's a girl!" that Stanton felt sorry for the new baby. She later wrote, "I did not understand at that time that girls were considered an inferior order of beings."

When Stanton was 11, her only brother died. Her father said, "Oh, my daughter, I wish you were a boy!" That sealed Stanton's determination to prove that girls were just as important as boys.

How did Stanton's childhood experiences motivate her to help other people besides herself?

The Seneca Falls Convention

Stanton and Mott held the <u>Seneca Falls Convention</u> for women's rights in Seneca Falls, New York, on July 19 and 20, 1848. The convention attracted between 100 and 300 women and men, including Frederick Douglass.

Before the meeting opened, a small group of planners debated how to present their complaints. One woman read aloud the Declaration of Independence. This inspired the planners to write a document modeled on it. The women called their document the Declaration of Sentiments and Resolutions. Just as the Declaration of Independence said that "All men are created equal," the Declaration of Sentiments stated that "All men and women are created equal." It went on to list several complaints or resolutions. Then it concluded with a demand for rights.

A VOICE FROM THE PAST

Now, in view of this entire disenfranchisement [denying the right to vote] of one-half the people of this country, their social and religious degradation—in view of the unjust laws above mentioned, and because women do feel themselves aggrieved, oppressed, and fraudulently deprived of their most sacred rights, we insist that they have immediate admission to all the rights and privileges which belong to them as citizens of the United States.

Seneca Falls Declaration of Sentiments and Resolutions, 1848

*Reading***History**
E. Using Primary Sources Why did the women at the Seneca Falls Convention believe they deserved rights and privileges?

Every resolution won unanimous approval from the group except **suffrage,** or the right to vote. Some argued that the public would laugh at women if they asked for the vote. But Elizabeth Cady Stanton and Frederick Douglass fought for the resolution. They argued that the right to vote would give women political power that would help them win other rights. The resolution for suffrage won by a slim margin.

The women's rights movement was ridiculed. In 1852, the *New York Herald* poked fun at women who wanted "to vote, and to hustle with the rowdies at the polls" and to be men's equals. The editorial questioned what would happen if a pregnant woman gave birth "on the floor of Congress, in a storm at sea, or in the raging tempest of battle."

Continued Calls for Women's Rights

In the mid-1800s, three women lent powerful voices to the growing women's movement. Sojourner Truth, Maria Mitchell, and Susan B. Anthony each offered a special talent.

In 1851, Sojourner Truth rose to speak at a convention for women's rights in Ohio. Some participants hissed their disapproval. Because Truth supported the controversial cause of abolition, they feared her

appearance would make their own cause less popular. But Truth won applause with her speech that urged men to grant women their rights.

> ### A VOICE FROM THE PAST
>
> I have heard much about the sexes being equal. I can carry as much as any man, and can eat as much too, if I can get it. I am as strong as any man. . . . If you have woman's rights give it to her and you will feel better. You will have your own rights, and they won't be so much trouble.
>
> **Sojourner Truth,** quoted by Marius Robinson, convention secretary

THE DISCORD.

This drawing shows a husband and wife fighting over who will "wear the pants in the family"— that is, who will rule the household.

The scientist Maria Mitchell fought for women's equality by helping to found the Association for the Advancement of Women. Mitchell was an astronomer who discovered a comet in 1847. She became the first woman elected to the American Academy of Arts and Sciences.

Susan B. Anthony was a skilled organizer who worked in the temperance and antislavery movements. She built the women's movement into a national organization. Anthony argued that a woman must "have a purse [money] of her own." To this end, she supported laws that would give married women rights to their own property and wages. Mississippi passed the first such law in 1839. New York passed a property law in 1848 and a wages law in 1860. By 1865, 29 states had similar laws. (Anthony also fought for suffrage. See Chapter 22.)

But women's suffrage stayed out of reach until the 1900s, and the U.S. government did not fully abolish slavery until 1865. As you will read in the next chapter, the issue of slavery began to tear the nation apart in the mid-1800s.

Section 4 Assessment

1. Terms & Names

Explain the significance of:
- abolition
- Frederick Douglass
- Sojourner Truth
- Underground Railroad
- Harriet Tubman
- Elizabeth Cady Stanton
- Seneca Falls Convention
- suffrage

2. Using Graphics

On a time line like the one below, record significant individuals and events in the historical development of the abolition movement.

1807   1865

Why does the time line end in 1865?

3. Main Ideas

a. Why were freedom of speech and freedom of the press important to the abolitionist movement?

b. What were Frederick Douglass's contributions to the abolitionist movement?

c. What were Elizabeth Cady Stanton's contributions to the women's rights movement?

4. Critical Thinking

Drawing Conclusions
Why do you think that many of the people who fought for abolition also fought for women's rights?

THINK ABOUT
- why they opposed slavery
- the social and economic position of women
- what the two causes had in common

ACTIVITY OPTIONS

TECHNOLOGY

DRAMA

With a partner, act out a meeting between a reformer from Section 3 and one from Section 4. **Videotape** their conversation or **perform** it for the class.

The Underground Railroad

The Underground Railroad was a network of people and places that hid escaping slaves and helped them reach safety in the North or in Canada. One reason slaves often went to Canada is that a U.S. federal law required people to return runaway slaves to their owners. Defying this law, both whites and blacks helped slaves to escape.

The map on page 447 shows the main escape routes. As the map shows, most of the slaves who escaped came from states bordering free states, such as Kentucky and Virginia. Distances from there to the North were relatively short, increasing the chances of reaching freedom. However, the number of slaves who escaped from the Deep South, such as Georgia and South Carolina, was very small, because of the long distances that had to be traveled. While no one knows the exact number, historians estimate that 40,000 to 100,000 people may have used the Underground Railroad on their journey from slavery to freedom.

Among the many people who helped slaves to freedom was former slave Harriet Tubman (far left). She became a well-known guide on the Underground Railroad. She is pictured with her husband (third from left), along with other formerly enslaved people.

ARTIFACT FILE

Identity Tag Enslaved persons were forced to wear tags that identified to whom they belonged.

Freedom Marker The "P" on the rock shown here told slaves that they were in Pennsylvania, a free state.

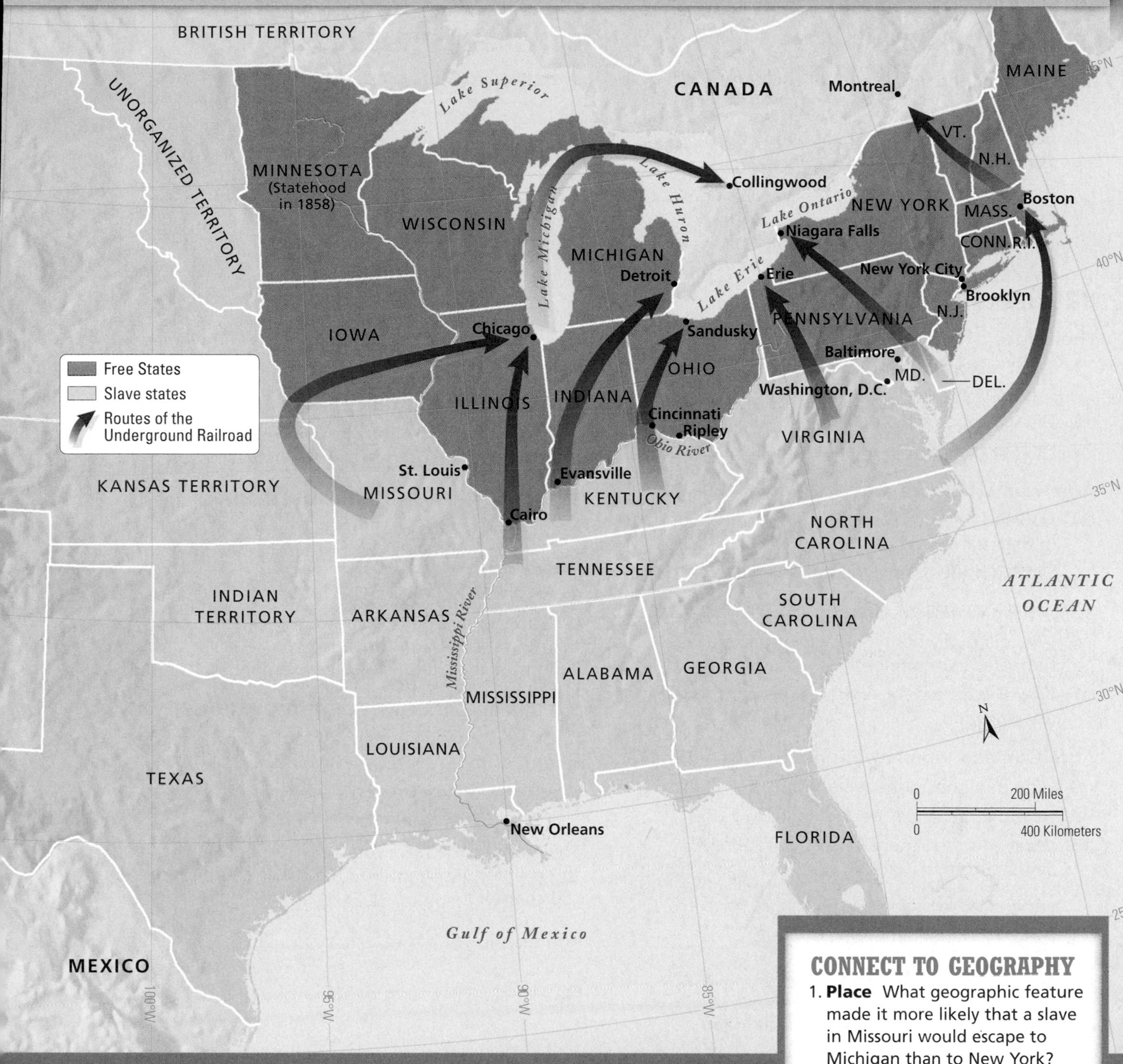

Map

BRITISH TERRITORY

UNORGANIZED TERRITORY

Lake Superior

CANADA

Montreal

MAINE

45°N

VT.

N.H.

MINNESOTA
(Statehood in 1858)

WISCONSIN

Lake Huron

Collingwood

Lake Ontario

NEW YORK

MASS.

Boston

Lake Michigan

MICHIGAN

Detroit

Niagara Falls

CONN. R.I.

40°N

IOWA

Chicago

Lake Erie

Erie

New York City

Brooklyn

Sandusky

PENNSYLVANIA

N.J.

ILLINOIS

INDIANA

OHIO

Baltimore

Washington, D.C.

MD.

DEL.

St. Louis

MISSOURI

Evansville

Cincinnati

Ripley

Ohio River

VIRGINIA

KANSAS TERRITORY

Cairo

KENTUCKY

35°N

NORTH CAROLINA

ATLANTIC OCEAN

INDIAN TERRITORY

ARKANSAS

Mississippi River

TENNESSEE

SOUTH CAROLINA

ALABAMA

GEORGIA

MISSISSIPPI

30°N

LOUISIANA

N

TEXAS

0   200 Miles

0   400 Kilometers

MEXICO

100°W   95°W   90°W   85°W

New Orleans

FLORIDA

25°N

Gulf of Mexico

Legend

- Free States
- Slave states
- Routes of the Underground Railroad

On-Line Field Trip

The National Underground Railroad Freedom Center is being built in Cincinnati, Ohio. Its collections will include artifacts and primary sources like this poster, which shows that substantial rewards were offered for the recapture of slaves.

For more about the Underground Railroad . . .

RESEARCH LINKS
CLASSZONE.COM

STOP THE THIEF!

One Hundred Dollars Reward.

Stolen from the Plantation of Mrs. E. S. FARRAR, on the night of Saturday last, two Negro Girls. One, MARY, low stature, heavy and squarely formed, very straight, black hair—a very bright Mulatto.

The other named CINTA or CINDERILLA, dark Copper, common height, has a flesh mole, near the left ear, and is well formed. Mary is twenty years old and CINTA nineteen.

I will pay a reward of $25 for the apprehension of each, if taken in the State, and $50 if taken out of it.

My address is Howardsville, Albemarle County, or Rocklish Depot, Nelson County.

September 15, 1862.   **RICHARD T. FARRAR.**

CONNECT TO GEOGRAPHY

1. **Place** What geographic feature made it more likely that a slave in Missouri would escape to Michigan than to New York?

2. **Movement** In what way did the Underground Railroad differ from other migrations?

   See Geography Handbook, pages 4–5.

CONNECT TO HISTORY

3. **Drawing Conclusions** How did the Underground Railroad reflect the American people's division over slavery?

TERMS & NAMES

Briefly explain the significance of each of the following.

1. immigrant
2. push-pull factors
3. civil disobedience
4. revival
5. Second Great Awakening
6. labor union
7. abolition
8. Underground Railroad
9. Seneca Falls Convention
10. suffrage

REVIEW QUESTIONS

The Hopes of Immigrants (pages 423–428)

1. What factors influenced so many immigrants to come to America in the 1800s?
2. What did Germans contribute to U.S. identity?
3. How did the potato famine affect Irish emigration?

American Literature and Art (pages 429–432)

4. How did American artists display the love of nature in their paintings?
5. What did the transcendentalists believe?

Reforming American Society (pages 433–439)

6. Why did many business owners support the temperance movement?
7. Why was it hard for African Americans to receive an education?

Abolition and Women's Rights (pages 440–447)

8. Who published antislavery writings?
9. How did the Underground Railroad work?
10. What was the Seneca Falls Declaration of Sentiments and Resolutions?

CRITICAL THINKING

1. USING YOUR NOTES: COMPARING

How People Influenced America in the mid-1800s	
Immigrants	
Writers	
Reformers	
Abolitionists	
Women	

Using your chart, answer the questions below.

a. Who influenced America to make reforms?

b. Compare the goals of abolitionists and women. How are they alike?

2. ANALYZING LEADERSHIP

Who is someone from this chapter who exercised leadership by standing up for an unpopular position?

3. THEME: IMPACT OF THE INDIVIDUAL

Judging from what you read in this chapter, what methods can individuals use to influence their society?

4. APPLYING CITIZENSHIP SKILLS

Who in this chapter displayed good citizenship by taking responsibility for their own behavior or by providing for their families? Give examples.

5. FORMING AND SUPPORTING OPINIONS

If someone asked you what was the most important reform of this period, what would you say? Why?

Interact *with* History

Think about the laws you proposed before you read the chapter. Has your opinion changed since you read the chapter?

VISUAL SUMMARY

A New Spirit of Change

The Hopes of Immigrants
Immigrants came to America from many European countries. They strongly influenced American life and culture.

Reforming American Society
Inspired by a religious revival, a reform movement swept the country. It aided schools, the workplace, and the disabled.

IMPACT OF THE INDIVIDUAL

American Literature and Art
American writers and artists of the 1800s produced some of America's greatest works, which are still studied.

Abolition and Women's Rights
Whites and blacks united to fight slavery. Women abolitionists expanded their fight to include women's rights as well.

STANDARDS-BASED ASSESSMENT

Use the graph and your knowledge of U.S. history to answer questions 1 and 2.

Additional Test Practice, pp. S1–S33.

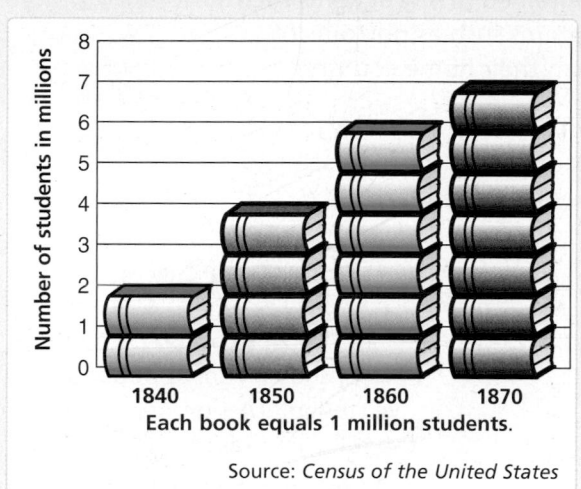

School Enrollment, *1840–1870*

Number of students in millions

1840   1850   1860   1870

Each book equals 1 million students.

Source: *Census of the United States*

1. On the graph, what does each book stand for?
   A. 100 students
   B. 1,000 students
   C. 100,000 students
   D. 1,000,000 students

2. What is the difference in school enrollment between 1840 and 1870?
   A. 2 million students
   B. 4 million students
   C. 5 million students
   D. 7 million students

Henry David Thoreau is discussing individuality in this quotation. Use the quotation and your knowledge of U.S. history to answer question 3.

PRIMARY SOURCE

If a man does not keep pace with his companions, perhaps it is because he hears a different drummer. Let him step to the music which he hears, however measured or far away.

Henry David Thoreau, *Walden*

3. Which sentence best states Thoreau's perspective?
   A. People should be able to enjoy whatever type of music they want.
   B. People should do what they believe is right, regardless of what others think.
   C. People should always comply with the wishes of those around them.
   D. People should understand that there is only one right way to behave.

TEST PRACTICE
CLASSZONE.COM

ALTERNATIVE ASSESSMENT

1. ✎ WRITING ABOUT HISTORY

You are a reporter interviewing immigrants as they arrive in the United States after an ocean voyage. Decide what country your interviewee is from, and write questions and answers that would come from an **interview**. Ask questions about the voyage, as well as questions that reveal why they immigrated.

• Use books about U.S. immigrants to research your interview.

2. COOPERATIVE LEARNING

Working with other students, make an annotated map of the Underground Railroad. Divide the work of researching to find accounts of slaves who escaped along the Underground Railroad. Type short summaries of their stories and identify their location on the map.

INTEGRATED TECHNOLOGY

DOING BIOGRAPHICAL INTERNET RESEARCH

Biographical information can be obtained from many on-line sources. Use the Internet to find facts about one of the following people: Horace Mann, Elizabeth Blackwell, Alexander Twilight, or Maria Mitchell.

• Use your subject's name as a keyword in your research.

• Use a minimum of three different online sources and record the Web sites you used in your research.

• Once you have conducted your research, write a fact sheet about the person you chose.

For more about these individuals . . .

INTERNET ACTIVITY
CLASSZONE.COM

Pack Your Trunk

For immigrants, packing up to go to a new land required making hard decisions. Wealthy people could ship belongings ahead. Most immigrants, though, carried their belongings in burlap bags, knotted sheets, large baskets, or small trunks. Even children carried small bundles. Only the very basic items or very precious ones could be taken to the United States. Baggage contained practical items such as tools and household items. But some had personal items such as portraits of loved ones. A few people even carried bags of dirt from their home country!

ACTIVITY Pack a trunk with items needed for a new life in the United States. Explain why you chose the items that you have packed. Finally, write a letter to a friend or relative back in Europe about your journey to the United States.

TOOLBOX

Each group will need:

a shoebox	markers or colored pencils
assorted magazines (optional)	3 x 5 note cards
craft sticks	masking tape
drawing paper or posterboard	styrofoam (optional)

STEP BY STEP

1 **Form groups.** Each group should consist of about four or five students. Assign group members the following tasks:

- Do research on what people brought with them when immigrating to the United States.

- Choose ten items that you will need for your new life.

- Present your items in class and give reasons for selecting them.

2 **Research what immigrants brought with them.** In the library or on the Internet (see Researching Your Project on the next page), research what immigrants brought with them to the United States. Make a list of everything you think you'll need for a new life in the United States. Some basic items included

- books
- favorite or special clothing
- toys
- important documents

Real immigrants brought these items to the United States: a mortar and pestle (used to grind spices or medicines), a shoe brush, a coffee grinder, and a paisley shawl.

3 **Create your items.** From your list, choose ten items that you think will be most important to starting a new life. Then draw pictures of the selected items or cut pictures of them out of a magazine. Attach a craft stick to the back of the picture with masking tape.

4 **Write reasons.** Think of why you selected each of the ten items. Write the reasons for each item on a separate 3 x 5 note card. Attach each note card to the back of the corresponding picture.

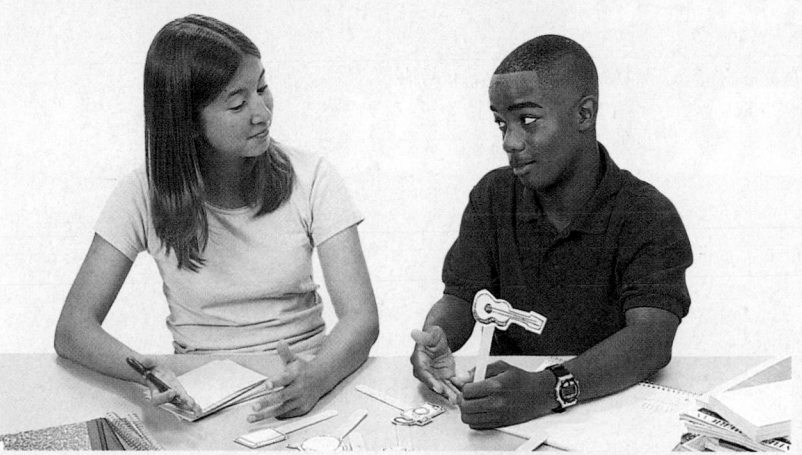

5 **Decorate the shoebox to look like a trunk.** Using the masking tape, affix your pictures to the rim of the shoebox, or use styrofoam in the bottom of the box to insert the pictures.

6 **Examine other groups' trunks.** Walk around the room and examine the contents of the other groups' trunks. Compare your trunk with that of your classmates. Share your reasons for selecting certain items.

WRITE AND SPEAK

Write a descriptive letter. Use the point of view of an immigrant. Write a letter to someone in your homeland describing your journey to the United States. Your letter might also describe what you miss most (personal belongings or people, for example) since the move. Read the letters to others in your class.

HELP DESK

For related information, see pages 423–428 in Chapter 14.

Researching Your Project

- *They Sought a New World* by William Kurdek and Margaret S. Englehart
- *American Immigration* by Edward G. Hartmann

For more about immigration . . .

RESEARCH LINKS CLASSZONE.COM

Did You Know?

Most immigrants traveled in **steerage** or third class. It was the lowest area of the ship, where a steering mechanism was located. A family "berth," or space allotted, in steerage was about six feet square.

Before World War I, fares in steerage to the United States from Europe were never more than $35 and by 1900 were as low as $10.

Shipping companies often fed herring (a kind of fish) to the immigrants. Herring was cheap and nourishing. It was also thought to help prevent seasickness.

REFLECT & ASSESS

- What priorities did you use in selecting items for your trunk?

- Which items would have to be left behind if you only had a small bag for your belongings?

- Why do you think other groups selected items different from yours?

A Nation Divided and Rebuilt

"I have a dream that my four little children . . . will not be judged by the color of their skin, but by the content of their character."

—Dr. Martin Luther King, Jr.

CHAPTER
29

The Civil Rights Era 1954–1975

Section 1
Origins of the Civil Rights Movement

Section 2
Kennedy, Johnson, and Civil Rights

Section 3
The Equal Rights Struggle Expands

People of many races participated in the March on Washington.

Civil rights marchers sing at the March on Washington in 1963.

1954
The Supreme Court decides *Brown* v. *Board of Education.*

1955
Montgomery bus boycott begins.

1957
Federal troops are sent to desegregate Little Rock Central High School.

1963
The March on Washington takes place.
Kennedy is assassinated, and Johnson becomes president.

1964
Congress passes Civil Rights Act of 1964.

USA
World   1954

1957
African nation of Ghana wins independence.

1959
Fidel Castro comes to power in Cuba.

1962
African National Congress leader Nelson Mandela is imprisoned.

It is 1960, and you live in a southern city. For decades, African Americans in the South have endured racial segregation. Now they are protesting against it—in spite of the risk of being attacked. You must decide whether or not you will participate in the protests and in what way.

How would you stop injustice in society?

What Do You Think?

• How far would you be willing to go to help the protesters?

• In what ways, besides protesting, could you help to end segregation?

RESEARCH LINKS
CLASSZONE.COM
Visit the Chapter 29 links for more information about the Civil Rights era.

1965
Congress passes the Voting Rights Act.

1968
Dr. Martin Luther King, Jr., is assassinated.

1970
La Raza Unida is founded.

1972
Members of AIM occupy the Bureau of Indian Affairs.

1975

1967
Civil war rages in Nigeria.

1971
India and Pakistan go to war.

Reading Strategy: Analyzing Causes

What Do You Know?

What do you think of when people talk about civil rights? Why have some people in the United States been denied their civil rights? Why are civil rights important in a democratic society?

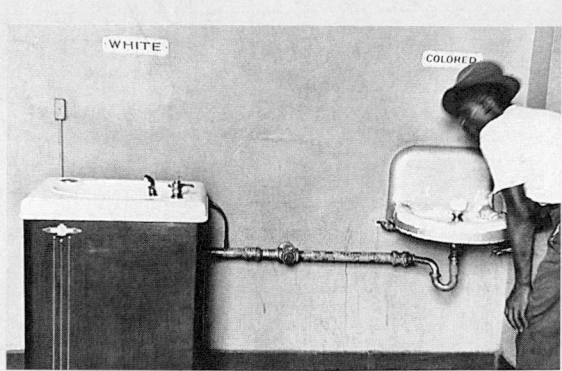

Think About

- what you have learned about racism, segregation, and discrimination in earlier chapters
- what you have learned about famous civil rights leaders from your parents or teachers
- your responses to the Interact with History about stopping injustice in society (see page 811)

What Do You Want to Know?

 What questions do you have about civil rights? Write those questions in your notebook before you read the chapter.

Analyzing Causes

For most historical events there are reasons, or causes, for that event. Copy the chart below in your notebook. Use it to take notes on the cause of each event listed in the chart.

 S See Skillbuilder Handbook, page R11.

✏️ Taking Notes

Causes	Events
	Brown v. Board of Education of Topeka
	Montgomery bus boycott
	Civil Rights Act of 1964
	Voting Rights Act of 1965
	La Raza Unida
	Publication of *The Feminine Mystique*, by Betty Friedan
	The federal government ends its "termination policy."

Origins of the Civil Rights Movement

MAIN IDEA	WHY IT MATTERS NOW	TERMS & NAMES
Changes after World War II helped African Americans make progress in their struggle for equality.	The African-American struggle for equality became a model for modern protest movements.	Thurgood Marshall *Brown v. Board of Education of Topeka* Montgomery bus boycott Dr. Martin Luther King, Jr. SCLC sit-in SNCC

ONE AMERICAN'S STORY

On December 1, 1955, Rosa Parks, an African-American woman from Montgomery, Alabama, boarded a bus to go home after work. Along the way, a group of white people climbed aboard. The bus driver told Parks and a few other African Americans to give up their seats for the whites and move to the back of the bus. All of them except Parks got up to move. She described what happened next.

A VOICE FROM THE PAST

The driver of the bus saw me still sitting there, and he asked was I going to stand up. I said, "No." He said, "Well, I'm going to have you arrested." Then I said, "You may do that."

Rosa Parks, *Rosa Parks: My Story*

Rosa Parks rides a bus in Montgomery, Alabama, in 1956.

Parks was arrested. As Section 1 explains, that event would spark a movement that began to tear down segregation in America.

Postwar Changes Strengthen Protests

Since the Civil War, African Americans had fought for equality. Their goals included full political rights, better job opportunities, and an end to segregation. But before World War II, they had had little success. Several changes made their efforts more successful after the war.

First, more Americans began to see racism as evil. Racist attitudes had supported the discrimination that oppressed African Americans. Many white Americans saw that racist beliefs had contributed to the rise of Adolf Hitler and the Holocaust. As a result, they began to recognize that racism had no place in the United States.

In addition, the war made African Americans more determined than ever to win equality at home. Having fought for freedom in Europe, African Americans wanted a share of it in the United States, too.

Taking Notes

Use your chart to take notes about *Brown v. Board of Education of Topeka* and the Montgomery bus boycott.

Causes	Events
	Brown v. Board of Education of Topeka
	Montgomery bus boycott
	Civil Rights Act of 1964
	Voting Rights Act of 1965
	La Raza Unida
	Publication of *The Feminine Mystique*
	The federal government ends its "termination policy."

The Civil Rights Era **813**

African Americans also gained important resources to help them fight segregation. More blacks had moved into cities to work. They made more money and formed more contacts with one another at work, on the street, and in churches. These changes helped to make the civil rights protests successful.

Background
Churches played a key role in the movement. They offered spiritual and moral support, buildings for meetings, and ministers as leaders.

Brown Overturns *Plessy*

The NAACP, the oldest civil rights organization in the United States, benefited from these changes. Before the war, it had established a fund to pay for legal challenges to segregation. Even so, the "separate but equal" doctrine remained in effect well into the 1950s. This doctrine had been established by *Plessy* v. *Ferguson* in 1896.

In the early 1950s, African Americans in several states sued to end segregation in, or integrate, public schools. Up to this point, white-controlled school boards had provided white children with better schoolhouses and newer books and equipment than they provided to black children. **Thurgood Marshall,** the NAACP counsel, led the attorneys who challenged the segregation laws in the courts.

Vocabulary
integrate: to open to people of all races or ethnic groups; to desegregate

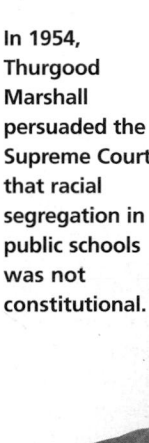

In 1954, Thurgood Marshall persuaded the Supreme Court that racial segregation in public schools was not constitutional.

In the early 1950s, the Supreme Court heard these cases under the name ***Brown v. Board of Education of Topeka***. On May 17, 1954, Chief Justice Earl Warren delivered the Court's historic opinion on these cases.

> **A VOICE FROM THE PAST**
>
> We conclude that in the field of public education the doctrine of "separate but equal" has no place. Separate educational facilities are inherently unequal.
>
> **Chief Justice Earl Warren,** *Brown* v. *Board of Education of Topeka*

The *Brown* decision was limited to public schools. But many people hoped that it would eventually end segregation in other public facilities. In the meantime, civil rights supporters hoped that black children would receive the same educational opportunities as white children. But the Supreme Court did not say how desegregation was to occur until a year later.

Reading **History**

A. Making Inferences Why might the *Brown* decision lead to the end of segregation in other public facilities?

At that time, the Court ordered public schools to desegregate "with all deliberate speed." This ruling, which was known as *Brown II,* actually gave segregated school districts *more* time to desegregate. A few places, such as Washington, D.C., desegregated quickly. But in most places, white-controlled schools resisted desegregation.

Montgomery Bus Boycott

In 1955, about six months after the *Brown II* decision, Rosa Parks was arrested, as you read in One American's Story on page 813. News of her arrest quickly reached

the other members of her church. The church members issued a notice to other African-American churches and local groups. It said, "If Negroes did not ride the buses, they [the buses] could not operate. We are, therefore, asking every Negro to stay off the buses Monday in protest of the arrest and trial." This protest, called the **Montgomery bus boycott,** began that day.

Background
African Americans made up 70 percent of the riders on Montgomery's buses.

That evening, local NAACP leaders held a meeting to decide whether to continue the boycott. A 26-year-old Baptist minister from Atlanta, Georgia, named **Dr. Martin Luther King, Jr.,** spoke to the group.

A VOICE FROM THE PAST

There comes a time that people get tired. We are here this evening to say to those who have mistreated us so long that we are tired—tired of being segregated and humiliated; tired of being kicked about by the brutal feet of oppression.

Martin Luther King, Jr., quoted in *Stride Toward Freedom*

The church members vowed to continue the boycott. It went on for 13 months. Boycotters, including some whites, organized car pools, rode bikes, or walked to their jobs and schools. King and other leaders endured death threats, bombings, and jailings. The violent reactions of whites to the nonviolent boycott gained the attention of the national media.

Meanwhile, the Montgomery bus segregation law had been challenged in court. On November 13, 1956, the Supreme Court ruled that the law was unconstitutional. African Americans once again boarded the buses in Montgomery. This time they sat wherever they pleased.

Reading **History**
B. Recognizing Effects What were the most important results of the Montgomery bus boycott?

The boycott had several important results. First, it ended segregation on Montgomery buses. Second, it led to the founding of the Southern Christian Leadership Conference (**SCLC**). SCLC coordinated civil rights protests across the South. Third, the boycott made Dr. King one of the best-known civil rights leaders in the nation.

MARTIN LUTHER KING, JR.
1929–1968
Fresh out of school, King had been in Montgomery about a year when he became leader of the bus boycott. But his courage and brilliant speaking abilities made him the ideal leader for the civil rights movement.

King learned about nonviolence by studying writers and thinkers such as Mohandas Gandhi. He came to believe that only love could convert people to the side of justice. He described the power of nonviolent resisters: "We will wear you down by our capacity to suffer. And in winning our freedom . . . we will win you in the process."

Why do you think King was well-suited to lead a nonviolent protest?

Massive Resistance

Civil rights victories upset many Southern whites. Polls showed that more than 80 percent opposed school desegregation. Segregationists fought back against African Americans and civil rights organizations. The Ku Klux Klan used beatings, arson, and murder to threaten African Americans who pursued their civil rights.

Many whites, especially among the middle class, organized groups known as White Citizens Councils to prevent desegregation. The opposition of whites to desegregation became known as massive resistance. It was very effective in delaying desegregation.

Showdown in Little Rock

Massive resistance threatened the desegregation of schools in Little Rock, Arkansas, in 1957. Following the *Brown* case, the Little Rock school board made plans to integrate. It called for nine African-American students to enroll at Central High School in September 1957.

As the start of the school year neared, segregationists tried to block the integration of the school. Arkansas governor Orval Faubus sided with the segregationists. On September 3, he ordered National Guard troops to prevent the African-American students from entering the school the next morning.

Eight of the students had received phone calls saying someone would drive them to the high school for their safety. When they arrived, the National Guard troops turned them away. The family of the ninth student, Elizabeth Eckford, had no telephone. She took a bus to school alone that morning. When she arrived, a mob of angry whites followed her toward the school's doors.

She saw a guard let some white students pass, so she went up to him. But he did not move out of the way. Later Eckford wrote, "When I tried to squeeze past him, he raised his bayonet. . . . Somebody started yelling, 'Lynch her! Lynch her!'" Finally, a white woman guided Eckford away from the mob and took her home.

For three weeks, Faubus refused to allow the African-American students into the school—even after meeting with President Dwight Eisenhower. The president did not want to force the governor to obey the law, but he eventually realized that it was his only choice.

Background
The nine African-American students chosen to integrate Central High School became known as the Little Rock Nine.

Vocabulary
lynch: to execute illegally, especially by hanging

HISTORY through ART

Elizabeth Eckford faced an angry mob as she walked to Little Rock Central High School on September 4, 1957. She had made her black-and-white dress especially for her first day of school at Central High.

How does the photograph show the emotions stirred by desegregation?

On September 24, Eisenhower ordered the 101st Airborne Division into Little Rock. The Little Rock Nine rode to school, escorted by jeeps armed with machine guns. Paratroopers lined the streets and protected the students as they entered Central High.

Sit-Ins Energize the Movement

Victories like the one in Little Rock encouraged civil rights supporters to continue their fight. In February 1960, four African-American college students began a sit-in to desegregate a lunch counter at a store in Greensboro, North Carolina. A **sit-in** is a protest in which people sit in a place and refuse to move until their demands are met. The students sat down at the lunch counter and ordered coffee. The waitress refused to serve them because they were African Americans.

"The doctrine of 'separate but equal' has no place."

From Brown v. Board of Education

That first day, the students stayed for 45 minutes. They came back each day that week with more protesters. By Thursday, there were more than 100 protesters, including some whites. Over the following weeks, thousands of protesters took part in sit-ins across the South.

Reading **History**

C. Solving Problems How did African Americans end discrimination at many lunch counters?

As the sit-ins spread, segregationists began to abuse the protesters. They covered the protesters with ammonia and itching powder. They yelled at them, beat them, and burned them with cigarettes. Some protesters went to jail. But other protesters replaced them at the counters. The sit-ins were an effective protest tactic. They forced many stores with lunch counters to serve African Americans.

Many civil rights leaders saw the success of the sit-ins and supported an organization for young people. Out of this movement, the Student Nonviolent Coordinating Committee (**SNCC**) was formed. Through SNCC, SCLC, and other groups, the civil rights movement increased the pressure for change in the 1960s, as you will read in the next section.

Section 1 Assessment

1. Terms & Names

Explain the significance of:
- Thurgood Marshall
- *Brown v. Board of Education of Topeka*
- Montgomery bus boycott
- Dr. Martin Luther King, Jr.
- SCLC
- sit-in
- SNCC

2. Using Graphics

Use a cluster diagram to record details about the early civil rights movement.

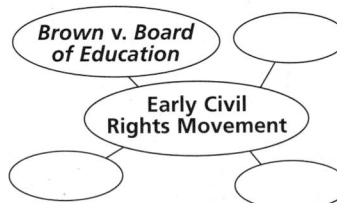

Brown v. Board of Education

Early Civil Rights Movement

3. Main Ideas

a. How did World War II help lead to the civil rights movement?

b. What role did Thurgood Marshall play in challenging segregation?

c. How did Martin Luther King, Jr., become a well-known civil rights leader?

4. Critical Thinking

Contrasting How did the tactics used by civil rights protesters differ from the response of many Southern whites?

THINK ABOUT
- the Montgomery bus boycott
- the events in Little Rock
- the nature of sit-ins

ACTIVITY OPTIONS

ART

TECHNOLOGY

You have been asked to honor people in the civil rights movement. Create a **wall of fame,** or plan a **Web page** that pays tribute to several of them.

2

Kennedy, Johnson, and Civil Rights

MAIN IDEA	WHY IT MATTERS NOW	TERMS & NAMES
The civil rights movement led to the end of legal segregation.	African Americans still face discrimination but now have more opportunities than before.	Freedom Ride · Freedom Summer CORE · Voting Rights Act March on Washington · Great Society Civil Rights Act of 1964 · Malcolm X

ONE AMERICAN'S STORY

Jim Zwerg, a white student from Wisconsin, joined a Freedom Ride in May 1961. **Freedom Rides** were protests against segregation on interstate busing in the South. During the rides, whites would sit in the back of a bus. African Americans would sit in the front and refuse to move. At bus terminals along the route, black riders would try to use "whites only" facilities.

In Alabama, segregationists savagely attacked the freedom riders. In this section, you will read how the Freedom Rides and other protests helped win support for civil rights.

John Lewis (left) and Jim Zwerg of SNCC are covered with blood after being beaten in Montgomery.

Taking Notes

Use your chart to take notes about the Civil Rights Act of 1964 and the Voting Rights Act of 1965.

Causes	Events
	Brown v. Board of Education of Topeka
	Montgomery bus boycott
	Civil Rights Act of 1964
	Voting Rights Act of 1965
	La Raza Unida
	Publication of The Feminine Mystique
	The federal government ends its "termination policy."

Kennedy and Civil Rights

In 1960, Americans elected a new president. Although civil rights was not the main issue in the campaign, it played an important role. The Democrats nominated John F. Kennedy, a senator from Massachusetts. The Republicans nominated Vice-President Richard Nixon. During the campaign, the candidates had similar positions on most issues. But many Americans thought that Kennedy was more dynamic.

Late in the campaign, police arrested Martin Luther King, Jr. Kennedy called King's wife, and Robert Kennedy, the candidate's brother, arranged for King's release. Those actions increased African-American support for Kennedy. Kennedy won a very close election.

As president, Kennedy had to work with a Congress that was reluctant to act on civil rights issues. In the early 1960s, Southern Democrats supported segregation. Kennedy did not want to anger Southern Democrats because they could weaken his presidency.

Even so, activists continued to pressure the federal government. In May 1961, the Congress of Racial Equality (**CORE**) planned Freedom Rides to desegregate interstate buses, or buses that travel between states.

Despite attacks on the freedom riders by segregationists along the route, the riders would not give up. Kennedy had to do something. Finally, he sent a group of federal marshals to protect the riders. Four months later, the federal government issued an order integrating interstate bus facilities. The riders had achieved their goal.

Protests in Birmingham

In the early 1960s, the civil rights movement gained strength across the South. African Americans in Birmingham, Alabama, wanted to integrate public facilities and gain better job and housing opportunities. Local civil rights leaders invited King and SCLC to join the protests.

Reading **History**
A. Drawing Conclusions Why did civil rights leaders choose to protest in cities where they were likely to face violence?

Birmingham was a great opportunity for protesters to expose the evils of segregation. They knew that Eugene "Bull" Connor, the city's Public Safety commissioner, was likely to use violence to stop the protests. They also knew that the sight of segregationists attacking nonviolent protesters would increase the pressure for change.

The protests began in April 1963. After about a week, the police arrested King, who had traveled to Birmingham for the protests. From jail, King wrote an eloquent defense of the protests.

A VOICE FROM THE PAST

I guess it is easy for those who have never felt the stinging darts of segregation to say, "Wait." . . . [But] there comes a time when the cup of endurance runs over, and men are no longer willing to be plunged into an abyss [a bottomless pit] of injustice.

Martin Luther King, Jr., "Letter from Birmingham Jail"

SCLC recruited children for the Birmingham marches. The police used dogs and firehoses on the marchers. People across the nation saw this on television and were horrified. Soon, Birmingham's white leaders agreed to

The firehoses used on Birmingham protesters had enough force to tear people's clothes and send small children skidding down the street.

desegregate lunch counters, remove segregation signs, and employ more African Americans in downtown stores.

The March on Washington

The events in Birmingham caused many Americans to support passage of new laws to protect the civil rights of all people. Civil rights organizations planned a huge demonstration in Washington, D.C., to build support for civil rights legislation.

On August 28, 1963, about 250,000 people took part in the **March on Washington,** as the demonstration became known. The march ended at the Lincoln Memorial. The high point of the march came when King delivered his "I Have a Dream" speech. (For a section from King's speech, see page 828.) During this speech, King spoke these famous words.

Reading **History**
B. Making Inferences Why might marchers have chosen the Lincoln Memorial as the place to end their march?

> ### A VOICE FROM THE PAST
> I have a dream that my four little children will one day live in a nation where they will not be judged by the color of their skin but by the content of their character.
> **Martin Luther King, Jr.,** from "I Have a Dream"

The March on Washington united many groups that called for passage of civil rights laws. President Kennedy promised support.

New Civil Rights Laws

Tragically, though, President Kennedy did not live long enough to fulfill this promise. On November 22, 1963, Kennedy and Vice-President Lyndon Baines Johnson went to Texas to campaign. As the presidential motorcade passed through Dallas, thousands of people greeted the president. Suddenly, shots rang out. Kennedy slumped forward; he'd been hit. The president died within an hour.

The tragedy deeply saddened the nation. Schools, factories, and businesses closed as citizens mourned their slain leader. The assassination of President Kennedy would remain a central event in the memories of many Americans in the decades to come.

Background
The man accused of shooting Kennedy, Lee Harvey Oswald, was killed two days later by another assassin.

Lyndon Johnson became president after Kennedy's death. He promised to continue Kennedy's policies. Johnson moved quickly on civil rights. He argued that "no memorial oration or eulogy could more eloquently honor President Kennedy's memory than the earliest possible passage of the civil rights bill." The nation's grief led to broad support for the bill.

In July, the **Civil Rights Act of 1964** was signed into law. The law banned segregation in public places, such as hotels, restaurants, and theaters. It also created the Equal Employment Opportunity Commission to prevent job discrimination. At long last, segregation was officially illegal throughout the United States.

Kennedy's flag-draped casket is drawn through the streets of Washington, D.C., during the slain leader's funeral procession.

Fighting for Voting Rights

White Southerners had long used literacy tests, poll taxes, and violence to keep African Americans from voting. The Civil Rights Act of 1964 barred states from using different voting standards for blacks and whites. In the same year, the states ratified the Twenty-Fourth Amendment. It outlawed poll taxes. Even so, African Americans in the South still found it difficult to vote. As a result, they lobbied Congress to pass a strong voting rights law.

In 1964, SNCC organized a voter-registration drive for Southern blacks. The program was called **Freedom Summer**. It brought Northern college students into Mississippi to work with SNCC organizers. The young volunteers endured bombings, beatings, arrests, and murder while performing their work. Even so, they managed to add about 1,200 African Americans to voter registration rolls.

Early in 1965, King and SCLC organized voter-registration drives in Selma, Alabama, including a protest march to Montgomery. On March 7, as the marchers crossed a bridge at the edge of Selma, state troopers on horseback attacked them. Americans watched as the violence was broadcast on national television. Pressure for federal action rose.

President Johnson told Alabama Governor George Wallace that he would not tolerate any more violence. When the march to Montgomery resumed, the president sent troops to protect it. He also used the public's anger at the incident to push for action on voting rights.

Johnson used the considerable political skills he had acquired when he was a senator to push a voting rights bill through Congress. On August 6, 1965, he signed the **Voting Rights Act** into law. It banned literacy tests and other laws that kept blacks from registering to vote. It also sent federal officials to register voters. Within weeks, the percentage of African Americans in Selma who registered to vote increased from 10 percent to 60 percent.

Reading **History**

C. Drawing Conclusions How did television help to advance the civil rights movement?

Reading **History**

D. Reading a Map Use the map below to see how the registration of African-American voters increased throughout the South.

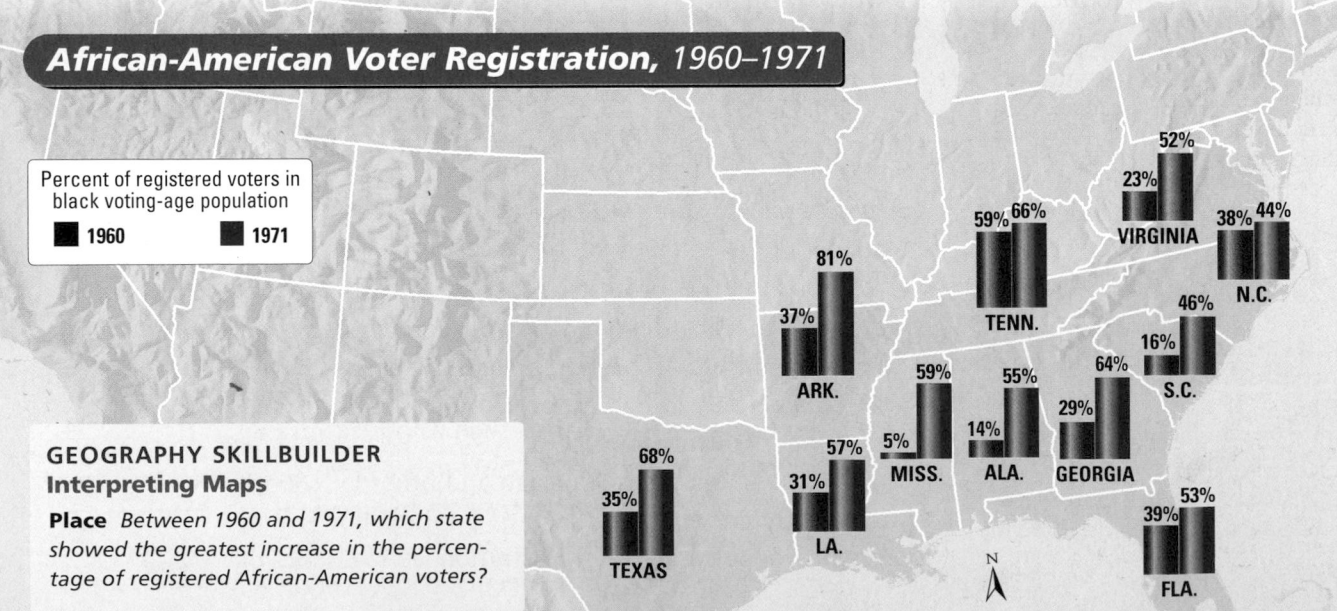

African-American Voter Registration, 1960–1971

Percent of registered voters in black voting-age population
■ 1960   ■ 1971

VIRGINIA 23% 52%
N.C. 38% 44%
TENN. 59% 66%
ARK. 37% 81%
S.C. 16% 46%
GEORGIA 29% 64%
MISS. 5% 59%
ALA. 14% 55%
LA. 31% 57%
TEXAS 35% 68%
FLA. 39% 53%

GEOGRAPHY SKILLBUILDER
Interpreting Maps

Place *Between 1960 and 1971, which state showed the greatest increase in the percentage of registered African-American voters?*

Source: *Voter Mobilization and the Politics of Race*

821

President Johnson signs the Medicare bill into law on July 30, 1965.

The Great Society

Civil Rights Act (1964)

Outlawed discrimination in public places, created the Equal Employment Opportunity Commission, and barred states from using different standards for voter registration for whites and blacks

Voting Rights Act (1965)

Banned literacy tests and used federal registrars to register voters

Medical Care Act (1965)

Established Medicare and Medicaid programs to assist the aged and the poor with medical care

Elementary and Secondary School Act (1965)

Provided federal aid to education

SKILLBUILDER
Interpreting Charts

1. *What act created the Equal Employment Opportunity Commission?*
2. *What acts helped to increase the number of African-American voters?*

Johnson and the Great Society

The Civil Rights Act and the Voting Rights Act were important parts of the reform plan supported by President Johnson. Shortly after taking office, Johnson asked Americans to seek a "great society [that] demands an end to poverty and racial injustice." His program was called the **Great Society**. It provided a series of programs to help the disenfranchised, the poor, the elderly, and women. It also included legislation to promote education, end discrimination, and protect the environment.

Many of the programs were passed and still exist today, such as Medicare and Medicaid. Medicare provides health insurance for senior citizens, while Medicaid provides medical care for the poor.

In addition, Congress passed the Elementary and Secondary School Act, which provided new federal funds for education. Laws were also passed to protect the environment. Congress strengthened the 1960 Clean Water and 1963 Clean Air acts. And it passed legislation to protect endangered species and to preserve millions of acres of wilderness.

Vocabulary
disenfranchised: people deprived of the rights of citizenship, especially the right to vote

Divisions in the Civil Rights Movement

In the late 1960s, with the civil rights laws of Johnson's Great Society already passed, civil rights leaders disagreed about what steps to take next. The SCLC and other organizations wanted to expand the nonviolent struggle. But some groups wanted the movement to become more aggressive.

In 1966, King and the SCLC joined protests in Chicago. In the North, there were no laws that denied African Americans their civil rights—white people simply discriminated against them. Whites would not sell property in certain areas to African Americans, and some white employers refused to hire black workers.

In spite of the protests, most white Chicagoans were no more interested in desegregation than Southern whites had been. Chicago mayor Richard J. Daley made only a few minor changes before SCLC abandoned its campaign.

African Americans in Chicago and other U.S. cities were frustrated with their lack of political power and economic opportunity. This frustration led to a series of

Reading **History**
E. Forming Opinions Why did race riots take place in Northern cities?

riots in the late 1960s. Nationwide, 164 riots broke out in the first 9 months of 1967. Then, on April 4, 1968, Martin Luther King, Jr., was assassinated in Memphis, Tennessee. As the nation mourned the slain civil rights leader, African-American neighborhoods across the country exploded in anger. Over 45 people died in the rioting.

Some African Americans had begun to reject nonviolence and cooperation with whites. In 1966, SNCC's black members forced white members out of the organization. Stokely Carmichael, the new leader of SNCC, began to call for "black power." Carmichael and others wanted blacks to create their own organizations under their own control to fight white racism.

The Nation of Islam, a branch of Islam founded in the United States, also urged African Americans to separate from whites. In the 1960s, the Nation was led by Elijah Muhammad, but the group's most popular personality was **Malcolm X**.

Malcolm X speaks at a rally in Harlem in 1963.

Background Mecca is the holiest city for Muslims.

By the mid-1960s, Malcolm X rejected the separatist ideas of the Nation of Islam and left the group. During a trip to Mecca, in Saudi Arabia, he had met Muslims of all races. He began to picture a world where all races could live together in peace. But he had little time to spread his new message. In 1965, he was gunned down by members of the Nation of Islam.

From the late 1960s on, civil rights progress came slowly for African Americans. But the African-American struggle for equality encouraged civil rights movements among other oppressed groups, as you will read in the next section.

Section **2** Assessment

1. Terms & Names

Explain the significance of:
- Freedom Ride
- CORE
- March on Washington
- Civil Rights Act of 1964
- Freedom Summer
- Voting Rights Act
- Great Society
- Malcolm X

2. Using Graphics

Use a time line like the one shown to record important events of the civil rights movement.

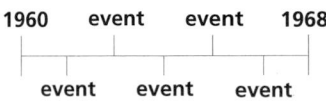

In what year was the voter registration drive in Selma?

3. Main Ideas

a. Why did civil rights workers believe that Birmingham was a good place to protest?

b. How did civil rights workers fight to improve African-American voting rights?

c. Why did the movement begin to break apart?

4. Critical Thinking

Making Inferences Why do you think African Americans placed so much importance on the right to vote?

THINK ABOUT
- who and what they might want to vote for
- what they were willing to endure to win voting rights
- how Southern whites kept them from voting

ACTIVITY OPTIONS

ART

SPEECH

Imagine that you are taking part in the March on Washington. Design a **poster** you could carry, or deliver a **speech** in favor of civil rights.

The Equal Rights Struggle Expands

MAIN IDEA	WHY IT MATTERS NOW	TERMS & NAMES
The African-American struggle for equality inspired other groups to fight for equality.	Nonwhites and women continue to fight for equality today.	César Chávez National Congress of American Indians Betty Friedan NOW ERA

ONE AMERICAN'S STORY

In the 1940s, **César Chávez** and his family worked as migrant laborers in California. (Migrant workers travel from place to place in search of work.) One time the whole family, parents and six children, worked picking peas. Chávez described the poor pay.

A VOICE FROM THE PAST

They [the managers] would take only the peas they thought were good, and they only paid you for those. The pay was twenty cents a hamper, which had to weigh in at twenty-five pounds. So in about three hours, the whole family made only twenty cents.

César Chávez, *César Chávez: Autobiography of* La Causa

In 1962, Chávez decided to start a union for farm workers. But the owners refused to recognize the union. Responding to Chávez's call, workers went on strike. Then Chávez asked people not to buy produce harvested by nonunion workers. The tactics worked. In 1970, 26 major California growers signed a contract with the union. It gave the workers higher wages. Section 3 explains how the fight for equal rights spread beyond African Americans.

César Chávez, head of the National Farm Workers Association, marches with striking grape pickers in the 1960s. (*Huelga* is the Spanish word for strike.)

Taking Notes

Use your chart to take notes about *La Raza Unida*, *The Feminine Mystique*, and the "termination" policy.

Causes	Events
	Brown v. Board of Education of Topeka
	Montgomery bus boycott
	Civil Rights Act of 1964
	Voting Rights Act of 1965
	La Raza Unida
	Publication of *The Feminine Mystique*
	The federal government ends its "termination policy."

Mexican Americans Organize

The farm workers' struggle inspired other Mexican Americans. By the 1960s, most Mexican Americans lived in cities in the Southwest and California. In 1970, Mexican Americans formed *La Raza Unida* (lah RAH•sah oo•NEE•dah)—"the united people." *La Raza* fought for better jobs, pay, education, and housing. It also worked to elect Mexican Americans to public office.

Mexican-American students also began to organize. They wanted reform in the school system. The students demanded such changes as

Background
Many Mexican Americans prefer to be called Chicanos, or Chicanas if they are female.

better facilities, more courses on the Mexican-American experience, and more Mexican-American teachers.

In 1968, students in Los Angeles walked out of classes to press their demands. At first, school authorities reacted harshly to the walkouts and arrested many of the protesters. Even so, they eventually admitted to the poor conditions of many schools and met with protesters to discuss solutions. By the early 1970s, many of the reforms that the students demanded had been made.

Hispanic Diversity

Hispanics, including Mexican Americans, trace their roots to Spanish-speaking countries and cultures. Because these countries are commonly known as Latin America, some people from these areas refer to themselves as Latinos.

Because Hispanic Americans come from many different countries, they sometimes have little in common. For example, among Mexican Americans, immigration and citizenship are important issues. Puerto Ricans, however, are already U.S. citizens and are not troubled by such issues.

Reading **History**
A. Summarizing
What are the factors that unite and separate Hispanics?

Similarly, many Cubans came to the United States as political refugees after Communists took power in Cuba. They tend to be more politically conservative than other Hispanics. Such differences make it difficult for Hispanic Americans to achieve political unity.

Native Americans Unite

Native Americans, like Hispanics, often had difficulty uniting to address common problems. But in the 1950s, that began to change. In 1953, the federal government began a "termination policy" that ended federal protection of land and other assets held by Native American tribes. One result of this policy was the decline of traditional Native American cultures.

Native Americans protested against these policies. The **National Congress of American Indians** (NCAI)—founded in 1944 to promote the "common welfare" of Native Americans—led the protests. Under pressure, the federal government changed the policy in 1958.

The success of these protests inspired a new generation of Native American activists to fight for their rights. In 1961, more than 400 Native Americans from dozens of tribes met in Chicago. They issued a statement they titled the Declaration of Indian Purpose. In it, they demanded the "right to choose our own way of life" and the "responsibility of preserving precious heritage."

In 1968, a group of Native Americans founded the American Indian Movement (AIM). AIM was more aggressive than other organizations in demanding rights for people on reservations and greater recognition of

America's HERITAGE

CINCO DE MAYO

During the civil rights era, many Americans learned to appreciate the variety of cultural traditions that make their nation unique.

For example, many Americans now join in the celebration of the Mexican holiday Cinco de Mayo (5th of May). This holiday commemorates the 1862 victory of Mexican troops over the French Army in Puebla, Mexico.

The holiday reflects the national pride of Mexicans over the defeat of a superior fighting power. But the holiday has also taken on a broader meaning for all Americans as a celebration of the right of all people to self-determination. A Cinco de Mayo gathering is shown below.

Native Americans petition for the return of tribal artifacts at the state capital in Albany, New York, in 1970.

tribal laws. In 1972, members of AIM occupied the Bureau of Indian Affairs in Washington, D.C., for seven days. Russell Means, one of the group's leaders, declared, "We don't want civil rights in the white man's society—we want our own sovereign rights."

In the early 1970s, Native Americans protested to force the government to provide them with more federal aid. In addition, the Indian Self-Determination Act of 1975 gave tribal governments more control over social programs, law enforcement, and education. Other victories came through winning court cases. Native Americans won back some of their lands. They have also gone to court over rights to water, hunting, and fishing.

Reading **History**
B. Comparing Did any African-American organizations during the civil rights era have goals similar to AIM's?

The Women's Movement

In the 1960s, women also demanded equal rights. Early in the decade, women were kept out of many jobs. They faced discrimination in many male-dominated businesses. For example, there were few female police officers. The military also limited the jobs open to women.

Women also had limited legal rights. Married women, for example, faced problems in signing contracts, selling property, and getting credit. A woman could lose her job if she became pregnant. In addition, society pressured women to quit their jobs when they married. Women who wanted to work at jobs outside their homes were seen as "unnatural." **Betty Friedan** described the problems women faced in her 1963 book, *The Feminine Mystique.*

A VOICE FROM THE PAST

We can no longer ignore that voice within women that says: "I want something more than my husband and my children and my home."

Betty Friedan, *The Feminine Mystique*

Friedan's words helped give direction to a movement for women's liberation. In 1966, Friedan helped to found the National Organization for Women (**NOW**). Some of NOW's major goals were to help women get good jobs and equal pay for their work.

In response to women's groups, Congress passed the Equal Rights Amendment (**ERA**) in 1972 and sent it to the states for ratification. The proposed amendment stated, "Equality of rights under the law shall not be denied or abridged by the United States or any State on account of sex." Supporters of the amendment argued that it would protect women against discrimination. They also said it would help women achieve equality with men, including such things as equal opportunity for jobs and education as well as equal pay for equal work.

Background
An Equal Rights Amendment was initially proposed in 1923, after women gained the right to vote.

Women's Rights Leaders, 1972

In July 1972, women's rights leaders met in Washington, D.C., to demand that women play a larger role in the upcoming presidential conventions.

1 **Bella Abzug** was a U.S. representative from New York.

2 **Gloria Steinem** was the founding editor of *Ms.* magazine.

3 **Shirley Chisholm** was a U.S. representative from New York and ran for president in 1972.

4 **Betty Friedan** wrote *The Feminine Mystique* and was the cofounder and first president of NOW.

For the amendment to be added to the Constitution, 38 of the 50 states had to ratify it. Within months, 22 states had done so. But by the 1982 deadline, only 35 states had ratified the amendment, and it died despite support by a majority of Americans. The amendment failed because it faced well-organized opposition, even from some women. Phyllis Schlafly, ERA's most famous opponent, argued that it would destroy American families and that the problems of women were not the government's business.

Other reforms, however, reduced the inequality between women and men. The Civil Rights Act of 1964 and the Higher Education Act of 1972 outlawed discrimination against women. These two laws helped to expand opportunities for women in education, sports, and the workplace.

The civil rights movements that followed World War II greatly changed life in the United States. As you will read in the next chapter, the war in Vietnam also changed the nation.

*Reading***History**
C. Analyzing Causes Why wasn't the ERA added to the Constitution even though it was passed in 1972?

Section 3 Assessment

1. Terms & Names

Explain the significance of:
- Cesar Chavez
- National Congress of American Indians
- Betty Friedan
- NOW
- ERA

2. Using Graphics

Use a chart like the one shown to record important details about the struggle for equal rights.

Mexican Americans	Native Americans	Women

How do the positions women hold today reflect changes won in the civil rights era?

3. Main Ideas

a. What was *La Raza Unida,* and what did it do?

b. What was the Declaration of Indian Purpose?

c. How did Betty Friedan help to launch the women's liberation movement?

4. Critical Thinking

Analyzing Points of View
What were the different opinions about the ERA?

THINK ABOUT
- what NOW and other women's groups would have thought of it
- what Phyllis Schlafly thought of it

ACTIVITY OPTIONS

TECHNOLOGY
LANGUAGE ARTS

Plan part of a **multimedia presentation** focusing on one of the groups mentioned in this section, or write a **pamphlet** explaining that group's goals.

I Have a Dream

Setting the Stage On August 28, 1963, Martin Luther King, Jr., gave his most famous speech at the March on Washington. In it, he shared his dream of equality for all. **See Primary Source Explorer**

A CLOSER LOOK

ABRAHAM LINCOLN

In his speech, King made references to Abraham Lincoln. He specifically referred to the Emancipation Proclamation and used the phrase "Five score years ago" to remind his listeners of the opening of the Gettysburg Address.

1. Why do you think King would refer to Lincoln's speeches?

A CLOSER LOOK

THE AMERICAN DREAM

The American dream can mean different things to different people. Usually, however, it refers to the freedom and opportunity for Americans to lead their own lives.

2. How do civil rights fit into the American dream?

A CLOSER LOOK

GOING TO JAIL

Dr. King—who was arrested 30 times for civil rights activities—said that, with the faith that some day all men will be treated as equals, people will be ready to go to jail together.

3. Why do you think civil rights workers were willing to go to jail?

I am happy to join with you today in what will go down in history as the greatest demonstration for freedom in the history of our nation.

Five score years ago, a great American, in whose symbolic shadow we stand today, signed the Emancipation Proclamation. . . . But one hundred years later, the Negro still is not free. One hundred years later, the life of the Negro is still sadly crippled by the **manacle**[1] of segregation and the chains of discrimination.

So we've come here today to dramatize a shameful condition. . . .

I say to you today, my friends, that even though we face the difficulties of today and tomorrow, I still have a dream. It is a dream deeply rooted in the American dream.

I have a dream that one day this nation will rise up and live out the true meaning of its **creed**[2] —we hold these truths to be self-evident that all men are created equal.

I have a dream that my four little children will one day live in a nation where they will not be judged by the color of their skin but by the content of their character.

I have a dream today!

This is our hope. This is the faith that I will go back to the South with. . . . With this faith we will be able to work together, to pray together, to struggle together, to go to jail together, to stand up for freedom together, knowing that we will be free one day. This will be the day, this will be the day when all of God's children will be able to sing with new meaning "My country 'tis of thee, sweet land of liberty, of thee I sing. Land where my fathers died, land of the Pilgrim's pride, from every mountainside, let freedom ring!" And if America is to be a great nation, this must become true.

And when this happens, when we allow freedom to ring, when we let it ring from every tenement and every hamlet, from every state and every city, we will be able to speed up that day when all of God's children, black men and white men, Jews and **Gentiles,**[3] Protestants and Catholics, will be able to join hands and sing in the words of the old Negro spiritual, "Free at last, free at last. Thank God Almighty, we are free at last."

Martin Luther King, Jr.

1. **manacle:** handcuff.   2. **creed:** statement of belief.   3. **Gentile:** Non-Jewish person.

An Open Letter

Setting the Stage In 1969, Cesar Chavez wrote a letter in which he denied accusations that he had used violence to win decent wages and better benefits for farm workers. **See Primary Source Explorer** ◎

Today . . . we remember the life and sacrifice of Martin Luther King, Jr., who gave himself totally to the nonviolent struggle for peace and justice. In his letter from Birmingham Jail, Dr. King describes better than I could our hopes for the strike and boycott: "Injustice must be exposed, with all the tension its exposure creates, to the light of human conscience and the air of national opinion before it can be cured." For our part, I admit that we have seized upon every tactic and strategy consistent with the morality of our cause to expose that injustice and thus to heighten the sensitivity of the American conscience so that farmworkers will have without bloodshed their own union and the dignity of bargaining with their **agribusiness**[1] employers. . . .

Our strikers here in **Delano**[2] and those who represent us throughout the world are well trained for this struggle. . . . They have been taught not to lie down and die or to flee in shame, but to resist with every ounce of human endurance and spirit. To resist not with retaliation in kind but to overcome with love and compassion, with **ingenuity**[3] and creativity, with hard work and longer hours, with stamina and patient **tenacity**[4], with truth and public appeal, with friends and allies, with mobility and discipline, with politics and law, and with prayer and fasting. They were not trained in a month or even a year; after all, this new harvest season will mark our fourth full year of strike and even now we continue to plan and prepare for the years to come. . . .

We shall overcome and change it not by retaliation or bloodshed but by a determined nonviolent struggle carried on by those masses of farmworkers who intend to be free and human.

Cesar E. Chavez

A CLOSER LOOK

AGRIBUSINESS

Farm workers were excluded from the National Labor Relations Act of 1935—the law that gives most Americans the right to organize a union. By 1975, pressure from Chavez had convinced lawmakers in California to allow farm workers in the state to organize unions.

1. Why do you think farm workers wanted to organize a union?

A CLOSER LOOK

TRAINING FOR PROTESTS

During the civil rights era, protesters often received extensive training before participating in marches, demonstrations, and sit-ins. Chavez explains that farm workers were also trained for the struggle.

2. Why do you think that training for nonviolent protest might be necessary?

---

1. **agribusiness:** farming as a large-scale business operation.
2. **Delano:** a farming city in California.
3. **ingenuity:** imagination or cleverness.
4. **tenacity:** persistence.

Interactive Primary Sources Assessment

1. Main Ideas

a. Why does King declare that the United States is not living up to its creed?

b. What does King say must happen before America can be considered a truly great nation?

c. Why do you think Cesar Chavez refers to King in his speech?

2. Critical Thinking

Comparing and Contrasting In what ways were the problems that King and Chavez wrote about similar and different?

THINK ABOUT
- the kinds of discrimination they faced
- their hopes for the future

The Civil Rights Era

1954

1954
Brown v. *Board of Education of Topeka*

1955
The Montgomery bus boycott begins.

1957
Federal troops are sent to desegregate Little Rock Central High School.

1960
John F. Kennedy is elected president.

1961
Native Americans issue the Declaration of Indian Purpose.

1962
Cesar Chavez starts a union for farm workers.

1963
March on Washington

Kennedy is assassinated, and Johnson becomes president.

1964
Civil Rights Act

1965
Voting Rights Act

Malcolm X is assassinated.

1968
Martin Luther King, Jr., is assassinated.

1970
La Raza Unida is founded.

1972
Congress passes the Equal Rights Amendment, but it is never ratified by the states.

1975

TERMS & NAMES

Briefly explain the significance of each of the following.

1. *Brown* v. *Board of Education of Topeka*
2. Montgomery bus boycott
3. Martin Luther King, Jr.
4. March on Washington
5. Civil Rights Act of 1964
6. Voting Rights Act
7. Great Society
8. Cesar Chavez
9. National Congress of American Indians
10. ERA

REVIEW QUESTIONS

Origins of the Civil Rights Movement (pages 813–817)

1. What factors helped to give strength to the demands of the civil rights movement?
2. What were the immediate and long-term effects of *Brown* v. *Board of Education of Topeka?*
3. How did white people react to civil rights protests?

Kennedy, Johnson, and Civil Rights (pages 818–823)

4. What factors made it difficult for Kennedy to act on civil rights?
5. Why did Congress eventually pass civil rights legislation?
6. What effects did Johnson's Great Society legislation have?

The Equal Rights Struggle Expands (pages 824–829)

7. How did farm workers participate in the equal rights movement?
8. What challenges did Hispanics face in their civil rights struggle?
9. Why did Native Americans protest U.S. government policy?
10. What kinds of discrimination did women challenge during the civil rights era?

CRITICAL THINKING

1. USING YOUR NOTES: ANALYZING CAUSES

Using your completed chart, answer the questions below.

Causes	Events
	Brown v. *Board of Education of Topeka*
	Montgomery bus boycott
	Civil Rights Act of 1964
	Voting Rights Act of 1965
	La Raza Unida
	Publication of *The Feminine Mystique*, by Betty Friedan
	The federal government ends its "termination policy."

a. What causes resulted in the Supreme Court decision *Brown* v. *Board of Education of Topeka?*
b. What forces led Betty Friedan to write *The Feminine Mystique?*

2. ANALYZING LEADERSHIP

What qualities do you think made Martin Luther King, Jr., an effective leader?

3. THEME: DEMOCRATIC IDEALS

How did participants in the civil rights movement advance the democratic ideals of the United States?

4. APPLYING CITIZENSHIP SKILLS

How did the nonviolent methods used by protesters during the civil rights movement demonstrate good citizenship?

5. MAKING GENERALIZATIONS

In what ways do you think the lives of Americans today might differ from the lives of Americans who lived before the civil rights movement?

Interact *with* History

How has your study of the civil rights era influenced your decision about the ways in which you would act to change injustices in society?

Use the graph and your knowledge of U.S. history to answer questions 1 and 2.

Additional Test Practice, pp. S1–S33.

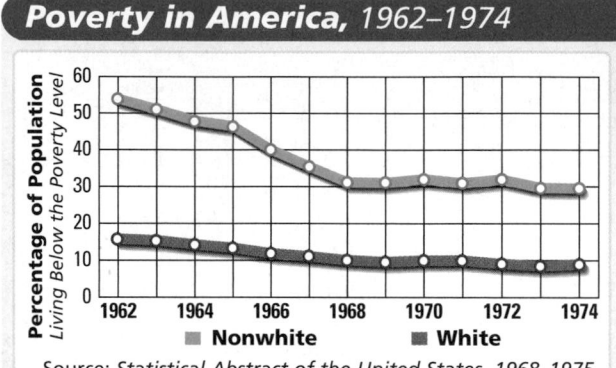

Poverty in America, *1962–1974*

Percentage of Population
Living Below the Poverty Level

Source: *Statistical Abstract of the United States, 1968–1975*

■ Nonwhite ■ White

1. What percentage of nonwhite people were living below the poverty level in 1962?

A. about 10 percent

B. about 16 percent

C. about 30 percent

D. about 54 percent

2. What was the difference between the poverty rates of whites and nonwhites in 1974?

A. about 9 percent

B. about 21 percent

C. about 30 percent

D. about 38 percent

This quotation from Rosa Parks describes her refusal to observe racial segregation on a public bus. Use the quotation and your knowledge of U.S. history to answer question 3.

PRIMARY SOURCE

The driver of the bus saw me still sitting there, and he asked was I going to stand up. I said, "No." He said, "Well, I'm going to have you arrested." Then I said, "You may do that."

Rosa Parks, *Rosa Parks: My Story*

3. Which of the following did Rosa Parks's refusal to stand represent?

A. disrespect for authority

B. an attempt to show off to the others

C. belief in her equal right to a seat

D. desire to instigate trouble

TEST PRACTICE
CLASSZONE.COM

ALTERNATIVE ASSESSMENT

1. 📝 WRITING ABOUT HISTORY

Imagine that the Voting Rights Act is under consideration in the House of Representatives. Write a **letter** to your representative in support of the bill.

• Use library resources to research the bill.

• Then, write a letter to your representative explaining why you believe the bill should be passed. Use your research to support your argument.

2. COOPERATIVE LEARNING

With a small group, create a plan for making your community a better place to live. Organize a march that will raise awareness of your group's plan. You should account for how to organize marchers, the best route for the march, if permission from officials is required, and if you need to provide food and sanitation facilities.

INTEGRATED TECHNOLOGY

DOING INTERNET RESEARCH

Many believe the civil rights movement reached its climax on August 28, 1963. On this date, about 250,000 people arrived in Washington, D.C., to peacefully protest racial discrimination and show support for civil rights legislation. Do research in order to create a radio broadcast of the March on Washington.

• Using the Internet and the library, find primary sources such as newspaper articles, memoirs, songs, poems, and books.

• You might also find oral history interviews online or in the library.

For more about the March on Washington . . .

INTERNET ACTIVITY
CLASSZONE.COM

The Vietnam War Years 1954–1975

Prowar rally in New York in 1970

PEACE WITH Honor

WITH AMERICANS LIKE JOHN LINDSAY.... HANOI CANT LOSE

1954
United States gives economic aid to South Vietnam.

North Vietnam

South Vietnam

USA World 1954

1954
Vietnam is divided into North and South.

1960
John F. Kennedy is elected president.

1960
National Liberation Front (Viet Cong) organizes in South Vietnam.

1963
Lyndon B. Johnson becomes president after Kennedy's assassination.

1962
Soviet Union places nuclear missiles in Cuba.

Antiwar rally in
Washington in 1969

You are a young person in 1969. Your country is at war to stop Communists from taking over South Vietnam. College students have organized huge protests against the war and the draft. Many people think such protests are unpatriotic and an insult to the soldiers who are fighting.

Would you support the war?

What Do You Think?

• Should the United States try to stop the spread of communism in Vietnam?

• Why are so many people against the war?

• Is it unpatriotic to criticize the government? To refuse army service?

 **RESEARCH LINKS**
CLASSZONE.COM
Visit the Chapter 30 links for more information about the Vietnam War.

1964
Johnson is reelected president.

    1965
    First U.S. ground troops go to Vietnam.

1968
Richard M. Nixon is elected president.

1970
Nixon orders invasion of Cambodia.
Four students are killed during an antiwar protest at Kent State University.

1973
U.S. involvement in war ends.

1975

    1966
ommunist leader Mao edong begins Cultural Revolution in China.

1968
Viet Cong launch Tet offensive.
Soviets invade Czechoslovakia to stop reforms.

1975
South Vietnam surrenders to Communists.

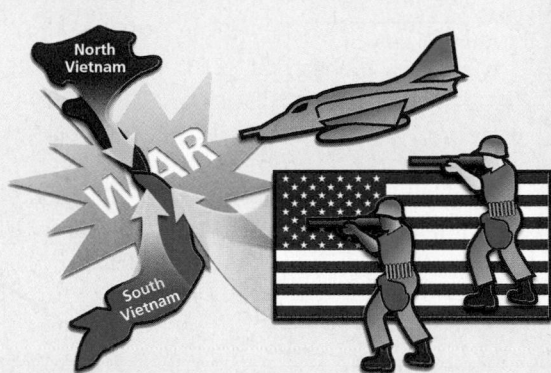

CHAPTER 30

Reading Strategy: Analyzing Points of View

What Do You Know?

What images spring to mind when you hear the word *Vietnam?* What have you learned about the Vietnam War from movies, books, or relatives' stories? Have you seen the Vietnam Veterans Memorial or any other Vietnam memorials?

Think About

- whether Americans seem proud of or ashamed of the war
- how this war differed from World War II or other wars you know about
- your responses to the Interact with History about supporting the war (see page 833)

What Do You Want to Know?

In your notebook, write down any questions you have about the war. Later, note the answers if you learn them in this chapter.

Analyzing Points of View

The Vietnam War bitterly divided Americans. Presidents, military strategists, ordinary soldiers, and college students, among others, all had their reasons for supporting or opposing the war. On a chart like the one below, note these reasons as you read. This will help you understand how the war split the country and why Americans still argue over it today.

S See Skillbuilder Handbook, page R9.

 Taking Notes

Reasons for Involvement in Vietnam	Reasons Against Involvement in Vietnam
French alliance	U.S. interests
Domino theory	Draft
Nation-building	Social programs
Cold War crises	Vietnamese civilians
U.S. weaponry	Domestic unrest

Cold War Roots of the Conflict

MAIN IDEA	WHY IT MATTERS NOW	TERMS & NAMES
The United States entered the Vietnam War to stop the spread of communism.	The United States still becomes involved in foreign struggles for political reasons.	Ngo Dinh Diem French Indochina Ho Chi Minh domino theory Viet Cong Ho Chi Minh Trail Cuban missile crisis

ONE AMERICAN'S STORY

Edward Lansdale, a U.S. military officer, went to South Vietnam in June 1954. His mission: to stop the spread of communism in Vietnam. He would try to do this by helping the non-Communist government of South Vietnam resist being taken over by Communist North Vietnam.

Lansdale became a trusted adviser to **Ngo Dinh Diem** (uhng•oh dihn zih•ehm), the leader of South Vietnam. At Lansdale's urging, the United States helped support Diem's unpopular government. Within a year, Lansdale reported, "The Free Vietnamese are now becoming unified and learning how to cope with the Communist enemy."

Lansdale was too optimistic. U.S. involvement in Vietnam grew into the longest war the United States ever fought—and one in which it failed. In this section, you will learn how the United States first became involved in Vietnam.

Edward Lansdale was one of the earliest U.S. military advisers sent to Vietnam.

Vietnam After World War II

From the late 1800s until World War II, France ruled Vietnam as part of its colony of **French Indochina**. The colony also included neighboring Laos (LAH•ohs) and Cambodia. (See the map on page 837.) During this colonial period, France increased its wealth by exporting rice and rubber from Vietnam. But Vietnamese peasants lost their land and grew poor.

The Vietnamese never accepted French rule. Various groups of nationalists, who wanted Vietnam to become an independent nation, staged revolts against the French. In 1930, a revolutionary leader named **Ho Chi Minh** (hoh chee mihn) united three Communist groups to form the Indochinese Communist Party (ICP). This new party called for an independent Vietnam controlled by peasants and other workers.

Taking Notes

Use your chart to take notes about reasons for and against U.S. involvement in Vietnam.

Reasons for	Reasons against
French alliance	U.S. interests
Domino theory	Draft
Nation building	Social programs
Cold War crises	Vietnamese civilians
U.S. weaponry	Domestic unrest

Ho Chi Minh speaks to a French audience in 1946.

The Indochinese Communist Party organized protests by peasants against the French government. The French responded by arresting suspected Communists and executing a number of leaders. Ho Chi Minh, who was living in China, was sentenced to death without being present.

In 1940, during World War II, Japan took over Indochina. The next year, Ho Chi Minh secretly returned to Vietnam and hid in a jungle camp. Under his direction, the ICP joined with other nationalists to form an organization called the Viet Minh. The Viet Minh trained soldiers to fight to make Vietnam independent of all foreign rulers. Because Japan was an enemy of the United States in World War II, the U.S. government aided Ho Chi Minh and the Viet Minh in their fight against the Japanese.

After the Japanese surrendered to the Allies in August 1945, Ho Chi Minh declared Vietnam's independence before a cheering crowd in Hanoi. But France soon tried to regain control of Vietnam. Ho Chi Minh sought a peaceful solution to the conflict with France.

Reading **History**

A. Analyzing Causes What was the original source of the conflict in Vietnam?

A VOICE FROM THE PAST

If they force us into war, we will fight. The struggle will be atrocious [terrible], but the Vietnamese people will suffer anything rather than renounce [give up] their freedom.

Ho Chi Minh, quoted in *Vietnam: A History* by Stanley Karnow

Reading **History**

B. Reading a Map Use the map on page 837 to find Haiphong and Hanoi.

In 1946, war broke out between the Viet Minh and France. The French bombed Haiphong, and the Viet Minh attacked Hanoi.

Truman and Eisenhower Aid the French

As France fought to hold on to power in Vietnam, the United States struggled against the Soviet Union in the Cold War. President Truman followed a policy of containment, working to prevent the spread of communism in Western Europe.

In the fall of 1949, Communists gained control of China. This event made American leaders worry about the spread of communism in Asia. When France asked the United States for aid to help them fight the Viet Minh, the United States agreed. One reason was that U.S. leaders needed French support in opposing the Soviets in Europe. Another reason was that the United States did not want Vietnam to become Communist.

The United States entered the conflict in Vietnam in 1950, when President Truman offered $10 million in military aid to the French. After Dwight D. Eisenhower became president in 1953, he continued aiding the French war effort in Vietnam.

*Reading*History
C. Analyzing Points of View
Why did Truman and Eisenhower support the French in Vietnam?

Both Truman and Eisenhower used the **domino theory** to explain the need to support anti-Communists in Vietnam. According to this theory, if a country fell to communism, nearby countries would also topple, like a row of dominoes standing on end. U.S. leaders feared that if Vietnam became Communist, the rest of Southeast Asia would follow.

Dividing North and South

Even with limited U.S. support, France could not defeat the Viet Minh. In 1954, the Viet Minh overran French forces at Dien Bien Phu, in northwestern Vietnam. In May 1954, France met with the Viet Minh for peace talks in Geneva, Switzerland. The two sides reached an agreement called the Geneva Accords. This agreement divided Vietnam into North and South along the 17th parallel, or at 17°N latitude. Surrounding this line was a demilitarized zone, or DMZ. The split was meant to be temporary, however. The two sides agreed to hold elections in 1956 for a single government that would reunify the country.

Until then, the Geneva Accords allowed for separate governments in the North and the South. Ho Chi Minh and the Communists controlled North Vietnam. Ngo Dinh Diem, an anti-Communist, became prime minister and, later, president of South Vietnam. Thousands of anti-Communists from the North fled to the South. The United States provided ships for their transportation.

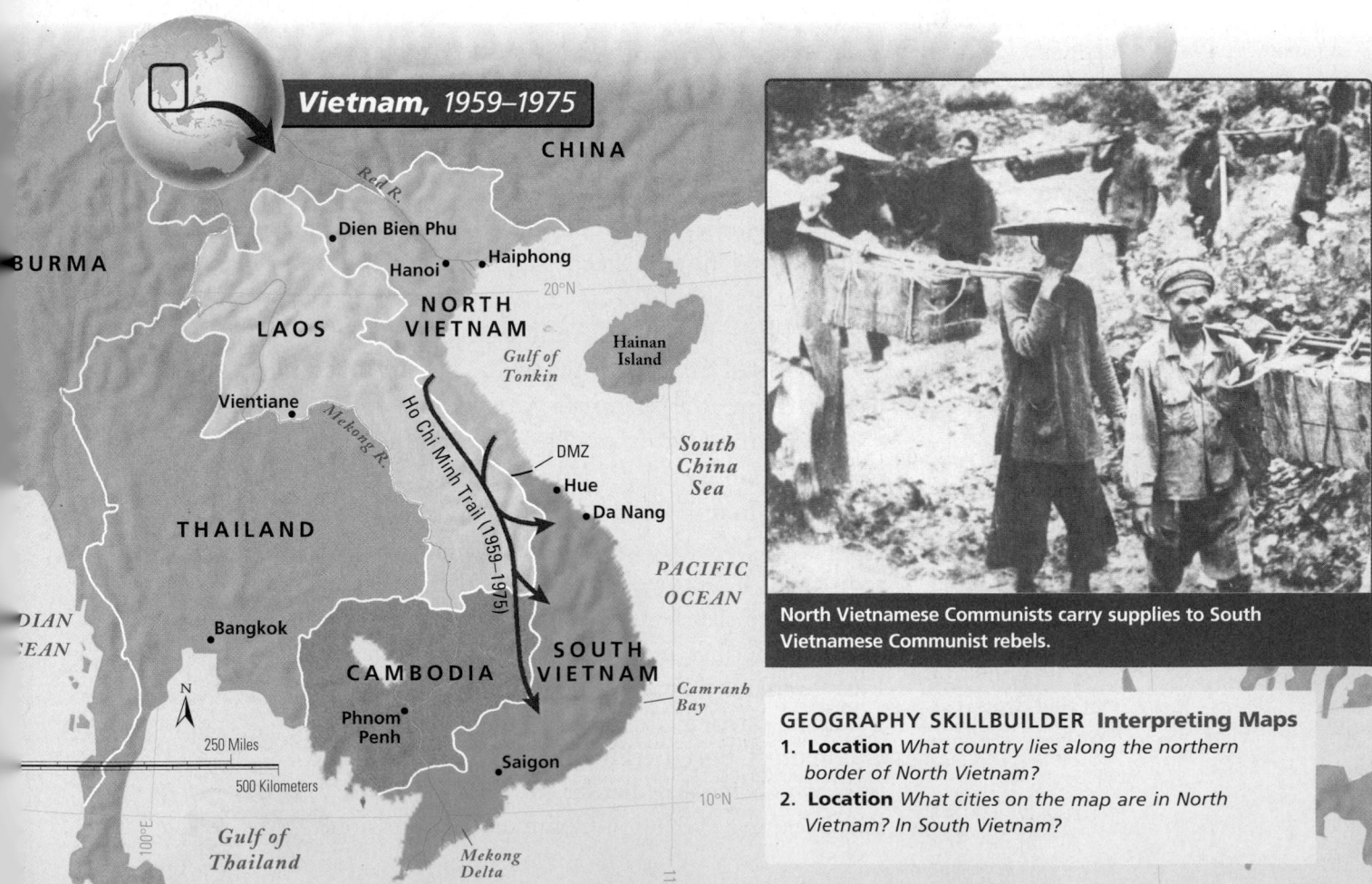

Vietnam, 1959–1975

North Vietnamese Communists carry supplies to South Vietnamese Communist rebels.

GEOGRAPHY SKILLBUILDER Interpreting Maps
1. **Location** *What country lies along the northern border of North Vietnam?*
2. **Location** *What cities on the map are in North Vietnam? In South Vietnam?*

Ho Chi Minh enjoyed great popularity in North Vietnam, while Diem had little support from the people of South Vietnam. As a result, Diem refused to hold national elections in 1956. President Eisenhower supported him, later saying, "If the elections had been held in 1956, Ho Chi Minh would have won 80% of the vote."

Instead, Eisenhower sent more aid and advisers to South Vietnam to help the Diem government. U.S. advisers described their mission as "nation-building."

The Viet Cong Oppose Diem

In spite of U.S. aid, Diem did not establish a democratic government in South Vietnam. Instead, his government was corrupt. In the countryside, for example, he let landlords take back land given to peasants. In addition, he jailed, tortured, and killed opponents.

Diem's opponents included South Vietnamese Communists. In 1960, they joined with other dissatisfied South Vietnamese to form the National Liberation Front. Diem ridiculed the group by calling them the **Viet Cong,** for Vietnamese Communists. This name became the commonly used term for the group.

The Viet Cong fought to overthrow the Diem government and reunite the country under Communist rule. North Vietnam supported the Viet Cong, sending soldiers and supplies along a network of paths called the **Ho Chi Minh Trail**. This supply line wove through the jungles and mountains of neighboring Laos and Cambodia. By 1963, when John F. Kennedy was in the White House, the Viet Cong were close to victory.

Kennedy Faces Communist Threats

President Kennedy continued to send military advisers and equipment to South Vietnam. By late 1963, the United States had more than 16,000 military personnel there. Kennedy faced a number of Cold War crises that influenced him to keep supporting the fight against communism in Vietnam.

The first was the Bay of Pigs invasion in April 1961. An army of Cuban exiles, trained by the United States, invaded Cuba. They planned to overthrow the country's Communist leader, Fidel Castro. Cuban troops easily crushed the invasion, humiliating the United States.

Then in June 1961, the Soviet Union threatened to close off Western access to West Berlin because so many East Germans were fleeing there to escape communism. Tensions rose when Kennedy insisted on West Berlin's independence. The Soviets and East Germans then built the Berlin Wall, a heavily guarded barrier dividing West Berlin from Communist East Berlin and East Germany. The wall, which made it harder for East Germans to flee, became a symbol of Communist oppression.

Reading **History**
D. Making Inferences Why was the Diem government unpopular?

Reading **History**
E. Reading a Map Find the Ho Chi Minh Trail on the map on page 837.

A woman in West Berlin talks across the Berlin Wall to her mother in East Berlin.

The **Cuban missile crisis** in October 1962 was Kennedy's most serious confrontation with the Soviets. Fidel Castro, believing the United States planned another attack on Cuba, had asked for more Soviet military aid. The United States learned that the Soviets had put nuclear missiles in Cuba. These missiles could reach U.S. cities within minutes. Kennedy weighed his choices. "The greatest danger of all," he told the country, "would be to do nothing." In a frightening showdown between the two superpowers, the Soviets agreed to remove the missiles, and the United States promised not to invade Cuba.

These Cold War crises fed American fears that the Soviet Union might become the strongest world power. In this climate of fear and suspicion, the United States made a greater effort to contain communism in Asia by sending more money and military advisers to South Vietnam.

The Diem Government Falls

As U.S. aid increased, so did South Vietnamese opposition to Diem. American officials told Diem to make political, economic, and military reforms. But he refused.

The Kennedy administration lost faith in Diem. With U.S. support, a military coup overthrew Diem on November 1, 1963. Against Kennedy's wishes, the coup's leaders killed Diem. In a terrible and unrelated turn of events, President Kennedy was assassinated three weeks later. Vice-President Lyndon Johnson became president. He deepened U.S. involvement in the Vietnam War, as you will see in the next section.

*Reading*History

F. Analyzing Causes What Cold War crises made Kennedy increase his commitment to fight communism in Asia?

Vocabulary
coup (koo): a sudden takeover by a small group

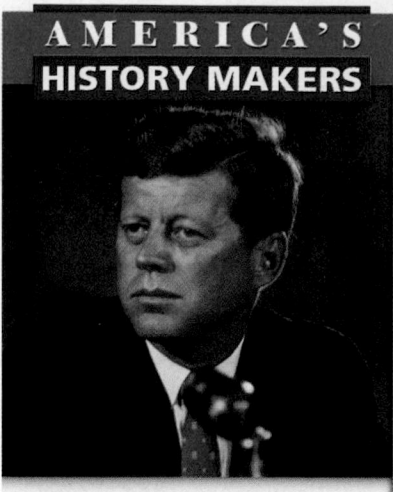

AMERICA'S HISTORY MAKERS

JOHN F. KENNEDY
1917–1963

In 1960, at age 43, John F. Kennedy became the youngest U.S. president ever elected. Handsome and energetic, he inspired belief in the country's capabilities.

Many Americans regard the Cuban missile crisis as Kennedy's finest moment of leadership. This conflict brought the United States to the brink of nuclear war. Kennedy considered bombing the Soviet missile sites in Cuba and invading the country before deciding it was safer to blockade Cuba and keep bargaining with Soviet leader Nikita Khrushchev.

How did the missile crisis show Kennedy's leadership?

Section 1 Assessment

1. Terms & Names

Explain the significance of:
- Ngo Dinh Diem
- French Indochina
- Ho Chi Minh
- domino theory
- Viet Cong
- Ho Chi Minh Trail
- Cuban missile crisis

2. Using Graphics

Review the section and identify a key event for each year on the time line.

1930	1945	1950	1960
1940	1946	1954	1963

What event brought the United States into the Vietnam conflict?

3. Main Ideas

a. What were Ho Chi Minh's goals for Vietnam?

b. How did the Cold War affect American decisions regarding Vietnam?

c. What level of involvement did the Truman, Eisenhower, and Kennedy administrations have in Vietnam?

4. Critical Thinking

Evaluating How did U.S. support of the Diem government involve a conflict of values?

THINK ABOUT
- American beliefs in democracy and individual rights
- the actions of the Diem government

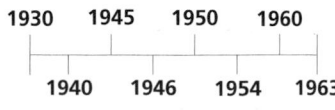

ACTIVITY OPTIONS

SPEECH
ART

Record imaginary **radio interviews** with Ho Chi Minh and Ngo Dinh Diem about Vietnam, or construct **signs** that their supporters might carry in a demonstration.

War Expands in Vietnam

MAIN IDEA	WHY IT MATTERS NOW	TERMS & NAMES
America sent ground troops to Vietnam expecting victory, but soldiers soon grew frustrated.	The Vietnam War taught Americans that superior military strength does not always ensure victory.	Gulf of Tonkin Resolution guerrilla warfare escalation napalm William Westmoreland Agent Orange Tet offensive

ONE AMERICAN'S STORY

Reginald Edwards landed in Vietnam in 1965. He was unprepared for the experience. It was nothing like his dream of "landing on this beach like they did in World War II." On night patrols, Edwards and his fellow marines shot at whatever moved. Their first large-scale attack on the enemy proved disastrous.

American soldiers take aim in the Vietnamese jungle.

A VOICE FROM THE PAST

We had received fire. All of a sudden we could see people in front of us. Instead of waiting for air [support], we returned the fire, and you could see people fall. . . . Come to find out it was Bravo Company. What the VC [Viet Cong] had done was [lure] Bravo Company in front of us. . . . It was our own people. That's the bodies we saw falling. . . . I think we shot up maybe 40 guys in Bravo Company.

Private Reginald "Malik" Edwards, quoted in *Bloods: An Oral History of the Vietnam War by Black Veterans*

In this section, you will learn why the Vietnam War created such confusion and why people questioned how the war was conducted.

Taking Notes

Use your chart to take notes about reasons for and against U.S. involvement in Vietnam.

Reasons for	Reasons against
French alliance	U.S. interests
Domino theory	Draft
Nation building	Social programs
Cold War crises	Vietnamese civilians
U.S. weaponry	Domestic unrest

Johnson Sends Combat Troops

The assassination of President Diem in 1963 brought chaos to South Vietnam. One ineffective leader after another headed the government. Meanwhile, the North Vietnamese kept shipping more aid to the Viet Cong. By late 1964, combined Viet Cong and North Vietnamese forces controlled much of the South Vietnamese countryside.

Like earlier presidents, Lyndon Johnson did not want to lose Vietnam to communism. As a result, he increased U.S. efforts in Vietnam.

In the summer of 1964, Johnson's military advisers made plans to bomb North Vietnam. Johnson and his advisors wanted to

pressure Ho Chi Minh to stop supporting the Viet Cong. But no bombing could start unless Congress approved the plan. A shooting incident off the coast of North Vietnam spurred Congress to give its approval.

The U.S. destroyer *Maddox* had been patrolling in the Gulf of Tonkin when North Vietnamese torpedo boats fired on it. Two days later, on August 4, the *Maddox* and another destroyer reported a second attack. However, no one could confirm this attack. There had been thunderstorms that night, and the weather could have affected the radar screens. U.S. jet pilots flying overhead said they had seen no North Vietnamese boats.

*Reading*History

A. Finding Main Ideas What did the Gulf of Tonkin Resolution do?

Despite doubts about the second attack, Johnson asked Congress to pass the **Gulf of Tonkin Resolution**. This gave the president the power to use military force in Vietnam. All but two senators voted for the resolution. The "yes" vote in the House was unanimous.

In March 1965, Johnson began bombing North Vietnam. At about the same time, he sent the first combat ground troops to Vietnam. Their numbers grew from 75,000 in the middle of 1965 to 184,000 by the end of 1965.

This policy of **escalation,** or increasing military involvement in Vietnam, continued over the next few years. General **William Westmoreland,** the commander of U.S. forces in South Vietnam, asked for more and more troops. By the end of 1968, there were more than 536,000 American military personnel in South Vietnam.

AMERICA'S HISTORY MAKERS

LYNDON JOHNSON
1908–1973

Lyndon Johnson wanted people to remember him as a social reformer. The Great Society was the name for his wide-ranging domestic programs, which included reforms in education, medical care for the elderly, aid to cities, and support for civil rights.

The Vietnam War overshadowed Johnson's achievements. He was tormented by the deaths and the social divisions the war brought. His goals for the country were blocked by the war, which still had not ended when he died.

How would you describe Johnson's presidency?

A Frustrating War

Many Americans thought that, with their superior weapons, U.S. ground forces would quickly defeat the Viet Cong and drive them out of the villages. Many conditions frustrated American soldiers, however. First of all, they could wage only a limited war, partly because the government feared drawing China into the conflict.

Background
The average World War II soldier was 26 and served for three years. Many soldiers in Vietnam had fathers who had fought in World War II.

Also, most U.S. soldiers in Vietnam were young and inexperienced. The average soldier was 19 and served a one-year tour of duty. Officers served even shorter tours, on average six months. The short tours meant that by the time soldiers and officers had gained enough experience, their tours of duty were over.

The Vietnam War differed from World War II in that there was no frontline. The Viet Cong mixed with the general population and operated everywhere, attacking U.S. troops in the countryside and in the cities. Even a shoeshine boy on a city street corner might toss a grenade into an army bus carrying American soldiers. Marine captain E. J. Banks described his frustration: "You never knew who was the enemy and who was the friend. . . . The enemy was all around you."

Booby Traps
The Viet Cong hid deadly booby traps made of sharpened sticks.

Guerrilla Warfare
In the jungles, surprise attacks could come at any moment. Helicopters quickly took the wounded to hospitals.

The style of fighting in Vietnam also differed from that in World War II. Because they could not match American firepower, the Viet Cong relied on **guerrilla warfare,** surprise attacks by small bands of fighters. Viet Cong guerrillas would suddenly emerge from networks of underground tunnels to fight. Then they would disappear back into the tunnels. They riddled the countryside and jungles with land mines and booby traps, such as bamboo stakes hidden in covered pits. They hung grenades from trees and hid them in bushes. Every day, U.S. Army and Navy nurses treated young soldiers with gruesome wounds.

Even the land and climate of Vietnam proved difficult. The heat was suffocating and the rain almost constant. Soldiers sweated through tangled jungles. After wading through flooded rice paddies, they had to pick leeches off their feet and legs. American soldier Warren Wooten said, "It seemed like the whole country was an enemy. The animals, the reptiles, the insects, the plants. And the people."

Finally, the Viet Cong were a very dedicated enemy. They took heavy losses, built up their ranks again, and kept on fighting year after year because they believed in their cause. An American who interviewed Viet Cong prisoners noted, "They see the war entirely as one of defense of their country against the invading Americans, who, in turn, are seen merely as successors to the French."

Background
Nearly 7,500 women served in Vietnam as nurses.

Reading **History**

B. Analyzing Causes Why was the war so hard for the United States to win?

Stripping the Jungle

One of the strengths of the Viet Cong was their ability to hide in the jungle and in underground tunnels. To reveal and destroy Viet Cong hideouts, American troops used chemicals that ruined the landscape.

Search-and-Destroy Missions
U.S. soldiers destroyed villages suspected of hiding Viet Cong.

Napalm
U.S. planes dropped fiery napalm bombs to wipe out Viet Cong bases. Napalm is jellied gasoline.

Over wide areas, U.S. planes dropped bombs of **napalm**, jellied gasoline that burns violently. Planes also sprayed **Agent Orange**, a chemical that kills plants, over the jungles.

Such chemicals helped destroy the hideouts and food supplies of the Viet Cong. But in the process, they also harmed innocent Vietnamese villagers. This undermined the villagers' support for the United States. Later, people learned that Agent Orange harmed U.S. soldiers as well. Veterans exposed to it have suffered from skin diseases and cancers.

Search-and-Destroy Missions

Search-and-destroy missions were another American war tactic that terrorized Vietnamese villagers. In such missions, soldiers hunted Viet Cong and burned or bombed villages thought to be sheltering them. Marine sergeant William Ehrhart described how search-and-destroy missions affected South Vietnamese peasants.

A VOICE FROM THE PAST

Their homes had been wrecked, their chickens killed, their rice confiscated [taken away]—and if they weren't pro-Vietcong before we got there, they sure . . . were by the time we left.

William Ehrhart, quoted in *Vietnam: A History* by Stanley Karnow

Reading **History**

C. Drawing Conclusions Why did Americans fail in "winning the hearts and minds" of the people in Vietnam?

These destructive methods defeated the purpose of "winning the hearts and minds" of the villagers and turning them against communism. Furthermore, even if the tactics did clear a village of Viet Cong temporarily, the Viet Cong usually returned later.

The Surprise Tet Offensive

By the end of 1967, the war had caused great destruction, but neither side was close to victory. Still, U.S. military officials claimed that they would soon win. Then, on January 30 and 31, 1968, the Communists launched the **Tet offensive.** This was a surprise attack on U.S. military bases and more than 100 cities and towns in South Vietnam. It came during Tet, the Vietnamese celebration of the lunar New Year.

In preparation for the Tet offensive, the Viet Cong hid weapons in vegetable trucks, food trucks, peddlers' carts, and even coffins. They smuggled these weapons into South Vietnamese cities. Soldiers dressed in civilian clothes entered the cities on buses, on motorcycles, and on foot. No one could tell them apart from the war refugees who streamed into the cities from the countryside or from visitors coming for the holiday.

The Viet Cong fought to take over the cities during the offensive. They killed not only enemy soldiers but also government officials, schoolteachers, doctors, and priests.

The Tet offensive was a military defeat for the Communists. They gained no cities and lost 45,000 soldiers, while the South Vietnamese lost 2,300 soldiers and the United States 1,100.

But the attack stunned Americans. General Westmoreland had recently declared, "We have turned the corner," suggesting that victory was in sight. The Tet offensive raised doubts that this was true. Many government and business leaders began to think that the United States could not win the war, except at too high a price.

The Tet offensive also made many Americans ask whether the U.S. mission in Vietnam was wise. To retake some cities, troops had to almost level them with bombing and shelling. Speaking of the city of Ben Tre, a U.S. major said, "It became necessary to destroy the town in order to save it." The quote became an example of what many considered the senselessness of the war.

Because of the doubts it raised, the Tet offensive became a turning point in the war. Afterward, President Johnson changed his war policy. When General Westmoreland asked for 206,000 more troops, to take advantage of the enemy's weakness, President Johnson said no. Then, on March 31, 1968, Johnson said that he would stop bombing most of North Vietnam and would seek to

Background
In the Tet offensive, enemy forces invaded the U.S. embassy compound in Saigon, killing five Americans.

Reading **History**

D. Drawing Conclusions How was the Tet offensive both a failure and a success for the Viet Cong?

GEOGRAPHY SKILLBUILDER Interpreting Maps
1. **Location** *In what country were the major battles?*
2. **Location** *What did the number and location of attacks suggest about the country's security?*

844

bargain for peace. In the same speech, he announced that he would not run for another term as president.

U.S. Morale Sinks

As the Vietnam War went on, it wore down American soldiers. They fought hard and bravely, but many were losing faith that the United States could win the war. The South Vietnamese government did not have the loyalty of the people. In addition, the South Vietnamese army often avoided fighting. American soldiers asked why they were fighting a war the Vietnamese did not want to fight themselves.

The low morale of American forces in Vietnam became clear when news of the My Lai (mee ly) massacre broke in 1969. The incident happened on March 16, 1968. A U.S. platoon led by Lieutenant William Calley, Jr., rounded up and shot between 175 and 500 unarmed civilians, mostly women, children, and old men. A U.S. helicopter pilot rescued some civilians by threatening to fire on the soldiers. To Americans, My Lai represented a horrifying breakdown in morality and discipline in the armed forces. In 1971, a colonel warned that U.S. forces were "in a state approaching collapse."

In the next section, you'll learn how the United States withdrew from the Vietnam War.

Background
Calley was jailed briefly, but many saw him as a scapegoat because charges were dropped against higher-ranking officers.

"I DON'T KNOW IF EITHER SIDE IS WINNING, BUT I KNOW WHO'S LOSING."

This 1968 cartoon by Herblock comments on the war's cost to civilians.

Section 2 Assessment

1. Terms & Names

Explain the significance of:
- Gulf of Tonkin Resolution
- escalation
- William Westmoreland
- guerrilla warfare
- napalm
- Agent Orange
- Tet offensive

2. Using Graphics

On a chart like the one below, note the war's effects on Vietnamese villagers and on U.S. soldiers.

Effects of War

Villagers	U.S. Soldiers

3. Main Ideas

a. How did President Johnson escalate U.S. involvement in the Vietnam War?

b. What made fighting the war so frustrating for American soldiers?

c. How was the Tet offensive a turning point in the war?

4. Critical Thinking

Analyzing Points of View
Were the Viet Cong right to see the Americans "merely as successors to the French"?

THINK ABOUT
- the goals of the French in Vietnam
- the goals of the Americans in Vietnam
- the actions of the French and the Americans

ACTIVITY OPTIONS

SCIENCE

HEALTH

Investigate the health effects of Agent Orange reported by Vietnam veterans.
Design a science **exhibit** or create a **warning label** to share your findings.

3

The Vietnam War Ends

MAIN IDEA	WHY IT MATTERS NOW	TERMS & NAMES
The Vietnam War divided Americans and had lasting effects in the United States and Southeast Asia.	Lessons of the Vietnam War still influence the United States whenever it gets involved in a foreign conflict.	doves hawks Richard Nixon Vietnamization	Cambodia Twenty-sixth Amendment War Powers Act

ONE AMERICAN'S STORY

Mary Ann Vecchio was just 14 when she became a symbol of anguish over the Vietnam War. A student journalist took Vecchio's picture as she knelt by a dead student at Kent State University in Ohio. The youth was Jeffrey Glenn Miller, one of four students killed by the National Guard during an antiwar demonstration on May 4, 1970. Later, Vecchio described her feelings.

Mary Ann Vecchio cries out in horror after the Kent State shootings in May 1970.

A VOICE FROM THE PAST

I couldn't believe that people would kill people over what they thought, just because he demonstrated against the Vietnam War.

Mary Ann Vecchio Gillum, conference at Emerson College, April 23, 1995

In this section, you will learn how growing opposition to the war eventually led the United States to pull its troops out of Vietnam.

Taking Notes

Use your chart to take notes about reasons for and against U.S. involvement in Vietnam.

Reasons for	Reasons against
French alliance	U.S. interests
Domino theory	Draft
Nation building	Social programs
Cold War crises	Vietnamese civilians
U.S. weaponry	Domestic unrest

A Growing Antiwar Movement

As the war escalated in the mid-1960s, antiwar feeling grew among Americans at home. Religious leaders, civil rights leaders, teachers, students, journalists, and others protested the war for a variety of reasons. Some believed that the United States had no business involving itself in another country's civil war. Others believed that the methods of fighting the war were immoral. Still others thought that the costs to American society were too high.

College students formed a large and vocal group of protesters. They particularly opposed the draft, which required young men to serve in the military. In demonstrations around the country, young men burned their

draft cards. About 50,000 people staged such a protest in front of the Pentagon on October 21, 1967.

Opponents of the draft pointed out its unfairness. Most draftees were poor. Middle- and upper-class youths could delay being drafted by enrolling in college. They also sought advice from draft counselors, doctors, and lawyers to help them avoid service. Certain medical conditions or religious beliefs, for example, could keep them out of the military.

Reading **History**
A. Analyzing Points of View
Why did people think the draft was unfair?

Another unfair aspect of the draft was the high number of African Americans called to serve. African Americans made up about 20 percent of combat troops in Vietnam. In 1965, they accounted for 24 percent of U.S. Army combat deaths. Yet they were only 11 percent of the male population in the United States.

For this and other reasons, the antiwar movement became linked with the civil rights movement. In 1967, civil rights leader Martin Luther King, Jr., spoke out against the Vietnam War. Noting that the war took money away from antipoverty programs, he declared, "I was increasingly compelled to see the war as an enemy of the poor."

By 1967, it was clear that the Vietnam War was dividing Americans into two camps. Even within families, people took opposite sides. Those who opposed the war were called **doves**. Those who supported it were known as **hawks**. Supporters of the war staged marches of their own. Believing that antiwar protesters were unpatriotic, they popularized such slogans as "America—love it or leave it."

1968—A Turning Point

As you learned in Section 2, the Tet offensive in January 1968 made Americans doubt that they could win the war. Walter Cronkite, a respected TV news anchorman, visited Vietnam in February. After returning, he ended a special report with his own opinion of the war. He concluded that the United States was not winning but was in a deadlock.

> **A VOICE FROM THE PAST**
>
> [T]he only rational way out, then, will be to negotiate, not as victors, but as an honorable people who lived up to their pledge to defend democracy, and did the best they could.
>
> **Walter Cronkite,** *A Reporter's Life*

President Johnson took Cronkite's words to heart. "If I've lost Cronkite, I've lost middle America," he reportedly said.

That summer, the Democratic National Convention in Chicago reflected the country's turmoil. Democrats chose Hubert Humphrey, Johnson's vice-president, as their nominee. Outside the convention hall, TV

daily *life*

THE "TELEVISION WAR"
The Vietnam War was the first "television war," broadcast each night on the evening news. Reports rarely showed actual battles, partly because much of the fighting occurred off and on and at night, between small units.

Networks also tried to avoid gruesome scenes because they did not want to offend viewers. In addition, the networks agreed not to show any American dead or wounded so that their families would not see them on the screen. Still, the images of war shocked TV audiences.

cameras showed police clubbing antiwar demonstrators and bystanders. The chaos helped Republican candidate **Richard Nixon** win the presidency in 1968. In his campaign, Nixon promised to "bring an honorable end to the war in Vietnam."

Nixon's Vietnam Strategy

In July 1969, Nixon announced his strategy of **Vietnamization.** It called for gradually withdrawing U.S. forces and turning the ground fighting over to the South Vietnamese. Nixon promised to withdraw 25,000 of the 543,000 U.S. ground troops in Vietnam by the end of the year. However, Nixon had already begun secret bombing raids of **Cambodia,** a country bordering Vietnam. This bombing was meant to stop North Vietnamese troops and supplies from moving along the Ho Chi Minh Trail. Many people grew angry when they learned that the government had widened the war and hidden its actions.

Background In 1970, a U.S. invasion of Cambodia sparked protests at Kent State and many other colleges.

Public anger and distrust of the government grew after Daniel Ellsberg released the Pentagon Papers to the *New York Times* in 1971. Ellsberg had helped research and write these secret Defense Department papers. They showed that the four previous presidential administrations had not been honest with the public about U.S. involvement and goals in Vietnam.

Withdrawal from Vietnam

Thousands try to escape during the fall of Saigon.

Promising that peace was at hand, Nixon was reelected by a landslide in 1972. On January 27, 1973, the United States and South Vietnam signed a peace agreement with North Vietnam and the Viet Cong. The United States agreed to withdraw all its troops, and North Vietnam agreed not to invade South Vietnam. On March 29, the last U.S. troops left Vietnam. For the United States, the war was over.

But for the Vietnamese, the war continued. In 1975, North Vietnam launched a massive invasion of South Vietnam. On April 30 of that year, Communist forces captured Saigon, which they renamed Ho Chi Minh City. The war then ended.

Reading **History** B. Making Inferences Why did fighting begin again after the peace agreement?

Legacy of the Vietnam War

The Vietnam War caused terrible destruction and suffering in Southeast Asia. More than 1.2 million North and South Vietnamese died in the conflict. American bombing and chemical spraying caused lasting damage to farmland and forests. The war ruined Vietnam's economy, leaving many in poverty. After the North Vietnamese set up Communist rule in the

848

reunited country, many Vietnamese fled. By 1980, almost 173,000 had come to the United States.

The Vietnam War also took a heavy toll on American soldiers. About 58,000 died, and more than 300,000 were wounded. Many suffered permanent, disabling injuries. Returning soldiers often had recurring nightmares and other stress-related problems. To make things worse, they came home to a public that treated them coldly.

Background
Although there is no draft now, 18-year-old men must still register with the Selective Service in case Congress orders a draft in the future.

The Vietnam War had far-reaching political effects in the United States. The **Twenty-sixth Amendment,** passed in 1971, lowered the voting age from 21 to 18. Its supporters argued persuasively that anyone old enough to be drafted should be allowed to vote. The government ended the draft in 1973 because so many people opposed it. The nation now relies on an all-volunteer military.

*Reading*History
C. Making Inferences Why did the Vietnam War influence Congress to pass the War Powers Act?

Another legacy of Vietnam is that Americans have been less willing to get involved in overseas wars. In 1973, Congress passed the **War Powers Act,** which limits the president's war-making powers. The president must report to Congress within 48 hours if troops have been sent into a hostile situation without a declaration of war. They can remain for no more than 90 days unless Congress permits them to.

Finally, the war made many Americans distrust government leaders, who sometimes misled the public about actions in Vietnam. In Chapter 31, you will read about the Watergate scandal, which further shook confidence in government and brought down Nixon's presidency.

America's HERITAGE

VIETNAM VETERANS MEMORIAL

The public finally honored those who served in Vietnam with the Vietnam Veterans Memorial, designed by Maya Lin and unveiled in Washington, D.C., on November 13, 1982. Etched into this V-shaped black granite wall are the names of all Americans killed in the war.

At the Wall, as it is known, visitors leave letters, flowers, and mementos. Many believe that the monument has helped heal the divisions created by the war. As the father of a veteran noted, "It doesn't say whether the war was right or wrong. . . . It just says, 'Here is the price we paid.'"

Section **3** Assessment

1. Terms & Names

Explain the significance of:
• doves
• hawks
• Richard Nixon
• Vietnamization
• Cambodia
• Twenty-sixth Amendment
• War Powers Act

2. Using Graphics

Use a chart like this one to review information about the antiwar movement.

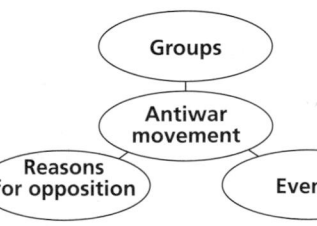

Groups

Antiwar movement

Reasons for opposition

Events

3. Main Ideas

a. Why did more and more Americans oppose the war after 1968?

b. How did the Vietnam War end?

c. In what major ways did the war affect Southeast Asia and the United States?

4. Critical Thinking

Forming and Supporting Opinions What is your opinion of the way the United States ended its involvement in the Vietnam War?

THINK ABOUT
• what happened to South Vietnam
• what options the United States had

ACTIVITY OPTIONS

LITERATURE

MATH

Compare the Vietnam War to World War II by writing an **essay** on two pieces of war literature or by presenting comparable **statistics.**

VISUAL SUMMARY

The Vietnam War Years

1946

1946
Communist-led Vietnamese nationalists struggle for independence from France.

1950
United States sends aid to the French.

1954
French are defeated. Vietnam divides into Communist North and non-Communist South.

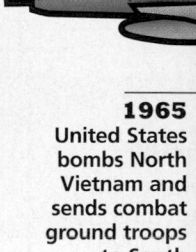

1965
United States bombs North Vietnam and sends combat ground troops to South Vietnam.

1973
United States withdraws its troops.

1975

1975
South Vietnam surrenders to the Communists.

850

TERMS & NAMES

Briefly explain the significance of each of the following.

1. Ho Chi Minh
2. domino theory
3. Viet Cong
4. Ho Chi Minh Trail
5. guerrilla warfare
6. Agent Orange
7. Tet offensive
8. Richard Nixon
9. Vietnamization
10. Twenty-sixth Amendment

REVIEW QUESTIONS

Cold War Roots of the Conflict (pages 835–839)

1. Why did the United States decide to support France in its fight against the Viet Minh?

2. What decisions about Vietnam were laid out in the 1954 Geneva Accords?

3. What Cold War crises made President Kennedy continue to aid Ngo Dinh Diem's government in South Vietnam?

War Expands in Vietnam (pages 840–845)

4. How was President Johnson's Vietnam policy different from President Kennedy's?

5. What kept U.S. troops from defeating the Viet Cong quickly?

6. How did American war tactics affect Vietnamese villagers?

7. How was the Tet offensive both a defeat and a victory for the Communists?

The Vietnam War Ends (pages 846–849)

8. Why did many Americans protest against the war?

9. What policies did President Nixon pursue in Vietnam?

10. What long-term political effects did the Vietnam War have on the United States?

CRITICAL THINKING

1. USING YOUR NOTES: ANALYZING POINTS OF VIEW

Reasons for involvement in Vietnam
French alliance
Domino theory
Nation building
Cold War crises
U.S. weaponry

Reasons against involvement in Vietnam
U.S. interests
Draft
Social programs
Vietnamese civilians
Domestic unrest

Using your completed chart from the beginning of this chapter, answer the questions.

a. Which do you consider the strongest reason in support of American involvement in the Vietnam War?

b. Which do you consider the strongest reason against American involvement in the Vietnam War?

c. Which side do you think is more persuasive? Why?

2. ANALYZING LEADERSHIP

How would you evaluate President Johnson's leadership during the Vietnam War and his decision not to seek a second term as president?

3. APPLYING CITIZENSHIP SKILLS

During the Vietnam War, many Americans had to choose between obeying laws and following their consciences. In your opinion, what is the right thing to do in such a situation?

4.THEME: AMERICA IN THE WORLD

How do you think involvement in the Vietnam War affected the reputation of the United States among other nations? Why?

5. DRAWING CONCLUSIONS

Would the United States have become involved in the Vietnam War if the Cold War had not been going on? Explain your opinion.

Interact with History

If you had lived during the Vietnam War, what would have determined whether you supported or opposed the war?

Use the table and your knowledge of U.S. history to answer questions 1 and 2.

Additional Test Practice, pp. S1–S33.

U.S. Deaths in Four Wars

WAR	BATTLE DEATHS	OTHER DEATHS
World War I	53,513	63,195
World War II	292,131	115,185
Korean War	33,629	20,617
Vietnam War	47,244	10,446

*accidents, diseases, etc.

Source: Harry G. Summers, Jr., *Vietnam War Almanac*

1. How many U.S. soldiers died in World War II?
A. 53,513
B. 63,195
C. 115,185
D. 292,131

2. Which war or wars caused more battle deaths than the Vietnam War?
A. World War I
B. World War I and II
C. Korean War
D. Korean War and World War II

This quotation from Walter Cronkite gives his opinion about ending the war in Vietnam. Use the quotation and your knowledge of U.S. history to answer question 3.

PRIMARY SOURCE

[T]he only rational way out, then, will be to negotiate, not as the victors, but as an honorable people who lived up to their pledge to defend democracy, and did the best they could.

Walter Cronkite, *A Reporter's Life*

3. Which of the following states Walter Cronkite's military assessment of the war?
A. The United States will win the war very soon.
B. The United States will win the war with more troops.
C. The war is deadlocked and neither side can win.
D. Vietnam is about to win the war.

TEST PRACTICE
CLASSZONE.COM

ALTERNATIVE ASSESSMENT

1. WRITING ABOUT HISTORY

Imagine the year is 1967 and you are writing an **editorial** to appear in your local newspaper. Decide whether to write the editorial supporting peace or supporting the war.

- Read more about the Vietnam War in books or in newspaper articles from 1967.
- Find editorials from 1967 and see if their arguments persuade you to support their point of view.

2. COOPERATIVE LEARNING

Work in a small group to create and present a video documentary about the Vietnam War and its impact on the country or on your community. As interview subjects, you might want to locate a soldier or nurse who served, someone who faced the draft but was not called to serve, or an antiwar demonstrator.

INTEGRATED TECHNOLOGY

DOING INTERNET RESEARCH

Most Americans know little about the country of Vietnam. Plan a Web site that describes geography, history, and culture of Vietnam. Use printed library resources and the Internet to locate a variety of information.

- Find detailed maps of Vietnam and its major cities.
- Locate photographs of its people, land, and art.
- Read biographies of important people in Vietnamese history and excerpts from stories, poetry and memoirs by Vietnamese writers.
- Colleges, museums, and Vietnamese organizations are good sources of additional information.

For more about Vietnam . . .

INTERNET ACTIVITY
CLASSZONE.COM

CHAPTER
31

Years of Doubt
1969–1981

Section 1
**Nixon
Confronts
Problems**

Section 2
**Watergate
Brings
Down Nixon**

Section 3
**Issues
of the
Seventies**

People outside the White House read
about Nixon's decision to resign.

Washington Star-News

ON TV AT 9 TONIGH

Nixon Resig

1972
Watergate
break-in occurs.

**Nixon is
reelected.**

1974
Nixon resigns

**Gerald Ford
becomes
president.**

1969
Richard M. Nixon is inaugurated as president.
U.S. astronauts land on moon.

USA
World 1969

1969
Golda Meir
becomes
prime minister
of Israel.

1970
Anwar el-Sadat
becomes
president of
Egypt.

1971
General Idi
Amin seizes
power
in Uganda.

1973
U.S. involvement in Vietnam
War ends.

Military overthrows government
of Chile.

It is the evening of August 8, 1974. You turn on the television to watch a speech from President Richard M. Nixon. Looking grim and tired, Nixon says that he will resign the next day. You wonder how the country will cope with the crisis.

How is America able to survive a crisis and move on?

What Do You Think?

- What happens when a president resigns from office? Has a president resigned before?

- How has the government functioned when a president has died?

RESEARCH LINKS
CLASSZONE.COM

Visit the Chapter 31 links for more information about Nixon and the 1970s.

1976
The U.S. celebrates its bicentennial.
Jimmy Carter is elected president.

1980
Ronald Reagan is elected president.

1981

1975
South Vietnam surrenders to North Vietnam.

1978
Camp David Accords are signed.

1979
Americans taken hostage in Iran.
Soviet Union invades Afghanistan.

1981
American hostages are released by Iran.

Reading Strategy: Finding Main Ideas

What Do You know?

What do you already know about the problems of the 1970s, such as inflation and the energy crisis? Were they different from problems the country faced at other times in its history?

Think About

- what you have learned about the 1970s from books, movies, television, and popular music
- how the nation has reacted to economic, political, and social problems in the past
- your responses to the Interact with History about America surviving a crisis and moving on (see page 853)

Gas shortages were one problem the United States faced in the 1970s.

What Do You Want to Know?

What would you like to know about Watergate and other crises of the 1970s? In your notebook, record what you hope to learn from this chapter.

Finding Main Ideas

To help you remember what you read, take notes on the main ideas about issues and events discussed in this chapter. Taking notes means writing down important information. The chart below lists the three presidents of the 1970s—Richard Nixon, Gerald Ford, and Jimmy Carter. As you read, use a chart like the one below to take notes on the issues and events of their presidencies.

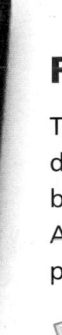 See Skillbuilder Handbook, page R5.

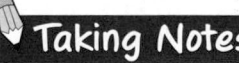 Taking Notes

President	Main Ideas: Issues and Events
Nixon	
Ford	
Carter	

Nixon Confronts Problems

MAIN IDEA	WHY IT MATTERS NOW	TERMS & NAMES
President Richard M. Nixon faced the challenge of governing a deeply divided America.	Social, economic, and political divisions are still part of American life.	Richard M. Nixon détente Henry Kissinger SALT revenue sharing

ONE AMERICAN'S STORY

After his election as president in November 1968, **Richard M. Nixon** picked **Henry Kissinger** to be his national security adviser. Kissinger was a professor at Harvard University and a Jewish refugee from Nazi Germany. He had become a well-known foreign-policy expert. Nixon felt that Kissinger had great intelligence, insight, and experience.

Nixon also found that he and Kissinger had very similar ideas about politics. Both men were practical politicians who did not let their ideologies, or beliefs, get in the way of their actions.

President Richard Nixon (left) with Henry Kissinger

> ### A VOICE FROM THE PAST
>
> The statesman manipulates [shrewdly manages] reality; his first goal is survival. . . . He is conscious of many great hopes which have failed, of many good intentions that could not be realized.
>
> **Henry A. Kissinger,** *American Foreign Policy*

In this section, you will learn how Nixon used a practical approach to try to solve problems at home and, with Kissinger's help, abroad.

A Divided America

As president, Richard M. Nixon would have liked to focus on foreign policy and leave domestic issues to his cabinet. But he became president at a time when America was being torn apart by inflation, racial problems, and conflict over the war in Vietnam. Also, he had won the presidency in 1968 by only a narrow margin. His major support came from conservatives. They wanted him to shrink the federal government and end Lyndon Johnson's Great Society programs.

Nixon hoped to cut the cost of running the federal government and turn some of its activities over to the states. But both houses of Congress were controlled by the Democrats. As a result, he took a more moderate

Taking Notes

Use your chart to take notes about Nixon's presidency.

President	
Nixon	
Ford	
Carter	

DESTINATION MOON

On July 20, 1969, with 600 million people viewing on television, Apollo 11 astronaut Neil Armstrong stepped onto the moon and said, "That's one small step for a man, one giant leap for mankind." Edwin Aldrin (shown below) soon joined him. The excitement of the first moon landing gave Americans a sense of unity during a troubled time.

On July 31, 1999, an American space probe was sent crashing into the moon's surface. Its purpose was to see whether there was water on the moon. This flight took place almost 30 years to the day after the historic first landing.

approach at first. But he did veto many spending bills passed by the Democratic Congress. Included were cuts in funds for education and low-income housing—Great Society programs.

In 1969, President Nixon attempted to change the existing welfare system, which had been criticized by conservatives. But he could not get congressional agreement. He was more successful in starting **revenue sharing**. Under revenue sharing, the federal government gave back some tax money it collected to state and local governments. These governments could spend the money on any number of different programs. The plan was supported by both parties and passed Congress in 1972.

Law-and-Order Politics

During the presidential campaign, Nixon had said that he would restore law and order. He promised an end to the social unrest and rioting of the late 1960s. Nixon also promised a return to traditional values.

One way to his goal, Nixon thought, was to appoint more conservative justices to the Supreme Court. He believed that these justices would rule against loose interpretations of the law. Such interpretations, Nixon and his supporters felt, were partly to blame for rising crime. During his first term, he appointed four new justices.

Nixon also used all the powers of the federal government to "crack down" on crime and protest. He directed the Central Intelligence Agency and the Federal Bureau of Investigation to investigate some of his political enemies. Nixon would later excuse any illegal acts by claiming they were needed for the nation's security.

A Troubled Economy

Civil unrest and crime were not the only problems President Nixon had to face. He inherited serious economic troubles. Under the Johnson administration, the government began spending huge amounts of money on programs to aid the poor *and* on fighting the Vietnam War. But taxes were not raised to cover these expenses. As a result, the government spent more money than it collected in taxes. This practice is called deficit spending.

Deficit spending put a great deal of money into circulation in the late 1960s. At the same time, the economy began to slow down. By 1970, the economy had gone into a recession. With the recession, fewer goods were produced. The increase in the money supply and the decrease in products to buy caused inflation. (See Economics in History on the next page.)

Inflation caused problems for all Americans, but especially the poor. One mother said, "I used to be able to go to the store with $50 and come back with six or seven bags of groceries. Now I'm lucky if I come back

Reading **History**

A. Recognizing Effects How did Nixon try to shrink the size of the federal government?

Reading **History**

B. Analyzing Causes What were causes of the nation's troubled economy?

with three." When Nixon took office in 1969, the inflation rate was about 5 percent. That was twice the rate it had been earlier in the decade. Increasing unemployment was another problem. It doubled from about 3 percent in 1969 to 6 percent in 1971.

Nixon tried different ways to help the economy. He cut spending. He also placed a temporary freeze on wage and price increases. Inflation dropped but only temporarily. Then, in 1973, the economy was jolted by the actions of the Organization of Petroleum Exporting Countries (OPEC).

OPEC raised its prices and cut its shipments of oil to the United States. OPEC, which was made up mainly of Arab nations, took these actions in part to protest America's support of Israel in the Yom Kippur War of 1973. That war was fought between Israel and its Arab neighbors. In a few months, gas prices quadrupled. Inflation and unemployment soared to new heights.

Vocabulary
quadrupled:
multiplied by four

Besides these serious economic problems at home, Nixon also faced tough challenges in foreign policy.

Economics *in* History

Inflation

Inflation is a rise in prices across the economy. When the price of milk goes up, that's a price increase. When the prices of gasoline, clothing, food, housing, and health care all go up, that's inflation.

Sometimes prices rise because there's more demand for goods than there are goods available to buy. This happened after World War II. During the war years, factories had produced weapons and supplies for the war effort. After the war, it took a while for factories to produce enough peacetime goods to meet consumer demand.

Sometimes prices rise because businesses increase their prices to cover their rising costs. This was the case in the 1970s, when the rising price of oil sent up the prices of many different goods and services.

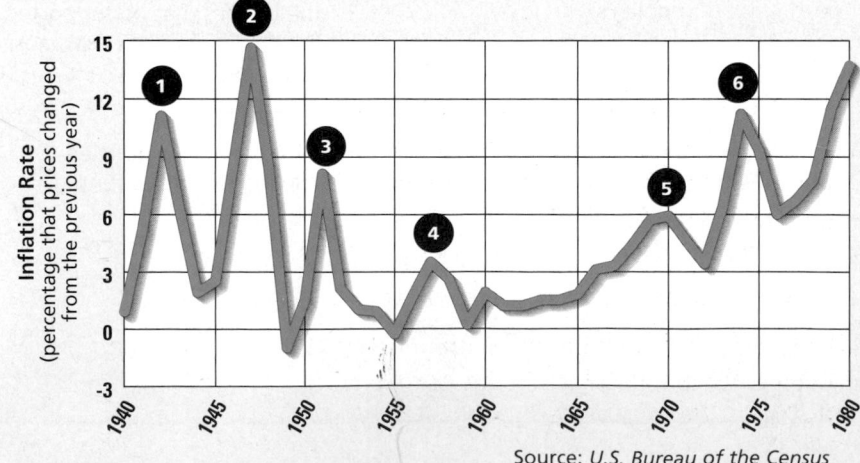

Source: *U.S. Bureau of the Census*

CONNECT TO HISTORY

1. **Making Inferences** Why do you think oil price increases had such a widespread effect on the economy?

   S See Skillbuilder Handbook, page R12.

CONNECT TO TODAY

2. **Researching** Find out what the rate of inflation has been in the most recent two years. How does today's inflation rate compare with that when Nixon came to office and when he left?

For more about inflation . . .

RESEARCH LINKS
CLASSZONE.COM

1. World War II
2. Postwar boom
3. Korean War
4. Suez crisis
5. Vietnam War
6. Arab oil embargo— oil prices increase

RICHARD M. NIXON

1913–1994

Richard Nixon entered politics in 1946 when he ran as a Republican for Congress. He was bright and ambitious. Some opponents, though, said that he would do anything to gain political power. Within seven years, he was vice-president of the United States.

In 1960, Nixon lost the presidential election to John Kennedy. In 1962, he was defeated for governor of California. Most thought his career over. But he battled back and was elected president in 1968. He is shown here in China in 1972 with his wife, Pat.

What characteristics did Nixon show as a leader?

Nixon Eases the Cold War

Nixon's main foreign-policy goal was world stability. During his 1968 presidential campaign, Nixon pledged to end the Vietnam War quickly and honorably. As you learned in Chapter 30, it took four years to negotiate a cease-fire with the North Vietnamese.

Nixon's most important triumph came in dealings with the People's Republic of China. He had long opposed the Communists, who took power in China in 1949. But Nixon believed a nation of a billion people could not be ignored. He asked Henry Kissinger to find a way to improve relations with China, even though they knew many Americans would be opposed. Kissinger arranged for Nixon to visit China in February 1972. This trip led to the opening of diplomacy and trade with the Chinese.

Nixon's China trip affected American relations with the Soviet Union, which was having conflicts with China. The Soviets feared closer relations between the United States and China. So they invited Nixon to Moscow in May 1972. As a result, Soviet-American relations improved. This easing of tensions between rivals is called **détente**—a French word. The policy of détente led the two nations to sign the Strategic Arms Limitation Treaty of 1972 (**SALT**). This pact limited the number of each country's nuclear weapons, easing fears of nuclear war.

Nixon's triumphs in foreign policy helped make him look like a sure winner for reelection in 1972. But, as you will read in the next section, events that occurred in that campaign eventually destroyed his presidency.

Reading **History**

C. Making Inferences What effect did improved American-Chinese relations have on Soviet-American relations?

Section 1 Assessment

1. Terms & Names

Explain the significance of:
- Richard M. Nixon
- Henry Kissinger
- revenue sharing
- détente
- SALT

2. Using Graphics

Use a spider diagram to describe problems Nixon faced in his first term.

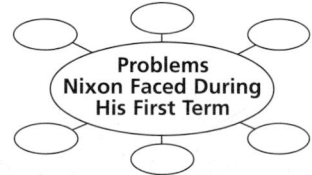

Problems Nixon Faced During His First Term

Which problems were linked?

3. Main Ideas

a. How did Nixon try to show support for law-and-order politics?

b. What economic problems developed during Nixon's first term as president?

c. How did Nixon change the country's relationship with China? with Russia?

4. Critical Thinking

Making Inferences Nixon often surprised Americans in the policies that he supported. Which do you think was most surprising? Why?

THINK ABOUT
- his economic policies, such as deficit spending
- his appointment of conservative justices
- the policy of détente

ACTIVITY OPTIONS

ART

LANGUAGE ARTS

Draw a **political cartoon** or write a **press release** describing one of Nixon's policies or achievements from his first term as president.

Watergate Brings Down Nixon

MAIN IDEA	WHY IT MATTERS NOW	TERMS & NAMES
Nixon's involvement in the Watergate scandal caused a political crisis that forced him to resign.	Watergate led many Americans to have less confidence in government and politicians.	Committee to Reelect the President Watergate scandal

ONE AMERICAN'S STORY

Barbara Jordan grew up in a poor home in Houston, Texas, in the 1940s. After graduating from Boston University Law School in 1959, she became interested in politics. She began her career as a volunteer worker for John Kennedy in his 1960 presidential campaign against Richard Nixon.

Jordan went on to become the first African-American woman from the South elected to the U.S. Congress. In 1974, at impeachment hearings in the House Judiciary Committee, Jordan warned that Nixon's actions during that campaign and his presidency were threats to the Constitution.

As a member of the House Judiciary Committee, Representative Barbara Jordan of Texas recommended the impeachment of President Nixon.

A VOICE FROM THE PAST

My faith in the Constitution is whole, it is complete, it is total, and I am not going to sit here and be an idle spectator to the diminution [lessening], the subversion [undermining], the destruction of the Constitution.

Barbara Jordan, speech in House Judiciary Committee, July 25, 1974

In this section, you will read about the events that led Nixon, Jordan, and the nation into the political nightmare that ended his presidency.

The 1972 Presidential Election

The 1972 presidential campaign did not appear to be much of a race for President Nixon. His diplomatic successes in China and the Soviet Union and Kissinger's negotiations to end the Vietnam War were triumphs for the president. The Republicans nominated him overwhelmingly for reelection.

Nixon's Democratic opponent was George McGovern. McGovern was a liberal senator from South Dakota who spoke out against the Vietnam War. McGovern had strong support from young people, African Americans, and members of the women's movement. But Nixon won with the largest victory of any Republican candidate to that time.

Taking Notes

Use your chart to take notes about Nixon's presidency.

President	
Nixon	
Ford	
Carter	

The Watergate scandal was the subject of thousands of political cartoons. Here, cartoonist Paul Conrad shows Nixon attempting to tap the telephones at the Democratic Party headquarters in the Watergate building.

What do you think the cartoon suggests about Nixon's involvement in the Watergate scandal?

"HE SAYS HE'S FROM THE PHONE COMPANY..."

The Watergate Scandal

An almost certain victory in the 1972 presidential election had not been enough for Nixon. He had wanted to win big. By doing so, he would help Republicans take control of Congress, and he would gain more power. To ensure this landslide victory, many people working for him engaged in various illegal activities.

These activities started coming to light on June 17, 1972. Five men were caught breaking into Democratic Party headquarters in the Watergate office-apartment complex in Washington, D.C. The burglars had cameras and listening devices for the telephones. They were linked to Nixon's reelection campaign staff, called the **Committee to Reelect the President**. Nixon may not have known in advance about the break-in. But in less than a week, he was talking to his aides about covering up any White House connection to the Watergate burglary to avoid a scandal.

The cover-up involved lies told by President Nixon and his aides. It involved payments to the Watergate burglars and others to lie. It involved using the CIA to halt an FBI investigation of Watergate. These illegal actions by Nixon and his aides to cover up Watergate and other related crimes came to be called the **Watergate scandal**.

The Watergate break-in stayed on the back pages of most newspapers in the 1972 campaign. But some reporters kept investigating. They found more evidence tying Nixon to Watergate. In February 1973, the Senate began an investigation. The threat to Nixon's presidency was building.

Nixon Resigns

The Senate Watergate investigation began with the questioning of members of the reelection committee and the White House staff. Within six weeks, the investigation was closing in on the president's closest advisers—H. R. Haldeman, John Ehrlichman, former Attorney-General John Mitchell, and John Dean. On March 21, 1973, Dean, one of the president's attorneys, spoke to Nixon about the worsening situation.

A VOICE FROM THE PAST

I think that there is no doubt about the seriousness of the problem we've got. We have a cancer within, close to the Presidency, that is growing. It is growing daily.

John Dean, quoted in *The White House Transcripts*

Dean was warning about money needed to keep the burglars quiet. Nixon agreed to pay the "hush money." He now clearly had committed a crime.

As more Watergate information was being uncovered, Dean decided to tell all to the Senate. He said that the president had been involved in the

*Reading*History
A. Making Inferences Why did Nixon want a big win in the 1972 presidential election?

Background Eventually, 25 members of the Nixon administration were convicted and served prison terms for crimes connected to Watergate.

cover-up for months. But Nixon denied any knowledge. It was Dean's word against Nixon's until mid-July. Then a White House aide revealed that Nixon had been taping conversations in his office. A long battle over the tapes began in the courts.

Meanwhile, more bad news came for Nixon. It was revealed that Vice-President Spiro Agnew had accepted bribes as governor of Maryland and continued taking them as vice-president. Not wanting to face impeachment, Agnew resigned in October 1973. Nixon then nominated Congressman Gerald Ford of Michigan as the new vice-president.

President Nixon put on an upbeat face as he left Washington after resigning on August 9, 1974.

Evidence of the president's role in the cover-up continued to grow, but he told the country that he had done nothing wrong. He said, "I am not a crook." Then, in January 1974, the House Judiciary Committee began an impeachment investigation. It reviewed court testimony, Senate transcripts, and documents from special prosecutors. Nixon did not give them his tapes but released edited transcripts. The committee felt it had a strong case even without the tapes. In July, both Democrats and Republicans on the committee approved impeachment charges.

On August 5, Nixon was forced by a court order to release full transcripts of the tapes. The evidence that he had been involved in the cover-up from the beginning—what investigators called "a smoking gun"—had been recorded on the tapes. On August 9, 1974, Richard Nixon resigned. Vice-President Gerald Ford was then sworn in as the next president.

Reading**History**

B. Recognizing Effects How did the Watergate scandal change many Americans' view of their government?

Watergate was one of the worst political scandals in the nation's history. Many Americans lost faith in the government and its leaders. This lack of confidence weakened the government, especially the president. As you will read in the following section, the next two presidents—Gerald Ford and Jimmy Carter—worked hard to try to restore the presidency.

Section 2 Assessment

1. Terms & Names

Explain the significance of:

- Committee to Reelect the President
- Watergate scandal

2. Using Graphics

Use a time line like the one below to trace the events of the Watergate scandal.

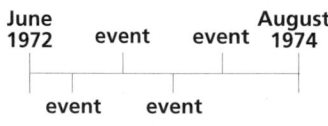

June 1972 — event — event — August 1974

event — event

Which event made Nixon's downfall almost certain?

3. Main Ideas

a. Why did Nixon want a big win in the 1972 election?

b. What kinds of illegal activities was Nixon involved with in the Watergate scandal?

c. What was the outcome of the Watergate scandal?

4. Critical Thinking

Forming and Supporting Opinions What do you think would have happened if President Nixon had apologized for Watergate rather than trying to cover it up?

THINK ABOUT

- when the break-in occurred
- how the nation reacted to past scandals

ACTIVITY OPTIONS

TECHNOLOGY

LANGUAGE ARTS

Interview someone who remembers Watergate. Either create a **radio broadcast** of the interview or write it as a **question-and-answer magazine feature**.

Issues of the Seventies

MAIN IDEA	WHY IT MATTERS NOW	TERMS & NAMES
Presidents Ford and Carter had a difficult time solving the nation's problems after Watergate.	These problems helped lead to a conservative mood in the United States.	Gerald Ford environmentalism Jimmy Carter Rachel Carson Camp David Accords Iran hostage crisis

ONE AMERICAN'S STORY

On August 9, 1974, Vice-President **Gerald Ford** became president after Richard Nixon resigned. During 25 years as a congressman from Michigan, Ford had gained a reputation for integrity and openness.

As president, Ford inherited a nation that had suffered through the years of Vietnam and Watergate. He tried to reassure Americans that the turmoil of the Nixon years was behind them.

A VOICE FROM THE PAST

My fellow Americans, our long national nightmare is over. Our Constitution works; our great Republic is a Government of laws and not of men. Here the people rule. . . . As we bind up the internal wounds of Watergate, more painful and more poisonous than those of foreign wars, let us restore the golden rule to our political process, and let brotherly love purge our hearts of suspicion and of hate.

Gerald Ford, speech on August 9, 1974

President Gerald Ford speaks to the nation from the White House.

Ford pardoned former President Nixon, a decision that brought him much criticism. In this section, you will learn more about the difficulties presidents Ford and Jimmy Carter faced in the 1970s.

Taking Notes

Use your chart to take notes about the presidencies of Ford and Carter.

President	
Nixon	
Ford	
Carter	

Ford Takes Over

In his first weeks in office, Ford set out to restore confidence in the presidency. He soothed the nation with his plain speaking, openness, and willingness to talk to the press and to work with Congress.

However, within a month, Ford lost the support of many Americans when he pardoned Richard Nixon for any crimes he might have committed during the Watergate scandal. It had been Ford's hope to spare the country the spectacle of a former president being brought to trial. But

Reading **History**

A. Drawing Conclusions
Why were many Americans upset with President Ford over Nixon's pardon?

many people felt strongly that Nixon should be charged with crimes because of the Watergate cover-up. Ford's popularity dropped sharply.

Making life even tougher for Ford was the fact that the economy was not in good shape. Inflation was spiraling higher while a recession was throwing more people out of work. Many Americans were having a hard time making ends meet. Ford proposed a voluntary campaign to "Whip Inflation Now." He asked Americans to cut spending and energy use. The WIN plan received much publicity but failed to help the economy.

In foreign affairs, Ford had mixed success. He asked Congress to help South Vietnam when the cease-fire in the Vietnam War broke down in 1974. But Congress refused. In 1975, he negotiated a treaty with European nations and Canada called the Helsinki Accords. This pact spelled out basic human rights for the citizens of the signer nations.

Vocabulary

human rights: basic rights and freedoms to which all human beings are entitled, such as freedom of speech

Ford's pardon of Nixon and his difficulty in improving the economy caused him problems in the 1976 presidential campaign. He only narrowly won his party's nomination over California governor Ronald Reagan. Then he lost the presidency in a close election to Democrat **Jimmy Carter**.

Carter was a former peanut farmer and governor of Georgia. He had run for president as a Washington outsider and one who would "never lie" to the American people. He promised honesty in government and support for human rights throughout the world.

Reading **History**

B. Making Inferences How did Jimmy Carter benefit from the Watergate scandal?

Carter as President

Many Americans were still suspicious of their government as Carter took office in 1977. Since Carter had never served in Washington, Americans hoped that he would bring fresh ideas to the presidency.

Carter immediately tried to show that he was one of the people. On inauguration day, he and his family walked from the Capitol to the White House rather than take the traditional limousine. However, being a Washington outsider would make political life difficult for Carter.

Carter and Congress often clashed. One point of conflict was the energy crisis. Early in 1977, shortages of oil and natural gas forced many schools and businesses to close. In response, Carter asked Americans to conserve energy. He also sent a national energy program to Congress. It would cut oil imports, increase production of oil and natural gas at home, and promote alternative energy sources like coal and nuclear and solar energy.

After months of debate, Congress passed some of the measures. But they were of little help when OPEC again sharply raised oil prices. Inflation surged beyond 10 percent. Unemployment rose. Like Nixon and Ford, Carter could not solve the nation's economic problems.

America's HERITAGE

THE BICENTENNIAL
On July 4, 1976, the United States celebrated the 200th anniversary of the Declaration of Independence. The Bicentennial, as it was called, was a year-long birthday party. People in every corner of the nation celebrated with special events.

Americans also used the time to reflect on the nation's progress. Women, African Americans, Hispanic Americans, Native Americans, and others still faced discrimination. Yet Americans were proud of what had been achieved, and the celebration helped the nation move beyond the turmoil of the early 1970s.

Connections TO WORLD HISTORY

MIDDLE EAST PEACE PROCESS

The signing of the Camp David Accords in 1978 by (left to right) Prime Minister Menachem Begin of Israel, President Carter, and President Anwar el-Sadat of Egypt was the first important step in the attempt to bring peace to the Middle East.

In 1998, another step was taken when President Bill Clinton brought Palestinian leader Yasir Arafat and Israeli Prime Minister Benjamin Netanyahu together to sign a peace agreement called the Wye River Accords.

Carter had more success in accomplishing his foreign-policy goals. He wanted to end the long-standing conflict with Panama over the Panama Canal. As you read in Chapter 23, the Panama Canal was built and controlled by the United States. Most Americans wanted it to stay that way. But Carter thought winning the good will of Latin America was worth losing control of the canal. Under treaties signed in 1977, the United States agreed to give the canal to Panama in 2000.

Carter also tried to reduce tensions in the Middle East. In 1978, he helped to negotiate the **Camp David Accords.** Under these agreements, Egypt and Israel signed the first peace treaty between Israel and an Arab nation, thus ending 30 years of conflict.

The Environmental Movement Begins

Protection of the environment was also a goal of Carter's. He supported a movement to save the environment that had gained momentum in the 1970s. Actually, the first laws to protect the nation's natural environment had been passed in the late 1800s. But **environmentalism,** or work toward protecting the environment, only began to attract wide public attention in the 1960s. In 1962, biologist **Rachel Carson** wrote of the dangers of heavy pesticide use in her bestseller, *Silent Spring.* She warned that some of these chemicals could kill animals, cause disease, and destroy the environment unless their use was limited or stopped.

In 1969, a huge oil spill near Santa Barbara, California, polluted miles of beaches and killed many marine animals. The cry for tougher laws to protect the environment grew. In the 1970s, Nixon, Ford, and Carter all proposed laws to restrict pesticide use, to regulate the cleanup of oil spills, and to curb air and water pollution. With these laws in effect, many polluted lakes began to recover, and high levels of some air pollutants began to drop. But environmental disasters continued to occur.

In 1979, an accident occurred at the Three Mile Island nuclear power plant in Pennsylvania. Radioactive water leaked out of the plant, causing

Reading **History**

C. Finding Main Ideas What role did Rachel Carson play in the environmental movement?

fears that the nuclear reactor might explode. Within a week, the reactor was shut down. Disaster was averted. To assure people it was safe, Carter visited Three Mile Island. But not long after, he faced another disaster—a political one—in Iran.

Reagan and the Conservatives Win

For decades, the United States had supported the Shah (king) of Iran. In 1979, Muslim leaders overthrew his government. When Carter allowed the Shah to come to the United States for medical treatment, Iranians struck back at the United States. On November 4, 1979, they overran the American embassy in Iran's capital of Tehran and took 52 Americans hostage. The **Iran hostage crisis** had begun.

*Reading*History
D. Reading a Map
Locate Tehran, the capital of Iran, in the map on this page.

Carter tried negotiating to get Iran's leaders to release the hostages but without success. He approved a secret military mission, but it failed. The continuing crisis affected the election in 1980. Americans blamed Carter for the plight of the hostages, for the nation's economic ills, and for making America look weak to the world.

Meanwhile, support for conservative ideas had been growing for more than a decade. The Republicans chose a conservative—Ronald Reagan, a former actor and California governor—to be their candidate in 1980. He vowed that, if elected president, he would not allow the United States to be pushed around. Reagan's get-tough talk appealed to many voters.

Carter eventually won release of the hostages. But the majority of voters had already decided that it was time for a change and elected Reagan president. The hostages left Iran on January 20, 1981, the day Reagan was inaugurated. In the next chapter, you will read how Ronald Reagan took the nation in a more conservative direction.

Section 3 Assessment

1. Terms & Names

Explain the significance of:
- Gerald Ford
- Jimmy Carter
- Camp David Accords
- environmentalism
- Rachel Carson
- Iran hostage crisis

2. Using Graphics

Use a chart to list the high and low points of both the Ford and Carter presidencies.

Presidency	High points	Low points
Gerald Ford		
Jimmy Carter		

Which do you think was the highest point of each? Why?

3. Main Ideas

a. Why did Carter win the 1976 election over Ford?

b. What were some problems related to energy use that occurred during Carter's term?

c. What progress did the environmental movement make during the 1960s and the 1970s?

4. Critical Thinking

Comparing How would you compare the strengths and weaknesses of Ford and Carter? Use events from their presidencies to support your answer.

THINK ABOUT
- actions each took to draw Americans together
- response to economic and foreign-policy issues

ACTIVITY OPTIONS

MATH
ART

Research inflation in the 1970s. Make a **graph** to show the annual rate change or create a **political cartoon** about inflation's effect on people's lives.

Save the Environment!

You are a citizen of the 1970s who has joined the fight against pollution, waste, and the destruction of the Earth's natural resources. Each year on Earth Day, you help out with community clean-ups. You are interested in finding ways to rally public opinion and help save the planet.

COOPERATIVE LEARNING On this page are three challenges you face as an American concerned about the environment. Working with a small group, decide how to deal with each challenge. Select an option, assign a task to each group member, and do the activity. You will find useful information in the Data File. Present your solutions to the class.

Renew the Earth

LANGUAGE ARTS CHALLENGE

"the community of living things"

You are worried that lack of concern about the environment may result in a permanently damaged world. The destruction of natural resources by individuals and industry continues. You decide to promote a campaign to save the environment. Present your ideas using one of these options:

• Write an editorial describing environmental dangers and promoting conservation.

• Make a speech to rally people in support of conservation.

Take Public Transportation

ART CHALLENGE

"the air we breathe for life"

Ozone alert! TV announcers warn families to keep small children at home. The elderly, especially those with lung and heart problems, must stay inside. You wish that people understood the terrible effects of air pollution better so they might start demanding cleaner air. You decide to take action. Present your ideas using one of these options:

- Design a public service ad for magazines explaining how air pollutants harm the body.
- Draw a cartoon asking people to use public transportation.

SCIENCE CHALLENGE

"the lakes and rivers and oceans"

News of an oil spill off California's shores has sparked your concern for the environment. You are sickened by pictures of oil-soaked beaches and thousands of injured and dead animals. You want to help rid the oceans of this menace. Use the Data File for information. Then present your ideas, using one of these options:

- Create a labeled diagram for your local paper showing why oil pollution harms most sea life.
- Role-play a community meeting in which you explain how offshore oil pollution damages sea life.

Prevent Pollution

ACTIVITY WRAP-UP

Present to the class Meet with the group to review your methods of helping to save the environment. Select a solution that best meets each challenge and then present it to the class.

DATA FILE

ENVIRONMENTAL PROBLEMS

Air and water pollution, acid rain, destruction of the ozone layer, toxic chemical disposal, extinction of wildlife, oil spills, destruction of forests, overpopulation

OCEAN LIFE ZONES

- Shorelines support crabs, oysters, shore birds, and other marine life.
- Open ocean over the continental shelf supports the largest amount of sea life, including algae, lobsters, thousands of fish species, turtles, seals, sharks, and whales.
- Deep ocean supports a smaller variety.

SOURCES OF OCEAN OIL POLLUTION

Offshore oil production, vessel accidents, natural seepage, non-tanker and tanker shipping operations, waste car oil

AIR POLLUTANTS

- sources—fossil fuels, cars, power plants, industry, ozone
- effects—smog; eye irritation; impaired judgment; chest pains; lung, nerve, and kidney damage; cancer; birth defects

WAYS TO CLEAN WATER

- Install oil pollution prevention equipment on ships.
- Car owners, cities, and industry recycle used oil.

REDUCE AIR POLLUTION

- Burn fewer fossil fuels.
- Take public transportation.
- Improve car efficiency.
- Use sun and wind power.

For more about the environment . . .

RESEARCH LINKS
CLASSZONE.COM

TERMS & NAMES

Briefly explain the significance of each of the following.

1. Richard M. Nixon
2. Henry Kissinger
3. revenue sharing
4. détente
5. Watergate scandal
6. Gerald Ford
7. Jimmy Carter
8. Camp David Accords
9. environmentalism
10. Iran hostage crisis

REVIEW QUESTIONS

Nixon Confronts Problems (pages 855–858)

1. What kinds of government programs did Nixon propose to deal with America's social problems?
2. How did Nixon try to promote "law and order"?
3. What were the economic problems Nixon faced?
4. How was Nixon's foreign policy toward China different from that of previous presidents?

Watergate Brings Down Nixon (pages 859–861)

5. What were the chief causes of the Watergate scandal?
6. What did reporters and others find when they looked more deeply into the Watergate burglary?
7. What were the events that caused Nixon to resign?

Issues of the Seventies (pages 862–867)

8. What were the main reasons people did not vote for Gerald Ford in the 1976 election?
9. What successes did Carter have with foreign policy and what problems did he have at home?
10. What appealed to voters about Ronald Reagan in the 1980 election?

CRITICAL THINKING

1. USING YOUR NOTES: FINDING MAIN IDEAS

President	Issues and Events
Nixon	
Ford	
Carter	

Use your completed chart to answer these questions.

a. What issues did all three presidents have to deal with during their terms? Which were the most frequently occurring issues of their presidencies?
b. Which of the presidents do you think faced the most difficult issues? Explain.

2. ANALYZING LEADERSHIP

What characteristics did Nixon, Ford, and Carter have that made them good leaders? Poor leaders?

3. THEME: CITIZENSHIP

What could Americans do to help their country during the 1970s?

4. FORMING AND SUPPORTING OPINIONS

Do you think Nixon's actions showed that his main goal was to survive during the events of Watergate? Explain your answer.

5. EVALUATING

Do you think that Ford made a good decision in pardoning Nixon? Explain why or why not.

Interact with History

Did your ideas about how the nation survives a crisis agree or disagree with what you read?

VISUAL SUMMARY

Years of Doubt

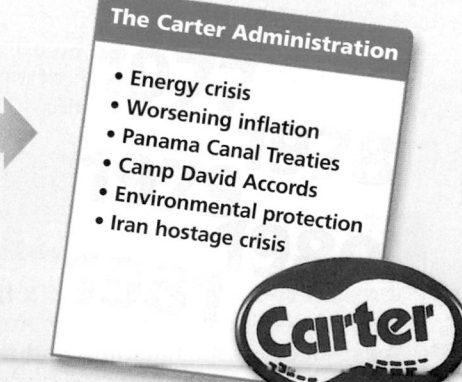

The Nixon Administration

- Revenue sharing
- Law-and-order politics
- Inflation, recession, and unemployment
- Opening to China
- Détente with the Soviet Union
- Watergate scandal
- Nixon resignation

The Ford Administration

- Unelected president
- Nixon pardon
- Whip Inflation Now program
- Helsinki Accords

The Carter Administration

- Energy crisis
- Worsening inflation
- Panama Canal Treaties
- Camp David Accords
- Environmental protection
- Iran hostage crisis

Use the graph and your knowledge of U.S. history to answer questions 1 and 2.

Additional Test Practice, pp. S1–S33.

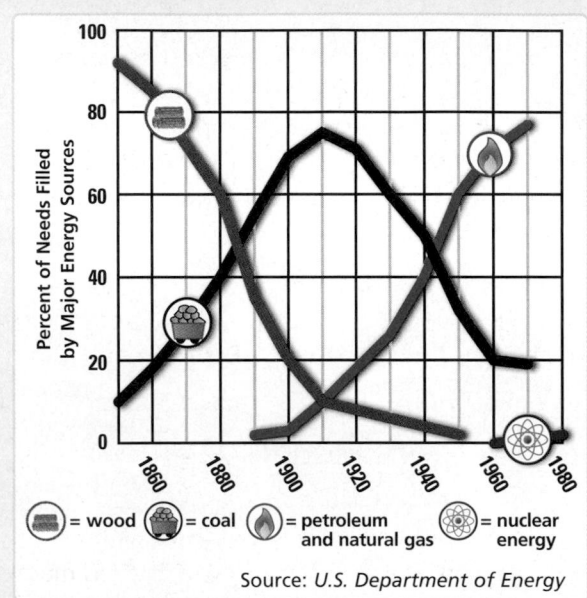

Major Energy Sources, 1850–1980

Percent of Needs Filled by Major Energy Sources

= wood = coal = petroleum and natural gas = nuclear energy

Source: *U.S. Department of Energy*

1. What fuel supplied most of the nation's energy between 1850 and 1880?

   A. wood

   B. coal

   C. petroleum

   D. natural gas

2. When did petroleum and natural gas begin being used as a major source of fuel?

   A. around 1860

   B. around 1880

   C. around 1885

   D. around 1945

This quotation comes from a conversation between attorney John Dean and President Nixon. Use the quotation and your knowledge of U.S. history to answer question 3.

PRIMARY SOURCE

I think there is no doubt about the seriousness of the problem we've got. We have a cancer within, close to the Presidency, that is growing. It is growing daily.

John Dean, quoted in *The White House Transcripts*

3. What problem is John Dean referring to in this conversation with Nixon?

   A. the oil spill near Santa Barbara, California

   B. the Vietnam War

   C. the Watergate investigation

   D. the Iran hostage crisis

TEST PRACTICE
CLASSZONE.COM

ALTERNATIVE ASSESSMENT

1. ✍ WRITING ABOUT HISTORY

Suppose you are a TV news reporter on August 9, 1974. Write a **script** to report that Richard Nixon has resigned as President.

• Use library resources to research your script.

• Explain the events that lead to his decision.

• Include quotes from key figures.

• Report on the new president, Gerald Ford.

2. COOPERATIVE LEARNING

Working in a small group, research President Nixon's last two years in office. Pick one event and work together to write a play about the incident. Use primary sources, such as diaries or tape transcripts, to create your dialogue. Present your play to the class.

INTEGRATED TECHNOLOGY

CREATING A WEB SITE

The 200th anniversary of independence was a cause for celebration for Americans everywhere. It was a time to reflect on how the nation began, where it was then, and what might happen next. Create a Bicentennial Web site that presents sight and sound of this important celebration.

• Use the library and the Internet to locate images of Bicentennial highlights and historical figures.

• Choose music that captures the spirit of the event.

• Select Web sites that would be good links for visitors to your site.

For more about the United States Bicentennial . . .

INTERNET ACTIVITY
CLASSZONE.COM

CHAPTER 32

Entering a New Millennium 1981–present

Section 1
Conservatives Reshape Politics

Section 2
Technological and Economic Changes

Section 3
The New Americans

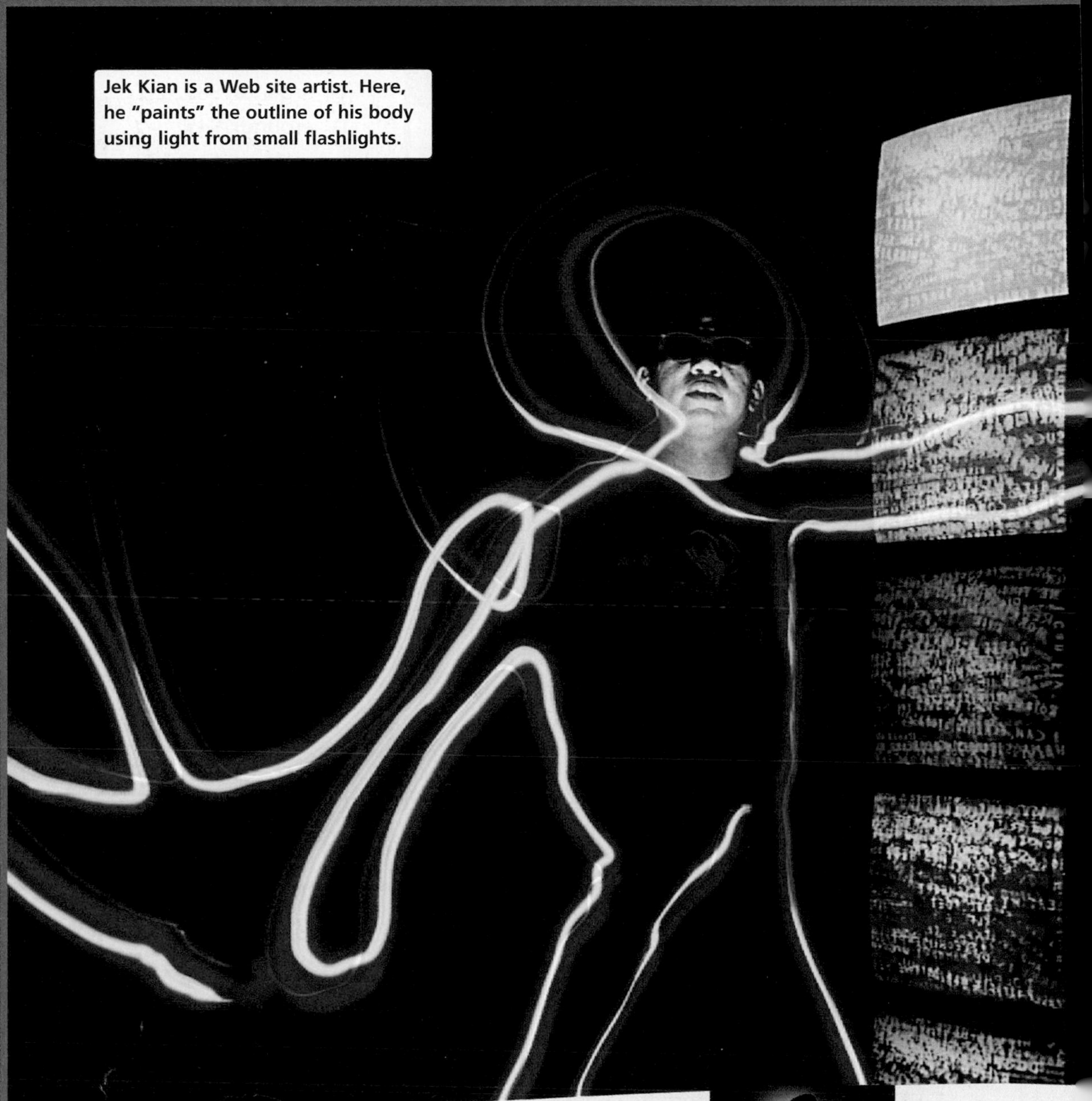

Jek Kian is a Web site artist. Here, he "paints" the outline of his body using light from small flashlights.

USA
World
1980

1982
Barney Clark receives first artificial heart.

1984
President Reagan is reelected.

1988
Reagan's vice-president, George H. W. Bush, is elected president.

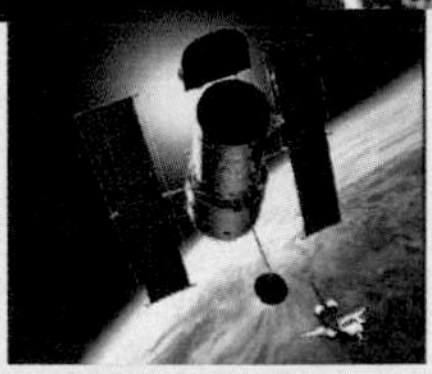

1990
The Hubble Space Telescope is launch

1982
Great Britain defeats Argentina in a war over the Falkland Islands.

1985
An earthquake in Mexico City kills thousands.

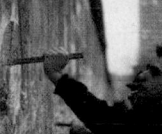

1989
The Berlin Wall is taken down.

1991
The Soviet Union breaks apart.

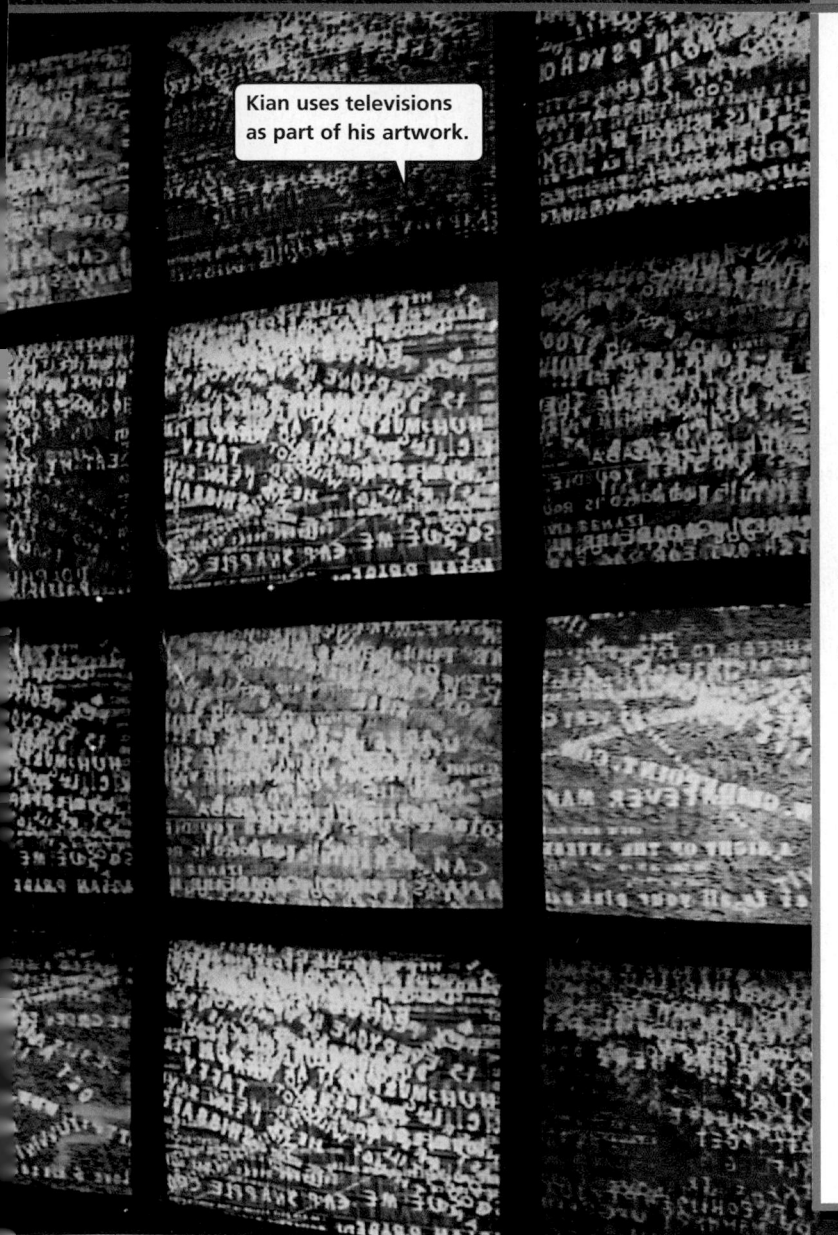

Kian uses televisions as part of his artwork.

The time is four years from now, and you're about to finish high school. Your friends ask about your plans for the future. At graduation, the speaker urges your class not just to focus on earning money but also to care about making the world a better place. How can you do that?

What can you contribute to the future?

What Do You Think?

- What are your talents, and how could you use them to benefit both yourself and society?
- What things do you really enjoy doing?
- What do you think the United States and the world need most from your generation?

RESEARCH LINKS
CLASSZONE.COM

Visit the Chapter 32 links for more information about America today.

1992
Democrat Bill Clinton is elected president.

1994
The Republicans gain control of both houses of Congress.

1996
Clinton is reelected.

1998
Clinton is impeached.

2000
Republican George W. Bush is elected president.

2004
Bush is reelected.

present

1994
In South Africa's first all-race election, Nelson Mandela is elected president.

2001
The World Trade Center in New York City is attacked by terrorists.

2003
Iraq War begins.

Reading Strategy: Recognizing Effects

What Do You Know?

How closely do you follow current events? What do you think are the major trends in the United States today?

Think About

- political events in the news
- the latest changes in technology
- how immigration is affecting the United States
- your responses to the Interact with History about contributing to the future (see page 871)

What Do You Want to Know?

 What would you like to know about our most recent presidents? What questions do you have about technology? What do you want to learn about recent patterns of immigration? Record your questions in your notebook before you read this chapter.

SPECIAL ISSUE

TIME

Take a good look at this woman. She was created by a computer from a mix of several races. What you see is a remarkable preview of . . .

THE NEW FACE OF AMERICA
How Immigrants Are Shaping the World's
First Multicultural Society

Recognizing Effects

The consequences of an event are its effects. As you read the chapter, look for major events in the categories of politics, technological and economic change, and immigration. Notice how these events affected U.S. society. Record your information on a chart like the one below.

S See Skillbuilder Handbook, page R11.

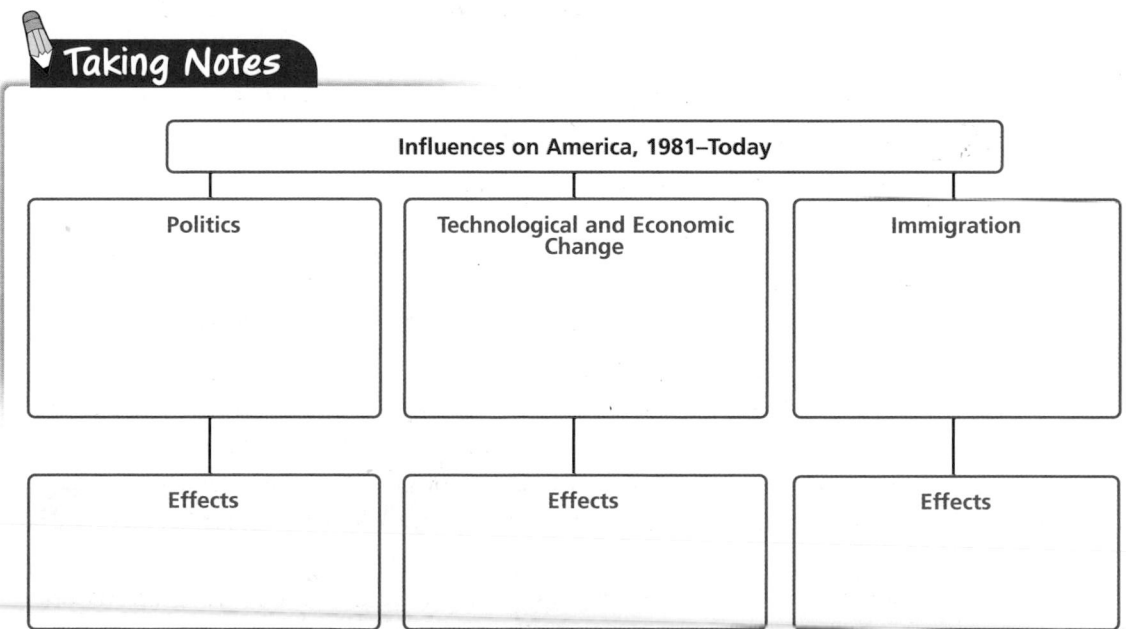

Taking Notes

Influences on America, 1981–Today

Politics	Technological and Economic Change	Immigration
Effects	Effects	Effects

Conservatives Reshape Politics

MAIN IDEA	WHY IT MATTERS NOW	TERMS & NAMES
The country became more conservative, leading to Republican political victories.	In response, the Democratic Party became less liberal and even adopted some conservative ideas.	Ronald Reagan / supply-side economics / Iran-Contra affair / George H. W. Bush / Persian Gulf War / Bill Clinton / NAFTA / George W. Bush

ONE AMERICAN'S STORY

Restaurant owner Mike Savic knew the mood in his working-class Chicago neighborhood. In the fall of 1980, most of his customers were frightened. Unemployment and inflation were rising. Most of Savic's neighbors had supported Carter in 1976, but now they turned to Carter's Republican opponent, former California governor **Ronald Reagan**.

A VOICE FROM THE PAST

People have been talking. . . . Some of them in this neighborhood have been laid off four, six months. . . . And they've been scared. . . . The ones who'd been talking that they were for Carter, well, they changed.

Mike Savic, quoted in the *Chicago Tribune*, November 6, 1980

This campaign button is from the 1980 debate between Jimmy Carter and Ronald Reagan.

In 1980, millions of Democrats voted for Reagan in the hope that he could fix the economy. With their help, Reagan won the election. This section covers the presidencies of Reagan and his successors.

Reagan's Conservative Goals

President Reagan was a conservative. In his 1981 inaugural address, he declared, "Government is not the solution to our problem. . . . It is time to check the growth of government." Reagan pursued the following conservative goals.

1. **Lower Taxes.** Reagan preached **supply-side economics.** This theory held that if taxes were lower, people would save more money. Banks could loan that money to businesses, which could invest in ways to improve productivity. The supply of goods would increase, driving down prices. At Reagan's urging, Congress lowered income taxes by 25 percent over three years.
2. **Deregulation.** The president deregulated, or eased restrictions on, many industries. Reagan believed that business would grow more rapidly if government interfered with it less.

Taking Notes

Use your chart to take notes about politics in the 1980s.

Entering a New Millennium **873**

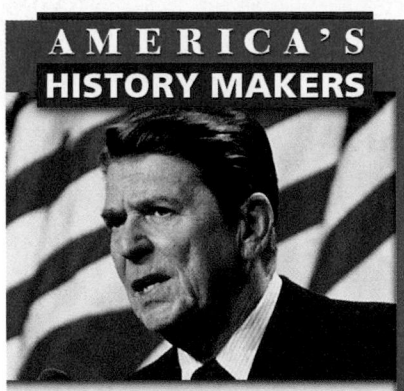

AMERICA'S HISTORY MAKERS

RONALD REAGAN
1911–2004

One reason for Ronald Reagan's popularity was his unfailing optimism at a time when many Americans felt uncertain. Not even an assassination attempt could dampen his spirits.

In 1981, a gunman shot the president. When Reagan's wife, Nancy, arrived at the hospital, Reagan told her, "Honey, I forgot to duck."

In addition, he remarked to the doctors who were about to operate on him, "I hope you're all Republicans."

Why might it be important for a leader to convey a sense of optimism and high spirits?

3. **Fewer Government Programs.** Reagan fought to end or weaken many government programs, from affirmative action to environmental regulations.

4. **A Conservative Supreme Court.** Reagan named three conservative judges to the Supreme Court. One of them, Sandra Day O'Connor, was the first woman to sit on the nation's highest court.

At first, inflation rose, and unemployment stayed high. But by 1983, inflation decreased, and more people found jobs. Business boomed. Even so, Reagan's policies created a problem. Because of the tax cut, the federal government took in less money and had to resort to deficit spending. As a result, the national debt doubled from 1981 to 1986.

Vocabulary
deficit spending: using borrowed money to fund government programs

A Tough Anti-Communist Stand

Reagan opposed communism. To compete militarily with the Soviet Union, he began the most expensive arms buildup in history. It cost more than $2 trillion.

In 1985, Mikhail Gorbachev became the leader of the Soviet Union. He and Reagan met four times to discuss improving U.S.-Soviet relations and easing the threat of nuclear war. They signed the Intermediate-Range Nuclear Forces (INF) Treaty in 1987. Under that treaty, the two countries agreed to destroy all of their medium-range missiles.

The Reagan administration also decided to support the anti-Communist side in several conflicts, including two Central American civil wars. In El Salvador, the United States backed the government against Communist-led rebels. In Nicaragua, the United States provided aid to anti-Communist rebels known as Contras.

This aid resulted in a scandal, known as the **Iran-Contra affair.** In 1986, Americans learned that the U.S. government had sold weapons to Iran in return for help in freeing American hostages in the Middle East. The money from these sales went to the Contras. This action violated a law that barred the U.S. government from funding the rebels. President Reagan claimed he never knew about the deal. But investigators concluded that he should have kept track of what his administration was doing.

*Reading*History
A. Analyzing Causes Why did investigators hold Reagan responsible for the Iran-Contra affair?

Bush and a Changing World

Despite the scandal, Reagan and his administration remained popular. In 1988, Reagan's vice-president, **George H. W. Bush,** ran for president and won. During his presidency, dramatic foreign events took place.

In 1989, several Eastern European countries ended Communist rule. This angered old-time Communists in the Soviet Union. In August 1991, a group of them tried to take over the Soviet government. Boris Yeltsin, a Russian reform leader, fought the takeover attempt and won.

Unlike Gorbachev, who wanted to reform communism, Yeltsin and others wanted to get rid of it. One by one, the republics that made up the Soviet Union declared their independence from it. In December 1991, Yeltsin and the leaders of these nations joined in a loose alliance called the Commonwealth of Independent States (CIS). The Soviet Union, once a superpower, was gone. Its breakup marked the end of the Cold War.

A crisis also erupted in the Middle East. In August 1990, Iraq invaded its neighbor Kuwait—a major supplier of oil. The United States, led by Bush, and the United Nations (UN) organized a group of 39 nations to free Kuwait by fighting the **Persian Gulf War**. In mid-January 1991, UN forces began bombing Iraqi military targets. A month later, UN ground forces moved into Kuwait and drove the Iraqis out of that country.

The war's success boosted George Bush's popularity, and he seemed certain to win reelection in 1992. Then the economy stalled. By the spring of 1992, the U.S. unemployment rate had climbed to around 7 percent—a six-year high. Americans began to think that Bush was good at foreign policy but ineffective with problems at home. In November, they elected his Democratic opponent, Arkansas governor **Bill Clinton**.

Clinton's Fights with Congress

One of President Clinton's first acts was to try to reform the health-care system. Clinton asked his wife, Hillary Rodham Clinton, to design a health-care plan. Opponents criticized the plan as costing too much, and Congress chose not to vote on it. But it did pass a law allowing workers to keep their insurance when they change jobs.

Clinton did win passage of the North American Free Trade Agreement (NAFTA) in 1993. NAFTA lifted tariffs in an effort to increase trade among Mexico, Canada, and the United States.

In 1994, Republicans won control of both houses of Congress. Clinton and the new Congress could not agree on a budget for 1995 and government agencies shut down twice in late 1995. Finally, Clinton and Congress reached a compromise on the budget.

The two sides did work together to pass a welfare reform bill, a long time conservative goal. The bill ended a guarantee of aid to needy families. It also cut the length of time people could receive benefits.

In 1996, Clinton was reelected. But his second term in office was marked by scandal. Clinton was investigated for a land deal he took part in during the 1970s. During that investigation, information emerged that Clinton had had an improper relationship with a White House intern. And he allegedly had lied about it under oath.

*Reading*History

B. Summarizing
What were two major world events that happened during George H. W. Bush's presidency?

Background
Most developed countries have nationalized health insurance, a government program that pays for the health care of most citizens. The United States does not.

Connections TO **WORLD HISTORY**

THE BERLIN WALL FALLS
Communists built the Berlin Wall in 1961 to separate Communist East Berlin from West Berlin. In November 1989, as communism began to fall, East Germans tore down the wall. The photograph below shows Germans celebrating the opening of the wall. Andreas Ramos witnessed the event.

The final slab was moved away. A stream of East Germans began to pour through. . . . Looking around, I saw an indescribable joy in people's faces. It was the end of the government telling people what not to do, it was the end of the Wall, the war, the East, the West.

The Washington Post

SUNDAY, DECEMBER 20, 1998

Clinton Impeached
House Approves Articles Charging Perjury, Obstruction

When the charges became public in January 1998, Clinton denied them. Later, he admitted to the relationship but denied lying under oath. In December 1998, the House of Representatives impeached President Clinton. In general, Republicans voted for impeachment while Democrats voted against it. In spite of the charges, Clinton remained popular. In January 1999, the Senate held its trial of President Clinton and acquitted him. Clinton remained in office to finish his second term.

Background
Clinton was the second president to be impeached, or formally charged with wrongdoing. The first was Andrew Johnson. (See Chapter 18.)

War in Kosovo

Despite his troubles at home, Clinton still had to act as a world leader. In 1999, he led a group of nations dealing with a crisis in Yugoslavia. The European country of Yugoslavia was created after World War I. Yugoslavia contained many ethnic and religious groups. Often, these groups fought with one another.

The Yugoslav republic of Serbia has a region called Kosovo (KAW-suh-VOH) inhabited mostly by people of Albanian descent. The Kosovars sought independence, but the Serbs opposed them. A vicious war broke out over Kosovo. The Serbian government tried to drive the Albanians out of Kosovo by using violence and murder.

*Reading***History**
C. Analyzing Causes What caused the violence in Kosovo?

In March 1999, the North Atlantic Treaty Organization (NATO) began bombing Serbia. In June 1999, the Serbs withdrew from Kosovo. After the troops pulled out, UN peacekeepers moved in. The United Nations has run Kosovo since then. In February 2003, Yugoslavia became a federation called Serbia and Montenegro. In 2006, both republics will vote on independence.

The 2000 Presidential Campaign

In 2000, the nation turned its attention to a presidential election as Clinton finished his second term. The Democrats nominated Vice-President Al Gore as their candidate. The Republicans chose Texas governor George W. Bush, the son of the former president. Other candidates included Ralph Nader of the Green Party and Pat Buchanan of the Reform Party. It was clear, however, that Bush and Gore were the leaders in the race.

*Reading***History**
D. Drawing Conclusions How was it helpful and harmful to Al Gore to be Clinton's vice-president?

In the campaign, Gore emphasized his experience as vice-president. Bush attacked Gore's connection with Clinton's administration. On the issue of taxes, Bush proposed a large income tax cut, which he said would stimulate economic growth. Gore argued that Bush's plan would mainly benefit wealthy Americans. Gore called for a smaller tax cut aimed to help lower- and middle-class Americans.

A Close Election

On Election Day, November 7, 2000, most people expected a very close race. The election ended up being one of the closest in U.S. history. As the day moved into night, it became clear that whichever candidate won Florida would win the presidency.

The next morning, Gore led the nationwide popular vote by more than 300,000 votes and also had a lead in electoral votes. But Bush led in Florida by a few hundred votes, which could still win the election for him.

The vote was so close in Florida that recounts were required. In addition, many Floridians claimed there were problems with the voting process. Some voters were confused by the way the names were listed on the ballots. They claimed this may have caused them to vote for the wrong candidate. In some cases, the voting machines did not work correctly.

*Reading*History

E. Analyzing Causes Why did Bush win the presidency even though he had fewer popular votes than Gore?

The Gore campaign asked for manual, or hand, recounts of ballots in four Florida counties. The Bush campaign opposed manual recounts and sued to stop them. The legal battles reached the U.S. Supreme Court. On December 12, the Court voted five to four to stop the recounts. The majority argued that there was no way to be sure the votes would be recounted in exactly the same way in all counties. This situation, they said, would be unfair to some voters. With the recounts stopped, Florida's electoral votes, and the presidency, went to George W. Bush.

The 2000 election raised issues about how elections are conducted in the United States. For example, Gore won the popular vote but lost the election. This led to renewed efforts to abolish the Electoral College. Americans also looked to improve the ways votes are cast and counted.

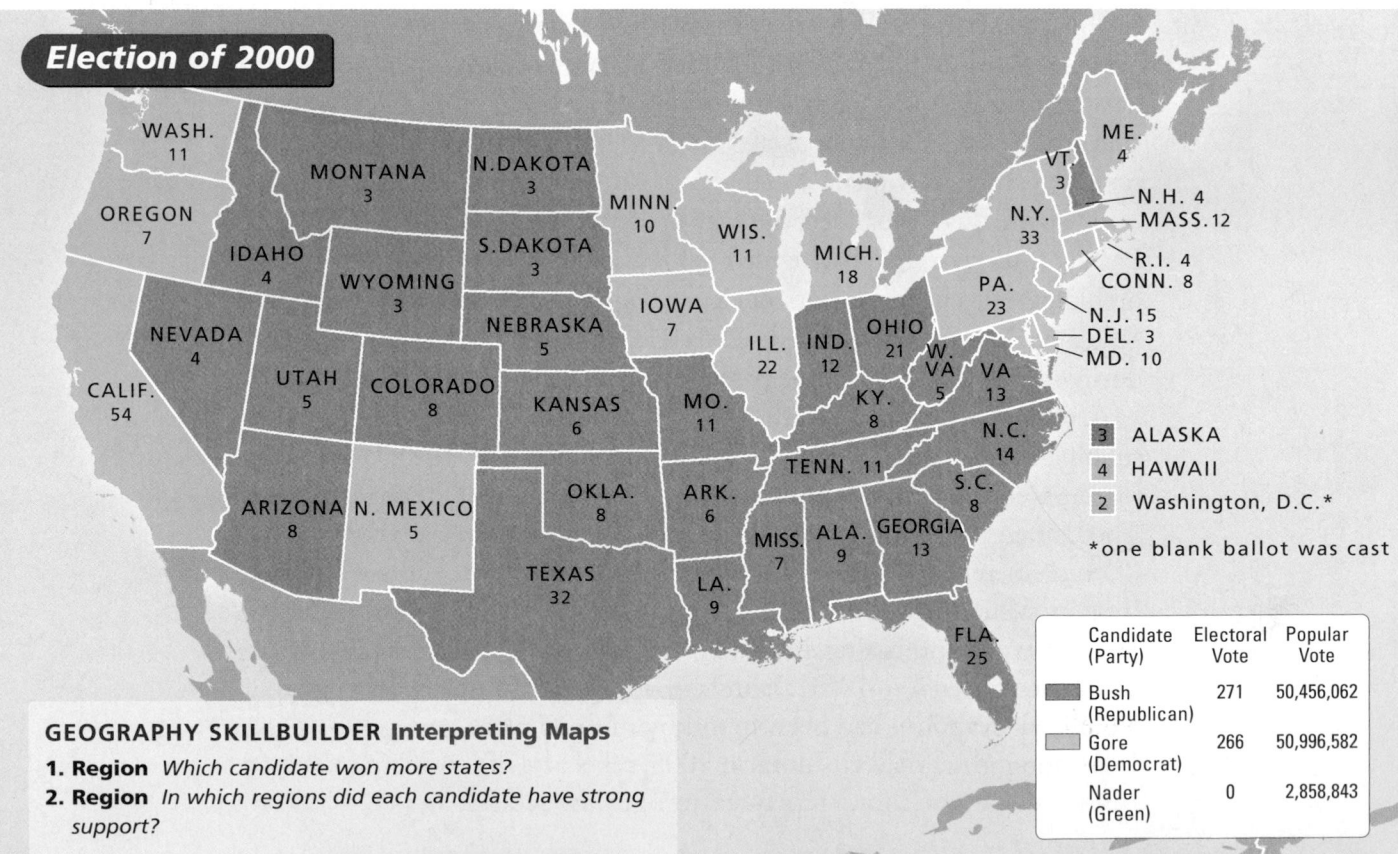

Election of 2000

Candidate (Party)	Electoral Vote	Popular Vote
Bush (Republican)	271	50,456,062
Gore (Democrat)	266	50,996,582
Nader (Green)	0	2,858,843

3 ALASKA
4 HAWAII
2 Washington, D.C.*

*one blank ballot was cast

GEOGRAPHY SKILLBUILDER Interpreting Maps

1. Region *Which candidate won more states?*
2. Region *In which regions did each candidate have strong support?*

Bush Fights Terrorism

The Pentagon after the September 11 attack

On September 11, 2001, Bush and the world faced a new challenge. A series of terrorist attacks against the United States cost thousands of people their lives and dramatically changed the world. As a result, the Bush administration began a war on terrorism. (For a special report, see pages 892–897.)

In October 2001, Bush signed an antiterrorism bill into law. The law, called the USA Patriot Act, allowed the government to detain foreigners suspected of terrorism. Bush also created the Department of Homeland Security to coordinate national efforts to combat terrorism. In addition, the federal government increased its involvement in aviation security.

In October 2001, the United States led forces from different countries in an attack on Afghanistan. The Afghan government was harboring Osama bin Laden and his al-Qaeda terrorist network believed responsible for the September 11 attacks. In 2002, it appeared that the coalition had successfully broken up the al-Qaeda network in Afghanistan, although Osama bin Laden remained at large. Afghanistan adopted a new constitution and elected a president. However, in mid-2005, coalition troops still remained, as al-Qaeda members slipped into the country to create more violence.

In 2003, Bush expanded the war on terrorism to Iraq. Following the Persian Gulf War, Iraq had agreed to UN demands to stop the production of biological, chemical, and nuclear weapons. The leader of Iraq was Saddam Hussein. Hussein refused to cooperate with UN arms inspectors during the 1990s and eventually stopped them from entering his country.

After the September 11 attacks, Bush maintained that Hussein might supply terrorists with weapons of mass destruction (WMDs). Bush called for renewed arms inspections in Iraq, but Hussein refused to cooperate fully. The United States and Great Britain ordered Hussein to leave the country.

Hussein refused to give up control. U.S. and British forces invaded Iraq in March 2003. Within a month, Iraq's military was defeated. Hussein went into hiding, but later was captured. U.S. forces then began an intensive search for WMDs in Iraq. However, no trace of chemical or biological weaponry had been found by mid-2005.

Although Iraq held elections in 2005, rebel acts of terrorism increased steadily. Coalition forces remained to fight the rebels.

The Bush Presidency at Home

During his first months as president, Bush began to work on his domestic policies. He signed into law an education reform plan entitled No Child Left Behind. This plan called for more accountability by states for students' success, mandatory achievement testing, and more school options for parents.

Bush also wanted to improve a slowing economy. But corporate scandals further damaged the economy. In the 1990s, Enron had established itself as one of the most successful companies in the world. In October 2001, the Security Exchange Commission began investigating Enron's financial records. Several months later, the company was charged with using illegal accounting practices and was fined $3 million. Enron's accounting firm, Arthur Andersen, was charged with obstruction of justice.

Political opinion remained deeply divided through Bush's first term. While Bush's antiterrorism policies initially gained wide support, many Americans began to question his handling of the invasion of Iraq.

In 2004, Massachusetts senator John Kerry challenged Bush. After both sides waged one of the most expensive campaigns in history, Bush was able to win a majority of the popular vote, but once again the electoral vote came down to one state. In Ohio, Bush held a lead of more than 130,000 votes, which would give him the state's 20 electoral votes and the presidency. After deciding that the uncounted absentee and paper ballots would not be enough to take the lead, Kerry conceded the race to Bush the day after the election.

In Bush's victory speech, he promised to revise the nation's tax code and reform Social Security in order to improve the economy. In the next section you will read more about the U.S. economy, including the impact of technology on it, at the start of the 21st century.

President George W. Bush campaigning for Republican candidates in 2002

Section 1 Assessment

1. Terms & Names

Explain the significance of:

- Ronald Reagan
- supply-side economics
- Iran-Contra affair
- George H. W. Bush
- Persian Gulf War
- Bill Clinton
- NAFTA
- George W. Bush

2. Using Graphics

Use a chart like the one shown to record important details about the terms of three presidents.

Reagan	
Bush	
Clinton	

What do you think was the greatest achievement by any of these presidents?

3. Main Ideas

a. What were the positive and negative effects of Reagan's economic policies?

b. Why did Clinton win the 1992 presidential election?

c. Why did it take five weeks to decide the winner of the 2000 presidential election?

4. Critical Thinking

Drawing Conclusions
What do you think was the stronger force shaping U.S. politics from 1981 to 2000—economics or foreign affairs?

THINK ABOUT

- Reagan's goals and actions
- the events of George H. W. Bush's presidency
- the events of Clinton's presidency

ACTIVITY OPTIONS

ART

TECHNOLOGY

You have been asked to summarize the politics of the years 1981–2001. Create an **illustrated time line,** or plan part of a **multimedia presentation.**

Technological and Economic Changes

MAIN IDEA	WHY IT MATTERS NOW	TERMS & NAMES
Advances in science and technology have improved daily life and created a global economy.	Technology continues to change American homes, leisure activities, and workplaces.	Internet · information revolution e-commerce · downsizing service economy

ONE AMERICAN'S STORY

In the late 1990s, technology transformed business. One reason was the **Internet**, a worldwide computer network. Some enterprising people developed **e-commerce**, business that is conducted over the Internet.

Jeff Bezos was a pioneer of e-commerce. In 1994, he decided to open a bookstore online. The idea caught on quickly. The number of Internet businesses exploded by the year 2000. Bezos's business also grew. Bezos doesn't define his job as selling books but as giving buyers more choice.

> *A VOICE FROM THE PAST*
>
> Our business is helping customers make purchasing decisions. . . . It all has to do with the balance of power shifting away from companies and toward consumers.
>
> **Jeff Bezos,** quoted in "Companies Wired for the Bottom Line," *Newsweek,* September 20, 1999

Jeff Bezos revolutionized the bookselling industry by putting it online.

Section 2 explains more about the ways technology has affected American life and the U.S. economy.

Taking Notes

Use your chart to take notes about technological and economic changes.

Influences on America, 1981–Today		
Politics	Technological and Economic Change	Immigration
Effects	Effects	Effects

Technology and Daily Life

As the 20th century drew to a close, thousands of institutions, from hospitals to airports to banks, relied on computers to perform essential tasks. Computer use also grew in homes and schools. By 2003, nearly 62 percent of all U.S. households had a personal computer. And from 1998 to 2004, the number of computers in classrooms leaped from 8 million to more than 14 million.

Computers and the Internet revolutionized communication and research. Using the Internet, a person can track down information on nearly any subject. Internet users can also send and receive electronic

messages called e-mail. In addition, they can shop at online stores.

Other forms of new technology have also transformed American life. One popular example is the battery-powered cellular telephone. People can carry these phones with them anywhere. Between 1995 and 2003, the number of cellular phone subscribers in the United States grew dramatically from 34 million to more than 159 million.

A Changing Economy

For much of the 20th century, manufacturing made up a major share of the U.S. economy. By the year 2000, that had changed drastically. The computer age fueled the growth of the service economy. In a **service economy,** most jobs provide services instead of producing goods. By 2003, about 84 percent of all workers had jobs in the service industry. Many of these jobs—such as lawyers, teachers, engineers, and Web-site designers—focused on providing knowledge and information.

Some experts said the United States was going through an **information revolution.** This meant that technology had radically changed the way information was delivered—and gave people access to far more information than ever before. This improved the productivity of many industries.

*Reading*History
A. Drawing Conclusions Why is the Internet an important part of the information revolution?

Computers changed not just industries but also the lives of most individual workers. For example, engineers began to use computers to test new car designs. In large companies, workers from many departments were able to share information through computer networks. Filmmakers used computers to create animated characters that would react on-screen with live actors.

Economic Change Affects Workers

The dramatic changes in the economy were both good news and bad news for U.S. workers. During the 1990s, high-tech industries created many new, high-paying jobs for skilled workers.

Yet other workers faced hard times. The decline of manufacturing meant the loss of factory jobs. The newly unemployed workers faced an uncertain future. They had earned good wages in the factory, although many of them were not highly skilled or educated. Most new jobs required specialized skills. As a result, job seekers had to obtain education and training, or they had to settle for lower-paying jobs.

Highly skilled workers also lost jobs. Many corporations engaged in **downsizing**—reducing the number of workers to increase company profits. During the mid-1990s, companies let go of hundreds of thousands of workers. In addition, many mergers—in which two companies

Background
Downsizing most often occurs during hard times but also can take place when the economy is strong.

STRANGE *but* True

INTERNET 911

In April 1997, 12-year-old Sean Redden was using the Internet at his home in Texas when he saw a startling message: "Hello, help me."

The message was from 20-year-old Tarja Laitinen of Finland. While using the Internet, she'd had a severe attack of asthma.

Sean's mother called 911. This led to a series of phone calls that ended up with Tarja's being rushed to a Finnish hospital. Sean, with the help of the Internet, had saved Tarja's life!

The Computer Revolution

Would you be impressed if a scientist came to you and said, "I can take a machine, reduce it to one-thousandth of its present size, and yet increase its power"? That is exactly what happened with computers during the last half of the 20th century. Today, personal computers can perform more operations more quickly than the first giant computers did. In addition, the first computers were very expensive and difficult to maintain. The development of inexpensive personal computers made it possible for small businesses and ordinary families to use the latest technology.

1940s

ENIAC One of the first general-purpose electronic computers, the ENIAC used 18,000 vacuum tubes (which looked a bit like light bulbs). ENIAC took up 1,500 square feet, about one-third of a basketball court. It was used for mathematical calculations and could do 5,000 additions a second.

1970s

Commodore PET Computer chips made the personal computer possible. The Commodore PET was the first personal computer designed to be sold to the public. It cost only $595—but had just 12K of memory.

Computer Chip Vacuum tubes were replaced first by transistors and later by tiny computer chips. By the 1970s, all of a computer's operations were contained on a small number of chips, wired to a control board.

1990s

Virtual Reality The personal computers of the 1990s grew increasingly powerful and were able to perform sophisticated jobs. Here, an interior designer uses a virtual-environment program to recreate a room. Computers were also used in engineering and film animation.

FUTURE

CONNECT TO HISTORY

1. **Recognizing Effects** Do you think the development of the personal computer had a positive or negative effect on the economy? Explain.

    See Skillbuilder Handbook, page R11.

CONNECT TO TODAY

2. **Identifying Problems** What problem might the computer industry try to solve next?

For more information about computers . . .

 RESEARCH LINKS
CLASSZONE.COM

join—took place. When two companies merge, it creates a situation in which people hold duplicate jobs, so mergers usually lead to layoffs.

Most laid-off workers found other jobs. But in an effort to cut costs, many companies hired people for part-time or temporary jobs. Such jobs generally offer lower pay and fewer benefits than full-time jobs.

In the late 1990s, however, many more jobs were created when the economy boomed. By late summer of 2000, the unemployment rate dipped below 4 percent—its lowest level in 30 years. In addition, the economy grew by a robust 5 percent in 2000. The growth of Internet companies contributed greatly to these numbers.

By the end of 2000, however, many Internet companies went out of business. Technology stocks collapsed. In March 2001, the nation fell into a recession. Unemployment climbed to 5.7 percent in November 2001. But the economy still managed to grow early in the year. By May 2005, unemployment had dropped to 5.4 percent.

A More Global Economy

Technology helped to build a more global economy—in which countries around the world are linked through business. Through the Internet, companies on different continents could do business as if they were in the same city. Trade and investment among nations expanded.

Corporations also built factories and offices in other countries. By 1995, for example, more than 3 million Japanese cars were made at U.S. plants. And businesses in different countries merged to form multinational corporations such as the worldwide auto giant, DaimlerChrysler AG.

President Clinton saw the growth of world trade as a chance for America to sell more goods and create more jobs. This was why he urged Congress to pass NAFTA.

The global economy caused problems for some U.S. workers. To cut costs, some businesses moved their operations from the United States to countries where wages were lower. In the mid-1990s, for example, a large U.S. clothing maker moved many of its sewing operations to Mexico, the Caribbean, and Central America. Thousands of U.S. workers lost their jobs. By 2015, an estimated 3.4 million U.S. jobs will have moved to other countries

Because of global trade, the economies of various countries had become more closely linked. Nations were more likely to suffer from each other's financial woes. For example, in October 1997, Hong Kong's stock market fell, which caused stock markets from Europe to North America to drop. In the summer of 1998, Russia temporarily experienced a financial crisis, which also caused markets to fall.

Reading **History**

B. Analyzing Causes Why did Americans fear that the U.S. economy was headed for a recession in 2001?

Background NAFTA is the North American Free Trade Agreement. (See Section 1.)

Now and **then**

PREPARING FOR TOMORROW'S JOBS

In the past, many workers spent their entire careers at one company. By the 1990s, workers were changing jobs often to gain more pay or more challenging assignments.

Workers today also have more chances to work overseas. For example, 27-year-old Anne Larlarb has already worked in England and Thailand. In the photo above, she uses e-mail to keep in touch with friends.

If these trends continue, future workers will need to be flexible, quick learners and be open to other cultures.

Scientific Breakthroughs

This firefighter has received an artificial arm with the ability to sense heat.

In the last decades of the 20th century, the world of medicine saw many breakthroughs. Engineers developed smaller, more precise surgical instruments. These and new technologies such as lasers allowed doctors to perform surgery through tiny incisions in the body, which heal more quickly than large cuts. New tests helped doctors to make better diagnoses.

Scientists developed new drugs that offer greater hope for a cure for cancer. New drugs and treatments also slowed the rate at which AIDS (acquired immune deficiency syndrome) kills infected people.

In 1997, Scottish scientists cloned the first mammal—a sheep. This set off a furious debate. Many feared that cloning human beings could be next. Some insisted that cloning would help to improve the human species. Others argued that the process is unethical.

Vocabulary
clone: to make a genetic duplicate of a living being

A VOICE FROM THE PAST

Creating life in the laboratory is totally inappropriate and so far removed from the process of marriage and parenting that . . . we must rebel against the very concept of human cloning. It is simply wrong to experiment with the creation of human life in this way.

U.S. Representative Vernon Ehlers, statement to U.S. Congress

Reading **History**
C. Identifying Facts and Opinions Is Representative Ehlers expressing a fact or an opinion? Explain.

In nonmedical science, the United States and other nations began to build an international space station. The station was scheduled to be finished in the early 2000s. Nations will use it to research the stars, planets, and galaxies. While technology and science shape the years to come, so too will people. Section 3 discusses the nation's diverse population and how these many groups are shaping American society.

Section 2 Assessment

1. Terms & Names

Explain the significance of:
- Internet
- e-commerce
- service economy
- information revolution
- downsizing

2. Using Graphics

Use a cluster diagram like the one shown to list changes in technology, the economy, and science.

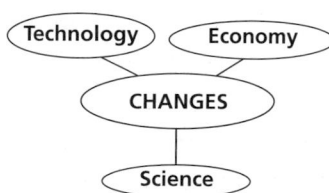

3. Main Ideas

a. How did the information revolution change jobs?

b. Why did the rise of the global economy cause some workers to worry?

c. What advances did scientists make in the field of medicine?

4. Critical Thinking

Forming and Supporting Opinions What job skills do you think you will need for the future? Why?

THINK ABOUT
- the changes in technology and science
- the changes in the economy

ACTIVITY OPTIONS

TECHNOLOGY

DRAMA

What technological marvel would you like to see invented? Design a **Web page** advertising the new technology, or perform a **skit** showing someone using it.

The New Americans

MAIN IDEA	WHY IT MATTERS NOW	TERMS & NAMES
Due to immigration, the United States grew more diverse.	Americans of all backgrounds share common goals: the desire for equal rights and economic opportunity.	Immigration Reform and Control Act of 1986

ONE AMERICAN'S STORY

Born in the Dominican Republic, Junot Díaz came to the United States with his family when he was seven. He started writing when he was just 13. In 1996, at the age of 28, he published his first book of stories. Díaz writes about being Dominican but believes his stories are universal; that is, they have meaning for everyone.

Díaz and millions of other recent immigrants have made important contributions to the nation's growth. This section discusses how these new Americans are making the United States a more diverse nation.

Junot Díaz

Immigrants Affect American Society

From 1981 to 2002, more than 18.5 million legal immigrants came to the United States. These immigrants increased U.S. diversity. Most of the immigrants who came to America during earlier periods had come from Europe. Nearly 85 percent of the arrivals since 1981 came from either Latin America or Asia. The Census Bureau predicts that the Hispanic population in the United States will continue to increase, from 14.1 percent in 2005 to 15.4 percent by 2010. The Asian population is expected to increase, from 4.2 percent in 2005 to about 4.6 percent in 2010.

Changes to immigration laws passed in 1965 have contributed to the recent surge in immigration. These changes allowed people from a greater variety of countries to enter the United States. The lure of America also plays a role. As earlier immigrants did, many of the newcomers came to the United States seeking economic opportunity and, in some cases, political freedom.

U.S. citizens have mixed feelings about immigration. Some argue that immigrants take jobs from citizens. Many Americans also worry about the number of immigrants who enter the United States illegally. Officials

Taking Notes

Use your chart to take notes about immigration.

Influences on America, 1981–Today		
Politics	Technological and Economic Change	Immigration
Effects	Effects	Effects

The American People

Ancestry of Americans, 2000	(descendants, in thousands)
1. German	42,800
2. Irish	30,500
3. African	24,900
4. English	24,500
5. Mexican	18,300
6. Italian	15,600
7. Polish	8,900
8. French	8,300
9. Native American	7,800
10. Scottish	4,800

Origins of Immigrants, 1981–2002	(immigrants, in thousands)
1. Mexico	4,300
2. Philippines	1,100
3. China*	930
4. Vietnam	890
5. India	790
6. Dominican Republic	640
7. Korea	550
8. El Salvador	490
9. Jamaica	420
10. Cuba	400

* China includes Taiwan.

SKILLBUILDER Interpreting Charts

1. Compare the origins of recent immigrants to the ancestry of Americans overall. Are any the same?
2. How might the list of top ten ancestry groups change in the future?

Source: *U.S. Bureau of the Census; U.S. Dept. of Homeland Security*

estimate that in 2002, between 8 and 12 million illegal immigrants lived in the United States. Roughly 5.3 million were thought to be from Mexico.

Because illegal immigrants are here secretly, they do not pay income taxes. However, they do pay sales taxes and often work for low wages in poor conditions because they fear being sent away. Even so, they receive some government services, such as education for their children. As a result, some people feel that they are a drain on the U.S. economy. Congress passed the **Immigration Reform and Control Act of 1986** to strengthen immigration laws and enforcement measures. But illegal immigrants continued to come to the United States.

Background
An illegal immigrant is someone who enters the United States secretly and without filling out the appropriate government forms.

Immigrant Contributions

Recent immigrants have brought, and continue to bring, many talents to the United States. The National Science Foundation estimates that 23 percent of all U.S. residents with doctorate degrees in engineering and science are foreign-born. High-tech industries, such as those located in Silicon Valley, California, have benefited from their skills.

In addition, immigrants are an important source of labor. Some studies indicate that without immigrants, the workforce might actually begin to shrink by 2015. In other words, U.S. businesses wouldn't be able to hire enough people to maintain their productivity.

Immigrants also make sports much more exciting. In 1998 and 1999, Dominican-born Sammy Sosa thrilled baseball fans by battling Mark McGwire for the home run record. Immigrants have also starred in other sports such as basketball, football, soccer, and golf.

Many immigrants enrich American arts and culture. Latin music, for example, has become very popular. Chinese-born author Bette Bao

Reading **History**
A. Drawing Conclusions
What have immigrants contributed to the economy?

Lord has written popular books for children and adults. In addition, immigrants, and their sons and daughters, are acting in a greater number of movies. "When immigrants come to America they bring their culture, and that culture becomes part of a new country," noted Cuban-born singer Gloria Estefan. "It makes everyone stronger."

What Americans Have in Common

While immigrants bring their culture to America, many of them also have embraced American ways. They wear American clothes, adopt American customs, and learn English.

They also share the American belief in democracy and freedom. Ken Burns, a documentary filmmaker, explained that these beliefs make America unique in the world.

*Reading*History

B. Making Inferences
Judging from this quotation, how do you think Ken Burns views the future of the United States?

A VOICE FROM THE PAST

There is no other country on Earth that is configured like ours. Every other nation is there because of race, religion, language, ethnicity, or geography. We are here only because we agreed to subscribe to the words on four pieces of paper—the U.S. Constitution. Unlike every other country which sees itself as an end unto itself, we see ourselves as evolving. We're not satisfied. We're not willing to rest on our laurels. We think we can do better. We think we have got someplace to go.

Ken Burns, quoted in *The West*

Today the United States is a very different nation from the one founded in 1776. Democratic rights have expanded to include more and more people. As the United States moves into the future, it will no doubt continue to change. Tolerance and cooperation will be essential.

Citizens of all backgrounds will play a vital role in shaping what America will be. So will today's students. You have a part to play in helping the United States embrace people from every culture and land. You are the generation that will create the America of the future.

Section **3** Assessment

1. Terms & Names

Explain the significance of:
• Immigration Reform and Control Act of 1986

2. Using Graphics

Use a diagram like the one shown to record the effects of recent immigration on the United States.

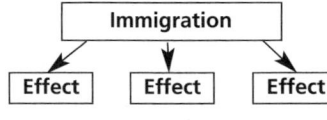

How has immigration affected your life?

3. Main Ideas

a. How did the changes to immigration laws in 1965 help create a more diverse population?

b. In which areas of American society have immigrants made contributions?

c. What ideals do both immigrant and native-born Americans believe in?

4. Critical Thinking

Comparing and Contrasting How was the immigration that occurred in the years 1981–2000 similar to and different from earlier waves of immigration?

THINK ABOUT
• the immigration you read about in Chapter 14
• the immigration you read about in Chapter 21

ACTIVITY OPTIONS

MATH

SPEECH

Survey ten people outside your class to learn their ethnic background. Present your findings as a **table** like the one on page 886 or in a **speech**.

VISUAL SUMMARY

Entering a New Millennium

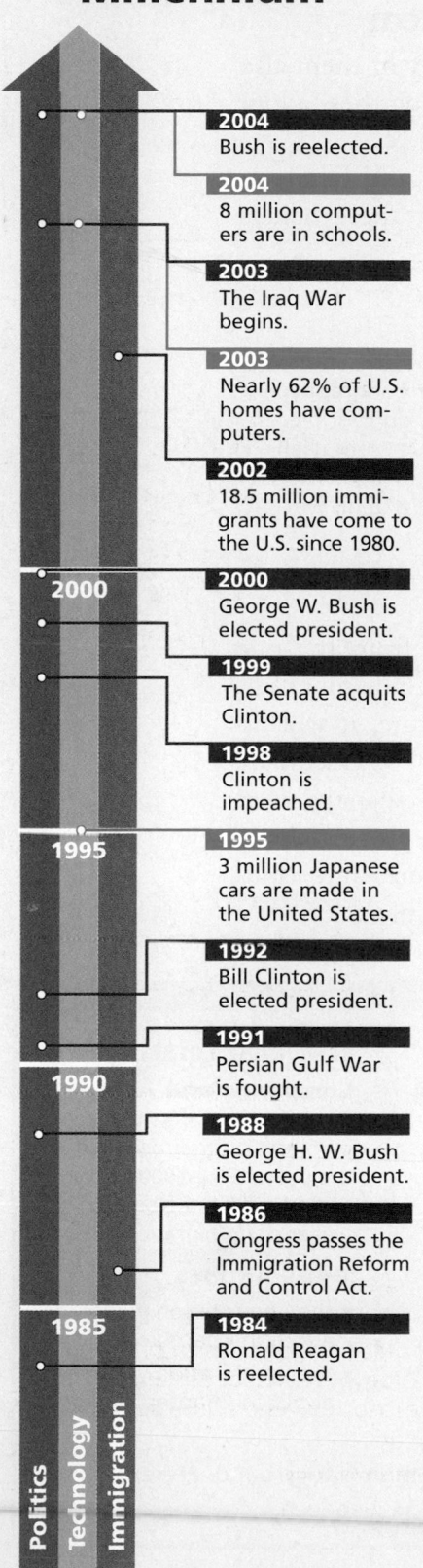

2004
Bush is reelected.

2004
8 million computers are in schools.

2003
The Iraq War begins.

2003
Nearly 62% of U.S. homes have computers.

2002
18.5 million immigrants have come to the U.S. since 1980.

2000
George W. Bush is elected president.

1999
The Senate acquits Clinton.

1998
Clinton is impeached.

1995
3 million Japanese cars are made in the United States.

1992
Bill Clinton is elected president.

1991
Persian Gulf War is fought.

1988
George H. W. Bush is elected president.

1986
Congress passes the Immigration Reform and Control Act.

1984
Ronald Reagan is reelected.

Politics Technology Immigration

TERMS & NAMES

Briefly explain the significance of each of the following.

1. Ronald Reagan
2. supply-side economics
3. Iran-Contra affair
4. George H. W. Bush
5. Persian Gulf War
6. Bill Clinton
7. Internet
8. service economy
9. information revolution
10. Immigration Reform and Control Act of 1986

REVIEW QUESTIONS

Conservatives Reshape Politics (pages 873–879)

1. How did Reagan try to improve the economy?
2. What happened in the Iran-Contra affair?
3. What role did the United States play during the Persian Gulf War?
4. What happened during the 2000 presidential election?

Technological and Economic Changes (pages 880–884)

5. What did the Internet allow its users to do?
6. How did corporate mergers affect individuals?
7. What were the different reactions to cloning?

The New Americans (pages 885–887)

8. Why did the recent wave of immigrants come to the United States?
9. What do immigrants contribute to the economy?
10. Why do experts think the United States will become more diverse?

CRITICAL THINKING

1. USING YOUR NOTES: RECOGNIZING EFFECTS

Using your completed chart, answer the questions below.

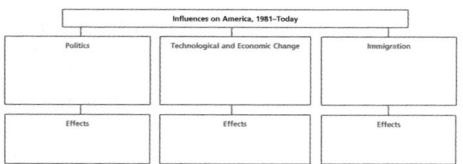

a. What were the effects of recent political events?
b. What were the main technological and economic changes?

2. ANALYZING LEADERSHIP

Judging from what you read in this chapter, what issues will a U.S. president face in the 21st century?

3. APPLYING CITIZENSHIP SKILLS

In what ways have recent immigrants demonstrated good citizenship here in the United States?

4. THEME: DIVERSITY AND UNITY

What ideas and goals help to unify Americans of different racial and ethnic backgrounds?

5. MAKING INFERENCES

Are U.S. citizens likely to be more or less welcoming to immigrants in good economic times? Explain.

Interact *with* History

Now that you have read about recent changes in the United States, what new ideas do you have about how you can contribute to the future?

Use the map and your knowledge of U.S. history to answer questions 1 and 2.

Additional Test Practice, pp. S1–S33.

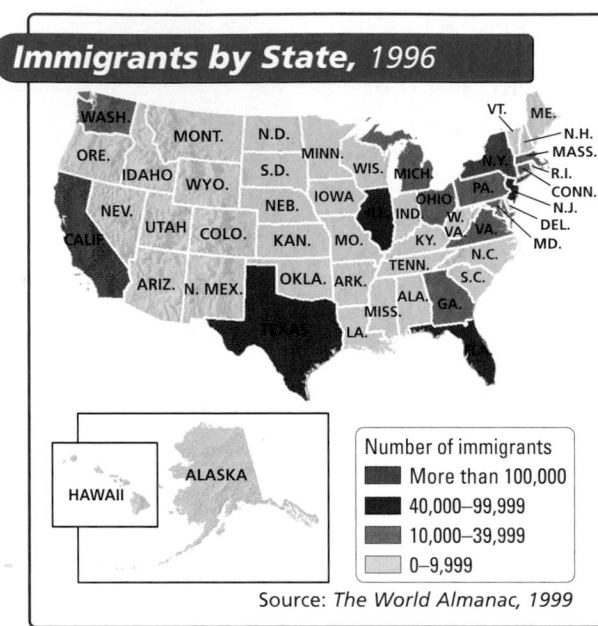

Immigrants by State, *1996*

Number of immigrants
More than 100,000
40,000–99,999
10,000–39,999
0–9,999

Source: *The World Almanac, 1999*

1. Which states have the highest numbers of immigrants?

A. Florida and Texas

B. Alaska and Texas

C. California and New York

D. California, New York, and Washington

2. How many states have between 10,000 and 39,999 immigrants?

A. 2

B. 4

C. 9

D. 35

This quotation from a restaurant owner describes what he heard in his restaurant. Use the quotation and your knowledge of U.S. history to answer question 3.

PRIMARY SOURCE

People have been talking. . . . Some of them in this neighborhood have been laid off four, six months . . . People don't like to see their neighbors out of work. And they've been scared. . . . The ones who'd been talking that they were for Carter, well, they changed.

Mike Savic, quoted in the *Chicago Tribune,* November 6, 1980

3. According to the passage, which of the following factors would affect the 1980 presidential election?

A. loyalty

B. good faith

C. unemployment

D. foreign affairs

TEST PRACTICE
CLASSZONE.COM

ALTERNATIVE ASSESSMENT

1. 📝 WRITING ABOUT HISTORY

In the late 1990s, the media focused on events such as the Clinton impeachment trial and the war in Kosovo. Write a radio news **report** about one of these issues.

- Use library resources to research your topic.

- Your report should be accurate and informative. It may also include quotes and stories from people at the scene of the event.

2. COOPERATIVE LEARNING

With four other students, create a newspaper front page that reports on the major events of the late 20th century. Three members of the group can write articles, with headlines, and the fourth can find the images for each article. Topics might include computers, immigration, or the presidential election.

INTEGRATED TECHNOLOGY

CREATING A WEB SITE

Think about what the United States will be like in ten years. Design a Web site that represents your vision. Research the Internet and the library to find out how to create a Web page with text, images, and links.

- Decide what kinds of images and descriptions you want to include on your Web page. Then draw a design of what the page will look like.

- Your Web page should include links to other sites that discuss technology, politics, or social issues. Provide written descriptions and addresses of the Web sites that are linked to yours.

For more about the designing a Web page . . .

INTERNET ACTIVITY
CLASSZONE.COM

Make a Time Capsule

A time capsule is a sealed container that preserves records and artifacts from the present for people in the future. Ancient Babylonians and Egyptians began this custom by carving messages inside their temples. These records give people today an idea of what life was like thousands of years ago. One of the first modern time capsules is in Oglethorpe, Georgia. Sealed in 1940, it is not due to be opened until 8113. It contains such things as a Donald Duck doll and 640,000 pages on microfilm.

ACTIVITY With a group, construct a time capsule. Write an explanation of the contents and your predictions or dreams for the future. Then record this explanation on a cassette tape.

A family from the 1960s poses in front of their house.

TOOLBOX

Each group will need:

posterboard	stapler
aluminum foil	markers
cellophane	3 x 5 notecards
scissors	blank cassette tape
duct or masking tape	cassette recorder

STEP BY STEP

1 **Form groups.** Meet with three to four students to create a time capsule. To complete this project, groups will be expected to

- do research on a particular decade
- identify artifacts from that decade to place in a time capsule
- construct a time capsule
- write an explanation of the contents, and record it on an audio cassette

2 **Choose the 1950s, 1960s, 1970s, 1980s, or 1990s.** Use the Internet, encyclopedias, or books about that decade to brainstorm ideas for the contents of your time capsule. Each person should jot down items on a piece of paper. A sample is shown below. With your group, discuss these items and decide which ones you'd like to use. Be sure to include enough items so that people opening the capsule many years from now will have a complete picture of your decade.

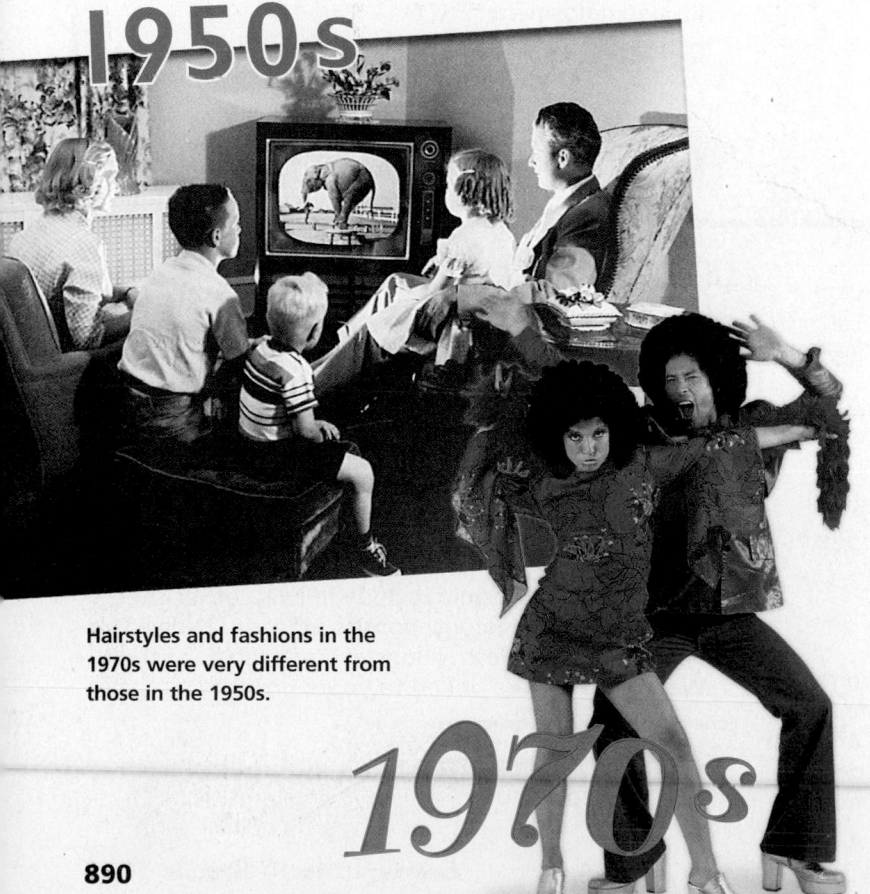

Hairstyles and fashions in the 1970s were very different from those in the 1950s.

1960s items
photo of Vietnam war
Beatles record
peace sign

3 **Build the time capsule.** First, cut a small square out of the middle of the posterboard to make a window. Using tape or a stapler, place the cellophane over the hole. Then roll the posterboard so that it forms a large cylinder. Tape or staple the ends of the posterboard together. Place aluminum foil over one end of your time capsule—using tape to secure it.

4 **Decorate the time capsule.** Use markers to decorate the outside of the time capsule. These decorations should reflect your decade. Also, include a message that is connected with your decade. Be sure to explain when the capsule should be opened.

5 **Select your items.** Use the actual item, or a picture. On each 3 x 5 card, write an explanation of the items you've selected and explain their purpose. Attach a card to each picture or item. Be sure to include the year the item was first used.

6 **Present the contents to the class.** Using your notecards, explain to the class why you chose these items. Place the notecards inside the time capsule. Wait until you make your audio cassette to seal the time capsule—and be sure to include it.

WRITE AND SPEAK

Write a paragraph describing your time capsule. Include your predictions and dreams for future generations. Then record your message on an audio cassette and place it inside the time capsule. After sealing the time capsule, put it on display with the other time capsules.

HELP DESK

For related information, see Chapters 29, 30, 31, and 32.

Researching Your Project

"Time Immemorial," *Popular Mechanics*, February 1999.

For more about time capsules . . .

RESEARCH LINKS
CLASSZONE.COM

Did You Know?

Westinghouse Electric Company coined the term *time capsule*. The company built one for the New York World's Fair of 1939–1940. The capsule is due to be opened in 6939. To preserve the capsule's contents, the company formed a new metal alloy called Cupaloy. It combined the durability of steel with the ability of copper to prevent corrosion.

The designers figured people living in the 70th century may not know the time capsule exists. So they created *The Book of Record*. It gives the time capsule's location and was placed in libraries all over the world.

REFLECT & ASSESS

- Why did you choose the particular artifacts in your time capsule?

- How do you think future generations might react to the articles in your time capsule?

- How well do your items represent the history, social issues, and culture of your decade?

The Attack: September 11, 2001

Terrorism is the use of violence against people or property to force changes in societies or governments. Acts of terrorism are not new. Throughout history, individuals and groups have used terror tactics to achieve political or social goals.

In recent decades, though, terrorist groups have carried out increasingly destructive and high-profile attacks. The growing threat of terrorism has caused many people to feel vulnerable and afraid. It also has prompted action from the governments of many nations, including the United States.

Many of the terrorist activities of the late 20th century occurred far from U.S. soil. As a result, most Americans felt safe from such violence. All that changed, however, on the morning of September 11, 2001.

A Surprise Strike

As the nation began another workday, 19 terrorists hijacked four airplanes heading from East Coast airports to California. The hijackers crashed two of the jets into the twin towers of the World Trade Center in New York City. They slammed a third plane into the Pentagon outside Washington, D.C. The fourth plane crashed into an empty field in Pennsylvania after passengers apparently fought the hijackers.

The attacks destroyed the World Trade Center and badly damaged a section of the Pentagon. In all, some 3,000 people died. Life for Americans would never be the same after that day. Before, most U.S. citizens viewed terrorism as something that happened in other countries. Now they knew it could happen on their soil as well.

Officials soon learned that those responsible for the attacks were part of a largely Islamic terrorist network known as al-Qaeda. Observers, including many Muslims, accuse al-Qaeda of preaching a false and extreme form of Islam. Its members believe, among other things, that the United States and other Western nations are evil.

U.S. president George W. Bush vowed to hunt down all those responsible for the attacks. In addition, he called for a greater international effort to combat global terrorism.

Securing the Nation

As the Bush Administration began its campaign against terrorism, it also sought to prevent any further attacks on America. In October 2001, the president signed into

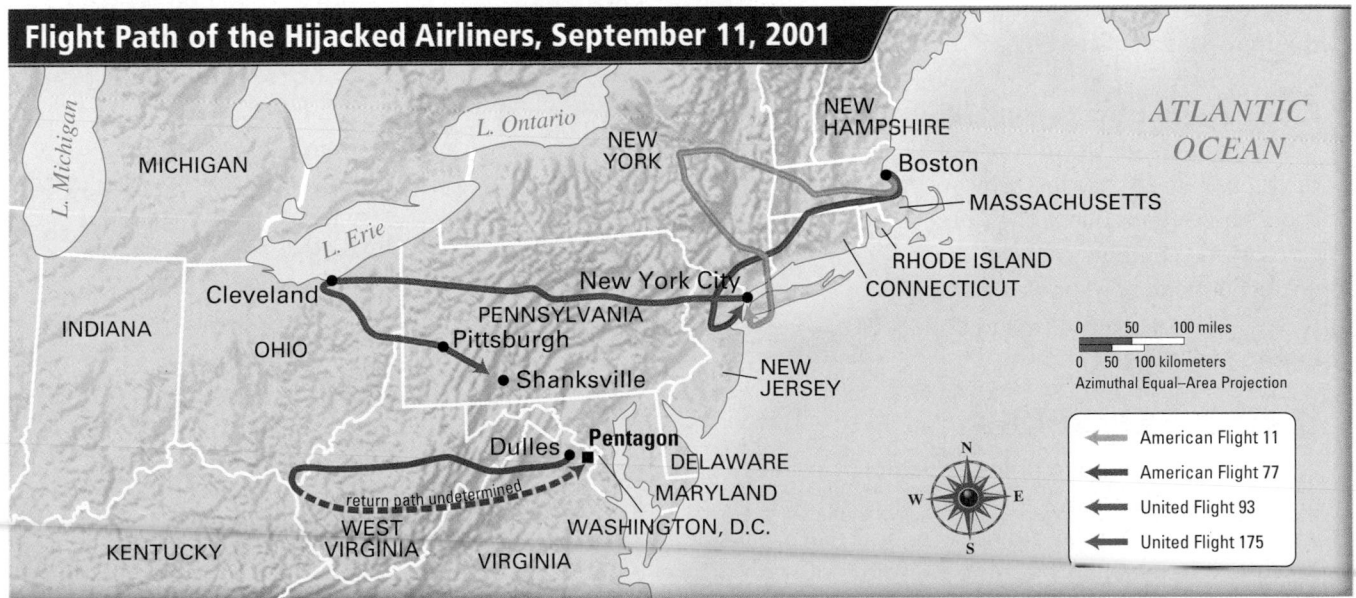

Flight Path of the Hijacked Airliners, September 11, 2001

⟵	American Flight 11
⟵	American Flight 77
⟵	United Flight 93
⟵	United Flight 175

0   50   100 miles
0   50   100 kilometers
Azimuthal Equal–Area Projection

law the USA Patriot Act. The new law enabled officials to detain foreigners suspected of terrorism for up to seven days without charging them with a crime. Officials could also monitor all phone and Internet use by suspects, and prosecute terrorist crimes without any time restrictions or limitations.

In addition, the government created the Department of Homeland Security. Its job is to coordinate national efforts against terrorism.

Some critics charged that a number of the government's new anti-terrorism measures violated people's civil rights. Supporters countered that occasionally limiting some civil liberties was justified to protect national security. In addition, U.S. treatment of terrorist suspects held at Guantanamo Bay, Cuba, resulted in widespread disapproval.

Underneath a U.S. flag posted amid the rubble of the World Trade Center, rescue workers search for survivors of the attack.

The federal government also stepped in to ensure greater security at the nation's airports. In November 2001, President Bush signed the Aviation and Transportation Security Act into law. The new law put the federal government in charge of airport security. Before, individual airports had been responsible for security. The new law created a federal security force to inspect passengers and carry-on bags. It also required the screening of checked baggage.

Meanwhile, the 9/11 Commission—a group appointed by President Bush in 2002—recommended ways to further strengthen national security. One suggestion resulted in the creation of a new Cabinet post—that of national intelligence director. In April 2005, John Negroponte became the first to hold the position.

While the September 11 attacks shook the United States, they also strengthened the nation's resolve. In 2003, officials approved plans to rebuild on the World Trade Center site. At 1,776 feet high, the Freedom Tower will be the center of the new complex. The plans also include a memorial.

Stunned bystanders look on as smoke billows from the twin towers of the World Trade Center moments after an airplane slammed into each one.

Fighting Back

The attack against the United States on September 11, 2001, represented the single most deadly act of terrorism in modern history. By that time, however, few regions of the world had been spared from terrorist attacks. Today, America and other nations are responding to terrorism in a variety of ways.

The Rise of Terrorism

The problem of modern international terrorism first gained world attention during the 1972 Summer Olympic Games in Munich, Germany. Members of a Palestinian terrorist group killed two Israeli athletes and took nine others hostage. Five of the terrorists, all the hostages, and a police officer were later killed in a bloody gun battle.

Since then, terrorist activities have occurred across the globe. In Europe, the Irish Republican Army (IRA) used terrorist tactics for decades against Britain. The IRA has long opposed British control of Northern Ireland. Since 1998, the two sides have been working toward a peaceful solution to their conflict. In South America, a group known as the Shining Path terrorized the residents of Peru throughout the late 20th century. The group sought to overthrow the government and establish a Communist state.

In Africa, officials have linked several major attacks against U.S. facilities to al-Qaeda. In 1998, for example, U.S. embassies in Kenya and Tanzania were bombed.

Most terrorists target high profile events or crowded places, such as subway stations, bus stops, restaurants, or shopping malls. Terrorists choose these spots carefully in order to gain the most attention and to achieve the highest level of intimidation.

Terrorists use bullets and bombs as their main weapons. In recent years, however, some terrorist groups have used biological and chemical agents in their attacks. These actions involve the release of bacteria or poisonous gas into the air. For example, in 1995, members of a Japanese religious cult, Aum Shinrikyo, released sarin, a deadly nerve gas, in subway stations in Tokyo. Twelve people were killed and more than 5,700 injured. The possibility of this type of terrorism is particularly worrisome, because biochemical agents are relatively easy to acquire.

Terrorism: A Global Problem

PLACE	YEAR	EVENT
Munich, Germany	1972	Palestinians take Israeli hostages at Summer Olympics; hostages and terrorists die in gun battle with police
Beirut, Lebanon	1983	Terrorists detonate truck bomb at U.S. marine barracks, killing 241
Tokyo, Japan	1995	Religious extremists release lethal gas into subway stations, killing 12
Omagh, Northern Ireland	1998	Faction of Irish Republican Army sets off car bomb, killing 29
New York City; Washington, D.C., USA	2001	Al-Qaeda flies airplanes into New York's Twin Towers and the Pentagon, killing about 3,000
Madrid, Spain	2004	Terrorists detonate bombs on 4 trains during morning rush hour, killing 202
Baghdad, Iraq	2005	Rumors of a terrorist attack cause a stampede that kills nearly 1,000
London, England	2005	Four bombs explode on London subway trains, killing 56

Hunting Down Terrorists

Most governments have adopted an aggressive approach to combating terrorism. This approach includes spying on terrorist groups to gather information and arresting individuals suspected of planning terrorist activities.

Another approach is to make it more difficult for terrorists to act. This involves eliminating terrorist sources of funding. President Bush issued an executive order freezing the U.S. assets of alleged terrorist organizations. He asked other nations to freeze such assets as well. Many cooperated. In spring of 2003, the White House reported that the United States and other countries had blocked or seized nearly $200 million in alleged terrorist assets.

Battling al-Qaeda

The United States quickly took military action against those it held responsible for the September 11 attacks. Americans widely supported these efforts.

U.S. officials had determined that members of the al-Qaeda terrorist group had carried out the assault under the direction of the group's leader, Osama bin Laden. Bin Laden was a Saudi Arabian millionaire who lived in Afghanistan. He directed al-Qaeda's activities under the protection of the country's extreme Islamic government, known as the Taliban.

The United States demanded that the Taliban turn over bin Laden. The Taliban refused. In October 2001, U.S. forces began bombing Taliban air defenses, airfields, and command centers. They also struck numerous al-Qaeda training camps. On the ground, the United States provided assistance to rebel groups opposed to the Taliban. By December, the United States had driven the Taliban from power and severely weakened the al-Qaeda network.

In 2003, Afghanistan adopted a constitution and, the following year, elected Hamid Karzai as president. As of 2005, though, bin Laden was still at large. Rebel groups—including some al-Qaeda members—continued to use violence and threats against the coalition soldiers and government.

Osama bin Laden delivers a videotaped message from a hidden location shortly after the U.S.-led strikes against Afghanistan began.

In the Afghanistan elections, the ballot included photographs of the candidates and symbols for each party to help voters who could not read.

The War in Iraq

In the ongoing battle against terrorism, the United States confronted the leader of Iraq, Saddam Hussein. The longtime dictator had concerned the world community for years. During the 1980s, Hussein had used chemical weapons to put down a rebellion in his own country. In 1990, he had invaded neighboring Kuwait—only to be pushed back by a U.S.-led military effort. In light of such history, many viewed Hussein as an increasing threat to peace and stability in the world. As a result, the Bush Administration led an effort in early 2003 to remove Hussein from power.

The Path to War

One of the main concerns about Saddam Hussein was his possible development of so-called weapons of mass destruction. These are weapons that can kill large numbers of people. They include chemical and biological agents as well as nuclear devices.

Bowing to world pressure, Hussein allowed inspectors from the United Nations to search Iraq for such outlawed weapons. Some investigators, however, insisted that the Iraqis were not fully cooperating with the inspections. U.S. and British officials soon threatened to use force to disarm Iraq.

Operation Iraqi Freedom

The UN Security Council debated what action to take. Some countries, such as France and Germany, called for letting the inspectors continue searching for weapons. British prime minister Tony Blair, however, accused the Iraqis of "deception and evasion" and insisted inspections would never work.

On March 17, President Bush gave Saddam Hussein and his top aides 48 hours to leave the country or face a military strike. The Iraqi leader refused. On March 19, a coalition led by the United States and Britain launched air strikes in and around the Iraqi capital, Baghdad. The next day, coalition forces marched into Iraq though Kuwait. The invasion of Iraq to remove Saddam Hussein, known as Operation Iraqi Freedom, had begun.

The military operation met with strong opposition from numerous countries. Russian president Vladimir Putin claimed the invasion could "in no way be justified." He and others criticized the policy of attacking a nation to prevent it from future misdeeds. Many Americans also protested the coming invasion. U.S. and British officials, however, argued that they would not wait for Hussein to strike first.

As coalition troops marched north to Baghdad, they met pockets of stiff resistance and engaged in fierce fighting in several southern cities. Meanwhile, coalition forces parachuted into northern Iraq and began moving south toward the capital city. By the end of April, Baghdad had fallen and the regime of Saddam Hussein had collapsed. The coalition had won the war. In the process, about 170 coalition soldiers lost their lives. Most were Americans. The number of Iraqi soldiers who died is not known, but it was probably in the thousands.

The Struggle Continues

Despite the coalition victory, much work remained to be done in Iraq. With the help of the United States, the Iraqis began rebuilding their nation. They established an interim government several months after the war. The new governing body

As the regime of Saddam Hussein collapsed, statues of the dictator toppled.

To prevent people from voting twice in the Iraqi election in 2005, officials marked a voter's finger with purple ink.

Meanwhile, numerous U.S. troops remained behind to help maintain order and battle pockets of resistance. In addition to fighters loyal to Saddam Hussein, an increasing number of Iraqis began to oppose the continued presence of coalition forces. As a result, violence often erupted. By mid-2005, more than 25,000 Iraqi civilians had been killed. As for the defeated dictator, he finally was captured on December 13, 2003.

The debate over the wisdom of the war continued. Critics pointed out that occupying Iraq was far more costly and deadly than the Bush administration had publicly predicted. By late 2005, over 1,900 Americans had died in Iraq and more than 14,000 had been wounded. In addition, no weapons of mass destruction had been found. U.S. treatment of Iraqi captives held in Abu Ghraib prison also caused widespread criticism.

The lack of dangerous weapons in Iraq did not change President Bush's view about the war. Instead, he defended the war for other reasons. He argued that it had strengthened democracy in the Middle East and global security.

While Americans agreed with President Bush on the importance of fighting terrorism, they were increasingly divided over the war in Iraq. In June 2005, for the first time, a majority of polled Americans expressed support for withdrawal from Iraq. President Bush, though, continued to pledge to keep American troops in Iraq until the Iraqi government could control the country.

President George W. Bush and British prime minister Tony Blair stood together throughout the war.

went to work creating a temporary constitution and planning democratic elections. Iraq held elections in February 2005. A party heavily supported by Shiite Muslims won the most votes. Leaders of various religions and ethnic factions in the country then began the difficult process of writing a permanent constitution.

Special Report Assessment

1. Main Ideas

a. What steps did the U.S. government take to make the nation more secure after the attacks on September 11, 2001?

b. Why did the United States take military action against the Taliban in Afghanistan?

c. What was the result of Operation Iraqi Freedom?

2. Critical Thinking

Analyzing Issues Is it important for the U.S. government to respect people's civil rights as it wages a war against terrorism? Why or why not?

THINK ABOUT

• what steps are necessary to protect the nation
• a government that grows too powerful

The Supreme Court

The task of the Supreme Court, according to Chief Justice John Marshall, is "to say what the law is." The Court reviews appeals of decisions by lower courts. It judges whether federal laws or government actions violate the Constitution. And it settles conflicts between state and federal laws.

By interpreting the law, the Supreme Court wields great power, for its decisions affect practically every aspect of life in the United States. In the following pages, you'll learn about some of the Supreme Court's landmark cases—decisions that altered the course of history or brought major changes to American life.

"When we have examined . . . the Supreme Court and the [rights] which it exercises, we shall readily admit that a more imposing judicial power was never constituted by any people."

— ALEXIS DE TOCQUEVILLE, *DEMOCRACY IN AMERICA* (1835)

Chief Justice John Marshall established the principle of judicial review.

The development of steamships led to Supreme Court decisions on interstate commerce.

McCulloch v. *Maryland* decided if a state had the power to tax a federal agency.

1803	1824	1896
Marbury v. *Madison*	*Gibbons* v. *Ogden*	*Plessy* v. *Ferguson*
Judicial Review	State Versus Federal Authority	Segregation

1819	1857
McCulloch v. *Maryland*	*Dred Scott* v. *Sandford*
Powers of Congress and States' Rights	Citizenship

Landmark decisions on school desegregation helped give rise to the civil rights movement.

Opinions written by Justice Oliver Wendell Holmes, Jr., helped to set standards for free speech.

TABLE OF CONTENTS

BEFORE YOU READ

Think About It Why is there a need for a judicial authority "to say what the law is"? How might the history of the United States have been different if the Supreme Court had not taken on this role?

Find Out About It Use library resources or the Internet to find out what issues the Supreme Court is presently reviewing. How might the Court's decisions on these issues affect you?

For more information on the Supreme Court . . .

 **RESEARCH LINKS**
CLASSZONE.COM

The Supreme Court has reviewed several affirmative-action cases in recent years.

1919
Schenck v. *United States*
Freedom of Speech

1954
Brown v. *Board of Education of Topeka*
School Desegregation

1964
Reynolds v. *Sims*
One Person, One Vote

1978
Regents of the University of California v. *Bakke*
Affirmative Action

Marbury v. Madison (1803)

THE ISSUE Judicial Review

ORIGINS OF THE CASE In 1801, just before he left office, President John Adams appointed dozens of Federalists as judges. Most of these "midnight justices" took their posts before Thomas Jefferson, Adams's Democratic-Republican successor, took office. Jefferson ordered his secretary of state, James Madison, to block the remaining appointees from taking their posts. One of these appointees, William Marbury, asked the Supreme Court to issue an order forcing Madison to recognize the appointments.

THE RULING The Court ruled that the law under which Marbury had asked the Supreme Court to act was unconstitutional.

The Legal Arguments

Chief Justice John Marshall wrote the Court's opinion, stating that Marbury had every right to receive his appointment. Further, Marshall noted, the Judiciary Act of 1789 gave Marbury the right to file his claim directly with the Supreme Court. But Marshall questioned whether the Court had the power to act. The answer, he argued, rested on the kinds of cases that could be argued directly in the Supreme Court without first being heard by a lower court.

Article 3 of the Constitution clearly identified those cases that the Court could hear directly. A case like Marbury's was not one of them. The Judiciary Act, therefore, was at odds with the Constitution. Which one should be upheld? Marshall's response was clear:

> . . . [T]he particular phraseology of the Constitution of the United States confirms and strengthens the principle . . . that a law repugnant to the Constitution is void; and that *courts* . . . are bound by that instrument.

Since Section 13 of the Judiciary Act violated the Constitution, Marshall concluded, it could not be enforced. The Court, therefore, could not issue the order. With this decision, Marshall appeared to limit the powers of the Supreme Court. In fact, the decision increased the Court's power because it established the principle of judicial review. This holds that the courts—most notably the Supreme Court—have the power to decide if laws are unconstitutional.

LEGAL *Sources*

U.S. CONSTITUTION/LEGISLATION

Article 3, Section 2 (1789)
"In all cases affecting ambassadors, other public ministers and consuls, and those in which a state shall be party, the Supreme Court shall have original jurisdiction. In all the other cases . . . the Supreme Court shall have appellate jurisdiction."

Judiciary Act, Section 13 (1789)
"The Supreme Court shall . . . have power to issue . . . writs of *mandamus,* in cases warranted by the principles and usages of law."

RELATED CASES

Fletcher v. Peck (1810)
For the first time, the Supreme Court ruled a state law unconstitutional.

Cohens v. Virginia (1821)
For the first time, the Court overturned a state court decision.

William Marbury received his appointment as a reward for his loyal support of John Adams in the 1800 presidential election.

Why Did It Matter Then?

The principle of judicial review had been set down in earlier state and lower federal court decisions. However, Marshall did not refer to those cases in *Marbury*. Rather, he based his argument on logic.

For a written constitution to have any value, Marshall stated, it is logical that any "legislative act [that is] contrary to the Constitution is not law." Only then could the Constitution be—as Article VI calls it—"the supreme law of the land." Who, then, decides that a law is invalid? Marshall declared that this power rests only with the courts:

> It is, emphatically, the province and duty of the judicial department to say what the law is. Those who apply the rule to particular cases must of necessity expound and interpret that rule. If [the Constitution and a law] conflict with each other, the courts must decide on the operation of each.

Not only did the courts have this power, Marshall said, it was "the very essence of judicial duty" for them to exercise it.

Why Does It Matter Now?

Over the years, judicial review has become a cornerstone of American government. The principle plays a vital role in the system of checks and balances that limits the powers of each branch of the federal government. For example, since 1803 the Court has struck down more than 125 acts of Congress as unconstitutional.

The Court has cited *Marbury* more than 250 times to justify its decisions. In *Clinton* v. *Jones* (1997), for example, the Court found that presidents are not protected by the Constitution from lawsuits involving actions in their private lives. The Court supported this finding by pointing to its power "to say what the law is." More recently, in *United States* v. *Morrison* (2000), the Court ruled that Congress went beyond its constitutional bounds by basing a federal law banning violence against women on the Fourteenth Amendment and the Commerce Clause of the Constitution. The opinion pointed out that "ever since *Marbury* this Court has remained the ultimate [explainer] of the constitutional text."

John Marshall, a Federalist, was practically a "midnight justice." John Adams appointed him chief justice in January 1801, just two months before Thomas Jefferson took office.

CONNECT TO HISTORY

1. **Making Decisions** Marshall was a Federalist, and many people expected him to act quickly on Marbury's case. What do you think might have been the consequences if Marshall had found for Marbury?

    See Skillbuilder Handbook, page R14.

CONNECT TO TODAY

2. **Researching** Find a recent instance of a law or administrative action that was ruled unconstitutional by the Supreme Court. What were the Court's reasons for the ruling, and what impact did the decision have? Prepare a summary of your findings.

   For more information on judicial review . . .

   RESEARCH LINKS
   CLASSZONE.COM

McCulloch v. Maryland
(1819)

THE ISSUES Balance of power between the federal and state governments

ORIGINS OF THE CASE The second Bank of the United States (BUS) was established by an act of Congress in 1816. It set up branches nationwide. But many states objected to the bank's policies and wanted to limit its operations. In fact, Maryland set a tax on the currency issued by the Baltimore branch. The bank could avoid the tax by paying an annual fee of $15,000. However, James McCulloch, the branch cashier, refused to pay either the tax or the fee. The state sued McCulloch, and the Maryland courts ordered him to pay. McCulloch appealed the case to the Supreme Court.

THE RULING The Court ruled that Congress had the power to establish a national bank and that the Maryland tax on that bank was unconstitutional.

The Legal Arguments

The Court first addressed Maryland's argument that the act establishing the BUS was unconstitutional. Chief Justice John Marshall wrote that the Constitution listed the specific powers of Congress. These included collecting taxes, borrowing money, and regulating commerce. In addition, the Elastic Clause gave Congress the authority to make all "necessary and proper" laws needed to exercise those powers. Establishing a bank, he concluded, was necessary for Congress to carry out its powers. The BUS, then, was constitutional.

Next, Marshall addressed whether Maryland had the power to tax the BUS. Marshall acknowledged that the states had the power of taxation. But he said:

> [T]he constitution and the laws made in pursuance thereof are supreme . . . they control the constitution and laws of the respective states, and cannot be controlled by them.

So, to give a state the power to tax a federal agency created under the Constitution would turn the Supremacy Clause, Article 6, Section 2, on its head. Further, Marshall observed, "the power to tax involves the power to destroy." If a state could tax one federal agency, it might tax others. This eventually "would defeat all the ends of government." He added that the framers of the Constitution certainly did not intend to make the national government subject to the states:

> [T]he States have no power, by taxation or otherwise, to retard, impede, burden, or in any manner control, the operations of the constitutional laws enacted by Congress to carry [out its] powers.

The Maryland tax, therefore, was unconstitutional.

LEGAL Sources

U.S. CONSTITUTION/LEGISLATION

Article 1, Section 8 (1789)
"The Congress shall have the power to . . . make all laws which shall be necessary and proper for carrying into execution the [specific powers given to Congress]."

Article 6, Section 2 (1789)
"This Constitution, and the laws of the United States . . . shall be the supreme law of the land; . . . anything in the Constitution or laws of any state to the contrary notwithstanding."

RELATED CASES

Fletcher v. Peck (1810)
Noting that the Constitution was the supreme law of the land, the Supreme Court ruled a state law unconstitutional.

Gibbons v. Ogden (1824)
The Court ruled that the federal Congress—not the states—had the power to regulate interstate commerce.

Why Did It Matter Then?

At the time of the *McCulloch* case, there was considerable debate over what powers Congress held. Some people took a very limited view. They suggested that Congress's powers should be restricted to those named in the Constitution. Others pointed out that the Elastic Clause implied that Congress had much broader powers.

The *McCulloch* opinion followed this second view. Marshall wrote:

> Let the end be [lawful], let it be within the scope of the Constitution, and all means which are appropriate, which are plainly adapted to that end, which are not prohibited, but consist with the letter and spirit of the Constitution, are constitutional.

In other words, Congress could exercise the powers it considered appropriate to achieve its lawful goals.

Marshall's broad view of congressional power strengthened the federal government. And this stronger government reflected and encouraged the growing nationalist spirit in the early 1800s.

Why Does It Matter Now?

Since Marshall's time, the United States has undergone many changes. Over the course of the 19th and 20th centuries, the country has grown dramatically. The population has increased and moved. In Marshall's day, the United States was predominantly rural. Today, most people live in urban areas, where economic and leisure activities abound.

The economy of the United States, too, has changed. The country has moved from an agricultural economy to one based on industry and, later, service and information.

During this time, the federal government has stretched its powers to meet the needs of the ever-changing American society. Programs like Franklin Roosevelt's New Deal and Lyndon Johnson's Great Society came about through this expanding of powers. Marshall's broad reading of the Elastic Clause in the *McCulloch* opinion, in large part, laid the groundwork for this growth in the size and power of the federal government.

The Bank of the United States had branches throughout the country, including this one in Philadelphia.

CONNECT TO HISTORY

1. **Forming and Supporting Opinions** Chief Justice John Marshall considered the *McCulloch* decision the most important that he made. Why do you think he considered it such an important decision? Give reasons for your answer.

 See Skillbuilder Handbook, page R17.

CONNECT TO TODAY

2. **Researching** One issue addressed in *McCulloch* was states' rights and federal authority. Do research to find a recent Supreme Court case that has dealt with this issue. Write a paragraph describing the basis of the case and the Court's decision.

For more information on states' rights and federal authority . . .

 RESEARCH LINKS
CLASSZONE.COM

Gibbons v. Ogden (1824)

THE ISSUE Federal power to regulate interstate commerce

ORIGINS OF THE CASE Aaron Ogden ran steamboats between New York City and New Jersey. The New York state legislature granted him a monopoly—the right to operate this service without any competition. However, Thomas Gibbons ran a competing service. He had a license to sail under the federal Coasting License Act of 1793. Ogden sued Gibbons for violating his monopoly. When the New York state courts found in Ogden's favor, Gibbons appealed to the United States Supreme Court.

THE RULING In a unanimous decision, the Court ruled that when state and federal laws on interstate commerce conflict, federal laws are superior.

LEGAL *Sources*

U.S. CONSTITUTION/LEGISLATION

Article 1, Section 8 (1789)
"The Congress shall have power to . . . regulate commerce with foreign nations, and among the several states, and with the Indian tribes."

Coasting License Act (1793)
All ships licensed under this act, "and no others, shall be deemed ships or vessels of the United States, entitled to the privileges of ships or vessels employed in the coasting trade or fisheries."

RELATED CASES

Fletcher v. Peck (1810)
Citing the Supremacy Clause, the Court ruled that a state law was unconstitutional.

McCulloch v. Maryland (1819)
The Court established that states had no authority to tax federal agencies.

The Legal Arguments

Chief Justice John Marshall wrote the Court's unanimous opinion, which found for Gibbons. Since the Constitution gave Congress the power to regulate commerce among the states, Marshall began, it would be useful to decide what the word *commerce* meant. In arguments before the Court, Ogden's lawyers had said that it simply referred to the buying and selling of goods. Marshall disagreed, suggesting that it also included the navigation necessary to move goods from one place to another. He wrote:

> The word used in the constitution comprehends . . . navigation within its meaning; and a power to regulate navigation is as expressly granted as if that term had been added to the word "commerce."

Marshall then pointed to the Supremacy Clause of the Constitution. This is Article 6, Section 2, which states, "This Constitution, and the laws of the United States . . . shall be the supreme law of the land."

The New York monopoly law denied Gibbons the right to sail in New York waters. The federal Coasting License Act, however, gave him the right to sail *all* U.S. waters. According to the Supremacy Clause, the Constitution and federal laws were the supreme law of the land. So, Marshall concluded, the Coasting License Act was "the supreme law of the land," and the New York monopoly was void.

Aaron Ogden obtained a monopoly on steamship operation between New York and New Jersey in 1815.

Why Did It Matter Then?

At the time of the *Gibbons* case, navigation of the waters around New York was difficult. To encourage companies to provide water transportation, New York granted monopolies to the companies. Some states set up their own. Other states passed laws preventing New York steamboats from entering their waters. Obviously, such a situation was not good for trade among the states. By making it clear that the federal government regulated commerce among the states, the *Gibbons* decision brought order to interstate commerce. And this helped the national economy to grow.

Unlike other decisions of the Marshall Court that strengthened the federal government, *Gibbons* proved popular. Most Americans—even New Yorkers—were opposed to the New York steamboat monopoly. They saw any kind of monopoly as a limit to economic competition. As a result, the *Gibbons* decision was well received throughout the country. One newspaper reported the following incident:

> **Yesterday the Steamboat *United States*, [commanded by] Capt. Bunker, from New Haven, entered New York in triumph, with streamers flying and a large company of passengers [celebrating] the decision of the United States Supreme Court against the New York monopoly. She fired a salute which was loudly returned by [cheers] from the wharves.**

After the first voyage of Robert Fulton's *Clermont* in 1807, it soon became clear that operating steamships could be a profitable business.

Why Does It Matter Now?

Marshall defined "commerce" very broadly in the *Gibbons* decision. Over the years, Congress has used Marshall's definition to expand its authority over interstate commerce. Today, Congress regulates practically every activity that affects or is connected to commerce.

In 1964, for example, Congress used the Commerce Clause to justify the passage of the Civil Rights Act. This law banned racial discrimination in hotels, restaurants, theaters, and other public places.

The Supreme Court rejected two challenges to the Civil Rights Act—in *Heart of Atlanta Motel, Inc.* v. *United States* (1964) and *Katzenbach* v. *McClung* (1964). In both cases, the Court noted that racial discrimination could harm interstate commerce.

CONNECT TO HISTORY

1. **Drawing Conclusions** Many of Chief Justice John Marshall's opinions contributed to the growth of the nationalist spirit in the early 1800s. How do you think the *Gibbons* v. *Ogden* decision might have helped to build national unity?

 See Skillbuilder Handbook, page R13.

CONNECT TO TODAY

2. **Researching** Use library resources and the Internet to find recent Supreme Court cases that involved interstate commerce. Write a brief summary of one of these cases, noting whether it expanded or contracted Congress's power to regulate commerce.

For more information on interstate commerce . . .

RESEARCH LINKS
CLASSZONE.COM

Dred Scott v. Sandford (1857)

THE ISSUE The definition of citizenship

ORIGINS OF THE CASE Dred Scott was an enslaved African American who had lived for a while in Illinois and in the Wisconsin Territory, both of which banned slavery. Scott sued for his freedom, arguing that since he had lived in a free state and a free territory, he was a free man. In 1854, a federal court found against Scott, ruling that he was still a slave. Scott's lawyers appealed to the Supreme Court, which heard arguments in 1856 and delivered its decision the following year.

THE RULING The Court ruled that no African American could be a citizen and that Dred Scott was still a slave. The Court also ruled that the Missouri Compromise of 1820 was unconstitutional.

The Legal Arguments

Chief Justice Roger Taney wrote the majority opinion for the Court. He began by addressing the issue of citizenship. He pointed out that since colonial times African Americans had been looked on as inferior and "had no rights which the white man was bound to respect." Taney added that where African Americans were mentioned in the Constitution, they were referred to as property—slaves. African Americans, whether enslaved or free, he continued:

> . . . are not included, and were not intended to be included, under the word 'citizens' in the Constitution, and can therefore claim none of the rights and privileges which that instrument provides for and secures to citizens of the United States.

Since Scott was not a citizen, Taney concluded, he had no right to use the courts to sue for his freedom.

Taney then went further, claiming Scott was still a slave because he had never been free. Congress had gone beyond its power when it passed the Missouri Compromise, he argued. The Constitution guaranteed the right to own property, and slaves were property. By banning slavery from the territories, Congress was, in effect, taking away private property without due process of the law. This action violated the Fifth Amendment. The Missouri Compromise was, Taney charged, "not warranted by the Constitution, and . . . therefore void." As a result, Scott remained a slave, regardless of where he lived.

Two justices disagreed with the majority on both grounds. They pointed to precedents—earlier legal rulings—that indicated that African Americans could, indeed, be citizens. They also argued that the Constitution gave Congress the power to establish rules and regulations for the territories.

LEGAL Sources

U.S. CONSTITUTION/LEGISLATION

Article 4, Section 3 (1789)
"No person held to service or labor in one state, . . . escaping into another, shall, in consequence of any law or regulation therein, be discharged from such service or labor. . . ."

Fifth Amendment (1791)
"No person shall be . . . deprived of life, liberty, or property, without due process of law."

Missouri Enabling Act (1820)
"[I]n all that territory . . . north of 36° 30' N latitude, . . . slavery . . . shall be . . . forever prohibited." Also known as the Missouri Compromise.

RELATED CASE

Ableman v. Booth (1858)
The Court ruled that laws passed in Northern states that prohibited the return of fugitive slaves were unconstitutional.

Why Did It Matter Then?

Dred Scott contributed to the growing dispute over slavery that led to the Civil War. White Southerners praised the ruling, seeing it as a spirited defense of their right to own slaves. Many Northerners, however, viewed it with alarm. They feared that if Congress could not ban slavery in the territories, slavery would spread. If this happened, slave states eventually would outnumber free states and would control Congress.

Stephen A. Douglas, a Northern Democrat, disagreed with the Court's finding. He favored leaving the issue of slavery to the voters in each territory. Most Southern Democrats, however, did not agree with him. As a result, the Democratic Party divided along sectional lines in the 1860 presidential election. Northern Democrats supported Douglas, while Southern Democrats backed a pro-slavery candidate. Because of this split, Abraham Lincoln of the anti-slavery Republican Party won the election. Soon after, many slave states seceded, and the Civil War began.

Northern abolitionists held meetings to show their support for Scott (shown here) and their opposition to the Supreme Court decision.

Why Does It Matter Now?

The issues addressed by *Dred Scott* were resolved by the Thirteenth and Fourteenth amendments to the Constitution. The Thirteenth Amendment, which was ratified in 1865, abolished slavery in the United States. The Fourteenth Amendment, ratified three years later, made it very clear who was a citizen:

> All persons born or naturalized in the United States, and subject to the jurisdiction thereof, are citizens of the United States and of the state wherein they reside.

This amendment went on to guarantee all citizens "equal protection of the laws" and the right to due process. These amendments meant the rulings in *Dred Scott* no longer had the force of law.

Today, *Dred Scott* is not used as a precedent. Instead, it is pointed to as an example of how the Supreme Court can make mistakes. In fact, many legal scholars think it is the worst decision the Court has ever handed down.

CONNECT TO HISTORY

1. **Forming and Supporting Opinions** The *Dred Scott* decision was just one in a long line of events that led to the Civil War. Write an editorial about the case in which you evaluate its importance in bringing about the war.

    See Skillbuilder Handbook, page R17.

CONNECT TO TODAY

2. **Researching** Use library sources and the Internet to research a contemporary Court decision that affects civil rights. Use newspaper indices, periodical guides, and library catalogs, for example, to locate sources of this information. Create a public service brochure to report your findings.

   For more information on citizenship . . .

   RESEARCH LINKS
   CLASSZONE.COM

Plessy v. Ferguson (1896)

THE ISSUE Segregation

ORIGINS OF THE CASE By the 1890s, most Southern states had begun to pass laws enforcing segregation—the separation of the races—in public places. One Louisiana law called for "equal but separate accommodations for the white and colored races" on trains. On June 7, 1892, Homer Plessy, who was part African American, took a seat in a train car reserved for whites. When a conductor told him to move, Plessy refused. Plessy was convicted of breaking the "separate car" law. He appealed the case, saying that the law violated his rights under the Thirteenth and Fourteenth amendments.

THE RULING The Court ruled that "separate but equal" facilities for blacks and whites did not violate the Constitution.

LEGAL Sources

U.S. CONSTITUTION/LEGISLATION

Thirteenth Amendment (1865)
"Neither slavery nor involuntary servitude . . . shall exist within the United States, or any place subject to their jurisdiction."

Fourteenth Amendment (1868)
"No state shall make or enforce any law which shall abridge the privileges or immunities of citizens of the United States; nor shall any state deprive any person of life, liberty, or property, without due process of law; nor deny to any person within its jurisdiction the equal protection of the laws."

RELATED CASE

Cumming v. Board of Education of Richmond County (1899)
The Court ruled that because education is a local issue, the federal government could not stop school districts from having separate facilities for black and white students.

The Legal Arguments

The Court's opinion, written by Justice Henry Billings Brown, rejected Plessy's appeal. Brown first answered Plessy's claim that the separate car law created a relationship between whites and blacks similar to that which existed under slavery. The Thirteenth Amendment simply ended the ownership of one person by another, Brown wrote. Louisiana's law did not reestablish this system of ownership.

Brown then turned to Plessy's claim that the Fourteenth Amendment was designed to ensure the equality of the races before the law. Brown wrote that the amendment "could not have been intended to abolish distinctions based on color." A law that treated the races differently did not brand one race as inferior. If a law made people feel inferior, it was because they chose to see it that way. Summing up, Brown stated:

> A [law] which implies merely a legal distinction between the white and colored races . . . has no tendency to destroy the legal equality of the two races.

Justice John Marshall Harlan strongly disagreed with the majority view. In a bitter dissent, he wrote that the "thin disguise" of separate but equal facilities would fool no one, "nor atone for the wrong this day done."

In his dissent, Justice Harlan stated that "our constitution is color-blind, and neither knows nor tolerates classes among citizens."

Why Did It Matter Then?

Plessy was one of several cases in the late 1800s involving the civil rights of African Americans. In these cases, the Court misread the Fourteenth Amendment and let stand state laws that denied African Americans their rights. *Plessy* has come to stand for all of these decisions because it said that "separate but equal" facilities for blacks and whites did not violate the Constitution.

Although the *Plessy* decision dealt only with public transportation, state governments across the South applied it to all areas of life. In time, "Jim Crow" laws forced African Americans to use separate restaurants, hotels, train cars, parks, schools, and hospitals. Signs reading "For Colored Only" and "Whites Only" ruled everyday life in the South for years to come.

Why Does It Matter Now?

After *Plessy*, many African Americans and some whites looked for ways to fight segregation. Some of these people helped to found the National Association for the Advancement of Colored People (NAACP).

Throughout the first half of the 20th century, lawyers working for the NAACP chipped away at segregation laws. Their greatest victory came in 1954, in *Brown* v. *Board of Education of Topeka*. In this decision, the Supreme Court ruled that separate educational facilities were "inherently unequal" and, therefore, unconstitutional. Southern state and local governments had used the *Plessy* decision to build a system of legal segregation. In the same way, civil rights workers used the *Brown* ruling to dismantle it.

After the *Plessy* decision, signs designating separate facilities for whites and African Americans became a common sight throughout the South.

CONNECT TO HISTORY

1. **Drawing Conclusions** Read the section of the Fourteenth Amendment reprinted in the "Legal Sources" section on page 908. Based on that passage, what do you think "equal protection of the laws" means? How does it apply to the *Plessy* case?

 See Skillbuilder Handbook, page R13.

CONNECT TO TODAY

2. **Researching** Use library resources and the Internet to find information on Supreme Court cases that dealt with segregation. Present your findings in a three-column chart. Use "Case," "Brief Description of Issues Involved," and "Decision" as column headings.

For more information on segregation and the law . . .

RESEARCH LINKS
CLASSZONE.COM

Schenck v. United States
(1919)

THE ISSUE Freedom of Speech

ORIGINS OF THE CASE In August 1917, Charles Schenck, a Socialist Party official, distributed several thousand antiwar leaflets throughout the city of Philadelphia. The leaflets called the draft a crime and urged people to work for the repeal of the Selective Service Act. Schenck was found guilty of violating the Espionage Act of 1917 and sentenced to prison. He appealed his conviction, arguing that the language in the leaflets was protected by the First Amendment.

THE RULING The Court upheld the verdict against Schenck, noting that the leaflets presented "a clear and present danger" to the country during wartime.

LEGAL Sources

U.S. CONSTITUTION/LEGISLATION

First Amendment (1791)
"Congress shall make no law . . . abridging the freedom of speech, or of the press."

The Espionage Act (1917)
"[Anyone who] shall wilfully obstruct . . . the recruiting or enlistment service of the United States . . . shall be punished by . . . fine . . . or imprisonment . . . or both."

RELATED CASES

Debs v. United States (1919)
Upheld the conviction of Socialist Party leader Eugene V. Debs for violating the Espionage Act.

Frohwerk v. United States (1919)
Confirmed the guilty verdict against a newspaper publisher for printing articles opposing U. S. involvement in World War I.

Abrams v. United States (1919)
Upheld convictions of five people under the Espionage Act. Holmes dissented, arguing that their action did not present "a clear and imminent danger."

The Legal Arguments

Justice Oliver Wendell Holmes, Jr., wrote the Court's unanimous opinion. In ordinary times, Holmes noted, Schenck's claim of First Amendment rights might well be valid. "But the character of every act depends upon the circumstances in which it is done," Holmes added. Schenck distributed the leaflets during wartime, when "many things that might be said in time of peace . . . will not be endured." Holmes suggested that Schenck's "impassioned" appeal for people to oppose the draft was just like someone "falsely shouting fire in a theatre and causing a panic." The First Amendment certainly did not protect such behavior.

Holmes then went on to offer a guide for judging when speech is protected by the First Amendment:

> The question in every case is whether the words used are used in such circumstances and are of such a nature as to create a clear and present danger that they will bring about the . . . evils that Congress has a right to prevent.

Schenck's words, Holmes charged, did pose "a clear and present danger" to the United States war effort. Therefore, they did not merit protection under the First Amendment.

Justice Holmes's opinions in the Espionage Act cases set the standard for free speech.

Why Did It Matter Then?

The Supreme Court decisions in *Schenck* and other Espionage Act cases considered the limits of free speech during wartime. In *Schenck,* Justice Holmes stated that speech that presented "a clear and present danger" to the country's well being was not protected. As he looked at other cases, however, Holmes began to refine this view.

In *Frohwerk* v. *United States* (1919), decided just a week after *Schenck,* the Court again upheld a conviction under the Espionage Act. However, Holmes noted that anti-government speech uttered during wartime is not always a crime. "We do not lose our right to condemn either measures or men because the country is at war," he wrote.

Holmes broadened this statement in his dissent to the majority opinion in *Abrams* v. *United States* (1919). The government's power to limit speech during wartime undoubtedly is greater, he noted, "because war opens dangers that do not exist at other times." However, the basic principles of free speech are the same in war as in peace:

> **It is only the present danger of immediate evil or an intent to bring it about that warrants Congress in setting a limit to the expression of opinion.**

All opinions, even ones we find hateful, should be heard, Holmes concluded.

During the Vietnam War, some Americans vigorously challenged government policies.

Why Does It Matter Now?

The Supreme Court has been asked to decide on free speech issues dozens of times since *Schenck.* In making these decisions, the Court has attempted to heed Justice Holmes's words and strike a balance between protecting free speech and maintaining political and social order.

Over the years, the Court has applied this balance test to free speech questions in many settings, including schools. In *Tinker* v. *Des Moines Independent Community School District* (1969), the Court upheld students' right to protest in school. However, the Court added that in certain circumstances school officials might limit the exercise of such rights—if the students' actions disrupt the work of the school, for example.

In two later cases, *Bethel School District No. 403* v. *Fraser* (1986) and *Hazelwood School District* v. *Kuhlmeier* (1988), the Court felt that such circumstances existed. In *Bethel,* the Court upheld the suspension of a student who, during a school assembly, gave a speech that included inappropriate language. The Court ruled that the school could punish behavior that "interferes with the educational process." In *Hazelwood,* the Court ruled that school officials could censor the content of a student newspaper if it was "inconsistent with [the school's] educational mission."

CONNECT TO HISTORY

1. Making Inferences The Supreme Court decided *Schenck* and other Espionage Act cases during the Red Scare. Do you think the timing of the cases influenced the Court's decisions? Why or why not?

 See Skillbuilder Handbook, page R12.

CONNECT TO TODAY

2. Researching Working with a group of two or three other students, identify and research recent court cases involving free speech issues. Present your findings in a brief oral report to the class.

For more information on free speech . . .

RESEARCH LINKS
CLASSZONE.COM

Brown v. Board of Education of Topeka (1954)

THE ISSUE School desegregation

ORIGINS OF THE CASE In September 1950, Oliver Brown tried to enroll his seven-year-old daughter, Linda, at the neighborhood grade school. The school principal rejected Brown's request because Linda was an African American. The school was for white students only. Linda ended up attending a school farther away from her home. Brown filed suit against the school board, demanding that Linda be allowed to go to the neighborhood school. The Supreme Court heard arguments in the *Brown* case in 1952 and 1953.

THE RULING A unanimous court ruled that segregation in education was unconstitutional.

LEGAL *Sources*

U.S. CONSTITUTION/LEGISLATION

Fourteenth Amendment (1868)
"No state shall . . . deprive any person of life, liberty, or property, without due process of law; nor deny to any person within its jurisdiction the equal protection of the laws."

RELATED CASES

Plessy v. Ferguson (1896)
Upheld Louisiana laws that segregated railroad passenger cars according to race. Established the doctrine of "separate but equal."

Brown v. Board of Education of Topeka (May, 1955)
Ordered that desegregation take place "with all deliberate speed." Often called "*Brown II*."

The Legal Arguments

Chief Justice Earl Warren wrote the Court's decision. He began by reviewing the history of the Fourteenth Amendment. Its equal protection clause was the basis for the decision. The Court had ruled in *Plessy* v. *Ferguson* (1896) that "separate but equal" facilities for blacks and whites did not violate this amendment. However, Warren pointed out that *Plessy* involved transportation, not education. He then stressed the importance of education for society:

> It is doubtful that any child may reasonably be expected to succeed in life if he is denied the opportunity of an education.

Warren went on to suggest that segregation denied African-American children that opportunity. He concluded with *Brown's* most famous statement:

> . . . [I]n the field of public education the doctrine of "separate but equal" has no place. Separate educational facilities are inherently unequal.

The Court expected whites in the South, where segregation was dominant, to resist the ruling. Therefore, it delayed orders on how to put the decision into action for several months.

Thurgood Marshall was one of the team of lawyers that represented Oliver Brown. In 1967, Marshall became the first African American appointed as a Supreme Court justice.

Why Did It Matter Then?

The Fourteenth Amendment had guaranteed African Americans equal rights as citizens. In the late 1800s, however, many Southern states passed "Jim Crow" laws, which enforced separation of the races in public places. In 1896, the Supreme Court upheld a "Jim Crow" law in *Plessy* v. *Ferguson.* In the Court's view, "separate but equal" rail cars did not violate the Fourteenth Amendment.

Brown, however, stated that segregated schools denied African Americans the "equal protection of the laws" guaranteed by the Fourteenth Amendment. Segregation, therefore, had no place in school systems.

As the Court expected, the decision met opposition. One Southern politician accused the Court of "a flagrant abuse of judicial power." Even after *Brown II,* many school districts, particularly in the South, dragged their feet on desegregation. Some 10 years later, segregation was still the rule in most Southern school districts. Even so, the impact of the *Brown* decision on American society was immense. It marked the beginning of the civil rights movement, which you read about in Chapter 29.

The *Brown* decision was a front-page story in newspapers across the United States.

Why Does It Matter Now?

Throughout the 1960s and 1970s, the Supreme Court continued to review the issue of school segregation. In *Green* v. *New Kent County* (1968), the Court called for the end of the dual school system—one white and one black. This involved integrating not only students, but also teachers, support staff, and services.

In *Swann* v. *Charlotte-Mecklenburg Board of Education* (1971), the Court ruled that busing could be used to achieve school desegregation. Later, in *Milliken* v. *Bradley* (1974), the Court ruled that students might be bused between school districts to achieve this goal. However, this step could be taken only in very exceptional circumstances.

In recent years, the Court has moved away from enforcing desegregation. Still, the *Brown* decision brought about far-reaching changes. The statement that separate facilities are "inherently unequal" proved a powerful weapon against segregation in all areas of American life. Indeed, the Court's opinion in *Brown* provided the basis for most of the civil rights laws passed in the late 1950s and 1960s.

CONNECT TO HISTORY

1. **Analyzing Points of View** Chief Justice Earl Warren wanted the *Brown* opinion to be unanimous. He even pressured Justice Stanley Reed, a southerner, not to file a dissenting opinion. Why do you think Warren insisted that all the justices agree to the *Brown* decision?

 See Skillbuilder Handbook, page R9.

CONNECT TO TODAY

2. **Researching** Working with a group of two or three other students, conduct research to find out about efforts to desegregate another part of American society, such as the military, the workplace, or colleges. Report your findings to the class.

For more information on civil rights today . . .

RESEARCH LINKS
CLASSZONE.COM

Reynolds v. Sims (1964)

THE ISSUE One Person, One Vote

ORIGINS OF THE CASE Most state constitutions require a redrawing of legislative districts every 10 years, based on the latest U.S. Census figures. By the 1960s, however, many states had not redrawn their districts for decades. For example, Alabama's last redrawing—in 1901—did not reflect the great population changes that had taken place. In 1962, a group of Alabama voters sued to have their legislative map redrawn. When a federal court found for the voters, the Alabama state legislature appealed to the Supreme Court.

THE RULING The Court firmly established the principle of "one person, one vote." It ruled that Alabama must redraw its legislative districts so that each district had about the same number of people.

LEGAL Sources

U.S. CONSTITUTION/LEGISLATION

Fourteenth Amendment (1868)
"No state shall . . . deprive any person of life, liberty, or property, without due process of law; nor deny to any person within its jurisdiction the equal protection of the laws."

Alabama Constitution, Article 9, Section 198 (1901)
"The members of the house of representatives shall be apportioned by the legislature among the several counties of the state, according to the number of inhabitants in them, respectively, as ascertained by the decennial census of the United States."

RELATED CASES

Baker v. Carr (1962)
Ruled that federal courts could intervene in state legislative districting issues.

Gray v. Sanders (1963)
Ruled that when counting votes in primary elections, states should follow the principle of "one person, one vote."

The Legal Arguments

The Court's ruling, written by Chief Justice Earl Warren, clearly stated the issue:

> The right to vote freely for the candidate of one's choice is of the essence of a democratic society, and any restrictions on that right strike at the heart of representative government.

Weakening the power of an individual's vote, Warren added, was as much a restriction as preventing that individual from voting.

"Legislators represent people, not trees or acres," Warren continued. Population, therefore, had to be the determining factor in redrawing legislative districts. Warren based his argument squarely on the Fourteenth Amendment:

Chief Justice Earl Warren considered *Reynolds* v. *Sims* one of the most important opinions he had written.

> We hold that as a basic constitutional standard, the Equal Protection Clause requires that seats in . . . a . . . state legislature must be apportioned on a population basis. . . . [T]he Equal Protection Clause requires that a State make an honest and good faith effort to construct districts . . . as nearly of equal population as is practicable.

John Marshall Harlan—the grandson of the justice who wrote the famous dissent to *Plessy* v. *Ferguson*—dissented. He claimed that the Constitution did not give the Court the power to interfere in how states decide on their legislative districts.

Why Did It Matter Then?

Reynolds was one of several voting rights cases that the Court heard in the 1960s. In the first, *Baker* v. *Carr* (1962), the Court broke with past decisions and said that federal courts had the power to make sure that states drew legislative districts fairly. A year later, in *Gray* v. *Sanders* (1963), the Court applied the principle of "one person, one vote" for the first time. The Court observed that the vote of someone living in one part of a state should count as much as that of someone living in another part.

In *Reynolds,* the court extended the "one person, one vote" principle to the drawing of state legislative districts. In time, the *Reynolds* ruling forced most states to draw new district boundaries. As a result, there was a shift in political power in state legislatures. The number of state representatives from cities, which had larger populations, increased. In contrast, the number from rural areas, where fewer people lived, declined.

Why Does It Matter Now?

During the 1990s, the Court faced a new redistricting issue. The Voting Rights Act of 1965 urged states to increase minority representation in the legislatures. To do so, many states created districts where minorities made up a voting majority. However, some white voters challenged these districts under the Fourteenth Amendment.

In several cases—*Bush* v. *Vera* (1996), for example—the Court ruled that such districts were unconstitutional. Since these districts were drawn *solely* based on race, the Court said, they violated the Fourteenth Amendment's equal protection clause. In *Lawyer* v. *Department of Justice* (1997), the Court upheld a Florida district drawn to include several African-American communities. The Court found that in this case, race was only one of several factors used to draw district boundary lines.

After the U.S. Census of 2000, the states began a new round of redistricting. As a result, the Supreme Court probably will revisit this issue over the next few years.

Representation in the Alabama State Legislature, 1962

COUNTY	POPULATION	NUMBER OF HOUSE REPRESENTATIVES
Bullock	13,462	2
Henry	15,286	2
Mobile	314,301	3
Jefferson	634,864	7

Source: *U.S. Supreme Court,* Reynolds v. Sims, *377 U.S. 533 (1964)*

In 1962, the rural counties of Bullock and Henry had less than one-thirtieth of the population of the urban counties of Mobile and Jefferson. Even so, they returned close to half as many state representatives as did the two urban counties.

CONNECT TO HISTORY

1. **Finding Main Ideas** Use library or Internet resources to locate a copy of the majority opinion in *Reynolds* v. *Sims.* Make a chart listing the main idea and details for each part of the opinion. Make a similar chart for Harlan's dissenting opinion in this case.

 See Skillbuilder Handbook, page R5.

CONNECT TO TODAY

2. **Researching** Conduct research to find news stories about a recent Supreme Court decision on the issue of redistricting. Write a summary of the background of the case, the ruling the Court made, and the legal reasoning behind that ruling.

For more information on the Supreme Court and redistricting . . .

RESEARCH LINKS
CLASSZONE.COM

Regents of the University of California v. Bakke (1978)

THE ISSUE Affirmative action

ORIGINS OF THE CASE In 1970, the medical school of the University of California at Davis adopted an "affirmative action" admissions policy. The policy set a quota calling for 16 percent of each year's incoming students to be minority students. Allan Bakke, a white applicant, had better test scores and grades than most of the students accepted under the affirmative-action plan. However, he was not admitted. Bakke sued, arguing that he had been rejected because of his race. The California Supreme Court ordered the school to admit Bakke. The school appealed the case to the U.S. Supreme Court.

THE RULING The Court ruled that the school could use race as one of several factors in making admissions decisions but that setting racial quotas was unconstitutional.

LEGAL Sources

U.S. CONSTITUTION/LEGISLATION

Fourteenth Amendment (1868)
"No state shall . . . deprive any person of life, liberty, or property, without due process of law; nor deny to any person within its jurisdiction the equal protection of the laws."

Civil Rights Act, Title VI (1964)
"No person in the United States shall, on the ground of race, color, or national origin, be excluded from participation in . . . any program or activity receiving Federal financial assistance."

RELATED CASE

Fullilove v. Klutznick (1980)
The Court upheld the Public Works Employment Act of 1977, which required that minority-owned businesses receive 10 percent of all federal funds for public works projects.

The Legal Arguments

The Court upheld the California Supreme Court decision in a 5–4 vote. Four of the five majority justices maintained that holding a set number of admission slots for minority students violated the Civil Rights Act of 1964. The fifth justice, Justice Lewis Powell, noted that racial quotas violated the Fourteenth Amendment. Powell wrote:

> The guarantee of equal protection cannot mean one thing when applied to one individual and something else when applied to a person of another color. If both are not accorded the same protection, then it is not equal.

However, the Court did not reject affirmative action completely. By a different 5-4 majority, the Court ruled that race could be used as one of several factors in college admissions. Powell, who again provided the deciding vote, thought that race should be considered in order to promote a "diverse student body."

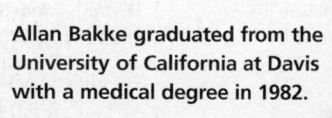

Allan Bakke graduated from the University of California at Davis with a medical degree in 1982.

Why Did It Matter Then?

African Americans made many gains in civil rights during the 1950s and 1960s. President Lyndon Johnson, however, thought more needed to be done. He explained why:

> You do not take a person who for years has been hobbled by chains and . . . bring him up to the starting line of a race and then say, "you are free to compete with all the others" and still justly believe that you have been completely fair.

In 1965, Johnson urged companies to increase the hiring and promoting of minorities.

In time, many businesses, colleges, and other organizations set up affirmative-action programs. Not everyone was happy with this development, however. Some whites felt that affirmative action amounted to little more than "reverse discrimination." That is, they felt that they would be denied jobs or college places because of their race.

With the Bakke ruling, the Supreme Court took a compromise position on affirmative-action programs. They were acceptable, the Court said, as long as they did not use strict racial quotas.

Why Does It Matter Now?

Since *Bakke,* the Court has ruled on several affirmative-action cases. In *Metro Broadcasting* v. *Federal Communications Commission* (1990), for example, the Court upheld a policy that gave preference to minority broadcasters. However, in *Adarand Constructors, Inc.* v. *Peña* (1995), the Court struck down a similar affirmative-action program.

The standing of affirmative action in college admissions is somewhat clearer, however. Some states have abandoned the policy altogether. In California, for example, voters approved a 1996 referendum banning the state's universities from using affirmative action in admissions.

Washington voters passed a similar measure in 1998. These and other states are looking for new ways to help minority students attend college. One method—adopted by California, Florida, and Texas—guarantees admission to state universities for the top students from each high school graduating class.

The affirmative-action debate, at times, has been quite bitter. Here, supporters and opponents of affirmative action confront each other at a demonstration on the campus of the University of California at Berkeley.

CONNECT TO HISTORY

1. **Making Inferences** In the *Bakke* case, the Supreme Court issued six separate opinions. Also, the voting on the two issues in the case was 5-4. From this information, what inferences can you draw on the Court's attitudes on affirmative action?

 See Skillbuilder Handbook, page R12.

CONNECT TO TODAY

2. **Researching** The state university system of Michigan recently has faced court challenges to its affirmative-action program. Track the progress of these challenges and write a few paragraphs comparing the arguments and court findings in Michigan to those in the *Bakke* case.

For more information on affirmative action . . .

 RESEARCH LINKS
CLASSZONE.COM

RAND McNALLY
World Atlas

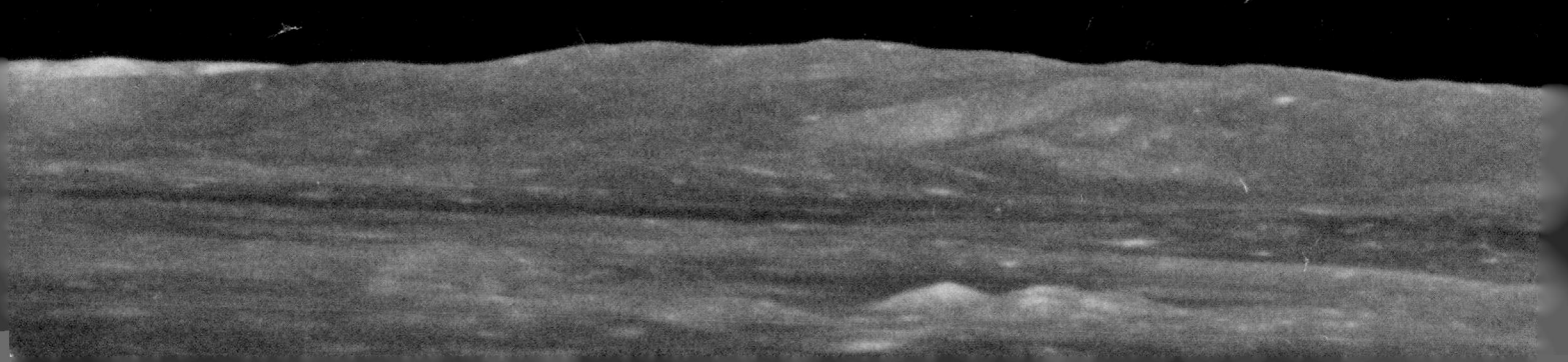

You are a reporter following Abraham Lincoln and Stephen A. Douglas on the campaign trail in 1858. The issue of slavery is causing heated debates. Respectable men have turned to violence to settle their differences. You worry that soon this violence may affect the entire nation.

How would you keep the nation together?

What Do You Think?

- Why do you think people feel so strongly about slavery?

- Do you think debates, such as those between Lincoln and Douglas, could settle emotional issues without leading to violence?

RESEARCH LINKS
CLASSZONE.COM
Visit the Chapter 15 links for more information about pre-war tension.

Although not allowed to vote, women clearly show an interest in politics.

"WESTWARD THE
THE GIRLS LINK
THEIR N

1854
Congress passes the Kansas–Nebraska Act.

1856
James Buchanan is elected president.

1857
Chief Justice Roger B. Taney delivers his opinion in the *Dred Scott* case.

1860
Abraham Lincoln is elected president.

1861
The Confederate States of America is formed.

1861

1856
War breaks out between Britain and Persia.

1861
Czar Alexander II frees the serfs in Russia.

CHAPTER 15

Reading Strategy: Analyzing Causes

What Do You Know?

What do you think about when you hear the terms *slavery* and *abolition*? Why do you think the issue of slavery caused so much anger and resentment?

Think About

- what you've learned about differences between the North and the South from books, travel, television, or movies
- reasons people have violent conflicts today
- your responses to the Interact with History about keeping the nation together (see page 455)

Slavery caused such strong emotions that fights sometimes broke out between members of Congress.

What Do You Want to Know?

 What questions do you have about the sectional crisis that led to the Civil War? Record them in your notebook before you read this chapter.

Analyzing Causes

Analyzing causes means looking closely at events and describing why they happened. The diagram below will help you analyze some of the causes of secession. Use the diagram to take notes on how each issue drove the North and the South farther apart.

[S] See Skillbuilder Handbook, page R11.

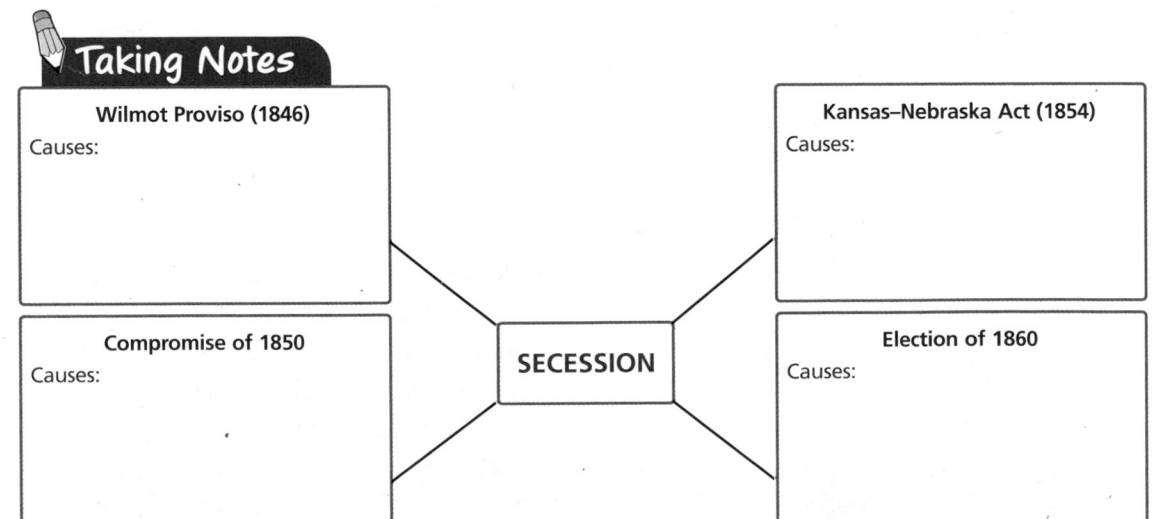

Taking Notes

Wilmot Proviso (1846)
Causes:

Kansas–Nebraska Act (1854)
Causes:

Compromise of 1850
Causes:

SECESSION

Election of 1860
Causes:

Growing Tensions Between North and South

MAIN IDEA	WHY IT MATTERS NOW	TERMS & NAMES
Disagreements between the North and the South, especially over the issue of slavery, led to political conflict.	Regional differences can make national problems difficult to resolve.	Wilmot Proviso Daniel Webster Free-Soil Party Stephen A. Douglas Henry Clay Compromise of 1850

ONE EUROPEAN'S STORY

During the 1830s, a French government official named Alexis de Tocqueville [TOHK•vihl] traveled down the Ohio River. The river was the border between Ohio, a free state, and Kentucky, a slave state. Tocqueville noted what he saw on both sides of the river.

A VOICE FROM THE PAST

The State of Ohio is separated from Kentucky just by one river; on either side of it the soil is equally fertile, and the situation equally favourable, and yet everything is different. Here [on the Ohio side] a population devoured by feverish activity, trying every means to make its fortune. . . . There [on the Kentucky side] are people who make others work for them and show little compassion, a people without energy, mettle or the spirit of enterprise. . . . These differences cannot be attributed to any other cause but slavery.

Alexis de Tocqueville, *Journey to America*

Alexis de Tocqueville

In this section, you will read about the differences between the North and the South.

North and South Take Different Paths

As you read in Chapter 11, the economies of the North and the South developed differently in the early 1800s. Although both economies were mostly agricultural, the North began to develop more industry and commerce. By contrast, the Southern economy relied on plantation farming.

The growth of industry in the North helped lead to the rapid growth of Northern cities. Much of this population growth came from immigration. In addition, immigrants and Easterners moved west and built farms in the new states formed from the Northwest Territory. Most canals and railroads ran east and west, helping the Eastern and Midwestern states develop strong ties with each other.

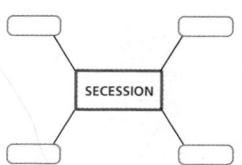

Taking Notes

Use your chart to take notes about the Wilmot Proviso and the Compromise of 1850.

SECESSION

Economics *in* History

Trade

Trade is based on a simple idea. If you have something someone else needs or wants, and that person has something you need or want, you exchange, or trade, those two things. After the trade, you should both be better off than before.

The concept of trade works similarly for groups of people. For example, in the early 1800s, the South had few factories. Planters who wanted manufactured goods usually had to buy them from manufacturers in the North or in Europe. To have the cash to buy those goods, Southerners sold other goods, such as cotton, to the North and other countries. Each sold the goods they could produce in order to get money to buy the goods they could not make.

CONNECT TO HISTORY
1. **Solving Problems** What problem does trade help a country solve? How else could a country solve this problem?
 See Skillbuilder Handbook, page R18.

CONNECT TO TODAY
2. **Comparing** What goods do Americans sell to other countries today? What goods do Americans buy from other countries?
For more about trade . . .

RESEARCH LINKS
CLASSZONE.COM

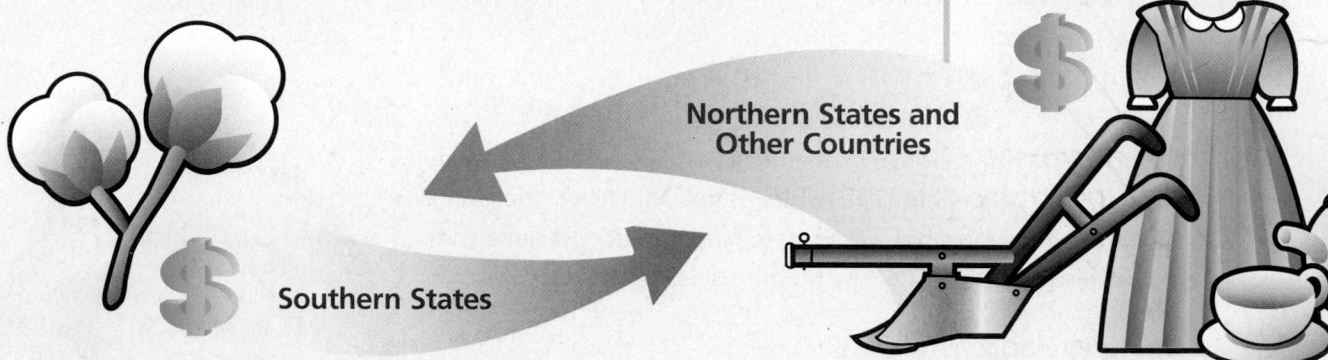

Northern States and Other Countries

Southern States

The South developed differently than the North. A few wealthy planters controlled Southern society. They made great profits from the labor of their slaves. Much of this profit came from trade. Planters relied on exports, especially cotton. Because these plantations were so profitable, planters invested in slaves instead of industry. As a result, the South developed little industry.

Most Southern whites were poor farmers who owned no slaves. But even many of the nonslaveholding whites supported slavery because it kept them off the bottom of society.

Reading **History**

A. Making Generalizations How did the economies of the North and the South differ?

Antislavery and Racism

The issue of slavery caused tension between the North and the South. In the North, the antislavery movement had slowly been gaining strength since the 1830s. Abolitionists believed that slavery was unjust and should be abolished immediately. Many Northerners who opposed slavery took a less extreme position. Some Northern workers and immigrants opposed slavery because it was an economic threat to them. Because slaves did not work for pay, free workers feared that managers would employ slaves rather than them. Some workers were even afraid that the expansion of slavery might force workers into slavery to find jobs.

Despite their opposition to slavery, most Northerners, even abolitionists, were racist by modern standards. Many whites refused to go to

school with, work with, or live near African Americans. In most states, even free African Americans could not vote.

Vocabulary
racist: having prejudice based on race

When Northern attacks on slavery increased, slaveholders defended slavery. Most offered the openly racist argument that white people were superior to blacks. Many also claimed that slavery helped slaves by introducing them to Christianity, as well as providing them with food, clothing, and shelter throughout their lives. Slaveholders were determined to defend slavery and their way of life. In this way, the different ideas about slavery brought the North and the South into conflict.

The Wilmot Proviso

After the Missouri Compromise in 1820, political disagreements over slavery seemed to go away. But new disagreements arose with the outbreak of the War with Mexico in 1846. Many Northerners believed that Southerners wanted to take territory from Mexico in order to extend slavery. To prevent that, Representative David Wilmot of Pennsylvania proposed a bill, known as the **Wilmot Proviso,** to outlaw slavery in any territory the United States might acquire from the War with Mexico.

But slaveholders believed that Congress had no right to prevent them from bringing slaves into any of the territories. They viewed slaves as property. The Constitution, they claimed, gave equal protection to the property rights of all U.S. citizens. The Wilmot Proviso removed the right of slaveholders to take their slaves, which they regarded as property, anywhere in the United States or its territories. Southerners claimed that the bill was unconstitutional.

The Wilmot Proviso divided Congress along regional lines. The bill passed the House of Representatives. But Southerners prevented it from passing the Senate.

Even though the Wilmot Proviso never became law, it had important effects. It led to the creation of the **Free-Soil Party,** a political party dedicated to stopping the expansion of slavery. The party's slogan expressed its ideals—"Free Soil, Free Speech, Free Labor, and Free Men." The Free-Soil Party won more than ten seats in Congress in the election of 1848. More important, the party made slavery a key issue in national politics. Politicians could ignore slavery no longer.

Reading **History**
B. Recognizing Effects What were the effects of the Wilmot Proviso?

Connections TO WORLD HISTORY

EXPANDING SLAVERY

William Walker, a Tennessee-born adventurer, wanted to take over land in Central America. In 1855, he joined an army of Nicaraguan rebels and seized power. Walker declared himself president of Nicaragua in 1856. As president, he legalized slavery there.

Troops from nearby countries drove him from power in 1857. The actions of men like Walker helped to convince Northerners that slaveholders were intent on expanding slavery beyond the U.S. South.

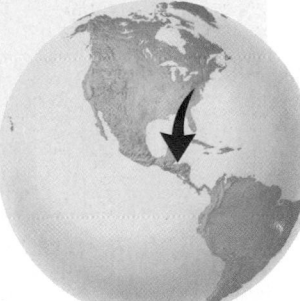

Controversy over Territories

By 1848, the nation's leaders had begun to debate how to deal with slavery in the lands gained from the War with Mexico. The proposed addition of new states threatened the balance in Congress between North and South. The discovery of gold in California brought thousands of people into that territory. There would soon be enough people in California for it to apply for statehood. Most California residents wanted their state to

be a free state. But this would tip the balance of power clearly in favor of the North. Southerners wanted to divide California in half, making the northern half a free state and the southern half a slave state.

In 1849, President Zachary Taylor—who opposed the extension of slavery—proposed that California submit a plan for statehood that year, without going through the territorial stage. Taylor's plan gave Southern slaveholders little time to move to California with their slaves.

In March 1850, California applied to be admitted as a free state. With California as a free state, slave states would become a minority in the Senate just as they were in the House. Jefferson Davis, a senator from Mississippi, warned, "For the first time, we are about permanently to destroy the balance of power between the sections."

The Compromise of 1850

California could not gain statehood, however, without the approval of Congress. And Congress was divided over the issue. Behind the scenes, statesmen sought compromise. Taking the lead was Senator **Henry Clay**

Background
U.S. land gains from the War with Mexico included all or parts of the future states of California, Nevada, Utah, Arizona, New Mexico, and Colorado.

This engraving dramatically portrays the Senate debate over the Compromise of 1850.

Henry Clay led the Congress in creating compromises on several important issues during his long career.

John C. Calhoun of South Carolina opposed the Compromise of 1850. He believed the South had no reason to compromise on the issue of slavery.

Daniel Webster spoke eloquently in favor of the compromise.

of Kentucky. Clay had helped create the Missouri Compromise in 1820. Now Clay crafted a plan to settle the California problem.

*Reading*History
C. Reading a Map
Look at the map on page 464 to see how the Compromise of 1850 affected the territories open to slavery.

1. To please the North, California would be admitted as a free state, and the slave trade would be abolished in Washington, D.C.
2. To please the South, Congress would not pass laws regarding slavery for the rest of the territories won from Mexico, and Congress would pass a stronger law to help slaveholders recapture runaway slaves.

Many people on both sides felt they had to give up too much in this plan. But others were tired of the regional bickering. They wanted to hold the Union together. **Daniel Webster,** senator from Massachusetts, supported the compromise for the sake of the Union.

A VOICE FROM THE PAST

I wish to speak today, not as a Massachusetts man, nor as a Northern man, but as an American. . . . I speak today for the preservation of the Union. Hear me for my cause.

Daniel Webster, quoted in *The Annals of America*

The job of winning passage of the plan fell to Senator **Stephen A. Douglas** of Illinois. By the end of September, Douglas succeeded, and the plan, now known as the **Compromise of 1850,** became law.

Some people celebrated the compromise, believing that it had saved the Union. But the compromise would not bring peace. In the next section, you will learn how sectional tensions continued to rise.

AMERICA'S HISTORY MAKERS

STEPHEN A. DOUGLAS
1813–1861

Stephen A. Douglas was one of the most powerful members of Congress in the mid-1800s. In fact, he was called the "Little Giant" because he commanded great respect even though he was only five feet four inches tall.

Perhaps the most important issue that Douglas faced during his career was the expansion of slavery into the territories. Douglas privately hated slavery. But he did not believe a debate on morality would do any good. He suggested that the people of each territory should decide whether or not to allow slavery.

What groups of Americans agreed with Douglas's position on slavery?

Section 1 Assessment

1. Terms & Names

Explain the significance of:
• Wilmot Proviso
• Free-Soil Party
• Henry Clay
• Daniel Webster
• Stephen A. Douglas
• Compromise of 1850

2. Using Graphics

Use a chart like the one below to explain the effects of each cause.

Causes	Effects
Abolitionism	
Wilmot Proviso	
California's application for statehood	

Which issue do you think most threatened national unity?

3. Main Ideas

a. What were two ways that the North and the South differed by the mid-1800s?

b. In what ways was racism common in both the North and the South?

c. How did the War with Mexico lead to conflict between the North and the South?

4. Critical Thinking

Comparing and Contrasting How was the Compromise of 1850 similar to and different from the Missouri Compromise?

THINK ABOUT
• the regional tensions at the time the compromises were proposed
• who proposed each bill
• the provisions of the bills

ACTIVITY OPTIONS

TECHNOLOGY

SPEECH

Imagine you are a television news director. Plan a five-minute **documentary** or organize a **panel discussion** on the Compromise of 1850.

The Crisis Deepens

MAIN IDEA	WHY IT MATTERS NOW	TERMS & NAMES
Turmoil over slavery led to acts of violence.	Violence can make compromise more difficult.	Harriet Beecher Stowe *Uncle Tom's Cabin* Fugitive Slave Act — popular sovereignty Kansas–Nebraska Act John Brown

ONE AMERICAN'S STORY

Harriet Beecher Stowe was outraged when she heard about the part of the Compromise of 1850 that would help slaveholders recapture runaway slaves. She stated that the Christian men who passed this law "cannot know what slavery is."

Stowe's anger motivated her to write **Uncle Tom's Cabin**, a novel that portrayed slavery as brutal and immoral. In this section, you will learn how the Compromise of 1850 deepened the division between the North and the South.

Harriet Beecher Stowe

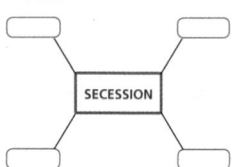

Taking Notes

Use your chart to take notes about the Kansas-Nebraska Act.

SECESSION

The Fugitive Slave Act

The 1850 law to help slaveholders recapture runaway slaves was called the **Fugitive Slave Act**. People accused of being fugitives under this law could be held without an arrest warrant. In addition, they had no right to a jury trial. Instead, a federal commissioner ruled on each case. The commissioner received five dollars for releasing the defendant and ten dollars for turning the defendant over to a slaveholder.

Southerners felt that the Fugitive Slave Act was justified because they considered slaves to be property. But Northerners resented the Fugitive Slave Act. It required Northerners to help recapture runaway slaves. It placed fines on people who would not cooperate and jail terms on people who helped the fugitives escape. In addition, Southern slave catchers roamed the North, sometimes capturing free African Americans.

The presence of slave catchers throughout the North brought home the issue of slavery to Northerners. They could no longer ignore the fact that, by supporting the Fugitive Slave Act, they played an important role in supporting slavery. They faced a moral choice. Should they

obey the law and support slavery, or should they break the law and oppose slavery?

Uncle Tom's Cabin

Reading History
A. Analyzing Points of View
How did the play *Uncle Tom's Cabin* affect the development of drama in the United States?

Stowe published *Uncle Tom's Cabin* in 1852. It dramatically portrayed the moral issues of slavery. In fact, a play based on the book increased the popularity of drama as well as abolitionism. The book's main character was Uncle Tom, a respected older slave. The plot centers on Tom's life under three owners. Two of the owners were kind, but the third was cruel. The novel includes dramatic scenes, such as the dangerous escape of a slave named Eliza and her baby across the Ohio River.

A VOICE FROM THE PAST

Eliza made her desperate retreat across the river just in the dusk of twilight. The gray mist of evening, rising slowly from the river, enveloped her as she disappeared up the bank, and the swollen current and floundering masses of ice presented a hopeless barrier between her and her pursuer.

Harriet Beecher Stowe, *Uncle Tom's Cabin*

Stowe's book was wildly popular in the North. But white Southerners believed the book falsely criticized the South and slavery.

The Kansas–Nebraska Act

While the Fugitive Slave Act and *Uncle Tom's Cabin* heightened the conflicts between the North and the South, the issue of slavery in the territories brought bloodshed to the West. In 1854, Senator Stephen A. Douglas of Illinois drafted a bill to organize territorial governments for the Nebraska Territory. He proposed that it be divided into two territories—Nebraska and Kansas.

To get Southern support for the bill, he suggested that the decision about whether to allow slavery in each of these territories be settled by popular sovereignty. **Popular sovereignty** is a system where the residents vote to decide an issue. If this bill passed, it would result in getting rid of the Missouri Compromise by

In 1854, Bostonians protested the capture of an African American by federal marshals under the Fugitive Slave Act.

Background
The Nebraska Territory was part of the Louisiana Purchase. It lay north of the 36° 30' line, so the Missouri Compromise banned slavery there.

463

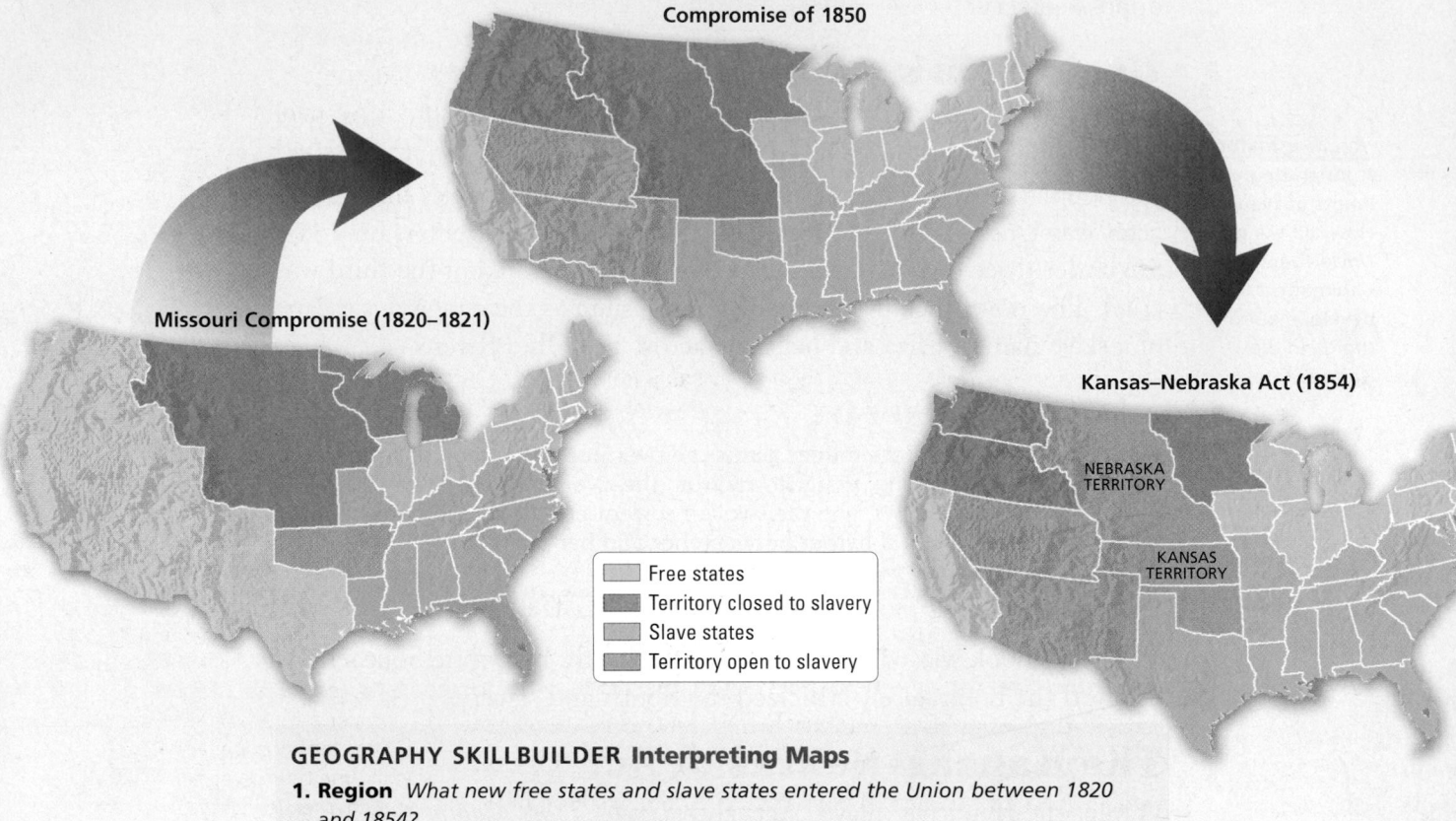

Compromise of 1850

Missouri Compromise (1820–1821)

Kansas–Nebraska Act (1854)

NEBRASKA TERRITORY

KANSAS TERRITORY

☐ Free states
■ Territory closed to slavery
☐ Slave states
■ Territory open to slavery

GEOGRAPHY SKILLBUILDER Interpreting Maps
1. **Region** *What new free states and slave states entered the Union between 1820 and 1854?*
2. **Region** *How did the Kansas–Nebraska Act change the amount of territory open to slavery?*

allowing people to vote for slavery in territories where the Missouri Compromise had banned it.

As Douglas hoped, Southerners applauded the repeal of the Missouri Compromise and supported the bill. Even though the bill angered opponents of slavery, it passed. It became known as the **Kansas–Nebraska Act**. Few people realized that the act would soon turn Kansas into a battleground over slavery.

"Bleeding Kansas"

Proslavery and antislavery settlers rushed into the Kansas Territory, just west of Missouri, to vote for the territorial legislature. At the time of the election in March 1855, there were more proslavery settlers than antislavery settlers in the territory. But the proslavery forces did not want to risk losing the election. Five thousand Missourians came and voted in the election illegally. As a result, the official Kansas legislature was packed with proslavery representatives.

Antislavery settlers boycotted the official government and formed a government of their own. With political authority in dispute, settlers on both sides armed themselves. In May, a proslavery mob attacked the town of Lawrence, Kansas. The attackers destroyed offices and the

Vocabulary
boycott: refuse to participate in

house of the governor of the antislavery government. This attack came to be known as the Sack of Lawrence.

Onto this explosive scene came **John Brown,** an extreme abolitionist. To avenge the Sack of Lawrence, Brown and seven other men went to the cabins of several of his proslavery neighbors and murdered five people. This attack is known as the Pottawatomie Massacre, after the creek near where the victims were found. As news of the violence spread, civil war broke out in Kansas. It continued for three years, and the territory came to be called "Bleeding Kansas."

*Reading*History

B. Sequencing Events What events in Kansas preceded the Pottawatomie Massacre?

Violence in Congress

While violence was spreading in Kansas in the spring of 1856, blood was also being shed in the nation's capital. In late May, Senator Charles Sumner of Massachusetts delivered a speech attacking the proslavery forces in Kansas. His speech was packed with insults. Sumner even made fun of A. P. Butler, a senator from South Carolina.

Preston Brooks, a relative of Butler, heard about Sumner's speech. To defend Butler and the South, he attacked Sumner, who was sitting at his desk. Brooks hit Sumner over the head with his cane. Sumner tried to defend himself, but his legs were trapped. Brooks hit him 30 times or more, breaking his cane in the assault. (The painting on page 455 shows this event.)

Many Southerners cheered Brooks's defense of the South. But most Northerners were shocked at the violence in the Senate. "Bleeding Kansas" and "Bleeding Sumner" became rallying cries for antislavery Northerners and slogans for a new political party. In the next section, you will learn about the creation of the Republican Party.

STRANGE *but* True

PRESTON BROOKS'S CANE
Many Americans, Northerners and Southerners alike, were ashamed of the behavior of Sumner and Brooks. But sectional tensions were so high at the time that a large number of Southerners cheered Brooks for his actions.

A number of Brooks's supporters sent him new canes to replace the one he had broken while hitting Sumner on the head. Some of the canes were inscribed with mottoes such as "Hit Him Again."

Section 2 Assessment

1. Terms & Names

Explain the significance of:
• Harriet Beecher Stowe
• *Uncle Tom's Cabin*
• Fugitive Slave Act
• popular sovereignty
• Kansas–Nebraska Act
• John Brown

2. Using Graphics

Use a chart like the one below to compare Northern and Southern views of the issues listed.

Northern View	Issue	Southern View
	Fugitive Slave Act	
	Kansas–Nebraska Act	
	"Bleeding Kansas"	

3. Main Ideas

a. How did the book *Uncle Tom's Cabin* influence national politics?

b. Why was the Kansas–Nebraska Act so controversial?

c. What was the cause of "Bleeding Kansas"?

4. Critical Thinking

Solving Problems What would you have done to prevent the violence in Kansas?

THINK ABOUT
• the repeal of the Missouri Compromise
• popular sovereignty
• the actions of John Brown

ACTIVITY OPTIONS

LITERATURE

ART

Read a chapter of *Uncle Tom's Cabin.* Write a **book review** or make a series of **drawings** illustrating the story.

Slavery Dominates Politics

MAIN IDEA	WHY IT MATTERS NOW	TERMS & NAMES
Disagreement over slavery led to the formation of the Republican Party and heightened sectional tensions.	The Democrats and the Republicans are the major political parties of today.	Republican Party John C. Frémont James Buchanan *Dred Scott* v. *Sandford* Roger B. Taney Abraham Lincoln Harpers Ferry

ONE AMERICAN'S STORY

Joseph Warren, editor of the Detroit *Tribune,* wanted the antislavery parties of Michigan to join forces.

A VOICE FROM THE PAST

[A convention should be called] irrespective of the old party organizations, for the purpose of agreeing upon some plan of action that shall combine the whole anti-Nebraska, anti-slavery sentiment of the State, upon one ticket [set of candidates endorsed by a political party].

Detroit *Tribune,* quoted in *The Origins of the Republican Party*

This medal shows an early motto of the Republican Party. It also makes clear the Republican connection to the antislavery position of the Free-Soil Party.

On July 6, 1854, antislavery politicians from various parties met to form a new party and called themselves Republicans. In this section, you will learn why the Republican Party was formed and how it changed American politics in the 1850s.

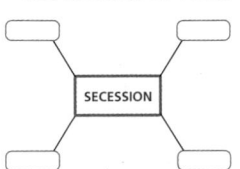

Taking Notes

Use your chart to take notes about the election of 1860.

SECESSION

The Republican Party Forms

The creation of the Republican Party grew out of the problems caused by the Kansas–Nebraska Act of 1854. The law immediately caused a political crisis for the Whig Party. Southern Whigs had supported the bill for the same reason that Northern Whigs had opposed it: the bill proposed to open new territories to slavery. There was no room for compromise, so the party split.

The Southern Whigs were destroyed by the split. A few joined the Democratic Party. But most searched for leaders who supported slavery and the Union. The Northern Whigs, however, joined with other opponents of slavery and formed the **Republican Party.**

The Republicans quickly gained strength in the North. "Bleeding Kansas" was the key to the Republican rise. Many people blamed the violence on the Democrats. With the 1856 elections nearing, the

Republicans believed that they had an excellent opportunity to gain seats in Congress and win the presidency.

The Republicans needed a strong presidential candidate in 1856 to strengthen their young party. They nominated **John C. Frémont**. Young and handsome, Frémont was a national hero for his explorations in the West, which earned him the nickname the "Pathfinder."

*Reading*History

A. Summarizing Why did the Republicans nominate Frémont for president in 1856?

Republicans liked Frémont for a couple of reasons. He had spoken in favor of admitting both California and Kansas as free states. Also, he had little political experience and did not have a controversial record to defend. Even so, the Republican position on slavery was so unpopular in the South that Frémont's name did not appear on the ballot there.

The Election of 1856

The Democrats nominated **James Buchanan** to run for the presidency in 1856. As minister to Great Britain, he had been in England since 1853 and had spoken neither for nor against the Kansas–Nebraska Act.

Buchanan took advantage of his absence from the country. He said little about slavery and claimed that his goal was to maintain the Union. Buchanan appealed to Southerners, to many people in the upper South and the border states, and to Northerners who were afraid that Frémont's election could tear the nation apart.

The American, or Know-Nothing, Party also nominated a presidential candidate in 1856. They chose Millard Fillmore, who had been president, following the death of Zachary Taylor, from 1850 until 1853. But the Know-Nothings were divided over slavery and had little strength.

The 1856 presidential election broke down into two separate races. In the North, it was Buchanan against Frémont. In the South, it was Buchanan against Fillmore. Buchanan won. He carried all the slave states except Maryland, where Fillmore claimed his only victory. Buchanan also won several Northern states.

Although he lost the election, Frémont won 11 Northern states. These results showed two things. First, the Republican Party was a major force in the North. Second, the nation was sharply split over slavery.

The Case of Dred Scott

The split in the country was made worse by the Supreme Court decision in the case of Dred Scott. Scott had been a slave in Missouri. His owner took him to live in territories where slavery was illegal. Then they returned to Missouri. After his owner's death, Scott sued for his freedom. He argued that he was a free man because he had lived in territories where slavery was illegal. His case, **_Dred Scott v. Sandford_**, reached the Supreme Court in 1856.

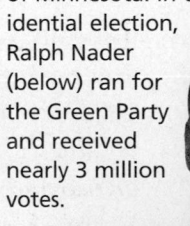

THIRD-PARTY CANDIDATES
American politics has usually been dominated by two parties. Most third-party candidates, such as the Republican Frémont in 1856, lose elections. Still, third parties are important. Women's right to vote, child labor laws, and the Social Security Act all began as third-party initiatives.

Modern third parties such as the Libertarian, Reform, and Green parties, continue to run candidates for office. In 1998, Reform Party candidate Jesse Ventura was elected governor of Minnesota. In the 2000 presidential election, Ralph Nader (below) ran for the Green Party and received nearly 3 million votes.

In 1857, the Court ruled against Scott. Chief Justice **Roger B. Taney** [TAW•nee] delivered his opinion in the case. In it, he said that Dred Scott was not a U.S. citizen. As a result, he could not sue in U.S. courts. Taney also ruled that Scott was bound by Missouri's slave code because he lived in Missouri. As a result, Scott's time in free territory did not matter in his case.

In addition, Taney argued that Congress could not ban slavery in the territories. To do so would violate the slaveholders' property rights, protected by the Fifth Amendment. In effect, Taney declared legislation such as the Missouri Compromise unconstitutional.

*Reading*History
B. Recognizing Effects How did Taney's opinion affect the Missouri Compromise?

Southerners cheered the Court's decision. Many Northerners were outraged and looked to the Republican Party to halt the growing power of Southern slaveholders.

Dred Scott (above) first sued for his freedom in 1846. The Supreme Court, led by Chief Justice Roger B. Taney (right), did not rule on the case until 1857.

Lincoln and Douglas Debate

After the *Dred Scott* decision, the Republicans charged that the Democrats wanted to legalize slavery not only in all U.S. territories but also in all the states. They used this charge to attack individual Democrats. Stephen A. Douglas, sponsor of the Kansas–Nebraska Act, was one of their main targets in 1858. That year, Illinois Republicans nominated **Abraham Lincoln** to challenge Douglas for his U.S. Senate seat. In his first campaign speech, Lincoln expressed the Northern fear that Southerners wanted to expand slavery to the entire nation. He set the stage for his argument by using a metaphor from the Bible.

A VOICE FROM THE PAST

"A house divided against itself cannot stand." I believe this government cannot endure, permanently half slave and half free. I do not expect the Union to be dissolved—I do not expect the house to fall—but I do expect it will cease to be divided. It will become all one thing, or all the other.

Abraham Lincoln, Springfield, Illinois, June 16, 1858

Later in the year, the two men held formal debates across Illinois. The Lincoln–Douglas debates are now seen as models of political debate. At the time, the debates allowed people to compare the short, stocky, well-dressed Douglas with the tall, thin, gawky Lincoln.

The two men squarely addressed the nation's most pressing issue: the expansion of slavery. For Lincoln, slavery was "a moral, a social and a political wrong." But he did not suggest abolishing slavery where it already existed. He argued only that slavery should not be expanded.

Douglas did not share Lincoln's belief that it was the national government's role to prevent the expansion of slavery. Instead, he argued

Debating Points of View

Debate has long been an important method of exploring public issues. The Lincoln-Douglas debates drew crowds from all over Illinois to hear Lincoln and Douglas discuss the issues of the day. Debates such as these can help people find out about candidates' views.

Today, the National Forensic League (NFL) sponsors Lincoln-Douglas Debates, competitions for high school students. Many judges, actors, news commentators, and talk show hosts began to develop their debating skills in such competitions.

High school students can benefit from learning to defend their positions in debates. One student explained what she learned from NFL debates. "I learned about how to think really fast and how to respond."

Jessica Bailey of Apple Valley High School in Minnesota won second place in the national Lincoln-Douglas Debates competition in 1998.

How Do You Debate an Issue?

1. Choose a debate opponent and an issue to debate. (One NFL topic for national competition was whether the federal government should establish an educational policy to increase academic achievement in secondary schools in the United States.)
2. Research the topic you chose.
3. Agree on a format for your debate—how many minutes for presentation, rebuttal, and closing.
4. Debate your opponent in front of the class.
5. Find out how many students in the audience agree with each side, then ask for their reasons.

 See Citizenship Handbook, page 285.

For more about debating . . .

 **RESEARCH LINKS** CLASSZONE.COM

that popular sovereignty was the best way to address the issue because it was the most democratic method to do so.

But popular sovereignty was a problem for Douglas. The Supreme Court decision in the *Dred Scott* case had made popular sovereignty unconstitutional. Why? It said that people could not vote to ban slavery, because doing so would take away slaveholders' property rights. In the debates, Lincoln asked Douglas if he thought people in a territory who were against slavery could legally prohibit it—despite the *Dred Scott* decision.

Douglas replied that it did not matter what the Supreme Court might decide about slavery because "the people have the lawful means to introduce it or exclude it as they please." Douglas won reelection. Lincoln, despite his loss, became a national figure and strengthened his standing in the Republican Party.

Reading **History**
C. Making Inferences Why were popular sovereignty and the opinion in the *Dred Scott* case inconsistent?

John Brown Attacks Harpers Ferry

In 1859, John Brown, who had murdered proslavery Kansans three years before, added to the sectional tensions. Brown had a plan. He wanted to inspire slaves to fight for their freedom. To do this, he planned to capture the weapons in the U.S. arsenal at **Harpers Ferry,** Virginia.

On October 16, 1859, Brown and 18 followers—13 whites and 5 blacks—captured the Harpers Ferry arsenal. They killed four people in the raid. Brown then sent out the word to rally and arm local slaves.

Vocabulary
arsenal: stock of weapons

John Steuart Curry painted *The Tragic Prelude* between 1937 and 1942. He shows a wild-eyed John Brown standing on the bodies of Civil War soldiers.

What do you think Curry's views were on John Brown's role in U.S. history?

But no slaves joined the fight. The U.S. Marines attacked Brown at Harpers Ferry. Some of his men escaped. But Brown and six others were captured, and ten men were killed.

Brown was then tried for murder and treason. He was convicted and sentenced to hang. On the day he was hanged, abolitionists tolled bells and fired guns in salute. Southerners were enraged by Brown's actions and horrified by Northern reactions to his death.

As the nation headed toward the election of 1860, the issue of slavery had raised sectional tensions to the breaking point. In the next section, you will read about the election of 1860 and its effect on the nation.

Section 3 Assessment

1. Terms & Names

Explain the significance of:

- Republican Party
- John C. Frémont
- James Buchanan
- *Dred Scott* v. *Sandford*
- Roger B. Taney
- Abraham Lincoln
- Harpers Ferry

2. Using Graphics

Use a chart like the one below to take notes on the major events discussed in this section.

Election of 1856	
Dred Scott v. *Sandford*	
Lincoln–Douglas debates	
Harpers Ferry	

3. Main Ideas

a. What issues led to the creation of the Republican Party?

b. What consequences did the *Dred Scott* decision have for free blacks?

c. How did John Brown's attack on Harpers Ferry increase tensions between the North and the South?

4. Critical Thinking

Identifying Facts and Opinions How did Lincoln and Douglas disagree about slavery? Which of their views were facts, and which were opinions?

THINK ABOUT

- Lincoln's speech at Springfield in 1858
- Douglas's support of popular sovereignty

ACTIVITY OPTIONS

MATH

GEOGRAPHY

Do research to find election returns from the 1856 presidential election. Make **graphs** or draw a **map** to illustrate the results.

Lincoln's Election and Southern Secession

MAIN IDEA	WHY IT MATTERS NOW	TERMS & NAMES
The election of Lincoln led the Southern states to secede from the Union.	This was the only time in U.S. history that states seceded from the Union.	platform — Jefferson Davis secede — Crittenden Plan Confederate States of America

ONE AMERICAN'S STORY

In 1860, most people assumed that William Seward of New York would win the Rebublican party's presidential nomination.

However, throughout the Republican convention, other candidates tried to win away Seward's delegates. Abraham Lincoln, a lesser-known candidate from Illinois, gained strength. The reporter Murat Halstead described the scene as Lincoln received the winning votes.

A VOICE FROM THE PAST

There was a moment's silence. The nerves of the thousands, which through the hours of suspense had been subjected to terrible tension, relaxed, and as deep breaths of relief were taken, there was a noise in the Wigwam [convention hall] like the rush of a great wind [just before] a storm—and in another breath, the storm was there. There were thousands cheering with the energy of insanity.

Murat Halstead, *Caucuses of 1860*

In 1860, the Republican delegates met in Chicago at a convention hall known as the Wigwam.

Having won the nomination, Lincoln could turn his attention to winning the general election. In this section, you will learn about the election of 1860 and its role in pushing the nation toward civil war.

Political Parties Splinter

In April, a few weeks before the Republicans nominated Abraham Lincoln, the Democrats held their convention in Charleston, South Carolina. Northern and Southern Democrats disagreed over what to say about slavery in the party's **platform,** or statement of beliefs.

The Southerners wanted the party to defend slavery in the platform.

Taking Notes

Use your chart to take notes about the election of 1860.

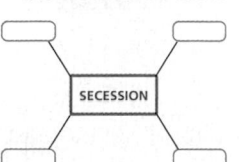

SECESSION

The Nation Breaking Apart **471**

But Northerners wanted the platform to support popular sovereignty as a way of deciding whether a territory became a free state or a slave state. The Northerners won the platform vote, causing 50 Southern delegates to walk out of the convention.

The remaining delegates tried to nominate a presidential candidate. Stephen A. Douglas was the leading contender, but the Southerners who stayed refused to back him because of his support for popular sovereignty. Douglas could not win enough votes to gain the nomination.

Finally, the Democrats gave up and decided to meet again in Baltimore in June to choose a candidate. But as the Baltimore convention opened, Northerners and Southerners remained at odds. This time, almost all the Southerners left the meeting.

With the Southerners gone, the Northern Democrats nominated Douglas. Meanwhile, the Southern Democrats decided to nominate their own candidate. They chose John Breckinridge of Kentucky, the current vice-president and a supporter of slavery.

As you read in One American's Story on page 471, the Republicans had already nominated Abraham Lincoln. In addition to Lincoln, Douglas, and Breckinridge, a candidate from a fourth party entered the race. This party was called the Constitutional Union Party, and its members had one aim—to preserve the Union. They nominated John Bell of Tennessee to run for president.

*Reading*History

A. Recognizing Effects How did slavery affect U.S. political parties in 1860?

The Election of 1860

The election of 1860 turned into two different races for the presidency, one in the North and one in the South. Lincoln and Douglas were the only candidates with much support in the North. Breckinridge and Bell competed for Southern votes.

Lincoln and Breckinridge were considered to have the most extreme views on slavery. Lincoln opposed the expansion of slavery into the territories. Breckinridge insisted that the federal government be required to protect slavery in any territory. Douglas and Bell were considered moderates because neither wanted the federal government to pass new laws on slavery.

The outcome of the election made it clear that the nation was tired of compromise. Lincoln defeated Douglas in the North. Breckinridge carried most of the South. Douglas and Bell managed to win only in the states between the North and the Deep South. Because the North had more people in it than the South, Lincoln won the election.

This cartoon of the long-legged Abe Lincoln shows him to be the fittest candidate in the 1860 presidential election.

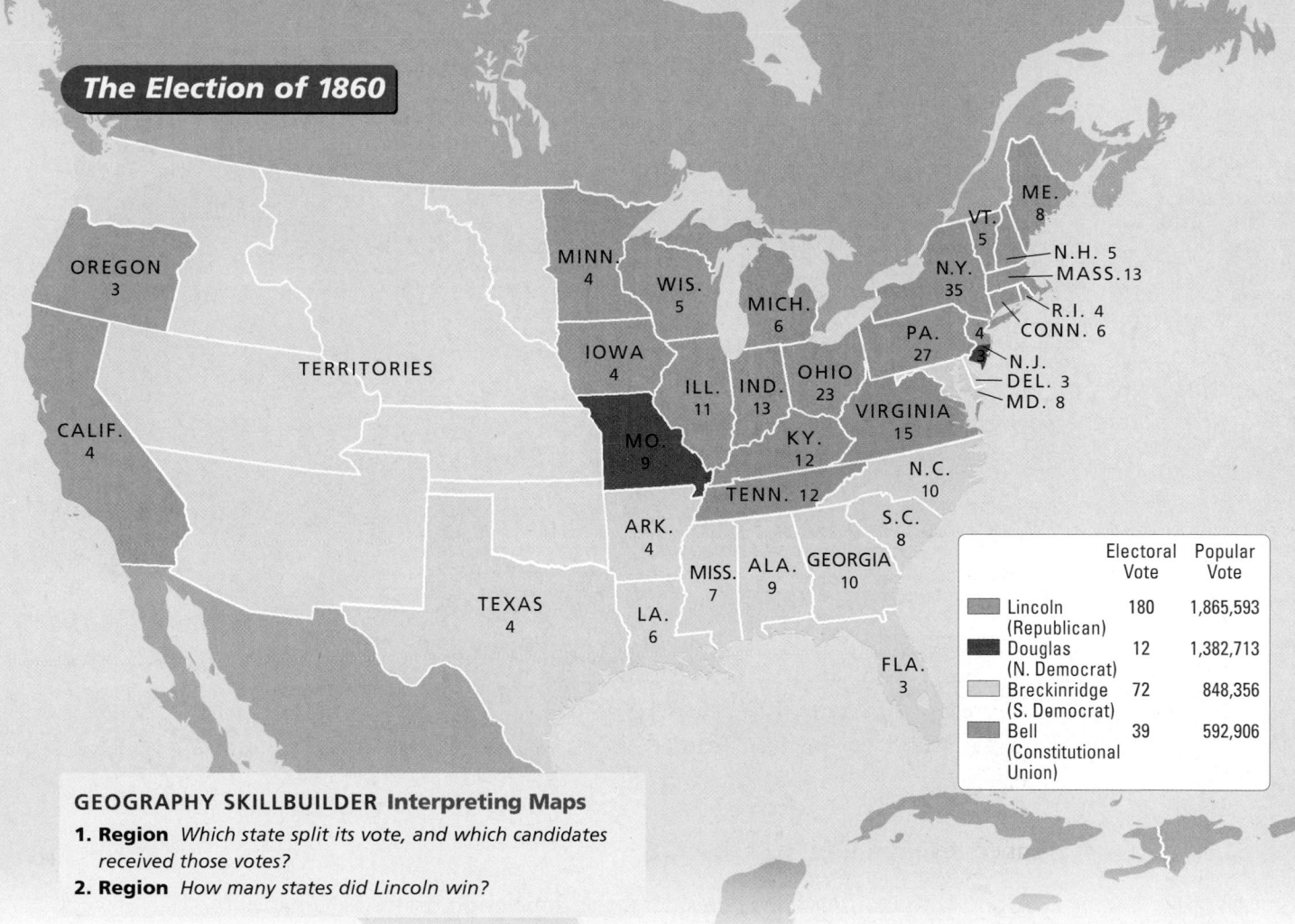

The Election of 1860

	Electoral Vote	Popular Vote
Lincoln (Republican)	180	1,865,593
Douglas (N. Democrat)	12	1,382,713
Breckinridge (S. Democrat)	72	848,356
Bell (Constitutional Union)	39	592,906

GEOGRAPHY SKILLBUILDER Interpreting Maps

1. **Region** *Which state split its vote, and which candidates received those votes?*
2. **Region** *How many states did Lincoln win?*

Despite Lincoln's statements that he would do nothing to abolish slavery in the South, white Southerners did not trust him. Many were sure that he and the other Republicans would move to ban slavery. As a result, white Southerners saw the Republican victory as a threat to the Southern way of life.

Southern States Secede

Before the 1860 presidential election, many Southerners had warned that if Lincoln won, the Southern states would **secede,** or withdraw from the Union. Supporters of secession based their arguments on the idea of states' rights. They argued that the states had voluntarily joined the Union. Consequently, they claimed that the states also had the right to leave the Union.

Background
Before becoming president of the Confederacy, Davis had been a hero during the War with Mexico and a U.S. senator.

On December 20, 1860, South Carolina became the first state to secede. Other states in the Deep South, where slave labor and cotton production were most common, also considered secession. During the next six weeks, Mississippi, Florida, Alabama, Georgia, Louisiana, and Texas joined South Carolina in secession.

In early February 1861, the states that had seceded met in Montgomery, Alabama. They formed the **Confederate States of America.** The convention named **Jefferson Davis** president of the Confederacy.

Along with naming Davis president, the convention drafted a constitution. The Confederate Constitution was modeled on the U.S. Constitution. But there were a few important differences. For example, the Confederate Constitution supported states' rights. It also protected slavery in the Confederacy, including any territories it might acquire.

Having formed its government, the Confederate states made plans to defend their separation from the Union. Some believed that war between the states could not be avoided. But everyone waited to see what the Union government would do in response.

In his First Inaugural Address, Lincoln argued passionately for the North and the South to preserve the Union.

The Union Responds to Secession

Northerners considered the secession of the Southern states to be unconstitutional. During his last months in office, President James Buchanan argued against secession. He believed that the states did not have the right to withdraw from the Union because the federal government, not the state governments, was sovereign. If secession were permitted, the Union would become weak, like a "rope of sand." He believed that the U.S. Constitution was framed to prevent such a thing from happening.

In addition to these issues, secession raised the issue of majority rule. Southerners complained that Northerners intended to use their majority to force the South to abolish slavery. But Northerners responded that Southerners simply did not want to live by the rules of democracy. They complained that Southerners were not willing to live with the election results. As Northern writer James Russell Lowell

Vocabulary
sovereign: supreme, self-governing authority

wrote, "[The Southerners'] quarrel is not with the Republican Party, but with the theory of Democracy."

Efforts to Compromise Fail

With the states in the lower South forming a new government in Montgomery, Alabama, some people continued to seek compromise. Senator John J. Crittenden of Kentucky developed a compromise plan. The **Crittenden Plan** was presented to Congress in late February 1861, but it did not pass.

With the hopes for compromise fading, Americans waited for Lincoln's inauguration. What would the new president do about the crisis? On March 4, Lincoln took the oath of office and gave his First Inaugural Address. He assured the South that he had no intention of abolishing slavery there. But he spoke forcefully against secession. Then he ended his speech with an appeal to friendship.

"We must not be enemies."
Abraham Lincoln

A VOICE FROM THE PAST

*Reading*History
B. Making Inferences What do you think Lincoln meant by "mystic chords of memory"?

We are not enemies, but friends. We must not be enemies. Though passion may have strained, it must not break our bonds of affection. The mystic chords of memory, stretching from every battle-field and patriot grave, to every living heart and hearthstone, all over this broad land, will yet swell the chorus of the Union, when again touched, as surely they will be, by the better angels of our nature.

Abraham Lincoln, *First Inaugural Address*

Lincoln would not press the South. He wanted no invasion. But he would not abandon the government's property there. Several forts in the South, including Fort Sumter in South Carolina, were still in Union hands. These forts would soon need to be resupplied. Throughout March and into April, Northerners and Southerners waited anxiously to see what would happen next. You will find out in the next chapter.

Section 4 Assessment

1. Terms & Names

Explain the significance of:
- platform
- secede
- Confederate States of America
- Jefferson Davis
- Crittenden Plan

2. Using Graphics

Use a time line to fill in the main events that occurred between April 1860 and March 1861.

April 1860   June 1860   Feb. 1861

May 1860   Nov. 1860   March 1861

Do you think secession could have been avoided? Why?

3. Main Ideas

a. Who were the candidates in the 1860 presidential election, and what policies did each candidate stand for?

b. Which states seceded right after Lincoln's election? How did they justify this action?

c. What attempts did the North and the South make to compromise? What were the results?

4. Critical Thinking

Analyzing Points of View
Do you think the Southern states seceded to protect slavery or states' rights?

THINK ABOUT
- the Southern view of the Fugitive Slave Act
- the Confederate Constitution
- slaveholders' views of the Republican Party

ACTIVITY OPTIONS

SPEECH

TECHNOLOGY

Read Lincoln's First Inaugural Address. Deliver a section of the **speech** before the class or plan an **electronic presentation** about that day and Lincoln's message.

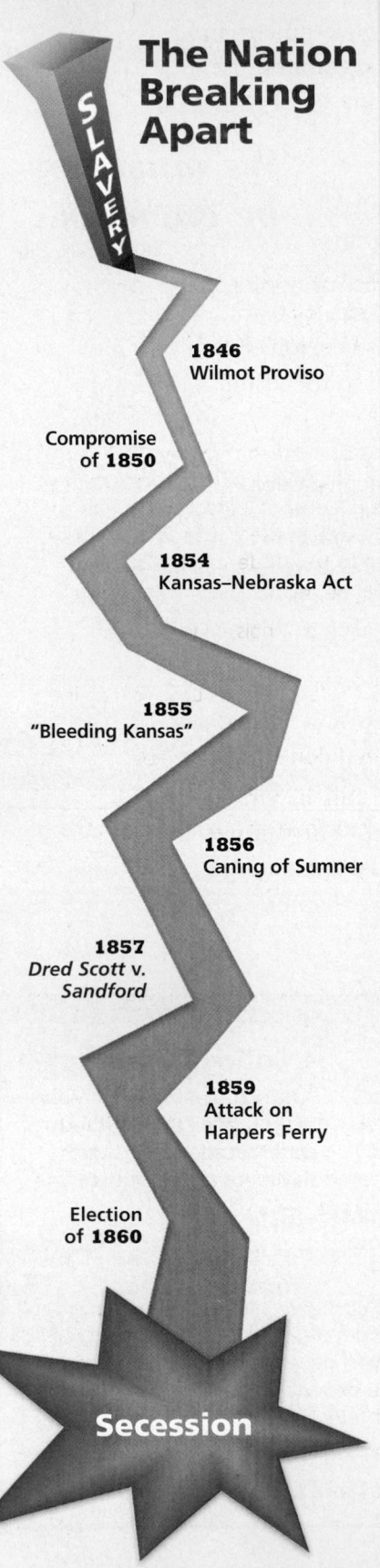

VISUAL SUMMARY

The Nation Breaking Apart

SLAVERY

1846
Wilmot Proviso

Compromise of 1850

1854
Kansas–Nebraska Act

1855
"Bleeding Kansas"

1856
Caning of Sumner

1857
Dred Scott v. Sandford

1859
Attack on Harpers Ferry

Election of 1860

Secession

TERMS & NAMES

Briefly explain the significance of each of the following.

1. Wilmot Proviso
2. Compromise of 1850
3. *Uncle Tom's Cabin*
4. popular sovereignty
5. Kansas–Nebraska Act
6. John Brown
7. John C. Frémont
8. *Dred Scott* v. *Sandford*
9. secede
10. Confederate States of America

REVIEW QUESTIONS

Growing Tensions Between North and South (pages 457–461)

1. How did the North and the South differ in the 1840s?
2. How did Southerners react to the Wilmot Proviso?
3. What was Stephen A. Douglas's role in passing the Compromise of 1850?

The Crisis Deepens (pages 462–465)

4. How did Northerners react to the Fugitive Slave Act?
5. Why did most Northerners and Southerners disagree about the Kansas–Nebraska Act?
6. How did "Bleeding Kansas" cause problems for Democrats?

Slavery Dominates Politics (pages 466–470)

7. What positions did Lincoln and Douglas take in their debates?
8. What was the result of John Brown's raid on Harpers Ferry?

Lincoln's Election and Southern Secession (pages 471–475)

9. What were the results of the election of 1860, and what did these results show?
10. How did Southerners justify secession?

CRITICAL THINKING

1. USING YOUR NOTES: ANALYZING CAUSES

Using your completed diagram, answer the questions below.

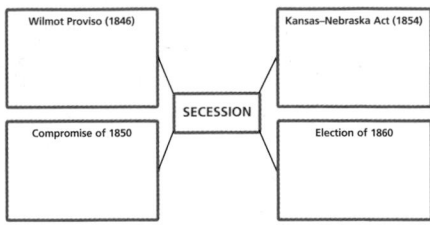

a. What did the Compromise of 1850 and the Kansas–Nebraska Act have in common?
b. Which event do you think caused the most damage to the relationship between the North and the South? Explain.

2. ANALYZING LEADERSHIP

Why were the nation's leaders in 1860 unable to compromise like the leaders in 1820 and 1850? Does their failure to compromise in 1860 mean that they were not as capable as earlier leaders?

3. APPLYING CITIZENSHIP SKILLS

What alternatives did the states in the lower South have to secession? Which of these alternatives do you think would have been the best choice?

4. SOLVING PROBLEMS

How did slavery divide Americans in the 1850s?

5. THEME: DIVERSITY AND UNITY

What could have been done in the 1850s to prevent the Southern states from seceding? What did Americans have in common that could have overcome their differences over slavery?

Interact *with* History

Now that you have read about the sectional crisis of the 1850s, do you think the solution you came up with at the start of the chapter would have helped keep the Union together? Explain.

Use the map and your knowledge of U.S. history to answer questions 1 and 2.

Additional Test Practice, pp. S1–S33.

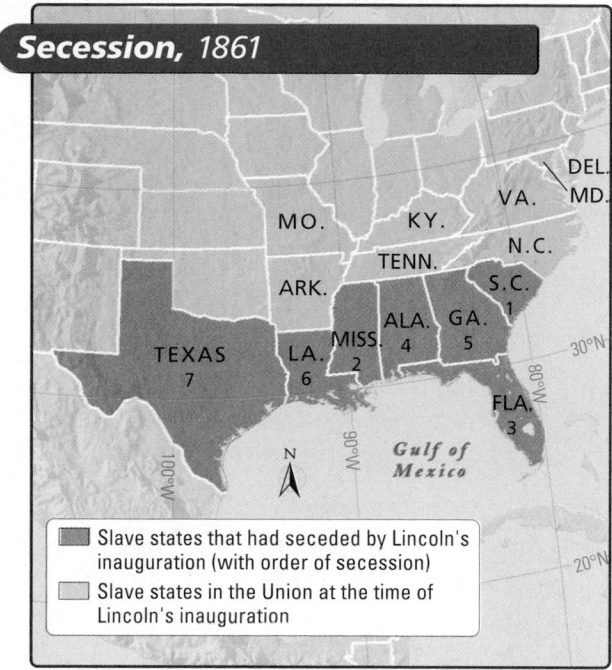

Secession, *1861*

■ Slave states that had seceded by Lincoln's inauguration (with order of secession)
□ Slave states in the Union at the time of Lincoln's inauguration

1. Of the following states, which was the last to secede before Lincoln's Inauguration?

A. South Carolina

B. Texas

C. Georgia

D. Louisiana

2. How many slave states were in the Union at the time of Lincoln's inauguration?

A. 6

B. 7

C. 8

D. 9

Abraham Lincoln is discussing the future of the United States regarding slavery in this quotation. Use the quotation and your knowledge of U.S. history to answer question 3.

PRIMARY SOURCE

"A house divided against itself cannot stand." I believe this government cannot endure, permanently half slave and half free. I do not expect the Union to be dissolved—I do not expect the house to fall—but I do expect it will cease to be divided. It will become all one thing, or all the other.

Abraham Lincoln, Springfield, Illinois, June 16, 1858

3. Which of the following best states Lincoln's point of view?

A. The states of the Union will be all free.

B. The states of the Union will be all slave.

C. The Union will remain intact.

D. The Union will be divided.

TEST PRACTICE
CLASSZONE.COM

ALTERNATIVE ASSESSMENT

1. ✎ WRITING ABOUT HISTORY

Imagine you work for a popular magazine and have been assigned to write an **article** about one of the important figures in this chapter. You might choose such figures such as Harriet Beecher Stowe or Stephen A. Douglas.

- Write a series of questions to ask this person.
- Use library resources to see how he or she might answer your questions.

2. COOPERATIVE LEARNING

Work with a small group to research the Dred Scott case and conduct a mock trial. In your research, look for information about the roles of Taney, the other justices, Scott, and other major participants. After you conduct the trial, have your class decide on a verdict.

INTEGRATED TECHNOLOGY

DOING INTERNET RESEARCH

Political parties in America changed a great deal during the 1840s and 1850s. Using the Internet or other library resources, research the election returns of the presidential elections from 1848 to 1860.

- Use an online or standard encyclopedia to find the election results.
- Prepare a presentation for your class. Create pie charts to show the percentage of votes that went to each political party in each election. Or use bar graphs to show the growth in total popular vote for each party for each election.

For more about these elections . . .

INTERNET ACTIVITY
CLASSZONE.COM

CHAPTER 16 The Civil War Begins 1861–1862

Section 1
War Erupts

Section 2
Life in the Army

Section 3
No End in Sight

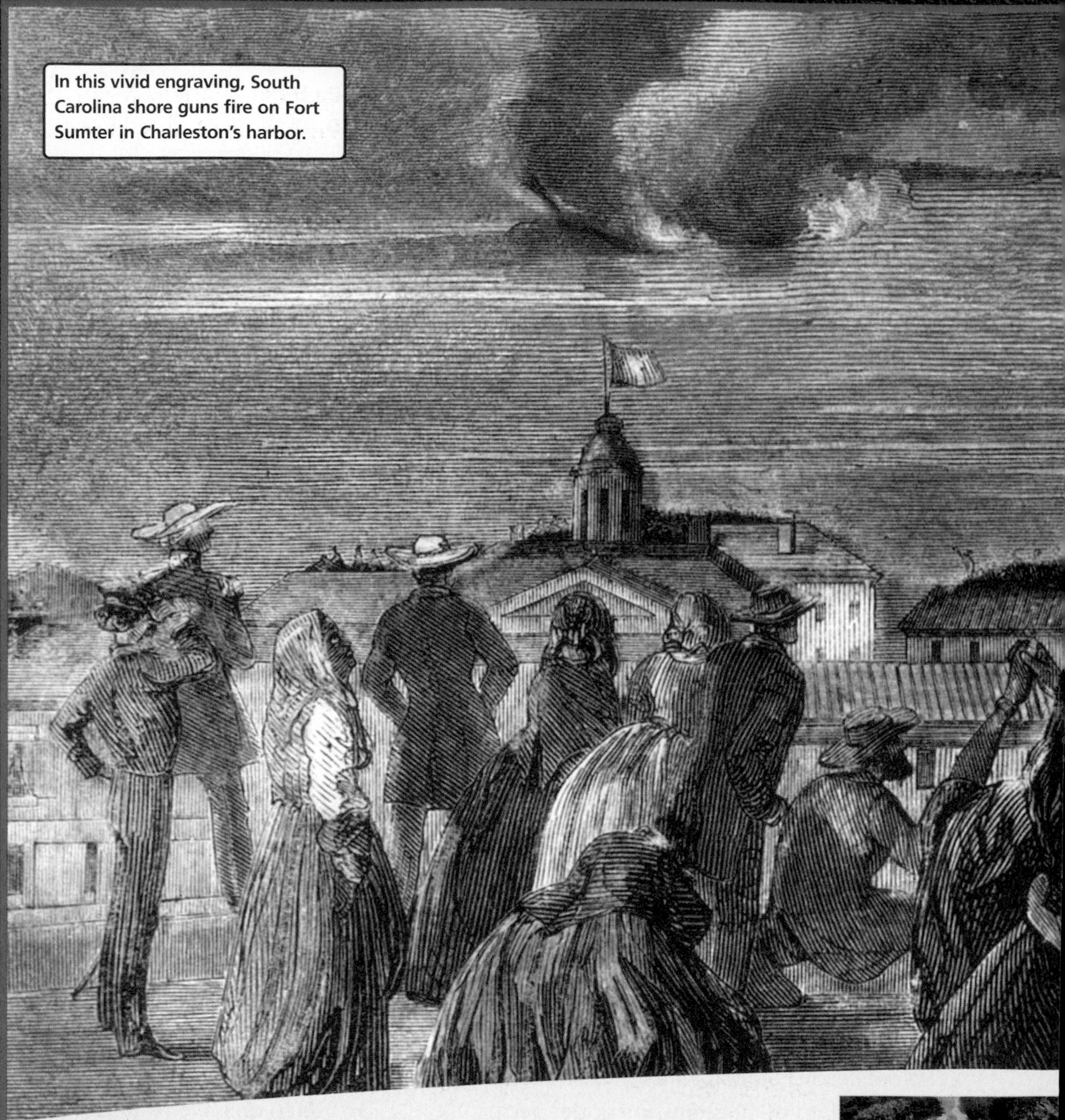

In this vivid engraving, South Carolina shore guns fire on Fort Sumter in Charleston's harbor.

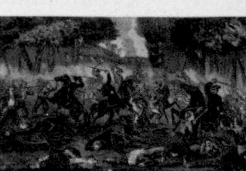

USA / World

1861

March 4, 1861
Abraham Lincoln inaugurated as president.

April 12, 1861
Confederate forces fire on Fort Sumter.

July 21, 1861
First Battle of Bull Run (Manassas) occurs.

March, 1861
Italy unified under King Victor Emmanuel II.

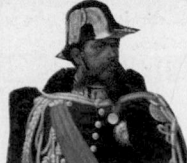

May 13, 1861
Britain declares neutrality in American Civil War.

The battle rages in the harbor.

People watch the bombardment from their rooftops.

The date is April 12, 1861. You and other residents of Charleston, South Carolina, watch the bombardment of Fort Sumter by Confederate forces. This event signals the beginning of the Civil War—a war between factions or regions of the same country.

How might a civil war be worse than other wars?

What Do You Think?

- What social, political, and economic problems might be likely to occur in a civil war?
- What might happen when a civil war breaks out?

RESEARCH LINKS
CLASSZONE.COM

Visit the Chapter 16 links for more information about the beginning of the Civil War.

March 9, 1862
The warships *Monitor* and *Merrimack* (or *Virginia*) clash.

April 6, 1862
Battle of Shiloh takes place.

April 25, 1862
New Orleans falls to Union forces.

September 17, 1862
Battle of Antietam (Sharpsburg) occurs.

April 13, 1862
France annexes Cochin China (southern Vietnam).

May 5, 1862
French troops are defeated at Puebla, Mexico.

June 25, 1862
Imperial decree expels foreigners from Japan.

September, 1862
Bismarck becomes prime minister of Prussia.

1862

CHAPTER 16

Reading Strategy: Comparing and Contrasting

What Do You Know?

What do you think of when you hear the phrase *civil war?* What would it be like to fight in a war of brother against brother? Where and how did the Civil War begin?

Think About

- what a civil war is
- what you've learned about the Civil War from movies, television, and books
- reasons that countries threaten to break apart in today's world
- your responses to the Interact with History about how a civil war is worse than other wars (see page 479)

These are the Union flag (left) and a Confederate battle flag (right).

What Do You Want to Know?

 What details do you need to help you understand the outbreak of the Civil War? Make a list of those details in your notebook before you read the chapter.

Comparing and Contrasting

When you compare, you look for similarities between two or more objects, ideas, events, or people. When you contrast, you look for differences. Comparing and contrasting can be a useful strategy for studying the two sides in a war. Use the chart shown here to compare and contrast the North and the South in the early years of the Civil War.

S See Skillbuilder Handbook, page R10.

 Taking Notes

	North	South
Reasons for fighting		
Advantages		
Disadvantages		
Military strategy		
Battle victories		

War Erupts

MAIN IDEA	WHY IT MATTERS NOW	TERMS & NAMES
The secession of the Southern states quickly led to armed conflict between the North and the South.	The nation's identity was in part forged by the Civil War.	Fort Sumter · Anaconda Plan Robert E. Lee · blockade border state · First Battle of King Cotton · Bull Run

ONE AMERICAN'S STORY

Like other South Carolinians, Emma Holmes got caught up in the passions that led her state to secede. In her diary, she wrote about South Carolina's attack on Fort Sumter, a federal fort in Charleston's harbor.

A VOICE FROM THE PAST

[A]t half past four this morning, the heavy booming of cannons woke the city from its slumbers. . . . Every body seems relieved that what has been so long dreaded has come at last and so confident of victory that they seem not to think of the danger of their friends. . . . With the telescope I saw the shots as they struck the fort and [saw] the masonry crumbling.

Emma Holmes, *The Diary of Emma Holmes 1861–1866*

Many Southerners expected a short war that they would easily win. Northerners expected the same. In this section, you will learn how the war started, how the states divided, and how each side planned to win.

This photograph of Emma Holmes was taken in 1900.

First Shots at Fort Sumter

As they seceded from the Union (the states loyal to the United States of America during the Civil War), the Southern states took over most of the federal forts inside their borders. President Abraham Lincoln had to decide what to do about the forts that remained under federal control. Major Robert Anderson and his garrison held on to **Fort Sumter** in the harbor of Charleston, South Carolina, but they were running out of supplies.

If Lincoln supplied the garrison, he risked war. If he ordered the troops to leave the fort, he would be giving in to the rebels. Lincoln informed South Carolina that he was sending supply ships to Fort Sumter. Leaders of the Confederacy (the nation formed by Southern states in 1861) decided to prevent the federal government from holding onto the fort by attacking before the supply ships arrived.

Taking Notes

Use your chart to take notes about military strategies and the advantages and disadvantages for both sides.

| Reasons for fighting |
| Advantages |
| Disadvantages |
| Military strategy |
| Battle victories |

At 4:30 A.M. on Aril 12, 1861, shore guns opened fire on the island fort. For 34 hours, the Confederates fired shells into the fort until Anderson was forced to surrender. No one was killed, but the South's attack on Fort Sumter was the beginning of the Civil War.

Lincoln Calls Out the Militia

Two days after the surrender of Fort Sumter, President Lincoln asked the Union states to provide 75,000 militiamen for 90 days to put down the uprising in the South. Citizens of the North responded with enthusiasm to the call to arms. A New York woman wrote, "It seems as if we never were alive till now; never had a country till now."

In the upper South, however, state leaders responded with anger. The governor of Kentucky said that the state would "furnish no troops for the wicked purpose of subduing her sister Southern States." In the weeks that followed, Virginia, North Carolina, Tennessee, and Arkansas voted to join the Confederacy.

As each state seceded, volunteers rushed to enlist, just as citizens did in the North. A young Arkansas enlistee wrote, "So impatient did I become for starting that I felt like ten thousand pins were pricking me in every part of the body, and started off a week in advance of my brothers." Some feared the war would be over before they got the chance to fight.

With Virginia on its side, the Confederacy had a much better chance for victory. Virginia was wealthy and populous, and the Confederacy in May of 1861 moved its capital to Richmond. Virginia also was the home of **Robert E. Lee,** a talented military leader. When Virginia seceded, Lee resigned from the United States Army and joined the Confederacy. Although Lee opposed slavery and secession, he explained, "I cannot raise my hand against my birthplace, my home, my children." He eventually became the commanding general of the Army of Northern Virginia.

Choosing Sides

After Virginia seceded, both sides knew that the border states would play a key role in the war's outcome. The **border states**—Delaware, Maryland, Kentucky, and Missouri—were slave states that bordered states in which slavery was illegal. Because of their location and resources, the border states could tip the scales toward one side.

Keeping Maryland in the Union was important for the North. If Maryland seceded, then Washington, D.C., would be cut off from the Union. To hold on to the state, Lincoln ordered the arrest of Maryland lawmakers who backed the South. Union forces arrested 31 secessionist

AMERICA'S HISTORY MAKERS

ABRAHAM LINCOLN
1809–1865

Today, Abraham Lincoln is considered one of the great men of all time. Yet early in his presidency, he was widely criticized and ridiculed. Critics labeled him ignorant, incompetent, and socially crude. As Lincoln grew into his job, however, he gained the respect and affection of many Northerners.

Even as a youth, Lincoln had displayed a gift for public speaking. During the Civil War, through his speeches and writings, Lincoln inspired fellow Americans to "dare to do our duty as we understand it."

Why would the ability to inspire people be important in a wartime leader?

Background
The state militias were armies of ordinary citizens rather than professional soldiers.

*Reading*History
A. Comparing
Why might citizens in both the North and the South have been eager to fight in the Civil War?

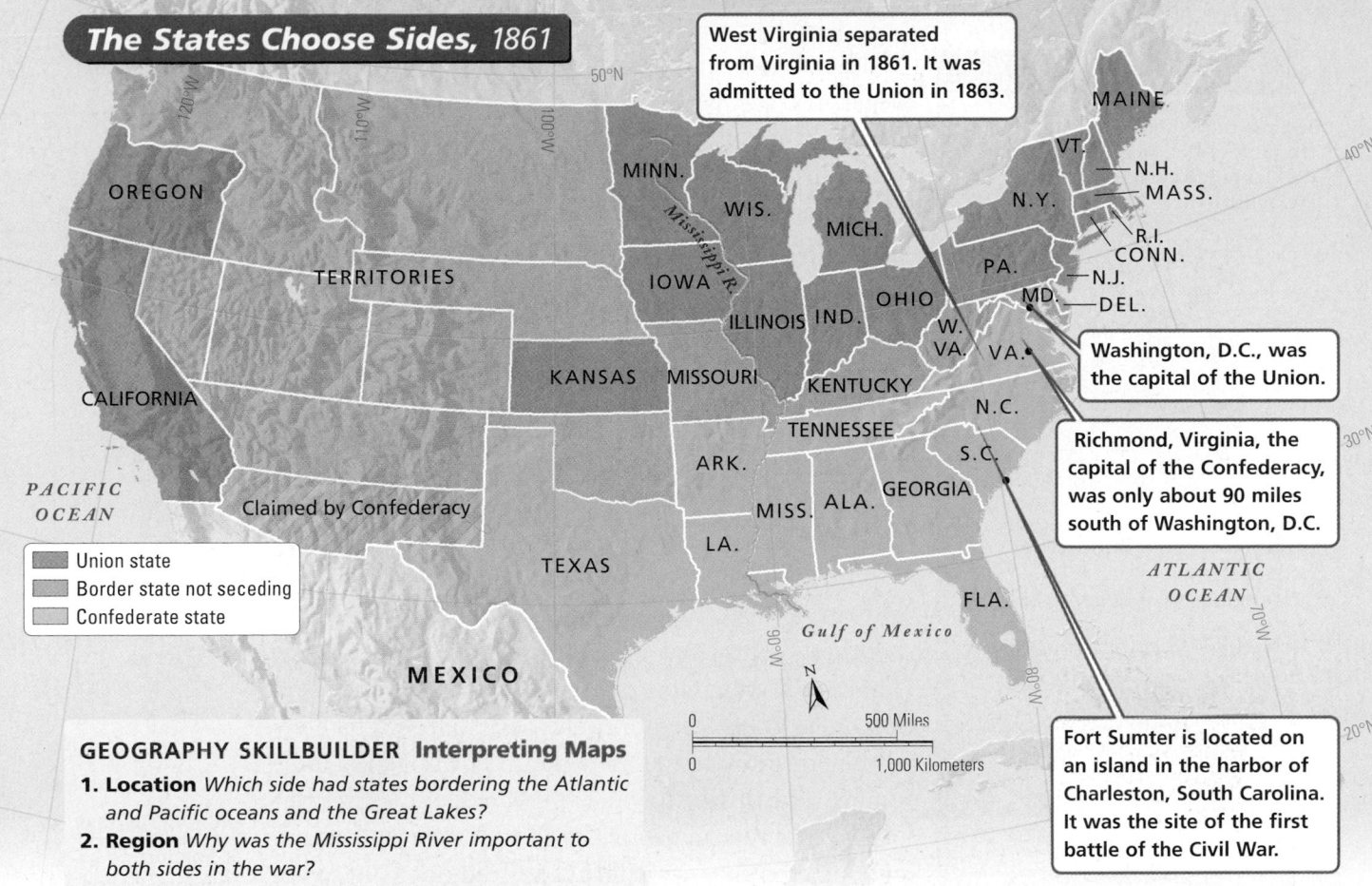

The States Choose Sides, 1861

West Virginia separated from Virginia in 1861. It was admitted to the Union in 1863.

Washington, D.C., was the capital of the Union.

Richmond, Virginia, the capital of the Confederacy, was only about 90 miles south of Washington, D.C.

Fort Sumter is located on an island in the harbor of Charleston, South Carolina. It was the site of the first battle of the Civil War.

OREGON

TERRITORIES

CALIFORNIA

PACIFIC OCEAN

Claimed by Confederacy

MINN.
WIS.
IOWA
ILLINOIS   IND.
KANSAS   MISSOURI
ARK.
TEXAS
LA.
MISS.   ALA.
GEORGIA
MICH.
OHIO
W. VA.   VA.
KENTUCKY
TENNESSEE
N.C.
S.C.
FLA.

MAINE
VT.
N.H.
MASS.
N.Y.
R.I.
CONN.
PA.
N.J.
MD.
DEL.

ATLANTIC OCEAN

MEXICO

Gulf of Mexico

Union state
Border state not seceding
Confederate state

0   500 Miles
0   1,000 Kilometers

N

GEOGRAPHY SKILLBUILDER Interpreting Maps

1. **Location** Which side had states bordering the Atlantic and Pacific oceans and the Great Lakes?
2. **Region** Why was the Mississippi River important to both sides in the war?

members of the legislature. They were held for at least two months—after the election of a new legislature.

Kentucky was also important to both sides because of its rivers. For the Union, the rivers could provide an invasion route into the South. For the South, the rivers could provide a barrier. Kentuckians were deeply divided over secession. However, a Confederate invasion in 1861 prompted the state to stay in the Union.

Both Missouri and Delaware also stayed in the Union. In Virginia, federal troops helped a group of western counties break away. These counties formed the state of West Virginia and returned to the Union. In the end, 24 states made up the Union and 11 joined the Confederacy.

Reading **History**

B. Summarizing Why were the border states critical to the war's outcome?

Strengths and Weaknesses

The Union had huge advantages in manpower and resources. The North had about 22 million people. The Confederacy had roughly 9 million, of whom about 3.5 million were slaves. About 85 percent of the nation's factories were located in the North. The North had more than double the railroad mileage of the South. Almost all the naval power and shipyards belonged to the North.

The Union's greatest asset, however, was President Abraham Lincoln. He developed into a remarkable leader. Lincoln convinced Northerners that democracy depended on preserving the Union.

The pie charts show the relative strength of the Union and the Confederacy in population and industry.

Total U.S. Population

29% | 71%

■ Union   ■ Confederacy

Total U.S. Railroad Mileage

29% | 71%

Total U.S. Manufacturing Plants

15%

85%

Total U.S. Industrial Workers

8%

92%

Source: *Encyclopedia Americana*

SKILLBUILDER
Interpreting Charts
1. *Which side had more resources?*
2. *How might the North's railways and factories have helped its armies?*

The Confederacy had some advantages, too. It began the war with able generals, such as Robert E. Lee. It also had the advantage of fighting a defensive war. This meant Northern supply lines would have to be stretched very far. In addition, soldiers defending their homes have more will to fight than invaders do.

The Confederate Strategy

At first, the Confederacy took a defensive position. It did not want to conquer the North—it only wanted to be independent. "All we ask is to be let alone," said Confederate President Jefferson Davis. Confederate leaders hoped the North would soon tire of the war and accept Southern independence.

The South also depended on **King Cotton** as a way to win foreign support. Cotton was king because Southern cotton was important in the world market. The South grew most of the cotton for Europe's textile mills. When the war broke out, Southern planters withheld cotton from the market. They hoped to force France and Britain to aid the Confederate cause. But in 1861, European nations had surplus cotton because of a big crop the year before. They did not want to get involved in the American war.

As the war heated up, the South soon moved away from its cautious plans. It began to take the offensive and try for big victories to wreck Northern morale.

The Union Strategy

The North wanted to bring the Southern states back into the Union. To do this, the North developed an offensive strategy based on General Winfield Scott's **Anaconda Plan.** This plan was designed to smother the South's economy like a giant anaconda snake squeezing its prey.

The plan called for a naval blockade of the South's coastline. In a **blockade,** armed forces prevent the transportation of goods or people into or out of an area. The plan also called for the Union to gain control of the Mississippi River. This would split the Confederacy in two.

One of the drawbacks of Scott's plan was that it would take time to work. But many people, eager for action, were calling for an immediate attack on Richmond, the Confederate capital. Lincoln ordered an invasion of Virginia in the summer of 1861.

Reading **History**
C. Supporting Opinions At the beginning of the Civil War, which side would you have predicted to win? Why?

Battle of Bull Run

To take Richmond, the Union army would first have to defeat the Confederate troops stationed at the town of Manassas, Virginia. This was a railway center southwest of Washington, D.C.

On July 21, 1861, Union forces commanded by General Irvin McDowell clashed with Confederate forces headed by General Pierre Beauregard near a little creek called Bull Run north of Manassas. In the North, this battle came to be known as the **First Battle of Bull Run**.

Background
In the South, the battle was called the First Battle of Manassas. In most cases, the South named a battle after a nearby town. The North used a landmark near the fighting, usually a stream.

At one point in the battle, a Confederate officer rallied his troops by pointing his sword toward Southern General Thomas J. Jackson. The officer cried, "There is Jackson standing like a stone wall! Rally behind the Virginians!" From this incident, Jackson won the nickname "Stonewall" Jackson. His men held fast against the Union assault.

The Confederate Army passes in review before General Pierre Beauregard.

As fresh troops arrived, the Confederates equaled the Union forces in number and launched a countercharge. Attacking the Union line, they let out a blood-curdling scream. This scream, later called the "rebel yell," caused the Union troops to panic. They broke ranks and scattered.

The Confederate victory in the First Battle of Bull Run thrilled the South and shocked the North. Many in the South thought the war was won. The North realized it had underestimated its opponent. Lincoln sent the 90-day militias home and called for a real army of 500,000 volunteers for three years. In the next section, you will learn what army life was like.

Section 1 Assessment

1. Terms & Names

Explain the significance of:
- Fort Sumter
- Robert E. Lee
- border state
- King Cotton
- Anaconda Plan
- blockade
- First Battle of Bull Run

2. Using Graphics

Use a Venn diagram to compare and contrast the strengths of the North and the South.

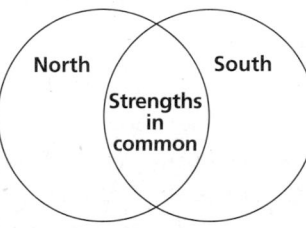

3. Main Ideas

a. How did citizens in the North and the South respond to the outbreak of the Civil War?

b. Why were the border states important to both sides in the Civil War?

c. What kind of military strategy did each side develop?

4. Critical Thinking

Comparing How was the South's situation in the Civil War similar to the situation of the Patriots in the Revolutionary War?

THINK ABOUT
- their reasons for fighting
- their opponents' strengths

ACTIVITY OPTIONS

LANGUAGE ARTS

TECHNOLOGY

Read an account of the First Battle of Bull Run. Use the information to write a **news article** or plan the battle's **home page** for the Internet.

from
Across Five Aprils
by Irene Hunt

At the beginning of the Civil War, nine-year-old Jethro Creighton and his family live on a farm in southern Illinois. Although Illinois is a free state that remains in the Union, many people in the area have ties to states where slavery is legal. For example, the Creightons have relatives in "Kaintuck," or Kentucky. When this excerpt begins, Jethro has already seen his brother Tom and his cousin Eb go off to fight for the Union. His other brothers, John and Bill, are trying to decide which side to fight for.

A line of wild geese flew southward far overhead, and Jethro stood motionless as he watched them disappear from sight. So **engrossed**[1] he was with the flight of the geese that he did not hear Bill's footsteps until his brother was quite near. He caught his breath at sight of Bill's face, which was swollen and beginning to grow discolored from a deep cut and many bruises.

"What's hurt you, Bill?" he asked, his voice barely **audible,**[2] for he was pretty sure he knew.

"We had a fight, Jeth, about an hour ago. We fit like two madmen, I guess."

"You and John?"

Bill's sigh was almost a moan. "Yes, me and John. Me and my brother John."

Jethro could not answer. He stared at the cut above Bill's right eye, from which blood still trickled down his cheek. Somewhere, far off in another field, a man shouted to his horses, and the shout died away in a cry that ran frightened over the brown water of the creek and into the darkening woods.

He had heard cries often that autumn, all through the countryside. They came at night, wakened him, and then lapsed into silence, leaving him in fear and **perplexity**.[3] Sounds once familiar were no longer as they had seemed in other days—his father calling cattle in from the pasture, the sheep dog's bark coming through the fog, the distant creak of the pulley as Ellen drew water for her chickens—all these once familiar sounds had taken on overtones of wailing, and he seemed to hear an echo of that wailing now. He shivered and looked away from his brother's face.

Bill sat down on the ground beside him. "Did ever Ma tell you, Jeth, about when John and me was little and was goin' to school fer the first time? At night I'd git a book and I'd say to Pa, 'What air that word, Pa?' and when he would tell me, I'd turn to John, jest a scant year older, and I'd say, 'Did Pa call it right, Johnny?' Ma and Pa used to laugh at that, but they was pleased to talk about it. They was always set up at John and me bein' so close."

"I know it." Jethro's words came from a tight throat. "What made you fight, Bill?"

"Hard feelin's that have been buildin' up fer weeks, hard feelin's that fin'ly come out in hard words." He held his hand across his eyes for a minute and then spoke quickly. "I'm leavin', Jeth; it ain't that I want to, but it's that I must. The day is comin' when I've got to fight, and I won't fight fer **arrogance**[4] and big money aginst the southern farmer. I won't do it. You tell Pa that. Tell him, too, that I'm takin' my brown mare—she's mine, and I hev the right. Still, it will leave him short, so you tell him that I'm leavin' money I

---

1. **engrossed:** absorbed; occupied.
2. **audible:** able to be heard.

3. **perplexity:** confusion.
4. **arrogance:** overbearing pride.

made at the sawmill and at corn shuckin'; it's inside the cover of his Bible. You tell him to take it and buy another horse."

Jethro was crying unashamedly in the face of his grief. "Don't go, Bill. Don't do it," he begged.

"Jeth . . ."

"I don't want you to go, Bill. I don't think I kin stand it."

"Listen to me, Jeth; you're gittin to be a sizable boy. There's goin' to be a lot of things in the years ahead that you'll have to stand. There'll be things that tear you apart, but you'll have to stand 'em. You can't count on cryin' to make 'em right."

The colors were beginning to fade on Walnut Hill. A light wind bent the dried grass and weeds. Jethro felt choked with grief, but he drew a sleeve across his eyes and tried to look at his brother without further weeping.

"Where will you go, Bill?"

"To Kaintuck. I'll go to Wilse's place first. From there—I don't know."

"Will you fight fer the Rebs?"

Bill hesitated a few seconds. "I've studied this thing, Jeth, and I've hurt over it. My heart ain't in this war; I've told you that. And while I say that the right ain't all on the side of the North, I know jest as well that it ain't all on the side of the South either. But if I hev to fight, I reckon it will be fer the South."

Jethro nodded. There were things you had to endure. After a while he asked, "Air you goin' tonight, Bill?"

"Right away. I've had things packed in that holler tree fer a couple days. I've knowed that this was comin' on, but I couldn't make myself leave. Now I'm goin'. The little mare is saddled and tied down at the molasses press. I'll go as fur as Newton tonight; in the morning I'll take out early."

He got to his feet. "There's lots of things I want to say, but I reckon I best not talk." Without looking at Jethro he laid his hand on the boy's shoulder. "Git all the larnin' you kin— and take keer of yoreself, Jeth," he said and turned abruptly away.

"Take keer of yoreself, Bill," Jethro called after him.

Across the prairies, through the woods, over the brown water of the creek, there was a sound of crying. Jethro ran to a tree and hid his face. He had heard his mother say that if you watch a loved one as he leaves you for a long journey, it's like as not to be the last look at him that you'll ever have.

Like the Creighton brothers, the Terrill brothers had different loyalties. William Rufus Terrill (left) fought for the Union as an artillery officer at Shiloh. His brother, James Terrill (right), was the commanding officer of a Virginia infantry regiment. Both men died in the war. William was killed at Perryville, Kentucky, in 1862; James was killed in battle in 1864. After the war, the family built a memorial to the brothers, which contained the words, "God Alone Knows Which Was Right."

CONNECT TO HISTORY
1. **Recognizing Effects** How has the Civil War affected the Creighton family? Discuss how the effect reflects what is happening in the country.

 See Skillbuilder Handbook, page R11.

CONNECT TO TODAY
2. **Researching** Where have civil wars or internal rebellions taken place in the recent past?

For more about other civil wars . . .

RESEARCH LINKS
CLASSZONE.COM

Life in the Army

MAIN IDEA	WHY IT MATTERS NOW	TERMS & NAMES
Both Union and Confederate soldiers endured many hardships serving in the army during the Civil War.	The hardships endured led to long-lasting bitterness on both sides.	hygiene minié ball rifle ironclad

ONE AMERICAN'S STORY

In 1862, Peter Vredenburgh, Jr., answered President Lincoln's call for an additional 300,000 soldiers. Nearly 26 years old, Vredenburgh became a major in the 14th Regiment New Jersey Volunteer Infantry. Less than two months after joining the regiment, he wrote a letter urging his parents to keep his 18-year-old brother from enlisting.

A VOICE FROM THE PAST

I am glad that Jim has not joined any Regt. [regiment] and I hope he never will. I would not have him go for all my pay; it would be very improbable that we could both go through this war and come out unharmed. Let him come here and see the thousands with their arms and legs off, or if that won't do, let him go as I did the other day through the Frederick hospitals and see how little account a man's life and limbs are held in by others.

Major Peter Vredenburgh, Jr., quoted in *Upon the Tented Field*

Major Peter Vredenburgh, Jr., was an officer in the Union army.

On September 19, 1864, Vredenburgh was killed in battle. In this section, you will learn more about other soldiers and what their experiences were like.

Taking Notes

Use your chart to take notes about the reasons for fighting the Civil War.

Reasons for fighting	
Advantages	
Disadvantages	
Military strategy	
Battle victories	

Those Who Fought

Like Peter Vredenburgh, the majority of soldiers in the Civil War were between 18 and 30 years of age. But both the Confederate and Union armies had younger and older soldiers. Charles Carter Hay was just 11 years old when he joined an Alabama regiment. William Wilkins was 83 when he became one of the Pennsylvania Home Guards.

Farmers made up the largest group among Civil War soldiers. About half the soldiers on both sides came from farms. Having rarely traveled far from their fields, many viewed going off to war as an exciting adventure. Some rode a train for the first time.

Although the majority of soldiers in the war were born in the United States, immigrants from other countries also served. German and Irish immigrants made up the largest ethnic groups. One regiment from New York had soldiers who were born in 15 foreign countries. The commanding officer gave orders in seven languages.

At the beginning of the war, African Americans wanted to fight. They saw the war as a way to end slavery. However, neither the North nor the South accepted African Americans into their armies. As the war dragged on, the North finally took African Americans into its ranks. Native Americans served on both sides.

In all, about 2 million American soldiers served the Union, and fewer than 1 million served the Confederacy. The vast majority were volunteers. Why did so many Americans volunteer to fight? Many sought adventure and glory. Some sought an escape from the boredom of farm and factory work. Some signed up because their friends and neighbors were doing it. Others signed up for the recruitment money offered by both sides. Soldiers also fought because they were loyal to their country or state.

Reading **History**
A. Summarizing
How did most men in the North and the South feel about going off to war?

Turning Civilians into Soldiers

After enlisting, a volunteer was sent to a nearby army camp for training. A typical camp looked like a sea of canvas tents. The tents were grouped by company, and each tent held from two to twenty men. In winter, the soldiers lived in log huts or in heavy tents positioned on a log base. In the Civil War, Confederate soldiers and soldiers in volunteer units in the Union Army elected their company officers. Both the Union and Confederate armies followed this practice.

A soldier in training followed a set schedule. A bugle or drum awakened the soldier at dawn. After roll call and breakfast, the soldier had the first of several drill sessions. In between drills and meals, soldiers performed guard duty, cut wood for the campfires, dug trenches for latrines (outdoor toilets), and cleaned up the camp.

Shortly after they came to camp, new recruits were given uniforms and equipment. Union soldiers wore blue uniforms, and Confederate soldiers wore gray or

daily *life*

DRILL SESSIONS

"The first thing in the morning is drill. Then drill, then drill again. Then drill, drill, a little more drill. Then drill, and lastly drill." That is the way one soldier described his day in camp.

A soldier in training might have as many as five drill sessions a day, each lasting up to two hours. The soldiers learned to stand straight and march in formation. They also learned to load and fire their guns. Shown drilling below are soldiers of the 22nd New York State Militia near Harpers Ferry, Virginia, in 1862.

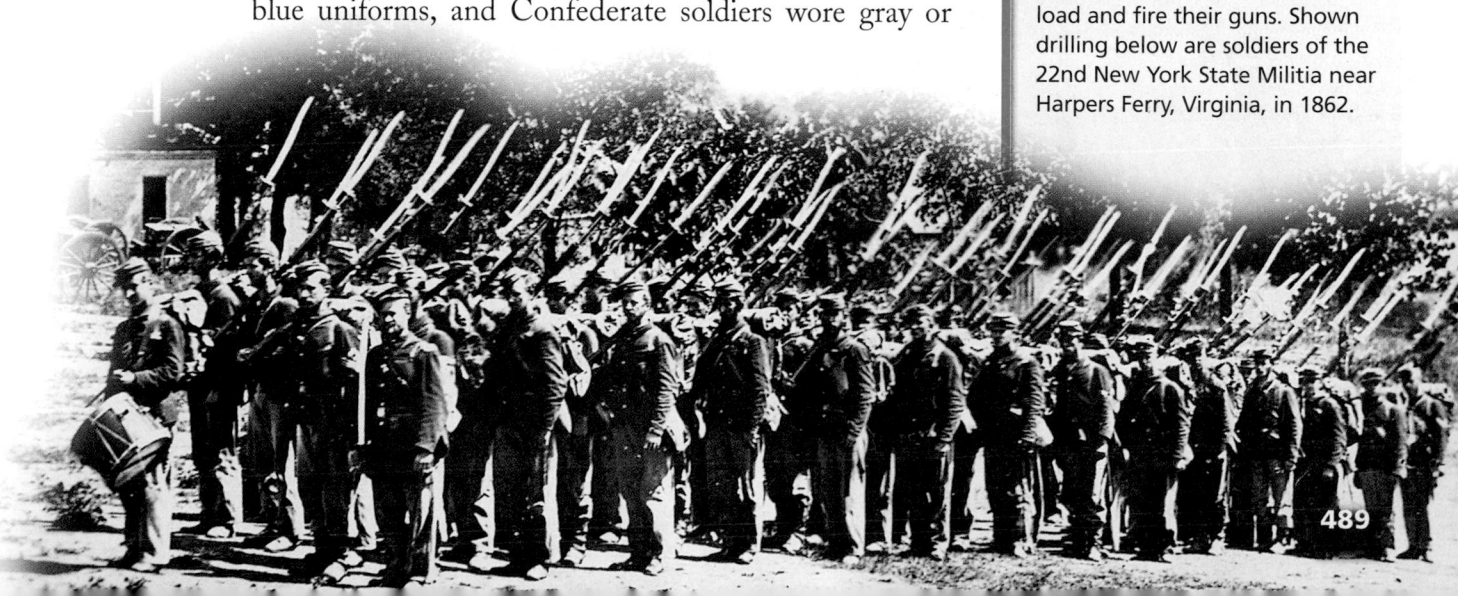

yellowish-brown uniforms. Getting a uniform of the right size was a problem, however. On both sides, soldiers traded items to get clothing that fit properly.

Early in the war, Northern soldiers received clothing of very poor quality. Contractors took advantage of the government's need and supplied shoddy goods. Shoes made of imitation leather, for example, fell apart when they got wet. In the Confederacy, some states had trouble providing uniforms at all, while others had surpluses. Because the states did not always cooperate and share supplies, Confederate soldiers sometimes lacked shoes. Like soldiers in the Revolutionary War, they marched over frozen ground in bare feet. After battles, needy soldiers took coats, boots, and other clothing from the dead.

At the beginning of the war, most soldiers in army camps received plenty of food. Their rations included beef or salt pork, flour, vegetables, and coffee. But when they were in the field, the soldiers' diet became more limited. Some soldiers went hungry because supply trains could not reach them.

Background
Before uniforms became standardized, soldiers dressed in outfits supplied from home. This caused confusion on the battlefield.

STRANGE *but* True

DEADLIER THAN BULLETS

"Look at our company—21 have died of disease, 18 have become so unhealthy as to be discharged, and only four have been killed in battle." So a Louisiana officer explained the high death rate in the Civil War.

More than twice as many men died of disease as died of battle wounds. Intestinal disorders, including typhoid fever, diarrhea, and dysentery, killed the most. Pneumonia, tuberculosis, and malaria killed many others. Bad water and food, poor diet, exposure to cold and rain, unsanitary conditions, and disease-carrying insects all contributed to the high rate of disease.

Hardships of Army Life

Civil War soldiers in the field were often wet, muddy, or cold from marching outdoors and living in crude shelters. Many camps were unsanitary and smelled from the odors of garbage and latrines. One Union soldier described a camp near Washington. In the camp, cattle were killed to provide the troops with meat.

A VOICE FROM THE PAST

The hides and [waste parts] of the [cattle] for miles upon miles around, under a sweltering sun and sultry showers, would gender such swarms of flies, armies of worms, blasts of stench and oceans of filth as to make life miserable.

William Keesy, quoted in *The Civil War Infantryman*

Not only were the camps filthy, but so were the soldiers. They often went weeks without bathing or washing their clothes. Their bodies, clothing, and bedding became infested with lice and fleas.

Poor **hygiene**—conditions and practices that promote health—resulted in widespread sickness. Most soldiers had chronic diarrhea or other intestinal disorders. These disorders were caused by contaminated water or food or by germ-carrying insects. People did not know that germs cause diseases. Doctors failed to wash their hands or their instruments. An observer described how surgeons "armed with long, bloody knives and saws, cut and sawed away with frightful rapidity, throwing the mangled limbs on a pile nearby as soon as removed."

*Reading***History**
B. Making Inferences What changes could have helped lower the spread of disease among soldiers?

Changes in Military Technology

While camp life remained rough, military technology advanced. Improvements in the weapons of war had far-reaching effects. Battle tactics changed, and casualties soared.

Rifles that used minié balls contributed to the high casualty rate in the Civil War. A **rifle** is a gun with a grooved barrel that causes a bullet to spin through the air. This spin gives the bullet more distance and accuracy. The **minié ball** is a bullet with a hollow base. The bullet expands upon firing to fit the grooves in the barrel. Rifles with minié balls could shoot farther and more accurately than old-fashioned muskets. As a result, mounted charges and infantry assaults did not work as well. Defenders using rifles could shoot more of the attackers before they got close.

Ironclads, warships covered with iron, proved to be a vast improvement over wooden ships. In the first ironclad battle, the Confederate *Virginia* (originally named the *Merrimack*) battled the Union *Monitor* off the coast of Virginia in 1862. After hammering away for about four hours, the battle ended in a draw. (See page 492 for more information on ironclads.)

Despite new technology and tactics, neither side gained a decisive victory in the first two years of the war, as you will see in the next section.

Vocabulary
casualties: number of people killed or injured

Reading **History**
C. Drawing Conclusions
Which changes in military technology had an effect on the average soldier? Why?

The naval duel between the Union *Monitor* and the Confederate *Merrimack* (or *Virginia*) took place on March 9, 1862.

Section 2 Assessment

1. Terms & Names
Explain the significance of:
- hygiene
- rifle
- minié ball
- ironclad

2. Using Graphics
Complete the chart below.

The Typical Civil War Soldier	
Age	
Occupation	
Training	
Hardships	

Which hardship do you think would have been most difficult to endure? Why?

3. Main Ideas
a. How were the wartime experiences of Northern and Southern soldiers alike?

b. What factors contributed to the spread of disease among soldiers?

c. How did the use of the rifle and minié ball change combat tactics in the Civil War?

4. Critical Thinking
Forming and Supporting Opinions What were the motives that led individual soldiers to fight in the Civil War?

THINK ABOUT
- the multiple reasons that people had for enlisting
- what you consider valid reasons for fighting

ACTIVITY OPTIONS

LANGUAGE ARTS

ART

Imagine you are a soldier in the Civil War. Write a **letter** home to your parents about your experience or draw an **illustrated map** of your training camp.

Ironclads

They moved through the water, as one observer put it, "like a huge, half-submerged crocodile." To crew members of traditional wooden ships, the ironclads indeed may have seemed like horrible mechanical monsters.

With a powerful iron hull almost entirely under water and a rotating gun turret, or short tower, an ironclad easily destroyed the older vessels it met. When the *Monitor* and the *Merrimack* (or *Virginia*) clashed during the Civil War in the first battle ever waged between ironclads, a new era of naval warfare had begun. Below is a closer look at the Union's *Monitor*.

> Steam engines powered the ship. They were connected by a propeller shaft to a four-blade propeller. Behind the propeller sat the vessel's rudder. This entire area was heavily protected so the ship could keep moving under heavy fire or ramming.

> The pilothouse, where the captain steered the ship, was a rectangular, reinforced iron box-like structure. A small opening all around the top allowed for full visibility.

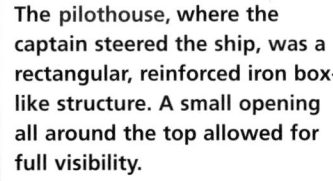

> The ship's weapons—two large cannons—were enclosed in a rotating iron turret. This allowed the guns to fire at an enemy from all directions. Ammunition was passed up to the gunners through a hatch in the floor.

SCALE AND SIZE OF WARSHIPS

Class, Name, Launch Date	Length	Weight	Number of Crew	Weaponry
Ironclad (USS *Monitor*) 1862	172 ft.	987 tons	49	two 11-inch smoothbore cannons
Battleship (USS *Maine*) 1889	319 ft.	6,682 tons	374	four 10-inch guns, six 6-inch guns, seven rapid-fire 6-pounders, four torpedo tubes
Nuclear Submarine (USS *Nautilus*) 1954	324 ft.	4,092 tons	105	six torpedo tubes
Aircraft Carrier (USS *Nimitz*) 1972	1,092 ft.	95,000 tons	6,000	24 F-14A Tomcat warplanes, 16 radar guided missiles, six-barrel, 20-millimeter Gatling gun

CONNECT TO HISTORY

1. **Drawing Conclusions** Why would a rotating gun be an advantage in a naval battle?

 See Skillbuilder Handbook, page R13.

CONNECT TO TODAY

2. **Researching** Find out more about modern battleships or aircraft carriers, and write a brief report about their capabilities in battle.

For more about military ships . . .

RESEARCH LINKS
CLASSZONE.COM

No End in Sight

ONE AMERICAN'S STORY

In the summer of 1861, President Lincoln gave George McClellan command of the Union army in the East. The army had recently been defeated at Bull Run. Within months, McClellan restored the soldiers' confidence and organized and trained an army that could defeat the Confederates. But while Lincoln kept urging him to attack Richmond, McClellan kept drilling his troops.

A VOICE FROM THE PAST

[S]oon as I feel that my army is well organized and well disciplined and strong enough, I will advance and force the Rebels to a battle on a field of my own selection. A long time must elapse before I can do that.

General George McClellan, quoted in *Civil War Journal: The Leaders*

President Lincoln (right) meets with General McClellan (left) on the Antietam battlefield in 1862.

Lincoln said McClellan had "the slows." While McClellan was stalling in the East, another general was winning victories in the West.

Union Victories in the West

That victorious Union general in the West was **Ulysses S. Grant**. In civilian life, he had failed at many things. But Grant had a simple strategy of war: "Find out where your enemy is, get at him as soon as you can, strike at him as hard as you can, and keep moving on."

In February 1862, Grant made a bold move to take Tennessee. Using ironclad gunboats, Grant's forces captured two Confederate river forts. These were Fort Henry on the Tennessee and Fort Donelson on the nearby Cumberland. (See map on next page.) The seizure of Fort Henry opened up a river highway into the heart of the South. Union gunboats could now travel on the river as far as northern Alabama. When the people of Nashville, Tennessee, heard the forts were lost, they fled the city in panic. A week later, Union troops marched into Nashville.

Taking Notes

Use your chart to take notes about the battle victories for both sides.

Reasons for fighting	
Advantages	
Disadvantages	
Military strategy	
Battle victories	

The Battle of Shiloh

After Grant's river victories, Albert S. Johnston, Confederate commander on the Western front, ordered a retreat to Corinth, Mississippi. Grant followed. By early April, Grant's troops had reached Pittsburg Landing on the Tennessee River. There he waited for more troops from Nashville. Johnston, however, decided to attack before Grant gained reinforcements. Marching his troops north from Corinth on April 6, 1862, Johnston surprised the Union forces near Shiloh Church. The **Battle of Shiloh** in Tennessee turned into the fiercest fighting the Civil War had yet seen.

Commanders on each side rode into the thick of battle to rally their troops. One Union general, William Tecumseh Sherman, had three horses shot out from under him. General Johnston was killed, and the command passed to General Pierre Beauregard. By the end of the day, each side believed that dawn would bring victory.

That night, there was a terrible thunderstorm. Lightning lit up the battlefield, where dead and dying soldiers lay in water and mud. During the night, Union boats ran upriver to ferry fresh troops to Grant's camp. Grant then led an attack at dawn and forced the exhausted Southern troops to retreat.

The cost of the Union victory was staggering. Union casualties at Shiloh numbered over 13,000, about one-fourth of those who had fought. The Confederates lost nearly 11,000 out of 41,000 soldiers. Describing

Reading **History**

A. Contrasting
How did Grant differ from McClellan as a military leader?

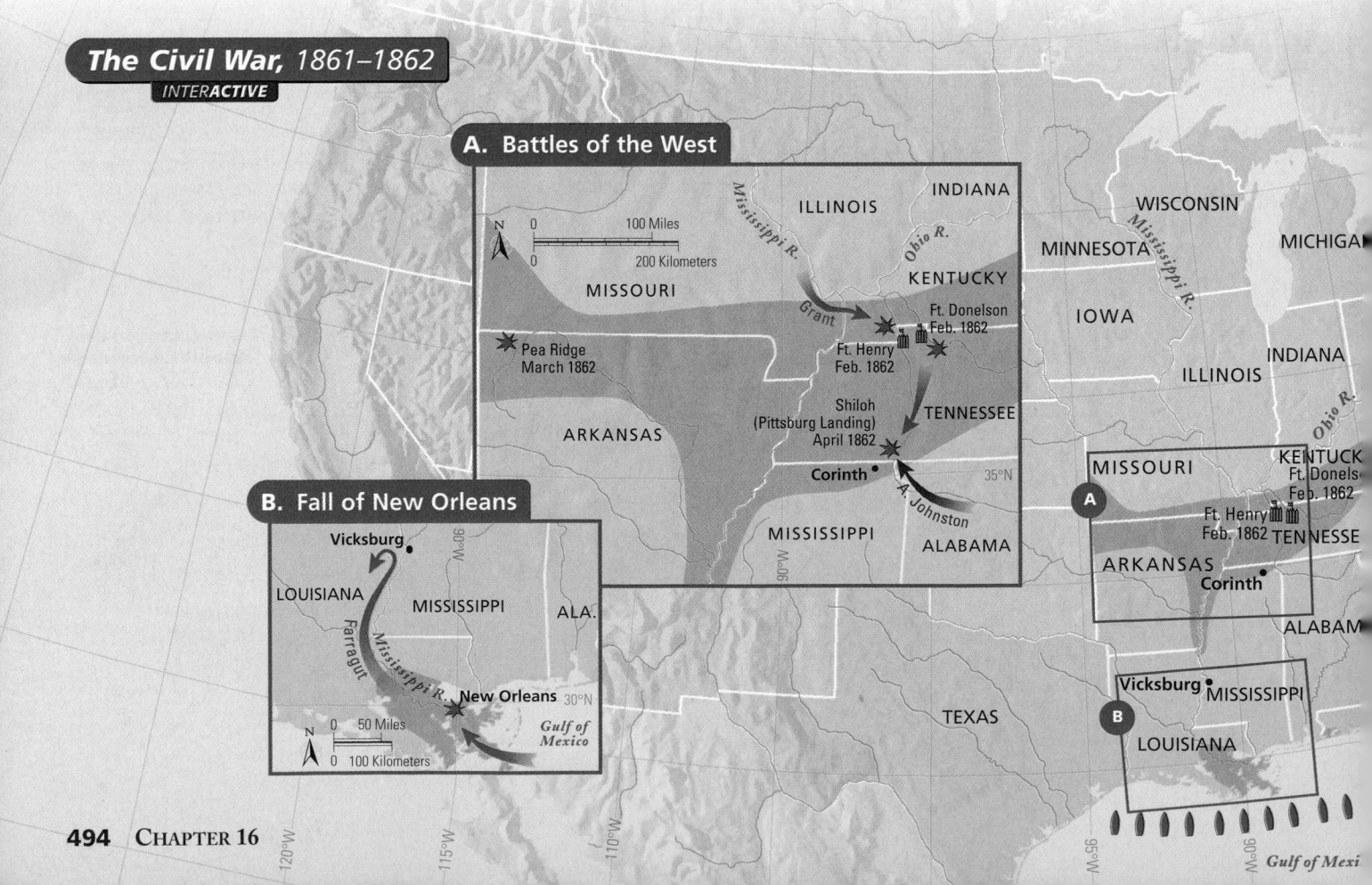

The Civil War, *1861–1862*
INTER**ACTIVE**

A. Battles of the West

B. Fall of New Orleans

the piles of mangled bodies, General Sherman wrote home, "The scenes on this field would have cured anybody of war." Congressmen criticized Grant for the high casualties and urged Lincoln to replace him. But Lincoln replied, "I can't spare this man—he fights."

> *"I can't spare this man—he fights."*
>
> **Abraham Lincoln, describing General Grant**

The Fall of New Orleans

The spring of 1862 brought other bad news for the Confederacy. On April 25, a Union fleet led by David Farragut captured New Orleans, the largest city in the South. Rebel gunboats tried to ram the Union warships and succeeded in sinking one. Farragut's ships had to run through cannon fire and then dodge burning rafts in order to reach the city. Residents stood on the docks and cursed the Yankee invaders, but they were powerless to stop them.

Reading **History**

B. Recognizing Effects Why was the fall of New Orleans significant?

The fall of New Orleans was a heavy blow to the South. Mary Chesnut of South Carolina, the wife of an aide to President Davis, wrote in her diary, "New Orleans gone—and with it the Confederacy. Are we not cut in two?" Indeed, after the victories of General Grant and Admiral Farragut, only a 150-mile stretch of the Mississippi remained in Southern hands. The Union was well on its way to achieving its goal of cutting the Confederacy in two. But guarding the remaining stretch of the river was the heavily armed Confederate fort at Vicksburg, Mississippi.

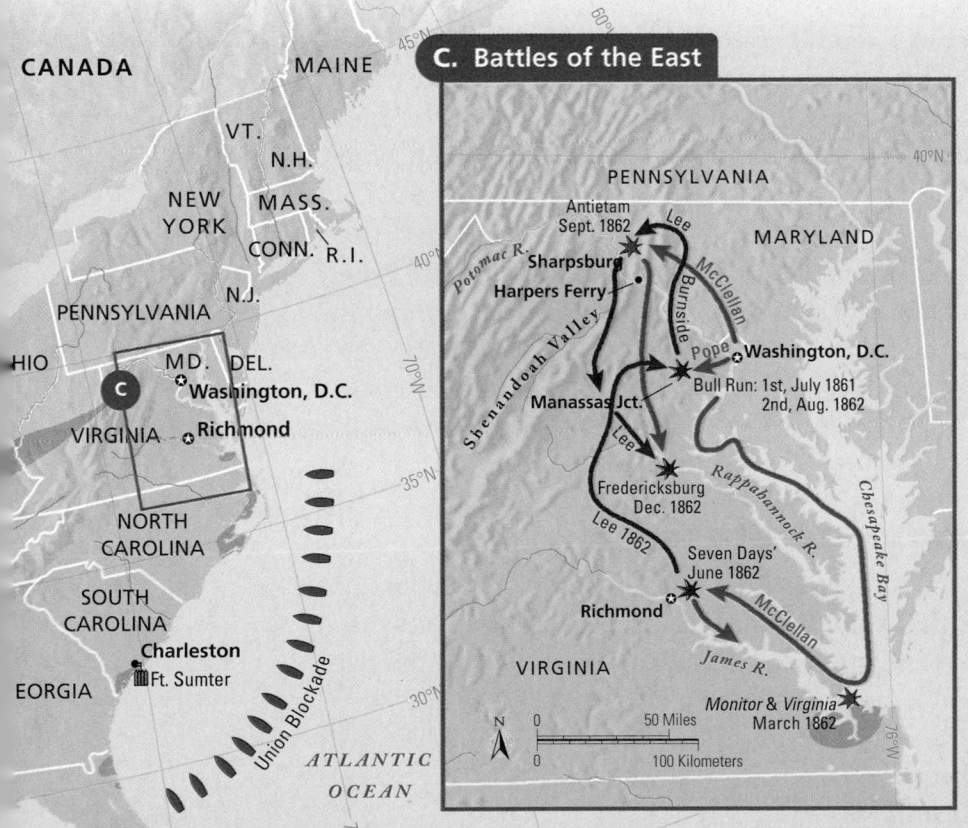

C. Battles of the East

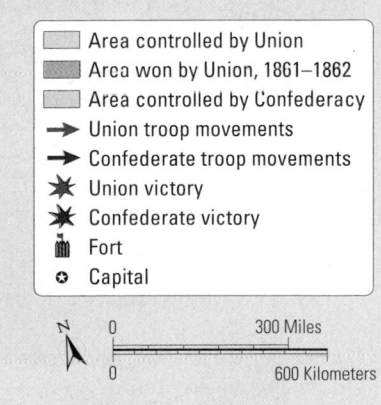

	Area controlled by Union
	Area won by Union, 1861–1862
	Area controlled by Confederacy
→	Union troop movements
→	Confederate troop movements
✸	Union victory
✸	Confederate victory
🏛	Fort
✪	Capital

0   300 Miles
0   600 Kilometers

GEOGRAPHY SKILLBUILDER

1. **Location** *Where did most of the early Union victories take place? Where did early Confederate victories take place?*

2. **Region** *Why did much of the fighting take place in the Virginia-Maryland region?*

Lee Claims Victories in the East

Meanwhile, also in the spring of 1862, McClellan finally made his move to try to capture Richmond. He planned to attack the Confederate capital by way of a stretch of land between the York and James rivers. McClellan succeeded in bringing his troops within a few miles of Richmond.

But in June 1862, Robert E. Lee took charge of the Army of Northern Virginia and proceeded to turn the situation around. Lee sent Jeb Stuart and his **cavalry**—soldiers on horseback—to spy on McClellan. With about 1,000 men, Stuart rode around the whole Union army in a few days and reported its size back to Lee. Lee then attacked McClellan's army. The two sides clashed for a week, from June 25 to July 1, 1862, in what became known as the **Seven Days' Battles.** The Army of Northern Virginia suffered heavier losses, but it forced McClellan's army to retreat.

In late August, the Confederates won a second victory at Bull Run, and Union troops withdrew back to Washington. Within just a few months, Lee had ended the Union threat in Virginia.

*Reading*History

C. Making Inferences How was Lee's appointment fortunate for the South?

Lee Invades the North

Riding a wave of victories, General Lee decided to invade the Union. He wrote to tell President Davis of his plan. Lee thought it was a crucial time, with the North at a low point. Without waiting for Davis's response, Lee crossed the Potomac with his army and invaded Maryland in early September 1862.

*Reading*History

D. Reading a Map Use the map on page 495 to follow Lee's movements into the North.

Lee had several reasons for taking the war to the North. He hoped a victory in the North might force Lincoln to talk peace. The invasion would give Virginia farmers a rest from war during the harvest season. The Confederates could plunder Northern farms for food.

Lee hoped the invasion would show that the Confederacy could indeed win the war, which might convince Europe to side with the South. By this time, both Britain and France were leaning toward recognizing the Confederacy as a separate nation. They were impressed by Lee's military successes, and their textile industry was now hurting from the lack of Southern cotton.

Bloody Antietam

Soon after invading Maryland, Lee drew up a plan for his campaign in the North. A Confederate officer accidentally left a copy of Lee's battle plans wrapped around three cigars at a campsite. When Union troops stopped to rest at the abandoned campsite, a Union soldier stumbled on the plans. The captured plans gave McClellan a chance to stop Lee and his army.

AMERICA'S HISTORY MAKERS

JEFFERSON DAVIS
1808–1889

Jefferson Davis expected to be given a military command when the Confederacy was formed in 1861. But Davis was chosen President of the Confederacy instead, which stunned and saddened him.

Because of his strong sense of duty and loyalty to the South, Davis accepted the unwelcome post. He had to immediately form a national government and prepare for war at the same time. Davis found it hard to compromise or accept disagreement with his opinions.

How do the qualities required in a military leader differ from those required in a political leader?

McClellan went on the attack, though he moved slowly as always. On September 17, 1862, at Antietam Creek near Sharpsburg, Maryland, McClellan's army clashed with Lee's. The resulting **Battle of Antietam** was the bloodiest day in all of American history. A Confederate officer later described the battle.

Confederate artillery soldiers lie dead after the Battle of Antietam.

A VOICE FROM THE PAST

Again and again . . . by charges and counter-charges, this portion of the field was lost and recovered, until the green corn that grew upon it looked as if it had been struck by a storm of bloody hail. . . . From sheer exhaustion, both sides, like battered and bleeding athletes, seemed willing to rest.

John B. Gordon, quoted in *Voices of the Civil War*

After fighting all day, neither side had gained any ground by nightfall. The only difference was that about 25,000 men were dead or wounded. Lee, who lost as much as one-third of his fighting force, withdrew to Virginia. The cautious McClellan did not follow, missing a chance to finish off the crippled Southern army. Lincoln was so fed up that he fired McClellan in November, 1862. In the next chapter, you will learn about the historic action Lincoln took after the Battle of Antietam.

Section Assessment

1. Terms & Names

Explain the significance of:
- Ulysses S. Grant
- Battle of Shiloh
- cavalry
- Seven Days' Battles
- Battle of Antietam

2. Using Graphics

Review the section and find five key events to place on a time line as shown.

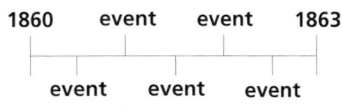

Which of these events do you think was most important?

3. Main Ideas

a. Why were Union victories in the West and the fall of New Orleans significant to the Union cause?

b. Why did Lee go on the offensive against the North?

c. How did the South's fortunes change after Lee took command of the Army of Northern Virginia?

4. Critical Thinking

Making Inferences What does Lee's invasion of the North suggest about his qualities as a general and a leader?

THINK ABOUT
- Lee's military skills and style
- the North's resources

ACTIVITY OPTIONS

GEOGRAPHY

ART

Develop a new military strategy for either the North or the South. Show your strategy on a **map** or in a **diagram** of troop movements.

TERMS & NAMES

Briefly explain the significance of each of the following.

1. Fort Sumter
2. Robert E. Lee
3. border state
4. blockade
5. hygiene
6. rifle
7. ironclad
8. Ulysses S. Grant
9. Battle of Shiloh
10. Battle of Antietam

REVIEW QUESTIONS

War Erupts (pages 481–487)

1. How and when did the Civil War start?
2. What advantages did the North have at the beginning of the war?
3. What were the war strategies of the two sides?

Life in the Army (pages 488–492)

4. What was the typical Civil War soldier like?
5. Why did so many people volunteer to fight in the Civil War?
6. Why was the incidence of disease so high among Civil War soldiers?
7. How did the use of rifles and minié balls change war tactics?

No End in Sight (pages 493–497)

8. What goal of the Union strategy did Grant further, and how did he do it?
9. Why did the North have such a hard time capturing Richmond, Virginia?
10. How did Lee's appointment to head the Army of Northern Virginia affect the course of the war?

CRITICAL THINKING

1. USING YOUR NOTES: COMPARING AND CONTRASTING

	North	South
Reasons for fighting		
Advantages		
Disadvantages		
Military strategy		
Battle victories		

Using your completed chart, answer the questions.

a. Which side seemed likelier to win the war? Why?
b. Which side followed more closely its original strategy in the first two years of the war?

2. ANALYZING LEADERSHIP

Think about the leaders discussed in this chapter. Choose one. What character traits helped make him an effective leader?

3. APPLYING CITIZENSHIP SKILLS

Which individuals or groups of people demonstrated good and poor citizenship during the war? Explain your choices.

4. THEME: CITIZENSHIP

How could people on both sides of the Civil War believe that they were being good citizens by fighting?

5. MAKING DECISIONS

In your opinion, was Lincoln correct in deciding to go to war to save the Union? Explain your answer.

Interact *with* History

How did the consequences and effects of civil war that you predicted before you read the chapter compare with the actual conditions you read about?

VISUAL SUMMARY

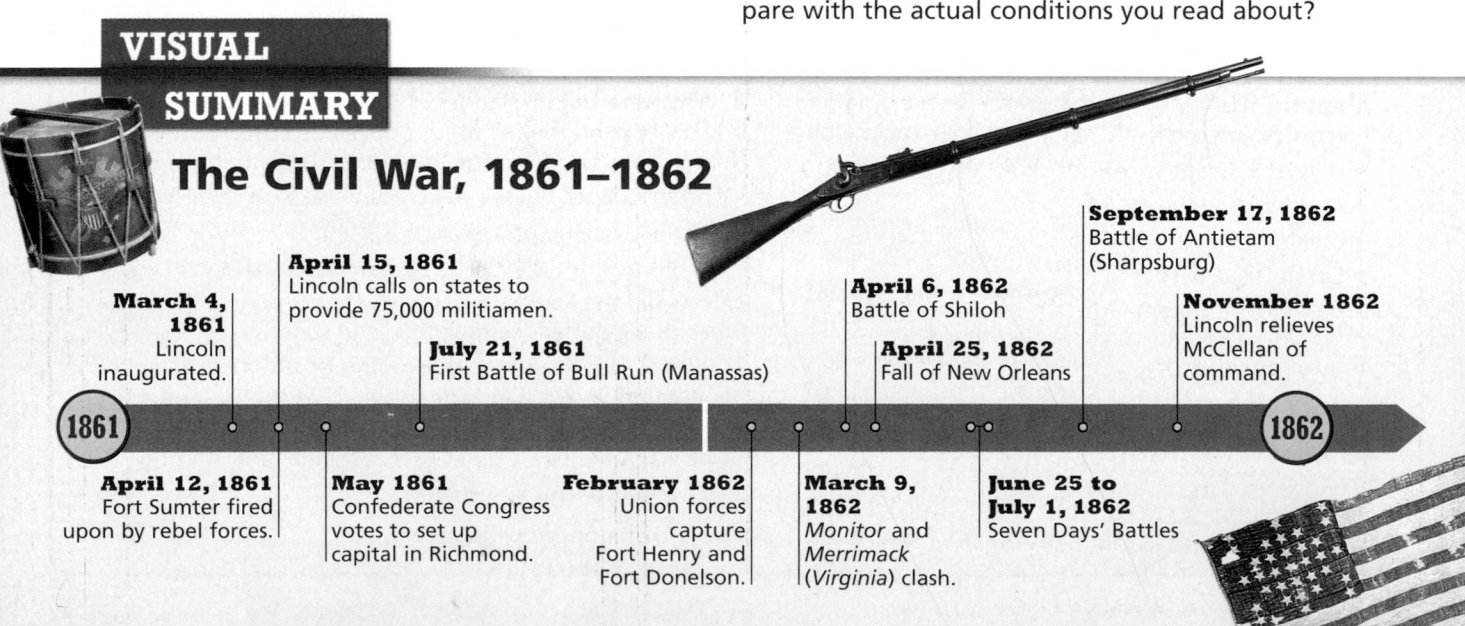

The Civil War, 1861–1862

March 4, 1861
Lincoln inaugurated.

April 15, 1861
Lincoln calls on states to provide 75,000 militiamen.

July 21, 1861
First Battle of Bull Run (Manassas)

April 6, 1862
Battle of Shiloh

April 25, 1862
Fall of New Orleans

September 17, 1862
Battle of Antietam (Sharpsburg)

November 1862
Lincoln relieves McClellan of command.

1861

1862

April 12, 1861
Fort Sumter fired upon by rebel forces.

May 1861
Confederate Congress votes to set up capital in Richmond.

February 1862
Union forces capture Fort Henry and Fort Donelson.

March 9, 1862
Monitor and *Merrimack* (*Virginia*) clash.

June 25 to July 1, 1862
Seven Days' Battles

Use the map and your knowledge of U.S. history to answer questions 1 and 2.

Additional Test Practice, pp. S1–S33.

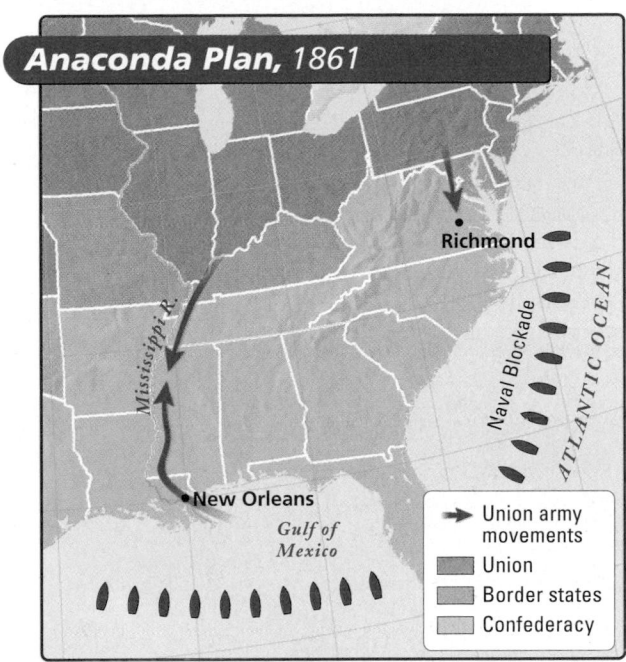

Anaconda Plan, 1861

Richmond

Naval Blockade

ATLANTIC OCEAN

Mississippi R.

New Orleans

Gulf of Mexico

→ Union army movements
■ Union
■ Border states
■ Confederacy

1. What does the arrow in the east indicate?
   A. movement of Union troops toward Richmond
   B. movement of resisting Confederate troops
   C. movement of Confederate troops to take New Orleans
   D. movement of Union troops up the Mississippi

2. Which of the following did the blockade prevent access to?
   A. border states
   B. Confederate states
   C. Union states
   D. Union troops

General George McClellan discusses his battle plan in this quotation. Use the quotation and your knowledge of U.S. history to answer question 3.

PRIMARY SOURCE

[S]oon as I feel that my army is well organized and well disciplined and strong enough, I will advance and force the Rebels to a battle on a field of my own selection. A long time must elapse before I can do that.

General George McClellan, quoted in Civil War Journal: The Leaders

3. Which of the following summarizes McClellan's priority in leading his army into battle?
   A. He will lead his troops into battle quickly.
   B. He refuses to go into battle without more troops.
   C. He wants to feel confident in his army's readiness for battle.
   D. He intends to make a surprise attack.

TEST PRACTICE
CLASSZONE.COM

ALTERNATIVE ASSESSMENT

1. ✎ **WRITING ABOUT HISTORY**

Assume the role of a soldier during the Civil War, either Union or Confederate, and write a **letter** home to your family.

- Use library resources to find written accounts from soldiers during the Civil War.
- Use what you learn to write your own letter. Include details about your daily life and your feelings about the war.

2. **COOPERATIVE LEARNING**

Work in a small group to develop a compromise that would have resolved the conflict between the North and the South. Have one member of your group take the position of a Northerner, another a Southerner, and a third the mediator between the two.

INTEGRATED TECHNOLOGY

DOING INTERNET RESEARCH

Life in the army training camps during the Civil War was difficult. Use the Internet to research army life. Then create a presentation about an aspect army life.

- Find primary sources about life in the army, such as diaries, letters, photographs, and news articles.
- Choose a specific topic for your presentation. For example, you might focus on drawings, maps, and photos that show the design of a typical army camp, items used for cooking, lodging, sanitation, military drilling, and recreation, or firsthand accounts of camp life from letters and diaries.

For more about Civil War armies . . .

INTERNET ACTIVITY
CLASSZONE.COM

The Tide of War Turns 1863–1865

Confederate and Union cavalry clash at Yellow Tavern, Virginia, on May 11, 1864.

The slight curve of the cavalry sword provided a better slashing motion when fighting on horseback.

January 1863
Lincoln issues the Emancipation Proclamation after presenting it to his cabinet.

July 1863
Battle of Gettysburg takes place.
Union takes Vicksburg.

March 1864
Grant is put in charge of all Union armies.

USA World 1863

January 1863
Polish nationalists revolt against Russian rule.

July 1863
Source of Nile River is found at Lake Victoria in present-day Uganda.

June 1864
Archduke Maximilian of Austria becomes emperor of Mexico.

The Confederate uniforms were gray and the Union's were blue. The two sides are often referred to by these colors.

In 1863, you have been a Civil War soldier for two years. The life of a soldier is a hard one. The food is awful. Disease is common. Worst of all is the horrible violence and death. Often you feel the urge to run away and go home.

What would inspire you to keep fighting?

What Do You Think?

- What would you be willing to sacrifice for your country? What if your country fought for something you did not believe in?
- How would the attitudes of fellow soldiers influence your decision?

RESEARCH LINKS
CLASSZONE.COM

Visit the Chapter 17 links for more information about the Civil War.

November 1864
Lincoln is reelected.

April 1865
Union takes Richmond.
Lee surrenders at Appomattox Court House.
Lincoln is assassinated.

1866

September 1864
First International Workingmen's Association is established, and Karl Marx becomes its leader.

September 1865
English officials arrest *Fenian* leaders of planned uprising in Ireland.

Reading Strategy: Comparing and Contrasting

What Do You Know?

What advantages and disadvantages did the North and the South have? Did particular individuals give either side an advantage during the Civil War?

Think About

- what qualities contribute to the success of military leaders
- the importance of obeying orders for soldiers even if it might mean death
- your responses to the Interact with History about what would inspire you to keep fighting (see page 502)

Robert E. Lee was the military genius at the head of the Confederate armies.

Ulysses S. Grant took charge of the Union armies in March 1864.

What Do You Want to Know?

What questions do you have about the later part of the Civil War and how it ended? Make a list of those questions before you read the chapter.

Comparing and Contrasting

When you study historical events, it is important to compare and contrast the effects that events had on different individuals and groups. A single event might affect two groups of people in completely different ways. Use the chart below to compare and contrast the impact of events on the Union and the Confederacy in the later years of the Civil War.

S See Skillbuilder Handbook, page R10.

 Taking Notes

	North	South
Emancipation Proclamation		
War's Impact		
Northern Victories in Battle		
Union Wins Civil War		

The Emancipation Proclamation

MAIN IDEA	WHY IT MATTERS NOW	TERMS & NAMES
In 1863, President Lincoln issued the Emancipation Proclamation, which helped to change the war's course.	The Emancipation Proclamation was an important step in ending slavery in the United States.	Emancipation Proclamation 54th Massachusetts Regiment

ONE AMERICAN'S STORY

During the Civil War, abolitionists like Frederick Douglass continued their bitter fight against slavery. Douglass urged President Lincoln to emancipate, or free, enslaved Americans.

A VOICE FROM THE PAST

To fight against slaveholders, without fighting against slavery, is but a half-hearted business, and paralyzes the hands engaged in it. . . . Fire must be met with water. . . . War for the destruction of liberty [by the South] must be met with war for the destruction of slavery.

Frederick Douglass, quoted in *Battle Cry of Freedom*

During the Civil War, Frederick Douglass urged President Lincoln to make the conflict a war against slavery.

Douglass pointed out that the Confederate war effort depended on slave labor. For both practical and moral reasons, Douglass said, Lincoln should free the slaves. In this section, you will learn how ending slavery became an important goal of the Civil War.

Calls for Emancipation

Throughout the war, abolitionists had been urging Lincoln to emancipate enslaved persons. Many criticized the president for being too cautious. Some even charged that Lincoln's lack of action aided the Confederate cause.

Still, Lincoln hesitated. He did not believe he had the power under the Constitution to abolish slavery where it already existed. Nor did he want to anger the four slave states that remained in the Union. He also knew that most Northern Democrats, and many Republicans, opposed emancipation.

Lincoln did not want the issue of slavery to divide the nation further than it already had. Although he disliked slavery, the president's first priority was to preserve the Union. "If I could save the Union without freeing

Taking Notes

Use your chart to take notes about the effects of the Emancipation Proclamation.

Emancipation Proclamation
War's Impact
Northern Victories in Battle
Union Wins Civil War

any slave I would do it," he declared. "If I could save it by freeing *all* the slaves I would do it; and if I could save it by freeing some and leaving others alone, I would also do that."

By the summer of 1862, however, Lincoln had decided in favor of emancipation. The war was taking a terrible toll. If freeing the slaves helped weaken the South, then he would do it. Lincoln waited, however, for a moment when he was in a position of strength. After General Lee's forces were stopped at Antietam, Lincoln decided to act.

The Emancipation Proclamation

On January 1, 1863, Lincoln issued the **Emancipation Proclamation,** which freed all slaves in Confederate territory. The proclamation had a tremendous impact on the public. However, it freed very few slaves. Most of the slaves that Lincoln intended to liberate lived in areas distant from the Union troops that could enforce his proclamation.

Background
In September 1862, Lincoln issued an early proclamation that gave rebellious states a chance to preserve slavery by rejoining the Union.

Lincoln presents the Emancipation Proclamation to his cabinet.

A VOICE FROM THE PAST

On the first day of January, in the year of our Lord one thousand eight hundred and sixty-three, all persons held as slaves within any State or designated part of a State, the people whereof shall then be in rebellion against the United States, shall be then, [thenceforth], and forever free.

Abraham Lincoln, from the *Emancipation Proclamation*

Why, critics charged, did Lincoln free slaves only in the South? The answer was in the Constitution. Because freeing Southern slaves weakened the Confederacy, the proclamation could be seen as a military action. As commander-in-chief, Lincoln had this authority. Yet the Constitution did not give the president the power to free slaves within the Union. But Lincoln did ask Congress to abolish slavery gradually throughout the land.

Reading **History**
A. Drawing Conclusions Why did Lincoln choose to limit his proclamation mostly to rebellious states?

Although the Emancipation Proclamation did not free many enslaved people at the time it was issued, it was important as a symbolic measure. For the North, the Civil War was no longer a limited war whose main goal was to preserve the Union. It was a war of liberation.

Response to the Proclamation

Abolitionists were thrilled that Lincoln had finally issued the Emancipation Proclamation. "We shout for joy that we live to record this righteous decree," wrote Frederick Douglass. Still, many believed the law should have gone further. They were upset that Lincoln had not freed *all* enslaved persons, including those in the border states.

*Reading*History

B. Summarizing
Why did
Northern
Democrats
oppose the
Emancipation
Proclamation?

Other people in the North, especially Democrats, were angered by the president's decision. Northern Democrats, the majority of whom were against emancipating even Southern slaves, claimed that the proclamation would only make the war longer by continuing to anger the South. A newspaperman in Ohio called Lincoln's proclamation "monstrous, impudent, and heinous . . . insulting to God as to man."

Most Union soldiers, though, welcomed emancipation. One officer noted that, although few soldiers were abolitionists, most were happy "to destroy everything that . . . gives the rebels strength."

White Southerners reacted to the proclamation with rage. Although it had limited impact in areas outside the reach of Northern armies, many slaves began to run away to Union lines. At the same time that these slaves deprived the Confederacy of labor, they also began to provide the Union with soldiers.

African-American Soldiers

In addition to freeing slaves, the Emancipation Proclamation declared that African-American men willing to fight "will be received into the armed service of the United States."

Frederick Douglass had argued for the recruitment of African-American soldiers since the start of the war. He declared, "Once [you] let the black man get upon his person the brass letters, U.S. . . . there is no power on earth which can deny that he has earned the right to citizenship."

Before the proclamation, the federal government had discouraged the enlistment of African Americans, and only a few regiments were formed. After emancipation, African Americans rushed to join the army. By war's end, about 180,000 black soldiers wore the blue uniform of the Union army.

African-American soldiers were organized in all-black regiments, usually led by white officers. They were often given the worst jobs

Thousands
of African
Americans, such
as these men of
the 4th U.S.
Colored Troops,
fought for the
Union during the
Civil War.

505

*Reading***History**
C. Identifying
Facts How did
many black sol-
diers protest
when they were
offered lower
pay than white
soldiers?

to do and were paid less than white soldiers. Despite these obstacles, African-American soldiers showed great courage on the battlefield and wore their uniforms with pride. More than one regiment insisted on fighting without pay rather than accepting lower pay than the white soldiers.

The 54th Massachusetts

One unit that insisted on fighting without pay was the **54th Massachusetts Regiment,** one of the first African-American regiments organized in the North. The soldiers of the 54th—among whom were two sons of Frederick Douglass—soon made the regiment the most famous of the Civil War.

The 54th Massachusetts earned its greatest fame in July 1863, when it led a heroic attack on Fort Wagner in South Carolina. The soldiers' bravery at Fort Wagner made the 54th a household name in the North and increased African-American enlistment.

The soldiers of the 54th Massachusetts and other African-American regiments faced grave dangers if captured. Rather than take African Americans as prisoners, Confederate soldiers often shot them or returned them to slavery.

The war demanded great sacrifices, not only from soldiers and prisoners, but also from people back home. In the next section, you will read about the hardships that the Civil War placed on the civilian populations in both the North and the South.

Now and **then**

AFRICAN AMERICANS IN THE MILITARY

During the Civil War, no African-American soldier was promoted above the rank of captain. But times have changed. In 1989, General Colin Powell (shown below) was made a four-star general and named chairman of the Joint Chiefs of Staff—the highest position in the military.

General Powell's appointment was the climax of a long struggle to fully integrate American armed forces. From the Civil War through World War II, African-American soldiers were kept apart from white soldiers and denied equal rights. However, in 1948, President Harry Truman ended segregation in the armed forces. Today the American military is fully integrated.

Section **1** Assessment

1. Terms & Names

Explain the significance of:
• Emancipation Proclamation
• 54th Massachusetts Regiment

2. Using Graphics

Use a chart to record responses to the Emancipation Proclamation.

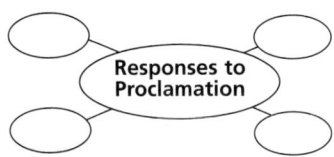

Responses to Proclamation

How did the proclamation change Northerners' views of the war?

3. Main Ideas

a. What was Lincoln's reason for not emancipating slaves when the war began?

b. Why was the immediate impact of the Emancipation Proclamation limited?

c. Why did black soldiers often face greater hardships than white soldiers?

4. Critical Thinking

Recognizing Effects How did the Emancipation Proclamation change the role of African Americans in the war?

THINK ABOUT
• how the proclamation changed military policy
• the response of many Southern slaves to the proclamation

ACTIVITY OPTIONS

TECHNOLOGY

MUSIC

Do research on the 54th Massachusetts Regiment. Create a **Web site** for the regiment or write a **song** about the soldiers' heroism at Fort Wagner.

War Affects Society

MAIN IDEA	**WHY IT MATTERS NOW**	**TERMS & NAMES**
The Civil War caused social, economic, and political changes in the North and the South.	Some changes, like the growth of industry, affected Americans long after the end of Civil War.	Copperhead income tax conscription greenback bounty Clara Barton

ONE AMERICAN'S STORY

As the Civil War moved into its third year, the constant demand for men and resources began to take its toll back home. Sometimes, the hardships endured by civilians resulted in angry scenes. On April 3, 1863, a resident of Richmond, Virginia, named Agnes came upon a group of hungry women and children, who had gathered in front of the capitol. She described the scene as these women and children were joined by other people who were upset by the shortage of food.

A VOICE FROM THE PAST

The crowd now rapidly increased, and numbered, I am sure, more than a thousand women and children. It grew and grew until it reached the dignity of a mob—a bread riot.

Agnes, quoted in *Reminiscences of Peace and War*

Food became scarce in many places during the Civil War. Here, women demand milk for their hungry families.

The mob then went out of control. It broke into shops and stole food and other goods. Only the threat of force ended the riot. In this section, you will read more about hardships that the Civil War caused on the home front.

Disagreement About the War

In the spring of 1863, riots like the one in Richmond broke out in a number of Southern towns. Southerners were growing weary of the war and the constant sacrifices it demanded.

Confederate soldiers began to leave the army in increasing numbers. By the end of the year, the Confederate army had lost nearly 40 percent of its men. Some of these men were on leave, but many others were deserters.

Taking Notes

Use your chart to take notes about the effects of the Civil War.

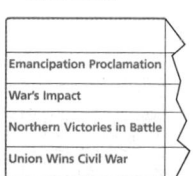

| Emancipation Proclamation |
| War's Impact |
| Northern Victories in Battle |
| Union Wins Civil War |

In this political cartoon, the Union defends itself against "Copperheads." This was the name given to Northerners who sympathized with the South.

Faced with the difficulties of waging war, the Confederate states fell into disagreement. The same principle of states' rights that led them to break with the Union kept them from coordinating their war effort. As one Southern governor put it, "I am *still* a rebel . . . no matter who may be in power."

Disagreements over the conduct of the war also arose in the North. Lincoln's main opponents were the **Copperheads,** Northern Democrats who favored peace with the South. (A copperhead is a poisonous snake that strikes without warning.) Lincoln had protesters arrested. He also suspended the writ of habeas corpus, which prevents the government from holding citizens without a trial.

Vocabulary
writ: a written order issued by a court of law

The Draft Laws

As the war dragged on, both the North and the South needed more soldiers. As a result, both sides passed laws of **conscription,** also known as the draft. These laws required men to serve in the military.

The Confederates had been drafting soldiers since the spring of 1862. By 1863, all able-bodied white men between the ages of 18 and 45 were required to join the army. However, there were a number of exceptions. Planters who owned 20 or more slaves could avoid military service. In addition, wealthy men could hire substitutes to serve in their place. By 1863, substitutes might cost as much as $6,000. The fact that wealthy men could avoid service caused poor Southerners to complain that it was a "rich man's war but a poor man's fight."

*Reading*History
A. Drawing Conclusions Why were many soldiers dissatisfied with the draft laws?

The Union draft law was passed in March 1863. Like the Confederacy, the Union allowed draftees to hire substitutes. However, the North also offered $300 **bounties,** or cash payments, to men who volunteered to serve. As a result, only a small percentage of men in the North were drafted. Most men volunteered and received the bounty.

Even so, the draft was extremely unpopular. In July 1863, anger over the draft and simmering racial tensions led to the New York City draft riots. For four days, rioters destroyed property and attacked people on the streets. Over 100 people were killed—many of them African Americans.

Economic Effects of the War

Many people suffered economic hardship during the war. The suffering was severe in the South, where most battles were fought, but the North also experienced difficulties.

Food shortages were very common in the South, partly because so many farmers were fighting in the Confederate army. Moreover, food sometimes could not get to market because trains were now being used to carry war materials. The Confederate army also seized food and other supplies for its own needs.

*Reading*History

B. Analyzing Causes Why were economic problems particularly bad in the South?

Another problem, especially in the South, was inflation—an increase in price and decrease in the value of money. The average family food bill in the South increased from $6.65 a month in 1861 to $68 by mid–1863. Over the course of the war, prices rose 9,000 percent in the South.

Inflation in the North was much lower, but prices still rose faster than wages, making life harder for working people. Some people took advantage of wartime demand and sold goods for high prices.

Overall, though, war production boosted Northern industry and fueled the economy. In the short term, this gave the North an economic advantage over the South. In the long term, industry would begin to replace farming as the basis of the national economy.

During the war, the federal government passed two important economic measures. In 1861, it established the first **income tax**—a tax on earnings. The following year, the government issued a new paper currency, known as **greenbacks** because of their color. The new currency helped the Northern economy by ensuring that people had money to spend. It also helped the Union to pay for the war.

Some Southerners in the border states took advantage of the stronger Union economy by selling cotton to Northern traders, in violation of Confederate law.

**Vocabulary
subjugate:** to bring under control or to conquer

"Yankee gold," wrote one Confederate officer, "is fast accomplishing what Yankee arms could never achieve—the subjugation of our people."

Resistance by Slaves

Another factor that affected the South was the growing resistance from slaves. To hurt the Southern economy, slaves slowed their pace of work or stopped working altogether. Some carried out sabotage, destroying crops and farm equipment to hurt the plantation economy. When white

daily *life*

INFLATION IN THE SOUTH
During the Civil War, inflation caused hardship in the North and the South. But inflation was especially severe in the Confederacy, where prices could become outrageously high.

The food prices shown below are from 1864. Consider how many days it took a Confederate soldier to earn enough money to buy each of these foods.

$6.00
Dozen Eggs

$6.25
Pound of Butter

$10.00
Quart of Milk

$12.00
Pound of Coffee

$18.00

Confederate Soldier's Monthly Pay

planters fled advancing Union armies, slaves often refused to go along. They stayed behind, waiting for Union soldiers to free them.

Some enslaved people even rose up in rebellion against their overseers. More commonly, though, slaves ran away from plantations to join the Union forces as they pushed farther into Confederate territory. One Union officer described a common sight.

A VOICE FROM THE PAST

It was very touching to see the vast numbers of colored [African-American] women following after us with babies in their arms, and little ones like our Anna clinging to their tattered skirts. One poor creature, while nobody was looking, hid two boys, five years old, in a wagon, intending, I suppose that they should see the land of freedom if she couldn't.

Union officer, quoted in *The Civil War*

After Lincoln issued the Emancipation Proclamation, the number of slaves fleeing Southern plantations greatly increased. By the end of the war, as many as half a million had fled to Union lines.

Women Aid the War Effort

With so many men away at war, women in both the North and the South assumed increased responsibilities. Women plowed fields and ran farms and plantations. They also took over jobs in offices and factories that had previously been done only by men.

Other social changes came about because of the thousands of women who served on the front lines as volunteer workers and nurses. Susie King Taylor was an African-American woman who wrote an account of her experiences as a volunteer with an African-American regiment. She asked her readers to remember that "many lives were lost,—not men alone but noble women as well."

Relief agencies put women to work washing clothes, gathering supplies, and cooking food for soldiers. Also, nursing became a respectable profession for many women. By the end of the war, around 3,000 nurses had worked under the leadership of Dorothea Dix in Union hospitals. Southern women were also active as nurses and as volunteers on the front.

Women also played a key role as spies in both the North and the South. Harriet Tubman served as a spy for Union forces along the coast of South Carolina. The most famous Confederate spy was Belle Boyd. Although she was arrested six times, she continued her work through much of the war. At one point, she even sent messages from her jail cell by putting them in little rubber balls and tossing them out the window.

AMERICA'S HISTORY MAKERS

CLARA BARTON
1821–1912

Trained as a schoolteacher, **Clara Barton** was working for the government when the Civil War began. She organized a relief agency to help with the war effort. "While our soldiers stand and fight," she said, "I can stand and feed and nurse them."

She also made food for soldiers in camp and tended to the wounded and dying on the battlefield. At Antietam, she held a doctor's operating table steady as cannon shells burst all around them. The doctor called her "the angel of the battlefield." After the war, Barton founded the American Red Cross.

How did Clara Barton demonstrate her leadership abilities?

*Reading*History
C. Summarizing
How did women participate in the Civil War?

Civil War Prison Camps

Women caught spying were thrown into jail, but soldiers captured in battle suffered far more. At prison camps in both the North and the South, prisoners of war faced terrible conditions.

*Reading*History

D. Making Inferences Why were death rates so high at many Civil War prison camps?

One of the worst prison camps in the North was in Elmira, New York. Perhaps the harshest feature of a prisoner's life at the camp was the New York winter. One prisoner called Elmira "an excellent summer prison for southern soldiers, but an excellent place for them to find their graves in the winter." In just one year, more than 24 percent of Elmira's 12,121 prisoners died of sickness and exposure to severe weather.

Conditions were also horrible in the South. The camp with the worst reputation was at Andersonville, Georgia. Built to hold 10,000 prisoners, at one point it housed 33,000. Inmates had little shelter from the heat or cold. Most slept in holes scratched in the dirt. Drinking water came from one tiny creek that also served as a sewer. As many as 100 men per day died at Andersonville from starvation, disease, and exposure.

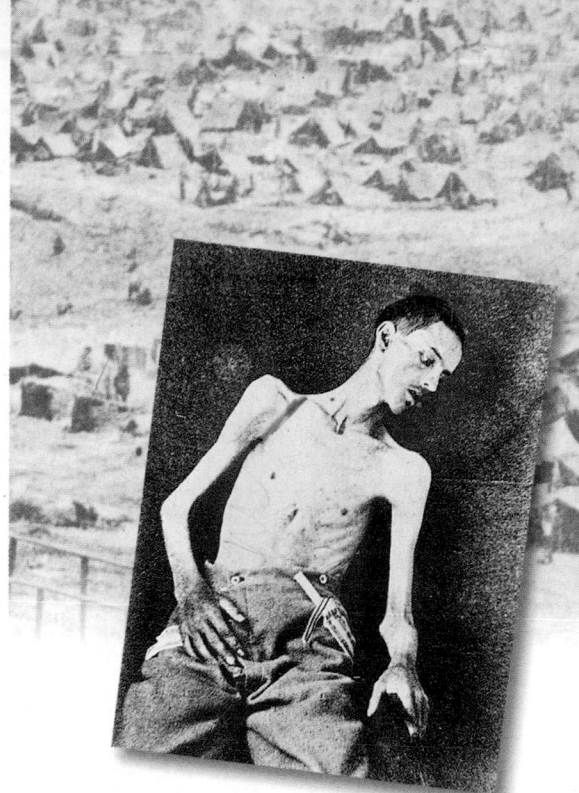

The terrible conditions at Civil War prison camps caused much suffering and death.

People who saw the camps were shocked by the condition of the soldiers. The poet Walt Whitman—who served as a Union nurse—described a group of soldiers who returned from a prison camp. He exclaimed, "Can those be *men?* . . . are they not really mummied, dwindled corpses?"

Around 50,000 men died in Civil War prison camps. But this number was dwarfed by the number of dead on the battlefronts and even more from disease in army camps. In the next section, you will read about the bloody battles that led to the end of the Civil War.

Section 2 Assessment

1. Terms & Names

Explain the significance of:
- Copperhead
- conscription
- bounty
- income tax
- greenback
- Clara Barton

2. Using Graphics

Use a diagram like the one below to compare conditions in the North and South during the later years of war.

Conditions During the War

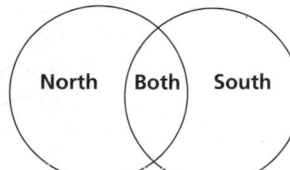

North | Both | South

3. Main Ideas

a. How did the South's principle of states' rights undermine the Confederate war effort?

b. How did the draft laws in the North and South differ?

c. What conditions at prison camps caused so many to suffer behind enemy lines?

4. Critical Thinking

Making Generalizations What economic changes took place during the Civil War?

THINK ABOUT
- the war's effect on prices
- industry and agriculture
- new economic measures begun by the government

ACTIVITY OPTIONS

GEOGRAPHY

SPEECH

Study Civil War prison camps. Make a **map** showing where they were located or give a **speech** explaining why prisoners should be treated better.

3

The North Wins

MAIN IDEA	WHY IT MATTERS NOW	TERMS & NAMES
Thanks to victories, beginning with Gettysburg and ending with Richmond, the Union survived.	If the Union had lost the war, the United States might look very different now.	Battle of Gettysburg / Siege of Vicksburg Pickett's Charge / William Tecumseh Sherman Ulysses S. Grant / Appomattox Court House Robert E. Lee

ONE AMERICAN'S STORY

Joshua Lawrence Chamberlain left his job as a college professor and took command of troops from his home state of Maine. His description of the aftermath of one battle shows how soldiers got used to the war's violence.

In 1862, Joshua Chamberlain was offered a year's travel with pay to study languages in Europe. He chose to fight for the Union instead.

A VOICE FROM THE PAST

It seemed best to [put] myself between two dead men among the many left there by earlier assaults, and to draw another crosswise for a pillow out of the trampled, blood-soaked sod, pulling the flap of his coat over my face to fend off the chilling winds, and still more chilling, the deep, many voiced moan [of the wounded] that overspread the field.

Joshua Lawrence Chamberlain, quoted in *The Civil War*

Chamberlain is best remembered for his courageous actions at the Battle of Gettysburg. In this section, you will read about that battle and others that led to the end of the Civil War.

Taking Notes

Use your chart to take notes about the military victories of the North.

> Emancipation Proclamation
> War's Impact
> Northern Victories in Battle
> Union Wins Civil War

The Road to Gettysburg

In September 1862, General McClellan stopped General Lee's Northern attack at the Battle of Antietam. But the cautious McClellan failed to finish off Lee's army, which retreated safely to Virginia.

President Lincoln, who was frustrated by McClellan, replaced him with Ambrose Burnside. But Burnside also proved to be a disappointment. At the Battle of Fredericksburg, Virginia, in December 1862, Burnside attacked Confederate troops who had dug trenches. The bloody result was 12,600 Union casualties. This disastrous attack led General Lee to remark, "It is well that war is so terrible—we should grow too fond of it!"

Lincoln replaced Burnside with General Joseph Hooker, who faced Lee the following May at Chancellorsville, Virginia. The result was yet another Union disaster. With half as many men as Hooker, Lee still managed to

cut the Union forces to pieces. However, the South paid a high price for its victory. As General "Stonewall" Jackson returned from a patrol on May 2, Confederate guards thought he was a Union soldier and shot him in the arm. Shortly after a surgeon amputated the arm, Jackson caught pneumonia. On May 10, Lee's prized general was dead.

In spite of Jackson's tragic death, Lee decided to head North once again. He hoped that a Confederate victory in Union territory would fuel Northern discontent with the war and bring calls for peace. He also hoped a Southern victory would lead European nations to give diplomatic recognition and aid to the Confederacy.

The Battle of Gettysburg

In late June 1863, Lee crossed into southern Pennsylvania. The Confederates learned of a supply of shoes in the town of Gettysburg and went to investigate. There, on July 1, they ran into Union troops. Both sides called for reinforcements, and the **Battle of Gettysburg** was on.

*Reading*History

A. Reading a Map Use the map and illustration on pages 514–515 to study Gettysburg's geography.

The fighting raged for three days. On the rocky hills and fields around Gettysburg, 90,000 Union troops, under the command of General George Meade, clashed with 75,000 Confederates.

During the struggle, Union forces tried to hold their ground on Cemetery Ridge, just south of town, while rebel soldiers tried to dislodge them. At times, the air seemed full of bullets. "The balls were whizzing so thick," said one Texan, "that it looked like a man could hold out a hat and catch it full."

The turning point came on July 3, when Lee ordered General George Pickett to mount a direct attack on the middle of the Union line. It was a deadly mistake. Some 13,000 rebel troops charged up the ridge into heavy Union fire. One soldier recalled "bayonet thrusts, sabre strokes, pistol shots . . . men going down on their hands and knees, spinning round like tops . . . ghastly heaps of dead men."

*Reading*History

B. Making Inferences Why might Lincoln have been disappointed after the Union victory at Gettysburg?

Pickett's Charge, as this attack came to be known, was torn to pieces. The Confederates retreated and waited for a Union counterattack. But once again, Lincoln's generals failed to finish off Lee's army. The furious Lincoln wondered when he would find a general who would defeat Lee once and for all.

Even so, the Union rejoiced over the victory at Gettysburg. Lee's hopes for a Confederate victory in the North were crushed. The North had lost 23,000 men, but Southern losses were even greater. Over one-third of Lee's army, 28,000 men, lay dead or wounded. Sick at heart, Lee led his army back to Virginia.

America's HERITAGE

THE GETTYSBURG ADDRESS

On November 19, 1863, President Lincoln spoke at the dedication of a cemetery in Gettysburg for the 3,500 soldiers buried there. His speech was short, and few who heard it were impressed. Lincoln himself called it "a flat failure."

Even so, the Gettysburg Address has since been recognized as one of the greatest speeches of all time. In it, Lincoln declared that the nation was founded on "the proposition that all men are created equal." He ended with a plea to continue the fight for democracy so that "government of the people, by the people, for the people shall not perish from the earth."

See page 524 for the full text of the Gettysburg Address.

Battle of Gettysburg

A monument stands today near a ridge at the Gettysburg battle-field. Labeled the "High Water Mark of the Rebellion," it shows how far Confederate troops advanced against Union lines. There, on July 3, 1863, the South came closest to winning the Civil War.

The fighting began on July 1. When a Confederate force captured Gettysburg, Union defenders took up new positions in the hills south of town. The next day, Confederate troops attacked across a wheat field and peach orchard in an attempt to seize the hill called Little Round Top. But Union forces held their ground.

July 3 was the decisive day. Lee, having failed to crack the side of General Meade's Union line, attacked its center. In an assault that came to be known as Pickett's Charge, some 13,000 men charged uphill across an open field toward the Union lines along Cemetery Ridge. Union soldiers covered the field with rifle and cannon fire. "Pickett's Charge" was a Confederate disaster.

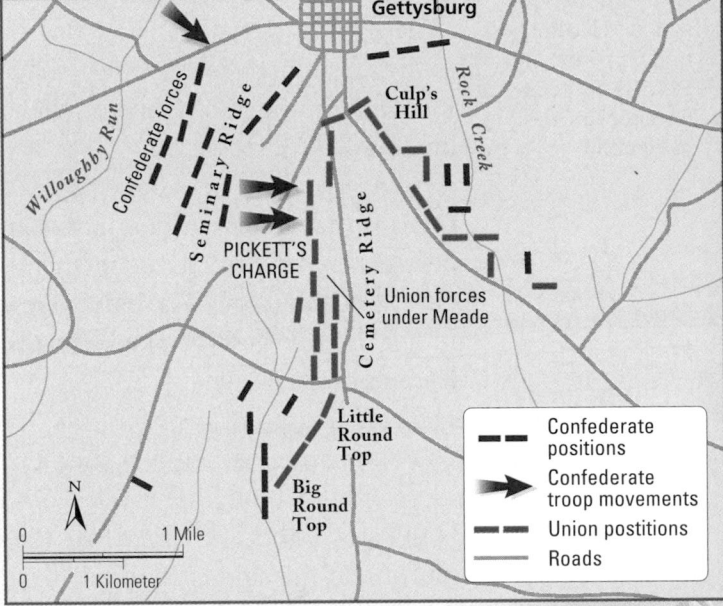

PENNSYLVANIA

• Gettysburg

Washington, D.C.

Gettysburg

Rock Creek

Culp's Hill

Seminary Ridge

Confederate forces

Willoughby Run

PICKETT'S CHARGE

Cemetery Ridge

Union forces under Meade

Little Round Top

Big Round Top

N

0   1 Mile
0   1 Kilometer

- - - Confederate positions
➤ Confederate troop movements
- - - Union postitions
—— Roads

Before beginning the charge named for him, Major General Pickett wrote to his fiancée, "My brave Virginians are to attack in front. Oh, may God in mercy help me."

ARTIFACT FILE

Soldiers' Diaries
Many Civil War soldiers wrote about their wartime experiences in personal diaries, such as this one belonging to Sergeant Alfred S. Rowe of Maryland.

MECHANICSVILLE
HANOVER
MANASSAS
CEDAR RUN
OX HILL
HARPERS FERRY
COLD HARBOR
FRAZIERS FARM

Regimental Flag Flags helped soldiers to identify the different sides during battle. Often, a regiment's flag would show the names of battles it had fought. This flag, which belonged to the 28th North Carolina, was captured at Pickett's Charge.

Gettysburg

Culp's Hill

Cemetery Hill

Cemetery Ridge

As in many battles of the Civil War, the outcome at Gettysburg was affected by the landscape. Both sides fought for control of the high ground. Union control of the two "Round Top" hills, Cemetery Ridge and Culp's Hill, gave Meade the advantage.

Peach Orchard

Wheat Field

Devil's Den

Little Round Top

Big Round Top

On-Line Field Trip

The Gettysburg National Military Park Museum contains many objects relating to the Battle of Gettysburg, including this federal bass drum. This heavy drum—two feet in diameter—was harnessed to the neck of a soldier, who beat time with leather-covered wooden mallets.

For more about Gettysburg . . .

RESEARCH LINKS
CLASSZONE.COM

CONNECT TO GEOGRAPHY

1. **Place** How might Confederate positions on low ground have put them at a disadvantage?

2. **Human-Environment Interaction** How might the attitudes of Union soldiers have been affected by fighting in their own territory?

G See Geography Handbook, pages 4–5.

CONNECT TO HISTORY

3. **Asking Questions** Ask and answer a question about how the geographic patterns of the Gettysburg area affected the battle.

ULYSSES S. GRANT

1822–1885

<u>General Ulysses S. Grant</u> was an unlikely war hero. Although educated at West Point Military Academy, he was a poor student and showed little interest in an army career. With his quiet manner and rumpled uniform, he often failed to impress his fellow officers.

Yet on the battlefield, Grant proved to be a brilliant general. Highly focused and cool under fire, he won the first major Union victories of the war.

Grant was willing to fight Lee—even if the costs were high. He told his generals, "Wherever Lee goes, there you will go also."

ROBERT E. LEE

1807–1870

<u>Robert E. Lee</u> seemed destined for greatness. In his crisp uniform and trim, white beard, Lee was a dashing figure on the battlefield.

Born to a leading Virginia family, Lee was a top student at West Point and won praise for his actions in the Mexican War. General Winfield Scott called him "the very best soldier I have ever seen in the field."

Lee did not want to fight the Union, but he felt he had to stand by Virginia. "I did only what my duty demanded," Lee said. "I could have taken no other course without dishonor."

How did the tough decisions made by Grant and Lee affect the Civil War?

The Siege of Vicksburg

On July 4, 1863, the day after Pickett's Charge, the Union received more good news. In Mississippi, General Ulysses S. Grant had defeated Confederate troops at the <u>**Siege of Vicksburg**</u>.

The previous year, Grant had won important victories in the West that opened up the Mississippi River for travel deep into the South. Vicksburg was the last major Confederate stronghold on the river. Grant had begun his attack on Vicksburg in May 1863. But when his direct attacks failed, he settled in for a long siege. Grant's troops surrounded the city and prevented the delivery of food and supplies. Eventually, the Confederates ran out of food. In desperation, they ate mules, dogs, and even rats. Finally, after nearly a month and a half, they surrendered.

The Union victory fulfilled a major part of the Anaconda Plan. The North had taken New Orleans the previous spring. Now, with complete control over the Mississippi River, the South was split in two.

With the victories at Vicksburg and Gettysburg, the tide of war turned in favor of the North. Britain gave up all thought of supporting the South. And, in General Grant, President Lincoln found a man who was willing to fight General Lee.

Sherman's Total War

In March 1864, President Lincoln named General Grant commander of all the Union armies. Grant then developed a plan to defeat the Confederacy. He would pursue Lee's army in Virginia, while Union forces under General <u>**William Tecumseh Sherman**</u> pushed through the Deep South to Atlanta and the Atlantic coast.

Vocabulary
siege: the surrounding of a city, town, or fortress by an army trying to capture it

Background
The Anaconda Plan called for blockading Southern ports, taking control of the Mississippi, and capturing Richmond.

Battling southward from Tennessee, Sherman took Atlanta in September 1864. He then set out on a march to the sea, cutting a path of destruction up to 60 miles wide and 300 miles long through Georgia.

Sherman waged total war: a war not only against enemy troops, but against everything that supports the enemy. His troops tore up rail lines, destroyed crops, and burned and looted towns.

Reading **History**
C. Drawing Conclusions How might the political situation in the North have been different if Sherman had not taken Atlanta?

Sherman's triumph in Atlanta was important for Lincoln. In 1864, the president was running for reelection, but his prospects were not good. Northerners were tired of war, and Democrats—who had nominated George McClellan—stood a good chance of winning on an antiwar platform.

Sherman's success changed all that. Suddenly, Northerners could sense victory. Lincoln took 55 percent of the popular vote and won re-election. In his second inaugural speech, Lincoln hoped for a speedy end to the war: "With malice towards none; with charity for all; . . . let us strive on to finish the work we are in; to bind up the nation's wounds; . . . to do all which may achieve and cherish a just, and a lasting peace." (See page 525 for more of Lincoln's Second Inaugural Address.)

In December, Sherman took Savannah, Georgia. He then sent a telegram to Lincoln: "I beg to present you, as a Christmas gift, the city of Savannah, with 150 heavy guns and . . . about 25,000 bales of cotton."

> ## *"Let us strive . . . to bind up the nation's wounds."*
> **Abraham Lincoln**

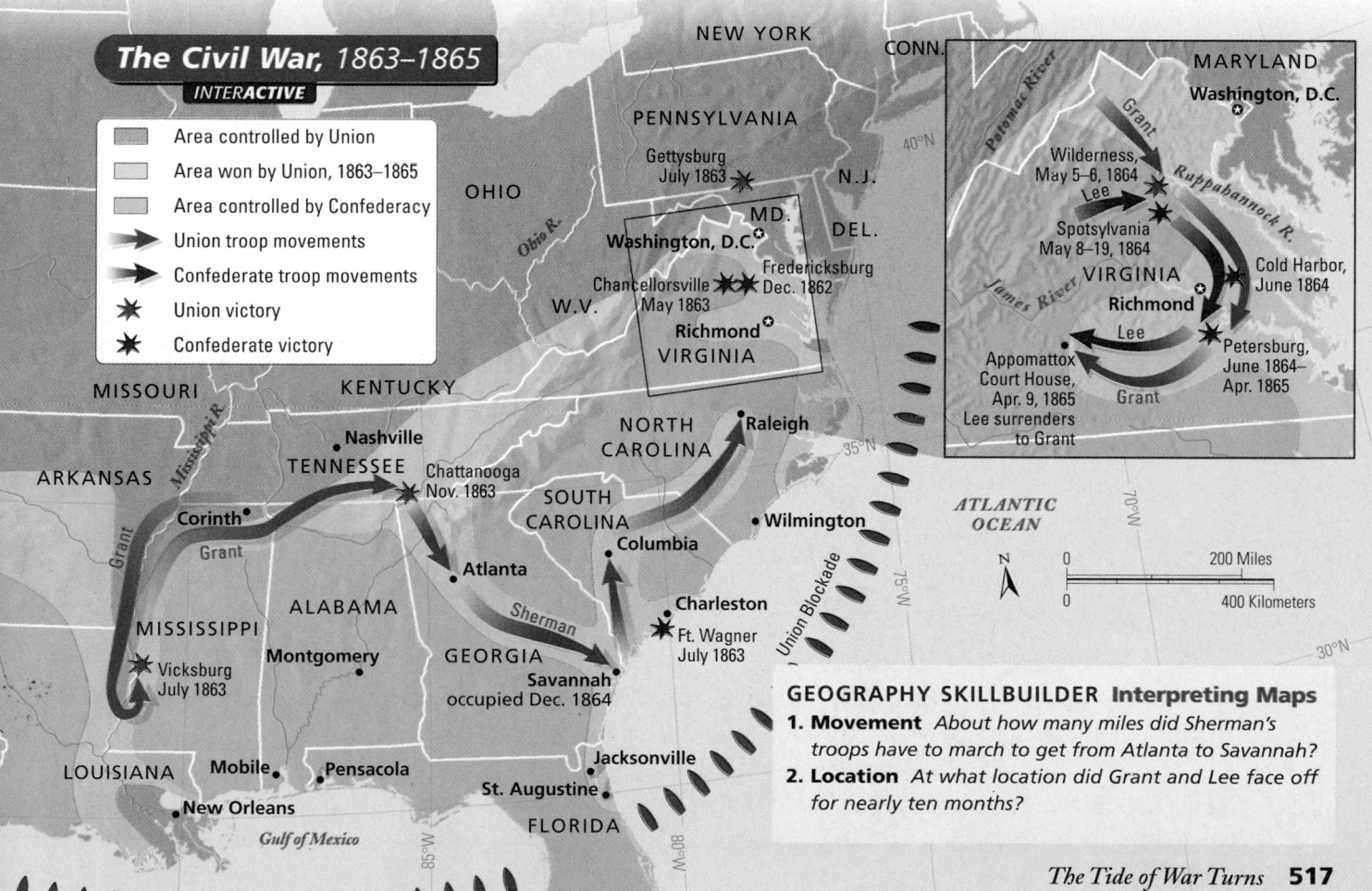

The Civil War, 1863–1865
INTERACTIVE

- Area controlled by Union
- Area won by Union, 1863–1865
- Area controlled by Confederacy
- Union troop movements
- Confederate troop movements
- ✹ Union victory
- ✹ Confederate victory

NEW YORK
CONN.
MARYLAND
Washington, D.C.
PENNSYLVANIA
Gettysburg July 1863
N.J.
OHIO
MD.
Washington, D.C.
DEL.
Chancellorsville May 1863
Fredericksburg Dec. 1862
W.V.
Richmond
VIRGINIA
MISSOURI
KENTUCKY
Raleigh
NORTH CAROLINA
Nashville
TENNESSEE
Chattanooga Nov. 1863
SOUTH CAROLINA
Wilmington
ARKANSAS
Corinth
Grant
Columbia
ATLANTIC OCEAN
Atlanta
ALABAMA
Sherman
Charleston
Ft. Wagner July 1863
MISSISSIPPI
Montgomery
GEORGIA
Savannah occupied Dec. 1864
Union Blockade
Vicksburg July 1863
LOUISIANA
Mobile
Pensacola
Jacksonville
St. Augustine
New Orleans
FLORIDA
Gulf of Mexico

Inset map — Virginia
Potomac River
MARYLAND
Washington, D.C.
Grant
Wilderness, May 5–6, 1864
Lee
Rappahannock R.
Spotsylvania May 8–19, 1864
VIRGINIA
Cold Harbor, June 1864
Richmond
James River
Lee
Appomattox Court House, Apr. 9, 1865 Lee surrenders to Grant
Petersburg, June 1864– Apr. 1865
Grant

N
0   200 Miles
0   400 Kilometers

GEOGRAPHY SKILLBUILDER Interpreting Maps
1. **Movement** *About how many miles did Sherman's troops have to march to get from Atlanta to Savannah?*
2. **Location** *At what location did Grant and Lee face off for nearly ten months?*

In 1861, Congress created the Medal of Honor to reward individual bravery in combat.

Grant's Virginia Campaign

After taking Savannah, Sherman moved north through the Carolinas seeking to meet up with Grant's troops in Virginia. Since May 1864, Grant and his generals had been fighting savage battles against Lee's forces. In battle after battle, Grant would attack, rest, then attack again, all the while moving south toward Richmond.

At the Battle of the Wilderness in May 1864, Union and Confederate forces fought in a tangle of trees and brush so thick that they could barely see each other. Grant lost over 17,000 men, but he pushed on. "Whatever happens," he told Lincoln, "we will not retreat."

At Spotsylvania and Cold Harbor, the fighting continued. Again, the losses were staggering. Grant's attack in June, at Cold Harbor, cost him 7,000 men, most in the first few minutes of battle. Some Union troops were so sure they would die in battle that they pinned their names and addresses to their jackets so their bodies could be identified later.

In June 1864, Grant's armies arrived at Petersburg, just south of Richmond. Unable to break through the Confederate defenses, the Union forces dug trenches and settled in for a long siege. The two sides faced off for ten months.

In the end, though, Lee could not hold out. Grant was drawing a noose around Richmond. So Lee pulled out, leaving the Confederate capital undefended. The Union army marched into Richmond on April 3. One Richmond woman recalled, "Exactly at eight o'clock the Confederate flag that fluttered above the Capitol came

*Reading*History
D. Reading a Map Use the map on page 517 to find the locations of the major battles of Grant's Virginia campaign.

HISTORY *through*ART

This photograph shows Union officers before the Battle of the Wilderness. Next to the tree on the right is the photographer Mathew Brady. Photography was still a new art when the Civil War began. Brady's Civil War photos represent one of the first examples of photojournalism.

How might people's attitudes toward war be affected when they can see pictures from the front lines?

518

down and the Stars and Stripes were run up. . . . We covered our faces and cried aloud."

Surrender at Appomattox

From Richmond and Petersburg, Lee fled west, while Grant followed in pursuit. Lee wanted to continue fighting, but he knew that his situation was hopeless. He sent a message to General Grant that he was ready to surrender.

On April 9, 1865, Lee and Grant met in the small Virginia town of **Appomattox Court House** to arrange the surrender. Grant later wrote that his joy at that moment was mixed with sadness.

A VOICE FROM THE PAST

I felt like anything rather than rejoicing at the downfall of a foe who had fought so long and valiantly, and had suffered so much for a cause, though that cause was, I believe, one of the worst for which a people ever fought, and one for which there was the least excuse. I do not question, however, the sincerity of the great mass of those who were opposed to us.

Ulysses S. Grant, *Personal Memoirs*

STRANGE *but* True

WILMER MCLEAN

The first major battle of the Civil War was fought on the property of Wilmer McLean. McLean lived in Manassas, Virginia, the site of the Battle of Bull Run. After the battle, McLean decided to move to a more peaceful place. He chose the village of Appomattox Court House (see map on page 517).

When Lee made the decision to surrender in April 1865, he sent Colonel Charles Marshall to find a location for a meeting with Grant. Marshall stopped the first man he saw in the deserted streets of Appomattox Court House. It was Wilmer McLean.

McLean reluctantly offered his home. Thus, the war that began in McLean's back yard ended in his parlor.

Grant offered generous terms of surrender. After laying down their arms, the Confederates could return home in peace, taking their private possessions and horses with them. Grant also gave food to the hungry Confederate soldiers.

After four long years, the Civil War was coming to a close. Its effects would continue, however, changing the country forever. In the next section, you will learn about the long-term consequences of the Civil War.

Section Assessment

1. Terms & Names

Explain the significance of:
- Battle of Gettysburg
- Pickett's Charge
- Ulysses S. Grant
- Robert E. Lee
- Siege of Vicksburg
- William Tecumseh Sherman
- Appomattox Court House

2. Using Graphics

Use a time line like the one below to record key events from Section 3.

1862　　　　　　　1866

Which event is considered the turning point of the war?

3. Main Ideas

a. Why was the Battle of Gettysburg important?

b. Why was Northern success in the Siege of Vicksburg important?

c. How did Grant treat Confederate soldiers after the surrender at Appomattox Court House?

4. Critical Thinking

Contrasting How was the Civil War different from wars that Americans had previously fought?

THINK ABOUT
- the role of civilians
- Sherman's military strategy

ACTIVITY OPTIONS

Research the Siege of Vicksburg. Make a **topographic map** of the area or write an **article** describing the soldiers' hardships during the siege.

4

The Legacy of the War

MAIN IDEA	WHY IT MATTERS NOW	TERMS & NAMES
The Civil War brought great changes and new challenges to the United States.	The most important change was the liberation of 4 million enslaved persons.	Thirteenth Amendment John Wilkes Booth

ONE AMERICAN'S STORY

In the spring of 1864, a year before the end of the Civil War, the Union army was running out of cemetery space to bury its war dead. The secretary of war ordered Quartermaster General Montgomery Meigs to find a new site for a cemetery. Without hesitation, Meigs chose Robert E. Lee's plantation in Arlington, Virginia, just across the Potomac River from Washington, D.C.

Meig's decision to turn Lee's plantation into a Union cemetery was highly symbolic. The Union soldiers who died fighting Lee's army would be buried in Lee's front yard. That site became Arlington National Cemetery.

During the Civil War, the government turned Robert E. Lee's Virginia plantation into a graveyard.

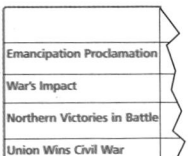

Taking Notes

Use your chart to take notes about the effects of the Union's victory in the Civil War.

> Emancipation Proclamation
> War's Impact
> Northern Victories in Battle
> Union Wins Civil War

Costs of the War

Many Northerners shared Montgomery Meigs's bitter feelings toward the South. At the same time, many Southerners felt great resentment toward the North. After the war, President Lincoln hoped to heal the nation and bring North and South together again. The generous terms of surrender offered to Lee were part of that effort. Hard feelings remained, however, in part because the costs of the war were so great.

The Civil War was the deadliest war in American history. In four years of fighting, approximately 620,000 soldiers died—360,000 for the Union and 260,000 for the Confederacy. Another 275,000 Union soldiers and 260,000 Confederate soldiers were wounded. Many suffered from their wounds for the rest of their lives.

Altogether, some 3,000,000 men served in the armies of the North and South—around 10 percent of the population. Along with the soldiers, many other Americans had their lives disrupted by the war.

ReadingHistory

A. Contrasting
How did government spending during the Civil War compare to that during previous years?

The war also had great economic costs. Together, the North and South spent more than five times the amount spent by the government in the previous eight decades. Many years after the fighting was over, the federal government was still paying interest on loans taken out during the war.

The Thirteenth Amendment

One of the greatest effects of the war was the freeing of millions of enslaved persons. As the Union army moved through the South during and after the war, Union soldiers released African Americans from bondage. One of those released was Booker T. Washington, who later became a famous educator and reformer. He recalled the day a Union officer came to his plantation to read the Emancipation Proclamation.

A VOICE FROM THE PAST

After the reading we were told that we were all free, and could go when and where we pleased. My mother, who was standing by my side, leaned over and kissed her children, while tears of joy ran down her cheeks. She explained to us what it all meant, that this was the day for which she had been so long praying, but fearing that she would never live to see.

Booker T. Washington, quoted in his autobiography, *Up from Slavery*

ReadingHistory

B. Making Inferences Why was an amendment needed to free enslaved persons even after the Emancipation Proclamation?

The Emancipation Proclamation applied primarily to slaves in the Confederacy, however. Many African Americans in the border states were still enslaved. In 1864, with the war still under way, President Lincoln had approved of a constitutional amendment to end slavery entirely, but it failed to pass Congress.

In January 1865, Lincoln urged Congress to try again to end slavery. This time, the measure—known as the **Thirteenth Amendment**—passed. By year's end, 27 states, including eight in the South, had ratified the amendment. From that point on, slavery was banned in the United States.

Lincoln's Assassination

Lincoln did not live to see the end of slavery, however. Five days after Lee's surrender at Appomattox, the president and his wife went to see a play at Ford's Theatre in Washington, D.C. During the play, a Confederate supporter, **John Wilkes Booth,** crept into the balcony where the president sat and shot him in the back of the head. Booth then jumped over the railing and landed on the stage. Although he broke his leg in the leap, he managed to escape the theater.

CONNECTIONS TO MATH
Costs of the Civil War

CONFEDERATE CASUALTIES

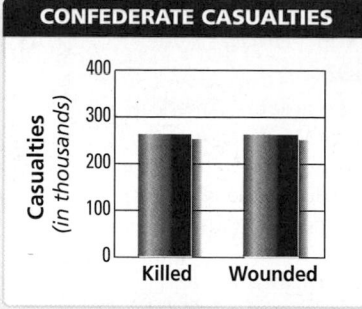

UNION CASUALTIES

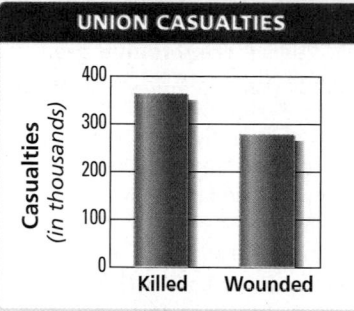

Source: *World Book; Historical Statistics of the United States; The United States Civil War Center*

ECONOMIC COSTS

- Federal loans and taxes to finance the war totaled $2.6 billion.
- Federal debt on June 30, 1865, rose to $2.7 billion.
- Confederate debt ran over $700 million.
- Union inflation reached 182% in 1864 and 179% in 1865.
- Confederate inflation rose to 9,000% by the end of the war.

SKILLBUILDER
Interpreting Graphs
1. *About how many Confederate soldiers were killed in the Civil War?*
2. *Approximately how many soldiers were wounded in the war?*

Connections TO LITERATURE

WALT WHITMAN

1819–1892

One of the greatest American poets, Walt Whitman (below) was a large, bearded man whose poetry captured the American spirit. His most famous book of poems, *Leaves of Grass,* praised the values of freedom and democracy.

Whitman was 41 when the Civil War began. Too old for the army, he offered his services as a nurse when his younger brother was wounded at Fredericksburg. He stayed on after that to help at hospitals in Washington, D.C.

Whitman wrote a book of poetry about war. Later editions of the book, which appeared after Lincoln's assassination, included several poems about the president.

That same evening, an accomplice of Booth stabbed Secretary of State William Seward, who later recovered. Another man was supposed to assassinate Vice-President Johnson, but he failed to carry out the attack.

Although Booth had managed to escape after shooting the president, Union troops found and killed him several days later. Soldiers also hunted down Booth's accomplices, whom they either hanged or imprisoned.

After Lincoln was shot, he was carried to a house across the street from the theater. The bullet in his brain could not be removed, however. The next morning, April 15, 1865, the president died. He was the first American president to be assassinated.

Lincoln's murder stunned the nation and caused intense grief. In Washington, D.C., people wept in the streets. One man who mourned the nation's loss was the poet Walt Whitman. In one poem, Whitman considered the president's legacy.

> **A VOICE FROM THE PAST**
>
> This dust was once the man,
> Gentle, plain, just and resolute, under whose cautious hand,
> Against the foulest crime in history known in any land or age,
> Was saved the Union of these States.
>
> **Walt Whitman,** *This Dust Was Once the Man*

The loss of Lincoln's vast experience and great political skills was a terrible setback for a people faced by the challenge of rebuilding their nation. In both the North and the South, life would never be the same after the Civil War.

Consequences of the War

In the North, the war changed the way people thought about the country. In fighting to defend the Union, people came to see the United States as a single nation rather than a collection of states. After 1865, people no longer said "the United States *are*" but "the United States *is.*"

The war also caused the national government to expand. Before the war, the government was relatively small and had limited powers. With the demands of war, however, the government grew larger and more powerful. Along with a new paper currency and income tax, the government established a new federal banking system. It also funded railroads, gave western land to settlers, and provided for state colleges. This growth of federal power continued long after the war was over.

The war also changed the Northern economy. New industries such as steel, petroleum, food processing, and manufacturing grew rapidly. By

Vocabulary

accomplice: someone who aids a lawbreaker

Reading **History**

C. Summarizing How did Americans react to the assassination of Lincoln?

Background In the 1850s, an improved way of making steel—the Bessemer process—had been perfected, allowing for the mass production of steel.

CAUSE AND EFFECT: The Civil War, 1861–1865

CAUSES	IMMEDIATE EFFECTS
Conflict over slavery in territories	Abolition of slavery
Economic differences between North and South	Devastation of South
	Reconstruction of South
Failure of Congress to compromise	**LONG-TERM EFFECTS**
Election of Lincoln as president	Growth of industry
Secession of Southern states	Government more powerful
Firing on Fort Sumter	Nation reunited

SKILLBUILDER Interpreting Charts
1. *What military event is among the causes of the Civil War?*
2. *What effect did the Civil War have on the federal government?*

Background
Some people have called the Civil War the first modern war because of the use of machines, the destructiveness, and the effects on civilians, which would be repeated in later wars.

the late 1800s, industry had begun to replace farming as the basis of the national economy.

For the South, however, the war brought economic disaster. Farms and plantations were destroyed. About 40 percent of the South's livestock was killed. Fifty percent of its farm machinery was wrecked. Factories were also demolished, and thousands of miles of railroad tracks were torn up. Also gone was the labor system that the South had used—slavery.

Before the war, the South accounted for 30 percent of the nation's wealth. After the war it accounted for only 12 percent. These economic differences between the North and the South would last for decades.

The country faced difficult challenges after the war. How would the South be brought back into the Union, and how would four million former slaves be integrated into national life? You will read more about these challenges in the next chapter.

Section 4 Assessment

1. Terms & Names
Explain the significance of:
- Thirteenth Amendment
- John Wilkes Booth

2. Using Graphics
Use a chart like the one below to record the social, economic, and political legacy of the Civil War.

Legacy of the Civil War

Society	Economy	Politics

Is the legacy of the Civil War still apparent today? How?

3. Main Ideas
a. What were some of the human costs of the Civil War?

b. What did the Thirteenth Amendment achieve?

c. What was the state of the Southern economy after the Civil War?

4. Critical Thinking
Making Inferences How do you think the assassination of President Lincoln affected the nation?

THINK ABOUT
- the reaction of ordinary citizens
- its impact on government

ACTIVITY OPTIONS
MATH

TECHNOLOGY

Read about the postwar economy. Create a **database** on industry in the North or make a **storyboard** for a video on the problems in the South.

The Gettysburg Address (1863)

Setting the Stage On November 19, 1863, officials gathered in Gettysburg, Pennsylvania. They were there to dedicate a national cemetery on the ground where the decisive Battle of Gettysburg had taken place nearly five months earlier. Following the ceremony's main address, which lasted nearly two hours, President Lincoln delivered his Gettysburg Address in just over two minutes. In this famous speech, Lincoln expressed his hopes for the nation. **See Primary Source Explorer**

Four **score**[1] and seven years ago our fathers brought forth on this continent a new nation, conceived in liberty, and dedicated to the proposition that all men are created equal.

Now we are engaged in a great civil war, testing whether that nation or any nation so conceived and so dedicated, can long endure. We are met on a great battlefield of that war. We have come to dedicate a portion of that field, as a final resting place for those who here gave their lives that that nation might live. It is altogether fitting and proper that we should do this.

But, in a larger sense, we cannot dedicate—we can not **consecrate**[2]—we can not hallow—this ground. The brave men, living and dead, who struggled here, have consecrated it, far above our poor power to add or **detract.**[3] The world will little note, nor long remember what we say here, but it can never forget what they did here. It is for us the living, rather, to be dedicated here to the unfinished work which they who fought here have thus far so nobly advanced. It is rather for us to be here dedicated to the great task remaining before us—that from these honored dead we **take increased devotion to**[4] that cause for which they **gave the last full measure of devotion**[5]—that we here highly resolve that these dead shall not have died **in vain**[6]—that this nation, under God, shall have a new birth of freedom—and that government of the people, by the people, for the people, shall not perish from the earth.

A CLOSER LOOK

LINCOLN'S MODESTY

Lincoln claimed that what he said at Gettysburg would not be long remembered. However, the address soon came to be recognized as one of the best speeches of all time.

1. What features of Lincoln's address make it so memorable?

A CLOSER LOOK

FIGHTING FOR A CAUSE

Different people fought for different causes during the Civil War. Sometimes, the causes for which people fought changed over the course of the war.

2. What cause is Lincoln referring to in the Gettysburg Address?

1. **score:** a group of 20.
2. **consecrate:** to declare as sacred.
3. **detract:** to take away from.
4. **take increased devotion to:** work harder for.
5. **gave the last full measure of devotion:** sacrificed their lives.
6. **in vain:** for nothing.

Second Inaugural Address (1865)

Setting the Stage President Lincoln delivered his Second Inaugural Address just before the end of the Civil War. In this excerpt, he recalled the major cause of the war and vowed to fight for the restoration of peace and unity. **See Primary Source Explorer** ◎

One-eighth of the whole population were colored slaves. . . . These slaves constituted a peculiar and powerful interest. All knew that this interest was somehow the cause of the war. To strengthen, perpetuate, and extend this interest was the object for which the **insurgents**[1] would rend the Union even by war, while the Government claimed no right to do more than to restrict the territorial enlargement of it. Neither party expected for the war the magnitude or the duration which it has already attained. Neither anticipated that the cause of the conflict might cease with or even before the conflict itself should cease. Each looked for an easier triumph, and a result less fundamental and astounding. Both read the same Bible and pray to the same God, and each invokes His aid against the other. . . . Fondly do we hope, fervently do we pray, that this mighty **scourge**[2] of war may speedily pass away. Yet, if God wills that it continue until all the wealth piled by the **bondsman's**[3] two hundred and fifty years of **unrequited**[4] toil shall be sunk, and until every drop of blood drawn with the lash shall be paid by another drawn with the sword, as was said three thousand years ago, so still it must be said "the judgments of the Lord are true and righteous altogether."

With malice toward none, with charity for all, with firmness in the right as God gives us to see the right, let us strive on to finish the work we are in, to bind up the nation's wounds, to care for him who shall have borne the battle and for his widow and his orphan, to do all which may achieve and cherish a just and lasting peace among ourselves and with all nations.

1. **insurgent:** one that revolts against civil authority.
2. **scourge:** a source of suffering and devastation.
3. **bondsman:** enslaved person.
4. **unrequited:** not paid for.

A CLOSER LOOK

SLAVERY IN TERRITORIES

Before the Civil War, Northern states wanted to prohibit slavery in territories that would eventually become new states. Southern states fought to expand slavery, fearing the prohibition would threaten slavery where it already existed.

1. Why did the Southerners fear that prohibiting slavery in new territories might threaten slavery where it already existed?

A CLOSER LOOK

MALICE TOWARD NONE

As Northerners became more confident in victory, many looked forward to punishing Southerners, whom they blamed for the war. Lincoln, however, urged citizens to care for one another and work for a just and lasting peace.

2. Why do you think that Lincoln believed it would be wiser for Americans not to place blame or seek revenge on one another?

Interactive Primary Sources Assessment

1. Main Ideas

a. Why might President Lincoln have begun the Gettysburg Address by noting that the country was "dedicated to the proposition that all men are created equal"?

b. According to Lincoln's Second Inaugural Address, why did the Confederacy go to war?

c. To what did Lincoln refer with the phrase "the bondsman's two hundred and fifty years of unrequited toil?"

2. Critical Thinking

Making Inferences In 1865, if the South had asked to rejoin the Union without ending slavery, do you think Lincoln would have agreed?

THINK ABOUT
- what Lincoln identifies as the cause of the war
- what might happen if the war ended but slavery did not

TERMS & NAMES

Briefly explain the significance of each of the following.

1. Emancipation Proclamation
2. 54th Massachusetts Regiment
3. conscription
4. Battle of Gettysburg
5. Ulysses S. Grant
6. Robert E. Lee
7. Siege of Vicksburg
8. William Tecumseh Sherman
9. Appomattox Court House
10. Thirteenth Amendment

REVIEW QUESTIONS

The Emancipation Proclamation (pages 503–506)

1. Why did Lincoln issue the Emancipation Proclamation?
2. How did black soldiers aid the war effort?

War Affects Society (pages 507–511)

3. How did events on the home front show the toll that war was taking there?
4. Why did some people say the Civil War was a "rich man's war but a poor man's fight"?
5. How did enslaved persons help the Union?

The North Wins (pages 512–519)

6. Why was the Battle of Gettysburg so important?
7. How did Sherman's march help the Union?
8. How did Grant defeat Lee?

The Legacy of the War (pages 520–523)

9. How was the Thirteenth Amendment different from the Emancipation Proclamation?
10. How did the war change the national economy?

CRITICAL THINKING

1. USING YOUR NOTES: COMPARING AND CONTRASTING

	North	South
Emancipation Proclamation		
War's Impact		
Northern Victories in Battle		
Union Wins Civil War		

a. How did white and black Southerners react to the Emancipation Proclamation?

b. How did inflation affect the North and the South?

2. ANALYZING LEADERSHIP

What qualities made Lincoln an effective leader?

3. THEME: IMPACT OF THE INDIVIDUAL

How did General Grant's actions in the war make a crucial difference to the outcome?

4. FORMING AND SUPPORTING OPINIONS

One Union relief worker said, "The suffering of men in battle is nothing next to the agony that women feel sending forth their loved ones to war." Do you agree with this statement? Explain why or why not.

5. APPLYING CITIZENSHIP SKILLS

How might the behavior of General Grant and President Lincoln toward the Confederacy have helped to begin healing the war-torn nation?

Interact *with* History

Having read about the ferocity of battle during the Civil War, do you still believe that you would be inspired to continue the fighting? Why or why not?

VISUAL SUMMARY

The Civil War, 1863–1865

January 1863 Emancipation Proclamation is issued.

July 1863 Battle of Gettysburg takes place. Union takes Vicksburg.

September 1864 Sherman takes Atlanta, Georgia.

May 1864 Battle of the Wilderness and Spotsylvania occur.

December 1864 Sherman takes Savannah, Georgia.

April 1865 Lee surrenders at Appomattox Court House. Lincoln is assassinated.

1863 ——— 1866

March 1863 Union passes the draft law.

March 1864 Grant is put in charge of all Union armies.

June 1864 Battle of Cold Harbor occurs.

November 1864 Lincoln is reelected.

January 1865 Thirteenth Amendment is passed by Congress.

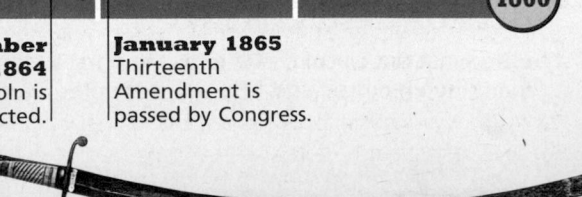

Use the map and your knowledge of U.S. history to answer questions 1 and 2.

Additional Test Practice, pp. S1–S33.

Siege of Vicksburg, 1863

Union state
Border state
Confederate state
Federal territory
+++ Railroad

1. Vicksburg was built next to which of the following bodies of water?
   A. Red River
   B. Ohio River
   C. Mississippi River
   D. Gulf of Mexico

2. Why might Vicksburg be important for Southerners supplying the Confederacy from Texas?
   A. Vicksburg was on a river and a rail line.
   B. Vicksburg was located in a border state.
   C. Vicksburg was an ocean port city.
   D. Vicksburg was located in Texas.

Frederick Douglass explains his views on the efforts to end slavery in this quotation. Use the quotation and your knowledge of U.S. history to answer question 3.

PRIMARY SOURCE

To fight against slaveholders, without fighting against slavery, is but a half-hearted business, and paralyzes the hands engaged in it . . . Fire must be met with water . . . War for the destruction of liberty [by the South] must be met with war for the destruction of slavery.

Frederick Douglass, quoted in *Battle Cry of Freedom*

3. What do you think Frederick Douglass meant when he said "Fire must be met with water?"
   A. He was referring to new military weapons.
   B. The Civil War must wipe out slavery just as water puts out a fire.
   C. Fire and water were symbols of the war against the Confederacy.
   D. He wanted an end to the "flames" of warfare.

TEST PRACTICE
CLASSZONE.COM

ALTERNATIVE ASSESSMENT

1. ✎ WRITING ABOUT HISTORY

Write a **report** about the advances of military technology during the Civil War. Your report should give a detailed description of the new or improved weapons that were used during the war.

- Research your report by reading books about military technology or books about the Civil War.

2. COOPERATIVE LEARNING

Work with a group to produce a newspaper that covers a specific period of the Civil War. Choose the period you want to cover and decide whether you will take a Northern or Southern viewpoint. Then, group members can select topics, such as important battles and military strategies, social or economic conditions, or important figures, to research and write about.

INTEGRATED TECHNOLOGY

DOING INTERNET RESEARCH

The Battle at Gettysburg was a turning point in the Civil War. Use the Internet and other library resources to create a presentation on the Battle at Gettysburg.

- Find primary sources about the battle, such as letters, diary entries, and journals.
- Another source of information might be Web sites for Civil War museums or archives.
- You might consider focusing your presentation on paintings or written descriptions of the battle, images of destruction caused by conflict, music from the time period, or statistics on casualties.

For more about the Battle of Gettysburg . . .

INTERNET ACTIVITY
CLASSZONE.COM

Create a Medal of Honor

In 1782, George Washington established the nation's first award to recognize the bravery of American soldiers. It was a purple heart made of cloth and was called the Badge of Military Merit. But the award was not used much after the Revolutionary War. Then, in 1861, Congress created a new award—the Medal of Honor. In the Civil War, 1,520 Union soldiers, including 20 African Americans, received the medal. Today, that medal is the highest United States military award for individual bravery and is commonly referred to as the Congressional Medal of Honor.

ACTIVITY Create a medal of honor for a hero or heroine from either side of the Civil War. Write a letter recommending your hero for the medal. Then read a speech in class as you award your medal to the deserving individual.

TOOLBOX

Each group will need:

tops of juice cans or cardboard	glue
	markers
aluminum foil	scissors
pieces of ribbon	writing paper
safety pins	

STEP BY STEP

1 **Form groups.** Each group should consist of three or four students. Each group will:

- identify a Civil War hero or heroine
- create a medal
- write a letter explaining why your group considers that person a hero
- award the medal and read a speech in class

2 **Research a hero.** First, brainstorm characteristics that you think a hero should have. Then, using this chapter, books on the Civil War, or the Internet, select an individual who you think was a hero for either side of the Civil War. Take notes on the actions of the person you selected. The actions should show how that person meets your standards for being a hero.

The Congressional Medal of Honor rewards military personnel who risked their lives, "above and beyond the call of duty." In the Civil War, 1,520 Union soldiers, including 20 African Americans, received the Medal of Honor.

HELP DESK

For related information, see page 518 in Chapter 17.

Researching Your Project

Visit the library to learn more about the history of military awards or go to your local historical museum to examine actual medals.

For more about military awards . . .

RESEARCH LINKS
CLASSZONE.COM

3 Design your medal.
Think about the shape, images, and words that you will use to make your medal of honor. You may want to look at the example from Chapter 17 and in Civil War books. Sketch a design of your medal in pencil.

4 Construct your medal.
Using art supplies, construct a medal based on your design. First, construct the medal itself by using a juice can lid or a cardboard pattern. Decorate the medal by using foil and markers. Then add a ribbon and pin.

Did You Know?

Since the Congressional Medal of Honor was created in 1861, 3,408 persons have received the award. Nineteen persons have received two such awards. Only one woman has received the award.

The Confederate States of America also awarded 43 of its finest men with the Confederate Medal of Honor.

The practice of awarding medals began in Europe during the Middle Ages. Kings realized that giving land to valued knights was too costly, so they gave medals instead.

5 Write a letter. The letter should be addressed to the Congress of the United States of America or the Congress of the Confederate States of America. Your letter should give reasons for recommending your hero based on the person's actions. Carefully recopy your letter after you have made any corrections.

6 Pin up the medal.
Create a Medal of Honor board with other groups in your class. Pin up all the medals you have created. Discuss with other groups the standards your group set for calling a person a hero.

REFLECT & ASSESS

- What requirements did you set for awarding a medal of honor?

- What reasons did your letter and speech give for awarding the medal?

- What symbols did you use for your medal? Why did you select them?

WRITE AND SPEAK

Write a Speech As a Civil War military leader, write a speech praising the courage and bravery of the individual who is receiving the medal. Choose another member of your group to act as the recipient of the award. Read your speech to the class as you award the medal to that person.

CHAPTER 18

Reconstruction

1865–1877

Section 1
Rebuilding the Union

Section 2
Reconstruction and Daily Life

Section 3
End of Reconstruction

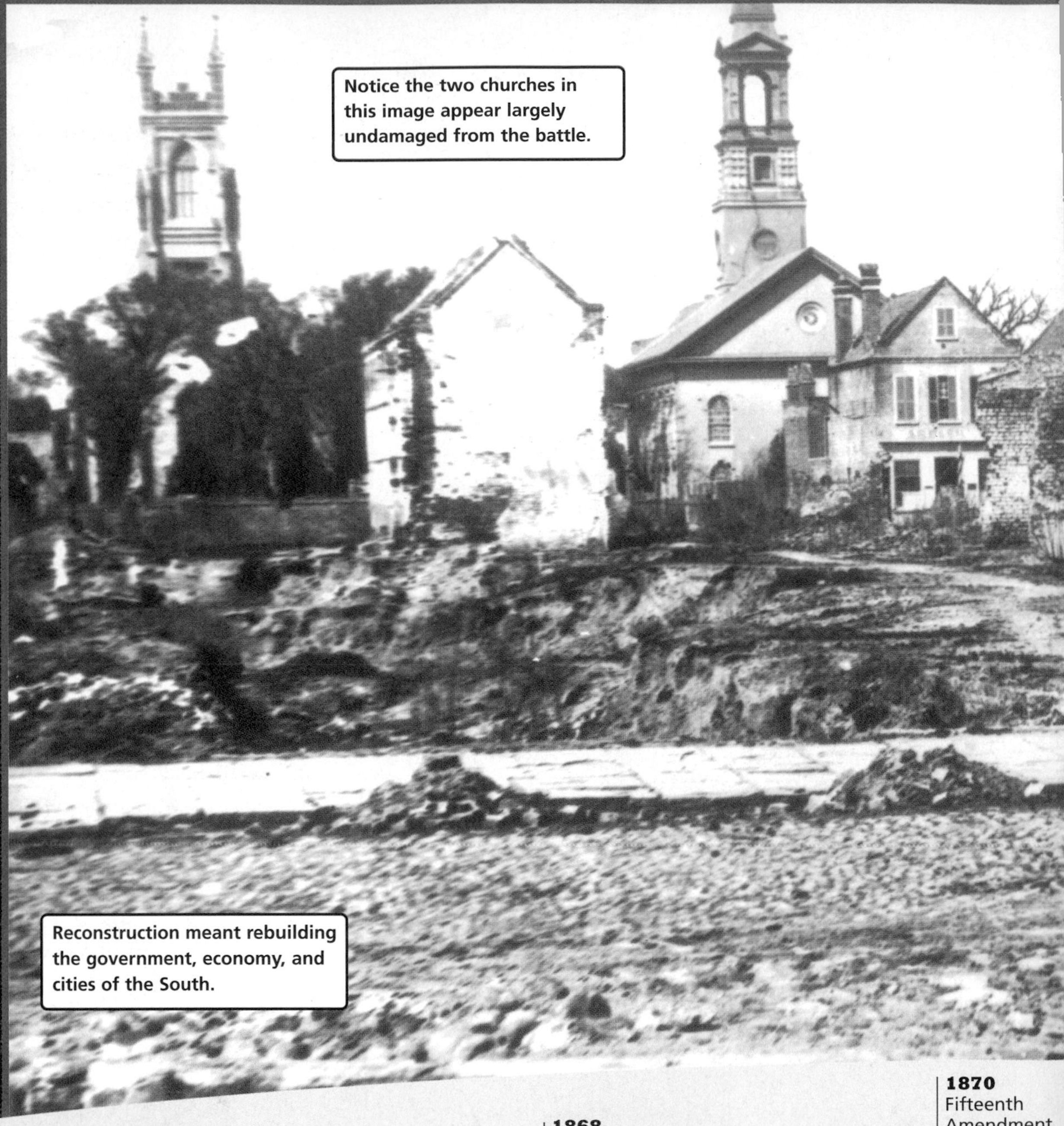

Notice the two churches in this image appear largely undamaged from the battle.
Reconstruction meant rebuilding the government, economy, and cities of the South.

USA

1865
Andrew Johnson becomes president after Lincoln's assassination.

1866
Civil Rights Act is passed.

1867
Reconstruction Acts are passed.

1868
Fourteenth Amendment extends full citizenship to African Americans.

Ulysses S. Grant is elected president.

1870
Fifteenth Amendment guarantees voting rights to African Americans.

World

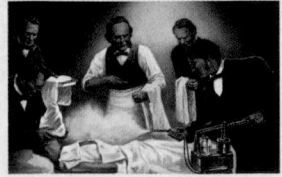

1865
Joseph Lister pioneers antiseptic surgery.

1867
Emperor Maximilian is executed in Mexico.

1870
Unification of Italy is completed.

The Civil War has just ended, and the Southern economy is in ruins. Slavery has been abolished. Northerners and Southerners feel deep anger toward one another. As a member of Congress, you must help the nation recover.

How would you rebuild the Union?

Freed African Americans sit in the ruins of Charleston, South Carolina, after the Civil War.

What Do You Think?

- What problems would you face in rebuilding the nation?
- How would you ease tensions between North and South?
- How would you help freed African Americans?

RESEARCH LINKS
CLASSZONE.COM

Visit the Chapter 18 links for more information about Reconstruction.

1872
Grant is reelected president.

1873
Financial panic leads to an economic depression.

1877
Rutherford B. Hayes is inaugurated as president and ends Reconstruction.

1877

1871
Unification of Germany is completed by Kaiser Wilhelm I.

1874
In England, the Factory Act limits the working week to 56.5 hours.

1876
Korea becomes an independent nation.

Reconstruction **531**

Reading Strategy: Identifying and Solving Problems

What Do You Know?

What do you think it means to reconstruct something? What kinds of things did the U.S. government need to reconstruct after the Civil War? Which of these issues do you think was most important?

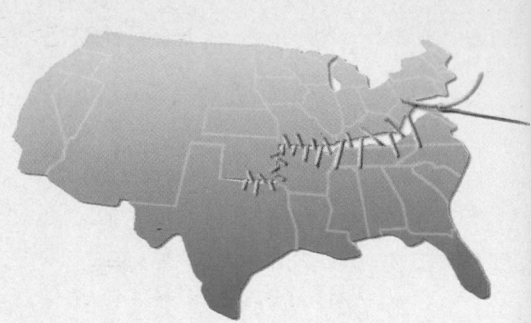

Think About

- what you learned about the Civil War in the last two chapters
- what you've learned about civil rights in the United States from television and movies
- your responses to the Interact with History about rebuilding the Union (see page 531)

What Do You Want to Know?

 What questions do you have about Reconstruction? Record those questions in your notebook before you read this chapter.

Identifying and Solving Problems

Sometimes, to understand what you read, you must learn to identify problems and solutions. As you read through this chapter, use a diagram like the one below to take notes on the problems the United States faced during Reconstruction and the actions the nation took to solve them.

S See Skillbuilder Handbook, page R18.

 Taking Notes

Problems	Solutions
Black codes	
President Johnson	
Education	
Economy	
Ku Klux Klan	
Voting	

Rebuilding the Union

MAIN IDEA	WHY IT MATTERS NOW	TERMS & NAMES
During Reconstruction, the president and Congress fought over how to rebuild the South.	Reconstruction was an important step in the African-American struggle for civil rights.	Radical Republicans Andrew Johnson Reconstruction black codes Freedmen's Bureau civil rights Fourteenth Amendment

ONE AMERICAN'S STORY

After the Civil War, Pennsylvania congressman Thaddeus Stevens became a leader of the Radical Republicans. This group of congressmen favored using federal power to create a new order in the South and to promote full citizenship for freed African Americans. Stevens stated that "the whole fabric of southern society must be changed."

In this section, you will learn how political leaders battled over how to bring the Southern states back into the Union.

Thaddeus Stevens addresses Congress.

Reconstruction Begins

After the Civil War ended in 1865, the South faced the challenge of building a new society not based on slavery. The process the federal government used to readmit the Confederate states to the Union is known as **Reconstruction**. Reconstruction lasted from 1865 to 1877.

In his Second Inaugural Address, in March 1865, Lincoln promised to reunify the nation "with malice [harm] toward none, with charity for all." Lincoln's plan included pardoning Confederate officials. It also called for allowing the Confederate states to quickly form new governments and send representatives to Congress.

To assist former slaves, the president established the **Freedmen's Bureau**. This federal agency set up schools and hospitals for African Americans and distributed clothes, food, and fuel throughout the South.

When Lincoln was killed in April 1865, Vice-President **Andrew Johnson** became president. Johnson was a Democrat. The Republicans

Taking Notes

Use your chart to take notes about black codes and President Johnson.

Problems

Black codes	➤
President Johnson	➤
Education	➤
Economy	➤
Ku Klux Klan	➤
Voting	➤

Andrew Johnson was a self-educated man whose strong will led to trouble with Congress.

As a former slaveholder from Tennessee, Johnson called for a mild program for bringing the South back into the Union. In particular, he let states decide whether to give voting rights to freed African Americans.

Johnson's policies led to a break with the Radical Republicans in Congress and, finally, to his impeachment trial (see page 537).

Why might Johnson have chosen not to punish the South?

had put him on the ticket in 1864 to help win support in the nation's border states. Johnson was a former slaveholder and, unlike Lincoln, a stubborn, unyielding man.

Johnson believed that Reconstruction was the job of the president, not Congress. His policies were based on Lincoln's goals. He insisted that the new state governments ratify the Thirteenth Amendment, which prohibited slavery. He also insisted that they accept the supreme power of the federal government.

Johnson offered amnesty, or official pardon, to most white Southerners. He promised to return their property. In return, they had to pledge loyalty to the United States. At first, the large plantation owners, top military officers, and ex-Confederate leaders were not included in this offer. But they, too, eventually won amnesty.

Rebuilding Brings Conflict

As the Southern states rebuilt, they set up new state governments that seemed very much like the old ones. Some states flatly refused to ratify the Thirteenth Amendment. "This is a white man's government," said the governor of South Carolina, "and intended for white men only."

The Southern states passed laws, known as **black codes,** which limited the freedom of former slaves. In Mississippi, for instance, one law said that African Americans had to have written proof of employment. Anyone without such proof could be put to work on a plantation. African Americans were forbidden to meet in unsupervised groups or carry guns. Because of such laws, many people in the North suspected that white Southerners were trying to bring back the "old South."

When Congress met in December 1865, its members refused to seat representatives from the South. Many of these Southern representatives had been Confederate leaders only months before.

Under the Constitution, Congress has the right to decide whether its members are qualified to hold office. So instead of admitting the Southerners, Congress set up a committee to study conditions in the South and decide whether the Southern states should be represented. By taking such action, Congress let the president know that it planned to play a role in Reconstruction.

Republicans outnumbered Democrats in both houses of Congress. Most Republicans were moderates who believed that the federal government should stay out of the affairs of individuals and the states.

The Radical Republicans, however, wanted the federal government to play an active role in remaking Southern politics and society. Led by Thaddeus Stevens and Massachusetts senator Charles Sumner, the

Background
Not all Confederate leaders were pardoned. Former Confederate president Jefferson Davis, for example, was imprisoned for two years awaiting trial for treason. But he was never tried.

*Reading***History**
A. Analyzing Causes What was the main reason Southern states passed black codes?

Vocabulary
moderates: people opposed to extreme views

group also demanded full and equal citizenship for African Americans. Their aim was to destroy the South's old ruling class and turn the region into a place of small farms, free schools, respect for labor, and political equality for all citizens.

The Civil Rights Act

Urged on by the Radicals, Congress passed a bill promoting **civil rights**—those rights granted to all citizens. The Civil Rights Act of 1866 declared that all persons born in the United States (except Native Americans) were citizens. It also stated that all citizens were entitled to equal rights regardless of their race.

Republicans were shocked when President Johnson vetoed the bill. Johnson argued that federal protection of civil rights would lead "towards centralization" of the national government. He also insisted that making African Americans full citizens would "operate against the white race." Congress voted to override Johnson's veto. That is, two-thirds of the House and two-thirds of the Senate voted for the bill after the president's veto, and the bill became law.

The Fourteenth Amendment

Reading **History**

B. Making Inferences How did the Fourteenth Amendment encourage states to give African Americans the vote?

Republicans were not satisfied with passing laws that ensured equal rights. They wanted equality to be protected by the Constitution itself. To achieve this goal, Congress proposed the **Fourteenth Amendment** in 1866. It stated that all people born in the United States were citizens and had the same rights. All citizens were to be granted "equal protection of the laws." However, the amendment did not establish black suffrage. Instead, it declared that any state that kept African Americans from voting would lose representatives in Congress. This meant that the Southern states would have less power if they did not grant black men the vote.

Johnson refused to support the amendment. So did every former Confederate state except Tennessee. This rejection outraged both moderate and Radical Republicans. As a result, the two groups agreed to join forces and passed the Reconstruction Acts of 1867. The passage of these

Radical Republicans pose for a formal portrait. Standing (left to right): James F. Wilson, George S. Boutwell, and John A. Logan. Seated: Benjamin F. Butler, Thaddeus Stevens, Thomas Williams, and John A. Bingham.

acts began a period known as Radical Reconstruction. From this point on, Congress controlled Reconstruction.

One of the Reconstruction Acts of 1867 divided the South into five military districts, each run by an army commander. Members of the ruling class before the war lost their voting rights. The law also stated that before the Southern states could reenter the Union, they would have to do two things:

1. They must approve new state constitutions that gave the vote to all adult men, including African Americans.
2. They must ratify the Fourteenth Amendment.

The New Southern Governments

In 1867, Southern voters chose delegates to draft their new state constitutions. About three-fourths of the delegates were Republicans. Many of the Republicans were poor white farmers. Angry at planters for starting what they called the "rich man's war," these delegates were called scalawags (scoundrels) for going along with Radical Reconstruction.

Another one-fourth of the Republican delegates were known as carpetbaggers—white Northerners who had rushed to the South after the war. Many Southerners accused them, often unfairly, of seeking only to get rich or gain political power.

African Americans made up the rest of the Republican delegates. Of these, half had been free before the war. Most were ministers, teachers, or skilled workers. About 80 percent of them could read.

The new constitutions written by these delegates set up public schools and gave the vote to all adult males. By 1870, voters in all the Southern states had approved their new constitutions. As a result, the former Confederate states were let back into the Union and allowed to send representatives to Congress.

During Reconstruction, more than 600 African Americans served in state legislatures throughout the South, and 14 of the new U.S. congressmen from the South were African Americans. Two African Americans served as U.S. senators during this time. One was Hiram Revels of Mississippi, a minister in the African Methodist Episcopal Church. He had recruited African Americans to fight for the Union during the Civil War.

His First Vote, an 1868 oil painting by Thomas Waterman Wood, shows a new African-American voter.

How do you think the man felt about voting?

Background
Attempts to secure voting rights for African Americans applied only to men. Women were not allowed to vote until 1919.

Background
Carpetbaggers were said to have headed south carrying only a cheap suitcase, known as a carpetbag.

*Reading***History**
C. Finding Main Ideas What political gains did African Americans make during Reconstruction?

536

For an activity about Johnson's impeachment . . .

NET SIMULATION
CLASSZONE.COM

Johnson Is Impeached

President Johnson fought against many of Congress's reform efforts during Radical Reconstruction. For instance, he chose people friendly to ex-Confederates to serve as military commanders in the South. The conflict between Johnson and Congress soon brought a showdown.

This is a ticket to the 1868 impeachment trial of President Johnson.

In 1867, Congress passed the Tenure of Office Act, which prohibited the president from firing government officials without the Senate's approval. In February 1868, Johnson fired his secretary of war, Edwin Stanton, over disagreements about Reconstruction. Three days later, the House of Representatives voted to impeach the president. This means that the House formally accused him of improper conduct while in office. By removing Johnson from office, they hoped to strengthen Congress's role in Reconstruction.

Reading **History**

D. Drawing Conclusions Why did Congress decide to impeach President Johnson?

The case moved to the Senate for a trial. After several weeks of testimony, the senators prepared to vote. George Julian, a 20-year congressman from Indiana, recalled the tension in the air.

A VOICE FROM THE PAST

The galleries were packed, and an indescribable anxiety was written on every face. Some of the members of the House near me grew pale and sick under the burden of suspense. Such stillness prevailed that the breathing in the galleries could be heard at the announcement of each Senator's voice.

George Julian, quoted in *Grand Inquests*

Vocabulary
acquitted: cleared of a charge

In the end, President Johnson was acquitted by a single vote. But much work remained to be done in rebuilding the South. In the next section, you will learn how African Americans in the South worked to improve their lives.

Section 1 Assessment

1. Terms & Names

Explain the significance of:
- Radical Republicans
- Reconstruction
- Freedmen's Bureau
- Andrew Johnson
- black codes
- civil rights
- Fourteenth Amendment

2. Using Graphics

Use a diagram to review the events that led to Johnson's impeachment.

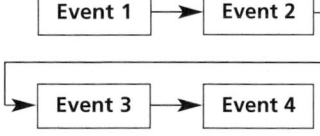

Which event seems most important and why?

3. Main Ideas

a. What was Lincoln's Reconstruction plan?

b. How did white Southerners plan to restore the "old South"?

c. What impact did the Reconstruction Acts of 1867 have on the South?

4. Critical Thinking

Evaluating Do you think the House was justified in impeaching President Johnson? Why or why not?

THINK ABOUT
- the clash over Reconstruction policies
- Congress's motives for impeaching Johnson

ACTIVITY OPTIONS

TECHNOLOGY

SPEECH

Research an African American who served in Congress during Reconstruction. Design his Internet **home page,** or make a **speech** about his accomplishments.

Rebuilding Richmond

You live in Richmond, Virginia, the capital of the Confederacy. It is 1865, and the South faces defeat in the Civil War. On April 2, Confederate officials set fire to supplies in Richmond to prevent the approaching Union army from using them. The fire spreads out of control and destroys downtown Richmond. The next day, Union troops march into the city and take command. You must now help rebuild the city.

COOPERATIVE LEARNING On this page are two challenges you face as a resident of Richmond. Working with a small group, decide how to solve one of these problems. Divide the work among the group members. You will find useful information in the Data File. Be prepared to present your solutions to the class.

This picture shows a street in Richmond before the fire.

ARTS CHALLENGE

"We want the burnt district of Richmond to . . . sit proudly again."

The smell of charred wood still floats in the breeze. However, spirit and determination fill the air. Warehouses are opening. Newly cleared streets bustle with activity. The rebuilding of Richmond has begun. How would you design one block of Richmond's new downtown business district? Use the Data File for help. Then present your plan using one of these options:

• Make a model of your new city block.

• Ask and answer questions about how buildings and services should be distributed on the model block.

THE BURNT DISTRICT

- about $30 million damage
- 20 city blocks destroyed, including 900 buildings

Destroyed Property
all banks, 20 law offices, 24 grocery stores, 36 merchant shops, 2 carriage factories, 2 paper mills, 7 book and stationery stores, 2 train depots, 3 bridges, a church, a machine shop, a tin shop, a pottery factory, several flour mills and printing offices

Surviving Property
capitol and city hall, residential areas, ironworks

EMERGENCY SERVICES

Union Army
- distributes 13,000 food rations
- provides medical help
- guards homes; patrols streets

American Union Commission
- hands out food tickets
- distributes 80,000 pounds of flour; feeds soup to 800 people a day
- provides garden seeds and sells shovels at cost to farmers

REBUILDING

April 1865
- rubble is cleared
- markets sell meat, fish, produce
- hotels and bakeries open
- one bridge is rebuilt

May 1865
- two banks open
- gas and telegraph service is restored
- river opens to steamboat traffic

Summer 1865
- horse-drawn buses operate
- city government is reinstated

Fall 1865
- ironworks reopens
- 100 buildings are now under construction

For more about Reconstruction . . .

RESEARCH LINKS
CLASSZONE.COM

CIVICS CHALLENGE

"Open robberies have been perpetrated."

Robberies and assaults are commonplace, especially in the burnt area of the downtown. Groups of orphaned children also roam the city, picking pockets to support themselves. Union military police supposedly protect the public. However, soldiers sometimes commit crimes themselves. What would you do to improve public safety? Use the Data File for help. Present your ideas using one of these options:

- Hold a town meeting to explore possible solutions.
- Create a set of emergency laws, with plans for publicizing them.

ACTIVITY WRAP-UP

Meet as a group to review your responses to rebuilding Richmond. Pick your most creative solution and present it to the class.

2

Reconstruction and Daily Life

MAIN IDEA	WHY IT MATTERS NOW	TERMS & NAMES
As the South rebuilt, millions of newly freed African Americans worked to improve their lives.	Many important African-American institutions, including colleges, began during Reconstruction.	freedmen's school Ku Klux Klan sharecropping lynch

ONE AMERICAN'S STORY

One day, as the Civil War came to a close, two enslaved women named Mill and Jule saw a fleet of Union gunboats coming up the Mississippi River. Yankee soldiers came ashore and offered them and other slaves passage aboard their boats. On that day, Mill and Jule left the plantation.

A VOICE FROM THE PAST

An' we all got on the boat in a hurry . . . we all give three times three cheers for the gunboat boys, and . . . three times three cheers for gov'ment.

Mill and Jule, quoted in *We Are Your Sisters*

The Union's victory in the Civil War spelled the end of slavery in America. In this section, you will learn about the gains and setbacks of former slaves during Reconstruction.

Freed people and a federal soldier pose on a South Carolina plantation.

Taking Notes

Use your chart to take notes about education, the economy, and the Ku Klux Klan.

Problems

- Black codes
- President Johnson
- Education
- Economy
- Ku Klux Klan
- Voting

Responding to Freedom

African Americans' first reaction to freedom was to leave the plantations. No longer needing passes to travel, they journeyed throughout the region. "Right off colored folks started on the move," recalled one freedman. "They seemed to want to get closer to freedom, so they'd know what it was—like it was a place or a city." Some former slaves returned to the places where they were born. Others went looking for more economic opportunity. Still others traveled just because they could.

African Americans also traveled in search of family members separated from them during slavery. One man walked 600 miles from Georgia to North Carolina to find his family. To locate relatives, people placed advertisements in newspapers. The Freedmen's Bureau helped many families reunite. A Union officer wrote in 1865, "Men are taking

*Reading*History

A. Analyzing Causes For what reasons did former slaves move?

their wives and children, families which had been for a long time broken up are united and oh! such happiness."

Freedom allowed African Americans to strengthen their family ties. Former slaves could marry legally. They could raise families without fearing that their children might be sold. Many families adopted children of dead relatives and friends to keep family ties strong.

Starting Schools

With freedom, African Americans no longer had to work for an owner's benefit. They could now work to provide for their families. To reach their goal of economic independence, however, most had to learn to read and write. As a result, children and adults flocked to **freedmen's schools** set up to educate newly freed African Americans. Such schools were started by the Freedmen's Bureau, Northern missionary groups, and African-American organizations. Freed people in cities held classes in warehouses, billiard rooms, and former slave markets. In rural areas, classes were held in churches and houses. Children who went to school often taught their parents to read at home.

*Reading*History

B. Finding Main Ideas Why did freed people desire an education?

In the years after the war, African-American groups raised more than $1 million for education. However, the federal government and private groups in the North paid most of the cost of building schools and hiring teachers. Between 1865 and 1870, the Freedmen's Bureau spent $5 million for this purpose.

Background
Most African Americans were illiterate because teaching slaves to read and write had been illegal.

More than 150,000 African-American students were attending 3,000 schools by 1869. About 10 percent of the South's African-American adults could read. A number of them became teachers. Northern teachers, black and white, also went South to teach freed people. Many white Southerners, however, worked against these teachers' efforts. White racists even killed teachers and burned freedmen's schools in some parts of the South. Despite these setbacks, African Americans kept working toward an education.

America's HERITAGE

BLACK COLLEGES

Some of today's African-American colleges and universities date back to Reconstruction. The Freedmen's Bureau and other societies raised funds to build many of the schools. Howard University, shown in this photograph, opened in 1867. It was named for General Oliver Otis Howard, head of the Freedmen's Bureau. During Reconstruction, these colleges offered courses ranging from basic reading and writing to medicine and law. They also trained much-needed teachers.

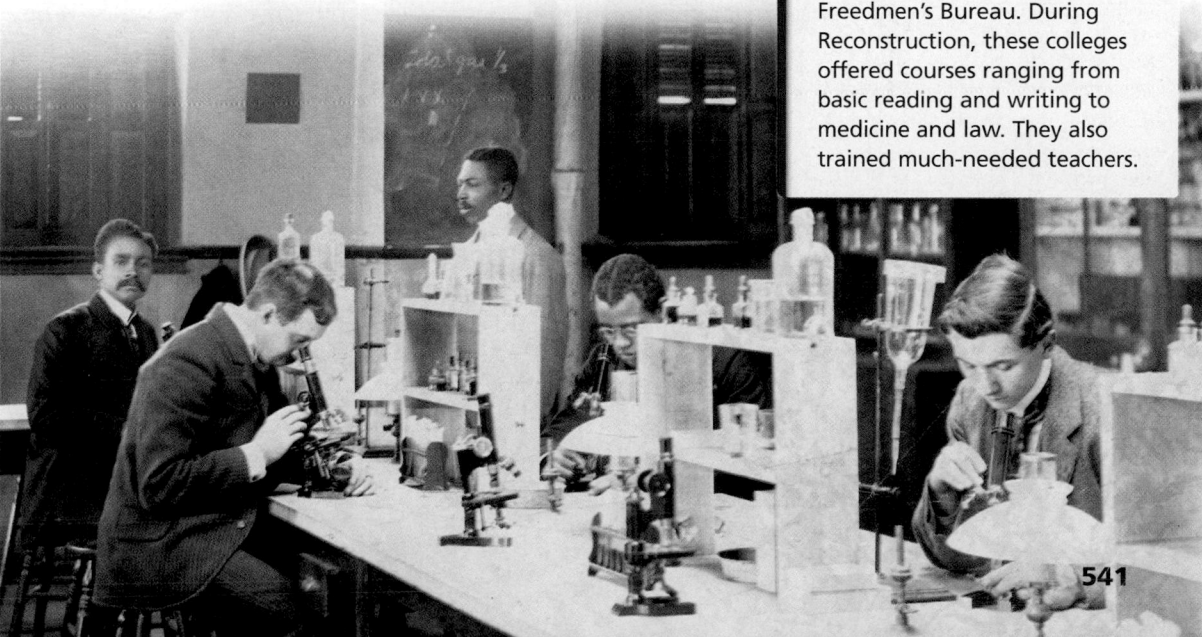

African–American families hoped to own land but were often disappointed.

40 Acres and a Mule

More than anything else, freed people wanted to own land. As one freedman said, "Give us our own land and we take care of ourselves, but without land, the old masters can hire us or starve us, as they please."

As the Civil War ended, General William T. Sherman suggested that abandoned land in coastal South Carolina be split into 40-acre parcels and given to freedmen. The rumor then spread that all freedmen would get 40 acres and a mule. Most African Americans thought they deserved at least that much. In the end, however, most freedmen never received land. Those who did often had to return it to its former owners after the owners were pardoned by President Johnson. One freedman, Bayley Wyat, protested.

A VOICE FROM THE PAST

Our wives, our children, our husbands, [have] been sold over and over again to purchase the lands we now [locate] upon; for that reason we have a divine right to the land. . . . And then didn't we clear the land, and raise the crops of corn, of cotton, of tobacco, of rice, of sugar, of everything.

Bayley Wyat, quoted in *Reconstruction: America's Unfinished Revolution*

Radical Republican leaders Thaddeus Stevens and Charles Sumner pushed to make land reform part of the Reconstruction Acts of 1867. Stevens proposed a plan to Congress that would have taken land from plantation owners and given it to freed people.

Many moderate Republicans and even some Radicals were against the plan. They believed that new civil and voting rights were enough to give African Americans a better life.

Supporters of the plan argued that civil rights meant little without economic independence. Land could provide that independence, they claimed. However, Congress did not pass the land-reform plan.

Reading **History**

C. Analyzing Points of View What were some arguments in favor of giving land to freed people?

The Contract System

Without their own property, many African Americans returned to work on plantations. They returned not as slaves but as wage earners. They and the planters both had trouble getting used to this new relationship. "It seems humiliating to be compelled to bargain and haggle with our own servants about wages," wrote the daughter of a Georgia plantation owner. For their part, many freed workers assumed that wages were extra. They thought that the planters still had to house and feed them.

After the Civil War, planters desperately needed workers to raise cotton, still the South's main cash crop. African Americans reacted to this demand for labor by choosing the best contract offers. The contract system was far better than slavery. African Americans could decide whom to work for, and planters could not abuse them or split up families.

The contract system still had drawbacks, however. Even the best contracts paid very low wages. Workers often could not leave the plantations

Background Civil War deaths and the departure of slaves from plantations created a labor shortage in the South.

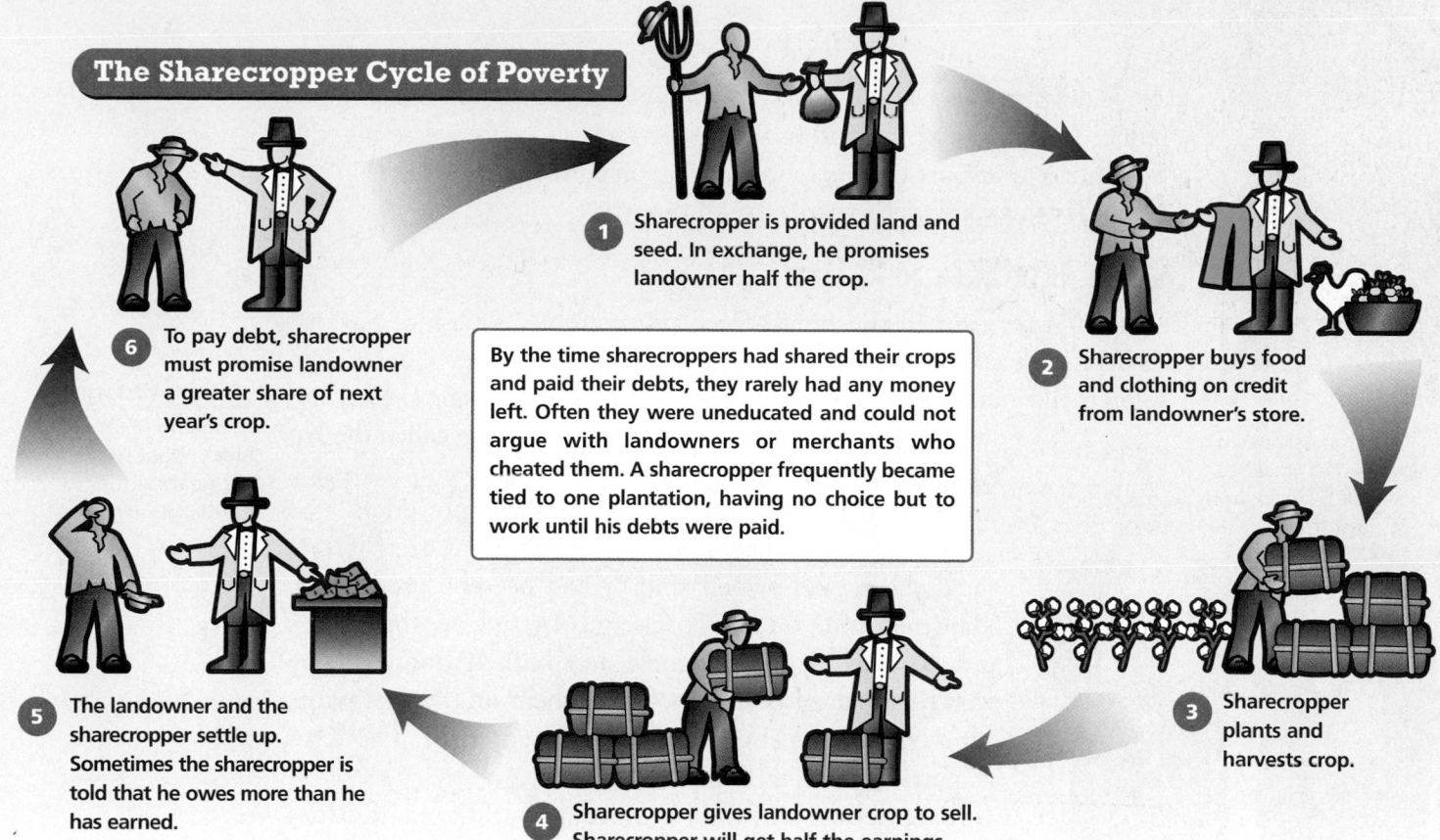

The Sharecropper Cycle of Poverty

1 Sharecropper is provided land and seed. In exchange, he promises landowner half the crop.

2 Sharecropper buys food and clothing on credit from landowner's store.

3 Sharecropper plants and harvests crop.

4 Sharecropper gives landowner crop to sell. Sharecropper will get half the earnings, minus the cost of his purchases for the year.

5 The landowner and the sharecropper settle up. Sometimes the sharecropper is told that he owes more than he has earned.

6 To pay debt, sharecropper must promise landowner a greater share of next year's crop.

By the time sharecroppers had shared their crops and paid their debts, they rarely had any money left. Often they were uneducated and could not argue with landowners or merchants who cheated them. A sharecropper frequently became tied to one plantation, having no choice but to work until his debts were paid.

without permission. Many owners cheated workers out of wages and other benefits. Worse yet, laws punished workers for breaking their contracts, even if the plantation owners were abusing or cheating them. These drawbacks made many African Americans turn to sharecropping.

Sharecropping and Debt

Under the **sharecropping** system, a worker rented a plot of land to farm. The landowner provided the tools, seed, and housing. When harvest time came, the sharecropper gave the landowner a share of the crop. This system gave families without land a place to farm and gave landowners cheap labor.

But problems soon arose with the sharecropping system. One cause of these problems was that farmers and landowners had opposite goals. Farmers wanted to grow food to feed their families, but landowners forced them to grow cash crops, such as cotton. As a result, farmers had to buy food from the local store—which was usually owned by the landlord. Most farmers did not have the money to pay for goods. As a result, many were caught in a cycle of debt, as shown in the diagram above. Often farmers had to use one year's harvest to pay the previous year's bills.

White farmers also became sharecroppers. Many had lost their land in the war. Others had lost it to taxes. By 1880, one-third of the white farmers in the Deep South worked someone else's land.

No matter who worked the plantations, much of what they grew was cotton. After the war, the value of cotton dropped. Southern planters responded by trying to produce more of the cash crop—a move that

*Reading*History
D. Recognizing Effects What were some problems with the sharecropping system?

drove down prices even further. Growing cotton exhausted the soil and reduced the amount of land available for food crops. As a result, the South had to import half its food. Relying on cotton was one reason the Deep South experienced years of rural poverty.

The Ku Klux Klan

African Americans in the South faced other problems besides poverty. They also faced violent racism. Many planters and former Confederate soldiers did not want African Americans to have more rights. In 1866,

such feelings spurred the rise of a secret group called the **Ku Klux Klan.** The Klan's goals were to restore Democratic control of the South and keep former slaves powerless.

*Reading*History
E. Finding Main Ideas What were the goals of the Ku Klux Klan?

The Klan attacked African Americans. Often it targeted those who owned land or had become prosperous. Klansmen rode on horseback and dressed in white robes and hoods. They beat people and burned homes. They even **lynched** some victims, killing them on the spot without a trial as punishment for a supposed crime. The Klan also attacked white Republicans.

Klan victims had little protection. Military authorities in the South often ignored the violence. President Johnson had appointed most of these authorities, and they were against Reconstruction.

The Klan's terrorism served the Democratic Party. As gun-toting Klansmen kept Republicans away from the polls, the Democrats increased their power.

In the next section you will see how planters took back control of the South. You also will learn how they blocked African Americans' attempts to win more rights.

These Ku Klux Klan members were arrested after an 1868 riot in Alabama.

Section 2 Assessment

1. Terms & Names
Explain the significance of:
- freedmen's school
- sharecropping
- Ku Klux Klan
- lynch

2. Using Graphics
Use a cluster diagram like the one below to review details about sharecropping.

For farmers, what were the advantages and disadvantages of sharecropping?

3. Main Ideas
a. How did freedom help strengthen African-American families?

b. How were African Americans educated during Reconstruction?

c. What were the main reasons African Americans wanted their own land?

4. Critical Thinking
Analyzing Causes
Despite greater civil rights, why did African Americans still face difficulty in improving their lives?

THINK ABOUT
- the defeat of the land-reform bill
- the Ku Klux Klan's rise
- the attitude of military authorities in the South

ACTIVITY OPTIONS

SPEECH

ART

Make a **speech** to President Johnson or design a **mural** explaining why land should be given to newly freed African Americans.

End of Reconstruction

MAIN IDEA	WHY IT MATTERS NOW	TERMS & NAMES
As white Southerners regained power, Reconstruction ended, as did black advances toward equality.	Reforms made during Reconstruction made later civil rights gains possible.	Fifteenth Amendment Compromise of 1877 Panic of 1873

ONE AMERICAN'S STORY

Robert B. Elliott was a U.S. congressman from South Carolina during Reconstruction. In 1874, he made a speech in favor of a civil rights bill that would outlaw racial discrimination in public service.

A VOICE FROM THE PAST

The passage of this bill will determine the civil status, not only of the negro but of any other class of citizens who may feel themselves discriminated against. It will form the capstone of that temple of liberty begun on this continent.

Robert B. Elliott, quoted in *The Glorious Failure*

Robert B. Elliott lost his political office when Reconstruction ended.

In 1877, federal troops left the South. White Southerners took back control of the region. Quickly, they forced African Americans, including Elliott, out of office. In Section 3, you will learn about the events that ended Reconstruction. You will also see how Reconstruction's end meant setbacks in the fight for civil rights.

The Election of Grant

The Republican Party seemed stronger than ever in 1868. That year, its candidate, General Ulysses S. Grant, won the presidency. During the campaign, the Democrats attacked the Republicans' Reconstruction policies. They blamed the party for granting rights to African Americans.

On Election Day, however, the Republicans won. Grant received 214 electoral votes. His Democratic opponent received only 80. The popular count was much closer. Grant had a majority of only 306,000 votes.

Grant would not have had such a majority without the freedmen's vote. Despite attacks by the Ku Klux Klan, about 500,000 African Americans voted in the South. Most cast their ballots for Grant.

Taking Notes

Use your chart to take notes about voting.

Problems

- Black codes
- President Johnson
- Education
- Economy
- Ku Klux Klan
- Voting

Now *and* **then**

AFRICAN AMERICANS IN CONGRESS

Between 1870 and 1877, 16 African Americans served in Congress. Seven are shown in the picture below. Two were senators: Hiram R. Revels and Blanche K. Bruce, both of whom were from Mississippi.

In 1999, there were 38 African Americans in Congress. The longest-serving member was John Conyers, a representative from Michigan elected in 1964. Only two African-American senators were elected in the 20th century. Massachusetts senator Edward W. Brooke served from 1967 to 1979. Illinois senator Carol Moseley-Braun served from 1993 to 1999.

The Fifteenth Amendment

After Grant's victory, Radical Republicans worried that the Southern states might try to keep African Americans from voting in future elections. To prevent this, Radical leaders proposed a new constitutional amendment.

The **Fifteenth Amendment** stated that citizens could not be stopped from voting "on account of race, color, or previous condition of servitude." (This amendment, like the Fourteenth Amendment, did not apply to Native Americans on tribal lands.) The amendment was ratified in 1870.

The Fifteenth Amendment was not aimed only at the South. African-American men could not vote in 16 states. "We have no moral right to impose an obligation on one part of the land which the rest will not accept," one Radical wrote. With the Fifteenth Amendment, the nation again turned toward democracy.

The Fifteenth Amendment did not apply to women. This made many white women angry. Why couldn't they vote when black men—former slaves—could? Suffragist Elizabeth Cady Stanton protested the idea of uneducated immigrants and freedmen "who never read the Declaration of Independence" making laws for educated white women. Most African-American women were not as angry. To Frances E. W. Harper, a black suffragist and writer, it was important for African Americans to gain voting rights, even if that meant only men at first.

*Reading*History

A. Comparing
How was the Fifteenth Amendment a step beyond the Fourteenth Amendment?

Vocabulary
suffragist: someone who favors equal voting rights, especially for women

Grant Fights the Klan

Despite gaining the vote, African Americans in the South continued to be terrorized by the Ku Klux Klan. In 1871, to stop the terror, President Grant asked Congress to pass a tough law against the Klan. Joseph Rainey, a black congressman from South Carolina, had received death threats from the Klan. He urged his fellow lawmakers to support the bill.

A VOICE FROM THE PAST

When myself and colleagues shall leave these Halls and turn our footsteps toward our southern home we know not but that the assassin may await our coming. Be it as it may we have resolved to be loyal and firm, and if we perish, we perish! I earnestly hope the bill will pass.

Joseph Rainey, quoted in *The Trouble They Seen*

Congress approved the anti-Klan bill. Federal marshals then arrested thousands of Klansmen. Klan attacks on African-American voters declined. As a result, the 1872 presidential election was both fair and peaceful in the South. Grant won a second term.

Scandal and Panic Weaken Republicans

Under the Grant administration, support for the Republicans and Reconstruction weakened. Scandals hurt the administration and caused divisions in the Republican Party. A financial panic further hurt the Republicans and turned the country's attention away from Reconstruction.

President Grant did not choose his advisers well. He put his former army friends and his wife's relatives in government positions. Many of these people were unqualified. Some Grant appointees took bribes. Grant's private secretary, for instance, took money from whiskey distillers who wanted to avoid paying taxes. Grant's secretary of war, General William Belknap, left office after people accused him of taking bribes.

*Reading*History
B. Making Inferences How did Republican scandals hurt Reconstruction?

Such scandals deeply outraged many Republicans. In 1872, some Republican officials broke away and formed the new Liberal Republican Party. The Republicans, no longer unified, became less willing to impose tough Reconstruction policies on the South.

In 1873, political corruption and Republican quarreling gave way to a more serious problem. When several powerful Eastern banks ran out of money after making bad loans, a financial panic swept the country. In the **Panic of 1873,** banks across the land closed. The stock market temporarily collapsed. The panic caused an economic depression, a time of low business activity and high unemployment. The railroad industry, which relied on banks for loans, suffered. Within a year, 89 of the country's 364 railroads went broke. Railroad failures left Midwestern farmers with no way to move their crops, and many farmers were ruined.

This cartoon from *Puck* magazine shows President Grant weighed down by corruption in his administration.

The depression, which lasted about five years, touched nearly all parts of the economy. By 1875, more than 18,000 companies had folded. Hundreds of workers had lost their jobs. Many Americans blamed the crisis on the Republicans—the party in power. As a result, Democrats won victories in the 1874 congressional and state elections. In the middle of the depression, Americans grew tired of hearing about the South's problems. The nation was losing interest in Reconstruction.

*Reading*History
C. Recognizing Effects What resulted from the Panic of 1873?

Supreme Court Reversals

To make matters worse for the Republicans, the Supreme Court began to undo some of the changes that had been made in the South. In an 1876 case, *U.S.* v. *Cruikshank,* the Court ruled that the federal government could not punish individuals who violated the civil rights of African Americans. Only the states had that power, the Court declared. Southern state officials often would not punish those who attacked African Americans. As a result, violence against them increased.

In the 1876 case *U.S.* v. *Reese,* the Court ruled in favor of white Southerners who barred African Americans from voting. The Court stated that the Fifteenth Amendment did not give everyone the right to vote—it merely listed the grounds on which states could not deny the vote. In other words, states could prevent African Americans from voting for other reasons. States later imposed poll taxes and literacy tests to restrict the vote. These Court decisions weakened Reconstruction and blocked African-American efforts to gain full equality.

*Reading*History

D. Recognizing Effects How did the Reese and Cruikshank rulings affect African Americans' efforts to gain civil rights?

Reconstruction Ends

The final blow to Reconstruction came with the 1876 presidential election. The Democrats nominated Samuel J. Tilden, governor of New York. The Republicans chose Rutherford B. Hayes, governor of Ohio. The race was very close. Victory depended on the electoral votes of South Carolina, Louisiana, and Florida. The votes in those states were so close that both the Democrats and the Republicans claimed victory. A special commission of eight Republicans and seven Democrats made a deal. Under the **Compromise of 1877,** Hayes became president. In return, the Republicans compromised with the Southern Democrats on several issues.

This cartoon from *Harper's Weekly* shows a federal soldier as the freedman's only defense against white Southerners.

1. The government would remove federal troops from the South.
2. The government would provide land grants and loans for the construction of railroads linking the South to the West Coast.
3. Southern officials would receive federal funds for construction and improvement projects.
4. Hayes would appoint a Democrat to his cabinet.
5. The Democrats promised to respect African Americans' civil and political rights.

*Reading*History

E. Summarizing What events led to a weakening of support for Reconstruction?

Abolitionist Wendell Phillips was against the compromise. He doubted that the South would respect black rights. "The whole soil of the South is hidden by successive layers of broken promises," he said. "To trust a Southern promise would be fair evidence of insanity."

After the 1876 presidential election, the Reconstruction governments in the South collapsed. The Democrats returned to power, believing that they were the redeemers, or rescuers, of the South.

Reconstruction: Civil Rights Amendments and Laws

Civil Rights Act of 1866	• Granted citizenship and equal rights to all persons born in the United States (except Native Americans)
Fourteenth Amendment (1868)	• Granted citizenship and equal protection of the laws to all persons born in the United States (except Native Americans)
Fifteenth Amendment (1870)	• Protected the voting rights of African Americans
Civil Rights Act of 1875	• Outlawed racial segregation in public services • Ensured the right of African Americans to serve as jurors

SKILLBUILDER Interpreting Charts

1. *Which amendment and law are most similar?*
2. *Which amendment specifically protects voting rights?*

The Legacy of Reconstruction

Historians still argue about the success of Reconstruction. The nation did rebuild and reunite. However, Reconstruction did not achieve equality for African Americans.

After Reconstruction, most African Americans still lived in poverty. Legally, they could vote and hold public office. But few took part in politics. They continued to face widespread violence and prejudice.

During this period, however, African Americans did make lasting gains. Protection of civil rights became part of the U.S. Constitution. The Fourteenth and Fifteenth amendments would provide a legal basis for civil rights laws of the 20th century. Black schools and churches begun during Reconstruction also endured. Reconstruction changed society, putting African Americans on the path toward full equality. In the next unit, you will learn about other changes in American society after the Civil War.

Section Assessment

1. Terms & Names

Explain the significance of:
- Fifteenth Amendment
- Panic of 1873
- Compromise of 1877

2. Using Graphics

Review the chapter and find five significant individuals and events to place on a time line as shown.

Which event or person was most important and why?

3. Main Ideas

a. What did the Fifteenth Amendment declare?

b. What effect did scandals in the Grant administration have on the Republican Party?

c. What demands did Southern Democrats make in the Compromise of 1877?

4. Critical Thinking

Drawing Conclusions
Why do you think the Republicans were willing to agree to the Compromise of 1877 and end Reconstruction?

THINK ABOUT
- the election of 1876
- the Panic of 1873
- the Supreme Court rulings

ACTIVITY OPTIONS

LANGUAGE ARTS

CIVICS

Research Ku Klux Klan activities barring African Americans from voting. Then write a protest **letter to the editor** or propose a **law** to protect voting rights.

TERMS & NAMES

Briefly explain the significance of each of the following.

1. Reconstruction
2. Andrew Johnson
3. black codes
4. civil rights
5. Fourteenth Amendment
6. sharecropping
7. lynch
8. Fifteenth Amendment
9. Panic of 1873
10. Compromise of 1877

REVIEW QUESTIONS

Rebuilding the Union (pages 533–539)

1. What was the Freedmen's Bureau?
2. What were the main parts of President Johnson's Reconstruction plan?
3. Who were scalawags and carpetbaggers?
4. What reason did the House give for impeaching President Johnson?

Reconstruction and Daily Life (pages 540–544)

5. Why did Congress not pass a land-reform plan?
6. What new systems of labor developed in the South after the Civil War?
7. How did the Ku Klux Klan serve the Democratic Party?

End of Reconstruction (pages 545–549)

8. Why did the Fifteenth Amendment arouse anger in many women?
9. What caused an economic depression in the 1870s?
10. How did Supreme Court rulings during Reconstruction help weaken African Americans' civil rights?

CRITICAL THINKING

1. USING YOUR NOTES: IDENTIFYING AND SOLVING PROBLEMS

Problems		Solutions
Black codes	➤	
President Johnson	➤	
Education	➤	
Economy	➤	
Ku Klux Klan	➤	
Voting	➤	

Using your diagram, answer the following questions.

a. What was the solution to the problem of educating African Americans?

b. What was the solution to the problem of Ku Klux Klan violence?

2. ANALYZING LEADERSHIP

Why might Reconstruction be considered a time in which the presidency was weak?

3. THEME: DEMOCRATIC IDEALS

How did the Fourteenth and Fifteenth amendments promote greater equality for African Americans? How were the amendments limited?

4. APPLYING CITIZENSHIP SKILLS

What were the different viewpoints of Elizabeth Cady Stanton and Frances E. W. Harper regarding the Fifteenth Amendment's failure to give women an important right of citizenship—the right to vote?

5. ANALYZING CAUSES

What aspect of the Compromise of 1877 likely played the greatest role in ending Reconstruction?

Interact with History

How did your solutions to rebuilding the nation compare with the actual solutions carried out?

VISUAL SUMMARY

Reconstruction

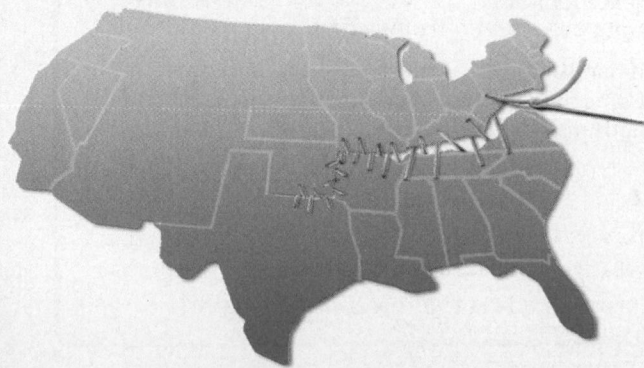

Rebuilding the Union

During Reconstruction, Congress decided how the Southern states would be readmitted to the Union and passed laws to improve conditions for freed people.

Reconstruction and Daily Life

After slavery ended, freed African Americans reunited their families, attended school, and began working for pay. Racist violence and lack of land slowed their progress.

End of Reconstruction

In the 1870s, hostile Supreme Court decisions, the Southern Democrats' return to power, and the withdrawal of federal troops from the South ended Reconstruction.

Use the map and your knowledge of U.S. history to answer questions 1 and 2.

Additional Test Practice, pp. S1–S33.

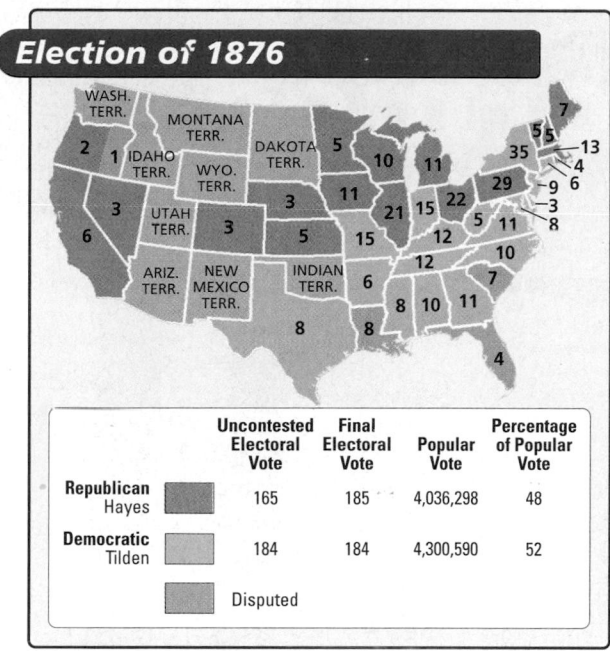

Election of 1876

WASH. TERR.
MONTANA TERR.
IDAHO TERR.
WYO. TERR.
DAKOTA TERR.
UTAH TERR.
ARIZ. TERR.
NEW MEXICO TERR.
INDIAN TERR.

2 1
3
6
3
3
5
5
10
11
11
21 15 22
15
12
6
8 8
4
7
5 5
35
29
5 11
12
7
8 10 11
13
4
9 6
3
8
10

		Uncontested Electoral Vote	Final Electoral Vote	Popular Vote	Percentage of Popular Vote
Republican Hayes		165	185	4,036,298	48
Democratic Tilden		184	184	4,300,590	52
		Disputed			

1. In what region of the country were most of the disputed votes located?
   A. the North
   B. the South
   C. the Northeast
   D. the Southwest

2. What regions voted mostly Republican?
   A. the North and East
   B. the South and East
   C. the South and West
   D. the North and West

Robert B. Elliott gives his views of the civil rights bill in this quotation. Use the quotation and your knowledge of U.S. history to answer question 3.

PRIMARY SOURCE

The passage of this bill will determine the civil status, not only of the negro but of any other class of citizens who may feel themselves discriminated against. It will form the capstone of that temple of liberty begun on this continent.

Robert B. Elliott, quoted in *The Glorious Failure*

3. This passage supports which point of view?
   A. African Americans would never gain freedom without the passage of the civil rights bill.
   B. The passage of the civil rights bill would be important to southern states only.
   C. The passage of the civil rights bill would help any group subject to discrimination.
   D. Failure to pass the civil rights bill would mean renewed war in the United States.

TEST PRACTICE
CLASSZONE.COM

ALTERNATIVE ASSESSMENT

1. 📝 WRITING ABOUT HISTORY

Write a **letter** to the editor of a newspaper stating your opinion of the freedmen's schools. You might write from the perspective of a plantation owner, or from that of a recently-freed African American.

- Use library resources to research the schools.
- Support your opinion with facts from your research.
- Try to persuade your reader to support your position.

2. COOPERATIVE LEARNING

Work with two classmates to research sharecropping. Each group member can choose a different perspective to research: a land owner; a white sharecropper, or an African-American sharecropper. Explain how their perspectives differ from each other.

INTEGRATED TECHNOLOGY

PARTICIPATING IN A NET SIMULATION

Go to *NetSimulations: The Impeachment of Andrew Johnson* at **classzone.com** to participate in the impeachment trial of the president. You must evaluate the evidence against President Johnson and vote to retain or remove him from office.

- Use the simulation to learn about the impeachment process, the conflicts between Congress and the president, and the events that led to the trial.
- Answer questions in the Senator's Journal, and use it to take notes.
- Before you cast your vote, carefully consider the closing arguments of each attorney.

NET SIMULATION
CLASSZONE.COM

America Transformed

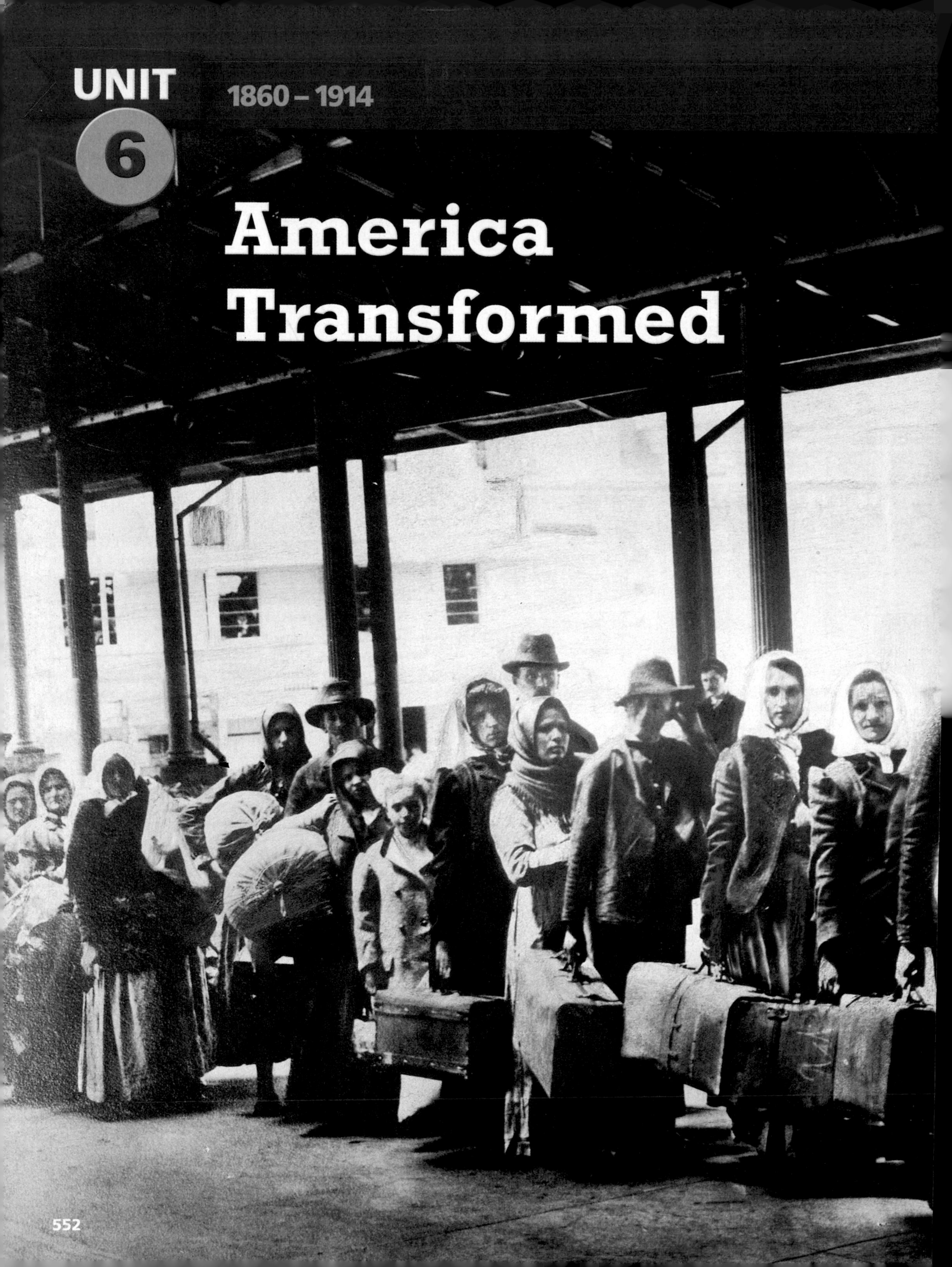

"Give me your tired, your poor,
Your huddled masses, yearning
to breathe free…"

—Emma Lazarus

European immigrants such as those
shown in this photograph (taken
around 1900) streamed into Ellis
Island at the turn of the century.

CHAPTER 19

Growth in the West 1860–1900

Section 1 **Miners, Ranchers, and Cowhands**

Section 2 **Native Americans Fight to Survive**

Section 3 **Life in the West**

Section 4 **Farming and Populism**

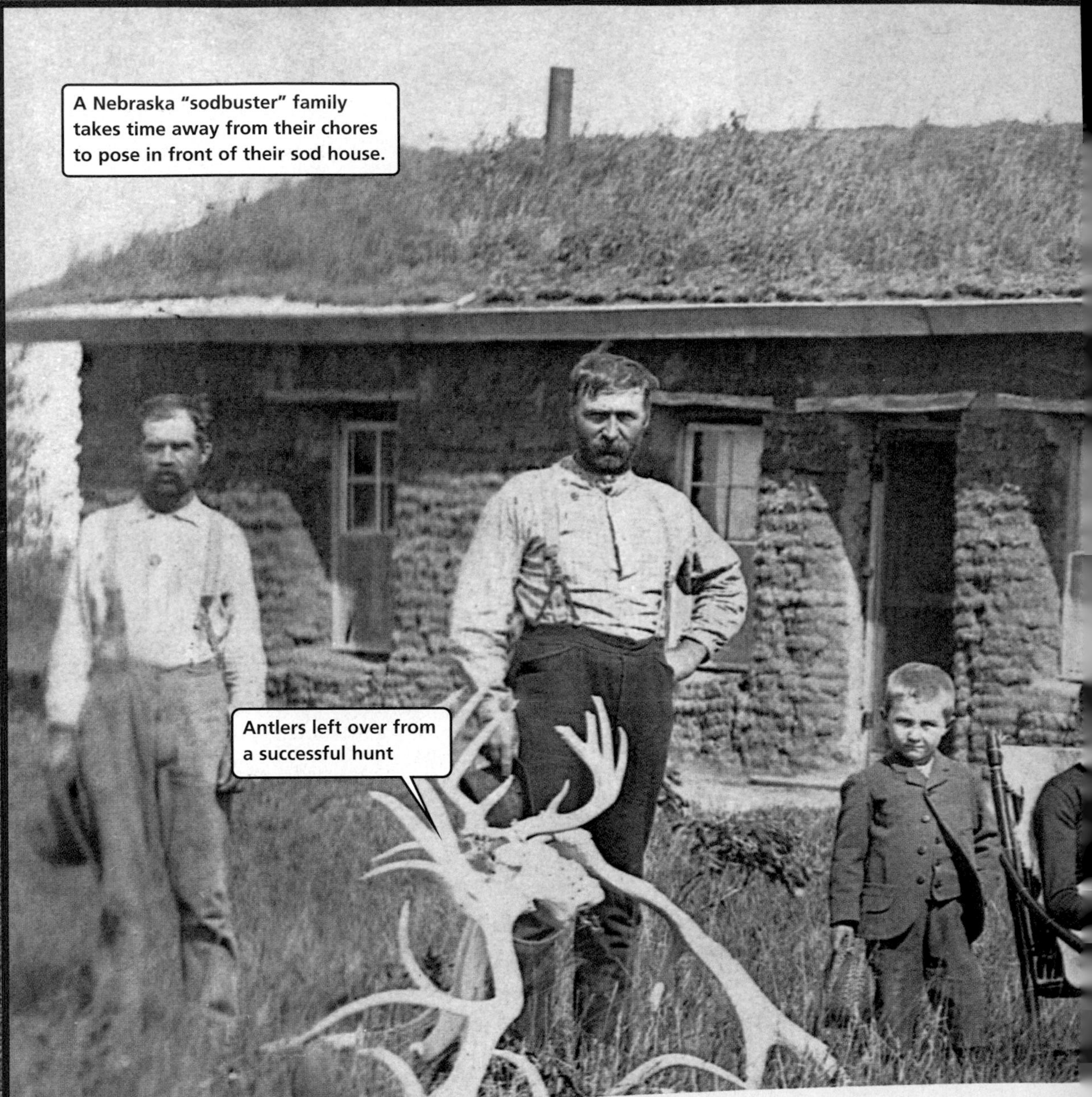

A Nebraska "sodbuster" family takes time away from their chores to pose in front of their sod house.

Antlers left over from a successful hunt

USA / World — 1860

1862 Congress passes the Homestead Act.

1864 Sand Creek Massacre

1867 The Grange is founded.

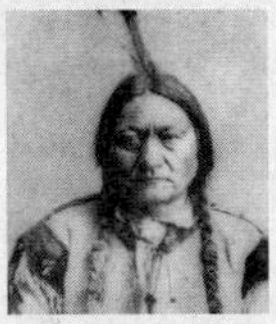

1876 Sitting Bull leads Native American warriors at the Battle of the Little Bighorn.

1880 James Garfield is electec president

1861 Serfs are freed in Russia.

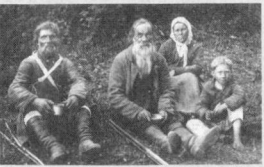

1871 Franco-Prussian War ends.

1876 Japan recognizes Korean independence.

The windows in this sod house are a real luxury.

It is 1865, and the Civil War has just ended. You are drawn to the West by stories of gold, silver, fertile soil, and free land, and by tales of adventure and new opportunities. Yet you know there would be hardships and unknown dangers. Your life would never be the same.

How might your life change in the West?

What Do You Think?

- What might be some of the ways to make a living in the West?

- What do you think your daily life would be like in the West?

- What would be the biggest difference in your life?

RESEARCH LINKS
CLASSZONE.COM
Visit the Chapter 19 links for more information about the American West.

1881
Chester Arthur becomes president after Garfield is assassinated.

1884
Grover Cleveland is elected president.

1889
Oklahoma land rush begins.

1890
Wounded Knee Massacre

1891
Farmers organize the Populist Party.

1896
William McKinley is elected president.

1900

1885
in Conference on African airs divides Africa among European nations.

1889
First Pan-American Conference is held.

1893
France takes over Indochina.

1900
Boxer Rebellion takes place in China.

Reading Strategy: Finding Main Ideas

What Do You Know?

What do you think about when you hear terms like *cowboy* and *Wild West?* What do you already know about the people, places, and events in the West in the last half of the 19th century?

Think About

- what you have learned about the West from books, movies, and television
- what happens when different cultures clash
- your responses to the Interact with History about how the West might change your life (see page 555)

What Do You Want to Know?

 What details do you need to help you understand the settling of the West? Make a list of those details in your notebook before you read the chapter.

Finding Main Ideas

To make it easier for you to understand what you read, learn to find the main idea of each paragraph, topic heading, and section. Remember that the supporting details help to explain the main ideas. On the chart below, write down the main ideas about the many diverse people who settled the West.

S See Skillbuilder Handbook, page R5.

 Taking Notes

Cowhands/Ranchers

Miners

Native Americans

Many diverse people settled the West!

African Americans

Women

Mexican Americans

Farmers

Miners, Ranchers, and Cowhands

MAIN IDEA	WHY IT MATTERS NOW	TERMS & NAMES
Miners, ranchers, and cowhands settled in the West seeking economic opportunities.	The mining and cattle industries that developed then still contribute to American economic growth.	frontier long drive Great Plains *vaquero* boomtown vigilante

ONE AMERICAN'S STORY

Nat Love was born a slave in Tennessee in 1854. After the Civil War, he was one of thousands of African Americans who left the South and went west. In 1869, Love headed for Dodge City, Kansas

Love's horse taming skills landed him a job as a cowhand. He became well known for his expert horsemanship and rodeo riding and roping. In his 1907 autobiography, Love offered a lively but exaggerated account of his life.

> *A VOICE FROM THE PAST*
>
> I carry the marks of fourteen bullet wounds on different parts of my body, most any one of which would be sufficient to kill an ordinary man. . . . Horses were shot from under me, men killed around me, but always I escaped with a trifling wound at the worst.
>
> **Nat Love,** *The Life and Adventures of Nat Love*

As you will read in this section, few cowhands led lives as exciting as that described by Nat Love, but they all helped to open a new chapter in the history of the American West.

Nat Love was an African-American cowhand who became a rodeo star.

Geography and Population of the West

In the mid-1800s, towns such as St. Joseph and Independence, Missouri, were jumping-off places for settlers going west. They were the last cities and towns before the frontier. The **frontier** was the unsettled or sparsely settled area of the country occupied largely by Native Americans.

Many white settlers thought of the **Great Plains**—the area from the Missouri River to the Rocky Mountains—as empty. (See map on page 558.) Few had been attracted to its rolling plains, dry plateaus, and deserts. However, west of the Rockies, on the Pacific Coast, settlers had followed miners streaming into California after the 1849 gold rush. By 1850, California had gained statehood. Oregon followed in 1859.

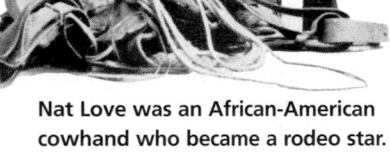

Taking Notes

Use your chart to take notes about miners, ranchers, and cowhands.

Many diverse people settled the West!

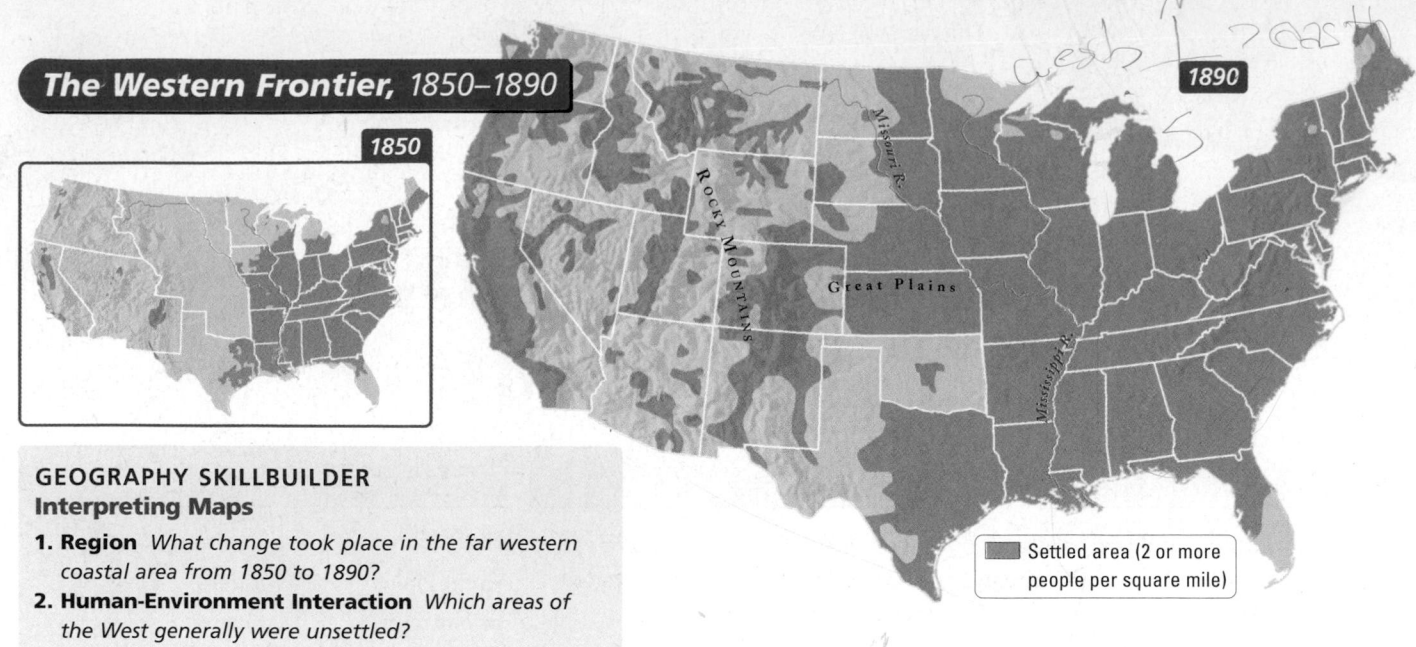

The Western Frontier, 1850–1890

1850

1890

GEOGRAPHY SKILLBUILDER
Interpreting Maps

1. **Region** What change took place in the far western coastal area from 1850 to 1890?
2. **Human-Environment Interaction** Which areas of the West generally were unsettled?

Settled area (2 or more people per square mile)

The Great Plains had few trees, but its grasslands were home to about 300,000 Native Americans in the mid-1800s. Most followed the buffalo herds that rumbled across the open plains. Despite the presence of these peoples, the United States claimed ownership of the area.

Railroads played a key role in settling the western United States. Trains carried the natural resources of the West—minerals, timber, crops, and cattle—to eastern markets. In turn, trains brought miners, ranchers, and farmers west to develop these resources further. As the railroads opened new areas to white settlement, they also helped to bring an end to the way of life of the West's first settlers—the Native Americans.

Reading **History**

A. Making Inferences Why were railroads so important to the West?

Mining in the West

In 1859, gold and silver strikes drew fortune seekers to Colorado and Nevada. As many as 100,000 miners raced to the Rocky Mountains in Colorado after gold was discovered near Pikes Peak. Also in 1859, prospectors hit "pay dirt" at the Comstock Lode in western Nevada. (A lode is a deposit of a valuable mineral buried in layers of rock.) From 1859 to 1880, the Comstock mine produced some $300 million in silver and gold.

Nearby Virginia City, Nevada, became a **boomtown,** a town that has a sudden burst of economic or population growth. Population jumped from 3,000 in the 1860s to over 20,000 in the 1870s. The writer Samuel Clemens, better known as Mark Twain, captured the excitement of life there.

Vocabulary
strike: valuable discovery of a precious mineral

A VOICE FROM THE PAST

The sidewalks swarmed with people. . . . Money was as plenty as dust; [everyone] considered himself wealthy. . . . There were . . . fire companies, brass bands, banks, hotels, theaters . . . gambling palaces . . . street-fights, murders, . . . riots, . . . and a half dozen jails . . . in full operation.

Mark Twain, *Roughing It*

Other major strikes took place in the Black Hills of South Dakota in 1874 and at Cripple Creek, Colorado, in 1891. In 1896, gold was discovered in

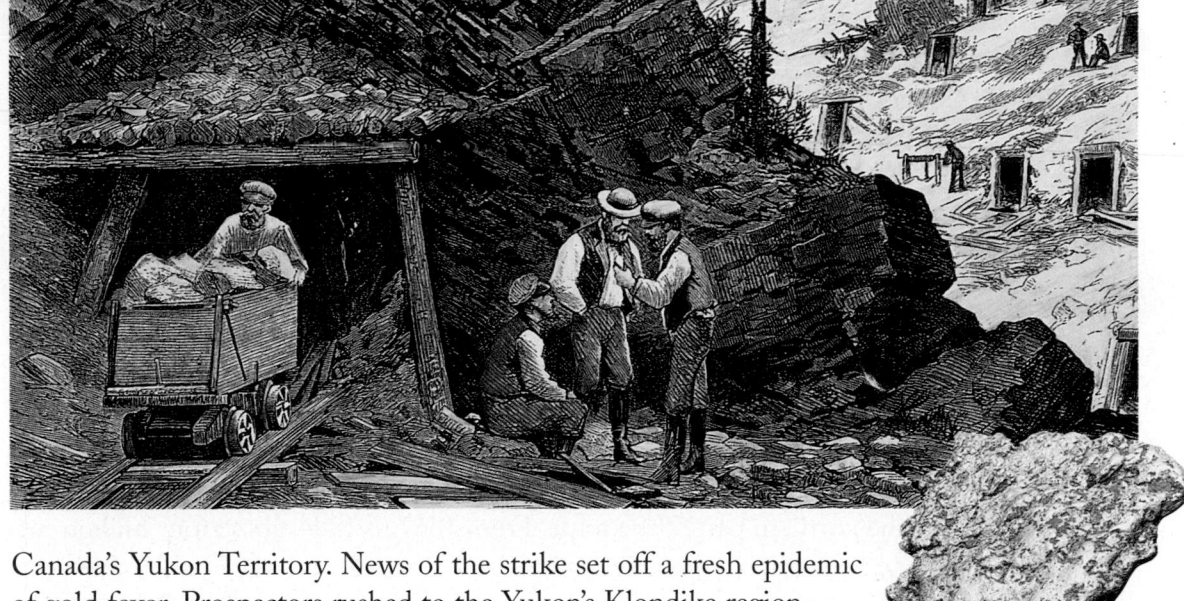

Canada's Yukon Territory. News of the strike set off a fresh epidemic of gold fever. Prospectors rushed to the Yukon's Klondike region.

The chance to strike it rich drew Americans from both East and West coasts. Gold fever also attracted miners from other parts of the world, including Europe, South America, Mexico, and China. Unfortunately, few prospectors became rich. Most left, disappointed and broke.

Early miners used panning and sluicing to wash sand and gravel from a stream to separate out any bits of precious metal, as you read in Chapter 13. Large mining companies moved in after surface mines no longer yielded gold or silver. Only they could buy the costly, heavy equipment needed to take the precious metals from underground. Water cannons blasted away hillsides to expose gold deposits. In other places, workers sank shafts thousands of feet into the ground to create underground mines. These new methods recovered more precious metals, but in the process stripped hillsides of vegetation and left rivers polluted.

Paid workers in company mines replaced independent prospectors. The work was hard and dangerous. Dust caused lung problems, and deadly cave-ins could trap miners hundreds of feet below the surface.

By the 1890s, the mining boom was over. Many mines closed because the costs had become too high, and the quality of the ore had dropped. Jobless workers moved elsewhere. Once-thriving communities became ghost towns. Still, the mining boom had lasting effects. Nevada, Colorado, and South Dakota all grew so rapidly that they soon gained statehood.

Reading **History**
B. Recognizing Effects Why did large mining companies replace individual prospectors?

Miners brought ore, like the gold nugget shown, from underground mines that dotted the hillsides.

The Rise of the Cattle Industry

The cattle trade had existed in the Southwest since the Spanish arrived there in the 1500s. But cattle herds remained small until the Civil War. There were few buyers for Western beef because there was no efficient way to get the beef to markets in the more heavily populated cities of the East. The ranchers mostly sold their cattle locally.

The extension of railroad lines from Chicago and St. Louis into Kansas by the 1860s brought changes. An Illinois livestock dealer named Joseph McCoy realized that railroads could bring cattle from Texas ranches to meat-hungry Eastern cities. Cowhands had only to drive cattle herds north from Texas to his stockyards in Abilene, Kansas. From there, the beef could be shipped to Chicago and points east by rail car.

McCoy's plan turned cattle ranching into a very profitable business. Cattle fed on the open range for a year or two and cost the rancher nothing. Ranchers then hired cowhands to round up the cattle and take them to Abilene. There they were sold for as much as ten times their original price. The success of the Abilene stockyards spurred the growth of other Kansas cow towns, including Wichita and Dodge City. The cattle drives to cow towns along the railways were called the **long drives**.

Over time, cowhands followed specific trails across the plains. The first was the Chisholm Trail, which stretched from San Antonio, Texas, to Abilene, Kansas. It was named for Jesse Chisholm, a trader who marked the northern part of the route. From 1867 to 1884, about four million cattle were driven to market on this trail. As cattle raising became more profitable, ranching spread north across the plains from Texas to Montana.

Reading **History**
C. Reading a Map
Use the map on page 581 to locate the Chisholm Trail.

Vaqueros and Cowhands

The first cowhands, or **vaqueros,** as they were known in Spanish, came from Mexico with the Spaniards in the 1500s. They settled in the Southwest. The *vaqueros* helped Spanish, and later Mexican, ranchers manage their herds. From the *vaquero*, the American cowhand learned to rope and ride. Cowhands also adapted the saddle, spurs, lariat (which they used to rope a calf or steer), and chaps of the *vaqueros*.

About one in three cowhands in the West was either Mexican or African-American. Many Mexican cowhands were descendants of the *vaqueros*. Some African-American cowhands were former slaves. They came west at the end of Reconstruction because the enactment of Black Codes in the South put restrictions on their freedom. Also among the cowhands were a large number of former Confederate and Union soldiers.

Background
Chaps, from the Spanish word *chaperejos,* were seatless leather pants worn over trousers to protect legs from scrub brush, snakes, and cactus.

daily *life*

LIFE OF A COWHAND: THE ROUNDUP

During some parts of the year, the cowhand's life was downright dull. While cattle grazed on the open range, cowhands sat around the ranch, repairing their gear and doing odd jobs. The pace quickened at roundup time in the spring and fall.

For several weeks, 150 to 250 cowhands from nearby ranches rode hundreds of miles locating cattle. Cowhands from each ranch collected their cattle, removed sick or weak animals, and branded new calves. Then the cowhands were ready for the long drive. A roundup by *vaqueros* is shown in this painting by James Walker.

The "Wild West"

At first, the rapidly growing cow towns had no local governments. There were no law officers to handle the fights that broke out as cowhands drank and gambled after a long drive. A more serious threat to law and order came from "con men." These swindlers saw new towns as places to get rich quick by cheating others.

Vocabulary
con man: a person who cheats victims by first gaining their confidence

Some Union and Confederate veterans were led to crime by hard feelings left over from the Civil War. Outlaws like John Wesley Hardin, "Billy the Kid," and Jesse and Frank James made crime a way of life. Some women became outlaws, too. Belle Starr, better known as the Bandit Queen, was a legendary horse thief.

For protection, citizens formed vigilante groups. **Vigilantes** were people who took the law into their own hands. They caught suspected criminals and punished them without a trial. Vigilante justice often consisted of hanging suspects from the nearest tree or shooting them on the spot. As towns became more settled, citizens elected a local sheriff or asked the federal government for a marshal. These law officers would arrest lawbreakers and hold them in jail until the time of trial.

Bandit Queen Belle Starr sits atop a horse she just might have stolen.

End of the Long Drives

For about 20 years, the cattle industry boomed. As the railroads extended farther west and south into Texas, the long drives grew shorter. The future looked bright. But by 1886, several developments had brought the cattle boom to an end. First, the price of beef dropped sharply as the supply increased in the early 1880s. It fell from more than $30 a head to $7. Then came the newly invented barbed wire. As more settlers moved to the Great Plains to farm or raise sheep, they fenced in their lands with barbed wire. The open range disappeared, and cattle could no longer pass freely over the trails. Finally, in the harsh winter of 1886–1887, thousands of cattle on the northern Plains froze to death. Many ranchers were put out of business.

Meanwhile, as the mining and cattle industries were developing, the Native Americans of the Great Plains were being pushed off their land, as you will read in the next section.

Reading **History**

D. Analyzing Causes What caused the decline of cattle ranching on the open range?

Section 1 Assessment

1. Terms & Names

Explain the significance of:
• frontier
• Great Plains
• boomtown
• long drive
• *vaquero*
• vigilante

2. Using Graphics

Use a diagram to review the rise and fall of the cattle industry.

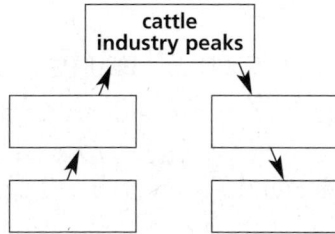

cattle industry peaks

3. Main Ideas

a. What economic opportunities drew large numbers of people to the West beginning in the 1860s?

b. How did the transcontinental railroad spur Western settlement?

c. What did cowhands learn from the *vaqueros*?

4. Critical Thinking

Evaluating Could cattle ranchers have stopped the decline of the cattle industry that occurred in the late 1880s?

THINK ABOUT
• economic causes
• impact of weather
• changing settlement patterns

ACTIVITY OPTIONS

LANGUAGE ARTS

MUSIC

Do research on a legendary figure of the West such as Wyatt Earp, "Calamity Jane," or Nat Love. Then write a **biographical sketch** or **song** about the person.

Native Americans Fight to Survive

MAIN IDEA	WHY IT MATTERS NOW	TERMS & NAMES
The Native Americans of the Great Plains fought to maintain their way of life as settlers poured onto their lands.	The taking of their lands led to social and economic problems for Native Americans that continue to this day.	reservation Sand Creek Massacre Sitting Bull George A. Custer Battle of the Little Bighorn Wounded Knee Massacre Dawes Act

ONE AMERICAN'S STORY

Buffalo Bird Woman was a Hidatsa who lived almost 100 years. She was born in 1840. As a child, she and her family made their home along the Missouri River. Later the federal government forced her family onto a reservation. A **reservation** is land set aside for Native American tribes.

The federal government attempted to "Americanize" Native American children, including Buffalo Bird Woman, by sending them away to boarding schools. But Buffalo Bird Woman struggled to hold on to Hidatsa customs. As an old woman, she looked back on her early years.

> ### A VOICE FROM THE PAST
>
> Sometimes at evening I sit, looking out on the . . . Missouri [River]. . . . In the shadows I seem . . . to see our Indian village, with smoke curling upward from the earth lodges; and in the river's roar I hear the yells of the warriors, the laughter of . . . children as of old.
>
> **Buffalo Bird Woman,** quoted in *Native American Testimony*, edited by Peter Nabokov

As white settlers claimed Native American lands, Plains peoples fought a losing battle to save not only their homes but their way of life.

Buffalo Bird Woman

Taking Notes

Use your chart to take notes about Native Americans.

Many diverse people settled the West!

Native American Life on the Plains

Before the arrival of Europeans in the 1500s, most Plains tribes lived in villages along rivers and streams. The women tended crops of beans, corn, and squash. The men hunted deer and elk and in the summer stalked the vast buffalo herds that inhabited the Plains.

In the early 1540s, the Spanish brought the first horses to the Great Plains. The arrival of horses changed the way of life of the Plains people. They quickly became expert riders. By the late 1700s, most Plains tribes kept their own herds of horses. Mounted on horseback, hunters traveled far from their villages seeking buffalo.

The buffalo was central to the life of Plains tribes. Its meat became the chief food in their diet, while its skins served as portable shelters called tepees. Plains women turned buffalo hides into clothing, shoes, and blankets and used buffalo chips (dried manure) as cooking fuel. Bones and horns became tools and bowls. Over time, many Plains tribes developed a nomadic way of life tied to buffalo hunting.

Vocabulary
nomadic: wandering from place to place

A Clash of Cultures

When the federal government first forced Native American tribes of the Southeast to move west of the Mississippi in the 1830s, it settled them in Indian Territory. This territory was a huge area that included almost all of the land between the Missouri River and Oregon Territory. Most treaties made by the government with Native Americans promised that this land would remain theirs "as long as Grass grows or water runs."

Unfortunately, these treaty promises would be broken. Government policy was based on the belief that white settlers were not interested in the Plains. The land was considered too dry for farming. However, as wagon trains bound for Oregon and California crossed the Great Plains in the 1850s, some pioneers saw possibilities for farming and ranching on its grasslands. Soon white settlers moved onto the prairies.

These settlers pressured the federal government for more land. They also wanted protection from Native Americans in the area. In 1851, the government responded by calling the Sioux, Cheyenne, Arapaho, and

Reading **History**

A. Analyzing Causes What was the major source of conflict between white settlers and Native Americans?

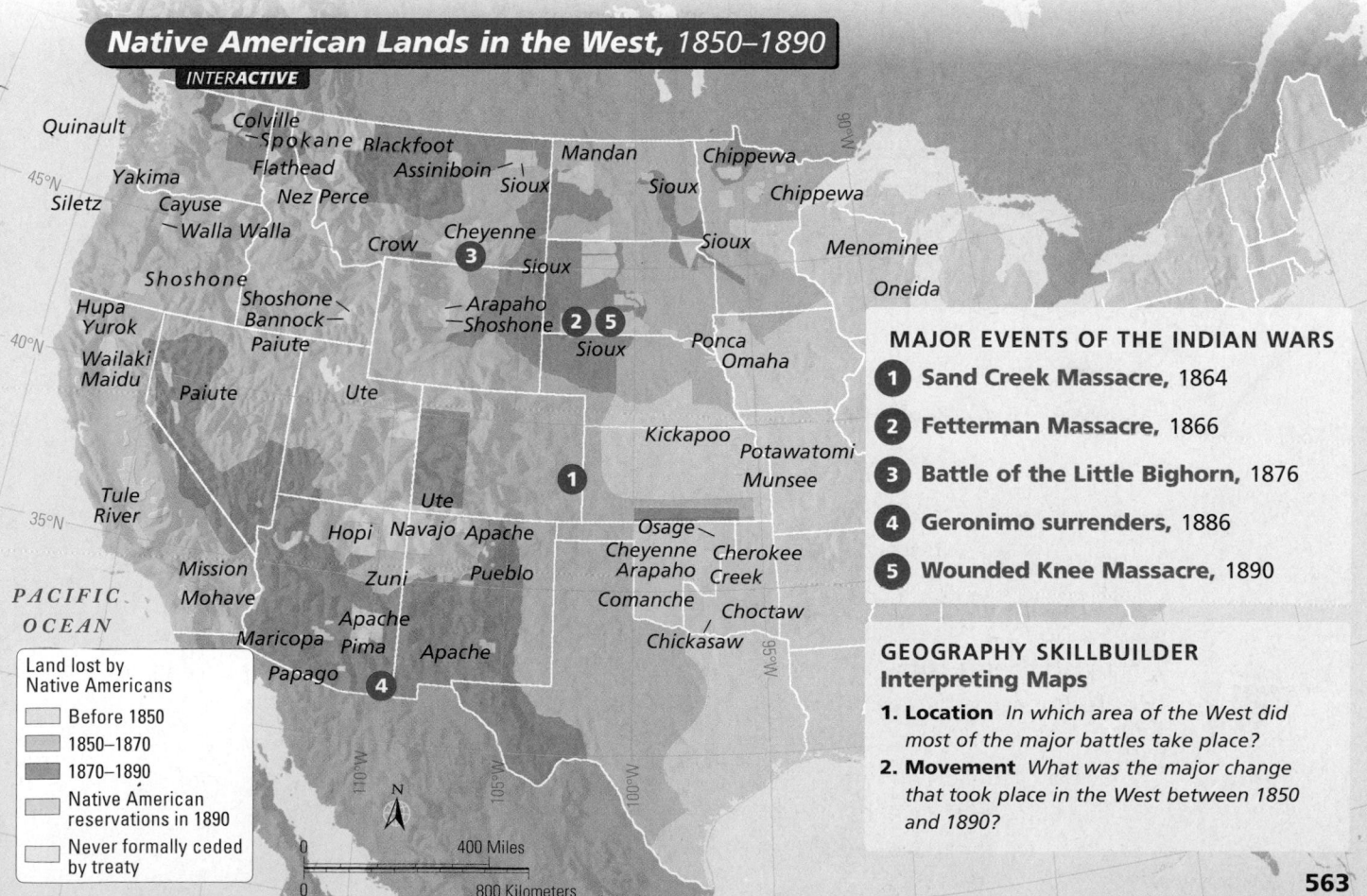

Native American Lands in the West, 1850–1890

INTER**ACTIVE**

MAJOR EVENTS OF THE INDIAN WARS

1 **Sand Creek Massacre, 1864**

2 **Fetterman Massacre, 1866**

3 **Battle of the Little Bighorn, 1876**

4 **Geronimo surrenders, 1886**

5 **Wounded Knee Massacre, 1890**

GEOGRAPHY SKILLBUILDER
Interpreting Maps

1. **Location** In which area of the West did most of the major battles take place?

2. **Movement** What was the major change that took place in the West between 1850 and 1890?

Land lost by Native Americans
- Before 1850
- 1850–1870
- 1870–1890
- Native American reservations in 1890
- Never formally ceded by treaty

0 | 400 Miles
0 | 800 Kilometers

other Plains tribes together near Fort Laramie in present-day Wyoming. Government officials tried to buy back some Native American land and also set boundaries for tribal lands. Many Plains tribes signed the First Treaty of Fort Laramie (1851)—they saw no other choice.

But some Cheyennes and Sioux resisted. They preferred conflict with settlers and soldiers to the restrictions of reservation life. In southeastern Colorado, bands of Cheyenne warriors attacked miners and soldiers. In response, about 1,200 Colorado militia led by Colonel John Chivington opened fire on a peaceful Cheyenne village along Sand Creek in 1864. More than 150 Cheyenne men, women, and children were killed in what came to be known as the **Sand Creek Massacre.**

Reading **History**

B. Reading a Map Locate the site of the Sand Creek Massacre on the map on page 563.

The Plains tribes reacted to such attacks by raiding white settlements. One of the fiercest battles took place in Montana. There the government had begun to build a road called the Bozeman Trail across Sioux hunting grounds. To stop construction, the Sioux attacked construction workers. In 1866, Captain W. J. Fetterman and 80 troopers stumbled into a deadly ambush set by the Sioux. All the soldiers were killed in what was called the Fetterman Massacre.

Such incidents finally forced the government to try to find a way to end the fighting. In 1868, U.S. officials signed the Second Treaty of Fort Laramie with the Sioux, Northern Cheyenne, and Arapaho. The treaty gave these tribes a large reservation in the Black Hills of South Dakota.

HISTORY *through* ART

Artist Edgar S. Paxson researched the Battle of the Little Bighorn for 20 years to try to accurately re-create the last moments of the fighting. Custer is at the center clutching at a bullet wound in his chest.

What do you think this painting shows about the fighting at the Little Bighorn?

INTER**ACTIVE**

Battle of the Little Bighorn

The Second Treaty of Fort Laramie did not end the trouble between the Sioux and white settlers, though. In 1874, white prospectors discovered gold in the Black Hills. Paying no attention to the Fort Laramie treaty, thousands of miners rushed onto Sioux land. Tribal leaders angrily rejected a government offer to buy back the land. Many Sioux warriors fled the reservation during the

winter of 1875–1876. They united under the leadership of two Sioux chiefs—**Sitting Bull** and Crazy Horse—to push back the intruders.

The Seventh Cavalry set out to return the Sioux to the reservations. It was commanded by Lieutenant Colonel **George A. Custer,** a hero of the Civil War and of other campaigns against Plains tribes. On June 25, his forces met several thousand Sioux and Cheyennes near the Little Bighorn River in Montana in the **Battle of the Little Bighorn.** In less than two hours, Custer and his men—211 in all—were wiped out.

News of Custer's defeat shocked the nation. The government responded by stepping up military action. As a result, Little Bighorn was the last major Native American victory. In 1877, Crazy Horse surrendered and Sitting Bull and his followers fled to Canada. In 1881, Sitting Bull's starving band surrendered to U.S. troops and were returned to the reservation.

Resistance in the Northwest and Southwest

The Nez Perce (nehz PURS) was a Northwest tribe that lived in eastern Oregon and Idaho. Until the 1860s, the Nez Perce lived peacefully on land guaranteed to them by an 1855 treaty. However, as white settlement increased, the government forced them to sell most of their land and move to a narrow strip of territory in Idaho. Most reluctantly agreed, but a group of Nez Perce led by Chief Joseph refused.

In 1877, Chief Joseph and his followers fled north to seek refuge in Canada. For four months, the Nez Perce traveled across 1,000 miles of rugged terrain with army troops in pursuit. About 40 miles from the Canadian border, the army caught up with them. Greatly outnumbered, the Nez Perce surrendered. Chief Joseph spoke for his people when he said, "I will fight no more, forever."

In the Southwest, both the Navajos and Apaches fought against being removed to reservations. U.S. troops ended Navajo resistance in Arizona in 1863 by burning Navajo homes and crops. Most Navajos surrendered. Nearly 8,000 took what they called the "Long Walk," a brutal journey of 300 miles to a reservation in eastern New Mexico. Hundreds died on the way. Their new home was a parched strip of land near the Pecos River. After four years, the government allowed the Navajos to return to Arizona, where many live today.

*Reading*History
C. Recognizing Effects What were the results of the Battle of the Little Bighorn?

Background
Nez Perce means "pierced nose" in French. French-Canadian trappers gave this name to these Native American people because some of them wore jewelry in their noses.

Native American Leaders

Sitting Bull ▶
(c. 1831–1890)
Sioux chief: "We did not give our country to you; you stole it."

◀ Chief Joseph
(1840–1904)
Nez Perce chief: "It makes my heart sick when I remember all the good words and all the broken promises."

Geronimo ▶
(1829–1909)
Apache leader: "Once I moved about like the wind. Now I surrender."

> *"Once I moved about like the wind. Now I surrender."*
> Geronimo

In the early 1870s, the government forced many Apaches to settle on a barren reservation in eastern Arizona. But a group led by Geronimo refused to remain. Escaping the reservation, these Apaches survived by raiding settlers' homes. Geronimo was captured many times but always managed to escape. In 1886, however, he finally surrendered and was sent to prison.

A Way of Life Ends

As the Native Americans of the Plains battled to remain free, the buffalo herds that they depended upon for survival dwindled. At one time, 30 million buffalo roamed the Plains. However, hired hunters killed the animals to feed crews building railroads. Others shot buffalo as a sport or to supply Eastern factories with leather for robes, shoes, and belts. From 1872 to 1882, hunters killed more than one million buffalo each year.

Background
In 1889, fewer than 100 buffalo remained.

By the 1880s, most Plains tribes had been forced onto reservations. With their hunting grounds fast disappearing, some turned in despair to a Paiute prophet named Wovoka. He preached a vision of a new age in which whites would be removed and Native Americans would once again freely hunt the buffalo. To prepare for this time, Wovoka urged Native Americans to perform the chants and movements of the Ghost Dance. Wovoka's hopeful vision quickly spread among the Plains peoples.

Many of Wovoka's followers, especially among the Sioux, fled their reservations and gathered at the Pine Ridge Reservation in South Dakota. White settlers and government officials began to fear that they were preparing for war. The army was sent to track down the Ghost Dancers. They rounded them up, and a temporary camp was made along Wounded Knee Creek in South Dakota, on December 28, 1890. The next day, as the Sioux were giving up their weapons, someone fired a shot. The troopers responded to the gunfire, killing about 300 men, women, and children. The **Wounded Knee Massacre,** as it was called, ended armed resistance in the West.

These Native American students in Oklahoma Territory in 1901 posed for a class picture at the school where they were sent to learn the culture of white people.

Reading **History**
D. Drawing Conclusions
What was the most important factor in the defeat of the Native Americans?

The Dawes Act Fails

Some white Americans had been calling for better treatment of Native Americans for years. In 1881, Helen Hunt Jackson published *A Century of Dishonor*, which listed the failures of the federal government's policies toward Native Americans. About the same time, Sarah Winnemucca, a Paiute reformer, lectured in the East about the injustices of reservation life.

*Reading*History

E. Analyzing Points of View
Why did reformers support assimilation?

Many well-meaning reformers felt that assimilation was the only way for Native Americans to survive. Assimilation meant adopting the culture of the people around them. Reformers wanted to make Native Americans like whites—to "Americanize" them.

The **Dawes Act**, passed in 1887, was intended to encourage Native Americans to give up their traditional ways and become farmers. The act divided reservations into individual plots of land for each family. The government sold leftover land to white settlers. The government also sent many Native American children to special boarding schools where they were taught white culture. In "One American's Story," you read about the effort to Americanize Buffalo Bird Woman. But these attempts to Americanize the children still did not make them part of white society.

In the end, the Dawes Act did little to benefit Native Americans. Not all of them wanted to be farmers. Those who did lacked the tools, training, and money to be successful. Over time, many sold their land for a fraction of its real value to white land promoters or settlers.

The situation of Native Americans at the end of the 1800s was tragic. Their lands had been taken and their culture treated with contempt. Not until decades later would the federal government recognize the importance of their way of life. In the next section, you will read about some of the people who settled on Native American lands.

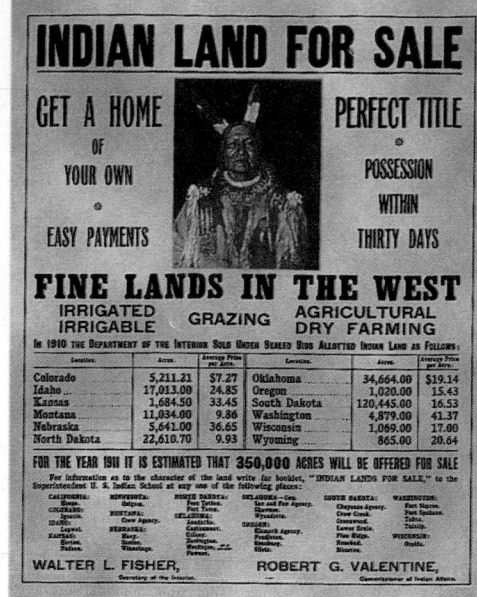

This poster advertised the sale of Native American lands to white settlers.

Section 2 Assessment

1. Terms & Names

Explain the significance of:
- reservation
- Sand Creek Massacre
- Sitting Bull
- George A. Custer
- Battle of the Little Bighorn
- Wounded Knee Massacre
- Dawes Act

2. Using Graphics

Use a chart to compare the life of Plains people before and after the arrival of white settlers.

	Before	After
Meeting survival needs		
Customs		
Land use		

3. Main Ideas

a. How did federal government policy toward Native Americans change as white settlers moved to the West?

b. How did the destruction of the buffalo affect Plains peoples?

c. Why was Wounded Knee a turning point in relations between Native Americans and the government?

4. Critical Thinking

Recognizing Effects How were the effects of the Dawes Act different from what was intended?

THINK ABOUT
- goals of the act
- impact on the land use, culture, and independence of the Plains peoples

---

ACTIVITY OPTIONS

TECHNOLOGY

SPEECH

Research the life of a Native American leader discussed in this section. Create that person's **Web page** or give a **speech** from this person's perspective.

Life in the West

ONE AMERICAN'S STORY

Abigail Scott was born in Illinois in 1834. At 17, she moved to Oregon by wagon train with her family. Her mother died on the journey. In Oregon, Abigail taught school until she married a farmer named Benjamin Duniway in 1853. When he was disabled in an accident, Abigail assumed the support of her family. She wrote about a day on a pioneer farm with its endless chores.

Like Abigail Scott Duniway, this pioneer woman worked long and hard. She is shown here with buffalo chips she has collected to use as fuel.

A VOICE FROM THE PAST

[W]ashing, scrubbing, churning . . . preparing . . . meals in our lean-to kitchen . . . [having] to bake and clean and stew and fry; to be in short, a general pioneer drudge, with never a penny of my own, was not pleasant business.

Abigail Scott Duniway, in her autobiography, *Path Breaking*

Later, Duniway grew committed to the cause of women's rights. Oregon honored Duniway for her part in the suffrage struggle by registering her as the state's first woman voter. As you will read in this section, women like Duniway helped to shape the West.

Taking Notes

Use your chart to take notes about women and Mexican Americans.

Many diverse people settled the West!

Women in the West

Women often were not given recognition for their efforts to turn scattered Western farms and ranches into settled communities. In their letters and diaries, many women recorded the harshness of pioneer life. Others talked about the loneliness. While men went to town for supplies or did farm chores with other men, women rarely saw their neighbors. Mari Sandoz lived in Nebraska on a **homestead,** a piece of land and the house on it. She wrote that women "had only the wind and the cold and the problems of clothing [and] shelter." Living miles from others, women were their family's doctors—setting broken bones and delivering babies—as well as cooks.

Despite its challenges, Western life provided opportunities for women. Most who worked held traditional jobs. They were teachers or servants or gave their families financial support by taking in sewing or laundry. However, a few became sheriffs, gamblers, and even outlaws. In mining camps and cow towns, some even ran dance halls and boarding houses.

Western lawmakers recognized the contributions women made to Western settlement by giving them more legal rights than women had in the East. In most territories, women could own property and control their own money. In 1869, Wyoming Territory led the nation in giving women the vote. Esther Morris, who headed the suffrage fight there, convinced lawmakers women would bring law and order to the territory.

When Wyoming sought statehood in 1890, many in Congress demanded that the state repeal its woman suffrage law. But Wyoming lawmakers stood firm. They told Washington, "We may stay out of the Union for 100 years, but we will come in with our women." Congress backed down. By 1900, women had also won the right to vote in Colorado, Utah, and Idaho.

Reading **History**
A. Making Inferences Why were women in the West the first to win the right to vote?

The Rise of Western Cities

Cities seemed to grow overnight in the West. Gold and silver strikes made instant cities of places like Denver in Colorado Territory and brought new life to sleepy towns like San Francisco in California. These cities prospered, while much of the area around them remained barely settled. San Francisco grew from a small town to a city of about 25,000 in just one year after the 1849 gold rush.

Miners who flocked to the "Pikes Peak" gold rush of 1859 stopped first in Denver to buy supplies. Not even a town in 1857, Denver was the capital of Colorado Territory by 1867. A decade later, it became the state capital when Colorado was admitted into the Union. The decision by Denver citizens to build a railroad to link their city with the transcontinental railroad sent population soaring. In 1870, it had about 4,800 residents. In 1890, it had nearly 107,000.

The railroads also brought rapid growth to other towns in the West. Omaha, Nebraska, flourished as a meat-processing center for cattle ranches in the area. Portland, Oregon, became a regional

Population of Western Cities		
CITY	1860	1890
Denver	2,603*	106,713
Omaha	1,883	140,452
Portland	2,874	46,385
San Francisco	56,802	298,997

SKILLBUILDER Interpreting Charts
Which city had the largest increase in numbers of people, 1860–1890?

*1861 Territorial Census
Sources: *Population Abstract of the United States; Colorado Republic*

San Francisco, 1847

San Francisco, 1850

569

"Billy the Kid" ▶
(Henry McCarty, 1859–1881)
He was an outlaw and hired gun who called himself William Bonney and was killed at 21.

▲ **Wyatt Earp (1848–1929)**
He was a frontier peace officer, gunfighter, and gambler in towns such as Dodge City, Kansas, and Tombstone, Arizona.

◀ **"Calamity Jane" (Martha Jane Canary, c. 1852–1903)**
She had a legendary career as a wagon driver, scout, and Wild West Show performer.

market for fish, grain, and lumber. While these cities were growing on the Great Plains and Pacific coast, the Southwest was also developing.

Mexicanos in the Southwest

The Southwest included what are now New Mexico, Texas, Arizona, and California. For centuries, it had been home to people of Spanish descent whose ancestors had come from Mexico. These Spanish-speaking southwesterners called themselves **Mexicanos**.

In the 1840s, the annexation of Texas and Mexico's defeat in the Mexican War brought much of the Southwest under the control of the United States. Soon after, English-speaking white settlers—called Anglos by the Mexicanos—began arriving. These pioneers were attracted to the Southwest by opportunities in ranching, farming, and mining. Their numbers grew in the 1880s and 1890s, as railroads connected the region with the rest of the country.

As American settlers crowded into the Southwest, the Mexicanos lost economic and political power. Many also lost land. They claimed their land through grants from Spain and Mexico. But American courts did not usually recognize these grants. One Mexicano remarked that "the North Americans . . . consider us unworthy to form with them one nation and one society." Only in New Mexico Territory did Hispanic society survive despite Anglo-American settlement.

The Myth of the Old West

America's love affair with the West began just as the cowboy way of life was vanishing in the late 1800s. To most Americans, the West had become a larger-than-life place where brave men and women tested themselves against hazards of all kinds and won. Easterners eagerly bought "dime novels" filled with tales of daring adventures. Sometimes the hero was a real person like Wyatt Earp or "Calamity Jane." But the plots were fiction or exaggerated accounts of real-life incidents.

Also adding to the myth were more serious works of fiction, like Owen Wister's bestselling novel about Wyoming cowhands, *The Virginian* (1902). Such works showed little of the drabness of daily life in the West. White settlers—miners, ranchers, farmers, cowhands, and law officers—played heroic roles not only in novels but also in plays and, later, in movies.

*Reading*History
B. Summarizing
Who were the Mexicanos?

Native Americans generally appeared as villains. African Americans were not even mentioned.

William "Buffalo Bill" Cody, a buffalo hunter turned showman, brought the West to the rest of the world through his Wild West show. Cody recognized people's fascination with the West. His show, with its reenactments of frontier life, played before enthusiastic audiences across the country and in Europe.

The Real West

Background
From 1866 to 1898, some 12,500 African Americans served in the West in the 9th and 10th Cavalry and the 24th and 25th Infantry regiments.

The myth of the Old West overlooked the contributions of many peoples. The first cowhands, as you read earlier, were the Mexican *vaqueros*. Native Americans and African Americans played a role in cattle ranching, too. Many African Americans also served in the U.S. Army in the West, where Native Americans nicknamed them **"buffalo soldiers."** And the railroads would not have been built without the labor of Chinese immigrants.

Western legends often highlighted the attacks by Native Americans on soldiers or settlers. But the misunderstandings and broken treaties that led to the conflicts were usually overlooked.

Reading **History**
C. Comparing How does the real West compare to the myth of the West?

Historians also say that the image of the self-reliant Westerner who tames the wild frontier ignores the important role played by the government in Western settlement. Settlers needed the help of the army to remove Native Americans. The government also aided in the building of the railroads and gave the free land that drew homesteaders to the West. You will read about these homesteaders and the problems that they faced in the next section.

Now and then

THE WEST IN POPULAR CULTURE

The distorted picture of life in the West that had been part of popular culture for decades eventually changed. Starting in the late 1970s, the view became more realistic, especially in motion pictures.

For example, the hardships of the cattle drives were shown in *Lonesome Dove* (1989). The sufferings of Native Americans were portrayed in *Dances With Wolves* (1990). The role of women in the West was dramatized in *Sarah, Plain and Tall* (1991). And the contributions of African Americans were noted in *Buffalo Soldiers* (1997), pictured below.

Section 3 Assessment

1. Terms & Names

Explain the significance of:
- homestead
- Mexicano
- William "Buffalo Bill" Cody
- buffalo soldier

2. Using Graphics

Use a chart to compare Wild West myths with the realities of Western life.

Myth	Real life

What do you think is the most well-known myth about the West?

3. Main Ideas

a. How were women's contributions to the West recognized by Western lawmakers?

b. Which factors led to the growth of such Western cities as Denver, Omaha, and San Francisco?

c. How did the arrival of Anglo-Americans change life for Spanish-speaking residents of the Southwest?

4. Critical Thinking

Making Inferences What changed the attitudes of Western lawmakers about giving women voting rights?

THINK ABOUT
- new roles for women
- need for stability in Western communities
- part played by women in settlement

ACTIVITY OPTIONS

MATH

SPEECH

Pick a Western city mentioned in this section. Create a **database** of information about the city or give a **short speech** describing its growth.

Stage a Wild West Show!

You are the manager of Buffalo Bill's Wild West, the biggest and most famous of the 50 outdoor circuses and shows performing in the United States in the 1880s. Your job is to keep the show running smoothly. You oversee publicity and keep performers and livestock housed, fed, and supplied with the gear they need. You also manage finances.

COOPERATIVE LEARNING On this page are three challenges you face as the manager of Buffalo Bill's Wild West show. Working with a small group, decide how to deal with each challenge. Choose an option, assign a task to each group member, and do the activity. You will find useful information in the Data File.

MATH CHALLENGE

"over $280,000"

What a season you had from May to September of 1886! The show took in more than $280,000. But you had big expenses, too. You want to compare income and expenses so you can make changes to increase profits. Use the Data File for more statistics. Then present your summary using one of these options:

• Make a line graph comparing income and expenses.

• Make a pie chart showing how you spent the income—that is, what your expenses were. Include one sector for profit (the difference between total income and total expenses). Label each sector with the percentage.

LANGUAGE ARTS CHALLENGE

"the thunder of hoofs"

Over the last three days, attendance at the show has slacked off. To meet expenses and generate a profit, you need to fill 15,000 seats. You decide to stir up interest using the local newspaper. Use the Data File for information. Then promote the show.

• Write an article dramatizing the Wild West show.

• Write a script to be used by the master of ceremonies.

BUFFALO BILL'S WILD WEST
AND CONGRESS OF ROUGH RIDERS OF THE WORLD.

COMPANY

CODY ... PERFORMANCE ... EXPLOITS OF BRAVERY

ART CHALLENGE

"History . . . in Living Legends"

You need more posters right away because splashy posters are your best advertising. They dazzle people with thrilling Western scenes. They also give show times and admission fees. Use the Data File for help. Then present your ideas using one of these options:

- Design a 2' x 3' poster showing the excitement of the Wild West show.
- Sketch two small action posters, each showing one event, for shop windows.

ACTIVITY WRAP-UP

Present to the class Meet as a group to review your methods of promoting and charting the success of your Wild West show. Evaluate which of your solutions is the best for each challenge. Once you have chosen one solution for each, make a class presentation. Each group member should take part.

DATA FILE

WILD WEST SHOW

- 3-hour show; admission, 50¢

Major Show Acts

- "Star-Spangled Banner" Overture
- Grand Review of Buffalo Bill Cody and cast on horseback
- Annie Oakley shoots card targets, apple off her poodle's head
- Reenactments of covered wagons crossing the prairie; a Native American buffalo hunt; outlaws attacking a mail coach; a battle between army and Native Americans
- Sharpshooting by Buffalo Bill

Show Crew and Gear

- crew of 700—including Buffalo Bill, Annie Oakley, Sitting Bull, cowhands, Native Americans, 36-piece band, cooks, blacksmiths, teams to set up grandstand and tents
- animals—including 500 horses, 10 mules, 5 steers, 18 buffalo
- gear—including covered wagons and tepees, guns and ammunition, living and dressing room tents, dining tents, booths selling popcorn, souvenirs, and canvas scenery backdrops, 26-car train for transport

INCOME AND EXPENSES

May 9–September 25, 1886

Total income: $287,000 (from attendance)

Total expenses: $285,000

Owners', managers', key performers' salaries: $55,000

Rents: $58,000

Advertising: $17,000

Printing: $4,000

Groceries/ammunition: $7,000

Miscellaneous expenses: $144,000 (other wages, livestock feed, electricity, medical, security, etc.)

For more about the Old West . . .

 **RESEARCH LINKS** CLASSZONE.COM

Farming and Populism

MAIN IDEA

A wave of farmers moved to the Plains in the 1800s and faced many economic problems.

WHY IT MATTERS NOW

Farmers are facing similar economic problems today.

TERMS & NAMES

Homestead Act
Exoduster
sodbuster
Grange
cooperative
Populist Party
gold standard
William Jennings Bryan

ONE AMERICAN'S STORY

From 1865 to 1900, about 800,000 Swedes left their homeland in northern Europe. Most Swedes were drawn to the United States by the promise of more and better land.

For Olaf Olsson, the acres of free land offered to settlers by the U.S. government was an unbelievable opportunity. Shortly after he arrived in 1869, Olsson wrote home to tell friends and family what awaited them in America.

A VOICE FROM THE PAST

We do not dig gold with pocket knives, we do not expect to become . . . rich in a few days or in a few years, but what we aim at is to own our own homes. . . . The advantage which America offers is not to make everyone rich at once, without toil or trouble, but . . . that the poor . . . can work up little by little.

Olaf Olsson, quoted in *The Swedish Americans,* by Allyson McGill

As you will read in this section, many Americans as well as immigrants from all parts of Europe shared Olsson's optimism.

Taking Notes

Use your chart to take notes about farmers and African Americans.

Many diverse people settled the West!

U.S. Government Encourages Settlement

For years, people had been calling on the federal government to sell Western land at low prices. Before the Civil War, Southern states fought such a policy. They feared that a big westward migration would result in more nonslave states. Once the South left the Union, however, the way was clear for a new land policy. To interest both American and immigrant families like the Olssons in going west, the federal government passed the **Homestead Act** in 1862. This law offered 160 acres of land free to anyone who agreed to live on and improve the land for five years.

After Reconstruction ended in 1877, African Americans in the South faced harsh new forms of discrimination. (See Chapter 18.) By 1879,

Railroad posters advertise lands in the West.

leaders like Benjamin "Pap" Singleton of Tennessee had convinced thousands to migrate to new homes in Kansas. They compared themselves to the biblical Hebrews led out of slavery in Egypt and called themselves **Exodusters.** One of them, John Solomon Lewis, remarked, "When I landed on the soil of Kansas, I looked on the ground and I says this is free ground." In all, some 50,000 African Americans settled in Kansas, Missouri, Indiana, and Illinois.

Thousands of European immigrants also sought a new start in the West. Swedes, like Olaf Olsson, joined Germans, Norwegians, Ukrainians, and Russians on the Great Plains. They often first learned about the West from land agents for American railroad companies. These salesmen traveled throughout Europe with pamphlets proclaiming "Land for the Landless! Homes for the Homeless."

From 1850 to 1870, the government gave millions of acres of public land to the railroads to promote railroad expansion. The railroads resold much of the land to settlers. This not only made the railroad companies rich, but it also supplied new customers for railroad services. The railroads' sales pitch worked. In the 1860s, so many Swedes and Norwegians settled in Minnesota that a local editor wrote, "It seems as if the Scandinavian Kingdoms were being emptied into this state."

*Reading***History**

A. Analyzing Causes How did the railroads help to settle the West?

Life on the Farming Frontier

Once pioneers reached their new homes on the plains, they faced many challenges never mentioned by the land agents. The plains were nearly treeless. So farmers were forced to build their first homes from blocks of sod. Sod is the top layer of prairie soil that is thickly matted with grass roots.

For fuel, the **sodbusters,** as the farmers were called, burned corn cobs or "cow chips" (dried manure). In many places, sodbusters had to dig wells more than 280 feet deep to reach the only water. Blizzards, prairie fires, hailstorms, tornadoes, grasshoppers, and drought added to the misery of life on the plains. Many settlers, such as Katherine Kirk of South Dakota, wondered whether they had the courage "to stick it out."

Connections TO SCIENCE

SOD HOUSES

To build their dwellings, Plains farmers, or sodbusters, like the Nebraska family pictured here, cut the tough buffalo grass of the prairie into two-or three-foot strips. Then they laid chunks of sod into two rows as walls. The walls were often 36 inches thick.

Prairie grass was thick. Its roots grew outward under the soil, often connecting with one another. This held the sod together. The roots also provided a layer of insulation. So sod houses, or soddies, stayed warm in the winter and cool in the summer. But their roofs leaked rain and dirt, and the walls housed mice, snakes, and insects.

New inventions helped farmers to meet some of these challenges. A steel plow invented by John Deere in 1838 and improved upon by James Oliver in 1868 sliced through the tough sod. Windmills adapted to the plains pumped water from deep wells to the surface. Barbed wire allowed farmers to fence in land and livestock. Reapers made the harvesting of crops much easier, and threshers helped farmers to separate grain or seed from straw. These inventions also made farm work more efficient. From 1860 to 1890, farmers doubled their production of wheat.

The Problems of Farmers

As farmers became more efficient, they grew more and more food. The result was that farmers in the West and South watched with alarm as prices for farm crops began to drop lower and lower in the 1870s.

Economics *in* History

Supply and Demand

Farmers in the West were having economic problems in the 1880s. The supply of food was increasing rapidly, but consumer demand was growing slowly. To attract more consumers, farmers had to drop the prices of their products.

The farmers were experiencing the **law of supply and demand**. The amount of economic goods available for sale is the **supply**. The willingness and ability of consumers to spend money for goods and services is **demand**. The price of goods is set by the supply of that good and the demand for that good.

At a lower price, businesses produce less of a good because they will make less money. As the price rises, they produce more. Consumer demand works in the opposite way. Consumers want to buy more of the good when the price is lower—after all, it costs them less. They buy less when the price is higher. The actual price of a good results from a compromise—how much consumers are willing to pay and how little businesses are willing to take for the good.

CONNECT TO HISTORY

1. **Recognizing Effects** Suppose farmers found a new market for their wheat—the people in another country, for instance. What effect would that have on price? Why?

   S See Skillbuilder Handbook, page R11.

CONNECT TO TODAY

2. **Comparing** How does the price of blue jeans show the law of supply and demand?

For more about supply and demand . . .

RESEARCH LINKS CLASSZONE.COM

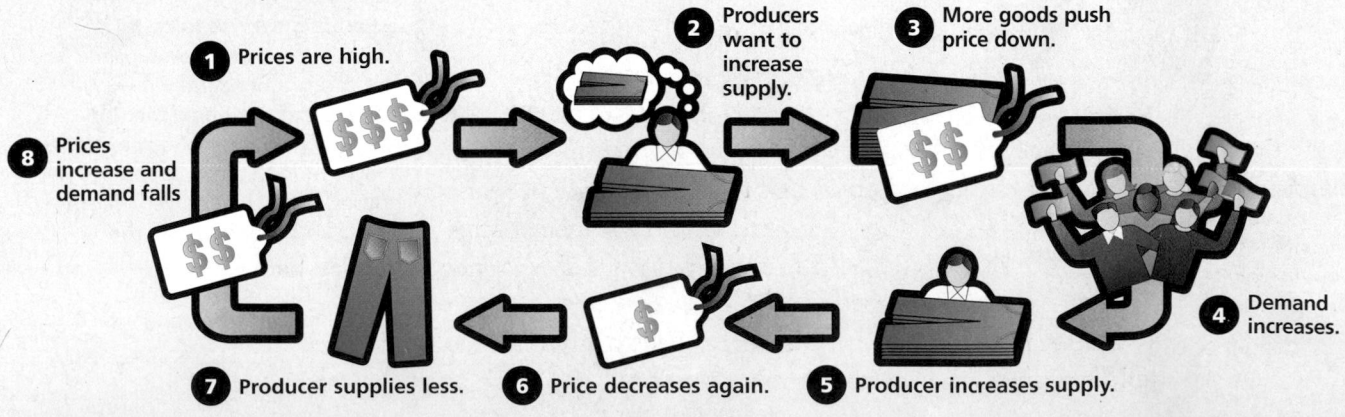

1 Prices are high.

2 Producers want to increase supply.

3 More goods push price down.

4 Demand increases.

5 Producer increases supply.

6 Price decreases again.

7 Producer supplies less.

8 Prices increase and demand falls

(See "Economics in History" on page 576.) Wheat that sold for $1.45 a bushel after the Civil War was 49 cents 30 years later. One reason for lower prices was overproduction. Farmers were growing more food because additional farmland had been opened up and farming methods and machines had improved.

Receiving less money for their crops was bad enough. But at the same time farmers had to spend more to run a farm. New farm machinery and railroad rates were especially costly. Railroads charged the farmers high fees to carry their crops to market. The railroads also usually owned the grain elevators where crops were stored until shipment. Farmers had no choice but to pay the high costs of storage that railroads charged.

"The Grange Awakening the Sleepers" (1873) shows a farmer trying to warn the country about the menace of the railroads.

Farmers were angry. They began to work together to seek solutions to their problems. In 1867, farmers had formed the **Grange**, officially known as the Patrons of Husbandry. The group's main purpose at first had been to meet the social needs of farm families who lived great distances from one another. However, as economic conditions got worse, Grange members took action. They formed **cooperatives.** These are organizations owned and run by their members. The cooperatives bought grain elevators and sold crops directly to merchants. This allowed farmers to keep more of their profits.

Farmers also began to demand action from the government to change their circumstances. For example, Grangers asked states to regulate railroad freight rates and storage charges. Illinois, Minnesota, Wisconsin, and Iowa did so. In 1877, the Supreme Court backed the farmers in their fight against the railroads. In *Munn* v. *Illinois*, the Court ruled that states and the federal government could regulate the railroads because they were businesses that served the public interest.

The Rise of Populism

In 1890, several farm groups joined together to try to gain political power. They formed the **Populist Party,** or People's Party. The Populists wanted the government to adopt a free silver policy, that is, the unlimited coining of silver. Since silver was plentiful, more money would be put in circulation. They believed that increasing the money supply would cause inflation. Inflation, in turn, would result in rising prices. Higher prices for crops would help farmers pay back the money that they had borrowed to improve their farms.

Opponents of free silver wanted to keep the gold standard. Under the **gold standard,** the government backs every dollar with a certain amount

*Reading*History

B. Summarizing What steps did farmers take to seek solutions to their problems?

WILLIAM JENNINGS BRYAN
1860–1925

William Jennings Bryan was known as the "silver-tongued orator from Nebraska." His powerful voice and his strong belief in the "common people" won him two terms in Congress and a presidential nomination at age 36. He made and lost two more bids for president in 1900 and 1908.

Although he never again held elective office, Bryan remained influential in the Democratic Party. Many reforms that he fought for, such as an eight-hour workday and woman suffrage, later became law.

How do you think Bryan was able to influence reform without being elected president?

of gold. Since the gold supply is limited, fewer dollars are in circulation. Inflation is less likely. This protects the value of money by keeping prices down.

In 1892, the Populist Party platform called for free silver to expand the money supply, government ownership of railroads, shorter working hours, and other political reforms. The Populist presidential candidate, James B. Weaver, lost to Grover Cleveland. But he won more than a million votes—a good showing for a third-party candidate.

The Election of 1896

By the next presidential campaign, money issues mattered much more to voters. The nation had suffered through a serious depression, the Panic of 1893. The Republican candidate, William McKinley, favored the gold standard. He warned that "free silver" would mean higher prices for food and other goods.

The Populists joined the Democratic Party in supporting **William Jennings Bryan** of Nebraska. Bryan urged the Democratic convention to support free silver in his stirring "Cross of Gold" speech.

A VOICE FROM THE PAST

Burn down your cities and leave our farms, and your cities will spring up again as if by magic; but destroy our farms and the grass will grow in the street of every city in the country. . . . [We] . . . answer . . . their demand for a gold standard by saying . . . : You shall not press down upon the brow of labor this crown of thorns. You shall not crucify mankind upon a cross of gold.

William Jennings Bryan, Democratic Convention speech, July 8, 1896

*Reading*History

C. Analyzing Points of View
What point was William Jennings Bryan making about the importance of farms?

Farmers in the South and the West voted overwhelmingly for Bryan. But McKinley, who was backed by industrialists, bankers, and other business leaders, won the East and the election by about half a million votes. This election was the beginning of the end for the Populist Party.

The Closing of the Frontier

By the late 1880s, fenced-in fields had replaced open plains. The last remaining open land was in Indian Territory. The Oklahoma land rush of 1889 symbolized the closing of the frontier. At the blast of the starting gun on April 22, thousands of white settlers rushed to claim two million acres of land that had once belonged to Native Americans. In May 1890, this part of Indian Territory officially became Oklahoma Territory. In 1890, 17 million people lived between the Mississippi and the Pacific. That year the Census Bureau declared that the country no longer had a continuous frontier line—the frontier no longer existed.

To many, the frontier was what had made America unique. In 1893, historian Frederick Jackson Turner wrote an influential essay on the frontier. Turner said that the frontier was a promise to all Americans, no matter how poor, that they could advance as far as their abilities allowed. To Turner the frontier meant opportunity, and its closing marked the end of an era.

Thousands of settlers rushed into Oklahoma Territory in 1889 to claim the last open land on the frontier.

*Reading***History**

D. Using Secondary Sources What did Frederick Jackson Turner believe about the frontier?

A VOICE FROM THE PAST

Up to our own day American history has been in a large degree the history of the colonization of the Great West. The existence of an area of free land, its continuous recession, and the advance of American settlement westward, explain American development.

Frederick Jackson Turner, "The Significance of the American Frontier"

Today many historians question Turner's view. They think he gave too much importance to the frontier in the nation's development and in shaping a special American character. These historians point out that the United States remains a land of opportunity long after the frontier's closing.

In the next chapter, you will learn how an industrial society developed in the East during the same period that the West was settled.

Section Assessment

1. Terms & Names

Explain the significance of:

- Homestead Act
- Exoduster
- sodbuster
- Grange
- cooperative
- Populist Party
- gold standard
- William Jennings Bryan

2. Using Graphics

Review the chapter and find five key events to place on a time line as shown.

```
1860    event    event    1890
  |_____|_____|_____|
      event   event   event
```

What do you think was the most important event?

3. Main Ideas

a. How did the federal government encourage and support settlement of the Plains?

b. Which groups of people moved onto the Plains in the late 1800s? Why did they come?

c. Which problems in the 1890s led farmers to take political action?

4. Critical Thinking

Drawing Conclusions Why did the Grange favor government regulation of the railroads?

THINK ABOUT

- powers of monopolies
- importance of railroads to farmers
- railroad freight and storage rates

ACTIVITY OPTIONS

Pick one invention that helped farmers on the Plains. Plan an **electronic presentation** on the invention or deliver a **sales pitch** to potential buyers.

Chapter 19 ASSESSMENT

Growth of the West

The West

Miners

Miners were attracted to the West by gold and silver strikes. Mining contributed to the population growth of many Western territories.

Cowhands & Ranchers

Ranchers and cowhands established a thriving cattle industry. New settlement, barbed wire, and bad weather ended the cattle boom.

Native Americans

Government policies, wars, and the destruction of the buffalo led to the defeat of the Plains peoples and to their placement on reservations.

Homesteaders

Hundreds of thousands of homesteaders settled on the Plains. Their life was hard, but they used new technologies to increase their output.

TERMS & NAMES

Briefly explain the significance of each of the following.

1. frontier
2. long drive
3. reservation
4. Battle of the Little Bighorn
5. Dawes Act
6. homestead
7. Mexicano
8. Homestead Act
9. sodbuster
10. Populist Party

REVIEW QUESTIONS

Miners, Ranchers, and Cowhands (pages 557–561)

1. What role did miners play in the settlement of the West?
2. What made cattle ranching so profitable in the late 1800s?
3. What ended the boom in the cattle business?

Native Americans Fight to Survive (pages 562–567)

4. What caused conflict between Native Americans and white settlers on the Great Plains?
5. How did Native Americans resist white settlement?

Life in the West (pages 568–573)

6. What rights did women in the West gain before women in Eastern states?
7. How has the myth of the "Wild West" been revised?

Farming and Populism (pages 574–579)

8. How did the federal government encourage people to settle on the Great Plains?
9. What were the goals of the Grange?
10. What marked the closing of the frontier?

CRITICAL THINKING

1. USING YOUR NOTES: FINDING MAIN IDEAS

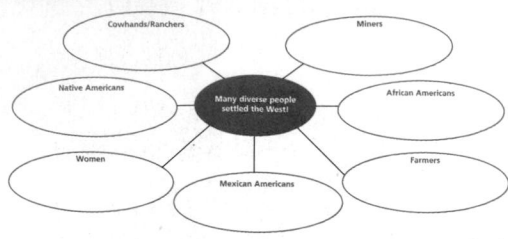

Using your completed chart, answer the questions below.

a. What were the main reasons that drew people to the West?
b. Which groups do you think benefited from being in the West and which groups did not? Explain.

2. APPLYING CITIZENSHIP SKILLS

What are the dangers of vigilante justice?

3. THEME: DIVERSITY AND UNITY

Why might the contributions of women and Native Americans, African Americans, and other ethnic groups have been overlooked in early books and films on the West?

4. ANALYZING LEADERSHIP

Why did the Nez Perce Chief Joseph decide to surrender? What other choices might he have made?

5. CONTRASTING

How did ranchers and sodbusters differ over land use? Why did these differences lead to conflict?

6. FORMING AND SUPPORTING OPINIONS

What do you think would be the most difficult challenge in starting a new life on the Great Plains? Give reasons for your answer.

Interact with History

Now that you have read the chapter, would you still make the same statements about how your life would change in the West? Explain.

Use the map and your knowledge of U.S. history to answer questions 1 and 2.

Additional Test Practice, pp. S1–S33.

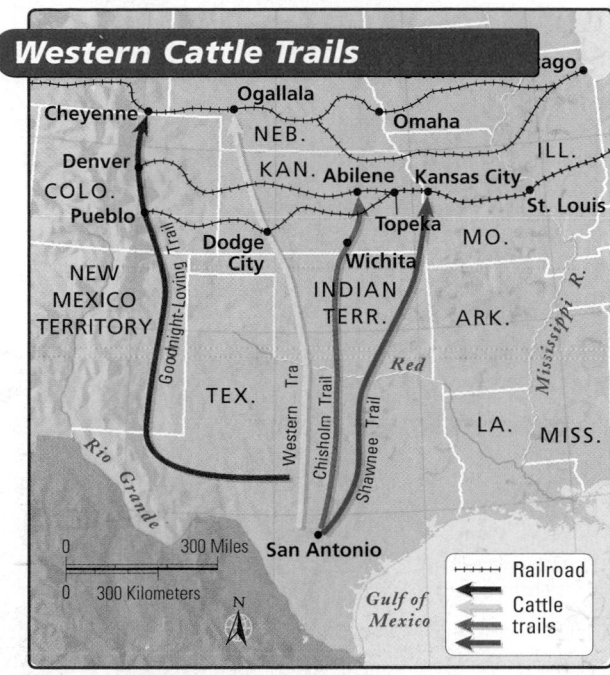

Western Cattle Trails

1. What is the longest cattle trail?
   A. Chisholm Trail
   B. Goodnight-Loving Trail
   C. Shawnee Trail
   D. Western Trail

2. How many miles did the longest trail cover?
   A. about 600 miles
   B. about 800 miles
   C. about 1,000 miles
   D. about 1,200 miles

This quotation from Olaf Olsson describes the advantage of America. Use the quotation and your knowledge of U.S. history to answer question 3.

PRIMARY SOURCE

We do not dig gold with pocket knives, we do not expect to become . . . rich in a few days or in a few years, but what we aim at is to own our own homes. . . . The advantage which America offers is not to make everyone rich at once, without toil or trouble, but . . . that the poor . . . [can] secure a large piece of good land almost without cost, that they can work up little by little.

Olaf Olsson, quoted in *The Swedish Americans,* by Alison McGill

3. What type of person is described in the passage?
   A. a person who has inherited land
   B. a person who hopes for instant wealth
   C. a person who has a strong work ethic
   D. a person who works well as part of a team

TEST PRACTICE
CLASSZONE.COM

ALTERNATIVE ASSESSMENT

1. ✍ WRITING ABOUT HISTORY

You are a biographer writing about Native American leaders of the West. Write a **biography** of a leader, such as Sitting Bull, Chief Joseph, or Geronimo.

• Use library resources to research your subject.

• Persuade your reader that your subject is an important historical figure.

2. COOPERATIVE LEARNING

Work with a small group to create a play based on the life of the sodbusters. Choose a topic, such as "the journey west," "first impressions," or "women's work and worries." Research and choose quotations related to your topic. Some group members can compose lines to introduce and make transitions between topics and others can perform the readings.

INTEGRATED TECHNOLOGY

DOING INTERNET RESEARCH

The "Wild West" of the late 1800s was a land of myth and legend. Use the Internet or library resources to find information in order to create a "Wild West" Web site.

• Find newspaper articles, advertisements, and stories about the "Wild West."

• You can also learn about this era from books, and from documentary films.

• Select legendary personalities to be featured in your Web site, and choose musical selections to add background.

For more about the "Wild West" . . .

INTERNET ACTIVITY
CLASSZONE.COM

CHAPTER 20

An Industrial Society 1860–1914

Section 1
The Growth of Industry

Section 2
Railroads Transform the Nation

Section 3
The Rise of Big Business

Section 4
Workers Organize

At the turn of the century, industrial strikes for better conditions often erupted in violence, as this illustration shows.

Most of the workers have only bricks, stones, or sticks for weapons.

There were no laws protecting children from dangerous work or long hours.

1863
Two companies begin to build a transcontinental railroad across the United States.

1879
Thomas Edison invents a practical lightbulb.

1882
Thomas Edison installs electric lights in New York City.

USA
World 1860

1869
Suez Canal opens in Egypt.

582

The year is 1894. You work in a factory that is unheated and badly lit. The machine that you operate is dangerous. The economy is doing poorly, so the factory has cut your wages. Some of your coworkers have gone out on strike. They want better pay and working conditions.

Would you join the strike? Why or why not?

What Do You Think?

- What are some risks you would be taking if you join the strike?

- What might you gain if you take part in the strike?

- What other methods might you use to persuade your employer to meet your demands?

RESEARCH LINKS
CLASSZONE.COM

Visit the Chapter 20 links for more information about U.S. industry.

1888
enjamin rison is elected esident.

1892
Grover Cleveland is elected president for the second time.

1894
Pullman Strike halts rail traffic across the nation.

1901
Oil drillers discover a huge oil field in Texas.

1905
Supreme Court overturns a New York law establishing a 60-hour workweek for bakers.

1914

1889
The world's tallest structure to date, the Eiffel Tower in Paris, is built of iron.

1896
The Italian engineer Guglielmo Marconi patents the radio.

1904
Russia finishes building the first Trans-Siberian railway across Asia.

Reading Strategy: Analyzing Causes and Effects

What Do You Know?

Do you know of any businesses that started back in the 1800s? How do businesses grow?

Think About
- businesses that you see in your community
- businesses that are advertised on television, in magazines or newspapers, or on the Internet
- your responses to the Interact with History about conflict with workers (see page 583)

What Do You Want to Know?

What facts and details would help you understand how a nation of small businesses became a nation of giant corporations? In your notebook, list the facts and details you hope to learn from this chapter.

Business leader John D. Rockefeller is shown as a wealthy king. Notice which industries are the "jewels in his crown."

Analyzing Causes and Effects

The conditions or actions that lead to a historical event are its causes. The consequences of an event are its effects. As you read the chapter, look for the causes and effects of industrial and railroad growth. Causes include geographical factors and actions by individuals and the government. Effects include both benefits and problems. Use the diagram below to record both causes and effects.

 See Skillbuilder Handbook, page R11.

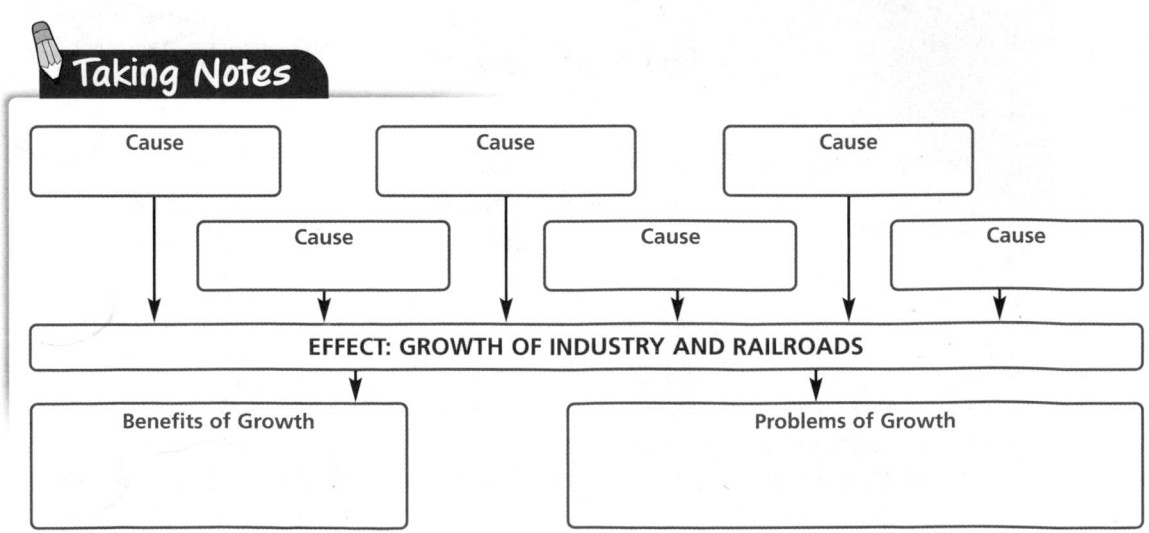

Taking Notes

Cause		Cause		Cause
	Cause		Cause	Cause

EFFECT: GROWTH OF INDUSTRY AND RAILROADS

Benefits of Growth	Problems of Growth

The Growth of Industry

MAIN IDEA	WHY IT MATTERS NOW	TERMS & NAMES
The growth of industry during the years 1860 to 1914 transformed life in America.	Modern businesses rely on many of the inventions and products developed during that time.	petroleum generator patent Thomas Edison business cycle Alexander Graham Bell Bessemer steel process Centennial Exhibition

ONE AMERICAN'S STORY

In the 1850s, most Americans lit their homes with oil lamps. They could have used kerosene, an oil made from coal, but it was expensive. Then, in 1855, a chemist reported that kerosene could be made more cheaply from an oily liquid called **petroleum**. However, people didn't know how to obtain petroleum from underground. They just gathered it slowly when it seeped to the surface.

In 1857, Edwin Drake visited a site in Pennsylvania where petroleum oozed to the surface.

Drake began drilling in 1859. He struck oil in August. This event launched the oil industry—one of many new industries that developed in the late 1800s, as this section explains.

The wooden structure is Drake's first oil well.

The Industrial Revolution Continues

Throughout the 1800s, factory production expanded in the United States. By the Civil War, factory production had spread beyond New England textiles to other regions and industries. Several factors encouraged this growth.

1. **Plentiful natural resources.** America had immense forests and large supplies of water. It also had vast mineral wealth, including coal, iron, copper, silver, and gold. Industry used these resources to manufacture a variety of goods.
2. **Growing population.** From 1860 to 1900, the U.S. population grew from 31.5 million to 76 million. This led to a growing need for goods. The demand for goods spurred the growth of industry.

Taking Notes

Use your chart to take notes about the growth of industry.

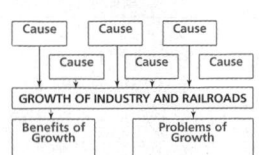

3. **Improved transportation.** In the early 1800s, steamboats, canals, and railroads made it possible to ship items long distances more quickly. Railroad building boomed after the Civil War. As shipping raw materials and finished goods to markets became even easier, industry grew.

4. **High immigration.** Between 1860 and 1900, about 14 million people immigrated to the United States. Many of them knew specialized trades, such as metalworking. Such knowledge was valuable to industries. In addition, unskilled immigrants supplied the labor that growing industry needed.

5. **New inventions.** New machines and improved processes helped industry produce goods more efficiently. Inventors applied for patents for the machines or processes they invented. A **patent** is a government document giving an inventor the exclusive right to make and sell his or her invention for a specific number of years.

6. **Investment capital.** When the economy was thriving, many businesses made large profits. Hoping to share in those profits, banks and wealthy people lent businesses money. The businesses used this capital to build factories and buy equipment.

7. **Government assistance.** State and federal governments used tariffs, land grants, and subsidies to help businesses grow.

Background
Some of these canals were built because of Henry Clay's American System. (See Chapter 11.)

Vocabulary
capital: money and property used in a business

The Business Cycle

American industry did not grow at a steady pace; it experienced ups and downs. This pattern of good and bad times is called the **business cycle.** During good times, called booms, people buy more, and some invest in business. As a result, industries and businesses grow. During bad times, called busts, spending and investing decrease. Industries lay off workers and make fewer goods. Businesses may shrink—or even close. Such a period of low economic activity is a depression.

America experienced depressions in 1837 and 1857. Both were eventually followed by periods of strong economic growth. In the late 1800s, there were two harsh depressions, also called panics. The depression of 1873 lasted five years. At its height, three million people were out of work. During the depression that began in 1893, thousands of businesses failed, including more than 300 railroads.

The Business Cycle

Change in volume of what businesses produce

Peak (high point)

Expansion (growth)

Contraction (decrease)

Trough (low point)

Expansion

Peak

Passage of time

SKILLBUILDER Interpreting Charts
1. *How does the amount of goods produced at the peak compare to the amount at the trough?*
2. *Are all peaks equally prosperous? Explain.*

Reading **History**
A. Recognizing Effects How do you think depressions affect ordinary people?

Even with these economic highs and lows, industries in the United States grew tremendously between 1860 and 1900. Overall, the amount of manufactured goods increased six times during these years.

Steel: The Backbone of Industry

The steel industry contributed to America's industrial growth. Before the mid-1800s, steel was very expensive to manufacture because the steel-making process used huge amounts of coal. In the 1850s, William Kelly in the United States and Henry Bessemer in England independently developed a new process for making steel. It used less than one-seventh of the coal that the older process used. This new manufacturing technique was called the **Bessemer steel process**.

Because the Bessemer process cut the cost of steel, the nation's steel output increased 500 times between 1867 and 1900. Industry began to make many products out of steel instead of iron. These products included plows, barbed wire, nails, and beams for buildings. But the main use of steel throughout the late 1800s was for rails for the expanding railroads. (See Section 2.)

Edison and Electricity

Another industry that grew during the late 1800s was the electric-power industry. By the 1870s, inventors had designed efficient generators. A **generator** is a machine that produces electric current. As a result, people grew eager to tap the power of electricity.

The inventor who found the most ways to use electricity was **Thomas Edison**. In 1876, he opened a laboratory in Menlo Park, New Jersey. He employed many assistants, whom he organized into teams to do research. Edison's laboratory invented so many things that Edison received more than 1,000 U.S. patents, more than any other individual inventor.

Edison would start with an idea for a possible invention. Then he would work hard to make that idea a reality—even if problems arose.

Reading **History**

B. Drawing Conclusions Which industries benefited from the steel products mentioned here?

Reading **History**

C. Finding Main Ideas According to Edison, is inventing easy?

Connections TO SCIENCE

IRON VS. STEEL
Why is the comic book hero Superman also called the man of steel? People often use the word *steel* as a synonym for strength.

Steel is an iron alloy—a blend of iron and other materials such as carbon. But steel is stronger and more durable than iron. That is why steel replaced iron in many industries in the late 1800s. A giant ladle (bucket) used to pour melted steel is pictured below.

Stainless steel, invented in the early 1900s, has an additional benefit: it doesn't rust. Stainless steel is used in tools, machines, and many household items, such as pots, pans, and utensils.

A VOICE FROM THE PAST

It has been just so in all my inventions. The first step is an intuition—and comes with a burst, *then* difficulties arise. . . . "Bugs"—as such little faults and difficulties are called—show themselves and months of anxious watching, study and labor are requisite [needed] before commercial success—or failure—is certainly reached.

Thomas Edison, quoted in *Edison* by Matthew Josephson

Edison's most famous invention was practical electric lighting. Other inventors had already created electric lights, but they were too bright and

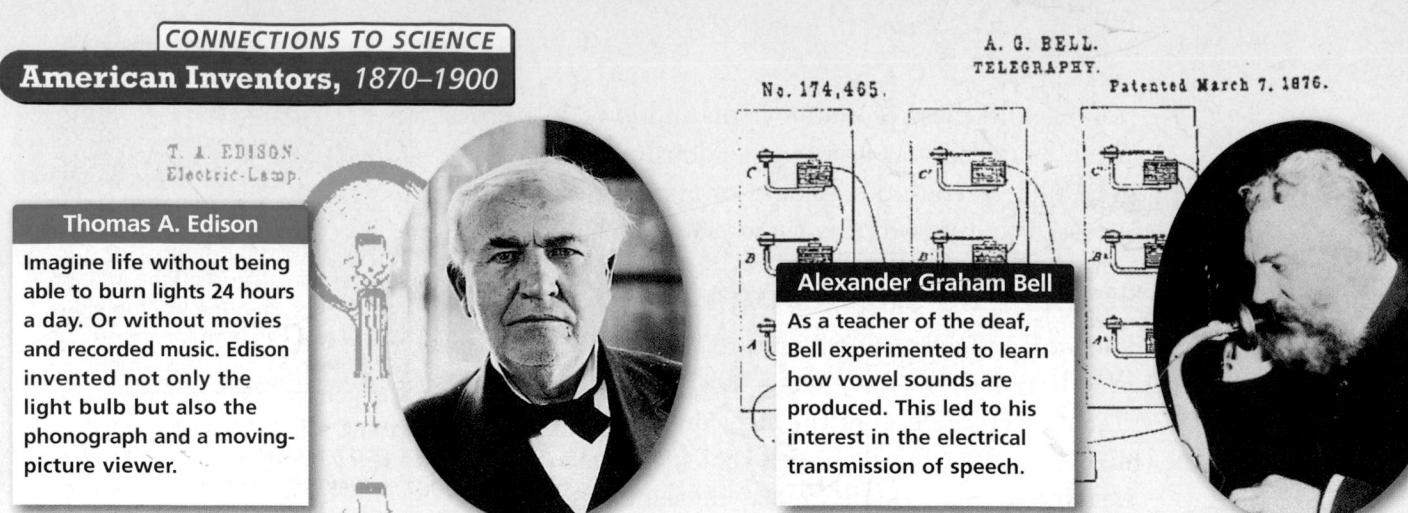

T. A. EDISON.
Electric-Lamp.

Thomas A. Edison

Imagine life without being able to burn lights 24 hours a day. Or without movies and recorded music. Edison invented not only the light bulb but also the phonograph and a moving-picture viewer.

A. G. BELL.
TELEGRAPHY.

No. 174,465.

Patented March 7, 1876.

Alexander Graham Bell

As a teacher of the deaf, Bell experimented to learn how vowel sounds are produced. This led to his interest in the electrical transmission of speech.

flickery for home use. Edison figured out how to make a safe, steady light bulb. He also invented a system to deliver electricity to buildings.

By 1882, he had installed electric lighting in a half-mile-square area of New York City. Electric lighting quickly replaced gaslights. By the late 1880s, Edison's factory produced about a million light bulbs a year.

Bell and the Telephone

Electricity played a role in communications devices invented during the 1800s. In 1835, Samuel Morse developed the telegraph. It allowed people to use electrical impulses to send messages over long distances.

The next step in communications was the telephone, invented by **Alexander Graham Bell**. He was a Scottish immigrant who taught deaf students in Boston. At night, Bell and his assistant, Thomas Watson, tried to invent a device to transmit human speech using electricity.

After years of experiments, Bell succeeded. One day in March 1876, he was adjusting the transmitter in the laboratory in his apartment. Watson was in another room with the receiver. The two doors between the rooms were shut. According to Watson's memoirs, Bell accidentally spilled acid on himself and said, "Mr. Watson, come here. I want you." Watson rushed down the hall. He burst into the laboratory, exclaiming that he had heard and understood Bell's words through the receiver.

Bell showed his telephone at the **Centennial Exhibition** in June 1876. That was an exhibition in Philadelphia to celebrate America's 100th birthday. There, several of the world's leading scientists and the emperor of Brazil saw his demonstration. Afterward, they declared, "Here is the greatest marvel ever achieved in electrical science."

Reading **History**

D. Analyzing Points of View Why do you think the scientists said this about the telephone?

Inventions Change Industry

The telephone industry grew rapidly. By 1880, more than 50,000 telephones had been sold. The invention of the switchboard allowed more and more people to connect into a telephone network. Women commonly worked in the new job of switchboard operator.

The typewriter also opened jobs for women. Christopher Latham Sholes helped invent the first practical typewriter in 1867. He also

J. E. MATZELIGER.
LASTING MACHINE.

Patented Mar. 20, 1883.

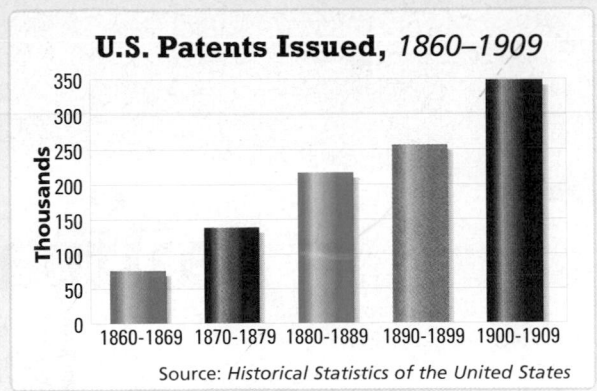

Jan Matzeliger

An immigrant from Dutch Guiana, Matzeliger worked in a shoe factory. To reduce the time needed to fasten shoe leather to the sole by hand, he invented a machine to do the job. It increased production by 1,400 percent!

U.S. Patents Issued, *1860–1909*

Source: *Historical Statistics of the United States*

SKILLBUILDER Interpreting Graphs

1. *How many more patents were issued from 1900 to 1909 than from 1860 to 1869?*
2. *Was this a time of increasing or decreasing inventiveness?*

improved the machine and sold his rights to it to a manufacturer who began to make typewriters in the 1870s.

The sewing machine also changed American life. Elias Howe first patented it in 1846. In the next few years, the sewing machine received many design improvements. Isaac Singer patented a sewing machine in 1851 and continued to improve it. It became a bestseller and led to a new industry. In factories, people produced ready-made clothes. Instead of being fitted to each buyer, clothes came in standard sizes and popular styles. Increasingly, people bought clothes instead of making their own.

Other inventors helped industry advance. African-American inventor Granville T. Woods patented devices to improve telephone and telegraph systems. Margaret Knight invented machines for the packaging and shoemaking industries and also improved motors and engines.

Of all the up-and-coming industries of the middle 1800s, one would have a larger impact on American life than any other. That was the railroad industry. You will read about railroads in Section 2.

Section 1 Assessment

1. Terms & Names

Explain the significance of:
• petroleum
• patent
• business cycle
• Bessemer steel process
• generator
• Thomas Edison
• Alexander Graham Bell
• Centennial Exhibition

2. Using Graphics

Use a cluster diagram like the one below to list some of the inventions of the late 1800s.

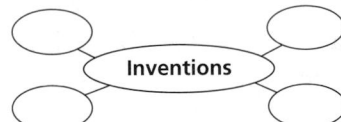

Inventions

How has one of these inventions recently been improved?

3. Main Ideas

a. What factors contributed to industrial growth in the United States?

b. What is the business cycle?

c. What caused the steel-making industry to boom and why?

4. Critical Thinking

Recognizing Effects How did the inventions of the late 1800s make it easier to do business?

THINK ABOUT
• electric generators and light bulbs
• the telephone
• the typewriter

ACTIVITY OPTIONS

SCIENCE

TECHNOLOGY

Choose an invention and learn more about it. Create a **display** explaining how it works or design a **Web page** linking to sites with more information.

2
Railroads Transform the Nation

ONE AMERICAN'S STORY

Ah Goong was one of thousands of Chinese workers on the Western railroads in the late 1800s. In some places, the workers had to blast rock from a cliff wall. The lightest Chinese were lowered in wicker baskets hundreds of feet to the blasting site. Years later, Ah Goong's granddaughter described her grandfather's job.

A VOICE FROM THE PAST

Swinging near the cliff, Ah Goong . . . dug holes, then inserted gunpowder and fuses. . . . The basketmen signaled one another to light the fuses. He struck match after match and dropped the burnt matches over the sides. At last his fuse caught; he waved, and the men above pulled hand over hand hauling him up, pulleys creaking.

Maxine Hong Kingston, *China Men*

This section discusses the building of the railroads.

Chinese immigrants—like the one at the lower left—helped build several railroads in the West.

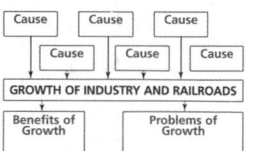
Taking Notes

Use your chart to take notes about the growth of railroads.

Deciding to Span the Continent

Americans had talked about building a **transcontinental railroad**—one that spanned the entire continent—for years. Such a railroad would encourage people to settle the West and develop its economy. In 1862, Congress passed a bill that called for two companies to build a transcontinental railroad across the center of the United States.

The Central Pacific, led by Leland Stanford, was to start in Sacramento, California, and build east. The Union Pacific was to start in Omaha, Nebraska, and build west. To build the railroad, these two companies had to raise large sums of money. The government lent them millions of dollars. It also gave them 20 square miles of public land for every mile of track they laid. The railroad companies could then sell the land to raise money.

With the guarantees of loans and land, the railroads attracted many investors. The Central Pacific began to lay its first track in 1863. The

Union Pacific laid its first rail in July 1865 (after the Civil War had ended).

Building the Railroad

The Central Pacific faced a labor shortage because most men preferred to try to strike it rich as miners. Desperate for workers, the Central Pacific's managers overcame the widespread prejudice against the Chinese and hired several dozen of them. The Chinese were small and weighed, on average, no more than 110 pounds. But they were efficient, fearless, and hard working.

They also followed their own customs, which led to an unexpected benefit for the railroad company. The Chinese drank tea instead of unboiled water, so they were sick less often than other workers. Pleased with the Chinese workers, the company brought more men over from China. At the peak of construction, more than 10,000 Chinese worked on the Central Pacific.

The Union Pacific hired workers from a variety of backgrounds. After the Civil War ended in 1865, former soldiers from both North and South flocked to work on the railroad. Freed slaves came, too. But one of the largest groups of Union Pacific workers was immigrants, many from Ireland.

Both railroads occasionally hired Native Americans. Washos, Shoshones, and Paiutes all assisted the race of the rails across the deserts of Nevada and Utah.

Background
Boiling water kills germs.

Reading **History**
A. Drawing Conclusions Why did the Union Pacific have a larger supply of workers?

daily *life*

RAILROAD CAMPS
Union Pacific workers often worked 12-hour days. Graders had the job of leveling the roadbed. After a day of hard labor, they slept in small dirt shanties like the one below.

Track layers lived together in groups of 100 to 135, in railroad cars with three layers of bunk beds. The cars were parked at the end of the just-finished track. Workers ate in a dining car with their plates nailed to the table. They gobbled a quick meal of beef, beans, and bread. As soon as one group of 125 workers was done, the next group filed in.

Railroads Tie the Nation Together

Only short, undergrown trees dotted the vast open space. To the south shimmered the Great Salt Lake. In the east rose the bluish shapes of the Rocky Mountains. Across that space, from opposite directions, the workers of the Central Pacific and the Union Pacific toiled. By May 10, 1869, Central Pacific workers had laid 690 miles of track. Union Pacific workers had laid 1,086 miles. Only one span of track separated the two lines at their meeting point at Promontory, Utah.

Hundreds of railroad workers, managers, spectators, and journalists gathered on that cool, windy day to see the transcontinental railroad completed. Millions of Americans waited to hear the news by telegraph. A band played as a Chinese crew and an Irish crew laid the last rails. The last spike, a golden one, was set in place. First, the president of the Central Pacific raised a hammer to drive in the spike. After he swung the hammer down, the crowd roared with laughter. He had missed. The vice-president of the Union Pacific took a turn and also missed. But the telegraph operator couldn't see and had already sent the message: "done." People across the nation celebrated.

Reading **History**
B. Reading a Map Using the map on page 592, find the Union Pacific and Central Pacific Railroads. Notice how they connect Omaha to Sacramento.

This golden spike united the Central Pacific and Union Pacific Railroads.

The Union Pacific-Central Pacific line was the first transcontinental railroad. By 1895, four more U.S. lines had been built across the continent. Between 1869 and 1890, the amount of money railroads earned carrying freight grew from $300 million to $734 million per year.

Background
Canada had also built a transcontinental railroad, so there were six altogether.

Railroad Time

The railroads changed America in a surprising way: they altered time. Before the railroads, each community determined its own time, based on calculations about the sun's travels. This system was called "solar time." Solar time caused problems for people who scheduled trains crossing several time zones and for travelers.

A VOICE FROM THE PAST

I have been annoyed and perplexed by the changes in the time schedules of connecting railroads. My watch could give me no information as to the arrival and departure of trains, nor of the time for meals.

John Rodgers, quoted in *Passage to Union*

To solve this problem, the railroad companies set up **standard time**. It was a system that divided the United States into four time zones. Although the plan went into effect on November 18, 1883, Congress did not adopt standard time until 1918. By then, most Americans saw its benefit because following schedules had become part of daily life.

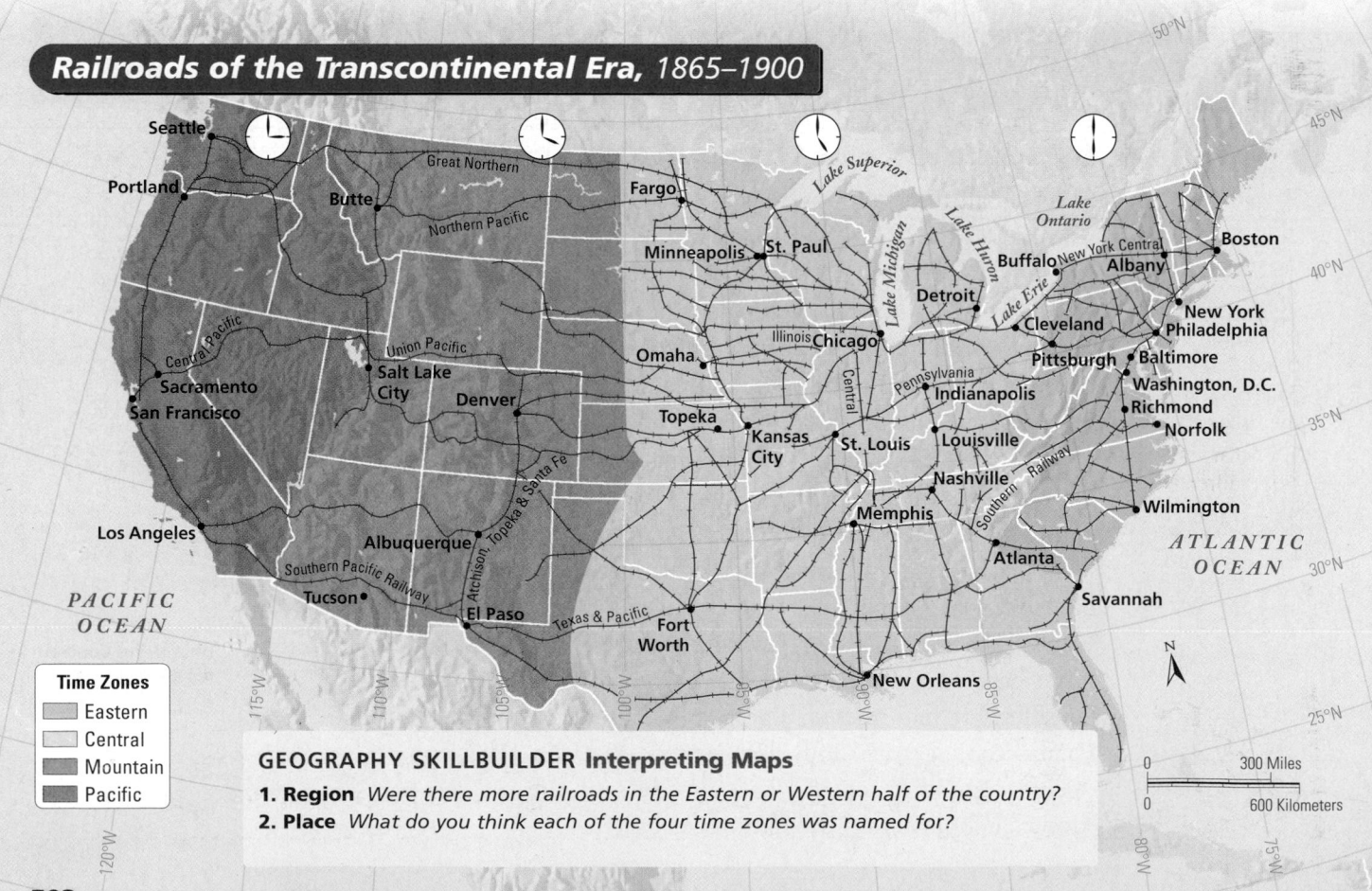

Railroads of the Transcontinental Era, 1865–1900

Time Zones
- Eastern
- Central
- Mountain
- Pacific

GEOGRAPHY SKILLBUILDER Interpreting Maps
1. **Region** *Were there more railroads in the Eastern or Western half of the country?*
2. **Place** *What do you think each of the four time zones was named for?*

Economic and Social Changes

The railroads changed people's lives in many other important ways. They helped create modern America.

1. **Linked the economies of the West and East.** From the West, the railroads carried eastward raw materials such as lumber, livestock, and grain. Materials like these were processed in Midwestern cities such as Chicago and Cleveland. (See Geography in History on pages 598–599.) From Eastern cities, in turn, came manufactured goods, which were sold to Westerners.

2. **Helped people settle the West.** Railroads were lifelines for settlers. Trains brought them lumber, farm equipment, food, and other necessities and hauled their crops to market.

3. **Weakened the Native American hold on the West.** As Chapter 19 explained, the railroads carried hunters who killed off the herds of buffalo. They also brought settlers and miners who laid claim to Native American land.

4. **Gave people more control of the environment.** Before railroads, people lived mainly where there were waterways, such as rivers. Roads were primitive. Railroads made possible cities such as Denver, Colorado, which had no usable waterways.

Just as railroads changed life for many Americans in the late 1800s, so did big business. You will read about big business in Section 3.

Reading **History**

C. Evaluating Which of these four changes do you think were positive, and which were negative?

Connections TO ART & MUSIC

RAILROAD HEROES

Several American songs celebrate railroad heroes. One tells of Casey Jones, an engineer who saved lives. He slammed on the brakes as his train rounded a bend and plowed into a stalled freight train. He died but slowed the train enough to save his passengers.

Another song tells of a mythical worker named John Henry, shown below. This ballad celebrates an African American's strength in a track-laying race against a steam-driven machine.

Section 2 Assessment

1. Terms & Names

Explain the significance of:
- transcontinental railroad
- standard time

2. Using Graphics

Using a chart like the one below, record which groups of people helped build the transcontinental railroad.

Central Pacific	Union Pacific

Which group worked on both railroads?

3. Main Ideas

a. Why did the federal government want a transcontinental railroad built?

b. How did the government encourage the building of the railroad?

c. Why was standard time created?

4. Critical Thinking

Recognizing Effects Which of the trends started by railroads are still part of the modern business world?

THINK ABOUT
- railroads' effect on time
- the way they linked the economy
- the way they changed where people settled

ACTIVITY OPTIONS

ART

TECHNOLOGY

You have been asked to honor those who built the transcontinental railroad. Design a **memorial** or create the opening screen of a **multimedia presentation**.

The Rise of Big Business

MAIN IDEA	WHY IT MATTERS NOW	TERMS & NAMES
Business leaders guided industrial expansion and created new ways of doing business.	These leaders developed the modern corporation, which dominates business today.	robber baron monopoly corporation trust John D. Rockefeller philanthropist Andrew Carnegie Gilded Age

ONE AMERICAN'S STORY

In 1853, when Jay Gould was 17, he visited New York. Big-city wealth impressed Gould. After returning to his small hometown, he told a friend, "Crosby, I'm going to be rich. I've seen enough to realize what can be accomplished by means of riches, and I tell you I'm going to be rich."

Gould achieved his goal. By the time he died in 1892, he was worth $77 million. He made a lot of his money using methods that are illegal today—such as bribing officials and selling fake stock. Most of his deals involved railroads.

Jay Gould was a robber baron. A **robber baron** was a business leader who became wealthy through dishonest methods. This section discusses other business leaders and their companies.

Jay Gould used methods such as trickery and false reports to "bowl over" his competition.

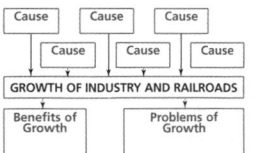

Taking Notes

Use your chart to take notes about the growth of big business.

Cause — Cause — Cause
Cause — Cause — Cause
GROWTH OF INDUSTRY AND RAILROADS
Benefits of Growth — Problems of Growth

The Growth of Corporations

Until the late 1800s, most businesses were owned directly by one person or by a few partners. Then advances in technology made many business owners want to buy new equipment. One way to raise money to do so was to turn their businesses into corporations. A **corporation** is a business owned by investors who buy part of the company through shares of stock. A corporation has advantages over a privately owned business:

1. By selling stock, a corporation can raise large amounts of money.
2. A corporation has a special legal status and continues to exist after its founders die. Banks are more likely to lend a corporation money.
3. A corporation limits the risks to its investors, who do not have to pay off the corporation's debts.

In the late 1800s, few laws regulated corporations. This led to the growth of a few giant corporations that dominated American industry. The oil and steel industries are examples of this process.

The Oil and Steel Industries

Vocabulary
refinery: a plant
that purifies oil

As Section 1 explained, the oil and steel industries began to grow in the late 1800s. Two men dominated these industries. **John D. Rockefeller** led the oil industry, and **Andrew Carnegie** controlled the steel industry.

John D. Rockefeller built his first refinery in 1863. He decided that the best way to make money was to put his competitors out of business. A company that wipes out its competitors and controls an industry is a **monopoly**. Rockefeller bought other refineries. He made secret deals with railroads to carry his oil at a lower rate than his competitors' oil. He also built and purchased his own pipelines to carry oil.

Rockefeller's most famous move to end competition was to develop the trust in 1882. A **trust** is a legal body created to hold stock in many companies, often in the same industry. Rockefeller persuaded other oil companies to join his Standard Oil Trust. By 1880, the trust controlled 95 percent of all oil refining in the United States—and was able to set a high price for oil. The public had to pay that price because they couldn't buy oil from anyone else. As head of Standard Oil, Rockefeller earned millions of dollars. He also gained a reputation as a ruthless robber baron.

*Reading***History**

A. Analyzing Points of View
Why do you think people thought monopolies were unfair?

Businessmen in other industries began to follow Rockefeller's example. Trusts were formed in the sugar, cottonseed oil, and lead-mining industries. Many people felt that these monopolies were unfair and hurt the economy. But the government was slow to regulate them.

Rockefeller tried to control all the companies in his industry. By contrast, Andrew Carnegie tried to beat his competition in the steel industry

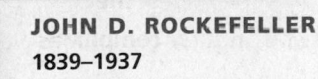

AMERICA'S HISTORY MAKERS

JOHN D. ROCKEFELLER
1839–1937

John D. Rockefeller was born to a poor family in upstate New York. From his mother, he learned the habit of frugality—he avoided unnecessary spending. "Willful waste makes woeful want" was a saying that Rockefeller's mother passed down to him.

By 1897, he had made millions and millions of dollars. Instead of keeping all that vast fortune for himself and his family, he spent the rest of his life donating money to several worthy causes.

ANDREW CARNEGIE
1835–1919

When Andrew Carnegie was 12, he and his family moved from Scotland to Pennsylvania. Carnegie's first job was in a cotton mill.

Later he worked in a telegraph office. There he was noticed by a railroad superintendent, who hired Carnegie as his assistant. Carnegie learned not only about running a big business but also about investing money. Eventually, he quit to start his own business.

Despite his fortune, Carnegie once wrote that none of his earnings gave him as much happiness as his first week's pay.

Compare the characters of Rockefeller and Carnegie. What do you think made each of them successful?

by making the best and cheapest product. To do so, he sought to control all the processes related to the manufacture of steel. He bought the mines that supplied his iron ore, and the ships and railroads that carried that ore to his mills. Carnegie's company dominated the U.S. steel industry from 1889 to 1901, when he sold it to J.P. Morgan, the nation's most prominent banker.

Rockefeller and Carnegie were multimillionaires. They also were both **philanthropists,** people who give large sums of money to charities. Rockefeller donated money to the University of Chicago and Rockefeller University in New York. Carnegie also gave money to universities, and he built hundreds of public libraries. During his life, Rockefeller gave away more than $500 million. Carnegie gave away more than $350 million.

*Reading***History**

B. Contrasting
How did the methods that Carnegie and Rockefeller used to eliminate competition differ?

The Gilded Age

The rags-to-riches stories of people such as Rockefeller and Carnegie inspired many Americans to believe that they too could grow rich. Stories like theirs also inspired writer Horatio Alger. He wrote popular stories about poor boys who worked hard and became quite successful.

Inspiring as these stories were, they hid an important truth. Most people who made millions of dollars had not been raised in poverty. Many belonged to the upper classes and had attended college. Most began their careers with the advantage of money or family connections.

For the rich, the late 1800s was a time of fabulous wealth. Writers Mark Twain and Charles Warner named the era the **Gilded Age.** To

HISTORY *through*ART

Artist Eastman Johnson painted this portrait of Alfredrick Smith Hatch's family, one of the wealthiest families in America, in 1870–1871. It shows the family in their New York mansion. Notice the expensive furnishings.

Photographer Jessie Tarbox Beals shot this photograph of a poor family in a tenement in 1910. A tenement is an apartment house that is usually rundown and overcrowded. This family probably had only this tiny space.

How do these two images reflect continuity and change in American life during the Gilded Age?

Vocabulary
gold leaf: gold that has been pounded into thin sheets

gild is to coat an object with gold leaf. Gilded decorations were popular during the era. But the name has a deeper meaning. Just as gold leaf can disguise an object of lesser value, so did the wealth of a few people mask society's problems, including corrupt politics and widespread poverty.

The South Remains Agricultural

One region that knew great poverty was the South. The Civil War had left the South in ruins. Industry did grow in some Southern areas, such as Birmingham, Alabama. Founded in 1871, Birmingham developed as an iron- and steel-producing town. In addition, cotton mills opened from southern Virginia to Alabama. Compared with the Northern economy, however, the Southern economy grew very slowly after the war.

Most of the South remained agricultural. As you have read, many Southern landowners rented their land to sharecroppers who paid a large portion of their crops as rent. Often sharecroppers had to buy their seed and tools on credit. The price of cotton, the South's main crop, was very low. Sharecroppers made little money from selling cotton and had difficulty paying what they owed. And because most sharecroppers had little education, merchants cheated them, increasing their debt.

Reading **History**
C. Making Inferences What is Fortune implying about the storekeeper?

A VOICE FROM THE PAST

My father once kept an account . . . of the things he "took up" at the store as well as the storekeeper. When the accounts were footed [added] up at the end of the year the thing became serious. The storekeeper had $150 more against my father than appeared on the latter's book. . . . It is by this means that [sharecroppers] are swindled and kept forever in debt.

T. Thomas Fortune, testimony to a Senate committee, 1883

At the same time that sharecroppers struggled to break free of debt, workers in the industrial North also faced injustices. In the next section, you will learn how labor unions tried to fight back.

Section **3** *Assessment*

1. Terms & Names

Explain the significance of:
- robber baron
- corporation
- John D. Rockefeller
- Andrew Carnegie
- monopoly
- trust
- philanthropist
- Gilded Age

2. Using Graphics

Use a Venn diagram like the one shown to compare and contrast Rockefeller and Carnegie.

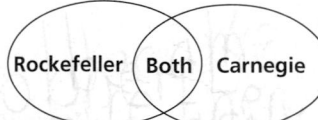

Whose business methods do you agree with more?

3. Main Ideas

a. Why did the number of corporations grow in the late 1800s?

b. Who is an example of a robber baron? Why?

c. Why was the South so much less industrial than the North?

4. Critical Thinking

Forming and Supporting Opinions Do you think that wealthy people have a duty to become philanthropists? Explain your opinion.

THINK ABOUT
- Carnegie and Rockefeller
- how most wealthy people gain their money
- the differences between the rich and the poor

ACTIVITY OPTIONS

MATH

SPEECH

In your local or school library, look up the business cycle. Create a **graph** of the cycle for the last century or prepare an **oral report** to Congress on the trends.

Industry in the Midwest

The Midwest is the region around the Great Lakes and the Upper Mississippi Valley. The region saw explosive growth during the 1800s. The first wave came after 1825, when the Erie Canal linked the East with the Great Lakes region. The second wave, caused by investments in products related to the Civil War (1861–1865), saw a boom in mining, farming, forestry, and meat-packing. By 1890, 29 percent of the country's manufacturing employment was in the Midwest, and the next big wave of growth was just beginning. New industries included steel and steel products, such as train rails and skyscraper beams.

Transportation and resources spurred the region's growth. Coal, oil, iron ore, limestone, and lumber were abundant, and the land was fertile. Trains, rivers, and lakes connected the Midwest to markets in the East and South and brought in raw materials from the West. The map on page 599 shows the resources of the lower Great Lakes and how transportation by rail and water joined regions.

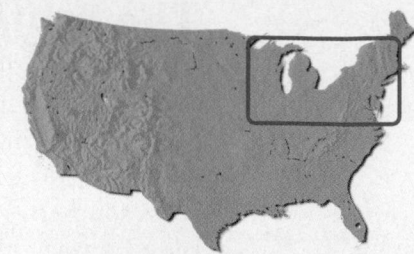

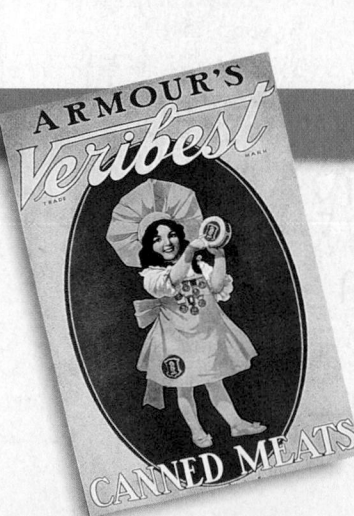

The industries of the Midwest used raw materials that came both from their own region and from other regions of the country. For example, the cattle in this photograph of the Chicago stockyards came by rail from the ranches of the West. In contrast, the logs being floated down the river came from the pine forests of Michigan and Wisconsin.

ARTIFACT FILE

A Quick Dinner Midwestern meat-packing companies advertised canned meats as a way to save time feeding a hungry family.

ARMOUR'S *Veribest* CANNED MEATS

Affordable Housing People began to build with wooden siding over a frame of wooden two-by-fours. These homes were cheap and quick to construct.

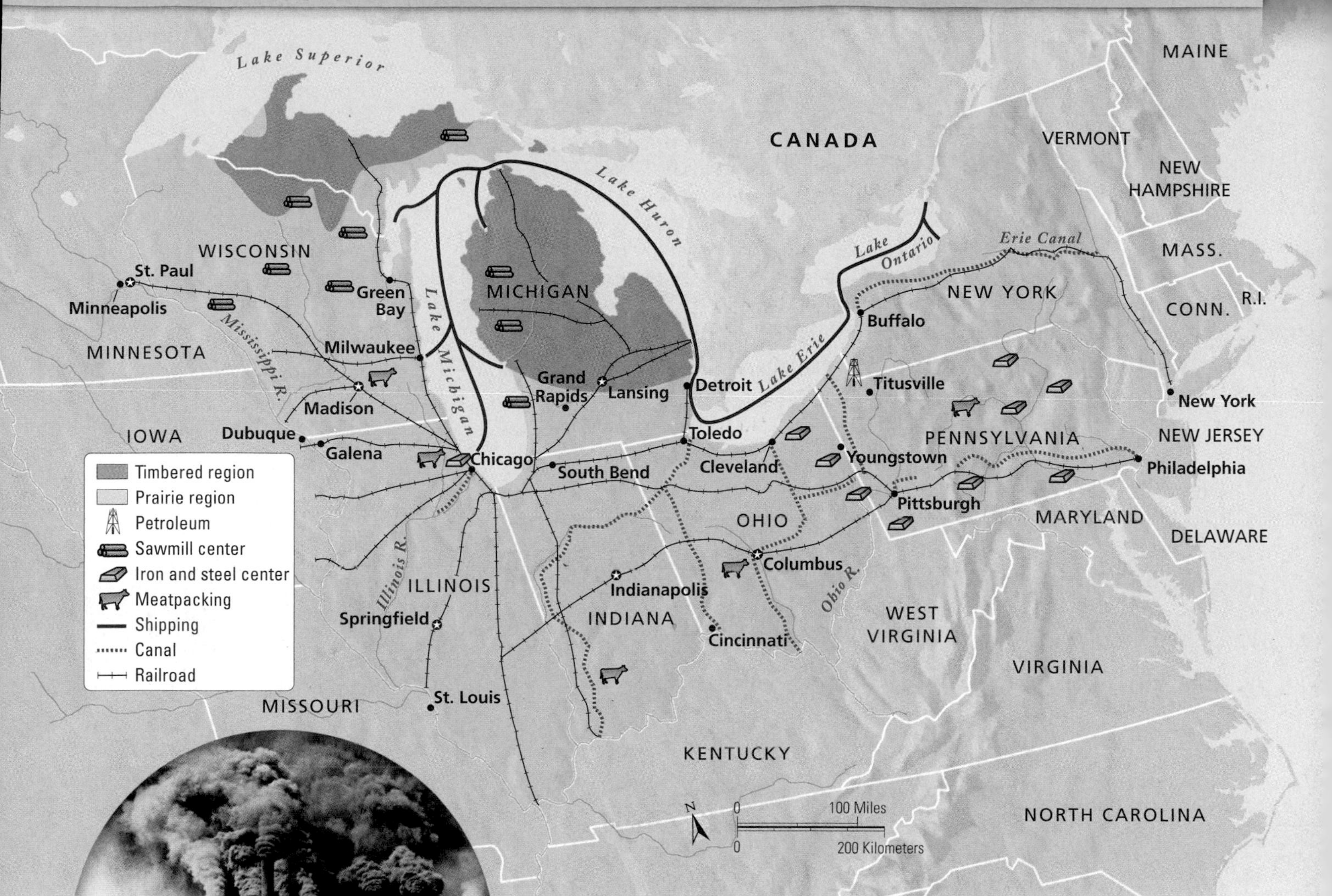

Map Legend

- Timbered region
- Prairie region
- ⚡ Petroleum
- Sawmill center
- Iron and steel center
- Meatpacking
- — Shipping
- ···· Canal
- ⊢⊣ Railroad

Lake Superior

CANADA

MAINE

VERMONT

NEW HAMPSHIRE

MASS.

CONN. **R.I.**

Lake Huron

Lake Ontario

Erie Canal

NEW YORK

WISCONSIN
- St. Paul
- Minneapolis
- Green Bay
- Milwaukee
- Madison

MINNESOTA

Mississippi R.

MICHIGAN
- Grand Rapids
- Lansing

Buffalo

Detroit **Lake Erie**

Titusville

PENNSYLVANIA

New York

NEW JERSEY

Philadelphia

IOWA
- Dubuque
- Galena

Chicago
- South Bend
- Toledo
- Cleveland
- Youngstown
- Pittsburgh

Illinois R.

OHIO

MARYLAND

DELAWARE

ILLINOIS
- Springfield
- Indianapolis

INDIANA
- Columbus
- Cincinnati

Ohio R.

WEST VIRGINIA

VIRGINIA

MISSOURI
- St. Louis

KENTUCKY

NORTH CAROLINA

N

| 0 | 100 Miles |
| 0 | 200 Kilometers |

Iron ore from the Lake Superior region and coal from southern Illinois were used to manufacture steel.

On-Line Field Trip

The Chicago Historical Society
in Chicago, Illinois, contains photographs, documents, and artifacts such as this Western Electric typewriter, made in 1900. Typewriters enabled office workers to produce neat, clean documents quickly.

For more about the Midwest . . .

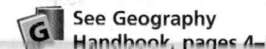
RESEARCH LINKS
CLASSZONE.COM

CONNECT TO GEOGRAPHY

1. **Region** What advantages did the Midwest have that helped it become highly industrialized?
2. **Human-Environment Interaction** How did the development of railroads add to the region's advantages?

   G See Geography Handbook, pages 4–5

CONNECT TO HISTORY

3. **Analyzing Causes** Chicago was a big meatpacking center. Why do you think that industry chose to locate there?

Workers Organize

MAIN IDEA	WHY IT MATTERS NOW	TERMS & NAMES
To increase their ability to bargain with management, workers formed labor unions.	Many of the modern benefits that workers take for granted were won by early unions.	sweatshop Pullman Strike Knights of Labor Eugene V. Debs socialism Samuel Gompers Haymarket affair American Federation of Labor (AFL)

ONE AMERICAN'S STORY

In 1867, Mary Harris Jones lost her husband and four children to yellow fever. Moving to Chicago, she started a dressmaking business. But the great Chicago fire of 1871 destroyed everything she owned. Instead of giving up in despair, Jones found a cause to fight for.

A VOICE FROM THE PAST

From the time of the Chicago fire I . . . decided to take an active part in the efforts of the working people to better the conditions under which they worked and lived.

Mary Harris Jones, *Autobiography of Mother Jones*

Jones became an effective labor leader. Workers loved her so much that they called her Mother Jones. In this section, you will learn about the labor movement of the late 1800s.

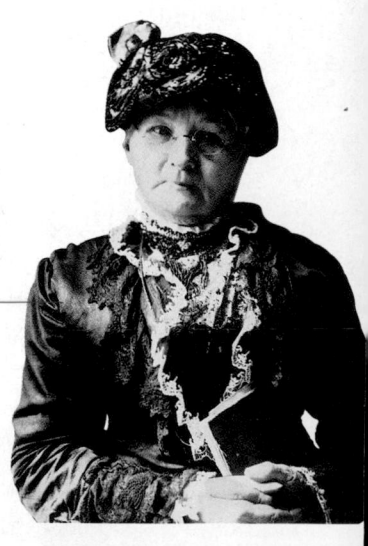

Mother Jones won the love of working people by fighting for their rights.

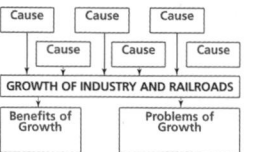

Taking Notes

Use your chart to take notes about organized labor.

[diagram: Cause / Cause / Cause → Cause / Cause / Cause → GROWTH OF INDUSTRY AND RAILROADS → Benefits of Growth / Problems of Growth]

Workers Face Hardships

Business owners of the late 1800s wanted to keep their profits high, so they ran their factories as cheaply as possible. Some cut costs by requiring workers to buy their own tools or to bring coal to heat the factories. Others refused to buy safety equipment. For example, railroads would not buy air brakes or automatic train-car couplers. Because of this, 30,000 railroad workers were injured and 2,000 killed every year.

If a factory became too crowded, the owner rarely built a larger one. Instead, the owner sent part of the work to be done by smaller businesses that critics called sweatshops. **Sweatshops** were places where workers labored long hours under poor conditions for low wages. Often both children and adults worked there.

Factory and sweatshop workers did the same jobs, such as sewing collars or making buttonholes, all day long. They grew bored and did not

experience the satisfaction that came from making an entire product themselves. Further, both factory and sweatshop owners kept wages low. In the 1880s, the average weekly wage was less than $10. This barely paid a family's expenses. If a worker missed work due to illness or had any unexpected bills, the family went into debt. Workers began to feel that only other working people could understand their troubles.

Child labor was common in the late 1800s, and as this boy's bare feet demonstrate, safety practices were rare.

A VOICE FROM THE PAST

They know what it is to bring up a family on ninety cents a day, to live on beans and corn meal week in and week out, to run in debt at the stores until you cannot get trusted [credit] any longer, to see the wife breaking down . . . , and the children growing sharp and fierce like wolves day after day because they don't get enough to eat.

A railroad worker, quoted in the *Philadelphia Inquirer,* July 23, 1877

So discontented workers joined together to try to improve their lives. They formed labor unions—groups of workers that negotiated with business owners to obtain better wages and working conditions.

Early Unions

As you read in Chapter 14, the first labor unions began in the mid-1800s but were unable to win many improvements for workers. After the Civil War, some unions started to form national organizations. One of these was the **Knights of Labor.** This was a loose federation of workers from all different trades. Unlike many labor organizations, the Knights allowed women and, after 1878, African-American workers to join their union. They inspired many people to support their cause.

Then, beginning in 1873, the United States fell into a serious economic depression. Over the next four years, millions of workers took pay cuts, and about one-fifth lost their jobs. In July 1877, the Baltimore and Ohio (B & O) Railroad declared a wage cut of 10 percent. The day the pay cut was to go into effect, B & O workers in Martinsburg, West Virginia, refused to run the trains. No labor union had called the strike. The workers themselves had stopped working on their own.

"[Working people] know what it is to bring up a family on ninety cents a day."
A railroad worker, 1877

This work stoppage was the Railroad Strike of 1877. As the news spread, workers in many cities and in other industries joined in. This threw the country into turmoil. In several cities, state militias battled angry mobs. President Rutherford B. Hayes called out federal troops. Before the two-week strike ended, dozens of people were killed.

The strike did not prevent the railroad pay cut, but it showed how angry American workers had become. In 1884–1885, railroaders again went out on strike. This time they went on strike against the Union

Pacific and two other railroads. The strikers, who were members of the Knights of Labor, gained nationwide attention when they won their strike. Hundreds of thousands of new workers joined the union.

Union Setbacks

The growth of labor unions scared many business leaders. They blamed the labor movement on socialists and anarchists. Socialists believe in **socialism**. In that economic system, all members of a society are equal owners of all businesses—they share the work and the profits. Anarchists are far more extreme. They want to abolish all governments.

Business and government leaders feared that unions might spread such ideas, so they tried to break union power. In Chicago in 1886, the McCormick Harvester Company locked out striking union members and hired strikebreakers to replace them. On May 3, union members, strikebreakers, and police clashed. One union member was killed.

The next day, a protest meeting was held at Haymarket Square. Held on a rainy evening, the rally was small. As police moved in to end the meeting, an unknown person threw a bomb. It killed 7 police and wounded about 60. The police then opened fire on the crowd, killing several people and wounding about a hundred. This conflict was called the **Haymarket affair**.

Afterward, the Chicago police arrested hundreds of union leaders, socialists, and anarchists. Opposition to unions increased. The membership in the Knights of Labor dropped rapidly—even though that wasn't the union that had called the meeting at Haymarket Square.

*Reading*History

B. Recognizing Effects Did the action of the bomber make it seem more or less likely that anarchists were behind union activity? Explain.

The Homestead and Pullman Strikes

Labor conflicts grew more bitter. In 1892, Andrew Carnegie reduced wages at his steel mills in Homestead, Pennsylvania, but the union refused to accept the cut. The company responded by locking out union workers from the mills and announcing that it would hire nonunion labor. The company also hired 300 armed guards. In response, the locked-out workers gathered weapons. The guards arrived on July 6, and a battle broke out that left ten people dead. The Pennsylvania state militia began to escort the nonunion workers to the mills. After four months, the strike collapsed, breaking the union.

Workers lost another dispute in 1894. In that depression year, many railroad companies went bankrupt. To stay in business, the Pullman Palace Car Company, which made railroad cars,

One night during the Pullman Strike, some 600 freight cars were burned.

*Reading*History

C. Analyzing Causes Why was it so difficult for early unions to win against big business?

cut workers' pay 25 percent. But Pullman did not lower the rent it charged workers to live in company housing. After their rent was deducted from the lower pay, many Pullman workers took home almost nothing.

The Pullman workers began the **Pullman Strike,** a strike which spread throughout the rail industry in 1894. When the Pullman Company refused to negotiate, American Railway Union president **Eugene V. Debs** called on all U.S. railroad workers to refuse to handle Pullman cars. Rail traffic in much of the country came to a halt. President Grover Cleveland called out federal troops, which ended the strike. Debs was put in jail.

Gompers Founds the AFL

Not all companies treated workers as harshly as Carnegie and Pullman did. For instance, in the 1880s, the soap company Procter & Gamble began to give its employees an extra half day off a week. It also began a profit-sharing plan, in which a company gives part of its profits to workers.

However, workers at most companies received low wages and few benefits. So in spite of the opposition to unions, the labor movement did not die. In 1886, labor leader **Samuel Gompers** helped found a new national organization of unions called the **American Federation of Labor (AFL).** Gompers served as AFL president for 37 years.

The AFL focused on improving working conditions. By using strikes, boycotts, and negotiation, the AFL won shorter working hours and better pay for workers. By 1904, it had about 1.7 million members.

In the next few decades, labor unions helped change the way all Americans worked. At the same time, city growth and immigration transformed America. You will read about that in Chapter 21.

Reading **History**
D. Identifying Problems What problems did the AFL try to solve?

Now and then

MODERN BENEFITS WON BY UNIONS

Today, many Americans work 40 hours per week—perhaps 9-to-5, Monday through Friday. Contrast this situation with the 10-to12-hour days of most 19th-century workers. The 8-hour day was one benefit won by labor unions. Other benefits unions won include workers' compensation (insurance that pays for injuries received on the job), pensions, and paid vacation.

Unions continue to fight to improve the lives of working Americans. In recent years they have tried to increase benefits for part-time and temporary workers. They have also fought for safety standards to prevent injuries, such as carpal tunnel syndrome, which affects many workers who use computers.

Section 4 Assessment

1. Terms & Names

Explain the significance of:
- sweatshop
- Knights of Labor
- socialism
- Haymarket affair
- Pullman Strike
- Eugene V. Debs
- Samuel Gompers
- American Federation of Labor (AFL)

2. Using Graphics

Review this section and find five key events to place on a time line like the one below.

1870   event   event   1910

event   event   event

What individuals played significant roles in these events?

3. Main Ideas

a. What hardships did workers face in the late 1800s?

b. What happened to unions after the protest at Haymarket Square?

c. How did Carnegie's company break the union at the Homestead mills?

4. Critical Thinking

Drawing Conclusions In your opinion, was the government more supportive of unions or business in the late 1800s? Explain.

THINK ABOUT
- the Railroad Strike of 1877
- the Homestead Strike
- the Pullman Strike

ACTIVITY OPTIONS

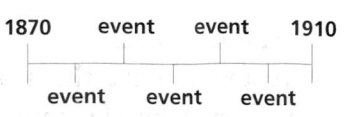
LANGUAGE ARTS
ART

Decide whether unions should be encouraged. Write an **editorial** or create a **public message poster** expressing your opinion.

VISUAL SUMMARY

An Industrial Society

Long-Term Causes
- plentiful natural resources
- building of canals and railroads in early 1800s

Immediate Causes
- continued building of railroads in late 1800s
- growing population and high immigration
- new inventions and industrial processes
- investment capital and development of corporations

GROWTH of INDUSTRY

Immediate Effects

- increased amount of manufactured goods
- growth of large corporations, monopolies, and trusts
- poor conditions for workers in factories and sweatshops
- labor unions and strikes

Long-Term Effects
- economies of East and West linked together
- labor movement wins permanent changes, such as reduced working hours

TERMS & NAMES

Briefly explain the significance of each of the following.

1. patent
2. business cycle
3. transcontinental railroad
4. standard time
5. corporation
6. John D. Rockefeller
7. Andrew Carnegie
8. Haymarket affair
9. Pullman Strike
10. American Federation of Labor (AFL)

REVIEW QUESTIONS

The Growth of Industry (pages 585–589)

1. How do inventors protect their rights to what they invent?
2. What did Thomas Edison and Alexander Graham Bell invent?

Railroads Transform the Nation (pages 590–593)

3. What geographic feature made building the Central Pacific difficult?
4. What took place when workers connected the Central Pacific and the Union Pacific?

The Rise of Big Business (pages 594–599)

5. What is a monopoly?
6. What are trusts, and why did some people think they were bad for the country?
7. Why did writers Mark Twain and Charles Warner name the late 1800s the Gilded Age?

Workers Organize (pages 600–603)

8. What ideas did business leaders fear that unions would spread?
9. How did the Pullman Strike begin and end?
10. Which unions were led by Eugene V. Debs and Samuel Gompers?

CRITICAL THINKING

1. USING YOUR NOTES: ANALYZING CAUSES AND EFFECTS

Using your completed chart, answer the questions below.

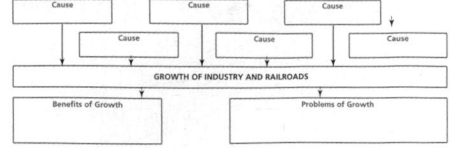

a. How did the growth of railroads act as a cause of industrial growth?
b. Who do you think benefited most from the growth of industry? Explain.

2. THEME: ECONOMICS IN HISTORY

Who is someone from this chapter that might view the United States as a land of economic opportunity? Explain your answer.

3. ANALYZING LEADERSHIP

What characteristics of a good leader did Mother Jones possess?

4. APPLYING CITIZENSHIP SKILLS

Were John D. Rockefeller and Andrew Carnegie good citizens? Support your answer with details from this chapter.

5. COMPARING

How were the problems of share-croppers, described on page 597, similar to those of Pullman workers, described on pages 602–603?

6. DRAWING CONCLUSIONS

Why do you think unions were more successful at attracting members in the late 1800s than in the early 1800s?

Interact with History

Now that you have read the chapter, would you change your mind about joining the strike? Explain.

Use the graph and your knowledge of U.S. history to answer questions 1 and 2.

Additional Test Practice, pp. S1–S22.

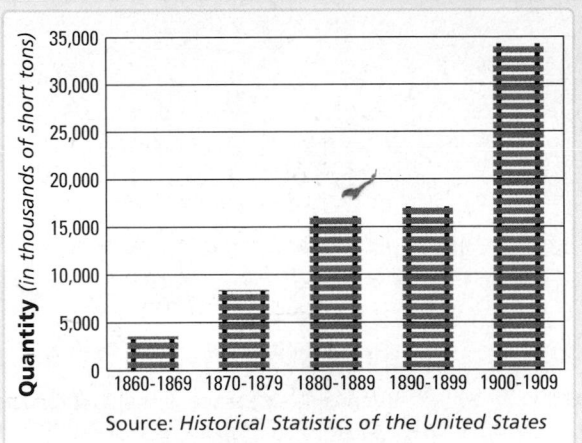

U.S. Rails Produced, 1860–1909

Quantity (in thousands of short tons)

35,000
30,000
25,000
20,000
15,000
10,000
5,000
0

1860-1869 1870-1879 1880-1889 1890-1899 1900-1909

Source: *Historical Statistics of the United States*

1. Which decade saw the biggest change in rail production?

A. 1870–1879
B. 1880–1889
C. 1890–1899
D. 1900–1909

2. What does this graph indicate about what was happening in the railroad industry?

A. The industry grew quickly and leveled off.
B. The industry was booming.
C. The industry was failing.
D. The industry grew in very small increments.

Thomas Edison describes the process of inventing in this quotation. Use the quotation and your knowledge of U.S. history to answer question 3.

PRIMARY SOURCE

It has been just so in all my inventions. The first step is an intuition—and comes with a burst, then difficulties arise. . . . "Bugs"—as such little faults and difficulties are called—show themselves and months of anxious watching, study and labor are requisite [needed] before commercial success—or failure—is certainly reached.

Thomas Edison, quoted in *Edison* by Matthew Josephson

3. According to Edison, what elements are common to the creation of his inventions?

A. idea, observation, study, and work
B. observation, energy, study, and work
C. study, observation, work, and energy
D. work, idea, energy, and luck

TEST PRACTICE
CLASSZONE.COM

ALTERNATIVE ASSESSMENT

1. WRITING ABOUT HISTORY

Assume the role of a labor leader, such as Mother Jones, and write a **speech** informing workers of their rights and urging them to unite.

• Use library resources to write your speech.

• Focus your speech by addressing one major issue, such as safe working conditions, shorter working hours, or increased wages.

2. COOPERATIVE LEARNING

With your group, research the life of a business or labor leader from this chapter. Write and perform a monologue in which the leader discusses his or her life. Group members can share the responsibilities for researching and writing the monologue, finding costumes and props, and acting out the monologue.

INTEGRATED TECHNOLOGY

DOING INTERNET RESEARCH

During different periods of U.S. history, scientific ideas have influenced technological developments. Use the Internet and the library to research how scientific ideas affected industrialization in the 19th century.

• Use keywords such as *industrialization + electricity* to do research on the Internet.

• Look for Web sites for museums of science and industry.

• In your research, consider how the Bessemer process affected industrialization. Compile your research into a report.

For more about science and technology . . .

INTERNET ACTIVITY
CLASSZONE.COM

CHAPTER 21

Changes in American Life 1880–1914

Section 1
Cities Grow and Change

Section 2
The New Immigrants

Section 3
Segregation and Discrimination

Section 4
Society and Mass Culture

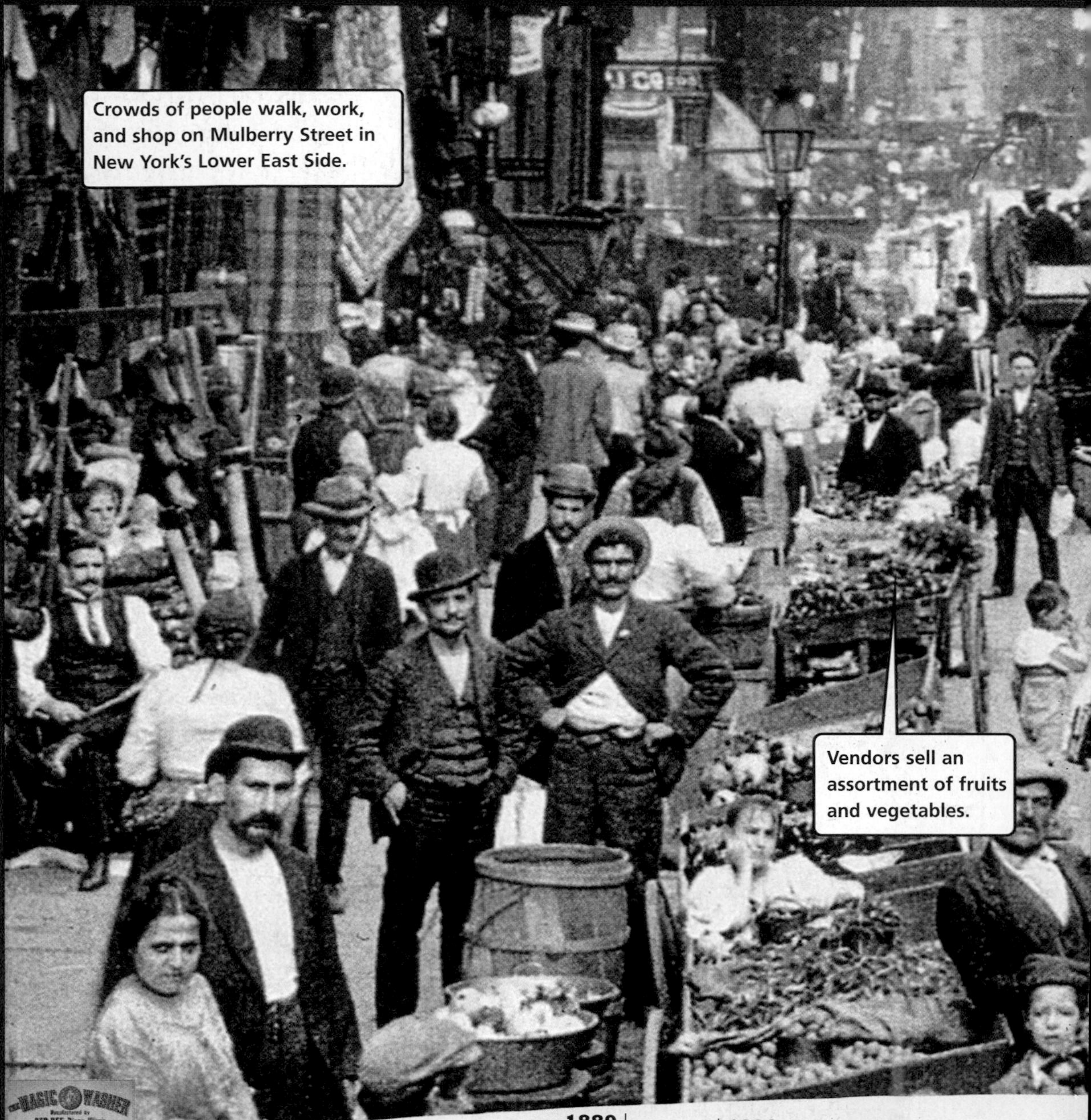

Crowds of people walk, work, and shop on Mulberry Street in New York's Lower East Side.

Vendors sell an assortment of fruits and vegetables.

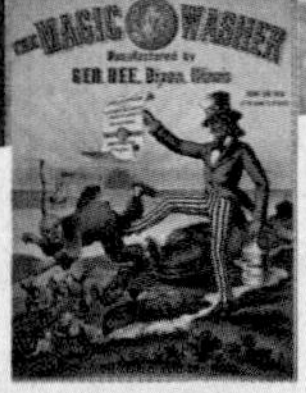

USA

1882
Congress passes the Chinese Exclusion Act.

1888
Electric trolleys are set up in Richmond, Virginia.

1889
The first electric elevator is installed.

Jane Addams founds Hull House.

1892
Immigration center opens on Ellis Island.

1893
Columbian Exposition opens in Chicago.

1880

World

1889
Brazil becomes a republic.

Barnum & Baily circus opens in London.

1893
Karl Benz invents the modern automobile.

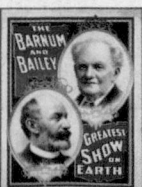

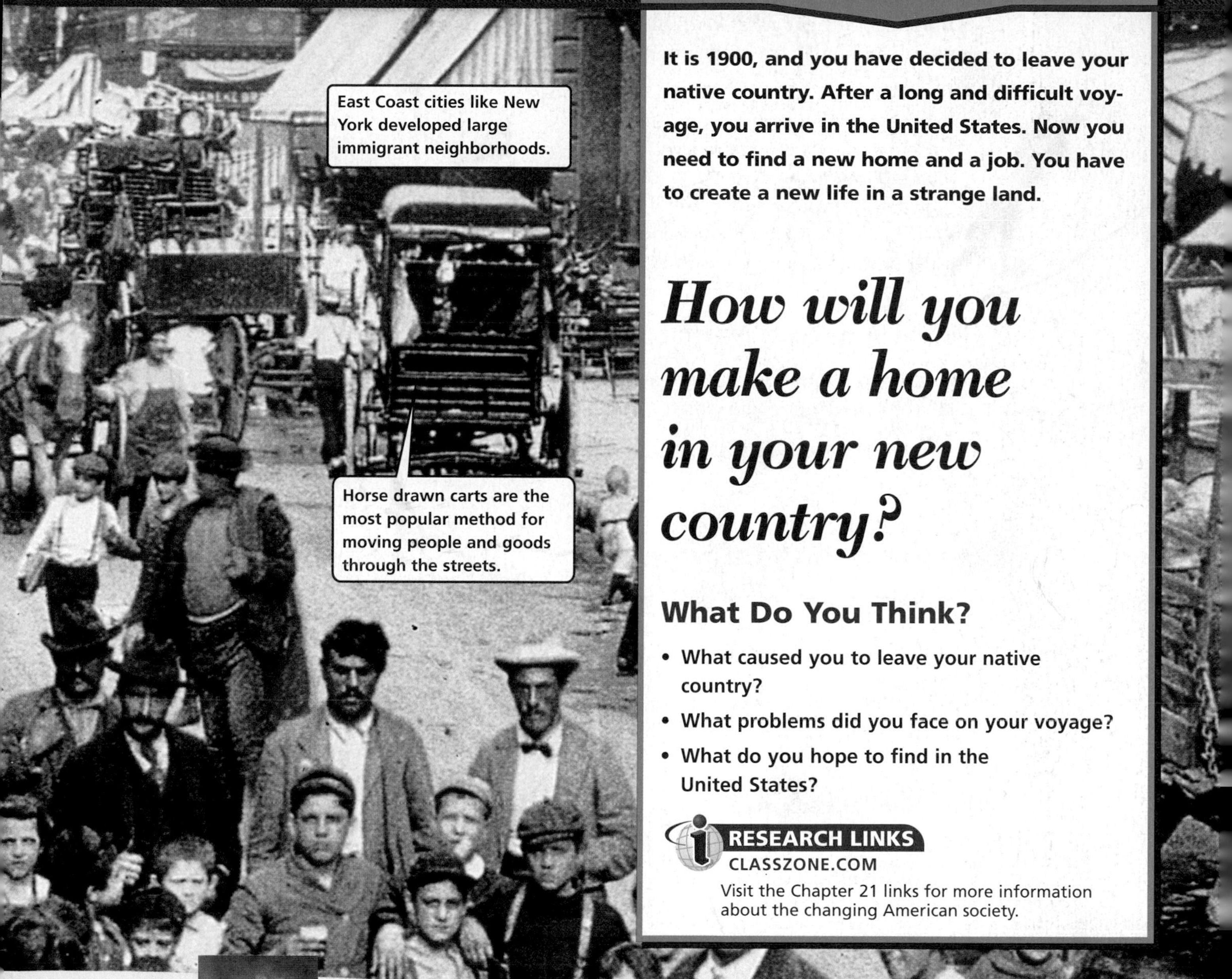

East Coast cities like New York developed large immigrant neighborhoods.

Horse drawn carts are the most popular method for moving people and goods through the streets.

Interact *with* History

It is 1900, and you have decided to leave your native country. After a long and difficult voyage, you arrive in the United States. Now you need to find a new home and a job. You have to create a new life in a strange land.

How will you make a home in your new country?

What Do You Think?

- What caused you to leave your native country?
- What problems did you face on your voyage?
- What do you hope to find in the United States?

 **RESEARCH LINKS**
CLASSZONE.COM

Visit the Chapter 21 links for more information about the changing American society.

896
preme Court
tablishes
eparate-but-
qual" doctrine
Plessy v.
rguson case.

1906
Earthquake
and fire
devastate
San Francisco.

1909
National Association for the
Advancement of Colored People
(NAACP) is founded.

1914

896
rst modern
lympic Games
e held in
hens, Greece.

1910
Mexican
Revolution
begins.

Changes in American Life **607**

Reading Strategy: Categorizing Information

What Do You Know?

What do you think about when you hear the term *immigration*? Why do people move to different countries? What kinds of challenges might immigrants face in their new country?

Think About

- what you know about immigration from the experience of your family
- what would make you want to move away from your home
- your responses to the Interact with History about making a home in a new country (see page 607)

Asia

Europe

Latin America

What Do You Want to Know?

What questions do you have about American life around 1900? Write them in your notebook before you read the chapter.

Categorizing Information

To help you make sense of what you read, learn to categorize. Categorizing means sorting information into groups. The chart below will help you take notes and categorize the changes in American life that occurred during the late 19th and early 20th centuries.

 S See Skillbuilder Handbook, page R6.

 Taking Notes

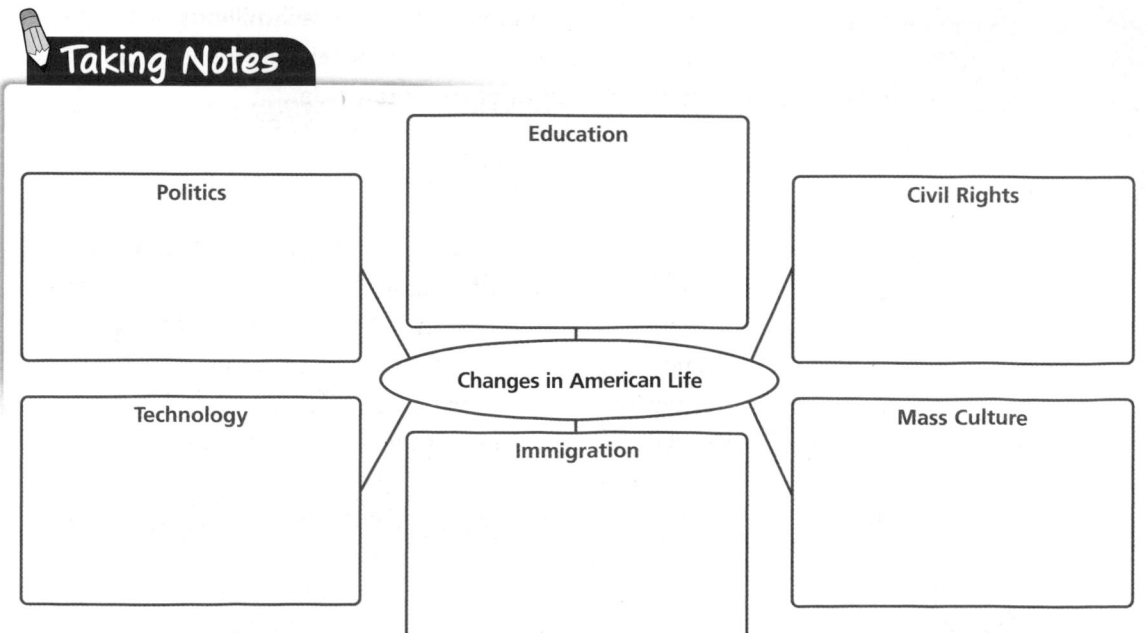

Education

Politics

Civil Rights

Changes in American Life

Technology

Immigration

Mass Culture

Cities Grow and Change

MAIN IDEA	WHY IT MATTERS NOW	TERMS & NAMES
Industrialization and immigration caused American cities to grow rapidly.	Modern American city life first emerged during this period.	urbanization Jane Addams tenement Hull House slum political machine social gospel Tammany Hall

ONE AMERICAN'S STORY

Carl Jensen came to the United States from Denmark in 1906. Like most of the millions of immigrants who came to America around the turn of the century, he immediately began to look for work.

A VOICE FROM THE PAST

I wandered in search of work . . . waiting through rain and sleet and snow with gangs of longshoremen [dockworkers] to reach the boss before he finished picking the men he wanted. . . . Strong men crushed each other to the ground in their passion for work.

Carl Jensen, quoted in *A Sunday Between Wars*

Shipyards in growing cities provided jobs for many Americans.

At the turn of the century, the promise of work drew millions of people like Carl Jensen from around the world to American cities. In this section, you will read about the rapid growth of American cities.

Industrialization Expands Cities

The Industrial Revolution, which had been changing how people worked, also changed *where* people worked. Since colonial days, most Americans had lived and worked in rural areas. But in the late 1800s, that began to change as more and more people moved to cities to find jobs.

Industries were drawn to cities because cities offered good transportation and plentiful workers. Increasing numbers of factory jobs appeared in America's cities, followed by more workers to fill those jobs. The growth of cities that resulted from these changes is called **urbanization**.

Many of the people who moved to American cities were immigrants like Carl Jensen. People also migrated from America's farms to the cities. Once there, even workers with few skills could usually find steady work.

Taking Notes

Use your chart to take notes about changes in technology and politics.

Changes in
American Life

Modern cities depend on skyscrapers to increase the space for people to live and work. Steel, electricity, and elevators make skyscrapers possible.

1 **STEEL FRAMES** Steel beams can carry much more weight than brick or stone walls. The strength of the steel allows architects to design extremely tall buildings.

2 **WINDOWS** In skyscrapers, the outer walls do not support the weight of the building; the steel beams do. As a result, many skyscrapers have outer walls made of glass to allow sunlight inside.

3 **ELEVATOR** Tall buildings would be useless if people could not reach all of the floors. Elevators powered by electricity make such tall buildings practical.

Technology Changes City Life

New technologies helped cities absorb the millions of people who flocked there. For example, new technologies made possible the construction of skyscrapers, buildings that looked tall enough to scrape the sky. Skyscrapers helped cities grow and made modern city life possible.

The elevator was a key invention for constructing tall buildings that could hold greater numbers of people. Before the 1860s, buildings rarely rose higher than four stories because it was hard for people to climb to the top. In 1889, the Otis Elevator Company installed the first electric elevator. Now buildings could be more than a few stories tall because people no longer had to walk up to the higher floors. As a result, buildings could hold more people.

The use of steel also helped to increase the height of buildings. In 1885, the Home Insurance Building in Chicago boasted an iron and steel skeleton that could hold the immense weight of the skyscraper's floors and walls. The building climbed to ten stories. Skyscrapers changed city skylines forever.

The Streetcar City

As electricity helped change the way people traveled inside buildings, it also changed how people traveled around cities. Before industrialization, people walked or used horse-drawn vehicles to travel over land. But by 1900, electric streetcars in American cities were carrying more than 5 billion passengers a year. Streetcars and trains changed the walking city into the streetcar city.

*Reading***History**
A. Recognizing Effects How did industry and technology help cities grow?

Background
Streetcars are also called trolleys.

In 1888, Richmond, Virginia, became the first American city to have a transportation system powered by electricity. Other cities soon installed their own electric streetcars. The streetcars could quickly carry people to work and play all over the city. Some cities, such as Chicago, moved their electric streetcars above the street level, creating elevated, or "el," lines. Other cities, like New York, placed their city rail lines in underground tunnels, making subways.

The streetcar city spread outward from the city's center in ways the walking city never could. The ability to live farther away from work helped new suburbs to develop around cities. Some people in the suburbs wanted to become part of the city they bordered. That way they also could be served by the city's transportation system. Largely due to public transportation, cities expanded. For example, in 1889, Chicago annexed several suburbs and more than doubled its population as well as its area.

Vocabulary
annex: to add

Urban Disasters and Slums

The concentration of people in cities increased the danger of disasters because people and buildings were packed closely together. For example, in 1906, a powerful earthquake rocked San Francisco. The tremors caused large fires to tear through the city. The central business district was destroyed. About 700 people died, and nearly $400 million in property was damaged. But natural disasters were not the only source of danger for the people of the cities. Poverty and disease also threatened their lives.

As people flocked to cities, overcrowding became a serious problem. It was especially serious for families who could not afford to buy a house. Such families usually lived in rented apartments or tenements. A **tenement** is an apartment house that is usually run-down and overcrowded.

Old buildings, landlord neglect, poor design, and little government control led to dangerous conditions in many tenements. Poor families who could not afford to rent a place of their own often needed to move in with other families. This resulted in severely overcrowded tenements. Inadequate garbage pick-up also caused problems. Tenants sometimes dumped their garbage into the narrow air shafts between tenements. There was little fresh air, and the smell was awful.

Many tenements had no running water. Residents had to collect water

*Reading*History
B. Summarizing
What was it like to live in a turn-of-the-century tenement?

HISTORY through ART

This photograph by Lewis Hine shows a family of Italian immigrants in their cramped, decaying tenement in New York City in 1912. Often photographers, such as Hine, had their subjects pose for their pictures to create the strongest effect.

What effect do you think Hine wanted this photograph to have?

from a faucet on the street. The water could be heated for bathing. But it was often unsafe for drinking. Sewage flowed in open gutters and threatened to spread disease among tenement dwellers.

A neighborhood with such overcrowded, dangerous housing was called a **slum**. The most famous example was New York City's Lower East Side. But every city had slums. After visiting Chicago's slums, the British writer Rudyard Kipling wrote in disgust, "Having seen it [Chicago], I urgently desire never to see it again."

Reformers Attack Urban Problems

Many Americans were also disgusted by poverty and slums. Some people fought to reform, or create changes, that would solve these problems. They were known as urban reformers.

The social gospel movement provided one basis for these beliefs. The **social gospel** movement aimed to improve the lives of the poor. Led by Protestant ministers, the ideas of the movement were based on Christian values. The most important concerns of the social gospel movement were labor reforms, such as abolishing child labor. Some reformers inspired by the movement opened settlement houses. They helped the poor and immigrants improve their lives. Settlement houses offered services such as daycare, education, and health care to needy people in slum neighborhoods.

*Reading*History
C. Making Inferences How did Christian values support the social gospel movement?

CITIZENSHIP TODAY

Community Service

Since the United States began, citizens have shared concerns about their communities. Many citizens, such as Jane Addams in 1889, have identified problems and proposed solutions to them.

In 1993, sixth-grader David Levitt asked his principal if the leftover food from the school cafeteria could be sent to a program to feed needy people. David was told that many restrictions prevented giving away the food.

Determined to get food to people who needed it, David talked to the school board, the state health department, and private companies to convince them to back his program. Today, more than 500,000 pounds of food from schools has been given to hungry people in the Seminole, Florida, area.

David Levitt carries supplies for his food pantry program.

How Do You Participate in Your Community?

1. In a small group, think about problems within your community. Make a list of those problems.

2. Choose one problem to work on.

3. Gather information about the problem. Keep a log of your sources to use again.

4. After you gather information, brainstorm solutions to the problem. Create a plan to carry out one solution.

5. Present the problem and your plan to the class.

 See the Citizenship Handbook, page 286.

For more about community service . . .

 RESEARCH LINKS
CLASSZONE.COM

Many settlement house founders were educated middle-class women. **Jane Addams** founded Chicago's **Hull House** in 1889 with Ellen Gates Starr. Hull House soon became a model for other settlement houses, including New York's Henry Street Settlement House, which Lillian D. Wald established in 1889.

Political Machines Run Cities

Political machines were another type of organization that addressed the problems of the city. A **political machine** is an organization that influences enough votes to control a local government.

Political machines gained support by trading favors for votes. For example, machine bosses gave jobs or food to supporters. In return, supporters worked and voted for the machine. Political machines also did many illegal things. They broke rules to win elections. They accepted bribes to affect government actions.

The most famous political machine was **Tammany Hall** in New York City. It was led by William Marcy Tweed. Along with his greedy friends, "Boss" Tweed stole enormous amounts of money from the city.

Despite such corruption, political machines did a number of good things for cities. They built parks, sewers, schools, roads, and orphanages in many cities. In addition, machine politicians often helped immigrants get settled in the United States by helping them find jobs or homes. Many immigrants gratefully supported the political machine after this kind of help. In the next section, you will learn more about immigration.

Reading **History**

D. Comparing and Contrasting How were settlement houses and political machines similar? How were they different?

AMERICA'S HISTORY MAKERS

JANE ADDAMS
1860–1935
Jane Addams founded Hull House as an "effort to aid in the solution of the social and industrial problems which are [caused] by the modern conditions of life in a great city."

In addition to Hull House, Addams was active in many other areas. She fought for the passage of laws to protect women workers and outlaw child labor. She also worked to improve housing and public health. In 1931, she was awarded a share of the Nobel Peace Prize for her efforts.

Why did Jane Addams found Hull House?

Section 1 Assessment

1. Terms & Names

Explain the significance of:

- urbanization
- tenement
- slum
- social gospel
- Jane Addams
- Hull House
- political machine
- Tammany Hall

2. Using Graphics

Use a chart like the one below to show the causes and effects of urban growth.

Cause	Effect
Steel	
Elevators	
Streetcars	
Immigration	

3. Main Ideas

a. Why did immigrants and farmers settle in big cities at the end of the 19th century?

b. What are two inventions that made modern city life possible?

c. What urban problems did reformers try to solve?

4. Critical Thinking

Evaluating What were some of the advantages and disadvantages of machine politics?

THINK ABOUT

- the problems faced by immigrants and cities
- Tammany Hall and "Boss" Tweed

ACTIVITY OPTIONS

LANGUAGE ARTS

ART

It is 1900, and you have just moved to an American city. Write a **letter** to friends back home or draw a **picture** that describes your new home.

The New Immigrants

MAIN IDEA	WHY IT MATTERS NOW	TERMS & NAMES
Millions of immigrants—mostly from southern and eastern Europe—moved to the United States.	The new immigrants had an important role in shaping American culture in the 20th century.	new immigrants melting pot Ellis Island assimilation Angel Island Chinese Exclusion Act

ONE AMERICAN'S STORY

In 1907, 10-year-old Edward Corsi left Italy to come to America. After two weeks at sea, he caught sight of the Statue of Liberty.

A VOICE FROM THE PAST

This symbol of America . . . inspired awe in the hopeful immigrants. Many older persons among us, burdened with a thousand memories of what they were leaving behind, had been openly weeping. . . . Now somehow steadied, I suppose, by the concreteness of the symbol of America's freedom, they dried their tears.

Edward Corsi, *In the Shadow of Liberty*

In this section, you will learn about the immigrants who came to the United States around 1900 and their effect on the nation.

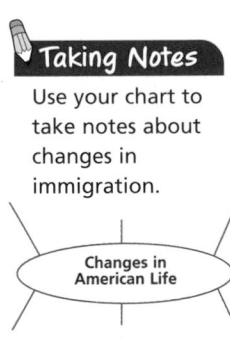

Taking Notes

Use your chart to take notes about changes in immigration.

Changes in American Life

The Statue of Liberty and Ellis Island were two of the first things many immigrants saw of the United States.

The New Immigrants

Until the 1890s, most immigrants to the United States had come from northern and western Europe. But after 1900, fewer northern Europeans immigrated, and more southern and eastern Europeans did. This later group of immigrants came to be known as the **new immigrants.** Southern Italy sent large numbers of immigrants. Many Jews from eastern Europe and Slavic peoples, such as Poles and Russians, also immigrated.

Ellis Island was the first stop for most immigrants from Europe. There, they were processed before they could enter the United States. First, they had to pass a physical examination. Those with serious health problems or diseases were sent home. Next, they were asked a series of questions: Name? Occupation? How much money do you have?

Slovenian immigrant Louis Adamic described the night he spent on Ellis Island. He and many other immigrants slept in a huge hall. Lacking a warm blanket, the young man "shivered, sleepless, all night, listening to snores" and dreams "in perhaps a dozen different languages."

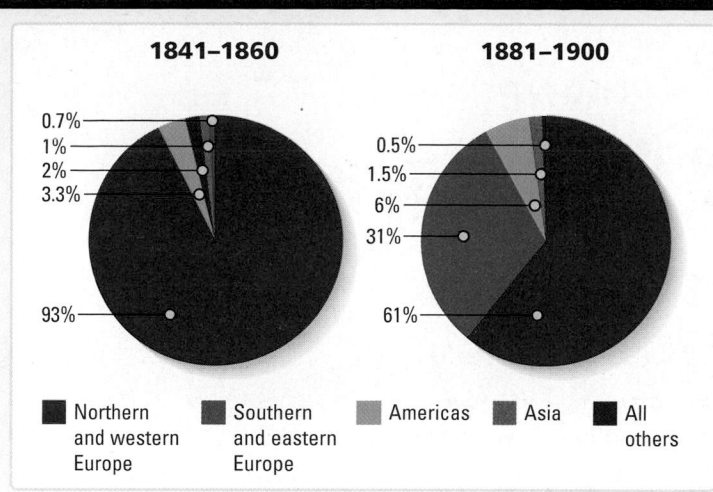

CONNECTIONS TO MATH

U.S. Immigration, *1841–1900*

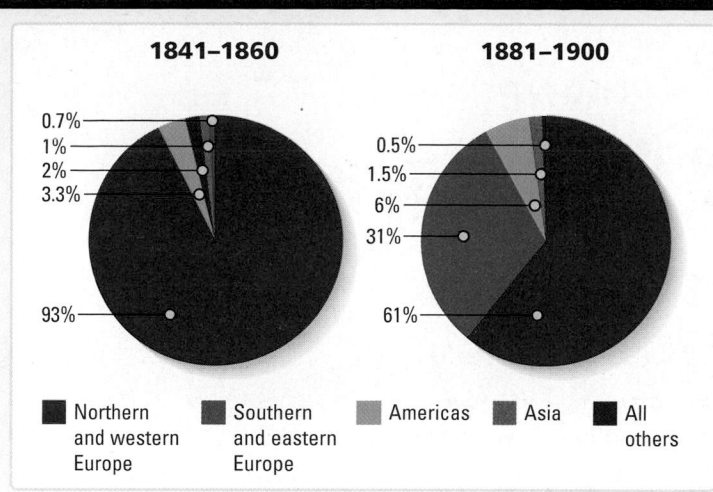

1841–1860

- 0.7%
- 1%
- 2%
- 3.3%
- 93%

1881–1900

- 0.5%
- 1.5%
- 6%
- 31%
- 61%

- ■ Northern and western Europe
- ■ Southern and eastern Europe
- ■ Americas
- ■ Asia
- ■ All others

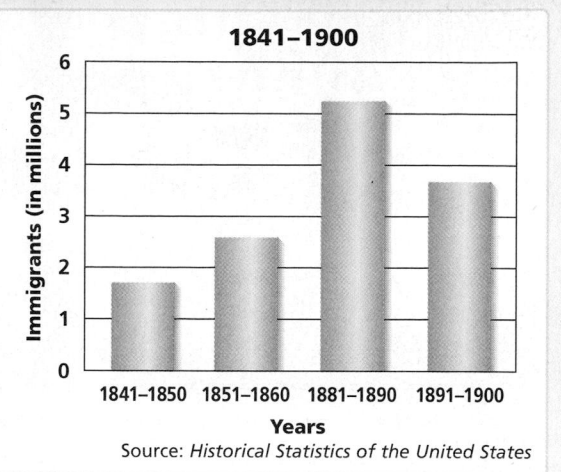

1841–1900

Immigrants (in millions)

1841–1850 1851–1860 1881–1890 1891–1900

Years

Source: *Historical Statistics of the United States*

SKILLBUILDER Interpreting Graphs

1. *About how many immigrants came to the United States from 1841 to 1860?*
2. *About how many southern and eastern European immigrants came to the United States from 1881 to 1900?*

While European immigrants passed through Ellis Island on the East Coast, Asians landed at **Angel Island** in San Francisco Bay. In Angel Island's filthy buildings, most Chinese immigrants were held for several weeks. One unhappy prisoner carved in the wall, "For what reason must I sit in jail? It is only because my country is weak and my family poor."

Many Mexican immigrants entered the United States through Texas. Jesús [heh•SOOS] Garza recalled how simple his journey was. "I paid my $8, passed my examination, then changed my Mexican coins for American money and went to San Antonio, Texas."

Settling in America

Immigrants settled where they could find jobs. Many found work in American factories. The immigrants contributed to the growth of cities such as New York, Boston, Philadelphia, Pittsburgh, and Chicago. About half of the new immigrants settled in four industrial states: Massachusetts, New York, Pennsylvania, and Illinois.

Once in America, newer immigrants looked for people from the same village in the old country to help them find jobs and housing. People with similar ethnic backgrounds often moved to the same neighborhoods. As a result, ethnic neighborhoods with names like "Little Italy" and "Chinatown" became common in American cities.

The immigrants living in these communities pooled money to build places of worship for their neighborhoods. They published newspapers in their native languages. They commonly supported political machines, often led by politicians who had also come from their country of origin. Such politicians could speak the native language and help new arrivals feel comfortable. Most importantly, politicians could help immigrants find jobs.

*Reading*History
A. Identifying Problems How did immigrants show creativity in solving problems?

"I paid my $8, passed my examination, . . . and went to San Antonio."

Jesús Garza

Changes in American Life **615**

Labor unions helped immigrants fit into American life. The various languages on the signs at this rally show the ethnic diversity in the labor movement.

Immigrants Take Tough Jobs

Immigrants took whatever jobs they could get. Many immigrants worked in Northern factories. As you read in Chapter 20, most factories offered low wages, long hours, and unsafe conditions. Many European immigrants who had settled in the East found jobs in sweatshops for about $10 a week. One observer of textile sweatshops noted, "The faces, hands, and arms to the elbows of everyone in the room are black with the color of the cloth on which they are working."

While European immigrants settled mostly in the East and Midwest, Asian immigrants settled mostly in the West. Many Chinese immigrants worked on the railroad. Others settled in Western cities where they set up businesses such as restaurants and stores. Large numbers of Japanese immigrants first came to Hawaii in 1885 to work on sugar plantations. Others settled on the mainland, where they fished, farmed, and worked in mines.

Immigrants from Mexico came to the Southwest. Mexican immigration increased after 1910 when revolution in that country forced people to flee. Growers and ranchers in California and Texas used the cheap labor Mexican immigrants offered. Owners of copper mines in Arizona hired Mexicans as well.

Reading **History**

B. Making Inferences What did all the immigrants seem to have in common?

Becoming Americans

Some Americans have described the United States as a **melting pot,** or a place where cultures blend. The new immigrants blended into American society as earlier immigrants had. This process of blending into society is called **assimilation.** Most new immigrants were eager to assimilate. To do so, they studied English and how to be American citizens.

Many workers began to assimilate at work. Employers and labor unions both tried to "Americanize" immigrant workers by offering classes in citizenship and English. A Lithuanian worker explained that his labor union helped him learn to "read and speak and enjoy life like an American." He then became an interpreter for the union to help other Lithuanians become Americans.

At the same time the immigrants were learning about America, they were also *changing* America. Immigrants did not give up their cultures right away. Bits and pieces of immigrant languages, foods, and music worked their way into the rest of American culture.

Despite their efforts to assimilate, immigrants faced prejudice from native-born Americans. Many Protestants feared the arrival of Catholics and Jews. Other native-born Americans thought immigrants would not fit into democratic society because they would be controlled by political machines. Such prejudices led some native-born Americans to push for restrictions to reduce the numbers of new immigrants coming to America.

Restrictions on Immigration

Many native-born Americans also feared they would have to compete with immigrants for jobs. Immigrants were desperate for jobs and would often take work for lower wages in worse conditions than other Americans. Some Americans worried that there would not be enough jobs for everyone. These fears led to an upsurge in nativist opposition to immigration. In 1882, Congress began to pass laws to restrict immigration. They placed taxes on new immigrants and banned specific groups, such as beggars and people with diseases. Nonwhites faced deeper prejudice than European immigrants, and Asians faced some of the worst. In 1882, Congress passed the **Chinese Exclusion Act.** It banned Chinese immigration for ten years.

The Chinese Exclusion Act was not the only example of prejudice in America around 1900. As you will read in the next section, racial discrimination was common throughout the United States.

Background
The Chinese Exclusion Act was renewed in 1892. In 1902, the ban was made permanent. It was not repealed until 1943.

Now and then

LATE 20TH-CENTURY IMMIGRATION

Historians refer to the people who came to the United States around 1900 as the "new immigrants." But an even newer wave of immigrants has been coming to the United States since the 1980s.

From 1981 to 1996, nearly 13.5 million people immigrated to the United States. About 6.5 million came from other nations in the Western Hemisphere. In the same period, 4.8 million people came from Asia.

Section 2 Assessment

1. Terms & Names

Explain the significance of:
- new immigrants
- Ellis Island
- Angel Island
- melting pot
- assimilation
- Chinese Exclusion Act

2. Using Graphics

Use a chart to take notes on immigrant experiences in the United States.

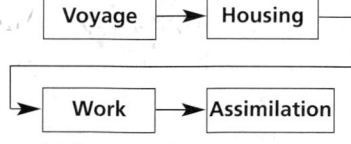

Which part of the immigrant experience was the most difficult?

3. Main Ideas

a. How were the new immigrants different from earlier immigrants?

b. How did immigrants support one another?

c. Why did nonwhite immigrants have a harder time assimilating than European immigrants did?

4. Critical Thinking

Making Generalizations
How well does the idea of the melting pot reflect U.S. immigration around 1900?

THINK ABOUT
- assimilation
- immigrant languages and cultures
- ethnic neighborhoods

ACTIVITY OPTIONS

MATH
GEOGRAPHY

Research immigration to your city or state. Create a **spreadsheet** of this information or draw a **map** showing immigration routes.

from

Dragonwings

by Laurence Yep

In 1903, eight-year-old Moon Shadow makes the long journey from China to join his father in San Francisco. After living for a time in Chinatown, the two move into a white neighborhood where Moon Shadow's father takes a job as a handyman working for Miss Whitlaw, who runs a boarding house for elderly people. Moon Shadow makes friends with Miss Whitlaw's niece Robin. In April of 1906, their world is turned upside down. As Moon Shadow goes outside to fetch water from the pump, an earthquake hits San Francisco, endangering rich and poor, young and old, American and immigrant alike.

The morning was filled with that soft, gentle twilight of spring, when everything is filled with soft, dreamy colors and shapes; so when the earthquake hit, I did not believe it at first. It seemed like a nightmare where everything you take to be the rock-hard, solid basis for reality becomes unreal.

Wood and stone and brick and the very earth became fluidlike. The pail beneath the pump jumped and rattled like a spider dancing on a hot stove. The ground deliberately seemed to slide right out from under me. I landed on my back hard enough to drive the wind from my lungs. The whole world had become unglued. Our stable and Miss Whitlaw's house and the tenements to either side heaved and bobbed up and down, riding the ground like ships on a heavy sea. Down the alley mouth, I could see the cobblestone street **undulate**[1] and twist like a red-backed snake.

From inside our stable, I could hear the cups and plates begin to rattle on their shelves, and the equipment on Father's work table clattered and rumbled **ominously**.[2]

Suddenly the door banged open and Father stumbled out with his clothes all in a bundle. "It's an earthquake, I think," he shouted. He had washed his hair the night before and had not had time to twist it into a **queue**,[3] so it hung down his back long and black.

He looked around in the back yard. It was such a wide, open space that we were fairly safe there. Certainly more safe than in the frame doorway of our stable. He got into his pants and shirt and then his socks and boots.

"Do you think one of the mean dragons is doing all this?" I asked him.

"Maybe. Maybe not." Father had sat down to stuff his feet into his boots. "Time to wonder about that later. Now you wait here."

He started to get to his feet when the second tremor shook and he fell forward flat on his face. I heard the city bells ringing. They were rung by no human hand—the earthquake had just shaken them in their steeples. The second tremor was worse than the first. From all over came an immense wall of noise: of metal tearing, of bricks crashing, of wood breaking free from wood nails, and all. Everywhere, what man had built came undone. I was looking at a tenement house to our right and it just seemed to shudder and then collapse. One moment there were solid wooden walls and the next moment it had fallen with the cracking of wood and the tinkling of glass and the screams of people inside.

---

1. **undulate:** to move like a wave.
2. **ominously:** threateningly.
3. **queue:** a long braid of hair hanging down the back.

Mercifully, for a moment, it was lost to view in the cloud of dust that rose up. The debris surged against Miss Whitlaw's fence and toppled it over with a creak and a groan and a crash. I saw an arm sticking up from the mound of rubble and the hand was twisted at an impossible angle from the wrist. Coughing, Father pulled at my arm. "Stay here now," he ordered and started for Miss Whitlaw's.

I turned. Her house was still standing, but the tenement house to the left had partially collapsed; the wall on our side and part of the front and back had just fallen down, revealing the apartments within: the laundry hanging from lines, the old brass beds, and a few lucky if astonished people just looking out dazedly on what had once been walls. I could see Jack sitting up in bed with his two brothers. His mother and father were standing by the bed holding on to Maisie. Their whole family crowded into a tiny two-room apartment. Then they were gone, disappearing in a cloud of dust and debris as the walls and floor collapsed. Father held me as I cried.

Miss Whitlaw came out onto her porch in her nightdress and a shawl. She pulled the shawl tighter about her shoulders. *"Are you all right?"*

"Yes," Father said, patting me on the back.

"Aren't we, Moon Shadow?"

"Yes." I wiped my eyes on my sleeves.

"Is everyone okay inside?" Father asked Miss Whitlaw.

She nodded. We joined her on the porch and walked with her into her house. Robin was sitting on the stairs that led up to the second floor. She huddled up, looking no longer like the noisy, **boisterous**[4] girl I knew. The front door was open before her. She must have gone outside to look. *"Just about the whole street's gone."*

From up the stairs we could hear the **querulous**[5] old voices of the boarders demanding to know what had happened. Miss Whitlaw shouted up the stairs, "Everything's all right."

"Are you sure?" Father asked quietly.

Miss Whitlaw laughed. *"From top to bottom. Papa always built well. He said he wanted a house that could hold a herd of thundering elephants—that was what he always called Mama's folks. He never liked them much."*

"It's gone," Robin repeated. *"Just about the whole street's gone."*

"Oh, really now." Miss Whitlaw walked past Robin. We followed her out the front door to the front porch. Robin was right.

---

4. **boisterous:** loud, noisy.

5. **querulous:** complaining.

San Franciscans watch the destruction caused by the 1906 earthquake and the resulting fire.

CONNECT TO HISTORY

1. **Finding Main Ideas** How does the earthquake affect the neighborhood that Moon Shadow lives in?

   S See Skillbuilder Handbook, page R5.

CONNECT TO TODAY

2. **Researching** What happened in San Francisco after the quake? Did it affect the immigrants differently than others?

For more about the San Francisco earthquake . . .

RESEARCH LINKS
CLASSZONE.COM

619

Segregation and Discrimination

MAIN IDEA	WHY IT MATTERS NOW	TERMS & NAMES
Racial discrimination ran through American society in the late 19th and early 20th centuries.	Modern American society continues to face the problems caused by racism and discrimination.	racial discrimination Booker T. Washington Jim Crow W. E. B. Du Bois segregation NAACP *Plessy* v. *Ferguson* Ida B. Wells

ONE AMERICAN'S STORY

African-American sisters Bessie and Sadie Delany grew up in North Carolina in the early 20th century. Almost 100 years later, they described their first taste of <u>racial discrimination</u>, different treatment on the basis of race.

A VOICE FROM THE PAST

We were about five and seven years old. . . . Mama and Papa used to take us to Pullen Park . . . and that particular day, the trolley driver told us to go to the back. We children objected loudly, because we always liked to sit in the front. . . . But Mama and Papa just gently told us to hush and took us to the back.

Sarah L. Delany and A. Elizabeth Delany, *Having Our Say*

Bessie (left) and Sadie Delany

    As you will read in this section, racial discrimination was common throughout the United States.

Taking Notes

Use your chart to take notes about changes in civil rights.

Changes in American Life

Racism Causes Discrimination

As you read in earlier chapters, racist attitudes had been developing in America since the introduction of slavery. The low social rank held by slaves led many whites to believe that whites were superior to blacks. Most whites held similar attitudes toward Asians, Native Americans, and Latin Americans. Even most scientists of the day believed that whites were superior to nonwhites. However, no scientists believe this today.

Such attitudes led whites to discriminate against nonwhites across the country. The most obvious example of racial discrimination was in the South. Southern blacks had their first taste of political power during Reconstruction. (See Chapter 18.) But when Reconstruction ended in 1877, Southern states began to restrict African Americans' rights.

Segregation Expands in the South

One way for whites to weaken African-American political power was to restrict their voting rights. For example, Southern states passed laws that set up literacy, or reading, tests and poll taxes to prevent African Americans from voting. White officials made sure that blacks failed literacy tests by giving unfair exams. For example, white officials sometimes gave blacks tests written in Latin. Poll taxes kept many blacks from voting because they didn't have enough cash to pay the tax.

Such laws threatened to prevent poor whites from voting, too. To keep them from losing the vote, several Southern states added grandfather clauses to their constitutions. Grandfather clauses stated that a man could vote if he or an ancestor, such as a grandfather, had been eligible to vote before 1867. Before that date, most African Americans, free or enslaved, did not have the right to vote. Whites could use the grandfather clause to protect their voting rights. Blacks could not.

In addition to voting restrictions, African Americans faced Jim Crow laws. **Jim Crow** laws were meant to enforce **segregation,** or separation, of white and black people in public places. As a result, separate schools, trolley seats, and restrooms were common throughout the South.

Plessy v. Ferguson

African Americans resisted segregation, but they had little power to stop it. In 1892, Homer Plessy, an African American, sued a railroad company, arguing that segregated seating violated his Fourteenth Amendment right to "equal protection of the laws."

In 1896, the case of ***Plessy v. Ferguson*** reached the Supreme Court. The Court ruled against Plessy. It argued that "separate but equal" facilities did not violate the Fourteenth Amendment. This decision allowed Southern states to maintain segregated institutions.

But the separate facilities were not equal. White-controlled governments and companies allowed the facilities for African Americans to decay. African Americans would have to organize to fight for equality.

Reading **History**
A. Recognizing Effects What was the purpose behind literacy tests, poll taxes, and grandfather clauses?

Reading **History**
B. Identifying Problems Why was a policy of "separate but equal" unfair?

Segregation forced African Americans to use separate entrances from whites and to attend separate, usually inferior, schools like the one shown below.

African Americans Organize

<u>Booker T. Washington</u> was an early leader in the effort to achieve equality. He had been born into slavery. But after the Civil War, he became a teacher. In 1881, he founded the Tuskegee Institute in Alabama to help African Americans learn trades and gain economic strength. Washington hired talented teachers and scholars, such as George Washington Carver.

Background
Carver made important discoveries to improve farming.

To gain white support for Tuskegee, Washington did not openly challenge segregation. As he said in an 1895 speech in Atlanta, in "purely social matters" whites and blacks "can be as separate as the fingers, yet one as the hand in all things essential to mutual progress."

However, some blacks disagreed with Washington's views. <u>W. E. B. Du Bois</u> (doo•BOYS) encouraged African Americans to reject segregation.

A VOICE FROM THE PAST

Is it possible . . . that nine millions of men can make effective progress in economic lines if they are deprived of political rights? . . . If history and reason give any distinct answer to these questions, it is an emphatic *No.*

W. E. B. Du Bois, *The Souls of Black Folk*

*Reading*History
C. Making Inferences In what way did Washington and Du Bois disagree about how to achieve African-American progress?

In 1909, Du Bois and other reformers founded the National Association for the Advancement of Colored People, or the **NAACP**. The NAACP played a major role in ending segregation in the 20th century.

Violence in the South and North

Besides discrimination, African Americans in the South also faced violence. The Ku Klux Klan, which first appeared during Reconstruction, used violence to keep blacks from challenging segregation. More than 2,500 African Americans were lynched between 1885 and 1900.

Ida B. Wells, an African-American journalist from Memphis, led the fight against lynching. After three of her friends were lynched in 1892, she mounted an anti-lynching campaign in her newspaper. When whites called for Wells herself to be lynched, she moved to Chicago. But she continued her work against lynching. (See Interactive Primary Sources, page 624.)

Like Wells, many blacks moved north to escape discrimination. Public facilities there were not segregated by law. But Northern whites still discriminated against blacks. Blacks could not get housing in white neighborhoods and usually were denied good jobs. Anti-black feelings among whites sometimes led to violence. In 1908, whites in Springfield, Illinois, attacked blacks who had moved there. The whites lynched two blacks within a half mile of Abraham Lincoln's home.

AMERICA'S HISTORY MAKERS

W. E. B. DU BOIS
1868–1963

W. E. B. Du Bois grew up in a middle-class home. He went to college and earned his doctorate at Harvard. Du Bois became one of the most distinguished scholars of the 20th century.

Du Bois fought against segregation. He believed that the best way to end it would be to have educated African Americans lead the fight. He referred to this group of educated African Americans as the "Talented Tenth"—the most educated 10 percent of African Americans.

Why do you think Du Bois believed the Talented Tenth should lead the fight against segregation?

Racism in the West

Chinese immigrants who came to the West in the 1800s also faced severe discrimination. Chinese laborers received lower wages than whites for the same work. Sometimes, Chinese workers faced violence. In 1885, white workers in Rock Springs, Wyoming, refused to work in the same mine as Chinese workers. The whites stormed through the Chinese part of town, shooting Chinese people and burning buildings. During the attack, 28 Chinese people were killed and 15 were wounded.

At the same time, Mexicans and African Americans who came to the American Southwest were forced into peonage (PEE•uh•nihj). In this system of labor, people are forced to work until they have paid off debts. Congress outlawed peonage in 1867, but some workers were still forced to work to repay debts. In 1911, the U.S. Supreme Court declared such labor to be the same as peonage. As a result, the Court struck down such forms of labor as a violation of the Thirteenth Amendment.

Despite the problems caused by racism, many Americans had new opportunities to enjoy their lives at the turn of the century. In the next section, you will learn about changes in people's daily lives.

Background
The Thirteenth Amendment banned "involuntary servitude"—another term for slavery.

The Workingmen's Party of California produced this anti-Chinese poster during the 1880s.

Section 3 Assessment

1. Terms & Names

Explain the significance of:
- racial discrimination
- Jim Crow
- segregation
- *Plessy* v. *Ferguson*
- Booker T. Washington
- W. E. B. Du Bois
- NAACP
- Ida B. Wells

2. Using Graphics

Use a chart to identify people and events related to racial discrimination at the turn of the century.

People	
Events	

Which person do you think did the most to end racial discrimination?

3. Main Ideas

a. What were Jim Crow laws?

b. How did discrimination against African Americans in the North differ from discrimination in the South?

c. What did Chinese immigrants and Mexican immigrants have in common?

4. Critical Thinking

Solving Problems What could have been done to end racial discrimination against nonwhites in the United States at the turn of the century?

THINK ABOUT
- attitudes of whites about nonwhites
- the efforts of nonwhites to find jobs and security
- competition for jobs

ACTIVITY OPTIONS

LANGUAGE ARTS
TECHNOLOGY

Research a civil rights leader from the turn of the century. Write a short **biography** of that person or design a **Web site** devoted to the work of that person.

from *Crusade for Justice* (1892)

Setting the Stage Ida B. Wells was the editor of the *Free Speech and Headlight,* a small Baptist newspaper in Memphis, Tennessee. She used the paper to attack the evils of Jim Crow, especially lynching. In her auto-biography, *Crusade for Justice,* she described the events that led to the lynching of three of her friends. **See Primary Source Explorer**

A CLOSER LOOK

ECONOMIC COMPETITION

Moss, McDowell, and Stewart were African Americans who opened a grocery store near a white-owned store in a black neighborhood.

1. Why might the opening of the black-owned grocery store lead to problems?

A CLOSER LOOK

LYNCHINGS

There was a sharp increase in the number of lynchings in the United States in the 1890s. From 1891 to 1900, more than 1,100 African Americans were lynched.

2. Why do you think the number of lynchings increased in this period?

A CLOSER LOOK

THE GREAT MIGRATION

Between 1890 and 1920, hundreds of thousands of African Americans left the South to escape racism. This movement is called the Great Migration.

3. Why does Wells's newspaper advise African Americans to move away in the wake of the lynching?

While I was thus carrying on the work of my newspaper . . . there came the lynching in Memphis which changed the whole course of my life. . . .

Thomas Moss, Calvin McDowell, and Henry Stewart owned and operated a grocery store. . . . There was already a grocery owned and operated by a white man who **hitherto**[1] had had a **monopoly**[2] on the trade of this thickly populated colored suburb. Thomas's grocery changed all that, and he and his **associates**[3] were made to feel that they were not welcome by the white grocer. . . .

About ten o'clock that [one Saturday] night, . . . shots rang out in the back room of the store. The men stationed there had seen several white men steal-ing through the rear door and fired on them without a moment's pause. Three of these men were wounded, and others fled and gave the alarm.

Sunday morning's paper came out with **lurid**[4] headlines telling how officers of the law had been wounded while in the **discharge**[5] of their duties. . . . The same newspaper told of the arrest and jailing of the **proprietor**[6] of the store and many of the colored people. . . .

On Tuesday following, . . . a body of picked [white] men was admitted to the jail. . . . This mob took out of their cells Thomas Moss, Calvin McDowell, and Henry Stewart. . . . They were loaded on a switch engine of the railroad which ran back of the jail, carried a mile north of the city limits, and horribly shot to death.

Although stunned by the events of that hectic week, the *Free Speech* [Wells's newspaper] felt that it must carry on. Its [lead article] for that week said:

The city of Memphis has demonstrated that neither character nor standing **avails**[7] the Negro if he dares to protect himself against the white man or become his rival. There is nothing we can do about the lynching now, as we are out-numbered and without arms. The white mob could help itself to ammunition without pay, but the order was rigidly enforced against the selling of guns to Negroes. There is therefore only one thing left that we can do; save our money and leave a town which will neither protect our lives and property, nor give us a fair trial in the courts, but takes us out and murders us in cold blood when accused by white persons.

1. **hitherto:** until this time.
2. **monopoly:** exclusive control by one person or group.
3. **associates:** friends or partners.
4. **lurid:** causing shock or horror.
5. **discharge:** performance of duty.
6. **proprietor:** owner.
7. **avails:** helps.

Like Country Pretty Much

Setting the Stage Kee Low was a Chinese immigrant. He had come to the United States in 1876. He was interviewed in 1924 as part of a project by scholars to create a "Survey of Race Relations." This is an excerpt from that interview. In it, Kee Low tells his story. Despite the racism, he still "like country pretty much." **See Primary Source Explorer** 💿

I arrived in San Francisco in 1876, 49 years ago. Come to San Francisco when country one hundred years old. People treat Chinese rotten then. Don't blame people much at that time. Chinese and European not educated as much then as today. More civilized today. People drive Chinese out of country. . . .

I was living on the waterfront, and they told me to get out one day. Sunday morning, they come together and drive Chinese out. . . . They want to get us out to San Francisco, to go on steamer, and we stayed on the **wharf**[1] all night, and they bring us little black coffee and little bread in morning. We pretty hungry. The last day, some of the citizens, Judge Greene, Judge Hanford, United States Attorney, nice fellow want to help us. . . . Judge Greene told the Chinese that those who wanted to stay and make good citizens could stay, and those who wanted to go could go. One half wanted to go, and one half wanted to stay. . . .

There were so many around the streets that they had to have somebody to protect these people. Some of the **hobos**[2] tried to make them go back to the wharf, but volunteers tried to keep these fellows away. They **commenced**[3] shooting and kill one of them. So Chinese people get excited when gun begin to sound, so they throw shoes, blankets and everything and run. I was uptown myself. I didn't intend to go. I ran outside to see what happened because I was so excited. . . . Call up one or two friends of mine and tell them get killed, and we better get out of the way. We run out in woods. Build fire. Pretty cold. I told friends, we got to protect ourselves. We got to get out of here.

1. **wharf:** landing place for ships.　2. **hobos:** homeless people.　3. **commenced:** began.

A CLOSER LOOK

RACIST ATTITUDES

Some people believe that racism is caused by ignorance.

4. Why does Kee Low believe that discrimination against the Chinese was worse in the 1870s than in the 1920s?

A CLOSER LOOK

REASONS TO STAY

Despite the violence that they faced for having Asian ancestry, half of the Chinese with Kee Low wanted to stay in the United States.

5. Why do you think Asian-Americans stayed in the United States despite discrimination?

Interactive Primary Sources Assessment

1. Main Ideas

a. What do the accounts of Wells and Low have in common?

b. How did the officers of the law behave differently in the report by Low than in the one by Wells?

c. What conclusions do Wells and Low come to about how someone should respond to discrimination?

2. Critical Thinking

Forming and Supporting Opinions Do you think Wells and Low were right to flee racism? Why?

THINK ABOUT
- the causes of racism
- the threat of violence to Wells and Low

Society and Mass Culture

MAIN IDEA	WHY IT MATTERS NOW	TERMS & NAMES
Industrialization and new technologies created a mass culture in the United States.	Modern American mass culture had its beginnings during this period.	mass culture mail-order catalog Joseph Pulitzer leisure William Randolph Hearst vaudeville department store ragtime

ONE AMERICAN'S STORY

Mary Ellen Chase dreaded her first day of teaching, but she did her best to control the class.

A VOICE FROM THE PAST

I stormed up and down. . . . This pathetic pretense of courage, aided by the mad flourishing of my razor strop, brought forth . . . the expression of respectful fear on the faces of the young giants.

Mary Ellen Chase, quoted in *The Good Old Days—They Were Terrible!*

Students work on their lessons in this New York City classroom in 1906.

In this section, you will learn how education helped create an American **mass culture**—a common culture experienced by large numbers of people.

Taking Notes

Use your chart to take notes about changes in education and mass culture.

Changes in American Life

Education and Publishing Grow

Immigration caused enormous growth in American schools. To teach citizenship and English to immigrants, new city and state laws required children to attend school. Between 1880 and 1920, the number of children attending school more than doubled. To serve the growing number of students, the number of public high schools increased from 2,526 in 1890 to 14,326 in 1920.

The growth of education increased American literacy. Reading became more popular. Americans read large numbers of novels. Dime novels were especially popular. They sold for ten cents each and told exciting tales of romance and adventure, often set in the West or on the high seas.

Americans also read more newspapers. Tough competition pushed newspaper publishers to try all sorts of gimmicks to outsell their rivals. For example, **Joseph Pulitzer,** owner of the *New York World,* and

William Randolph Hearst, owner of the *New York Morning Journal,* were fierce competitors. They filled the pages of their papers with spectacular stories. They also added special features, such as comics and sports.

Modern Advertising and New Products

Newspapers had a wide influence on American life, including the rise of modern advertising. Advertisers used images of celebrities in newspapers and magazines to tempt people to buy products. They advertised everything from cereal to jewelry to soap. Some ads played on people's fears. For example, advertisers might scare a young woman concerned about her appearance into buying a particular brand of face cream. Advertising was effective in turning brand names into household words.

Advertisements also helped people learn about new products. At the turn of the century, new inventions, such as the electric washing machine, promised to help people do their household chores more easily. Because women did most of these chores as well as most of the shopping, manufacturers marketed these new devices to women.

One of the places people could buy these—and many other—goods was in department stores. **Department stores** sold everything from clothing to furniture to hardware. The Chicago businessman Marshall Field discovered as a sales clerk that he could increase his sales by paying close attention to each woman customer. Field opened his own department store in downtown Chicago with the motto, "Give the lady what she wants."

People who did not live near a department store could order goods through the mail. Companies like Montgomery Ward and Sears Roebuck sent catalogs to customers. These **mail-order catalogs** included pictures and descriptions of merchandise. People could place their orders by mail, and the company would deliver the product. Richard Sears claimed that he sold 10,000 items a minute.

In 1896, the post office made it easier for people to receive goods through the mail by establishing a new delivery system. Rural free delivery brought packages directly to homes in rural areas. Now people in these areas could get the same goods as people in the cities.

*Reading***History**

A. Summarizing What developments changed American methods of selling at the turn of the century?

STRANGE *but* True

BICYCLES TO AIRPLANES

At the turn of the century, two bicycle mechanics invented a machine that would help advertisers and businessmen reach new customers. In 1892, Orville and Wilbur Wright opened a bicycle shop in Ohio. They used the profits to fund experiments in aeronautics, the construction of aircraft.

In 1903, the Wright brothers took a gasoline-powered airplane that they had designed to a sandy hill outside Kitty Hawk, North Carolina. On December 17 of that year, Orville made the first successful flight of a powered aircraft in history. By 1918, the U.S. Postal Service began airmail service that made it faster and easier for people to get goods.

Urban Parks and World's Fairs

Advertising and shopping were not the only daily activities changing at this time. **Leisure,** or free time, activities also changed. In cities, new parks provided people with entertainment. The increasing number of people working in factories and offices liked going to parks to get some sunshine and fresh air. Parks helped bring grass and trees back into city landscapes.

▼ Coney Island
Visitors to New York's Coney Island cool off in the Steeple-chase Pool.

▼ World's Fair
Visitors to the 1893 world's fair in Chicago saw exotic sights, such as elephants.

▼ Football
Excited fans watch the 1881 Harvard–Yale football game at the Polo Grounds in New York.

Central Park in New York City is the nation's best-known urban park. Opened in 1876, Central Park looked like the country. Trees and shrubs dotted its gently rolling landscape. Winding walkways let city dwellers imagine they were strolling in the woods. People could also ride bicycles and play sports in the park.

In addition to urban parks, amusement parks provided a place people could go for fun. The most famous amusement park was Coney Island in New York City. Completed in 1904, Coney Island had shops, food vendors, and exciting rides like roller coasters. One immigrant woman said Coney Island "is just like what I see when I dream of heaven!"

World's fairs provided another wildly popular form of entertainment for Americans. Between 1876 and 1916, several U.S. cities, including Philadelphia, Chicago, St. Louis, and San Francisco, hosted world's fairs. The fairs were designed to show off American technology. The 1876 fair in Philadelphia displayed Alexander Graham Bell's newly invented telephone. Millions of people attended these fairs. Nearly 10 million attended the Philadelphia fair alone. Visitors were drawn to foods, shows, and amusements. The historian Thomas Schlereth described the giant wheel built by George Ferris at the 1893 Chicago fair.

Reading **History**
B. Comparing and Contrasting What did urban parks and world's fairs have in common?

A VOICE FROM THE PAST

Chicago's answer to Paris's 1889 Eiffel Tower, Ferris's 264-foot bicycle wheel in the sky dominated the landscape. With thirty-six cars, each larger than a Pullman coach and capable of holding 60 people, the wheel, when fully loaded, rotated 2,160 people in the air.

Thomas Schlereth, *Victorian America*

Spectator Sports

During this time, spectator sports also became popular entertainment. Baseball, football, boxing, and many other sports drew thousands of people to fields and gyms around the country.

Baseball was the most popular sport. Summer games drew crowds of enthusiastic fans. By the 1890s, baseball had standardized rules and a published schedule of games. Racial discrimination kept African-American baseball players out of baseball's American and National Leagues. In order to compete, African Americans formed their own teams in

the Negro American League and the Negro National League. (See Geography in History, pages 722–723.)

Going to the Show

In addition to sports, other forms of live entertainment attracted large audiences. **Vaudeville,** for example, featured a mixture of song, dance, and comedy. A show would have a series of acts leading up to an exciting end, which advertisers billed as the "wow finish."

New types of music also began to be heard. **Ragtime,** a blend of African-American songs and European musical forms, was an important new musical form. African-American composer Scott Joplin heard ragtime while he traveled through black communities from New Orleans to Chicago. Joplin's "Maple Leaf Rag," published in 1899, became a hit in the first decade of the 20th century.

Early in the 20th century, movies began to compete with live entertainment. The first movies were silent and were added as the final feature of a vaudeville show. Soon storefront theaters appeared that showed only movies. After 1905, these movie theaters were called nickelodeons because they charged just a nickel for admission.

Reading **History**

C. Making Inferences How do you think movies contributed to mass culture?

Movies, music, sports, and advertising contributed to shaping modern American mass culture. People across the nation experienced many of these things. In the next chapter, you will learn about different nationwide changes—the reform movements of the Progressive era.

America's HERITAGE

RAGTIME

Tired of slow waltz music, young people eagerly embraced ragtime at the turn of the century. The name probably came from a description of the rhythm of black dance music as "ragged time." Ragtime's exciting beat inspired the names of such songs as "Irresistible Fox Trot Rag," "That Fascinating Rag," and "That Nifty Rag."

Ragtime had an enormous influence on American music. Throughout the 20th century, American musical styles such as jazz, blues, rock-and-roll, rap, and rhythm-and-blues built on the style of ragtime.

Scott Joplin

Section 4 Assessment

1. Terms & Names

Explain the significance of:
- mass culture
- Joseph Pulitzer
- William Randolph Hearst
- department store
- mail-order catalog
- leisure
- vaudeville
- ragtime

2. Using Graphics

Use a diagram like the one below to note the changes that created a mass culture at the turn of the century.

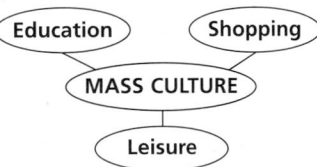

3. Main Ideas

a. What did dime novels and newspapers have in common?

b. How did new technologies change the way people bought goods?

c. What did visitors see at world's fairs?

4. Critical Thinking

Making Inferences Why did mass culture emerge during this period?

THINK ABOUT
- the impact of newspapers
- advertising and catalogs
- the development of leisure time

ACTIVITY OPTIONS

ART

LANGUAGE ARTS

Research a world's fair from the turn of the century. Then make a **poster** or write a **newspaper advertisement** that will attract people to the fair.

Chapter ㉑ ASSESSMENT

TERMS & NAMES

Briefly explain the significance of each of the following.

1. urbanization
2. Jane Addams
3. political machine
4. Ellis Island
5. assimilation
6. Jim Crow
7. *Plessy* v. *Ferguson*
8. W. E. B. Du Bois
9. Joseph Pulitzer
10. leisure

REVIEW QUESTIONS

Cities Grow and Change (pages 609–613)

1. How did public transportation change city life?
2. What dangers did urban overcrowding pose to tenement dwellers?
3. How did big-city political machines keep their power?

The New Immigrants (pages 614–619)

4. Where did most American immigrants come from around 1900?
5. How did immigrants enter the United States?
6. Why have some people described the United States as a melting pot?

Segregation and Discrimination (pages 620–625)

7. Why was *Plessy* v. *Ferguson* an important Supreme Court decision?
8. What did African-American leaders do to fight discrimination?

Society and Mass Culture (pages 626–629)

9. What is mass culture?
10. How did city parks improve city life?

CRITICAL THINKING

1. USING YOUR NOTES: CATEGORIZING INFORMATION

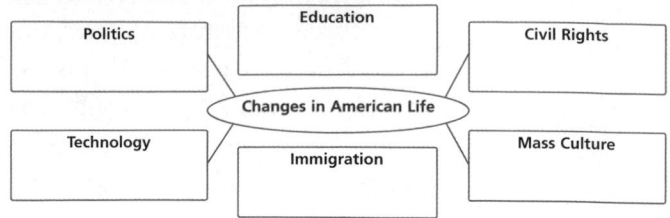

Using your completed chart, answer the questions below:

a. What changes did increased immigration cause?
b. How did the growing popularity of spectator sports and movies help bring about mass culture?
c. Which changes helped immigrants assimilate into American life?

2. ANALYZING LEADERSHIP

Think about the actions of Booker T. Washington and W. E. B. Du Bois. What approach did each take against discrimination? Whose approach do you think was the most likely to be effective?

3. THEME: DIVERSITY AND UNITY

How do you think the emergence of mass culture around 1900 affected immigrants and nonwhites?

4. APPLYING CITIZENSHIP SKILLS

What kinds of things prevented African Americans and immigrants from having full citizenship? How did they attempt to participate in American politics?

Interact *with* History

Have your ideas about how you'll make a home in the United States changed after reading the chapter? Explain

VISUAL SUMMARY

Changes in American Life

Cities Grow and Change
Industrialization caused American cities to grow.

The New Immigrants
Large numbers of immigrants, especially from southern and eastern Europe, came to the United States.

American Life Around 1900

Segregation and Discrimination
Racial and ethnic minorities faced discrimination across the country.

Society and Mass Culture
New leisure activities and mass culture emerged at this time.

630

STANDARDS-BASED ASSESSMENT

Use the graph and your knowledge of U.S. history to answer questions 1 and 2.

Additional Test Practice, pp. S1–S33.

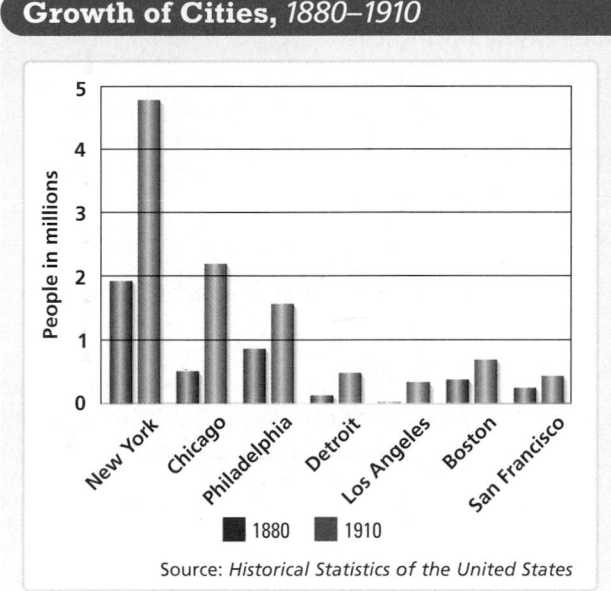

Growth of Cities, *1880–1910*

Source: *Historical Statistics of the United States*

1. Which city's population increased by the greatest amount between 1880 and 1910?
   A. Boston
   B. Chicago
   C. New York
   D. Philadelphia

2. For which city is no 1880 population information provided?
   A. Chicago
   B. Detroit
   C. Los Angeles
   D. New York

This quotation from teacher Mary Ellen Chase is about how she controlled a classroom. Use the quotation and your knowledge of U.S. history to answer question 3.

PRIMARY SOURCE

I stormed up and down. . . . This pathetic pretense of courage, aided by the mad flourishing of my razor strop, brought forth . . . the expression of respectful fear on the faces of the young giants.

Mary Ellen Chase, quoted in *The Good Old Days—They Were Terrible!*

3. Based on this passage, which of the following best states Mary Ellen Chase's view of what was important in a classroom?
   A. fear and punishment
   B. large classrooms
   C. a physically-strong teacher
   D. respect and discipline

TEST PRACTICE
CLASSZONE.COM

ALTERNATIVE ASSESSMENT

1. 📝 **WRITING ABOUT HISTORY**

Write a **guide** for new immigrants coming to the United States at the beginning of the 20th century.

- Include information about life in the cities, job opportunities, discrimination, and leisure activities.
- Include icons or other illustrations where possible as an aid to people who are just learning English.

2. COOPERATIVE LEARNING

Work with a few of your classmates to research city parks built in the late 1800s and design your own park. Include sports fields, areas for rest, places for nature and wildlife, and buildings for food and restrooms. Divide responsibilities for researching and designing the park.

INTEGRATED TECHNOLOGY

DOING INTERNET RESEARCH

Racial discrimination has been a tragic feature of American history. Conduct research to create a museum exhibit about discrimination and civil rights.

- Use the Internet to locate primary sources such as newspaper articles or autobiographies.
- Look for information on racial or ethnic groups that faced discrimination, as well as biographies of important civil rights leaders. Then prepare a presentation for your class that illustrates how beliefs and practices have changed.

For more about racial discrimination . . .

INTERNET ACTIVITY
CLASSZONE.COM

Create an Exhibit

In 1904 the Louisiana Purchase Exposition, better known as the St. Louis World's Fair, opened to great fanfare. The event celebrated the 100th anniversary of the U.S. purchase of the Louisiana Territory from France in 1803. Taking five years to plan and opening a year late, the fair focused on education and American technology. The automobile was among the most notable attractions at the fair. People from 63 countries and 43 states gathered in St. Louis.

People stroll down The Great Pike at the St. Louis World's Fair.

ACTIVITY Create an exhibit that reflects some aspect of technology at the end of the 19th century. Then make a classroom fair. Write an article about it and give a speech describing your favorite exhibit.

TOOLBOX

Each group will need:

bifold (type of poster board that folds open)	scissors
	pencils
poster board	glue
drawing paper	cardboard
markers	

STEP BY STEP

1 **Form groups.** Each group should consist of three or four students. During the workshop, each group will be expected to:

- research technology and inventions just prior to 1904
- design and create an exhibit for a classroom fair
- write a news report about the fair
- give a speech in praise of a favorite exhibit at the fair

2 **Research the fair.** Using this chapter, books on the St. Louis fair, or the Internet, find out what kinds of exhibits were displayed. Also research the technology and inventions of the time. Some themes of the fair's massive exhibit halls are listed below. Pick one theme on which to focus. Then brainstorm ideas for your exhibit and choose the best one.

World's Fair Themes	
transportation	education
technology	the arts

The New York-to-St. Louis Automobile Parade arrives at the St. Louis World's Fair.

3 Design your exhibit.
Think about what your group wants to create. Using drawing paper, sketch a design of the exhibit in pencil. Next to your sketch, list all the items you'll need for the exhibit. Assign each person in your group certain items to bring for the next class period.

4 Lay out your display.
Use the images and text you found to visually organize the three-panel display. Vary the size of the images, type-size of the text, and include color to make your layout clear and interesting. Remember to create a title.

HELP DESK

For related information, see pages 627–628 in Chapter 21.

Researching Your Project
- *The Song of the Molimo* by Jane Cutler

For more about world's fairs . . .

RESEARCH LINKS
CLASSZONE.COM

Did You Know?
One vender at the fair had difficulty selling tea in the hot St. Louis summer. As a result, he began putting ice cubes in the tea, and sales of his "iced tea" soared.

Though there has been some controversy over who invented the ice-cream cone, the St. Louis World's Fair was the place it became popular. One story states that a vendor at the fair rolled a waffle into a cone-shaped holder when another vendor ran out of dishes. However, Italo Marchiony of New York City claimed to have been selling ice-cream cones since 1896.

A Machine for the New Century

5 Create a mini St. Louis fair. Along with the other groups, arrange the exhibits around the classroom. Walk around the room and look at the other groups' exhibits. Discuss with other groups how you created your exhibit.

REFLECT & ASSESS
- How did your group come up with its idea?
- How does your design fit into the theme of the St. Louis fair?
- What criteria did you use when judging the exhibits?

WRITE AND SPEAK

Write a newspaper article. Cover the fair as a journalist from another city. Write an article about the classroom fair, describing the atmosphere as well as the exhibits. Then give a speech in praise of the outstanding exhibit of the fair.

Modern America Emerges

"Woman must not depend upon the protection of man, but must be taught to protect herself."

—Susan B. Anthony

Suffragists marched in Washington, D.C., in 1914 in support of a constitutional amendment giving women the right to vote.

CHAPTER 22

The Progressive Era 1890–1920

Section 1
Roosevelt and Progressivism

Section 2
Taft and Wilson as Progressives

Section 3
Women Win New Rights

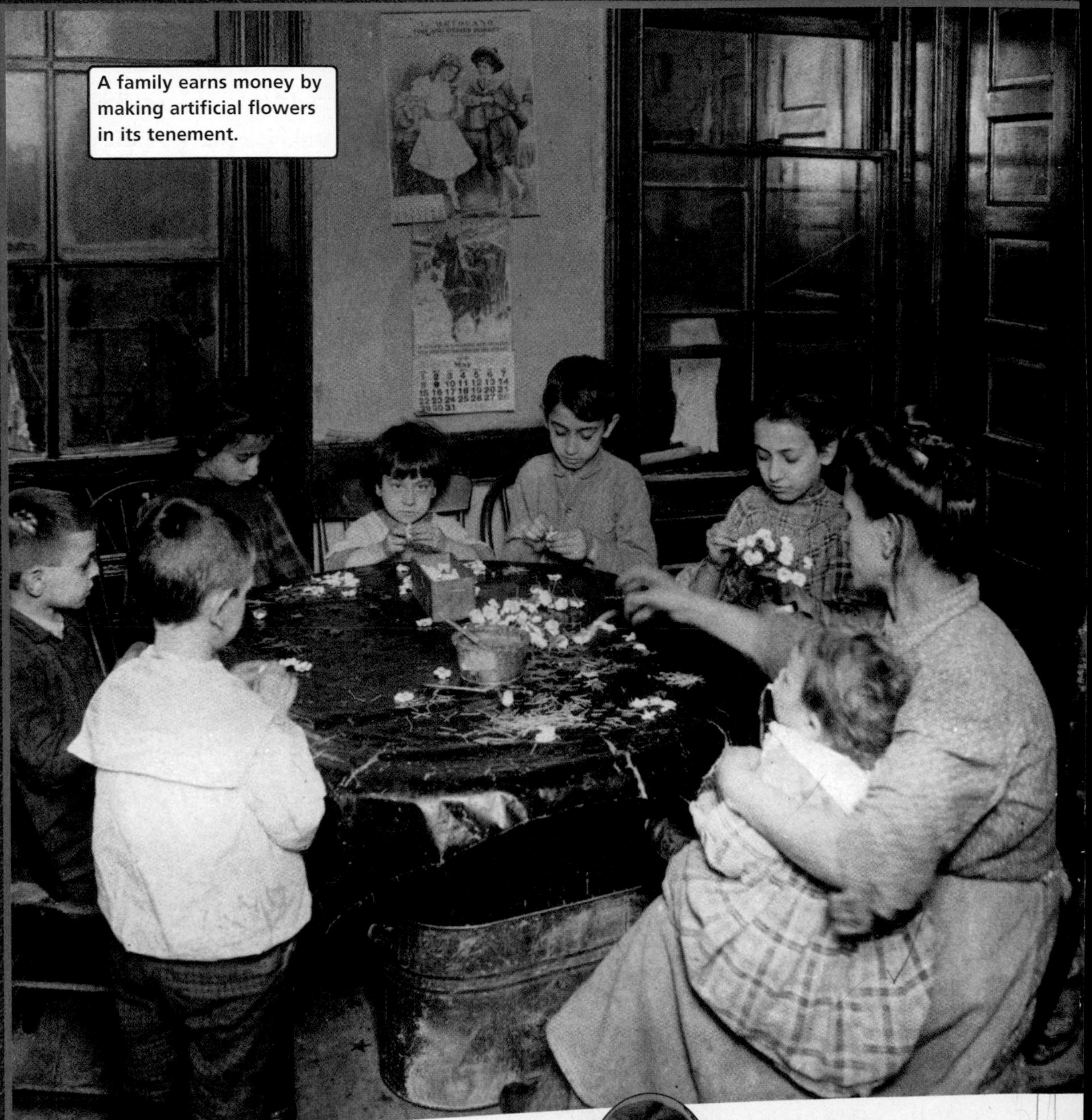

A family earns money by making artificial flowers in its tenement.

1890
Congress passes Sherman Antitrust Act.

1896
William McKinley is elected president.

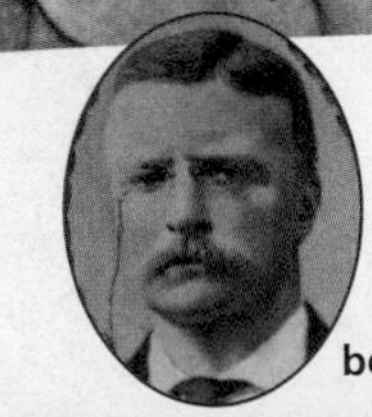

1901
McKinley is assassinated, and Theodore Roosevelt becomes president.

190
Roosevelt i reelecte presiden

USA
World
1890

1890
German leader Bismarck is dismissed by Kaiser Wilhelm II.

1894
Uganda becomes a British protectorate.

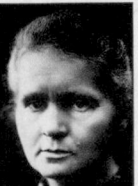

1898
Marie Curie discovers radium.

1900
Boxer uprising against foreigners begins in China.

Children play in the filth of the gutter.

It is 1901, and Theodore Roosevelt has suddenly become president. You and all Americans are counting on him to help end child labor, poverty, business abuses, and political corruption. You're anxious to see what actions the new president will take to address these problems.

How would you solve one of these problems?

What Do You Think?

- What problems do the photographs show?
- What qualities would a leader need to tackle such problems?
- What might be the cause of these problems?

RESEARCH LINKS
CLASSZONE.COM
Visit the Chapter 22 links for more information about the Progressive Era.

1908
William Howard Taft is elected president.

Henry Ford introduces the Model T automobile.

1912
Woodrow Wilson is elected president.

1913
17th Amendment provides for direct election of senators.

1919
18th Amendment outlaws alcohol.

1920
19th Amendment grants women the right to vote.

1920

1910
Union of South Africa is established.

1913
Gandhi, leader of Indian resistance movement, is arrested.

Reading Strategy: Identifying and Solving Problems

What Do You Know?

What do you know about life in American cities in the early 1900s? What problems plagued the cities? How have people living in cities overcome obstacles?

Think About

- what you've learned in previous chapters
- what you know about urban problems today
- your responses to the Interact with History about solving social problems (see page 637)

A social worker pays a visit to a poor family.

What Do You Want to Know?

 What questions do you have about the reform movements of the early 1900s? Record your questions in your notebook before you read the chapter.

Identifying and Solving Problems

This chapter focuses on the problems that Americans faced at the turn of the century and how they worked to solve those problems. A graphic organizer can help you keep track of problems and solutions. Major problems faced by the nation at the turn of the century are listed in the first column of the chart below. As you read, record solutions for these problems in the second column of the chart.

S See Skillbuilder Handbook, page R18.

 Taking Notes

PROBLEM	SOLUTION
Political: patronage; limited suffrage and democracy	
Social: poverty; alcohol abuse	
Economic: power of big corporations; unemployment	
Environmental: impure food and water; diminishing natural resources	

Roosevelt and Progressivism

MAIN IDEA	WHY IT MATTERS NOW	TERMS & NAMES
Reformers tried to solve the problems of the cities. They gained a champion in Theodore Roosevelt.	Many of the reforms of the Progressive Era have had an effect on life in America today.	progressivism referendum muckrakers recall direct primary Sherman Antitrust Act initiative Theodore Roosevelt

ONE AMERICAN'S STORY

In 1887, journalist Nellie Bly investigated an asylum—a place where people with mental illness can get help. She faked mental illness so that she could become a patient. Afterwords, Bly wrote about what she had witnessed. She described being forced to take ice cold baths.

A VOICE FROM THE PAST

My teeth chattered and my limbs were goose-fleshed and blue with cold. Suddenly I got, one after the other, three buckets of water over my head—ice-cold water, too—into my eyes, my ears, my nose and my mouth.

Nellie Bly, quoted in *Nellie Bly: Daredevil, Reporter, Feminist*

Nellie Bly

She reported that nurses choked and beat patients. Shortly after Bly's stories appeared, conditions at the asylum improved.

Like other reformers, Bly wanted to correct the wrongs in American society. All of these reformers made up the Progressive movement around the turn of the century.

The Rise of Progressivism

As you saw in Chapter 21, the rapid growth of cities and industries in the United States at the turn of the century brought many problems. Among them were poverty, the spread of slums, and poor conditions in factories. A depression in the 1890s made problems worse. In addition, corrupt political machines had won control of many city and state governments. Big corporations had gained power over the economy and government.

To attack these problems, individuals organized a number of reform movements. These reformers believed in the basic goodness of people. They also believed in democracy. The reformers were mostly native born and middle-class. They could be found in either political party. Their reform movements came to be grouped under the label **progressivism**.

Taking Notes

Use your chart to take notes about problems faced by Americans and their attempted solutions.

PROBLEM
Political: patronage; limited suffrage and de
Social: poverty; alcohol abuse
Economic: power of big corporations; unemploy
Environmental: impure food and water; diminishing

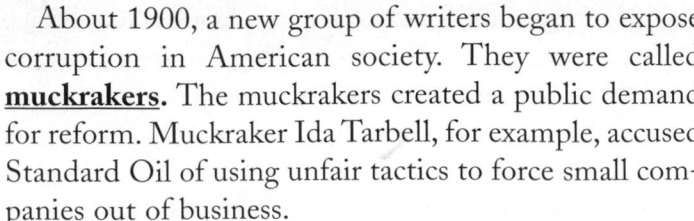
In the late 1800s, John D. Rockefeller made a fortune as he gained control of most of the nation's oil refineries, oil fields, and pipelines. In 1906, the government filed an antitrust suit against Rockefeller's Standard Oil. This resulted in its breakup in 1911. The cartoon below shows Standard Oil as an octopus.

In the 1990s, Bill Gates became the richest man in the world as he built Seattle-based Microsoft into a computer software giant. In 1998, the government filed an antitrust suit against Microsoft. It charged the company with using illegal tactics to gain a monopoly with its computer operating system and Web browser.

About 1900, a new group of writers began to expose corruption in American society. They were called **muckrakers**. The muckrakers created a public demand for reform. Muckraker Ida Tarbell, for example, accused Standard Oil of using unfair tactics to force small companies out of business.

The progressive reformers shared at least one of three basic goals: first, to reform government and expand democracy; second, to promote social welfare; third, to create economic reform.

Reforming Government and Expanding Democracy

In the 1870s and 1880s, elected officials often handed out government jobs and contracts. In return, they won political support. This practice was called patronage. It became a hot political issue during the presidencies of Rutherford B. Hayes, James Garfield, and Chester Arthur. Finally, Congress passed the Pendleton Civil Service Act in 1883. This law required people to take civil service exams for certain government jobs. It also prevented elected officials from firing civil service workers for political reasons.

In the 1890s and early 1900s, progressive leaders in a number of states sought to expand democracy. They wanted to give voters more control over their government. In 1903, under progressive governor Robert M. La Follette, Wisconsin became the first state to establish a direct primary. In a **direct primary,** voters, rather than party conventions, choose candidates to run for public office.

*Reading*History
A. Finding Main Ideas What was the main goal behind the progressive reforms of government?

In Oregon, newspaper editor William S. U'Ren promoted three reforms besides the direct primary.

1. **Initiative**—This reform allowed voters to propose a law directly.
2. **Referendum**—In this reform, a proposed law was submitted to the vote of the people.
3. **Recall**—This reform allowed people to vote an official out of office.

In the years that followed, many other states adopted one or more of these progressive reforms.

Promoting Social Welfare

This goal addressed such problems as poverty, unemployment, and poor working conditions. You read about the social gospel and settlement house movements in Chapter 21. Leaders in these movements promoted many social-welfare reforms. For example, Jane Addams provided social services

to the poor at Hull House. She also worked to help the unemployed. Florence Kelley, also from Hull House, pushed for minimum wage laws and limits on women's working hours.

Another group of reformers who wanted to improve social welfare were the prohibitionists. They worked to prevent alcohol from ruining people's lives. The prohibitionists built on the temperance movement of the 1800s.

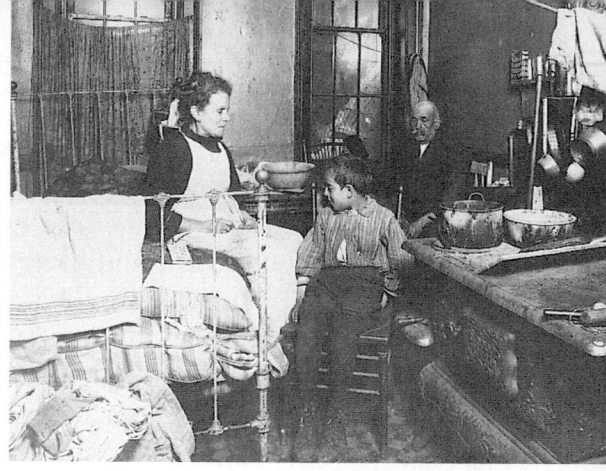

This photograph shows an immigrant family in a crowded tenement at the turn of the century.

Creating Economic Reform

The third progressive goal was to create economic reform. This meant limiting the power of big business and regulating its activities. By the late 1800s, business leaders in some major industries had formed trusts. These were combinations of businesses. The business firms in a trust worked together to cut prices and squeeze out competitors. Then the trust would raise prices and make larger profits.

Reading **History**

B. Summarizing How did progressives pursue their three basic goals?

The **Sherman Antitrust Act** of 1890 made it illegal for corporations to gain control of industries by forming trusts. However, the government did not enforce the law at first. Enforcement required a strong president.

Roosevelt and the Square Deal

Theodore Roosevelt—the first progressive president—provided this strength and leadership. He came to the presidency by accident, however. In 1898, Roosevelt won fame fighting in the Spanish-American War in Cuba. He returned from Cuba a war hero and was elected governor of New York. In 1900, Roosevelt ran on the Republican ticket as President McKinley's vice president.

Then an assassin shot McKinley, just six months after his inauguration. Roosevelt became president when McKinley died on September 14, 1901. At age 42, Roosevelt was the youngest person ever to become president. He brought his boundless energy to the office. The president often joined his six children in playing in the White House. Americans admired Roosevelt's zest for living. He gained the public's support for reform.

> *"I believe in a square deal."*
> Theodore Roosevelt

Roosevelt began his reforms with an effort to break up the corporate trusts. He thought industries should be regulated for the public interest.

A VOICE FROM THE PAST

When I say I believe in a square deal I do not mean, and nobody who speaks the truth can mean, that he believes it possible to give every man the best hand. If the cards do not come to any man, or if they do come, and he has not got the power to play them, that is his affair. All I mean is that there shall not be any crookedness in the dealing.

Theodore Roosevelt, speech on April 5, 1905

Roosevelt saw government as an umpire. Its purpose was to ensure fairness, or a "square deal," for workers, consumers, and big business.

To root out "crookedness," Roosevelt used the Sherman Antitrust Act. Since its passage in 1890, many corporations had ignored the law, which was intended to regulate the trusts. No one had enforced it—no one, that is, until Roosevelt became president in 1901.

At the end of 1901, the nation's railroads were run by a handful of companies. The power of railroads continued to grow. It was not surprising, therefore, that one of Roosevelt's first targets was the railroads. He used the Sherman Antitrust Act to bust up a railroad trust.

Roosevelt was not against big business as such. However, he opposed any trust he thought worked against the national interest. In addition to the railroad trust, Roosevelt broke up the Standard Oil Company and a tobacco trust. In all, the government filed suit against 44 corporations during Roosevelt's presidency.

*Reading*History
C. Making Inferences How do you think big business leaders regarded President Roosevelt? Why?

Roosevelt Leads Progressive Reforms

As president, Roosevelt had a great deal of power to push progressive ideas. To make such ideas into law, however, he needed help. Roosevelt got it as voters began pressuring their senators and representatives. As a result, Congress passed laws that helped change American society.

Roosevelt acted to regulate the meat-packing industry after reading Upton Sinclair's *The Jungle.* The novel describes a packing plant in which dead rats end up in the sausage. Sinclair focused attention on the poor sanitary conditions under which the meat-packers worked. "I aimed at the public's heart, and by accident I hit it in the stomach," he noted.

Roosevelt launched an investigation of the meat-packing industry. In 1906, he signed the Meat Inspection Act. This act created a government meat inspection program. Roosevelt also signed the Pure Food and Drug Act. This law banned the sale of impure foods and medicines.

While Roosevelt tried to win a square deal for most Americans, he did not push for civil rights for African Americans. He believed that discrimination was morally wrong. However, he did not take the political risk of leading a fight for civil rights.

Shown at the left is the cover of Upton Sinclair's novel, *The Jungle.* The photograph shows immigrant workers stuffing sausages in a Chicago meat-packing house.

642

Conservation

Roosevelt was a strong crusader for conservation—controlling how America's natural resources were used. As an outdoorsman and hunter, he had observed the gradual loss of natural resources. He camped with naturalist John Muir for four days in Yosemite, California. Because he loved the Yosemite Valley so much, he set out to preserve Yosemite and other areas for people's "children and their children's children."

Roosevelt preserved more than 200 million acres of public lands. He established the nation's first wildlife refuge at Pelican Island, Florida. He doubled the number of national parks in the United States. At one point, Congress refused to establish any more national parks. Roosevelt used the Antiquities Act to create national monuments instead. In this way, he preserved the Grand Canyon and the Petrified Forest in Arizona. Roosevelt spoke of the glories of the Grand Canyon while visiting the site in 1903.

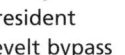

*Reading*History

D. Finding Main Ideas Why did President Roosevelt bypass Congress?

> **A VOICE FROM THE PAST**
>
> Leave it as it is. You cannot improve on it. The ages have been at work on it, and man can only mar it.
>
> **Theodore Roosevelt**, quoted in *Yellowstone*

Both the Grand Canyon and the Petrified Forest have since become national parks. America's next president, William Howard Taft, was not as interested in conservation. However, he did continue Roosevelt's progressive reforms, as you will read in the next section.

AMERICA'S HISTORY MAKERS

THEODORE ROOSEVELT
1858–1919

From his youth on, Theodore Roosevelt lived what he called the "strenuous life." He rode horses, hiked, boxed, wrestled, and played tennis. In winter, he swam in the icy Potomac River. He hunted rhinoceros in Africa, harpooned devilfish in Florida, and boated down the Amazon.

Americans loved reading of his exploits and affectionately referred to him as "Teddy" or "T.R." Once, on a hunting trip, he refused to shoot a bear cub. News of the event resulted in a new toy—the teddy bear.

How did Roosevelt's active style of living carry over into his presidency?

Section 1 Assessment

1. Terms & Names

Explain the significance of:

- progressivism
- muckrakers
- direct primary
- initiative
- referendum
- recall
- Sherman Antitrust Act
- Theodore Roosevelt

2. Using Graphics

Use a chart to list examples of progressive reforms.

Goals	Reforms
To expand democracy	
To protect social welfare	
To create economic reform	

Which reform was most important? Explain.

3. Main Ideas

a. What kinds of problems did progressives attempt to solve?

b. What did President Roosevelt mean by a "square deal," and how did he try to achieve it?

c. What were Roosevelt's achievements in the field of conservation?

4. Critical Thinking

Recognizing Effects In what ways do the reforms that President Roosevelt promoted affect your life today?

THINK ABOUT

- the quality of the food you eat
- natural resources that have been preserved

ACTIVITY OPTIONS

ART

GEOGRAPHY

Do research on one of the natural areas that President Roosevelt preserved. Create a **travel brochure** or an illustrated **map** of the area.

The National Parks Movement

As the United States expanded westward, two things became evident. First, this was a land of astonishing beauty. Second, this unspoiled beauty would not last if it wasn't protected.

President Theodore Roosevelt may have given the conservation movement its most significant boost. An outdoorsman, naturalist, and visionary, he established the U.S. Forest Service and set aside more than 200 million acres of public lands as national parks, forests, monuments, and wildlife refuges.

Creating parks was just the first step in protecting these lands. Problems arose that had not been foreseen. These problems included a lack of funds and growing numbers of tourists and researchers. In 1916, the National Park Service was established with the goal of saving the parks for future generations.

Alaska

In 1903, Teddy Roosevelt (left) joined conservationist John Muir (right) for a camping trip. Their trip took them from the "big trees" of the Sequoia forest to the wonders of the Yosemite Valley. This photo of Roosevelt and Muir was taken at Glacier Point in Yosemite. Both men wanted to protect the magnificent beauty of America's most spectacular regions.

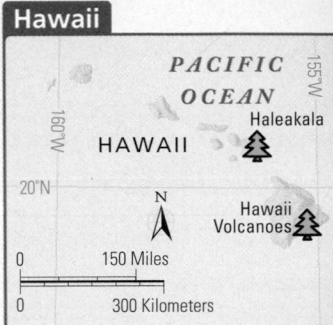

Hawaii

ARTIFACT FILE

Sequoia National Park is a land of giants. In a forest where many trees are more than 250 feet high, it is difficult to get a sense of scale when looking at the biggest of these giants. The General Sherman Tree, shown here, is the largest tree by volume in the world. A number of trees in Sequoia National Park are named for Civil War generals.

Everglades National Park in Florida is part of the approximately 1,500,000-acre Everglades region. This wetland habitat is home to birds, especially waders such as herons, egrets, and ibis, and is famous for its alligators.

The National Parks Today

Olympic
North Cascades
Mount Rainier
Glacier
Voyageurs
Isle Royale
Acadia
Theodore Roosevelt
Crater Lake
Yellowstone
Redwood
Grand Teton
Wind Cave
Badlands
Lassen Volcanic
Yosemite
Great Basin
Capitol Reef
Rocky Mountain
Shenandoah
Arches
Kings Canyon
Black Canyon of the Gunnison
Sequoia
Zion
Canyonlands
Mammoth Cave
Death Valley
Bryce Canyon
Mesa Verde
Great Smoky Mountains
Channel Islands
Grand Canyon
Joshua Tree
Petrified Forest
Hot Springs
ATLANTIC OCEAN
Saguaro
Carlsbad Caverns
Guadalupe Mountains
Big Bend
PACIFIC OCEAN
Gulf of Mexico
N
Everglades
Biscayne
Dry Tortugas

500 Miles
1000 Kilometers

National parks are identified on the map above. The National Park System includes many areas, all of which are under the management of the National Park Service (NPS).

On-Line Field Trip

Yellowstone National Park was designated the world's first national park in 1872. Covering about 2,200,000 acres, Yellowstone is still the largest national park in the United States. There are many geysers in Yellowstone, including Old Faithful (at right).

For more about national parks . . .

RESEARCH LINKS
CLASSZONE.COM

CONNECT TO GEOGRAPHY

1. **Region** What might be two reasons the national parks are concentrated where they are?
2. **Human-Environment Interaction** What effects might visits from many tourists have on a national park?

   See Geography Handbook, page 17.

CONNECT TO HISTORY

3. **Analyzing Causes** What general mood of the era made the late 1800s a likely time for successfully starting a national park?

2

Taft and Wilson as Progressives

MAIN IDEA	WHY IT MATTERS NOW	TERMS & NAMES
Progressive reforms continued under William Howard Taft and Woodrow Wilson.	Constitutional amendments passed during this time affect Americans today.	William Howard Taft Sixteenth Amendment Seventeenth Amendment Clayton Antitrust Act Federal Reserve Act

ONE AMERICAN'S STORY

During the Progressive Era, many Americans became disturbed by the problems caused by capitalism. Some even turned to socialism. This is a system in which business and industry are totally controlled by the state. Labor leader Eugene V. Debs became a socialist while serving time in prison for his role in an 1894 labor strike.

In the 1908 presidential election, Debs ran as the Socialist Party candidate. In his campaign, he urged American workers to consider what competition was like in a capitalist system.

A VOICE FROM THE PAST

Competition was natural enough at one time, but do you think you are competing today? . . . Against whom? Against Rockefeller? About as I would if I had a wheelbarrow and competed with the Santa Fe [railroad] from here to Kansas City.

Eugene V. Debs, quoted in *The Annals of America*

The forceful speeches of Eugene V. Debs attracted large audiences.

Debs made a decent showing in the election, winning more than 420,000 votes. However, the Republican candidate Taft did better and was elected.

Taking Notes

Use your chart to take notes about problems faced by Americans and how they were solved.

PROBLEM
Political: patronage; limited suffrage and den
Social: poverty; alcohol abuse
Economic: power of big corporations; unemploy
Environmental: impure food and water; diminishing

Taft and Progressivism

In the 1908 election, Debs ran against Republican **William Howard Taft** and Democrat William Jennings Bryan. Neither Debs nor Bryan stood much of a chance against Taft. He was Roosevelt's handpicked successor. Roosevelt's popularity swayed many people to vote for Taft, who promised to follow Roosevelt's progressive policies.

Taft continued Roosevelt's attack on trusts. During his four years in office, Taft pursued almost twice as many antitrust suits as Roosevelt had in nearly eight years in office. But Taft received less credit for his progressivism because he became allied with conservative Republicans rather

than Roosevelt's progressive Republicans. Nevertheless, Taft did move forward with progressive reforms. His reforms addressed the progressive goals of democracy, social welfare, and economic reform. Two of the major progressive achievements under President Taft were constitutional amendments.

Two Progressive Amendments

The **Sixteenth Amendment** was passed in 1909 and ratified in 1913. It gave Congress the power to create income taxes. The Constitution previously did not allow direct taxes on an individual's income. This amendment was intended to provide a means of spreading the cost of running the government among more people. The income tax soon became the main source of federal revenue.

Economics *in* History

Types of Taxes

The Sixteenth Amendment, ratified in 1913, made it constitutional for the federal government to have an income tax. Congress quickly passed an income tax law the same year. The income tax provides revenue to the federal government by taxing profits and earnings. In a graduated income tax, larger incomes are taxed at higher rates than smaller incomes. The income tax is only one of several taxes that governments use to raise money.

INCOME TAXES

1. **Individual:** You pay a percentage of what you earn at work or from investments. Under the payroll deduction plan, income taxes are deducted (taken out) from your wages or salary before you get your paycheck.
2. **Corporate:** Corporations pay a percentage of their profits in income tax.

PROPERTY TAXES

People pay taxes on property they own, such as land or a house. Property taxes are often used to support public services such as schools.

TYPES OF TAXES

SALES TAXES

Sales tax is imposed on the retail price of merchandise and collected by the retailer. For example, when you buy a pair of jeans, you pay sales tax, which will be listed on your receipt.

ESTATE TAXES

This tax is charged against the value of the property of a person who has died. It is also called the "death tax" because it is collected from the dead person's estate before the estate is passed on to the heirs.

CONNECT TO HISTORY

1. **Making Inferences** How might a corporate income tax fit the goals of the Progressive Era?

   S See Skillbuilder Handbook, page R12.

CONNECT TO TODAY

2. **Drawing Conclusions** Some states that have a sales tax do not charge that tax on the purchase of goods like food or clothing. Why do you think they make an exception for these purchases?

For more about taxes . . .

RESEARCH LINKS
CLASSZONE.COM

STRANGE but True

FROM PRESIDENT TO CHIEF JUSTICE

William Howard Taft was the only man in American history to serve first as president and then as chief justice of the U.S. Supreme Court. He had always wanted to be a Supreme Court justice. Even his mother said, "I do not want my son to be President. His is a judicial mind and he loves the law."

Taft was unhappy as president. When he left office, he said: "I'm glad to be going. This is the lonesomest place in the world." Eight years later, in 1921, President Warren G. Harding appointed Taft to the Supreme Court. Taft is shown here in his judicial robes.

The **Seventeenth Amendment** was ratified in 1913. It provided for the direct election of U.S. senators by voters in each state. Formerly, state legislatures had chosen U.S. senators. Under this system, many senators obtained their positions through corrupt bargains. Because of this, the Senate was called the "Millionaires' Club." The Seventeenth Amendment gave people a more direct voice in the government.

The Election of 1912

Taft achieved a number of progressive reforms. However, a deep split developed between him and progressive leaders in the Republican Party. Still, with the support of conservative Republicans, Taft won the party's nomination as its presidential candidate in 1912.

However, many progressive Republicans supported Theodore Roosevelt. He had entered the race and formed the Progressive Party, also known as the Bull Moose Party.

The Democrats chose Governor Woodrow Wilson of New Jersey as their presidential candidate. Eugene Debs again entered the race as the Socialist candidate. With the Republicans deeply divided, Wilson won the election.

The Wilson Presidency

As president, Wilson established a progressive record. Wilson believed that "bigness" itself was dangerous. He wanted the government to use its powers to break up monopolies—groups that sought complete control over an industry. He also wanted the government to help workers in their struggles against business owners.

At Wilson's urging, Congress passed the **Clayton Antitrust Act** of 1914. The new law laid down rules forbidding business practices that lessened competition. A business, for example, could no longer buy the stock of a competitor. The Clayton Act gave the government more power to regulate trusts. In addition, the Clayton Act was also prolabor:

1. It said labor unions and farm organizations could merge and expand.
2. It limited the ability of the courts to force workers to end strikes.
3. It legalized such labor tactics as strikes, picketing, and boycotts.

During Wilson's two terms, reforms to the nation's financial system occurred. In 1913, the **Federal Reserve Act** was passed. This improved the nation's monetary and banking system. The law created the modern banking system, which resembles a pyramid. At the top is the Federal Reserve Board, which is appointed by the president. Next are 12 Federal Reserve Banks for different regions of the country. These are "bankers'

Reading **History**

A. Drawing Conclusions Why are the Sixteenth and Seventeenth amendments considered progressive?

Vocabulary
boycott: an attempt to pressure a business by refusing to buy a product or use a service

banks." They serve the bottom level—the member banks.

The Federal Reserve Act created a more flexible currency system by allowing banks to control the money supply. To raise money, for example, the Federal Reserve Board, or "Fed," lowers the interest rate that it charges member banks. These banks then borrow more from the Fed and thus have more money to lend to people and businesses.

President Wilson throws out a baseball at the opening game of the 1916 season.

Reading**History**
B. Summarizing
What were some of Wilson's achievements as a progressive president?

Wilson did no more to advance civil rights for African Americans than Roosevelt did. In fact, Wilson approved the segregation, or separation, of African-American and white employees in the federal government. Throughout the Progressive Era, presidents Roosevelt, Taft, and Wilson did not actively promote civil rights for African Americans.

The Eighteenth Amendment

Another amendment passed during the Progressive Era was the Eighteenth Amendment. This is also called the Prohibition Amendment. During Wilson's administration, supporters of prohibition gained strength. Reformers thought an alcohol ban would reduce poverty. They argued that liquor added to unemployment and violence. Business leaders saw that alcohol made workers less efficient. Finally, in 1917, Congress passed a constitutional amendment. The Eighteenth Amendment prohibited the manufacture and sale of alcoholic beverages. The states ratified the amendment in 1919.

In the next section, you will read about the most important amendment of the era—the Nineteenth Amendment, which gave women the vote.

Section **2** Assessment

1. Terms & Names

Explain the significance of:
- William Howard Taft
- Sixteenth Amendment
- Seventeenth Amendment
- Clayton Antitrust Act
- Federal Reserve Act

2. Using Graphics

Complete the chart to review some of the major reforms of both the Taft and Wilson administrations.

Law	Description
Sixteenth Amendment	
Clayton Antitrust Act	
Federal Reserve Act	

3. Main Ideas

a. What caused the Republican Party to split in 1912?

b. What were the major progressive accomplishments of Wilson's presidency?

c. What did the Federal Reserve Act do?

4. Critical Thinking

Making Inferences Why did progressive presidents do little to advance civil rights for African Americans?

THINK ABOUT
- the goals of progressivism
- the groups of people that progressivism aimed to help

ACTIVITY OPTIONS

LANGUAGE ARTS
TECHNOLOGY

Research one of the people mentioned in this section. Then write the **script** for the first 10 minutes of his documentary or design his **Web page**.

Women Win New Rights

MAIN IDEA	WHY IT MATTERS NOW	TERMS & NAMES
Women became leaders in social reform movements and won the right to vote during the Progressive Era.	Today, American women enjoy the right to vote because of women reformers in the Progressive Era.	Susan B. Anthony Carrie Chapman Catt Nineteenth Amendment

ONE AMERICAN'S STORY

In the 1890s, Lillian Wald was teaching a home nursing class at a school for immigrants in New York City. One day a child asked Wald to help her sick mother. Following the child home, Wald was shocked by what she saw.

A VOICE FROM THE PAST

Over broken asphalt, over dirty mattresses and heaps of refuse we went. The tall houses reeked with rubbish. . . . There were two rooms and a family of seven not only lived here but shared their quarters with boarders.

Lillian Wald, quoted in *Always a Sister*

(Above left) Lillian Wald. (Above) A visiting nurse takes a shortcut between two tenements.

Inspired to help such poor immigrants, Wald founded the Nurses' Settlement. This was later called the Henry Street Settlement. The program mainly helped poor women and children. In this section, you will read about others like Wald who worked to make life better for all women.

Taking Notes

Use your chart to take notes about problems faced by Americans and their attempted solutions.

PROBLEM
Political: patronage; limited suffrage and de
Social: poverty; alcohol abuse
Economic: power of big corporations; unemploy
Environmental: impure food and water; diminishing

New Roles for Women

The social reform movements of the Progressive Era were led by educated, middle-class women. At the turn of the century, women like Wald were looking for new roles outside the home. The growth of industry had changed many urban, middle-class homes. These homes now had indoor running water and electric power for lamps and vacuum cleaners.

In addition, factories produced the products that women once made in the home, such as soap, clothing, and canned goods. Such technological advances reduced some of the unpleasant work of homemaking. At the same time, families were becoming smaller as women had fewer children.

As a result, the homemaker's role began to change. High schools, colleges, and women's clubs offered courses in home economics and domestic science. In these courses, women were encouraged to apply the latest methods to running their homes.

Other women responded to changes in the home by taking jobs in factories, offices, and stores. Women worked as telephone operators, store clerks, and typists. Those who gained a college education could pursue a profession. The choices were limited to such fields as teaching and nursing. Women who could afford to were expected to quit their jobs when they married. In 1890, approximately 30 percent of women between the ages of 20 and 24 worked outside the home. However, only about 15 percent between the ages of 25 and 44 did so.

*Reading*History
A. Finding Main Ideas How and why did women's roles begin to change around the turn of the century?

Women Progressives

The social reform movements that many middle-class, college-educated women took part in were focused on helping people. These included the settlement house and prohibition movements. A settlement house is a community center providing assistance to residents—particularly immigrants—in a slum neighborhood.

Jane Addams was a good example of the progressive female leader. After graduating from college, Addams sought a meaningful way to participate in society. She was financially independent. A visit to a settlement house in a London slum inspired her to start a similar program in Chicago. She was helped by her friend Ellen Starr.

With donations from wealthy Chicagoans, Addams and Starr rented an old mansion. Hull House was located in a poor, immigrant neighborhood. Within just a few years, they organized a full program of services, classes, and clubs. These were run by a group of young women residents and over 90 volunteers. Hull House served as an information bureau for new immigrants. It also helped the unemployed find jobs. It offered a kindergarten, a day nursery, after-school youth clubs, nutrition classes, and a concert program. Workers also pressured politicians for improved city services for the neighborhood.

Connections TO LITERATURE

WOMEN OUTSIDE THE HOME
Charlotte Perkins Gilman (shown below) was an influential writer on women's rights. She wanted to free women from housework to pursue careers. In *Women and Economics* (1898), Gilman argued that a wife's dependency on her husband limited her personal development.

In *Concerning Children* (1900) and *The Home* (1903), she proposed that families live in large apartments. These would have centralized nurseries and a staff devoted to cooking, cleaning, and child-care. This support would free women to work outside the home.

A VOICE FROM THE PAST

One function of the settlement to its neighborhood somewhat resembled that of the big brother whose mere presence in the playground protected the little ones from bullies.

Jane Addams, quoted in *Women and the American Experience*

The young women residents of Hull House received no salary and had to pay for their room and board. This meant that they had to be financially

independent. For some, Hull House provided training for other public service. Florence Kelley, for example, worked at Hull House from 1891 to 1898. She later became secretary of the National Consumers' League. This group promoted better working conditions in factories and stores.

Another prominent but controversial progressive leader was Carry Nation. She campaigned for prohibition. Nation had once been married to an alcoholic. Tall and strong, she adopted dramatic methods in her opposition to alcoholic beverages. In the 1890s, she smashed saloons with a hatchet. This caused law enforcement officials to arrest her for disturbing the peace. Although some people criticized Nation, her efforts helped bring about passage of the Eighteenth Amendment in 1919.

Suffrage for Women

Many women progressives were active in the struggle for woman suffrage, or the right to vote. American women fought longer for the right to vote than they did for any other reform. Some leaders in the fight died before realizing their goal.

In 1890, two separate woman suffrage groups merged to form the National American Woman Suffrage Association (NAWSA). Elizabeth Cady Stanton served as its first president. Two years later, in 1892, **Susan B. Anthony** became president. She held the position until 1900. Expressing their frustration over the difficulty of gaining suffrage, Elizabeth Cady Stanton and Susan B. Anthony wrote, "Words can not describe the indignation, the humiliation a proud woman feels for her sex in disfranchisement [being deprived of the right to vote]."

NAWSA at first focused on state campaigns to win the right to vote, since earlier efforts at passing a federal amendment had failed. But by 1896, only four states allowed women to vote. These were Wyoming, Utah, Idaho, and Colorado. Between 1896 and 1910, women did not gain the right to vote in a single state. Then, between 1910 and 1914, seven more Western states approved full suffrage for women.

Background
Because she helped organize the woman suffrage movement, Susan B. Anthony became the first woman to be pictured on a U.S. coin.

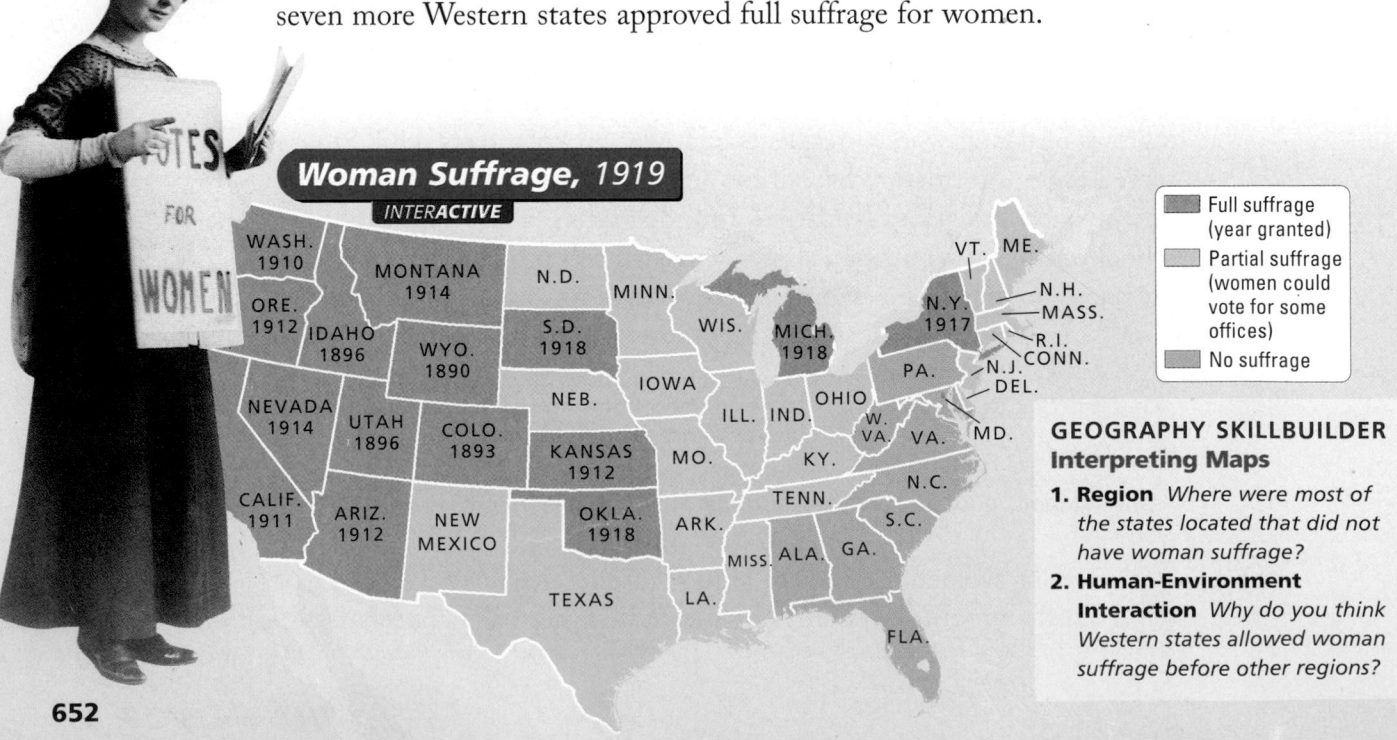

Woman Suffrage, 1919
INTER**ACTIVE**

- Full suffrage (year granted)
- Partial suffrage (women could vote for some offices)
- No suffrage

WASH. 1910
MONTANA 1914
N.D.
MINN.
VT. ME.
ORE. 1912
IDAHO 1896
WYO. 1890
S.D. 1918
WIS.
MICH. 1918
N.Y. 1917
N.H.
MASS.
R.I.
CONN.
NEVADA 1914
UTAH 1896
COLO. 1893
NEB.
IOWA
ILL. IND.
OHIO
PA.
N.J.
DEL.
CALIF. 1911
ARIZ. 1912
NEW MEXICO
KANSAS 1912
MO.
KY.
W. VA.
VA.
MD.
OKLA. 1918
ARK.
TENN.
N.C.
S.C.
TEXAS
LA.
MISS.
ALA.
GA.
FLA.

GEOGRAPHY SKILLBUILDER
Interpreting Maps

1. **Region** Where were most of the states located that did not have woman suffrage?

2. **Human-Environment Interaction** Why do you think Western states allowed woman suffrage before other regions?

The Progressive Amendments, 1909–1920

Number	Description	Passed by Congress	Ratified by States
16th	Federal income tax	1909	1913
17th	Senators elected by people rather than state legislatures	1912	1913
18th	Manufacture, sale, or transport of alcohol prohibited	1917	1919
19th	Woman suffrage	1919	1920

SKILLBUILDER Interpreting Charts

1. *For which amendment was there the longest gap between passage by Congress and ratification by states?*
2. *What do the dates 1909 and 1920 represent in this chart?*

The Nineteenth Amendment

The Western successes turned the tide in favor of woman suffrage. The United States' entry into World War I in 1917 made the final difference. During the war, membership in NAWSA reached 2 million. **Carrie Chapman Catt,** president of NAWSA, argued that the nation could no longer deny the right to vote to women, who were supporting the war effort by selling war bonds and organizing benefits. President Wilson urged the Senate to pass a women's suffrage amendment. He called passage "vital to the winning of the war."

In 1918, the House passed the **Nineteenth Amendment,** which gave women full voting rights. The Senate approved the amendment in 1919. In 1920, the states ratified it. In the final state campaigns, women staged marches, parades, and rallies around the country. Charlotte Woodard had attended the first women's rights convention in 1848 at Seneca Falls as a teenager. In 1920, the 91-year-old Woodard voted in a presidential election for the first time.

*Reading*History

B. Recognizing Effects What factors helped women gain the right to vote?

Section ❸ Assessment

1. Terms & Names

Explain the significance of:
- Susan B. Anthony
- Carrie Chapman Catt
- Nineteenth Amendment

2. Using Graphics

Use a chart to record the achievements of some women leaders of the era.

Progressive Achievements	
Lillian Wald	
Jane Addams	
Florence Kelley	

Which achievement seems greatest and why?

3. Main Ideas

a. How did women's roles expand near the turn of the century?

b. What was the background of many women who became leaders in social reform movements?

c. How did World War I influence the passage of the Nineteenth Amendment?

4. Critical Thinking

Comparing and Contrasting In what ways was the struggle for woman suffrage similar to and different from African Americans' struggle for equal rights?

THINK ABOUT
- the restrictions that both groups faced
- how long they struggled for basic rights

ACTIVITY OPTIONS

LANGUAGE ARTS

TECHNOLOGY

Research one of the women reformers discussed in this chapter. Then write the **script** for the first 10 minutes of her documentary or design her **Web page.**

TERMS & NAMES

Briefly explain the significance of each of the following.

1. progressivism
2. muckrakers
3. referendum
4. Theodore Roosevelt
5. William Howard Taft
6. Sixteenth Amendment
7. Seventeenth Amendment
8. Susan B. Anthony
9. Carrie Chapman Catt
10. Nineteenth Amendment

REVIEW QUESTIONS

Roosevelt and Progressivism (pages 639–645)

1. What problems did progressivism address?
2. How did progressive reformers expand democracy in the states?
3. What was Roosevelt's "square deal"?
4. What were Roosevelt's achievements in the area of conservation?

Taft and Wilson as Progressives (pages 646–649)

5. In what area did Taft achieve a more impressive progressive record than Roosevelt?
6. What progressive goals did the Sixteenth and Seventeenth amendments address?
7. How did Wilson's position on big business differ from Roosevelt's?

Women Win New Rights (pages 650–653)

8. How did women's lives change around 1900?
9. What was the background of many women progressives?
10. What helped further the passage of the Nineteenth Amendment in 1918?

CRITICAL THINKING

1. USING YOUR NOTES: IDENTIFYING AND SOLVING PROBLEMS

PROBLEM	SOLUTION
Political: patronage; limited suffrage and democracy	
Social: poverty; alcohol abuse	
Economic: power of big corporations; unemployment	
Environmental: impure food and water; diminishing natural resources	

Use your completed chart from the beginning of this chapter to answer these questions.

a. Which solution to a problem do you think was most effective? Why?
b. Which solution was least effective and why?
c. To which problem on the chart might you offer a different solution, and what is your solution?

2. ANALYZING LEADERSHIP

Based on their domestic record, which president—Roosevelt, Taft, or Wilson—was most effective? Why?

3. APPLYING CITIZENSHIP SKILLS

Why might women at the turn of the century consider the right to vote important enough to devote their lives to fighting for it?

4. THEME: IMPACT OF THE INDIVIDUAL

In what ways did individuals affect the political, social, and economic life of the country during the Progressive Era?

Interact *with* History

How did your solution to one of the social problems of the Progressive Era compare to the solutions proposed by reformers?

VISUAL SUMMARY

The Progressive Era

Corruption plagues the government.

Congress passes the Pendleton Civil Service Act (1883).

Theodore Roosevelt becomes president.

Roosevelt breaks up trusts, establishes "square deal," and advocates national parks.

Abuses in industry, politics, business, and labor are widespread.

Congress passes the Pure Food and Drug Act (1906), progressive amendments, Federal Reserve Act (1913), and the Clayton Antitrust Act (1914).

Women lack social justice and equality.

Vote for WOMEN
Women work to establish settlement houses, fight for woman suffrage, and gain 19th Amendment (1920).

Use the chart and your knowledge of U.S. history to answer questions 1 and 2.

Additional Test Practice, pp. S1–S33.

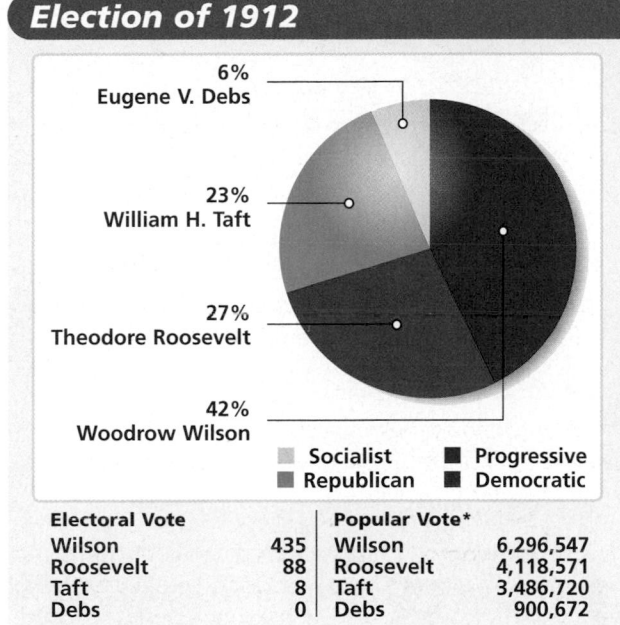

Election of 1912

6%
Eugene V. Debs

23%
William H. Taft

27%
Theodore Roosevelt

42%
Woodrow Wilson

■ Socialist   ■ Progressive
■ Republican   ■ Democratic

Electoral Vote		Popular Vote*	
Wilson	435	Wilson	6,296,547
Roosevelt	88	Roosevelt	4,118,571
Taft	8	Taft	3,486,720
Debs	0	Debs	900,672

*Other candidates received about 2% of the popular vote.

1. To which political party did Theodore Roosevelt belong?
   A. Democratic
   B. Progressive
   C. Republican
   D. Socialist

2. How many electoral votes did Eugene Debs receive?
   A. 0
   B. 6
   C. 8
   D. 88

This quotation from Eugene V. Debs describes his feelings about capitalism. Use the quotation and your knowledge of U.S. history to answer question 3.

PRIMARY SOURCE

Competition was natural enough at one time, but do you think you are competing today? . . . Against whom? Against Rockefeller? About as I would if I had a wheelbarrow and competed with the Santa Fe [railroad] from here to Kansas City.

Eugene V. Debs, quoted in *The Annals of America*

3. Which of the following best summarizes Debs' opinion of capitalism?
   A. Capitalism creates fair markets.
   B. Capitalism creates unfair markets.
   C. Capitalism creates competitive railroads.
   D. Capitalism creates competitive farms.

TEST PRACTICE
CLASSZONE.COM

ALTERNATIVE ASSESSMENT

1. ✎ WRITING ABOUT HISTORY

Jane Addams established Hull House with the help of donations from wealthy Chicago residents. Write a **letter** that Jane Addams might have written to people asking them to donate money to her project.

- Research your letter by reading books about Jane Addams or about Hull House.
- Explain why people should donate money.

2. COOPERATIVE LEARNING

Working in a group, research the problems that African Americans faced during the Progressive Era and investigate President Wilson's attitudes toward civil rights. Write a script for a meeting in which African-American leaders confront Wilson about his voting record regarding civil rights.

INTEGRATED TECHNOLOGY

DOING INTERNET RESEARCH

Use the Internet to find information about national parks that interest you. Then choose one of these as the subject of a classroom presentation.

- Begin your research on <u>nationalparks.com</u> where you can find information about all the parks. Use that information to decide on one park to research.
- Each national park has its own Web site. Use these sites to gather information.
- Include a map, a description of park features and recreational activities, photographs, and a database of facts in your presentation.

For more about national parks . . .

INTERNET ACTIVITY
CLASSZONE.COM

Becoming a World Power 1880–1917

The "Great White Fleet" of the United States symbolized the nation's presence as a global power at the beginning of the 20th century.

1893
Planters overthrow the Hawaiian queen, Liliuokalani.

1887
Hawaii grants United States exclusive use of Pearl Harbor.

1892
Grover Cleveland is elected president.

1896
William McKinley is elected president.

USA
World 1880

1884
European nations meet at the Berlin Conference to divide Africa.

1895
Sino-Japanese War ends with Japanese victory over China.

> The fleet was made up of 16 new battleships of the Atlantic Fleet that sailed around the world between 1907 and 1909.

In 1907, the United States launches one of the greatest naval fleets in history—the Great White Fleet. With this fleet, the United States has the military might to enforce political decisions involving foreign countries. Now you, the U.S. president, need to decide where and how to best use this fleet.

When should you get involved in the affairs of another country?

What Do You Think?

- What interests does the United States have in other countries?
- How important is protecting those interests?

RESEARCH LINKS
CLASSZONE.COM

Visit the Chapter 23 links for more information about the growth of the United States.

> The ships were manned by 14,000 sailors and covered 43,000 miles.

1898
Spanish-American War takes place.

1901
Theodore Roosevelt becomes president after McKinley is assassinated.

1904
Roosevelt is elected president.

1908
William Howard Taft is elected president.

1912
Woodrow Wilson is elected president.

1914
Panama Canal opens.

1917

00
xer
ion
s in
na.

1903
Republic of Panama established.

1904
Russo-Japanese War begins.

1910
Mexican Revolution begins.

1916
Pancho Villa makes a raid in the United States.

Reading Strategy: Finding Main Ideas

What Do You Know?

Was expansion something new, or was it a force that you have seen before in the history of the United States?

Think About

- the idea of Manifest Destiny
- the Louisiana Purchase
- the War with Mexico
- your responses to the Interact with History about getting involved in the affairs of another country (see page 657)

What Do You Want to Know?

 What do you think might have caused the United States to expand overseas at the end of the 1800s? Make a list of the possible reasons before you read the chapter.

The American eagle spreads its wings over Asia and Latin America in this political cartoon from 1904.

Finding Main Ideas

An important skill for reading history is the ability to find main ideas. Identifying main ideas helps you to organize and understand the variety of details and examples that support those ideas. Use a chart like the one below to write main ideas about U.S. expansion overseas.

S See Skillbuilder Handbook, page R5.

Taking Notes

Economic Interests

Military Interests

Reasons for
U.S. Expansion
Overseas

Belief in Cultural
Superiority

The United States Continues to Expand

MAIN IDEA

The United States expanded its interest in world affairs and acquired new territories.

WHY IT MATTERS NOW

During this period, the United States acquired Alaska and Hawaii as territories.

TERMS & NAMES

imperialism
William Seward
Queen Liliuokalani

ONE AMERICAN'S STORY

Alfred T. Mahan served in the U.S. Navy for nearly 40 years. In the 1890s, he wrote several books on the historical importance of sea power, trading stations, and colonies.

A VOICE FROM THE PAST

The trading-station . . . [was] the same as the . . . colony. In both cases the mother-country had won a foothold in a foreign land, seeking a new outlet for what it had to sell, a new sphere for its shipping, more employment for its people, and more comfort and wealth for itself.

A. T. Mahan, *The Influence of Sea Power upon History, 1660–1805*

Mahan encouraged government officials to build up American naval forces. In this section you will learn how the United States began to extend its influence beyond the national boundaries.

Naval historian Alfred Thayer Mahan at the turn of the century

Reasons for U.S. Expansion

Use your chart to take notes about the reasons for U.S. expansion overseas.

Americans had always sought to expand the size of their nation. Throughout the 19th century, they extended their control toward the Pacific Coast. By the 1880s, however, many leaders became convinced that the United States should join the imperialist powers of Europe and establish colonies overseas. **Imperialism**—the policy by which stronger nations extend their economic, political, or military control over weaker territories—was a trend around the world.

European nations had been establishing colonies for centuries. In the late 19th century, Africa became a major area of European expansion. By the early 20th century, only two countries in Africa—Ethiopia and Liberia—remained independent.

Imperialist countries also competed for territory in Asia, especially in China. There, European nations had to compete with Japan, which had also become a world power by the end of the 1800s.

Most Americans gradually came to approve of the idea of expansion overseas. Three factors helped to fuel the development of American imperialism.

1. **Economic Interests.** Economic leaders argued that expansion would increase U.S. financial prosperity. Industry had greatly expanded after the Civil War. Many industrialists saw new colonies as a potential source of cheap raw materials. Agriculture had also expanded. Farmers pointed out that colonies would mean new markets for their products.

2. **Military Interests.** In his books, Alfred T. Mahan had argued that economic interests went hand-in-hand with military interests. Foreign policy experts agreed. They urged U.S. leaders to follow the European example and establish a military presence overseas.

3. **Belief in Cultural Superiority.** Many Americans believed that their government, religion, and even race were superior to those of other societies. Some people hoped to spread democratic ideas overseas. Others saw a chance to advance Christianity. Racist ideas about the inferiority of the nonwhite populations in many foreign countries were also used to justify American imperialism.

Each of these developments—economic interests, military interests, and a belief in cultural superiority—led the United States to a larger role on the world stage.

Reading **History**
A. Making Inferences Why might economic and military interests go hand in hand?

Seward and Alaska

A strong backer of expansion was **William Seward,** Secretary of State under presidents Abraham Lincoln and Andrew Johnson. Seward made his biggest move in 1867, when he arranged the purchase of Alaska from Russia.

Not everyone was pleased by Seward's move, though. At the time, the $7.2-million deal was widely criticized. Newspapers called Alaska a "Polar Bear Garden" and "Seward's Icebox." Even so, the purchase of the resource-rich territory turned out to be a great bargain for the United States.

Throughout his career, Seward continued to pursue new territory. Before he retired in 1869, he considered acquiring the Hawaiian Islands, a group of volcanic and coral islands in the central Pacific Ocean. That would not happen, however, for almost 30 more years.

Background
In the late 1800s, large gold fields were discovered in Alaska. The territory was also rich in fur-bearing animals, timber, copper, coal, and oil.

Alaska, 1867 & Hawaii, 1898

United States and its possessions

RUSSIA
Arctic Circle

Alaska, 1867

180°
160°W
140°W
120°W
100°W

60°N

PACIFIC OCEAN

Hawaiian Islands, 1898
Kauai
Oahu
Molokai
Pearl Harbor
Maui
Hawaii

NORTH AMERICA

UNITED STATES

40°N

Tropic of Cancer

20°N

N

0   2,000 Miles
0   4,000 Kilometers

GEOGRAPHY SKILLBUILDER
Interpreting Maps
1. **Location** *What country lies to the west of Alaska?*
2. **Location** *On which Hawaiian island is Pearl Harbor?*

The Annexation of Hawaii

*Reading*History

B. Reading a Map
Locate the Hawaiian Islands on the map on page 660.

In the early 1800s, Christian missionaries from the United States had moved to the Kingdom of Hawaii to convert the local population. Some of the missionaries' descendants started sugar plantations. By the late 1800s, wealthy planters dominated Hawaii's economy.

In 1891, **Queen Liliuokalani** (lee•LEE•oo•oh•kah• LAH•nee) became the leader of Hawaii. Believing that planters had too much influence, she wanted to limit their power. Around the same time, U.S. trade laws changed to favor sugar grown exclusively in American states.

American planters in Hawaii were upset by these threats to their political and economic interests. In January 1893, they staged a revolt. With the help of U.S. Marines, they overthrew the queen and set up their own government. They then asked to be annexed by the United States.

Vocabulary
annex: to add

U.S. leaders already understood the value of the islands. In 1887, they had pressured Hawaii to allow a U.S. naval base at Pearl Harbor, the kingdom's best port. The base became an important refueling station for American merchant and military ships bound for Asia.

Thus, when President Benjamin Harrison received the planters' request in 1893, he gave his approval and sent a treaty to the Senate. But before the Senate could act, Grover Cleveland became president. He did not approve of the planters' actions and withdrew the treaty. Hawaii would not be annexed until 1898, during the Spanish-American War. In the next section, you will read about the events that led to that war.

AMERICA'S HISTORY MAKERS

QUEEN LILIUOKALANI
1838–1917

As a young princess, Liliuokalani received a Western education and toured the world. Although she learned about many cultures, she remained committed to Hawaii. An excellent musician, she wrote the famous Hawaiian song "Aloha Oe [Farewell to Thee]."

She was the first queen of Hawaii and proved to be a good leader. She resisted the foreign takeover of Hawaii and inspired a revolt against the planters. Only in 1895, when the safety of her supporters was threatened, did she agree to give up her throne.

How did Queen Liliuokalani protect her followers after planters seized power?

Section 1 Assessment

1. Terms & Names

Explain the significance of:

• imperialism
• William Seward
• Queen Liliuokalani

2. Using Graphics

Use a chart like the one shown to record causes of U.S. expansion overseas in the late 1800s.

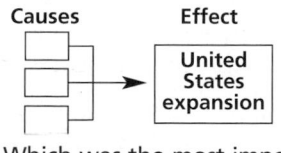

Which was the most important cause?

3. Main Ideas

a. Where was the focus of U.S. expansion before the late 1800s?

b. How did William Seward contribute to U.S. expansion?

c. Why did the American planters' request for the annexation of Hawaii fail in the early 1890s?

4. Critical Thinking

Making Inferences What benefits were American planters looking for when they staged a revolt in 1893?

THINK ABOUT

• the new policies of Queen Liliuokalani
• changes in U.S. trade laws

ACTIVITY OPTIONS

TECHNOLOGY

ART

Read more about Hawaii's Queen Liliuokalani. Outline a **video presentation** on the overthrow of the queen or plan a **mural** that depicts the event.

The Spanish-American War

MAIN IDEA	WHY IT MATTERS NOW	TERMS & NAMES
Independence movements in Spanish colonies led to the Spanish-American War in 1898.	U.S. involvement in Latin America and Asia expanded greatly after the Spanish-American War.	yellow journalism Rough Riders U.S.S. *Maine* Platt Amendment Spanish-American Anti-Imperialist League War Luis Muñoz Rivera

ONE AMERICAN'S STORY

José Martí was forced to leave Cuba in the 1870s. In those years, Cuba was a Spanish colony, and he had spoken out for independence. Martí later described the terrible conditions suffered under Spanish rule.

A VOICE FROM THE PAST

Cuba's children . . . suffer in indescribable bitterness as they see their fertile nation enchained and also their human dignity stifled . . . all for the necessities and vices of the [Spanish] monarchy.

José Martí, quoted in *José Martí, Mentor of the Cuban Nation*

In New York City, Martí began to plan a revolt against Spain that began in 1895. Martí's lifelong struggle for Cuban independence made him a symbol of liberty throughout Latin America. In this section, you will read how U.S. disapproval of Spain's treatment of Cubans led to the Spanish-American War.

José Martí dedicated his life to the Cuban struggle for independence from Spain.

Taking Notes

Use your chart to take notes about the reasons for U.S. expansion overseas.

Reasons for U.S. Expansion Overseas

Rebellion Against Spain

The Spanish empire was crumbling at the end of the 19th century. Spain had once controlled most of the Americas, including land that became part of the United States. By the 1890s, however, it owned only a few colonies. Among them were the Philippine Islands in the Pacific and the Caribbean islands of Cuba and Puerto Rico. (See the maps on page 665.) Many of the inhabitants of these colonies had begun to demand independence.

Cubans had revolted against Spain several times in the second half of the nineteenth century. Each time, Spanish soldiers defeated the rebels. In 1895, an ongoing economic depression had increased Cubans' anger over Spanish rule, and they rebelled again. José Martí, who had helped to organize the rebellion from New York, returned to Cuba. He was killed in a skirmish with Spanish troops shortly after, but the revolt continued.

Spain sent General Valeriano "the Butcher" Weyler to crush the rebels. Weyler's methods were harsh. He forced many Cubans from their homes and placed them in camps guarded by Spanish troops. Thousands died of starvation and disease in the camps.

The revolt in Cuba caused alarm in the United States. Business leaders were concerned because the fighting disrupted U.S. trade with Cuba. Most Americans, however, became outraged when the press began to describe the brutality of Spanish officials. Two New York City newspapers, in particular, stirred up people's emotions.

Reading **History**
A. Forming Opinions How can newspapers affect public opinion?

The *World,* owned by Joseph Pulitzer, and the *New York Journal,* owned by William Randolph Hearst, were battling for customers. Both owners were able to attract readers by printing stories that described—and often exaggerated—news about Spanish cruelty. This sensational style of writing was known as **yellow journalism.** It was named after "The Yellow Kid," a popular comic strip that ran in the two New York papers.

The United States Goes to War

William McKinley, the U.S. president in 1898, did not want war. "I have been through [the Civil War]," he told a friend. "I have seen the dead piled up, and I do not want to see another."

Even so, public opinion—stirred up by sensational newspaper reports—forced McKinley to take action. He demanded that Spain halt its harsh treatment of Cubans. Spain did bring General Weyler home, but conditions remained severe.

In January 1898, McKinley sent the **U.S.S. *Maine*** to Cuba. Riots had broken out in the capital, Havana, and the battleship was dispatched to protect U.S. citizens. Then, the following month, the *Maine* exploded and sank in Havana's harbor, killing 260 sailors.

No one knows what caused the explosion. Most historians today believe that it was an accident. For example, a spark might have set off an explosion in the ship's coal bunker. Even so, Americans blamed Spain.

The explosion of the *Maine* and accounts of the event by yellow journalists led many Americans to favor war against Spain.

Detecting Bias in the Media

Modern journalists try to report the news without bias—that is, without letting their personal opinions or those of their employer influence what they write. Unbiased reporting is one of the responsibilities of a free press. It allows citizens to weigh the facts and come to their own understanding of issues and events.

As you have read, journalists and their employers do not always avoid bias. In fact, in the 1890s, journalists were not concerned with bias. Before the United States declared war on Spain in 1898, 'yellow journalists' exaggerated stories to help sell newspapers. These stories helped turn U.S. public opinion in favor of war against Spain. They used words and images to reflect their bias that the United States should declare war on Spain—and sell more papers along the way.

William Randolph Hearst ran this headline in his *New York Journal* before authorities had a chance to determine the cause of the *Maine*'s explosion.

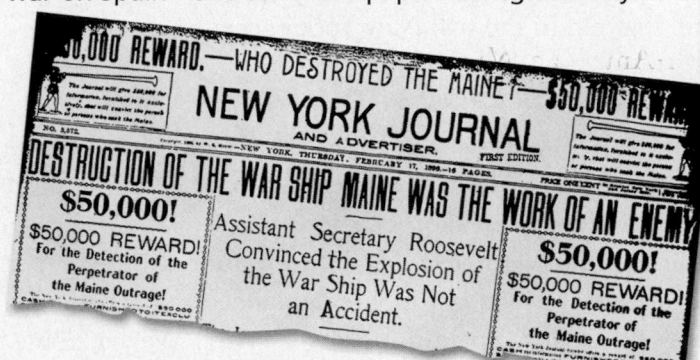

Can You Find Bias in the Media?

1. With a small group, collect news stories from different sources that cover the same issue or event.

2. Record any differences in the way a specific issue or event is covered by the oral, written, or visual sources you have selected.

3. Review the differences and decide whether any of the authors of the sources showed bias in their coverage.

4. Write a report that describes any bias you might detect. Explain why the biased source might have reported the story the way it did.

See Citizenship Handbook, page 284.

For more about the news media . . .

RESEARCH LINKS
CLASSZONE.COM

"Remember the Maine!" became a call to arms. On April 20, 1898, President McKinley signed a congressional resolution that called for Cuba's independence and demanded a withdrawal of Spanish forces. He gave Spain three days to respond. Spain refused, and the **Spanish-American War** began.

The War in the Philippines

The United States went to war to fight for Cuban freedom. But the first major battle of the Spanish-American War took place in a Spanish colony on the other side of the world—the Philippine Islands. Many Filipinos, as the inhabitants of the islands were called, had also revolted against Spanish rule in the 1890s.

Before the war began, the Filipino independence movement had attracted the attention of Theodore Roosevelt. At that time, Roosevelt was assistant secretary of the navy. He put a fleet of American ships in Hong Kong on alert. Their leader, Commodore George Dewey, prepared his forces and made contact with the head of the Filipino rebel forces, Emilio Aguinaldo (eh•MEE•lyoh AH•gee•NAHL•doh).

When the war began, Dewey set out for Manila, the Philippine capital, where part of the Spanish fleet was located. The battle in Manila Bay began early on the morning of May 1, 1898. By a little past noon,

*Reading*History
B. Making Inferences Why did Theodore Roosevelt put the U.S. fleet in Hong Kong on alert?

Dewey's forces had destroyed the Spanish fleet. About 380 Spanish sailors were dead or wounded. No Americans died. U.S. troops, aided by Filipino rebels, took control of Manila in August.

Dewey became an instant hero in the United States. Thousands of babies born at the time of the victory in Manila Bay were named for him, and a chewing gum called "Dewey's Chewies" became popular.

The War in the Caribbean

When the Spanish-American War began, the U.S. Army had only 28,000 men. Within four months, over 200,000 more joined up. Among the new recruits was Theodore Roosevelt, who had resigned from the Navy Department to volunteer.

Roosevelt helped to organize the First United States Volunteer Cavalry. This unit was nicknamed the **Rough Riders.** Its recruits included cowboys, miners, college students, New York policemen, athletes, and Native Americans.

In June, the Rough Riders and about 16,000 other soldiers—nearly a quarter of them African American—gathered in Tampa, Florida. They then set out for Santiago, a Spanish stronghold in southern Cuba. When the Rough Riders arrived, their dark-blue wool uniforms were too hot for the Cuban climate. Also, many of the soldiers came down with tropical diseases. Even so, they fought their way toward Santiago.

In order to gain control of Santiago's port, American troops had to capture San Juan Hill. They attacked the Spanish on July 1.

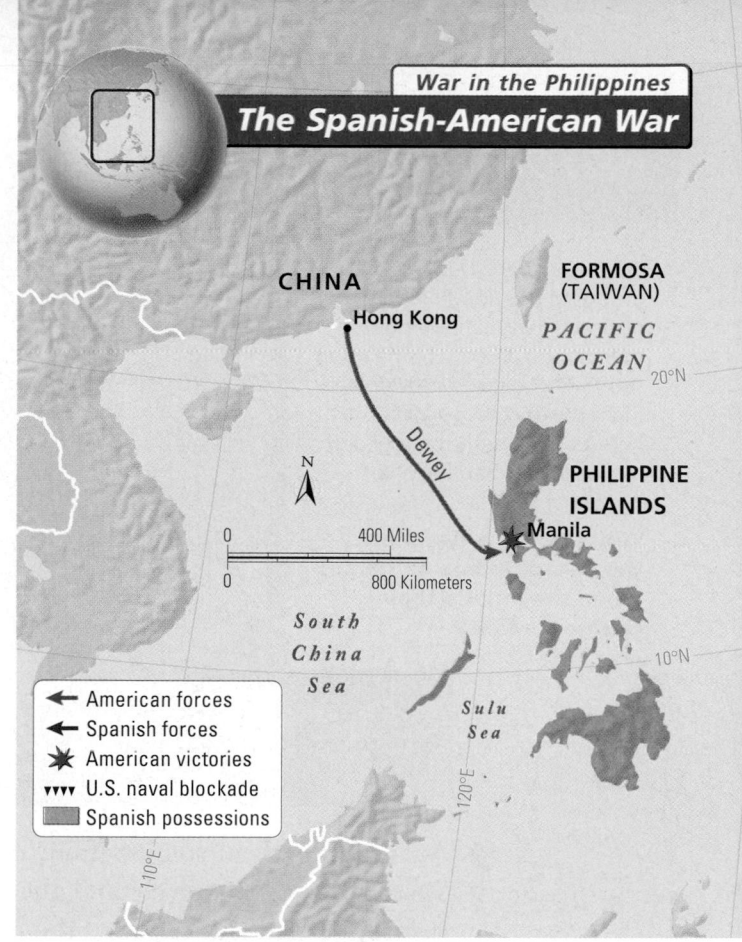

War in the Philippines
The Spanish-American War

CHINA
Hong Kong

FORMOSA (TAIWAN)

PACIFIC OCEAN

20°N

PHILIPPINE ISLANDS

Manila

Dewey

N

0   400 Miles
0   800 Kilometers

South China Sea

Sulu Sea

10°N

120°E

110°E

← American forces
← Spanish forces
✹ American victories
▼▼▼ U.S. naval blockade
▨ Spanish possessions

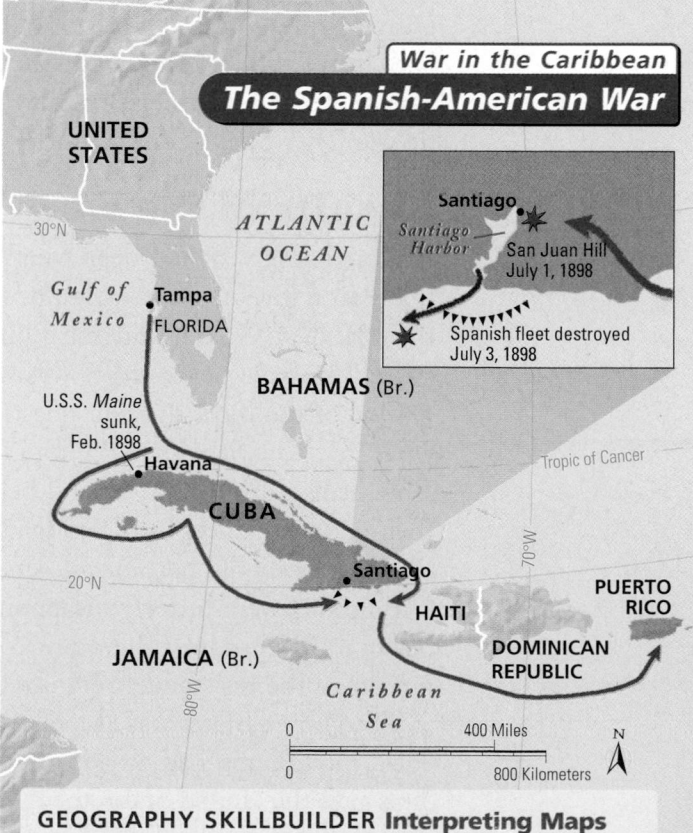

War in the Caribbean
The Spanish-American War

UNITED STATES

30°N

ATLANTIC OCEAN

Santiago

Santiago Harbor

San Juan Hill July 1, 1898

Spanish fleet destroyed July 3, 1898

Gulf of Mexico

Tampa
FLORIDA

BAHAMAS (Br.)

U.S.S. *Maine* sunk, Feb. 1898

Havana

Tropic of Cancer

CUBA

20°N

Santiago

70°W

HAITI

PUERTO RICO

JAMAICA (Br.)

DOMINICAN REPUBLIC

80°W

Caribbean Sea

0   400 Miles
0   800 Kilometers

N

GEOGRAPHY SKILLBUILDER Interpreting Maps

1. **Movement** Where was Dewey's fleet before it steamed toward the Philippines?
2. **Location** About how far is Havana from the tip of southern Florida?

HISTORY through ART

On July 1, 1898, U.S. troops, including the Rough Riders, attacked San Juan Hill outside of Santiago, Cuba. This painting shows Theodore Roosevelt leading a cavalry charge up the hill—even though the regiment's horses had been left behind in Florida.

Why did the artist show the Rough Riders on horses when they made their charge on foot?

African-American soldiers from the Tenth Cavalry began to drive the Spanish back. Roosevelt and the Rough Riders joined them as they rushed forward and captured the hill.

Two days later, American ships destroyed Spain's fleet as it tried to escape Santiago Harbor. On July 17, the city surrendered. A week later, U.S. forces took Puerto Rico. Finally, on August 12, 1898, Spain signed a truce. To U.S. Secretary of State John Hay, it had been "a splendid little war." For Spain, four centuries of glory had come to an end.

Results of the War

Although the war had been fought over Cuba, U.S. leaders demanded that Spain give up other colonies after the war—including Puerto Rico, the island of Guam, and the Philippines. Spain had no choice but to agree. The final peace treaty was signed in Paris in December 1898.

One of the most difficult questions for U.S. leaders after the war was what to do with the Philippines. Filipinos had fought alongside Americans during the war and believed that Spain's defeat would bring them independence. But President McKinley eventually decided that the Philippines should become an American colony.

Filipinos were bitterly disappointed. Led by Emilio Aguinaldo, they began to fight against their new colonial rulers. American troops sent to put down the resistance were not able to restore order until 1902.

The United States was also reluctant to grant Cuba complete independence. First, Cuba had to add the **Platt Amendment** to its constitution. This gave the United States the right to intervene in Cuban affairs anytime there was a threat to "life, property, and individual liberty." Cuba also had to allow a U.S. naval base at Guantánamo Bay.

Puerto Rico became an American territory. The United States set up a government and appointed the top officials. Puerto Ricans had little to

Reading **History**

C. Making Inferences Why did the United States demand that Spain give up territories in addition to Cuba?

say in their own affairs. Only in 1917 would the United States agree to make Puerto Rico a self-governing territory and grant U.S. citizenship to all Puerto Ricans.

The Anti-Imperialist League

U.S. treatment of Spain's former colonies after the Spanish-American War disappointed many people in the United States.

Several well-known Americans, including businessman Andrew Carnegie, reformer Jane Addams, and writer Mark Twain, joined with others to form the **Anti-Imperialist League**. Members of the League believed that Americans should not deny other people the right to govern themselves.

*Reading*History

D. Finding Main Ideas Why did the Anti-Imperialist League oppose U.S. efforts to collect colonies?

A VOICE FROM THE PAST

We hold that the policy known as imperialism is hostile to liberty. . . . We regret that it has become necessary in the land of Washington and Lincoln to reaffirm that all men, of whatever race or color, are entitled to life, liberty, and the pursuit of happiness.

From the *Platform of the American Anti-Imperialist League*

The voice of the Anti-Imperialist League was lost, however, in the roar of popular approval of the Spanish-American War.

Many Americans hoped that their nation would surpass the glory of the old Spanish empire. In the next section, you will read more about how the United States continued its involvement overseas.

AMERICA'S HISTORY MAKERS

LUIS MUÑOZ RIVERA
1859–1916

Luis Muñoz Rivera devoted his life to obtaining self-government for Puerto Rico—first from Spain and then from the United States.

After Spain granted Puerto Rico self-rule in 1897, Muñoz Rivera joined the government. He resigned and renewed his struggle when Puerto Rico became a U.S. territory.

Muñoz Rivera died just before the United States granted Puerto Ricans U.S. citizenship and a large measure of self-government.

In what ways did Muñoz Rivera use his leadership skills to help his country?

Section 2 Assessment

1. Terms & Names

Explain the significance of:
- yellow journalism
- U.S.S. *Maine*
- Spanish-American War
- Rough Riders
- Platt Amendment
- Anti-Imperialist League
- Luis Muñoz Rivera

2. Using Graphics

Use a time line to record the major events of the Spanish-American War.

Spanish-American War, 1898

About how long did the Spanish-American War last?

3. Main Ideas

a. What led to the Cuban rebellion against Spain in 1895?

b. What was the first major military event of the Spanish-American War?

c. What happened in the Philippines after the war?

4. Critical Thinking

Forming Opinions Did the United States betray its democratic principles when it made the Philippines a colony?

THINK ABOUT
- the public's response to yellow journalists and U.S. military victories
- the work of the Anti-Imperialist League

ACTIVITY OPTIONS

LANGUAGE ARTS
MATH

Research the Spanish-American War. Write a **television news script** covering a major battle or create a **database** of wartime casualties.

U.S. Involvement Overseas

MAIN IDEA	WHY IT MATTERS NOW	TERMS & NAMES
In the early 1900s, the United States expanded its involvement in Asia and Latin America.	The United States still trades extensively with Asian and Latin American countries.	sphere of influence Open Door Policy Boxer Rebellion Panama Canal Roosevelt Corollary

ONE AMERICAN'S STORY

In 1852, President Millard Fillmore sent Commodore Matthew Perry on a mission to open Japan to U.S. trade. For over two centuries, Japan's rulers had kept the country closed to most foreigners. Perry wanted to break Japan's traditional policy.

A VOICE FROM THE PAST

[I was determined] to adopt an entirely contrary plan of proceedings from that of all others who had . . . visited Japan on the same errand [to open up trade]: to demand as a right and not to [ask] as a favor those acts of courtesy which are due from one civilized nation to another.

Commodore Matthew Perry, *Personal Journal*

A Japanese artist portrayed Commodore Matthew Perry's meeting with Japanese officials in 1853.

Under the threat of force, Japan signed a treaty in 1854 giving American ships access to its ports. In this section, you will read more about U.S. involvement in Asia, as well as in Latin America.

Taking Notes

Use your chart to take notes about the reasons for U.S. expansion overseas.

Reasons for U.S. Expansion Overseas

A Power in the Pacific

Throughout the 1800s, the United States continued to expand its involvement in Asia. Toward the end of the century, the United States acquired a chain of islands—including Hawaii and Guam—that stretched across the Pacific Ocean to Asia.

During the Spanish-American War, Americans fought in the Philippine Islands, a Spanish colony in eastern Asia. After the war, the United States annexed the islands and put down the Filipino independence movement.

Some Americans objected to the annexation of the Philippines. However, supporters of imperialism, such as Indiana senator Albert Beveridge, applauded U.S. actions. Beveridge boasted, "The Philippines

are ours forever. And just beyond the Philippines are China's [unlimited] markets. We will not retreat from either. . . . The power that rules the Pacific is the power that rules the world."

Many Americans looked forward to the profits promised by Asian markets and resources. Others saw a chance to extend U.S. democracy and culture in the region. The Philippines would provide a base for these activities.

"The power that rules the Pacific . . . rules the world."

Albert Beveridge

The United States in China

As Senator Beveridge noted, control of the Philippines gave Americans greater access to China. However, by the time the United States acquired the islands, other imperialist nations, including Japan, were already deeply involved in China.

When Commodore Perry opened Japan to U.S. trade in the 1850s, he also opened the nation to Western ideas. After Perry's voyages, Japan began to modernize and soon emerged as a world power. In the 1890s, Japan demonstrated its strength in a successful war against China.

After the war, both Japan and the major European powers expanded their **spheres of influence** in China. These were areas where foreign nations claimed special rights and economic privileges. By the late 1890s, France, Germany, Britain, Japan, and Russia had established prosperous settlements along the coast of China. They also claimed exclusive rights to railroad construction and mining development in the nation's interior.

The competition for spheres of influence worried U.S. leaders who wanted access to China's markets and resources. In 1899, Secretary of State John Hay asked nations involved in the region to follow an **Open Door Policy**. This meant that no single country should have a monopoly on trade with China. Eventually, most of the nations accepted Hay's proposal.

Many Chinese people were not pleased by the presence of foreigners. One group, called the "Boxers," was angered by the privileges given to foreigners and the disrespect they showed toward Chinese traditions. In 1900, Chinese resentment toward foreigners' attitude of cultural superiority led to a violent uprising known as the **Boxer Rebellion**. Many foreigners were killed before the uprising was put down by an international force.

*Reading*History
A. Analyzing Causes Why did John Hay propose the Open Door Policy?

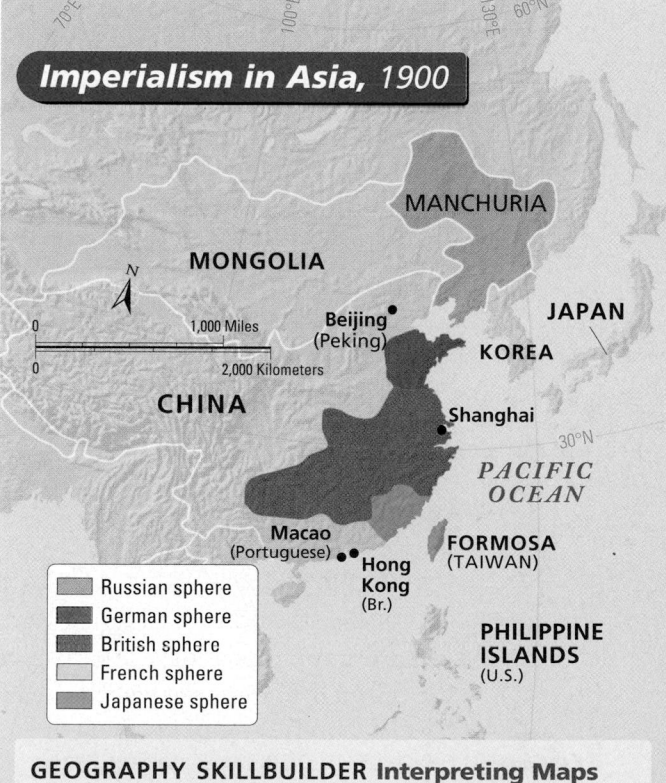

Imperialism in Asia, *1900*

MANCHURIA

MONGOLIA

Beijing (Peking)

JAPAN

KOREA

CHINA

Shanghai

30°N

PACIFIC OCEAN

Macao (Portuguese)

FORMOSA (TAIWAN)

Hong Kong (Br.)

PHILIPPINE ISLANDS (U.S.)

0   1,000 Miles
0   2,000 Kilometers

- ☐ Russian sphere
- ☐ German sphere
- ☐ British sphere
- ☐ French sphere
- ☐ Japanese sphere

GEOGRAPHY SKILLBUILDER Interpreting Maps

1. **Place** *What country controlled the port of Macao?*
2. **Region** *What country had the largest sphere of influence in the coastal region of China?*

669

The Panama Canal

As American interests in the Pacific expanded, easy access to the region became vital. For that reason, U.S. leaders proposed a canal to connect the Atlantic and Pacific oceans. A canal would mean that U.S. ships would not have to travel around South America. The Spanish-American War, fought in both oceans, also made clear the need for such a shortcut.

The South American nation of Colombia controlled the best spot for the canal—the Isthmus of Panama. But Colombia was unwilling to give up this land. Ignoring Colombia's right to control its territory, President Roosevelt sent the U.S. Navy to support a revolution on the isthmus. Out of this revolution, the new nation of Panama was created in 1903.

The new Panamanian leaders granted the U.S. government rights to a ten-mile-wide strip of land called the Canal Zone. In return, the United States paid Panama $10 million and an annual fee of $250,000. There, the United States would build the **Panama Canal,** the shortcut that would connect the Atlantic and Pacific oceans.

Some people in Latin America and the United States opposed Roosevelt's actions. They believed that he had interfered in Colombia's affairs in order to cheat it out of land. In 1921, the United States finally paid Colombia $25 million for the loss of Panama.

Vocabulary
isthmus: a narrow strip of land connecting two larger masses of land

Reading **History**
B. Summarizing What political difficulty faced U.S. leaders who wanted to build the Panama Canal?

Building the Canal

Building the canal was extremely difficult. The land was swampy and full of mosquitoes that carried the organism that causes malaria. In spite of the difficulties, the project moved forward. When Roosevelt visited Panama in 1906, he wrote a letter describing the work.

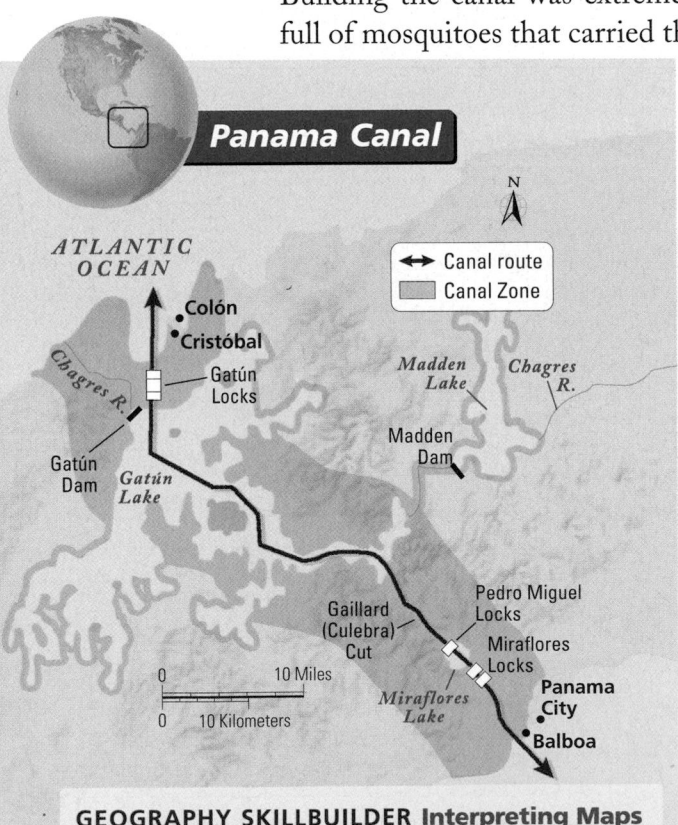

Panama Canal

ATLANTIC OCEAN

Colón
Cristóbal
Gatún Locks
Chagres R.
Madden Lake
Chagres R.
Madden Dam
Gatún Dam
Gatún Lake
Gaillard (Culebra) Cut
Pedro Miguel Locks
Miraflores Locks
Panama City
Miraflores Lake
Balboa

← Canal route
Canal Zone

N

0   10 Miles
0   10 Kilometers

GEOGRAPHY SKILLBUILDER Interpreting Maps
1. **Location** Which locks are closest to Panama City?
2. **Movement** In which direction do ships move through the canal from the Atlantic Ocean to the Pacific Ocean?

A VOICE FROM THE PAST

Steam shovels are hard at it; scooping huge masses of rock and gravel and dirt previously loosened by the drillers and dynamite blasters, loading it on trains which take it away. . . . They are eating steadily into the mountain cutting it down and down. . . . It is an epic feat.

Theodore Roosevelt, from a letter sent to his son

More than 45,000 workers, including many black West Indians, labored for years on the canal. They did not finish the work until 1914. The canal cost $352 million, the most expensive project up to that time. It was expensive in human terms, too. More than 5,000 workers died from diseases or accidents.

Background In 1977, the United States signed a treaty that transferred ownership of the canal to Panama on December 31, 1999.

How the Panama Canal Works

Engineers faced a problem in building the Panama Canal. Because of the region's different landscape elevations, no waterway would remain level. They solved this dilemma by building three sets of *locks*—water-filled chambers that raise or lower ships to match a canal's different water levels.

1 The lock gates open on one end to allow the ship to enter.

2 The gates close, and water is pumped in or out depending on whether the ship is moving up or down.

3 Once the water in the chamber and the canal ahead is level, the second gate opens and the ship moves on.

The locks, whose steel gates rise six stories high, can hold as much as 26 million gallons of water—enough to supply a major U.S. city for one day.

Gatún Locks   Culebra Cut   Pedro Miguel Locks
Gatún Lake   Miraflores Lake
Atlantic Ocean   Miraflores Locks   Pacific Ocean

◄——— 51 miles ———►

This cross-section shows the different elevations and locks that a ship moves through on the 8–9 hour trip through the canal. Before the canal was built, a trip around South America could take two months.

CONNECT TO HISTORY

1. **Drawing Conclusions** Why did the United States want a shorter route between the Atlantic and Pacific oceans?

CONNECT TO TODAY

2. **Researching** What is the economic and political status of the Panama Canal today?

For more about the Panama Canal . . .

RESEARCH LINKS
CLASSZONE.COM

INTERACTIVE

PACIFIC
OCEAN

ATLANTIC
OCEAN

U.S. troops, 1898–1902, 1906–1909, 1912, 1917–1922;
Platt Amendment, 1901-1934

U.S. troops, 1915–1934;
Financial supervision, 1916–1941

UNITED STATES

Columbus

U.S. troops, 1916–1917

U.S. troops, 1916–1924;
Financial supervision,
1905–1941

Gulf of
Mexico

U.S. troops, 1914

MEXICO

Havana

CUBA Guantánamo

PUERTO
RICO

HAITI

U.S. naval base, 1903

DOMINICAN
REPUBLIC

Mexico City   Veracruz

BR. HONDURAS

Caribbean
Sea

HONDURAS

U.S. possession
after 1898

GUATEMALA
EL SALVADOR

NICARAGUA

PANAMA

U.S. troops, 1909–1910, 1912–1925, 1926–1933;
Financial supervision, 1911–1924

COSTA RICA

Equator

U.S. acquired Canal Zone, 1903;
Canal completed, 1914

GEOGRAPHY SKILLBUILDER
Interpreting Maps
1. **Location** On what island is the U.S. naval base at Guantánamo?
2. **Place** To how many Latin American countries did the United States send troops?

U.S. Involvement in Latin America

The Panama Canal was only one sign of U.S. involvement in Latin America. As the U.S. economy continued to grow, so did Americans' interest in the resources of their southern neighbors.

Businesses in the United States found that they could cheaply buy food and raw materials—for example, bananas, coffee, and copper—from Latin America. They shipped these goods to the United States and sold them for higher prices. U.S. companies also bought large amounts of land in the region for farming and mining.

As economic interests drew the United States deeper into Latin American affairs, U.S. leaders became concerned about political stability in the region. They were especially worried that instability might tempt European nations to intervene in the region.

Reading **History**
C. Making Inferences Why was the United States interested in the political stability of Latin America?

Policing the Hemisphere

During his presidency, Theodore Roosevelt made it clear that the United States would remain the dominant power in the Western Hemisphere. He summed up his foreign policy toward the region with an African saying: "Speak softly, but carry a big stick." Roosevelt, however, rarely spoke softly. He made sure that everyone knew the United States would use military force if its interests were threatened.

Roosevelt reminded European powers of the Monroe Doctrine—the policy that prevented other nations from intervening in Latin America. In 1904, he added the **Roosevelt Corollary**. Now, the doctrine would not only prevent European intervention in Latin America; it also authorized the United States to act as a "policeman" in the region. That is, U.S. leaders would now intervene in Latin America's domestic affairs

Vocabulary
corollary: a statement that follows logically from an earlier statement

when they believed that such action was necessary to maintain stability.

In 1905, the United States used the Roosevelt Corollary to take control of the Dominican Republic's finances after the country failed to pay its foreign debts. A year later, when a revolt threatened Cuba's government, the policy was used to send troops there.

Later presidents expanded on Roosevelt's "big stick diplomacy." William Howard Taft urged American businesses to invest in Latin America, promising military action if anything threatened these investments. He kept his word. In 1912, Taft sent marines to Nicaragua to restore order.

Background
Taft's policy was known as "dollar diplomacy."

President Taft's successor, Woodrow Wilson, also intervened in Latin America. When a revolution in Mexico began to threaten U.S. interests, Wilson took action. In 1914, he sent a fleet to Veracruz after U.S. sailors were arrested. Two years later, he sent troops into Mexico after a Mexican revolutionary named Pancho Villa (PAHN•choh VEE•yah) raided New Mexico and killed 19 Americans in the town of Columbus.

Americans rarely questioned U.S. actions in Latin America. They saw their nation as a good police officer, maintaining peace and preventing disorder. But many Latin Americans saw the United States as an imperial power that cared only about its own interests. This mistrust continues to trouble U.S. relations with its neighbors. In the next chapter, you will read about U.S. involvement in another part of the world—Europe.

Now and then

GLOBO COP?

In the early 1900s, the United States used its "police powers" in the Western Hemisphere. Today, U.S. forces participate in police actions all over the globe. This fact has led some journalists to call the United States the "Globo Cop."

In the 1990s, U.S. forces helped lead international police actions in Somalia (see photo below), Yugoslavia, and other areas in crisis. The United States also led the Gulf War forces that liberated Kuwait after it was seized by Iraq.

The United States continues to patrol its own hemisphere, too. In 1989, U.S. troops invaded Panama to overthrow dictator Manuel Noriega.

Section 3 Assessment

1. Terms & Names

Explain the significance of:
- sphere of influence
- Open Door Policy
- Boxer Rebellion
- Panama Canal
- Roosevelt Corollary

2. Using Graphics

Use a chart like the one below to record details about U.S. involvement in Asia and Latin America.

Asia	Latin America

How was U.S. involvement in Asia different from that in Latin America?

3. Main Ideas

a. Why was the United States interested in the Philippines?

b. Why was the nation of Panama created in 1903?

c. How did the Roosevelt Corollary change U.S. foreign policy?

4. Critical Thinking

Drawing Conclusions
Why did the United States become so heavily involved in Asia and Latin America?

THINK ABOUT
- U.S. economic growth
- American military interests

ACTIVITY OPTIONS

SCIENCE

MATH

Research the Panama Canal. Build a simple **model** of the canal or create a **graph** that shows how many ships use the canal each year.

VISUAL SUMMARY

Becoming a World Power

The United States Continues to Expand

In the late 1800s, the United States began to expand overseas.
- Alaska was purchased from Russia.
- Planters took over Hawaii's government.

The Spanish-American War

Events in Cuba, a Spanish colony in the Caribbean, led to the Spanish-American War.
- U.S. forces won victories in the Caribbean and in Asia.
- Spain gave up its colonies in Cuba, Puerto Rico, the Philippines, and Guam.

U.S. Involvement Overseas

In both Asia and Latin America, the United States began to play a larger role.
- U.S. leaders insisted on an Open Door Policy in China.
- The United States built the Panama Canal.

TERMS & NAMES

Briefly explain the significance of each of the following.

1. imperialism
2. Queen Liliuokalani
3. yellow journalism
4. Spanish-American War
5. Rough Riders
6. Anti-Imperialist League
7. Open Door Policy
8. Boxer Rebellion
9. Panama Canal
10. Roosevelt Corollary

REVIEW QUESTIONS

The United States Continues to Expand (pages 659–661)

1. Why did Americans become interested in overseas expansion in the late 1800s?
2. How did the public react when William Seward negotiated the purchase of Alaska in 1867?
3. Why did the United States take an interest in Hawaii?
4. Why might President Cleveland have wanted to restore Liliuokalani to the Hawaiian throne?

The Spanish-American War (pages 662–667)

5. How did the Spanish-American War begin?
6. What were the most important battles of the war?
7. What territories did the United States take control of as a result of its victory over the Spanish?

U.S. Involvement Overseas (pages 668–673)

8. Why did U.S. leaders want access to China's markets after the Spanish-American War?
9. Why was there an interest in building a canal across Latin America?
10. How were the Latin American policies of Roosevelt, Taft, and Wilson similar?

CRITICAL THINKING

1. USING YOUR NOTES: FINDING MAIN IDEAS

Using your completed chart, answer the questions below.

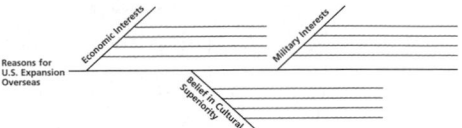

a. How did U.S. economic interests in Latin America influence the foreign policy of the United States?

b. In what ways was the Boxer Rebellion a reaction to the attitude of foreigners in China?

2. ANALYZING LEADERSHIP

What qualities made Theodore Roosevelt an effective leader?

3. THEME: EXPANSION

How did U.S. expansion at the end of the 19th century compare with expansion that occurred earlier? Discuss both similarities and differences.

4. APPLYING CITIZENSHIP SKILLS

How might the activities of the Anti-Imperialist League have helped to remind citizens of their democratic responsibilities?

5. FORMING OPINIONS

The "yellow journalism" of major newspapers influenced U.S. foreign policy at the turn of the century. How does modern media, such as television, shape public opinion today?

Interact *with* History

How has your study of U.S. involvement overseas at the turn of the century influenced your opinion about getting involved in the affairs of another country?

Use the graph and your knowledge of U.S. history to answer questions 1 and 2.

Additional Test Practice, pp. S1–S33.

U.S. Trade Expansion, *1865–1915*

Source: *Historical Statistics of the United States*

1. In what year was the value of U.S. imports approximately $1,500,000,000?

A. 1885

B. 1895

C. 1905

D. 1915

2. In what time period did the value of U.S. exports remain nearly the same?

A. 1875–1885

B. 1885–1895

C. 1895–1905

D. 1905–1915

This quotation from the Anti-Imperialist League is about imperialism. Use the quotation and your knowledge of U.S. history to answer question 3.

PRIMARY SOURCE

We hold that the policy known as imperialism is hostile to liberty. . . . We regret that it has become necessary in the land of Washington and Lincoln to reaffirm that all men, of whatever race or color, are entitled to life, liberty, and the pursuit of happiness.

From the *Platform of the American Anti-Imperialist League*

3. Which conclusion best sums up this passage?

A. The League believed people of all nations should be free to make their own choices.

B. The League believed American freedoms should be brought to the world.

C. The League believed imperialism was more important than liberty.

D. The League believed all nations of the world wanted American help to become free.

TEST PRACTICE
CLASSZONE.COM

ALTERNATIVE ASSESSMENT

1. 📝 **WRITING ABOUT HISTORY**

Suppose that you are a construction worker building the Panama Canal. Write a **letter** home that describes your work and living conditions.

• Research your letter using library resources.

• Include a map or a diagram in your letter.

• Decide if you believe the canal is a good or a bad project and make your letter reflect your opinion.

2. COOPERATIVE LEARNING

Work with three or four other students to help to plan, write, and illustrate a news story that features an important event from the Spanish-American War. Remember to use a journalistic style, presenting information in an unbiased manner.

INTEGRATED TECHNOLOGY

DOING INTERNET RESEARCH

When the United States annexed the Philippines after the Spanish-American War, Filipinos rose in rebellion. Prepare a multimedia presentation on the Philippine-American War that resulted from that rebellion.

• Find quotes that express views of the Filipino and American soldiers, including African-American troops. Use online encyclopedias in your research.

• Use presentation software to show descriptions or images of the battle. Record any quotes you've found and play them along with your presentation.

• Prepare a datasheet or a chart indicating casualties on both sides during the conflict.

For more about the Philippine-American war . . .

INTERNET ACTIVITY
CLASSZONE.COM

World War I
1914–1920

This photograph shows a battlefield view of trench warfare during World War I.

The soldiers "go over the top" and charge the enemy lines.

August 15, 1914
U.S.-built Panama Canal officially opens.

May 7, 1915
Many Americans die as a German U-boat sinks *Lusitania*.

November 7, 1916
Woodrow Wilson is reelected president.

USA
World 1914

June 28, 1914
Austria-Hungary's Archduke Franz Ferdinand is assassinated, starting World War I.

COME AND DO
YOUR BIT

JOIN NOW

February– December, 1915
Allies and Central Powers clash at Gallipoli in the Ottoman Empire.

July– November, 1916
French, British, and Germans suffer huge losses at the Battle of the Somme.

The year is 1917, and the United States has been drawn into World War I. Each citizen is called upon to help the war effort. Some will join the American armed forces and go to fight in Europe. Others will work in factories at home, producing weapons and supplies. Even children will do their part.

How will you support the war effort?

What Do You Think?

- How can Americans at home help win the war?
- What might U.S. soldiers experience in Europe?
- How might being at war affect the country?

RESEARCH LINKS
CLASSZONE.COM

Visit the Chapter 24 links for more information about World War I.

Artillery shells pound the battlefield, killing soldiers and leaving great destruction behind.

April 2, 1917
Wilson asks Congress to declare war on Germany.

I WANT YOU
FOR U.S. ARMY
NEAREST RECRUITING STATION

January 8, 1918
President Wilson proposes League of Nations.

November 2, 1920
Warren G. Harding is elected president.

1920

March 3, 1918
Russia withdraws from the war.

November 11, 1918
The Allies defeat the Central Powers, ending World War I.

June 28, 1919
The Allies and Germany sign the Treaty of Versailles.

World War I **677**

Reading Strategy: Recognizing Effects

What Do You Know?

What do you think of when you hear the phrase "world war"? What were the major countries in the war? Where did most of the fighting take place?

Think About

- what you've learned about World War I from movies or television
- reasons that millions of people might choose to risk their lives in a global conflict
- your responses to the Interact with History about supporting the war effort (see page 677)

What Do You Want to Know?

What details do you need to help you understand what is involved in waging a world war? Make a list of these details in your notebook before you read the chapter.

This 1918 poster urged Americans not to waste food during the war.

Recognizing Effects

To help you make sense of what you read, learn to analyze the effects of important historical events. The chart below will help you analyze some of the effects of World War I, both on the world and on the United States. In each box, fill in a different effect. Add more boxes if you need to.

See Skillbuilder Handbook, page R11.

Taking Notes

EFFECTS ON THE WORLD

EFFECTS ON THE UNITED STATES

World War I

War Breaks Out in Europe

MAIN IDEA	WHY IT MATTERS NOW	TERMS & NAMES
After World War I broke out, the United States eventually joined the Allied side.	This was the first time that the United States was involved in a European conflict.	militarism U-boat Central Powers Woodrow Wilson Allies neutrality trench warfare Zimmermann telegram

ONE AMERICAN'S STORY

In the late 1800s and early 1900s, European nations competed to expand their empires. Rivalry caused tension among these nations. In 1914, President Woodrow Wilson sent Colonel Edward M. House to study the situation.

House gave the president a troubling report. He compared Europe to an open keg of gunpowder that only needed a spark to explode. He was right. On June 28, 1914, a Serbian shot and killed Archduke Franz Ferdinand, the heir to the throne of Austria-Hungary. Soon Austria declared war on Serbia. The nations of Europe chose sides and the Great War, later called World War I, began.

Archduke Franz Ferdinand and his wife are murdered at Sarajevo on June 28, 1914.

Causes of World War I

A single action, the assassination of the archduke, started World War I. But the conflict had many underlying causes.

1. **Imperialism.** Britain, France, Germany, and Italy competed for colonies in Africa and Asia. Because it had fewer colonies than Britain and France, Germany felt it deserved more colonies to provide it with resources and buy its goods.

2. **Nationalism.** Europeans were very nationalistic, meaning that they had strong feelings of pride, loyalty, and protectiveness toward their own countries. They wanted to prove their nations were the best. They placed their countries' interests above all other concerns. In addition, some ethnic groups hoped to form their own separate nations and were willing to fight for such a cause.

3. **Militarism.** The belief that a nation needs a large military force is <u>militarism</u>. In the decades before the war, the major powers built up their armies and navies.

Taking Notes

Use your chart to take notes about the effects of World War I.

EFFECTS ON THE WORLD	EFFECTS ON THE UNITED STATES

World War I

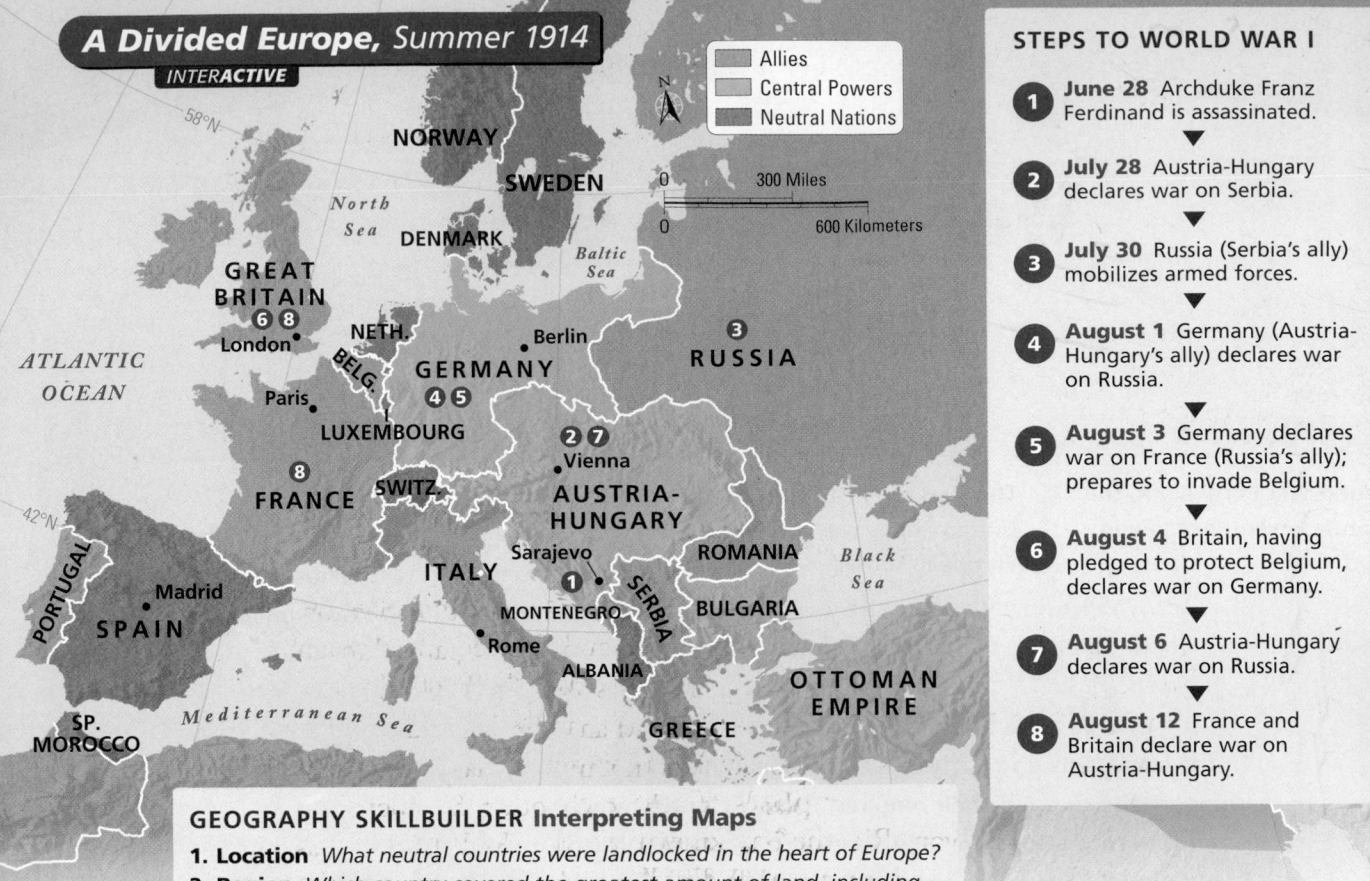

A Divided Europe, Summer 1914
INTERACTIVE

Allies
Central Powers
Neutral Nations

N

0   300 Miles
0   600 Kilometers

NORWAY
SWEDEN
North Sea
DENMARK
Baltic Sea
GREAT BRITAIN ❻❽
London
NETH.
Berlin
BELG.
GERMANY ❹❺
RUSSIA ❸
Paris
LUXEMBOURG
ATLANTIC OCEAN
❽
FRANCE
SWITZ.
❷❼
Vienna
AUSTRIA-HUNGARY
Sarajevo
ITALY
❶
MONTENEGRO
Rome
SERBIA
ROMANIA
Black Sea
BULGARIA
ALBANIA
OTTOMAN EMPIRE
PORTUGAL
Madrid
SPAIN
SP. MOROCCO
Mediterranean Sea
GREECE

58°N
42°N

STEPS TO WORLD WAR I

1 **June 28** Archduke Franz Ferdinand is assassinated.

2 **July 28** Austria-Hungary declares war on Serbia.

3 **July 30** Russia (Serbia's ally) mobilizes armed forces.

4 **August 1** Germany (Austria-Hungary's ally) declares war on Russia.

5 **August 3** Germany declares war on France (Russia's ally); prepares to invade Belgium.

6 **August 4** Britain, having pledged to protect Belgium, declares war on Germany.

7 **August 6** Austria-Hungary declares war on Russia.

8 **August 12** France and Britain declare war on Austria-Hungary.

GEOGRAPHY SKILLBUILDER Interpreting Maps
1. **Location** *What neutral countries were landlocked in the heart of Europe?*
2. **Region** *Which country covered the greatest amount of land, including territory in both Europe and Asia?*

4. **Alliances** In 1914, a tangled network of competing alliances bound European nations together. An attack on one nation forced all its allies to come to its aid. Any small conflict could become a larger war. European nations had divided into two opposing alliances. The **Central Powers** were made up of Austria-Hungary, Germany, the Ottoman Empire, and Bulgaria. They faced the Allied Powers, or **Allies,** consisting of Serbia, Russia, France, Great Britain, Italy, and seven other countries.

Stalemate in the Trenches

When the war began in August, most people on both sides assumed it would be over within a few months. With France as its goal, the German army invaded Belgium on August 4, 1914. Despite stiff resistance, the Germans fought their way west into France. They reached the Marne River about 40 miles from Paris. There the French, supported by the British, rallied and prepared to fight back. The First Battle of the Marne, in September 1914, stopped the German advance.

Instead of one side quickly defeating the other, the two sides stayed stuck in the mud for more than three years. The soldiers were fighting a new kind of battle, **trench warfare**. Troops huddled at the bottom of rat-infested trenches. They fired artillery and machine guns at each other. Lines of trenches stretched across France from the English Channel to the border with Switzerland. (See pages 684–685 for an

Background
The Ottoman Empire included modern-day Turkey and Syria.

Reading **History**
A. Reading a Map On the map on page 688, find the site of the first Battle of the Marne.

Vocabulary
trench: a long, deep ditch dug for protection

illustration of the trenches.) For more than three years, the battle lines remained almost unchanged. Neither side could win a clear victory.

In the trenches, soldiers faced the constant threat of sniper fire. Artillery shelling turned the area between the two opposing armies into a "no man's land" too dangerous to occupy. When soldiers left their trenches to attack enemy lines, they rushed into a hail of bullets and clouds of poison gas.

When battles did take place, they cost many thousands of lives, often without gaining an inch for either side. The Battle of the Somme (SAHM), between July and November 1916, resulted in more than 1.2 million casualties. British dead or wounded numbered over 400,000. German losses totaled over 600,000, and French nearly 200,000. Despite this, the Allies gained only about seven miles.

Reading **History**

B. Reading a Map
Find the site of the Battle of the Somme on the map on page 688.

A War of New Technology

New technology raised the death toll. The tank, a British invention, smashed through barbed wire, crossed trenches, and cleared paths through no man's land. Soldiers also had machine guns that fired 600 bullets a minute. Poison gas, used by both sides, burned and blinded soldiers.

World War I was the first major conflict in which airplanes were used in combat. By 1917, fighter planes fought each other far above the clouds. Manfred von Richthofen, known as the Red Baron, was Germany's top ace. An ace was an aviator who had downed five or more enemy aircraft. Von Richthofen shot down over 80 enemy planes.

Background
U-boat was short for "undersea boat."

At sea, the Germans used submarines, which they called **U-boats,** to block trade. They were equipped with both guns and torpedoes. German U-boats sank over 11 million tons of Allied shipping.

New Technology of War

First used effectively during World War I, these new weapons caused high casualties.

Airplane

Poison Gas

Machine Gun

Tank

681

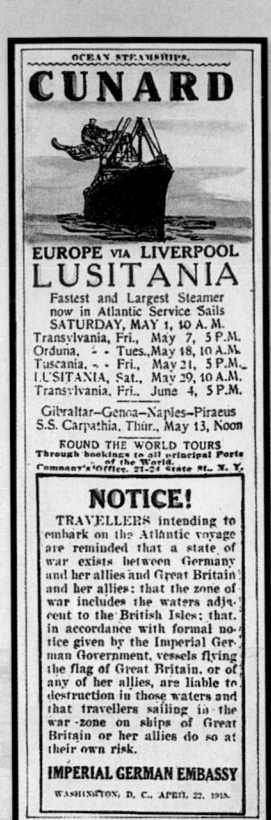

OCEAN STEAMSHIPS.

CUNARD

EUROPE VIA LIVERPOOL

LUSITANIA

Fastest and Largest Steamer
now in Atlantic Service Sails
SATURDAY, MAY 1, 10 A.M.
Transylvania, Fri., May 7, 5 P.M.
Orduna, - - Tues., May 18, 10 A.M.
Tuscania, - - Fri., May 21, 5 P.M.
LUSITANIA, Sat., May 29, 10 A.M.
Transylvania, Fri., June 4, 5 P.M.

Gibraltar—Genoa—Naples—Piraeus
S.S. Carpathia, Thur., May 13, Noon

ROUND THE WORLD TOURS
Through bookings to all principal Ports
of the World.
Company's Office, 21-24 State St., N.Y.

NOTICE!

TRAVELLERS intending to
embark on the Atlantic voyage
are reminded that a state of
war exists between Germany
and her allies and Great Britain
and her allies; that the zone of
war includes the waters adja-
cent to the British Isles; that,
in accordance with formal notice given by the Imperial German Government, vessels flying
the flag of Great Britain, or of
any of her allies, are liable to
destruction in those waters and
that travellers sailing in the
war zone on ships of Great
Britain or her allies do so at
their own risk.

IMPERIAL GERMAN EMBASSY
WASHINGTON, D.C., APRIL 22, 1915.

The British liner *Lusitania* is sunk off the Irish coast by a German submarine on May 7, 1915.

America's Path to War

When the war started in 1914, President <u>Woodrow Wilson</u> announced a policy of <u>neutrality,</u> refusing to take sides in the war. A popular song, "I Didn't Raise My Boy to Be a Soldier," expressed the antiwar sentiment of many Americans.

Over time, however, German attacks shifted public opinion to the Allied cause. In the fall of 1914, Britain set up a naval blockade of German ports, seizing all goods bound for Germany. In response, German submarines sank all Allied merchant ships they found off the British coast. In May 1915, a German U-boat torpedoed the British passenger ship *Lusitania*, killing 1,198 people, including 128 Americans. The sinking turned many Americans against Germany.

But President Wilson kept the United States neutral. He demanded that the German government halt unrestricted submarine warfare, and it agreed. In the election of 1916, the Democratic Party's campaign slogan, "He kept us out of war," appealed to voters. Wilson won reelection.

Desperate to defeat Britain, Germany resumed unrestricted submarine warfare at the end of January 1917. Its military leaders knew this action would bring the United States into the war. However, they hoped to win the war before the Americans arrived.

The next month, another blow to German-American relations came from the <u>Zimmermann telegram.</u> The telegram was discovered by the British, who passed it on to the Americans. In it, Arthur Zimmermann, the German foreign minister, told the German ambassador in Mexico to propose that Mexico join the Germans. In exchange, Germany would help Mexico get back its "lost" territories of Texas, New Mexico, and Arizona. Americans were furious.

Reading **History**

C. Making Inferences Why did the sinking of the *Lusitania* turn Americans against Germany?

In March, German submarines sank three American ships. President Wilson asked for a declaration of war.

> ***"The world must be made safe for democracy."***
> Woodrow Wilson

A VOICE FROM THE PAST

The world must be made safe for democracy. . . . We desire no conquest. . . . We are but one of the champions of the rights of mankind. We shall be satisfied when those rights have been made . . . secure.

Woodrow Wilson, message to Congress, April 2, 1917

Six senators and 50 representatives, including the first woman in Congress, Jeannette Rankin of Montana, voted against going to war. But the majority shared the president's commitment to join the Allies.

Revolution in Russia

Events in Russia made U.S. entry into the war more urgent for the Allies. By early 1915, the huge Russian army had been outfought by a smaller German army led by better-trained officers. In August 1915, Czar Nicholas II insisted on taking control of the troops himself. His poor leadership was blamed for more deaths. By 1917, food shortages led to riots, and soaring inflation led to strikes by angry workers in Russia.

In March 1917, Czar Nicholas II was forced to step down. A temporary government continued the unpopular war until November. In that month the Bolsheviks, a communist group led by Vladimir Ilich Lenin, took power. Communism is a political system in which the government owns key parts of the economy, and there is no private property.

*Reading***History**

D. Analyzing Causes What led Russia to pull out of the war?

Because the war had devastated Russia, Lenin at once began peace talks with Germany. In March 1918, Russia withdrew from the war by signing the Treaty of Brest-Litovsk. German troops could now turn from Russia to the Western front. The Allies urged American troops to come quickly, as you will read in the next section.

Section 1 Assessment

1. Terms & Names

Explain the significance of:
- militarism
- Central Powers
- Allies
- trench warfare
- U-boat
- Woodrow Wilson
- neutrality
- Zimmermann telegram

2. Using Graphics

Write at least four events that brought the United States into World War I.

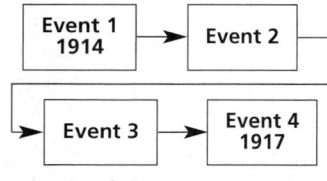

Which of these events was most important? Why?

3. Main Ideas

a. What were the long-term causes of World War I?

b. Why were Americans divided over the issue of remaining neutral?

c. Why was Russia's withdrawal from the war in 1917 a blow to Allies?

4. Critical Thinking

Analyzing Causes How did imperialism, nationalism, and militarism work to reinforce each other?

THINK ABOUT
- the goals of each
- how nationalism might encourage military buildup
- how nationalism contributed to the race for colonies

ACTIVITY OPTIONS

SCIENCE

ART

Research one of the new weapons of World War I. Explain how it works using a **model,** or draw an illustrated **diagram** of a defense against the weapon.

Survive Trench Warfare

You are a platoon leader assigned to a section of the front in central France. You have 60 men under your command. Day and night, through constant rain, earthen trenches full of sticky mud serve as your only protection. Sometimes, you think, the cold, rain, mud, rats, and fatigue are tougher to endure than a German bombardment.

COOPERATIVE LEARNING On this page are two challenges you face as a soldier during World War I. Working with a small group, decide how to deal with each challenge. Choose an option, assign a task to each group member, and do the activity. You will find useful information in the Data File. Be prepared to present your solutions to the class.

PHYSICAL EDUCATION CHALLENGE

"They must have 20 or 30 pounds of mud on them."

Until now, no one thought the trenches would be a permanent part of this war. So you, like the other soldiers along the front, weren't trained to cope with heavy, thick mud, 70-pound backpacks, and the other demands of living and fighting in these conditions. You learned on the job. Now you've been ordered to contribute ideas for a training program that will prepare recruits for the trenches. Look at the Data File for help. Then present your ideas using one of these options:

• Design an exercise regimen to strengthen troops for the trenches.
• Write a booklet of survival tips based on your platoon's experiences.

HEALTH CHALLENGE

"Your feet swell to two or three times . . . normal size."

You're worried about your men getting trench foot. You've heard horror stories about men whose feet swelled so much they couldn't pull off their boots. Some of these men developed gangrene and had their feet amputated. The key to preventing trench foot is staying dry. What will you do? Use the Data File for help. Then present your solution using one of these options:

• Come up with a way to keep the men's feet dry.
• Role-play a conversation with veteran soldiers about preventing trench foot.

ACTIVITY WRAP-UP

Present to the Class As a group, review your methods of surviving the trenches. Pick the most creative solution for each challenge, and present these solutions to the class.

📁 DATA FILE

THE TRENCHES

• Trenches covered about 450 miles between the North Sea and the Swiss border.

• In France, ten-foot-deep trenches were dug into the ground and topped with sandbag parapets.

• Inside was a fire step, a ledge two or three feet up from bottom of the trench, used by sentries or troops firing.

• The sides were held up by sandbags and timber.

A SOLDIER'S GEAR

60–75 pounds of gear, including blankets, waterproof ground-sheet, extra boots and occasionally waterproof gum boots, quilted coat, shovel for digging trenches, helmet, wire clippers, pail for rations, 2 quarts of water, 4 days' food, 200 cartridges, 6 hand grenades, gas mask, 3 pairs of socks, soap, toothbrush, bottle of whale oil, towel, rifle, bayonet

TRENCH FOOD

beef stew, corned beef, bread, hard biscuits, pork and beans, tins of jam, butter, sugar, tea

PROBLEMS

• **trench foot:** condition caused by feet staying wet 24 hours a day; feet swell, turn numb and blue; if not treated, gangrene sets in and feet must be amputated; helped by rubbing whale oil on feet, changing to dry socks three times daily

• **mud:** mud traps the wounded until some drown, clogs rifles and gear, weighs men down, causes trench walls to fall in

• **rats:** huge rats, as big as rabbits, infest the trenches

For more about trench warfare . . .

RESEARCH LINKS
CLASSZONE.COM

America Joins the Fight

MAIN IDEA	WHY IT MATTERS NOW	TERMS & NAMES
U.S. forces helped the Allies win World War I.	For the first time, the United States asserted itself as a world power.	John J. Pershing American Expeditionary Force convoy system Second Battle of the Marne Alvin York armistice

ONE AMERICAN'S STORY

Eddie Rickenbacker was America's most famous flying ace. He was one of the first Americans to get a look at the trenches from the cockpit of an airplane.

A VOICE FROM THE PAST

[T]here appeared to be nothing below but these old battered ditches . . . and billions of shell holes. . . . [N]ot a tree, a fence . . . nothing but . . . ruin and desolation. The whole scene was appalling.

Eddie Rickenbacker, *Fighting the Flying Circus*

As you will read in this section, Rickenbacker and other U.S. soldiers helped the Allies win the war.

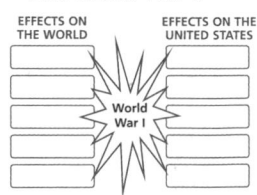

Taking Notes

Use your chart to take notes about the effects of America's entrance into World War I.

```
EFFECTS ON          EFFECTS ON THE
THE WORLD           UNITED STATES
   [ ]  \           /  [ ]
   [ ]   \  World  /   [ ]
   [ ]   /  War I  \   [ ]
         /          \
```

Raising an Army and a Navy

The U.S. Army was not ready for war. American fighting forces consisted of fewer than 200,000 soldiers, many of them recent recruits. To meet its need for troops, the government began a draft. This system of choosing people for forced military service was first used during the Civil War. In May 1917, Congress passed the Selective Service Act. This act required all males between the ages of 21 and 30 to sign up for military service. By the end of 1918, nearly 3 million men had been drafted.

About 2 million American soldiers went to France. They served under General **John J. Pershing** as the **American Expeditionary Force,** or AEF. British commanders asked the U.S. government to have AEF troops join existing French and British combat units. Wilson refused. He believed that having "distinct and separate" American combat units would guarantee the United States a major role in the peace talks at war's end. Most U.S. troops fought separately, but some fought under Allied command.

An American gun crew advances against German positions in 1918.

Close to 50,000 American women also served in World War I. Some volunteered for overseas duty with the American Red Cross. However, for the first time in American history, women also served in the military. The Navy, desperate for clerical workers, took about 12,000 female volunteers. The Marine Corps accepted 305 female recruits, known as Marinettes. Over 1,000 women went overseas for the Army. Nurses made up the largest group of females in the armed forces. However, women also acted as interpreters, operated switchboards, entertained troops, and drove ambulances for the AEF.

Reading **History**
A. Finding Main Ideas How did women serve in the U.S. armed forces?

Around 400,000 African Americans served in the armed forces. More than half of them served in France. As they had at home, African-American troops overseas faced discrimination. However, it came from white American soldiers rather than from their European allies. At first, the Army refused to take black draftees. However, responding to pressure from African-American groups, the military eventually created two African-American combat divisions.

American Ships Make a Difference

In the first years of the war, German U-boat attacks on supply ships were a serious threat to the Allied war effort. American Rear Admiral William S. Sims convinced the Allies to adopt a system of protection. In a **convoy system,** a heavy guard of destroyers escorted merchant ships across the Atlantic in groups. Begun in May 1917, this strategy quickly reduced the loss rate.

Vocabulary
mines: hidden explosive devices

Another American tactic gave the Allies added protection from the U-boat menace. Beginning in June 1918, the Allies laid a barrier of 70,000 mines in the North Sea. The 180-mile-long minefield made U-boat access to the North Atlantic almost impossible. Admiral Sims called the North Sea minefield "one of the wonders of the war."

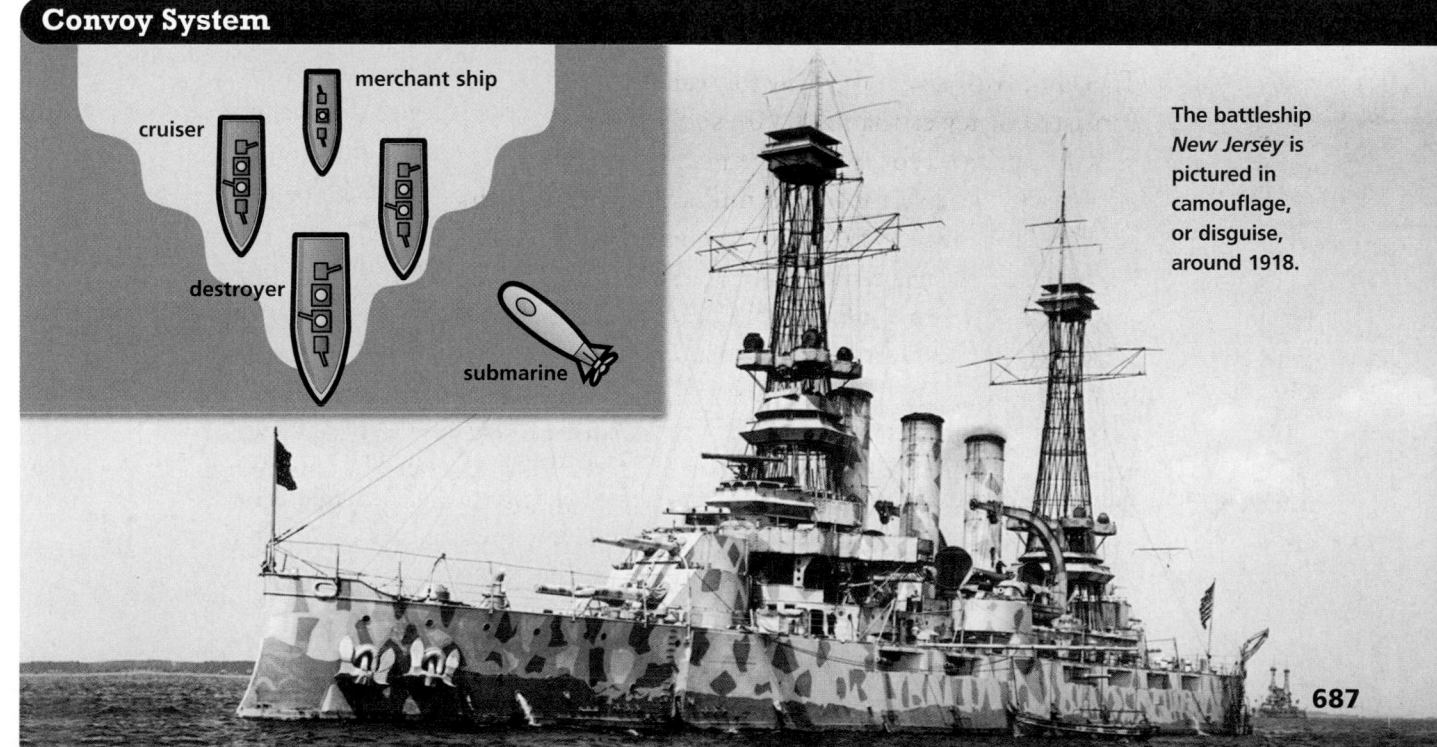

Convoy System

cruiser

merchant ship

destroyer

submarine

The battleship *New Jersey* is pictured in camouflage, or disguise, around 1918.

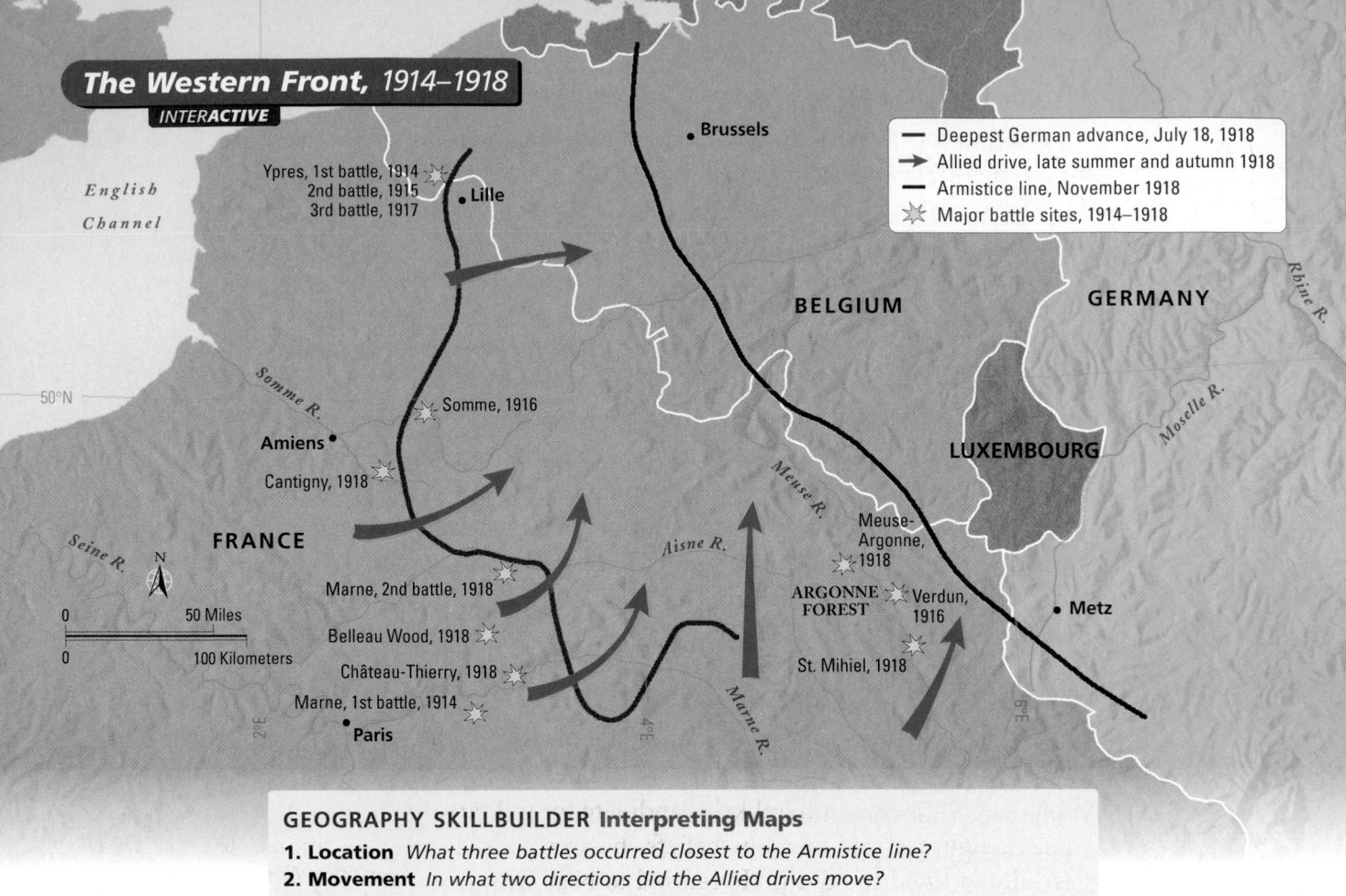

The Western Front, 1914–1918
INTERACTIVE

English Channel

Ypres, 1st battle, 1914
2nd battle, 1915
3rd battle, 1917

Lille

• Brussels

— Deepest German advance, July 18, 1918
→ Allied drive, late summer and autumn 1918
— Armistice line, November 1918
✹ Major battle sites, 1914–1918

BELGIUM

GERMANY

Rhine R.

50°N

Somme R.

✹ Somme, 1916

Amiens •

Cantigny, 1918 ✹

Meuse R.

Moselle R.

LUXEMBOURG

FRANCE

Aisne R.

Seine R.

Meuse-
Argonne,
1918 ✹

Metz •

Marne, 2nd battle, 1918 ✹

ARGONNE
FOREST ✹ Verdun,
1916

0   50 Miles

0   100 Kilometers

Belleau Wood, 1918 ✹

St. Mihiel, 1918 ✹

Château-Thierry, 1918 ✹

Marne, 1st battle, 1914 ✹

Marne R.

• Paris

2°E   4°E   6°E

GEOGRAPHY SKILLBUILDER Interpreting Maps
1. **Location** *What three battles occurred closest to the Armistice line?*
2. **Movement** *In what two directions did the Allied drives move?*

American Troops Enter the War

By the time the first American troops arrived in France in June 1917, the Allies had been at war for almost three years. The small force of 14,000 Yanks boosted the morale of the battle-weary Allies. However, almost a year would pass before the bulk of the American troops landed in Europe.

After their Russian opponents withdrew from the war, the Germans and the other Central Powers prepared to finish the fight in France. In March 1918, the Germans launched an offensive to end the war before the Americans arrived in force. Within two months, they had smashed through the French lines, reaching the Marne River only 50 miles from Paris. Just in time, in May 1918, one million fresh American troops arrived ready for action.

On May 28, American soldiers attacked the French town of Cantigny (kahn•tee•NYEE), which was occupied by the Germans. The soldiers advanced into the town, blasting enemy soldiers out of trenches and dragging them from cellars. Within two hours, the Yanks had taken control of Cantigny. The American victory lifted Allied morale.

When the Germans moved against the town of Château-Thierry (shah•toh•tyeh•REE), the Americans held their ground. They helped the French stop the German advance. Encouraged by these successes, French General Ferdinand Foch, commander of the Allied forces, ordered General Pershing's American forces to retake Belleau (beh•LOH) Wood.

Background
American soldiers were also called *doughboys*. This term was used even during the Civil War.

This was a forest near the Marne River well defended by German troops. American soldiers succeeded, but at a fearful cost. One unit lost 380 of its 400 men. However, the Americans had proved themselves in combat.

Pushing the Germans Back

The **Second Battle of the Marne** in the summer of 1918 was the turning point of the war. It began with a German drive against the French line. During three days of heavy fighting, about 85,000 Americans helped the Allies halt the German advance. The Allies then took the initiative. They cut the enemy off from its supply lines and forced the Germans back.

For the rest of the war, the Allies advanced steadily. By early September, the Germans had lost all the territory they had gained since the spring. September 26, 1918, marked the beginning of the final Meuse-Argonne (myooz•ahr•GAHN) offensive. Around 1.2 million U.S. soldiers took part in a massive drive to push back the German line between the Argonne Forest and the Meuse River. The war's final battle left 26,000 Americans dead. But by November, the Germans were retreating.

The Meuse-Argonne offensive made a hero of American soldier **Alvin York.** At first, Tennessee-born Sergeant York seemed an unlikely candidate for military fame. Because of his religious beliefs, he tried unsuccessfully to avoid the draft. He refused to bear arms on religious grounds. An army captain convinced him to change his mind. In October 1918, in the Argonne Forest, York attacked German machine gunners, killing 25 of them. Other German soldiers surrendered, and York returned to the American lines with 132 captives.

Another American hero was pilot Eddie Rickenbacker. He won fame as the U.S. "ace of aces" for shooting down a total of 26 enemy planes. Just before the Meuse-Argonne offensive, he attacked seven German planes, sending two of them crashing to the ground. This action won him the Medal of Honor.

Four African-American combat units also received recognition for their battlefield valor. Fighting under French commanders, the 369th, 371st, and 372nd regiments (and part of the 370th) were awarded France's highest honor, the Croix de Guerre. The 369th spent more continuous time on the front lines than any other American unit. Although under intense fire for 191 days, it never lost a foot of ground.

*Reading*History
B. Recognizing Effects What was the effect of the Meuse-Argonne offensive?

*Reading*History
C. Evaluating What was heroic about Sergeant York?

Connections TO LITERATURE

LITERATURE OF WORLD WAR I

Several notable American writers served in World War I. They included Ernest Hemingway, the poet E. E. Cummings, and John Dos Passos. Hemingway drove an ambulance for the Italian army. He put this experience into his war novel *A Farewell to Arms.* Cummings wrote of his time in France in *The Enormous Room.*

Dos Passos, who also worked as an ambulance driver, once explained what attracted him to the battlefront: "What was war like, we wanted to see with our own eyes. I wanted to see the show."

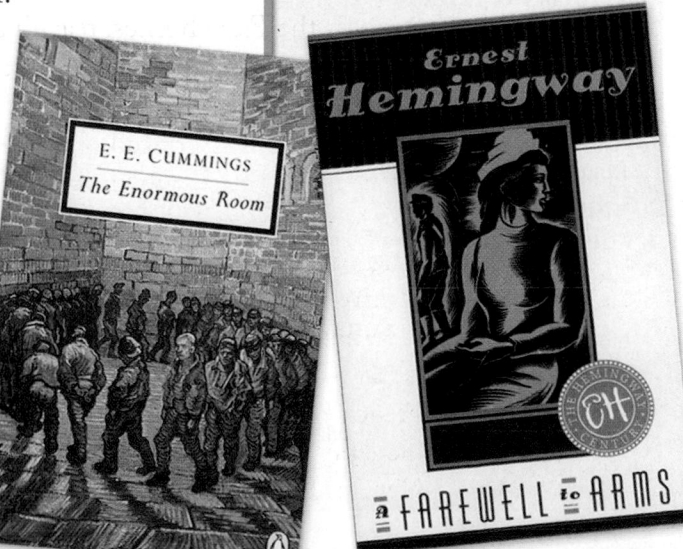

Americans were proud of the contribution their troops made to the war effort. They helped shift the balance in favor of the Allies.

Germany Stops Fighting

After the defeat of the Meuse-Argonne, General Erich Ludendorff advised the German government to seek peace. In early November, Germany's navy mutinied and its allies dropped out. On November 9, the Kaiser stepped down. Two days later Germany agreed to an **armistice,** an end to fighting. On November 11, 1918, at 11:00 A.M.—the 11th hour of the 11th day of the 11th month—all fighting ceased.

About 8.5 million soldiers died in the war, and about 21 million were wounded. Before he was killed in battle, one British soldier summed up the war's tragic costs.

Background
For many years after the war, Americans celebrated Armistice Day as a national holiday.

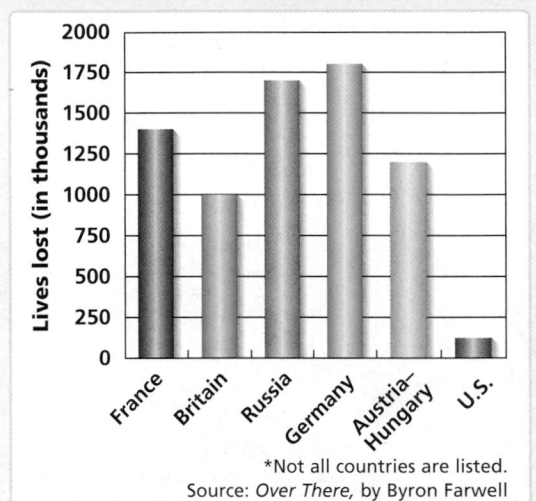

CONNECTIONS TO MATH

Military Deaths in World War I*

*Not all countries are listed.
Source: *Over There*, by Byron Farwell

SKILLBUILDER
Interpreting Graphs

1. *Which two nations on the chart suffered the most deaths?*
2. *U.S. deaths were about what percentage of combined French and British deaths?*

A VOICE FROM THE PAST

The sufferings of the men at the Front, of the wounded whose flesh and bodies are torn in a way you cannot conceive; the sorrow of those at home. . . . What a cruel and mad diversion of human activity!

William John Mason, quoted in *The Lost Generation of 1914*

Millions of civilians in Europe, Asia, and Africa also died in the war—from starvation and disease. In the next section, you will learn how the war affected U.S. civilians.

Section **Assessment**

1. Terms & Names

Explain the significance of:
- John J. Pershing
- American Expeditionary Force
- convoy system
- Second Battle of the Marne
- Alvin York
- armistice

2. Using Graphics

Create a web to show how American groups or individuals helped fight the war.

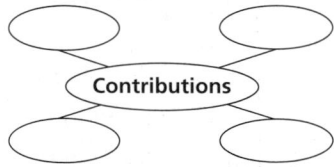

Contributions

Whose contribution was most surprising?

3. Main Ideas

a. Why did Wilson want U.S. forces to fight as a separate American combat unit?

b. What were two ways the U.S. Navy countered the U-boat threat?

c. Why was the Meuse-Argonne offensive a turning point in the war?

4. Critical Thinking

Recognizing Effects How important was America's entry into the war to the Allied cause?

THINK ABOUT
- the morale of Allied troops
- troop strength
- performance in battle

ACTIVITY OPTIONS

MUSIC

LANGUAGE ARTS

Make an **audiotape** of music or sounds that suggest the stages of the war, or write a **letter** in the voice of a soldier in the war.

Life on the Home Front

MAIN IDEA	WHY IT MATTERS NOW	TERMS & NAMES
The war required sacrifice for Americans at home and changed life in other ways.	Some wartime changes were permanent, such as black migration to Northern cities.	war bonds propaganda Espionage Act Sedition Act Oliver Wendell Holmes Great Migration

ONE AMERICAN'S STORY

On the home front, the war opened up new jobs for women. But when the war ended, female workers were laid off. Carrie Fearing wrote to her boss, hoping to keep her job.

A VOICE FROM THE PAST

We never took a soldier's place, a soldier would not do the work we did . . . such as sweeping, picking up waste and paper. . . . We . . . like our job very much and I hope you will . . . place us back at the shop.

Carrie Fearing, quoted in *Women, War, and Work*

In May 1918, these women worked in the Union Pacific Railroad freight yard in Cheyenne, Wyoming.

Like Fearing, many women were proud of the part they played in getting the country ready for war. In this section. you will learn more about wartime life at home.

Mobilizing for War

To prepare for war, the government needed money. World War I cost the United States $35.5 billion. Americans helped pay almost two-thirds of that amount by buying government war bonds. **War bonds** were low-interest loans by civilians to the government, meant to be repaid in a number of years. To sell the bonds, officials held Liberty Loan drives. Posters urged citizens to "Come Across or the Kaiser Will." Hollywood actors like Charlie Chaplin toured the country selling bonds to starstruck audiences.

Schoolchildren rolled bandages and collected tin cans, paper, toothpaste tubes, and apricot pits. The pits were burned and made into charcoal for gas mask filters. Some Boy Scout troops even sold war bonds. So that more food could be sent to soldiers, people planted "victory gardens" in backyards and vacant lots. Women's groups came together in homes and churches to knit socks and sweaters and sew hospital gowns.

Taking Notes

Use your chart to take notes about the effects of World War I on the home front.

EFFECTS ON THE WORLD		EFFECTS ON THE UNITED STATES
	World War I	

To persuade women to buy war bonds, this poster appealed to their love of family.

Patriotic citizens also saved food by observing wheatless Mondays and Wednesdays, when they ate no bread, and meatless Tuesdays. To save gas, they stopped their Sunday pleasure drives. The government limited civilian use of steel and other metals. Women donated their corsets with metal stays to scrap drives. Manufacturers stopped making tin toys for children and removed metal from caskets.

The war brought more government control of the economy. To produce needed war supplies, in 1917 President Wilson set up the War Industries Board. The board had great power. It managed the buying and distributing of war materials. It also set production goals and ordered construction of new factories. With the president's approval, the board also set prices. Another government agency, the National War Labor Board, settled conflicts between workers and factory owners.

Reading **History**
A. Finding Main Ideas What were civilians asked to do for the war effort?

To rally citizen support, Wilson created the Committee on Public Information. The committee's writers, artists, photographers, and film-makers produced **propaganda,** opinions expressed for the purpose of influencing the actions of others. The committee sold the war through posters, pamphlets, and movies. One popular pamphlet, "How the War Came to America," came out in Polish, German, Swedish, Bohemian, and Spanish. In movie houses, audiences watched such patriotic films as *Under Four Flags* and *Pershing's Crusaders.*

Intolerance and Suspicion

Patriotic propaganda did much to win support for the war. But its anti-German, anti-foreign focus also fueled prejudice. Suddenly people distrusted anything German. A number of towns with German names changed their names. Berlin, Maryland, became Brunswick. People called sauerkraut "liberty cabbage," and hamburger became "Salisbury steak." Owners of German shepherds took to calling their pets "police dogs."

Reading **History**
B. Recognizing Effects How did war propaganda fuel prejudice?

On June 15, 1917, Congress passed the **Espionage Act.** The **Sedition Act** followed in May 1918. These laws set heavy fines and long prison terms for such antiwar activities as encouraging draft resisters. The laws made it illegal to criticize the war. U.S. courts tried more than 1,500 pacifists, socialists, and other war critics. Hundreds went to jail. Socialist Party leader Eugene Debs gave a speech arguing that the war was fought by poor workingmen for the profit of wealthy business owners. For this talk, a judge sentenced him to ten years in prison.

The government ignored complaints that the rights of Americans were being trampled. In the 1919 decision in *Schenck* v. *United States,* the Supreme Court upheld the Espionage Act. Schenck, convicted of

distributing pamphlets against the draft, had argued that the Espionage Act violated his right to free speech. Justice **Oliver Wendell Holmes, Jr.,** wrote the court's opinion.

A VOICE FROM THE PAST

The most stringent [strict] protection of free speech would not protect a man in falsely shouting fire in a theater and causing a panic. . . . The question in every case is whether the words used . . . are of such a nature as to create a clear and present danger that they will bring about . . . evils that Congress has a right to prevent.

Oliver Wendell Holmes, Jr., *Schenck* v. *United States,* 1919

*Reading*History

C. Analyzing Points of View
Why did Justice Holmes believe that free speech could be limited?

Justice Holmes argued that free speech, guaranteed by the First Amendment, could be limited, especially in wartime.

New Jobs and the Great Migration

As soldiers went off to battle, the United States faced a labor shortage. Northern factories gearing up for war were suddenly willing to hire workers they had once rejected. Throughout the South, African Americans heeded the call. Between 1910 and 1920, about 500,000 African Americans moved north to such cities as New York, Chicago, Detroit, Cleveland, and St. Louis. This movement became known as the **Great Migration.** African Americans left to escape the bigotry, poverty, and racial violence of the South. They hoped for a better life in the North.

HISTORY *through* **ART**

The Migration of the Negro, Panel No. 1 (1940–41), by Jacob Lawrence, shows three of the most common destinations for African Americans leaving the South.

How does Lawrence's painting reflect continuity and change in American life?

693

New jobs were opening up in the American Southwest. These jobs were fueled by the growth of railroads and irrigated farming. A revolution was under way in Mexico, and the chaos led many Mexicans to flee across the border after 1910. Many immigrants settled in Texas, Arizona, Colorado, and California. Most became farm workers. During the war years, some went to Northern cities to take better-paying factory jobs.

The wartime labor shortage also meant new job choices for women. Women replaced male workers in steel mills, ammunition factories, and assembly lines. Women served as streetcar conductors and elevator operators. The war created few permanent openings for women, but their presence in these jobs gave the public a wider view of their abilities. Women's contributions during the war helped them win the vote.

Now and then

THE FLU EPIDEMIC

In 1918, flu victims often came down with pneumonia and died within a week. Today, bacterial infections such as pneumonia resulting from the flu can be controlled with antibiotics.

The 1998 discovery of the frozen remains of a 1918 flu victim in an Alaskan cemetery may one day lead to a better understanding of the virus. Scientists have found a genetic link between the 1918 flu virus and swine flu, a virus first found in pigs. The Alaskan find may help scientists develop vaccines to protect against future flu outbreaks.

Reading **History**

D. Recognizing Effects What groups gained new jobs as a result of the war?

The Flu Epidemic of 1918

Another result of the war was a deadly flu epidemic that swept the globe in 1918. It killed more than 20 million people on six continents by the time it disappeared in 1919. It had no known cure. Spread around the world by soldiers, the virus took some 500,000 American lives. People tried desperately to protect themselves. Everywhere, schools and other public places shut down to limit the flu's spread.

In the army, more than a quarter of the soldiers caught the disease. In some AEF units, one-third of the troops died. Germans fell victim in even larger numbers than the Allies. World War I brought death and disease to millions. It would also have longer-term effects, as you will read in Section 4.

Section 3 Assessment

1. Terms & Names
Explain the significance of:
- war bonds
- propaganda
- Espionage Act
- Sedition Act
- Oliver Wendell Holmes
- Great Migration

2. Using Graphics
Make a chart like the one below to show reasons for wartime shifts in population.

	Shift	Reason(s)
African Americans		
Mexicans		

How similar were the two groups' reasons for moving?

3. Main Ideas
a. What were three ways American families could contribute to the war effort?

b. What was the purpose of the Espionage and Sedition Acts? What groups were most affected by them?

c. What kinds of new job opportunities did the war create for women and minorities?

4. Critical Thinking
Making Inferences What were the positive and the negative consequences of American wartime propaganda?

THINK ABOUT
- contributions to war effort
- effect on opponents of war and on German-Americans

ACTIVITY OPTIONS

SPEECH

MATH

Deliver a **radio broadcast** on the importance of conserving food, or make a **calculation** of the amount of food your class wastes monthly.

The Legacy of World War I

MAIN IDEA	WHY IT MATTERS NOW	TERMS & NAMES
After the war, Americans were divided over foreign policy and domestic issues.	The war affected the role the United States played in the world during the rest of the century.	League of Nations reparations Fourteen Points Red Scare Treaty of Versailles Palmer raids

ONE AMERICAN'S STORY

Senator Henry Cabot Lodge opposed President Wilson's idea that the United States join the **League of Nations**—an organization set up to settle conflicts through negotiation. Lodge felt that joining such an alliance would require the United States to guarantee the freedom of other nations.

A VOICE FROM THE PAST

If we guarantee any country . . . its independence . . . we must [keep] at any cost . . . our word. . . . I wish [the American people] carefully to consider . . . whether they are willing to have the youth of America ordered to war by other nations.

Henry Cabot Lodge, speech to the Senate, February 28, 1919

Lodge's speech helped turn the public against the League. In this section, you will learn how the United States and Europe adjusted to the end of the war.

Senator Henry Cabot Lodge (1850–1924) opposed U.S. entry into the League of Nations.

Wilson's Fourteen Points

In January 1918, ten months before the war ended, President Wilson told Congress his goals for peace. His speech became known as the **Fourteen Points** (see page 699). It called for smaller military forces, an end to secret treaties, freedom of the seas, free trade, and changes in national boundaries. Most of these changes gave independence to peoples that Austria-Hungary or the Ottoman Empire had ruled.

For Wilson, the fourteenth point mattered most. He called for an association of nations to peacefully settle disputes. This association was to become the League of Nations, which Republicans like Lodge opposed. Wilson firmly believed that acceptance of his Fourteen Points by the warring parties would bring about what he called a "peace without victory."

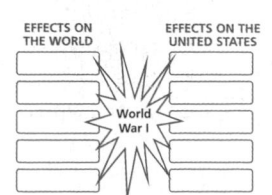

Taking Notes

Use your chart to take notes about the effects of World War I.

EFFECTS ON THE WORLD | EFFECTS ON THE UNITED STATES

World War I

Treaty of Versailles

Wilson led the U.S. delegation to the peace conference in France. Though many Europeans considered him a hero, conference leaders did not. The leaders of Britain, France, and Italy did not share Wilson's vision of "peace without victory." They wanted Germany to pay heavily for its part in the war.

The **Treaty of Versailles** (vuhr•SY) forced Germany to accept full blame for the war. Germany was stripped of its colonies and most of its armed forces. It was also burdened with $33 billion in **reparations**—money that a defeated nation pays for the destruction caused by a war. The treaty divided up the empires of Austria-Hungary and the Ottomans. It created Yugoslavia and Czechoslovakia and recognized Poland's independence.

*Reading*History

A. Recognizing Effects How were the Central Powers punished by the Treaty of Versailles?

Wilson managed to include the League of Nations in the treaty. He firmly believed the League would help to keep the peace. He returned home to seek Senate approval for the treaty. But the Republican-run Senate was dead set against it. Senator Henry Cabot Lodge kept delaying a vote on the treaty.

After weeks of delay, Wilson decided to make his case to the public. In September of 1919, he began a cross-country speaking trip to build support for the League. In about 21 days, he traveled almost 10,000 miles and gave over 30 speeches.

A VOICE FROM THE PAST

In the covenant [agreement] of the League of Nations, the moral forces of the world are mobilized . . . . They consent . . . to submit every matter of difference between them to the judgment of mankind, and just so certainly as they do that, . . . war will be pushed out of the foreground of terror in which it has kept the world.

Woodrow Wilson, speech in Pueblo, Colorado, on September 25, 1919

AMERICA'S HISTORY MAKERS

WOODROW WILSON

1856–1924

A gifted speaker, Woodrow Wilson had a strong sense of duty, and he inspired great loyalty. Yet he could be a harsh judge of others, stiff and unbending in his relations with people. Sculptor Jo Davidson remarked that "He invoked fear and respect . . . but not affection." Though not America's best-loved president, he still commands respect. When historians list the nation's best presidents, Wilson often ranks in the top ten.

How might Wilson's character have worked against approval of the Treaty of Versailles?

Shortly after giving this speech, Wilson collapsed from strain. Later, he suffered a stroke from which he never fully recovered.

Negotiations to get the treaty through Congress continued, but Americans were not eager for more foreign commitments. Lodge and his supporters offered to accept the treaty if major changes were made in the League. Wilson refused to compromise. As a result, the United States did not ratify the treaty. The League of Nations was formed without the United States.

*Reading*History

B. Analyzing Causes Why didn't the United States ratify the Treaty of Versailles?

The war and the Treaty of Versailles failed to make Europe "safe for democracy." In the next decades, Germany's resentment of the treaty grew. The treaty planted the seeds of World War II, an even more deadly conflict to come.

Postwar Europe, 1919

New nations

0   400 Miles
0   800 Kilometers

ATLANTIC OCEAN

North Sea

Baltic Sea

NORWAY   FINLAND
SWEDEN   ESTONIA   SOVIET RUSSIA
LATVIA
IRELAND   DENMARK   LITHUANIA
GREAT BRITAIN   NETH.
GERMANY
BELGIUM   POLAND
LUX.   CZECHOSLOVAKIA
FRANCE   SWITZ.   AUSTRIA
HUNGARY
YUGOSLAVIA   ROMANIA
PORTUGAL
SPAIN   ITALY   BULGARIA   Black Sea
ALBANIA   GREECE
Mediterranean Sea

GEOGRAPHY SKILLBUILDER Interpreting Maps
1. **Region** What new nations were created after the war?
2. **Region** In what part of Europe were most of the new nations located?

EFFECTS OF WORLD WAR I ON EUROPE

IMMEDIATE EFFECTS	LONG-TERM EFFECTS
Revolution in Russia	Breakup of empires
Allied victory	Formation of League of Nations
Destruction in Europe	Resentments leading to World War II

Strikes and the Red Scare

Background
In 1919, police, steelworkers, and coal miners also went on strike.

The Treaty of Versailles was not the only issue that divided Americans after the war. Shortly after the war ended, the United States experienced a number of labor strikes. For example, in Seattle, Washington, in February 1919, more than 55,000 workers took part in a peaceful general strike. The shutdown paralyzed the city.

Some Americans saw efforts to organize labor unions as the work of radicals, people who favor extreme measures to bring about change. The strikes sparked fears of a communist revolution like the one that toppled the Russian czar. In 1919–1920, this fear created a wave of panic called the **Red Scare** (communists were called *reds*). Public fear was heightened by the discovery of mail bombs sent to government officials. Many believed the bombs were the work of anarchists. Anarchists are radicals who do not believe in any form of government.

Reading **History**
C. Recognizing Effects What resulted from the Red Scare?

In January 1920, Attorney General A. Mitchell Palmer took action. He ordered federal agents and local police to raid the homes and headquarters of suspected radicals. His agents arrested at least 6,000 people in the **Palmer raids.** Without search warrants, agents burst into homes and offices and dragged citizens off to jail.

The Red Scare was not only antiradical but also antiforeign. During the Red Scare, two Italian-born anarchists, Nicola Sacco and Bartolomeo Vanzetti, were arrested for killing two men in an armed robbery in

Massachusetts. They claimed they were innocent, but both were found guilty and executed. Their trial attracted worldwide attention.

Racial Tensions Increase

Americans also saw a rise in racial tensions after the war. Between 1910 and 1920, the Great Migration brought a half million African Americans to Northern cities. In the cities where African Americans had settled in large numbers, whites and blacks competed for factory jobs and housing.

On July 2, 1917, tensions erupted into a race riot in East St. Louis, Illinois. The trouble began when blacks were brought in to take the jobs of white union members who had gone on strike. A shooting incident touched off a full-scale riot.

Two years later, African-American soldiers returning from the war found their social plight unchanged. They had fought to make the world "safe for democracy." At home, though, they were still second-class citizens.

Simmering resentments over housing, job competition, and segregation exploded during the summer of 1919. In 25 cities around the country, race riots flared. In Chicago, a black man swimming in Lake Michigan drifted into the white section of a beach. Whites stoned him until he drowned. Thirteen days of rioting followed. Before it ended, 38 people were dead.

Reading **History**
D. Analyzing Causes How did the war contribute to racial tensions?

Longing for "Normalcy"

By the time campaigning began for the 1920 election, Americans felt drained. Labor strikes, race riots, the Red Scare, and the fight over the Treaty of Versailles and the League of Nations had worn them out. Voters were ready for a break. Republican candidate Warren G. Harding of Ohio offered them one. His promise to "return to normalcy" appealed to voters. Harding won a landslide victory. In the next chapter, you will learn about American life after his election.

Section **4** Assessment

1. Terms & Names

Explain the significance of:
- League of Nations
- Fourteen Points
- Treaty of Versailles
- reparations
- Red Scare
- Palmer raids

2. Using Graphics

Create a diagram to examine the war's effects on Europe and America.

Effects of World War I	
Europe	United States

Which effects were positive and which were negative?

3. Main Ideas

a. Why did Germany resent the Treaty of Versailles?

b. Why did Lodge and other Republicans oppose joining the League of Nations?

c. What caused the Red Scare? Who was most affected by it?

4. Critical Thinking

Analyzing Points of View
Why was Wilson unable to get other powers to accept his goals for the peace conference?

THINK ABOUT
- conflicting goals
- practicality of Wilson's aims
- attitudes of other nations toward U.S. contributions during the war

ACTIVITY OPTIONS

LANGUAGE ARTS

ART

Imagine that you work for a newspaper. Write an **editorial** about the Palmer raids, or draw a political **cartoon** about the raids.

The Fourteen Points

Setting the Stage Nine months after the United States entered World War I, President Wilson delivered to Congress a statement of war aims. This statement became known as the "Fourteen Points." In the speech, President Wilson set forth 14 proposals for reducing the risk of war in the future. Numbers have been inserted to help identify the main points, as well as those omitted. **See Primary Source Explorer**

All the peoples of the world are in effect partners . . . , and for our own part we see very clearly that unless justice be done to others it will not be done to us. The program of the world's peace, therefore, is our program; and that program, . . . as we see it, is this:

[1] Open **covenants**[1] of peace, openly arrived at, after which there shall be no private international understandings of any kind but diplomacy shall proceed always frankly and in the public view.

[2] Absolute freedom of navigation upon the seas . . . in peace and in war. . . .

[3] The removal, so far as possible, of all economic barriers and the establishment of an equality of trade conditions among all the nations. . . .

[4] Adequate guarantees given and taken that national **armaments**[2] will be reduced. . . .

[5] A free, open-minded, and absolutely impartial adjustment of all colonial claims, based upon . . . the principle that . . . the interests of the populations concerned must have equal weight with the . . . claims of the government whose title is to be determined.

[6–13: These eight points deal with specific boundary changes.]

[14] A general association of nations must be formed under specific covenants for the purpose of affording mutual guarantees of political independence and territorial **integrity**[3] to great and small states alike.

—*Woodrow Wilson*

A CLOSER LOOK

THE VALUE OF OPENNESS

The first of Wilson's points attempts to solve one of the problems that caused the outbreak of World War I—agreements between nations arrived at in secret.

1. How might agreements arrived at in public prevent another world war?

A CLOSER LOOK

BALANCING CLAIMS

Wilson frequently appeals to fairness, balance, and impartiality in settling competing claims.

2. What might be unusual about a leader such as Wilson calling for an impartial adjustment of colonial claims?

A CLOSER LOOK

LEAGUE OF NATIONS

Wilson proposes that nations join a formal organization to protect one another.

3. Why did Wilson believe that such an organization would benefit the world?

1. **covenants:** binding agreements.
2. **armaments:** weapons and supplies of war.
3. **integrity:** the condition of being whole or undivided; completeness.

Interactive Primary Source Assessment

1. Main Ideas

a. Why should diplomacy avoid private dealings and proceed in public view?

b. How might equality of trade be important to keeping the peace?

c. What must nations join together to guarantee?

2. Critical Thinking

Evaluating The first five points address issues that Wilson believed had caused the war. How successful do you think Wilson's ideas have been in the rest of the 20th century?

THINK ABOUT

• other conflicts since World War I
• peacekeeping efforts around the world

TERMS & NAMES

Briefly explain the significance of each of the following.

1. militarism
2. Allies
3. trench warfare
4. Zimmermann telegram
5. American Expeditionary Force
6. convoy system
7. propaganda
8. Great Migration
9. Treaty of Versailles
10. Red Scare

REVIEW QUESTIONS

War Breaks Out in Europe (pages 679–685)

1. What were the sources of tension between the European powers that led to war?
2. Why did the United States at first remain neutral in the war between the Allies and the Central Powers?
3. What brought the United States into the war on the Allied side?

America Joins the Fight (pages 686–690)

4. How did the Allies fight the German U-boat threat?
5. How did U.S. entry into the war affect the Allies?
6. What led Germany to agree to an armistice?

Life on the Home Front (pages 691–694)

7. How did U.S. civilians aid the war effort?
8. How did Congress contribute to increased prejudice and intolerance on the home front?

The Legacy of World War I (pages 695–699)

9. How did Wilson's goals for the peace conference differ from those of his European allies?
10. Why did the Senate reject the Treaty of Versailles?

CRITICAL THINKING

1. USING YOUR NOTES: RECOGNIZING EFFECTS

Using your chart, answer the questions below.

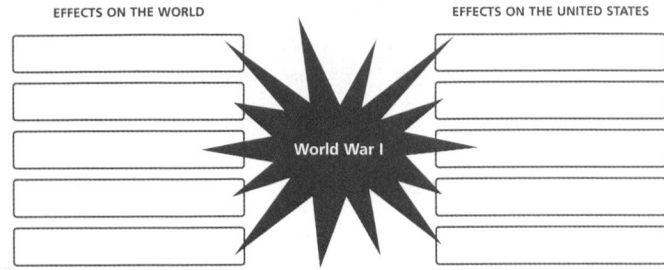

EFFECTS ON THE WORLD   World War I   EFFECTS ON THE UNITED STATES

a. Were the effects of the war greater in Europe or the United States?
b. What political effects did the war have on the United States?
c. How did the war affect African-American civilians?

2. APPLYING CITIZENSHIP SKILLS

Are limitations on freedom of speech justified by war? Explain your opinion.

3. THEME: AMERICA IN THE WORLD

How did Wilson's view of the role the United States should play in world affairs compare with Theodore Roosevelt's view of America's role?

4. ANALYZING LEADERSHIP

Do you think Wilson's refusal to compromise to get the Treaty of Versailles through Congress was a good decision? Why?

Interact *with* History

How accurately did you predict the ways in which American citizens might support the war effort?

VISUAL SUMMARY

World War I

War Breaks Out in Europe
When the Allies and the Central Powers went to war in Europe, the United States reluctantly joined the Allies.

America Joins the Fight
Millions of U.S. soldiers and civilian volunteers went abroad and helped the Allies win the war.

Life on the Home Front
The war required Americans to sacrifice many things, even political freedoms. The war also brought new jobs.

The Legacy of World War I
The war broke up European empires and left lasting social changes in the United States.

Use the map and your knowledge of U.S. history to answer questions 1 and 2.

Additional Test Practice, pp. S1–S33.

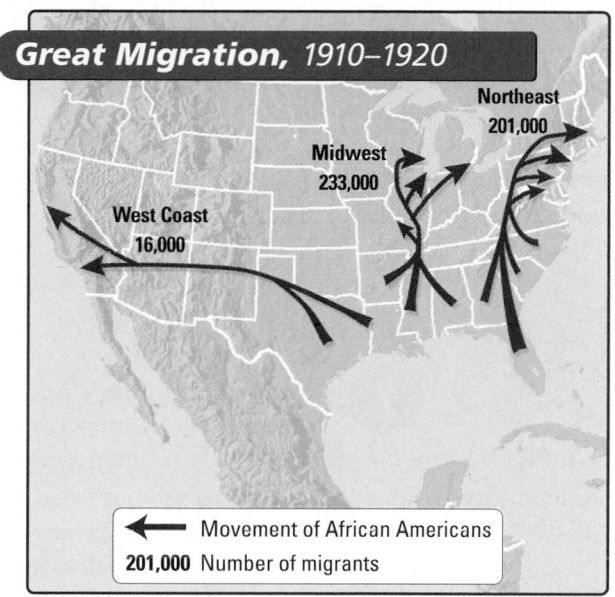

Great Migration, 1910–1920

Northeast
201,000

Midwest
233,000

West Coast
16,000

← Movement of African Americans
201,000 Number of migrants

Source: *Historical Statistics of the United States*

1. How many African Americans migrated to the Northeast?

A. 16,000

B. 201,000

C. 233,000

D. 450,000

2. To which region did the fewest number of African Americans move?

A. Northwest

B. Northeast

C. Midwest

D. West Coast

This quotation from Senator Henry Cabot Lodge supports his opposition to the United States entering the League of Nations. Use the quotation and your knowledge of U.S. history to answer question 3.

PRIMARY SOURCE

If we guarantee any country . . . its independence . . . we must [keep] at any cost . . . our word. I wish [the American people] carefully to consider . . . whether they are willing to have the youth of America ordered to war by other nations.

Henry Cabot Lodge, speech to the Senate, February 28, 1919

3. What was Lodge's major opposition to U.S. entry into the League of Nations?

A. The U.S. would have to pay the expenses.

B. U.S. soldiers would have to fight foreign wars.

C. The League of Nations would not be effective.

D. Deals with a foreign country would lead to war.

TEST PRACTICE
CLASSZONE.COM

ALTERNATIVE ASSESSMENT

1. ✍ WRITING ABOUT HISTORY

Write a **newspaper article** on the new technologies being used in World War I. Choose one type of technology, such as airplanes, submarines, or tanks, and explain its use, advantages, and disadvantages.

• Look for and include primary sources from soldiers.

• Include a section on why you believe or do not believe that these new weapons are necessary.

2. COOPERATIVE LEARNING

Working in one of seven groups, research the conference that created the Treaty of Versailles. Your group will represent one of these nations: Germany, France, Britain, the United States, Italy, Japan, or Poland. Make a list of goals and issues you want discussed. Then choose a spokesperson to represent your group in a mock conference.

INTEGRATED TECHNOLOGY

DOING INTERNET RESEARCH

Research the posters that were used to influence public opinion during World War I. Use a search engine to find pictures of these posters on the Internet.

• View as many posters as possible.

• Print images of the two posters you find most interesting. Try to find some background information about the purpose and audience for each poster.

• Write your reactions to the posters including what actions you think the posters were trying to promote, how the posters made you feel, and how effective you think they were.

For more about World War I posters . . .

INTERNET ACTIVITY
CLASSZONE.COM

Campaign for Liberty Bonds

To rally Americans to support World War I, the government set up the Committee on Public Information (CPI). This agency called on creative individuals to join "the world's greatest adventure in advertising." Speakers gave patriotic speeches in theaters, hotels, and restaurants. Artists designed posters persuading Americans to buy Liberty Bonds. These loans to the government helped fund the war effort. Liberty Bonds were actually sold through four Liberty Loan drives in 1917 and 1918.

ACTIVITY Create a poster to help the government raise money for World War I. In addition, write and present a patriotic speech that wins public support of the war.

TOOLBOX

Each group will need:

poster board	drawing paper
colored markers	glue
pencils	scissors

Posters such as this one appealed to patriotism and love of family to sell Liberty Bonds.

STEP BY STEP

1 **Form an imaginary ad agency.** Meet with three or four other students to discuss your latest contract: The CPI has hired your agency to create a poster as part of a nationwide campaign to sell Liberty Bonds and promote World War I. Your group will:

- do research on Liberty Bonds
- design and create a poster advertising Liberty Bonds
- write and deliver a "pep talk" persuading people to buy Liberty Bonds

2 **Research Liberty Bonds.** Look on the Internet, in this chapter, or in books about World War I to find out more about Liberty Bonds and to see actual posters. As you look over the posters, think about the feelings the posters bring out. What images and words seem most powerful or persuasive?

3 **Choose a theme for your poster.** Persuading people to buy Liberty Bonds means that you need to show that winning World War I is important. One way is to appeal to people's emotions. For example, the poster can appeal to their sense of fear, pride, or love of family.

4 **Sketch out your idea.** Write out a slogan and choose images based on the theme of your poster. Make sure your words and pictures communicate the same feeling and message. Draw an outline of the images and the letters. Then cut both the letters and images out. Be sure that they're large enough to be seen from several yards away.

5 **Create the poster.** Decide where the art and writing will appear. Experiment with the arrangement of the art and the writing. Move them around. Do not overwhelm your viewers with too many images or too many words. Use vivid, patriotic colors for your poster.

6 **Create a bulletin board display.**
Pin or tape your poster on the wall, along with the posters of the other groups. As you examine the other posters, compare and contrast your poster with the others.

WRITE AND SPEAK

Write a patriotic speech. As a group, write a two-minute "pep talk" persuading people to buy Liberty Bonds and to support the soldiers fighting overseas. Include reasons why the war is worth fighting. Each group member should be prepared to deliver the speech, using the poster you made as a visual aid.

 **HELP DESK**

For related information, see pages 691–692 in Chapter 24.

Researching Your Project
- *World War I* by Gail Stewart
- *Causes and Consequences of World War I* by Stewart Ross

For more about World War I . . .

 **RESEARCH LINKS**
CLASSZONE.COM

Did You Know?
The CPI used about 75,000 lecturers. They gave around 755,190 speeches to about 300 million people in 5,000 towns.

Even children were moved by advertising slogans to help fund the war: "Lick a stamp and lick the kaiser." Children filled books with war stamps, each worth 25 cents. These stamps were then converted into government bonds.

Even President Wilson helped to raise money for the war effort. He sold wool from sheep raised on the White House lawn.

REFLECT & ASSESS
- What aspects of your poster do you think will inspire people to buy Liberty Bonds?
- How well does your speech inspire patriotic feeling about the war?
- Which do you think is a more powerful means of persuasion—your poster or your speech?

Depression, War, and Recovery

This panel of a WPA mural shows California workers picking oranges, tilling the soil, and collecting flowers during the 1920s and 1930s.

"The test of our progress . . . is whether we provide enough for those who have too little."

—Franklin Delano Roosevelt

CHAPTER 25

The Roaring Twenties 1919–1929

Section 1 **The Business of America**

Section 2 **Changes in Society**

Section 3 **The Jazz Age and the Harlem Renaissance**

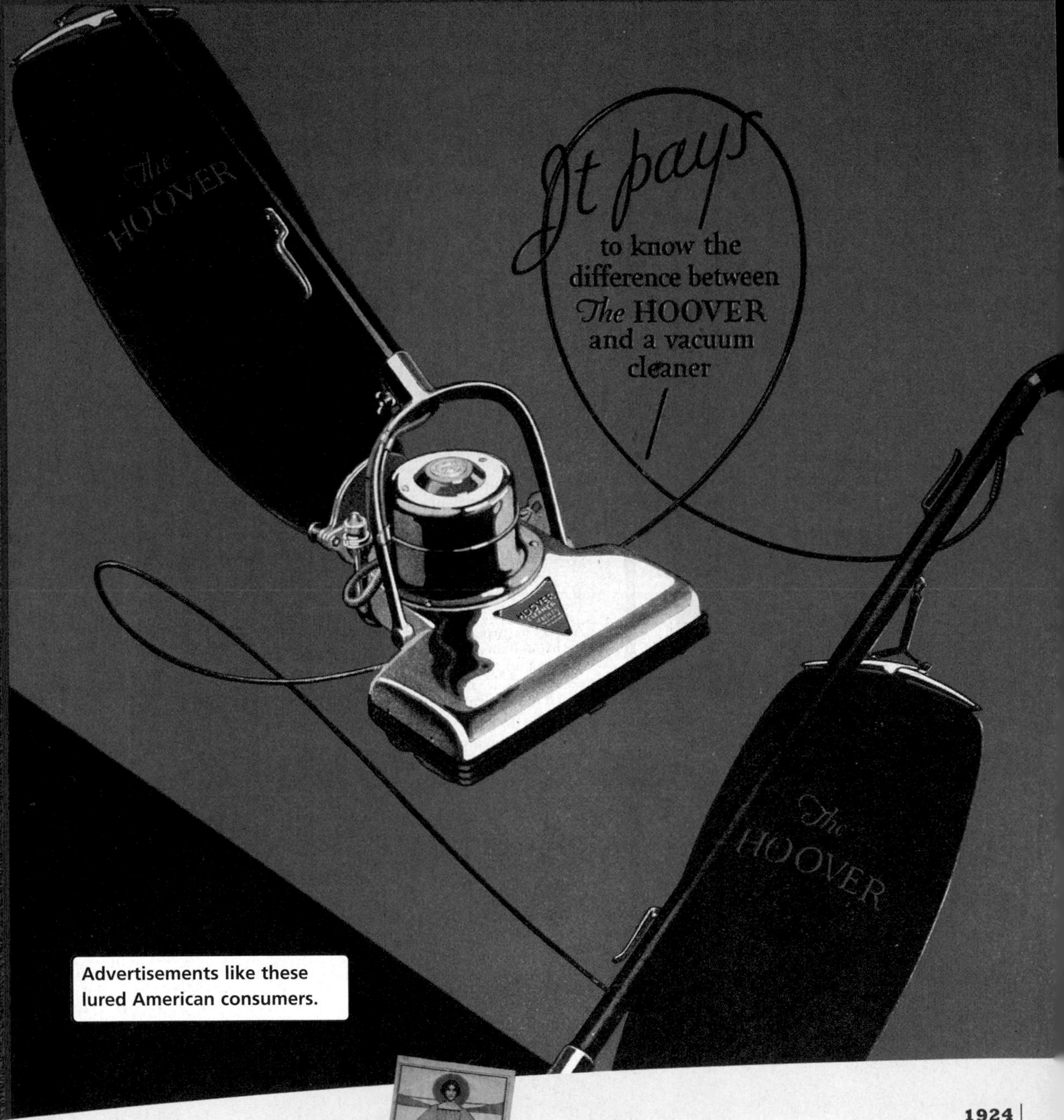

The HOOVER
It pays
to know the difference between The HOOVER and a vacuum cleaner
The HOOVER

Advertisements like these lured American consumers.

1920
Warren G. Harding is elected president.

1920
Ninteenth Amendment gives women the right to vote.

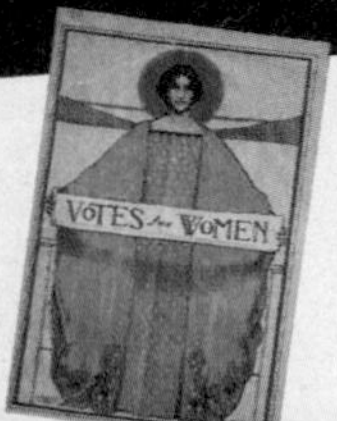

VOTES for WOMEN

1923
Calvin Coolidge becomes president.

1924
Coolidge is elected president.
Nellie Tayloe Ross is first woman elected governor.

USA
World
1919

1921
Chinese Communist Party is founded.

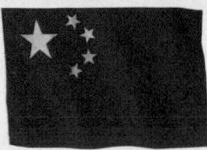

1922
Benito Mussolini is named Italy's prime minister.

1923
Adolf Hitler tries but fails to gain power in southern Germany.

LET THE KOHLER ELECTRIC SINK

NOW you will wash the dishes electrically—with a cheer! There is a wonderful new sink—the Kohler Electric Sink—which washes dishes so gleaming clean, and does it so smoothly and easily, that the old, forbidding, thrice-daily drudgery becomes a thrice-daily pleasure.

This is the *modern* sink which you knew was bound to come some day. And the fact that it has come from KOHLER OF KOHLER will tell you that it is beautifully designed and beauti-

electrical dishwasher to its snow immaculately white Kohler enamel.

There is a Kohler Electric Sir kitchen, be it large or small. Ther hand and left-hand models, with o drainboard; and there is a separate unit, if you prefer, to install alor present sink.

Ask your plumbing dealer about the Kohler And mail the coupon below for descriptive booklet.

World War I is over, and a new decade has begun. There is peace in the world and prosperity at home. It is a time of exciting social, cultural, economic, and technological change. You see new products and new ideas coming into your life.

Which changes in technology and culture will affect your life the most?

What Do You Think?

- How will these new ideas and products change your life?
- Will these changes make life better and easier? How?

RESEARCH LINKS
CLASSZONE.COM

Visit the Chapter 25 links for more information about the 1920s.

1925
opes Trial is held.
rlem Renaissance flourishes.

1927
Lindbergh makes first transatlantic solo flight.

First movie with sound, *The Jazz Singer,* released.

1928
Herbert Hoover is elected president.

1929

1926
Hirohito becomes emperor of Japan.

1928
Kellogg-Briand Pact signed.

1929
National Revolutionary Party organized in Mexico.

Reading Strategy: Finding Main Ideas

What Do You know?

What do you already know about the Roaring Twenties? What were the issues and who were the personalities that made this decade "roar"?

Think About

- how the 1920s have been portrayed in movies, television, and historical fiction
- what happens to a country when rapid changes take place
- your responses to the Interact with History about changes in culture or technology (see page 707)

What Do You Want to Know?

What additional information do you want about the issues and personalities of the 1920s? Record questions you may have in your notebook before you read the chapter.

The carefree spirit of the Roaring Twenties is captured on this magazine cover from 1926.

Finding Main Ideas

To understand what you read, learn to find the main idea of each paragraph, topic heading, and section. Remember that the supporting details help to explain the main idea. On the chart below, write down the main idea in this chapter for each category of American life.

See Skillbuilder Handbook, page R5.

Taking Notes

Categories	Main Ideas
Government	
Business	
Agriculture	
Technology	
Society	
Popular Culture	

The Business of America

MAIN IDEA	**WHY IT MATTERS NOW**	**TERMS & NAMES**

The government supported business and kept a hands-off policy in other matters.

How involved the government should be in the economy remains an issue today.

Warren G. Harding
Teapot Dome Scandal
Calvin Coolidge
laissez faire

isolationist
Kellogg-Briand Pact
assembly line
installment buying

ONE AMERICAN'S STORY

Warren G. Harding was a pleasant man of whom it was said he "looked like a president." He was happiest relaxing or playing cards with his friends. But urged on by his ambitious wife, Florence Kling Harding, he rose from small-town newspaper publisher, to U.S. senator from Ohio, to Republican presidential candidate.

The advice from Republican Party leaders in 1920 was "Keep Warren at home. Don't let him make any speeches." Even so, Harding was what the voters wanted. He promised them prosperity at home and peace abroad, and they elected him president.

In this section, you will read about presidents Warren G. Harding and Calvin Coolidge, the booming economy of the Roaring Twenties, and the new technologies that helped businesses to grow.

Warren G. Harding and his wife, Florence Kling Harding

Harding and the "Return to Normalcy"

After some 20 years of reform and war, Americans were ready for the "normalcy" promised by Harding in the election and at his inauguration.

A VOICE FROM THE PAST

Our supreme task is the resumption of our onward, normal way. Reconstruction, readjustment, restoration all these must follow. I would like to hasten them.

Warren G. Harding, Inaugural Address, March 4, 1921

Taking Notes

Use your chart to take notes about government, business, agriculture, and technology.

Categories	Main Ideas
Government	
Business	
Agriculture	
Technology	
Society	
Popular Culture	

As president, Harding wanted to lift the burden of taxes and regulations from the shoulders of Americans. To do this, he proposed lower taxes and "less government in business and more business in government." He also sought higher tariffs on foreign goods to help American companies.

Harding chose a pro-business cabinet. The secretary of the treasury was Andrew W. Mellon, one of the wealthiest men in the United States.

STRANGE *but* True

PRESIDENT SWORN IN BY FATHER

On August 2, 1923, Vice-President Calvin Coolidge went to bed early at his family home in Plymouth Notch, Vermont. During the night, Coolidge's father received news by telegram that Harding had died. He then woke his son. The U.S. attorney general urged Coolidge to take the oath of office as soon as possible. At 2:47 A.M. on August 3, 1923, John Coolidge, a justice of the peace, administered the oath to his son.

Mellon persuaded Congress to lower taxes and balance the budget. Herbert Hoover, an engineer who organized aid to Europe in World War I, was secretary of commerce. He worked to cut federal government waste.

While some of Harding's cabinet choices, like Mellon and Hoover, were excellent, a number were unqualified, and even corrupt. These men had been Harding's friends back in Ohio and were known as the "Ohio Gang." They used their government positions to make money illegally. Their actions helped to wreck the Harding presidency. The worst scandal involved Secretary of the Interior Albert Fall. It was called the **Teapot Dome Scandal.** Fall took bribes and made illegal deals with oil executives to drill on oil-rich government land in Teapot Dome, Wyoming.

Rumors of corruption in the Harding administration began to be heard in 1923. Harding, who was politically and personally honest, was alarmed. He had once said, "I knew that this job would be too much for me." Tired and depressed, Harding went on a speaking tour in the summer of 1923. It was then that he learned the full extent of the corruption. He died suddenly while on the trip, on August 2, 1923. The American people mourned his death, but they were shocked when the scandals became public.

*Reading***History**
A. Drawing Conclusions How did members of the Ohio Gang take advantage of their friendship with Harding?

Coolidge Takes Over

Vice-President **Calvin Coolidge** became president when Harding died. He moved quickly to try to clean up the scandals. His efforts limited the political damage to the Republican Party, and Coolidge was elected president in his own right in 1924. He defeated Democrat John W. Davis and Robert M. La Follette, the Progressive Party nominee.

Coolidge and those who voted for him felt that prosperity would be the reward of those who worked hard. As a friend of business, Coolidge agreed with the economic theory of **laissez faire.** It stated that business, if left unregulated by the government, would act in a way that would benefit the nation. In 1925, Coolidge stated his belief that "the chief business of the American people is business." He said that Americans were concerned with "prospering in the world." Under the Coolidge administration, business prospered and so did many Americans.

Vocabulary
laissez faire: to allow to do (French)

Coolidge also believed that it was not the government's job to help people with social and economic problems. Farmers were one group that Coolidge refused to help. Because new machinery had been introduced, farmers were producing more food than the nation needed. So food prices were dropping.

"The chief business of the American people is business."

Calvin Coolidge

Congress passed a bill that required the government to buy the extra food. This would have raised prices. But Coolidge vetoed the bill.

Like Harding, Coolidge was an **isolationist.** Both believed that the United States should stay out of other nations' affairs except in matters of self-defense. Both supported efforts to avoid war.

Coolidge's major peace effort was the **Kellogg-Briand Pact** of 1928. This pact, or treaty, was signed by 15 nations who pledged not to make war against one another except in self-defense. Most Americans supported the treaty. They hoped that if war were outlawed, it would disappear. Then they could concentrate on their own lives.

Technology Changes American Life

The economy was booming in the 1920s. Both Harding and Coolidge kept government regulation to a minimum, and business flourished. Part of the "roar" in the Roaring Twenties was the growth in the nation's wealth. The average annual income per person rose more than 35 percent during the period—from $522 to $716. This increase in income gave Americans more money to buy goods and to spend on leisure activities.

Automobiles had the greatest impact on life during the 1920s. Henry Ford, who built his first successful automobile in 1896, was determined to make a car that most people could afford. At the Ford Motor Company in Detroit, his dream came true with a car called the Model T. In 1920, Ford produced more than a million automobiles, at a rate of one per minute. Each car cost the consumer $335.

*Reading***History**
B. Recognizing Effects What effect did the assembly line have on the price of cars?

To speed up production and lower costs and prices, Ford used an **assembly line.** In an assembly line, the product moves along a conveyor belt across the factory. Workers at various stations add parts as the belt moves past them. By the mid-1920s, a Model T came off a Ford assembly line every ten seconds.

1923 Model T Ford

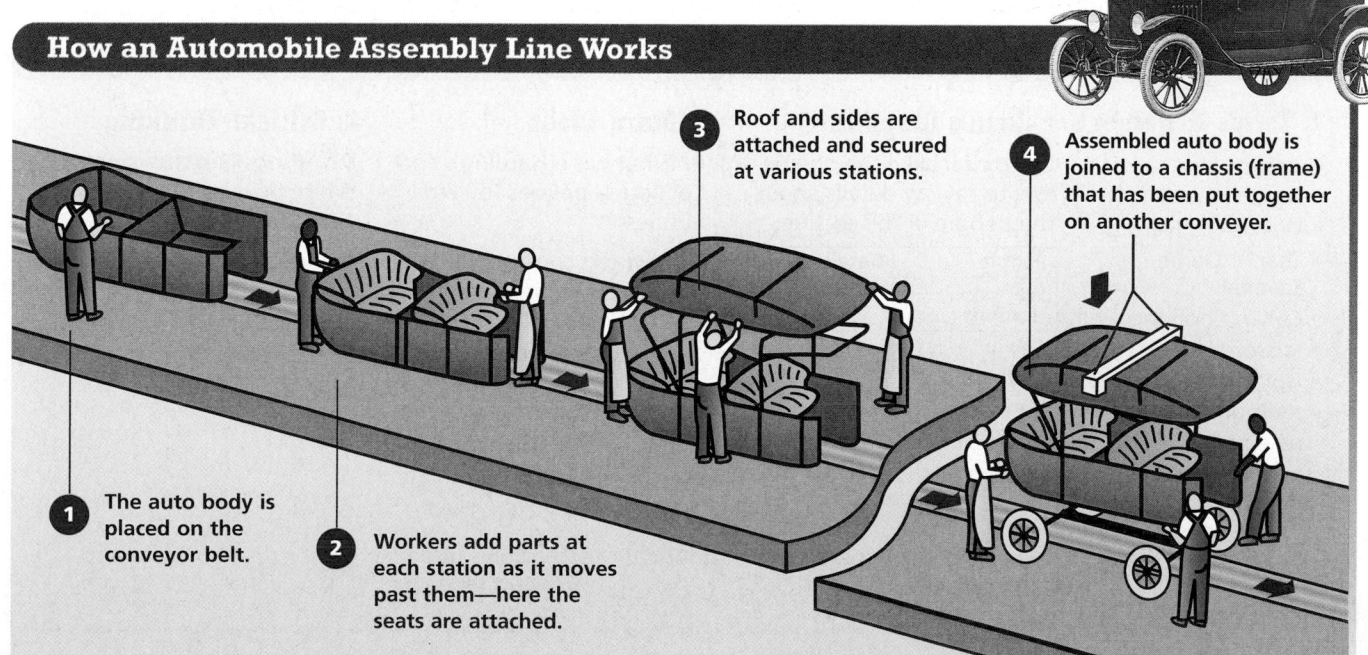

How an Automobile Assembly Line Works

3 Roof and sides are attached and secured at various stations.

4 Assembled auto body is joined to a chassis (frame) that has been put together on another conveyer.

1 The auto body is placed on the conveyor belt.

2 Workers add parts at each station as it moves past them—here the seats are attached.

OIL HEAT
FOR
small homes

$50
DOWN—*balance on liberal terms*

WILLIAMS
DIST·O·MATIC
HEATING

Credit allowed consumers to buy the latest products—$50 down and small monthly payments bought this new oil heater.

Other advances in technology improved life. New machines turned out products faster and cheaper. Once-costly items were now available to many consumers. Some consumers used credit and paid for their purchases through **installment buying.** This allowed repaying the amount borrowed in small monthly payments. National advertising also got its start at this time, as a way of helping to promote new products.

Cheap fuel powered the new prosperity. Petroleum and electricity became widely available. These power sources made possible new inventions and advances in technology that made life easier, such as electric vacuum cleaners, washers, sewing machines, toasters, and fans. However, it was mostly only the white middle class that could afford these new products.

*Reading*History
C. Summarizing
How did advances in technology change the lives of Americans?

The Air Age Begins

The 1920s also marked the beginning of the air age. After World War I, many former military pilots bought old war planes and worked as crop-dusters, stunt fliers, and flight instructors. In 1918, the Post Office Department began air mail service. Airplanes had found new uses.

Transatlantic flights by Charles A. Lindbergh in 1927 and Amelia Earhart in 1928 and 1932 helped to promote the idea of commercial air transportation. Pan American Airways, founded in 1927, became the nation's first passenger airline. By the end of the decade, its operations were drawing distant cities closer together both in North and South America.

In the next section, you will read about more changes in life in the United States and the conflicts these changes caused.

Section 1 Assessment

1. Terms & Names

Explain the significance of:
- Warren G. Harding
- Teapot Dome Scandal
- Calvin Coolidge
- laissez faire
- isolationist
- Kellogg-Briand Pact
- assembly line
- installment buying

2. Using Graphics

Use a chart like the one below to review details about the people in this section.

People	Details
Warren G. Harding	
Calvin Coolidge	
Henry Ford	

3. Main Ideas

a. What were Harding's and Coolidge's policies toward business?

b. How did corruption affect the Harding administration?

c. How did new technology help business to grow during the 1920s?

4. Critical Thinking

Drawing Conclusions
Which developments in the 1920s added to prosperity?

THINK ABOUT
- government's role in the economy
- advances made in technology

ACTIVITY OPTIONS

TECHNOLOGY
ART

Research an aspect of the American automobile industry. Either draw a **diagram** of how a car works or design an **advertisement** for an automobile.

Changes in Society

MAIN IDEA	WHY IT MATTERS NOW	TERMS & NAMES
Changes in society in the 1920s brought new attitudes and lifestyles but also caused divisions and conflict.	Many of the social issues of the 1920s continue to challenge American society today.	flapper Marcus Garvey Prohibition fundamentalism Al Capone Ku Klux Klan NAACP

ONE AMERICAN'S STORY

Poet Edna St. Vincent Millay was one of many young people who rebelled against traditional values in the 1920s. She lived among artists and writers whose ideas challenged those traditionally held by society. She wrote poems about love and the carefree lifestyle of the 1920s.

Edna St. Vincent Millay became a bestselling poet and a symbol of her time.

A VOICE FROM THE PAST

My candle burns at both ends;
It will not last the night;
But ah, my foes, and oh, my friends—
It gives a lovely light!

Edna St. Vincent Millay, "First Fig," from *A Few Figs from Thistles*

In this section, you will read about changing social roles during the 1920s and the problems facing African Americans.

Youth in the Roaring Twenties

The 1920s were called the Roaring Twenties. According to author F. Scott Fitzgerald, "The uncertainties of 1919 were over. America was going on the greatest, gaudiest spree in history." During the decade, youth and its culture were celebrated. For the first time, young people as a group rebelled against the values of the past and the authority of their elders. The under-25 generation wanted fun and freedom. Many of them experimented with new fashions, attitudes, and ways of behavior.

Young people stayed in school longer, and more went to college. School became a place for socializing as well as learning. Young people expressed their new freedom in daring new clothes, lively songs and dances, and silly fads. Men wore extra-wide floppy pants and sported hair slicked down close to the head. Women wore a shorter hairstyle called a *bob* to match the shorter dresses of the period.

Taking Notes

Use your chart to take notes about society.

Categories	Main Ideas
Government	
Business	
Agriculture	
Technology	
Society	
Popular Culture	

COSMO HAMILTON'S New Serial "Daughters of Folly"

McCLURE'S

August

25 Cents

The flapper appeared on many magazine covers during the 1920s.

The Charleston was a favorite dance. It involved wild, flailing movements of the arms and legs. Dance marathons became the rage. In these contests, couples would dance nonstop for days. Songs also captured the high spirits of the decade. Among the most popular tunes were "Runnin' Wild" and "Ain't We Got Fun." Many young people imitated the behavior of favorite stars from Hollywood movies. Other fads included crossword puzzles, mah-jongg, and flagpole sitting (sitting on a platform on top of a flagpole for days).

The spirited behavior of young women during the decade was just one way women's lives changed.

Background
Mah-jongg was a game from China played with small painted tiles.

New Roles for Women

The symbol of the 1920s American woman was the **flapper.** The flapper was the creation of John Held, Jr., a magazine illustrator. Flappers often wore bobbed hair, makeup, and dresses that fell to just below the knee. They were always eager to try something new, whether it was a new fashion, behavior, dance, or fad.

During the 1920s, women took more active roles in their life than ever before. They had more personal freedom. They drove cars, played sports, went to college, and took jobs. Margaret Sanger, a reformer who focused on women's health issues, described these women.

A VOICE FROM THE PAST

Today women are on the whole much more individual. They possess as strong likes and dislikes as men. They live more and more on the plane of social equality with men . . . [and] there is more enjoyable companionship and real friendship between men and women.

Margaret Sanger, quoted in *A More Perfect Union*

The prosperity of the 1920s opened new job opportunities for women in business offices, retail stores, factories, and various professions. College graduates most often became teachers and nurses, but also librarians, social workers, and bankers. Women with less education worked in factories or in offices as typists and secretaries or in stores as clerks and cashiers. Attitudes toward marriage also changed. Men and women came to view marriage as more of an equal partnership. Women still had the responsibility of housework and child rearing. But labor-saving appliances and timesaving convenience foods made life easier.

The 19th Amendment ensured women the right to vote. Some women even ran for political office. In 1924, two were elected governor—Nellie Tayloe Ross in Wyoming and Miriam "Ma" Ferguson in Texas. In 1923, an equal rights amendment was introduced in Congress. It would be almost 50 years, however, before such an amendment would pass Congress.

Reading **History**
A. Recognizing Effects What were some of the effects of women's greater opportunities?

Prohibition and Lawlessness

Another change in American society came on January 16, 1920. That was the date when the 18th Amendment went into effect. The amendment was commonly called **Prohibition,** the ban on the manufacture and sale of alcohol. Many people saw Prohibition as a victory of small-town, Protestant Americans over city dwellers. Supporters felt that Prohibition would promote morality and good health. To enforce the ban, Congress had passed the Volstead Act in 1919.

Saloons were forced to close their doors. But many Americans did not consider drinking harmful or sinful. They resented government interference. People who wanted alcohol found endless ways to get it. For instance, illegal nightclubs known as speakeasies sold liquor. People called bootleggers made their living by transporting and selling liquor illegally. Others simply brewed their own homemade liquor.

Background
Bootlegger came from the old smugglers' practice of carrying liquor in the legs of boots.

One unfortunate result of Prohibition was the growth of organized crime. In nearly every major city, criminal gangs battled for control of bootlegging operations. The most ruthless crime boss of the era was **Al Capone** in Chicago. With a private army of 700 criminals, he violently seized control of the city's 10,000 speakeasies. By the late 1920s, most Americans had come to see Prohibition as a failure. It was repealed by the 21st Amendment in 1933. Prohibition ended, but organized crime did not end with it.

Marcus Garvey led a Back-to-Africa movement in the 1920s.

Changes for African Americans

Reading **History**
B. Reading a Map Locate cities with significant African-American populations on the map on page 723.

The 1920s also brought major changes to the lives of many African Americans. To find better jobs, African Americans had begun moving north in the early 1900s. As you read in Chapter 24, this movement was called the Great Migration. The jobs that they held in industries during World War I raised their expectations for a better life.

In the North, African Americans gained some economic and political power. But they still faced discrimination in jobs and housing. Rising tensions between African Americans and whites in Northern cities led to over 25 race riots in 1919 alone. The movement of an additional 1.5 million African Americans to these cities during the 1920s increased tensions even more.

The National Association for the Advancement of Colored People **(NAACP)** tried to protect the constitutional rights of African Americans. The NAACP worked to make people aware of crimes against African Americans. But it was unable to get Congress to pass legislation to help African Americans fight against discrimination.

Reading **History**
C. Analyzing Points of View What action did Marcus Garvey believe would improve the lives of African Americans?

Daily threats and discrimination made some African Americans lose faith in America. **Marcus Garvey,** the founder of the Universal Negro Improvement Association, called for a return to Africa and the formation of a separate nation there. He said, "If Europe is for the Europeans, then Africa shall be for the black peoples of the world." Few African Americans migrated to Africa. But Garvey set an example for future black political movements.

More than 40,000 Ku Klux Klan members march in Washington, D.C., in 1925, to show their growing political power.

A Divided Society

Some groups felt threatened by the changes in society in the 1920s. Conflicts developed over ideas and values. Divisions between groups resulted—between African Americans and whites, the native-born and immigrants, and the urban and rural communities. Science and religion also were in conflict.

In religion, a movement called **fundamentalism** gained both recognition and political power. Fundamentalists believed in a literal, or word-for-word, interpretation of the Bible. They did not want the theory of evolution taught in public schools because it opposed their belief in the biblical story of creation. Evolution is the scientific theory that living things developed over millions of years from earlier and simpler forms of life.

Fundamentalists succeeded in banning the teaching of evolution in Tennessee and 12 other states. In 1925, in Dayton, Tennessee, biology teacher John Scopes broke this law. He took this action to test whether the law could be enforced. Scopes's trial attracted national attention. The jury found Scopes guilty, but the Tennessee Supreme Court reversed the decision. Controversy over the teaching of evolution continues today.

Another reaction to changes in society was the rebirth of the **Ku Klux Klan.** The Klan called for a "racially and morally pure" America. It became strong in several states, including some outside the South. By 1924, the Klan claimed as many as five million members. It tried to influence national, state, and local politics by using violence against African Americans and other groups. Its power began to decrease by the end of the decade because of personal and financial scandals in the organization.

In this section, you read about divisions in society. In the next, you will learn how mass media and popular culture brought Americans together.

*Reading*History

D. Analyzing Causes What action taken by fundamentalists caused John Scopes to break the law in Tennessee?

Section 2 Assessment

1. Terms & Names

Explain the significance of:
- flapper
- Prohibition
- Al Capone
- NAACP
- Marcus Garvey
- fundamentalism
- Ku Klux Klan

2. Using Graphics

Use a cluster diagram to review the fads of the Roaring Twenties.

Which fads of the 1920s had lasting influence?

3. Main Ideas

a. How did the Roaring Twenties change the lives of young people?

b. What factors were responsible for the changes in women's lives?

c. What were the conflicts that divided society?

4. Critical Thinking

Recognizing Effects How was American society transformed in the 1920s?

THINK ABOUT
- roles of young people and women
- migration of African Americans
- conflicts between groups

ACTIVITY OPTIONS

ART

MUSIC

Draw a **poster** with an image that represents the Roaring Twenties or write a **song** capturing the spirit of the times.

The Jazz Age and the Harlem Renaissance

MAIN IDEA	WHY IT MATTERS NOW	TERMS & NAMES
Popular culture was influenced by the mass media, sports, and the contributions of African Americans.	Much of today's popular culture had its origins in this period.	jazz mass media popular culture Harlem Renaissance Lost Generation expatriate

ONE AMERICAN'S STORY

The Roaring Twenties was also called the Jazz Age, because the lively, loose beat of **jazz** captured the carefree spirit of the times. Jazz was developed by African-American musicians in New Orleans. That city was the home of Louis Armstrong, who became one of the world's great jazz musicians. As a child, Armstrong had a job collecting junk in a horse-drawn wagon. While in the wagon, he often played a small tin horn.

A VOICE FROM THE PAST

I had a little tin horn, the kind the people celebrate with. I would blow this long tin horn without the top on it. Just hold my fingers close together. Blow it as a call for old rags, bones, bottles or anything that people had to sell. . . . The kids loved the sounds of my tin horn!

Louis Armstrong, quoted in *Louis Armstrong* by Sandford Brown

Louis Armstrong brought New Orleans jazz to the North in the 1920s.

Later, Armstrong learned to play the trumpet. With other jazz musicians, he spread this new music to other parts of the country and to Europe.

In this section, you will read more about the spread of popular culture, the Harlem Renaissance, and the artists of the Lost Generation.

More Leisure Time for Americans

Laborsaving appliances and shorter working hours gave Americans more leisure time. Higher wages also gave them money to spend on leisure activities. People wanted more fun, and they were willing to spend money to have it. Americans paid 25 cents or more to see a movie—an increase of at least 5 times the price in the previous decade. By the end of the 1920s, there were more than 100 million weekly moviegoers.

In addition to attending movies, some Americans went to museums and public libraries. Others bought books and magazines. Sales rose by

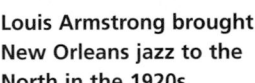

Taking Notes

Use your chart to take notes about popular culture.

Categories	Main Ideas
Government	
Business	
Agriculture	
Technology	
Society	
Popular Culture	

Celebrities of the 1920s

◀ **Charlie Chaplin** was the most popular male film star during the 1920s. He was known as the "great comedian."

Babe Ruth ▶ helped to popularize baseball. In 1927, he became the first player to hit 60 home runs in one year.

◀ **Helen Wills** dominated women's tennis in the 1920s.

▼ **Duke Ellington** was a world-famous jazz pianist and composer. His band played at the Cotton Club in Harlem in the 1920s.

50 percent. Americans also spent time listening to the radio, talking on the telephone, playing games, and driving their cars. In 1929, Americans spent about $4 billion on entertainment—a 100 percent jump in a decade.

But not all Americans were able to take part equally in leisure-time activities or in the consumer culture of the 1920s. Some, like African Americans and Hispanic Americans, had their time and choices limited by factors such as income and race.

Mass Media and Popular Culture

New types of **mass media**—communications that reach a large audience—began to take hold in the 1920s. Radio and movies provided entertainment and spread the latest ideas about fashions and lifestyles.

The first commercial radio broadcast took place in Pittsburgh at station KDKA in 1920. Other radio stations soon emerged. The number of households with radios jumped from about 60,000 in 1922 to 10 million in 1929. Radio stations broadcast news, sports, music, comedy, and commercials. Not only were Americans better informed than before, but listening to the same radio programs united the nation.

Of all the powerful new influences of the 1920s, none shaped the ideas and dreams of Americans more than motion pictures. The moviemaking industry was centered in Hollywood, California.

Movies gave people an escape into worlds of glamour and excitement they could never enter. Audiences flocked to movie theaters to see their favorite actors and actresses. These included Charlie Chaplin, Mary Pickford, Douglas Fairbanks, Clara Bow, and Rudolph Valentino. Movies also spread American popular culture to Europe. **Popular culture** included songs, dances, fashions, and even slang expressions like *scram* (leave in a hurry) and *ritzy* (elegant).

Moviemakers like Samuel Goldwyn, the Warner brothers, and Louis B. Mayer made fortunes overnight. For most of the 1920s, films were silent. In 1927, *The Jazz Singer* introduced sound. Another *talkie* caused a sensation in 1928—Walt Disney's cartoon *Steamboat Willie,* featuring Mickey Mouse. Within a few years, all movies were talkies.

Reading **History**

A. Recognizing Effects What was the main effect that laborsaving devices and reduced working hours had on Americans' lives?

A Search for Heroes

Another leisure activity was watching sporting events and listening to them on the radio. Sporting events of all types—baseball, football, hockey, boxing, golf, and tennis—enjoyed rising attendance. Boxing became very popular. Fans who could not attend the fights listened to matches on the radio or saw them on newsreels shown at movie theaters. The Jack Dempsey–Gene Tunney boxing match of 1926 drew 120,000 fans.

Reading **History**

B. Summarizing
What were some of the changes that came about in popular entertainment in the 1920s?

In the 1920s, professional baseball gained many new fans because games were broadcast on radio. As a result, fans flocked to major league ballparks. In New York City, fans went to Yankee Stadium, which opened in 1923, to watch the "Bronx Bombers"—the nickname for the New York Yankees. Even college football and basketball attracted huge crowds.

Sports figures captured the imagination of the American public. They became heroes because they restored Americans' belief in the power of the individual to improve his or her life. Babe Ruth of the Yankees was baseball's top home-run hitter. Someone once asked Ruth why his $80,000 salary was higher than the president's. Ruth supposedly replied, "Well, I had a better year."

Baseball players weren't the only sports heroes. Golfers idolized Bobby Jones. People cheered Helen Wills and Bill Tilden on the tennis courts. In 1926, New York City threw a huge homecoming parade for Gertrude Ederle, the first woman to swim the English Channel. Americans also made national heroes of two daring young fliers—Charles A. Lindbergh and Amelia Earhart.

AMERICA'S HISTORY MAKERS

CHARLES A. LINDBERGH
1902–1974

Charles A. Lindbergh took flying lessons in 1922 and bought his first airplane in 1923. Four years later, in May 1927, he became the first person to fly nonstop alone across the Atlantic Ocean.

Lindbergh had heard about an offer of $25,000 to anyone who could fly nonstop from New York to Paris. Piloting his single engine monoplane, the *Spirit of St. Louis,* without radio or parachute, Lindbergh flew some 3,600 miles in 33 ½ hours. "Lucky Lindy" became an instant hero.

AMELIA EARHART
1897–1937

Amelia Earhart was often called "Lady Lindy" because of both her physical resemblance to Charles Lindbergh and her similar accomplishments as a pilot.

Earhart took flying lessons in 1921 and bought her first plane in 1922. Noted for her courage and independence, she flew where no women had gone before. She was the first woman to cross the Atlantic in a plane (as a passenger) in 1928 and the first to fly solo across the Atlantic in 1932. She disappeared on a round-the-world flight in 1937. What happened remains a mystery to this day.

Why do you think Lindbergh and Earhart became American heroes?

Artists of the Harlem Renaissance celebrated the cultural traditions and the life experiences of African Americans. This painting by Lois Mailou Jones is entitled *The Ascent of Ethiopia*.

How does the artist show the link between African and American cultures?

The Harlem Renaissance

Wartime military service and work in war industries had given African Americans a new sense of freedom. They migrated to many cities across the country, but it was New York City that turned into the unofficial capital of black America. In the 1920s, Harlem, a neighborhood on New York's West Side, was the world's largest black urban community.

The migrants from the South brought with them new ideas and a new kind of music called jazz. Soon Harlem produced a burst of African-American cultural activity known as the **Harlem Renaissance,** which began in the 1920s and lasted into the 1930s. It was called a renaissance because it symbolized a rebirth of hope for African Americans.

Harlem became home to writers, musicians, singers, painters, sculptors, and scholars. There they were able to exchange ideas and develop their creativity. Among Harlem's residents were poets Langston Hughes, James Weldon Johnson, and Countee Cullen and novelists Claude McKay and Zora Neale Hurston. Hughes was perhaps Harlem's most famous writer. He wrote about the difficult conditions under which African Americans lived.

Jazz became widely popular in the 1920s. It was a form of music that combined African rhythms, blues, and ragtime to produce a unique sound. Jazz spread from its birthplace in New Orleans to other parts of the country and made its way into the nightclubs of Harlem. These nightclubs featured popular jazz musicians such as Louis Armstrong and Duke Ellington, and singers such as the jazz and blues great, Bessie Smith. Harlem's most famous nightclub was the Cotton Club. It made stars of many African-American performers, but only white customers were allowed in the club.

Vocabulary
renaissance: rebirth (French)

*Reading*History
C. Recognizing Effects What changes to popular culture resulted from the migration of African Americans to the North?

The Lost Generation

For some artists and writers, the decade after the war was not a time of celebration but a time of deep despair. They had seen the ideas of the Progressives end in a senseless war. They were filled with resentment and they saw little hope for the future. They were called the **Lost Generation**.

Reading History

D. Analyzing Causes Why did many American writers become expatriates and live in Paris?

For many of them, only one place offered freedom and tolerance. That was Paris. The French capital became a gathering place for American **expatriates**, people who choose to live in a country other than their own. Among the American expatriates living in Paris was the young novelist Ernest Hemingway. As an ambulance driver in Europe during World War I, he had seen the war's worst. His early novels, *The Sun Also Rises* and *A Farewell to Arms*, reflected the mood of despair that followed the war.

Novelists F. Scott Fitzgerald and Sinclair Lewis were two other members of the Lost Generation. Fitzgerald and his wife, Zelda, lived the whirlwind life of the Jazz Age—fast cars, nightclubs, wild parties, and trips to Paris. His masterpiece, *The Great Gatsby*, is a tragic story of wealthy New Yorkers whose lives spin out of control. The novel is a portrait of the dark side of the Roaring Twenties.

Lewis wrote *Babbitt*, a novel that satirized, or made fun of, the American middle class and its concern for material possessions.

F. Scott Fitzgerald is pictured here in France with his wife, Zelda. He published his masterpiece, The Great Gatsby, while living there.

A VOICE FROM THE PAST

It's the fellow with four to ten thousand a year . . . and an automobile and a nice little family in a bungalow . . . that makes the wheels of progress go round! . . . That's the type of fellow that's ruling America today; in fact, it's the ideal type to which the entire world must tend, if there's to be a decent, well-balanced . . . future for this little old planet!

Sinclair Lewis, *Babbitt*

The social values and materialistic lifestyles criticized by Lewis soon came to an end. As you will read in the next chapter, the soaring economy that brought prosperity in the 1920s came to a crashing halt. It was followed by a worldwide economic depression in the 1930s.

Section 3 Assessment

1. Terms & Names

Explain the significance of:
- jazz
- mass media
- popular culture
- Harlem Renaissance
- Lost Generation
- expatriate

2. Using Graphics

Use the chart to review facts about mass media.

Radio	Movies

How did mass media change the lives of Americans?

3. Main Ideas

a. Which two factors gave Americans more leisure time?

b. What effect did radio have on sports?

c. Why was Harlem called the unofficial capital of black America?

4. Critical Thinking

Evaluating What contributions to popular culture occurred in the 1920s?

THINK ABOUT
- the impact of World War I
- the power of mass media
- new social values

ACTIVITY OPTIONS

ART

TECHNOLOGY

Find an image and important facts about a noted person in this section. Draw a **trading card** or plan that person's **home page** for the Internet.

African-American Baseball Leagues

More than a million African Americans left the South from 1917 to 1929. They were lured to large cities by the offer of higher wages and the increased demand for labor. It was during this period of growing urbanization that the Negro baseball leagues were formed. The map on the next page shows cities with notable teams in the 1920s and 1930s. Each city had an African-American population large enough and wealthy enough to support a team.

Most teams were owned by African Americans. To raise money for expenses, teams needed to play as many games as possible. Thus, they traveled constantly. Stopping in big cities and small towns, they played other African-American teams or white amateur and professional teams. Eventually, teams of African-American all-stars played exhibitions against professional white all-stars.

In 1920, Andrew "Rube" Foster persuaded owners of seven other teams to join him in forming the first Negro baseball league—the Negro National League. Foster (pictured in suit at right) was a former player and then owner of the Chicago American Giants. The Negro American League got started in 1937. After major league baseball was integrated by Jackie Robinson in 1947, the Negro leagues began to decline.

ARTIFACT FILE

Memorabilia
The baseball jersey and shoes pictured here are part of the uniform worn by a player from one of the traveling teams of the period.

Pittsburgh Crawfords
The Pittsburgh Crawfords, shown here with the team's bus, was one of the best teams in the Negro leagues in the 1930s. The success of traveling teams helped to boost revenues of African-American-owned hotels and restaurants in every city that they played.

Cities with Notable African-American Baseball Teams, 1920s–1930s

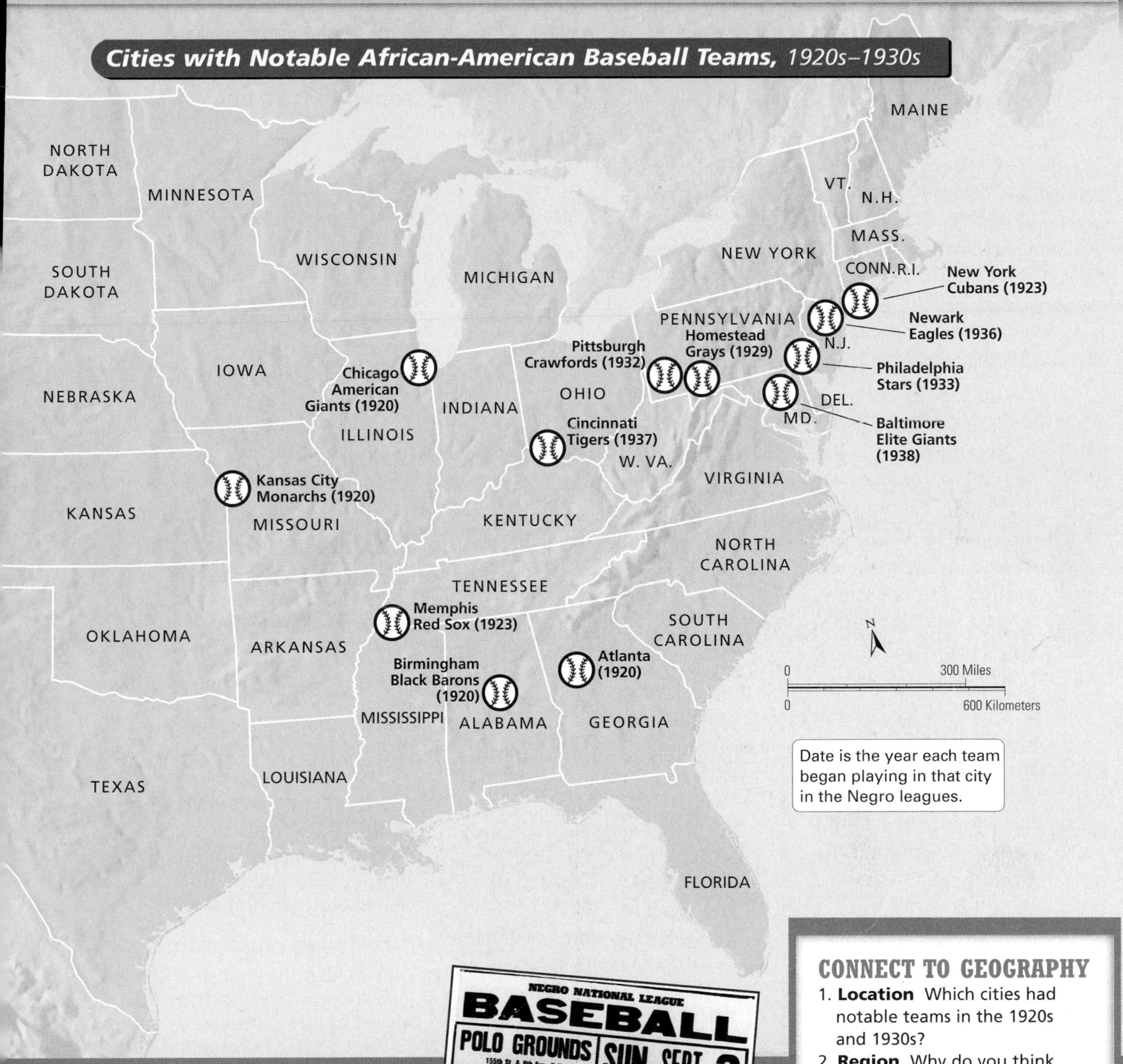

MAINE

NORTH DAKOTA

MINNESOTA

VT.

N.H.

SOUTH DAKOTA

WISCONSIN

MICHIGAN

MASS.

NEW YORK

CONN. R.I.

New York Cubans (1923)

IOWA

Chicago American Giants (1920)

PENNSYLVANIA
Homestead Grays (1929)

Newark Eagles (1936)

N.J.

NEBRASKA

INDIANA

OHIO

Pittsburgh Crawfords (1932)

Philadelphia Stars (1933)

ILLINOIS

Cincinnati Tigers (1937)

MD.

DEL.

Baltimore Elite Giants (1938)

Kansas City Monarchs (1920)

W. VA.

VIRGINIA

KANSAS

MISSOURI

KENTUCKY

NORTH CAROLINA

TENNESSEE

N

OKLAHOMA

ARKANSAS

Memphis Red Sox (1923)

SOUTH CAROLINA

0   300 Miles

Birmingham Black Barons (1920)

Atlanta (1920)

0   600 Kilometers

MISSISSIPPI

ALABAMA

GEORGIA

TEXAS

LOUISIANA

Date is the year each team began playing in that city in the Negro leagues.

FLORIDA

On-Line Field Trip

National Baseball Hall of Fame and Museum

The Negro leagues have been widely honored. This poster is from the National Baseball Hall of Fame and Museum in Cooperstown, New York. In Kansas City, Missouri, the Negro Leagues Baseball Museum also keeps the memory of these teams alive.

For more about the Negro leagues . . .

RESEARCH LINKS
CLASSZONE.COM

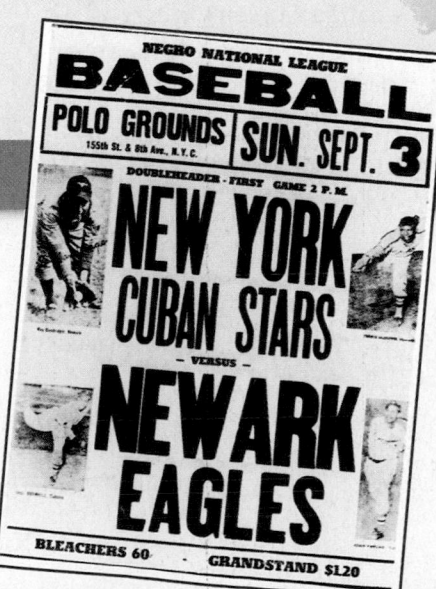

NEGRO NATIONAL LEAGUE
BASEBALL
POLO GROUNDS SUN. SEPT. 3
155th St. & 8th Ave., N.Y.C.
DOUBLEHEADER · FIRST GAME 2 P.M.
NEW YORK CUBAN STARS
— VERSUS —
NEWARK EAGLES
BLEACHERS 60   GRANDSTAND $1.20

CONNECT TO GEOGRAPHY

1. **Location** Which cities had notable teams in the 1920s and 1930s?

2. **Region** Why do you think that African-American teams were located mainly in cities in the East?

See Geography Handbook, pp. 4–5.

CONNECT TO HISTORY

3. **Evaluating** How did the migration of African Americans from the South to Northern cities lead to the rise of Negro baseball leagues?

VISUAL SUMMARY

The Roaring Twenties

Politics

Republican presidents Warren G. Harding and Calvin Coolidge supported business in the United States and isolationism in foreign relations.

Economics

Business prospered in the 1920s, helped by government support and the development of new technologies. But some groups, notably farmers, faced hardships.

Technology

Technological developments, such as the assembly line, and cheap, available sources of power, such as electricity and petroleum, powered the new prosperity.

Society and Culture

Changes in society brought new attitudes and lifestyles, especially for young people and women. Movies, radio, jazz, and sports became popular forms of entertainment.

TERMS & NAMES

Briefly explain the significance of each of the following.

1. Warren G. Harding
2. Calvin Coolidge
3. isolationist
4. Kellogg-Briand Pact
5. NAACP
6. Marcus Garvey
7. fundamentalism
8. mass media
9. Harlem Renaissance
10. Lost Generation

REVIEW QUESTIONS

The Business of America (pages 709–712)

1. How was the foreign policy of Harding and Coolidge isolationist?
2. What was the economic theory of laissez faire?
3. Which factors contributed to the nation's growing wealth during the 1920s?

Changes in Society (pages 713–716)

4. What changes took place in the behavior and values of young people during the 1920s?
5. What was the image of the *flapper?*
6. How did the 19th Amendment change women's lives?
7. What were some of the divisions in society in the 1920s?

The Jazz Age and the Harlem Renaissance (pages 717–723)

8. What were three examples of American popular culture?
9. Which factors contributed to the popularity of sports?
10. Why are the 1920s also called the Jazz Age?

CRITICAL THINKING

1. USING YOUR NOTES: FINDING MAIN IDEAS

Categories	Main Ideas
Government	
Business	
Agriculture	
Technology	
Society	
Popular Culture	

Using your completed chart, answer the questions below.

a. What role did government choose to play in the economy?
b. How did technology affect life during the 1920s?
c. How did popular culture change the habits of society?

2. ANALYZING LEADERSHIP

Think about the political leaders discussed in this chapter. Which of their characteristics made them good or poor leaders?

3. APPLYING CITIZENSHIP SKILLS

In what other ways could people have protested Prohibition besides disregarding the law?

4. THEME: SCIENCE AND TECHNOLOGY

How did advances in technology contribute to the prosperity of the United States during the 1920s?

5. DRAWING CONCLUSIONS

Explain how the African-American migration to the North and the spread of jazz contributed to the cultural diversity of the United States.

Interact *with* History

In your opinion, which changes in American life discussed in this chapter would have affected you the most?

STANDARDS-BASED ASSESSMENT

Use the chart and your knowledge of U.S. history to answer questions 1 and 2.

Additional Test Practice, pp. S1–S33.

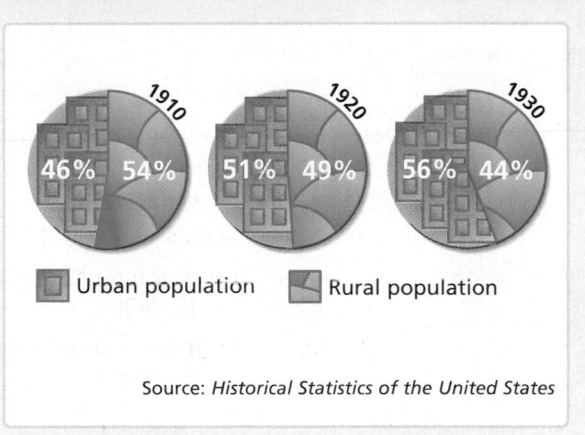

Urbanization of America, *1910–1930*

1910   46% 54%
1920   51% 49%
1930   56% 44%

Urban population   Rural population

Source: *Historical Statistics of the United States*

1. What was the total percentage increase in the urban population from 1910 to 1930?

A. 8 percent

B. 10 percent

C. 46 percent

D. 54 percent

2. By what year was the percentage of urban and rural populations closest to equal in the United States?

A. 1900

B. 1910

C. 1920

D. 1930

This quotation from Margaret Sanger is about women and men in the 1920s. Use the quotation and your knowledge of U.S. history to answer question 3.

PRIMARY SOURCE

Today women are on the whole much more individual. They posses as strong likes and dislikes as men. They live more and more on the plane of social equality with men . . . [and] there is more enjoyable companionship and real friendship between men and women.

Margaret Sanger, quoted in *A More Perfect Union*

3. According to Sanger, what is the status of women compared to men in the 1920s?

A. Men are superior to women.

B. Women are superior to men.

C. an increasing equality between the two

D. Men and women will never be equal.

TEST PRACTICE
CLASSZONE.COM

ALTERNATIVE ASSESSMENT

1. ✎ WRITING ABOUT HISTORY

Choose a sports hero from the 1920s. Then write an **article** about one of their competitions.

- Research your article in biographies or books about the history of sports. Include some biographical information about the person.
- You should also provide a persuasive argument about why your subject is so important.

2. COOPERATIVE LEARNING

Many inventions, such as refrigerators, vacuum cleaners, toasters, fans, and washing machines made life easier during the 1920s. Work in a group to create a 1920s ad for one of these products. Include how it will improve people's lives, and how much it costs. Divide the work of researching, writing, and illustrating the ad.

INTEGRATED TECHNOLOGY

DESIGNING A WEB SITE

In the 1920s, American popular culture was being spread throughout the country and abroad by radio and movies. Use the library or search the Internet for information about music, fashion, fads, and celebrities of the time. Then create a Roaring Twenties Web page.

- Select images of personalities, fashions, and fads. Include biographical information and quotations from celebrities.
- Choose music that captures the spirit of the era.
- Identify Web sites that would be good links for visitors to your page.

For more about the 1920s . . .

INTERNET ACTIVITY
CLASSZONE.COM

CHAPTER 26

The Great Depression and New Deal 1929–1940

Section 1
Hoover and the Crash

Section 2
Roosevelt and the New Deal

Section 3
Life During the Depression

Section 4
The Effects of the New Deal

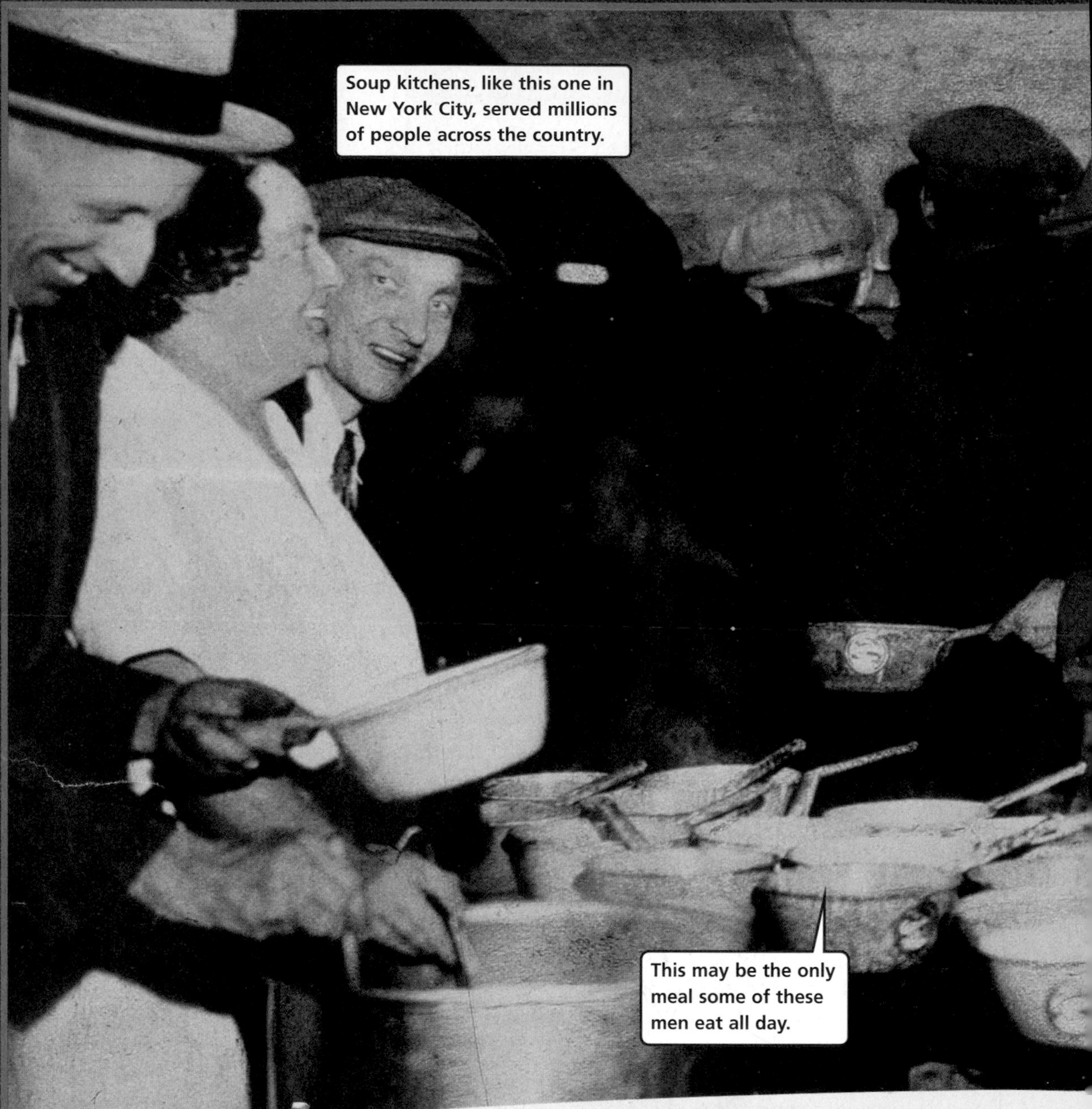

Soup kitchens, like this one in New York City, served millions of people across the country.

This may be the only meal some of these men eat all day.

USA

1929
U.S. stock market crashes. Great Depression begins.

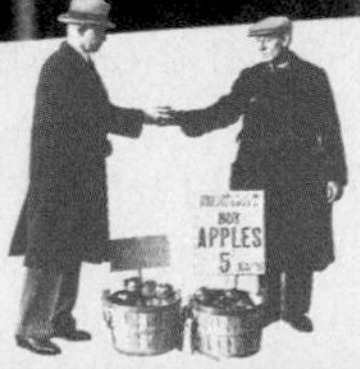

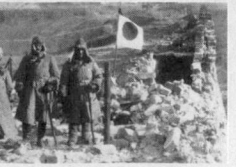

1931
Over eight million Americans are unemployed.

1932
Americans turn against Hoover. Franklin Delano Roosevelt is elected president.

1933
Roosevelt initiates government programs to help the economy.

World

1931
Affected by the Depression, Japan invades Manchuria, partially to expand its economy.

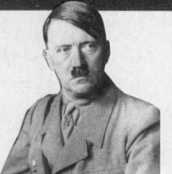

1933
Adolf Hitler becomes dictator of Germany.

It's 1932. The economy is bad, and millions of people are out of work. Some are starving.

Two men are running for president. One says the government should give money to the poor. The other says this will make people stop looking for jobs. He wants charity groups to help people in need.

Who do you think should help the poor?

What Do You Think?

- Is the government responsible for everyone's well-being?

- What responsibility do individuals have to help others?

- What is the best way to help people out of poverty?

RESEARCH LINKS
CLASSZONE.COM

Visit the Chapter 26 links for more information about the Great Depression and the New Deal.

> Notice that some of the men appear well-dressed. Hard times fell on rich and poor alike.

1935
ongress passes the ocial Security Act.

1936
Roosevelt is reelected.

1936
Léon Blum, Socialist premier of France, introduces reforms such as the 40-hour workweek.

1937
Roosevelt tries but fails to add justices to the Supreme Court.

1939
John Steinbeck publishes *The Grapes of Wrath* about migrant workers.

1939
Germany invades Poland, starting World War II.

1940

Reading Strategy: Evaluating

What Do You Know?

What do people do to get by when they are unable to find work? Where can they turn for help besides the government?

Think About

- stories you may have heard about the Great Depression
- movies and books about people with economic struggles
- your responses to the Interact with History about helping the poor (see page 727)

What Do You Want to Know?

ROOSEVELT'S NEW DEAL PROSPERITY

Needle~Book

What questions do you have about how the Great Depression affected Americans? What facts and details would you like to learn about government actions during that period? In your notebook, list the things you hope to learn from this chapter.

Evaluating

To evaluate is to make a judgment about something. As you read this chapter, look for details about how the following people responded to the Great Depression: President Herbert Hoover, President Franklin Delano Roosevelt, and ordinary citizens (civilians). Record those details in a chart like the one below. Then evaluate how effective those responses were at making the situation better.

S See Skillbuilder Handbook, page R19.

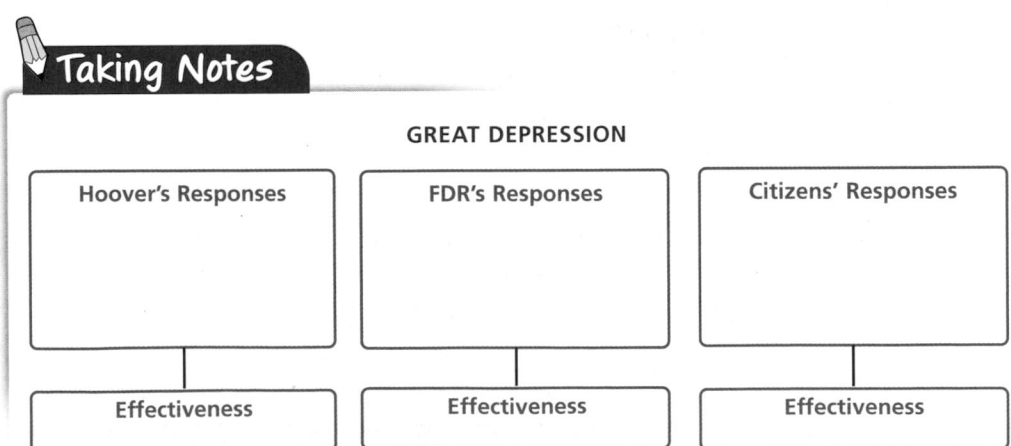

✎ *Taking Notes*

GREAT DEPRESSION

Hoover's Responses	FDR's Responses	Citizens' Responses
Effectiveness	Effectiveness	Effectiveness

Hoover and the Crash

MAIN IDEA	WHY IT MATTERS NOW	TERMS & NAMES
After the stock market crash of 1929, the U.S. economy sank into the worst depression in its history.	Today the government regulates banking and the stock exchange to prevent such severe depressions.	Herbert Hoover — Crash of 1929 speculation — Great Depression buying on margin — public works projects Black Tuesday — Bonus Army

ONE AMERICAN'S STORY

In the 1920s, many farmers suffered poverty because farm prices stayed low. Republican senator George Norris from Nebraska criticized bankers for not caring about farmers' problems.

A VOICE FROM THE PAST

When the great leaders of banking and industry can see no further than the artificial prosperity that comes to Big Business while those who toil on farms are getting no return for their labor, then indeed we have a right to question the wisdom of our financial leaders.

George Norris, "The Farmers' Situation, a National Danger"

George Norris

Norris was unusual because most Republicans supported business. Section 1 explains what the Republicans did when business failed.

Problems in the Economy

Secretary of Commerce **Herbert Hoover** became the Republican candidate for president in 1928. In a speech, he stated, "We shall soon . . . be in sight of the day when poverty will be banished from this nation." But the overall prosperity of the 1920s hid the fact that some industries were in trouble. These included agriculture, railroads, textile mills, and mines.

The growing wealth of the richest Americans also hid the struggle of the majority. By 1929, 71 percent of American families earned less than $2,500 per year, the minimum needed to live decently. Some people had no jobs. African Americans in particular had high jobless rates.

During the 1920s, industries had improved efficiency and begun to produce more goods. But the income of middle-class and poor people didn't rise enough for them to purchase the extra goods. Products piled up in warehouses, causing a problem. Unless businesses sold their products, they couldn't pay for materials, salaries, equipment, or shipping.

Taking Notes

Use your chart to take notes about Hoover's responses to the Great Depression.

GREAT DEPRESSION

Hoover's Responses	FDR's Responses	Citizens' Responses
Effectiveness	Effectiveness	Effectiveness

Economic Problems, *1920–1929*

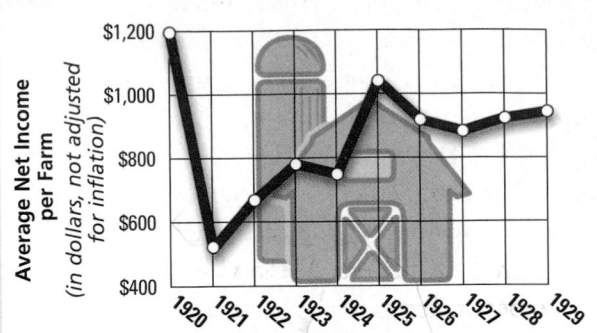

Average Net Income per Farm Notice the big drop in average farm income between 1920 and 1921. Although farm income generally rose during the decade, it did not reach the 1920 level.

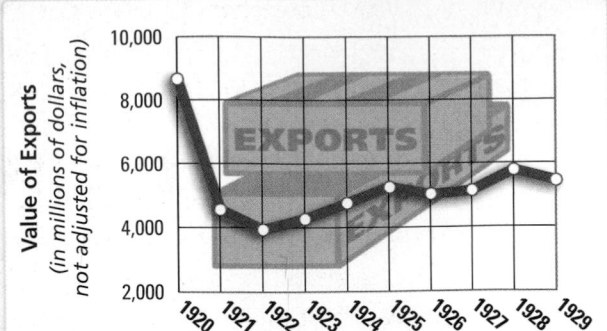

Value of Exports Notice the drop between 1920 and 1921. For the next eight years, exports remained generally the same. U.S. businesses barely increased the amount they sold overseas.

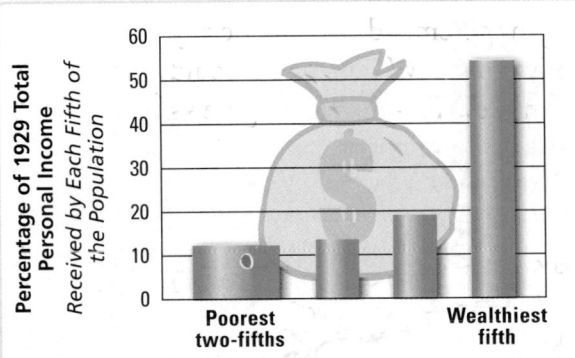

Income Distribution In 1929, the wealthiest fifth of the population had more income than the other four-fifths combined. Poor and middle-class people could not afford to buy many consumer goods. This hurt business.

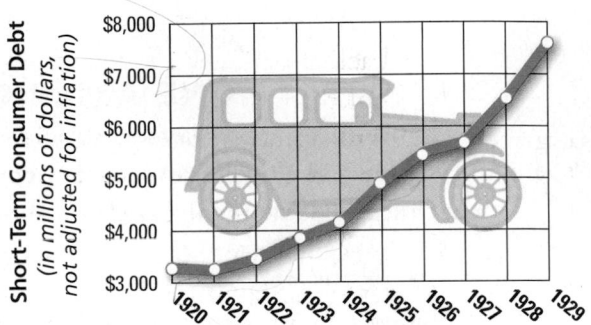

Short-Term Consumer Debt If people do not earn enough to buy what they want, they may take out loans or buy on credit. Short-term consumer debt skyrocketed from 1920 to 1929.

Sources: *Historical Statistics of the United States; A Study of Saving in the United States*

SKILLBUILDER Interpreting Graphs

1. *Which of these problems affected individuals, and which affected businesses?*

2. *By how much did short-term consumer debt rise from 1920 to 1929?*

Some consumers bought goods anyway—on credit. But when their debt grew higher than they could repay, they stopped buying new items. Unsold goods piled up even more.

Yet stock market prices kept climbing. Americans who could afford it rushed to buy stocks. Increasingly, investors bought on **speculation**, buying and selling stocks in the hope of making a quick profit.

Investors also began **buying on margin**—they paid a small part of a stock's price as a down payment and borrowed the rest. When they sold the stock, they repaid the loan and kept the profit. The system worked as long as prices rose. But if prices fell, borrowers couldn't repay their loans because they had to sell the stock for less than they paid for it.

Despite these problems, people believed Hoover when he predicted growing prosperity. In 1928, he won the presidency by a landslide.

Vocabulary
credit: an agreement to pay over time, instead of all at once

The Crash and the Great Depression

On September 3, 1929, the value of stocks on the New York Stock Exchange reached a high point. Then prices drifted downward. On October 23, prices dropped sharply. The next morning, people tried to sell thousands of shares before their value dropped further. Many of those who had bought on margin were forced to sell stocks to pay off their loans.

This heavy selling drove prices even lower. Because more people wanted to sell stocks than to buy them, prices had to go down to attract purchasers. But the quickly falling prices scared off buyers. Meanwhile, sellers hurried to unload their shares at the best price they could get.

On October 24, a record 12.9 million shares were traded. But the worst was yet to come. On October 29, **Black Tuesday,** investors sold 16.4 million shares of stocks at prices much lower than they had been selling for a month earlier. The plunge in stock market prices, called the **Crash of 1929,** was the first event of a terrible economic depression.

After the stock market crash, banks began to demand that people pay back the money they had borrowed to buy stocks. When people could not repay these loans, banks ran short of money. This frightening news sent people running to the banks to withdraw their savings. But banks typically do not keep enough cash on hand to pay all of their depositors at once. Unable to pay their depositors, many banks simply closed. By March 1933, about 9,000 banks had gone out of business.

Background
This pattern of selling stocks and withdrawing deposits because of fear is the reason the depressions of the 1800s are also called panics.

Businesses felt the impact next. Many already had warehouses filled with more goods than they could sell. Because the economy's problems scared people, they stopped buying new goods. As a result, businesses sold less and less. Tens of thousands of businesses went bankrupt.

To survive, many businesses fired workers. Unemployment grew to 25 percent by 1933. As more people lost jobs, they bought fewer products—and companies laid off even more workers. Unable to pay their bills, thousands of people lost their homes, and millions went hungry.

The United States had experienced economic depressions before. But no depression caused as much suffering or lasted as long as this one—from 1929 to World War II. Therefore, it is called the **Great Depression**.

The Great Depression also affected millions of people around the world. For example, many European countries had borrowed money from U.S. banks to rebuild after World War I. When the American economy failed, so did Europe's. Hard times spread around the globe.

Hoover Acts Conservatively

Reading **History**
A. Analyzing Causes Why do you think people expected Hoover to end the Depression?

Americans looked to the president to end the hard times. Along with most Republicans, Hoover feared that government interference might hurt the economy even more. Even so, he did try to fight the Depression, but his actions often backfired. For example, he tried to balance the

Economics *in* History

Recession and Depression

Many people hoped the economy would fix itself because they believed depressions were a natural part of the business cycle (shown below). Economies go through ups and downs. The period when an economy is at its worst is a trough. There are two kinds of troughs—recessions and depressions. A depression is more severe.

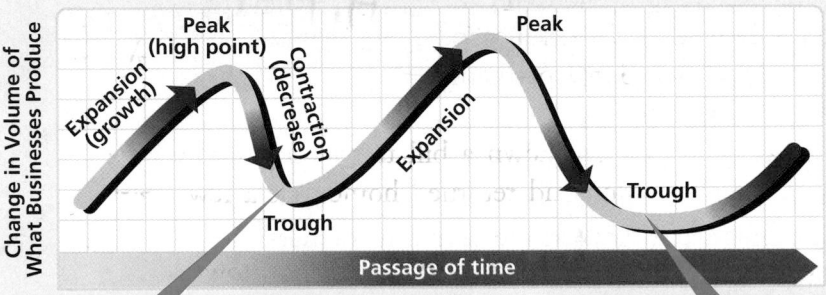

Change in Volume of What Businesses Produce

Peak (high point)

Expansion (growth)

Contraction (decrease)

Trough

Expansion

Peak

Trough

Passage of time

Recession

- The production of a nation's goods and services goes down each month for six months.
- Business owners produce less and invest less in new equipment and facilities. They also lay off workers.
- Consumers buy fewer goods.

Depression

- The production of goods and services drops lower than in a recession.
- The period of no economic growth is longer than in a recession. Unemployment is higher.
- The slowdown may spread to other countries; international trade declines dramatically.

CONNECT TO HISTORY

1. **Evaluating** Why were the hard times of the 1930s a depression, not a recession?

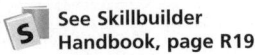 See Skillbuilder Handbook, page R19.

CONNECT TO TODAY

2. **Making Inferences** How would today's world be affected differently by a depression in the United States than by one in Holland? Explain.

For more about economics . . .

 RESEARCH LINKS
CLASSZONE.COM

federal budget by cutting government spending and raising taxes. This pulled money out of the economy, which made the slump worse.

Some of Hoover's actions made him very unpopular. For example, he believed that federal relief—aid to the poor—would make people too dependent on government. So he would not support giving relief. In his view, one answer to the hard times was a quality he called "rugged individualism." In 1931, Hoover said, "We cannot legislate ourselves out of a world economic depression. We can and will work ourselves out."

Hoover also stressed the value of volunteer efforts. He encouraged churches and private charities such as the Salvation Army and the Red Cross to help needy Americans. In 1932, private giving did reach a record level—but it still wasn't enough to help everyone in need.

As unemployment, hunger, and homelessness grew, people became bitter toward the president. They blamed him for their suffering. They called empty pockets turned inside out "Hoover flags." And they called villages of wretched huts that housed homeless people "Hoovervilles."

Finally, Hoover softened his stand against government relief. States received some federal money to give to the needy. And in 1932, Hoover set up an agency to lend money to states, cities, and towns. This money would be used for **public works projects**—government-funded projects to build public resources such as roads and dams. These projects would create jobs. But Hoover's actions proved to be too little and too late.

Reading **History**

B. Solving Problems What were Hoover's solutions to the problems caused by the Depression, and did they succeed?

Hoover Loses to Roosevelt

In the summer of 1932, a dramatic event made Hoover even more unpopular. Congress had promised World War I veterans a bonus for wartime service. The bonuses were not due to be paid until the 1940s. But many of the ex-soldiers were jobless and wanted early payment. Some decided to march to Washington, D.C., to ask Congress to pass such a law. Through May and June, the **Bonus Army** of 12,000 to 15,000 veterans poured into Washington and set up camps around the city. Some of them were accompanied by their families.

U.S. troops used tanks and grenades to force the Bonus Army from their camps.

The Senate, backed by Hoover, voted down a bill that called for a bonus payment. Most veterans gave up and returned home, but a few thousand remained to protest.

At the end of July, General Douglas MacArthur decided on his own to drive the Bonus Army from Washington. MacArthur's troops threw tear gas and prodded the veterans and their children with bayonets. One veteran was shot to death. The American public reacted angrily.

Reading **History**
C. Making Inferences Why do you think Evalyn McLean became so angry?

A VOICE FROM THE PAST

I saw in a news reel the tanks, the cavalry, and the gas-bomb throwers running those wretched Americans out of our capital. I was so raging mad I could have torn the theater down.

Evalyn Walsh McLean, *Father Struck It Rich*

Because of the attack, Americans turned against Hoover more than ever. In the 1932 presidential election, Democratic candidate Franklin Delano Roosevelt carried all but six states. Section 2 explains how Roosevelt tried to end the Depression with new federal programs.

Section ❶ Assessment

1. Terms & Names

Explain the significance of:
- Herbert Hoover
- speculation
- buying on margin
- Black Tuesday
- Crash of 1929
- Great Depression
- public works projects
- Bonus Army

2. Using Graphics

Use a diagram like the one below to show the sequence of events that led from the stock market crash to massive unemployment.

```
stock market    →    [        ]
   crash

[        ]    →    [        ]
```

3. Main Ideas

a. What weaknesses existed in the economy during the 1920s?

b. What is buying on margin, and how was it a problem?

c. Why did Hoover become unpopular with many Americans?

4. Critical Thinking

Contrasting How did Hoover's view of the federal government and that of most Americans differ?

THINK ABOUT
- Hoover's attitude about federal relief
- why Americans blamed Hoover for their suffering
- what Americans might have expected from Hoover

ACTIVITY OPTIONS

MATH
SPEECH

Research the changes in stock market value from September through October 1929. Create a **graph** or give a series of **radio news bulletins** about the changes.

Roosevelt and the New Deal

MAIN IDEA	WHY IT MATTERS NOW	TERMS & NAMES
After becoming president, Franklin D. Roosevelt took many actions to fight the Great Depression.	Roosevelt increased government's role in helping needy Americans and regulating the financial industry.	Franklin Delano Roosevelt fireside chat New Deal Hundred Days Social Security Act Second New Deal deficit spending

ONE AMERICAN'S STORY

Dynamite Garland's father had worked for the railroad. When the Depression struck, Dynamite's father lost his job, and her family moved into a rent-free garage.

A VOICE FROM THE PAST

We had a coal stove, and we had to each take turns, the three of us kids, to warm our legs. It was awfully cold when you opened those garage doors. . . . In the morning, we'd get out and get some snow and put it on the stove and melt it and wash around our faces.

Dynamite Garland, quoted in *Hard Times*

Children such as Dynamite Garland and the girls in this photograph suffered greatly from hunger and poverty during the Depression.

Starting in 1933, **Franklin Delano Roosevelt**, the new Democratic president, created a number of programs to help the economy and people like Dynamite. This section describes those programs.

Taking Notes

Use your chart to take notes about Roosevelt's responses to the Great Depression.

GREAT DEPRESSION

Hoover's Responses	FDR's Responses	Citizens' Responses
Effectiveness	Effectiveness	Effectiveness

Roosevelt Takes Charge

Millions of people lacked food and shelter. Yet the country had to endure a frustrating four-month wait from the November election to Roosevelt's inauguration. The Twentieth Amendment, which moved the inauguration date to January, was not ratified until 1933. President Roosevelt, nicknamed FDR, was finally inaugurated on March 4, 1933.

Roosevelt differed from Hoover in two important ways. First, he gave Americans hope, beginning with his inaugural address: "Let me assert my firm belief that the only thing we have to fear is fear itself." Second, he was willing to try new ideas and change the way government worked. Though he had no fixed plan to end the Depression, he set up a "brain trust" of advisers, including college professors and economists.

Roosevelt took three immediate steps that boosted public confidence. First, he declared a "bank holiday"—a temporary shutdown of all banks.

*Reading***History**

A. Drawing Conclusions Did Roosevelt's first fireside chat affect the public the way he wanted? Explain.

Second, he promised that only the banks that were in good shape would be allowed to reopen.

Third, the day before the banks reopened, FDR gave the first of many **fireside chats.** In these radio talks, he explained his policies in a warm, friendly style. He said it was safer to "keep your money in a reopened bank than under the mattress." The next day, people deposited more money into the banks than they withdrew.

The Hundred Days

During the campaign, FDR had pledged a "new deal" for Americans. This snappy phrase, the **New Deal,** came to stand for FDR's programs to fight the Depression.

In the session of Congress lasting from March 9 to mid-June 1933, Roosevelt sent Congress a pile of new bills. Many of them passed with little debate in this famous session of Congress, called the **Hundred Days.**

The laws passed during the Hundred Days had three major goals, known as the "three Rs."

1. **relief** for the hungry and jobless
2. **recovery** for agriculture and industry
3. **reforms** to change the way the economy worked

FDR wanted not only to ease suffering but also to try to prevent such a severe depression from happening again. The major programs passed during the Hundred Days included relief, recovery, and reform plans that related to jobs, banking, wages, and agriculture. The chart on page 737 lists several major programs and explains what those programs accomplished.

Responses to the New Deal

Some conservatives thought the New Deal went too far. They opposed the growth of the federal government and questioned how it would pay for all the new programs. They also feared that the New Deal was moving the country toward socialism.

Vocabulary
socialism: an economic system in which businesses are owned by the government, not individuals

Yet, other critics charged that the New Deal didn't go far enough. Louisiana senator Huey Long declared, "Unless we provide for redistribution of wealth in this country, the country is doomed." But Long's motives were far from noble. For years, he had ruled his state like a dictator. Attacking FDR was a way to increase his own power.

Father Charles Coughlin, a priest with a popular radio program, also argued for changing the economy to help the poor. He eventually began to blame Jews for the nation's problems. In the 1940s, the Catholic Church stopped his broadcasts. Another critic, Francis Townshend, proposed giving $200 a month to every American over age 60. He said a sales tax would pay for the pension, but economists disputed his figures.

AMERICA'S HISTORY MAKERS

FRANKLIN DELANO ROOSEVELT
1882–1945

A distant cousin of Theodore Roosevelt, Franklin D. Roosevelt became a New York state senator when he was 29. Later, he served as assistant secretary of the Navy.

At the age of 39, FDR caught polio. For the rest of his life, he walked with braces or rode in a wheelchair. Despite this, he continued in politics and was elected governor of New York in 1928.

The public rarely saw photos revealing FDR's disability. Even so, many Americans sensed that he was a man who understood trouble. This quality helped him as a leader during the Depression.

How would an understanding of trouble help Roosevelt to lead?

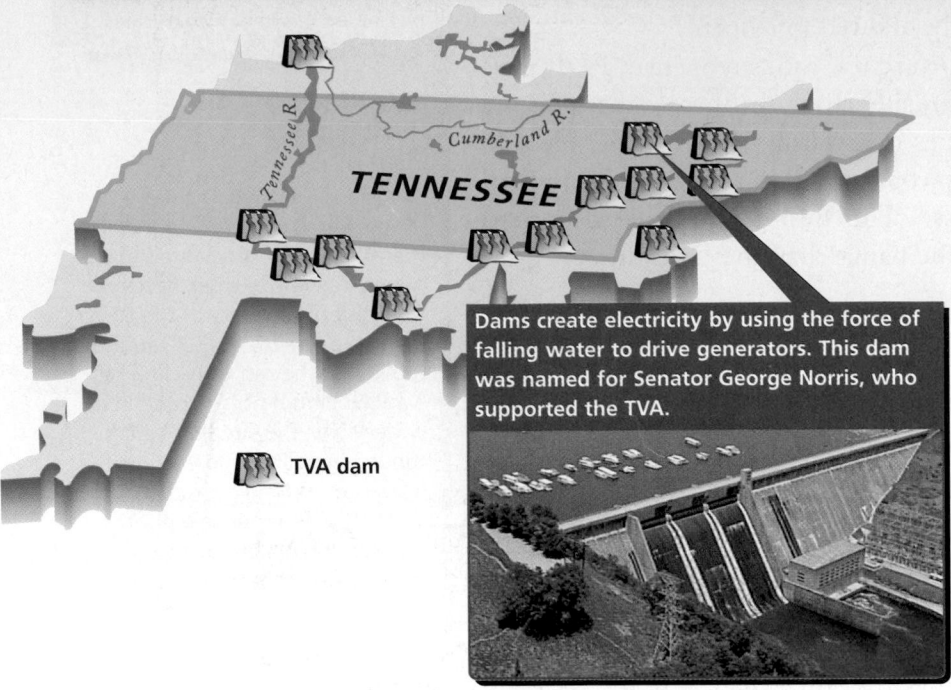

Dams create electricity by using the force of falling water to drive generators. This dam was named for Senator George Norris, who supported the TVA.

TVA dam

FACTS ABOUT THE TVA

- The TVA supplies power to an area of about 80,000 square miles, shown in dark and light green to the left. The region uses more than 100 billion kilowatt-hours of electricity. This is 65 times as much as in 1933.

- There are more than 40 TVA dams.

- Users of TVA power pay about a third less for their electricity than other Americans.

- The TVA dams also help control flooding on the Tennessee River.

In the 1934 congressional elections, voters had a chance to react to these criticisms. The party in power usually loses seats in a nonpresidential election. But, indicating their support for Roosevelt, voters in this election sent even more Democrats to Congress.

The Second New Deal

Although he rejected Townshend's plan, FDR did want to help the elderly. Bank failures and the stock market crash had stolen the savings of many old people. Some had lost their homes or had to beg for food.

In August 1935, Congress passed one of the most important bills of the century. Under the **Social Security Act,** workers and employers made payments into a special fund, from which they would draw a pension after they retired. The act also gave help to laid-off workers, disabled workers, and needy families with dependent children.

Background
Townshend's plan had been very popular with the public. FDR knew his own popularity would increase if he proposed a pension.

> **A VOICE FROM THE PAST**
>
> We have tried to frame a law which will give some measure of protection to the average citizen and to his family against the loss of a job and against poverty-ridden old age.
>
> **Franklin D. Roosevelt,** quoted in *Promises to Keep*

Social Security was part of a set of programs passed in 1935. These became known as the **Second New Deal.** Other programs of the Second New Deal are listed in the chart on the next page.

In 1936, the Democrats nominated Roosevelt for a second term. Business leaders opposed his reelection because they feared higher taxes. They also thought he was increasing government power at their expense. But a widespread alliance of working-class Americans supported FDR.

Major Programs of the New Deal

	PROGRAMS	ACCOMPLISHMENTS
Hundred Days, 1933	**FERA** (Federal Emergency Relief Administration)	Provided federal money for relief projects to the roughly 13 million unemployed
	PWA (Public Works Administration)	Created jobs by having people build highways, bridges, and other public works
	AAA (Agricultural Adjustment Administration)	Regulated farm production and promoted soil conservation
	TVA (Tennessee Valley Authority)	Planned development of the Tennessee Valley region
	CCC (Civilian Conservation Corps)	Hired young men to plant trees, build dams, and work on other conservation projects
	FDIC (Federal Deposit Insurance Corporation)	Protected the money of depositors in insured banks
	NRA (National Recovery Administration)	Regulated industry and raised wages and prices
Second New Deal, 1935	**WPA** (Works Progress Administration)	Established large-scale national works programs to create jobs
	REA (Rural Electrification Administration)	Brought electricity to rural areas
	NYA (National Youth Administration)	Set up job programs for young people and helped them continue their education
	Wagner Act	Protected labor's right to form unions and set up a board to hear labor disputes
	Social Security Act	Provided workers with unemployment insurance and retirement benefits

SKILLBUILDER Interpreting Charts

1. *How did the PWA and the CCC help both those who were hired and the nation as a whole?*
2. *How did the Second New Deal help both young and old workers?*

*Reading*History

B. Analyzing Causes Why did many African Americans switch to the Democratic Party?

They included African Americans, who until then had remained loyal to the Republican Party—the party of Lincoln, who had issued the Emancipation Proclamation during the Civil War. However, FDR's programs to help the poor convinced many African Americans to vote Democrat. On Election Day, FDR won every state except Maine and Vermont.

Roosevelt Fights the Supreme Court

From the high point of his 1936 victory, Roosevelt's presidency took a downward turn. Most of the nine justices of the Supreme Court didn't support FDR's programs. Using the power of judicial review (see Chapter 10), in 1935 the Court struck down laws that it believed gave the federal government too much power. These actions threatened to destroy the New Deal.

In 1937, FDR asked Congress to pass a bill allowing him to add up to six justices to the Supreme Court. He planned to appoint justices who shared his ideas about government. This would give him the majority he

"Dr. Roosevelt" reassures the Constitution that the New Deal won't harm it. Instead, FDR blames "Nurse Supreme Court" for any problems.

(speech bubble) THERE'S NOTHING THE MATTER WITH YOU—YOUR NURSE IS NOT GIVING YOU PROPER TREATMENT!

needed to save his programs from being overturned. Both Republicans and Democrats harshly criticized FDR's Court-packing bill. They said it interfered with the system of checks and balances that were set up by the U.S. Constitution. Congress agreed and voted it down.

In the end, Roosevelt did achieve his goal of a more sympathetic Court. Within the next two and a half years, retirements and deaths allowed Roosevelt to name five liberal justices to the bench. But the president may have lost more than he won. His clumsy attempt to pack the Court with allies damaged his image and gave ammunition to his critics.

Reading **History**

C. Recognizing Effects What was the outcome of Roosevelt's attempt to pack the Court?

The New Deal Slows Down

Opposition to Roosevelt grew after the Court-packing attempt. Then in late 1937, the economy worsened again. The amount of goods produced by industry fell, and unemployment rose. Many Americans blamed Roosevelt for the downturn.

Critics also attacked Roosevelt's use of **deficit spending,** or using borrowed money to fund government programs. Roosevelt himself had doubts about it. Even though some economists said that huge amounts of deficit spending were needed to boost the economy, FDR hesitated to take that course. He proposed few new programs in his second term. Meanwhile, as Section 3 explains, Americans continued to suffer from harsh economic conditions.

Section 2 Assessment

1. Terms & Names

Explain the significance of:
- Franklin Delano Roosevelt
- fireside chat
- New Deal
- Hundred Days
- Social Security Act
- Second New Deal
- deficit spending

2. Using Graphics

Use a chart like the one below to list FDR's major programs and whether you think each program's goal was relief, recovery, or reform (or a combination of these).

Program	Goal

Which programs created jobs?

3. Main Ideas

a. How did Roosevelt give Americans hope?

b. What happened during the period known as the Hundred Days?

c. What were the consequences of FDR's attempt to increase the size of the Supreme Court?

4. Critical Thinking

Analyzing Points of View What were some of the different reasons that people criticized FDR?

THINK ABOUT
- the conservatives
- Huey Long, Father Coughlin, and Francis Townshend
- those who opposed the Court-packing bill

ACTIVITY OPTIONS

ART

TECHNOLOGY

Choose one aspect of the New Deal that you have an opinion about. Create a **political cartoon** or design a **Web page** expressing your opinion.

Life During the Depression

MAIN IDEA	WHY IT MATTERS NOW	TERMS & NAMES
During the Depression, most Americans knew great hardship.	Because of this, a generation was scarred by suffering in ways that later generations were not.	Dust Bowl Eleanor Roosevelt	Congress of Industrial Organizations (CIO) sit-down strike

ONE AMERICAN'S STORY

Born to freed slaves, Mary McLeod Bethune founded Bethune-Cookman College. In 1936, FDR named her director of the Division of Negro Affairs at the National Youth Administration. Because of her health, her doctor told her to stop working so hard.

A VOICE FROM THE PAST

I promise to reform, but in an hour the promise is forgotten. . . . The drums of Africa still beat in my heart. They will not let me rest while there is a single Negro boy or girl without a chance to prove his worth.

Mary McLeod Bethune, "Faith That Moved a Dump Heap"

Mary McLeod Bethune was the first African-American woman to head a federal agency.

   Section 3 discusses the difficulty of living during the Depression— and the efforts of people like Bethune to make the hard times easier.

The Dust Bowl Destroys Lives

In the early 1930s, a drought hit the Great Plains and lasted for several years. Even before then, the overgrazing of livestock and the overplowing of fields had damaged the land by destroying the natural grasses whose roots anchored the soil. A journalist wrote, "You could hear the fields crack and dry, and the only movement in the down-driving heat was the dead withering of the dry blighted leaves on the twigs."

   Winds picked up dirt from the dry, exposed fields. During dust storms, noon turned into night as walls of dust filled the air and hid the sun. Dust damaged farms across a 150,000-square-mile region called the **Dust Bowl,** which covered parts of Kansas, Oklahoma, Texas, Colorado, and New Mexico. Dust storms ripped through the plains for years until rain and improved farming methods finally brought relief.

   With their crops buried under layers of dirt, ruined farmers loaded their belongings onto trucks and set off with their families to find work.

Taking Notes

Use your chart to take notes about citizens' responses to the Great Depression.

GREAT DEPRESSION

Hoover's Responses	FDR's Responses	Citizens' Responses
Effectiveness	Effectiveness	Effectiveness

Dust Bowl Migration, 1930–1940

Legend:
- Area of severe damage
- Other areas damaged by dust storms
- ← Migration route

This photograph demonstrates why the dust storms were often called "black blizzards."

GEOGRAPHY SKILLBUILDER Interpreting Maps

1. **Place** Which states suffered the most damage from the dust storms?
2. **Movement** What were the main highways that people took to leave the Dust Bowl, and where did they lead?

Many drove west on Route 66, the main highway to California. They had heard that California's farms needed workers.

But as the newcomers poured in, California farm towns quickly became overcrowded. Families lived in tiny shacks. By 1940, about 2.5 million people fleeing the Dust Bowl had made their way to California and other Pacific coast states. Because many had come from Oklahoma, they were sometimes called "Okies."

Living Through Hard Times

Not just in the Dust Bowl, but all over the country, families suffered. Even after the recovery measures of the New Deal, unemployment remained high. In 1936, for example, 9 million people had no jobs.

Without work, families couldn't afford to buy food. Bread lines offering food to the hungry appeared across the country. In January 1931, New York's 82 bread lines served an average of 85,000 small meals a day: bread and soup or bread and stew. Men, women, and children waited in these lines for their daily food. Some fainted from hunger while they waited.

Many people also lost their homes. Thousands of homeless people sought shelter under bridges and overpasses. One woman remembered "people living in old, rusted out car bodies. . . . There were people living in shacks made of orange crates. One family with a whole lot of kids were living in a piano box."

Reading **History**

A. Reading a Map
Look at the map above. Notice the three states that most Dust Bowl migrants went to.

Children had to grow up fast during the Depression. To add to their family's income, boys worked after school or even dropped out of school. Often girls had to stay home to look after younger children. Sometimes teenagers who failed to find jobs ran away from home to avoid burdening their families. By late 1932, perhaps a quarter million teens roamed the country. They sneaked onto freight trains, begged for food, and lived in squatter camps along the railroad tracks.

Family life suffered as many unemployed men felt a loss of status. They sometimes became irritable and quarreled with their families. Working women came under pressure to give up their jobs to jobless men. In fact, some New Deal projects would hire a woman only if her husband had a job. Even so, poverty forced many women to work as servants or at other low-paying jobs that men didn't want.

*Reading*History
B. Summarizing
What were the various hardships suffered by families during the Depression?

Artists Portray the Struggle

Many books of the period described the hard times. *Let Us Now Praise Famous Men* (1941) by James Agee and Walker Evans reported on the harsh lives of tenant farmers. John Steinbeck's novel *The Grapes of Wrath* (1939) told of Okies who had been evicted from their farms.

Vocabulary
evicted: forced to leave property

A VOICE FROM THE PAST

Carloads, caravans, homeless and hungry; twenty thousand and fifty thousand and a hundred thousand and two hundred thousand. They streamed over the mountains, hungry and restless—restless as ants, scurrying to find work to do—to lift, to push, to pull, to pick, to cut—anything, any burden to bear, for food. The kids are hungry. We got no place to live. Like ants scurrying for work, for food, and most of all for land.

John Steinbeck, *The Grapes of Wrath*

The African-American writer Richard Wright was one of many writers who were hired by the Works Progress Administration. Freed from his economic worries, he also wrote creatively in his spare time and produced the novel *Native Son* (1940). It depicts one African American's anger about society's racism.

daily *life*

HAVING FUN DURING HARD TIMES

To forget life's troubles, people went to the movies. At first, the Depression caused attendance to decline. But audiences soon grew as hard times made people eager for entertainment.

Viewers flocked to escapist movies such as *The Wizard of Oz.* People also saw realistic movies about the times, such as *The Grapes of Wrath,* based on John Steinbeck's novel.

Reading comic books about superheroes also was a popular pastime. Comic books were first published in 1933. *Superman* was introduced in 1938.

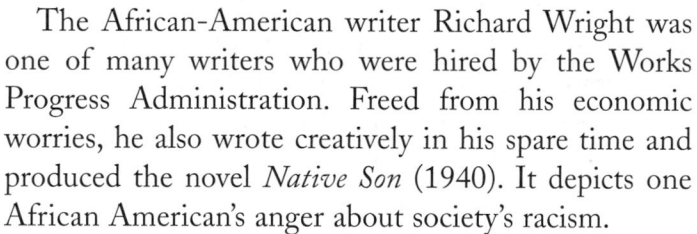

▼ *The Grapes of Wrath*

▼ *Gone with the Wind*

◄ *The Wizard of Oz*

Eleanor Roosevelt had an un-happy childhood. Her parents died when she was young, and the grandmother who raised her criticized Eleanor frequently.

In 1905, she married her distant cousin Franklin. When FDR entered politics, she was shy and disliked attending public events.

During World War I, Eleanor did volunteer work and discov-ered the joy of helping others. This gave her confidence. By the time FDR became governor of New York, Eleanor was actively working for social reform. She continued to do so as first lady.

How did Eleanor Roosevelt change from an insecure person to a leader for social reform?

Photographers also captured Depression-era suffer-ing. Dorothea Lange was one of several photographers whom the government hired to document the times. Her pictures show the hard lives of poor people during the Depression. (See pages 745 and 751.)

Women in the New Deal

The first lady, **Eleanor Roosevelt,** worked to help poor Americans. Because her husband had a disability, Mrs. Roosevelt acted as his "eyes and ears." She toured the country, visiting coal mines, work camps, and hospitals to find out how programs were working. Then she told the president what she learned and made suggestions.

In March 1933, Eleanor Roosevelt began to hold regular press conferences for women reporters. At these, the first lady introduced the women who ran New Deal programs. During Roosevelt's presidency, more women held positions with the government than ever before.

In 1933, the president named Frances Perkins secre-tary of labor, which made her the first female cabinet officer. Years earlier, Perkins had assisted Jane Addams at Chicago's Hull House. As secretary of labor, she supported laws granting a minimum wage, a limit on child employment, and unemployment compensation.

Minorities and the Depression

Mary McLeod Bethune was one of several African Americans who played a role in the government. They were called FDR's "Black Cabinet." This group included William Hastie and Robert C. Weaver. Hastie was a brilliant young lawyer who worked in the Department of the Interior. Weaver, an economist who had graduated from Harvard, became the president's adviser on racial issues.

Though he included more African Americans in government, FDR failed to back civil rights laws. For example, he did not support an anti-lynching bill. FDR opposed lynching but feared upsetting Southern white congressmen. Roosevelt said, "If I come out for the antilynching bill now, [the Southerners] will block every bill I ask Congress to pass to keep America from collapsing." In spite of this, African Americans remained loyal to the president because of his efforts to help the poor.

The Depression also greatly affected Mexican Americans. Many lived in rural areas, especially in the Southwest. Increasingly, migrants from other areas competed with them for jobs. Mexican Americans liv-ing in cities also had difficulty finding scarce jobs. While many Mexican Americans did benefit from New Deal programs, in general they received less aid than other groups.

*Reading*History
C. Making Inferences Why do you think Eleanor Roosevelt publicized the women who worked in government?

*Reading*History
D. Contrasting How did African Americans and Mexican Americans bene-fit differently from the New Deal?

During the 1930s, immigration from Mexico declined. In addition, many immigrants returned to Mexico. Some left on their own; the federal government deported others. Some of those who were forced to leave were U.S. citizens whose rights were ignored. Because they feared deportation, many Mexican Americans stopped applying for aid.

Life improved somewhat for Native Americans. In 1934, Congress passed the Indian Reorganization Act, which restored some reservation lands to Indian ownership. It also created the Indian Arts and Crafts Board to promote native arts.

Unions Gain Strength

Background
John L. Lewis had been president of the United Mine Workers of America since 1920.

Some minorities joined a new labor organization. The country's largest labor organization was the American Federation of Labor (AFL). It was open only to skilled workers, such as plumbers and electricians. Labor leader John L. Lewis wanted industrywide unions that included both skilled and unskilled workers. He and other leaders founded the **Congress of Industrial Organizations (CIO),** which broke from the AFL in 1938. It was more open to women and minorities than the AFL.

In the 1930s, the labor movement used an effective bargaining tactic called the **sit-down strike.** Instead of walking off their jobs, striking workers remained idle inside the plant. As a result, factory owners could not hire strikebreakers to do the work.

The Wagner Act, passed in 1935, gave unions the ability to negotiate better working conditions. Union membership jumped from 2.7 million in 1933 to 7.0 million in 1937. The growing strength of labor unions was just one legacy of the New Deal. Section 4 discusses other legacies of the Great Depression and the New Deal.

In early 1939, a women's group refused to rent a hall for opera star Marian Anderson's performance because of her race. So Mrs. Roosevelt asked her to sing at the Lincoln Memorial.

Section 3 Assessment

1. Terms & Names

Explain the significance of:
- Dust Bowl
- Eleanor Roosevelt
- Congress of Industrial Organizations (CIO)
- sit-down strike

2. Using Graphics

Use a cluster diagram like the one below to record details about life during the Depression.

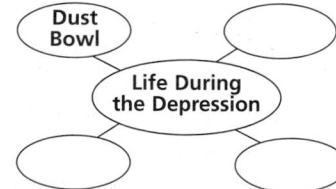

3. Main Ideas

a. How did storms in the Dust Bowl contribute to economic problems?

b. What effect did the Depression have on families?

c. How did Eleanor Roosevelt help her husband, the president?

4. Critical Thinking

Recognizing Effects What were some positive and negative results of the government's policies toward minorities during the Depression?

THINK ABOUT
- African Americans
- Mexican Americans
- Native Americans

ACTIVITY OPTIONS

SPEECH

ART

You have been asked to teach young children about life during the Depression. Write and perform a **monologue** or create a **comic strip** about it.

from
ROLL OF THUNDER, HEAR MY CRY

by Mildred D. Taylor

Even before the Depression, many African Americans struggled with poverty. When the Depression began, hard times made it more difficult for them to get ahead—or to keep what they had. Because the Logan family owns land in Mississippi, they are better off than their sharecropper neighbors. But they also have more to lose.

"Little Man, would you come on? You keep it up and you're gonna make us late."

My youngest brother paid no attention to me. Grasping more firmly his newspaper-wrapped notebook and his tin-can lunch of cornbread and oil sausages, he continued to concentrate on the dusty road. He lagged several feet behind my other brothers, Stacey and Christopher-John, and me, attempting to keep the rusty Mississippi dust from swelling with each step and drifting back upon his shiny black shoes and the cuffs of his corduroy pants by lifting each foot high before setting it gently down again. Always meticulously neat, six-year-old Little Man never allowed dirt or tears or stains to mar anything he owned. Today was no exception.

"You keep it up and make us late for school, Mama's gonna wear you out," I threatened, pulling with exasperation at the high collar of the Sunday dress Mama had made me wear for the first day of school—as if that event were something special. It seemed to me that showing up at school at all on a bright August-like October morning made for running the cool forest trails and wading barefoot in the forest pond was concession enough; Sunday clothing was asking too much. Christopher-John and Stacey were not too pleased about the clothing or school either. Only Little Man, just beginning his school career, found the prospects of both intriguing.

"Y'all go ahead and get dirty if y'all wanna," he replied without even looking up from his studied steps. "Me, I'm gonna stay clean."

"I betcha Mama's gonna 'clean' you, you keep it up," I grumbled.

"Ah, Cassie, leave him be," Stacey admonished, frowning and kicking testily at the road.

"I ain't said nothing but—"

Stacey cut me a wicked look and I grew silent. His disposition had been irritatingly sour lately. If I hadn't known the cause of it, I could have forgotten very easily that he was, at twelve, bigger than I, and that I had promised Mama to arrive at school looking clean and ladylike. "Shoot," I mumbled finally, unable to restrain myself from further comment, "it ain't my fault you gotta be in Mama's class this year."

Stacey's frown deepened and he jammed his fists into his pockets, but said nothing.

Christopher-John, walking between Stacey and me, glanced uneasily at both of us but did not interfere. A short, round boy of seven, he took little interest in troublesome things, preferring to remain on good terms with everyone. Yet he was always sensitive to others and now, shifting the handle of his lunch can from his right hand to his right wrist and his smudged notebook from his left hand to his left armpit, he stuffed his free hands into his pockets and attempted to make his face as moody as Stacey's and as cranky as mine. But after a few moments he seemed to forget that he was supposed to be grouchy and began whistling cheerfully. There was little that could make Christopher-John unhappy for very long, not even the thought of school.

I tugged again at my collar and dragged my feet in the dust, allowing it to sift back onto my socks and shoes like gritty red snow. I hated the dress. And the shoes. There was little I could do in a dress, and as for shoes, they imprisoned freedom-loving feet accustomed to the feel of the warm earth.

"Cassie, stop that," Stacey snapped as the dust billowed in swirling clouds around my feet. I looked up sharply, ready to protest. Christopher-John's whistling increased to a raucous, nervous shrill, and grudgingly I let the matter drop and trudged along in moody silence, my brothers growing as pensively quiet as I.

Before us the narrow, sun-splotched road wound like a lazy red serpent dividing the high forest bank of quiet, old trees on the left from the cotton field, forested by giant green-and-purple stalks, on the right. A barbed-wire fence ran the length of the deep field, stretching eastward for over a quarter of a mile until it met the sloping green pasture that signaled the end of our family's four hundred acres. An ancient oak tree on the slope, visible even now, was the official dividing mark between Logan land and the beginning of a dense forest. Beyond the protective fencing of the forest, vast farming fields, worked by a multitude of sharecropping families, covered two thirds of a ten-square-mile plantation. That was Harlan Granger land.

Once our land had been Granger land too, but the Grangers had sold it during Reconstruction to a Yankee for tax money. In 1887, when the land was up for sell again, Grandpa had bought two hundred acres of it, and in 1918, after the first two hundred acres had been paid off, he had bought another two hundred. It was good rich land, much of it still virgin forest, and there was no debt on half of it. But there was a **mortgage**[1] on the two hundred acres bought in 1918 and there were taxes on the full four hundred, and for the past three years there had not been enough money from the cotton to pay both and live on too.

That was why Papa had gone to work on the railroad.

---

1. **mortgage:** the transfer of a deed to property, usually in exchange for a loan.

In 1930 the price of cotton dropped. And so, in the spring of 1931, Papa set out looking for work, going as far north as Memphis and as far south as the Delta country. He had gone west too, into Louisiana. It was there he found work laying track for the railroad. He worked the remainder of the year away from us, not returning until the deep winter when the ground was cold and barren. The following spring after the planting was finished, he did the same. Now it was 1933, and Papa was again in Louisiana laying track.

I asked him once why he had to go away, why the land was so important. He took my hand and said in his quiet way: "Look out there, Cassie girl. All that belongs to you. You ain't never had to live on nobody's place but your own and long as I live and the family survives, you'll never have to. That's important. You may not understand that now, but one day you will. Then you'll see."

I looked at Papa strangely when he said that, for I knew that all the land did not belong to me. Some of it belonged to Stacey, Christopher-John, and Little Man, not to mention the part that belonged to Big Ma, Mama, and Uncle Hammer, Paper's older brother who lived in Chicago. But Papa never divided the land in his mind; it was simply Logan land. For it he would work the long, hot summer pounding steel; Mama would teach and run the farm; Big Ma, in her sixties, would work like a woman of twenty in the fields and keep the house; and the boys and I would wear threadbare clothing washed to dishwater color; but always, the taxes and the mortgage would be paid.

This Dorothea Lange photograph shows sharecroppers like the Logans' neighbors.

CONNECT TO HISTORY

1. **Analyzing Causes** Which of the economic problems shown in the graphs on page 730 has been making life hard for the Logan family?

 See Skillbuilder Handbook, page R11.

CONNECT TO TODAY

2. **Researching** What are current interest rates on mortgages?

For more about the Great Depression . . .

 **RESEARCH LINKS**
CLASSZONE.COM

The Effects of the New Deal

MAIN IDEA	WHY IT MATTERS NOW	TERMS & NAMES
The Depression and the New Deal had many long-term effects on U.S. government and society.	Politicians still debate how large a role government should play in American life.	Securities and Exchange Commission liberal conservative

ONE AMERICAN'S STORY

Until 1935, Ward James worked as a writer for a New York publisher. Then he lost his job. Eventually, he got a writing job with the WPA. Still, James continued to worry about what would happen next.

A VOICE FROM THE PAST

Everyone was emotionally affected. We developed a fear of the future which was very difficult to overcome. Even though I eventually went into some fairly good jobs, there was still this constant dread: everything would be cut out from under you and you wouldn't know what to do.

Ward James, quoted in *Hard Times*

The fear and despair described by Ward James was felt by many unemployed people during the Depression.

As this section explains, both the Depression and the New Deal had lasting effects on Americans and their government.

Taking Notes

Use your chart to take notes about the effects of the New Deal.

GREAT DEPRESSION

Hoover's Responses	FDR's Responses	Citizens' Responses
Effectiveness	Effectiveness	Effectiveness

Lasting Effects of the Depression

Americans like Ward James who lived through the Depression often saw themselves as the survivors of a terrible battle. For the rest of their lives, many feared losing their money and property again. One elderly government worker bought land whenever she could afford it so that if the Depression returned, she would "have something to live off."

Virginia Durr, who had worked for the federal government under FDR, said that the Depression affected people in two ways. "The great majority reacted by thinking money is the most important thing in the world. . . . And there was a small number of people who felt the whole system was lousy. You have to change it."

The New Deal did not end the Depression. Even with all the new programs, the government still wasn't spending enough money to jump-start a stalled economy. Then, in the 1940s, World War II changed the situation. To fight in that war, the government had to purchase guns,

tanks, ships, airplanes, and other military equipment. The defense industry hired many people, who then had more money to spend. The U.S. economy started growing again.

Although the New Deal didn't end the Depression, it forever changed the U.S. government. As Supreme Court justice John Clarke told FDR, "You have put a new face upon the social and political life of our country."

> **"We developed a fear of the future."**
> **Ward James**

A Larger Role for Government

*Reading*History

A. Recognizing Effects How did FDR increase the president's power?

President Roosevelt increased the president's power. Under FDR, the White House became the center of government. More than other early-20th-century presidents, Roosevelt proposed bills and programs for Congress to consider instead of waiting for Congress to act.

Other nations also saw the rise of strong leaders. But at the same time, those nations saw a loss of freedom. For example, during the Depression, Germany elected Adolf Hitler, who became a dictator. The United States did have some leaders who abused power—such as Huey Long—but they never became president. FDR's leadership and his concern for the poor helped Americans keep their faith in democracy.

As well as increasing the president's power, Roosevelt also expanded the federal government. Because of the New Deal, the federal government became directly responsible for people's well-being in a way it had not

---

CONNECTIONS TO MATH

Effects of the New Deal, *1929–1941*

Although Franklin Roosevelt's New Deal programs did not end the Depression, they did make some economic conditions better. Use these graphs to determine how the New Deal—begun in 1933—affected the unemployment rate, the number of bank closings, and the number of business failures.

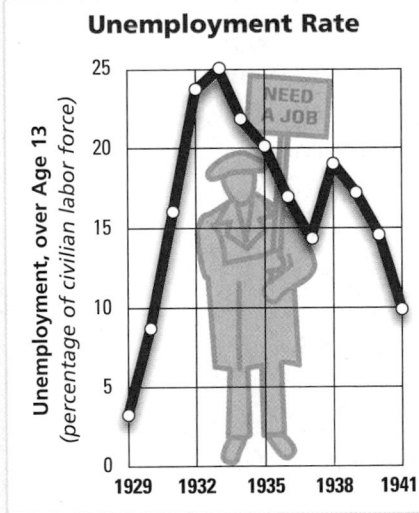

Unemployment Rate

Unemployment, over Age 13 (percentage of civilian labor force)

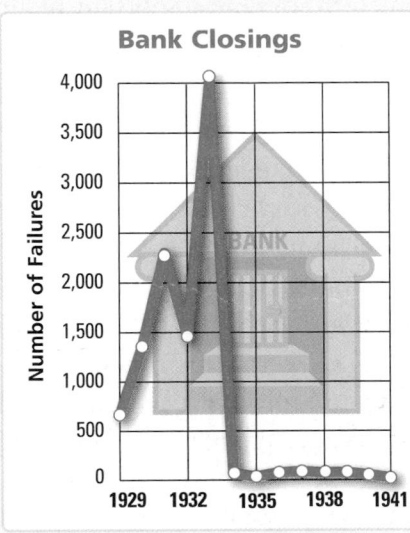

Bank Closings

Number of Failures

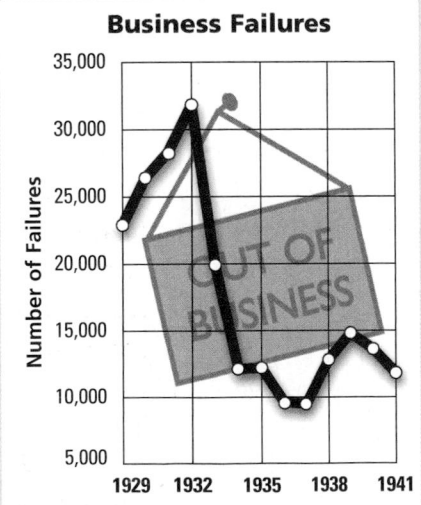

Business Failures

Number of Failures

Sources: *Historical Statistics of the United States*

SKILLBUILDER Interpreting Graphs

1. *Judging from these graphs, did the Depression's negative effects on business improve after FDR took office in 1933? Explain.*
2. *In which area was there the biggest change for the better?*

HISTORY through ART

The Works Progress Administration (WPA) created many jobs. One of the WPA's most enduring legacies is the art that it commissioned. Much WPA art was used to decorate public places, such as post offices and government buildings. This mural by William Gropper shows the building of a dam.

What attitude did Gropper want to convey about laborers?

been before. It now made relief payments, served school lunches, and ran a program providing pensions. People came to see the federal government, not their state or local governments, as the protector of their welfare.

The federal government went into debt to provide this aid. FDR used deficit spending both to fund the New Deal and to pay for the war. Since then, deficit spending has often been part of the federal budget.

New Deal Programs Today

Several of FDR's New Deal programs continue to help Americans today. Some of the more important programs that still exist offer the following benefits and protections.

1. **A National Pension System.** The Social Security system pays out old-age pensions (and has been expanded to include aid to other groups). It is funded through taxes on employers and employees.

2. **Oversight of Labor Practices.** Created by the Wagner Act, the National Labor Relations Board (NLRB) oversees labor unions. It also investigates disputes between management and labor.

3. **Agricultural Price Supports.** This program pays farmers to raise crops for domestic use rather than export. To receive payments, farmers must agree to limit the space they devote to certain crops.

4. **Protection for Savings.** After the bank holiday of 1933, the Federal Deposit Insurance Corporation (FDIC) was created. The FDIC insures bank deposits up to $100,000. It replaces the deposits of individuals if banks close.

5. **Regulation of the Stock Market.** A federal agency called the **Securities and Exchange Commission** watches the stock market. It makes sure companies follow fair practices for trading stocks.

Reading **History**
B. Analyzing Causes Why do you think FDR wanted to create an agency to oversee the stock market?

An Ongoing Political Debate

The issues that came out of the New Deal continue to shape American politics. For example, Democrats and Republicans still argue about whether federal or local government should be responsible for various programs. In addition, Democrats are more likely to be liberal and Republicans are more likely to be conservative in their political beliefs. A **liberal** in politics favors government action to bring about social and economic reform. A **conservative** favors fewer government controls and more individual freedom in economic matters.

Despite these lingering disagreements, some New Deal programs are still so popular that everyone supports them. For example, neither party wants to end Social Security, although both agree that it needs to be reformed. Payroll taxes are too low to pay all future benefits.

In 1999, President Clinton proposed using money from the federal budget to strengthen Social Security. The Republicans accepted his plan. They recognized that voters wanted Social Security protected, not turned into the subject of a political fight.

FDR probably would have approved. "The great public," Roosevelt said, "is interested more in government than in politics." Roosevelt felt that party labels mattered little as long as politicians "did the big job that their times demanded to be done."

In the 1940s, President Roosevelt would face another big job. He had to lead the country in fighting a world war. Chapter 27 discusses World War II and America's role in it.

*Reading***History**

C. Analyzing Points of View How would you summarize FDR's view of government's role?

Now *and* then

SOCIAL SECURITY

Social Security has changed since the 1930s. Since people are living longer and families are smaller, the percentage of the population receiving benefits has increased. In addition, benefits have increased. To keep the system strong has required higher payroll taxes. In 2004, President Bush proposed a furthur change that would allow people to divert part of their Social Security contributions into private retirement accounts.

Section 4 Assessment

1. Terms & Names

Explain the significance of:
- Securities and Exchange Commission
- liberal
- conservative

2. Using Graphics

Use a bulleted list like the one shown below to list the legacy of the Depression and New Deal.

Legacy of the Depression and New Deal
- _____
- _____
- _____
- _____

What part of the legacy affects politics today?

3. Main Ideas

a. What psychological impact did the Depression have on many Americans?

b. What finally pulled the United States out of its economic depression?

c. How do today's political differences date back to the Depression?

4. Critical Thinking

Drawing Conclusions Of the following New Deal programs, which one do you think affects your life the most? Explain.

THINK ABOUT
- Social Security
- Federal Deposit Insurance Corporation
- Securities and Exchange Commission

ACTIVITY OPTIONS

LANGUAGE ARTS
TECHNOLOGY

Ask your grandparents or other older relatives what they think the legacy of the Depression and New Deal is. Prepare a **written interview** or an **audio recording.**

The Great Depression and New Deal

CAUSES

- problems in agriculture and some industries
- unequal income distribution
- too much inventory
- too much debt
- stock market speculation

BROOKLYN DAILY EAGLE
And Complete Long Island News

WALL ST. IN PANIC AS STOCKS CRASH

DEPRESSION

- stock market crash
- bank and business failures
- high unemployment
- hunger and homelessness

NEW DEAL

- relief for the hungry and jobless
- recovery for agriculture and industry
- reforms to change the way the economy worked

SWEEPING THE DEPRESSION OUT

LONG-TERM EFFECTS

- fear of future
- more influence by federal government
- more presidential power
- long-term government programs
- debate between conservatives and liberals

TERMS & NAMES

Briefly explain the significance of each of the following.

1. Herbert Hoover
2. Crash of 1929
3. Great Depression
4. Franklin Delano Roosevelt
5. New Deal
6. deficit spending
7. Dust Bowl
8. Eleanor Roosevelt
9. liberal
10. conservative

REVIEW QUESTIONS

Hoover and the Crash (pages 729–733)

1. Why did stock prices fall so quickly during the stock market crash?
2. Who did President Hoover think should help the needy?
3. How did MacArthur's attack on the Bonus Army affect the 1932 election?

Roosevelt and the New Deal (pages 734–738)

4. What was the "brain trust"?
5. What were fireside chats, and how did they affect the country?
6. Why didn't Roosevelt propose many new programs during his second term?

Life During the Depression (pages 739–745)

7. How did writers and filmmakers respond to the hard times?
8. What new bargaining tactic did labor unions use, and how did it work?

The Effects of the New Deal (pages 746–749)

9. How did the New Deal change the role of the federal government in American life?
10. What New Deal program remains popular even though it is in financial trouble?

CRITICAL THINKING

1. USING YOUR NOTES: EVALUATING

Using your completed chart, answer the questions below.

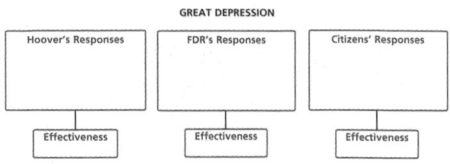

GREAT DEPRESSION

Hoover's Responses	FDR's Responses	Citizens' Responses
Effectiveness	Effectiveness	Effectiveness

a. What do you think was Hoover's most successful response to the Depression?
b. Judging from his responses to the Depression, do you think that FDR was one of our greatest presidents? Explain.

2. ANALYZING LEADERSHIP

During the Depression, many countries turned to strong leaders. How did the Depression-era leadership of Germany differ from that of the United States?

3. ANALYZING CAUSES

Review the economic problems that led to the Depression. What similar problems exist in the economy today?

4. THEME: ECONOMICS IN HISTORY

What reforms did FDR make to ensure that the United States would never again experience such a severe depression?

5. APPLYING CITIZENSHIP SKILLS

How were each of the following citizenship skills important during the Depression: voting, staying informed about issues, and community service?

Interact *with* History

Now that you have read the chapter, would you give the same answer to the question, "Who do you think should help the poor?" Explain why or why not.

Use the table and your knowledge of U.S. history to answer questions 1 and 2.

Additional Test Practice, pp. S1–S33.

Roosevelt's Presidential Elections		
ELECTION YEAR	TOTAL VOTES	VOTES FOR FDR
1932	39,749,382	22,825,016
1936	45,642,303	27,747,636
1940	49,840,443	27,263,448
1944	47,974,819	25,611,936

Source: *New York Times Almanac*

1. How many votes were cast for FDR in the election of 1940?

A. 22,825,016

B. 27,747, 636

C. 27,263, 448

D. 49,840,443

2. FDR's programs gained him popularity with voters. Based on these election results, during what years did he introduce most of his programs?

A. between 1932 and 1936

B. between 1936 and 1940

C. between 1936 and 1944

D. between 1940 and 1944

This quotation from Franklin D. Roosevelt describes one of his legislative efforts. Use the quotation and your knowledge of U.S. history to answer question 3.

PRIMARY SOURCE

We have tried to frame a law which will give some measure of protection to the average citizen and to his family against the loss of a job and against poverty-ridden old age.

Franklin D. Roosevelt, quoted in *Promises to Keep*

3. What is FDR referring to in this quote?

A. public works projects

B. the Wagner Act

C. Works Progress Administration

D. the Social Security Act

TEST PRACTICE
CLASSZONE.COM

ALTERNATIVE ASSESSMENT

1. **WRITING ABOUT HISTORY**

Imagine that you are a farmer living in Oklahoma, Kansas, Texas, Colorado, or New Mexico in the early 1930s. Write a **diary** entry that describes your struggle to make a living during the "Dust Bowl" years.

• Use library resources to research your entry.

• Use primary sources such as letters, journals, and diaries and use them as models for your writing.

2. COOPERATIVE LEARNING

Working in a group, have each group member take on the role of a depression-era leader and hold a debate on the following question: Should the government go into debt to help the poor? Research and present the beliefs of Herbert Hoover, FDR, Eleanor Roosevelt, Huey Long, Father Coughlin, or Francis Townshend.

INTEGRATED TECHNOLOGY

CREATING A MULTIMEDIA PRESENTATION

Choose an aspect of the Great Depression that you would like to learn more about. Using books, the Internet, and presentation software, research your topic and create a Multimedia Presentation.

• Locate oral histories and depression-era photographs and excerpts from literature to include in your presentation.

• Consider videotaping interviews with older relatives who have stories about the Depression years.

For more about the Great Depression . . .

INTERNET ACTIVITY
CLASSZONE.COM

A man shoes a horse in part of the mural shown above.

Paint a WPA Mural

Franklin Roosevelt once remarked that "the very soundness of our democratic institutions depends on the determination of our government to give employment to idle [people]." Indeed, one of Roosevelt's New Deal programs, the Works Progress Administration's (WPA) Federal Art Project (FAP), provided creative work for artists during the Great Depression. These artists created more than 2,500 murals and 100,000 paintings. Many of the works celebrate American workers. The paintings mainly appeared in schools, post offices, and other public buildings.

ACTIVITY Create your own WPA mural, as artists did during the Great Depression. Then write an exhibit note that tells viewers about your mural. Finally, give a speech dedicating your mural to your school.

TOOLBOX

Each group will need:

pencils	poster-sized/over-sized sheets of art paper
drawing paper	
newspapers to protect desks and floor	water-based paints
yardstick	paintbrushes

Warren Hunter painted this mural in 1939 on the wall of the post office in Alice, Texas.

STEP BY STEP

1 **Form artist groups.** Meet with three or four other students to discuss your new art project. Imagine that you have all signed a work contract with the WPA. Your job is to create a mural to show Americans at work during the Great Depression.

2 **Research the WPA and the FAP.** Use the Internet, encyclopedias, or books about the Great Depression to brainstorm ideas for your mural. Jot down the types of work people were doing, the structures they were building, and the machinery they were using. With your group, discuss these ideas and answer these questions to help plan your mural:

• Who should be in the mural?

• What should they look like?

• What should they be doing?

• What colors would best represent the subject of your mural?

3 **Sketch your mural.** Using a pencil, accurately sketch your mural on drawing paper. This drawing should be a much smaller version of the mural you will paint later.

4 **Draw a grid over the sketch.** A grid consists of lines drawn across and down a drawing to form squares. Like individual puzzle pieces, each square contains a part of the picture. Use a yardstick to make your grid lines straight.

5 **Transfer the design to larger paper.** Draw another grid on oversized paper that has the same number of squares as the scale drawing. This time, though, the grid should be much larger—as large as the oversized paper. Make sure the grid lines are faint. Now copy the original drawing one square at a time.

6 **Paint the mural.** Each group member can paint one grid area at a time. This process is like filling in the outlines of a gigantic coloring book. When your mural is completed, hang it on a wall along with the other groups' paintings.

WRITE AND SPEAK

Write an exhibit note about how the mural reflects the type of work people did during the Great Depression. Attach the explanation to the back of the mural. Then, in a classroom dedication ceremony, deliver a speech dedicating your mural to your school.

📖 HELP DESK

For related information, see page 748 in Chapter 26.

Researching Your Project
- *Life During the Great Depression* by Dennis Nishi
- *The New Deal* by Gail Stewart

For more about the Great Depression . . .

RESEARCH LINKS
CLASSZONE.COM

Did You Know?

Between 1935 and 1943, the WPA employed 8.5 million people and spent $11 billion. The average wage was $55 a month. The government poverty level at the time was $100 a month.

The agency built
- 651,087 miles of roads
- 125,110 public buildings
- 8,192 parks
- 853 airports

Among these projects were New York City's famed Lincoln Tunnel and the Fort Knox gold depository, located in Kentucky.

REFLECT & ASSESS
- Compare and contrast your image with those of the other groups.
- Why did you choose the particular image in your mural?
- How well does your mural represent the history, social issues, and culture of the time?

CHAPTER 27

The Rise of Dictators and World War II 1931–1945

Section 1 **Steps to War**

Section 2 **War in Africa and Europe**

Section 3 **War in the Pacific**

Section 4 **The Home Front**

Section 5 **The Legacy of the War**

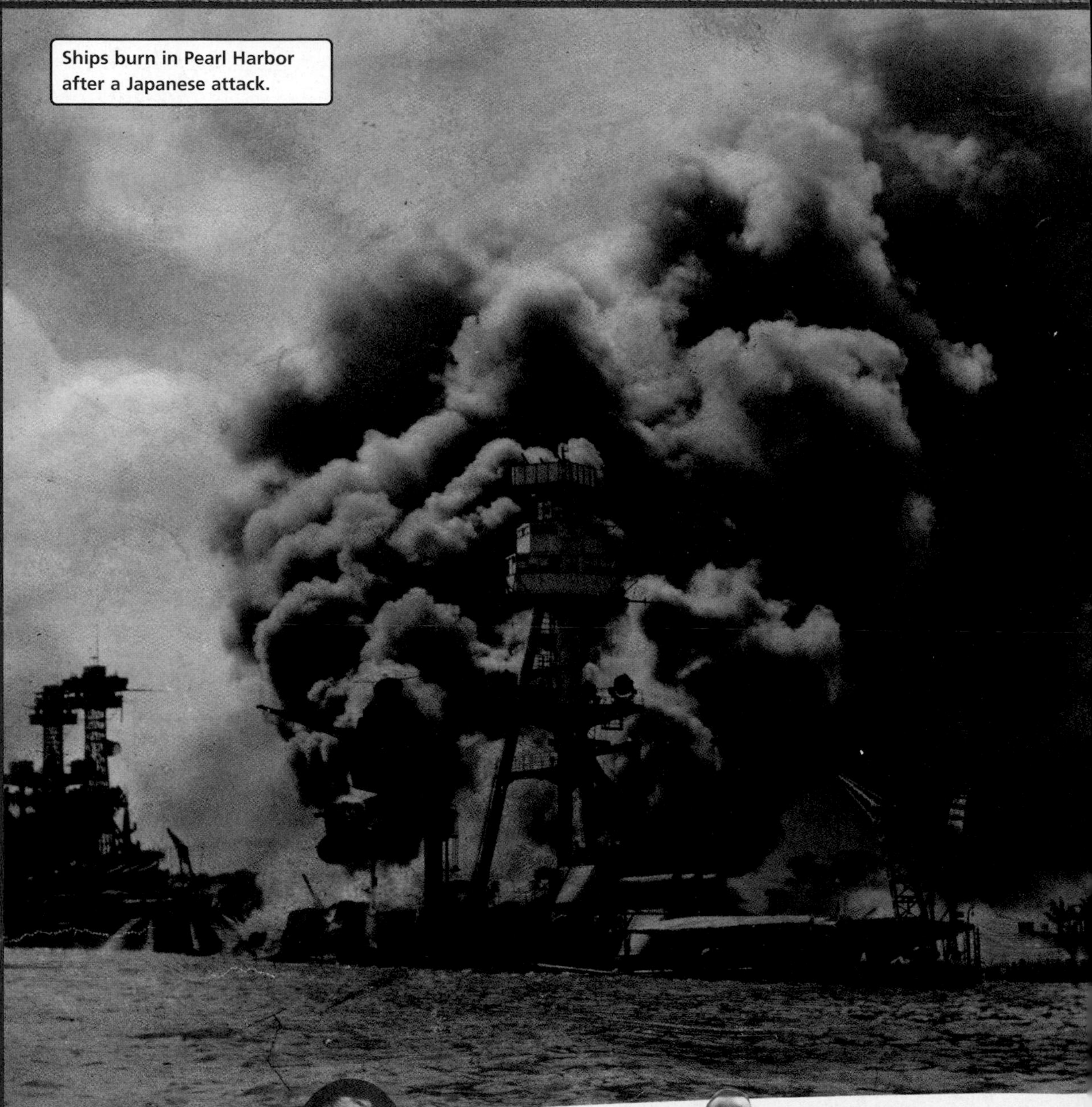

Ships burn in Pearl Harbor after a Japanese attack.

USA / World

1931

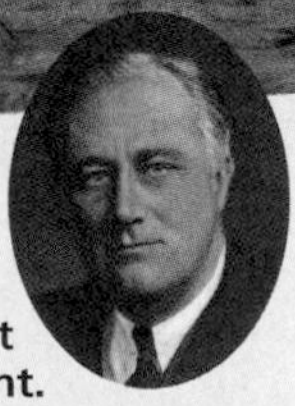

1932 Franklin Roosevelt is elected president.

1935 Congress passes first Neutrality Act.

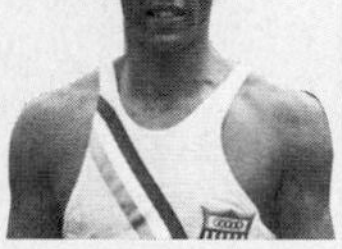

1936 Franklin Roosevelt is elected to a second term.

Jesse Owens wins four gold medals at the Olympics in Berlin, Germany.

1931 Japan invades Manchuria.

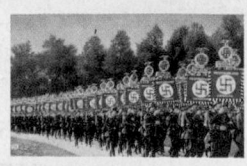

1933 The Nazi government announces its withdrawl from the League of Nations.

1935 Italy invades Ethiopia.

193 Japan invade China

President Roosevelt addresses the country after Pearl Harbor and asks Congress to declare war.

The year is 1941, and the American naval base at Pearl Harbor has been bombed. Now the United States has joined the Allies in World War II. The Allies face dangerous opponents in leaders such as Hitler, Mussolini, and Tojo. You must do your part to help defeat them.

Would you risk your life to fight against dictators?

What Do You Think?

- What threat do dictators pose to the world?
- What would you be willing to sacrifice to defeat dictators?

RESEARCH LINKS
CLASSZONE.COM
Visit the Chapter 27 links for more information about World War II.

1940
Roosevelt is elected to a third term.

1941
Japan bombs American naval base at Pearl Harbor, Hawaii.

1944
Roosevelt is elected to a fourth term.

1945
United States drops two atomic bombs on Japan.

1945

1939
Germany invades Poland.

1941
The Nazis force Jews to wear the Star of David in public to terrorize them.

1943
Soviets defeat Germans at Stalingrad.

1944
Allies invade Europe at Normandy.

1945
Germany and Japan surrender.

Reading Strategy: Sequencing Events

What Do You Know?

What do you think of when you hear the word *dictator* and the phrase *World War II*? Where did the fighting take place in this war?

Think About

- what you've heard about dictators from the news
- what you have learned about World War II from books, movies, or television
- your responses to the Interact with History about risking your life to fight against dictators (see page 755)

War in Europe and Africa

War in the Pacific

What Do You Want to Know?

What questions do you have about World War II? Record these questions in your notebook before you read the chapter.

Sequencing Events

Sequencing means putting events in the order in which they occurred. In learning about World War II, you will find it useful to list important events in order. For example, you might record important battles and their dates in a graphic organizer such as the one shown below. Copy this organizer in your notebook. Fill it in as you read the chapter.

S See Skillbuilder Handbook, page R4.

 Taking Notes

IMPORTANT BATTLES IN EUROPE, AFRICA, AND THE PACIFIC

September 1, 1939—Germany invades Poland → →

↓

→ →

↓

→ → April 1945—U.S. Marines invade Okinawa

Steps to War

MAIN IDEA	WHY IT MATTERS NOW	TERMS & NAMES
The rise of dictators in Europe and Asia led to World War II.	Aggressive rulers still threaten peace today.	fascism Axis Adolf Hitler appeasement Nazi Party Lend-Lease Act Joseph Stalin Pearl Harbor

ONE AMERICAN'S STORY

One of George Messersmith's duties as a U.S. diplomat in Austria in the 1930s was to watch events in Central Europe closely. What he saw happening in Germany worried him.

A VOICE FROM THE PAST

The National Socialist [Nazi] regime in Germany is based on a program of ruthless force, which program has for its aim, first, the enslavement of the German population to a National Socialist social and political program, and then to use the force of these 67 million people for the extension of German political and economic sovereignty over South-Eastern Europe—thus putting it into a position to dominate Europe completely.

George Messersmith, quoted in *The Making of the Second World War*

Adolf Hitler in a Harvest Festival crowd, 1937

As you will read in Section 3, Messersmith's predictions would prove true.

The Rise of Dictators

By the mid-1930s, dictators, or absolute rulers, had seized control in several countries—Italy, Germany, Japan, and the Soviet Union. Their rise to power was due to economic and political factors that dated back to the end of World War I.

The treaties that ended the war had left many nations feeling betrayed. Japan and Italy, for example, had helped to win the war. However, both were dissatisfied by the peace treaties. Italy gained less territory than it wanted. Japan felt ignored by the European powers. Of the losing countries, Germany was treated the most severely. The winners stripped Germany of more than 10 percent of its territory and all of its overseas colonies. The winners also forced Germany to disarm. And they made Germany pay for war damages and accept responsibility for the war.

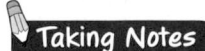

Taking Notes

Use your chart to take notes about conflicts leading to World War II.

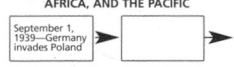

IMPORTANT BATTLES IN EUROPE, AFRICA, AND THE PACIFIC

September 1, 1939—Germany invades Poland ➤ ☐ ➤

The Rise of Dictators and World War II **757**

Many scientists left Germany or gave up their German citizenship after the Nazis took power. The most famous German scientist to do so was the physicist Albert Einstein (below).

Einstein, a German Jew, was visiting the United States when Hitler took control of Germany in 1933. Einstein announced he would not return home. "I shall live only in a country where civil liberty, tolerance, and equality of all citizens before the law prevail," he said. Einstein played a key role in convincing President Roosevelt to support research that would lead to the development of nuclear weapons.

Meanwhile, World War I had left the economies of Europe in ruins. Both sides emerged from the war heavily in debt. There was some economic growth in the 1920s. But the world economic situation collapsed with the Great Depression of the 1930s. Mass unemployment caused widespread unrest. Many Europeans turned to new leaders to solve these problems.

Mussolini, Hitler, and Stalin

One new leader was Benito Mussolini of Italy. Shortly after World War I, Mussolini began a political movement known as **fascism** (FASH•IZ•uhm). Fascists preached an extreme form of patriotism and nationalism that was often linked to racism. They oppressed people who did not share their views. In 1922, Mussolini became prime minister of Italy. In 1925, he established a dictatorship and took the title *Il Duce* (eel DOO•chay), or "the Leader."

In Germany, **Adolf Hitler** led the fascist National Socialist German Workers' Party, or **Nazi Party**. Throughout the early 1930s, the Nazis gained power by preaching German racial superiority. They also promised to avenge the nation's defeat in World War I. In 1933, the Nazis won control of the government. Hitler then overthrew the constitution. He called himself *der Führer* (duhr FYUR•uhr), or "the Leader."

In the Soviet Union, the Communists tightened their grip on power during the 1920s and 1930s. V.I. Lenin, who led the Communist takeover of Russia in 1917, died in 1924. His successor was **Joseph Stalin**. Under Stalin, the government tried to control every aspect of life in the nation. It crushed any form of opposition.

Dictators Seek to Expand Territory

While dictators were gaining power in Europe, the military was gaining increasing power in Japan. By 1931, the Japanese military pushed the island nation to grab more land and resources. That year, the Japanese attacked Manchuria, a province in northern China rich in natural resources. They conquered the region within months.

Both Italy and Germany also sought new territory. In 1935, Italy attacked Ethiopia, one of the few independent African nations. Italian troops roared in with machine guns, tanks, and airplanes. By the spring of 1936, *Il Duce* had his first conquest.

That same year, Hitler moved troops into the Rhineland, a region of Germany along the French border. Under the Treaty of Versailles, the Rhineland was to remain free of German forces. The French government was outraged by the treaty violation. However, it took no action. Nor did the League of Nations.

Reading **History**
A. Finding Main Ideas What factors led to the rise of dictators after World War I?

Vocabulary
avenge: to get revenge

Background
In theory, Communists and fascists have opposing ideas about government and society. Despite these differences, Stalin and Hitler were both brutal dictators.

Spanish artist Pablo Picasso expresses the horrors of war in his painting *Guernica* (GUAHR•nih•keh), shown above. Picasso created this work after German planes destroyed much of the Spanish town of Guernica in April 1937, during the Spanish Civil War. Through Picasso's painting, the town became a symbol of the destructiveness of air warfare.

What characteristics of war does the painting bring out?

In 1936, Hitler and Mussolini formed an alliance known as the Rome-Berlin Axis. After this treaty, Germany, Italy, and their allies became known as the **Axis.** That year, a civil war erupted in Spain. The conflict pitted Spain's fascist-style military against the country's elected government. Hitler and Mussolini supplied the fascist forces with troops, weapons, and aircraft. In April 1939, Spain's army declared victory over the government and established a dictatorship.

In 1938, Hitler invaded Austria, home to mostly German-speaking peoples. He insisted that the Austrians wanted to be part of Germany. Many residents of Austria and Germany welcomed the unification.

Background
Some Americans went to Spain to fight against the fascists. They were known as the Abraham Lincoln Battalion.

Appeasement at Munich

After taking over Austria, Hitler set his sights on the Sudetenland. This was a region of Czechoslovakia where many people of German descent lived. Czechoslovakia, though, did not want to give up the region.

France and Russia pledged their support to Czechoslovakia if Germany attacked. Suddenly, Europe teetered on the brink of another war. Britain's prime minister, Neville Chamberlain, stepped in. He met with Hitler in an attempt to calm the situation. But their talks made little progress.

On September 29, 1938, Hitler and Chamberlain met in Munich, Germany. By the next day, the two sides had made a breakthrough and signed an agreement. Germany gained control of the Sudetenland. In return, Hitler promised to stop seeking any more territory.

The Munich Agreement was an example of the British and French policy known as **appeasement.** Under this policy, they met Germany's demands in order to avoid war. Chamberlain returned home from Munich and triumphantly announced that he had achieved "peace in our time."

Others, however, disagreed with appeasement. Winston Churchill reportedly wrote of the agreement: "[Britain and France] had to choose between war and shame. They chose shame. They will get war, too."

*Reading***History**
B. Analyzing Points of View What were the different points of view about the policy of appeasement?

Germany Starts the War

Hitler soon broke the promise he had made in Munich. In March 1939, his troops moved in and conquered the rest of Czechoslovakia. The *Führer* then declared his intent to seize territory from Poland. Britain and France warned that an attack on Poland would mean war.

Britain and France assumed they had an ally in Stalin. After all, the Soviet Union and Germany were bitter enemies. However, in August 1939, Germany and the Soviet Union signed a nonaggression pact. In it, they agreed not to declare war on each other. On September 1, 1939, Germany invaded Poland. Great Britain and France declared war on Germany two days after the invasion of Poland. World War II had begun.

The Germans introduced a new method of warfare known as *blitzkrieg* ("lightning war"). It stressed speed and surprise in the use of tanks, troops, and planes. German forces drove deep into Poland. As Germany conquered western Poland, the Soviet Union invaded from the east. In less than a month, Poland fell to the invading armies.

In April 1940, Hitler conquered Denmark and overran Norway. A month later, Germany launched a *blitzkrieg* against Belgium, Luxembourg, and the Netherlands. British and French troops could do little to stop the advancing Germans.

Reading **History**

C. Making Inferences Why do you think Stalin signed a nonaggression pact with Hitler?

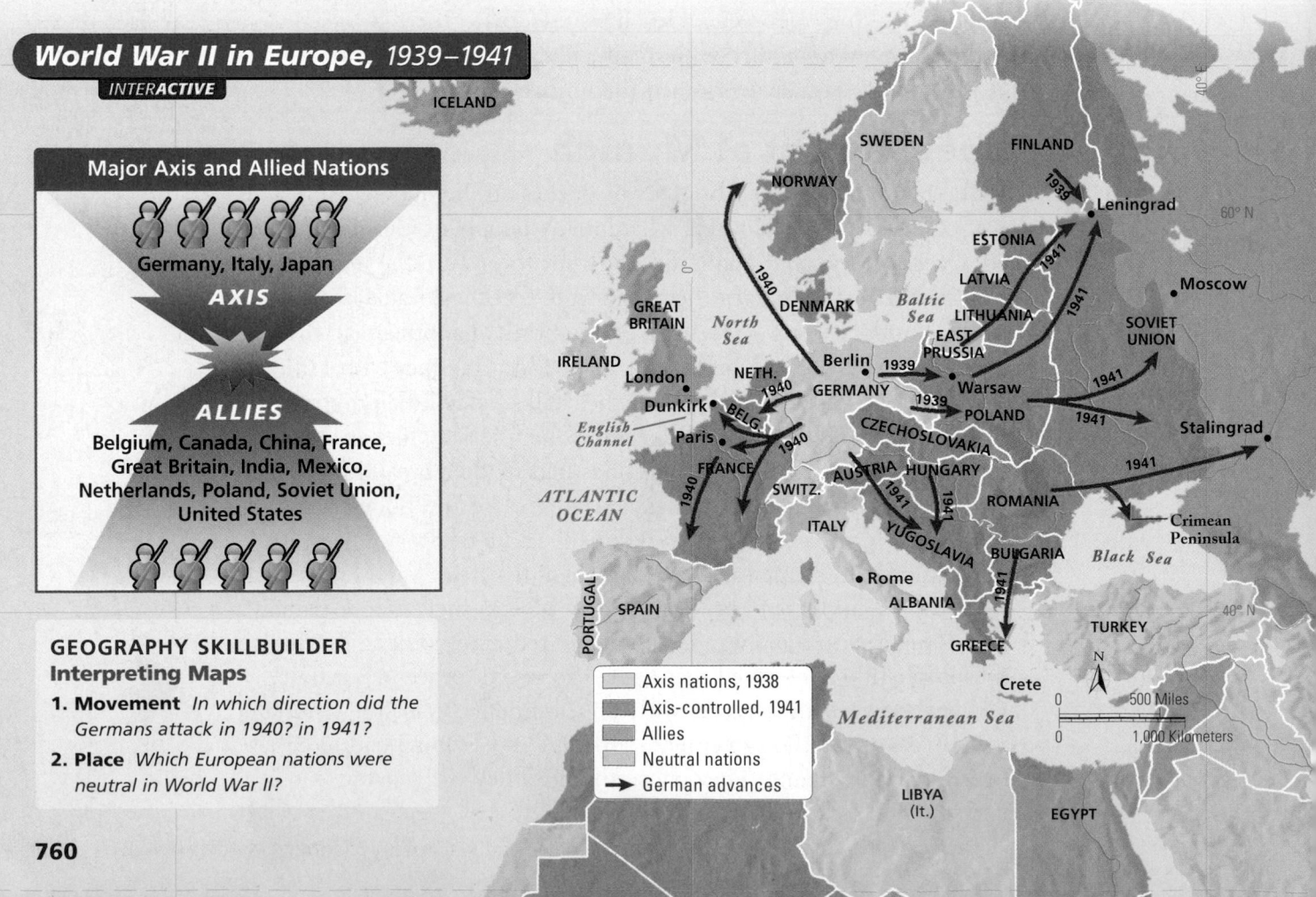

World War II in Europe, 1939–1941
INTER*ACTIVE*

Major Axis and Allied Nations

Germany, Italy, Japan
AXIS

ALLIES
Belgium, Canada, China, France, Great Britain, India, Mexico, Netherlands, Poland, Soviet Union, United States

GEOGRAPHY SKILLBUILDER
Interpreting Maps

1. **Movement** In which direction did the Germans attack in 1940? in 1941?

2. **Place** Which European nations were neutral in World War II?

Axis nations, 1938
Axis-controlled, 1941
Allies
Neutral nations
→ German advances

0   500 Miles
0   1,000 Kilometers

As each nation surrendered, British soldiers retreated to the French seaport of Dunkirk on the English Channel. Under heavy German bombardment, British vessels evacuated nearly 340,000 British, French, and Belgian troops.

In June 1940, the Germans launched a major offensive against France. In less than two weeks, they reached Paris. Days later, France surrendered. Hitler believed that Great Britain would seek peace after France fell.

Even though France had fallen, the British had no intention of quitting. Churchill, the new British prime minister, declared, "We shall defend every village, every town, and every city." Hitler soon made plans to invade Britain. To do so, however, he needed to destroy Britain's Royal Air Force, often called the RAF. In the summer of 1940, the German air force, or Luftwaffe (LUFT•VAHF•eh), and the RAF fought in the skies over Britain.

German planes also unleashed massive bombing attacks on London and other civilian targets. By September, however, the Battle of Britain had left Hitler frustrated. The RAF was holding off the Luftwaffe. And despite constant bombing, the British people did not surrender.

British civilians sleep in a subway station being used as an air raid shelter during the Battle of Britain in 1940.

Germany Attacks the Soviet Union

While Hitler's forces conquered Western Europe, Stalin's troops invaded Finland in November 1939. The Soviets then seized the countries of Estonia, Latvia, and Lithuania along the Baltic Sea. Despite their partnership, Hitler and Stalin distrusted each other. Hitler feared Soviet ambitions in Europe. He also wanted Soviet wheat and oil fields.

Reading **History**

D. Making Inferences Why did Hitler attack the Soviet Union just months after signing the non-aggression pact?

As a result, Hitler invaded the Soviet Union in June 1941. German forces moved easily through the giant country. They inflicted heavy casualties on Soviet troops. Then Hitler made a major mistake. He decided not to concentrate all his forces against Moscow. Instead, he reinforced his armies heading north toward Leningrad and south toward the Crimean Peninsula. The Germans tried to capture Leningrad from September 1941 to January 1944. About one million citizens died, many from starvation. But the city never fell to the Germans.

As German troops approached Moscow in December 1941, they ran into the harshest Russian winter in decades. Many German soldiers suffered frostbite. German tanks and weapons broke down in the cold. The Nazi advance had ground to a halt, and Soviet forces drove the Germans back.

The Rise of Dictators and World War II **761**

The United States Aids the Allies

While the Nazis advanced, President Roosevelt tried to help the Allies by supplying them with arms and other materials. "We must be the great arsenal of democracy," he declared. He proposed the **Lend-Lease Act** to address this issue. This measure allowed the United States to lend or lease raw materials, equipment, and weapons to the Allied nations. Congress approved the act in 1941. Under Lend-Lease, the United States sent about $50 billion worth of war goods to the Allies.

Japan Attacks Pearl Harbor

In 1940, Japan joined the alliance with Germany and Italy. In 1941, an even more warlike government came to power in Japan. Its leader was Hideki Tojo (HEE•deh•kee TOH•JOH), an army general. The Tojo government made plans to invade the Dutch East Indies—a source of oil—and Asian territories.

In the eyes of Japan's rulers, only one thing stood in their way—the United States Navy. On December 7, 1941, Japanese warplanes bombed the huge American naval base at **Pearl Harbor** in Hawaii. Before the day was over, about 2,400 Americans—both servicemen and civilians—died. Many of the American warplanes and ships were destroyed or damaged.

President Roosevelt asked Congress to declare war on Japan. He called December 7, 1941, "a date which will live in infamy." The nation quickly united behind him. On December 11, Germany and Italy declared war on the United States. In the next section, you will read about U.S. participation in the war in Europe.

America's HERITAGE

U.S.S. *ARIZONA* MEMORIAL

The U.S.S. *Arizona* suffered extensive damage during the attack on Pearl Harbor. The ship sank, and 1,177 of its crew died. The nation chose not to raise the ship. Instead, officials created a memorial (shown below) that sits above the sunken hull.

The names of all the crewmen who perished aboard the ship are carved on the memorial. To commemorate the 50th anniversary of the attack, President George Bush visited the site and dropped flowers in the water above the ship.

Reading **History**

E. Analyzing Causes What was the main source of conflict between Japan and the United States?

Section 1 Assessment

1. Terms & Names

Explain the significance of:
- fascism
- Adolf Hitler
- Nazi Party
- Joseph Stalin
- Axis
- appeasement
- Lend-Lease Act
- Pearl Harbor

2. Using Graphics

Use a diagram to review events that led to American participation in World War II.

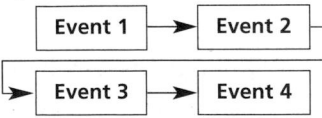

Which of these events do you think was the most important? Why?

3. Main Ideas

a. Who were the main Axis powers? Who were the main Allied powers?

b. Why was Hitler unable to conquer Great Britain?

c. What event prompted U.S. entry into the war?

4. Critical Thinking

Analyzing Causes Why do you think dictators such as Hitler and Mussolini were able to gain such power in the years before World War II?

THINK ABOUT
- the peace treaties of World War I
- the worldwide depression

ACTIVITY OPTIONS

LANGUAGE ARTS

GEOGRAPHY

Imagine that you are a citizen of one of the countries invaded by Germany. Write a **journal entry** describing the invasion or draw a **map** of the invasion route.

War in Africa and Europe

MAIN IDEA	WHY IT MATTERS NOW	TERMS & NAMES
The Allies defeated the Axis powers in Europe and Africa.	During World War II, the United States assumed a leading role in world affairs that continues today.	Dwight D. Eisenhower / Yalta Conference D-Day / Holocaust Battle of the Bulge

ONE AMERICAN'S STORY

Private First Class Richard Courtney could hardly believe it. Finally, his 26th Infantry Division was heading overseas to fight the Nazis in Europe. As his ship pulled out of New York Harbor, Courtney described his feelings.

A VOICE FROM THE PAST

I was eager to see all the ships in the harbor and to look up at the *Statue of Liberty,* which I had seen two years before on a trip to New York with my father. . . . For a moment I considered missing Mass and staying on deck with the others to see the statue. Then my better sense took over, and I headed down the stairs to Mass. As soon as Mass ended, I hurried up the stairs and rushed out on deck to see water, nothing but water. Well, Old Girl [Statue of Liberty], I will just have to wait for the return trip to see you again.

Richard Courtney, *Normandy to the Bulge*

U.S. troops wait to travel overseas for duty in World War II.

In this section, you will learn how American troops, along with those of its allies, defeated Germany and Italy and freed Europe.

Mobilizing for War

The Japanese attack on Pearl Harbor pulled the United States into World War II. Now, there was little time to waste. The nation quickly had to build up its armed forces. Millions of Americans volunteered for duty. Millions more were drafted, or selected for military service. Under the Selective Service Act, all men between the ages of 18 and 38 had to register for military service.

Those who served represented many of the nation's ethnic and racial groups. For example, more than 300,000 Mexican Americans fought in Europe as well as Asia. Nearly one million African Americans served in

Taking Notes

Use your chart to take notes about battles in Africa and Europe.

IMPORTANT BATTLES IN EUROPE, AFRICA, AND THE PACIFIC

September 1, 1939—Germany invades Poland ▶ ☐ ▶

the armed forces. Native Americans and Asian Americans also took part in the struggle. African-American and some Japanese-American soldiers fought in segregated, or separate, units. For example, the 99th Fighter Squadron, known as the Tuskegee Airmen, consisted of African-American pilots. They served in North Africa and Italy.

More than 300,000 women also served in the U.S. armed forces. Many worked for the Women's Army Corps (WAC) as mechanics, drivers, and clerks. Others joined the Army and Navy Nurse Corps. Thousands of women also joined the U.S. Navy and Coast Guard, where they performed important noncombat duties.

Battles in Africa and Italy

The Allies began making plans to invade Europe. The Americans wanted to land in France as soon as possible. Stalin agreed. But Churchill believed the Allies were not prepared for such an invasion. He convinced the Americans that the Allies should first drive the Germans out of North Africa. This action would help the Allies gain control of the Mediterranean and open the way to invade Europe through Italy.

Since the summer of 1940, Britain had been battling Axis forces for control of northern Africa—especially Egypt. Without Egypt, the British would lose access to the Suez Canal. The canal was the shortest sea route to Asia and the Middle Eastern oil fields.

Reading **History**
A. Making Decisions Why did the Allies decide to attack the Nazis in North Africa before invading France?

World War II in Europe and Africa, 1942–1945
INTERACTIVE

The Tuskegee Airmen were an all-black unit of pilots that fought in North Africa and Italy.

GEOGRAPHY SKILLBUILDER
Interpreting Maps

1. **Movement** *Which Allied power captured Berlin?*
2. **Place** *What was the last territory in North Africa held by the Axis?*

Axis nations, 1938
Axis-controlled, 1941
Allies
Neutral nations
→ Allied advances

0   500 Miles
0   1,000 Kilometers

British troops in northern Africa faced a tough opponent in Germany's General Erwin Rommel. Rommel's skills had earned him the nickname "The Desert Fox." He commanded Germany's Afrika Korps, including two powerful tank divisions. In June 1942, Rommel's tanks pushed the British lines to the Egyptian town of El Alamein. The Desert Fox was just 200 miles from the Suez Canal.

He would go no further, however. The British stopped the German advance at El Alamein and then forced them to retreat. A wave of Allied troops, led by American General **Dwight D. Eisenhower,** landed in northern Africa in November 1942. They advanced toward Rommel's army in Tunisia. In February 1943, the two sides clashed. The inexperienced Americans fell to Rommel's forces. However, the Allies regrouped and continued attacking. In May, the Axis powers in northern Africa surrendered. The Allies now could establish bases from which to attack southern Europe.

The invasion of Italy got under way with an attack on the island of Sicily in July 1943. Allied and German forces engaged in a month of bitter fighting. American nurse June Wandrey recalled trying to help the wounded.

AMERICA'S HISTORY MAKERS

DWIGHT D. EISENHOWER
1890–1969
If ever there was a general who cared about his troops, it was General Dwight Eisenhower. As Allied forces battled in Italy, Eisenhower learned that he and another general were scheduled to stay in two large villas. He was not happy. He exploded.

That's *not* my villa! And that's not General Spaatz' villa! None of those will belong to any general as long as I'm Boss around here. This is supposed to be a rest center—for combat men—not a playground for the Brass!

How might Eisenhower's concern for the common soldier have affected his standing with the troops?

A VOICE FROM THE PAST

Many wounded soldiers' faces still haunt my memory. I recall one eighteen year old who had just been brought in from the ambulance to the shock ward. I went to him immediately. He looked up at me trustingly, sighed and asked, "How am I doing, Nurse?" . . . I put my hands around his face, kissed his forehead and said, "You are doing just fine, soldier." He smiled sweetly and said, "I was just checking up." Then he died. Many of us shed tears in private.

June Wandrey, quoted in *We're in This War, Too*

The Allies forced the Germans out of Sicily and then swept into Italy. By this time, the Italians had turned on Mussolini. Officials had imprisoned their leader. However, he escaped. The new Italian government surrendered to the Allies in September 1943.

The Allied Advance and D-Day

Meanwhile, Germany's difficulties in the Soviet Union had grown worse. In September 1942, German forces attacked the Russian city of Stalingrad, an important industrial center. A brutal battle took place. The Soviet army fiercely defended the city. As winter approached, the German commander begged Hitler to let him retreat. The *Führer* refused.

*Reading*History
B. Summarizing
What prevented the Germans from conquering the Soviet Union?

Fighting continued through the winter. The trapped Germans had no food or supplies. Many thousands of Nazi soldiers froze or starved to death. In February 1943, the remaining German troops surrendered.

American troops storm Omaha Beach in Normandy in northern France on June 6, 1944.

Each side had suffered staggering losses. With Germany's defeat at Stalingrad, its hopes of conquering the Soviet Union appeared gone.

Hitler soon had other things to worry about in the West. In June 1944, the Allies' plan to invade France got under way. On the morning of June 6, more than 5,000 ships and landing craft carried more than 130,000 soldiers across the English Channel to a region in northern France called Normandy. The attackers included American, British, and Canadian forces. The day of this historic assault became known as **D-Day.** It was the largest seaborne invasion in history.

The attack surprised the German forces positioned along the beach. Nonetheless, they defended the region fiercely. As Allied troops hit the shore, they endured a hail of gun and mortar fire. More than 10,000 Allied soldiers were killed or wounded as they attempted to move inland. By the end of the day, however, the Allies had secured the beaches.

By the end of June 1944, 850,000 Allied troops had poured into France. They moved inland toward Paris, battling German troops along the way. On August 25, Allied forces liberated, or freed, the French capital. As they continued fighting to recapture the rest of France from the Germans, numerous American heroes emerged. One of them was Audie Murphy, the most decorated U.S. soldier of World War II. In January 1945, German troops attacked Murphy's unit in France. The 20-year-old Murphy climbed on a burning tank destroyer and used its machine gun to kill about 50 enemy troops. The U.S. government awarded him the Medal of Honor, the nation's highest military award.

As Allied forces advanced through Europe from the west, Soviet troops were beating back Hitler's army in the East. In December 1944, the German leader launched one final assault. In what became known as the **Battle of the Bulge,** German troops attacked Allied forces in the Ardennes region in Belgium and Luxembourg. The Nazi troops overwhelmed the Allies and pushed them back. U.S. forces regrouped and defeated the Germans. The Battle of the Bulge was costly. German casualties totalled 120,000. Meanwhile, nearly 80,000 Americans were killed, captured, or wounded.

Background
The Germans were surprised by the attack at Normandy because many, including Hitler, thought it would occur at Calais— 150 miles away— where the English Channel is narrowest.

Victory in Europe

By February 1945, the Germans were retreating everywhere. That month, Allied leaders met in the Soviet resort of Yalta. Attending the **Yalta Conference** were the "Big Three" as they were called—Roosevelt, Churchill, and Stalin. During the conference, these leaders made plans for the end of the war and the future of Europe.

*Reading*History
C. Finding Main Ideas What was the purpose and outcome of the Yalta Conference?

Stalin promised to declare war on Japan after Germany surrendered. The three leaders also agreed to establish a postwar international peace-keeping organization. In addition, they discussed the type of governments that would be set up in Eastern Europe after the war.

By the time of the Yalta Conference, President Roosevelt was in poor health. In April 1945, just months after being sworn in for a fourth term, the president died. Roosevelt's vice-president, Harry S. Truman, succeeded him. As the nation mourned Roosevelt's death, the new president continued the war effort.

In late April 1945, the Russians reached Berlin. Deep inside his air-raid bunker, Adolf Hitler sensed the end was near. On April 30, the man who had conquered much of Europe committed suicide.

On May 2, the Soviet Army captured Berlin. Five days later, German leaders officially signed an unconditional surrender at General Eisenhower's headquarters in France. The Allies declared the next day, May 8, as V-E Day, or Victory in Europe Day. The war in Europe was finally over.

Churchill, Roosevelt, and Stalin meet during the Yalta Conference in 1945.

The Horrors of the Holocaust

Vocabulary
concentration camp: place where Germans held persecuted groups during World War II

As the Allies fought toward Berlin, they made a shocking discovery. Scattered throughout German-occupied Europe were concentration camps where Jews and people of other persecuted groups had been murdered. The world would soon learn of the horrifying events that took place behind German lines during the war. In what has become known as the **Holocaust**, the Nazis killed about 6 million Jewish men, women, and children—more than two-thirds of the Jews in Europe. The Nazis also killed millions of people of other ethnic groups, including Gypsies, Russians, and Poles. An estimated 11 million people were killed in all.

The roots of the Holocaust lay in Adolf Hitler's intense racism. He preached that other groups, particularly the Jews, were inferior to Germans. As he rose to power in the 1930s, Hitler blamed the Jews for many of Germany's troubles. After becoming leader of Germany, Hitler enforced anti-Semitism, prejudice against Jews, in numerous ways. He denied Jews many of their rights and possessions.

Survivors of the concentration camp at Buchenwald in central Germany stand behind a fence in April 1945.

Soon after war broke out, Germany's anti-Semitic policies took an even darker turn. In a policy decision labeled "The Final Solution," Nazi leaders set out to murder every Jew under German rule. To accomplish this evil scheme, the Germans built huge facilities known as concentration camps. Officials crammed Jews into railroad boxcars and sent them to these camps. They forced able-bodied people to work. All others were slaughtered. The Germans carried out their killings with terrible efficiency. For example, they killed hundreds of people at a time in gas chambers disguised as showers. They then burned the bodies in large ovens or open pits. The largest concentration camp was Auschwitz in Poland. More than 1 million people are thought to have been murdered there.

On reaching the camps, the advancing Allies were outraged by what they saw. The Allies would battle this type of hate and bias by bringing German leaders to trial for what they had done. First, however, they had to defeat the Japanese. In the next section, you will read about the war in the Pacific.

Section 2 Assessment

1. Terms & Names

Explain the significance of:

- Dwight D. Eisenhower
- D-Day
- Battle of the Bulge
- Yalta Conference
- Holocaust

2. Using Graphics

Use a cluster diagram like the one shown below to identify the key battles and events that led to the Allies' victory in Europe.

Victory in Europe

3. Main Ideas

a. How did the United States build an army for the war?

b. Why did the Allies try to conquer North Africa before attacking southern Europe?

c. Why was the Battle of Stalingrad considered the turning point of the war in the east?

4. Critical Thinking

Supporting Opinions How might the war have been different if Hitler had decided to fight alongside the Soviet Union instead of against it?

THINK ABOUT

- the difficulties of fighting a two-front war
- the resources of Germany and the Soviet Union

ACTIVITY OPTIONS

GEOGRAPHY
TECHNOLOGY

Research the El Alamein battle. Draw a **map** of the battle or make a **database** showing the resources, such as the weapons and troops, of each side.

A Voice from the Holocaust

Setting the Stage Elie Wiesel (EHL•ee vee•ZEHL) was a Jewish boy from Romania. In 1944, when Wiesel was just 15, the Nazis sent the Jews of his town to Auschwitz in Poland. Wiesel's mother and one of his sisters died there. Wiesel and his father were sent to the Buchenwald concentration camp, where Wiesel's father died just a few months before the camp was liberated. In this excerpt from *Night,* Wiesel describes the terror he experienced on his way to Auschwitz. **See Primary Source Explorer**

The train stopped at Kaschau, a little town on the **Czechoslovak frontier.**[1] We realized then that we were not going to stay in Hungary. Our eyes were opened, but too late.

The door of the car slid open. A German officer, accompanied by a Hungarian lieutenant-interpreter, came up and introduced himself.

"From this moment, you come under the authority of the German army. Those of you who still have gold, silver, or watches in your possession must give them up now. Anyone who is later found to have kept anything will be shot on the spot. Secondly, anyone who feels ill may go to the hospital car. That's all."

The Hungarian lieutenant went among us with a basket and collected the last possessions from those who no longer wished to taste the bitterness of terror. "There are eighty of you in this wagon," added the German officer. "If anyone is missing, you'll all be shot, like dogs. . . ."

They disappeared. The doors were closed. We were caught in a trap, right up to our necks. The doors were nailed up; the way back was finally cut off. The world was a cattle wagon **hermetically**[2] sealed.

—*Elie Wiesel*

1. **Czechoslovak frontier:** the border of Czechoslovakia, a former European country occupied by Germany during World War II.

2. **hermetically:** thoroughly.

A CLOSER LOOK

A REIGN OF TERROR

The Germans attempt to rule their captives with a combination of brutality and terror.

1. What does the narrator mean when he describes "those who no longer wished to taste the bitterness of terror"?

A CLOSER LOOK

A CLOSED WORLD

The Jews as well as others were transported to the death camps in railway wagons.

2. What might be the effect of sealing people up in railway cars?

Interactive Primary Source Assessment

1. Main Ideas

a. What does the narrator mean when he says, "Our eyes were opened, but too late"?

b. What would be the effect on people of uprooting them from their homes?

c. This excerpt is from a book called *Night.* What might be the meaning of the title?

2. Critical Thinking

Analyzing Causes The horrors of the Holocaust followed from viewing and treating other people as less than human. What elements in this excerpt show the Germans treating the Jews this way?

THINK ABOUT

• the words and images used, both by the narrator and those he quotes

• the relations between those with power and those without

War in the Pacific

MAIN IDEA	WHY IT MATTERS NOW	TERMS & NAMES
After early losses, the Allies defeated the Japanese in the Pacific.	Since the war, the United States has continued to play a major role in Asia.	Bataan Death March Battle of Midway island hopping Manhattan Project Hiroshima

ONE AMERICAN'S STORY

In April 1942, more than 70,000 Filipino and American troops surrendered to the Japanese on the Bataan Peninsula in the Philippines. From there, the Japanese marched the soldiers about 60 miles to a prison camp. On the way, about 10,000 prisoners died from shootings, beatings, or starvation. Sidney Stewart was a U.S. soldier in the **Bataan Death March**.

Thousands of American prisoners endure the Bataan Death March.

A VOICE FROM THE PAST

The sun beat down on my throbbing head. I thought only of bringing my feet up, putting them down, bringing them up. . . .

A great many of the prisoners reached the end of their endurance. The drop-outs . . . fell by the hundreds in the road. . . .

There was a crack of a pistol. . . . There was another shot, and more shots, and I knew that, straggling along behind us, was a clean-up squad of Japanese, killing their helpless victims. . . . I gritted my teeth. "Oh, God, I've got to keep going. I can't stop. I can't die like that."

Sidney Stewart, *Give Us This Day*

As you will read in this section, the fighting was brutal before the Allies emerged victorious.

Taking Notes

Use your chart to take notes about battles in the Pacific.

IMPORTANT BATTLES IN EUROPE, AFRICA, AND THE PACIFIC

September 1, 1939—Germany invades Poland →☐→

Japan Expands Its Empire

At the same time as the attack on Pearl Harbor, Japanese forces launched attacks throughout the Pacific. By Christmas, Japan controlled Hong Kong, Thailand, and the U.S. islands of Guam and Wake.

The Japanese also pushed further into Southeast Asia, attacking Malaya and Burma. Great Britain, which ruled these lands and Hong Kong, fought back. But British forces proved to be no match for the Japanese invaders. Japan conquered the region within a few months.

But it took Japan longer to conquer the Philippines. They invaded the islands in December 1941 and pushed the Allied forces from the capital city of Manila onto the Bataan Peninsula. American and Filipino troops, led by U.S. General Douglas MacArthur, then fought the Japanese to a standstill for several months.

As fighting raged in the Philippines, the Allies feared that the Japanese might invade Australia. President Roosevelt ordered MacArthur to withdraw to Australia in March 1942. But MacArthur promised, on reaching Australia, "I shall return." Shortly after MacArthur left, the Japanese mounted an offensive. The U.S. troops on Bataan surrendered and endured the brutal Bataan Death March. The situation looked bleak for the Allies. But the momentum would soon turn.

"I shall return."
Gen. Douglas MacArthur

The Allies Turn the Tide at Midway

In the spring of 1942, the Allies began to turn the tide against the Japanese. The push began in April, with a daring air raid on Japanese cities, including Tokyo. Lieutenant Colonel James Doolittle led 16 bombers in the attack. Doolittle's raid caused little damage. But it shocked Japan's leaders and boosted the Allies' morale.

Reading **History**

A. Evaluating What was the significance of the Battle of the Coral Sea?

In May, the U.S. Navy clashed with Japanese forces in the Coral Sea off Australia. For the first time in naval history, enemy ships fought a battle without seeing each other. Instead, war planes launched from aircraft carriers fought the battle. Neither side won a clear victory in the Battle of the Coral Sea. However, the Americans had successfully blocked Japan's push toward Australia.

The opposing navies clashed again in June off the island of Midway in the central Pacific. The U.S. Navy destroyed four Japanese carriers and at least 250 planes. America lost one carrier and about 150 planes. The **Battle of Midway**, in June 1942, was a turning point in the war.

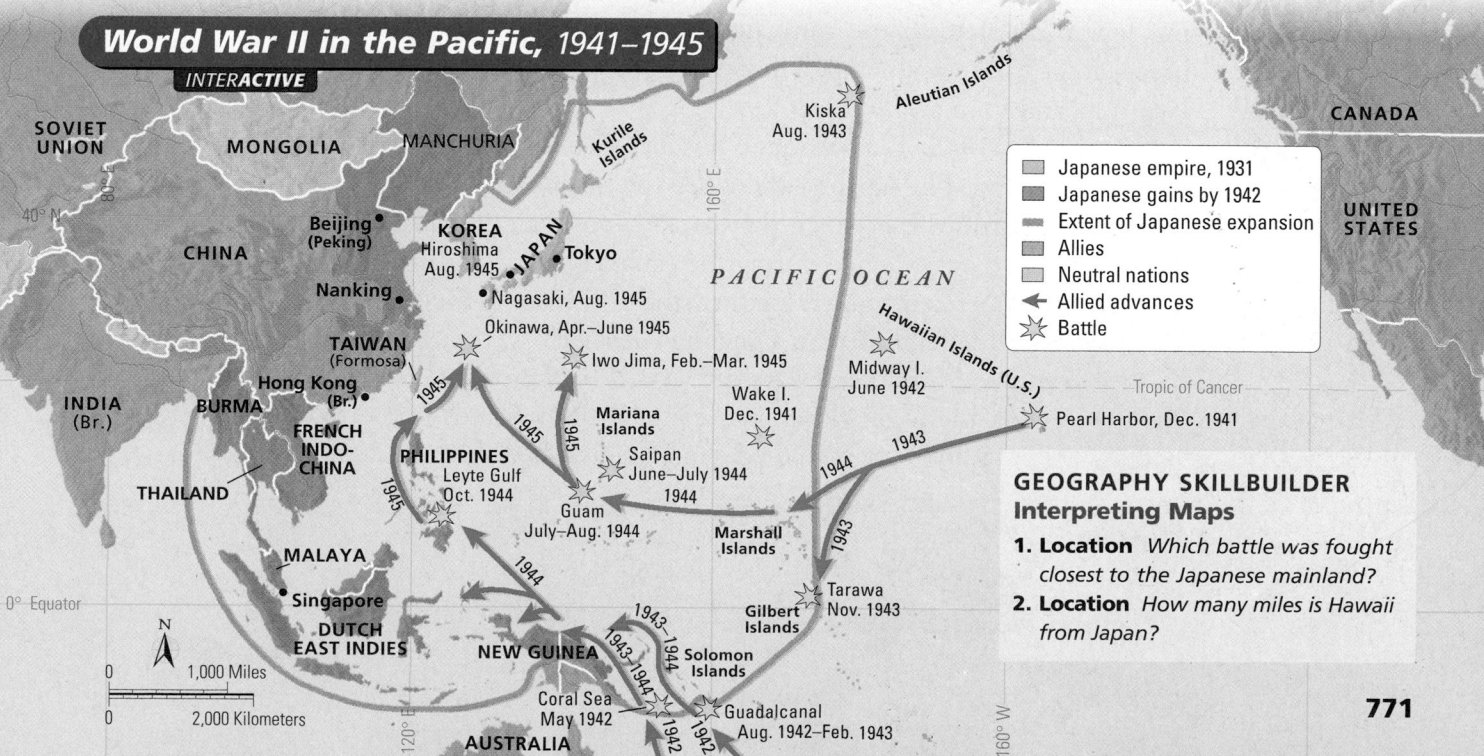

World War II in the Pacific, *1941–1945*
INTER*ACTIVE*

Japanese empire, 1931
Japanese gains by 1942
Extent of Japanese expansion
Allies
Neutral nations
Allied advances
Battle

Kiska Aug. 1943
Aleutian Islands
Kurile Islands
SOVIET UNION
MONGOLIA
MANCHURIA
CANADA
UNITED STATES
KOREA
Hiroshima Aug. 1945
JAPAN Tokyo
CHINA
Beijing (Peking)
Nanking
PACIFIC OCEAN
Nagasaki, Aug. 1945
Okinawa, Apr.–June 1945
TAIWAN (Formosa)
Iwo Jima, Feb.–Mar. 1945
Hong Kong (Br.)
Hawaiian Islands (U.S.)
Midway I. June 1942
Tropic of Cancer
INDIA (Br.)
BURMA
FRENCH INDO-CHINA
PHILIPPINES Leyte Gulf Oct. 1944
Wake I. Dec. 1941
Mariana Islands
Saipan June–July 1944
Pearl Harbor, Dec. 1941
THAILAND
Guam July–Aug. 1944
Marshall Islands
MALAYA
Singapore
Tarawa Nov. 1943
Gilbert Islands
DUTCH EAST INDIES
NEW GUINEA
Solomon Islands
Guadalcanal Aug. 1942–Feb. 1943
Coral Sea May 1942
AUSTRALIA
0° Equator

N
0   1,000 Miles
0   2,000 Kilometers

GEOGRAPHY SKILLBUILDER
Interpreting Maps

1. **Location** *Which battle was fought closest to the Japanese mainland?*
2. **Location** *How many miles is Hawaii from Japan?*

The Allies Advance

After the Battle of Midway, the Allies went on the attack to liberate the lands Japan had conquered. Rather than attempt to retake every Japanese-held island, the Allies decided to invade islands that were not heavily defended by the Japanese. The Allies could then use the captured islands to stage further attacks. This strategy was known as **island hopping**.

The two sides fought an important battle on the island of Guadalcanal. U.S. Marines marched ashore in August 1942. Six months of bitter fighting followed. In February 1943, the Allies finally won. They had gained their first major land victory against the Japanese.

Playing a role in this victory—and many others throughout the Pacific—was a group of Navajo Indians. To keep Japanese intelligence from breaking its codes, the U.S. military had begun using the Navajo language to transmit important messages. The marines recruited about 400 Navajos to serve as Code Talkers. They accompanied troops into battle and helped them communicate safely.

In October 1944, Allied forces invaded the Philippines. The effort included a massive naval battle off the Philippine island Leyte (LAY•tee). About 280 ships participated. The Allies won the three-day battle. Japan's navy was so badly damaged that it was no longer a threat. Allied forces came ashore. They liberated Manila in March 1945. General MacArthur, three years after leaving the Philippines, had returned.

Although they lost the fight in the Philippines, the Japanese increased their use of a new weapon—the *kamikaze* (KAH•mih• KAH•zee), or suicide pilot. *Kamikazes* filled their planes with explosives and crashed them into Allied warships. Japanese pilots volunteered for these suicide missions. But they couldn't stop Allied advances.

Reading **History**

B. Finding Main Ideas What was the Allies' strategy in the Pacific?

U.S. Marines raise a flag atop Mount Suribachi on Iwo Jima.

Iwo Jima and Okinawa

By early 1945, with Japan's defenses weakened, the Allies began bombing Japan. To step up the campaign, however, they had to establish bases closer to the mainland. They chose the Japanese-held islands of Iwo Jima and Okinawa.

In February 1945, U.S. marines invaded Iwo Jima. In April, they invaded Okinawa. The Japanese defended the islands fiercely. The Allies had to fight hard for every inch they took. More than 23,000 U.S. soldiers were killed or wounded during the campaign for Iwo Jima. In late February, American soldiers planted the U.S. flag at the top of the island's Mount Suribachi, signaling their victory, though fighting continued for several days afterward. In the several months it took the U.S. Marines to conquer both islands, more than 18,000 U.S. men died. Japanese deaths exceeded 120,000.

Reading **History**

C. Summarizing What happened during the battles for Iwo Jima and Okinawa?

Atomic Weapons End the War

In the summer of 1945, Japan continued to fight. The Allies planned to invade Japan in November 1945. American military leaders feared that an invasion of mainland Japan might cost 200,000 American casualties. Therefore, American officials considered the use of an atomic bomb.

Shortly after entering the war, the United States set up the **Manhattan Project** in 1942. This was a top-secret program to build an atomic bomb. Led by American scientist J. Robert Oppenheimer, the project team worked for three years to construct the weapon.

For an activity about the decision to drop the atomic bomb . . .

NET SIMULATION
CLASSZONE.COM

Background
By the end of 1945, another 70,000 people had died due to injuries and radiation caused by the atomic bomb dropped on Hiroshima.

The Japanese city of Hiroshima was leveled by the atomic bomb.

Soon after officials successfully tested the bomb, Truman told Japan that if it did not surrender, it faced destruction. The Japanese refused to give in. On August 6, 1945, the B-29 bomber *Enola Gay* dropped an atomic bomb on the city of **Hiroshima.** The explosion killed more than 70,000 people and turned five square miles into a wasteland. Still, the Japanese refused to surrender. On August 9, the United States dropped a second atomic bomb on Nagasaki, killing another 40,000. On August 14, Japan surrendered.

On September 2, 1945, Japanese and Allied leaders met aboard the U.S. battleship *Missouri* in Tokyo Bay. There, Japanese officials signed an official letter of surrender.

The war changed forever the lives of the soldiers who fought in it. In the next section, you will learn about how the war affected Americans back home.

Section 3 Assessment

1. Terms & Names

Explain the significance of:
- Bataan Death March
- Battle of Midway
- island hopping
- Manhattan Project
- Hiroshima

2. Using Graphics

Use a diagram like the one shown to list events that led to the defeat of Japan.

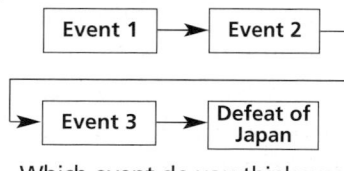

Which event do you think was most important, and why?

3. Main Ideas

a. Why was the Battle of Midway considered such an important victory for the Allies?

b. Why did the Allies want to conquer the islands of Iwo Jima and Okinawa?

c. What event finally prompted Japan to surrender?

4. Critical Thinking

Forming Opinions What might be the arguments for and against using the atomic bomb on Japan?

THINK ABOUT
- the consequences of invading Japan
- the bomb's destructive power

ACTIVITY OPTIONS

LANGUAGE ARTS
SCIENCE

Research the Manhattan Project. Write a **biography** of one of the scientists on the project or draw a **diagram** explaining how the atomic bomb worked.

The Home Front

MAIN IDEA	WHY IT MATTERS NOW	TERMS & NAMES
Americans at home made great contributions to the Allied victory.	World War II caused lasting changes in the lives of civilians.	War Production Board A. Philip Randolph *bracero* program rationing Rosie the Riveter Japanese-American internment

ONE AMERICAN'S STORY

During World War II, Margaret took a job as an "incoming inspector" at an aircraft plant. She often described her work in her letters to a friend serving with the Pacific fleet.

A VOICE FROM THE PAST

Gosh, we have been working hard at work lately. Just rushed to death and never getting through. Our production schedule has been doubled and still we work harder and put out more all the time. . . .

You had better be careful how you talk to me 'cause I have developed a big muscle in my right arm and a good strong one in my left arm, so take it easy, kid.

Margaret Hooper, quoted in *Since You Went Away*

Women factory workers rivet the interior of an airplane during World War II.

Americans on the home front worked together to help achieve an Allied victory, as you will read in this section.

Taking Notes

Use your chart to take notes about important events on the home front.

IMPORTANT BATTLES IN EUROPE, AFRICA, AND THE PACIFIC

September 1, 1939—Germany invades Poland

Wartime Production

The effort to defeat the Axis powers took more than just soldiers. American forces needed planes, tanks, weapons, parachutes, and other supplies. Under the guidance of the **War Production Board** (WPB), factories churned out materials around the clock. By 1945, the country had built about 300,000 aircraft and 75,000 ships. The United States was producing 60 percent of all Allied ammunition.

With so many factories in need of workers, jobs became easy to find. In effect, the war ended the Great Depression. Shortly after the war began, the nation's unemployment rate fell. The country's yearly gross national product (GNP) rose to new heights during the war. The GNP is the total value of all the goods and services produced by a nation

during a year. Between 1939 and 1945, the U.S. GNP soared from $90.5 billion to nearly $212 billion.

Because the armed forces needed so many materials, some of the items Americans took for granted became scarce. For example, American auto makers did not produce any cars between 1942 and 1945. Instead, they built tanks, jeeps, and airplanes. Items such as gasoline, tires, shoes, meat, and sugar were also in short supply. To divide these scarce goods among its citizens, the government established a system of **rationing**. Under this system, families received a fixed amount of a certain item.

The war was expensive. To help pay the cost, the government raised income taxes and sold war bonds. These bonds were loans that the government promised to repay with interest. Movie stars urged people to buy war bonds. Americans bought billions of dollars worth of bonds.

*Reading*History
A. Recognizing Effects How did World War II affect the U.S. economy?

Opportunities for Women and Minorities

With so many men fighting overseas, the demand for women workers rose sharply. In 1940, about 14 million women worked—about 25 percent of the nation's labor force. By 1945, that number had climbed to more than 19 million—roughly 30 percent of the work force. Women worked in munitions factories, shipyards, and offices.

Much of the nation welcomed the growing numbers of women into the workplace. The country promoted "**Rosie the Riveter**"—an image of a strong woman hard at work at an arms factory—as its cherished symbol for its new group of wage earners.

The war also created new job opportunities for minorities. More than 1 million African Americans worked in the defense industry during the war years. Many of these jobs were along the West Coast and in the North. As a result, more than 1 million African Americans migrated from the South during the war. Many traveled to California and such Northern cities as Detroit and Chicago. The inflow of African Americans often inflamed racial tensions. In 1943, a terrible race riot broke out in Detroit. Federal troops had to restore order after 34 people were killed.

On paper, at least, African Americans enjoyed equal rights in some workplaces. **A. Philip Randolph,** an African-American labor leader, had helped achieve these rights in 1941. Randolph had threatened to lead an African-American protest march for better jobs through Washington, D.C. President Roosevelt sought to avoid such a march. As a result, he issued Executive Order 8802. It outlawed job discrimination in defense industries working for the federal government.

Other minorities lent their hand to the home-front effort. Some 46,000 Native Americans left their reservations to work in the nation's

Background
A. Philip Randolph was the leader of the Brotherhood of Sleeping Car Porters, a powerful African-American labor union.

A. Philip Randolph and Eleanor Roosevelt chat at a labor rally in 1946.

war industries. Tens of thousands of Hispanics—people with ancestors from Spanish-speaking lands—also joined the ranks of the country's war-related laborers. Included in this group were thousands of Mexicans who migrated to the United States at the government's request. During the war years, the nation faced a serious shortage of farm workers. The government responded by hiring Mexicans to perform the much-needed labor. This policy was known as the ***bracero* program**. By mid-1945, more than 120,000 *braceros* worked on farms throughout the country.

Meanwhile, Mexican Americans struggled against prejudice and sometimes violence. In Los Angeles, for example, U.S. sailors often fought with "zoot suiters." These were young Mexican-American men who wore zoot suits—an outfit consisting of a broad-brimmed hat, a knee-length jacket, and baggy-legged pants. In what became known as the zoot-suit riots, groups of American servicemen attacked Mexican Americans. Beginning the night of June 3, 1943, the violence lasted 10 days before it was brought under control by police.

*Reading*History
B. Comparing and Contrasting What did the African-American and Hispanic-American experiences during World War II have in common?

The Internment of Japanese Americans

In the aftermath of Pearl Harbor, a growing number of Americans began to direct their anger toward people of Japanese ancestry. Many Americans saw Asian immigrants as a threat to their jobs. Many also believed that Asians could never fit into American society. As a result,

CITIZENSHIP TODAY

Writing to Government Officials

In the late 1970s, Japanese Americans asked the government to redress, or make up for, the injustice of the World War II internment. A letter-writing campaign by Japanese Americans helped secure passage of the Civil Liberties Act of 1988. This act included a formal apology and authorized payments of $20,000 each to Japanese Americans who were interned. The act also established a public-education program to prevent such discrimination in the future.

President Ronald Reagan signs the Civil Liberties Act of 1988.

How Do You Write to Government Officials?

1. Think about public issues that are important to you.

2. Choose one issue about which you would like the government to adopt a certain policy or take a certain action.

3. Gather information about the issue.

4. Refine your position on the issue in terms of a specific policy or action that you would like the government to follow.

5. Write a letter to your congressional representative or senator in which you urge him or her to take a particular stand on the issue.

 See Citizenship Handbook, page 284.

For more about contacting elected officials . . .

 RESEARCH LINKS
CLASSZONE.COM

Congress banned practically all immigrants from Asia in 1942.

In the days and weeks after Pearl Harbor, several newspapers declared Japanese Americans to be a security threat. President Roosevelt eventually responded to the growing anti-Japanese hysteria. In February 1942, he signed an order that allowed for the removal of Japanese and Japanese Americans from the Pacific Coast. This action came to be known as the **Japanese-American internment.** More than 110,000 men, women, and children were rounded up. They had to sell their homes and possessions and leave their jobs.

Soldiers stand by as Japanese Americans in San Francisco board a bus to take them to an internment camp.

These citizens were placed in internment camps, areas where they were kept under guard. In these camps, families lived in single rooms with little privacy. About two-thirds of the people interned were *Nisei* (NEE•say), Japanese Americans born in the United States.

The nation's fear of disloyalty from Japanese Americans was unfounded. Many of the camp internees raised the American flag each morning. In addition, thousands of young men in the camps volunteered to fight for the United States. The all-*Nisei* units, the 442nd Infantry and the 100th Infantry, fought in Europe. They were among the most highly decorated units in the war. One member, Daniel Inouye, showed extreme courage. After being severely wounded, he continued to lead his platoon in an attack in Italy. He lost his right arm, but earned the Distinguished Service Cross. In the next section, you will learn about other effects that World War II had on both the United States and the world.

Background
Daniel Inouye later became a U.S. senator from the state of Hawaii.

Section 4 Assessment

1. Terms & Names

Explain the significance of:
- War Production Board
- rationing
- Rosie the Riveter
- A. Philip Randolph
- *bracero* program
- Japanese-American internment

2. Using Graphics

Use a cluster diagram like the one shown to review the ways in which Americans at home contributed to the war effort.

Effort on Home Front

3. Main Ideas

a. How did the war lift the nation out of the Great Depression?

b. How did the war spur an African-American migration at home?

c. What action did the U.S. government take against many Japanese Americans during the war?

4. Critical Thinking

Comparing and Contrasting How were the war years a time of both opportunity and struggle for American women and minorities?

THINK ABOUT
- Rosie the Riveter
- African-American migrants
- zoot-suit riots

ACTIVITY OPTIONS

LANGUAGE ARTS
ART

Research the wartime life of one of the groups mentioned in this section. Write a **report** or design a **mural** about its members' experiences during the war.

Build Morale on the Home Front

You are an American helping to fight the war from the home front. You have friends and family stationed in Europe and the Pacific. You worry about them every day. To help them and the rest of your family and friends through the war, you do everything you can to keep morale high.

COOPERATIVE LEARNING On this page are three challenges you face as an American on the home front during World War II. Working with a small group, decide how to meet each challenge. Choose an option, assign a task to each group member, and do the activity. You will find useful information in the Data File. Be prepared to present your solutions to the class.

MUSIC CHALLENGE

"Jukebox Saturday Night"

Everybody loves the Andrews Sisters and Glenn Miller's big band sound. People whistle tunes like "Jukebox Saturday Night," a favorite of jitterbugging bobbysoxers. You want to write a snappy song with catchy lyrics to brighten people's moods in these tough times. Present your song using one of these options:

- **Sing your song in an audition for the bandleader.**
- **Tape record your song to send to the bandleader.**

HOME ECONOMICS CHALLENGE

"Make it do, or do without"

It's up to you to help with the war effort. How will you do it? You know that factories need certain materials to manufacture supplies for the war effort. And the troops need food. What can you do to help the troops fighting overseas? Use the Data File for help. Then present your ideas using one of these options:

- Create a list of activities that you and your friends can participate in to help the war effort, both by collecting materials and saving food.
- Write a letter to a relative serving in the armed forces explaining how the activities of you and your friends have helped him and his fellow soldiers.

Save Waste Paper

GIVE OR SELL IT!
CALL YOUR SALVAGE COMMITTEE TODAY!

Sort and Bundle
1 BROWN PAPER, BAGS, CORRUGATED BOXES
2 WASTEBASKET SCRAPS
3 OLD NEWSPAPERS
4 OLD MAGAZINES

ART CHALLENGE

"POW!"... "OW!!"

These days, battle stories crackle over the radio and fill the daily papers, bringing worry into every waking hour. The comic book adventures of Captain America help you cope with all the frightening news. This bold superpatriot and his pal Bucky find and defeat Nazis working in American factories, radio stations, and transportation systems. A recent Captain America tale gave you the idea for a super-spy character who helps the troops fighting overseas. You decide to send your idea to Joe Simon and Jack Kirby, creators of Captain America. Present your idea using one of these options:

• Create a short comic book of your hero's exploits.
• Design a cover illustrating your comic superhero.

ACTIVITY WRAP-UP

Present to the class As a group, review your methods of boosting wartime morale. Evaluate which of your solutions is the best.

Present your solutions to the class.

Captain America™ © 1999 Marvel Characters, Inc. Used with permission.

📁 DATA FILE

Life on the Home Front

• People collect tinfoil, old tools, scrap metal, lard, and bacon grease for making arms and ammunition.

• Rationed gas and tires force workers to rise early and take buses, trolleys, and trains to work. People stay home at night.

• People share housing to cut costs and provide child care for working mothers. Neighbors use one another's appliances.

• Bobby pins, can openers, flash-light batteries, boxed candy, lawn mowers, alarm clocks, and other everyday items are scarce.

• People save fuel by keeping houses at 65 degrees.

Victory Gardens

• Americans plant gardens on rooftops, in backyards, and on vacant lots, producing beans, radishes, carrots, squash, corn, and tomatoes.

• Housewives preserve corn relish, stewed tomatoes, and fruit jams.

Popular Music

Big Bands The Glenn Miller Orchestra is one of the most popular bands. It creates a special sound, mixing a clarinet and saxophones. The band's hits include "Don't Sit Under the Apple Tree (With Anyone Else But Me)," "When Johnny Comes Marching Home," "My Prayer," "Moonlight Serenade," and "A String of Pearls."

Andrews Sisters These three sisters harmonize on songs, including "I'll Be with You in Apple Blossom Time" and "Boogie Woogie Bugle Boy of Company B."

For more about the home front . . .

RESEARCH LINKS
CLASSZONE.COM

The Legacy of the War

MAIN IDEA	WHY IT MATTERS NOW	TERMS & NAMES
World War II had deep and lasting effects on the United States and the world.	As a result of World War II, the United States became the dominant power in the world.	Marshall Plan Nuremberg trials G.I. Bill of Rights United Nations

ONE AMERICAN'S STORY

When the end of the war came, Elliot Johnson was excited. He was finally going home. However, one of his captains told the troops that it might not be so easy to put the war behind them.

A VOICE FROM THE PAST

"You guys are anxious to get home and put this all behind you," he said. "But you don't understand how big a part of your life this has been. "You'll put it all behind you for about ten years, and then someday you'll hear a marching band. You'll pick up the beat and it will all come back to you and you'll be right back here on the parade ground marching again." And he was right.

Elliot Johnson, quoted in *The Homefront*

Soldiers celebrate being discharged from the service on May 12, 1945, at Fort Dix, New Jersey.

World War II affected millions of Americans. The great struggle also touched the United States and the world in many other ways, as you will read in this section.

Taking Notes

Use your chart to take notes about important events that resulted from World War II.

IMPORTANT BATTLES IN EUROPE, AFRICA, AND THE PACIFIC

September 1, 1939—Germany invades Poland	➤		➤

The War's Human Cost

No war has claimed so many lives or caused so much destruction as World War II. The human cost on both sides was immense. About 20 million soldiers were killed, and millions more were wounded. The Soviet Union suffered the greatest losses, with at least 7.5 million military deaths and another 5 million people wounded. More than 400,000 American soldiers died and more than 600,000 were wounded.

Civilian casualties also numbered in the millions. Both the Allied and Axis powers had fought a war without boundaries. They bombed cities, destroyed villages, and brought destruction to civilian life. Again, the Soviet Union experienced the worst losses. All told, about 20 million

Soviet citizens died in the struggle. China, which also endured years of attack from Japan in the 1930s, lost about 10 million civilians.

The war also created an enormous wave of refugees. They included orphans, prisoners of war, survivors of Nazi concentration camps, and those who fled advancing armies. After the war, 21 million refugees, most starving and homeless, tried to put their lives back together amid the ruins of Europe and Asia.

World War II Military Casualties, *1939–1945*		
NATION	DEAD	WOUNDED
Soviet Union	7,500,000	5,000,000
Germany	3,500,000	7,250,000
China	2,200,000	1,762,000
Japan	1,219,000	295,247
United States	405,399	671,278
Great Britain	329,208	348,403
France	210,671	390,000
Italy	77,494	120,000

Source: *World Book*

SKILLBUILDER Interpreting Charts
1. Which two nations suffered the most casualties in World War II?
2. Which of the major combatants suffered the fewest casualties?

Economic Winners and Losers

*Reading*History

A. Finding Main Ideas Why did the United States emerge from World War II so strong?

The war left many of the world's economies in ruins. Bombing campaigns had destroyed factories, transportation centers, and other important buildings. Only the United States—where no major battles were fought (except for Pearl Harbor)—came out of the war with a strong economy. The boom in industry during the war had pulled the nation out of the Great Depression. After the war, the U.S. economy continued to grow.

With the world's strongest economy, the United States set out to help rebuild the shattered economies of Europe and Japan. U.S. forces occupied Japan for several years after the war. During that time, they introduced programs that put Japan on the road to recovery. In 1948, Congress approved the **Marshall Plan** to help boost the economies of Europe. The plan was named after the man who came up with it, Secretary of State George C. Marshall. Under the plan, the United States gave more than $13 billion to help the nations of Europe get back on their feet.

Changes in American Society

The nation faced important social changes in the years following the war. For one thing, the country had to deal with the return of millions of soldiers. With so many servicemen suddenly back home, the competition for jobs and education was great. The government responded by passing a law that is commonly known as the **G.I. Bill of Rights** or G.I. Bill. This measure provided educational and economic help to veterans. The government paid for returning soldiers' schooling and provided them with a living allowance. More than 7.8 million World War II veterans attended school under the G.I. Bill.

The return of so many fighting men also created a great demand for housing. The Truman administration took steps to address the country's housing shortage. However, many Americans had to live in crowded urban slums or in country shacks.

The U.S. soldiers who returned home found an America that had changed. During the war, millions of Americans had moved to find war-related jobs in California and in the cities. Included in this group was a large number of African Americans. By war's end, hundreds of thousands of African Americans had moved from the South to various Northern cities and California. There, they lived in overcrowded ghettos and experienced prejudice. However, many also found economic opportunity.

Now *and* then

WAR CRIMES

More than 40 years after the Nuremberg trials (shown below), the world community once again brought army officials to trial for war crimes. These crimes were committed during brutal civil wars in the former Yugoslavia from 1991 to 1999. An international tribunal met in The Hague in 1996 to begin trying persons for their role in the conflicts.

These civil wars pitted Serbs, Croats, Bosnians, and Albanians against each other. Many people, especially Serbs, were accused of undertaking a policy of "ethnic cleansing"—the systematic attempt to rid a region of people from certain ethnic groups, often by killing them.

The Nuremberg Trials

As the United States dealt with important matters at home, the nation also joined the world in dealing with war crimes. The international community put together a court to try Nazi leaders for their role in World War II.

The trial opened in November 1945 in Nuremberg, Germany. The original 24 defendants included some of Hitler's top officials. The charges against them included crimes against humanity. These crimes referred to the Nazis' murder of millions of Jews and others. In his opening argument, the U.S. chief counsel at Nuremberg spelled out why a trial was necessary.

A VOICE FROM THE PAST

What makes this inquest significant is that these prisoners represent sinister influences that will lurk in the world long after their bodies have returned to dust. They are living symbols of racial hatreds, of terrorism and violence, and of the arrogance and cruelty of power.

Robert H. Jackson, *The Nürnberg Case*

After nearly a year-long trial, 19 of the defendants were found guilty. Twelve were sentenced to death. About 185 other Nazi leaders were found guilty in later trials. The **Nuremberg trials** upheld an important idea: People are responsible for their actions, even in wartime.

Creation of the United Nations

The war helped to establish another principle—nations must work together in order to secure world peace. The outbreak of World War II demonstrated the weakness of the League of Nations, the international peacekeeping body created after the First World War. The League was weak in large part because the United States had refused to join out of a strong desire to stay out of foreign affairs. Toward the end of World War II, President Roosevelt urged his fellow Americans not to turn their backs on the world again.

The country listened. In April 1945, delegates from 50 nations—including the United States—met in San Francisco to discuss creating a new international peace organization. In June, all 50 nations approved

Reading **History**

B. Solving Problems Why did President Roosevelt support U.S. participation in the United Nations?

the charter creating the new peacekeeping body known as the **United Nations,** or UN.

International Tensions

The horrors of World War II had caused many countries to work together toward lasting peace. However, tensions still arose among nations in the wake of the war. For example, in 1948 the United Nations helped found the nation of Israel to create a homeland for the Jews in Palestine. Fighting immediately broke out as neighboring Arab nations attacked Israel. In addition, colonies around the world began fighting for their independence.

Reading **History**
C. Reading a Map Look at the map on page R33 to find out where Israel is.

The United States, however, was more concerned with the rise of the Soviet Union. Despite suffering so much damage and loss of life, the Soviet Union emerged from World War II as a great power. It had conquered much of Eastern Europe.

During the war, the United States and the Soviet Union had been uneasy partners. After the war, Stalin angered the United States by breaking a wartime promise to promote democracy in the nations he had occupied in Eastern Europe. Instead, Stalin forced the countries to live under Communist regimes. The Soviet Union wanted to spread communism. The United States wanted to halt it. This led to future conflict.

Background
An important reason for U.S. leaders to drop the atomic bombs on Japan was to make the Soviets fear U.S. power.

Finally, the end of the war marked the beginning of the atomic age. The atomic bombs dropped on Japan showed the world a powerful new weapon. In the next chapter, you will learn how atomic weapons increased tensions between the United States and the Soviet Union.

D.R. Fitzpatrick drew this cartoon, entitled " . . . Shall Not Have Died In Vain." He hoped the memory of U.S. losses would push Americans to support the UN and preserve peace.

Section 5 Assessment

1. Terms & Names
Explain the significance of:
- Marshall Plan
- G.I. Bill of Rights
- Nuremberg trials
- United Nations

2. Using Graphics
Use a cluster diagram like the one shown to review the effects of World War II.

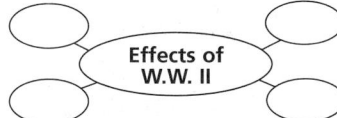

Effects of W.W. II

Which effect seems the most important to you?

3. Main Ideas
a. What was the Marshall Plan?

b. How did the G.I. Bill of Rights help World War II veterans?

c. What principles did the Nuremberg trials establish?

4. Critical Thinking
Analyzing Causes Why did the United States emerge from the war so much better off than other nations?

THINK ABOUT
- the geographic location of the United States
- the role of American industry

ACTIVITY OPTIONS

LANGUAGE ARTS

SPEECH

As a reporter, research and write a **news article** on a defendant at the Nuremberg trials or, as a lawyer, deliver a closing **speech** against a defendant.

The Rise of Dictators and World War II

■ Asia and the Pacific   ■ Europe and Africa

1931–1941

- ■ 1931 Japan invades Manchuria.
- ■ 1933 Hitler comes to power in Germany.
- ■ 1936 Germany and Italy form Axis.
- ■ 1938 Germany takes over Austria.
- ■ 1939 Germany invades Poland. World War II begins.
- ■ 1940 Germany invades France. Battle of Britain fought.
- ■ 1941 Japanese attack Pearl Harbor.

1942

- ■ Japanese stopped at Battle of Coral Sea.
- ■ Japanese defeated at Battle of Midway.

1943

- ■ Soviets defeat Germans at Stalingrad.
- ■ Allies stop Axis advance in North Africa.
- ■ Allies invade Italy. Italy surrenders.

1944

- ■ Allies invade Europe at Normandy.
- ■ Allies invade the Philippines.

1945

- ■ Allies invade Iwo Jima and Okinawa.
- ■ Germany surrenders.
- ■ United States drops atomic bombs on Hiroshima and Nagasaki.
- ■ Japan surrenders.

TERMS & NAMES

Briefly explain the significance of each of the following.

1. Adolf Hitler
2. Pearl Harbor
3. D-Day
4. Holocaust
5. Battle of Midway
6. Hiroshima
7. rationing
8. Japanese-American internment
9. G.I. Bill of Rights
10. Nuremberg trials

REVIEW QUESTIONS

Steps to War (pages 757–762)

1. Why did Hitler attack the Soviet Union?
2. What was the Lend-Lease program?

War in Africa and Europe (pages 763–769)

3. What role did women play in the war?
4. What was D-Day and why was it significant?

War in the Pacific (pages 770–773)

5. What was the strategy of island hopping?
6. What was the Manhattan Project?

The Home Front (pages 774–779)

7. In what ways did Americans at home contribute to the war effort?
8. Why did the nation put thousands of Japanese Americans in internment camps during the war?

The Legacy of the War (pages 780–783)

9. Which nation lost the most soldiers and civilians in the war?
10. What international tensions arose after World War II?

CRITICAL THINKING

1. USING YOUR NOTES: SEQUENCING EVENTS

IMPORTANT BATTLES IN EUROPE, AFRICA, AND THE PACIFIC

September 1, 1939—Germany invades Poland	→		→	
	→		→	
	→		→	April 1945—U.S. Marines invade Okinawa

Use your chart to answer these questions.

a. Which battle that you listed occurred first?
b. Which battle was the most important?

2. ANALYZING LEADERSHIP

Do you agree or disagree with Neville Chamberlain's policy of appeasement? Explain.

3. APPLYING CITIZENSHIP SKILLS

Imagine you are a Japanese American in an internment camp. If you were to write a letter of protest to the government, what violations of your rights would you describe in the letter?

4. THEME: AMERICA IN THE WORLD

Why do you think the United States joined the United Nations after World War II, when it had refused to join the League of Nations after World War I?

5. COMPARING AND CONTRASTING

What role did racism play in the Holocaust and the internment of Japanese Americans? How was the level of racism different?

Interact with History

After reading the chapter, would you make the same choice about whether to risk your life to fight against dictators that you made at the beginning of the chapter? Explain.

Use the map and your knowledge of U.S. history to answer questions 1 and 2.

Additional Test Practice, pp. S1–S33.

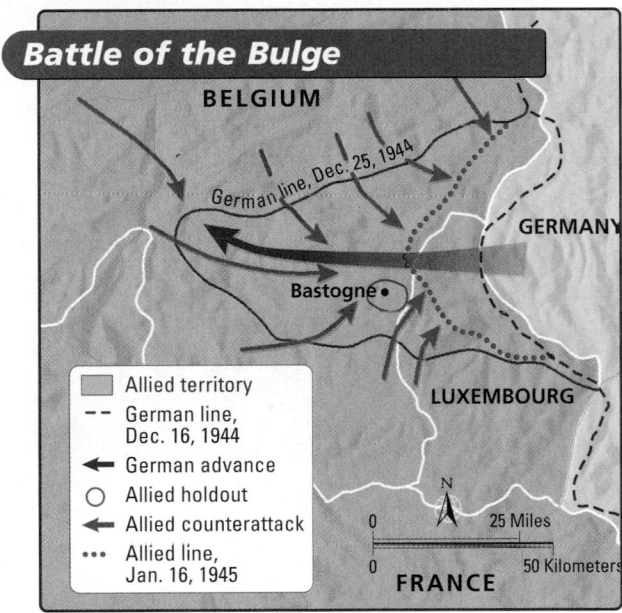

Battle of the Bulge

BELGIUM

German line, Dec. 25, 1944

GERMANY

Bastogne •

LUXEMBOURG

Allied territory
-- German line, Dec. 16, 1944
◄— German advance
○ Allied holdout
◄— Allied counterattack
••• Allied line, Jan. 16, 1945

N

0   25 Miles
0   50 Kilometers

FRANCE

1. About how many miles westward had the Germans advanced by Christmas 1944?

   A. about 25 miles

   B. about 50 miles

   C. about 75 miles

   D. about 100 miles

2. Why was this battle called the Battle of the Bulge?

   A. The Germans made a bulge in the Allied lines.

   B. There was a bulge in the German border.

   C. The Allies' attack was called the "bulge."

   D. The Allied attack "bulged" into France.

This quotation from Robert H. Jackson is about the Nazis on trial after World War II. Use the quotation and your knowledge of U.S. history to answer question 3.

PRIMARY SOURCE

What makes this inquest significant is that these prisoners represent sinister influences that will lurk in the world long after their bodies have returned to dust. They are living symbols of racial hatreds, of terrorism and violence, and of the arrogance and cruelty of power.

Robert H. Jackson, the Nürnberg Case

3. The passage best supports which point of view?

   A. The Nazis had a great deal of influence all over the world.

   B. The perpetrators of the crimes and the hatred they represented were on trial.

   C. The trial was significant in that the prisoners were guilty of terrorism.

   D. The prisoners deserved to be executed for the severity of their crimes.

TEST PRACTICE
CLASSZONE.COM

ALTERNATIVE ASSESSMENT

1. 📝 **WRITING ABOUT HISTORY**

During World War II, women took on jobs previously not available to them. Imagine you are a woman who has found a job as a welder in a shipyard. Write a series of brief **diary** entries.

* Include details about your daily life.

* Include reasons why women should or should not be allowed to keep their jobs once the war is over.

2. COOPERATIVE LEARNING

With a group of three to five students, create a news show about the experiences of American civilians during World War II. Choose a year between 1941 and 1945 and a specific location, such as a hospital, factory, or farm. Share the roles of anchor, reporter, or interviewees. Each student can write a script for his or her role.

INTEGRATED TECHNOLOGY

PARTICIPATING IN A NET SIMULATION

Go to *NetSimulations: World War II and the Atomic Bomb* at **classzone.com** and become President Truman as he decides how to end the war with Japan.

* Learn about the strategies and strengths of Japan and of the Allies.

* Meet with your advisers to learn about the development of the atomic bomb.

* Use the President's Diary to consider your war options: invasion; negotiate a peace plan; show the bomb's force and demand surrender; or drop the bomb in a surprise attack.

* Make your decision.

NET SIMULATION
CLASSZONE.COM

The Cold War and the American Dream
1945–1960

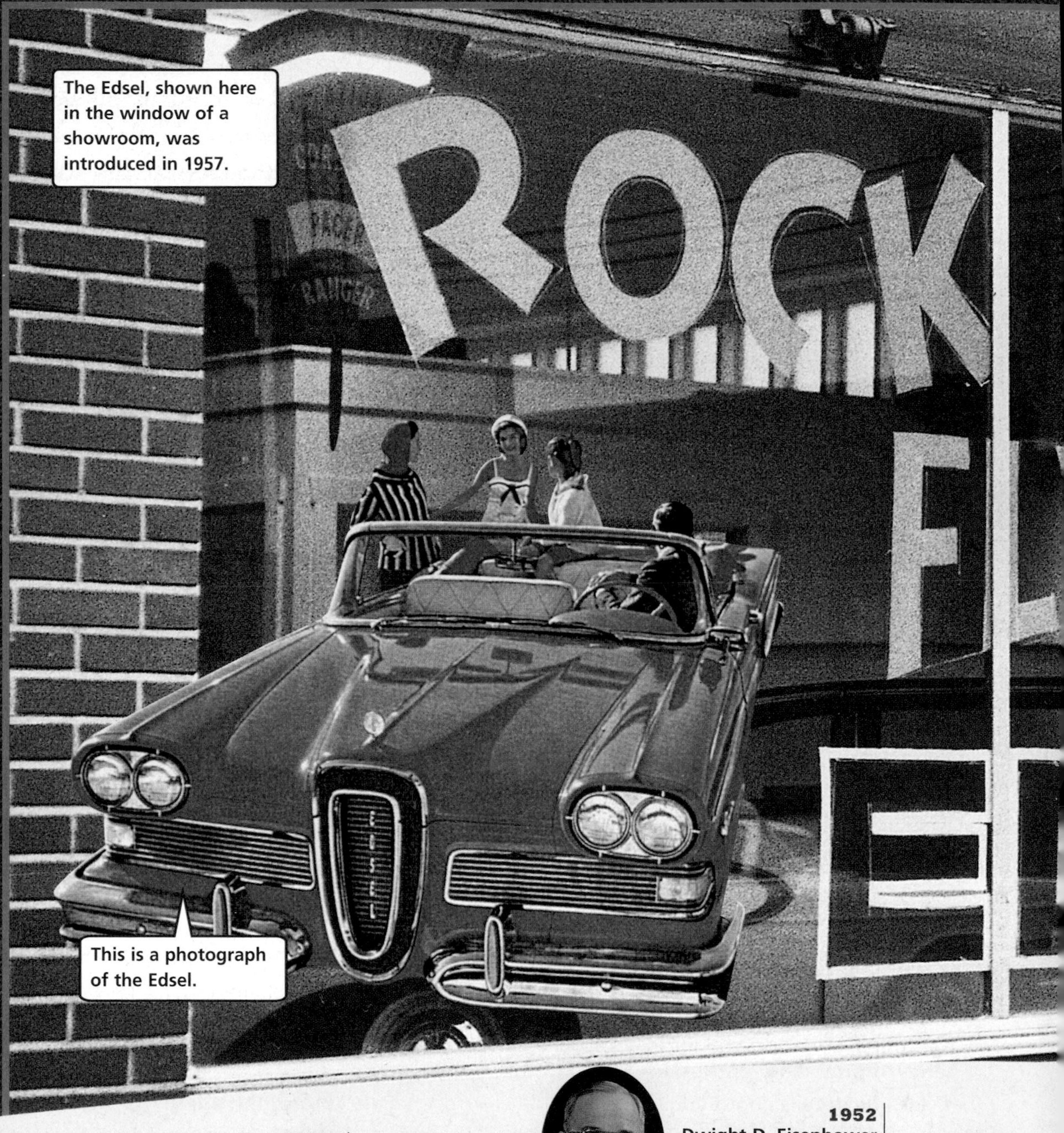

The Edsel, shown here in the window of a showroom, was introduced in 1957.

ROCK

This is a photograph of the Edsel.

1945
United Nations is established.

1947
Truman Doctrine and Marshall Plan are established.

1948
Harry S. Truman is elected president.

1952
Dwight D. Eisenhower is elected president.
United States explodes first hydrogen bomb.

1953
Rosenbergs are executed as spies.

USA
World 1945

1946
Churchill gives "Iron Curtain" speech.

1948
Berlin Airlift begins.

1949
Germany is partitioned.
China becomes Communist.

1950
Korean War begins.

1952
Mau Mau revolt shakes Kenya.

1953
Korean War cease-fire is agreed to.

The dealer tries to make the Edsel seem futuristic by comparing it to Russian satellites and flying saucers.

In the 1950s, American technology produced a flood of consumer goods. These included cars and houses in suburbs springing up across the country. You and your family have moved to a new house in a growing suburb, which some people think of as the American Dream.

What is the American Dream to you?

What Do You Think?

• How might the American Dream be connected to prosperity?

• How might the American Dream be connected to democracy, equality, and justice?

RESEARCH LINKS
CLASSZONE.COM

Visit the Chapter 28 links for more information about the Cold War and the 1950s.

1954
Senator Joseph McCarthy claims Communist influence in U.S. Army.

1956
Highway Act is passed.

Eisenhower is reelected president.

1960
John F. Kennedy is elected president.

1960

1956
Soviets suppress Hungarian Revolution.

1957
Soviets launch *Sputnik*.

Reading Strategy: Categorizing Information

What Do You Know?

What do you think of when you hear the phrase *the American Dream*? What sorts of dreams might a people and a nation have?

Think About
- what you have learned about the 1950s from television and movies
- hopes and dreams that might be achieved through politics and through other means
- your responses to the Interact with History about the American Dream (see page 787)

Early televisions looked very different from those of today.

What Do You Want to Know?

What additional information do you want to know about the Cold War and the American Dream? Record the sort of information you want in your notebook before you read the chapter.

Categorizing Information

The presidencies of Harry S. Truman and Dwight D. Eisenhower spanned the years between 1945 and 1960. There were a number of important issues, foreign and domestic, that both presidents had to deal with. Use the chart below to categorize each president's policy or action on the issues.

S See Skillbuilder Handbook, page R6.

Taking Notes

ISSUES	PRESIDENTS	
Domestic	Truman	Eisenhower
Labor unions and big business		
Communist threat at home		
Foreign		
Korea		
Communism in Europe		

Peacetime Adjustments and the Cold War

MAIN IDEA	WHY IT MATTERS NOW	TERMS & NAMES
Americans looked for prosperity after World War II. They also fought communism in the Cold War.	The U.S. economy grew rapidly, and the nation's role in the world expanded after World War II.	Harry S. Truman Truman Doctrine Fair Deal NATO Cold War Marshall Plan containment

ONE AMERICAN'S STORY

Harold Russell was a soldier, not an actor. Even so, in 1946 he won an Academy Award for best supporting actor in the film *The Best Years of Our Lives.* Russell played an amputee struggling to adjust to civilian life after World War II. It was a role he knew well. Russell had lost both hands in a grenade explosion and was fitted with hooks.

Sergeant Harold Russell demonstrates to other disabled veterans how to drink a cup of coffee.

A VOICE FROM THE PAST

I was all right. My problem was to make the people I met feel at ease. I just acted myself and didn't sulk in corners hiding the hooks. When my neighborhood friends saw I was okay and laughing they said to themselves, "Why should we feel sorry for him? He's getting along better than we are."

Harold Russell, quoted in *Life,* December 16, 1946

As you will read in this section, millions of returning soldiers like Russell had to restart their lives at the end of World War II.

Adjusting to Peace

The United States had spent the years 1941–1945 fighting World War II. Now, the country was at peace. The aircraft industry and other defense plants were changing over to making goods for peacetime. As part of this process, most industries reduced their work force. Factories shut down, and more than 10 million returning war veterans were looking for work.

Returning servicemen flooded the job market. Veterans won out over female workers in the competition for jobs in the first years after the war. In the aircraft industry, more than 800,000 workers—mostly women—were laid off. Several years after the war ended, as the economy boomed, employment rates for women began to return to wartime peaks. However, these jobs were often in traditional women's fields, such as teaching.

Taking Notes

Use your chart to take notes about labor unions, big business, and communism.

ISSUES
Domestic
Labor unions and big business
Communist threat at home
Foreign
Korea
Communism in Europe

A Changing Economy

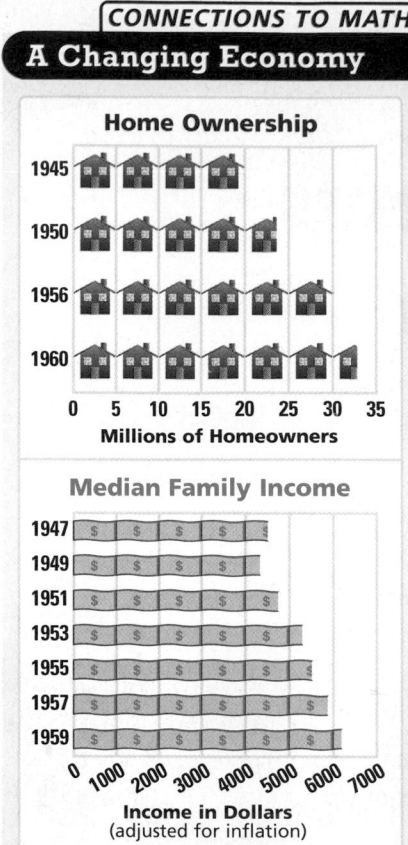

Home Ownership

1945
1950
1956
1960

0   5   10   15   20   25   30   35
Millions of Homeowners

Median Family Income

1947
1949
1951
1953
1955
1957
1959

0 1000 2000 3000 4000 5000 6000 7000
Income in Dollars
(adjusted for inflation)

Source: *Historical Statistics of the United States*

SKILLBUILDER
Interpreting Charts

1. *What period showed the biggest increase in home ownership?*
2. *About how much did family income increase in the years 1947 to 1959?*

The Postwar Economy

Instead of slowing down, as many had feared, the nation's economy boomed. During the war years, few consumer goods had been produced. After the war, people were starting families and buying new homes. They wanted cars, washing machines, toasters, and all the other goods they had put off buying during wartime. American factories were fitted out with new machinery and tools to make different products.

The spending spree led to inflation, or a rise in prices. During the war, the government had put controls on prices and wages. After the war, in 1946, the controls on prices were lifted. Consumer goods were still in short supply. People had plenty of money to spend, but few goods to buy. As a result, the demand for goods increased, and prices skyrocketed.

After the war, the number of marriages increased. At first, a housing shortage forced many newlyweds to move in with relatives. Government-guaranteed housing loans for veterans under the G.I. Bill spurred the demand for new houses. Businessman William Levitt saw a way to meet this demand. He applied assembly-line techniques to home building. His mass-produced houses were so cheap that many people could afford them. He built Levittown in 1947 on Long Island, New York. Three years later, 17,500 homes had turned the farmland into an instant suburb. However, not everyone benefited from the postwar boom.

Reading **History**

A. Making Inferences Why did Levitt's houses become so popular?

Labor Unrest and Civil Rights

During the war, unions had agreed to give up pay raises. When the government put controls on wages, the unions agreed not to strike. But with the war over, workers faced with rising prices demanded better pay. In 1946, the United States entered one of the most strike-torn years in its history. More than one million workers joined strikes in the automobile, steel, meatpacking, and electrical industries.

Later that year, both miners and railway workers also went out on strike. Although President **Harry S. Truman** was a friend of labor, he feared these strikes would cripple the nation. During the railroad strike, he threatened to draft all railroad workers into the army. He said he would have the army run the trains. But the strike was settled before Truman could carry out his threat.

African Americans were still excluded from prosperity and full equality in the postwar world. World War II had raised the hopes of African Americans for greater equality. Many African-American veterans expected their wartime service to be recognized. Particularly in the

South, however, little had changed. In many Southern states, African Americans who attempted to vote were threatened, fired from their jobs, and even murdered.

To deal with these problems, President Truman created a commission on civil rights. He issued an executive order in July 1948 ending racial segregation and discrimination in the armed forces. Truman also asked Congress for an anti-lynching law and an end to the poll tax as a requirement for voting. However, when Southern Democrats in Congress balked at the proposals, Truman backed off. Nonetheless, he was the first president to make equal rights a national issue. The action he took began the federal government's effort to deal with racial issues.

Background
In some Southern states a poll tax had to be paid in order to vote.

The Fair Deal

In 1946, fears about the economy hurt the Democrats. Voters sent a Republican majority to Congress. The new Congress wanted to block Truman's programs. Congress turned down his plans to provide federal funds for housing, education, and health care. Congress also limited the power of unions by passing the 1947 Taft-Hartley Act. This act outlawed the closed shop, a workplace that hired only union members. The act also gave the president the power to require an 80-day cooling-off period before a strike.

As the 1948 presidential election campaign opened, few political experts believed President Truman would keep his job. Polls showed the Republican candidate, New York governor Thomas E. Dewey, to be the clear favorite. Even within his own party, few of Truman's supporters thought that he could win.

Ignoring politicians and pollsters, Truman took his campaign to the people. Hiring a special train, he made a tour through hundreds of cities and small towns. Wherever his train stopped, Truman blasted the "do-nothing" Republican Congress because it passed little legislation. His strategy worked. When the votes were counted, he had won an upset victory over Dewey. The Democrats had also regained control of Congress.

After his victory, Truman presented Congress with a package of reforms he called the Fair Deal. He hoped to extend the social programs begun with FDR's New Deal. The **Fair Deal** called for new projects to create jobs, build public housing, and end racial discrimination in hiring. Many Republicans and Southern Democrats worked together to block his plans. Congress passed few of his proposals. Only his low-cost public housing measure became law. In addition to problems at home, Truman faced major problems abroad.

AMERICA'S HISTORY MAKERS

HARRY S. TRUMAN
1884–1972
During Harry Truman's 1948 whistle-stop campaign, he traveled many thousands of miles in eight weeks. He was often accompanied by his daughter and wife.

Audiences enjoyed his straightforward manner and his spirited attacks on the Republicans. He blamed the Republicans for the nation's problems. When the votes were counted, Truman won an upset victory over his opponent, Thomas Dewey. A Chicago newspaper (above) mistakenly declared Dewey the winner in the close contest.

What might Truman's whistle-stop campaign suggest about his character?

Origins of the Cold War

After World War II, the capitalist Western democracies came into increasing conflict with the communist Soviet Union. Their differing economic and political systems resulted in misunderstandings. During the war, the Western democracies were allied with the Soviet Union. They were united in the struggle to defeat Nazi Germany. However, as victory grew nearer, the West and the Soviet Union distrusted each other.

The most difficult issue was the political future of Eastern Europe. In the final battles of the war, the Soviets freed Eastern European states from Nazi rule. Then Soviet forces occupied those states, including the eastern sector of Germany. The Soviet leader Joseph Stalin promised free elections to the nations of Eastern Europe. However, when the war ended, Stalin installed pro-Soviet governments throughout Eastern Europe.

Stalin feared that free elections in Eastern Europe might result in the election of anti-Soviet governments on its borders. The Western democracies saw Stalin's occupation of Eastern Europe differently. President Truman believed that Stalin intended to spread communism worldwide.

Truman was determined to protect Western Europe from the threat of Soviet expansion. As the gap between the Soviet Union and the Western democracies widened, tensions developed. The resulting **Cold War** was a conflict that pitted the United States against the Soviet Union. The two nations never directly confronted each other on the battlefield. However, the threat of deadly conflict lasted for decades.

Reading **History**

B. Comparing and Contrasting How did the Soviet Union and the West view Eastern Europe?

Europe after World War II, *1955*

Member of NATO, 1955
Member of Warsaw Pact, 1955

GEOGRAPHY SKILLBUILDER Interpreting Maps
1. **Location** *What westernmost country in Europe was a member of NATO?*
2. **Region** *Which NATO members directly bordered the Warsaw Pact countries?*

Containing Communism Abroad

As tensions between the United States and the Soviet Union were increasing, Britain's Winston Churchill visited the United States in 1946. He warned the world of Soviet aims.

"An iron curtain has descended across the continent."
Winston Churchill

> **A VOICE FROM THE PAST**
>
> From Stettin in the Baltic to Trieste in the Adriatic, an iron curtain has descended across the continent. Behind that line lie all the . . . states of Central and Eastern Europe. . . . All these . . . populations . . . lie in the Soviet sphere and all are subject . . . not only to Soviet influence but to . . . increasing . . . control from Moscow.
>
> **Winston Churchill,** "Iron Curtain" speech, Fulton, Missouri

Background
Truman's containment policy was first announced in 1947 in response to Soviet pressure on Greece and Turkey.

The Truman Administration's main strategy in the Cold War was its containment policy. The goal of **containment** was to stop the spread of communism. This meant that the United States would work in military and nonmilitary ways to contain communism. Next, Truman announced the **Truman Doctrine,** which promised aid to people struggling to resist threats to democratic freedom.

In 1948, there was alarm over communist control of Eastern Europe. This led to formation of the North Atlantic Treaty Organization (NATO). The **NATO** alliance included the United States, Canada, and ten Western European nations. In response, the Soviet Union and Eastern European nations formed the Warsaw Pact (see map on page 792).

Marshall Plan and Berlin Airlift

Hoping to prevent the spread of communism, the United States came up with a plan to revive the war-torn economies of Europe. The plan was named for Truman's Secretary of State, George C. Marshall. The **Marshall Plan** offered $13 billion in aid to western and southern Europe. The plan helped the nations of Europe rebuild.

Reading **History**

C. Reading a Map
Use the map on page 792 to see how Berlin was divided among the four nations.

The European nation in which the Cold War almost turned hot was Germany. In June of 1945, the Allies had agreed to a temporary division of Germany into four zones. These were controlled by the Soviet Union, France, Great Britain, and the United States. The Western powers merged their zones and made plans to unite them as West Germany. Stalin feared a united Germany might threaten the Soviet Union.

An American plane brings supplies to Berlin during the airlift.

Berlin, Germany's former capital, lay within the eastern zone, still held by the Soviet Union. Like Germany, it too had been divided into East and West Berlin. In 1948, Stalin hoped to force the Western powers to abandon the city. His forces blocked access to Berlin.

Truman responded by approving a huge airlift of food, fuel, and equipment into the city. For nearly a year,

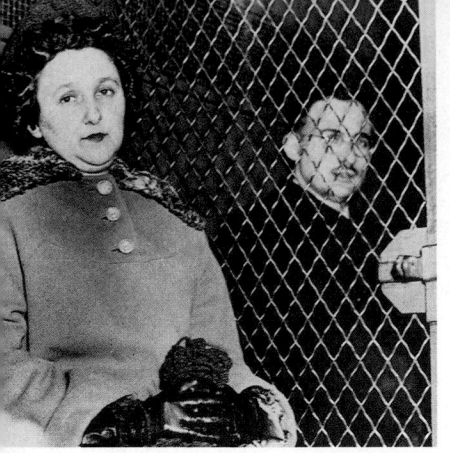

Ethel and Julius Rosenberg were executed despite numerous pleas to spare their lives.

British cargo planes made 275,000 flights into Berlin. They carried supplies to the city's residents. In 1949, Stalin called off the blockade. By May 1949, Germany had been divided into communist East Germany and democratic West Germany.

Fear of Communism at Home

After World War II, a growing number of Americans feared that communism would gain strength within the United States. In part this was a response to the Soviet occupation of Eastern Europe. At first, attention focused on Americans who belonged to the U.S. Communist Party who, it was feared, might spy for Russia.

Two famous spy trials made such fears believable. Alger Hiss was a former State Department official. He was accused of passing military information to the Soviet Union. Tried for lying under oath, he was sentenced to five years in prison in 1950. Ethel and Julius Rosenberg were members of the American Communist Party. In 1951, they were convicted of passing atomic secrets to the Russians. They were executed in 1953.

Truman fought Republican charges that his administration was soft on communism. He issued an executive order requiring 3 million government workers to undergo loyalty checks. Federal workers who objected to signing loyalty oaths lost their jobs. Between 1947 and 1951, loyalty boards forced over 3,000 government workers to resign.

The anticommunist crusade gave new life to the House Un-American Activities Committee (HUAC). In 1947, HUAC began targeting actors, directors, and writers in the movie industry for suspected communist ties. Within the entertainment industry, lists of names circulated among the Hollywood movie studios. These were blacklists—unofficial lists of people thought to be communists. The careers of the people on these lists were ruined. As you will read in the next section, fear of communism dominated American life in the early 1950s.

Section Assessment

1. Terms & Names

Explain the significance of:

- Harry S. Truman
- Fair Deal
- Cold War
- containment
- Truman Doctrine
- NATO
- Marshall Plan

2. Using Graphics

In a chart, explain the goals of these Cold War programs.

Program	Goal
Containment policy	
Truman Doctrine	
Marshall Plan	
NATO	

3. Main Ideas

a. Why was inflation a concern in the early postwar period?

b. What were the causes of the Cold War?

c. Why did the United States experience fear of communism after the war?

4. Critical Thinking

Forming Opinions Do you think an exaggerated fear of communism could occur again? Explain.

THINK ABOUT

- relations between the United States and Russia today
- American attitudes toward opposing views
- beliefs about communism

ACTIVITY OPTIONS

LANGUAGE ARTS

ART

Imagine that you were a child in Berlin during the airlift. Write a **letter** to a pen pal in the United States, or draw a **picture** describing your experiences.

2

The Korean War and McCarthyism

MAIN IDEA	**WHY IT MATTERS NOW**	**TERMS & NAMES**
The Cold War and the Korean War produced a far-reaching form of anticommunism.	Reckless charges damaged personal lives and set up a climate of suspicion that affected Americans for years.	Mao Zedong brinksmanship 38th parallel arms race Korean War H-bomb Joseph McCarthy space race

ONE AMERICAN'S STORY

Statesman John Stewart Service was one of thousands of Americans whose lives were turned upside down by the anticommunism of the postwar era. As a China expert, he warned the State Department of the weakness of China's anticommunist Nationalist Party.

In 1949, the Communists took control of China. Angry Americans wanted someone to blame. Service's good advice was forgotten. He became one of the first State Department officials blamed for the loss of China to the Communists. Although a loyalty board cleared him of charges of disloyalty, he lost his job. As you will read in this section, many innocent Americans suffered a similar fate.

John Stewart Service defends himself before the Senate Foreign Relations Committee.

Origins of the Korean War

In September 1949, the Communists defeated the anticommunist Nationalists in a civil war in China. The Nationalists were supported by the United States. **Mao Zedong** became head of the new Communist state. The Nationalist government, headed by Chiang Kai-shek, fled to the island of Taiwan, formerly Formosa, off the coast of the Chinese mainland. Many Americans were shocked by the fall of the Nationalist government. They viewed the takeover as part of a Communist plot to rule the world. They blamed the State Department for failing to stop the Communist revolution. American fear of communism grew. Events in Korea contributed to this fear.

Korea had been a Japanese colony for half a century when Japan surrendered to the Allies at the end of World War II. In 1945, Soviet troops occupied Korea north of the **38th parallel,** or line of latitude. American forces took control south of this line. Aided by the Soviets, a Communist government came to power in North Korea. In South Korea, a noncommunist leader supported by the United States governed.

Taking Notes

Use your chart to take notes about Korea and the communist threat at home.

ISSUES		
Domestic		
Labor unions and big business		
Communist threat at home		
Foreign		
Korea		
Communism in Europe		

Fighting Breaks Out in Korea

In June 1950, North Korean forces crossed the 38th parallel into South Korea. The conflict that followed became known as the **Korean War**. President Truman viewed Korea as a test case for his containment policy. He responded promptly. The United States appealed to the United Nations (UN) to stop the Communist move into South Korea. Sixteen nations provided soldiers for a UN force. However, U.S. troops made up most of the force and did most of the fighting. General Douglas MacArthur, former World War II hero in the Pacific, served as commander of all UN forces.

In early fighting, the North Koreans pushed the South Koreans back almost to Pusan. This city was on the southeastern tip of the Korean peninsula. MacArthur reversed the situation by landing his troops at Inchon. This was a port city behind the North Korean lines. It was a daring, dangerous plan, but it worked.

Squeezed between enemy troops coming at them from the north and south, the North Koreans soon retreated across the 38th parallel. General MacArthur requested permission of his superiors to pursue the enemy into North Korea. The UN and President Truman agreed. The president hoped the invasion might lead to a reunion of the two Koreas. The UN forces pushed northward beyond the 38th parallel (latitude) toward the Yalu

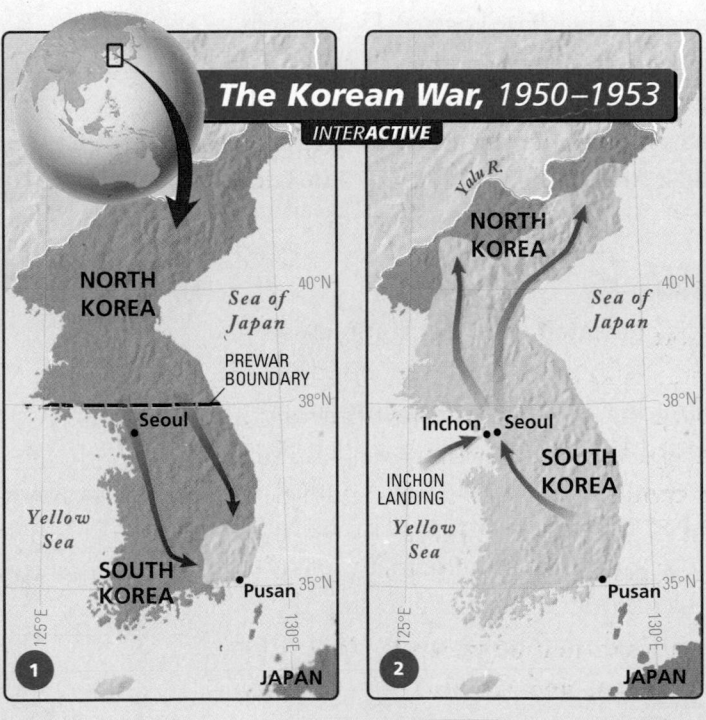
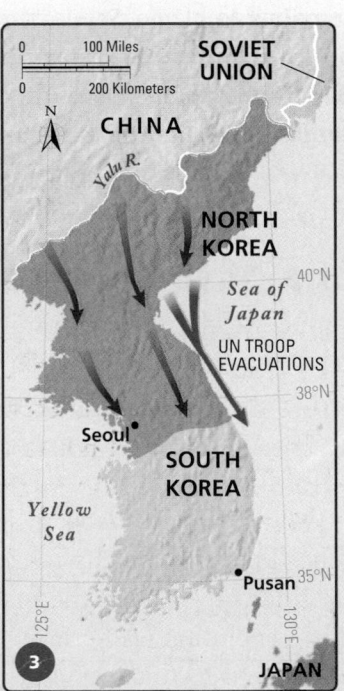
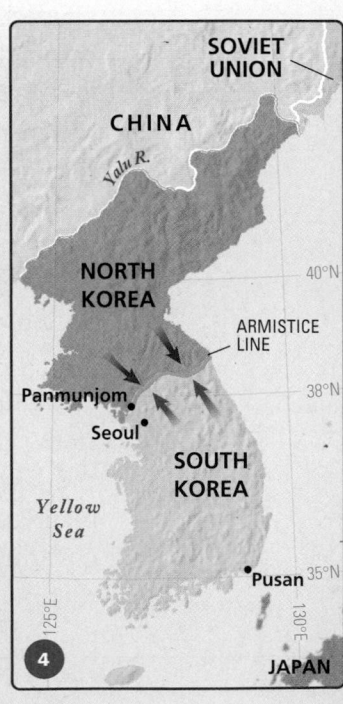

The Korean War, 1950–1953
INTERACTIVE

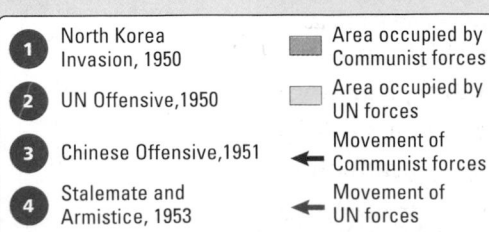

1. North Korea Invasion, 1950
2. UN Offensive, 1950
3. Chinese Offensive, 1951
4. Stalemate and Armistice, 1953

Area occupied by Communist forces
Area occupied by UN forces
Movement of Communist forces
Movement of UN forces

GEOGRAPHY SKILLBUILDER Interpreting Maps

1. **Movement** In map 1, which forces moved south almost to Pusan?
2. **Region** Compare the prewar boundary in map 1 with the armistice line in map 4. Which side gained slightly more territory?

River, the boundary separating China from North Korea. The Chinese warned them to stop.

China Enters the Conflict

Reading History
A. Reading a Map Find the 38th parallel on the maps on page 796. Notice the movement of Communist and UN forces back and forth across this parallel.

Communist China saw the movement of UN forces into North Korea as a threat to China's security. Chinese leaders warned that a further advance would force them to enter the war. Ignoring this warning, UN forces pushed on toward the Yalu River. On November 25, 1950, hundreds of thousands of Chinese Communist troops attacked in human waves across the Yalu River into North Korea. They drove UN troops back to South Korea. By early 1951, the two sides were deadlocked along the 38th parallel.

American and South Korean troops search prisoners after the Inchon landing.

General MacArthur requested permission to blockade China's coastline and bomb China. Truman refused. The president feared that such action would draw the Soviet Union in and make the conflict a world war. The general went over the president's head to win support for his war aims. He spoke and wrote to newspaper and magazine publishers. He also wrote to Republican leaders.

Reading History
B. Making Inferences What effect might MacArthur's actions have had on the idea of civilian control of the military?

As president, Truman was commander in chief of the armed forces. He viewed MacArthur's public criticism of his orders as undermining civilian control of the military. As a result, Truman fired MacArthur and ordered him home. When MacArthur returned to the United States, his admirers treated him as a hero. His farewell speech to Congress won the sympathy of many. "I now close my military career and just fade away—an old soldier who tried to do his duty as God gave him the light to see that duty. Good-bye." Despite support for MacArthur, Truman refused to back down. Most Americans came to agree with the president's actions.

War Ends in Stalemate

As the war dragged on, it became more unpopular. In July 1951, Truman accepted a Soviet suggestion that truce talks begin. The talks dragged on for two years. They continued through the 1952 presidential campaign. When Truman decided not to run again, the Democrats chose Illinois governor Adlai Stevenson as their candidate. The Republicans picked World War II hero General Dwight D. Eisenhower. Ike, as voters liked to call him, criticized the unpopular war. He promised to go to Korea to seek a speedy end to the conflict.

Eisenhower made good on his promise when he won a landslide victory. During talks with the North Koreans and Chinese, he agreed to compromise to end the war. But he also warned privately that he was ready to use nuclear weapons and carry the war into China. A cease-fire ended the fighting in July 1953. The two Koreas were left more or less where they had been in 1950 with a border near the 38th parallel. Communism had been contained in Korea. However, Americans felt frustrated by the indecisive war. Some politicians selfishly made use of this frustration.

McCarthy and Communism

One such politician was **Joseph McCarthy,** a Republican senator from Wisconsin. He used the Korean War to fan Americans' fears of communism. In February 1950, McCarthy declared that he had a list of 205 State Department officials who belonged to the Communist Party. These charges were never proven. Nonetheless, McCarthy's claim launched a hunt for Communists that wrecked the careers of thousands of people. The term *McCarthyism* came to stand for reckless charges against innocent citizens.

In the spring of 1954, the Senate held hearings. During these nationally televised Army-McCarthy hearings, McCarthy accused the U.S. Army of "coddling Communists." Army spokesmen then charged McCarthy's staff with improper conduct. McCarthy responded with unsupported charges against a young lawyer helping to represent the Army. Joseph Welch, the Army counsel, spoke out against McCarthy.

Senator Joseph McCarthy during the 1954 Army-McCarthy hearings

A VOICE FROM THE PAST

Until this moment, Senator, I think I never really gauged your cruelty or your recklessness. . . . Senator. You have done enough. Have you no sense of decency, sir, at long last? Have you left no sense of decency?

Joseph Welch, Army-McCarthy hearings, April 22, 1954

Americans watching the exchange between McCarthy and Welch were shocked by McCarthy's conduct. After the Senate issued a statement censuring, or criticizing, his conduct, he faded from public view.

*Reading*History
C. Summarizing What were some of McCarthy's charges?

Eisenhower and the Cold War

Like Truman, President Eisenhower waged the Cold War. Eisenhower's Secretary of State was John Foster Dulles. Dulles rejected Truman's containment policy. He favored a more aggressive stand. He urged the overthrow of Communist governments. In 1956, Dulles announced that the United States would go to the brink of war to combat communism. This approach was known as **brinksmanship.**

In August 1949, Americans learned that the Soviet Union had produced an atomic bomb, in part by using information stolen by Soviet spies. The two superpowers were soon locked in an **arms race**, developing weapons with more destructive power. In 1952, the United States built a hydrogen bomb, or **H-bomb.** Three years later the Soviets tested their H-bomb. Fear led both sides to build up huge nuclear stockpiles.

In the 1950s, both the United States and the Soviet Union helped allies and weakened enemies around the world. In 1953 in Iran, the U.S. government's Central Intelligence Agency (CIA) helped topple a leader whom they thought might seek Soviet aid. In 1954, the CIA trained an army that succeeded in overthrowing Guatemala's President Jacobo Arbenz Guzmán. The United States believed he favored communism.

During Eisenhower's presidency, the Suez Canal in Egypt, which connected the Mediterranean Sea and the Red Sea, was at the center of another Cold War conflict. In 1955, Egypt's ties with the Soviet Union angered Britain and the United States. The two Western powers withdrew aid to Egypt. Gamal Abdel Nasser, Egypt's leader, reacted by seizing the canal, which was owned by France and Britain. France, Britain, and Israel jointly attacked Egypt. The Soviet Union threatened to support Egypt. The United States, along with the Soviets and the rest of the UN, pressured France, Britain, and Israel to withdraw from Egypt. The UN imposed a cease-fire.

In 1957, the superpowers began a **space race.** The Soviet Union stunned the world by launching the world's first space satellite. They sent *Sputnik* into orbit around the earth. This meant that the Soviet Union had a missile powerful enough to reach the United States. American scientists raced to launch a satellite. Congress set aside billions of dollars for space research.

Eisenhower suggested easing tensions through face-to-face talks. A setback to such efforts occurred in May 1960. The president was to meet in Paris with Soviet Premier Nikita Khrushchev. Two weeks before the meeting, the Soviets shot down an American U-2 plane. The spy plane had been flying over the Soviet Union. Eisenhower denied the aircraft was a spy plane until the pilot was captured. Khrushchev demanded an apology. When the president refused, the talks collapsed. Meanwhile, America was changing at home, as you will read in the next section.

Connections TO SCIENCE

SPUTNIK

The 184-pound *Sputnik 1* (shown below), whose name means "traveling companion," was the first man-made object to orbit the Earth. Circling every 96 minutes, it remained in orbit until early 1958. *Sputnik 2* carried a dog into space.

In 1961, the Soviet Union sent Yuri Gagarin into space to orbit the earth. The Americans lagged behind because the rockets that carried U.S. satellites were smaller and less powerful. The early Soviet lead disappeared, however, as American scientists and engineers found ways to improve rocket design, construction, and testing.

Section 2 Assessment

1. Terms & Names

Explain the significance of:

- Mao Zedong
- 38th parallel
- Korean War
- Joseph McCarthy
- brinksmanship
- arms race
- H-bomb
- space race

2. Using Graphics

Create a time line of up to five events that played a part in the Korean War from its beginning to end.

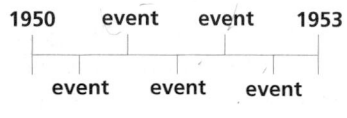

1950   event   event   1953

event   event   event

Which event do you think was most important? Why?

3. Main Ideas

a. Why did war break out in Korea? How did it end?

b. Why was McCarthy able to wield so much power during the 1950s?

c. How did Eisenhower's approach to the Cold War differ from Truman's?

4. Critical Thinking

Drawing Conclusions
How was U.S. involvement in Korea an example of the Truman Doctrine in action?

THINK ABOUT

- U.S. concerns about North Korean leadership
- U.S. goals for ending conflict
- the conflict's outcome

ACTIVITY OPTIONS

SCIENCE

ART

Research the problems of putting a satellite in orbit. Prepare a **report** explaining how these problems were solved, or draw a **design** of a rocket.

The Fifties

3

MAIN IDEA	WHY IT MATTERS NOW	TERMS & NAMES
While the United States was locked in a Cold War, social and economic changes took place in American life.	The American economy and popular culture continue to spread their influence around the globe.	suburb sunbelt baby boom rock 'n' roll

ONE AMERICAN'S STORY

LaVern Baker was one of many talented African-American artists to play a part in the popular music of the 1950s. Her records at first sold mostly to African-American teenagers. White singers covered, or copied, her songs. Baker was annoyed that remakes of her songs by white singers outsold her originals. She made the following comment about one such singer.

A VOICE FROM THE PAST

When I went to Australia with Bill Haley, Big Joe Turner, the Platters, and Freddy Bell and the Bellboys, I left her my [flight] insurance policy. I sent it to her with a letter, "Since I'll be away and you won't have anything new to copy, you might as well take this."

LaVern Baker, quoted in *USA Today*, March 12, 1997

This is the cover of a long-playing record album by LaVern Baker.

In 1990, Baker was admitted to the Rock and Roll Hall of Fame. The following section describes social, political, and cultural changes during the 1950s.

The Domestic Scene in the Fifties

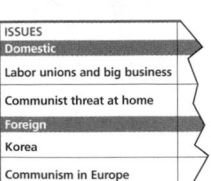
Taking Notes

Use your chart to take notes about big business.

ISSUES
Domestic
Labor unions and big business
Communist threat at home
Foreign
Korea
Communism in Europe

Not everyone prospered in the 1950s. In 1957, nearly one out of every five Americans lived in poverty. Many of the nation's poorest were in cities. In his book *The Other America* (1962), Michael Harrington called attention to the forgotten poor. They were the people left behind as more well-to-do Americans headed for the **suburbs**—residential areas surrounding a city. Shops and businesses moved to suburbia as well.

Fewer people remained in the city to pay taxes for such services as garbage collection, firefighting, and road repair. Often those most affected by urban decay were African Americans and Latinos. Many could not afford homes in the suburbs.

In the 1950s, immigration from Mexico increased greatly. Many people crossed the border illegally. Others came through the government-sponsored *bracero,* or temporary worker, program. The *braceros* found jobs on farms in the Southwest and Midwest. There they often earned low wages and endured difficult living and working conditions.

Despite this, when the program ended, many stayed on illegally. Employers took advantage of them. Fearful of being sent back to Mexico, workers were forced to work longer hours for lower pay.

When Eisenhower ran for president, he promised to steer a middle course. Once elected, Eisenhower pleased business leaders and conservatives without upsetting moderates and liberals. Although he disliked big government spending programs, Eisenhower kept most New Deal programs. He agreed to expand Social Security. He increased the minimum wage for workers. He also created the Department of Health, Education, and Welfare. He even backed some new spending. For example, Congress passed the Highway Act of 1956. This act provided $32 billion to build 41,000 miles of highway.

Changes Sweep America

In the postwar period, Americans began to feel more prosperous. The Depression and World War II had led many couples to put off marrying and starting a family. Now with the economy booming, Americans were getting married and having children. During the 1950s, the United States grew by almost 30 million people. This increase was mostly because of the **baby boom,** a sharp increase in the U.S. birthrate following World War II (from about 1946 through 1961). The number of families with three or four children increased dramatically.

The baby boom also spurred the growth of suburbs. Growing families left crowded city apartments for a house in the suburbs. Irving, Texas, a suburb of Dallas, was typical. In 1950, it had around 2,600 residents. Ten years later, 45,000 people lived there. To serve the suburbs, shopping centers, movie theaters, and restaurants sprouted up on what was once farmland. As suburbs grew, car sales exploded. In the suburbs, owning a car was a necessity. Few buses or other forms of public transportation existed.

In the 1950s, Americans not only moved from city to suburb. They also moved from the north and east to the south and west. The movement of people to the **sunbelt** increased the population of the warmer states of the South and Southwest. In the 1960s, California surpassed New York as the nation's most populous state.

STRANGE *but* True

FROM AUTOBAHN TO INTERSTATE

In the 1930s, Germany began to build a vast network of limited access, four-lane highways called *autobahns.* Germans believed these roads would have great military value.

During World War II, General Eisenhower saw the German road system firsthand. He was impressed by the way these highways enabled Germans to quickly move troops and supplies. President Eisenhower remembered Germany's *autobahns* when he called on Congress to pass the Highway Act of 1956. This act created the nation's first interstate highway system. A cloverleaf interchange is shown below.

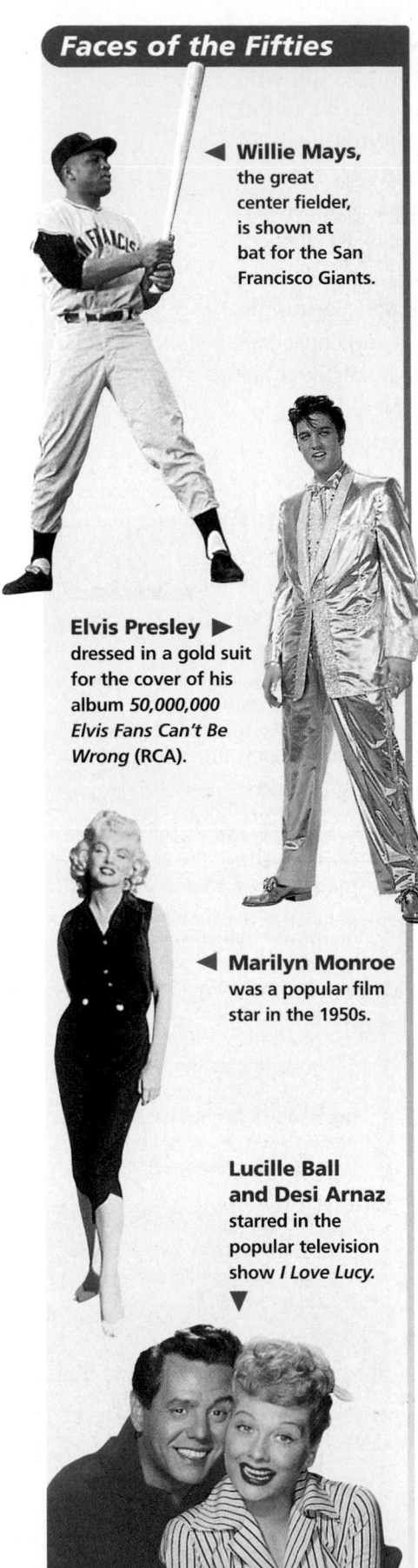

◄ **Willie Mays,** the great center fielder, is shown at bat for the San Francisco Giants.

Elvis Presley ► dressed in a gold suit for the cover of his album *50,000,000 Elvis Fans Can't Be Wrong* (RCA).

◄ **Marilyn Monroe** was a popular film star in the 1950s.

Lucille Ball and Desi Arnaz starred in the popular television show *I Love Lucy.*
▼

The American Dream in the Fifties

For millions of mainly white Americans, life in the suburbs was the American dream. They were happy to live in affordable, single-family houses. People welcomed the chance to send their children to good schools. Americans shopped in malls where parking was free and easy to find. They didn't care if their houses looked alike. Parents wanted a safe place in which to raise their children.

Many critics worried that Americans were being forced to fit into suburban life. Some argued that in business offices and suburbs, people felt pressured to conform—that is, to agree with the beliefs and ideas of the majority. Yet most Americans seemed willing to conform for the rewards of a comfortable life.

In the 1950s, popular magazines, films, and television programs praised women for their roles as homemakers. *Time* magazine called women the "keeper[s] of the suburban dream." But not all women felt fulfilled in this role. Some felt bored or isolated. Those working outside the home had limited job choices. Openings were largely in nursing, teaching, and office work.

By the mid-1950s, American industry was churning out goods for consumers to buy. The economy was booming. Americans filled their houses with dishwashers, washing machines, clothes dryers, and vacuum cleaners. The suburban living room or den showed off the family's television, tape recorder, and high-fidelity record player. The garage held a lawn mower. Barbecue equipment and patio furniture filled the backyard. Owning the latest car or appliance came to be a symbol of social standing and success. The advertising industry encouraged consumers to join the spending spree. Television helped advertisers lure buyers to stores and car showrooms.

Pop Culture and Rock 'n' Roll

In the 1950s, Hollywood cranked out westerns, musicals, and romances. However, movie attendance plummeted as more and more people stayed home to watch TV. By 1960, nine out of ten households owned a set. One of the most popular shows of the decade was the situation comedy (sitcom) *I Love Lucy.* It starred Lucille Ball as the zany wife of bandleader Desi Arnaz. In *Father Knows Best* and many other Fifties sitcoms,

*Reading***History**

A. Drawing Conclusions What might be some of the advantages and disadvantages of fitting in?

*Reading*History

B. Making Inferences Do you think such television shows reflected life in the average American family? Why?

cheerful moms kept the house spotless. The dads worked to support the family. On *Father Knows Best*, Mr. Anderson exercised kindly but firm control over his children, who seldom rebelled.

Young children watched *Lassie, The Lone Ranger, The Howdy Doody Show,* and the *Mickey Mouse Club*. Their teenage sisters and brothers had fallen head over heels for another form of entertainment—**rock 'n' roll** music. In 1955, Bill Haley and His Comets hit it big with "Rock Around the Clock." By the mid-1950s, Chuck Berry, Little Richard, Fats Domino, and other black musicians held the spotlight with white rockers like Jerry Lee Lewis. But the largest fan club belonged to Elvis Presley. With such songs as "Heartbreak Hotel" and "Don't Be Cruel," he became the king of rock 'n' roll. His onstage bumps and shakes delighted teenagers.

In the mid-1950s, Allen Ginsberg and Jack Kerouac led a group of poets and writers. They protested what they saw as the shallowness and conformity of American society. Known as "beatniks," their followers filled coffeehouses to hear their heated attacks on "square" society. A Democratic presidential candidate, John F. Kennedy, also wanted to shake up the dullness of the Eisenhower years.

The Election of 1960

The 1960 presidential election was one of the closest in U.S. history. John Fitzgerald Kennedy, Democratic senator from Massachusetts, defeated Richard M. Nixon, Eisenhower's vice president. At age 43, Kennedy was the nation's youngest elected president. He was also the first Catholic president. Kennedy had campaigned to "get this country moving again" after the Eisenhower years. Kennedy and Nixon staged the first televised presidential debates. Kennedy's youthful energy and confidence helped him to win. In the next chapter, you will read about Kennedy's role in setting domestic policy, including civil rights.

Section Assessment

1. Terms & Names

Explain the significance of:
• suburb
• baby boom
• sunbelt
• rock 'n' roll

2. Using Graphics

Create a web like the one below to examine the way life was changing the United States in the 1950s.

1950s American Life

3. Main Ideas

a. How did the movement to the suburbs affect the urban poor?

b. What caused the 1950s baby boom? How did the baby boom contribute to suburban growth?

c. How did television affect American life in the 1950s?

4. Critical Thinking

Contrasting Do you think the American Dream for most Americans today would be the same as it was in the 1950s? Why?

THINK ABOUT
• expectations about suburban/urban living
• changes in transportation and workplace

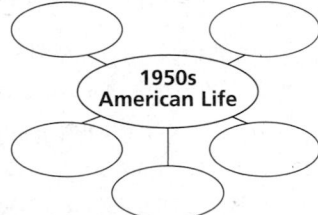

ACTIVITY OPTIONS

TECHNOLOGY

MUSIC

Research one aspect of music in the 1950s, and either plan a **Web page** to share your information, or write your own **song** that fits this time period.

The Cold War and the American Dream **803**

Route 66

America was changing, and few things contributed more to that change than U.S. Highway Route 66. Completed in the summer of 1926, this road connected small towns from Chicago to Los Angeles. Its course across the Heartland enabled farmers to move grain and produce to the big cities.

In the 1930s, farmers escaping the Great Plains' Dust Bowl fled westward along this highway. The first service stations—full-service gas stations—were built along Route 66. In the 1940s, it became an important route for the movement of troops and supplies. By the 1950s, a culture had developed along the highway. This roadside culture included the motor hotel (or motel), roadside diners, and tourist traps.

So many people were on the road that bigger, faster, wider highways were needed. These highways didn't go through the small towns connected by Route 66. With the new superhighways bypassing them, many of the well-known sights along Route 66 vanished.

WYOMING

COLORADO

CALIFORNIA

NEVADA

SLEEP in a Wigwam

ARIZONA

ROUTE 66

SANTA MONICA, CA

SAN BERNARDINO, CA

LOS ANGELES, CA

NEEDLES, CA

FLAGSTAFF, AZ

ALBUQUERQUE, NM

NEW MEXICO

PACIFIC OCEAN

SNOW CAP

·MALTS· *Creamy Root Beer* ·SHAKES·

ARTIFACT FILE

America's Main Street
Many of the towns, tourist traps, and beauty spots along Route 66 became popular destinations. Route 66 was often called "America's Main Street" because it ran through the centers of the small towns it connected.

GREETINGS from US 66 *Scenic* MISSOURI

Roadside Drive-In
Roadside food stands such as this one in Seligman, Arizona, were found all along Route 66.

804

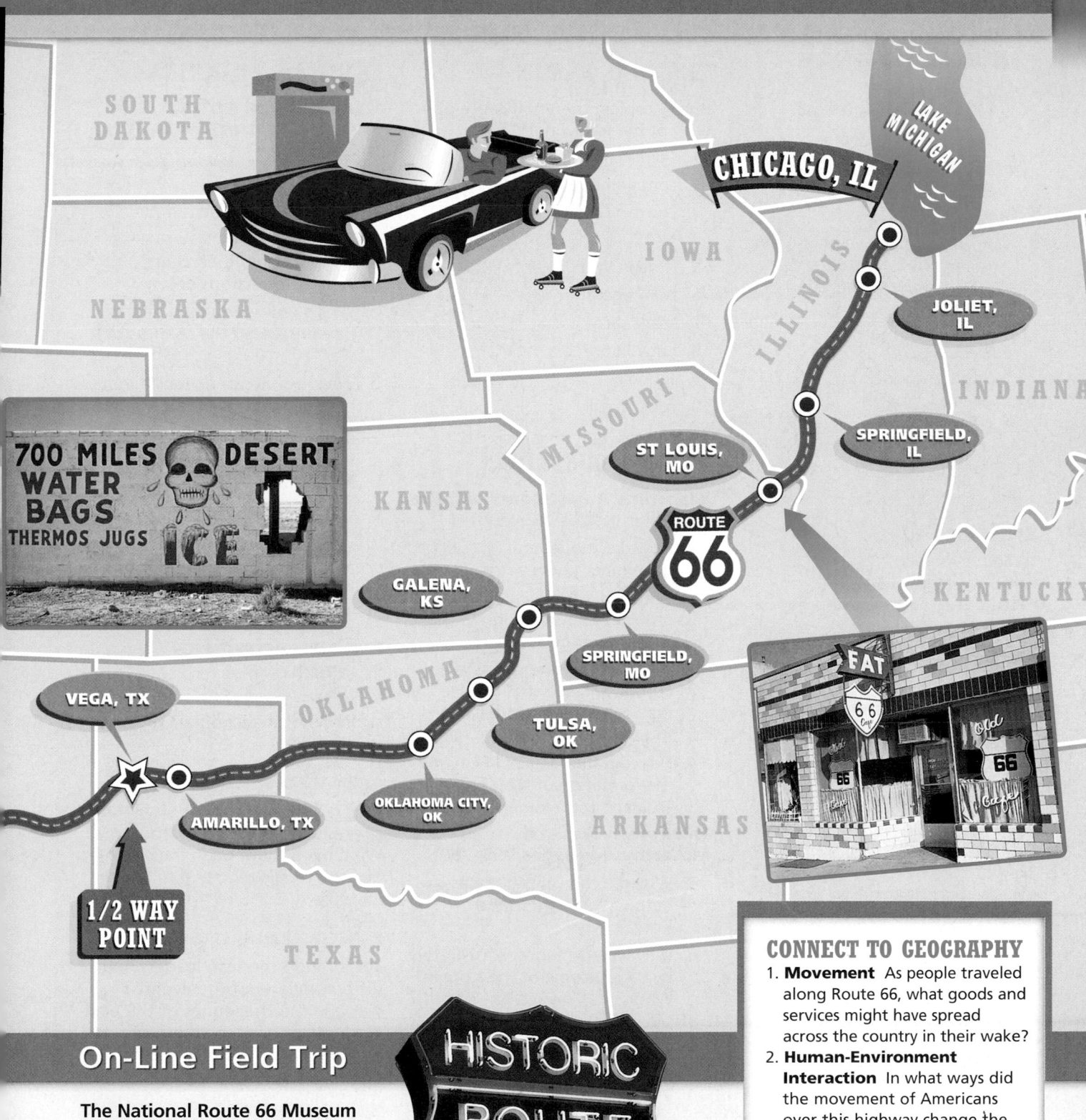

SOUTH DAKOTA

NEBRASKA

IOWA

CHICAGO, IL

LAKE MICHIGAN

ILLINOIS

INDIANA

JOLIET, IL

SPRINGFIELD, IL

MISSOURI

ST LOUIS, MO

KANSAS

700 MILES DESERT, WATER BAGS THERMOS JUGS ICE

ROUTE 66

GALENA, KS

SPRINGFIELD, MO

KENTUCKY

EAT 66

OKLAHOMA

TULSA, OK

VEGA, TX

AMARILLO, TX

OKLAHOMA CITY, OK

ARKANSAS

1/2 WAY POINT

TEXAS

On-Line Field Trip

HISTORIC ROUTE 66

The National Route 66 Museum is in Elk City, Oklahoma. Many such organizations preserve historic landmarks along Route 66. Each of the states along the road has its own Route 66 Association. There is also a National Historic Route 66 Federation.

For more about Route 66 . . .

RESEARCH LINKS
CLASSZONE.COM

CONNECT TO GEOGRAPHY

1. **Movement** As people traveled along Route 66, what goods and services might have spread across the country in their wake?
2. **Human-Environment Interaction** In what ways did the movement of Americans over this highway change the environment?

   See Geography Handbook, page 5.

CONNECT TO HISTORY

3. **Drawing Conclusions** In what ways did Route 66 contribute to the American Dream?

VISUAL SUMMARY

The Cold War and the American Dream

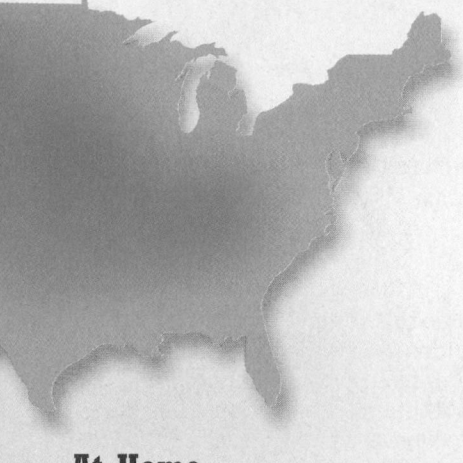

At Home

1940s:
- Truman faces labor unrest.
- Fear of communism spreads.
- Fair Deal is proposed.
- Equal rights for all remains a problem.

1950s:
- The economy booms under Eisenhower.
- McCarthy gains and loses power.
- Billions are spent on space research.
- Rock 'n' roll transforms popular culture.

Abroad

1940s:
- Truman Doctrine is announced.
- Marshall Plan offers aid to Europe.
- Berlin airlift takes place.
- NATO is formed.

1950s:
- Korean War ends in stalemate.
- Dulles practices brinksmanship.
- *Sputnik* is launched.
- Arms race takes place between superpowers.

TERMS & NAMES

Briefly explain the significance of each of the following.

1. Cold War
2. containment
3. Truman Doctrine
4. NATO
5. Korean War
6. brinksmanship
7. space race
8. baby boom
9. sunbelt
10. rock 'n' roll

REVIEW QUESTIONS

Peacetime Adjustments and the Cold War (pages 789–794)

1. How did the federal government help veterans?
2. Why was inflation a bigger problem than recession in the postwar period?
3. Why was the fate of Eastern Europe an issue that divided the Soviet Union from its former allies?
4. How did the Marshall Plan and the formation of NATO reflect Truman's containment policy?

The Korean War and McCarthyism (pages 795–799)

5. Why did the United States become involved in the Korean War?
6. Why were Americans frustrated by the outcome of the Korean War?
7. How was McCarthy able to gain such a powerful hold on the government and the American public?

The Fifties (pages 800–805)

8. What groups were left out of postwar prosperity?
9. What factors boosted the growth of suburbs?
10. Why did Americans become bigger consumers in the 1950s?

CRITICAL THINKING

1. USING YOUR NOTES: CATEGORIZING INFORMATION

ISSUES	PRESIDENTS	
Domestic	Truman	Eisenhower
Labor unions and big business		
Communist threat at home		
Foreign		
Korea		
Communism in Europe		

Using your completed chart, answer the questions below.

a. Which policy or action might have increased the chances of war?
b. What policies or actions might have led to a stalemate?
c. In your opinion, could anything have been done to end the Korean War sooner?

2. APPLYING CITIZENSHIP SKILLS

Was McCarthyism or communism a greater threat to the American way of life? Explain (or support) your opinion.

3. THEME: ECONOMICS IN HISTORY

What factors contributed most strongly to the economic prosperity of the 1950s?

4. ANALYZING LEADERSHIP

Why did Truman consider it his duty as president to fire MacArthur? What might have been the consequences of allowing him to remain in Korea?

5. RECOGNIZING EFFECTS

Soviet and American leaders had different views of the events of war and the challenges of the postwar period. How did these different views contribute to the mistrust and fear of the Cold-War era?

Interact *with* History

How did the American Dream you discussed before you read the chapter compare with the dreams that people actually pursued?

STANDARDS-BASED ASSESSMENT

Use the graph and your knowledge of U.S. history to answer questions 1 and 2.

Additional Test Practice, pp. S1–S33.

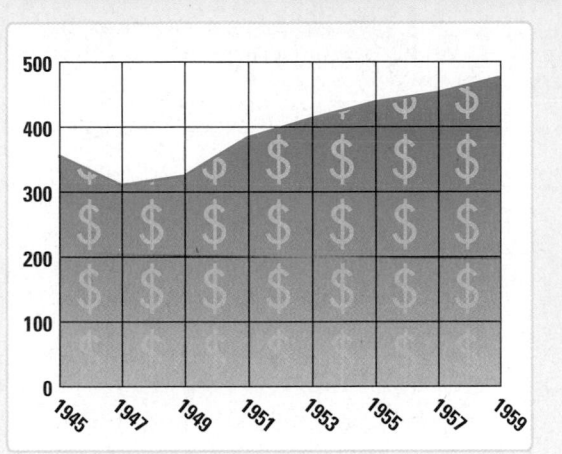

Gross National Product, 1945–1959

1. In dollars, approximately how much did the GNP increase between 1945 and 1951?
   A. about $10 billion
   B. about $30 billion
   C. about $50 billion
   D. about $100 billion

2. About how much did the GNP increase between 1951 and 1959?
   A. about $20 billion
   B. about $50 billion
   C. about $90 billion
   D. about $150 billion

This quotation from Winston Churchill is about Europe after World War II. Use the quotation and your knowledge of U.S. history to answer question 3.

PRIMARY SOURCE

From Stettin in the Baltic to Trieste in the Adriatic, an iron curtain has descended across the continent. Behind that line lie all the . . . states of Central and Eastern Europe. . . . All these . . . population . . . lie in the Soviet sphere and all are subject . . . not only to Soviet influence but to . . . increasing . . . control from Moscow.

Winston Churchill, "Iron Curtain" speech, Fulton, Missouri

3. According to Churchill, what significant danger did the "iron curtain" present?
   A. Europe would be separated by it.
   B. Communism could expand behind it.
   C. Food would not be accessible behind it.
   D. Travelers could not get around it.

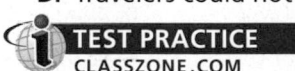
TEST PRACTICE
CLASSZONE.COM

ALTERNATIVE ASSESSMENT

1. WRITING ABOUT HISTORY

Since the collapse of the Soviet Union, many former Warsaw Pact nations have wanted to become NATO members. Write an **essay** for or against NATO expansion.

• Use library resources to learn more about NATO and its goals.

• Use your research to support your opinion.

2. COOPERATIVE LEARNING

With a group of classmates, examine images of the American family and family life in the media of the 1950s. Look at advertisements in magazines and books of the era, and if possible view TV reruns of 1950s sitcoms. Then prepare a short TV show about a 1950s family. Group members can take on the roles of writers, actors, director, and a narrator.

INTEGRATED TECHNOLOGY

DOING INTERNET RESEARCH

Popular culture in the 1950s included music, television, and movies. Prepare an electronic presentation about one aspect of popular culture of the Fifties.

• Use the Internet and the library to find articles and pictures about popular shows, music, and celebrities of the period.

• Possible topics for your presentation include bands or record companies; popular films, movie stars, or drive-in theaters; clothing, hairstyles, or teen life; or television shows and viewing habits of the American public.

For more about the 1950s . . .

INTERNET ACTIVITY
CLASSZONE.COM

Tensions at Home and Abroad

Dr. Martin Luther King, Jr., waves to demonstrators at the March on Washington in 1963.

CHAPTER 15

The Nation Breaking Apart 1846–186

Section 1
Growing Tensions Between North and South

Section 2
The Crisis Deepens

Section 3
Slavery Dominates Politics

Section 4
Lincoln's Election and Southern Secession

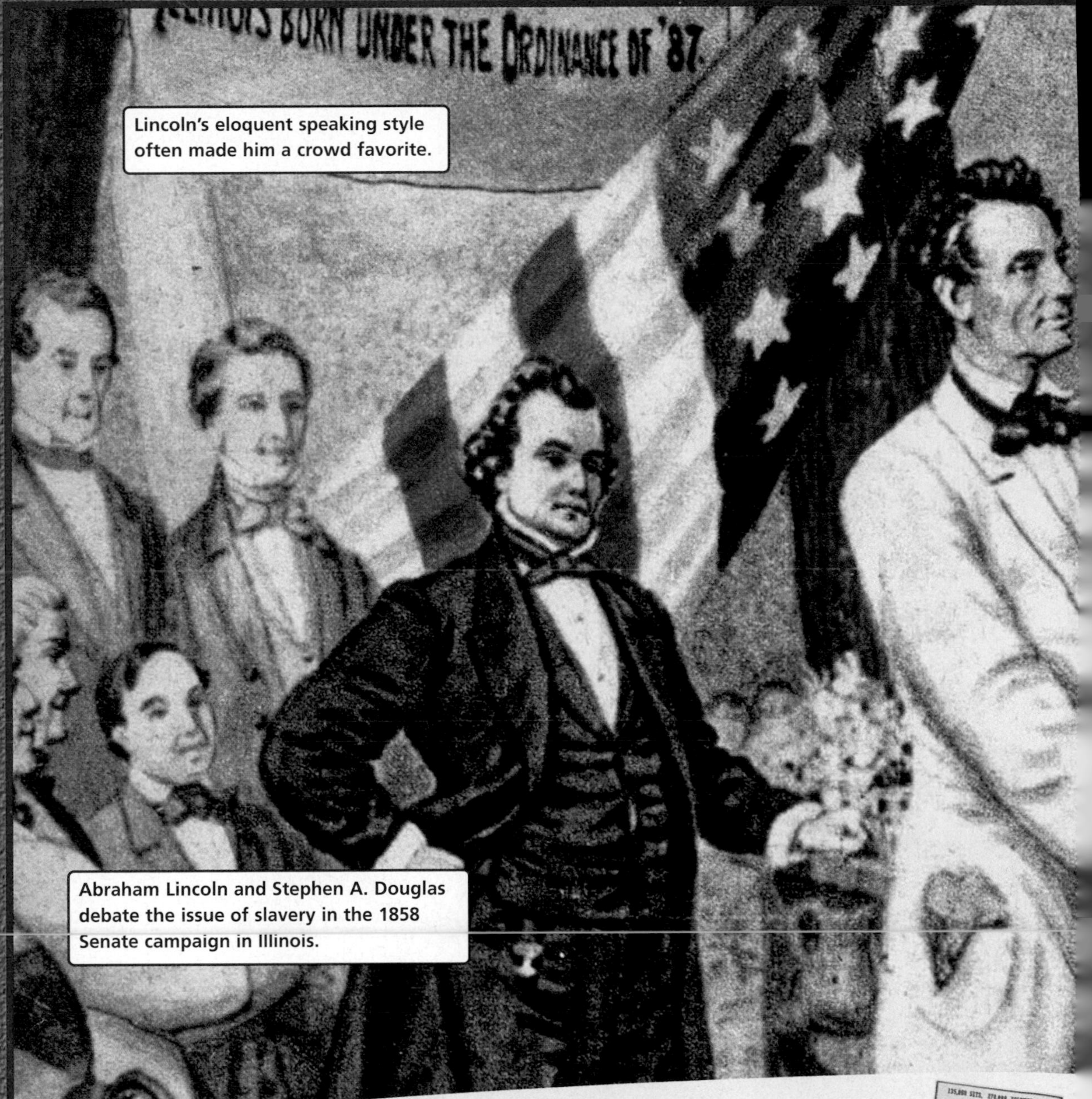
BORN UNDER THE ORDINANCE OF '87.

Lincoln's eloquent speaking style often made him a crowd favorite.

Abraham Lincoln and Stephen A. Douglas debate the issue of slavery in the 1858 Senate campaign in Illinois.

USA

1846
War with Mexico begins.
Wilmot Proviso is introduced.

1848
Zachary Taylor is elected president.

1850
President Taylor dies. Millard Fillmore becomes president.
Congress passes the Compromise of 1850.

1852
Uncle Tom's Cabin is published.
Franklin Pierce is elected president.

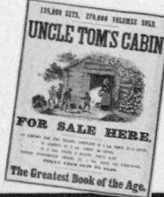

UNCLE TOM'S CABIN
FOR SALE HERE.
The Greatest Book of the Age.

World

1848
Rebellions erupt across Europe.

1850
Taiping Rebellion begins in China.

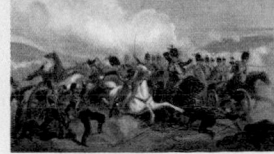

1853
Crimean Wa
begins.

"*Government of the people, by the people, for the people, shall not perish from the earth.*"

—*Abraham Lincoln, Gettysburg Address*

Gettysburg, Pennsylvania, was the site of the most decisive battle of the Civil War.

INDEX

An *i* preceding a page reference in italics indicates that there is an illustration, and usually text information as well, on that page. An *m* or a *c* preceding an italic page reference indicates a map or a chart, as well as text information on that page.

A

Abilene, Kan., 559, 560
abolition of slavery, 440–441
  amendments to Constitution for, 270
  Emancipation Proclamation and, 503–505
absolute location, 4
Abzug, Bella, *i827*
Acadians, *i149*
Across Five Aprils, 486–487
Adams, Abigail, *i176*
Adams, John, 165, *i166, i212,* R36
  in Continental Congress, 171
  death of, 371
  and Declaration of Independence, 159
  Jefferson and, 313, 316
  as president, 305–307
Adams, John Quincy, 359, 369–370, *i370,* R36
  abolition and, 441
  defense of *Amistad* rebels, 441
Adams, Samuel, 164, 165, *i166,* 172
Adams-Onis Treaty, 357
Addams, Jane, 612, *i613,* 640, 651–652
Adena people, 31
adobe, 35
affirmation, 257
affirmative action
  in college admissions, 910–911
Afghanistan
  terrorists and, 878, 895
  U.S. military action in, 878, 895, *i895*
AFL, 603, 743
Africa
  early civilizations in, 39–43, *m40*
  exploration of, 49
  Garvey's movement and, 715
  killer bees in, *i75*
  slave trade in, 77–79
  in World War II, 763–765, *m764*
African Americans
  abolition movement and, 440–441
  in American Revolution, 194
  as artists, 431
  in baseball, 628–629, 722–723, *i722, i723*
  as "buffalo soldiers," 571
  in cattle industry, 560
  civil rights, 903, 907, 911

civil rights movement and, 812, 813–817, 818–823
in Civil War, 489, 505–506, *i506*
Constitutional Convention and, 229
in Great Depression, 742–743, 744
Great Migration of, 693, 698, 715
Harlem Renaissance and, 720
Ku Klux Klan and, 716
and music, 717, 720, 800
obstacles to education of, 435
peonage and, 623
population in pre-Civil War South, 350–351
Reconstruction and, 533–536, 545–549
segregation and, 620–623, *i811,* 902–903, 906–907
slavery of, 118, 119, 121, 122, 123, 349–350, 351–353, *i351,* 446–447, 462–463, 503–505, 900–901
in sports, 628
Thirteenth Amendment and, 270, 521
in Vietnam War, 847
voting rights of, 271, 535, *i536*
in World War I, 687, 689
after World War II, 790–791
in World War II, 763–764, 775
African Diaspora, 78
Agee, James, 741
Agent Orange, 843
Agnew, Spiro, 861
AIM, 825–826
airline industry. *See* industry, airline.
airplanes, *i627, i681,* 712
  hijacking of, 892, *m892*
  as terrorist weapons, *i878,* 892, *i893*
Alabama, R34, R39
  secession of, 473
Alabama State Legislature
  representation in 1962, *c909*
Alamo, 129
Alamo, Battle of the, 402–404, *i403*
Alaska, *i10*
  facts about, R34, R39
  national parks in, *m644*
  purchase of, *m660*

Albania, 876
Albany Plan of Union, 149
Alden v. *Maine,* 317
Aldrin, Edwin, *i856*
Aleut people, 33–34
Alexander VI (pope), 61
Alger, Horatio, 596
Algeria, *m764*
Algonquin people, 147
Alien and Sedition Acts, 306, 313, 316
Allen, Ethan, 176–177
Allen, Richard, 215
Allies
  in World War I, 680
  in World War II, *i760,* 762, *m764,* 765–766, 771–773, 780
almanacs, 138
al-Qaeda, 878, 892, 894, 895
amendments, constitutional. *See also* Bill of Rights; *individual amendments by number.*
  procedure for proposal and adoption of, 263, *c263*
  text of, 266–277
American Crisis, The, 196, 198
American Expeditionary Force, 686
American Federation of Labor, 603, 743
American Indian Movement, 825–826
American Railway Union, 646
American Red Cross, *i510,* 687
American Revolution
  beginning of, *m172*
  early years of, 190–199
  events leading to, 157, 159–162, 163–167, 170–173, *m186*
  expansion of, 200–205
  on frontier, *m203*
  in Middle States, 195
  mortality in, *c213*
  in North, *m197*
  people and events of, *c216*
  results of, 211–215, *m213*
  in South, *m209*
  victory in, 206–211
American Samoa, R35
Americans with Disabilities Act, *i270*
American System, 354–355
Amistad, 441

Vietnamization [vietnamización] *s.* estrategia de la guerra de Vietnam de retirar las fuerzas estadounidenses gradualmente y dejar la lucha terrestre en manos de los vietnamitas del Sur. (p. 848)

vigilante [vigilante] *s.* persona dispuesta a tomar la ley en sus propias manos. (p. 561)

Virginia Plan *s.* plan presentado por Edmund Randolph, delegado a la Convención Constitucional de 1787, que proponía un gobierno de tres ramas y una legislatura bicameral en la que la representación se basaría en la población o la riqueza de un estado. (p. 231)

Voting Rights Act of 1965 [ley de los Derechos al Voto] *s.* esta ley prohibía las pruebas de lectura y escritura y otras leyes que impedían que los afroamericanos se anotaran para votar. (p. 821)

war bond [bono de guerra] *s.* préstamo de interés bajo de la población civil al gobierno, que se pagaría dentro de un número de años. (p. 691)

War Hawk *s.* habitante de las regiones del oeste que apoyaba la guerra de 1812. (p. 329)

War Powers Act [ley de Poderes de Guerra] *s.* aprobada en 1973, esta ley limita los poderes del presidente para declarar la guerra sin consultar el Congreso. (p. 849)

War Production Board [Junta de Producción Bélica] *s.* agencia establecida durante la segunda guerra mundial para coordinar la producción de suministros militares por las empresas estadounidenses. (p. 772)

Watergate scandal [escándalo de Watergate] *s.* escándalo que resultó de los esfuerzos del gobierno de Nixon por encubrir su participación en el allanamiento de la Sede Central del Partido Demócrata en el edificio de apartamentos Watergate. (p. 860)

Webster-Hayne debate [debate Webster-Hayne] *s.* debate de 1830 entre Daniel Webster y Robert Hayne sobre la doctrina de la invalidación. (p. 382)

Whig Party [Partido Whig] *s.* partido político organizado en 1834 en oposición a las políticas de Andrew Jackson. (p. 387)

Whiskey Rebellion [rebelión del Whisky] *s.* protesta de 1794 contra el impuesto que impuso el gobierno al whisky, valioso medio económico de los granjeros de la frontera. (p. 301)

Wilderness Road [Camino al Desierto] *s.* sendero a Kentucky que ayudó a construir el pionero Daniel Boone. (p. 221)

Wilmot Proviso [Claúsula de Wilmot] *s.* propuesta de 1846 que excluía la esclavitud de cualquier territorio adquirido como resultado de la guerra con México. (p. 459)

Wounded Knee Massacre [masacre de Wounded Knee] *s.* masacre de 1890 por soldados estadounidenses de 300 amerindios desarmados, en Wounded Knee Creek, Dakota del Sur. (p. 566)

writ of assistance [mandato judicial de transferencia] *s.* orden de registro que permitía a los oficiales británicos entrar en los hogares o comercios coloniales en busca de contrabando. (p. 164)

XYZ Affair [asunto XYZ] *s.* incidente de 1797 en que funcionarios franceses demandaron que los diplomáticos estadounidenses les pagaran un soborno. (p. 306)

Y2K [año 2000] *s.* problema de computadora causado por programas de computadoras que usan sólo los dos últimos dígitos de un año; complicado por la llegada del año 2000. (p. 878)

Yalta Conference [Conferencia de Yalta] *s.* en 1945 Franklin Roosevelt, Winston Churchill y Joseph Stalin discutieron planes para el fin de la segunda guerra mundial y el futuro de Europa. (p. 765)

yellow journalism [periodismo amarillo] *s.* estilo de periodismo que usa la exageración y el sensacionalismo para presentar las noticias. (p. 663)

Yoruba [Yoruba] *s.* gente de África Occidental que constituyó varios estados al sudoeste del río Níger. (p. 42)

Zimmermann telegram [telegrama de Zimmerman] *s.* mensaje enviado en 1917 por el ministro de Relaciones Exteriores alemán al embajador alemán en México proponiendo una alianza entre México y Alemania y prometiendo ayudar a México a recuperar Texas, New Mexico y Arizona si Estados Unidos entraba en la guerra. (p. 682)

temperance movement [movimiento de la templanza] *s.* campaña para acabar con el consumo de las bebidas alcohólicas. (p. 434)

tender *s.* dinero (p. 255)

tenement [casa de vecindad] *s.* edificio de apartamentos generalmente en muy malas condiciones y atestado. (p. 611)

Tet offensive [ofensiva del Tet] *s.* en 1968, ataque sorpresa por las tropas del Vietcong contra las bases militares estadounidenses y más de 100 ciudades y pueblos de Vietnam del Sur durante el Tet, la celebración del año nuevo lunar vietnamita. (p. 844)

Thirteenth Amendment [Enmienda Decimotercera] *s.* enmienda a la Constitución de Estados Unidos adoptada en 1865 que abolía la esclavitud y la servidumbre involuntaria en Estados Unidos. (p. 521)

38th parallel *s.* la región al norte de esta latitud ocupada por las tropas soviéticas en 1945. (p. 795)

Three-Fifths Compromise [Acuerdo de los Tres Quintos] *s.* acuerdo de la Convención Constitucional que establecía que, para efectos de la representación y del cobro de impuestos, se contarían como parte de la población tres quintos de los esclavos de un estado. (p. 232)

Townshend Acts [leyes de Townshend] *s.* serie de leyes aprobadas por el Parlamento en 1767 que suspendieron la Asamblea de Nueva York y establecieron impuestos a las mercancías importadas a las colonias británicas. (p. 163)

Trail of Tears [Sendero de las Lágrimas] *s.* trágica marcha del pueblo cherokee desde sus tierras hasta el Territorio Indio, entre 1838 y 1839; miles de cherokees murieron. (p. 377)

transcendentalism [trascendentalismo] *s.* filosofía del siglo XIX que enseñaba que el mundo espiritual es más importante que el mundo físico y que las personas pueden hallar la verdad dentro de sí mismas mediante los sentimientos y la intuición. (p. 431)

transcontinental railroad [ferrocarril transcontinental] *s.* ferrocarril que se extendía por todo el continente. (p. 590)

Treaty of Ghent [Tratado de Gante] *s.* tratado firmado en 1814 que puso fin a la guerra de 1812; no cambió de dueño ningún territorio ni se resolvieron los conflictos comerciales. (p. 333)

Treaty of Greenville [Tratado de Greenville] *s.* acuerdo de 1795 por el cual 12 tribus amerindias cedieron al gobierno de Estados Unidos gran parte de lo que hoy son los estados de Ohio e Indiana. (p. 300)

Treaty of Guadalupe Hidalgo [Tratado de Guadalupe Hidalgo] *s.* tratado de 1848 que puso fin a la guerra estadounidense con México; México cedió California y Nuevo México a los Estados Unidos. (p. 410)

Treaty of Paris [Tratado de París] *s.* tratado de 1763 que puso fin a la guerra Francesa y Amerindia; Inglaterra entregó toda norteamérica del este del río Mississippi. (p. 150)

Treaty of Paris of 1783 [Tratado de París de 1783] *s.* tratado que puso fin a la guerra Revolucionaria, confirmó la independencia de Estados Unidos y estableció los límites de la nueva nación. (p. 212)

Treaty of Tordesillas [Tratado de Tordesillas] *s.* tratado de 1494 por el cual España y Portugal acordaron repartirse las tierras del hemisferio occidental y movieron la línea de demarcación hacia el oeste. (p. 61)

Treaty of Versailles [Tratado de Versalles] *s.* tratado de 1919 que puso fin a la primera guerra mundial. (p. 696)

trench warfare [guerra de trincheras] *s.* clase de guerra durante la primera guerra mundial en que los combatientes se apiñaban en zanjas fortificadas y se disparaban artillería y fuego de ametralladora. (p. 680)

triangular trade [comercio triangular] *s.* sistema de comercio transatlántico en que se intercambiaban mercancías, incluso esclavos, entre África, Inglaterra, Europa, las Antillas y las colonias de Norte América. (p. 111)

tribunal [tribunal] *s.* corte. (p. 253)

Truman Doctrine [Doctrina Truman] *s.* política que prometía ayuda a la gente que luchaba por resistir las amenazas a la libertad democrática. (p. 793)

trust *s.* cuerpo legal creado para tener una cartera de acciones de varias empresas, con frecuencia en la misma industria. (p. 595)

tundra [tundra] *s.* pradera sin árboles que está permanentemente helada debajo de su capa de superior de tierra. (p. 33)

Twenty-sixth Amendment [Enmienda Vigésima Sexta] *s.* enmienda a la Constitución de Estados Unidos, adoptada en 1971, redujo la edad del derecho a votar de los 21 a los 18 años. (p. 849)

U

unanimous consent [consentimiento unánime] *s.* acuerdo completo. (p. 264)

Uncle Tom's Cabin [*La cabaña del tío Tom*] *s.* novela publicada por Harriet Beecher Stowe en 1852, que mostraba la esclavitud como brutal e inmoral. (p. 462)

unconstitutional [inconstitucional] *adj.* que contradice la ley de la constitución. (p. 317)

Underground Railroad [ferrocarril clandestino] *s.* serie de rutas de escape que usaban los esclavos para escaparse del Sur. (p. 442)

United Nations [Naciones Unidas] *s.* organización internacional para mantener la paz a la que pertenecen la mayoría de las naciones del mundo, creada en 1945 para promover la paz, seguridad y desarrollo económico del mundo. (p. 781)

urbanization [urbanización] *s.* crecimiento de las ciudades como resultado de la industrialización. (p. 609)

U.S.S. *Maine* *s.* barco de guerra estadounidense que explotó misteriosamente y se hundió en el puerto de La Habana, Cuba, el 15 de febrero de 1898. (p. 663)

V

vaquero [vaquero] *s.* peón de ganado que vino de México con los españoles en el siglo XVI. (p. 560)

vaudeville [vodevil] *s.* tipo de espectáculo teatral en vivo con mezcla de canciones, baile y comedia. (p. 629)

viceroyalty [virreinato] *s.* provincia regida por un virrey, que gobernaba en nombre del rey. (p. 71)

Viet Cong *s.* comunista vietnamita. (p. 838)

Sixteenth Amendment [Enmienda Decimosexta] *s.* enmienda a la Constitución de Estados Unidos, ratificada en 1913, que dio al Congreso el poder de crear impuestos a las rentas. (p. 647)

slash-and-burn agriculture [agricultura de corte y quema] *s.* método agrícola en que la gente preparaba los campos cortando y quemando árboles y pastos, cuyas cenizas fertilizaban la tierra. (p. 37)

slave code [código de los esclavos] *s.* ley pasada para reglamentar el tratamiento de los esclavos. (p. 79)

slavery [esclavitud] *s.* sistema de servidumbre humana involuntaria. (p. 76)

slum [barrio bajo] *s.* barrio de casas abarrotadas de gente y peligrosas. (p. 612)

smuggle [contrabandear] *v.* importar o exportar mercancías ilegalmente. (p. 112)

SNCC *s.* organizado en 1960, el Comité Coordinador No Violento de Estudiantes se creó para dar a los jóvenes un papel más importante en el movimiento por los derechos civiles. (p. 817)

social gospel [evangelio social] *s.* movimiento cuyo objetivo era mejorar la vida de los pobres. (p. 612)

socialism [socialismo] *s.* sistema económico en que todos los miembros de una sociedad son propietarios por igual de todas las empresas; los miembros comparten el trabajo y las ganancias (p. 602)

Social Security Act [ley de Seguridad Social] *s.* según esta ley aprobada en 1935, los empleados y los empresarios hacían pagos a un fondo especial, del cual podían recibir una jubilación después de retirarse. (p. 736)

sodbuster *s.* granjero de la frontera. (p. 575)

Songhai *s.* imperio de África Occidental que sucedió a Malí y controló el comercio desde el siglo XV hasta fines del XVI. (p. 42)

Sons of Liberty [Hijos de la Libertad] *s.* grupo de colonos que formaron una sociedad secreta para oponerse a las políticas británicas en los tiempos de la revolución norteamericana. (p. 161)

space race [carrera para conquistar el espacio] *s.* empezando en 1957, la Unión Soviética y Estados Unidos comenzaron a competir en la exploración del espacio. (p. 799)

Spanish-American War *s.* guerra de 1898 que comenzó cuando Estados Unidos demandó que España le concediera la independencia a Cuba. (p. 664)

Spanish Armada [Armada española] *s.* flota de buques enviada en 1588 por el rey español Felipe Segundo para invadir a Inglaterra y restaurar allí el catolicismo romano. (p. 69)

speculation [especulación] *s.* comprar y vender acciones con la esperanza de obtener una ganancia rápida. (p. 730)

sphere of influence [esfera de influencia] *s.* región donde las naciones extranjeras demandan derechos especiales y privilegios económicos. (p. 669)

spiritual [canción espiritual] *s.* canción folklórica religiosa. (p. 351)

spoils system [sistema de prebendas] *s.* práctica de otorgar los candidatos elegidos empleos gubernamentales a los simpatizantes políticos. (p. 373)

Stamp Act [ley del Timbre] *s.* ley aprobada por el Parlamento en 1765 que requería que todos los documentos comerciales y legales llevaran un timbre oficial que indicaba que se había pagado un impuesto. (p. 160)

standard time [hora oficial] *s.* sistema adoptado en 1918 que dividió a Estados Unidos en cuatro zonas horarias. (p. 592)

states' rights [derechos estatales] *s.* teoría que sostenía que los estados tenían el derecho a decidir cuándo el gobierno federal había pasado una ley inconstitucional. (p. 307)

steerage [tercera clase] *s.* nivel o lugar más barato de un barco. (p. 423)

Stono Rebellion [Rebelión de Stono] *s.* sublevación de esclavos de 1739, en Carolina del Sur, que resultó en que se hicieran aún más estrictas las leyes que controlaban a los esclavos. (p. 123)

strategy [estrategia] *s.* plan general de acción. (p. 196)

strike [declararse en huelga] *v.* suspender los obreros el trabajo para tratar de conseguir condiciones de trabajo mejores. (p. 434)

subsistence farm *v.* una granja que produce bastante alimento para la familia con sólo una pequeña cantidad para vender. (p. 110)

suburb [barrio residencial] *s.* área residencial que rodea a una ciudad. (p. 800)

suffrage [sufragio] *s.* derecho a votar. (pp. 262, 444)

Sugar Act [ley del Azúcar] *s.* ley aprobada por el Parlamento en 1764 que impuso impuestos al azúcar, la melaza y otros productos que llegaban a las colonias; también establecía severos castigos para los contrabandistas. (p. 160)

sunbelt *s.* estados más cálidos del sur y el suroeste. (p. 801)

supply-side economics [economía de la oferta] *s.* idea de que si se reducen los impuestos aumenta el número de empleos así como los ahorros y las inversiones, todo lo cual hace que aumenten las entradas del gobierno. (p. 873)

sweatshop *s.* lugar donde los obreros trabajaban largas horas en condiciones muy malas por salarios muy bajos. (p. 600)

Tammany Hall *s.* famosa maquinaria política de la ciudad de Nueva York de fines del siglo XIX. (p. 613)

tariff [arance aduanero] *s.* impuesto a las mercancías importadas. (p. 296)

Tariff of Abominations [arancel de las Abominaciones] *s.* ley de 1828 que subió los aranceles de las materias primas y las manufacturas; alteró a los sureños, quienes sentían que la política económica nacional la estaban determinando los intereses económicos del noreste. (p. 381)

Teapot Dome Scandal [escándalo de Teapot Dome] *s.* episodio causado por el ministro del Interior Albert B. Fall quien arrendó ricas reservas públicas de petróleo a compañías privadas a cambio de dinero y tierras. (p. 710)

technology [tecnología] *s.* uso de herramientas y conocimiento para satisfacer las necesidades humanas. (p. 32)

Tejano [tejano] *s.* persona de ascendencia española que consideraba a Texas su hogar. (p. 400)

revenue [rentas públicas] *s.* entradas que recibe un gobierno para cubrir sus gastos. (pp. 160, 252)

revenue sharing [reparto de las rentas públicas] *s.* la distribución de dinero federal a los estados y gobiernos locales con pocas o no restricciones en la manera cómo se gasta. (p. 856)

revival [renacimiento religioso] *s.* reunión diseñada para revivir la fe religiosa. (p. 433)

rifle [rifle] *s.* arma de barril estriado que hace que la bala vaya girando por el aire. (p. 491)

robber baron [capitalista inescrupuloso] *s.* líder industrial que se hizo acaudalado usando medios deshonestos. (p. 594)

rock 'n' roll *s.* tipo de música popular caracterizada por ritmos pesados y melodías simples que se desarrolló del rhythm and blues en los años cincuenta. (p. 803)

romanticism [romanticismo] *s.* movimiento artístico europeo que acentuaba al individuo, la imaginación, la creatividad y la emoción. (p. 429)

Roosevelt Corollary [Corolario de Roosevelt] *s.* la adición en 1904 a la Doctrina Monroe permitiendo a los Estados Unidos a actuar de "policía" en Latinoamérica. (p. 672)

Rosie the Riveter [Rosita la Remachadora] *s.* imagen de una mujer fuerte trabajando duro en una fábrica de armas durante la segunda guerra mundial. (p. 773)

Rough Rider *s.* miembro del Primer Regimiento Estadounidense de Voluntarios de Caballería que organizó Theodore Roosevelt y que luchó en la guerra entre España y Estados Unidos. (p. 665)

royal colony [colonia real] *s.* colonia regida por gobernadores nombrados por un rey. (p. 103)

salutary neglect [indiferencia beneficiosa] *s.* política de no interferir Inglaterra en los asuntos de sus colonias norteamericanas durante la primera mitad del siglo XVIII. (p. 144)

SALT *s.* Tratado sobre Limitación de Armas Estratégicas firmado en 1972 entre Estados Unidos y la Unión Soviética; limitaba las armas nucleares. (p. 858)

Sand Creek Massacre [masacre de Sand Creek] *s.* un ataque en 1864, en el que más de 150 hombres, mujeres y niños del pueblo cheyene murieron a manos de la milicia de Colorado. (p. 564)

Santa Fe Trail [Camino de Santa Fe] *s.* camino hacia el oeste que iba de Missouri a Santa Fe, New Mexico. (p. 395)

SCLC *s.* Conferencia de Líderes Cristianos del Sur, grupo que coordinó por todo el sur las protestas para promover los derechos civiles. (p. 815)

secede [separarse] *v.* retirarse. (p. 473)

secession [secesión] *s.* separarse como parte de Estados Unidos. (p. 383)

Second Battle of the Marne [segunda batalla del Marne] *s.* en 1918 esta batalla de la primera guerra mundial marcó el cambio decisivo en el curso de la guerra; las tropas aliadas junto con las estadounidenses detuvieron el avance alemán hacia el interior de Francia. (p. 689)

Second Continental Congress [segundo Congreso Continental] *s.* organismo de gobierno cuyos delegados acordaron en mayo de 1775 organizar el Ejército Continental y aprobar la Declaración de Independencia. (p. 177)

Second Great Awakening [segundo Gran Despertar] *s.* renovación de la fe religiosa durante fines del siglo XVIII y comienzos del XIX. (p. 433)

Second New Deal [segundo Nuevo Trato] *s.* conjunto de programas que se pasaron en 1935 para luchar contra la depresión. (p. 736)

sectionalism [seccionalismo] *s.* colocar los intereses de la región propia por encima de los de la nación como unidad. (p. 357)

Securities and Exchange Commission *s.* [Comisión de Valores y Bolsa] *s.* agencia que vigila la bolsa de valores y hace que las empresas sigan procedimientos honestos en la venta de acciones. (p. 748)

Sedition Act [ley de Sedición] *s.* ley aprobada en 1918 que hacía ilegal la crítica de la guerra. Imponía fuertes multas y largos períodos de encarcelamiento para los que participaran en actividades contra la guerra. (p. 692)

segregation [segregación] *s.* separación. (p. 621)

Seneca Falls Convention [convención de Seneca Falls] *s.* convención sobre los derechos de la mujer llevada a cabo en Seneca Falls, New York, en 1848. (p. 444)

separation of powers [separación de poderes] *s.* división de las funciones básicas del gobierno en tres ramas. (p. 246)

service economy [economía de servicios] *s.* economía en que la mayoría de los empleos suministran servicios en lugar de producir mercancías. (p. 881)

servitude [servitud] *s.* práctica de pertenecer a un dueño o amo. (p. 270)

Seven Days' Battles [batallas de los Siete Días] *s.* batalla de 1862 de la guerra civil en que la Confederación forzó a la Unión a retroceder después de un intento fracasado de capturar la capital sureña de Richmond. (p. 496)

Seventeenth Amendment [Enmienda Decimoséptima] *s.* enmienda a la Constitución estadounidense, ratificada en 1913, que autorizaba la elección directa de los senadores estadounidenses por el electorado de cada estado. (p. 648)

sharecropping [aparcería] *s.* sistema en que los terratenientes daban a los agricultores tierra, semilla y herramientas a cambio de parte de la cosecha. (p. 543)

Shays's Rebellion [revuelta de Shay] *s.* sublevación de granjeros adeudados de Massachusetts en 1787. (p. 225)

Sherman Antitrust Act [ley Antitrust Sherman] *s.* ley aprobada en 1890 que declaró ilegal que las corporaciones obtuvieran control de las industrias formandos trusts. (p. 641)

Siege of Vicksburg [sitio de Vicksburg] *s.* victoria unionista de 1863, durante la guerra civil que le permitió a la Unión controlar todo el río Misisipí. (p. 516)

sit-down strike *s.* [huelga de brazos caídos] huelga en que los obreros permanecen dentro de la fábrica pero se niegan a trabajar. (p. 743)

Pontiac's Rebellion [rebelión de Pontiac] *s.* rebelión de 1763 contra los fuertes británicos y los colonos norteamericanos, dirigida en parte por el líder ottawa Pontiac, en reacción a los colonos que demandaban las tierras de los amerindios, así como a la severidad con que trataban a éstos los soldados británicos. (p. 151)

popular culture [cultura popular] *s.* cosas como la música, la moda y las películas que son populares dentro de una cantidad grande de personas. (p. 718)

popular sovereignty [soberanía popular] *s.* gobierno en que gobierna la gente (p. 244); sistema en que los ciudadanos votan para decidir un asunto. (p. 463)

Populist Party [Partido Populista] *s.* también conocido como el Partido del Pueblo y constituido en 1890, este grupo quería una política que aumentara el precio de lo que cultivaban los granjeros. (p. 577)

prejudice [prejuicio] *s.* opinión negativa no basada en los hechos. (p. 427)

printing press [imprenta] *s.* máquina inventada por Johannes Gutenberg alrededor de 1455. (p. 47)

privateer [corsario] *s.* barco de propiedad particular autorizado por un gobierno que está en guerra a atacar los barcos de la marina mercante enemiga. (p. 204)

Proclamation of 1763 [Proclama de 1763] *s.* orden por la cual Gran Bretaña les prohibía a los colonos norteamericanos establecer asentamientos al oeste de los montes Apalaches. (p. 151)

profit [ganancia] *s.* cantidad de dinero que saca una empresa depués de descontar a las entradas los gastos empresariales. (p. 48)

progressivism [progresismo] *s.* movimiento reformista de principios del siglo XX que buscaba devolver el control del gobierno al pueblo, restablecer oportunidades económicas y corregir las injusticias de la vida estadounidense. (p. 639)

prohibition [prohibición] *s.* proscripción de la fábrica, venta y posesión de bebidas alcohólicas. (p. 715)

propaganda [propaganda] *s.* opinión expresada con el propósito de influir en las acciones de otras personas. (p. 692)

proprietary colony [colonia de propietario] *s.* colonia de un único dueño. (p. 101)

pro tempore *adv.* latín para "por el momento". (p. 250)

public works project [proyecto de obras públicas] *s.* proyecto patrocinado por el gobierno para construir recursos públicos, como caminos y diques. (p. 732)

Pullman Strike [huelga de Pullman] *s.* huelga nacional de ferrocarriles que se extendió por toda la industria ferroviaria en 1894. (p. 603)

Puritan [puritano] *s.* miembro de un grupo de Inglaterra que se asentó en la Colonia de la bahía de Massachusetts en 1630 y trató de reformar las prácticas de la Iglesia de Inglaterra. (p. 94)

push-pull factor *s.* factor que empuja a la gente a irse de su tierra natal y las atrae a un lugar nuevo. (p. 424)

Quaker [cuáquero] *s.* persona que creía que todas las personas debieran vivir en paz y armonía; aceptaba a religiones y grupos étnicos diferentes. (p. 101)

quarter [acuartelar] *v.* dar alojamiento. (p. 267)

Quartering Act [ley de Acuartelamiento] *s.* ley aprobada por el Parlamento en 1765 que requería que las colonias alojaran a los soldados británicos y los aprovisionaran. (p. 160)

quorum [quórum] *s.* número mínimo de miembros que deben estar presentes para que pueda empezar a deliberar oficialmente una asamblea. (p. 251)

racial discrimination [discriminación racial] *s.* tratamiento diferente por motivos de raza. (p. 620)

racism [racismo] *s.* creencia de que alguna gente es inferior a causa de su raza. (p. 79)

radical [radical] *s.* persona que adopta posiciones políticas extremas. (p. 313)

Radical Republican [republicano radical] *s.* diputado que después de la guerra civil estaba a favor de usar el gobierno para crear un nuevo orden en el Sur y dar la ciudadanía total y derecho al voto a los afroamericanos. (p. 533)

ragtime *s.* mezcla de canciones afroamericanas y formas musicales europeas. (p. 629)

ratification [ratificación] *s.* aprobación oficial. (p. 264)

ration [racionar] *v.* distribuir una cantidad fija de cierto artículo. (p. 773)

recall [destituir] *v.* votar para sacar a un funcionario de su cargo. (p. 640)

Reconstruction [Reconstrucción] *s.* proceso que usó el gobierno de Estados Unidos para readmitir a los estados confederados a la Unión después de la guerra civil. (p. 533)

Red Scare [Terror Rojo] *s.* entre 1919 y 1920, ola de pánico sobre una posible revolución comunista. (p. 697)

referendum [referéndum] *s.* cuando una ley que se ha propuesto se somete al voto del pueblo. (p. 640)

Reformation [Reforma] *s.* movimiento religioso del siglo XVI para corregir los problemas de la Iglesia Católica Romana. (p. 47)

Renaissance [Renacimiento] *s.* período de la historia europea que duró desde el siglo XIV hasta comienzos del XVII y que acrecentó el interés por el arte y el saber. (p. 46)

rendezvous [encuentro] *s.* reunión. (p. 197)

reprieve [indultar] *n.* cancelación de un castigo. (p. 259)

republic [república] *s.* gobierno en que el pueblo elige representantes para que lo gobiernen. (p. 222)

republicanism [republicanismo] *s.* creencia de que el gobierno se debe basar en el consentimiento del pueblo; el pueblo ejercita su poder votando por representantes políticos. (pp. 214, 245)

Republican Party [Partido Republicano] *s.* el partido político constituído en 1854 por los que se oponían a la esclavitud en los territorios. (p. 466)

reservation [reserva] *s.* tierras destinadas por el gobierno de Estados Unidos para las tribus amerindias. (p. 562)

New Deal [Nuevo Trato] *s.* programas de Franklin Roosevelt para luchar contra la depresión. (p. 735)

New France [Nueva Francia] *s.* puesto para el comercio de las pieles establecido en 1608 que se convirtió en el primer asentamiento francés permanente en Norteamérica. (p. 70)

new immigrant [inmigrante nuevo] *s.* persona del sur y el este de Europa que entró a Estados Unidos después de 1900. (p. 614)

New Jersey Plan [Plan de Nueva Jersey] *s.* plan de gobierno propuesto en 1787 en la Convención Constitucional que proponía una cámara legislativa única en que cada estado tendría un solo voto. (p. 231)

Nineteenth Amendment [Enmienda Decimonovena] *s.* enmienda a la Constitución de Estados Unidos ratificada en 1920 que dio a las mujeres el derecho absoluto a votar. (p. 653)

Nisei [nisei] *s.* estadounidense japonés nacido en Estados Unidos. (p. 775)

Northwest Ordinance [Ordenanza del Noroeste] *s.* describe cómo se iba a gobernar el territorio del Noroeste y establecía las condiciones para el asentamiento, así como los derechos de los colonos. (p. 223)

Northwest Territory [territorio del Noroeste] *s.* territorio organizado por la Ordenanza de Tierras de 1785, que incluía tierras que formaron los estados de Ohio, Indiana, Michigan, Illinois, Wisconsin y parte de Minnesota. (p. 223)

NOW *s.* fundada en 1966, la Organización Nacional de la Mujer adelantó una campaña para que las mujeres consiguieran empleos con paga igual a la de los hombres. (p. 826)

Nuremberg Trials [Juicios de Nuremberg] *s.* procesos judiciales que tuvieron lugar en Nuremberg, Alemania, después de la segunda guerra mundial, en que se enjuició a líderes nazis por sus crímenes de guerra. (p. 780)

O

Open Door Policy [política de puertas abiertas] *s.* en 1899 Estados Unidos instó a las naciones que tenían intereses en China a que siguieran una política según la cual ningún país controlaría el comercio con China. (p. 669)

Oregon Trail [Camino de Oregón] *s.* camino hacia el oeste que iba de Independence, Missouri, al territorio de Oregón. (p. 396)

overseer [capataz] *s.* persona contratada por el dueño de una plantación para vigilar a los esclavos y dirigir su trabajo. (p. 122)

P

pacifist [pacifista] *s.* persona moralmente opuesta a la guerra. (p. 209)

Palmer raids [allanamientos de Palmer] *s.* en 1920 agentes federales y la policía allanaron los hogares de personas que se sospechaba que eran radicales. (p. 697)

Panama Canal [canal de Panamá] *s.* atajo a través de Panamá que conecta los océanos Atlántico y Pacífico. (p. 670)

Panic of 1837 [pánico de 1837] *s.* crisis financiera con clausura de bancos y colapso del sistema crediticio, que resultó en muchas quiebras y serio desempleo. (p. 386)

Panic of 1873 [pánico de 1873] *s.* crisis financiera en que los bancos se clausuraron y la bolsa de comercio se derrumbó. (p. 547)

Parliament [Parlamento] *s.* el cuerpo legislativo principal de Inglaterra. (p. 142)

patent [patente] *s.* documento del gobierno que otorga a un inventor el derecho exclusivo a hacer o vender su invención durante un determinado número de años. (p. 586)

Patriot [patriota] *s.* colono norteamericano que durante la Revolución norteamericana estaba a favor de los rebeldes. (p. 173)

patroon [patrono] *s.* persona que traía 50 colonos a Nueva Holanda y a cambio recibía una gran concesión de tierras y otros privilegios especiales. (p. 101)

Pearl Harbor *s.* base naval en Hawai atacada de sorpresa por Japón el 7 de diciembre de 1941. (p. 760)

Persian Gulf War [guerra del Golfo Pérsico] *s.* en 1991 Estados Unidos y las Naciones Unidas echaron a Iraq de Kuwait, país que los iraquíes habían invadido en 1990. (p. 875)

petroleum [petróleo] *s.* líquido aceitoso e inflamable. (p. 585)

philanthropist [filántropo] *s.* persona que da grandes sumas de dinero a las organizaciones benéficas. (p. 596)

Pickett's Charge [carga de Pickett] *s.* en 1863 el general George Pickett dirigió una carga frontal contra las fuerzas de la Unión durante la batalla de la guerra civil en Gettysburg; el ataque fracasó. (p. 513)

piedmont [tierras bajas] *s.* ancha extensión de tierra llana al pie de una cadena de montañas. (p. 126)

Pilgrim [peregrino] *s.* miembros del grupo que rechazó la Iglesia de Inglaterra, viajó a América y fundó la colonia de Plymouth en 1620. (p. 92)

Pinckney's Treaty [Tratado de Pinckney] *s.* tratado de 1795 con España que otorgaba a Estados Unidos el uso del río Mississippi y el derecho a depositar bienes en Nueva Orleans; creó el paralelo 31 como el límite sur de Estados Unidos. (p. 302)

plantation [plantación] *s.* finca grande para cultivos comerciales. (p. 73)

platform [plataforma] *s.* declaración de creencias. (p. 471)

Platt Amendment [Enmienda Platt] *s.* resultado de la guerra entre Estados Unidos y España, dio a Estados Unidos el derecho a intervenir en los asuntos de Cuba cuando existiera amenaza a la "vida, propiedad y libertad individual". (p. 666)

Plessy v. Ferguson [Plessy contra Ferguson] *s.* caso de 1896 en que el Tribunal Supremo dictaminó que la separación de las razas en las instalaciones públicas era legal. (p. 621)

political machine [maquinaria política] *s.* organización que logra votos suficientes para controlar un gobierno local. (p. 613)

political party [partido político] *s.* grupo de personas que trata de promover sus ideas y ejercer su influencia sobre el gobierno, y que también apoya a candidatos a los cargos públicos. (p. 304)

mass media [medios de comunicación de masas] *s.* comunicaciones que alcanzan a un público muy grande. (p. 718)

matrilineal [por línea materna] *adj.* sociedad en que la ascendencia se determina mediante la madre. (p. 36)

Mayflower Compact [Pacto del Mayflower] *s.* acuerdo firmado por los hombres que viajaron a América en el Mayflower, que requería leyes para el bien de la colonia y establecía el concepto de autogobierno. (p. 93)

melting pot [crisol de culturas] *s.* lugar donde las culturas se amalgaman. (p. 616)

mercantilism [mercantilismo] *s.* sistema económico en que las naciones tratan de aumentar su riqueza y poder obteniendo oro y plata y estableciendo una balanza comercial favorable. (p. 61)

mercenary [mercenario] *s.* soldado profesional contratado para luchar por un país extranjero. (p. 195)

Mexican Cession [Cesión mexicana] *s.* extensa región cedida por México después de la guerra con México; incluía los actuales estados de California, Nevada, Utah, la mayor parte de Arizona y partes de Nuevo México, Colorado y Wyoming. (p. 411)

Mexicano [mexicano] *s.* persona de ascendencia española cuyos antepasados habían venido de México y se habían establecido en el sudoeste. (p. 570)

middle passage [travesía intermedia] *s.* parte intermedia de la ruta del comercio triangular (el viaje de África a las Américas) que traía africanos capturados a la esclavitud. (p. 78)

migrate [migrar] *v.* mudarse de un lugar a otro. (p. 27)

militarism [militarismo] *s.* creencia de que una nación necesita una fuerza militar grande. (p. 679)

militia [milicia] *s.* fuerza de civiles armados comprometidos a defender su comunidad durante la Revolución norteamericana. (p. 170); fuerza militar de emergencia, que no es parte del ejército profesional. (p. 254)

minié ball [bala minié] *s.* bala con base hueca. (p. 491)

Minuteman [minutero] *s.* miembro de la milicia colonial entrenado para responder "con un minuto de aviso". (p. 170)

misdemeanor [fechoría] *s.* violación de la ley. (p. 259)

mission [misión] *s.* asentamiento creado por la Iglesia con el propósito de convertir a los amerindios al cristianismo. (p. 72)

missionary [misionero] *s.* persona enviada por la Iglesia para predicar, enseñar y convertir a los indígenas al cristianismo. (p. 61)

Missouri Compromise [Acuerdo de Missouri] *s.* serie de leyes aprobadas en 1820 para mantener el equilibrio del poder político entre los estados esclavistas y los libres. (p. 358)

monopoly [monopolio] *s.* compañía que elimina a sus competidores y controla una industria. (p. 595)

Monroe Doctrine [Doctrina Monroe] *s.* política de oposición estadounidense a cualquier interferencia europea en el hemisferio occidental, proclamada por el presidente Monroe en 1823. (p. 359)

Montgomery bus boycott [Boicoteo al transporte público de Montgomery] *s.* en 1955 los afroamericanos boicotearon el transporte público de Montgomery, Alabama, en respuesta al arresto de Rosa Parks, quien se había negado a dejar su asiento a una persona blanca. (p. 815)

Mormon [mormón] *s.* miembro de una iglesia fundada por Joseph Smith en 1830. (p. 397)

Mound Builder [constructor de túmulos] *s.* amerindio primitivo que construía grandes estructuras de tierra. (p. 31)

mountain man [hombre de las montañas] *s.* trampero o explorador que abrió el oeste hallando sendas a través de las montañas Rocosas. (p. 393)

muckraker [revuelve estiércol] *s.* hacia comienzos del siglo XX, periodista que exponía la corrupción dentro de la sociedad estadounidense. (p. 640)

Muslim [musulmán] *s.* adherente del islam. (p. 41)

N

NAACP *s.* constituida en 1909, la Asociación Nacional para el Progreso de la Gente de Color. (pp. 622, 715)

NAFTA [Tratado Norteamericano de Libre Comercio] *s.* aprobado en 1993, el Tratado Norteamericano de Libre Comercio o zona de libre comercio entre Estados Unidos, México y Canadá. (p. 875)

napalm [napalm] *s.* gasolina gelatinosa que arde violentamente. (p. 843)

nationalism [nacionalismo] *s.* sentido de orgullo, lealtad y protección hacia el país de uno. (p. 354)

nativist [nativista] *s.* estadounidense nativo que quería eliminar toda influencia extranjera. (p. 428)

NATO [OTAN] *s.* la Organización del Tratado del Atlántico Norte es una alianza militar constituida en 1949 por diez países de la Europa occidental, Estados Unidos y Canadá. (p. 793)

natural-born citizen [ciudadano nato] *s.* ciudadano nacido en Estados Unidos o en un estado asociado o dependencia de Estados Unidos, o a padres que son ciudadanos estadounidenses que viven fuera del país. (p. 257)

naturalization [naturalización] *s.* manera de darle ciudadanía completa a una persona nacida en otro país. (pp. 253, 270)

Navigation Acts [Actas de Navegación] *s.* serie de leyes aprobadas por el Parlamento, empezando en 1651, para asegurarse Inglaterra de que el comercio de sus colonias le rindiera ganancias económicas. (p. 112)

navigator [oficial de derrota] *s.* persona que planea el rumbo de un barco mientras está en el mar. (p. 49)

Nazi Party [Partido Nazi] *s.* partido Alemán Nacionalsocialista de los Trabajadores, llegó al poder bajo Adolfo Hitler en 1930. (p. 756)

NCAI *s.* Congreso Nacional de Amerindios, fundado en 1944 para promover el "bienestar común" de los amerindios. (p. 825)

neutral [neutral] *adj.* que no apoya ni a un país ni al otro. (p. 302)

neutrality [neutralidad] *s.* rechazo de la idea de apoyar a un país u otro durante una guerra. (p. 682)

K

Kansas-Nebraska Act [ley de Kansas-Nebraska] *s.* ley de 1854 que estableció los territorios de Kansas y Nebraska y otorgó a sus habitantes el derecho a decidir si querían o no permitir la esclavitud. (p. 464)

kayak [kayak] *s.* embarcación pequeña hecha de piel de animales. (p. 33)

Kellogg-Briand Pact [Pacto Kellogg-Briand] *s.* en 1928 firmaron este pacto muchas naciones que prometieron no declararse en guerra entre ellas excepto en defensa propia. (p. 711)

King Cotton [rey Algodón] *s.* al algodón se lo llamaba rey porque era importante en el mercado mundial y el Sur cultivaba la mayor parte del algodón que usaban las fábricas textiles de Europa. (p. 484)

King Philip's War [guerra del rey Felipe] *s.* guerra entre las colonias puritanas y los amerindios que se libró entre 1675 y 1676. (p. 96)

Knights of Labor [Caballeros del Trabajo] *s.* organización de obreros de oficios diferentes formada después de la guerra civil. (p. 601)

Korean War [guerra de Corea] *s.* conflicto entre Corea del Norte y Corea del Sur que duró desde 1950 a 1953; Estados Unidos, junto con otros países de las Naciones Unidas, luchó del lado de los coreanos del Sur y China luchó del lado de los coreanos del Norte. (p. 796)

Ku Klux Klan *s.* grupo constituido en 1866 que quería restaurar el control del Sur a los demócratas y mantener sumisos a los antiguos esclavos. (p. 544)

L

labor union [sindicato laboral] *s.* obreros que se unen para tratar de conseguir mejores condiciones de trabajo. (p. 434)

laissez faire [dejad hacer] *s.* teoría que declaraba que el comercio no sujeto a regulaciones actuaría de manera beneficiosa a la nación. (p. 710)

Land Ordinance of 1785 [Ordenanza de Tierras de 1785] *s.* ley que establecía un plan para la agrimensura y venta de las tierras públicas al oeste de los montes Apalaches. (p. 223)

land speculator [especulador en tierras] *s.* persona que compra grandes extensiones de terreno a precio bajo y luego vende secciones pequeñas a precios altos. (p. 394)

League of Nations [Sociedad de Naciones] *s.* organización establecida después de la primera guerra mundial para resolver conflictos internacionales. (p. 695)

leisure *s.* tiempo libre. (p. 627)

Lend-Lease [ley de Préstamo y Arriendo] *s.* ley que le permitió a Estados Unidos mandar a las naciones que luchaban contra el Eje armas y suministros sin requerir pago inmediato. (p. 760)

Lewis and Clark expedition [expedición de Lewis y Clark] *s.* grupo dirigido por Meriwether Lewis y William Clark que exploró las tierras de la Compra de Luisiana empezando en 1803. (p. 320)

Lexington and Concord *s.* escenarios, en Massachusetts, de las primeras batallas de la Revolución norteamericana. (p. 173)

liberal [liberal] *s.* persona que favorece acción por parte del gobierno para lograr la reforma social y económica. (p. 749)

limited government [gobierno limitado] *s.* principio que requiere que todos los ciudadanos estadounidenses, incluso los líderes gubernamentales, obedezcan la ley. (p. 247)

lode [veta] *s.* mineral enterrado entre capas de roca. (p. 558)

Lone Star Republic [República de la Estrella Solitaria] *s.* apodo de la República de Texas, que se le dio en 1836. (p. 405)

long drive [largo arreo] *s.* arreo de ganado al ferrocarril. (p. 560)

Lost Generation [generación perdida] *s.* la generación de los años veinte, después de la primera guerra mundial cuando hombres y mujeres veían pocas esperanzas para el futuro. (p. 720)

Louisiana Purchase [Compra de Luisiana] *s.* en 1803, la compra a Francia del Territorio de Luisiana. (p. 319)

Lowell mills [fábricas de Lowell] *s.* fábricas textiles ubicadas en el pueblo manufacturero de Lowell, Massachusetts, fundado en 1826. (p. 342)

Loyalist [realista]. *s.* colono norteamericano que apoyaba a los británicos durante la Revolución norteamericana. (p. 173)

M

mail-order catalog [catálogo de venta por correo] *s.* publicación que contenía fotografías y la descripción de los artículos para que la gente encargara por correo. (p. 627)

Magna Carta [Carta Magna] *s.* "Gran Cédula Real"; documento que garantizaba los derechos políticos básicos en Inglaterra, aprobada por el rey Juan en el año 1215. (p. 141)

Mali [Malí] *s.* imperio del África Occidental desde el siglo XIII hasta el siglo XVI y que se enriqueció gracias al comercio. (p. 41)

Manhattan Project [Proyecto Manhattan] *s.* programa ultrasecreto establecido en 1942 para construir una bomba atómica. (p. 771)

manifest destiny [destino manifiesto] *s.* creencia de que era el destino de Estados Unidos extenderse por todo el continente, desde al océano Atlántico al océano Pacífico. (p. 407)

manor system [sistema señorial] *s.* sistema en que los nobles dividían sus tierras en propiedades, cultivadas mayormente por los siervos, quienes recibían la protección del noble. (p. 45)

Marbury* v. *Madison [Marbury contra Madison] *s.* caso de 1803 en que el Tribunal Supremo dictaminó que tenía el poder de invalidar leyes declarándolas inconstitucionales. (p. 317)

March on Washington [Marcha a Washington] *s.* enorme manifestación por los derechos civiles en Washington, D.C. en 1963. (p. 820)

Marshall Plan [Plan Marshall] *s.* aprobado en 1948, autorizó a Estados Unidos a dar más de trece mil millones de dólares para ayudar a la recuperación de las naciones de Europa después de la segunda guerra mundial. (p. 779)

mass culture [cultura de masas] *s.* cultura común compartida por grandes números de personas. (p. 626)

Immigration Reform and Control Act of 1986 [ley de Reforma y Control de la Inmigración] s. ley pasada para reforzar las leyes de inmigración y las medidas para su cumplimiento. (p. 886)

immunity [inmunidad] s. protección legal. (p. 262)

impeachment [imputación] s. proceso de acusar a un funcionario público de un delito en el desempeño de sus funciones. (p. 249)

imperialism [imperialismo] s. política por la cual las naciones más poderosas extienden su control económico, político o militar sobre territorios o naciones más débiles. (p. 659)

impressment [secuestro] s. el acto de capturar personas a la fuerza. (p. 327)

inaugurate [investir] v. conferir un cargo oficial en una ceremonia formal. (p. 293)

income tax [impuesto sobre la renta] s. impuesto sobre los ingresos. (p. 509)

indentured servant [siervo escriturado] s. persona que vendía su trabajo a cambio de pasaje a Norteamérica. (p. 88)

Indian Removal Act [ley del Traslado de los Indígenas] s. esta ley de 1830 requería que el gobierno negociara tratados para el traslado de los amerindios al oeste. (p. 376)

Indian Territory [territorio Indio] s. lo que hoy son Oklahoma y partes de Kansas y Nebraska a la cual se trasladó a los amerindios bajo la ley del Traslado de los Indígenas de 1830. (p. 376)

indictment [acusación] s. declaración escrita dictada por un jurado de acusación que inculpa a una persona de un delito. (p. 250)

indigo [añil] s. planta que cultivaban las colonias sureñas de la cual se obtiene un colorante azul oscuro. (p. 121)

individual right [derecho individual] s. libertad y privilegio personal que garantiza a los ciudadanos estadounidenses la Carta de Derechos. (p. 247)

Industrial Revolution [revolución industrial] s. en la Inglaterra de fines del siglo XVIII, las maquinarias de fábrica empezaron a reemplazar las herramientas manuales, y la producción de bienes manufacturados reemplazó la agricultura como el principal modo de trabajo. (p. 341)

inferior court [tribunal inferior] s. corte con autoridad menor que la del Tribunal Supremo. (p. 260)

inflation [inflación] s. subida en el precio de los productos y los servicios y disminución del valor del dinero. (p. 386)

information revolution [revolución de la información] s. proceso tecnológico que ha cambiado radicalmente el volumen y el modo de transmitir información. (p. 881)

initiative [iniciativa] s. el procedimiento que permite a los votantes proponer una ley directamente. (p. 640)

inoperative [inoperante] adj. que no está vigente. (p. 274)

installment buy [comprar a cuotas] v. comprar algo haciendo pequeños pagos mensuales. (p. 712)

insurrection [insurrección] s. levantamiento abierto contra un gobierno. (p. 271)

interchangeable part [parte intercambiable] s. parte que es exactamente igual a otra parte. (p. 343)

Internet [Internet] s. interconexión mundial de redes informáticas. (p. 880)

Intolerable Acts [leyes Intolerables] s. serie de leyes aprobadas en 1774 por el Parlamento para castigar a Massachusetts por el Motín del Té de Boston. (p. 170)

Iran-Contra affair [asunto Irán-Contra] s. en 1986 el gobierno de Estados Unidos vendió armas a Irán a cambio de ayuda para liberar a los rehenes estadounidenses en el Oriente Medio y el dinero de la venta fue a los rebeldes Contra de El Salvador. (p. 874)

Iran hostage crisis [crisis de los rehenes de Irán] s. el 4 de noviembre de 1979 un grupo de iraníes invadieron la embajada de Estados Unidos en Teherán, capital de Irán, y tomaron de rehenes a 52 estadounidenses. (p. 865)

ironclad [acorazado] s. buque de guerra cubierto de hierro. (p. 491)

Iroquois League [Liga Iroquesa] s. alianza del siglo XVI entre los pueblos amerindios cayuga, mohawk, oneida, onondaga y seneca, que vivían en la región oriental de los Grandes lagos. (p. 37)

irrigation [irrigación] s. práctica de llevar agua a los cultivos. (p. 29)

Islam [islam] s. religión fundada por el profeta Mahoma en el siglo VII, que enseña que hay un solo Dios: Alá. (p. 41)

island hopping [brincar de isla a isla] v. estrategia usada durante la segunda guerra mundial según la cual los aliados invadían islas débilmente defendidas por los japoneses para así lanzar nuevos ataques. (p. 770)

isolationist [aislacionista] s. persona que creía que Estados Unidos debía mantenerse apartado de los asuntos de las otras naciones, excepto en defensa propia. (p. 711)

J

Jacksonian Democracy [democracia jacksoniana] s. idea de extender el poder político a toda la gente asegurando de ese modo el gobierno de la mayoría. (p. 370)

Jamestown. s. primer asentamiento inglés permanente en Norteamérica. (p. 87)

Jay's Treaty [Tratado de Jay] s. el acuerdo que puso fin a la disputa sobre los derechos marítimos estadounidenses durante la Revolución francesa. (p. 302)

jazz [jazz] s. tipo nuevo de música en los años veinte que capturó el despreocupado espíritu de la época. (p. 717)

Jim Crow [ley Jim Crow] s. ley que imponía la separación entre la gente blanca y la de piel negra en los lugares públicos del Sur. (p. 621)

joint-stock company [sociedad por acciones] s. empresa en que los inversionistas colocan su dinero en un fondo común con la intención de sacar ganancias. (p. 86)

judicial review [revisión judicial] s. principio de que el Tribunal Supremo tiene la última palabra en la interpretación de la Constitución. (p. 317)

Judiciary Act of 1801 [ley Judicial de 1801] s. ley que aumentó el número de jueces federales, permitiéndole al presidente John Adams cubrir la mayoría de los puestos nuevos con federalistas. (p. 316)

French Revolution [Revolución francesa] *s.* en 1789 los franceses iniciaron un movimiento por la libertad y la igualdad. (p. 301)

fundamentalist [fundamentalista] *s.* persona que cree en la interpretación textual, o palabra por palabra, de la Biblia. (p. 716)

Fundamental Orders of Connecticut [Órdenes Fundamentales de Connecticut] *s.* conjunto de leyes establecidas en 1639 por una congregación puritana que se había asentado en el valle del río Connecticut y que ampliaban la idea de un gobierno representativo. (p. 95)

generator [generador] *s.* máquina que produce corriente eléctrica. (p. 587)

Ghana [Ghana] *s.* imperio del África Occidental entre los siglos VIII y XI d.de C. (p. 39)

G.I. Bill of Rights [Carta de Derechos del Soldado] *s.* aprobada en 1944, esta ley ofrecía ayuda educacional y económica a los veteranos. (p. 779)

Gilded Age [Edad Dorada] *s.* época de fines del siglo XIX de fabulosa riqueza. (p. 596)

"Glorious Revolution" [Revolución gloriosa] *s.* derrocamiento, en 1688, del rey inglés Jacobo II y su substitución por Guillermo y María. (p. 144)

gold standard [patrón oro] *s.* sistema en que el gobierno garantiza cada dólar con una cierta cantidad de oro. (p. 577)

Grange [La Quinta] *s.* creada en 1867 por un grupo de agricultores para tratar de satisfacer las necesidades sociales de las familias granjeras. (p. 577)

Great Awakening [Gran Despertar] *s.* renovación del sentimiento religioso en las colonias norteamericanas durante las décadas de 1730 a 1750. (p. 139)

Great Compromise [Gran Compromiso] *s.* acuerdo en la Convención Constitucional que estableció una legislatura nacional de dos cámaras; en una de estas cámaras, todos los estados tendrían representación igual, en la otra, cada estado tendría representación basada en su población. (p. 232)

Great Depression [gran depresión] *s.* período que duró desde 1929 hasta 1941, en que la economía de Estados Unidos declinó severamente y millones de estadounidenses estaban sin empleo. (p. 731)

Great Migration [Gran Emigración] *s.* movimiento de puritanos que salieron de Inglaterra para establecer asentamientos por todo el mundo, incluyendo a 20,000 que partieron para América (p. 94); el movimiento de afroamericanos entre 1910 y 1920 del Sur hacia las ciudades del Norte. (p. 693)

Great Plains [Grandes Llanuras] *s.* región desde el río Missouri hasta las montañas Rocosas. (p. 557)

Great Society [gran sociedad] *s.* programa iniciado por Lyndon Johnson para ayudan a los pobres, los ancianos y las mujeres y también promovía la educación, prohibía la discriminación racial y protegía el medio ambiente. (p. 822)

greenback [billete verde] *s.* papel moneda emitido por el gobierno federal durante la guerra civil. (p. 509)

gristmill [molino harinero] *s.* molino en que el grano se muele para producir cualquier tipo de harina. (p. 115)

guerrilla [guerrillero] *s.* soldado que debilita al enemigo con asaltos inesperados y ataques relámpagos. (p. 207)

guerrilla warfare [guerra de guerrillas] *s.* ataques inesperados por bandas pequeñas de guerrilleros. (p. 842)

Gulf of Tonkin Resolution [Resolución del golfo de Tonkín] *s.* resolución del Congreso que dio al presidente el poder de usar fuerza militar en Vietnam. (p. 841)

hacienda [hacienda] *s.* granja grande o finca. (p. 72)

Harlem Renaissance [renacimiento de Harlem] *s.* florecimiento de la creatividad artística afroamericana durante los años veinte, centrada en la comunidad de Harlem de la ciudad de Nueva York. (p. 720)

Harpers Ferry *s.* arsenal federal en Virginia, capturado en 1859 durante un levantamiento de esclavos. (p. 469)

Hausa [hausa] *s.* gente de África Occidental que después del año 1000 d.C. vivió en lo que ahora es la región norte de Nigeria. (p. 42)

hawk [halcón] *s.* persona que apoya la guerra. (p. 847)

Haymarket affair [asunto Haymarket] *s.* mitín de protesta sindicalista que resultó aproximadamente en un centenar de muertes después de que un desconocido tiró una bomba y la policía abrió fuego contra la multitud. (p. 602)

H-bomb [bomba H] *s.* bomba de hidrógeno. (p. 798)

Hiroshima [Hiroshima] *s.* primera ciudad del Japón contra la cual se lanzó la bomba atómica el 6 de agosto de 1945 durante la segunda guerra mundial. (p. 771)

Ho Chi Minh Trail [ruta de Ho Chi Minh] *s.* red de sendas que usó el Vietcong para mover soldados y provisiones durante la guerra de Vietnam. (p. 838)

Holocaust [Holocausto] *s.* matanza sistemática en Alemania, durante la segunda guerra mundial, de unos seis millones de judíos así como millones de otros grupos étnicos. (p. 765)

homestead [residencia] *s.* tierra para asentarse y construir una casa. (p. 568)

Homestead Act [ley de Residencia] *s.* aprobada en 1862, esta ley ofrecía 160 acres de tierra gratis a cualquiera que acordara ocuparla y trabajarla por cinco años. (p. 574)

House of Burgesses [Cámara de los Burgueses] *s.* creada en 1619, la primera asamblea representativa de las colonias norteamericanas. (p. 88)

Hudson River School [Escuela del río Hudson] *s.* grupo de artistas que vivían en el valle del río Hudson del estado de New York. (p. 430)

Hull House [Casa Hull] *s.* fundada en 1889, fue modelo para otras casas de acogida de la época. (p. 613)

Hundred Days [Cien Días] *s.* durante sus cien primeros días, del 9 de marzo a mediados de junio de 1933, Franklin Roosevelt mandó al Congreso muchos proyectos de ley nuevos. (p. 735)

hygiene [higiene] *s.* condiciones y prácticas que fomentan la buena salud. (p. 490)

immigrant [inmigrante] *s.* persona que se establece en un país nuevo. (p. 423)

escalation [escalada] *s.* política de aumentar la intervención militar en Vietnam. (p. 841)

Espionage Act [ley sobre el Espionaje] *s.* aprobada en 1917, esta ley establecía multas severas y muchos años de prisión para quienes participaran en actividades contra la guerra o alentaran a los que resistían la conscripción. (p. 692)

European Middle Ages [Edad Media europea] *s.* período desde fines del siglo V hasta aproximadamente el siglo XIV, durante el cual los europeos adoptaron el feudalismo y el sistema señorial. (p. 44)

exodusters *s.* afroamericanos que abandonaron el Sur para irse al Oeste y se comparaban a los hebreos bíblicos que habían escapado la esclavitud de Egipto. (p. 575)

expatriate [expatriado] *s.* ciudadano de un país que establece su residencia en otro país. (p. 721)

ex post facto law [ley ex post facto] *s.* ley que hace que un acto sea una ofensa criminal aprobada después de cometido el acto. (p. 255)

factory system [sistema fabril] *s.* un método de producción que juntó a obreros y máquinas en el mismo edificio. (p. 341)

Fair Deal [Trato Justo] *s.* programa presentado por Harry Truman que proponía proyectos nuevos para crear trabajos, construir viviendas públicas y acabar con la discriminación racial en el empleo. (p. 791)

fall line *s.* punto a partir del cual una catarata impide que los barcos grandes continúen río arriba. (p. 126)

famine [hambruna] *s.* severa escasez de alimentos. (p. 426)

fascism [fascismo] *s.* filosofía política que propugna un fuerte gobierno nacionalista centralizado, con un dictador poderoso a la cabeza. (p. 756)

federalism [federalismo] *s.* sistema de gobierno en que el poder está dividido entre el gobierno central (o federal) y los estados. (pp. 234, 245)

Federalists [federalistas] *s.* partidarios de la Constitución. (p. 234)

Federalist Papers [*El federalista*] *s.* serie de ensayos que defienden y explican la Constitución, escritos por Alexander Hamilton, James Madison y John Jay. (p. 235)

Federal Judiciary Act [ley de la Judicatura Federal] *s.* ayudó a establecer un sistema de tribunales; le dio al Tribunal Supremo seis miembros. (p. 294)

Federal Reserve Act [ley de la Reserva Federal] *s.* ley aprobada en 1913 que creó el sistema bancario de la nación e instituyó un sistema monetario flexible. (p. 648)

felony [felonía] *s.* delito grave. (p. 253)

feudalism [feudalismo] *s.* sistema político en que el rey concedía a sus nobles el uso de sus tierras a cambio de su prestación militar y la protección de la gente que vivía en esas tierras. (p. 44)

Fifteenth Amendment [Enmienda Decimoquinta] *s.* aprobada en 1870, esta enmienda a la Constitución de Estados Unidos declaraba que a los ciudadanos no se les podía impedir que votaran "por motivo de raza, color ni condición anterior de esclavitud". (p. 546)

54th Massachusetts Regiment [54.° Regimiento de Massachusetts] *s.* regimientos afroamericano organizado para luchar por la Unión en la guerra civil. (p. 506)

fireside chats [charlas al calor de la lumbre] *s.* nombre dado a las radioemisiones de Franklin Roosevelt en las que explicaba sus medidas. (p. 735)

First Battle of Bull Run [primera batalla de Bull Run] *s.* una batalla de la guerra civil, de 1861, en que el Sur horrorizó al Norte con una victoria. (p. 485)

flapper *s.* jovencita librepensadora que abrazaba las modas y actitudes urbanas nuevas de los años veinte. (p. 714)

foreign policy [política exterior] *s.* relaciones con los gobiernos de otros países. (p. 304)

Fort Sumter [fuerte Sumter] *s.* fuerte federal ubicado en el puerto de Charleston, Carolina del Sur; el ataque sureño al fuerte Sumter marcó el comienzo de la guerra civil. (p. 481)

forty-niner [buscador de ventura del 49] *s.* persona que fue a California en búsqueda de oro, empezando en 1849. (p. 412)

Fourteen Points [Catorce puntos] *s.* los objetivos del presidente Woodrow Wilson para la paz que siguió a la primera guerra mundial. (p. 695)

Fourteenth Amendment [Enmienda Decimocuarta] *s.* enmienda a la Constitución de Estados Unidos, aprobada en 1868, que hizo ciudadanos del país a todas las personas nacidas en Estados Unidos o naturalizadas, incluso a los antiguos esclavos. (p. 535)

First Continental Congress [primer Congreso Continental] *s.* reunión en 1774 de delegados de todas las colonias, excepto Georgia, para defender los derechos coloniales. (p. 171)

Freedmen's Bureau [Agencia de Manumisos] *s.* agencia federal establecida para ayudar a los antiguos esclavos después de la guerra civil. (p. 533)

freedmen's school [escuela para los manumisos] *s.* escuela establecida por la Agencia de Manumisos para educar a los recientes libertos afroamericanos. (p. 541)

Freedom Ride [Viaje por la Libertad] *s.* protesta contra la segregación racial en los autobuses interestatales del Sur. (p. 818)

Freedom Summer [Verano de la Libertad] *s.* en 1964 el Comité de Estudiantes no Violentos organizó una campaña de registro de votantes. (p. 821)

Free Soil Party [Partido del Suelo Libre] *s.* partido político dedicado a parar la expansión de la esclavitud. (p. 459)

French and Indian War [guerra Francesa y Amerindia] *s.* conflicto en Norteamérica, entre 1754 y 1763, que fue parte de una lucha mundial entre Francia y Gran Bretaña y que terminó con la derrota de Francia y el traspaso del Canadá francés a Gran Bretaña. (p. 147)

French Indochina [Indochina Francesa] *s.* colonia francesa que incluía lo que es hoy Vietnam, Laos y Camboya. (p. 835)

frontier [frontera] *s.* región sin o con muy pocos asentamientos ocupada mayormente por amerindios. (p. 557)

Fugitive Slave Act [ley de los Esclavos Fugitivos] *s.* ley de 1850 para ayudar a los dueños de esclavos a recapturar los esclavos fugados. (p. 462)

Copperheads [víboras cobrizas] *s.* los principales adversarios políticos de Abraham Lincoln; abogaban por la paz con el Sur. (p. 508)

CORE [Congreso para la Igualdad Racial] *s.* grupo que planeó freedom rides o viajes en autobús por todo el Sur para eliminar la segregación racial en los autobuses interestatales. (p. 818)

corporation [corporación] *s.* empresa propiedad de inversionistas que compran parte de la compañía mediante acciones. (p. 594)

cotton gin [desmontadora de algodón] *s.* máquina inventada en 1793 que limpiaba el algodón con mucha más rapidez y eficiencia que los obreros humanos. (p. 348)

Crash of 1929 [Crack de 1929] *s.* el desplome de los precios de las acciones. (p. 731)

Crittenden Plan [Plan de Crittenden] *s.* acuerdo presentado en 1861 que podría haber evitado la secesión. (p. 475)

Crusades [cruzadas] *s.* serie de guerras para capturar la Tierra Santa, iniciada en 1096 por cristianos europeos. (p. 45)

Cuban Missile Crisis [crisis de los misiles cubanos] *s.* en 1962 casi estalló la guerra entre Estados Unidos y la Unión Soviética porque ésta había instalado misiles nucleares en Cuba. (p. 839)

culture [cultura] *s.* manera de vida compartida por gente que tiene artes, creencias y costumbres semejantes. (p. 28)

D

Dawes Act [ley Dawes] *s.* ley, aprobada en 1887, que distribuía la tierra de las reservas amerindias a dueños individuales. (p. 567)

D-Day [día D] *s.* 6 de junio de 1944, día en que los aliados invadieron a Francia durante la segunda guerra mundial. (p. 764)

Declaration of Independence [Declaración de Independencia] *s.* documento, escrito en 1776, en que las colonias declararon su independendia de Gran Bretaña. (p. 180)

deficit [déficit] spend *v.* usar dinero prestado para financiar programas del gobierno. (p. 738)

department store [almacén departamental] *s.* tienda que vende de todo, desde ropa a muebles a artículos de ferretería. (p. 627)

depression [depresión] *s.* aguda crisis económica. (p. 386)

desert [desertar] *v.* abandonar el servicio militar sin intenciones de regresar. (p. 203)

détente [distensión] *s.* disminución de las tensiones entre EE. UU. y la Unión Soviética durante la guerra fría. (p. 858)

direct primary [elecciones primarias directas] *s.* el electorado, y no las convenciones de partido, eligen a los candidatos para los cargos públicos. (p. 640)

diversity [diversidad] *s.* variedad de gente. (p. 117)

doctrine of nullification [doctrina de la invalidación] *s.* derecho de un estado a rechazar una ley federal que considerase inconstitucional. (p. 381)

domestication [domesticación] *s.* práctica de criar plantas o amansar animales para satisfacer las necesidades humanas. (p. 28)

domino theory [teoría del dominó] *s.* teoría que sostenía que si un país caía en la órbita comunista, los países vecinos también caerían en el comunismo. (p. 837)

dove [paloma] *s.* persona opuesta a la guerra. (p. 847)

downsize [reducir el tamaño] *v.* disminuir una empresa el número de sus empleados para incrementar las ganancias. (p. 881)

Dred Scott v. Sandford [Dred Scott contra Sandford] *s.* caso de 1865 de la Corte Suprema en que un esclavo, Dred Scott, entabló juicio por su libertad porque su amo lo había llevado a vivir en territorios donde la esclavitud era ilegal; la Corte dictaminó contra Scott. (p. 467)

due process of law [proceso legal debido] *s.* tratamiento justo bajo la ley. (p. 267)

dust bowl [cuenca de polvo] *s.* fincas arruinadas por el polvo a comienzos de los años treinta, en una región de unas 150,000 millas cuadradas. (p. 739)

E

e-commerce [comercio electrónico] *s.* negocios que se realizan por Internet. (p. 880)

elector [elector] *s.* votante. (p. 249)

Ellis Island [isla Ellis] *s.* para la mayoría de los inmigrantes que vienen de Europa, la primera parada en Estados Unidos. (p. 614)

Emancipation Proclamation [Proclama de Emancipación] *s.* orden ejecutiva dictada por Abraham Lincoln el 1.° de enero de 1863, que liberaba a los esclavos de todas las regiones insurgentes contra la Unión. (p. 504)

Embargo Act of 1807 [ley de Embargo de 1807] *s.* ley que dictaminaba que los barcos estadounidenses ya no estaban autorizados para ir a puertos extranjeros y que también cerraba los puertos de Estados Unidos a los barcos británicos. (p. 328)

emigrant [emigrante] *s.* persona que abandona un país. (p. 423)

encomienda [encomienda] *s.* concesión del trabajo de los amerindios. (p. 72)

English Bill of Rights [Carta de Derechos Ingleses] *s.* acuerdo firmado por Guillermo y María por el que prometían respetar los derechos del Parlamento y los ciudadanos ingleses, incluso el derecho a elecciones libres. (p. 144)

enlightenment [Ilustración] *s.* movimiento del siglo XVIII que enfatizaba el uso de la razón y el método científico para obtener conocimiento. (p. 140)

enumeration [enumeración] *s.* recuento oficial, como un censo. (p. 249)

environmentalism [ecologismo] *s.* trabajo dedicado a proteger el medio ambiente. (p. 864)

equity [equidad] *s.* sistema de justicia no cubierto bajo la ley común. (p. 269)

ERA *s.* Enmienda para la Igualdad de Derechos, enmienda constitucional propuesta para dar igualdad de derechos sin consideración de sexo; la propuesta murió en 1982. (p. 826)

Erie Canal [canal de Erie] *s.* completado en 1825, esta vía navegable conectaba a la ciudad de Nueva York con Buffalo, New York. (p. 355)

California gold rush [fiebre del oro de California] s. en 1849 gran cantidad de gente se fue a California porque allí se había descubierto oro. (p. 413)

Cambodia [Camboya] s. país fronterizo de Vietnam. (p. 848)

Camp David Accords [acuerdos de Camp David] s. en 1979, basados en estos acuerdos, Egipto e Israel firmaron un tratado de paz que puso fin a 30 años de conflicto. (p. 864)

caravel [carabela] s. barco con velas triangulares que le permitían navegar hacia el viento y con velas cuadradas que lo llevaban hacia delante cuando soplaba viento en popa. (p. 49)

cash crop [cultivo comercial] s. cultivo que produce un agricultor para venderlo por dinero y no para su uso personal. (p. 115)

cavalry [caballería] s. soldados montados a caballo. (p. 496)

Centennial Exhibition [Exposición del Centenario] s. exposición de 1876 en Filadelfia que celebró el centésimo cumpleaños de Estados Unidos. (p. 588)

Central Powers [Potencias Centrales] s. alianza de Austria-Hungría, Alemania, el Imperio otomano y Bulgaria durante la primera guerra mundial. (p. 680)

charter [cédula] s. contrato escrito que concede un gobierno otorgando al que lo recibe el derecho a establecer una colonia. (p. 87)

checks and balances [frenos y cortapisas] s. capacidad de cada rama del gobierno de usar frenos o controles sobre las otras ramas. (p. 246)

Chinese Exclusion Act [ley de Exclusión para chinos] s. aprobada en 1882, esta ley prohibía la inmigración china por diez años. (p. 617)

civil disobedience [desobediencia civil] s. negarse pacíficamente a obedecer leyes que uno considera injustas. (p. 431)

civilization [civilización] s. forma de cultura caracterizada por ciudades con centros de comercio, trabajadores especializados, formas de gobierno y religión organizadas, sistemas de mantener registros, y herramientas avanzadas. (p. 29)

civil rights [derechos civiles] s. derecho otorgado a todos los ciudadanos. (p. 535)

Civil Rights Act of 1964 [ley de Derechos Civiles de 1964] s. esta ley prohibía la segregación racial en los lugares públicos y creó la Comisión para la Igualdad de Oportunidades de Empleo. (p. 820)

clan [clan] s. grupo grande de familias procedentes de un antepasado común. (p. 127)

Clayton Antitrust Act [ley Anti-trust Clayton] s. ley aprobada en 1914 que establecía reglas que prohibían prácticas comerciales que disminuyeran la competencia y le daba al gobierno más poder para reglamentar los trusts. (p. 648)

Cold War [guerra fría] s. estado de hostilidad, sin conflicto militar directo, que se desarrolló entre Estados Unidos y la Unión Soviética después de la segunda guerra mundial. (p. 792)

Columbian Exchange [transferencia colombina] s. transferencia de plantas, animales y enfermedades entre el hemisferio occidental y el oriental. (p. 74)

committee of correspondence [comité de correspondencia] s. grupo de personas de las colonias que se intercambiaban cartas sobre asuntos coloniales. (p. 166)

Committee to Reelect the President [Comité de Reelección del Presidente] s. organización cuya conexión con el allanamiento de la Sede Central del Partido Demócrata hizo estallar el escándalo Watergate. (p. 860)

common law [derecho consuetudinario] s. sistema de leyes desarrollado en Inglaterra, basado en costumbres y decisiones jurídicas anteriores. (p. 268)

Compromise of 1850 [Acuerdo de 1850] s. serie de medidas del Congreso para resolver los desacuerdos principales entre los estados libres y los esclavistas. (p. 461)

Compromise of 1877 [Acuerdo de 1877] s. acuerdo que resolvió la disputa sobre las elecciones de 1876: se declaró presidente a Rutherford B. Hayes, quien entonces retiró las tropas federales que quedaban en el Sur. (p. 548)

compulsory process [proceso obligatorio] s. procedimiento requerido. (p. 267)

Conestoga wagon [carreta conestoga] s. vehículo que tenía ruedas anchas, caja de carro curvada y capota de lona y se usaba para transportar gente y artículos. (p. 117)

Confederate States of America [Estados Confederados de América] s. confederación constituida en 1861 por los estados sureños después de separarse de la Unión. (p. 473)

Congress of Industrial Organizations (CIO) [Congreso de Organizaciones Industriales] s. organización sindical que en 1938 se separó de la Federación Norteamericana del Trabajo. (p. 743)

conquistador [conquistador] s. español que en el siglo XVI viajó a las Américas para explorar y conquistar. (p. 63)

conscription [conscripción] s. ley que requería que los hombres sirvieran en las fuerzas armadas o que fueran reclutados. (p. 508)

conservative [conservador] s. persona que está a favor de menos controles gubernamentales y más libertad individual en cuestiones de la economía. (p. 749)

Constitutional Convention [Convención Constitucional] s. reunión realizada en 1787 para considerar cambios a los Artículos de Confederación, que resultó en la redacción de la Constitución. (p. 229)

containment [contención] s. bloqueo de una nación en la expansión de la influencia de otras naciones, especialmente los esfuerzos de Estados Unidos por bloquear la expansión de la influencia soviética hacia fines de los años cuarenta y comienzos de los cincuenta. (p. 793)

Continental Army [Ejército Continental] s. fuerzas coloniales autorizadas en 1775 por el segundo Congreso Continental, con George Washington como su comandante en jefe. (p. 177)

convene [convocar] v. llamar a reunión. (p. 259)

convoy system [sistema de convoyes] s. fuerte flotilla de destructores que escolta a los barcos mercantes durante épocas de guerra. (p. 687)

cooperative [cooperativa] s. organización propiedad de los asociados que la dirigen. (p. 577)

Battle of Gettysburg [batalla de Gettysburg) *s.* batalla de 1863 de la guerra civil en que la Unión derrotó a la Confederación, poniendo fin a la esperanza de una victoria confederada en el Norte. (p. 513)

Battle of Midway *s.* victoria de Estados Unidos sobre los japoneses en una batalla naval de 1942 que señaló un cambio decisivo en la segunda guerra mundial. (p. 770)

Battle of Quebec [batalla de Quebec] *s.* batalla en la que los británicos derrotaron a los franceses y cambio decisivo en la guerra Francesa y Amerindia. (p. 150)

Battle of Shiloh [batalla de Shiloh] *s.* batalla de 1862 en que la Unión obligó a la Confederación a retroceder; fue una de las batallas más encarnizadas de la guerra civil. (p. 494)

Battle of Yorktown [batalla de Yorktown] *s.* última batalla importante de la guerra Revolucionaria que resultó en la capitulación de las fuerzas británicas en 1781. (p. 210)

Battle of the Alamo [batalla de El Álamo] *s.* en 1836 los texanos defendieron contra el ejército mexicano una misión llamada El Álamo; sobrevivieron sólo cinco texanos (p. 403)

Battle of the Bulge [batalla del Bolsón] *s.* batalla de la segunda guerra mundial de un mes de duración en que los aliados lograron rechazar la última gran ofensiva alemana de la guerra. (p. 764)

Battle of the Little Bighorn [batalla del Little Bighorn] *s.* batalla de 1876 en que los sioux y los cheyennes aniquilaron toda una partida militar estadounidense. (p. 565)

Battle of the Thames [batalla de Thames] *s.* victoria estadounidense sobre los británicos en la guerra de 1812 que puso fin a la amenaza británica en el Territorio del Noroeste. (p. 332)

Battles of Saratoga [batallas de Saratoga] *s.* serie de conflictos en 1777, entre soldados británicos y el Ejército Continental que resultó en un cambio decisivo en la guerra Revolucionaria. (p. 199)

bayonet [bayoneta] *s.* largo cuchillo de acero colocado en el extremo de un arma de fuego. (p. 202)

Bear Flag Revolt [revuelta de la Bandera del Oso] *s.* rebelión de 1846 por los estadounidenses contra el dominio mexicano en California. (p. 409)

Benin [Benín] *s.* reino de África Occidental que se estableció cerca del delta del río Níger en el siglo XIV y se transformó en un estado importante en el siglo XV. (p. 43)

Bessemer steel process [proceso siderúrgico Bessemer] *s.* manera nueva de producir acero desarrollada hacia 1850 que causó un gran incremento en la producción side rúrgica. (p. 587)

bill of attainder [decreto de proscripción] *s.* ley que condena a una persona sin juicio ante un tribunal. (p. 255)

Bill of Rights [Carta de Derechos] *s.* diez primeras enmiendas a la Constitución de Estados Unidos, adoptadas en 1791, que consisten en una lista formal de los derechos y libertades de los ciudadanos. (p. 237)

black code [código negro] *s.* ley pasada por los estados sureños que limitaba la libertad de los antiguos esclavos. (p. 534)

Black Tuesday [martes negro] *s.* nombre que se le da al 29 de octubre de 1929, cuando se desplomó el precio de las acciones. (p. 731)

blockade [bloqueo] *s.* acción de las fuerzas armadas que impide la entrada o salida de mercaderías o personas. (p. 484)

Bonus Army [Ejército de la Prima] *s.* en 1932 miles de veteranos marcharon a Washington demandando el pago de una prima que nunca habían recibido. (p. 733)

boomtown [pueblo en auge] *s.* pueblo que tiene una explosión repentina de crecimiento económico o demográfico. (p. 558)

border state [estado fronterizo] *s.* estados esclavistas fronterizos a estados en que la esclavitud era ilegal. (p. 482)

Boston Massacre [Matanza de Boston] *s.* choque en 1770 entre soldados británicos y colonos de Boston en que perecieron cinco de los colonistas, incluso Crispus Attucks. (p. 165)

Boston Tea Party [Motín del Té de Boston] *s.* como protesta contra el Acta del té, en 1773 los colonos arrojaron al puerto de Boston 342 cajones de té. (p. 167)

bounty [gratificación] *s.* recompensa o pago en dinero que da un gobierno. (pp. 271, 508)

Boxer Rebellion [Rebelión bóxer] *s.* en 1900 el resentimiento chino contra la actitud de superioridad cultural de los extranjeros resultó en este violento levantamiento. (p. 669)

boycott [boicot] *v.* negarse a comprar ciertos productos. (p. 161)

bracero program [programa bracero] *s.* uso de trabajadores mexicanos en la época de escasez de labriegos durante la segunda guerra mundial. (p. 774)

brinksmanship *s.* política internacional, el acto de empujar al límite una situación peligrosa; por ejemplo: los Estados Unidos yendo al borde de la guerra para parar el comunismo. (p. 798)

Brown v. Board of Education of Topeka, Kansas [Brown contra el Consejo de Educación de Topeka, Kansas] *s.* caso de 1954 en que la Corte Suprema declaró que la doctrina educativa de "iguales pero separados" para los blancos y los afroamericanos no era constitucional. (p. 814)

buck [ciervo] gamuza obtenida de la piel de un ciervo adulto, o unidad de dinero de los colonos. (p. 127)

buffalo soldier [soldado búfalo] *s.* apodo que los amerindios les dieron a los afroamericanos que servían en el ejército estadounidense del oeste. (p. 571)

business cycle [ciclo económico] *s.* serie de períodos de la economía buenos y malos. (p. 586)

buy on margin [comprar valores a crédito] *s.* pagar una pequeña parte del precio de una acción y pagar el resto con un préstamo. (p. 730)

cabinet [gabinete ministerial] *s.* grupo de ministros que actúan como los asesores princpales del presidente. (p. 294)

A

abolition [abolición] *s.* movimiento para eliminar la esclavitud. (p. 440)

abridge [abreviar] *v.* reducir. (p. 266)

AEF *s.* Fuerza Expedicionaria Estadounidense, fuerzas de EE. UU. durante la primera guerra mundial. (p. 686)

affirmation [afirmación] *s.* declaración de que algo es cierto. (p. 257)

African Diaspora [diáspora africana] *s.* traslado forzado de los africanos, desde su patria a las Américas para trabajar allí como esclavos. (p. 78)

Agent Orange [agente naranja] *s.* herbicida que mata las plantas. (p. 843)

Albany Plan of Union [Plan de la Unión de Albany] *s.* primera propuesta formal para unir las colonias norteamericanas, presentado por Benjamín Franklin. (p. 149)

Alien and Sedition Acts [leyes de Extranjeros y Sedición] *s.* serie de cuatro leyes promulgadas en 1798 para reducir el poder político de inmigrantes recién llegados a Estados Unidos. (p. 306)

allies [aliados] *s.* alianza de Serbia, Rusia, Francia, Gran Bretaña, Italia y otros siete países durante la primera guerra mundial. (p. 680)

ally [aliado] *s.* país que acuerda ayudar a otro país a alcanzar un objetivo común. (p. 200)

American Federation of Labor (AFL) [Federación Norteamericana del Trabajo] *s.* organización nacional de sindicatos obreros fundada en 1886. (p. 603)

American System [Sistema Americano] *s.* plan presentado en 1815 para hacer autosuficiente a Estados Unidos. (p. 354)

Anaconda Plan [Plan Anaconda] *s.* estrategia de tres pasos mediante la cual la Unión se proponía derrotar a la Confederación durante la guerra civil estadounidense. (p. 484)

Angel Island [isla del Ángel] *s.* primera parada en Estados Unidos para la mayoría de los inmigrantes que venían de Asia. (p. 615)

Antifederalist [antifederalista] *s.* persona que se oponía a la ratificación de la Constitución de los Estados Unidos. (p. 234)

Anti-Imperialist League [Liga Antiimperialista] *s.* grupo de estadounidenses importantes que creían que Estados Unidos no debía negarle a otras personas el derecho de gobernarse a sí mismas. (p. 667)

Appalachian Mountains [montes Apalaches] *s.* cadena de montañas que se extiende desde el este de Canadá hacia el sur, hasta Alabama. (p. 126)

appeasement [apaciguamiento] *s.* otorgamiento de concesiones a una potencia hostil con el fin de mantener la paz. (p. 757)

appellate [de apelación] *adj.* que tiene el poder de reexaminar decisiones de las cortes. (p. 260)

Appomattox Court House [Appomattox] *s.* pueblo de Virginia donde Robert E. Lee se rindió a Ulysses s. Grant en 1865, finalizando así la guerra civil. (p. 519)

apprentice [aprendiz] *s.* joven que aprende un oficio o una artesanía de un maestro experto. (p. 137)

appropiation [apropiación] *s.* fondos públicos que se reservan para un propósito específico. (p. 253)

archaeologist [arqueólogo] *s.* científico que estudia el pasado humano examinando artículos que dejó la gente. (p. 27)

armistice [armisticio] *s.* suspención de la lucha en una guerra. (p. 690)

arms race [carrera de armamento] *s.* desde fines de los años cuarenta hasta fines de los años ochenta, Estados Unidos y la Unión Soviética trataron de superarse una a la otra desarrollando armas de mayor poder destructivo. (p. 798)

Articles of Confederation [Artículos de Confederación] *s.* documento, adoptado por el Congreso Continental en 1777 y finalmente aprobado por los estados en 1781, que delineaba la forma de gobierno de los nuevos Estados Unidos. (p. 222)

artifact [artefacto] *s.* herramienta u otro artículo hecho por seres humanos. (p. 27)

artillery [artillería] *s.* cañon o arma grande. (p. 177)

artisan [artesano] *s.* obrero especializado, como un tejedor a telar o un alfarero, que hace artículos a mano; artífice. (p. 117)

assimilation [asimilación] *s.* proceso de integrarse a una sociedad. (p. 616)

Axis [Eje] *s.* Alemania, Italia y sus aliados durante la segunda guerra mundial. (p. 757)

B

baby boom *s.* término para la generación que nació en Estados Unidos entre 1946 y 1961, cuando el índice de natalidad aumentó marcadamente después de la segunda guerra mundial. (p. 801)

Backcountry [tierras fronterizas] *s.* región colonial que se extendía a lo largo de los montes Apalaches a través de la sección oeste de Nueva Inglaterra y las colonias del centro y del sur. (p. 109)

Bacon´s Rebellion [Rebelión de Bacon] *s.* levantamiento contra la poderosa autoridad colonial de Jamestown por Nathaniel Bacon y un grupo de habitantes de la frontera que resultó en la quema de Jamestown en 1676. (p. 89)

bail [fianza] *s.* dinero que pagan como fianza las personas arrestadas para garantizar que van a regresar para el juicio. (p. 268)

Bataan Death March [Marcha de la Muerte de Bataan] *s.* en 1942 los japoneses forzaron a 70,000 soldados filipinos y estadounidenses a marchar 60 millas a un campo de prisioneros. (p. 768)

Battle of Antietam [batalla de Antietam] *s.* batalla de la guerra civil, en 1862, en que murieron o resultaron heridos 25,000 hombres. (p. 497)

Battle of Fallen Timbers *s.* en 1794 el ejército estadounidense derrotó a 2,000 amerindios en un enfrentamiento por el control del territorio del Noroeste. (p. 299)

with three branches and a two-house legislature in which representation would be based on a state's population or wealth. (p. 231)

Voting Rights Act of 1965 *n.* this law banned literacy tests and other laws that kept African Americans from registering to vote. (p. 821)

W

war bond *n.* a low-interest loan by civilians to the government, meant to be repaid in a number of years. (p. 691)

War Hawk *n.* a westerner who supported the War of 1812. (p. 329)

War Powers Act *n.* passed in 1973, this limits the president's war-making powers without consulting Congress. (p. 849)

War Production Board *n.* an agency established during World War II to coordinate the production of military supplies by U.S. industries. (p. 772)

Watergate scandal *n.* a scandal resulting from the Nixon administration's attempt to cover up its involvement in the 1972 break-in at the Democratic National Committee headquarters in the Watergate apartment complex in Washington, D.C. (p. 860)

Webster-Hayne debate *n.* an 1830 debate between Daniel Webster and Robert Hayne over the doctrine of nullification. (p. 382)

Whig (hwig) **Party** *n.* a political party organized in 1834 to oppose the policies of Andrew Jackson. (p. 387)

Whiskey Rebellion *n.* a 1794 protest against the government's tax on whiskey, which was valuable to the livelihood of backcountry farmers. (p. 301)

Wilderness Road *n.* the trail into Kentucky that woodsman Daniel Boone helped to build. (p. 221)

Wilmot (WIL muht) **Proviso** (pruh VY zoh) *n.* an 1846 proposal that outlawed slavery in any territory gained from the War with Mexico. (p. 459)

Wounded Knee Massacre *n.* the massacre by U.S. soldiers of 300 unarmed Native Americans at Wounded Knee Creek, South Dakota, in 1890. (p. 566)

writ (rit) **of assistance** *n.* a search warrant that allowed British officers to enter colonial homes or businesses to search for smuggled goods. (p. 164)

X

XYZ Affair *n.* a 1797 incident in which French officials demanded a bribe from U.S. diplomats. (p. 306)

Y

Y2K *n.* a computer problem caused by computer programs using only the last two digits of a year and complicated by the arrival of the year 2000. (p. 878)

Yalta (YAWL tuh) **Conference** *n.* in 1945, Franklin Roosevelt, Winston Churchill, and Joseph Stalin discussed plans for the end of World War II and the future of Europe. (p. 765)

yellow journalism *n.* a style of journalism that exaggerates and sensationalizes the news. (p. 663)

Yoruba (YOH roo bah) *n.* a West African people who formed several states southwest of the Niger River. (p. 42)

Z

Zimmermann telegram *n.* a message sent in 1917 by the German foreign minister to the German ambassador in Mexico, proposing a German-Mexican alliance and promising to help Mexico regain Texas, New Mexico, and Arizona if the United States entered World War I. (p. 682)

Tet (tet) **offensive** *n.* in 1968, a surprise attack by the Viet Cong on U.S. military bases and more than 100 cities and towns in South Vietnam during Tet, the Vietnamese celebration of the lunar New Year. (p. 844)

Thirteenth Amendment *n.* an amendment to the U.S. Constitution, adopted in 1865, banning slavery and involuntary servitude in the United States. (p. 521)

38th parallel *n.* the area north of this latitude in Korea occupied by Soviet troops in 1945. (p. 795)

Three-Fifths Compromise *n.* the Constitutional Convention's agreement to count three-fifths of a state's slaves as population for purposes of representation and taxation. (p. 232)

Townshend (TOWN zuhnd) **Acts** *n.* a series of laws passed by Parliament in 1767 that suspended New York's assembly and established taxes on goods brought into the British colonies. (p. 163)

Trail of Tears *n.* the tragic journey of the Cherokee people from their homeland to Indian Territory between 1838 and 1839; thousands of Cherokee died. (p. 377)

transcendentalism (TRAN sen DEN tl ɪz uhm) *n.* a 19th-century philosophy that taught the spiritual world is more important than the physical world and that people can find truth within themselves through feeling and intuition. (p. 431)

transcontinental (TRANS kon tuh NEN tl) **railroad** *n.* a railroad that spanned the entire continent. (p. 590)

Treaty of Ghent (gent) *n.* treaty, signed in 1814, which ended the War of 1812; no territory exchanged hands and trade disputes were not resolved. (p. 333)

Treaty of Greenville *n.* a 1795 agreement in which 12 Native American tribes surrendered much of present-day Ohio and Indiana to the U.S. government. (p. 300)

Treaty of Guadalupe Hidalgo (GWAHD loop hi DAH goh) *n.* the 1848 treaty ending the U.S. war with Mexico; Mexico ceded nearly one-half of its land to the United States. (p. 410)

Treaty of Paris *n.* the 1763 treaty that ended the French and Indian War; Britain gave up all of North America east of the Mississippi River. (p. 150)

Treaty of Paris of 1783 *n.* the treaty that ended the Revolutionary War, confirming the independence of the United States and setting the boundaries of the new nation. (p. 212)

Treaty of Tordesillas (TAWR duh SEE uhs) *n.* the 1494 treaty in which Spain and Portugal agreed to divide the lands of the Western Hemisphere between them and moved the Line of Demarcation to the west. (p. 61)

Treaty of Versailles (vuhr SY) *n.* the 1919 treaty that ended World War I. (p. 696)

trench warfare *n.* a kind of warfare during World War I in which troops huddled at the bottom of trenches and fired artillery and machine guns at each other. (p. 680)

triangular trade *n.* the transatlantic system of trade in which goods, including slaves, were exchanged between Africa, England, Europe, the West Indies, and the colonies in North America. (p. 111)

tribunal (try BYOO nuhl) *n.* a court. (p. 253)

Truman Doctrine *n.* a policy that promised aid to people struggling to resist threats to democratic freedom. (p. 793)

trust *n.* a legal body created to hold stock in many companies, often in the same industry. (p. 595)

tundra (TUN druh) *n.* a treeless plain that remains frozen under its top layer of soil. (p. 33)

Twenty-sixth Amendment *n.* an amendment to the U.S. Constitution, adopted in 1971 and lowering the voting age from 21 to 18. (p. 849)

U

unanimous (yoo NAN uh muhs) **consent** *n.* complete agreement. (p. 264)

Uncle Tom's Cabin *n.* a novel published by Harriet Beecher Stowe in 1852 that portrayed slavery as brutal and immoral. (p. 462)

unconstitutional *n.* something that contradicts the law of the Constitution. (p. 317)

Underground Railroad *n.* a series of escape routes used by slaves escaping the South. (p. 442)

United Nations *n.* an international peacekeeping organization to which most nations in the world belong, founded in 1945 to promote world peace, security, and economic development. (p. 781)

urbanization *n.* growth of cities resulting from industrialization. (p. 609)

U.S.S. *Maine* *n.* a U.S. warship that mysteriously exploded and sank in the harbor of Havana, Cuba, on February 15, 1898. (p. 663)

V

vaquero (vah KAIR oh) *n.* a cowhand that came from Mexico with the Spaniards in the 1500s. (p. 560)

vaudeville (VAWD vil) *n.* a form of live stage entertainment with a mixture of songs, dance, and comedy. (p. 629)

viceroyalty (VYS ROI uhl tee) *n.* a province ruled by a viceroy, who ruled in the king's name. (p. 71)

Viet Cong *n.* a Vietnamese Communist. (p. 838)

Vietnamization (vee ET nuh mi ZAY shuhn) *n.* a strategy of gradually withdrawing U.S. forces and turning the ground fighting over to the South Vietnamese during the Vietnam War. (p. 848)

vigilante (vij uh LAN tee) *n.* a person willing to take the law into his or her own hands. (p. 561)

Virginia Plan *n.* a plan proposed by Edmund Randolph, a delegate to the Constitutional Convention in 1787, that proposed a government

slave code *n.* a law passed to regulate the treatment of slaves. (p. 79)

slavery *n.* the practice of holding a person in bondage for labor. (p. 76)

slum *n.* a neighborhood with overcrowded and dangerous housing. (p. 612)

smuggle *v.* to illegally import or export goods. (p. 112)

SNCC *n.* formed in 1960, the Student Nonviolent Coordinating Committee was created to give young people a larger role in the civil rights movement. (p. 817)

social gospel (GAHS puhl) *n.* a movement aimed at improving the lives of the poor. (p. 612)

socialism *n.* an economic system in which all members of a society are equal owners of all businesses; members share the work and the profits. (p. 602)

Social Security Act *n.* a law, passed in 1935, that requires workers and employers to make payments into a fund, from which they draw a pension after they retired. (p. 736)

sodbuster *n.* a farmer on the frontier. (p. 575)

Songhai (SAWNG HY) *n.* a West African empire that succeeded Mali and controlled trade from the 1400s to 1591. (p. 42)

Sons of Liberty *n.* a group of colonists who formed a secret society to oppose British policies at the time of the American Revolution. (p. 161)

space race *n.* a competition, beginning in 1957, between the Soviet Union and the United States in the exploration of space. (p. 799)

Spanish-American War *n.* a war in 1898 that began when the United States demanded Cuba's independence from Spain. (p. 664)

Spanish Armada (ahr MAH duh) *n.* a fleet of ships sent in 1588 by Philip II, the Spanish king, to invade England and restore Roman Catholicism. (p. 69)

speculation (SPEHK yuh LAY shuhn) *n.* buying and selling of a stock in the hope of making a quick profit. (p. 730)

sphere of influence *n.* an area where foreign nations claim special rights and economic privileges. (p. 669)

spiritual *n.* a religious folk song. (p. 351)

spoils system *n.* the practice of winning candidates giving government jobs to political backers or supporters. (p. 373)

Stamp Act *n.* a 1765 law passed by Parliament that required all legal and commercial documents to carry an official stamp showing a tax had been paid. (p. 160)

standard time *n.* a system adopted in 1918 that divided the United States into four time zones. (p. 592)

states' rights *n.* theory that said that states had the right to judge when the federal government had passed an unconstitutional law. (p. 307)

steerage *n.* the cheapest deck or place on a ship. (p. 423)

Stono (STOH noh) **Rebellion** *n.* a 1739 uprising of slaves in South Carolina, leading to the tightening of already harsh slave laws. (p. 123)

strategy *n.* an overall plan of action. (p. 196)

strike *v.* to stop work to demand better working conditions. (p. 434)

subsistence farm *n.* a farm that produces enough food for the family with a small additional amount for trade. (p. 110)

suburb *n.* a residential area that surrounds a city. (p. 800)

suffrage *n.* the right to vote. (pp. 262, 444)

Sugar Act *n.* a law passed by Parliament in 1764 that placed a tax on sugar, molasses, and other products shipped to the colonies; also called for harsh punishment of smugglers. (p. 160)

sunbelt *n.* the warmer states of the South and Southwest. (p. 801)

supply-side economics *n.* the idea that lowering taxes will lead to increases in jobs, savings, investments, and so lead to an increase in government revenue. (p. 873)

sweatshop *n.* a place where workers labored long hours under poor conditions for low wages. (p. 600)

Tammany (TAM uh nee) **Hall** *n.* a famous political machine, located in New York City in the late 19th century. (p. 613)

tariff *n.* a tax on imported goods. (p. 296)

Tariff of Abominations *n.* an 1828 law that raised the tariffs on raw materials and manufactured goods; it upset Southerners who felt that economic interests of the Northeast were determining national economic policy. (p. 381)

Teapot Dome Scandal *n.* episode caused by Secretary of the Interior Albert B. Fall's leasing of oil-rich public land to private companies for money and land. (p. 710)

technology *n.* the use of tools and knowledge to meet human needs. (p. 32)

Tejano (tuh HAH noh) *n.* a person of Spanish heritage who considered Texas to be home. (p. 400)

temperance movement *n.* a campaign to stop the drinking of alcohol. (p. 434)

tender *n.* money. (p. 255)

tenement *n.* an apartment building that is usually run-down and overcrowded. (p. 611)

revenue sharing *n.* the distribution of federal money to state and local governments with few or no restrictions on how it is spent. (p. 856)

revival (rih VY vuhl) *n.* a meeting designed to reawaken religious faith. (p. 433)

rifle *n.* a gun with a grooved barrel that causes a bullet to spin through the air. (p. 491)

robber baron *n.* a business leader who became wealthy through dishonest methods. (p. 594)

rock 'n' roll *n.* a form of popular music, characterized by heavy rhythms and simple melodies, that developed from rhythm and blues in the 1950s. (p. 803)

romanticism (roh MAN tih SIHZ uhm) *n.* a European artistic movement that stressed the individual, imagination, creativity, and emotion. (p. 429)

Roosevelt Corollary (KAWR uh lehr ee) *n.* a 1904 addition to the Monroe Doctrine allowing the United States to be the "policeman" in Latin America. (p. 672)

Rosie the Riveter (RIHV iht uhr) *n.* an image of a strong woman hard at work at an arms factory during World War II. (p. 773)

Rough Rider *n.* a member of the First United States Volunteer Cavalry, organized by Theodore Roosevelt during the Spanish-American War. (p. 665)

royal colony *n.* a colony ruled by governors appointed by a king. (p. 103)

salutary (SAL yuh TEHR ee) **neglect** *n.* a hands-off policy of England toward its American colonies during the first half of the 1700s. (p. 144)

SALT *n.* the Strategic Arms Limitation Treaty, a treaty signed in 1972 between the United States and the Soviet Union; it limited nuclear weapons. (p. 858)

Sand Creek Massacre (MAS uh kuhr) *n.* an 1864 attack in which more than 150 Cheyenne men, women, and children were killed by the Colorado militia. (p. 564)

Santa Fe (SAN tuh FAY) **Trail** *n.* a trail that began in Missouri and ended in Santa Fe, New Mexico. (p. 395)

SCLC *n.* the Southern Christian Leadership Conference, a group that coordinated civil rights protests across the South. (p. 815)

secede (sih SEED) *v.* to withdraw. (p. 473)

secession (sih SEHSH uhn) *n.* withdrawal. (p. 383)

Second Battle of the Marne (mahrn) *n.* a 1918 battle during World War I that marked the turning point in the war; allied troops along with Americans halted the German advance into France. (p. 689)

Second Continental Congress *n.* a governing body whose delegates agreed, in May 1775, to form the Continental Army and to approve the Declaration of Independence. (p. 177)

Second Great Awakening *n.* the renewal of religious faith in the 1790s and early 1800s. (p. 433)

Second New Deal *n.* a set of programs passed in 1935 to fight the Great Depression. (p. 736)

sectionalism (SEHK shuh nuh LIHZ uhm) *n.* the placing of the interests of one's own region ahead of the interests of the nation as a whole. (p. 357)

Securities and Exchange Commission *n.* an agency that watches the stock market and makes sure companies follow fair practices for trading stocks. (p. 748)

Sedition (sih DIHSH uhn) **Act** *n.* a 1918 law that made it illegal to criticize the war; it set heavy fines and long prison terms for those who engaged in antiwar activities. (p. 692)

segregation (SEHG rih GAY shuhn) *n.* separation, especially of races. (p. 621)

Seneca (SEHN ih kuh) **Falls Convention** *n.* a women's rights convention held in Seneca Falls, New York, in 1848. (p. 444)

separation of powers *n.* the division of basic government roles into branches. (p. 246)

service economy *n.* an economy in which most jobs provide services instead of producing goods. (p. 881)

servitude (SUR vih TOOD) *n.* a state of belonging to an owner or master. (p. 270)

Seven Days' Battles *n.* an 1862 Civil War battle in which the Confederacy forced the Union to retreat before it could capture the Southern capital of Richmond. (p. 496)

Seventeenth Amendment *n.* an amendment to the U.S. Constitution, ratified in 1913, that provided for the direct election of U.S. senators. (p. 648)

sharecropping *n.* a system in which landowners gave farm workers land, seed, and tools in return for a part of the crops they raised. (p. 543)

Shays's (SHAY zuhz) **Rebellion** *n.* an uprising of debt-ridden Massachusetts farmers in 1787. (p. 225)

Sherman Antitrust Act *n.* a law passed in 1890 that made it illegal for corporations to gain control of industries by forming trusts. (p. 641)

Siege (seej) **of Vicksburg** *n.* an 1863 Union victory in the Civil War that enabled the Union to control the entire Mississippi River. (p. 516)

sit-down strike *n.* a strike in which workers remain idle inside the plant or factory. (p. 743)

Sixteenth Amendment *n.* an amendment to the U.S. Constitution, ratified in 1913, that gave Congress the power to create income taxes. (p. 647)

slash-and-burn agriculture (ag rih kuhl chuhr) *n.* a farming method in which people clear fields by cutting and burning trees and grasses, the ashes of which fertilize the soil. (p. 37)

Populist Party *n.* also known as the People's Party and formed in the 1890s, this group wanted a policy that would raise crop prices. (p. 577)

prejudice (PREJ uh dis) *n.* a negative opinion that is not based on facts. (p. 427)

printing press *n.* a machine invented about 1455 by Johannes Gutenberg. (p. 47)

privateer (PRY vuh TEER) *n.* a privately owned ship that has government permission during wartime to attack an enemy's merchant ships. (p. 204)

Proclamation (PRAHK luh MAY shuhn) **of 1763** *n.* an order in which Britain prohibited its American colonists from settling west of the Appalachian Mountains. (p. 151)

profit *n.* money a business makes, after subtracting the costs of doing business from the income. (p. 48)

progressivism (pruh GREHS ih VIHZ uhm) *n.* an early 20th-century reform movement seeking to return control of the government to the people, to restore economic opportunities, and to correct injustices in American life. (p. 639)

prohibition (PROH uh BIHSH uhn) *n.* the banning of the manufacture, sale, and possession of alcoholic beverages. (p. 715)

propaganda (PRAHP uh GAN duh) *n.* an opinion expressed for the purpose of influencing the actions of others. (p. 692)

proprietary (pruh PRY ih TEHR ee) **colony** *n.* a colony with a single owner. (p. 101)

pro tempore (proh TEHM puh ree) *adv.* Latin phrase meaning "for the time being." (p. 250)

public works project *n.* a government-funded project to build public resources such as roads and dams. (p. 732)

Pullman Strike *n.* a nationwide railway strike that spread throughout the rail industry in 1894. (p. 603)

Puritan *n.* a member of a group from England that settled the Massachusetts Bay Colony in 1630 and sought to reform the practices of the Church of England. (p. 94)

push-pull factor *n.* a factor that pushes people out of their native lands and pulls them toward a new place. (p. 424)

Quaker (KWAY kuhr) *n.* a person who believed all people should live in peace and harmony; accepted different religions and ethnic groups. (p. 101)

quarter *v.* to give a place to stay. (p. 267)

Quartering Act *n.* a law passed by Parliament in 1765 that required the colonies to house and supply British soldiers. (p. 160)

quorum (KWAWR uhm) *n.* the minimum number of members that must be present for official business to take place. (p. 251)

racial (RAY shuhl) **discrimination** (dih SKRIHM uh NAY shuhn) *n.* different treatment based on a person's race. (p. 620)

racism (RAY SIHZ uhm) *n.* the belief that some people are inferior because of their race. (p. 79)

radical (RAD ih kuhl) *n.* a person who takes extreme political positions. (p. 313)

Radical Republican (rih PUHB lih kuhn) *n.* a congressman who, after the Civil War, favored using the government to create a new order in the South and to give African Americans full citizenship and the right to vote. (p. 533)

ragtime *n.* a blend of African-American songs and European musical forms. (p. 629)

ratification (RAT uh fih KAY shuhn) *n.* official approval. (p. 264)

ration (RASH uhn) *v.* to distribute a fixed amount of a certain item. (p. 773)

recall *v.* to vote an official out of office. (p. 640)

Reconstruction *n.* the process the U.S. government used to readmit the Confederate states to the Union after the Civil War. (p. 533)

Red Scare *n.* in 1919–1920, a wave of panic from fear of a Communist revolution. (p. 697)

referendum (REHF uh REHN duhm) *n.* when a proposed law is submitted to a vote of the people. (p. 640)

Reformation *n.* a 16th-century religious movement to correct problems in the Roman Catholic Church. (p. 47)

Renaissance (REHN ih SAHNS) *n.* a period of European history, lasting from the 1300s to 1600, that brought increased interest in art and learning. (p. 46)

rendezvous (RAHN day VOO) *n.* a meeting. (p. 197)

reprieve (rih PREEV) *n.* a delay or cancellation of punishment. (p. 259)

republic (rih PUHB lihk) *n.* a government in which people elect representatives to govern for them. (p. 222)

republicanism (rih PUHB lih keh NIHZ uhm) *n.* the belief that government should be based on the consent of the people; people exercise their power by voting for political representatives. (pp. 214, 245)

Republican Party *n.* the political party formed in 1854 by opponents of slavery in the territories. (p. 466)

reservation *n.* land set aside by the U.S. government for Native American tribes. (p. 562)

revenue (REHV uh noo) *n.* income a government collects to cover expenses. (pp. 160, 252)

New France *n.* a fur-trading post established in 1608 that became the first permanent French settlement in North America. (p. 70)

new immigrant *n.* a person from southern or eastern Europe who entered the United States after 1900. (p. 614)

New Jersey Plan *n.* a plan of government proposed at the Constitutional Convention in 1787 that called for a one-house legislature in which each state would have one vote. (p. 231)

Nineteenth Amendment *n.* an amendment to the U.S. Constitution, ratified in 1920, which gave women full voting rights. (p. 653)

Nisei (NEE say) *n.* a Japanese American born in the United States. (p. 775)

Northwest Ordinance *n.* it described how the Northwest Territory was to be governed and set conditions for settlement and settlers' rights. (p. 223)

Northwest Territory *n.* territory covered by the Land Ordinance of 1785, which included land that formed the states of Ohio, Indiana, Michigan, Illinois, Wisconsin, and part of Minnesota. (p. 223)

NOW *n.* founded in 1966, the National Organization for Women pushed to get women good jobs at equal pay. (p. 826)

Nuremberg (NOOR uhm BURG) **Trials** *n.* the court proceedings held in Nuremberg, Germany, after World War II, in which Nazi leaders were tried for war crimes. (p. 780)

Open Door Policy *n.* in 1899, the United States asked nations involved in Asia to follow a policy in which no one country controlled trade with China. (p. 669)

Oregon Trail *n.* a trail that ran westward from Independence, Missouri, to the Oregon Territory. (p. 396)

overseer *n.* a worker hired by a planter to watch over and direct the work of slaves. (p. 122)

pacifist (PAS uh fist) *n.* a person morally opposed to war. (p. 209)

Palmer raids *n.* in 1920, federal agents and police raided the homes of suspected radicals. (p. 697)

Panama (PAN uh MAH) **Canal** *n.* a shortcut through Panama that connects the Atlantic and the Pacific oceans. (p. 670)

Panic of 1837 *n.* a financial crisis in which banks closed and the credit system collapsed. (p. 386)

Panic of 1873 *n.* a financial crisis in which banks closed and the stock market collapsed. (p. 547)

Parliament (PAHR luh muhnt) *n.* England's chief lawmaking body. (p. 142)

patent *n.* a government document giving an inventor the exclusive right to make or sell his or her invention for a specific number of years. (p. 586)

Patriot *n.* an American colonist who sided with the rebels in the American Revolution. (p. 173)

patroon (puh TROON) *n.* a person who brought 50 settlers to New Netherland and in return received a large land grant and other special privileges. (p. 101)

Pearl Harbor *n.* a naval base in Hawaii that was hit in a surprise attack by Japan on December 7, 1941. (p. 760)

Persian (PUR zhen) **Gulf War** *n.* in 1990–1991, the United States and the UN drove Iraq out of Kuwait, a country the Iraqis had invaded in 1990. (p. 875)

petroleum *n.* an oily, flammable liquid. (p. 585)

philanthropist (fil LAN thruh pist) *n.* a person who gives large sums of money to charities. (p. 596)

Pickett's Charge *n.* General George Pickett led a direct attack on Union troops during the 1863 Civil War battle at Gettysburg; the attack failed. (p. 513)

piedmont *n.* a broad plateau that leads to the foot of a mountain range. (p. 126)

Pilgrim *n.* a member of the group that rejected the Church of England, sailed to America, and founded the Plymouth Colony in 1620. (p. 92)

Pinckney's (PINGK neez) **Treaty** *n.* a 1795 treaty with Spain that allowed Americans to use the Mississippi River and to store goods in New Orleans; made the 31st parallel the southern U.S. border. (p. 302)

plantation *n.* a large farm that raises cash crops. (p. 73)

platform *n.* a statement of beliefs. (p. 471)

Platt Amendment *n.* a result of the Spanish-American War, which gave the United States the right to intervene in Cuban affairs when there was a threat to "life, property, and individual liberty." (p. 666)

Plessy v. *Ferguson* *n.* an 1896 case in which the Supreme Court ruled that separation of the races in public accommodations was legal. (p. 621)

political machine *n.* an organization that influences enough votes to control a local government. (p. 613)

political party *n.* a group of people that tries to promote its ideas and influence government, and also backs candidates for office. (p. 304)

Pontiac's (PON tee AKS) **Rebellion** *n.* a revolt against British forts and American settlers in 1763, led in part by Ottawa war leader Pontiac, in response to settlers' claims of Native American lands and to harsh treatment by British soldiers. (p. 151)

popular culture *n.* items such as music, fashion, and movies that are popular among a large number of people. (p. 718)

popular sovereignty (SOV uhr in tee) *n.* a government in which the people rule (p. 244); a system in which the residents vote to decide an issue. (p. 463)

Mayflower Compact *n.* an agreement established by the men who sailed to America on the *Mayflower*, which called for laws for the good of the colony and set forth the idea of self-government. (p. 93)

melting pot *n.* a place where cultures blend. (p. 616)

mercantilism (MUHR kuhn tee LIZ uhm) *n.* an economic system in which nations increase their wealth and power by obtaining gold and silver and by establishing a favorable balance of trade. (p. 61)

mercenary (MUR suh NER ee) *n.* a professional soldier hired to fight for a foreign country. (p. 195)

Mexican Cession (sesh uhn) *n.* a vast region given up by Mexico after the War with Mexico; it included the present-day states of California, Nevada, Utah, most of Arizona, and parts of New Mexico, Colorado, and Wyoming. (p. 411)

Mexicano (may hi KAH noh) *n.* a person of Spanish descent whose ancestors had come from Mexico and settled in the Southwest. (p. 570)

Middle Passage *n.* the middle leg of the triangular trade route—the voyage from Africa to the Americas—that brought captured Africans into slavery. (p. 78)

migrate *v.* to move from one location to another. (p. 27)

militarism *n.* the belief that a nation needs a large military force. (p. 679)

militia (muh LISH uh) *n.* a force of armed civilians pledged to defend their community during the American Revolution. (p. 170); an emergency military force that is not part of the regular army. (p. 254)

minié (MIN ee) **ball** *n.* a bullet with a hollow base. (p. 491)

Minuteman *n.* a member of the colonial militia who was trained to respond "at a minute's warning." (p. 170)

misdemeanor (mis di MEE nuhr) *n.* a violation of the law. (p. 259)

mission *n.* a settlement created by the Church in order to convert Native Americans to Christianity. (p. 72)

missionary *n.* a person sent by the Church to preach, teach, and convert native peoples to Christianity. (p. 61)

Missouri Compromise *n.* a series of laws enacted in 1820 to maintain the balance of power between slave states and free states. (p. 358)

monopoly *n.* a company that eliminates its competitors and controls an industry. (p. 595)

Monroe Doctrine *n.* a policy of U.S. opposition to any European interference in the Western Hemisphere, announced by President Monroe in 1823. (p. 359)

Montgomery bus boycott *n.* in 1955, African Americans boycotted the public buses in Montgomery, Alabama, in response to the arrest of Rosa Parks, who refused to give up her seat to a white person. (p. 815)

Mormon *n.* a member of a church founded by Joseph Smith in 1830. (p. 397)

Mound Builder *n.* an early Native American who built large earthen structures. (p. 31)

mountain man *n.* a fur trapper or explorer who opened up the West by finding the best trails through the Rocky Mountains. (p. 393)

muckraker *n.* around 1900, the term for a journalist who exposed corruption in American society. (p. 640)

Muslim (MUZ luhm) *n.* a follower of Islam. (p. 41)

N

NAACP *n.* formed in 1909, the National Association for the Advancement of Colored People. (pp. 622, 715)

NAFTA *n.* passed in 1993, the North American Free Trade Agreement created a free trade block among the United States, Mexico, and Canada. (p. 875)

napalm (NAY PAHM) *n.* a jellied gasoline that burns violently. (p. 843)

nationalism *n.* a feeling of pride, loyalty, and protectiveness toward one's country. (p. 354)

nativist *n.* a native-born American who wanted to eliminate foreign influence. (p. 428)

NATO *n.* the North Atlantic Treaty Organization is a military alliance formed in 1949 by ten Western European countries, the United States, and Canada. (p. 793)

natural-born citizen *n.* a citizen born in the United States or a commonwealth of the United States or to parents who are U.S. citizens living outside the country. (p. 257)

naturalization *n.* a way to give full citizenship to a person born in another country. (pp. 253, 270)

Navigation Acts *n.* a series of laws passed by Parliament, beginning in 1651, to ensure that England made money from its colonies' trade. (p. 112)

navigator *n.* a person who plans the course of a ship while at sea. (p. 49)

Nazi (NAHT see) **Party** *n.* the National Socialist German Workers' Party; came to power under Adolf Hitler in the 1930s. (p. 756)

NCAI *n.* the National Congress of American Indians was founded in 1944 and aimed to promote the "common welfare" of Native Americans. (p. 825)

neutral (NOO truhl) *adj.* not siding with one country or the other. (p. 302)

neutrality (noo TRAL i tee) *n.* refusing to take sides in a war. (p. 682)

New Deal *n.* President Franklin Roosevelt's programs to fight the Great Depression. (p. 735)

Kansas-Nebraska Act *n.* an 1854 law that established the territories of Kansas and Nebraska and gave their residents the right to decide whether to allow slavery. (p. 464)

kayak (KY AK) *n.* a small boat made of animal skins. (p. 33)

Kellogg-Briand Pact *n.* in 1928, this pact was signed by many nations who pledged not to make war against each other except in self-defense. (p. 711)

King Cotton *n.* cotton was called king because cotton was important to the world market, and the South grew most of the cotton for Europe's mills. (p. 484)

King Philip's War *n.* a war between the Puritan colonies and Native Americans in 1675–1676. (p. 96)

Knights of Labor *n.* an organization of workers from all different trades formed after the Civil War. (p. 601)

Korean War *n.* a conflict between North Korea and South Korea, lasting from 1950 to 1953; the United States, along with other UN countries, fought on the side of the South Koreans, and China fought on the side of the North Koreans. (p. 796)

Ku Klux Klan *n.* a group formed in 1866 that wanted to restore Democratic control of the South and to keep former slaves powerless; the group called for a "racially and morally pure" America. (pp. 544, 716)

labor union *n.* a group of workers who band together to seek better working conditions. (p. 434)

laissez faire (LES ay FAIR) *n.* a theory that stated that business, if unregulated, would act in a way that would benefit the nation. (p. 710)

Land Ordinance of 1785 *n.* a law that established a plan for surveying and selling the federally owned lands west of the Appalachian Mountains. (p. 223)

land speculator *n.* a person who buys huge areas of land for a low price and then sells off small sections of it at high prices. (p. 394)

League of Nations *n.* an organization set up after World War I to settle international conflicts. (p. 695)

leisure (LEE zhuhr) *n.* free time. (p. 627)

Lend-Lease *n.* a 1941 law that allowed the United States to ship arms and supplies, without immediate payment, to nations fighting the Axis powers. (p. 760)

Lewis and Clark expedition *n.* a group led by Meriwether Lewis and William Clark who explored the lands of the Louisiana Purchase beginning in 1803. (p. 320)

Lexington and Concord *n.* sites in Massachusetts of the first battles of the American Revolution. (p. 173)

liberal *n.* a person who favors government action to bring about social and economic reform. (p. 749)

limited government *n.* the principle that requires all U.S. citizens, including government leaders, to obey the law. (p. 247)

lode *n.* a deposit of mineral buried in rock. (p. 558)

Lone Star Republic *n.* the nickname of the republic of Texas, given in 1836. (p. 405)

long drive *n.* taking cattle by foot to a railway. (p. 560)

Lost Generation *n.* the generation of the 1920s after World War I, when men and women saw little hope for the future. (p. 720)

Louisiana (loo EE zee AN uh) **Purchase** *n.* the 1803 purchase of the Louisiana Territory from France. (p. 319)

Lowell mills *n.* textile mills located in the factory town of Lowell, Massachusetts, founded in 1826. (p. 342)

Loyalist *n.* an American colonist who supported the British in the American Revolution. (p. 173)

mail-order catalog *n.* a publication that contains pictures and descriptions of items so that people can order by mail. (p. 627)

Magna Carta *n.* "Great Charter;" a document guaranteeing basic political rights in England, approved by King John in 1215. (p. 141)

Mali (MAH lee) *n.* a West African empire from the 13th–15th centuries that grew rich from trade. (p. 41)

Manhattan Project *n.* the top-secret program set up in 1942 to build an atomic bomb. (p. 771)

manifest destiny *n.* the belief that the United States was destined to stretch across the continent from the Atlantic Ocean to the Pacific Ocean. (p. 407)

manor system *n.* a system in which lords divided their lands into estates, which were farmed mostly by serfs who received protection from the lord in return. (p. 45)

Marbury* v. *Madison *n.* an 1803 case in which the Supreme Court ruled that it had the power to abolish laws by declaring them unconstitutional. (p. 317)

March on Washington *n.* a huge civil rights demonstration in Washington, D.C., in 1963. (p. 820)

Marshall Plan *n.* approved in 1948, the United States gave more than $13 billion to help the nations of Europe after World War II. (p. 779)

mass culture *n.* a common culture experienced by large numbers of people. (p. 626)

mass media *n.* communications that reach a large audience. (p. 718)

matrilineal (MAT ruh LIN ee uhl) *adj.* a society in which ancestry is traced through the mother. (p. 36)

immigrant *n.* a person who settles in a new country. (p. 423)

Immigration Reform and Control Act of 1986 *n.* a law that is designed to strengthen immigration laws and enforcement measures. (p. 886)

immunity *n.* legal protection. (p. 262)

impeachment *n.* the process of accusing a public official of wrongdoing. (p. 249)

imperialism *n.* the policy by which stronger nations extend their economic, political, or military control over weaker nations or territories. (p. 659)

impressment *n.* the act of seizing by force. (p. 327)

inaugurate (in AW gyuh RAYT) *v.* to swear in or induct into office in a formal ceremony. (p. 293)

income tax *n.* a tax on earnings. (p. 509)

indentured servant *n.* a person who sold his or her labor in exchange for passage to America. (p. 88)

Indian Removal Act *n.* this 1830 act called for the government to negotiate treaties that would require Native Americans to relocate west. (p. 376)

Indian Territory *n.* present-day Oklahoma and parts of Kansas and Nebraska to which Native Americans were moved under the Indian Removal Act of 1830. (p. 376)

indictment (in DYT muhnt) *n.* a written statement issued by a grand jury charging a person with a crime. (p. 250)

indigo *n.* a plant grown in the Southern colonies that yields a deep blue dye. (p. 121)

individual right *n.* a personal liberty and privilege guaranteed to U.S. citizens by the Bill of Rights. (p. 247)

Industrial Revolution *n.* in late 18th-century Britain, factory machines began replacing hand tools and manufacturing replaced farming as the main form of work. (p. 341)

inferior court *n.* a court with less authority than the Supreme Court. (p. 260)

inflation *n.* an increase in the price of goods and services and a decrease in the value of money. (p. 386)

information revolution *n.* a time when technology has radically changed how much information and the way information is delivered. (p. 881)

initiative (i NISH uh tiv) *n.* the procedure that allows voters to propose a law directly. (p. 640)

inoperative *adj.* no longer in force. (p. 274)

installment buy *v.* to buy something by making small monthly payments. (p. 712)

insurrection (IN suh REK shuhn) *n.* open revolt against a government. (p. 271)

interchangeable part *n.* a part that is exactly like another part. (p. 343)

Internet *n.* a worldwide computer network. (p. 880)

Intolerable Acts *n.* a series of laws enacted by Parliament in 1774 to punish Massachusetts colonists for the Boston Tea Party. (p. 170)

Iran-Contra affair *n.* in 1986, the U.S. government sold weapons to Iran for help in freeing American hostages in the Middle East, and the money from the sale went to the Contra rebels in El Salvador. (p. 874)

Iran hostage crisis *n.* on November 4, 1979, a group of Iranians overran the American embassy in Iran's capital of Tehran and took 52 Americans hostage. (p. 865)

ironclad *n.* a warship covered with iron. (p. 491)

Iroquois (IR uh KWOH) **League** *n.* a 16th-century alliance of the Cayuga, Mohawk, Oneida, Onondaga, and Seneca Native American groups living in the eastern Great Lakes region. (p. 37)

irrigation *n.* the practice of bringing water to crops. (p. 29)

Islam (is LAHM) *n.* a religion founded by the prophet Muhammad in the 600s, which teaches that there is one God, named Allah. (p. 41)

island hopping *n.* a World War II strategy in which the Allies invaded islands that the Japanese weakly defended in order to stage further attacks. (p. 770)

isolationist *n.* a person who believed that the United States should stay out of other nations' affairs except in self-defense. (p. 711)

Jacksonian Democracy *n.* the idea of spreading political power to all the people, thereby ensuring majority rule. (p. 370)

Jamestown *n.* the first permanent English settlement in North America. (p. 87)

Jay's Treaty *n.* the agreement that ended dispute over American shipping during the French Revolution. (p. 302)

jazz *n.* a new kind of music in the 1920s that captured the carefree spirit of the times. (p. 717)

Jim Crow *n.* laws meant to enforce separation of white and black people in public places in the South. (p. 621)

joint-stock company *n.* a business in which investors pool their wealth in order to turn a profit. (p. 86)

judicial (joo DISH uhl) **review** *n.* the principle that the Supreme Court has the final say in interpreting the Constitution. (p. 317)

Judiciary (joo DISH ee ER ee) **Act of 1801** *n.* a law that increased the number of federal judges, allowing President John Adams to fill most of the new spots with Federalists. (p. 316)

French Revolution *n.* in 1789, the French launched a movement for liberty and equality. (p. 301)

fundamentalist *n.* a person who believes in a literal, or word-for-word, interpretation of the bible. (p. 716)

Fundamental Orders of Connecticut *n.* a set of laws that were established in 1639 by a Puritan congregation who had settled in the Connecticut Valley and that expanded the idea of representative government. (p. 95)

G

generator *n.* a machine that produces electric current. (p. 587)

Ghana (GAH nuh) *n.* a West African empire in the 8th–11th centuries A.D. (p. 39)

G.I. Bill of Rights *n.* passed in 1944, this bill provided educational and economic help to veterans. (p. 779)

Gilded (gil did) **Age** *n.* an era during the late 1800s of fabulous wealth. (p. 596)

"Glorious Revolution" *n.* the overthrow of English King James II in 1688 and his replacement by William and Mary. (p. 144)

gold standard *n.* a policy under which the government backs every dollar with a certain amount of gold. (p. 577)

Grange (graynj) *n.* formed in 1867, the Patrons of Husbandry tried to meet the social needs of farm families. (p. 577)

Great Awakening *n.* a revival of religious feeling in the American colonies during the 1730s and 1740s. (p. 139)

Great Compromise *n.* the Constitutional Convention's agreement to establish a two-house national legislature, with all states having equal representation in one house and each state having representation based on its population in the other house. (p. 232)

Great Depression *n.* a period, lasting from 1929 to 1941, in which the U.S. economy was in severe decline and millions of Americans were unemployed. (p. 731)

Great Migration *n.* the movement of Puritans from England to establish settlements around the world, including 20,000 who sailed for America (p. 94); the movement of African Americans between 1910 and 1920 to northern cities from the South. (p. 693)

Great Plains *n.* the area from the Missouri River to the Rocky Mountains. (p. 557)

Great Society *n.* a program started by President Lyndon Johnson that provided help to the poor, the elderly, and women, and also promoted education and outlawed discrimination. (p. 822)

greenback *n.* paper currency issued by the federal government during the Civil War. (p. 509)

gristmill (GRIST MIL) *n.* a mill in which grain is ground to produce flour or meal. (p. 115)

guerrilla (guh RIL uh) *n.* a soldier who weakens the enemy with surprise raids and hit-and-run attacks. (p. 207)

guerrilla warfare *n.* surprise attacks by small bands of fighters. (p. 842)

Gulf of Tonkin Resolution *n.* congressional resolution that gave the president power to use military force in Vietnam. (p. 841)

H

hacienda (HAH see EN duh) *n.* a large farm or estate. (p. 72)

Harlem Renaissance *n.* a flowering of African-American artistic creativity during the 1920s, centered in the Harlem community of New York City. (p. 720)

Harpers Ferry *n.* a federal arsenal in Virginia that was captured in 1859 during a slave revolt. (p. 469)

Hausa (HOW suh) *n.* a West African people who lived in what is now northern Nigeria after A.D. 1000. (p. 42)

hawk *n.* a person who supports war. (p. 847)

Haymarket affair *n.* in 1886, a union protest resulted in about 100 dead after an unknown person threw a bomb, and police opened fire on the crowd. (p. 602)

H-bomb *n.* a hydrogen bomb. (p. 798)

Hiroshima (HEER uh SHEE muh) *n.* the first city in Japan that was hit by an atomic bomb on August 6, 1945. (p. 771)

Ho Chi Minh (HOH CHEE MIN) **Trail** *n.* a network of paths that the Viet Cong used to move soldiers and supplies during the Vietnam War. (p. 838)

Holocaust (HOL uh KAWST) *n.* the systematic killing by Germany during World War II of about six million Jews as well as millions from other ethnic groups. (p. 765)

homestead *n.* land to settle on and farm. (p. 568)

Homestead Act *n.* passed in 1862, this law offered 160 acres of land free to anyone who agreed to live on and improve the land for five years. (p. 574)

House of Burgesses *n.* created in 1619, the first representative assembly in the American colonies. (p. 88)

Hudson River school *n.* a group of artists living in the Hudson River Valley in New York. (p. 430)

Hull House *n.* founded in 1889, a model for other settlement houses of the time. (p. 613)

Hundred Days *n.* in his first hundred days, from March 9 to mid-June 1933, Franklin Roosevelt sent Congress many new bills. (p. 735)

hygiene (HY JEEN) *n.* conditions and practices that promote health. (p. 490)

Erie (EER ee) **Canal** *n.* completed in 1825, this water-way connected New York City and Buffalo, New York. (p. 355)

escalation (ES kuh LAY shuhn) *n.* the policy of increasing military involvement, as in Vietnam. (p. 841)

Espionage (ES pee uh NAHZH) **Act** *n.* passed in 1917, this law set heavy fines and long prison terms for antiwar activities and for encouraging draft resisters. (p. 692)

European Middle Ages *n.* a period from the late 400s to about the 1300s, during which Europeans turned to feudalism and the manor system. (p. 44)

exoduster (EKS suh duhs tuhr) *n.* an African American who left the South for the West and compared himself or herself to Biblical Hebrews who left slavery in Egypt. (p. 575)

expatriate (ek SPAY tree it) *n.* a citizen of one country who takes up residence in another country. (p. 721)

ex post facto (EKS pohst FAK toh) **law** *n.* a law that would make an act a criminal offense after it was committed. (p. 255)

F

factory system *n.* a method of production that brought many workers and machines together into one building. (p. 341)

Fair Deal *n.* a program under Harry Truman that called for new projects to create jobs, new public housing, and an end to racial discrimination in hiring. (p. 791)

fall line *n.* the point at which a waterfall prevents large boats from moving farther upriver. (p. 126)

famine (FAM in) *n.* a severe food shortage. (p. 426)

fascism (FASH iz uhm) *n.* a political philosophy that advocates a strong, centralized, nationalistic government headed by a powerful dictator. (p. 756)

federalism *n.* a system of government where power is shared among the central (or federal) government and the states. (pp. 234, 245)

Federalists *n.* supporters of the Constitution. (p. 234)

Federalist Papers *n.* a series of essays defending and explaining the Constitution. (p. 235)

Federal Judiciary (joo DISH ee ER ee) **Act** *n.* it helped create a court system and gave the Supreme Court six members. (p. 294)

Federal Reserve Act *n.* a law passed in 1913 that "created" the nation's banking system and instituted a flexible currency system. (p. 648)

felony (FEL uh nee) *n.* a serious crime. (p. 253)

feudalism (FYOOD l iz uhm) *n.* a political system in which the king allows nobles the use of his land in exchange for their military service and their protection of people living on the land. (p. 44)

Fifteenth Amendment *n.* passed in 1870, this amendment to the U.S. Constitution stated that citizens could not be stopped from voting "on account of race, color, or previous condition of servitude." (p. 546)

54th Massachusetts Regiment *n.* one of the first African-American regiments organized to fight for the Union in the Civil War. (p. 506)

fireside chat *n.* the name of Franklin Roosevelt's radio broadcasts in which he explained his policies. (p. 735)

First Battle of Bull Run *n.* an 1861 battle of the Civil War in which the South shocked the North with a victory. (p. 485)

flapper *n.* a young woman who embraced the fashions and urban attitudes of the 1920s. (p. 714)

foreign (FAWR in) **policy** *n.* relations with the governments of other countries. (p. 304)

Fort Sumter *n.* a federal fort located in the harbor of Charleston, South Carolina; the Southern attack on Fort Sumter marked the beginning of the Civil War. (p. 481)

forty-niner *n.* a person who went to California to find gold, starting in 1849. (p. 412)

Fourteen Points *n.* President Woodrow Wilson's goals for peace after World War I. (p. 695)

Fourteenth Amendment *n.* an amendment to the U.S. Constitution, passed in 1868, that made all persons born or naturalized in the United States—including former slaves—citizens of the country. (p. 535)

First Continental Congress *n.* a meeting of delegates in 1774 from all the colonies except Georgia to uphold colonial rights. (p. 171)

Freedmen's Bureau *n.* a federal agency set up to help former slaves after the Civil War. (p. 533)

freedmen's school *n.* a school set up to educate newly freed African Americans. (p. 541)

Freedom Ride *n.* a protest against segregation on interstate busing in the South. (p. 818)

Freedom Summer *n.* in 1964, the SNCC organized a voter-registration drive. (p. 821)

Free Soil Party *n.* a political party dedicated to stopping the expansion of slavery. (p. 459)

French and Indian War *n.* a conflict in North America from 1754 to 1763 that was part of a worldwide struggle between France and Britain; Britain defeated France and gained French Canada. (p. 147)

French Indochina (IN doh CHY nuh) *n.* a French colony that included present-day Vietnam, Laos, and Cambodia. (p. 835)

frontier (frun TEER) *n.* unsettled or sparsely settled area occupied largely by Native Americans. (p. 557)

Fugitive Slave Act *n.* an 1850 law to help slaveholders recapture runaway slaves. (p. 462)

Copperheads *n.* Abraham Lincoln's main political opponents; they favored peace with the South. (p. 508)

CORE *n.* the Congress of Racial Equality, a group that planned Freedom Rides to desegregate interstate buses. (p. 818)

corporation *n.* a business owned by investors who buy part of the company through shares of stock. (p. 594)

cotton gin *n.* a machine invented in 1793 that cleaned cotton much faster and far more efficiently than human workers. (p. 348)

counsel (KOWN suhl) *n.* a lawyer. (p. 267)

Crash of 1929 *n.* the plunge in stock market prices. (p. 731)

Crittenden (KRIT uhn duhn) **Plan** *n.* a compromise introduced in 1861 that might have prevented secession. (p. 475)

Crusades (kroo SAYDZ) *n.* a series of wars to capture the Holy Land, launched in 1096 by European Christians. (p. 45)

Cuban Missile Crisis *n.* in 1962, the United States and the Soviet Union almost went to war because the Soviets had placed nuclear missiles in Cuba. (p. 839)

culture (KUL chuhr) *n.* a way of life shared by people with similar arts, beliefs, and customs. (p. 28)

Dawes (dawz) **Act** *n.* a law, enacted in 1887, that distributed reservation land to individual owners. (p. 567)

D-Day *n.* June 6, 1944, the day the Allies invaded France during World War II. (p. 764)

Declaration of Independence *n.* the document, written in 1776, in which the colonies declared independence from Britain. (p. 180)

deficit (DEF i sit) **spend** *v.* to use borrowed money to fund government programs. (p. 738)

department store *n.* a store that sells everything from clothing to furniture to hardware. (p. 627)

depression *n.* a severe economic slump. (p. 386)

desert (di ZURT) *v.* to leave military duty without intending to return. (p. 203)

détente (day TAHNT) *n.* an easing of tensions between the United States and the Soviet Union during the Cold War. (p. 858)

direct primary *n.* voters, rather than party conventions, choose candidates to run for public office. (p. 640)

diversity (di VUR si tee) *n.* a variety of people. (p. 117)

doctrine of nullification (NUL uh fi KAY shuhn) *n.* a right of a state to reject a federal law that it considers unconstitutional. (p. 381)

domestication (doh MES ti KAY shuhn) *n.* the practice of breeding plants or taming animals to meet human needs. (p. 28)

domino (DOM uh NOH) **theory** *n.* a theory stating that if a country fell to communism, nearby countries would also fall to communism. (p. 837)

dove *n.* a person opposed to war. (p. 847)

downsize *v.* to reduce the number of workers in order to increase company profits. (p. 881)

Dred Scott* v. *Sandford *n.* an 1856 Supreme Court case in which a slave, Dred Scott, sued for his freedom because he had been taken to live in territories where slavery was illegal; the Court ruled against Scott. (p. 467)

due process of law *n.* fair treatment under the law. (p. 267)

dust bowl *n.* the area of dust-damaged farms across a 150,000-square-mile region during the early 1930s. (p. 739)

e-commerce *n.* business that is conducted over the Internet. (p. 880)

elector *n.* a voter. (p. 249)

Ellis Island *n.* the first stop in the United States for most immigrants coming from Europe. (p. 614)

Emancipation (i MAN suh PAY shuhn) **Proclamation** *n.* an executive order issued by Abraham Lincoln on January 1, 1863, freeing the slaves in all regions in rebellion against the Union. (p. 504)

Embargo (em BAHR goh) **Act of 1807** *n.* an act that stated that American ships were no longer allowed to sail to foreign ports, and it also closed American ports to British ships. (p. 328)

emigrant (EM i gruhnt) *n.* a person who leaves a country. (p. 423)

encomienda (en koh mee YEN duh) *n.* a grant of Native American labor. (p. 72)

English Bill of Rights *n.* an agreement signed by William and Mary to respect the rights of English citizens and of Parliament, including the right to free elections. (p. 144)

enlightenment (en LYT n muhnt) *n.* an 18th-century movement that emphasized the use of reason and the scientific method to obtain knowledge. (p. 140)

enumeration (i NOO muh RAY shuhn) *n.* an official count, such as a census. (p. 249)

environmentalism (en vy ruhn MEN tl iz uhm) *n.* work toward protecting the environment. (p. 864)

equity (EK wi tee) *n.* a system of justice not covered under common law. (p. 269)

ERA *n.* the Equal Rights Amendment, a proposed amendment that would give equality of rights regardless of sex; the amendment died in 1982. (p. 826)

California gold rush *n.* in 1849, large numbers of people moved to California because gold had been discovered there. (p. 413)

Cambodia (kam BOW dee uh) *n.* a country bordering Vietnam. (p. 848)

Camp David Accords *n.* in 1979, under these agreements, Egypt and Israel signed a peace treaty that ended 30 years of conflict. (p. 864)

caravel (KAR uh VEL) *n.* a ship with triangular sails that allowed it to sail into the wind and with square sails that carried it forward when the wind was at its back. (p. 49)

cash crop *n.* a crop grown by a farmer to be sold for money rather than for personal use. (p. 115)

cavalry *n.* soldiers on horseback. (p. 496)

Centennial (sen TEN ee uhl) **Exhibition** *n.* an exhibition in Philadelphia in 1876 that celebrated America's 100th birthday. (p. 588)

Central Powers *n.* an alliance of Austria-Hungary, Germany, the Ottoman Empire, and Bulgaria during World War I. (p. 680)

charter *n.* a written contract issued by a government giving the holder the right to establish a colony. (p. 87)

checks and balances *n.* the ability of each branch of government to exercise checks, or controls, over the other branches. (p. 246)

Chinese Exclusion Act *n.* enacted in 1882, this law banned Chinese immigration for ten years. (p. 617)

civil disobedience (DIS uh BEE dee uhns) *n.* peacefully refusing to obey laws one considers unjust. (p. 431)

civilization (SIV uh li ZAY shuhn) *n.* a form of culture characterized by city trade centers, specialized workers, organized forms of government and religion, systems of record keeping, and advanced tools. (p. 29)

civil rights *n.* rights granted to all citizens. (p. 535)

Civil Rights Act of 1964 *n.* this act banned segregation in public places and created the Equal Employment Opportunity Commission. (p. 820)

clan *n.* a large group of families that claim a common ancestor. (p. 127)

Clayton Antitrust Act *n.* a law passed in 1914 that laid down rules forbidding business practices that lessened competition; it gave the government more power to regulate trusts. (p. 648)

Cold War *n.* the state of hostility, without direct military conflict, that developed between the United States and the Soviet Union after World War II. (p. 792)

Columbian (kuh LUM bee uhn) **Exchange** *n.* the transfer of plants, animals, and diseases between the Western and the Eastern hemispheres. (p. 74)

committee of correspondence *n.* a group of people in the colonies who exchanged letters on colonial affairs. (p. 166)

Committee to Reelect the President *n.* an organization linked to the break-in at the Democratic National Committee headquarters that set off the Watergate scandal. (p. 860)

common law *n.* a system of law developed in England, based on customs and previous court decisions. (p. 268)

Compromise of 1850 *n.* a series of Congressional laws intended to settle the major disagreements between free states and slave states. (p. 461)

Compromise of 1877 *n.* the agreement that resolved an 1876 election dispute: Rutherford B. Hayes became president and then removed the last federal troops from the South. (p. 548)

compulsory process *n.* a required procedure. (p. 267)

Conestoga (KON i STOW guh) **wagon** *n.* a vehicle with wide wheels, a curved bed, and a canvas cover used by American pioneers traveling west. (p. 117)

Confederate States of America *n.* the confederation formed in 1861 by the Southern states after their secession from the Union. (p. 473)

Congress of Industrial Organizations (CIO) *n.* a labor organization that broke away from the American Federation of Labor in 1938. (p. 743)

conquistador (kon KWIS tuh DAWR) *n.* a Spaniard who traveled to the Americas as an explorer and a conqueror in the 16th century. (p. 63)

conscription (kuhn SKRIP shuhn) *n.* a law that required men to serve in the military or be drafted. (p. 508)

conservative *n.* a person who favors fewer government controls and more individual freedom in economic matters. (p. 749)

Constitutional Convention *n.* a meeting held in 1787 to consider changes to the Articles of Confederation; resulted in the drafting of the Constitution. (p. 229)

containment (kuhn TAYN muhnt) *n.* the blocking by one nation of another nation's attempts to spread influence—especially the efforts of the United States to block the spread of Soviet Communism during the late 1940s and early 1950s. (p. 793)

Continental Army *n.* a colonial force authorized by the Second Continental Congress in 1775, with George Washington as its commanding general. (p. 177)

convene (kuhn VEEN) *v.* to call together. (p. 259)

convoy system *n.* a heavy guard of destroyers that escorts merchant ships during wartime. (p. 687)

cooperative (koh OP uhr uh tiv) *n.* an organization owned and run by its members. (p. 577)

Battle of Antietam (an TEE tuhm) *n.* a Civil War battle in 1862 in which 25,000 men were killed or wounded. (p. 497)

Battle of Fallen Timbers *n.* in 1794, an American army defeated 2,000 Native Americans in a clash over control of the Northwest Territory. (p. 299)

Battle of Gettysburg (GET eez BURG) *n.* an 1863 battle in the Civil War in which the Union defeated the Confederacy, ending hopes for a Confederate victory in the North. (p. 513)

Battle of Midway *n.* a victory for the United States over the Japanese in a 1942 naval battle that was a turning point of World War II. (p. 770)

Battle of Quebec (kwi BEK) *n.* a battle won by the British over the French, and the turning point in the French and Indian War. (p. 150)

Battle of Shiloh (SHY loh) *n.* an 1862 battle in which the Union forced the Confederacy to retreat in some of the fiercest fighting in the Civil War. (p. 494)

Battle of Yorktown *n.* the last major battle of the Revolutionary War, which resulted in the surrender of British forces in 1781. (p. 210)

Battle of the Alamo (AL uh MOH) *n.* in 1836, Texans defended a church called the Alamo against the Mexican army; all but five Texans were killed. (p. 403)

Battle of the Bulge *n.* a month-long battle of World War II in which the Allies turned back the last major German offensive of the war. (p. 764)

Battle of the Little Bighorn *n.* an 1876 battle in which the Sioux and the Cheyenne wiped out an entire force of U.S. troops. (p. 565)

Battle of the Thames (temz) *n.* an American victory over the British in the War of 1812, which ended the British threat to the Northwest Territory. (p. 332)

Battles of Saratoga (SAR uh TOH guh) *n.* a series of conflicts between British soldiers and the Continental Army in 1777 that proved to be a turning point in the Revolutionary War. (p. 199)

bayonet (BAY uh net) *n.* a long steel knife attached to the end of a gun. (p. 202)

Bear Flag Revolt *n.* the 1846 rebellion by Americans against Mexican rule in California. (p. 409)

Benin (buh NIN) *n.* a West African kingdom that arose near the Niger River delta in the 1300s. (p. 43)

Bessemer (BES uh muhr) **steel process** *n.* a new way of making steel that was developed in the 1850s and caused steel production to soar. (p. 587)

bill of attainder (uh TAYN duhr) *n.* a law that condemns a person without a trial in court. (p. 255)

Bill of Rights *n.* the first ten amendments to the U.S. Constitution, added in 1791, and consisting of a formal list of citizens' rights and freedoms. (p. 237)

black code *n.* a law passed by Southern states that limited the freedom of former slaves. (p. 534)

Black Tuesday *n.* a name given to October 29, 1929, when stock prices fell sharply. (p. 731)

blockade *n.* when armed forces prevent the transportation of goods or people into or out of an area. (p. 484)

Bonus Army *n.* in 1932, thousands of veterans streamed into Washington demanding bonuses that they never received. (p. 733)

boomtown *n.* a town that has a sudden burst of economic or population growth. (p. 558)

border state *n.* a slave state that bordered states in which slavery was illegal. (p. 482)

Boston Massacre (MAS uh kuhr) *n.* a clash between British soldiers and Boston colonists in 1770, in which five of the colonists, including Crispus Attucks, were killed. (p. 165)

Boston Tea Party *n.* the dumping of 342 chests of tea into Boston Harbor by colonists in 1773 to protest the Tea Act. (p. 167)

bounty (BOWN tee) *n.* a reward or cash payment given by a government. (pp. 271, 508)

Boxer Rebellion *n.* in 1900, Chinese resentment toward foreigners' attitude of cultural superiority resulted in this violent uprising. (p. 669)

boycott (BOI KOT) *n.* a refusal to buy certain goods. (p. 161)

bracero (bruh SAIR oh) **program** *n.* the hiring of Mexicans to perform much-needed labor during World War II. (p. 774)

brinksmanship (BRINGKS muhn SHIP) *n.* in international politics, the act of pushing a dangerous situation to the limits; for example, the United States going to the brink of war to stop Communism. (p. 798)

Brown v. Board of Education of Topeka, Kansas *n.* a 1954 case in which the Supreme Court ruled that "separate but equal" education for black and white students was unconstitutional. (p. 814)

buck *n.* a buckskin from an adult male deer was a unit of money for settlers. (p. 127)

buffalo soldier *n.* a name given by Native Americans to African Americans serving in the U.S. army in the West. (p. 571)

business cycle *n.* the pattern of good times and bad times in the economy. (p. 586)

buy on margin *v.* to pay a small part of a stock's price and then borrow money to pay for the rest. (p. 730)

cabinet *n.* a group of department heads who serve as the president's chief advisers. (p. 294)

A

abolition (AB uh LIHSH uhn) *n.* the movement to end slavery. (p. 440)

abridge (uh BRIHJ) *v.* to reduce. (p. 266)

AEF *n.* the American Expeditionary Force, U.S. forces during World War I. (p. 686)

affirmation (AF uhr MAY shuhn) *n.* a statement declaring that something is true. (p. 257)

African Diaspora (AF rih kuhn dy AS puhr uh) *n.* the forced removal of Africans from their homelands to serve as slave labor in the Americas. (p. 78)

Agent Orange *n.* a chemical that kills plants. (p. 843)

Albany Plan of Union *n.* the first formal proposal to unite the American colonies, put forth by Benjamin Franklin. (p. 149)

Alien and Sedition (si DISH uhn) **Acts** *n.* a series of four laws enacted in 1798 to reduce the political power of recent immigrants to the United States. (p. 306)

allies (AL yz) *n.* an alliance of Serbia, Russia, France, Great Britain, Italy, and seven other countries during World War I. (p. 680)

ally (AL eye) *n.* a country that agrees to help another country achieve a common goal. (p. 200)

American Federation of Labor (AFL) *n.* a national organization of labor unions founded in 1886. (p. 603)

American System *n.* a plan introduced in 1815 to make the United States economically self-sufficient. (p. 354)

Anaconda (AN uh KAH duh) **Plan** *n.* a strategy by which the Union proposed to defeat the Confederacy in the Civil War. (p. 484)

Angel Island *n.* the first stop in the United States for most immigrants coming from Asia. (p. 615)

Antifederalist (AN tee FED uhr uh list) *n.* a person who opposed the ratification of the U.S. Constitution. (p. 234)

Anti-Imperialist (AN tee im PEER y uh LIZT) **League** *n.* a group of well-known Americans that believed the United States should not deny other people the right to govern themselves. (p. 667)

Appalachian (AP uh LAY chee uhn) **Mountains** *n.* a mountain range that stretches from eastern Canada south to Alabama. (p. 126)

appeasement (uh PEEZ muhnt) *n.* the granting of concessions to a hostile power in order to keep the peace. (p. 757)

appellate (uh PEL it) *adj.* having power to review court decisions. (p. 260)

Appomattox (AP uh MAT uhks) **Court House** *n.* the Virginia town where Robert E. Lee surrendered to Ulysses S. Grant in 1865, ending the Civil War. (p. 519)

apprentice (uh PREN tis) *n.* a beginner who learns a trade or a craft from an experienced master. (p. 137)

appropriation (uh PROH pree AY shuhn) *n.* public funds set aside for a specific purpose. (p. 253)

archaeologist (AHR kee AHL uh jist) *n.* a scientist who studies the human past by examining the things people left behind. (p. 27)

armistice (AHR mi stis) *n.* an end to fighting. (p. 690)

arms race *n.* from the late 1940s to the late 1980s, the United States and the Soviet Union tried to top each other by developing weapons with great destructive power. (p. 798)

Articles of Confederation *n.* a document, adopted by the Continental Congress in 1777 and finally approved by the states in 1781, that outlined the form of government of the new United States. (p. 222)

artifact (AHR tuh FAKT) *n.* a tool or other object made by humans. (p. 27)

artillery (ahr TIL uhr ee) *n.* a cannon or large gun. (p. 177)

artisan (AHR ti zuhn) *n.* a skilled worker, such as a weaver or a potter, who makes goods by hand; a craftsperson. (p. 117)

assimilation (uh SIM uh LAY shuhn) *n.* the process of blending into society. (p. 616)

Axis (AK sis) *n.* Germany, Italy, and their allies during World War II. (p. 757)

B

baby boom *n.* the term for the generation born between 1946 and 1961, when the U.S. birthrate sharply increased following World War II. (p. 801)

Backcountry *n.* a colonial region that ran along the Appalachian Mountains through the far western part of the New England, Middle, and Southern colonies. (p. 109)

Bacon's Rebellion *n.* a revolt against powerful colonial authority in Jamestown by Nathaniel Bacon and a group of landless frontier settlers that resulted in the burning of Jamestown in 1676. (p. 89)

bail (bayl) *n.* money paid as security by arrested persons to guarantee they will return for trial. (p. 268)

Bataan (buh TAN) **Death March** *n.* in 1942, the Japanese marched 70,000 Filipino and American soldiers 60 miles to a prison camp. (p. 768)

Potomac River historic river separating Virginia from Maryland and Washington, D.C. 496, *m495*

Puerto Rico Caribbean island that has been U.S. territory since 1898. 667, *m665*

Quebec major early Canadian city; also a province of eastern Canada. 146, *m148*

Rhode Island 13th state. Capital: Providence. *Atlas*

Richmond Virginia capital that was also the capital of the Confederacy. (38°N 77°W), 482, *m483*

Rio Grande river that forms part of the border between the United States and Mexico. *Atlas*

Roanoke Island island off the coast of North Carolina; 1585 site of the first English colony in the Americas. (36°N 76°W), 85, *m87*

Rocky Mountains mountain range in the western United States and Canada. *Atlas*

Russia large Eurasian country, the major republic of the former Soviet Union (1922–1991). 680, *m680*

St. Augustine oldest permanent European settlement (1565) in the United States, on Florida's northeast coast. (30°N 81°W), 68, *m63*

St. Lawrence River Atlantic-to-Great Lakes waterway used by early explorers of mid-North America. 146, *m148*

St. Louis Missouri city at the junction of the Missouri and Mississippi rivers. (39°N 90°W), 320, *Atlas*

San Antonio Texas city and site of the Alamo. (29°N 99°W), 402, *m405*

San Francisco major port city in northern California. (38°N 123°W), 416, *m592*

San Salvador West Indies island near the Bahamas where Columbus first landed in the Americas. (24°N 74°W), 52, *m51*

Santa Fe Trail old wagon route from Missouri to Santa Fe in Mexican province of New Mexico. 395, *m395*

Songhai early West African trading empire succeeding Mali empire. 42, *m40*

South America continent of Western Hemisphere south of Panama-Colombia border. *Atlas*

South Carolina 8th state. Capital: Columbia. *Atlas*

South Dakota 40th state. Capital: Pierre. *Atlas*

South Korea East Asian country bordering North Korea. 795, *m796*

South Vietnam southern region of Vietnam, established in 1954; reunified with North Vietnam in 1975 after Vietnam War. 837, *m837*

Soviet Union country created in 1922 by joining Russia and other republics; in 1991, broken into independent states. 757, *m760*

Spain nation in southwestern Europe; early empire builder in the Americas. 50, *m51*

Tennessee 16th state. Capital: Nashville. *Atlas*

Tenochtitlán Aztec Empire capital; now site of Mexico City. 64, *m63*

Texas 28th state. Capital: Austin. *Atlas*

Utah 45th state. Capital: Salt Lake City. *Atlas*

Valley Forge village in southeast Pennsylvania and site of Washington's army camp during winter of 1777–1778. (40°N 75°W), 202, *m209*

Vermont 14th state. Capital: Montpelier. *Atlas*

Vicksburg Mississippi River site of major Union victory (1863) in Civil War. (32°N 91°W), 516, *m517*

Vietnam country in Southeast Asia; divided into two regions (1954–1975), North and South, until end of Vietnam War. 835, *m837*

Virginia 10th state. Capital: Richmond. *Atlas*

Washington 42nd state. Capital: Olympia. *Atlas*

Washington, D.C. capital of the United States since 1800; makes up whole of District of Columbia (D.C.). (39°N 77°W), 305, *Atlas*

West Africa region from which most Africans were brought to the Americas. 39, *m40*

Western Hemisphere the half of the world that includes the Americas. 75, *m74*

West Indies numerous islands in the Caribbean Sea, between Florida and South America. 111, *m111*

West Virginia 35th state. Capital: Charleston. *Atlas*

Wisconsin 30th state. Capital: Madison. *Atlas*

Wounded Knee South Dakota site that was scene of 1890 massacre of Sioux. (43°N 102°W), 566, *m563*

Wyoming 44th state. Capital: Cheyenne. *Atlas*

Yorktown Virginia village and site of American victory that sealed British defeat in Revolutionary War. (37°N 77°W), 209, *m209*

Louisiana 18th state. Capital: Baton Rouge. *Atlas*

Louisiana Purchase land west of the Mississippi River purchased from France in 1803. 319, *m320*

Lowell Massachusetts city built in early 1800s as planned factory town. (43°N 71°W), 342

Maine 23rd state. Capital: Augusta. *Atlas*

Mali early West African trading empire succeeding Ghana empire. 41, *m40*

Maryland 7th state. Capital: Annapolis. *Atlas*

Massachusetts 6th state. Capital: Boston. *Atlas*

Mexico nation sharing U.S. southern border. *Atlas*

Michigan 26th state. Capital: Lansing. *Atlas*

Middle East eastern Mediterranean region that includes countries such as Iran, Iraq, Syria, Kuwait, Jordan, Saudi Arabia, Israel, and Egypt. 864, *m764, m865*

Minnesota 32nd state. Capital: St. Paul. *Atlas*

Mississippi 20th state. Capital: Jackson. *Atlas*

Mississippi River second longest U.S. river, south from Minnesota to the Gulf of Mexico. 146, *m153*

Missouri 24th state. Capital: Jefferson City. *Atlas*

Missouri River longest U.S. river, east from the Rockies to the Mississippi River. 321, *m320*

Montana 41st state. Capital: Helena. *Atlas*

Montgomery Alabama capital and site of 1955 African-American bus boycott. (32°N 86°W), 813, *m350*

Nagasaki Japanese port city, one-third of which was destroyed by U.S. atomic bomb dropped to end World War II. (33°N 130°E), 773, *m771*

Nebraska 37th state. Capital: Lincoln. *Atlas*

Nevada 36th state. Capital: Carson City. *Atlas*

New England northeast U.S. region made up of Maine, New Hampshire, Vermont, Massachusetts, Rhode Island, and Connecticut. 109, *m110*

New France first permanent French colony in North America. 70, *m148*

New Hampshire 9th state. Capital: Concord. *Atlas*

New Jersey 3rd state. Capital: Trenton. *Atlas*

New Mexico 47th state. Capital: Santa Fe. *Atlas*

New Netherland early Dutch colony that became New York in 1664. 70

New Orleans Louisiana port city at mouth of the Mississippi River. *Atlas*

New Spain former North American province of the Spanish Empire, made up mostly of present-day Mexico and the southwest United States. 71, *m72*

New York 11th state. Capital: Albany. *Atlas*

New York City largest U.S. city, at the mouth of the Hudson River; temporary U.S. capital, 1785–1790. *Atlas*

Normandy region of northern France where Allied invasion in 1944 turned tide of World War II. 766, *m766*

North America continent of Western Hemisphere north of Panama-Colombia border. *Atlas*

North Carolina 12th state. Capital: Raleigh. *Atlas*

North Dakota 39th state. Capital: Bismarck. *Atlas*

North Korea Communist country in Asia, bordering eastern China. 795, *m796*

North Vietnam northern region of Vietnam, established in 1954; reunified with South Vietnam in 1975 after Vietnam War. 837, *m837*

Northwest Territory U.S. land north of the Ohio River to the Great Lakes and west to the Mississippi River; acquired in 1783. 223, *m226*

Ohio 17th state. Capital: Columbus. *Atlas*

Ohio River river that flows from western Pennsylvania to the Mississippi River. *Atlas*

Oklahoma 46th state. Capital: Oklahoma City. *Atlas*

Oregon 33rd state. Capital: Salem. *Atlas*

Oregon Country former region of northwest North America claimed jointly by Britain and the United States until 1846. 318, *m320*

Oregon Trail pioneer wagon route from Missouri to the Oregon Territory in the 1840s and 1850s. *m395*, 396

Pacific Ocean world's largest ocean, on the west coast of the United States. *Atlas*

Panama Canal ship passageway cut through Panama in Central America, linking Atlantic and Pacific oceans. (8°N 80°W), 670, *m670*

Pearl Harbor naval base in Hawaii; site of surprise Japanese aerial attack in 1941. (21°N 158°W), 661 *m660*

Pennsylvania 2nd state. Capital: Harrisburg. *Atlas*

Persian Gulf waterway between Saudi Arabia and Iran, leading to Kuwait and Iraq. 875, *m865*

Philadelphia large port city in Pennsylvania; U.S. capital, 1790–1800. (40°N 76°W), 229, *Atlas*

Philippine Islands Pacific island country off the southeast coast of China. 662, *m665*

Plymouth town on Massachusetts coast and site of Pilgrim landing and colony. (42°N 71°W), 93, *m95*

Portugal nation in southwestern Europe; leader in early oceanic explorations. 49, *m51*

District of Columbia (D.C.) self-governing federal district between Virginia and Maryland, made up entirely of the city of Washington, the U.S. capital. (39°N 77°W), 305, *Atlas*

Dominican Republic nation sharing the island of Hispaniola with Haiti. 673, *m672*

England southern part of Great Britain. *Atlas*

English Channel narrow waterway separating Great Britain from France. 69, *m764*

Erie Canal all-water channel dug out to connect the Hudson River with Lake Erie. 355, *m355*

Europe second smallest continent, actually a peninsula of the Eurasian landmass. *Atlas*

Florida 27th state. Capital: Tallahassee. *Atlas*

Fort McHenry fort in Baltimore harbor where 1814 British attack inspired U.S. national anthem. (39°N 77°N), 332, *m331*

Fort Sumter fort in Charleston, South Carolina, harbor where 1861 attack by Confederates began the Civil War. (33°N 80°W), 481, *m483*

France nation in western Europe; it aided America in the Revolutionary War. *Atlas*

Gadsden Purchase last territory (from Mexico, 1853) added to continental United States. 411, *m410*

Georgia 4th state. Capital: Atlanta. *Atlas*

Germany nation in central Europe; once divided into West and East Germany, 1949–1990. *Atlas*

Gettysburg Pennsylvania town and site of 1863 Civil War victory for the North that is considered war's turning point. (40°N 77°W), 513, *m514*

Ghana first powerful West African trading empire. 40, *m40*

Great Britain European island nation across from France; it consists of England, Scotland, and Wales. *Atlas*

Great Lakes five connected lakes—Ontario, Erie, Huron, Michigan, and Superior—on the U.S. border with Canada. 355, *m355*

Great Plains vast grassland region in the central United States. 393, *m395*

Gulf of Mexico body of water forming southern U.S. boundary from east Texas to west Florida. *Atlas*

Haiti nation sharing the island of Hispaniola with Dominican Republic. *Atlas*

Harpers Ferry village today in extreme eastern West Virginia where John Brown raided stored U.S. weapons in 1859. (39°N 78°W), 469, *m495*

Hawaii 50th state. Capital: Honolulu. *Atlas*

Hiroshima Japanese city destroyed by U.S. atomic bomb dropped to end World War II. (34°N 132°E), 771, *m771*

Hispaniola West Indies island (shared today by Dominican Republic and Haiti) that Columbus mistook for Asia. 52, *m51*

Hudson River large river in eastern New York. 100, *m95*

Idaho 43rd state. Capital: Boise. *Atlas*

Illinois 21st state. Capital: Springfield. *Atlas*

Indiana 19th state. Capital: Indianapolis. *Atlas*

Indian Territory area, mainly of present-day Oklahoma, that in the 1800s became land for relocated Native Americans. 376, *m376*

Iowa 29th state. Capital: Des Moines. *Atlas*

Iran Middle East nation. 865, *m865*

Iraq Middle East nation whose 1990 invasion of Kuwait led to the Persian Gulf War. 875, *m865*

Ireland island country west of England whose mid-1800s famine caused more than one million people to emigrate to America. 426, *Atlas*

Israel Jewish nation in the Middle East. 864, *Atlas*

Italy nation in southern Europe. *Atlas*

Jamestown community in Virginia that was the first permanent English settlement in North America. 87, *m87*

Japan island nation in east Asia. *Atlas*

Kansas 34th state. Capital: Topeka. *Atlas*

Kentucky 15th state. Capital: Frankfort. *Atlas*

Kosovo province of the Yugoslavian republic of Serbia. 876, *m877*

Kuwait tiny, oil-rich Middle East nation. 875, *m865*

Latin America region made up of Mexico, Caribbean Islands, and Central and South America, where Latin-based languages of Spanish, French, or Portuguese are spoken. 359, *m672*

Lexington Massachusetts city and site of first Revolutionary War battle in 1775. (42°N 71°W), 173, *m172*

Little Bighorn River Montana site of Sioux and Cheyenne victory over Custer. (46°N 108°W), 565, *m563*

Little Rock capital of Arkansas and site of 1957 school-desegregation conflict. 816, *Atlas*

Los Angeles 2nd largest U.S. city, on California's coast. 824, *m804*

The Gazetteer identifies important places and geographical features in this book. Entries include a short description, often followed by two page numbers. The first number refers to a text page on which the entry is discussed, and the second, in italics, refers to a map where the place appears. (The reference *Atlas* is to the section of U.S. and world maps on pages R32–R37.) In addition, some entries include rounded-off geographical coordinates. There are entries for all U.S. states (with capital cities).

Africa world's second largest continent. *Atlas*

Alabama 22nd state. Capital: Montgomery. *Atlas*

Alamo Texas mission in San Antonio captured by Mexico in 1836. (29°N 98°W), 402, *m405*

Alaska 49th state. Capital: Juneau. *Atlas*

Antarctica continent at the South Pole. *Atlas*

Antietam Maryland creek; site of bloodiest day's fighting in the Civil War. (39°N 77°W), 497, *m495*

Appalachian Mountains mountain range running from Alabama into Canada. 126, *m127*

Appomattox Court House town near Appomattox, Virginia, where Lee surrendered to Grant on April 9, 1865. (37°N 79°W), 519, *m517*

Arizona 48th state. Capital: Phoenix. *Atlas*

Arkansas 25th state. Capital: Little Rock. *Atlas*

Asia world's largest continent. *Atlas*

Atlantic Ocean ocean forming east boundary of the United States. *Atlas*

Australia island country between Indian and Pacific oceans; also the world's smallest continent. *Atlas*

Austria-Hungary one of the Central Powers in World War I; after the war, divided into smaller countries. 680, *m680*

Aztec Empire former region of Mexico once under Aztec control. 63, *m63*

Backcountry identification for former undeveloped region beginning in the Appalachian Mountains and extending west. 126, *m127*

Baltimore Maryland city on Chesapeake Bay. (39°N 77°W), 332, *m331*

Bay of Pigs (Bahía de Cochinos) inlet on south coast of Cuba; site of 1961 ill-fated, U.S.-backed Cuban invasion attempt. (22°N 81°W), 838

Beringia former land bridge connecting Asia with North America and now under waters of Bering Strait. (66°N 169°W), 27, *m28*

Berlin capital of Germany; divided into East and West Berlin, 1948–1989. (53°N 13°E), 793, *m792*

Boston capital of Massachusetts; site of early colonial unrest and conflict. (42°N 71°W), 165, *m172*

Bull Run stream 30 miles southwest of Washington, D.C.; site of first land battle of Civil War. (39°N 78°W), 485, *m495*

Bunker Hill hill now part of Boston; its name misidentifies Revolutionary War battle fought at nearby Breed's Hill. (42°N 71°W), 177

Cahokia Illinois Mound Builders site; village taken from British by Clark in 1778. (39°N 90°W), 31, *m203*

California 31st state. Capital: Sacramento. *Atlas*

Canada nation sharing northern U.S. border. *Atlas*

Caribbean Sea expanse of the Atlantic Ocean between the Gulf of Mexico and South America. *Atlas*

Central America area of North America between Mexico and South America. *m72, Atlas*

Charleston as Charles Town, largest Southern colonial city; South Carolina site of first Civil War shots, at offshore Fort Sumter. (33°N 80°W), 481, *m483*

Charlestown former town, now part of Boston; site of both Bunker and Breed's hills. (42°N 71°W), 177, *m172*

Chicago large Illinois city on Lake Michigan. (42°N 88°W), 602, *Atlas*

China large nation in Asia. *Atlas*

Colorado 38th state. Capital: Denver. *Atlas*

Concord Massachusetts city and site of second battle of the Revolutionary War. (42°N 71°W), 172, *m172*

Confederate States of America nation formed by 11 Southern states during the Civil War. Capital: Richmond, Virginia. 473 and 482, *m483*

Connecticut 5th state. Capital: Hartford. *Atlas*

Cuba Caribbean island south of Florida. 662, *m665*

Delaware 1st state. Capital: Dover. *Atlas*

PRESIDENTS of the UNITED STATES

30 **Calvin Coolidge**
1923–1929
Republican
Birthplace: Vermont
Born: July 4, 1872
Died: January 5, 1933

31 **Herbert C. Hoover**
1929–1933
Republican
Birthplace: Iowa
Born: August 10, 1874
Died: October 20, 1964

32 **Franklin D. Roosevelt**
1933–1945
Democrat
Birthplace: New York
Born: January 30, 1882
Died: April 12, 1945

33 **Harry S. Truman**
1945–1953
Democrat
Birthplace: Missouri
Born: May 8, 1884
Died: December 26, 1972

34 **Dwight D. Eisenhower**
1953–1961
Republican
Birthplace: Texas
Born: October 14, 1890
Died: March 28, 1969

35 **John F. Kennedy**
1961–1963
Democrat
Birthplace: Massachusetts
Born: May 29, 1917
Died: November 22, 1963

36 **Lyndon B. Johnson**
1963–1969
Democrat
Birthplace: Texas
Born: August 27, 1908
Died: January 22, 1973

37 **Richard M. Nixon**
1969–1974
Republican
Birthplace: California
Born: January 9, 1913
Died: April 22, 1994

38 **Gerald R. Ford**
1974–1977
Republican
Birthplace: Nebraska
Born: July 14, 1913

39 **James E. Carter, Jr.**
1977–1981
Democrat
Birthplace: Georgia
Born: October 1, 1924

40 **Ronald W. Reagan**
1981–1989
Republican
Birthplace: Illinois
Born: February 6, 1911
Died: June 5, 2004

41 **George H. W. Bush**
1989–1993
Republican
Birthplace: Massachusetts
Born: June 12, 1924

42 **William J. Clinton**
1993–2001
Democrat
Birthplace: Arkansas
Born: August 19, 1946

43 **George W. Bush**
2001–
Republican
Birthplace: Texas
Born: July 6, 1946

13 Millard Fillmore
1850–1853
Whig
Birthplace: New York
Born: January 7, 1800
Died: March 8, 1874

14 Franklin Pierce
1853–1857
Democrat
Birthplace: New Hampshire
Born: November 23, 1804
Died: October 8, 1869

15 James Buchanan
1857–1861
Democrat
Birthplace: Pennsylvania
Born: April 23, 1791
Died: June 1, 1868

16 Abraham Lincoln
1861–1865
Republican
Birthplace: Kentucky
Born: February 12, 1809
Died: April 15, 1865

17 Andrew Johnson
1865–1869
National Union
Birthplace: North Carolina
Born: December 29, 1808
Died: July 31, 1875

18 Ulysses S. Grant
1869–1877
Republican
Birthplace: Ohio
Born: April 27, 1822
Died: July 23, 1885

19 Rutherford B. Hayes
1877–1881
Republican
Birthplace: Ohio
Born: October 4, 1822
Died: January 17, 1893

20 James A. Garfield
1881
Republican
Birthplace: Ohio
Born: November 19, 1831
Died: September 19, 1881

21 Chester A. Arthur
1881–1885
Republican
Birthplace: Vermont
Born: October 5, 1829
Died: November 18, 1886

22 24 Grover Cleveland
1885–1889, 1893–1897
Democrat
Birthplace: New Jersey
Born: March 18, 1837
Died: June 24, 1908

23 Benjamin Harrison
1889–1893
Republican
Birthplace: Ohio
Born: August 20, 1833
Died: March 13, 1901

25 William McKinley
1897–1901
Republican
Birthplace: Ohio
Born: January 29, 1843
Died: September 14, 1901

26 Theodore Roosevelt
1901–1909
Republican
Birthplace: New York
Born: October 27, 1858
Died: January 6, 1919

27 William H. Taft
1909–1913
Republican
Birthplace: Ohio
Born: September 15, 1857
Died: March 8, 1930

28 Woodrow Wilson
1913–1921
Democrat
Birthplace: Virginia
Born: December 28, 1856
Died: February 3, 1924

29 Warren G. Harding
1921–1923
Republican
Birthplace: Ohio
Born: November 2, 1865
Died: August 2, 1923

Here are some little-known facts about the presidents of the United States:

- Only former president to serve in Congress: John Quincy Adams
- First president born in the new United States: Martin Van Buren (eighth president)
- Only president who was a bachelor: James Buchanan
- First left-handed president: James A. Garfield
- Largest president: William H. Taft (6 feet 2 inches, 326 pounds)
- Youngest president: Theodore Roosevelt (42 years old)
- Oldest president: Ronald Reagan (77 years old when he left office in 1989)
- First president born west of the Mississippi River: Herbert Hoover (born in West Branch, Iowa)
- First president born in the 20th century: John F. Kennedy (born May 29, 1917)

1 George Washington
1789–1797
No Political Party
Birthplace: Virginia
Born: February 22, 1732
Died: December 14, 1799

2 John Adams
1797–1801
Federalist
Birthplace: Massachusetts
Born: October 30, 1735
Died: July 4, 1826

3 Thomas Jefferson
1801–1809
Democratic-Republican
Birthplace: Virginia
Born: April 13, 1743
Died: July 4, 1826

4 James Madison
1809–1817
Democratic-Republican
Birthplace: Virginia
Born: March 16, 1751
Died: June 28, 1836

5 James Monroe
1817–1825
Democratic-Republican
Birthplace: Virginia
Born: April 28, 1758
Died: July 4, 1831

6 John Quincy Adams
1825–1829
Democratic-Republican
Birthplace: Massachusetts
Born: July 11, 1767
Died: February 23, 1848

7 Andrew Jackson
1829–1837
Democrat
Birthplace: South Carolina
Born: March 15, 1767
Died: June 8, 1845

8 Martin Van Buren
1837–1841
Democrat
Birthplace: New York
Born: December 5, 1782
Died: July 24, 1862

9 William H. Harrison
1841
Whig
Birthplace: Virginia
Born: February 9, 1773
Died: April 4, 1841

10 John Tyler
1841–1845
Whig
Birthplace: Virginia
Born: March 29, 1790
Died: January 18, 1862

11 James K. Polk
1845–1849
Democrat
Birthplace: North Carolina
Born: November 2, 1795
Died: June 15, 1849

12 Zachary Taylor
1849–1850
Whig
Birthplace: Virginia
Born: November 24, 1784
Died: July 9, 1850

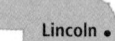

Nebraska
1,729,180 people
77,353 sq. mi.
Rank in area: 16
Entered Union in 1867

Ohio
11,421,267 people
44,825 sq. mi.
Rank in area: 34
Entered Union in 1803

Texas
21,779,893 people
267,256 sq. mi.
Rank in area: 2
Entered Union in 1845

Nevada
2,173,491 people
110,560 sq. mi.
Rank in area: 7
Entered Union in 1864

Oklahoma
3,493,714 people
69,898 sq. mi.
Rank in area: 20
Entered Union in 1907

Utah
2,316,256 people
84,898 sq. mi.
Rank in area: 13
Entered Union in 1896

New Hampshire
1,275,056 people
9,282 sq. mi.
Rank in area: 44
Entered Union in 1788

Oregon
3,521,515 people
97,126 sq. mi.
Rank in area: 10
Entered Union in 1859

Vermont
616,592 people
9,614 sq. mi.
Rank in area: 43
Entered Union in 1791

New Jersey
8,590,300 people
8,214 sq. mi.
Rank in area: 46
Entered Union in 1787

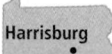

Pennsylvania
12,335,091 people
46,055 sq. mi.
Rank in area: 33
Entered Union in 1787

Virginia
7,293,542 people
42,328 sq. mi.
Rank in area: 35
Entered Union in 1788

New Mexico
1,855,059 people
121,589 sq. mi.
Rank in area: 5
Entered Union in 1912

Rhode Island
1,069,725 people
1,231 sq. mi.
Rank in area: 50
Entered Union in 1790

Washington
6,068,996 people
70,634 sq. mi.
Rank in area: 19
Entered Union in 1889

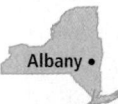

New York
19,157,532 people
54,077 sq. mi.
Rank in area: 27
Entered Union in 1788

South Carolina
4,107,183 people
31,190 sq. mi.
Rank in area: 40
Entered Union in 1788

West Virginia
1,801,873 people
24,230 sq. mi.
Rank in area: 41
Entered Union in 1863

North Carolina
8,320,146 people
52,670 sq. mi.
Rank in area: 29
Entered Union in 1789

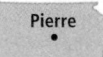

South Dakota
761,063 people
77,116 sq. mi.
Rank in area: 17
Entered Union in 1889

Wisconsin
5,441,196 people
65,498 sq. mi.
Rank in area: 22
Entered Union in 1848

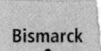

North Dakota
634,110 people
70,699 sq. mi.
Rank in area: 18
Entered Union in 1889

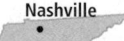

Tennessee
5,797,289 people
42,143 sq. mi.
Rank in area: 36
Entered Union in 1796

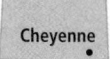

Wyoming
498,703 people
97,813 sq. mi.
Rank in area: 9
Entered Union in 1890

United States: Major Dependencies

- American Samoa—68,688 people; 90 sq. mi.
- Guam—160,796 people; 217 sq. mi.
- Commonwealth of Puerto Rico—3,957,988 people; 5,324 sq. mi.
- Virgin Islands of the United States—123,498 people; 171 sq. mi.
- Midway Atoll—no indigenous inhabitants; 2 sq. mi.
- Wake Atoll—no indigenous inhabitants; 3 sq. mi.

Alabama
4,486,508 people
52,218 sq. mi.
Rank in area: 30
Entered Union in 1819

Montgomery

Tallahassee
Florida
16,713,149 people
59,909 sq. mi.
Rank in area: 23
Entered Union in 1845

Baton Rouge
Louisiana
4,482,646 people
49,650 sq. mi.
Rank in area: 31
Entered Union in 1812

Juneau
Alaska
643,786 people
616,240 sq. mi.
Rank in area: 1
Entered Union in 1959

Atlanta
Georgia
8,560,310 people
58,970 sq. mi.
Rank in area: 24
Entered Union in 1788

Augusta
Maine
1,294,464 people
33,738 sq. mi.
Rank in area: 39
Entered Union in 1820

Phoenix
Arizona
5,456,453 people
113,998 sq. mi.
Rank in area: 6
Entered Union in 1912

Honolulu
Hawaii
1,244,898 people
6,641 sq. mi.
Rank in area: 47
Entered Union in 1959

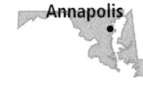
Annapolis
Maryland
5,458,137 people
12,297 sq. mi.
Rank in area: 42
Entered Union in 1788

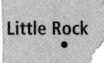
Little Rock
Arkansas
2,710,079 people
53,178 sq. mi.
Rank in area: 28
Entered Union in 1836

Boise
Idaho
1,341,131 people
83,570 sq. mi.
Rank in area: 14
Entered Union in 1890

Boston
Massachusetts
6,427,801 people
9,240 sq. mi.
Rank in area: 45
Entered Union in 1788

Sacramento
California
35,116,033 people
158,854 sq. mi.
Rank in area: 3
Entered Union in 1850

Springfield
Illinois
12,600,620 people
57,914 sq. mi.
Rank in area: 25
Entered Union in 1818

Lansing
Michigan
10,050,446 people
96,716 sq. mi.
Rank in area: 11
Entered Union in 1837

Denver
Colorado
4,506,542 people
104,093 sq. mi.
Rank in area: 8
Entered Union in 1876

Indianapolis
Indiana
6,159,068 people
36,418 sq. mi.
Rank in area: 38
Entered Union in 1816

St. Paul
Minnesota
5,019,720 people
86,938 sq. mi.
Rank in area: 12
Entered Union in 1858

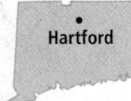
Hartford
Connecticut
3,460,503 people
5,543 sq. mi.
Rank in area: 48
Entered Union in 1788

Des Moines
Iowa
2,936,760 people
56,271 sq. mi.
Rank in area: 26
Entered Union in 1846

Jackson
Mississippi
2,871,782 people
48,282 sq. mi.
Rank in area: 32
Entered Union in 1817

Dover
Delaware
807,385 people
2,396 sq. mi.
Rank in area: 49
Entered Union in 1787

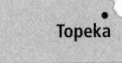
Topeka
Kansas
2,715,884 people
82,276 sq. mi.
Rank in area: 15
Entered Union in 1861

Jefferson City
Missouri
5,672,579 people
69,704 sq. mi.
Rank in area: 21
Entered Union in 1821

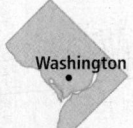
Washington
District of Columbia
570,898 people
68 sq. mi.

Frankfort
Kentucky
4,092,891 people
40,409 sq. mi.
Rank in area: 37
Entered Union in 1792

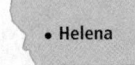
Helena
Montana
909,453 people
147,042 sq. mi.
Rank in area: 4
Entered Union in 1889

Sources: U.S. Bureau of the Census, July 1 2002 population estimates.
World Almanac and Book of Facts, 2003
Statistical Abstract of the United States, 2002

4.4 Creating a Multimedia Presentation

Defining the Skill

Movies, CD-ROMs, television, and computer software are different kinds of media. To **create a multimedia presentation,** you need to collect information in different media and organize them into one presentation.

Applying the Skill

The scene below shows students using computers to create a multimedia presentation. Use the strategies listed below to help you create your own multimedia presentation.

How to Create a Multimedia Presentation

Strategy ❶ Identify the topic of your presentation and decide which media are best for an effective presentation. For example, you may want to use slides or posters to show visual images of your topic. Or, you may want to use CDs or audiotapes to provide music or spoken words.

Strategy ❷ Research the topic in a variety of sources. Images, text, props, and background music should reflect the historical period of the event you choose.

Strategy ❸ Write the script for the oral portion of the presentation. You could use a narrator and characters' voices to tell the story. Primary sources are an excellent source for script material. Make sure the recording is clear so that the audience will be able to understand the oral part of the presentation.

Strategy ❹ Videotape the presentation. Videotaping the presentation will preserve it for future viewing and allow you to show it to different groups of people.

Practicing the Skill

Turn to Chapter 24, "World War I." Choose a topic from the chapter and use the strategies listed above to create a multimedia presentation about it.

4.3 Using the Internet

Defining the Skill

The Internet is a computer network that connects to universities, libraries, news organizations, government agencies, businesses, and private individuals throughout the world. Each location on the Internet has a home page with its own address, or URL (universal resource locator). With a computer connected to the Internet, you can reach the home pages of many organizations and services. The international collection of home pages, known as the World Wide Web, is a good source of up-to-date information about current events as well as research on subjects in history.

Applying the Skill

The Web page below shows the links for Chapter 6 of *Creating America*. Use the strategies listed below to help you understand how to use the Web page.

How to Use the Internet

Strategy ❶ Go directly to a Web page. For example, type http://www.mcdougallittell.com in the box at the top of the screen and press ENTER (or RETURN). The Web page will appear on your screen. Then click on ClassZone and find the link to *Creating America*.

Strategy ❷ Explore the *Creating America* links. Click on any one of the links to find out more about a specific subject. These links take you to other pages at this Web site. Some pages include links to related information that can be found at other places on the Internet.

Strategy ❸ When using the Internet for research, you should confirm the information you find. Web sites set up by universities, government agencies, and reputable news sources are more reliable than other sources. You can often find information about the creator of a site by looking for copyright information.

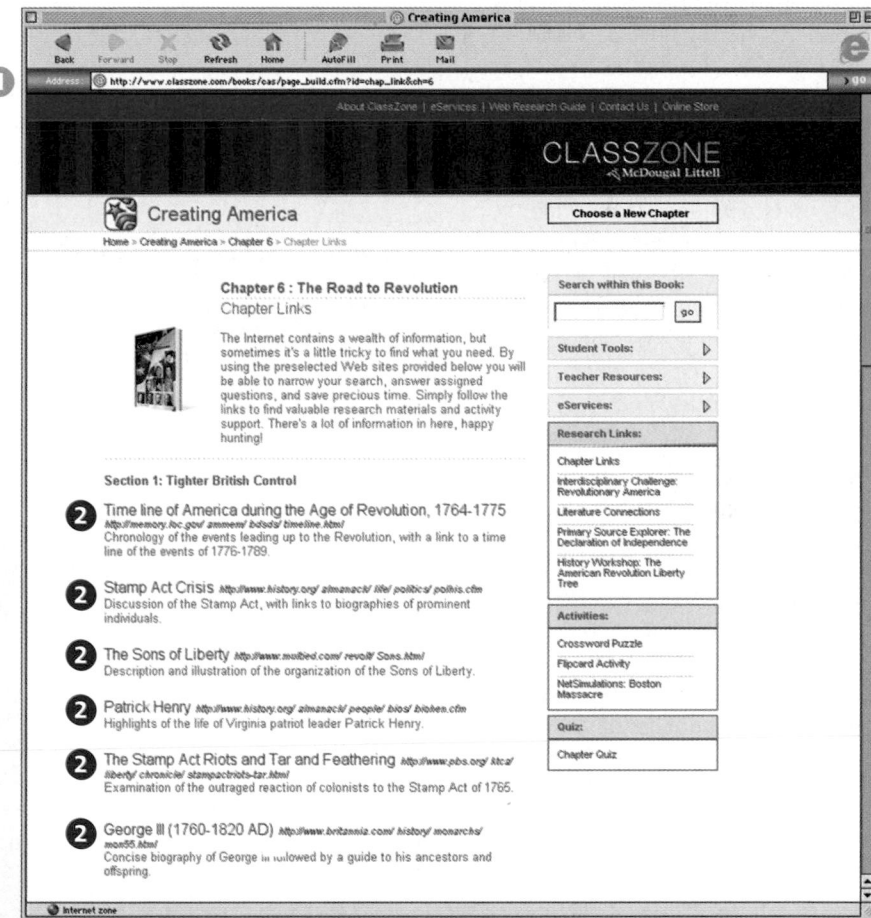

Practicing the Skill

Turn to Chapter 14, Section 2, "American Literature and Art." Read the section and make a list of topics you would like to research. If you have Internet access, go to the McDougal Littell home page at http://www.mcdougallittell.com and click on ClassZone. There you will find links that provide more information about the topics in the section.

4.2 Creating a Database

Defining the Skill

A **database** is a collection of data, or information, that is organized so that you can find and retrieve information on a specific topic quickly and easily. Once a computerized database is set up, you can search it to find specific information without going through the entire database. The database will provide a list of all information in the database related to your topic. Learning how to use a database will help you learn how to create one.

Applying the Skill

The chart below is a database for the significant battles of the Civil War. Use the strategies listed below to help you understand and use the database.

How to Create a Database

Strategy ① Identify the topic of the database. The keywords, or most important words, in this title are *Civil War* and *Battles*. These words were used to begin the research for this database.

Strategy ② Ask yourself what kind of data you need to include. For example, what geographic patterns and distributions will be shown? Your choice of data will provide the column headings for your database. The key words *Battle, Date, Location,* and *Significance* were chosen to focus the research.

Strategy ③ Identify the entries included under each heading.

Strategy ④ Use the database to help you find information quickly. For example, in this database you could search for "Union victories" to find a list of significant battles won by the North.

① LOCATION OF SIGNIFICANT CIVIL WAR BATTLES

② BATTLE	DATE	② LOCATION	SIGNIFICANCE
③ Fort Sumter	April 12, 1861	Charleston, SC	Beginning of the Civil War
First Battle of Bull Run (Manassas)	July 21, 1861	Virginia	Confederate victory
Shiloh	April 6–7, 1862	Tennessee (near Shiloh Church)	④ Union victory
Antietam	September 17, 1862	Sharpsburg, MD	No clear victory; considered bloodiest battle of war
Gettysburg	July 1–3, 1863	Gettysburg, PA	Retreat of Confederacy
Vicksburg	Three-month siege ending July 3, 1863	Vicksburg, MS	Union gained control of Mississippi River
Chattanooga	November 23–25, 1863	Chattanooga, TN	④ Union victory
Atlanta	September 2, 1864	Atlanta, GA	④ Union victory; helped convince Confederacy of defeat

Practicing the Skill

Create a database for U.S. presidents through the Civil War that shows each president's home state, political party, and years served as president. Use the information in "Presidents of the United States" on pages R36–R38 to provide the data. Use a format like the one above for your database.

4.1 Using an Electronic Card Catalog

Defining the Skill

An **electronic card catalog** is a library's computerized search program that will help you find information about the books and other materials in the library. You can search the catalog by entering a book title, an author's name, or a subject of interest to you. The electronic card catalog will give you information about the materials in the library. This information is called bibliographic information. You can use an electronic card catalog to create a bibliography (a list of books) on any topic you are interested in.

Applying the Skill

The screen shown below is from an electronic search for information about Thomas Jefferson. Use the strategies listed below to help you use the information on the screen.

How to Use an Electronic Card Catalog

Strategy ❶ Begin searching by choosing either subject, title, or author, depending on the topic of your search. For this search, the user chose "Subject" and typed in the words "Jefferson, Thomas."

Strategy ❷ Once you have selected a book from the results of your search, identify the author, title, city, publisher, and date of publication.

Strategy ❸ Look for any special features in the book. This book is illustrated, and it includes bibliographical references and an index.

Strategy ❹ Locate the call number for the book. The call number indicates the section in the library where you will find the book. You can also find out if the book is available in the library you are using. If not, it may be in another library in the network.

Search Request:
❶ Subject   Title   Author

Find Options Locations Backup Startover Help

❷ Miller, Douglas T. Thomas Jefferson and the creation of America. New York: Facts on File, 1997.
   ❷ AUTHOR: Miller, Douglas T.
      TITLE: Thomas Jefferson and the creation of America/Douglas T. Miller.
❷ PUBLISHED: New York: Facts on File, ©1997.
  ❸ PAGING: vi, 122p. : ill ; 24 cm.
    SERIES: Makers of America.
  ❸ NOTES: Includes bibliographical references (p. 117-118) and index.
❹ CALL NUMBER: 1. 973.46 N61T 1997–Book Available–

Practicing the Skill

Turn to Chapter 10, "The Jefferson Era," and find a topic that interests you, such as the Federalists, the Louisiana Purchase, the Lewis and Clark expedition, or the War of 1812. Use the SUBJECT search on an electronic card catalog to find information about your topic. Make a bibliography of books about the subject. Be sure to include the author, title, city, publisher, and date of publication for all the books included.

3.9 Creating a Model

Defining the Skill

When you **create a model**, you use information and ideas to show an event or a situation in a visual way. A model might be a poster or a diagram that explains how something happened. Or, it might be a three-dimensional model, such as a diorama, that depicts an important scene or situation.

Applying the Skill

The following sketch shows the early stages of a model of three ways that people could have traveled from the eastern United States to California during the gold rush. Use the strategies listed below to help you create your own model.

How to Create a Model

Strategy ❶ Gather the information you need to understand the situation or event. In this case, you need to be able to show the three routes and their dangers.

Strategy ❷ Visualize and sketch an idea for your model. Once you have created a picture in your mind, make an actual sketch to plan how it might look.

Strategy ❸ Think of symbols you may want to use. Since the model should give information in a visual way, think about ways you can use color, pictures, or other visuals to tell the story.

Strategy ❹ Gather the supplies you will need and create the model. For example, you will need a globe and art supplies, such as yarn, for this model.

Strategy ❺ Write and answer a question about the California gold rush, as shown in this model.

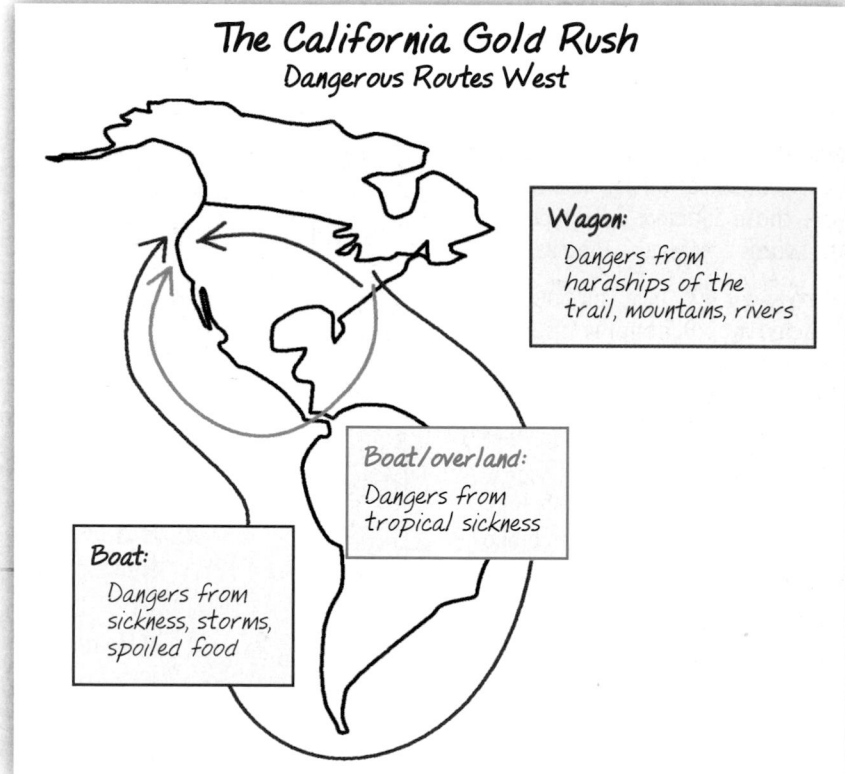

The California Gold Rush
Dangerous Routes West

Wagon:
Dangers from hardships of the trail, mountains, rivers

Boat/overland:
Dangers from tropical sickness

Boat:
Dangers from sickness, storms, spoiled food

Practicing the Skill

Read the History Workshop called "Pack Your Trunk" on pages 450–451. Follow the step-by-step directions to create a model of a trunk that shows what immigrants might have decided to bring with them when they came to America.

3.8 Interpreting Political Cartoons

Defining the Skill

Political cartoons are cartoons that use humor to make a serious point. Political cartoons often express a point of view on an issue better than words do. Understanding signs and symbols will help you to interpret political cartoons.

Applying the Skill

The cartoon below shows Abraham Lincoln and the other candidates running for the presidency in 1860. Use the strategies listed below to help you understand the cartoon.

How to Interpret a Political Cartoon

Strategy ❶ Identify the subject by reading the title of the cartoon and looking at the cartoon as a whole.

Strategy ❷ Identify important symbols and details. The cartoonist uses the image of a running race to discuss a political campaign. The White House is the finish line.

Strategy ❸ Interpret the message. Why is Lincoln drawn so much taller than the other candidates? How does that make him the fittest candidate?

Make a Chart

Making a chart will help you summarize information from a political cartoon. The chart below summarizes the information from the cartoon above.

Subject	"A Political Race" (The Election of 1860)
Symbols and Details	Running is a symbol for a political campaign. Lincoln is the tallest and fastest candidate.
Message	❸ Lincoln is pulling ahead of the other candidates in the campaign for the presidency.

Practicing the Skill

Turn to Chapter 18, Section 3, "End of Reconstruction." Look at the political cartoon on page 547. It shows a cartoonist's view of corruption in President Grant's administration. Use a chart like the one above and the strategies outlined to interpret the cartoon.

3.7 Creating a Map

Defining the Skill

Creating a map involves representing geographical information. When you draw a map, it is easiest to use an existing map as a guide. On the map you draw, you can show geographical information. You can also show other kinds of information, such as data on climates, population trends, resources, or routes. Often, this data comes from a graph or a chart.

Applying the Skill

Below is a map that a student created to show information about the number of slaves in 1750. Read the strategies listed below to see how the map was created.

How to Create a Map

Strategy ❶ Select a title that identifies the geographical area and the map's purpose. Include a date in your title.

Strategy ❷ Draw the lines of latitude and longitude using short dashes.

Strategy ❸ Create a key that shows the colors.

Strategy ❹ Draw the colors on the map to show information.

Strategy ❺ Draw a compass rose and scale.

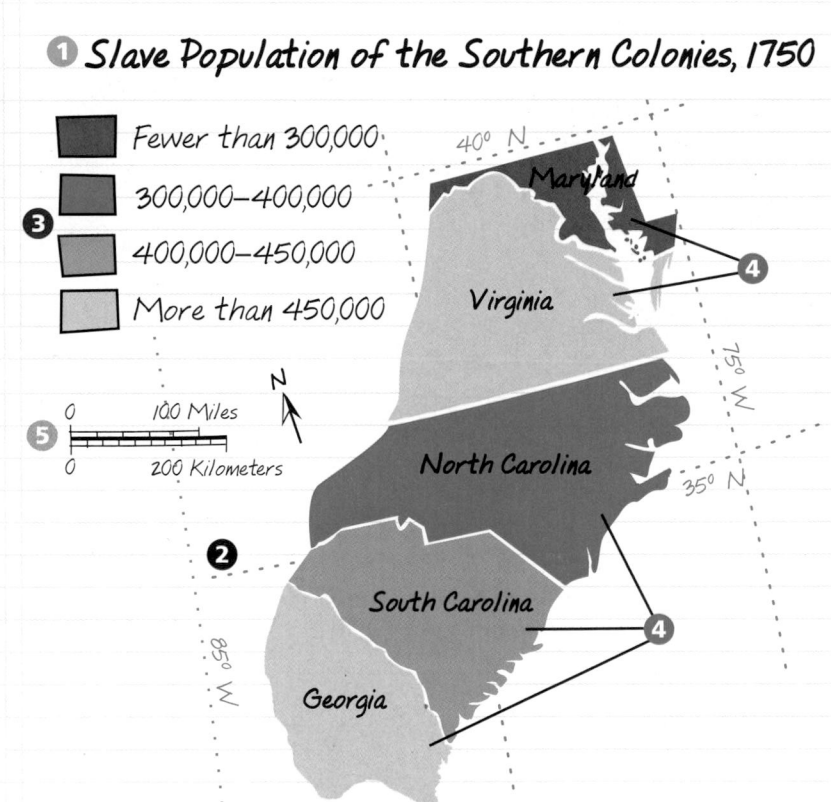

❶ Slave Population of the Southern Colonies, 1750

❸
■ Fewer than 300,000
■ 300,000–400,000
■ 400,000–450,000
■ More than 450,000

❺ 0   100 Miles   0   200 Kilometers

N

Maryland   40° N

Virginia

75° W

North Carolina   35° N

❷

85° W

South Carolina

Georgia

❹

Practicing the Skill

Make your own map. Turn to page 104 in Chapter 3 and study the graph entitled "The 13 Colonies." Use the strategies described above to create a map that shows the 13 colonies and the dates that they were founded. You can use the map on page 102 of that chapter as a guide.

3.6 Reading a Special-Purpose Map

Defining the Skill

Special-purpose maps help people focus on a particular aspect of a region, such as economic development in the South. These kinds of maps often use symbols to indicate information.

Applying the Skill

The following special-purpose map indicates the products of the Southern colonies. Use the strategies listed below to help you identify the information shown on the map.

How to Read a Special-Purpose Map

Strategy ❶ Read the title. It tells you what the map is intended to show.

Strategy ❷ Read the legend. This tells you what each symbol stands for. This legend shows the crops that were grown in various Southern colonies.

Strategy ❸ Look for the places on the map where the symbols appear. These tell you the places where each crop was grown.

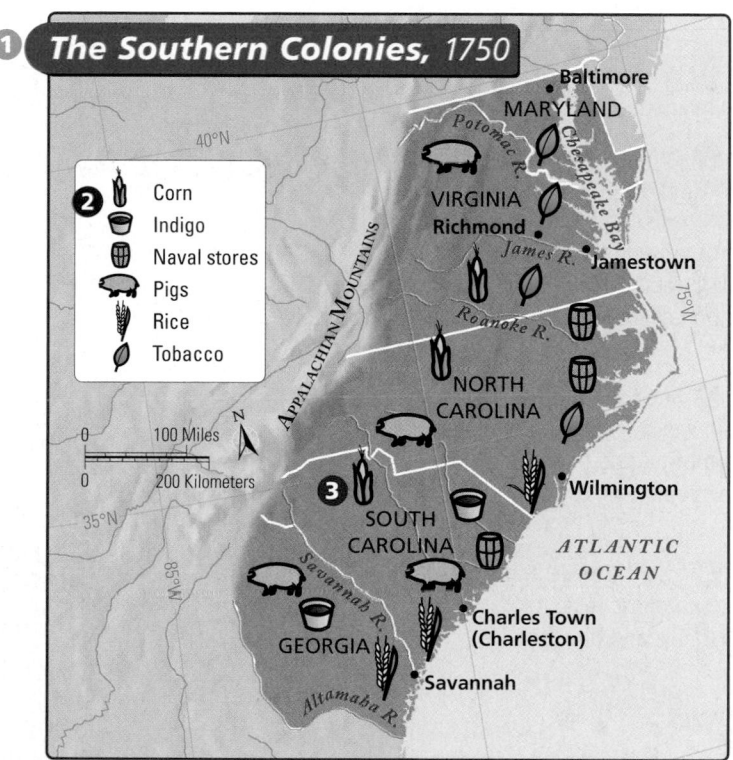

❶ **The Southern Colonies, 1750**

❷ Legend:
- Corn
- Indigo
- Naval stores
- Pigs
- Rice
- Tobacco

Make a Chart

A chart can help you understand special-purpose maps. The chart below shows information about the special-purpose map you just studied.

	Corn	Indigo	Naval stores	Pigs	Rice	Tobacco
Maryland						x
Virginia	x			x		x
North Carolina	x		x	x	x	x
South Carolina	x	x	x	x	x	
Georgia		x		x	x	

Practicing the Skill

Turn to Chapter 4, Section 1, "New England: Commerce and Religion." Look at the special-purpose map entitled "The New England Colonies, 1750" and make a chart that shows information about products from New England.

3.5 Reading a Map

Defining the Skill

Maps are representations of features on the earth's surface. Some maps show political features, such as national borders. Other maps show physical features, such as mountains and bodies of water. By learning to use map elements and math skills, you can better understand how to read maps.

Applying the Skill

The following map shows the Battle of Yorktown during the Revolution. Use the strategies listed below to help you identify the elements common to most maps.

How to Read a Map

Strategy 1 Read the title. This identifies the main idea of the map.

Strategy 2 Look for the grid of lines that forms a pattern of squares over the map. These numbered lines are the lines of latitude (horizontal) and longitude (vertical). They indicate the location of the area on the earth.

Strategy 3 Read the map key. It is usually in a box. This will give you the information you need to interpret the symbols or colors on the map.

Strategy 4 Use the scale and the pointer, or compass rose, to determine distance and direction.

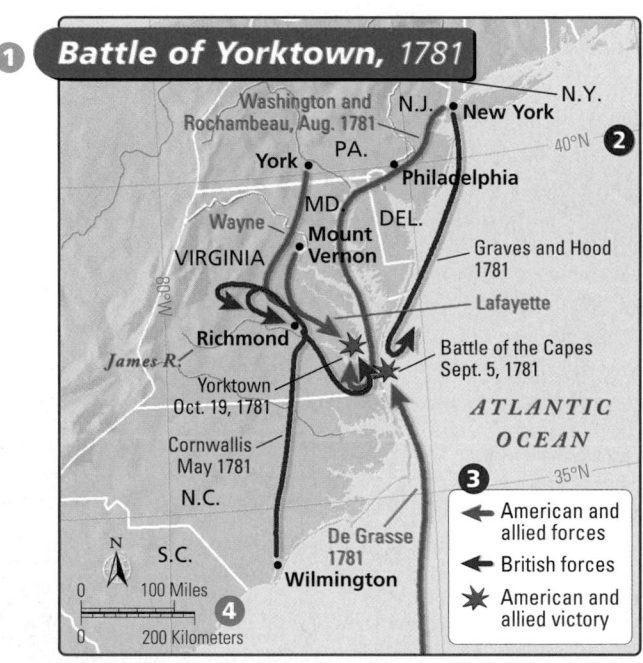

Make a Chart

A chart can help you organize information given on maps. The chart below summarizes information about the map you just studied.

Title	Battle of Yorktown, 1781
Location	between latitude 40° N and 35° N, just east of longitude 80° W
Map Key Information	blue = American and allied forces, red = British forces
Scale	7/16 in. = 100 miles, 9/16 in. = 200 km
Summary	British commanders Graves and Hood sailed south from New York. They were defeated by De Grasse at the Battle of the Capes. British commander Cornwallis marched north from Wilmington, North Carolina, to Virginia, where he was defeated by American forces.

Practicing the Skill

Turn to Chapter 1, Section 5, "Early European Explorers." Read the map entitled "Exploration Leads to New Sea Routes" and make a chart to identify information on the map.

3.4 Interpreting Time Lines

Defining the Skill

A **time line** is a visual list of events and dates shown in the order in which they occurred. Time lines can be horizontal or vertical. On horizontal time lines, the earliest date is on the left. On vertical time lines, the earliest date is often at the top.

Applying the Skill

The time line below lists dates and events during the presidencies of John Adams, Andrew Jackson, and Martin Van Buren. Use the strategies listed below to help you interpret the information.

How to Read a Time Line

Strategy ❶ Read the dates at the beginning and end of the time line. These will show the period of history that is covered. The time line below is a dual time line. It includes items related to two topics. The labels show that the information covers U.S. events and world events.

Strategy ❷ Read the dates and events in sequential order, beginning with the earliest one. Pay particular attention to how the entries relate to each other. Think about which events caused later events.

Strategy ❸ Summarize the focus, or main idea, of the time line. Try to write a main idea sentence that describes the time line.

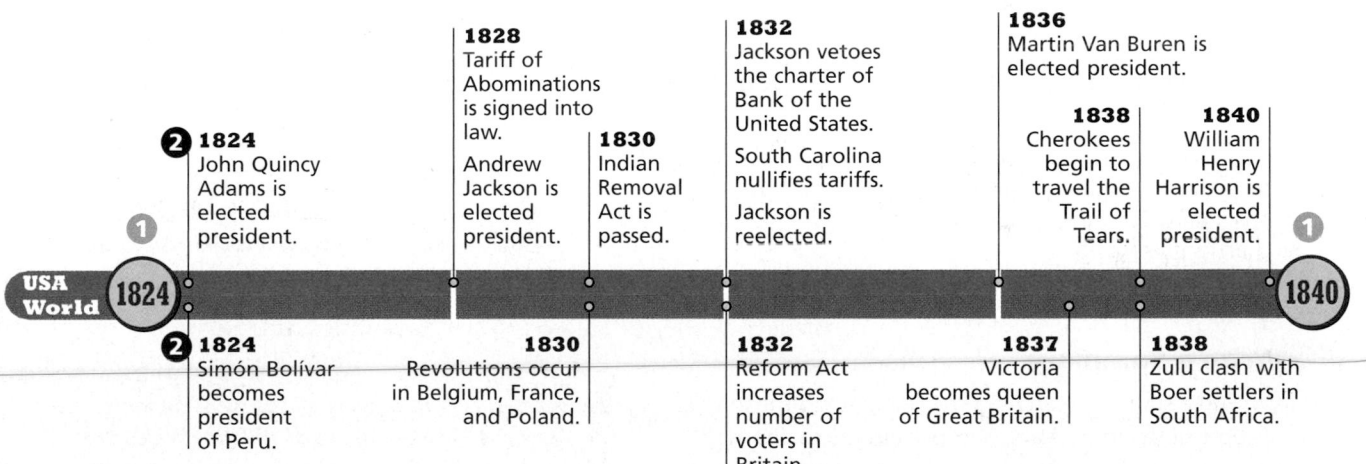

1828
Tariff of Abominations is signed into law.

1830
Andrew Jackson is elected president.

1830
Indian Removal Act is passed.

1832
Jackson vetoes the charter of Bank of the United States.
South Carolina nullifies tariffs.
Jackson is reelected.

1836
Martin Van Buren is elected president.

1838
Cherokees begin to travel the Trail of Tears.

1840
William Henry Harrison is elected president.

❷ **1824**
John Quincy Adams is elected president.

USA / World ❶ 1824 · · · · · · · · · · 1840 ❶

❷ **1824**
Simón Bolívar becomes president of Peru.

1830
Revolutions occur in Belgium, France, and Poland.

1832
Reform Act increases number of voters in Britain.

1837
Victoria becomes queen of Great Britain.

1838
Zulu clash with Boer settlers in South Africa.

Write a Summary

Writing a summary can help you understand information shown on a time line. The summary to the right states the main idea of the time line and tells how the events are related.

Practicing the Skill

Turn to Chapter 15, page 455, and write a summary of the information shown on the time line.

❸ *The time line covers the period between 1824, when John Quincy Adams was elected president, and 1840, when William Henry Harrison was elected president. During that period of time, Andrew Jackson and Martin Van Buren also served as president. The time line shows that the important issues in the United States were tariffs, banking, and relations with Native Americans.*

3.3 Interpreting Charts

Defining the Skill

Charts, like graphs, present information in a visual form. Charts are created by organizing, summarizing, and simplifying information and presenting it in a format that makes it easy to understand. Tables and diagrams are examples of commonly used charts.

Applying the Skill

The chart below shows the number of slaves who were imported to the Americas between 1601 and 1810. Use the strategies listed below to help you interpret the information in the chart.

How to Interpret a Chart

Strategy ① Read the title. It will tell you what the chart is about. Ask yourself what kinds of information the chart shows. For example, does it show chronological information, geographic patterns and distributions, or something else?

Strategy ② Read the labels to see how the information in the chart is organized. In this chart, it is organized by region and years.

Strategy ③ Study the data in the chart to understand the facts that the chart intends to show.

Strategy ④ Summarize the information shown in each part of the chart. Use the title to help you focus on what information the chart is presenting.

1601–1810

① Slaves Imported to the Americas *(in thousands)*

② REGION/COUNTRY	**1601–1700**	**1701–1810**
③ British N. America	*	348
British Caribbean	263.7	1,401.3
French Caribbean	155.8	1,348.4
Spanish America	292.5	578.6
Dutch Caribbean	40	460
Danish Caribbean	4	24
Brazil (Portugal)	560	1,891.4

*= less than 1,000

Source: Philip D. Curtin, *The Atlantic Slave Trade*

Write a Summary

Writing a summary can help you understand the information given in a chart. The paragraph to the right summarizes the information in the chart "Slaves Imported to the Americas, 1601–1810."

④ *The chart shows how many slaves were imported to the Americas between 1601 and 1810. It divides the Americas into seven regions. It also divides the time period into two parts: 1601–1700 and 1701–1810. The number of slaves imported increased greatly from the 1600s to the 1700s. More slaves were imported to Brazil than to any other region.*

Practicing the Skill

Turn to Chapter 27, Section 5, and look at the chart entitled "World War II Military Casualties, 1939–1945." Study the chart and ask yourself what geographic patterns and distributions are shown in it. Then write a paragraph in which you summarize what you learned from the chart.

3.2 Interpreting Graphs

Defining the Skill

Graphs use pictures and symbols, instead of words, to show information. Graphs are created by taking information and presenting it visually. The graph on this page takes numerical information on immigration and presents it as a bar graph. There are many different kinds of graphs. Bar graphs, line graphs, and pie graphs are the most common. Bar graphs compare numbers or sets of numbers. The length of each bar shows a quantity. It is easy to see how different categories compare on a bar graph.

Applying the Skill

The bar graph below shows numbers of immigrants coming to the United States between 1821 and 1860. Use the strategies listed below to help you interpret the graph.

How to Interpret a Graph

Strategy ❶ Read the title to identify the main idea of the graph. Ask yourself what kinds of information the graph shows. For example, does it show chronological information, geographic patterns and distributions, or something else?

Strategy ❷ Read the vertical axis (the one that goes up and down) on the left side of the graph. This one shows the number of immigrants in thousands. Each bar represents the number of immigrants during a particular decade.

Strategy ❸ Read the horizontal axis (the one that runs across the bottom of the graph). This one shows the four decades from 1821 to 1860.

Strategy ❹ Summarize the information shown in each part of the graph. Use the title to help you focus on what information the graph is presenting.

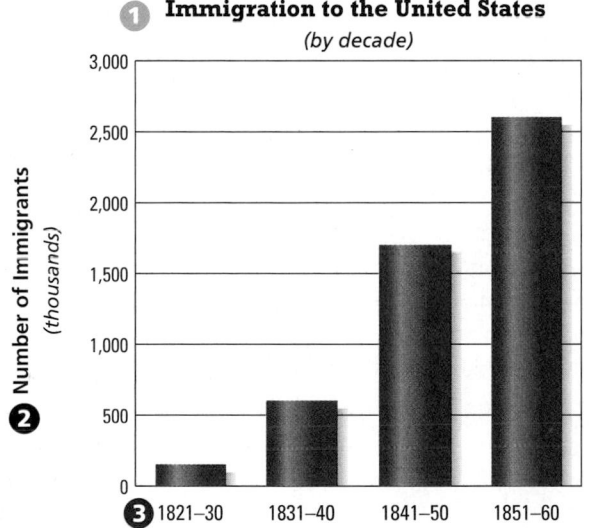

❶ **Immigration to the United States**
(by decade)

Write a Summary

Writing a summary will help you understand the information in the graph. The paragraph to the right summarizes the information from the bar graph.

Practicing the Skill

Turn to Chapter 2, Section 4, "Beginnings of Slavery in the Americas." Look at the graph entitled "Slaves Imported to the Americas, 1493–1810" and write a paragraph in which you summarize what you learned from it.

❹ Immigration to the United States increased between 1821 and 1860. Between 1821 and 1830, fewer than 200,000 immigrants arrived. In the next decade, more than 500,000 immigrants came. During the 1840s, more than 1.5 million immigrants arrived, and that number increased to more than 2.5 million in the 1850s.

3.1 Using Primary and Secondary Sources

Defining the Skill

Primary sources are materials written or made by people who lived during historical events and witnessed them. Primary sources can be letters, journal entries, speeches, autobiographies, or artwork. Other kinds of primary sources are government documents, census surveys, and financial records. **Secondary sources** are materials written by people who did not participate in an event. History books are secondary sources.

Applying the Skill

The following passage contains both a primary source and a secondary source. Use the strategies listed below to help you read them.

How to Read Primary and Secondary Sources

Strategy ❶ Distinguish secondary sources from primary sources. The first paragraph is a secondary source. The Declaration of Independence is a primary source. The secondary source explains something about the primary source.

Strategy ❷ Analyze the primary source and consider why the author produced it. Consider what the document was supposed to achieve and who would read it.

Strategy ❸ Identify the author of the primary source and note when and where it was written.

> ❶ The core idea of the Declaration is based on the philosophy of John Locke. This idea is that people have unalienable rights, or rights that government cannot take away. Jefferson stated this belief in what was to become the Declaration's best-known passage.
>
> ❷ We hold these truths to be self-evident, that all men are created equal, that they are endowed by their Creator with certain unalienable Rights, that among these are Life, Liberty and the pursuit of Happiness.
>
> ❸ —Thomas Jefferson, *The Declaration of Independence*, 1776

Make a Chart

Making a chart will help you summarize information from primary sources and secondary sources. The chart below summarizes the information from the passage you just read.

Author	Thomas Jefferson
Document	The Declaration of Independence
Notes on Primary Source	The Declaration says that "all men are created equal." It also says that people have "unalienable rights." These rights include the right to life and the right to liberty, as well as a right to pursue happiness.
Notes on Secondary Source	Jefferson based his ideas on those of John Locke. Locke had written about rights that governments could not take away from the people.

Practicing the Skill

Turn to Chapter 6, Section 3, "The Road to Lexington and Concord." Read "Between War and Peace" and make a chart like the one above to summarize the information in the primary source and the secondary source.

2.12 Making Generalizations

Defining the Skill

To **make generalizations** means to make broad judgments based on information. When you make generalizations, you should gather information from several sources.

Applying the Skill

The following three passages contain different views on George Washington. Use the strategies listed below to make a generalization about these views.

How to Make Generalizations

Strategy ❶ Look for information that the sources have in common. These three sources all discuss George Washington's ability as a military leader.

Strategy ❷ Form a generalization that describes Washington in a way that all three sources would agree with. State your generalization in a sentence.

> ### WASHINGTON'S LEADERSHIP
>
> ❶ Washington learned from his mistakes. After early defeats, he developed the strategy of dragging out the war to wear down the British. ❶ Despite difficulties, he never gave up.
> —*Creating America*
>
> ❶ [Washington] was no military genius. . . . But he was a great war leader. Creating an army out of unpromising material, he kept it in being against great odds.
> —*The Limits of Liberty*
>
> ❶ [Washington] certainly deserves some merit as a general, that he . . . can keep General Howe dancing from one town to another for two years together, with such an army as he has.
> —*The Journal of Nicholas Cresswell, July 13, 1777*

Make a Chart

Using a chart can help you make generalizations. The chart below shows how the information you just read can be used to generalize about people's views of Washington.

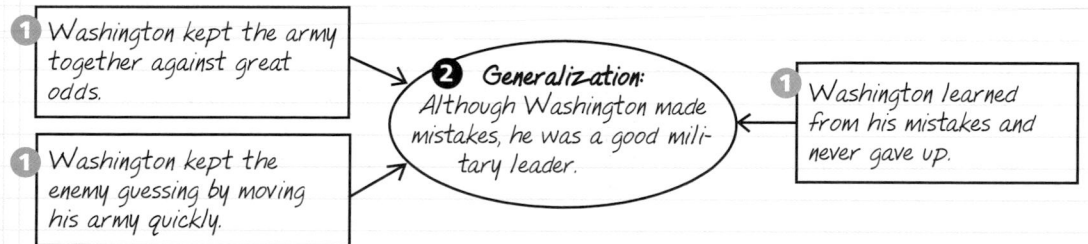

❶ Washington kept the army together against great odds.

❶ Washington kept the enemy guessing by moving his army quickly.

❷ Generalization: Although Washington made mistakes, he was a good military leader.

❶ Washington learned from his mistakes and never gave up.

Practicing the Skill

Turn to Chapter 16, Section 1, "War Erupts." Read "Choosing Sides." Also read the excerpt from *Across Five Aprils* on pages 486–487. Then use a chart like the one above to make a generalization about how the outbreak of the Civil War affected Americans.

2.11 Evaluating

Defining the Skill

To **evaluate** is to make a judgment about something. Historians evaluate the actions of people in history. One way to do this is to examine both the positives and negatives of a historical action, then decide which is stronger—the positive or the negative.

Applying the Skill

The following passage describes Susan B. Anthony's fight for women's rights. Use the strategies listed below to evaluate how successful she was.

How to Evaluate

Strategy ① Before you evaluate a person's actions, first determine what that person was trying to do. In this case, think about what Anthony wanted to accomplish.

Strategy ② Look for statements that show the positive, or successful, results of her actions. For example, Did she achieve her goals?

Strategy ③ Also look for statements that show the negative, or unsuccessful, results of her actions. Did she fail to achieve something she tried to do?

Strategy ④ Write an overall evaluation of the person's actions.

SUSAN B. ANTHONY

① Susan B. Anthony was a skilled organizer who fought for women's rights. ② She successfully built the women's movement into a national organization. Anthony believed that a woman must have money of her own. To this end, she supported laws that would give married women rights to control their own property and wages. ② Mississippi passed the first such law in 1839. New York passed a property law in 1848 and a wages law in 1860. ③ Anthony also wanted to win the vote for women but failed to convince lawmakers to pass this reform in her lifetime. This reform did go through in 1920, 14 years after her death.

Make a Diagram for Evaluating

Using a diagram can help you evaluate. List the positives and negatives of the historical person's actions and decisions. Then make an overall judgment. The diagram below shows how the information from the passage you just read can be diagrammed.

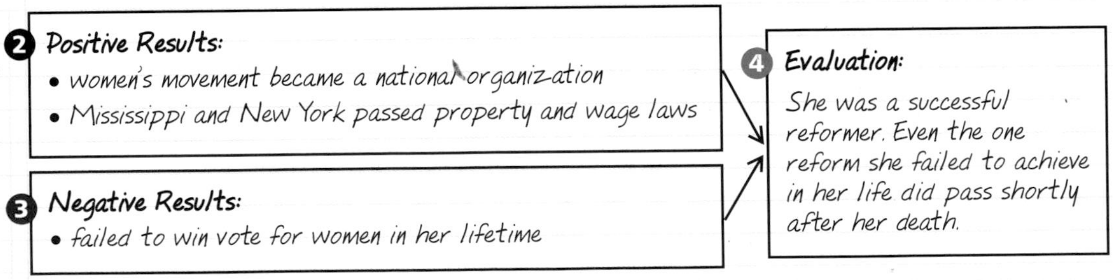

② **Positive Results:**
- women's movement became a national organization
- Mississippi and New York passed property and wage laws

③ **Negative Results:**
- failed to win vote for women in her lifetime

④ **Evaluation:**
She was a successful reformer. Even the one reform she failed to achieve in her life did pass shortly after her death.

Practicing the Skill

Turn to Chapter 2, Section 3, "The Spanish and Native Americans." Read "The Columbian Exchange" and make a diagram in which you evaluate whether the Columbian Exchange had mainly a positive or negative impact on the world.

2.10 Identifying and Solving Problems

Defining the Skill

Identifying problems means finding and understanding the difficulties faced by a particular group of people during a certain time. **Solving problems** means understanding how people tried to remedy those problems. By studying how people solved problems in the past, you can learn ways to solve problems today.

Applying the Skill

The following paragraph describes problems that the Constitutional Convention faced on the issues of taxation, representation, and slavery. Use the strategies listed below to help you see how the Founders tried to solve these problems.

How to Identify Problems and Solutions

Strategy ❶ Look for the difficulties, or problems, people faced.

Strategy ❷ Consider how the problem affected people with different points of view. For example, the main problem described here was how to count the population of each state.

Strategy ❸ Look for solutions people tried to deal with each problem. Think about whether the solution was a good one for people with differing points of view.

SLAVERY AND THE CONSTITUTION

Because the House of Representatives would have members according to the population of each state, ❶ the delegates had to decide who would be counted in the population of each state. The Southern states had many more slaves than the Northern states had. ❷ Southerners wanted the slaves to be counted as part of the general population for representation but not for taxation. ❷ Northerners argued that slaves were not citizens and should not be counted for representation, but that slaves should be counted for taxation. ❸ The delegates decided that three-fifths of the slave population would be counted in the population to determine both representation and taxes.

Make a Chart

Making a chart will help you identify and organize information about problems and solutions. The chart below shows problems and solutions included in the passage you just read.

❶ Problem	❷ Differing Points of View	❸ Solution
Northerners and Southerners couldn't agree on how to count population because of slavery in the South.	Southerners wanted slaves counted for representation but not for taxation. Northerners wanted slaves counted for taxation but not for representation.	Delegates decided that three-fifths of the slave population should be counted.

Practicing the Skill

Turn to Chapter 8, Section 2, "Creating the Constitution." Read "The Delegates Assemble" and "The Virginia Plan." Then make a chart that summarizes the problems faced by the delegates at the Constitutional Convention and the solutions they agreed on.

2.9 Forming and Supporting Opinions

Defining the Skill

When you **form opinions,** you interpret and judge the importance of events and people in history. You should always **support your opinions** with facts, examples, and quotes.

Applying the Skill

The following passage describes events that followed the gold rush. Use the strategies listed below to form and support your opinions about the events.

How to Form and Support Opinions

Strategy ❶ Look for important information about the events. Information can include facts, quotations, and examples.

Strategy ❷ Form an opinion about the event by asking yourself questions about the information. For example, How important was the event? What were its effects?

Strategy ❸ Support your opinions with facts, quotations, and examples. If the facts do not support the opinion, then rewrite your opinion so it is supported by the facts.

THE IMPACT OF THE GOLD RUSH

By 1852, the gold rush was over. ❶ While it lasted, about 250,000 people flooded into California. ❶ This huge migration caused economic growth that changed California. ❶ The port city San Francisco grew to become a center of banking, manufacturing, shipping, and trade. ❶ However, the gold rush ruined many *Californios. Californios* are the Hispanic people of California. The newcomers did not respect *Californios,* their customs, or their legal rights. ❶ In many cases, Americans seized their property.

Native Americans suffered even more. ❶ Thousands died from diseases brought by the newcomers. ❶ Miners hunted down and killed thousands more. ❶ By 1870, California's Native American population had fallen from 150,000 to only about 30,000.

Make a Chart

Making a chart can help you organize your opinions and supporting facts. The following chart summarizes one possible opinion about the impact of the gold rush.

❷	Opinion	The effects of the gold rush were more negative than positive.
❸	Facts	Californios were not respected, and their land was stolen.
		Many Native Americans died from diseases, and others were killed by miners. Their population dropped from 150,000 to about 30,000.

Practicing the Skill

Turn to Chapter 11, Section 3, "Nationalism and Sectionalism." Read "The Missouri Compromise" and form your own opinion about the compromise and its impact. Make a chart like the one above to summarize your opinion and the supporting facts and examples.

2.8 Identifying Facts and Opinions

Defining the Skill

Facts are events, dates, statistics, or statements that can be proved to be true. **Opinions** are the judgments, beliefs, and feelings of a writer or speaker. By identifying facts and opinions, you will be able to think critically when a person is trying to influence your own opinion.

Applying the Skill

The following passage tells about the Virginia Plan for legislative representation offered at the Constitutional Convention of 1787. Use the strategies listed below to help you distinguish facts from opinions.

How to Recognize Facts and Opinions

Strategy ① Look for specific information that can be proved or checked for accuracy.

Strategy ② Look for assertions, claims, and judgments that express opinions. In this case, one speaker's opinion is expressed in a direct quote.

Strategy ③ Think about whether statements can be checked for accuracy. Then, identify the facts and opinions in a chart.

> **ANTIFEDERALIST VIEWS**
>
> ① Antifederalists published their views about the Constitution in newspapers and pamphlets. ① They thought the Constitution took too much power away from the states and did not protect the rights of the people. They charged that the Constitution would destroy American liberties. As one Antifederalist wrote, ② "It is truly astonishing that a set of men among ourselves should have had the [nerve] to attempt the destruction of our liberties."

Make a Chart

The chart below analyzes the facts and opinions from the passage above.

Statement	③ Can It Be Proved?	③ Fact or Opinion
Antifederalists published their views in newspapers and pamphlets.	Yes. Check newspapers and other historical documents.	Fact
They thought the Constitution took too much power away from the states.	Yes. Check newspapers and other historical documents.	Fact
It is astonishing that some Americans would try to destroy American liberties.	No. This cannot be proved. It is what one speaker believes.	Opinion

Practicing the Skill

Turn to Chapter 11, Section 3, and read the section entitled "The Missouri Compromise." Make a chart in which you analyze key statements to determine whether they are facts or opinions.

2.7 Recognizing Propaganda

Defining the Skill

Propaganda is communication that aims to influence people's opinions, emotions, or actions. Propaganda is not always factual. Rather, it uses one-sided language or striking symbols to sway people's emotions. Modern advertising often uses propaganda. By thinking critically, you will avoid being swayed by propaganda.

Applying the Skill

The following political cartoon shows Andrew Jackson dressed as a king. Use the strategies listed below to help you understand how it works as propaganda.

How to Recognize Propaganda

Strategy ① Identify the aim, or purpose, of the cartoon. Point out the subject and explain the point of view.

Strategy ② Identify those images on the cartoon that viewers might respond to emotionally and identify the emotions.

Strategy ③ Think critically about the cartoon. What facts has the cartoon ignored?

BORN TO COMMAND.

OF VETO MEMORY.

HAD I BEEN CONSULTED.

KING ANDREW THE FIRST.

Make a Chart

Making a chart will help you think critically about a piece of propaganda. The chart below summarizes the information from the anti-Jackson cartoon.

①	Identify Purpose	The cartoon portrays Jackson negatively by showing him as a king.
②	Identify Emotions	The cartoonist knows that Americans like democracy. So he portrays Jackson as a king because kings are not usually supporters of democracy. He also shows Jackson standing on a torn U.S. Constitution—another thing that Americans love.
③	Think Critically	The cartoon shows Jackson vetoing laws. But it ignores the fact that those actions were not against the Constitution. The president has the power to veto legislation. In this case, Jackson was exercising the power of the presidency, not acting like a king.

Practicing the Skill

Turn to Chapter 6, Section 2, "Colonial Resistance Grows," and look at the engraving *The Bloody Massacre* on page 165. Use a chart like the one above to think critically about the engraving as an example of propaganda.

2.6 Making Decisions

Defining the Skill

Making decisions involves choosing between two or more options, or courses of action. In most cases, decisions have consequences, or results. Sometimes decisions may lead to new problems. By understanding how historical figures made decisions, you can learn how to improve your decision-making skills.

Applying the Skill

The following passage describes Lincoln's decisions regarding federal forts after the Southern states seceded. Use the strategies listed below to help you analyze his decisions.

How to Make Decisions

Strategy ❶ Identify a decision that needs to be made. Think about what factors make the decision difficult.

Strategy ❷ Identify possible consequences of the decision. Remember that there can be more than one consequence to a decision.

Strategy ❸ Identify the decision that was made.

Strategy ❹ Identify actual consequences that resulted from the decision.

FIRST SHOTS AT FORT SUMTER

❶ Lincoln had to decide what to do about the forts in the South that remained under federal control. A Union garrison still held **Fort Sumter**, but it was running out of supplies. ❷ If Lincoln supplied the garrison, he risked war. ❷ If he withdrew the garrison, he would be giving in to the rebels. ❸ Lincoln informed South Carolina that he was sending supply ships to Fort Sumter. ❹ Confederate leaders decided to prevent the federal government from holding on to the fort by attacking before the supply ships arrived. No one was killed, but ❹ the South's attack on Fort Sumter signaled the beginning of the Civil War.

Make a Flow Chart

A flow chart can help you identify the process of making a decision. The flow chart below shows the decision-making process in the passage you just read.

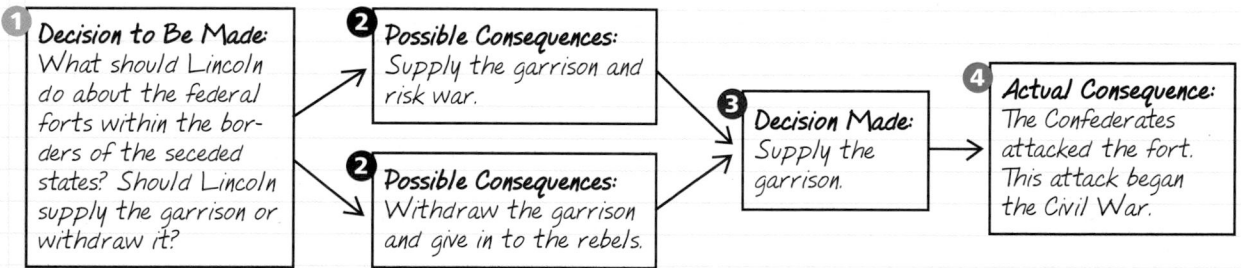

❶ Decision to Be Made: What should Lincoln do about the federal forts within the borders of the seceded states? Should Lincoln supply the garrison or withdraw it?

❷ Possible Consequences: Supply the garrison and risk war.

❷ Possible Consequences: Withdraw the garrison and give in to the rebels.

❸ Decision Made: Supply the garrison.

❹ Actual Consequence: The Confederates attacked the fort. This attack began the Civil War.

Practicing the Skill

Turn to Chapter 6, Section 1, "Tighter British Control." Read "The Colonies Protest the Stamp Act" and make a flow chart to identify a decision and its consequences described in that section.

2.5 Drawing Conclusions

Defining the Skill

Drawing conclusions means analyzing what you have read and forming an opinion about its meaning. To draw conclusions, look at the facts and then use your own common sense and experience to decide what the facts mean.

Applying the Skill

The following passage presents information about the Intolerable Acts and the colonists' reactions to them. Use the strategies listed below to help you draw conclusions about those acts.

How to Draw Conclusions

Strategy ❶ Read carefully to identify and understand all the facts, or statements, that can be proven true.

Strategy ❷ List the facts in a diagram and review them. Use your own experiences and common sense to understand how the facts relate to each other.

Strategy ❸ After reviewing the facts, write down the conclusion you have drawn about them.

> ### THE INTOLERABLE ACTS
>
> ❶ In 1774, Parliament passed a series of laws to punish the Massachusetts colony and serve as a warning to other colonies.
>
> ❶ These laws were so harsh that colonists called them the **Intolerable Acts.** One of the acts closed the port of Boston. Others banned committees of correspondence and allowed Britain to house troops wherever necessary.
>
> In 1773, Sam Adams had written, "I wish we could arouse the continent." ❶ The Intolerable Acts answered his wish. Other colonies immediately offered Massachusetts their support.

Make a Diagram

Making a diagram can help you draw conclusions. The diagram below shows how to organize facts and inferences to draw a conclusion about the passage you just read.

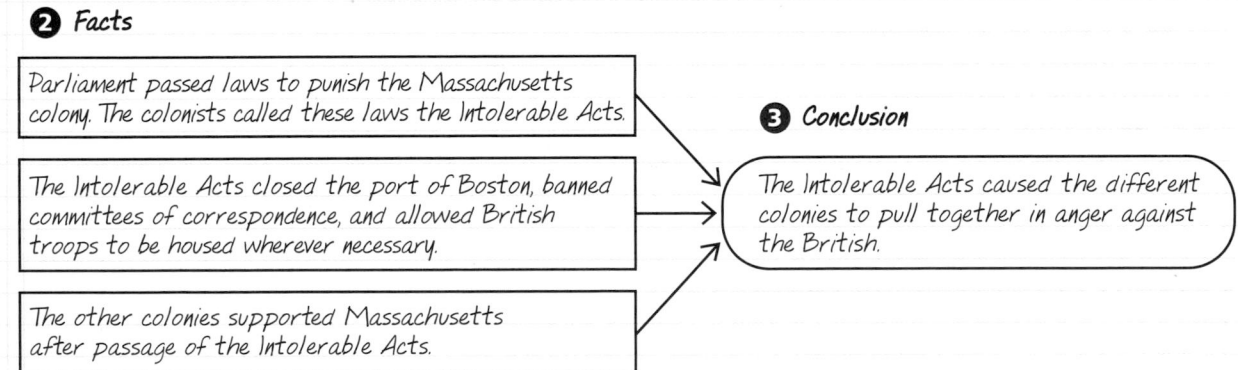

❷ Facts

| Parliament passed laws to punish the Massachusetts colony. The colonists called these laws the Intolerable Acts. |

❸ Conclusion

| The Intolerable Acts closed the port of Boston, banned committees of correspondence, and allowed British troops to be housed wherever necessary. |

| The Intolerable Acts caused the different colonies to pull together in anger against the British. |

| The other colonies supported Massachusetts after passage of the Intolerable Acts. |

Practicing the Skill

Turn to Chapter 3, Section 2, "New England Colonies." Read "The Salem Witchcraft Trials" and use the diagram above as a model to draw conclusions about the trials.

2.4 Making Inferences

Defining the Skill

Inferences are ideas that the author has not directly stated. **Making inferences** involves reading between the lines to interpret the information you read. You can make inferences by studying what is stated and using your common sense and previous knowledge.

Applying the Skill

The passage below describes the strengths and weaknesses of the North and the South as the Civil War began. Use the strategies listed below to help you make inferences from the passage.

How to Make Inferences

Strategy ① Read to find statements of facts and ideas. Knowing the facts will give you a good basis for making inferences.

Strategy ② Use your knowledge, logic, and common sense to make inferences that are based on facts. Ask yourself, "What does the author want me to understand?" For example, from the facts about population, you can make the inference that the North would have a larger army than the South. See other inferences in the chart below.

> ### ADVANTAGES OF THE NORTH AND THE SOUTH
>
> The North had more people and resources than the South. ① The North had about 22 million people. ① The South had roughly 9 million, of whom about 3.5 million were slaves. In addition, ① the North had more than 80 percent of the nation's factories and almost all of the shipyards and naval power. The South had some advantages, too. ① It had able generals, such as Robert E. Lee. ① It also had the advantage of fighting a defensive war. Soldiers defending their homes have more will to fight than invaders do.

Make a Chart

Making a chart will help you organize information and make logical inferences. The chart below organizes information from the passage you just read.

① Stated Facts and Ideas	② Inferences
The North had about 22 million people. The Confederacy had about 9 million.	The North would have a larger army than the South.
The North had more factories, naval power, and shipyards.	The North could provide more weapons, ammunition, and ships for the war.
The Confederacy had excellent generals.	The Confederacy had better generals, which would help it overcome other disadvantages.
The Confederacy was fighting a defensive war.	Confederate soldiers would fight harder because they were defending their homes and families.

Practicing the Skill

Turn to Chapter 11, Section 1, "Early Industry and Inventions." Read "Free Enterprise and Factories" and use a chart like the one above to make inferences about early industry.

2.3 Analyzing Causes; Recognizing Effects

Defining the Skill

A **cause** is an action in history that makes something happen. An **effect** is the historical event that is the result of the cause. A single event may have several causes. It is also possible for one cause to result in several effects. Historians identify cause-and-effect relationships to help them understand why historical events took place.

Applying the Skill

The following paragraph describes events that caused changes in Puritan New England. Use the strategies listed below to help you identify the cause-and-effect relationships.

How to Analyze Causes and Recognize Effects

Strategy ❶ Ask why an action took place. Ask yourself a question about the title and topic sentence, such as, "What caused changes in Puritan society?"

Strategy ❷ Look for effects. Ask yourself, "What happened?" (the effect). Then ask, "Why did it happen?" (the cause). For example, What caused the decline of Puritan religion in New England?

Strategy ❸ Look for clue words that signal causes, such as *cause* and *led to*.

Strategy ❹ One way to practice recognizing effects is to make predictions about the consequences that will result from particular actions. Then, as you read, look to see if your predictions were accurate.

> ❶ **CHANGES IN PURITAN SOCIETY**
>
> ❶ The early 1700s saw many changes in New England society.
>
> ❷ One of the most important changes was the gradual decline of the Puritan religion in New England. There were a number of reasons for that decline.
>
> ❸ One *cause* of this decline was the increasing competition from other religious groups. Baptists and Anglicans established churches in Massachusetts and Connecticut, where Puritans had once been the most powerful group. ❸ Political changes also *led to* a weakening of the Puritan community. In 1691, a new royal charter for Massachusetts granted the vote based on property ownership instead of church membership.

Make a Diagram

Using a diagram can help you understand causes and effects. The diagram below shows two causes and an effect for the passage you just read.

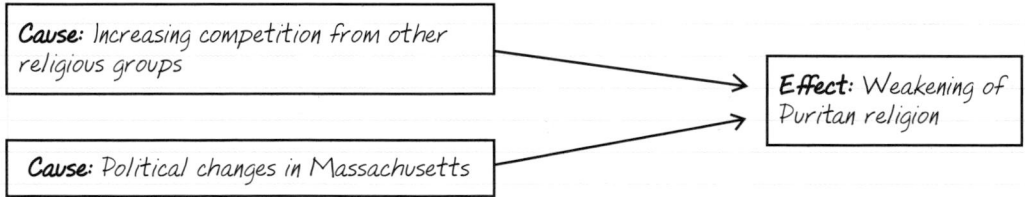

Cause: Increasing competition from other religious groups → **Effect:** Weakening of Puritan religion
Cause: Political changes in Massachusetts →

Practicing the Skill

Turn to Chapter 2, Section 1, "Spain Claims an Empire." Read "Reasons for Spanish Victories" and make a diagram about the causes and effects of the Spanish conquest of the Americas.

2.2 Comparing and Contrasting

Defining the Skill

Comparing means looking at the similarities and differences between two or more things. **Contrasting** means examining only the differences between them. Historians compare and contrast events, personalities, behaviors, beliefs, and situations in order to understand them.

Applying the Skill

The following paragraph describes the American and British troops during the Revolutionary War. Use the strategies listed below to help you compare and contrast these two armies.

How to Compare and Contrast

Strategy ① Look for two aspects of the subject that may be compared and contrasted. This passage compares the British and American troops to show why the Americans won the war.

Strategy ② To contrast, look for clue words that show how two things differ. Clue words include *by contrast, however, except,* and *yet.*

Strategy ③ To find similarities, look for clue words indicating that two things are alike. Clue words include *both, like, as,* and *similarly.*

> ### WHY THE AMERICANS WON
>
> ① By their persistence, the Americans defeated the British even though they faced many obstacles. The Americans lacked training and experience. They were often short of supplies and weapons. ② *By contrast,* the British forces ranked among the best trained in the world. They were experienced and well-supplied professional soldiers. ② *Yet,* the Americans also had advantages that enabled them to win. These advantages over the British were better leadership, foreign aid, a knowledge of the land, and motivation. Although ③ *both* the British and the Americans were fighting for their lives, ② the Americans were also fighting for their property and their dream of liberty.

Make a Venn Diagram

Making a Venn diagram will help you identify similarities and differences between two things. In the overlapping area, list characteristics shared by both subjects. Then, in the separate ovals, list the characteristics of each subject not shared by the other. This Venn diagram compares and contrasts the British and American soldiers.

American Soldiers:
- lacked experience and training
- short of supplies and weapons
- had better leadership
- received foreign aid
- had knowledge of the land
- fought for liberty and property

Both:
fought for their lives

British Soldiers:
- best trained in the world
- experienced
- well-supplied

Practicing the Skill

Turn to Chapter 5, Section 1, "Early American Culture." Read "Young People at Work" and make a Venn diagram showing the similarities and differences between the roles of boys and girls in colonial America.

2.1 Analyzing Points of View

Defining the Skill

Analyzing points of view means looking closely at a person's arguments to understand the reasons behind that person's beliefs. The goal of analyzing a point of view is to understand a historical figure's thoughts, opinions, and biases about a topic.

Applying the Skill

The following passage describes the Panic of 1837 and two politicians' points of view about it. Use the strategies listed below to help you analyze their points of view.

How to Analyze Points of View

Strategy ❶ Look for statements that show you a person's view on an issue. For example, Van Buren said he believed the economy would improve if he took no action. Clay thought the government should do something to help the people.

Strategy ❷ Use information about people to validate them as sources and understand why they might disagree. What do you know about Clay and Van Buren that might explain their own biases and disagreements with each other?

Strategy ❸ Write a summary that explains why different people took different positions on the issue.

> ### THE PANIC OF 1837
>
> The Panic of 1837 caused severe hardship. People had little money, so manufacturers had few customers for their goods. Almost 90 percent of factories in the East closed. Jobless workers could not afford food or rent. Many people went hungry.
>
> ❶ Whig senator Henry Clay wanted the government to do something to help the people. ❶ President Van Buren, a Democrat, disagreed. He believed that the economy would improve if left alone. He argued that "the less government interferes with private pursuits the better for the general prosperity." Many Americans blamed Van Buren for the Panic, though he had taken office only weeks before it started. The continuing depression made it difficult for him to win reelection in 1840.

Make a Diagram

Using a diagram can help you analyze points of view. The diagram below analyzes the views of Clay and Van Buren in the passage you just read.

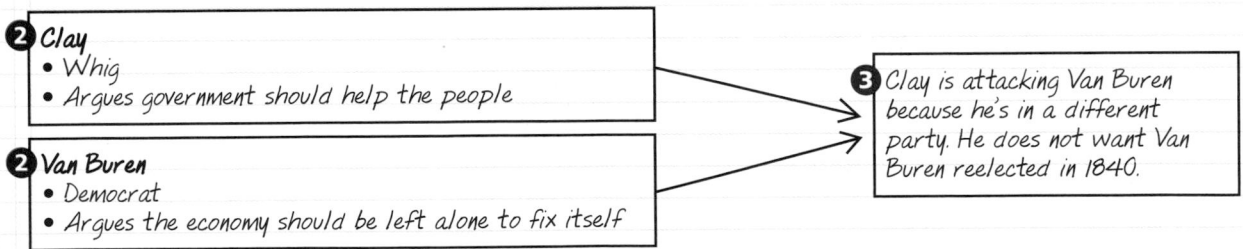

❷ Clay
- Whig
- Argues government should help the people

❷ Van Buren
- Democrat
- Argues the economy should be left alone to fix itself

❸ Clay is attacking Van Buren because he's in a different party. He does not want Van Buren reelected in 1840.

Practicing the Skill

Turn to the Interactive Primary Sources on pages 238 and 239. Read the selections by James Madison and George Mason. Use their language, information from other sources, and information about each man to validate them as sources. Then make a chart to analyze their different points of view on the Constitution.

1.7 Writing for Social Studies

Defining the Skill

Writing for social studies requires you to describe an idea, situation, or event. Often, social studies writing takes a stand on a particular issue or tries to make a specific point. To successfully describe an event or make a point, your writing needs to be clear, concise, and factually accurate.

Applying the Skill

The following passage describes Stephen A. Douglas. Notice how the strategies below helped the writer explain Douglas's historical importance.

How to Write for Social Studies

Strategy ❶ Focus on your topic. Be sure that you clearly state the main idea of your piece so that your readers know what you intend to say.

Strategy ❷ Collect and organize your facts. Collect accurate information about your topic to support the main idea you are trying to make. Use your information to build a logical case to prove your point.

Strategy ❸ To express your ideas clearly, use standard grammar, spelling, sentence structure, and punctuation when writing for social studies. Proofread your work to make sure it is well organized and grammatically correct.

STEPHEN A. DOUGLAS, 1813–1861

❶ Stephen A. Douglas was one of the most powerful members of Congress in the 1850s. In fact, ❷ he was called the "Little Giant" because he commanded great respect even though he was only five feet four inches tall. The most important issue that Douglas faced in his career was slavery in the territories. ❷ He played a key role in the passage of the Compromise of 1850 as well as the Kansas–Nebraska Act, which addressed this issue. In 1858, his famous debates with Abraham Lincoln also focused on slavery in the territories. ❷ When Douglas ran for president in 1860, his position on slavery was critical to his defeat.

Practicing the Skill

Turn to Chapter 15, Section 1, "Growing Tensions Between North and South." Read the section and use the strategies above to write your answer to Question 4 on page 461.

1.6 Making Public Speeches

Defining the Skill

A speech is a talk given in public to an audience. Some speeches are given to persuade the audience to think or act in a certain way, or to support a cause. You can learn how to **make public speeches** effectively by analyzing great speeches in history.

Applying the Skill

The following is an excerpt from the "I Have a Dream" speech delivered by Martin Luther King, Jr., in 1963 in Washington, D.C. Use the strategies listed below to help you analyze King's speech and prepare a speech of your own.

How to Analyze and Prepare a Speech

Strategy ❶ Choose one central idea or theme and organize your speech to support it. King organized his speech around his dream of equality.

Strategy ❷ Use words or images that will win over your audience. King referred to the Declaration of Independence when he used the words "all men are created equal."

Strategy ❸ Repeat words or images to drive home your main point—as if it is the "hook" of a pop song. King repeats the phrase "I have a dream."

I HAVE A DREAM

❶ I have a dream that one day this nation will rise up and live out the true meaning of its creed—we hold these truths to be

❷ self-evident that all men are created equal.

❸ I have a dream that one day on the red hills of Georgia the sons of former slaves and the sons of former slave owners will be able to sit down together at the table of brotherhood.

❸ I have a dream that my four little children will one day live in a nation where they will not be judged by the color of their skin but by the content of their character.

❸ I have a dream today!

Make an Outline

Making an outline like the one to the right will help you make an effective public speech.

Practicing the Skill

Turn to Chapter 12, Section 2, "Jackson's Policy Toward Native Americans." Read the section and choose a topic for a speech. First, make an outline like the one to the right to organize your ideas. Exchange your outline with a partner. Organize and interpret information from that outline to write a speech.

Title: I Have a Dream

I. Introduce Theme: I have a dream
   A. This nation will live up to its creed
   B. Quote from the Declaration of Independence:
      that all men are created equal

II. Repeat theme: I have a dream
   A. Sons of former slaves and slave owners will sit
      together in brotherhood
   B. My four children will be judged by their character,
      not by their skin color

III. Conclude: I have a dream

1.5 Categorizing

Defining the Skill

To **categorize** is to sort people, objects, ideas, or other information into groups, called categories. Historians categorize information to help them identify and understand patterns in historical events.

Applying the Skill

The following passage contains information about the reasons people went west during the mid-1800s. Use the strategies listed below to help you categorize information.

How to Categorize

Strategy ❶ First, decide what kind of information needs to be categorized. Decide what the passage is about and how that information can be sorted into categories.
For example, find the different motives people had for moving west.

Strategy ❷ Then find out what the categories will be. To find why many different groups of people moved west, look for clue words such as *some, other,* and *another.*

Strategy ❸ Once you have chosen the categories, sort information into them. Of the people who went west, which ones had which motives?

> ## THE LURE OF THE WEST
>
> ❶ People had many different motives for going west. ❷ One motive was to make money. ❷ *Some* people called speculators bought huge areas of land and made great profits by selling it to thousands of settlers. ❷ *Other* settlers included farmers who dreamed of owning their own farms in the West because land was difficult to acquire in the East. ❷ *Another* group to move west was merchants. They hoped to earn money by selling items that farmers needed. Finally, ❷ *some* people went west for religious reasons. These people included ❷ missionaries, who wanted to convert the Native Americans to Christianity, and Mormons, who wanted a place where they could practice their faith without interference.

Make a Chart

Making a chart can help you categorize information. You should have as many columns as you have categories. The chart below shows how the information from the passage you just read can be categorized.

Motives	Money	Land	Religion
Groups	• speculators • merchants	• farmers	• missionaries • Mormons

❸

Practicing the Skill

Turn to Chapter 14, Section 3, "Reforming American Society." Read "Improving Education" and make a chart in which you categorize the changes happening in elementary, high school, and college education.

1.4 Finding Main Ideas

Defining the Skill

The **main idea** is a statement that summarizes the main point of a speech, an article, a section of a book, or a paragraph. Main ideas can be stated or unstated. The main idea of a paragraph is often stated in the first or last sentence. If it is the first sentence, it is followed by sentences that support that main idea. If it is the last sentence, the details build up to the main idea. To find an unstated idea, you must use the details of the paragraph as clues.

Applying the Skill

The following paragraph describes the role of women in the American Revolution. Use the strategies listed below to help you identify the main idea.

How to Find the Main Idea

Strategy ❶ Identify what you think may be the stated main idea. Check the first and last sentences of the paragraph to see if either could be the stated main idea.

Strategy ❷ Identify details that support that idea. Some details explain the main idea. Others give examples of what is stated in the main idea.

> **WOMEN IN THE REVOLUTION**
>
> ❶ Many women tried to help the army. Martha Washington and other wives followed their husbands to army camps. ❷ The wives cooked, did laundry, and nursed sick or wounded soldiers. ❷ A few women even helped to fight. ❷ Mary Hays earned the nickname "Molly Pitcher" by carrying water to tired soldiers during a battle. ❷ Deborah Sampson dressed as a man, enlisted, and fought in several engagements.

Make a Chart

Making a chart can help you identify the main idea and details in a passage or paragraph. The chart below identifies the main idea and details in the paragraph you just read.

Main Idea: Women helped the army during the Revolution.

Detail: They cooked and did laundry.
Detail: They nursed the wounded and sick soldiers.
Detail: They helped to fight.
Detail: One woman, Molly Pitcher, carried water to soldiers during battles.

Practicing the Skill

Turn to Chapter 5, Section 1, "Early American Culture." Read "Women and the Economy" and create a chart that identifies the main idea and the supporting details.

1.3 Sequencing Events

Defining the Skill

Sequence is the order in which events follow one another. By being able to follow the sequence of events through history, you can get an accurate sense of the relationship among events.

Applying the Skill

The following passage describes the sequence of events involved in Britain's plan to capture the Hudson River Valley during the American Revolution. Use the strategies listed below to help you follow the sequence of events.

How to Find the Sequence of Events

Strategy ➊ Look for specific dates provided in the text. If several months within a year are included, the year is usually not repeated.

Strategy ➋ Look for clues about time that allow you to order events according to sequence. Words such as *day, week, month,* or *year* may help to sequence the events.

> **BRITAIN'S STRATEGY**
>
> Burgoyne captured Fort Ticonderoga in ➊ July 1777. From there, it was 25 miles to the Hudson River, which ran to Albany. ➋ Burgoyne took three weeks to reach the Hudson. On ➊ August 3, Burgoyne received a message from Howe. He would not be coming north, Howe wrote, because he had decided to invade Pennsylvania to try to capture Philadelphia and General Washington. "Success be ever with you," Howe's message said. But General Burgoyne needed Howe's soldiers, not his good wishes. Howe did invade Pennsylvania. In ➊ September 1777, he defeated —but did not capture—Washington at the Battle of Brandywine.

Make a Time Line

Making a time line can help you sequence events. The time line below shows the sequence of events in the passage you just read.

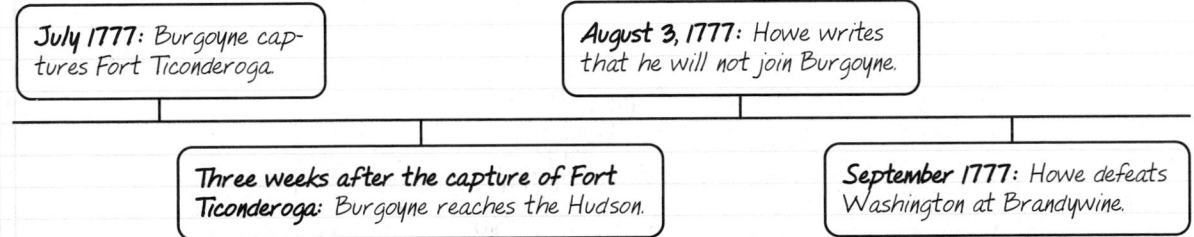

July 1777: Burgoyne captures Fort Ticonderoga.

August 3, 1777: Howe writes that he will not join Burgoyne.

Three weeks after the capture of Fort Ticonderoga: Burgoyne reaches the Hudson.

September 1777: Howe defeats Washington at Brandywine.

Practicing the Skill

Turn to Chapter 2, Section 1, "Spain Claims an Empire." Read "Europeans Explore Foreign Lands" and make a time line showing the sequence of events in that passage.

1.2 Taking Notes

Defining the Skill

When you **take notes,** you write down the important ideas and details of a paragraph, passage, or chapter. A chart or an outline can help you organize your notes to use in the future.

Applying the Skill

The following passage describes President Washington's cabinet. Use the strategies listed below to help you take notes on the passage.

How to Take and Organize Notes

Strategy ❶ Look at the title to find the main topic of the passage.

Strategy ❷ Identify the main ideas and details of the passage. Then summarize the main idea and details in your notes.

Strategy ❸ Identify key terms and define them. The term *cabinet* is shown in boldface type and underlined; both techniques signal that it is a key term.

Strategy ❹ In your notes, use abbreviations to save time and space. You can abbreviate words such as *department (dept.), secretary (sec.), United States (U.S.),* and *president (pres.)* to save time and space.

---

❶ **WASHINGTON'S CABINET**

❷ The Constitution gave Congress the task of creating departments to help the president lead the nation. The ❷ president had the power to appoint the heads of these departments, which became his ❸ <u>cabinet.</u>

Congress created three departments. Washington chose talented people to run them. ❷ For secretary of war, he picked Henry Knox, a trusted general during the Revolution. ❷ For secretary of state, Washington chose Thomas Jefferson. He had been serving as ambassador to France. The State Department oversaw U.S. foreign relations. For secretary of the treasury, Washington turned to the brilliant ❷ Alexander Hamilton.

Make a Chart

Making a chart can help you take notes on a passage. The chart below contains notes from the passage you just read.

❷ Item	Notes
1. ❸ cabinet	heads of ❹ depts; ❹ pres. appoints heads
a. War Dept.	Henry Knox; ❹ sec. of war; former Revolutionary War general
b. State Dept.	Thomas Jefferson; sec. of state; oversees relations between ❹ U.S. and other countries
c. Treasury Dept.	Alexander Hamilton; sec. of the treasury

Practicing the Skill

Turn to Chapter 3, Section 3, "Founding the Middle and Southern Colonies." Read "Maryland and the Carolinas" and use a chart to take notes on the passage.

1.1 Summarizing

Defining the Skill

When you **summarize,** you restate a paragraph, passage, or chapter in fewer words. You include only the main ideas and most important details. It is important to use your own words when summarizing.

Applying the Skill

The passage below tells about Harriet Tubman, a prominent member of the Underground Railroad. She helped runaway slaves to freedom. Use the strategies listed below to help you summarize the passage.

How to Summarize

Strategy ① Look for topic sentences stating the main idea. These are often at the beginning of a section or paragraph. Briefly restate each main idea—in your own words.

Strategy ② Include key facts and any numbers, dates, amounts, or percentages from the text.

Strategy ③ After writing your summary, review it to see that you have included only the most important details.

HARRIET TUBMAN

① One of the most famous conductors on the Underground Railroad was Harriet Tubman. ② Born into slavery in Maryland, the 13-year-old Tubman once tried to save another slave from punishment. The angry overseer fractured Tubman's skull with a two-pound weight. She suffered fainting spells for the rest of her life but did not let that stop her from working for freedom. When she was 25, Tubman learned that her owner was about to sell her. Instead, ② she escaped.

After her escape, ② Harriet Tubman made 19 dangerous journeys to free enslaved persons. The tiny woman carried a pistol to frighten off slave hunters and medicine to quiet crying babies. Her enemies offered $40,000 for her capture, but ② no one caught her. "I never run my train off the track and I never lost a passenger," she proudly declared. Among the people she saved were her parents.

Write a Summary

You can write your summary in a paragraph. The paragraph at right summarizes the passage you just read.

Practicing the Skill

Turn to Chapter 6, Section 2, "Colonial Resistance Grows." Read "The Boston Tea Party" and write a paragraph summarizing the passage.

③ *Harriet Tubman was one of the most famous conductors on the Underground Railroad. She had been a slave, but she escaped. She later made 19 dangerous journeys to free other slaves. She was never captured.*

Skillbuilder HANDBOOK

Table of Contents

Reference Section

Creating America
A History of the United States

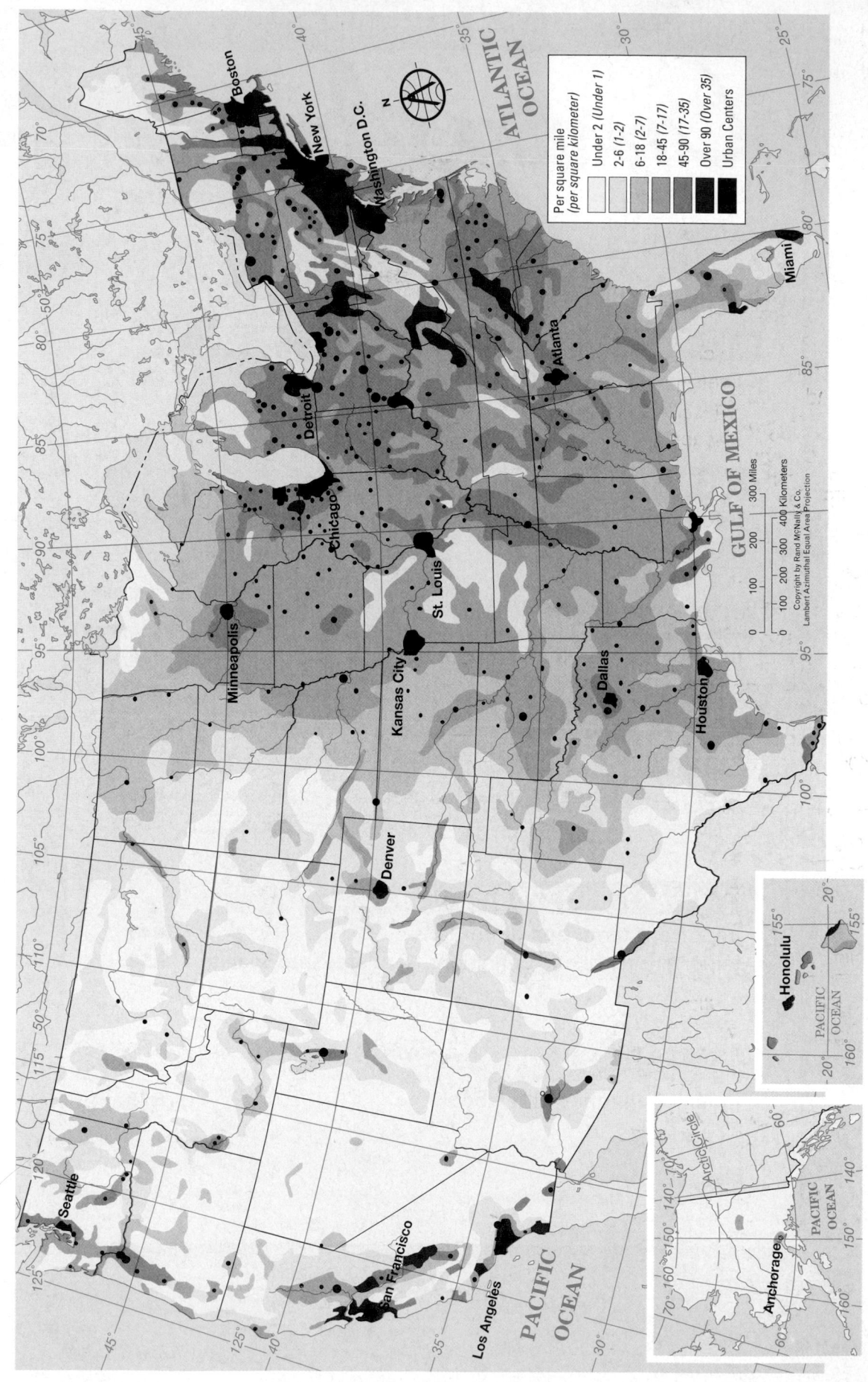

Per square mile
(per square kilometer)

Under 2 (Under 1)
2-6 (1-2)
6-18 (2-7)
18-45 (7-17)
45-90 (17-35)
Over 90 (Over 35)
Urban Centers

ATLANTIC OCEAN

Boston
New York
Washington D.C.
Miami

Atlanta

Detroit

Chicago

St. Louis

Minneapolis

Kansas City

Dallas

Houston

GULF OF MEXICO

Denver

0   100   200   300 Miles
0   100   200   300   400 Kilometers

Copyright by Rand McNally & Co.
Lambert Azimuthal Equal Area Projection

Seattle

San Francisco

Los Angeles

PACIFIC OCEAN

Honolulu
PACIFIC OCEAN

Anchorage
Arctic Circle
PACIFIC OCEAN

RAND McNALLY

A39

African-American Migration 1940–1970

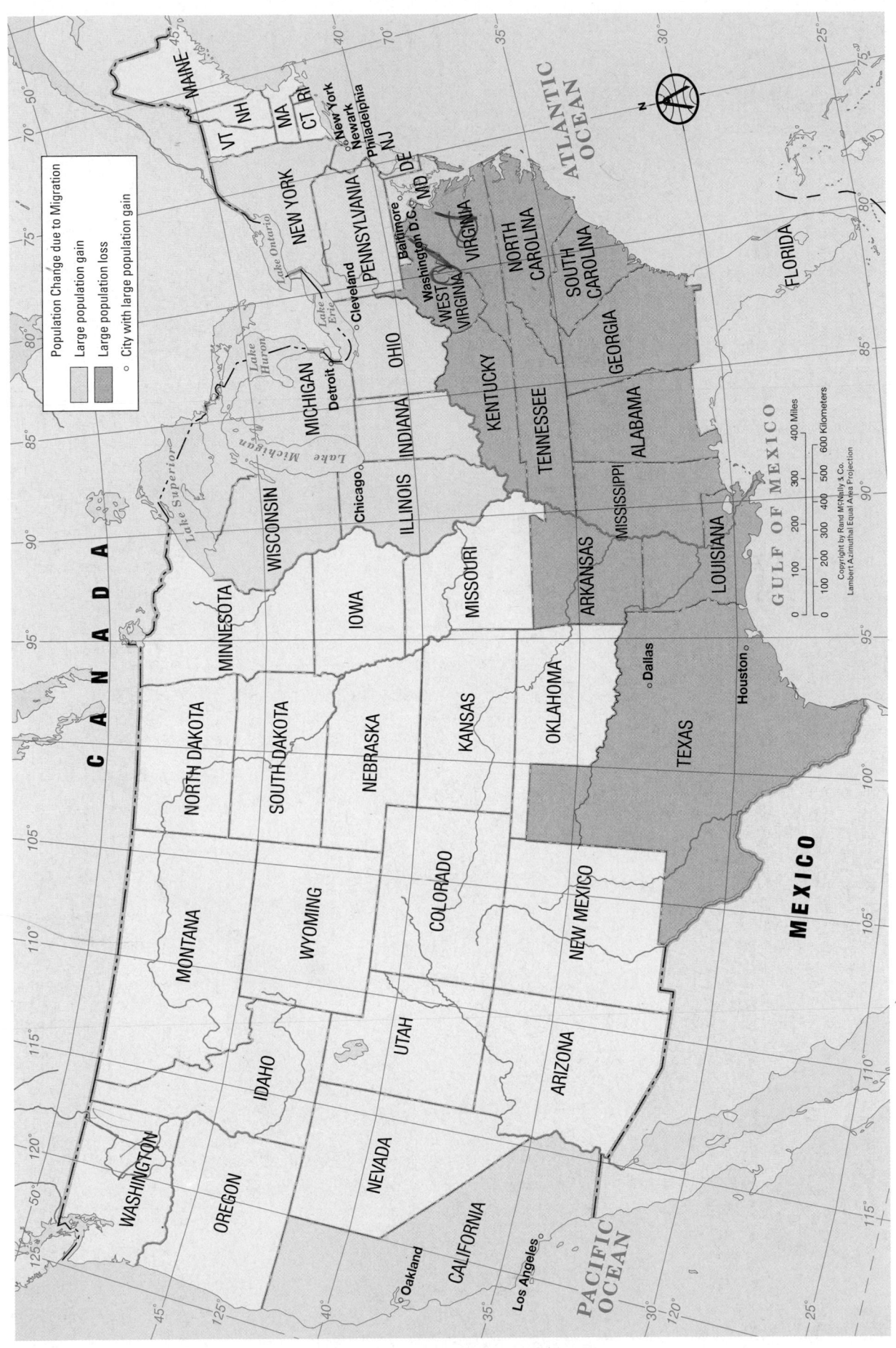

Population Change due to Migration
- Large population gain
- Large population loss
- City with large population gain

0 100 200 300 400 Miles
0 100 200 300 400 500 600 Kilometers

Copyright by Rand McNally & Co.
Lambert Azimuthal Equal Area Projection

ATLANTIC OCEAN

PACIFIC OCEAN

GULF OF MEXICO

CANADA

MEXICO

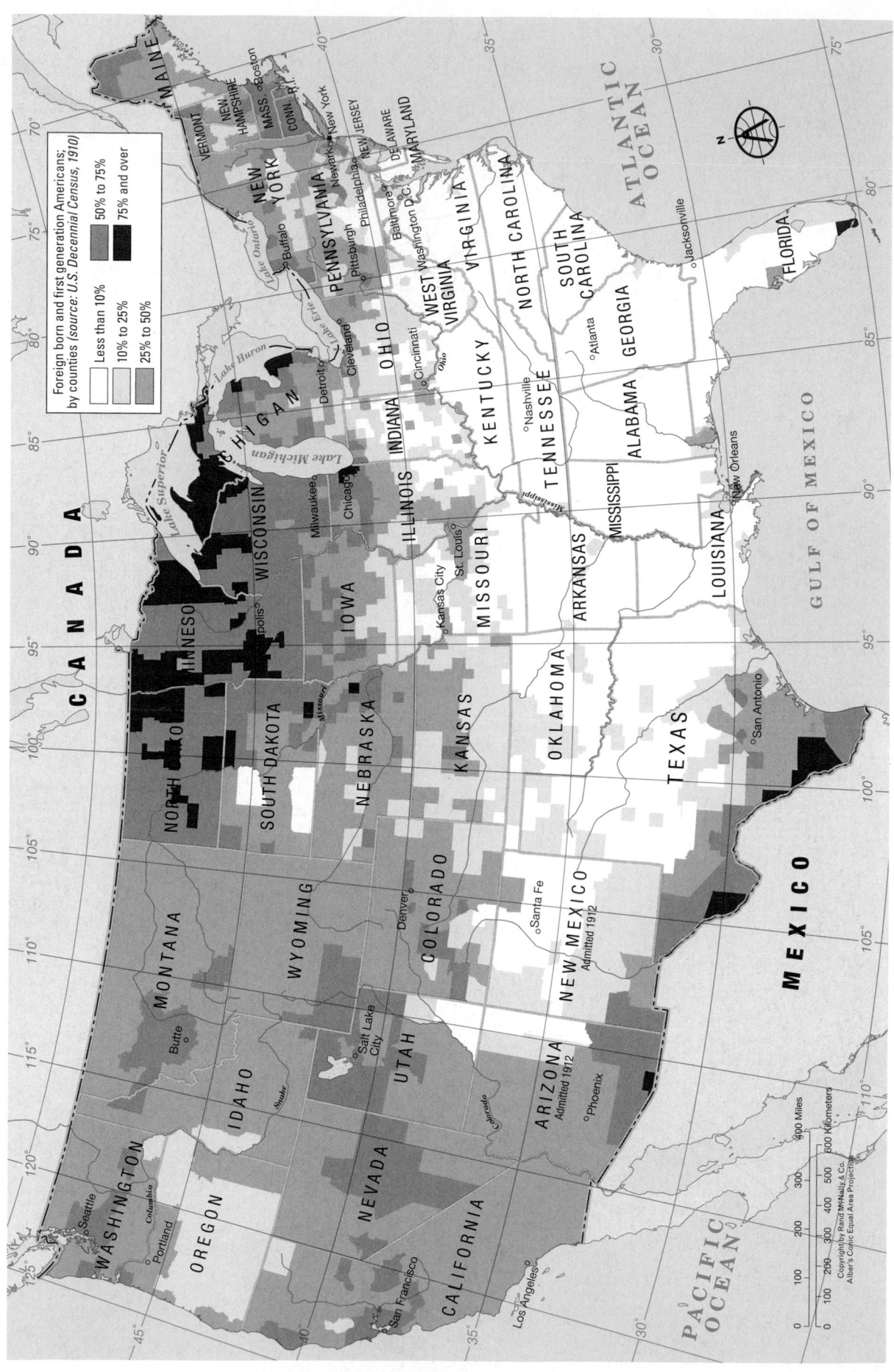

**Foreign born and first generation Americans;
by counties** (source: *U.S. Decennial Census, 1910*)

- Less than 10%
- 10% to 25%
- 25% to 50%
- 50% to 75%
- 75% and over

N

CANADA

ATLANTIC OCEAN

MAINE
VERMONT
NEW HAMPSHIRE
MASS.
CONN. R.I.
NEW YORK
New York
Buffalo
PENNSYLVANIA
Newark
Philadelphia
NEW JERSEY
DELAWARE
MARYLAND
Baltimore
Washington D.C.
Pittsburgh
WEST VIRGINIA
VIRGINIA
NORTH CAROLINA
SOUTH CAROLINA
Jacksonville
FLORIDA

Lake Ontario
Lake Erie
Detroit
Cleveland
OHIO
Cincinnati
Ohio
INDIANA
KENTUCKY
Nashville
TENNESSEE
GEORGIA
Atlanta
ALABAMA

MICHIGAN
Lake Huron
Lake Michigan
Lake Superior
WISCONSIN
Milwaukee
Chicago
ILLINOIS
St. Louis
MISSOURI
Kansas City
ARKANSAS
MISSISSIPPI
LOUISIANA
New Orleans

MINNESOTA
polis
IOWA
NEBRASKA
KANSAS
OKLAHOMA
TEXAS
San Antonio

GULF OF MEXICO

NORTH DAKOTA
SOUTH DAKOTA
Missouri
WYOMING
COLORADO
Denver
NEW MEXICO
Admitted 1912
Santa Fe

MONTANA
Butte
Snake
IDAHO
UTAH
Salt Lake City
ARIZONA
Admitted 1912
Phoenix
Colorado

MEXICO

WASHINGTON
Seattle
Columbia
Portland
OREGON
NEVADA
CALIFORNIA
San Francisco
Los Angeles

PACIFIC OCEAN

0   100   200   300   400 Miles
0 100 200 300 400 500 600 Kilometers

Copyright by Rand McNally & Co.
Alber's Conic Equal Area Projection

RAND McNALLY

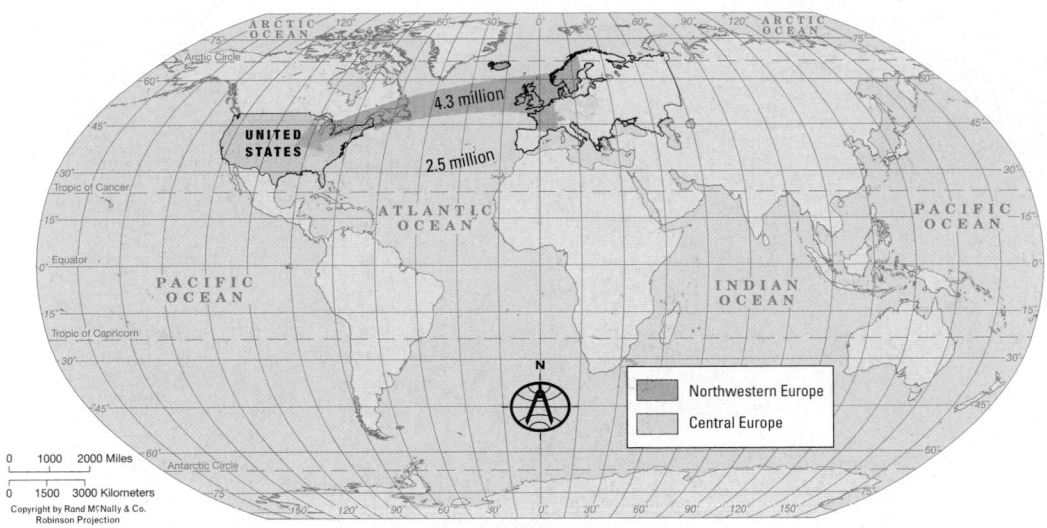

Immigration 1820–1870

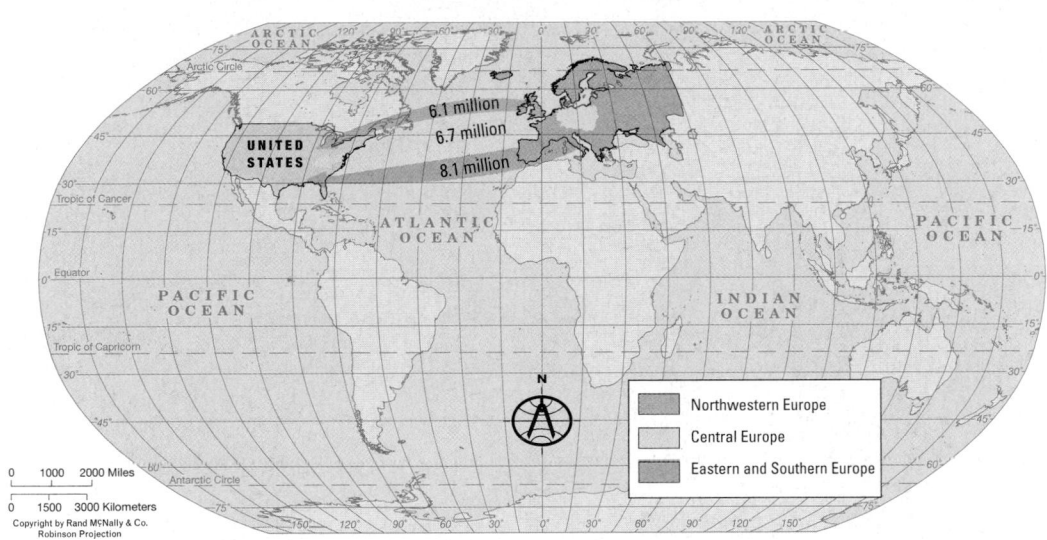

Immigration 1880–1920

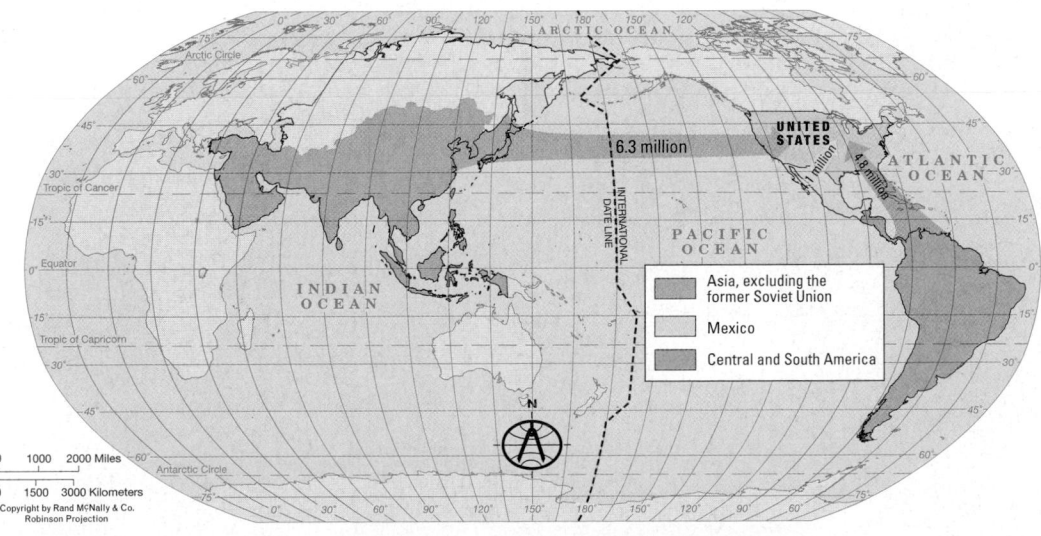

Immigration 1960s–1990s

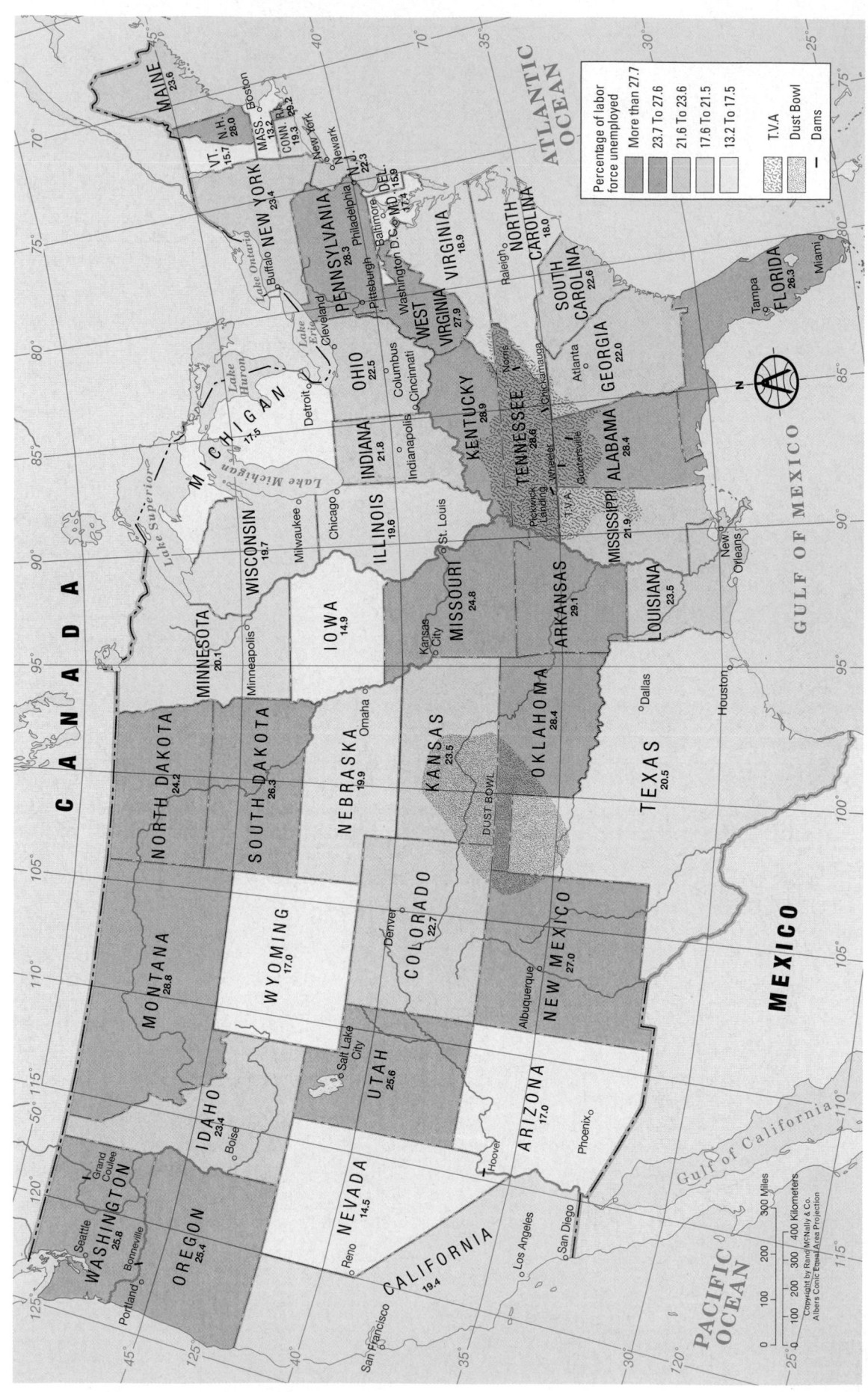

Percentage of labor force unemployed

	More than 27.7
	23.7 To 27.6
	21.6 To 23.6
	17.6 To 21.5
	13.2 To 17.5

T.V.A
Dust Bowl
— Dams

ATLANTIC OCEAN

MAINE 23.6
N.H. 28.0
VT. 15.7
MASS. 13.2
CONN. R.I. 19.3 29.2
NEW YORK 23.4
New York
Boston
Buffalo
Cleveland
PENNSYLVANIA 28.3
Pittsburgh
Philadelphia
N.J. 22.3
Baltimore
Washington D.C.
DEL. 15.9
MD. 17.4
WEST VIRGINIA 27.9
VIRGINIA 18.9
Raleigh
NORTH CAROLINA 18.0
SOUTH CAROLINA 22.6
FLORIDA 26.3
Tampa
Miami
OHIO 22.5
Columbus
Cincinnati
Detroit
MICHIGAN 17.5
Lake Ontario
Lake Erie
Lake Huron
Lake Superior
Lake Michigan
KENTUCKY 28.9
TENNESSEE 28.6
Norris
Chickamauga
Atlanta
GEORGIA 22.0
ALABAMA 28.4
Guntersville
Wheeler
Pickwick Landing
T.V.A.
MISSISSIPPI 21.9
INDIANA 21.8
Indianapolis
ILLINOIS 19.6
Chicago
St. Louis
MISSOURI 24.8
Kansas City
ARKANSAS 29.1
LOUISIANA 23.5
New Orleans
GULF OF MEXICO
WISCONSIN 19.7
Milwaukee
IOWA 14.9
MINNESOTA 20.1
Minneapolis
NORTH DAKOTA 24.2
SOUTH DAKOTA 26.3
NEBRASKA 19.9
Omaha
KANSAS 23.5
OKLAHOMA 28.4
TEXAS 20.5
Dallas
Houston
DUST BOWL
COLORADO 22.7
Denver
WYOMING 17.0
NEW MEXICO 27.0
Albuquerque
MONTANA 28.8
IDAHO 23.4
Boise
UTAH 25.6
Salt Lake City
ARIZONA 17.0
Phoenix
Hoover
NEVADA 14.5
Reno
CALIFORNIA 19.4
Los Angeles
San Diego
San Francisco
WASHINGTON 25.8
Seattle
Portland
Grand Coulee
Bonneville
OREGON 25.4
CANADA
MEXICO
Gulf of California
PACIFIC OCEAN

N

0 100 200 300 Miles
0 100 200 300 400 Kilometers
Copyright by Rand McNally & Co.
Albers Conic Equal Area Projection

RAND McNALLY

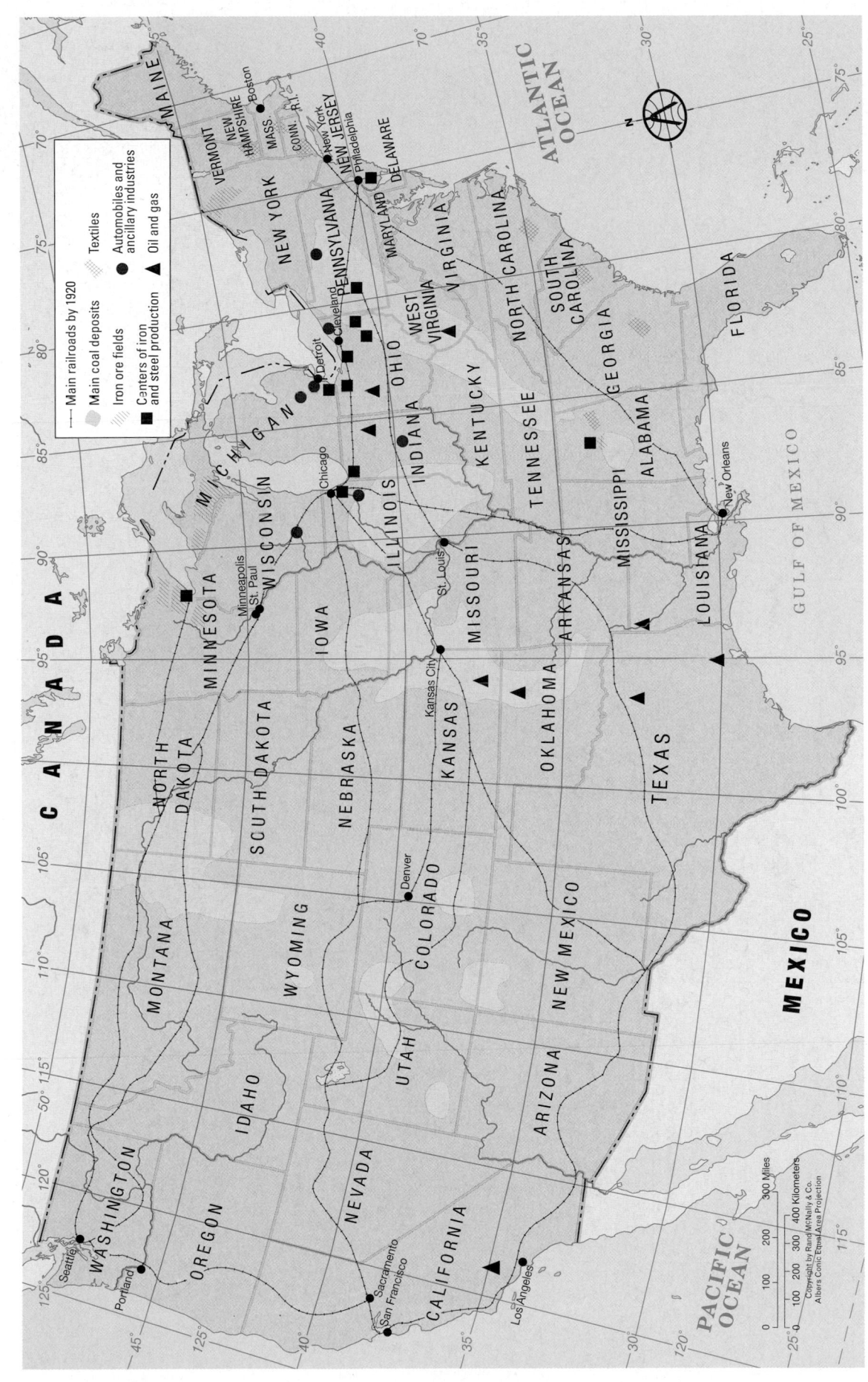

U.S. Industries 1920

RAND McNALLY

Legend:
- Main railroads by 1920
- Main coal deposits
- Iron ore fields
- Centers of iron and steel production ■
- Textiles
- Automobiles and ancillary industries ●
- Oil and gas ▲

Copyright by Rand McNally & Co.
Albers Conic Equal Area Projection

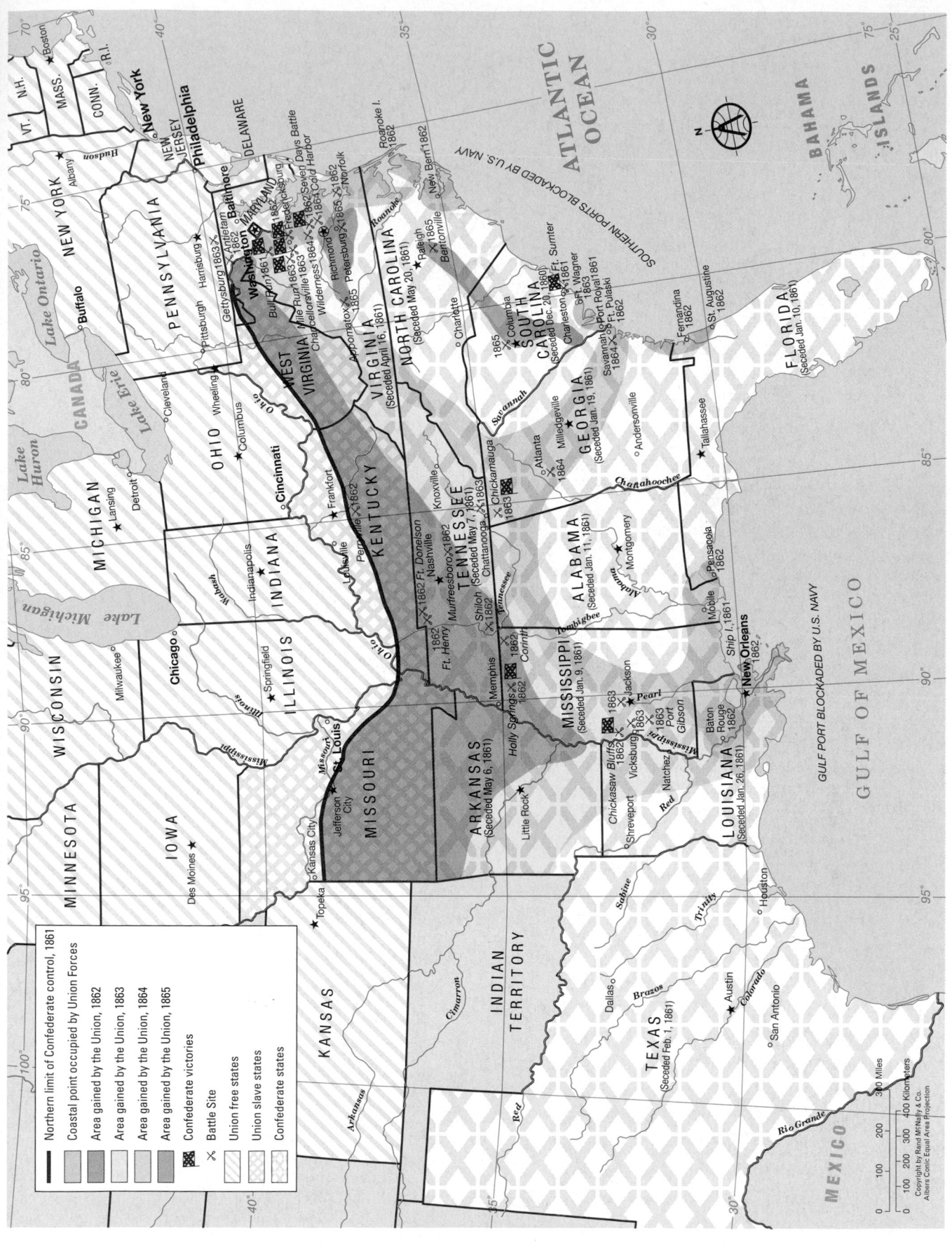

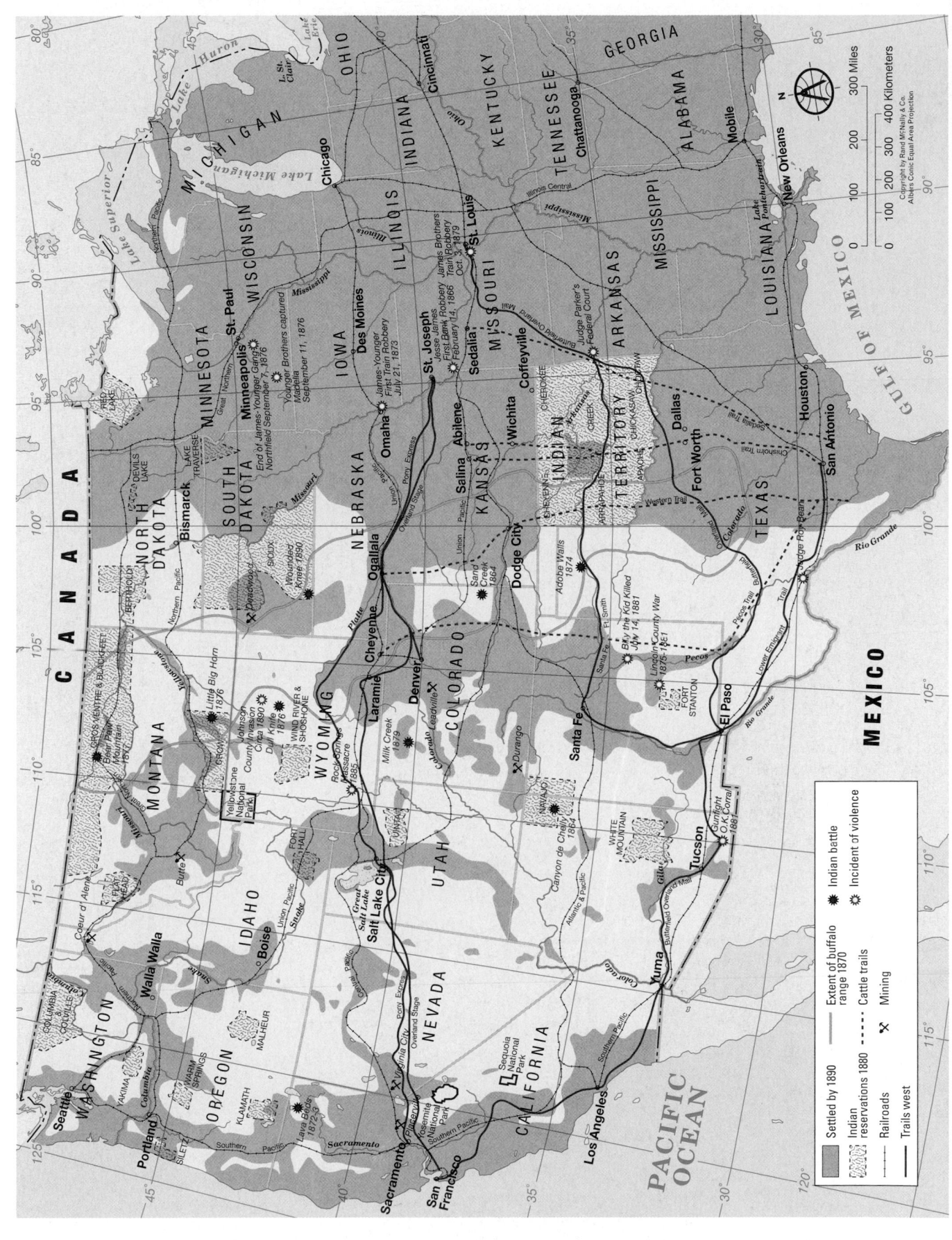

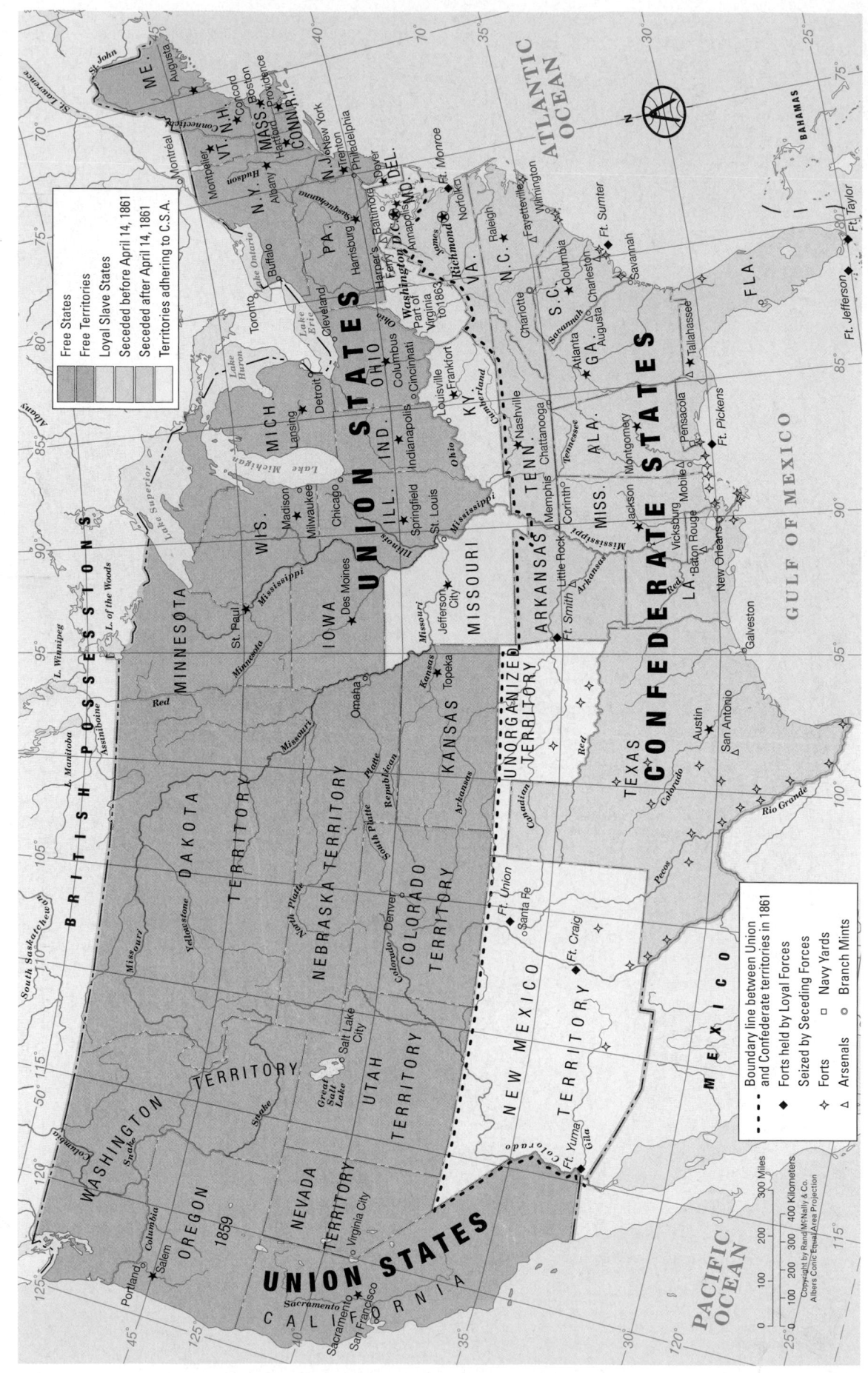

RAND McNALLY

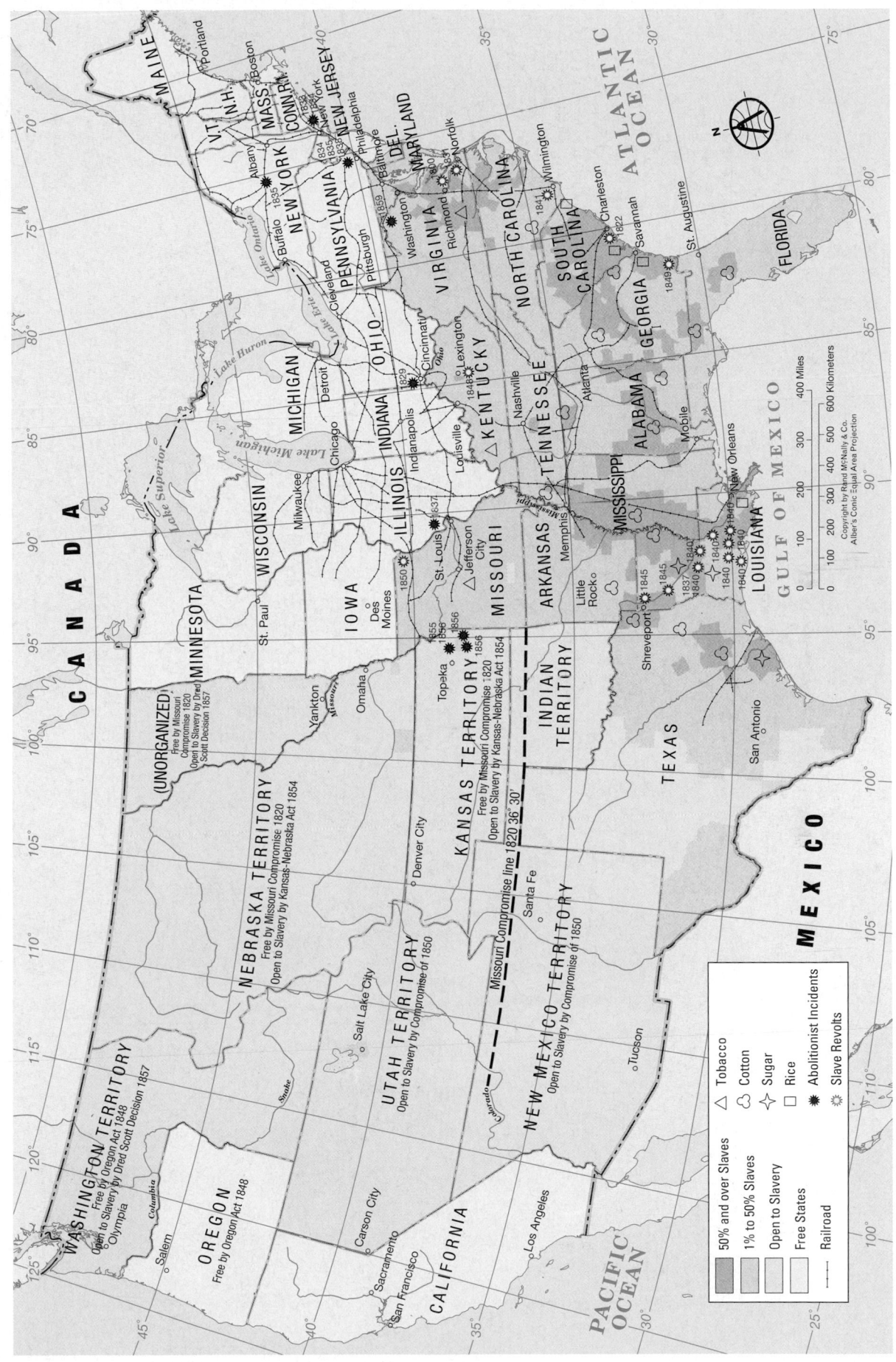

Slavery in the United States 1820–1860

Legend:
- 50% and over Slaves
- 1% to 50% Slaves
- Open to Slavery
- Free States
- Railroad
- Tobacco
- Cotton
- Sugar
- Rice
- Abolitionist Incidents
- Slave Revolts

CANADA

MAINE
Portland
Boston
N.H.
V.T.
MASS.
CONN. R.I.
NEW YORK
Albany
Buffalo
NEW JERSEY
New York
Philadelphia
PENNSYLVANIA
Pittsburgh
DEL.
MARYLAND
Baltimore
Washington
VIRGINIA
Richmond
Norfolk
NORTH CAROLINA
SOUTH CAROLINA
Charleston
Wilmington
GEORGIA
Savannah
St. Augustine
FLORIDA
ATLANTIC OCEAN

Lake Ontario
Lake Erie
Lake Huron
Lake Superior
Lake Michigan

MICHIGAN
Detroit
Cleveland
OHIO
Cincinnati
Lexington
KENTUCKY
Nashville
TENNESSEE
Atlanta
ALABAMA
Mobile
MISSISSIPPI
New Orleans
LOUISIANA
GULF OF MEXICO

Chicago
Milwaukee
WISCONSIN
MINNESOTA
St. Paul
INDIANA
Indianapolis
ILLINOIS
Louisville
IOWA
Des Moines
Yankton
Omaha
St. Louis
Jefferson City
MISSOURI
Memphis
ARKANSAS
Little Rock
Shreveport
Topeka
KANSAS TERRITORY
Free by Missouri Compromise 1820
Open to Slavery by Kansas-Nebraska Act 1854

(UNORGANIZED)
Free by Missouri Compromise 1820
Open to Slavery by Dred Scott Decision 1857

NEBRASKA TERRITORY
Free by Missouri Compromise 1820
Open to Slavery by Kansas-Nebraska Act 1854

INDIAN TERRITORY

TEXAS
San Antonio

NEW MEXICO TERRITORY
Open to Slavery by Compromise of 1850
Santa Fe
Tucson

UTAH TERRITORY
Open to Slavery by Compromise of 1850
Salt Lake City
Denver City

WASHINGTON TERRITORY
Free by Oregon Act 1848
Open to Slavery by Dred Scott Decision 1857
Olympia

OREGON
Free by Oregon Act 1848
Salem

CALIFORNIA
Sacramento
San Francisco
Carson City
Los Angeles

PACIFIC OCEAN

MEXICO

Missouri Compromise line 1820 36° 30'

ATLANTIC OCEAN

Columbia R.
Snake R.
Colorado R.
Mississippi R.
Missouri R.
Ohio R.

400 Miles
600 Kilometers
Copyright by Rand McNally & Co.
Alber's Conic Equal Area Projection

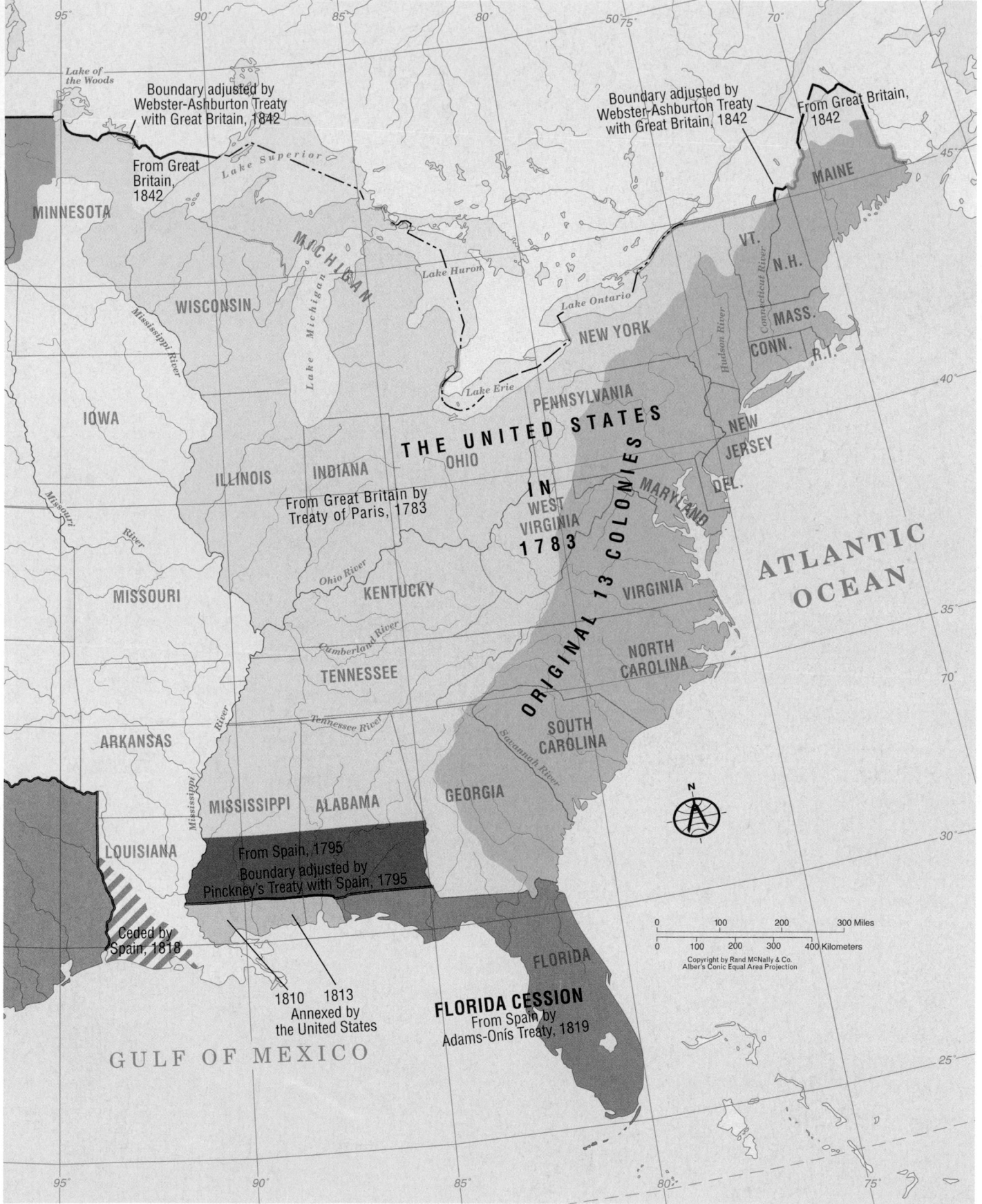

Boundary adjusted by
Webster-Ashburton Treaty
with Great Britain, 1842

From Great
Britain,
1842

Lake of
the Woods

Boundary adjusted by
Webster-Ashburton Treaty
with Great Britain, 1842

From Great Britain,
1842

MAINE

Lake Superior

MINNESOTA

MICHIGAN

Lake Huron

WISCONSIN

Lake Michigan

VT.

N.H.

MASS.

CONN.

R.I.

Lake Ontario

NEW YORK

Hudson River

Connecticut River

IOWA

Lake Erie

Mississippi River

Missouri River

ILLINOIS

INDIANA

OHIO

PENNSYLVANIA

NEW
JERSEY

DEL.

THE UNITED STATES

IN

WEST
VIRGINIA

1783

MARYLAND

ORIGINAL 13 COLONIES

From Great Britain by
Treaty of Paris, 1783

ATLANTIC
OCEAN

MISSOURI

Ohio River

KENTUCKY

VIRGINIA

Cumberland River

TENNESSEE

NORTH
CAROLINA

Tennessee River

ARKANSAS

SOUTH
CAROLINA

Savannah River

River

MISSISSIPPI

ALABAMA

GEORGIA

N

LOUISIANA

From Spain, 1795
Boundary adjusted by
Pinckney's Treaty with Spain, 1795

Mississippi River

Ceded by
Spain, 1818

FLORIDA

1810   1813
Annexed by
the United States

FLORIDA CESSION
From Spain by
Adams-Onís Treaty, 1819

0   100   200   300 Miles

0   100   200   300   400 Kilometers

Copyright by Rand McNally & Co.
Alber's Conic Equal Area Projection

GULF OF MEXICO

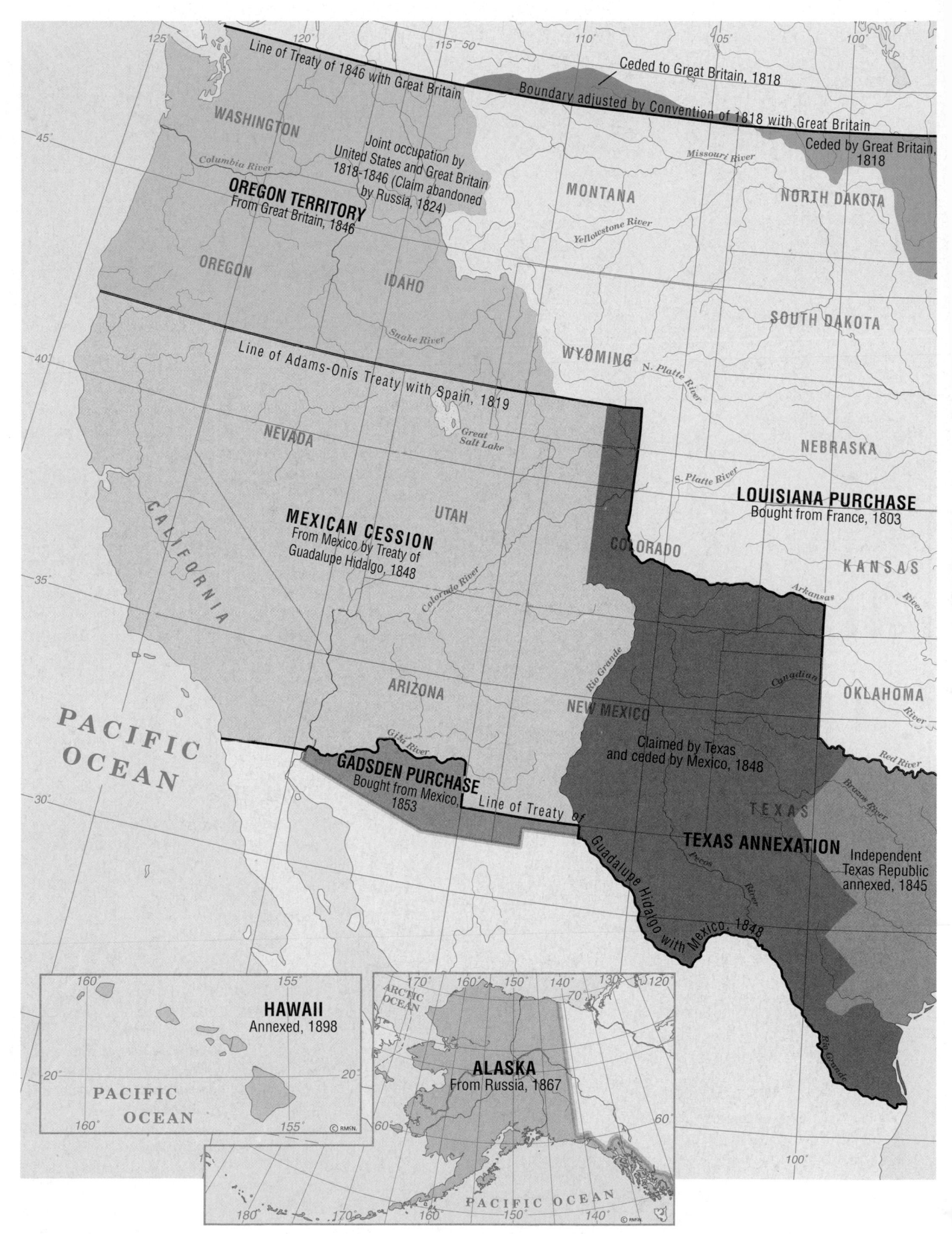

Line of Treaty of 1846 with Great Britain

Ceded to Great Britain, 1818

Boundary adjusted by Convention of 1818 with Great Britain

Ceded by Great Britain, 1818

WASHINGTON

Joint occupation by United States and Great Britain 1818-1846 (Claim abandoned by Russia, 1824)

OREGON TERRITORY
From Great Britain, 1846

Columbia River

MONTANA

Missouri River

NORTH DAKOTA

Yellowstone River

OREGON

IDAHO

Snake River

WYOMING

SOUTH DAKOTA

N. Platte River

Line of Adams-Onís Treaty with Spain, 1819

NEVADA

Great Salt Lake

S. Platte River

NEBRASKA

LOUISIANA PURCHASE
Bought from France, 1803

MEXICAN CESSION
From Mexico by Treaty of Guadalupe Hidalgo, 1848

UTAH

COLORADO

KANSAS

Arkansas River

CALIFORNIA

Colorado River

ARIZONA

NEW MEXICO

Rio Grande

Canadian River

OKLAHOMA

Red River

Brazos River

PACIFIC OCEAN

Gila River

GADSDEN PURCHASE
Bought from Mexico, 1853

Line of Treaty of

Claimed by Texas and ceded by Mexico, 1848

TEXAS

Pecos River

TEXAS ANNEXATION

Independent Texas Republic annexed, 1845

Guadalupe Hidalgo with Mexico, 1848

Rio Grande

HAWAII
Annexed, 1898

PACIFIC OCEAN

ARCTIC OCEAN

ALASKA
From Russia, 1867

PACIFIC OCEAN

© RMcN

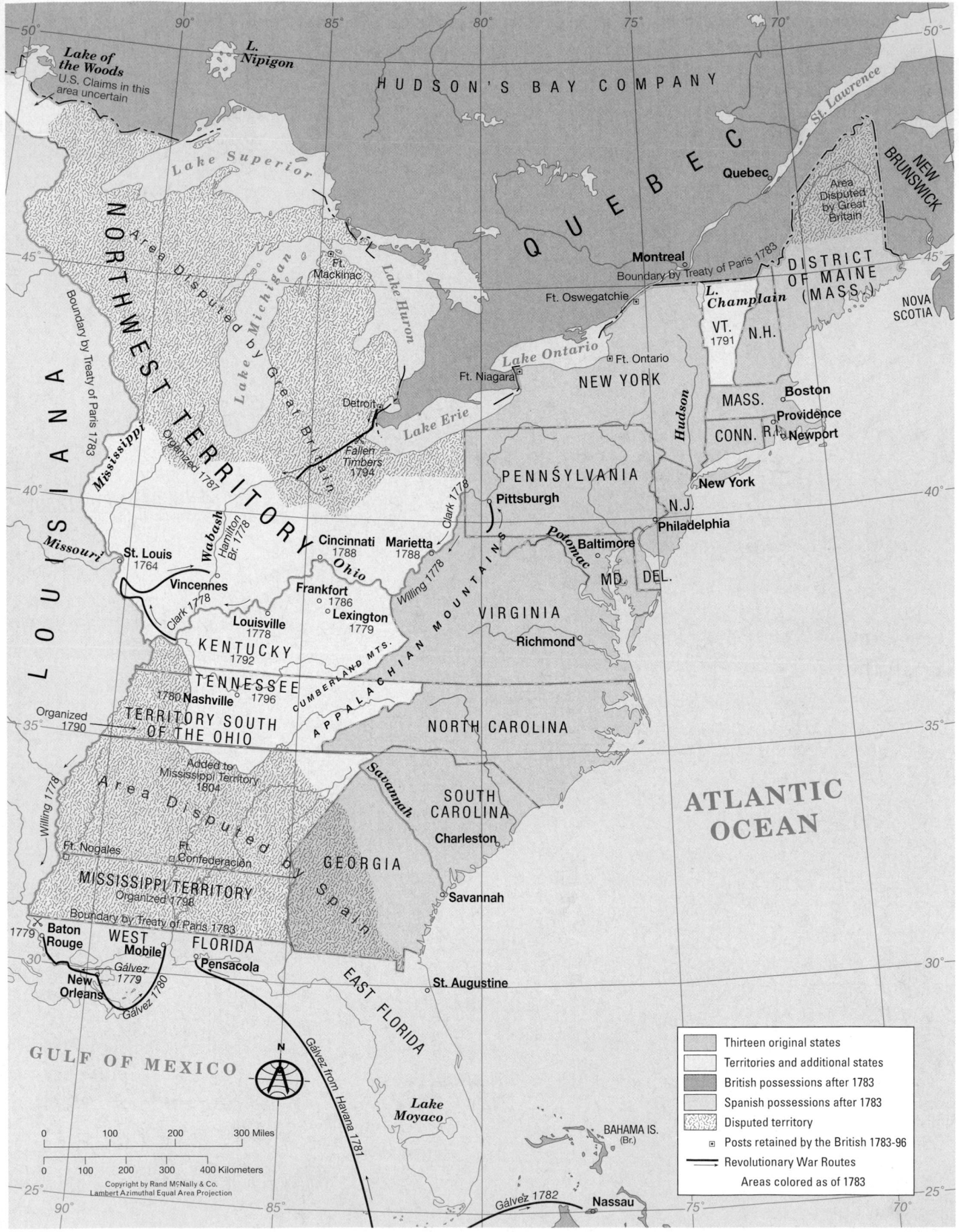

50°

Lake of the Woods
U.S. Claims in this area uncertain

L. Nipigon

HUDSON'S BAY COMPANY

St. Lawrence

Lake Superior

Quebec

QUEBEC

Area Disputed by Great Britain

NEW BRUNSWICK

NOVA SCOTIA

45°

Boundary by Treaty of Paris 1783

Ft. Mackinac

Lake Huron

Lake Michigan

Montreal

Ft. Oswegatchie

DISTRICT OF MAINE (MASS.

NORTHWEST TERRITORY

Area Disputed by Great Britain

VT. 1791

N.H.

L. Champlain

Organized 1787

Lake Ontario

Ft. Ontario

Boundary by Treaty of Paris 1783

Ft. Niagara

NEW YORK

MASS.

Boston

Providence

Hudson

LOUISIANA

Mississippi

Detroit

Lake Erie

CONN.

R.I.

Newport

Fallen Timbers 1794

40°

Missouri

St. Louis 1764

Wabash

Hamilton Br. 1778

Cincinnati 1788

Marietta 1788

Clark 1778

PENNSYLVANIA

Pittsburgh

New York

N.J.

Philadelphia

Vincennes

Clark 1778

Ohio

Frankfort 1786

Willing 1778

Potomac

Baltimore

MD.

DEL.

Louisville 1778

Lexington 1779

APPALACHIAN MOUNTAINS

VIRGINIA

Richmond

KENTUCKY 1792

TENNESSEE 1796

CUMBERLAND MTS.

Organized 1790

35°

TERRITORY SOUTH OF THE OHIO

1780 Nashville

NORTH CAROLINA

35°

Willing 1778

Area Disputed by Spain

Added to Mississippi Territory 1804

Savannah

SOUTH CAROLINA

ATLANTIC OCEAN

Ft. Nogales

Ft. Confederación

GEORGIA

Charleston

MISSISSIPPI TERRITORY
Organized 1798

Savannah

Boundary by Treaty of Paris 1783

1779

Baton Rouge

WEST FLORIDA

Mobile

Pensacola

Gálvez 1779

New Orleans

Gálvez 1780

St. Augustine

30°

EAST FLORIDA

GULF OF MEXICO

N

Gálvez from Havana 1781

Lake Moyaco

BAHAMA IS. (Br.)

0   100   200   300 Miles

0 100 200 300 400 Kilometers

Copyright by Rand McNally & Co.
Lambert Azimuthal Equal Area Projection

25°

Gálvez 1782

Nassau

25°

	Thirteen original states
	Territories and additional states
	British possessions after 1783
	Spanish possessions after 1783
	Disputed territory
⊡	Posts retained by the British 1783-96
	Revolutionary War Routes
	Areas colored as of 1783

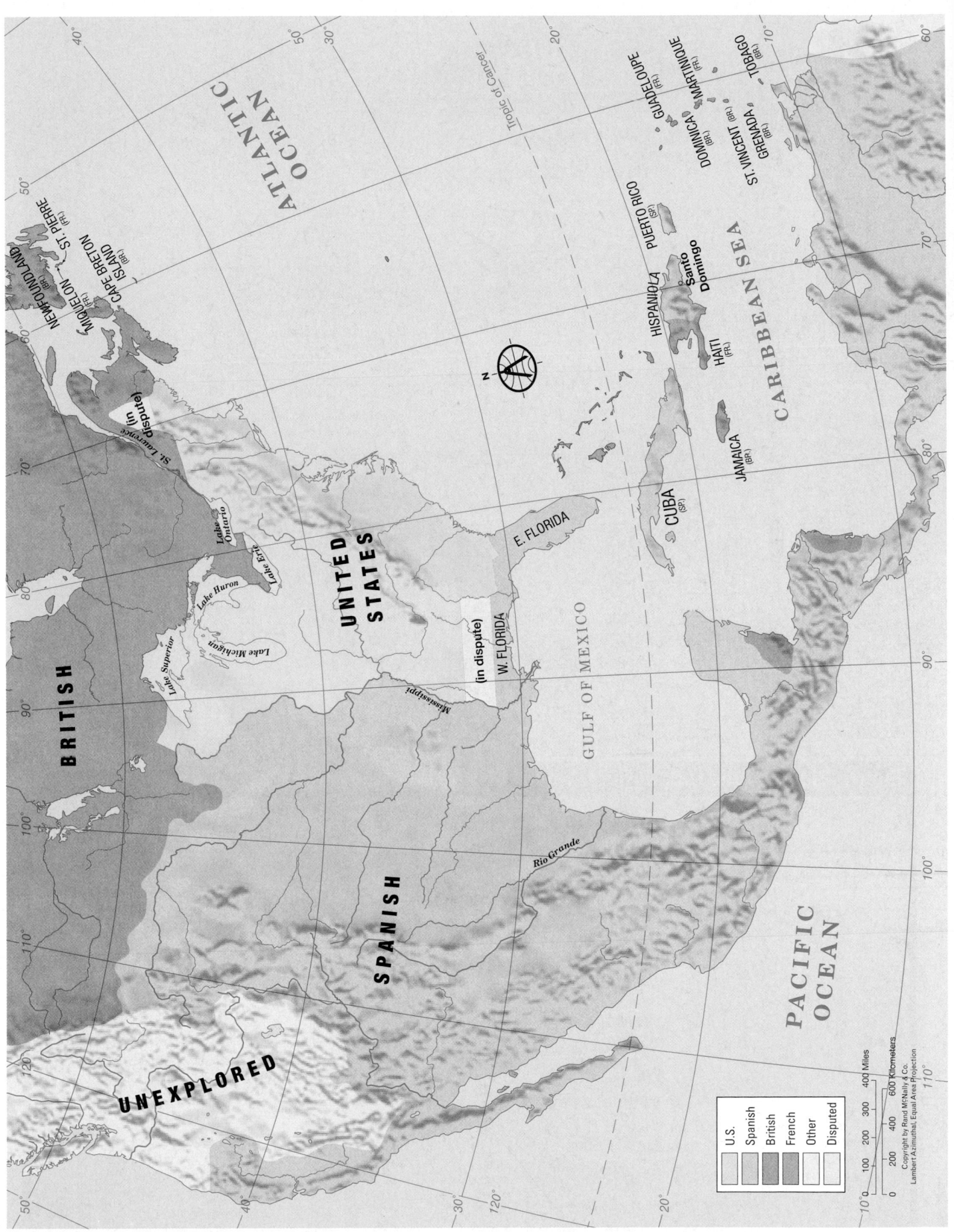

North America 1783

ATLANTIC OCEAN

BRITISH

UNITED STATES

SPANISH

UNEXPLORED

PACIFIC OCEAN

GULF OF MEXICO

CARIBBEAN SEA

Rio Grande

Mississippi

W. FLORIDA (in dispute)

E. FLORIDA

Tropic of Cancer

St. Lawrence (in dispute)

NEWFOUNDLAND (BR.)

MIQUELON (FR.)

ST. PIERRE (FR.)

CAPE BRETON ISLAND (BR.)

Lake Superior
Lake Michigan
Lake Huron
Lake Erie
Lake Ontario

CUBA (SP.)

JAMAICA (BR.)

HISPANIOLA
HAITI (FR.)
Santo Domingo

PUERTO RICO (SP.)

GUADELOUPE (FR.)

DOMINICA (BR.)
MARTINIQUE (FR.)

ST. VINCENT (BR.)
GRENADA (BR.)
TOBAGO (BR.)

U.S.
Spanish
British
French
Other
Disputed

0   100   200   300   400 Miles
0   200   400   600 Kilometers
Lambert Azimuthal Equal Area Projection
Copyright by Rand McNally & Co.

RAND McNALLY

A26

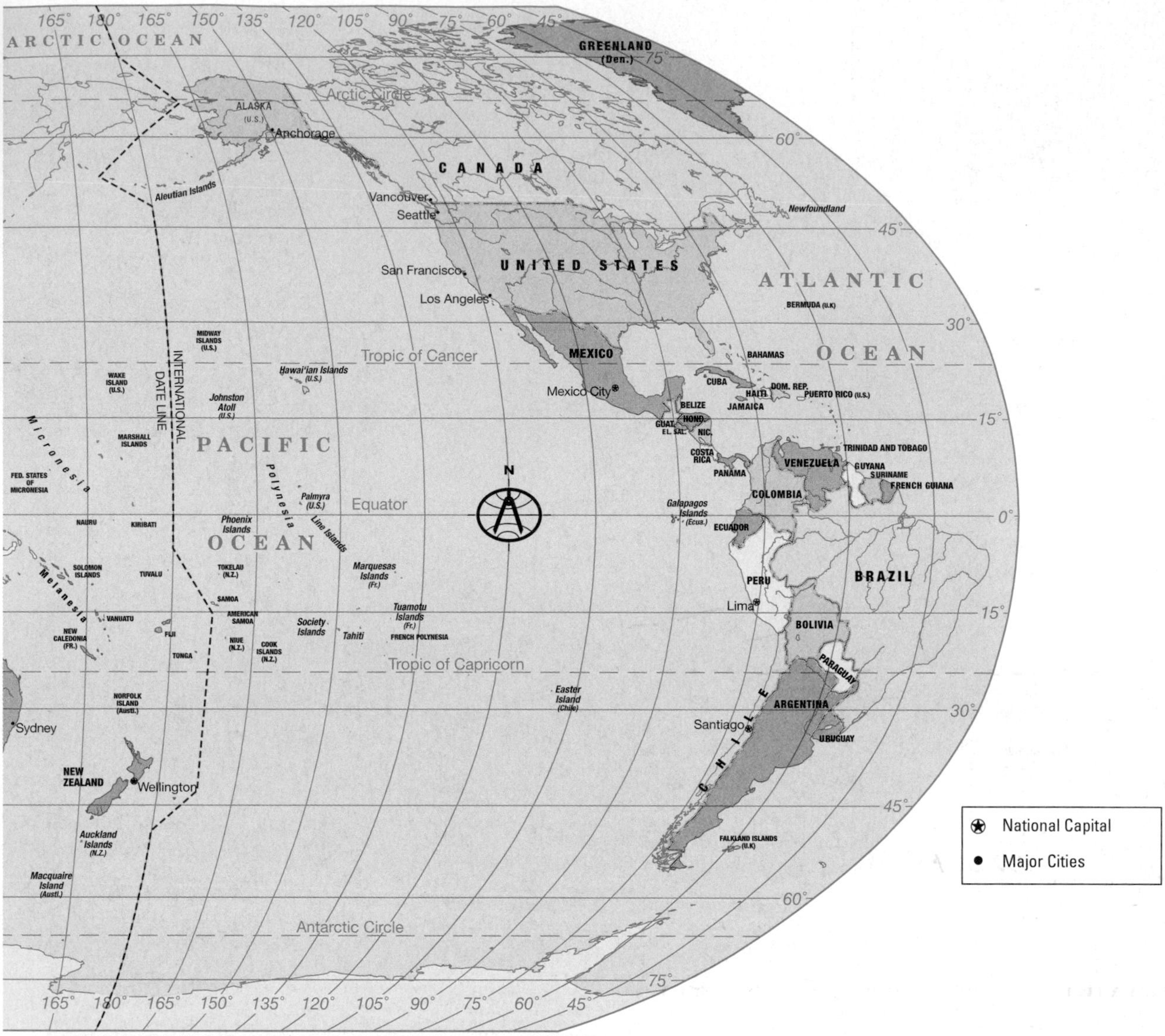

Puerto Rico and the U.S. Virgin Islands

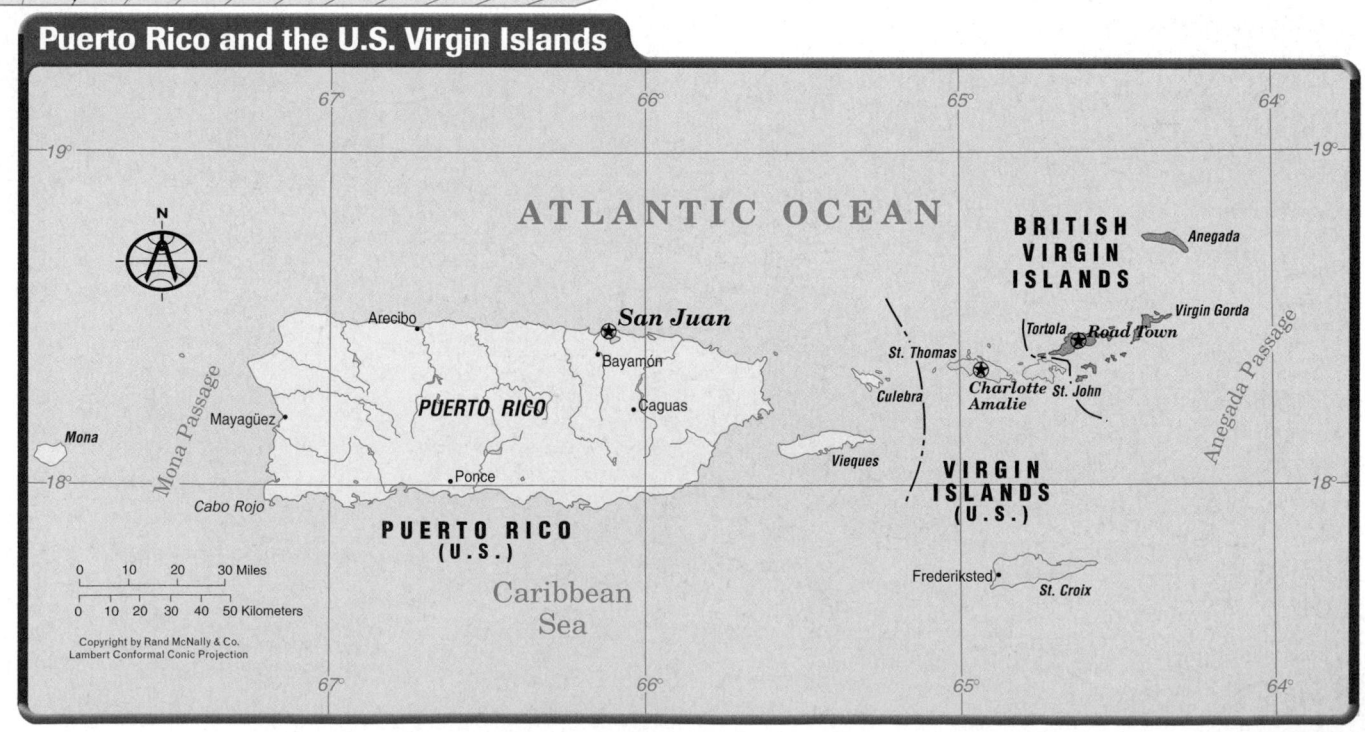

RAND McNALLY

Guam

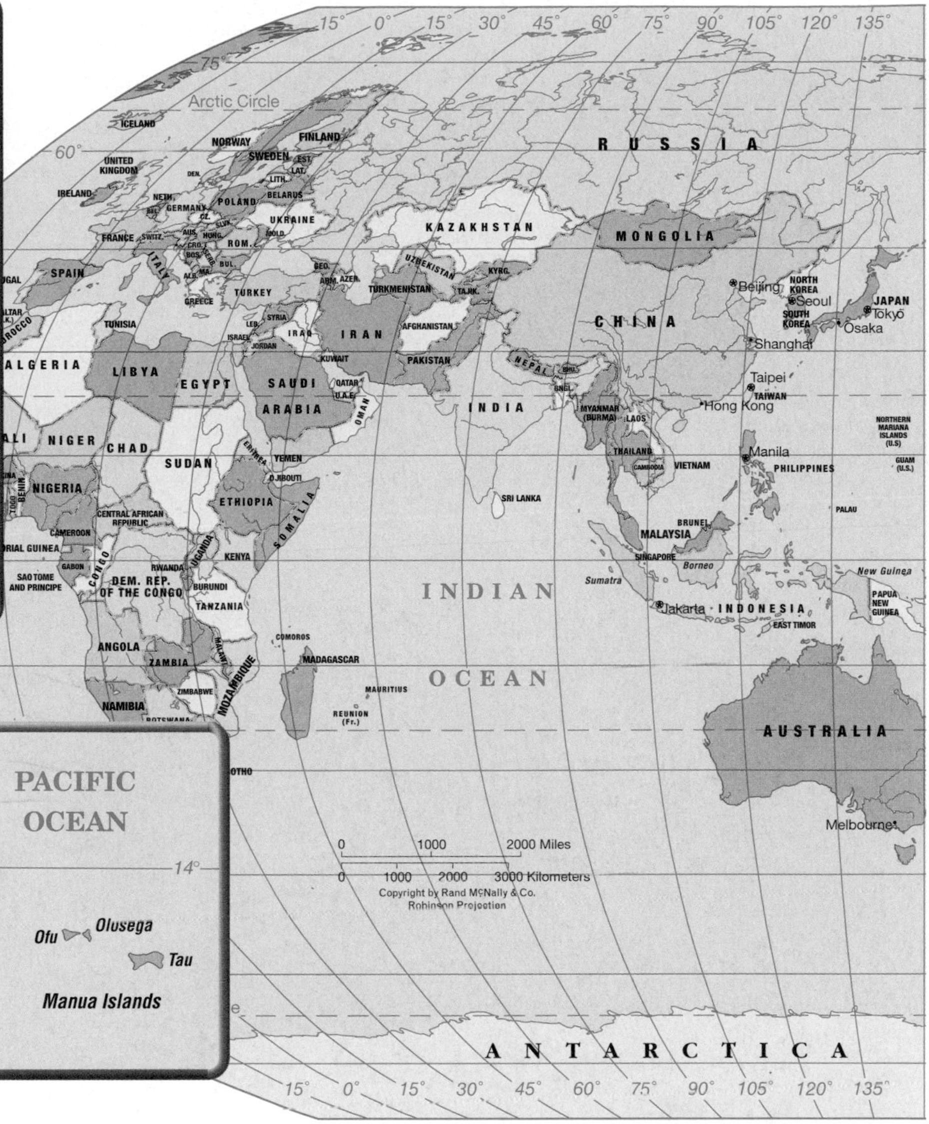

Philippine Sea

N

144°45'
145°

Agana • Tamuning

13°30'

GUAM
(U.S.)

PACIFIC
OCEAN

13°15'

| 0 | 2 | 4 | 6 | 8 | 10 Miles |

| 0 | 5 | 10 | 15 Kilometers |

Copyright by Rand McNally & Co.
Lambert Conformal Conic Projection

144°45'
145°

Samoa

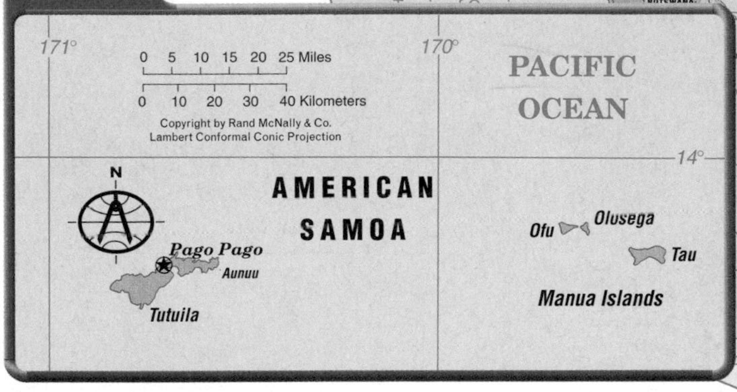

171°
170°

| 0 | 5 | 10 | 15 | 20 | 25 Miles |
| 0 | 10 | 20 | 30 | 40 Kilometers |

Copyright by Rand McNally & Co.
Lambert Conformal Conic Projection

PACIFIC
OCEAN

N

AMERICAN
SAMOA

14°

Ofu ⋈ *Olusega*

Tau

Pago Pago
Aunuu

Tutuila

Manua Islands

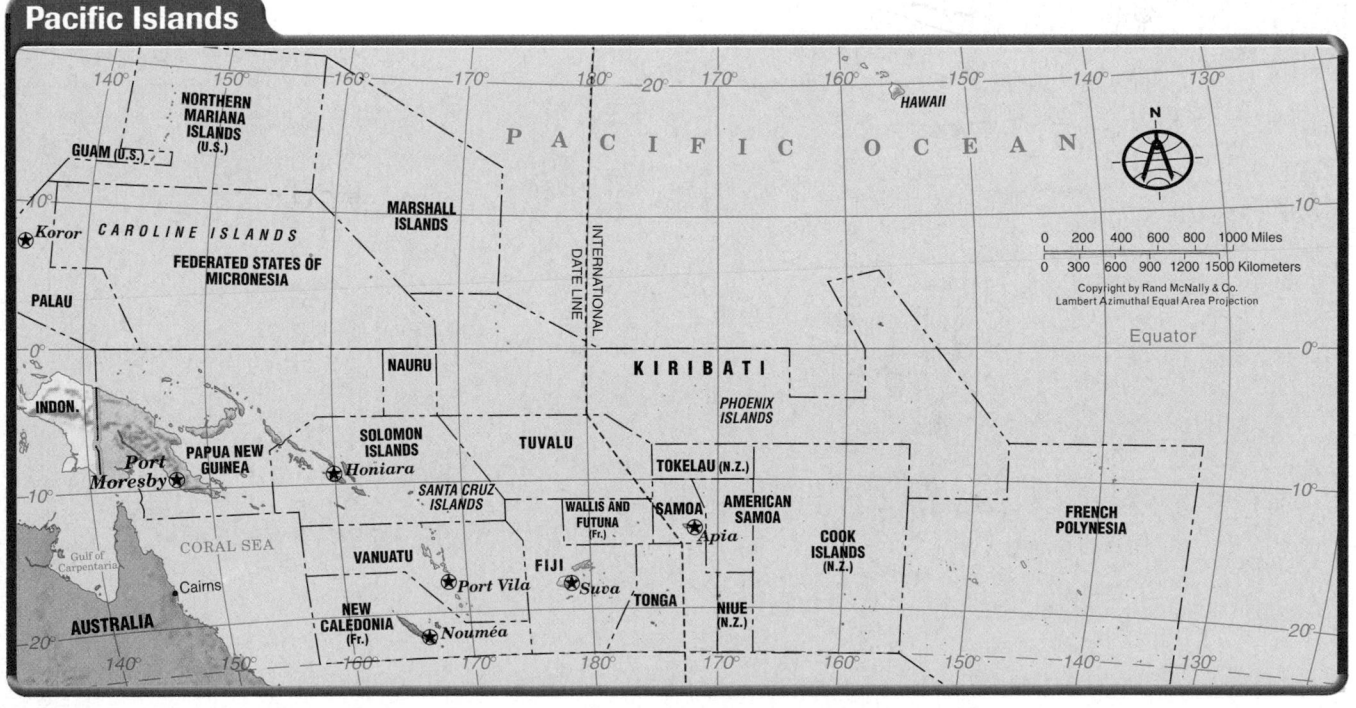

Arctic Circle

ICELAND
NORWAY SWEDEN FINLAND EST.
UNITED DEN. LAT.
KINGDOM LITH.
IRELAND NETH. GERMANY POLAND BELARUS
FRANCE SWITZ. CZ. UKRAINE
PORTUGAL SPAIN ITALY AUS. CRO. ROM. GEO. ARM. AZER.
GIBRALTAR GREECE BUL. TURKEY
MOROCCO TUNISIA LEB. SYRIA IRAQ
ALGERIA LIBYA ISRAEL JORDAN KUWAIT
EGYPT SAUDI QATAR
NIGER ARABIA U.A.E. OMAN
MALI CHAD SUDAN YEMEN
BENIN NIGERIA D.JIBOUTI
CENTRAL AFRICAN ETHIOPIA
CAMEROON REPUBLIC
EQUATORIAL GUINEA SOMALIA
SAO TOME GABON CONGO DEM. REP. RWANDA KENYA
AND PRINCIPE OF THE CONGO BURUNDI TANZANIA
ANGOLA ZAMBIA ZIMBABWE MOZAMBIQUE
NAMIBIA BOTSWANA

RUSSIA

KAZAKHSTAN

MONGOLIA

UZBEKISTAN KYRG.
TURKMENISTAN TAJIK.
AFGHANISTAN
IRAN PAKISTAN
NEPAL
INDIA
BANGLADESH

CHINA

NORTH KOREA
Beijing SOUTH KOREA JAPAN
Seoul Tōkyō
Shanghai Osaka

Taipei
Hong Kong TAIWAN

MYANMAR LAOS
(BURMA)
THAILAND VIETNAM
CAMBODIA
SRI LANKA MALAYSIA Manila
SINGAPORE BRUNEI PHILIPPINES
Borneo

NORTHERN MARIANA ISLANDS (U.S.)
PALAU
GUAM (U.S.)

New Guinea
Sumatra
Jakarta INDONESIA PAPUA NEW GUINEA
EAST TIMOR

INDIAN
OCEAN

COMOROS
MADAGASCAR
MAURITIUS
REUNION (Fr.)

AUSTRALIA

LESOTHO
Melbourne

| 0 | 1000 | 2000 Miles |
| 0 | 1000 | 2000 | 3000 Kilometers |

Copyright by Rand McNally & Co.
Robinson Projection

ANTARCTICA

75°
60°
15° 0° 15° 30° 45° 60° 75° 90° 105° 120° 135°
15° 0° 15° 30° 45° 60° 75° 90° 105° 120° 135°

Pacific Islands

140° 150° 160° 170° 180° 170° 160° 150° 140° 130°

PACIFIC OCEAN

HAWAII

N

NORTHERN MARIANA ISLANDS (U.S.)

GUAM (U.S.)

10°

CAROLINE ISLANDS
MARSHALL ISLANDS

FEDERATED STATES OF MICRONESIA

Koror

PALAU

INTERNATIONAL DATE LINE

| 0 | 200 | 400 | 600 | 800 | 1000 Miles |
| 0 | 300 | 600 | 900 | 1200 | 1500 Kilometers |

Copyright by Rand McNally & Co.
Lambert Azimuthal Equal Area Projection

Equator 0°

INDON.

NAURU

KIRIBATI

PHOENIX ISLANDS

TUVALU

TOKELAU (N.Z.)

Port Moresby
PAPUA NEW GUINEA

SOLOMON ISLANDS
Honiara

SANTA CRUZ ISLANDS

WALLIS AND FUTUNA (Fr.)

SAMOA
Apia

AMERICAN SAMOA

FRENCH POLYNESIA

10°

Gulf of Carpentaria

CORAL SEA

VANUATU

Port Vila

FIJI
Suva

TONGA

NIUE (N.Z.)

COOK ISLANDS (N.Z.)

AUSTRALIA

Cairns

NEW CALEDONIA (Fr.)
Nouméa

20°

140° 150° 160° 170° 180° 170° 160° 150° 140° 130°

MINNESOTA

Minneapolis

WISCONSIN

IOWA

Chicago

MICHIGAN

INDIANA

OHIO

ILLINOIS

STATES

MISSOURI

St. Louis

Lake of
the Ozarks

Ozark Plateau

KENTUCKY

TENNESSEE

KANSAS

Boston
Mts.

ARKANSAS

Ouachita Mts.

MISSISSIPPI

ALABAMA

GEORGIA

Atlanta

LOUISIANA

Houston

New
Orleans

Mississippi
Delta

GULF OF MEXICO

FLORIDA

Lake
Okeechobee

The
Everglades

Miami

Florida Keys

Cape Sable

Cape Canaveral

Tampa Bay

Great
Lakes

Lake Superior

Isle Royale

Keweenaw
Peninsula

Whitefish
Point

Upper Peninsula

ONTARIO

QUEBEC

MAINE

Mt. Katahdin
5,268 Ft
1,606m

Moosehead
Lake

NEW
BRUNSWICK

St. Lawrence

Montréal

VERMONT

White
Mts.

Mt. Washington
6,288 Ft.
1,917m

NEW
HAMPSHIRE

Gulf of
Maine

Lake
Champlain

Green Mts.

Adirondack
Mountains

MASS.

Boston

Cape Cod

Nantucket
Island

Lake Nipigon

Lake of
the
Woods

Lake
Winnipeg

CANADA

Georgian
Bay

Bruce
Peninsula

Lake Huron

Saginaw Bay

Lower Peninsula

Lake Michigan

Green Bay

Chippewa

Minnesota

Des Moines

Mississippi

Lake
Winnebago

Wisconsin

Muskegon

Grand

Maumee

Detroit

Lake Erie

Niagara
Falls

Allegheny

PENNSYLVANIA

Plateau

Catskill
Mts.

Hudson

Toronto

Lake Ontario

NEW YORK

Connecticut

CONNECTICUT R.I.

Long Island

New York

Philadelphia

NEW JERSEY

Delaware Bay

DELAWARE

MARYLAND

Susquehanna

Ohio

WEST
VIRGINIA

Allegheny

Appalachian Mountains

Washington D.C.

VIRGINIA

James

Chesapeake Bay

ATLANTIC
OCEAN

Scioto

White

Wabash

Illinois

Green

Lake
Cumberland

Cumberland

Kentucky
Lake

Kentucky

Ohio

Cumberland
Plateau

Mt. Mitchell
6,684 Ft.
2,037m

Blue Ridge

Piedmont

NORTH
CAROLINA

Roanoke

Albemarle
Sound

Cape Hatteras

Pamlico Sound

Cape Lookout

Tennessee

Tennessee

Clarks
Hill
Lake

SOUTH
CAROLINA

Pee Dee

Cape Fear

Santee

Cape Fear

Coastal Plain

Savannah

Sea Islands

Altamaha

Chattahoochee

Flint

Tombigbee

Alabama

Pearl

Yazoo

Mississippi

Ouachita

Arkansas

Red

Sabine

Trinity

Sam
Rayburn
Res.

Toledo
Bend
Res.

Atchafalaya
Bay

Cape
San Blas

Apalachee
Bay

Suwannee

Flint Hills

Neosho

Missouri

Neosho

Land Elevation	
Meters	Feet
3,000	9,840
2,000	6,560
500	1,640
200	656
0	0

Water Depth	
0	0
200	656
2,000	6,560

N

0   100   200   300 Miles

0   100 200 300 400 Kilometers

Copyright by Rand McNally & Co.
Alber's Conic Equal Area Projection

ATLANTIC
OCEAN

PUERTO RICO
(U.S.)

San Juan

Arecibo

Mayagüez

Ponce

Caguas

Caribbean
Sea

N

0   25   50 Miles

0   25   50 Kilometers

RAND M°NALLY

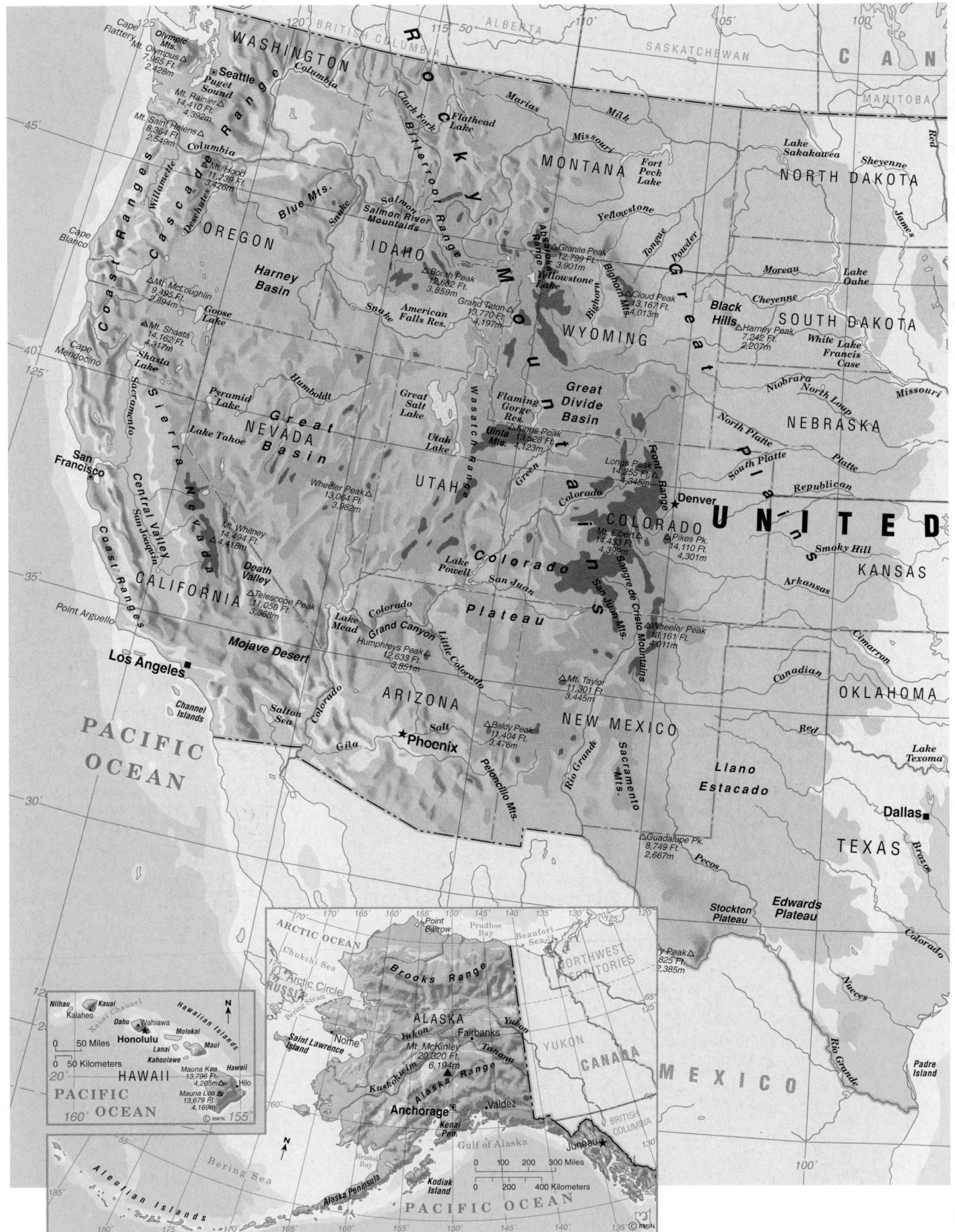

PACIFIC
OCEAN

WASHINGTON
Cape Flattery
Olympic Mts.
Mt. Olympus △ 7,965 Ft. 2,428m
Seattle ■
Puget Sound
Mt. Rainier △ 14,410 Ft. 4,392m
Mt. Saint Helens △ 8,364 Ft. 2,549m
Columbia
Mt. Hood △ 11,239 Ft. 3,426m
OREGON
Cascade Range
Coast Ranges
Blue Mts.
Deschutes
Willamette
Columbia
Harney Basin
Cape Blanco
△Mt. McLoughlin 9,495 Ft. 2,894m
Goose Lake
△Mt. Shasta 14,162 Ft. 4,317m
Cape Mendocino
Shasta Lake
Sacramento
Pyramid Lake
Humboldt
Great
NEVADA
Basin
Lake Tahoe
Wheeler Peak △ 13,064 Ft. 3,982m
San Francisco
Sierra Nevada
Central Valley
San Joaquin
Mt. Whitney △ 14,494 Ft. 4,418m
Death Valley
△Telescope Peak 11,050 Ft. 3,368m
Point Arguello
CALIFORNIA
Coast Ranges
Mojave Desert
Los Angeles ■
Channel Islands
Salton Sea
Colorado
ARIZONA
Gila
Salt
Phoenix ★
Colorado
Lake Mead
Grand Canyon
Humphreys Peak △ 12,633 Ft. 3,851m
Little Colorado
△Baldy Peak 11,404 Ft. 3,476m
Peloncillo Mts.

BRITISH COLUMBIA
ALBERTA
SASKATCHEWAN
CAN
MANITOBA
Columbia
Clark Fork
Bitterroot Range
Flathead Lake
Marias
Missouri
Milk
Lake Sakakawea
Red
Sheyenne
NORTH DAKOTA
MONTANA
Fort Peck Lake
Yellowstone
Moreau
Lake Oahe
Snake
Salmon River Mountains
IDAHO
△Borah Peak 12,662 Ft. 3,859m
ROCKY
Absaroka Range
△Granite Peak 12,799 Ft. 3,901m
Yellowstone Lake
Grand Teton △ 13,770 Ft. 4,197m
Bighorn Mts.
△Cloud Peak 13,167 Ft. 4,013m
Tongue
Powder
Cheyenne
Black Hills
△Harney Peak 7,242 Ft. 2,207m
SOUTH DAKOTA
White
Lake Francis Case
Snake
American Falls Res.
MOUNTAINS
WYOMING
Great Divide Basin
Niobrara
North Loup
Missouri
Great Salt Lake
Utah Lake
Flaming Gorge Res.
Uinta Mts.
△Kings Peak 13,528 Ft. 4,123m
Green
North Platte
South Platte
NEBRASKA
Platte
Wasatch Range
UTAH
Front Range
Longs Peak △ 14,255 Ft. 4,345m
Denver ★
COLORADO
Mt. Elbert △ 14,433 Ft. 4,399m
Pikes Pk. △ 14,110 Ft. 4,301m
UNITED
Republican
Smoky Hill
KANSAS
Lake Powell
Colorado
San Juan
Colorado
Plateau
Lake Powell
San Juan Mts.
Sangre de Cristo Mountains
△Wheeler Peak 13,161 Ft. 4,011m
Arkansas
Cimarron
Mt. Taylor △ 11,301 Ft. 3,445m
NEW MEXICO
Canadian
OKLAHOMA
Rio Grande
Sacramento Mts.
Red
Llano Estacado
Lake Texoma
Dallas ■
△Guadalupe Pk. 8,749 Ft. 2,667m
Pecos
TEXAS
Brazos
Stockton Plateau
Edwards Plateau
Colorado
MEXICO
Nueces
Rio Grande
Padre Island

HAWAII
Niihau
Kauai
Kalaheo
Oahu
Wahiawa
Honolulu ★
Molokai
Lanai
Maui
Kahoolawe
Hawaii
Mauna Kea △ 13,796 Ft. 4,205m
Hilo
Mauna Loa △ 13,679 Ft. 4,169m
Hawaiian Islands
Kauai Channel
N
0 50 Miles
0 50 Kilometers
PACIFIC OCEAN
20°
160°
155°
© RMN.

ARCTIC OCEAN
Chukchi Sea
Point Barrow
Prudhoe Bay
Beaufort Sea
Arctic Circle
RUSSIA
Bering Strait
Brooks Range
NORTHWEST TERRITORIES
ry Peak 825 Ft. 2,385m
Saint Lawrence Island
Nome
ALASKA
Yukon
Fairbanks
Yukon
Tanana
Kuskokwim
Mt. McKinley △ 20,320 Ft. 6,194m
Alaska Range
YUKON
CANADA
BRITISH COLUMBIA
Anchorage ■
Valdez
Juneau ★
Kenai Pen.
N
Bristol Bay
Gulf of Alaska
Kodiak Island
0 100 200 300 Miles
0 200 400 Kilometers
Bering Sea
Aleutian Islands
PACIFIC OCEAN
© RMN.

Legend

- ⊛ National Capital
- ★ Secondary Capital (State, Province, or Territory)
- ■ City over 1,000,000 population
- ▣ City of 250,000 to 1,000,000 population
- • City under 250,000 population

Copyright by Rand McNally & Co.
Alber's Conic Equal Area Projection

ATLANTIC OCEAN
San Juan
Arecibo
Mayagüez
Caguas
Ponce
PUERTO RICO (U.S.)
Caribbean Sea

RAND McNALLY

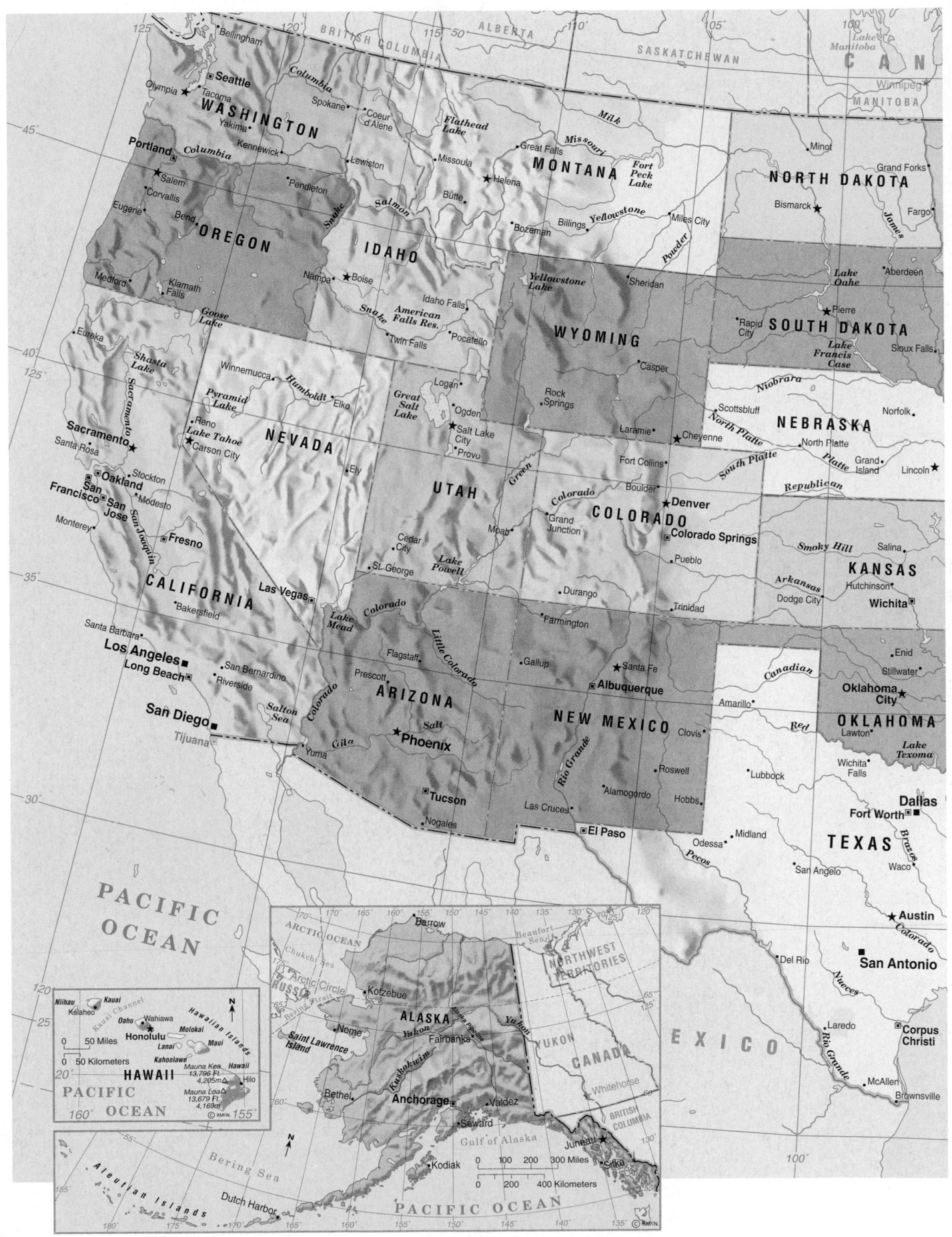

RAND McNALLY

A20

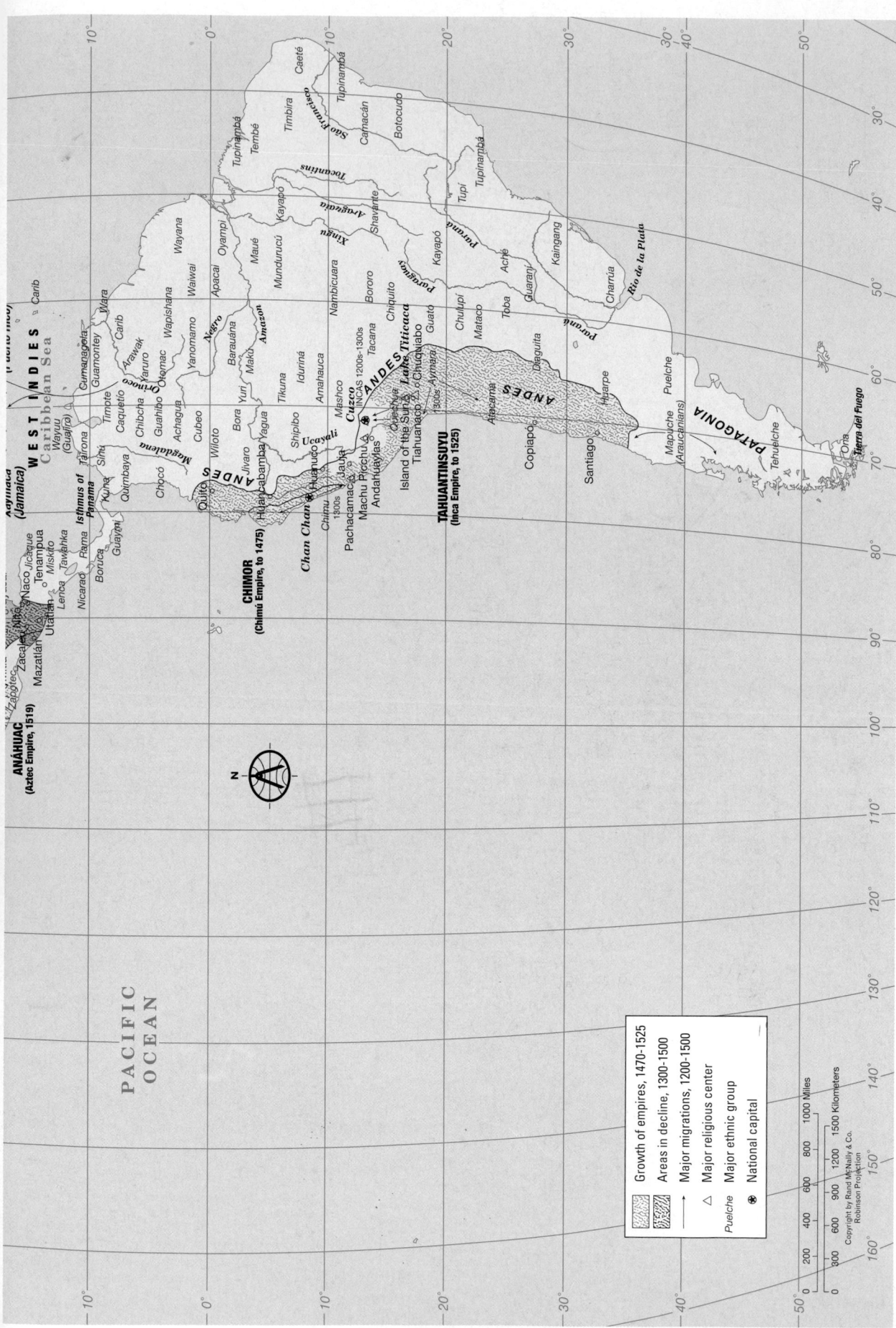

PACIFIC
OCEAN

WEST INDIES
Caribbean Sea

ANAHUAC
(Aztec Empire, 1519)

Zapotec
Zacateco
Mazatlán
Utatlán
Nicarao
Boruca
Guaymí
Rama
Lenca
Tawahka
Miskito
Tenampua
Jicaque
Naco
Quiché
Mixteca

Aguilillá
(Jamaica)

Cumanagota
Guamontey
Tairona
Kuna
Qûimbaya
Chocó
Magdalena
Chibcha
Achagua
Guahibo
Cubeo
Quito
Otomac
Wiloto
Yaruro
Arawak
Carib
Carib
Wara
Timote
Caquetío
Sihá
Orinoco
Negro
Yanomamo
Baraúana
Yuri
Maku
Bora
Jívaro
Yagua

ANDES

CHIMOR
(Chimú Empire, to 1475)

Chan Chan
Chimú
1300s
Huánuco
Jauja
Machu Picchu
Pachacamac
Andahuaylas
Huancabamba

TAHUANTINSUYU
(Inca Empire, to 1525)

Cuzco
INCAS 1200s–1300s
Quechua
Island of the Sun
Tiahuanaco
1300s Aymara
Lake Titicaca
Chuquiabo

Shipibo
Ucayali
Mashco
Amahuaca
Idurina
Tikuna
Amazon
Madeira
Munducurú
Nambicuara
Bororo
Tacana
Chiquito
Guato
Chulupi
Mataco
Guaporé
Xingu
Shavante
Araguaia
Kayapó
Tocantins
São Francisco
Tembé
Tupinambá
Timbira
Camacán
Botocudo
Caeté
Tupinambá

Tupi
Tupinambá
Atacama
Diaguita
Copiapó
Santiago
Huarpe
Aché
Guaraní
Kaingang
Toba
Charrúa
Rio de la Plata
Puelche
Mapuche
(Araucanians)
Tehuelche
PATAGONIA
Ona
Tierra del Fuego

Growth of empires, 1470–1525
Areas in decline, 1300–1500
Major migrations, 1200–1500
△ Major religious center
Puelche Major ethnic group
⊛ National capital

Copyright by Rand McNally & Co.
Robinson Projection

0   200   400   600   800   1000 Miles
0 300 600 900 1200 1500 Kilometers

⊛ RAND McNALLY

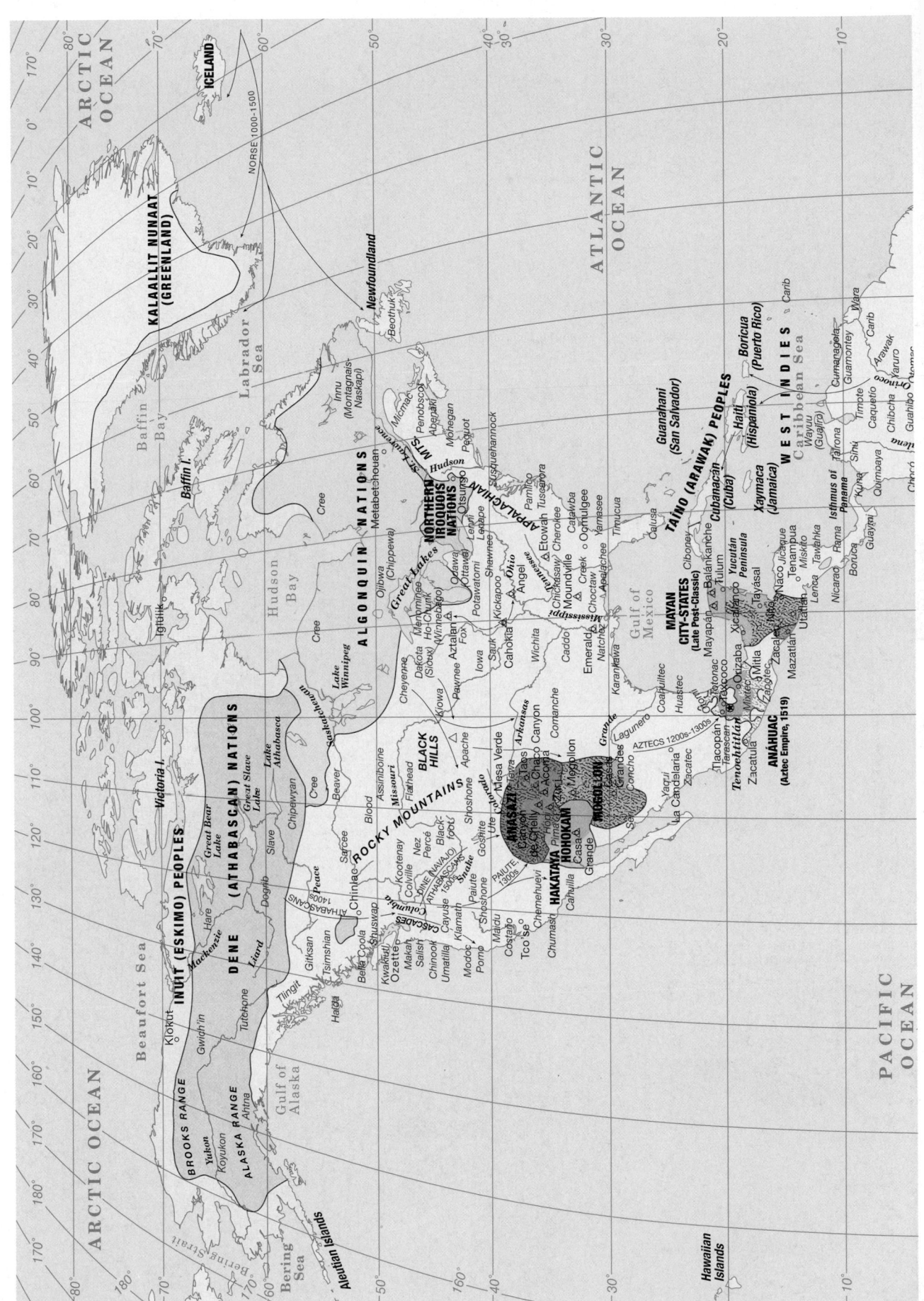

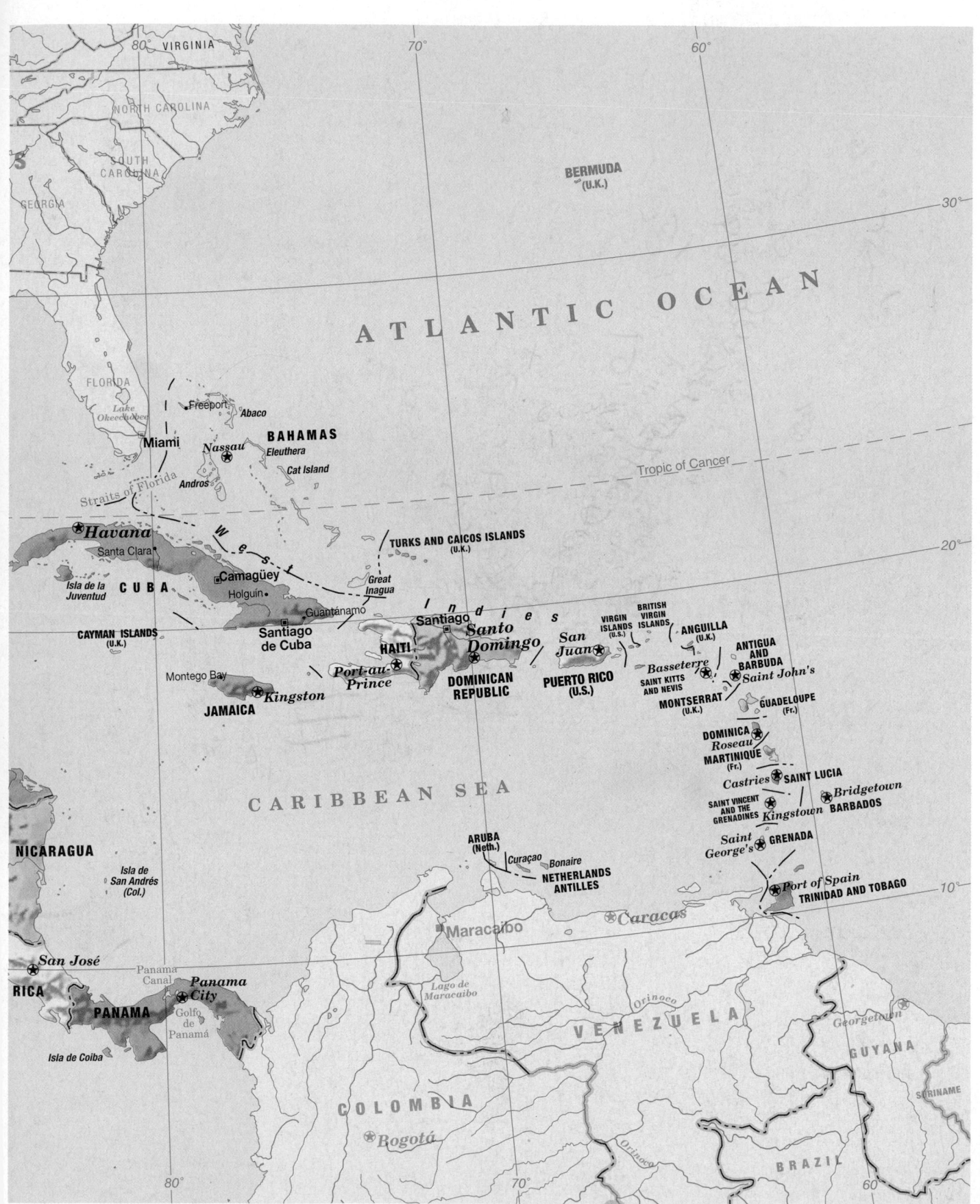

VIRGINIA

NORTH CAROLINA

SOUTH CAROLINA

GEORGIA

30°

FLORIDA

Lake Okeechobee

Miami

Straits of Florida

Havana

Santa Clara

CUBA

Isla de la Juventud

CAYMAN ISLANDS
(U.K.)

Montego Bay

Kingston

JAMAICA

Freeport

Abaco

BAHAMAS

Nassau

Eleuthera

Cat Island

Andros

West

Camagüey

Holguín

Guantánamo

Santiago de Cuba

HAITI

Port-au-Prince

BERMUDA
(U.K.)

ATLANTIC OCEAN

Tropic of Cancer

TURKS AND CAICOS ISLANDS
(U.K.)

Great Inagua

Indies

Santiago

Santo Domingo

DOMINICAN REPUBLIC

San Juan

PUERTO RICO
(U.S.)

VIRGIN ISLANDS
(U.S.)

BRITISH VIRGIN ISLANDS

ANGUILLA
(U.K.)

Basseterre

SAINT KITTS AND NEVIS

MONTSERRAT
(U.K.)

ANTIGUA AND BARBUDA

Saint John's

GUADELOUPE
(Fr.)

DOMINICA

Roseau

MARTINIQUE
(Fr.)

Castries

SAINT LUCIA

SAINT VINCENT AND THE GRENADINES

Kingstown

Bridgetown

BARBADOS

Saint George's

GRENADA

30°

20°

CARIBBEAN SEA

NICARAGUA

Isla de San Andrés
(Col.)

ARUBA
(Neth.)

Curaçao

Bonaire

NETHERLANDS ANTILLES

Caracas

Port of Spain

TRINIDAD AND TOBAGO

10°

San José

Panama Canal

RICA

PANAMA

Panama City

Golfo de Panamá

Isla de Coiba

Maracaibo

Lago de Maracaibo

Orinoco

VENEZUELA

Georgetown

GUYANA

SURINAME

COLOMBIA

Bogotá

Orinoco

BRAZIL

80°

70°

60°

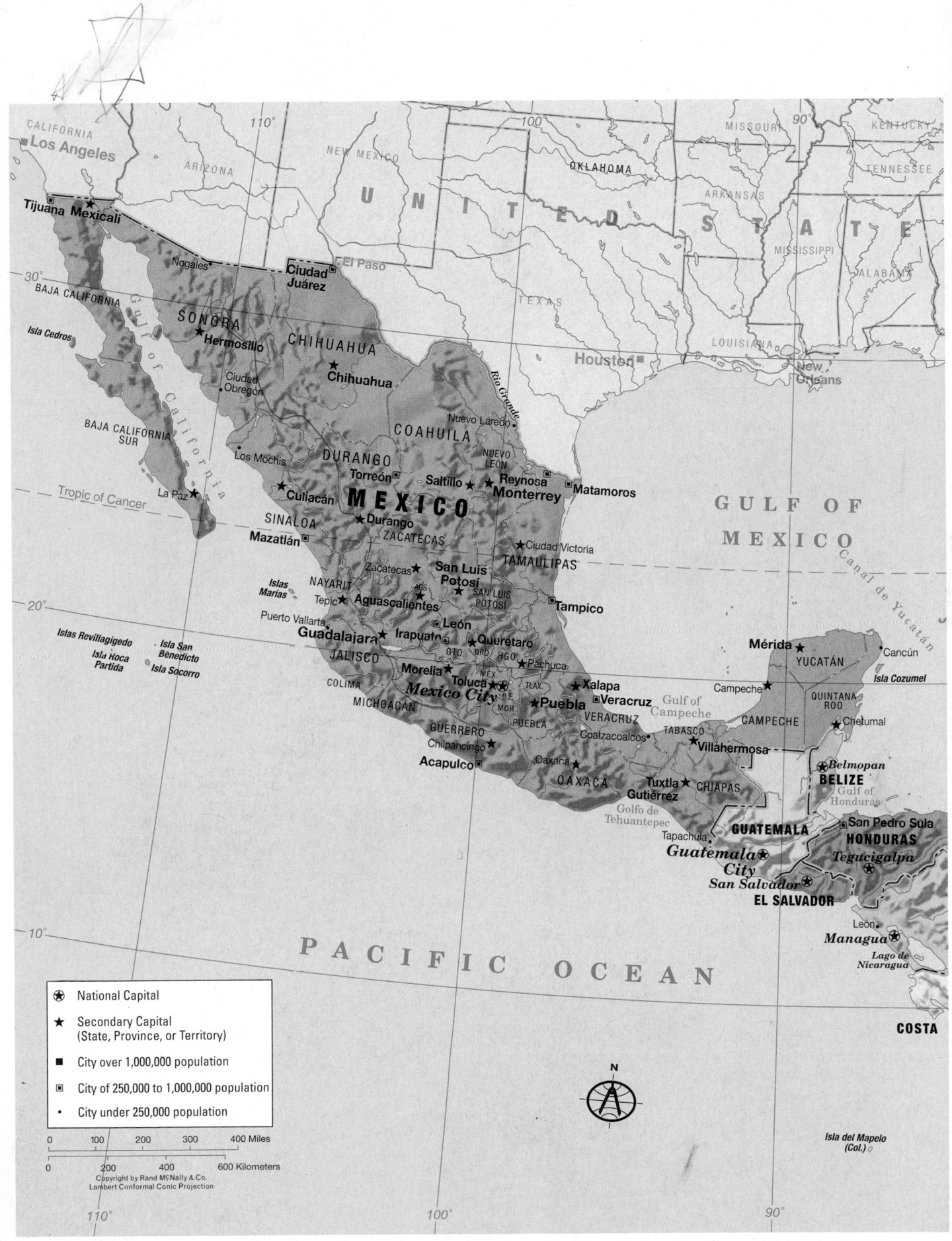

Legend

⊛ National Capital

★ Secondary Capital
(State, Province, or Territory)

■ City over 1,000,000 population

▣ City of 250,000 to 1,000,000 population

• City under 250,000 population

0   100   200   300   400 Miles

0   200   400   600 Kilometers

Copyright by Rand McNally & Co.
Lambert Conformal Conic Projection

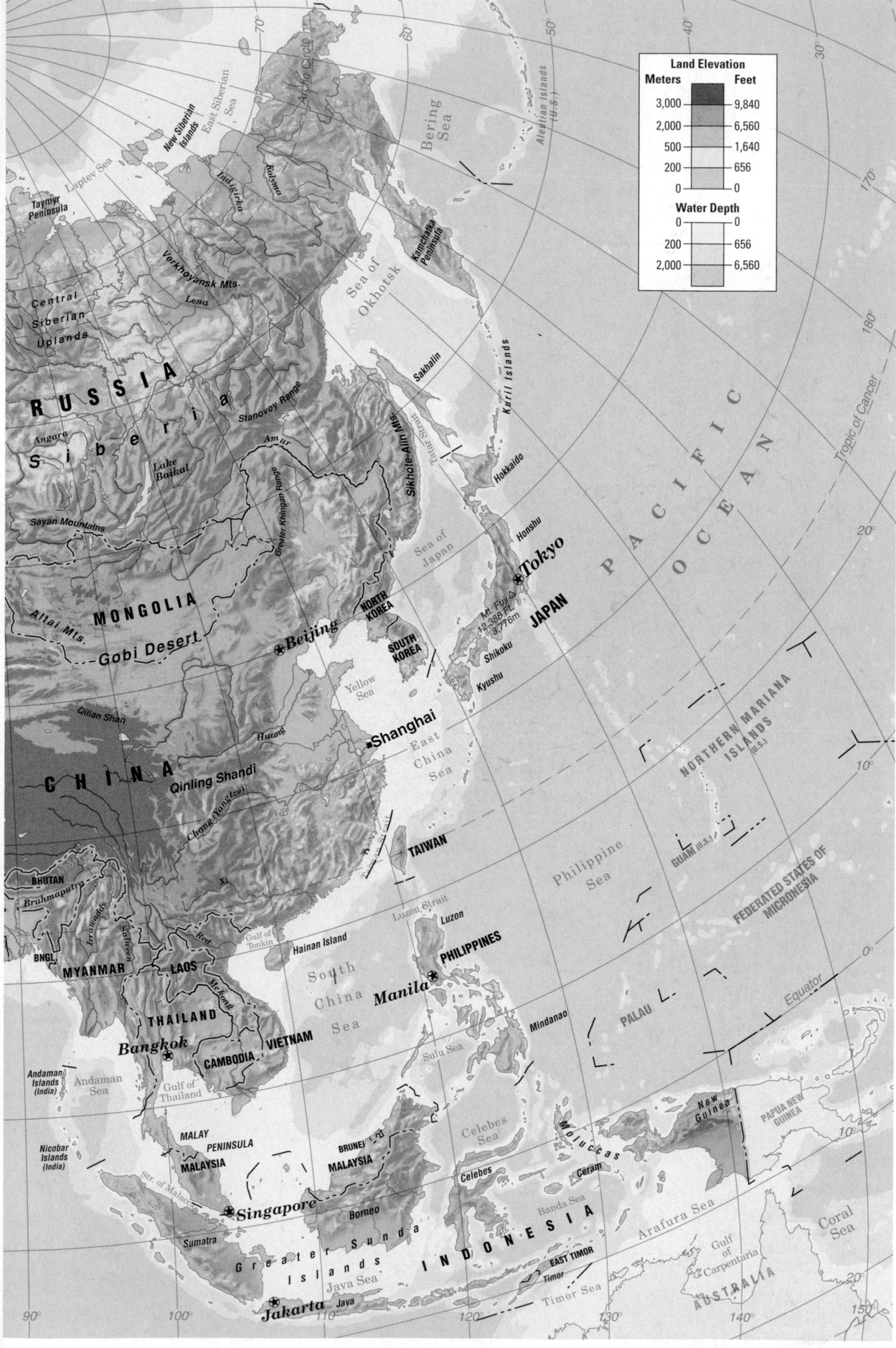

Land Elevation

Meters	Feet
3,000	9,840
2,000	6,560
500	1,640
200	656
0	0

Water Depth

0	0
200	656
2,000	6,560

Taymyr Peninsula
New Siberian Islands
East Siberian Sea
Laptev Sea
Indigirka
Kolyma
Bering Sea
Aleutian Islands (U.S.)
Arctic Circle
Central Siberian Uplands
Verkhoyansk Mts.
Lena
Kamchatka Peninsula
Sea of Okhotsk
Sakhalin
Kuril Islands
RUSSIA
Angara
Siberia
Stanovoy Range
Amur
Sikhote-Alin Mts.
Tatar Strait
Hokkaido
Sayan Mountains
Lake Baikal
Greater Khingan Range
Sea of Japan
Honshu
PACIFIC OCEAN
Tropic of Cancer
MONGOLIA
Altai Mts.
Gobi Desert
NORTH KOREA
Tokyo
JAPAN
Mt. Fuji 12,388 ft. 3,776m
Qilian Shan
Beijing
SOUTH KOREA
Shikoku
Kyushu
Yellow Sea
NORTHERN MARIANA ISLANDS (U.S.)
CHINA
Qinling Shandi
Huang
Shanghai
East China Sea
Chang (Yangtze)
TAIWAN
Xi
Philippine Sea
GUAM (U.S.)
BHUTAN
Brahmaputra
Luzon Strait
Luzon
FEDERATED STATES OF MICRONESIA
BNGL
MYANMAR
Irrawaddy
Salween
Red
Hainan Island
Gulf of Tonkin
PHILIPPINES
LAOS
South China Sea
Manila
Mekong
Equator
THAILAND
VIETNAM
Mindanao
PALAU
Bangkok
CAMBODIA
Sulu Sea
Andaman Islands (India)
Andaman Sea
Gulf of Thailand
Celebes Sea
Moluccas
New Guinea
PAPUA NEW GUINEA
MALAY PENINSULA
BRUNEI
MALAYSIA
Celebes
Ceram
Nicobar Islands (India)
MALAYSIA
Str. of Malacca
Singapore
Borneo
Banda Sea
Arafura Sea
Gulf of Carpentaria
Coral Sea
Sumatra
Greater Sunda Islands
Java Sea
INDONESIA
EAST TIMOR
Jakarta
Java
Timor
Timor Sea
AUSTRALIA

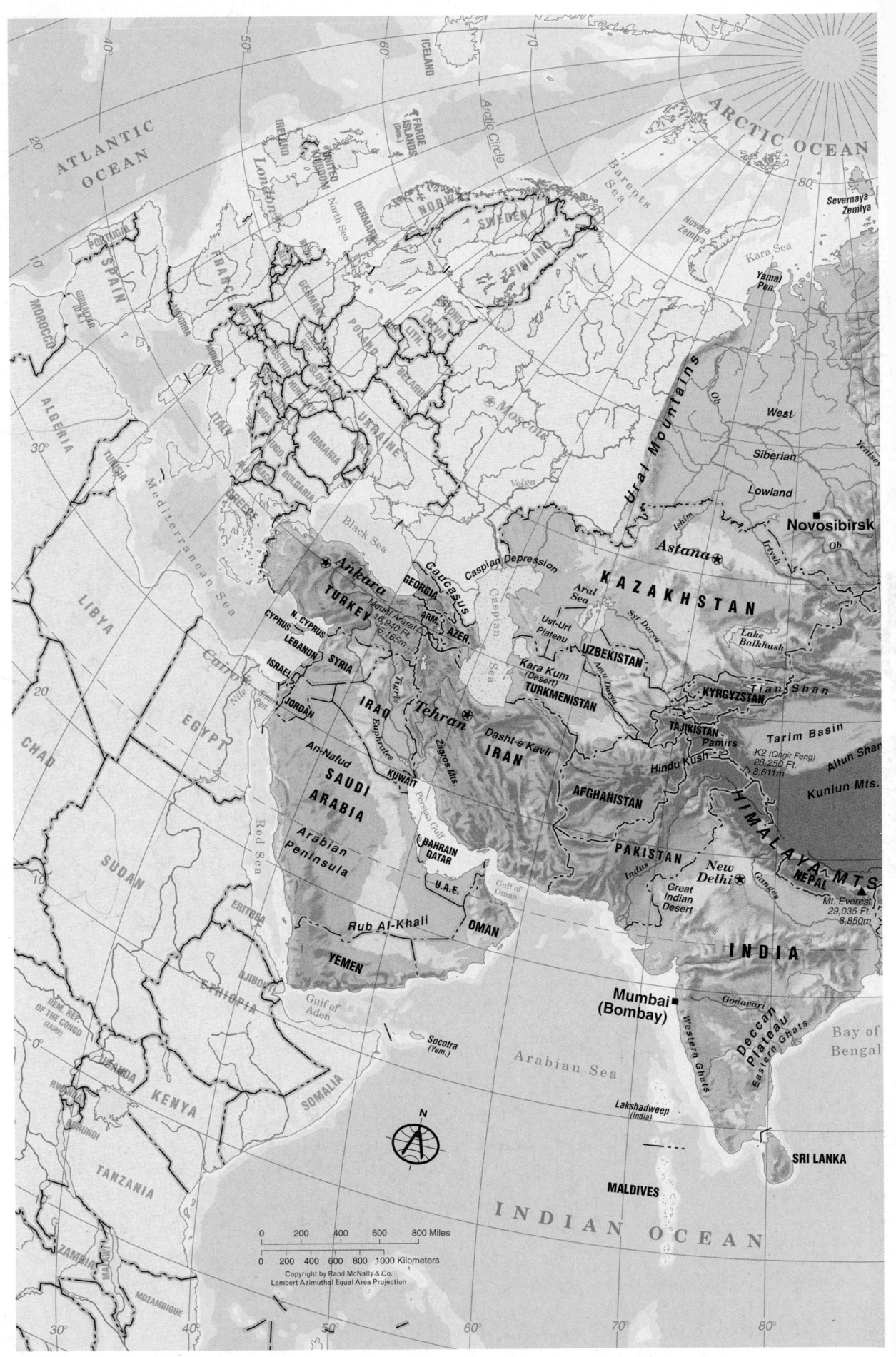

ATLANTIC OCEAN

ARCTIC OCEAN

ICELAND

FAROE ISLANDS (Den.)

IRELAND

UNITED KINGDOM

London

North Sea

NORWAY

SWEDEN

FINLAND

Barents Sea

Arctic Circle

Severnaya Zemlya

Novaya Zemlya

Kara Sea

Yamal Pen.

Ural Mountains

Ob

West Siberian Lowland

Yenisey

Novosibirsk

PORTUGAL

SPAIN

FRANCE

GERMANY

DENMARK

POLAND

BELARUS

Moscow

Volga

Astana

KAZAKHSTAN

Lake Balkhash

Irtysh

Ob

Ishim

GIBRALTAR

MOROCCO

ALGERIA

TUNISIA

ITALY

AUSTRIA

HUNGARY

SLOVAKIA

UKRAINE

ROMANIA

Mediterranean Sea

GREECE

BULGARIA

Black Sea

Ankara

TURKEY

Mount Ararat 16,940 Ft. 5,165m

GEORGIA

Caucasus

ARM.

AZER.

Caspian Depression

Aral Sea

Ust-Urt Plateau

UZBEKISTAN

Syr Darya

Tian Shan

KYRGYZSTAN

LIBYA

EGYPT

Nile

N. CYPRUS

CYPRUS

LEBANON

SYRIA

ISRAEL

Sinai Pen.

JORDAN

IRAQ

Tigris

Euphrates

Tehran

Caspian Sea

Kara Kum (Desert)

TURKMENISTAN

Amu Darya

TAJIKISTAN

Pamirs

Tarim Basin

K2 (Qogir Feng) 28,250 Ft. 8,611m

Altun Shan

CHAD

SUDAN

An-Nafud

SAUDI ARABIA

Arabian Peninsula

KUWAIT

Zagros Mts.

Dasht-e Kavir

IRAN

AFGHANISTAN

Hindu Kush

HIMALAYA MTS.

Kunlun Mts.

Red Sea

Persian Gulf

BAHRAIN

QATAR

U.A.E.

Gulf of Oman

PAKISTAN

Indus

New Delhi

Great Indian Desert

Ganges

NEPAL

Mt. Everest 29,035 Ft. 8,850m

ERITREA

DJIBOUTI

ETHIOPIA

Rub Al-Khali

OMAN

YEMEN

Gulf of Aden

Socotra (Yem.)

Arabian Sea

INDIA

Mumbai (Bombay)

Godavari

Deccan Plateau

Western Ghats

Eastern Ghats

Bay of Bengal

DEM. REP. OF THE CONGO (ZAIRE)

UGANDA

RWANDA

BURUNDI

KENYA

SOMALIA

TANZANIA

Lakshadweep (India)

N

MALDIVES

SRI LANKA

INDIAN OCEAN

ZAMBIA

MALAWI

MOZAMBIQUE

0   200   400   600   800 Miles

0   200 400 600 800 1000 Kilometers

Copyright by Rand McNally & Co.
Lambert Azimuthal Equal Area Projection

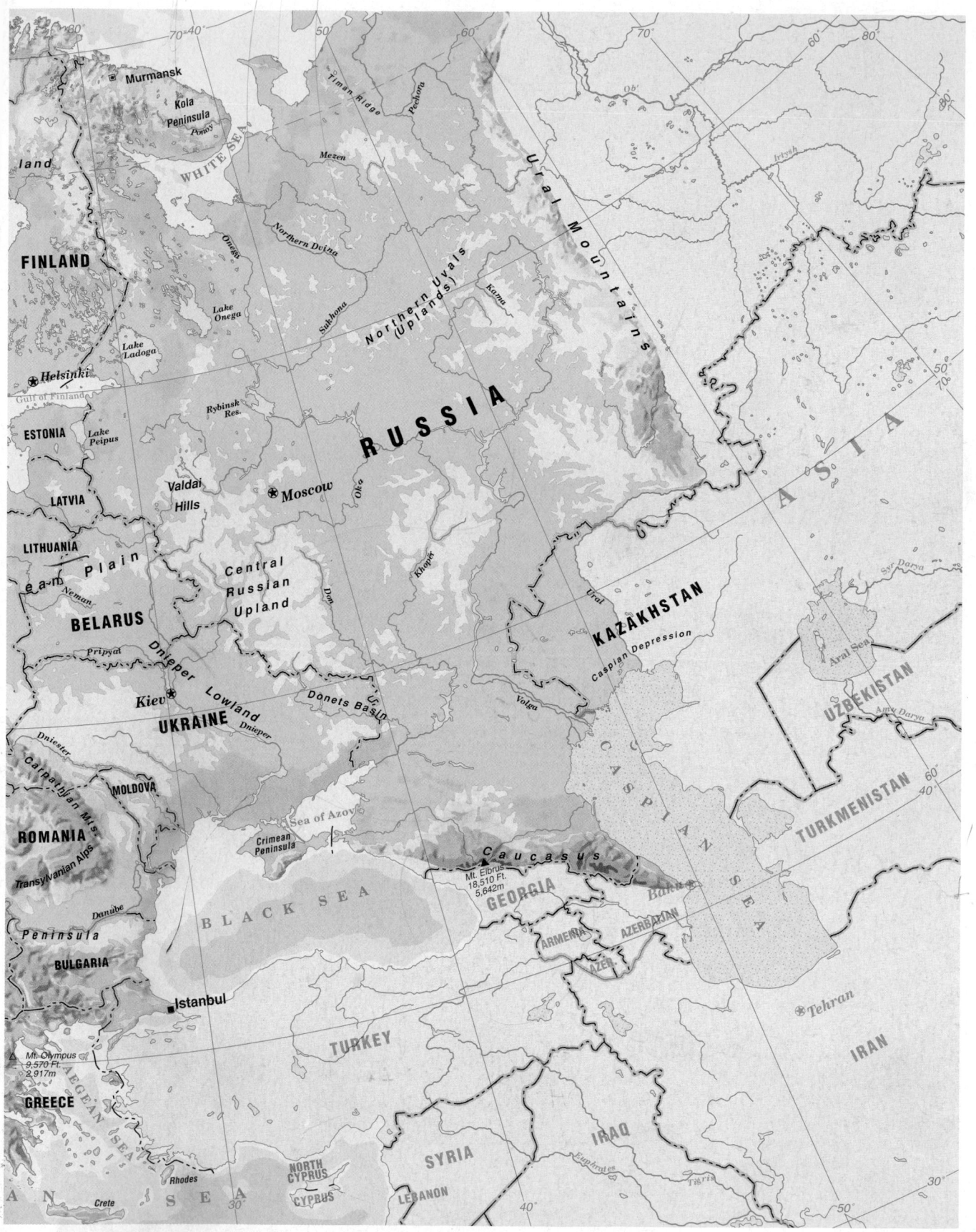

Murmansk
Kola
Peninsula
Ponoy
WHITE
SEA
land
Timan Ridge
Pechora
Mezen
Northern Dvina
Ob'
Irtysh
FINLAND
Onega
Sukhona
Kama
Northern Uvals
(Uplands)
Lake
Onega
RUSSIA
A S I A
Helsinki
Gulf of Finland
Rybinsk
Res.
Lake
Ladoga
ESTONIA
Lake
Peipus
Valdai
Hills
Moscow
Oka
LATVIA
Central
Russian
Upland
Don
LITHUANIA
Plain
Khoper
KAZAKHSTAN
Syr Darya
ea-n
Neman
Ural
Caspian Depression
BELARUS
Pripyat
Dnieper
Lowland
Volga
Aral Sea
UZBEKISTAN
Kiev
UKRAINE
Dnieper
Donets Basin
Amu Darya
Dniester
Carpathian Mts.
MOLDOVA
TURKMENISTAN
Sea of Azov
Crimean
Peninsula
ROMANIA
C a u c a s u s
Baku
Transylvanian Alps
Mt. Elbrus
18,510 Ft.
5,642m
GEORGIA
CASPIAN
SEA
Danube
B L A C K   S E A
ARMENIA
AZERBAIJAN
Peninsula
AZER.
BULGARIA
Istanbul
Tehran
IRAN
Mt. Olympus
9,570 Ft.
2,917m
TURKEY
GREECE
IRAQ
Euphrates
AEGEAN SEA
SYRIA
NORTH
CYPRUS
LEBANON
Tigris
AN
SEA
Rhodes
Crete
CYPRUS

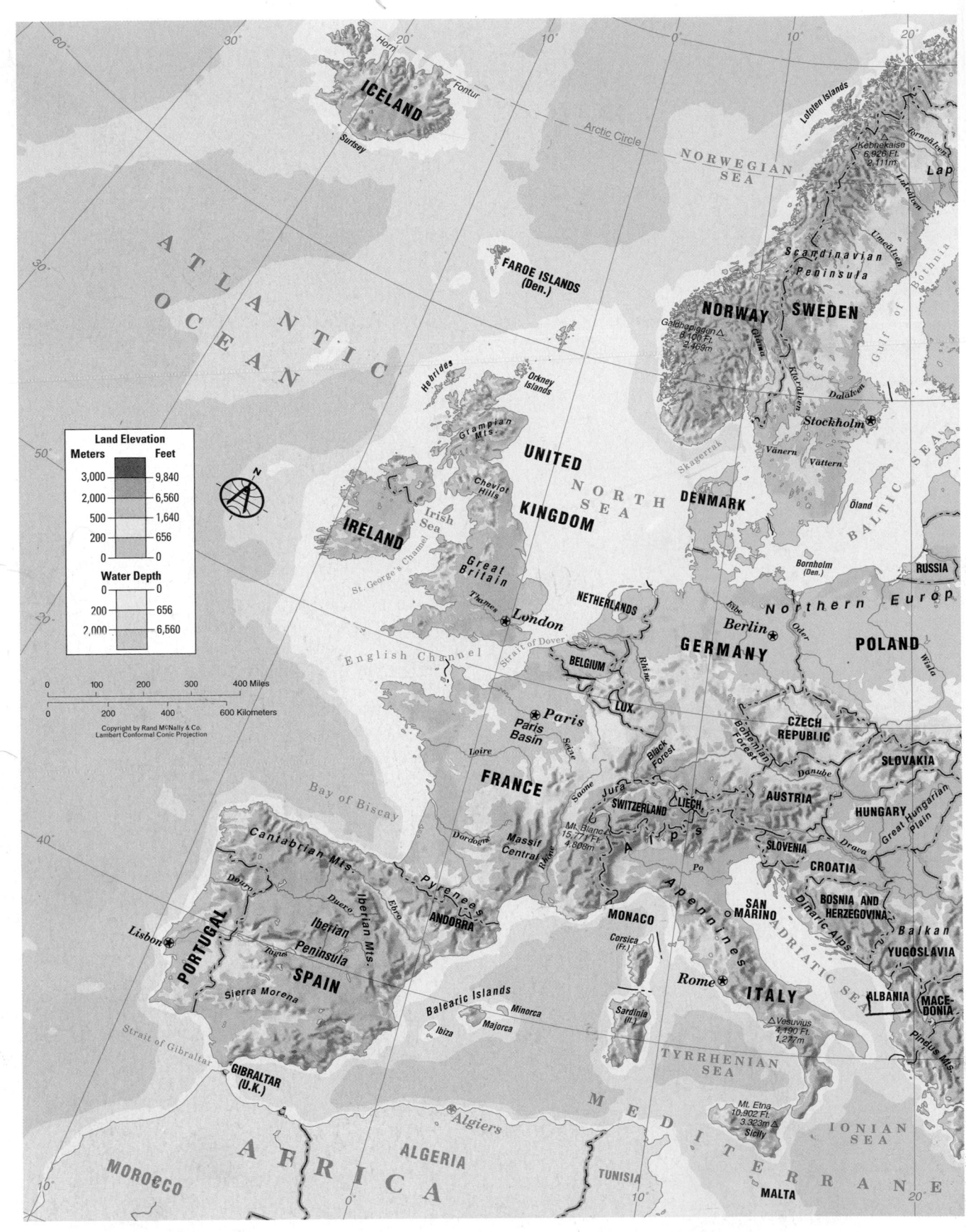

Land Elevation

Meters		Feet
3,000		9,840
2,000		6,560
500		1,640
200		656
0		0

Water Depth

0		0
200		656
2,000		6,560

0 100 200 300 400 Miles

0 200 400 600 Kilometers

Copyright by Rand McNally & Co.
Lambert Conformal Conic Projection

ICELAND
Surtsey
Horn
Fontur

ATLANTIC
OCEAN

Arctic Circle

NORWEGIAN
SEA

Lofoten Islands

Kebnekaise
6,926 Ft.
2,111m

Lap

Scandinavian
Peninsula

FAROE ISLANDS
(Den.)

NORWAY   SWEDEN

Galdhøpiggen
8,100 Ft.
2,469m

Gulf of Bothnia

Hebrides
Orkney
Islands

Grampian
Mts.

Stockholm

Vänern   Vättern

Öland

Cheviot
Hills

UNITED

NORTH
SEA

DENMARK

BALTIC SEA

IRELAND
Irish
Sea

KINGDOM

Skagerrak

Bornholm
(Den.)

RUSSIA

Great
Britain

St. George's Channel

Thames
London

NETHERLANDS

Elbe
Berlin
Oder

Northern   Europ

POLAND

English Channel

Strait of Dover

BELGIUM

Rhine

GERMANY

Wisla

Paris
Paris
Basin

LUX.

Seine

CZECH
REPUBLIC

SLOVAKIA

Loire

Black
Forest

Danube

FRANCE

Saone

Jura

SWITZERLAND

LIECH.

AUSTRIA

HUNGARY

Bohemian
Forest

Great Hungarian
Plain

Bay of Biscay

Dordogne

Massif
Central

Mt. Blanc
15,771 Ft.
4,808m

Rhone

A l p s

Po

Drava

SLOVENIA

CROATIA

Cantabrian Mts.

Douro

Pyrenees

Apennines

SAN
MARINO

Dinaric Alps

BOSNIA AND
HERZEGOVINA

Balkan

Duero
Iberian Mts.
Ebro

ANDORRA

MONACO

YUGOSLAVIA

Lisbon

Ibiza

Iberian
Peninsula

Tagus

SPAIN

Corsica
(Fr.)

Rome

ITALY

ADRIATIC SEA

ALBANIA

MACE-
DONIA

Pindus Mts.

PORTUGAL

Sierra Morena

Balearic Islands

Minorca

Majorca

Sardinia
(It.)

Vesuvius
4,190 Ft.
1,277m

Strait of Gibraltar

GIBRALTAR
(U.K.)

Algiers

TYRRHENIAN
SEA

IONIAN
SEA

AFRICA

ALGERIA

Mt. Etna
10,902 Ft.
3,323m
Sicily

MOROCCO

TUNISIA

MEDITERRANE

MALTA

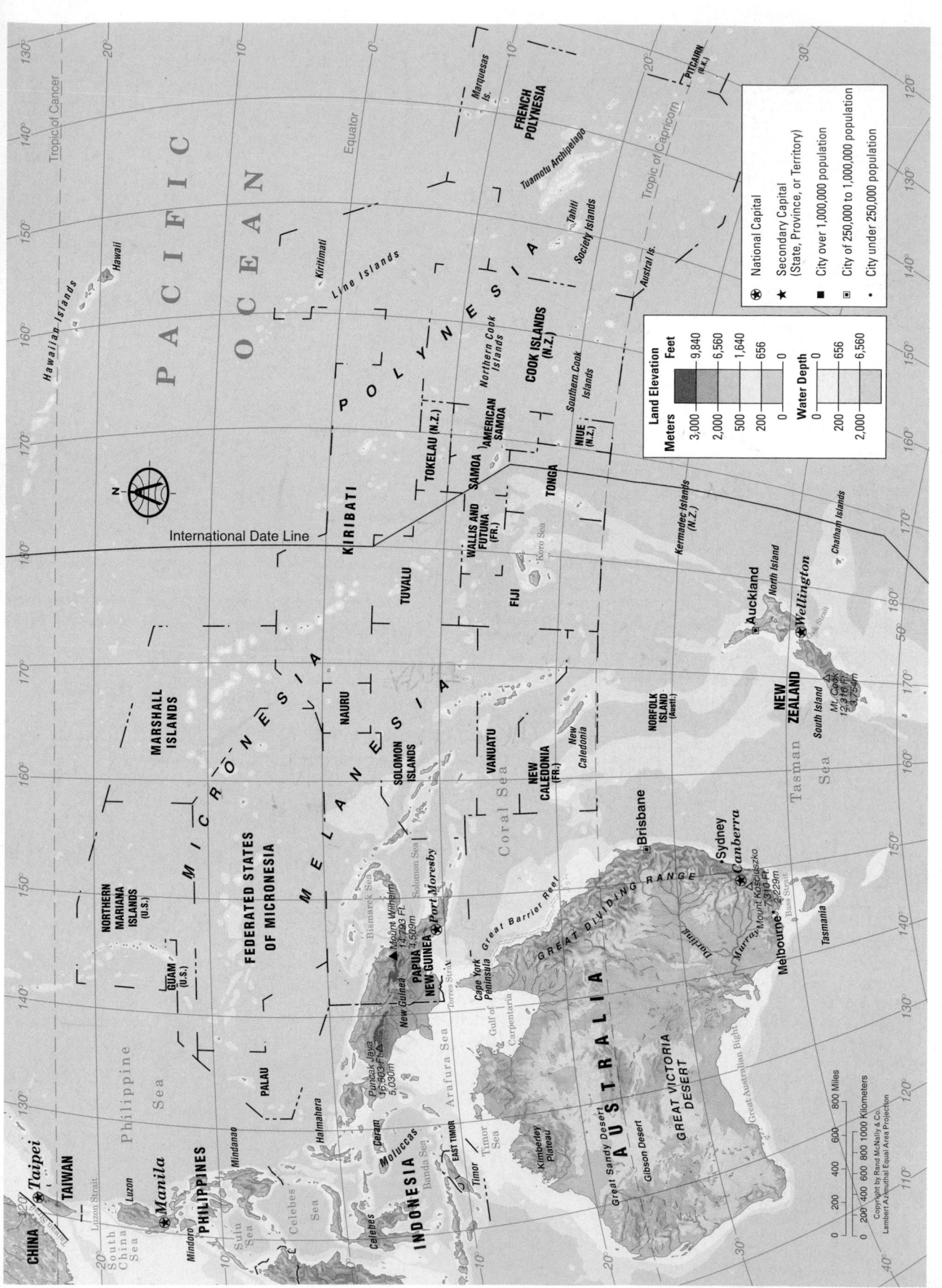

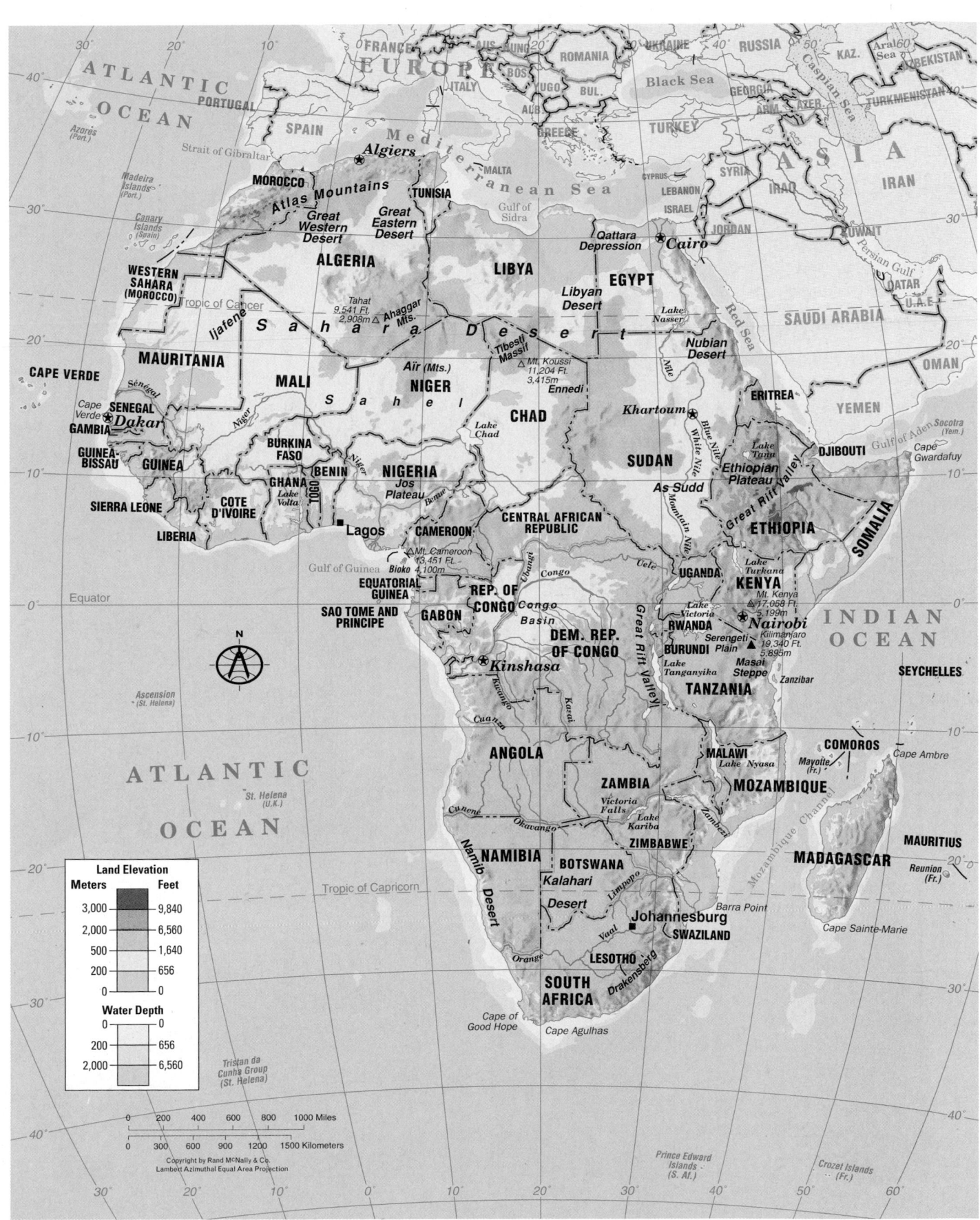

ATLANTIC OCEAN

PORTUGAL

Azores
(Port.)

Strait of Gibraltar

Madeira
Islands
(Port.)

Canary
Islands
(Spain)

CAPE VERDE

Cape
Verde

EUROPE

FRANCE
AUS. HUNG.
ROMANIA
ITALY
BOS.
YUGO.
BUL.
ALB.
GREECE
SPAIN

Mediterranean Sea

MALTA

Algiers

MOROCCO
Atlas Mountains
Great
Western
Desert
TUNISIA
Great
Eastern
Desert
Gulf of
Sidra

CYPRUS
LEBANON
ISRAEL
JORDAN

TURKEY

SYRIA
IRAQ

Black Sea

GEORGIA
ARM. AZER.

UKRAINE

RUSSIA

KAZ.

Aral 60°
Sea

UZBEKISTAN

TURKMENISTAN

Caspian Sea

ASIA

IRAN

KUWAIT

Persian Gulf

SAUDI ARABIA

QATAR

U.A.E.

OMAN

WESTERN
SAHARA
(MOROCCO)

Tropic of Cancer

Ijafene

ALGERIA

Sahara

Tahat
9,541 Ft.
2,908m
Ahaggar
Mts.

LIBYA

Libyan
Desert

EGYPT

Qattara
Depression

Cairo

Lake
Nasser

Red Sea

Desert

MAURITANIA

MALI

Sahel

Aïr (Mts.)

NIGER

Tibesti
Massif

Mt. Koussi
11,204 Ft.
3,415m

Ennedi

Nubian
Desert

ERITREA

YEMEN

Gulf of Aden

Socotra
(Yem.)

Cape
Gwardafuy

Senegal

SENEGAL

Dakar

GAMBIA

GUINEA-
BISSAU

GUINEA

Niger

BURKINA
FASO

Niger

BENIN

NIGERIA

Jos
Plateau

Benue

Lake
Chad

CHAD

SUDAN

As Sudd

Khartoum

White Nile

Blue Nile

Lake
Tana

Ethiopian
Plateau

Great Rift Valley

DJIBOUTI

SIERRA LEONE

LIBERIA

COTE
D'IVOIRE

GHANA

TOGO

Lake
Volta

Lagos

CAMEROON

Mt. Cameroon
13,451 Ft.
Bioko 4,100m

CENTRAL AFRICAN
REPUBLIC

Ubangi

Uele

Mountain Nile

ETHIOPIA

Lake
Turkana

KENYA

Mt. Kenya
17,058 Ft.
5,199m

SOMALIA

Gulf of Guinea

EQUATORIAL
GUINEA

SAO TOME AND
PRINCIPE

GABON

REP. OF
CONGO

Congo

Congo
Basin

DEM. REP.
OF CONGO

Congo

UGANDA

RWANDA

BURUNDI

Lake
Victoria

Great Rift Valley

Nairobi

Kilimanjaro
19,340 Ft.
5,895m

Serengeti
Plain

Masai
Steppe

Equator

N

INDIAN
OCEAN

Kinshasa

Kwango

Kasai

TANZANIA

Lake
Tanganyika

Zanzibar

SEYCHELLES

Ascension
(St. Helena)

Cuanza

ATLANTIC

St. Helena
(U.K.)

OCEAN

Cunene

ANGOLA

Okavango

ZAMBIA

Victoria
Falls

Lake
Kariba

MALAWI

Lake Nyasa

MOZAMBIQUE

Zambezi

COMOROS

Mayotte
(Fr.)

Cape Ambre

Mozambique Channel

MAURITIUS

Reunion
(Fr.)

MADAGASCAR

Namib
Desert

NAMIBIA

Tropic of Capricorn

Kalahari
Desert

BOTSWANA

ZIMBABWE

Limpopo

Barra Point

Cape Sainte-Marie

Orange

Vaal

Johannesburg

SWAZILAND

LESOTHO

Drakensberg

SOUTH
AFRICA

Cape of
Good Hope

Cape Agulhas

Land Elevation

Meters	Feet
3,000	9,840
2,000	6,560
500	1,640
200	656
0	0

Water Depth

0	0
200	656
2,000	6,560

Tristan da
Cunha Group
(St. Helena)

0   200   400   600   800   1000 Miles

0   300   600   900   1200   1500 Kilometers

Copyright by Rand McNally & Co.
Lambert Azimuthal Equal Area Projection

Prince Edward
Islands
(S. Af.)

Crozet Islands
(Fr.)

GULF OF MEXICO

90°   80°   CUBA   70°   60°   50°   40°

20°   20°
NORTH AMERICA   DOMINICAN REPUBLIC   ATLANTIC
MEXICO   BELIZE   HAITI   PUERTO RICO (U.S.)   OCEAN
GUATEMALA HONDURAS   Greater Antilles   JAMAICA
EL SALVADOR   NICARAGUA   CARIBBEAN SEA   Lesser Antilles

COSTA RICA   Cristóbal Colón Peak   Caracas   TRINIDAD AND TOBAGO
PANAMA   Gulf of Panama   18,948 Ft. 5,775m   VENEZUELA
10°   Magdalena   Llanos   Orinoco   GUYANA   10°
        Bogotá   SURINAME   FRENCH GUIANA   Cape Orange
        COLOMBIA

Galapagos Islands (Ec.)   Chimborazo   Putumayo   Japurá   Negro   Ilha de Marajó
ECUADOR   20,703 Ft.   Amazon   Belém   Equator
0°   6,310m   Amazon   Basin   Manaus   Amazon   Tocantins   0°
                Juruá   Madeira   Tapajós
        Selvas   B R A Z I L
        Mt. Huascarán   Ucayali
        22,133 Ft.   Recife
        6,746m   PERU   Mato Grosso
10°   Lima   Mt. Illampu   Plateau   10°
        Lake Titicaca   21,066 Ft.   Brasília   São Francisco
                6,421m   BOLIVIA
                Cordillera Oriental   Serra do Espinhaço
                Mt. Sajama
Tropic of Capricorn   21,463 Ft.   Paraná   Tropic of Capricorn
        Isla San Ambrosio   6,542m   Gran Chaco
        (Chile)   Atacama Desert   PARAGUAY
20°   Isla San Félix   PARAGUAY   São Paulo   Rio de   20°
        (Chile)   Paraná   Janeiro
PACIFIC   Mt. Ojos del Salado
OCEAN   22,615 Ft.   URUGUAY
        Archipiélago   6,893m
        Juan Fernández   Mt. Aconcagua
30°   (Chile)   22,831 Ft.   30°
        Santiago   6,959m   Buenos Aires
                Pampas   Río de la Plata   N

Land Elevation   San Matías Gulf
Meters   Feet   Península Valdés
3,000   9,840   Chiloé   ATLANTIC
2,000   6,560   San Jorge Gulf   OCEAN
500   1,640   Patagonia   Point Medanoso   40°
200   656
0   0   Grand   FALKLAND ISLANDS
Water Depth   Bay   West   (U.K.)
0   0   Falkland   East
                Strait of Magellan   Falkland
200   656   Tierra del
2,000   6,560   Fuego   Cape Horn   South Georgia (U.K.)   50°

0   200   400   600   800   1000 Miles
0   300   600   900   1200   1500 Kilometers   Drake Passage   South Sandwich Islands (U.K.)
Copyright by Rand McNally & Co.   South Shetland   South Orkney
Lambert Azimuthal Equal Area Projection   Islands (U.K.)   Islands (U.K.)

110°   100°   90°   80°   70°   60°   50°   40°   30°   20°   10°

CHILE   ARGENTINA   Andes

RAND MCNALLY

A9

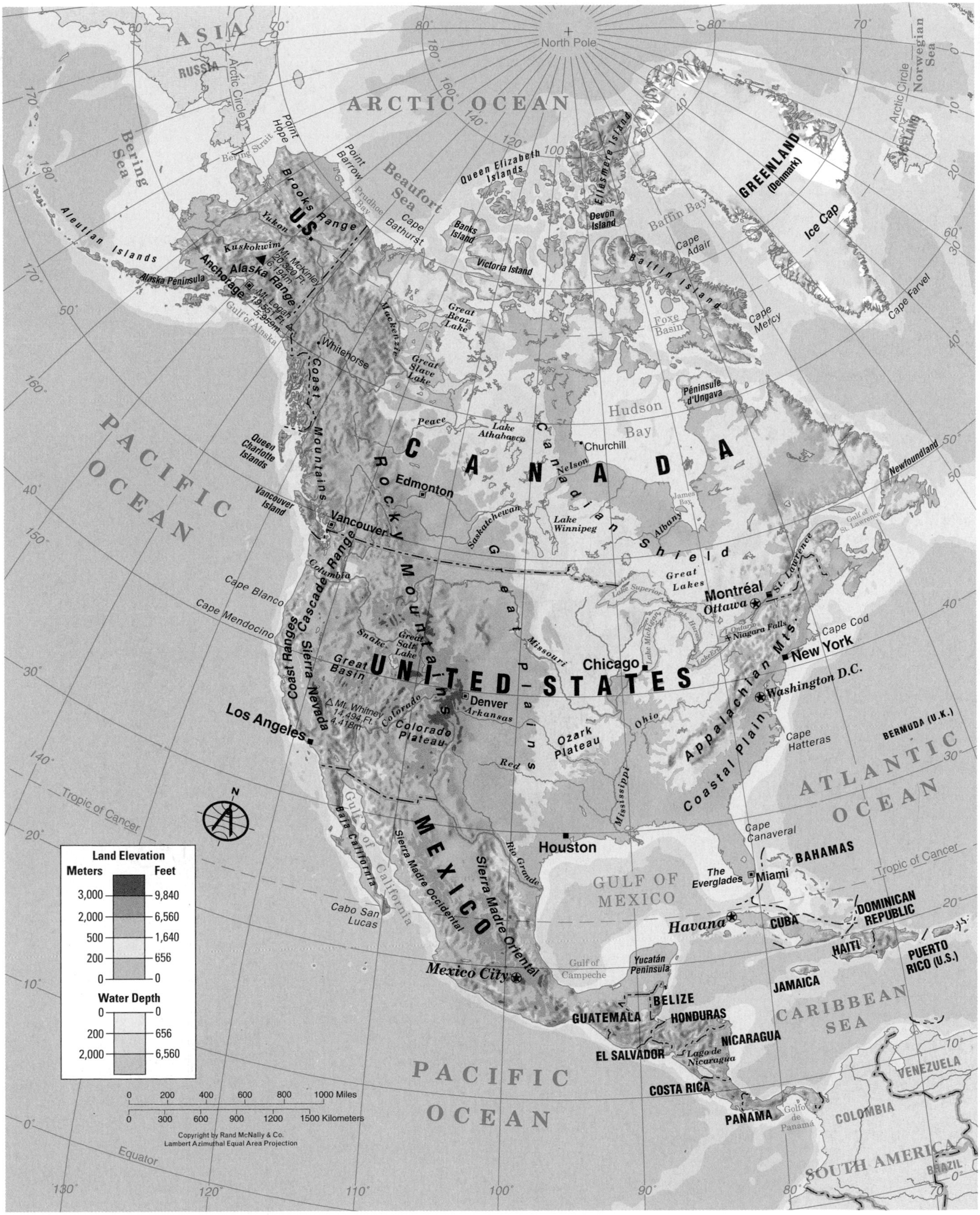

ASIA
RUSSIA
Arctic Circle
Bering Strait
Bering Sea
Aleutian Islands
Alaska Peninsula
Point Hope
Point Barrow
Prudhoe Bay
Brooks Range
Yukon
Kuskokwim
Anchorage
Alaska Range
Mt. McKinley 20,320 Ft. 6,194m
Mt. Logan 19,551 Ft. 5,959m
Gulf of Alaska
Whitehorse
Mackenzie
Peace

ARCTIC OCEAN
North Pole
Beaufort Sea
Cape Bathurst
Banks Island
Victoria Island
Queen Elizabeth Islands
Ellesmere Island
Devon Island
Baffin Bay
Cape Adair
Baffin Island
Cape Mercy
Foxe Basin
GREENLAND (Denmark)
Ice Cap
ICELAND
Arctic Circle
Norwegian Sea
Cape Farvel

CANADA
Great Bear Lake
Great Slave Lake
Lake Athabasca
Churchill
Nelson
Hudson Bay
Péninsule d'Ungava
Canadian Shield
James Bay
Newfoundland
Gulf of St. Lawrence

PACIFIC OCEAN
Queen Charlotte Islands
Vancouver Island
Vancouver
Coast Mountains
Columbia
Cascade Range
Coast Ranges
Sierra Nevada
Cape Blanco
Cape Mendocino
Edmonton
Saskatchewan
Rocky Mountains
Lake Winnipeg
Lake Superior
Great Lakes
Lake Michigan
Lake Huron
Lake Erie
Lake Ontario
Montréal
Ottawa
St. Lawrence
Niagara Falls
Cape Cod
New York
Washington D.C.

UNITED STATES
Snake
Great Salt Lake
Great Basin
Mt. Whitney 14,494 Ft. 4,418m
Colorado
Denver
Arkansas
Colorado Plateau
Los Angeles
Missouri
Chicago
Ohio
Ozark Plateau
Mississippi
Red
Great Plains
Appalachian Mts.
Coastal Plain
Cape Hatteras
BERMUDA (U.K.)

ATLANTIC OCEAN

Gulf of California
Baja California
Cabo San Lucas
Sierra Madre Occidental
Sierra Madre Oriental
MEXICO
Rio Grande
Houston
Cape Canaveral
The Everglades
Miami
GULF OF MEXICO
Havana
CUBA
BAHAMAS
Tropic of Cancer
DOMINICAN REPUBLIC
HAITI
PUERTO RICO (U.S.)
Mexico City
Gulf of Campeche
Yucatán Peninsula
JAMAICA
CARIBBEAN SEA
BELIZE
GUATEMALA
HONDURAS
EL SALVADOR
NICARAGUA
Lago de Nicaragua
COSTA RICA
PANAMA
Golfo de Panamá
VENEZUELA
COLOMBIA
SOUTH AMERICA
BRAZIL

PACIFIC OCEAN
Tropic of Cancer
Equator

Land Elevation

Meters	Feet
3,000	9,840
2,000	6,560
500	1,640
200	656
0	0

Water Depth

0	0
200	656
2,000	6,560

0 200 400 600 800 1000 Miles
0 300 600 900 1200 1500 Kilometers

Copyright by Rand McNally & Co.
Lambert Azimuthal Equal Area Projection

RAND McNALLY

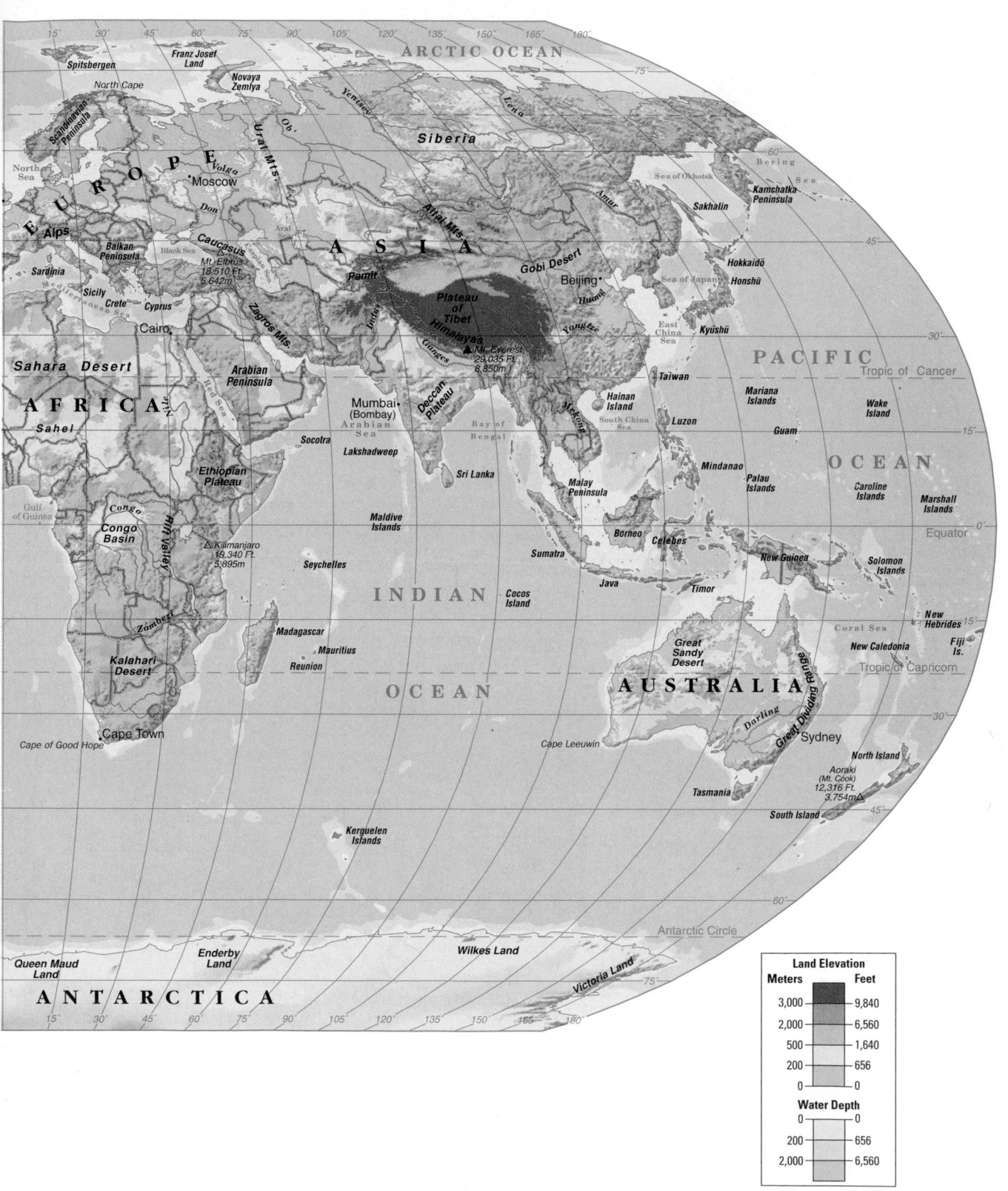

ARCTIC OCEAN

Spitsbergen
Franz Josef Land
Novaya Zemlya
North Cape
Scandinavian Peninsula
EUROPE
North Sea
Ob'
Yenisey
Lena
Siberia
Bering Sea
Sea of Okhotsk
Moscow
Volga
Ural Mts.
Kamchatka Peninsula
Sakhalin
Don
Aral
Altai Mts.
Amur
Alps
Caucasus
Mt. Elbrus 18,510 Ft. 5,642m
ASIA
Gobi Desert
Hokkaidō
Honshū
Sea of Japan
Balkan Peninsula
Black Sea
Pamir
Beijing
Huang
Sardinia
Sicily
Crete
Cyprus
Mediterranean Sea
Zagros Mts.
Indus
Plateau of Tibet
Yangtze
Kyūshū
East China Sea
Cairo
Himalayas
Ganges
Mt. Everest 29,035 Ft. 6,850m
Mekong
Taiwan
PACIFIC
Sahara Desert
AFRICA
Red Sea
Arabian Peninsula
Deccan Plateau
Hainan Island
Mariana Islands
Wake Island
Tropic of Cancer
Sahel
Nile
Mumbai (Bombay)
Arabian Sea
Bay of Bengal
South China Sea
Luzon
Guam
OCEAN
Socotra
Lakshadweep
Mindanao
Palau Islands
Caroline Islands
Marshall Islands
Ethiopian Plateau
Sri Lanka
Malay Peninsula
Gulf of Guinea
Congo
Congo Basin
Maldive Islands
Borneo
Celebes
New Guinea
Solomon Islands
Rift Valley
Kilimanjaro 19,340 Ft. 5,895m
Seychelles
Sumatra
Java
Timor
INDIAN
Cocos Island
Equator
Zambezi
Madagascar
Mauritius
Reunion
Coral Sea
New Hebrides
New Caledonia
Fiji Is.
Kalahari Desert
Great Sandy Desert
Tropic of Capricorn
OCEAN
AUSTRALIA
Cape Town
Cape of Good Hope
Cape Leeuwin
Darling
Great Dividing Range
Sydney
North Island
Aoraki (Mt. Cook) 12,316 Ft. 3,754m
Tasmania
South Island
Kerguelen Islands
Queen Maud Land
Enderby Land
Wilkes Land
Victoria Land
ANTARCTICA
Antarctic Circle

Land Elevation

Meters		Feet
3,000		9,840
2,000		6,560
500		1,640
200		656
0		0

Water Depth

0		0
200		656
2,000		6,560

RAND McNALLY

ARCTIC OCEAN

Baffin
Island

Baffin
Bay

Greenland

Jan Mayen

Arctic Circle

Iceland

Faroe Is.

Mt. McKinley △
20,320 Ft.
6,194m

Yukon

Mackenzie

Canadian Shield

Hudson
Bay

British
Isles

London

Aleutian Islands

NORTH

Vancouver

Rocky Mountains

Great Plains

Newfoundland

AMERICA

St. Lawrence

Los Angeles

Colorado

Appalachian Mts.

Washington D.C.

Mississippi

Cape Hatteras

Azores

Iberian
Peninsula

Midway Is.

ATLANTIC

Canary
Islands

Atlas
Mts.

Tropic of Cancer

Baja
California

Gulf of Mexico

Hawaiian
Islands

Yucatan
Peninsula

Cuba

Hispaniola

Cape
Verde
Islands

Jamaica

Puerto Rico

Caribbean
Sea

Cape Verde

Niger

PACIFIC

Trinidad

OCEAN

Orinoco

Palmyra

Galapagos Islands

Equator

Amazon

Amazon

Kiribati

SOUTH

Basin

Marquesas Is.

Andes

AMERICA

Samoa
Islands

Mato Grosso
Plateau

St. Helena

OCEAN

Cook
Islands

Tahiti

Tonga
Is.

Rio de Janeiro

Tropic of Capricorn

Easter Island

Andes

Paraná

N

△ Mt. Aconcagua
22,831 Ft.
6,959m

Archipiélago
Juan Fernández

Buenos Aires

Patagonia

Falkland Is.

South
Georgia

0   1000   2000 Miles

Chatham Is.

0   1000   2000   3000 Kilometers

Tierra del Fuego

South
Sandwich Is.

Copyright by Rand McNally & Co.
Robinson Projection

Cape Horn

South
Orkney Is.

Antarctic Circle

South
Shetland Is.

Antarctic
Peninsula

Weddell
Sea

Ross
Sea

Marie
Byrd
Land

△ Vinson Massif
16,066 Ft.
4,897m

RAND MCNALLY

ARCTIC OCEAN

Spitsbergen (Nor.)
Franz Josef Land
Novaya Zemlya

NORWAY
FINLAND
SWEDEN
North Sea
DEN.
EST.
LAT.
LITH.
Volga
Moscow
RUSSIA
Novosibirsk
Ob'
Yenisey
Lena
Bering Sea
Sea of Okhotsk

NETH.
BEL.
GERMANY
POLAND
BELARUS
UKRAINE
CZ.
SWITZ.
AUS.
HUNG.
SLVK.
MOLD.
ROM.
BUL.
KAZAKHSTAN
MONGOLIA
NORTH KOREA
SOUTH KOREA
JAPAN
Tokyo
ITALY
SLO.
CRO.
BOS.
YUGO.
GREECE
ALB.
MA.
Black Sea
GEO.
ARM.
AZER.
UZBEKISTAN
KYAG.
TAJIK.
Beijing
CHINA
Sea of Japan
Rome
Crete
TURKEY
CYPRUS
LEB.
ISRAEL
SYRIA
IRAQ
JORDAN
IRAN
AFGHANISTAN
TURKMENISTAN
KUWAIT
Chang Jiang
Yangtze
Shanghai
PACIFIC
TAIWAN
Tropic of Cancer
Mediterranean Sea
TUNISIA
ALGERIA
LIBYA
EGYPT
Cairo
SAUDI ARABIA
QATAR
U.A.E.
OMAN
NEPAL
Ganges
BHU.
BNGL.
PAKISTAN
Guangzhou
NORTHERN MARIANA ISLANDS (U.S.)
WAKE ISLAND (U.S.)
Red Sea
Nile
YEMEN
Kolkata (Calcutta)
MYANMAR
LAOS
GUAM (U.S.)
NIGER
CHAD
SUDAN
ERITREA
DJIBOUTI
Mumbai (Bombay)
Arabian Sea
INDIA
THAILAND
Bay of Bengal
South China Sea
VIETNAM
PHILIPPINES
OCEAN
BENIN
NIGERIA
Lagos
CENTRAL AFRICAN REPUBLIC
Addis Ababa
ETHIOPIA
SOMALIA
Bangkok
CAMBODIA
PALAU
FED. STATES OF MICRONESIA
MARSHALL ISLANDS
CAMEROON
EQUATORIAL GUINEA
GABON
Congo
UGANDA
RWANDA
KENYA
SRI LANKA
MALDIVES
BRUNEI
MALAYSIA
SINGAPORE
Borneo
REP. OF CONGO
DEM. REP. OF CONGO
BURUNDI
TANZANIA
SEYCHELLES
Sumatra
Jakarta
INDONESIA
Java
New Guinea
PAPUA NEW GUINEA
EAST TIMOR
SOLOMON ISLANDS
Equator
ANGOLA
ZAMBIA
COMOROS
INDIAN
Darwin
Coral Sea
VANUATU
NEW CALEDONIA (Fr.)
FIJI
NAMIBIA
ZIMBABWE
MALAWI
MOZAMBIQUE
MADAGASCAR
MAURITIUS
REUNION (Fr.)
OCEAN
AUSTRALIA
Tropic of Capricorn
BOTSWANA
Perth
Darling
Sydney
SWAZILAND
SOUTH AFRICA
LESOTHO
Cape Town
Kerguelen Islands (Fr.)
Melbourne
NEW ZEALAND
Wellington
Tasmania

Antarctic Circle

ANTARCTICA

* National Capital
• Major Cities

ARCTIC OCEAN

Baffin
Bay

GREENLAND
(Den.)

Arctic Circle

ICELAND

FAROE IS.
(Den.)

RUSSIA   ALASKA
Yukon (U.S)
Anchorage

UNITED
KINGDOM

IRELAND
London

Hudson
Bay

CANADA

Aleutian Islands

Newfoundland

FRANCE

Vancouver

Missouri

Montréal
Ottawa

Chicago

New York
Washington D.C.

Azores
(Port.)

Madrid

PORTUGAL   SPAIN

UNITED STATES

Colorado

Los Angeles

Mississippi

ATLANTIC

Casablanca

MOROCCO

Houston

MIDWAY IS.
(U.S.)

Tropic of Cancer

MEXICO

Gulf of Mexico

BAHAMAS

Canary
Islands
(Sp.)

W. SAHARA

Hawaiian
Islands
(U.S)

Mexico City

CUBA

DOM. REP.

PUERTO RICO (U.S.)

CAPE
VERDE

MAURITANIA

MALI

HAITI
JAMAICA

Caribbean
Sea

SENEGAL

Niger

BELIZE
GUAT. HOND.
EL. SAL. NIC.

GAMBIA
GUINEA-BISSAU

BURK.
FASO

PACIFIC

GUINEA

Caracas

TRINIDAD AND TOBAGO

SIERRA LEONE

COTE
D'IVOIRE

GHANA

COSTA
RICA

VENEZUELA   GUYANA

LIBERIA

PANAMA

SURINAME
FRENCH GUIANA

COLOMBIA

Galapagos Islands
(Ecuador)

ECUADOR

Amazon

0°   Equator

KIRIBATI

PERU

BRAZIL

OCEAN

OCEAN

Lima

SAMOA

AMERICAN
SAMOA

15°

COOK
ISLANDS (N.Z.)

TONGA

BOLIVIA

ST. HELENA
(U.K.)

FRENCH POLYNESIA

Tropic of Capricorn

PARAGUAY

Rio de Janeiro

Easter Island
(Chile)

ARGENTINA

30°

URUGUAY

Santiago

Buenos
Aires

N

CHILE

45°

0   1000   2000 Miles

0   1000   2000   3000 Kilometers

Copyright by Rand McNally & Co.
Robinson Projection

FALKLAND IS.
(U.K.)

South
Georgia
(U.K.)

South
Orkney Is.
(U.K.)

60°

Antarctic Circle

South
Shetland Is.
(U.K.)

W e d d e l l
S e a

75°

RAND McNALLY

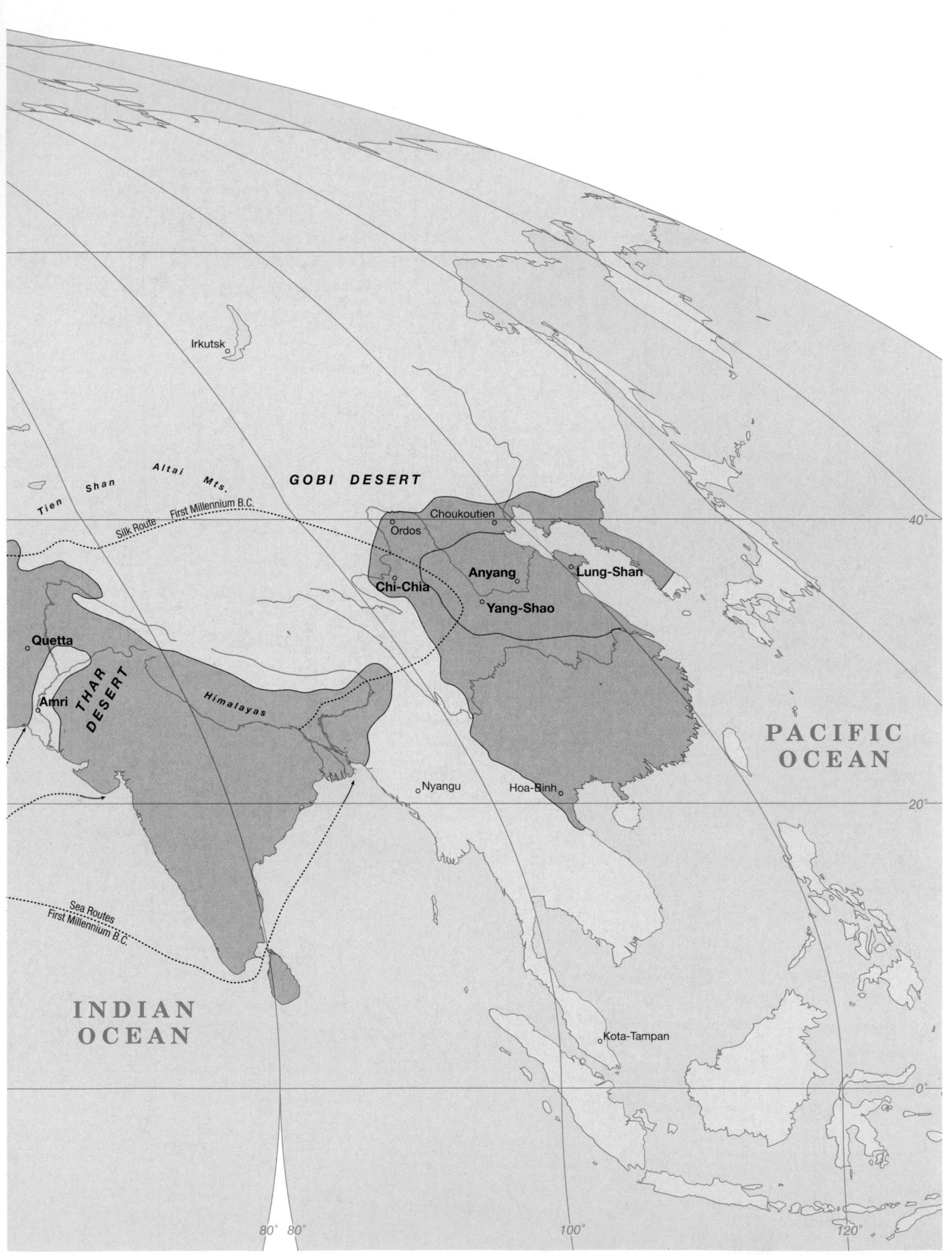

Irkutsk

Tien Shan *Altai Mts.* **GOBI DESERT**

Silk Route
First Millennium B.C.

Ordos
Choukoutien

Chi-Chia **Anyang** **Lung-Shan**

Yang-Shao

40°

Quetta

THAR DESERT *Himalayas*

Amri

PACIFIC OCEAN

Nyangu Hoa-Binh

20°

Sea Routes
First Millennium B.C.

INDIAN OCEAN

Kota-Tampan

0°

80° 80° 100° 120°

RAND McNALLY

A3

ARCTIC OCEAN

ATLANTIC
OCEAN

60°

Gagarino
Kiev

St. Acheul
Chelles   Hallstadt
Solutré   La Tène
Le Moustier
Villanova
Aurignac
Altamira   Pyrenees

Alps

Black Sea   Caucasus   Caspian Sea

40°

Troy   Anau

Mersin   Tell Halaf
Cnossus   Judeidah   Hassuna   Jarmo   Hissar
MEDITERRANEAN   Sialk
Gafsa   Mt. Carmel   Susa
SEA   Al-Ubaid
Atlas   Mountains   Jericho   Eridu
                                                          Bakun
Merimde
                                                          Kulli
SAHARA   Badari
DESERT   Naqada
Kharga Oasis   ARABIAN

DESERT

20°

N

La Tène   European Iron Age Sites

Judeidah   Early Agricultural Communities

Le Moustier   Palaeolithic Sites

⬜   Civilized areas in Third Millennium B.C.

🟦   Civilized areas in Second Millennium B.C.

🟦   Civilization 1000 B.C. - 200 A.D.

0   200   400   600   800 Miles

0   300   600   900   1200 Kilometers

Copyright by Rand McNally & Co.
Goodes Projection

20°   20°   40°   60°

RAND McNALLY

CONTENTS

Complete Legend for Physical and Political Maps

Symbols

- Lake
- Salt Lake
- Seasonal Lake
- River
- \ Waterfall
- — Canal
- △ Mountain Peak
- ▲ Highest Mountain Peak

Cities

- ■ Los Angeles   City over 1,000,000 population
- ▣ Calgary   City of 250,000 to 1,000,000 population
- • Haifa   City under 250,000 population
- ✪ Paris   National Capital
- ★ Vancouver   Secondary Capital (State, Province, or Territory)

Type Styles Used to Name Features

- CHINA   Country
- ONTARIO   State, Province, or Territory
- PUERTO RICO (U.S.)   Possession
- ATLANTIC OCEAN   Ocean or Sea
- *Alps*   Physical Feature
- *Borneo*   Island

Boundaries

- International Boundary
- Secondary Boundary

Land Elevation and Water Depths

Land Elevation

Meters	Feet
3,000 and over	9,840 and over
2,000 - 3,000	6,560 - 9,840
500 - 2,000	1,640 - 6,560
200 - 500	656 - 1,640
0 - 200	0 - 656

Water Depth

Less than 200	Less than 656
200 - 2,000	656 - 6,560
Over 2,000	Over 6,560

inventions for, 345
migrant workers and, 824, 828
New Deal and, 748
westward expansion and,
574–577
fascism, 758–759
Father Knows Best, 802–803
Faubus, Orval, 816
Federal Bureau of Investigation
(FBI), 856
Federal Deposit Insurance
Corporation (FDIC), 748
federal government
after Civil War, 522
aviation security and, 893
Great Depression and, 732
and Homestead Act, 574–575
and interstate commerce,
898–899
Native American resettlement
policy of, 376–377
New Deal and, 747–749
Nixon and, 855
power of, 235
progressive reforms of, *c647*
Reagan and, 874
and states' rights, 896–897
strengthening of, 356
supremacy of, 264
and transcontinental railroad,
590–592
federalism, 234, 245, *c262,* 306
Federalist Papers, The, 235, 238
Federalists
Adams and, 305, 313–314, 316
at Constitutional Convention,
234–237, *c235*
opposition to Democratic-
Republican Party, *c304,* 307
Federal Judiciary Act, 294
federal law
versus state law, 898
federal relief, 732
Federal Reserve Act, 648–649
Federal Reserve Bank, 648–649
felonies, 252, 253
Feminine Mystique, The, 826
Ferdinand (Spanish monarch),
50–51
ferris wheel, 628
Fetterman, W. J., 564
Fetterman Massacre, *m563,* 564
feudalism, 44–48, *i46*
Field, Marshall, 627
Fifteenth Amendment, *i243,* 271,
546, 549
Fifth Amendment, 267
"Fifty-four forty or fight!" 407
54th Massachusetts Regiment, 506
filibustering, 251
Fillmore, Millard, 467, 668, R37
"Final Solution," 768
fireside chats, 735
First Amendment, 266, 904
First Continental Congress, 171

fishing, 111
Fitzgerald, F. Scott, 713, *i721*
Fitzpatrick, D. R., *i783*
five freedoms, 282
Flag Day, *i199*
flappers, *i714*
flood plain, *i14*
Florida
acquisition from Spain, 357
expansionism and, *m410*
exploration of, 66
facts about, R34, R40
in French and Indian War, 150
human movement and, *m18*
Seminole resistance in, 378
Stono Rebellion in, 123
flu epidemic of 1918, 694
Foch, Ferdinand, 688
Folger, Peleg, 108
Fontaine, John, 126
Ford, Gerald R., 861, *i862,* R38
Ford, Henry, 711
Foreign Miners Tax, 416
forests, *m17,* 111
Forest Service, U.S., 644
Fort Duquesne, 148
Forten, James, 204
Fort Knox, 753
Fort Laramie, treaties of, 564
Fort McHenry, 332
Fort Necessity, 148
forts, 129
Fort Sumter, 475, *i478, i479,* 481,
m483
Fort Ticonderoga, 176, 196
Fortune, T. Thomas, 597
Fort Wagner, 506
Fort Wayne, Treaty of, 328
forty-niners, 412, 413–414, *i415*
Foster, Andrew "Rube," *i722*
442nd Infantry, 777
Fourteen Points, 695–696
text of, *i699*
Fourteenth Amendment, 270–271,
535, 549, 621, 901, 902, 906,
907, 909
Fourth Amendment, 267
4th U.S. Colored Troops, *i505*
France
in American Revolution, 200–201
balance of trade and, 62
in Civil War, 496
conflicts with England, 129, 301
control of New Orleans by, 319
and Convention of 1800, 307
exploration of Americas by, 68,
70
in French and Indian War,
146–151, *m148*
Jefferson and, 327
and postwar Germany, 793
revolution in, 301–302
and Suez Canal, 799
Vietnam and, 835–837

in World War I, 680–682,
684–685, 688–690
in World War II, 758, 759, *m760,*
761, *m764,* 766
and XYZ Affair, 305–306
Franklin, Benjamin, *i140,* 149,
i200, i212, i219, 229
Franz Ferdinand, *i679*
Fredericksburg, Battle of, 512
Free African Society, 215
free blacks, 351
in Reconstruction, 532, 533, 534,
536, 540–542, *i540*
Freedmen's Bureau, 533, 540–541
freedmen's schools, 540–541
freedom of assembly, *c266*
freedom of religion, *c266*
freedom of speech, 198, *c266*
Alien and Sedition Acts and, 306
protection of, 904–905
in schools, 905
freedom of the press, *c266*
Alien and Sedition Acts and, 306
Zenger Trial and, 145
Freedom Rides, 818
Freedom Summer, 821
freedom to petition, *c266*
free enterprise, *c214*
Freeman, Elizabeth, *i215*
free silver, 577–578
Free-Soil Party, 459, *i466*
Free Speech and Headlight, 624
Frémont, John C., 409, 467
French and Indian War, 146–150,
m148
results of, 150–151, *m150,* 159, 200
French Indochina, 835–837
French Revolution, 301–302, *i301*
Friedan, Betty, 826, *i827*
frontier
American Revolution on, 203
closing of, 578–579, *i579*
conflicts with Native Americans
on, 562–567
farming and populism on,
574–579
life on western, 568–573
miners, ranchers, and cowhands
on, 557–562
settlement of, *m558*
Fugitive Slave Act, 462
Fuller, Margaret, 431
Fulton, Robert, 344–345, *i344*
fundamentalism, 716
Fundamental Orders of
Connecticut, 95
text of, 98–99
fur trade
in Backcountry, 129
Lewis and Clark Expedition and,
c323
mountain men and, 394
in New France, 146–147

urbanization, 609–611, *c725*
U.S. v. Cruikshank, 548
U.S. v. Reese, 548
USA Patriot Act, 878, 893
Utah, 397, R35, R42
utopian communities, 437
U-2, 799

V

Vallejo, Mariano, 412, *i417*
valley, *i15*
Valley Forge, Pa., *i190*, 202–203, *i202*, *m209*
Van Buren, Martin, 386, R36
Vanderbilt family, *i596*
vaqueros, 560, *i560*, 571
vaudeville, 629
Vecchio, Mary Ann, *i846*
V-E Day, 767
vegetation, 13
Vermont, R35, R42
Verrazzano, Giovanni da, 68
Versailles, Treaty of, 696, 758
Vesey, Denmark, 353
Vespucci, Amerigo, 62
veto, 252, *c253*
vice-president
   constitutional provisions for, 250, 257
   election of, 269
   lame duck sessions and, 273
Vicksburg, Miss., 516, *m527*
victory gardens, 779
Viet Cong, 838, 840, 841, 842
Viet Minh, 836
Vietnamese immigrants, 427
Vietnamization, 848
Vietnam Veterans Memorial, *i832*, *i849*
Vietnam War, *c834*, *m837*, *m844*, *c851*
   background of, 835–839
   demonstrations against, 846–847
   end of, 847–848, 858, 863
   under Johnson, 840–845, *i84*
   legacy of, 848–849
   veterans of, 849
vigilantes, 561
Villa, Pancho, 673
Vincennes, Ill., 204
Virginia, 143
   in American Revolution, 209
   Antifederalists from, 236–237
   facts about, R35, R42
   plantation life in, *i121*
   secession of, 482
   and states' rights, 307
Virginia, University of, 316
Virginia City, Nev., 558
Virginian, The, 570
Virginia Plan, 230–231, *c232*

Virginia Resolution, 307
Virgin Islands, U.S., R35
virtual reality, *i882*
volcano, *i14*
Volstead Act, 715
volunteerism, 732
voter registration, *m821*
voting. *See also* suffrage.
   in District of Columbia, 275
   expansion of rights, 371
   individuals' rights, 908–909
   mock elections for students, *i372*
Voting Rights Act of 1965, 271, 821, 822, 909
Vredenburgh, Peter, Jr., *i488*

W

WAC, 764
Wagner Act, 743
wagon train, 396
Waikiki Beach, *i13*
Wake Atoll, R35
Wald, Lillian D., 613, *i650*
Walden Pond, 431
Walker, David, 440–441
Walker, Felix, 221
Walker, James, *i560*
Wallace, George, 821
Waltham, Mass., 342–343
war, declaration of, 253
war against terrorism,
   in Afghanistan, 878, 895–897
   George W. Bush Administration and, 878, 895–897
war bonds, 691, *i692*, *i702–703*, 775
war crimes, *i782*
war debts, 264, 295
War Hawks, 329
War Industries Board, 692
War of 1812, *m7*, 330–333, *c333*, 342
War Powers Act, 849
War Production Board, 774
Warren, Earl, 814, *i900*, 908
Warren, Joseph, 466
Warsaw Pact, *m792*, 793
War with Mexico, 406–409, *m408*, 459–460
Washington (state), R35, R42
Washington, Booker T., 521, 622
Washington, D.C.
   in Civil War, *m483*
   design of, *i305*
   voting in, 275
Washington, George, R36
   in American Revolution, 177, 178, *i190*, *i194*, *i196*, 202–203, 211
   at Constitutional Convention, *i219*, 229, 230
   farewell address of, 303
   in French and Indian War, 148

as president, *i291*, 293–295, 298–302
Watergate scandal, *i852*, 859–861, *i860*
Waterman, Thomas, *i536*
Watson, Thomas, 588
Wayne, Anthony, *i298*, 299
weapons
   in American Revolution, *i204*, *i208*
   atomic, 773, 783, 798
   in Civil War, 491–492, *i492*
   in Vietnam War, *i842–843*
   in World War I, *i681*
weapons of mass destruction, 878, 896, 897
Weaver, Robert C, 742
Webster, Daniel, 372, *i382*, *i460*, 461
Webster, Noah, 430
Welch, Joseph, 798
Weld, Theodore, 441
Wells, Ida B., 622, 624
West, Benjamin, *i212*
West, *i2*
   artists in, 430–431
   farming and populism in, 574–578
   immigrants in, 457
   Jackson and, 379, 380
   Kansas-Nebraska Act and, 463
   land claims in, *m223*
   Lewis and Clark Expedition to, 318–325
   life in, 568–571
   manifest destiny and, 392–399, 406–407
   miners, ranchers, and cowhands in, 557–561
   mountain men in, 394
   Native American lands in, 34, *m563*
   railroads in, 593
   sectionalism and, 357
   settlement of, *m558*
West Africa, *mR33*
Westinghouse Electric Company, 891
Westmoreland, William, 841
West Virginia
   in Civil War, *m483*
   facts about, R35, R42
West Virginia, U.S.S., *i754*
westward expansion. *See* expansionism.
Weyler, Valeriano "the Butcher," 663
whaling, *i108*, *i125*
wheat, 576–577
Wheatley, Phillis, *i178*
Whig Party, 386–387, 466
Whiskey Rebellion, 300–301
White, John, 85, 86
White Citizens Councils, 815

ACKNOWLEDGMENTS

TEXT ACKNOWLEDGMENTS

Chapter 1, page 28: map, "New Paths to the Americas," *U.S. News & World Report,* October 12, 1998, page 62. Copyright © October 12, 1998, U.S. News and World Report. Visit us at our Web site at www.usnews.com for additional information. Adapted by permission of U.S. News & World Report.

page 33: Excerpt from "Navajo Blessing Way," from *Language and Art in the Navajo Universe* by Gary Witherspoon, page 26 (Ann Arbor: The University of Michigan Press, 1977). Reprinted by permission of The University of Michigan Press.

Chapter 6, pages 174–175: Excerpt from *Johnny Tremain* by Esther Forbes. Copyright © 1943 by Esther Forbes Hoskins, copyright renewed by Linwood M. Erskine, Jr., executor of the Estate of Esther Forbes Hoskins. Reprinted by permission of Houghton Mifflin Company. All rights reserved.

Chapter 9, page 300: "Obeying Rules and Laws," from *Government in America* by Richard J. Hardy. Copyright © 1995 by Houghton Mifflin Company. All rights reserved. Reprinted by permission.

Chapter 16, pages 486–487: Excerpt from *Across Five Aprils* by Irene Hunt. Copyright © 1964 by Irene Hunt. All rights reserved. Reprinted by permission of Shirley Beem on behalf of the author.

Chapter 17, pages 508, 509, 510, 512, 513, 516, 518, 519: Excerpts from *The Civil War* by Kenneth Burns, Ric Burns, and Geoffrey Ward. Copyright © 1990 by American Documentaries, Inc. Reprinted by permission of Alfred A. Knopf, a division of Random House, Inc.

Chapter 19, page 562: Excerpt from "Wahenee: An Indian Girl's Story Told by Herself to Gilbert L. Wilson," *North Dakota History,* Vol. 38, Nos. 1 & 2. Copyright © 1971 State Historical Society of North Dakota. Used by permission.

Chapter 21, pages 618–619: Excerpt from *Dragonwings* by Laurence Yep. Copyright © 1975 by Laurence Yep. Used by permission of HarperCollins Publishers.

pages 624–625: Excerpt from *Crusade for Justice: The Autobiography of Ida B. Wells,* edited by Alfreda M. Duster. Copyright © 1970 by The University of Chicago. All rights reserved. Reprinted by permission of The University of Chicago Press.

Chapter 25, page 713: "First Fig" by Edna St. Vincent Millay, from *Collected Poems,* HarperCollins Publishers. Copyright 1922, 1950 by Edna St. Vincent Millay. All rights reserved. Reprinted by permission of Elizabeth Barnett, literary executor.

page 725: "I, Too," from *Collected Poems* by Langston Hughes. Copyright © 1994 by the Estate of Langston Hughes. Reprinted by permission of Alfred A. Knopf, a division of Random House, Inc.

Chapter 26, page 744–745: Excerpt from *Roll of Thunder, Hear My Cry* by Mildred D. Taylor. Copyright © 1976 by Mildred D. Taylor. Used by permission of Dial Books for Young Readers, a division of Penguin Putnam Inc.

Chapter 27, page 767: Excerpt from *Night* by Elie Wiesel, translated by Stella Rodway. Copyright © 1960 by MacGibbon & Kee. Copyright renewed 1988 by The Collins Publishing Group. Reprinted by permission of Hill and Wang, a division of Farrar, Straus & Giroux, Inc.

Chapter 28, page 800: Excerpt from "Remembering LaVern Baker, a strong-willed R&B original" by Steve Jones, *USA Today,* March 12, 1997. Copyright © 1997 USA Today. Reprinted with permission.

Chapter 29, page 815: Excerpt from *Stride Toward Freedom: The Montgomery Story* by Martin Luther King, Jr. Copyright © 1958 by Martin Luther King, Jr., copyright renewed 1986 by Coretta Scott King. Reprinted by arrangement with The Heirs to the Estate of Martin Luther King, Jr., c/o Writers House, Inc., as agent for the proprietor.

page 819: Excerpt from "Letter from Birmingham Jail" by Martin Luther King, Jr. Copyright © 1963 by Martin Luther King, Jr., copyright renewed 1991 by Coretta Scott King. Reprinted by arrangement with The Heirs to the Estate of Martin Luther King, Jr., c/o Writers House, Inc., as agent for the proprietor.

pages 820, 828: Excerpts from "I Have a Dream" by Martin Luther King, Jr. Copyright © 1963 by Martin Luther King, Jr., copyright renewed 1991 by Coretta Scott King. Reprinted by arrangement with The Heirs to the Estate of Martin Luther King, Jr., c/o Writers House, Inc., as agent for the proprietor.

Copyright © César E. Chávez Foundation. Reprinted by permission of the César E. Chávez Foundation.

Chapter 32, page 873: Excerpt from "Election no surprise to ordinary folk" by Anne Keegan, *Chicago Tribune,* November 6, 1980. Copyright © 1980 by the Chicago Tribune Company. All rights reserved. Used with permission.

page 883: Excerpt from "Dominican Dominion" by Maximo Zeledon, *Frontera Magazine,* Issue 5. Reprinted by permission of Frontera Magazine.

Maps created by Mapping Specialists.

ART CREDITS

Cover and Frontispiece

cover background Copyright © Bob Gelberg/SharpShooters. *frontispiece background* The Granger Collection, New York. **Amelia Earhart:** Copyright © Albert L. Bresnik. **Maya Lin:** Copyright © 1999 Richard Howard/Black Star. **Juan Seguín:** Detail of *Juan Seguin* (1838), Jefferson Wright. Texas State Library and Archives Commission. **Harry S. Truman:** White House Collection. Copyright © White House Historical Association. Courtesy of the Harry S. Truman Library. **Ida Bell Wells:** The Granger Collection, New York. **Abigail Adams:** *Portrait traditionally said to be Abigail Adams* (about 1795), artist unknown. Oil on canvas, 30 1/4" x 26 1/2", N-150.55. Photo by Richard Walker. Copyright © New York State Historical Association, Cooperstown, New York. **Zitkala-Sa:** Negative no. Mss 299, Tom Perry Special Collections, Harold B. Lee Library, Brigham Young University, Provo, Utah. **Benjamin Franklin:** Copyright © Joseph-Siffrede Duplessis/Wood River Gallery/PNI. **Abraham Lincoln:** The Library of Congress. **Martin Luther King, Jr:** Photo by Howard Sochrer/Life Magazine, copyright © Time Inc.

Table of Contents

viii–xvii *background* The Granger Collection, New York; **viii** *top* Benin *Horn-Blower* (about 1550–1680) unknown African artist. Nigeria, Court of Benin, Bini Tribe. Bronze, 24 7/8" x 11 5/8" x 6 3/4" (63 cm x 29.4 cm x 17.2 cm). The Metropolitan Museum of Art, The Michael C. Rockefeller Memorial Collection, gift of Nelson A. Rockefeller, 1972 (1978.412.310). Photograph copyright © 1983 The Metropolitan Museum of Art; *bottom* The Granger Collection, New York; **ix** *top* Copyright © Michael Gadomski/Photo Researchers, Inc.; *center* The Granger Collection, New York; *bottom* Library of Congress; **x** *top* Copyright © R. Kord/H. Armstrong Roberts; *center* Detail of *George Washington in the Uniform of a British Colonial Colonel* (1772), Charles Willson Peale. Washington-Custis-Lee Collection. Washington and Lee University, Lexington,

Virginia; *bottom* Corbis; **xi** *top* Copyright © 1998 North Wind Pictures; *center* National Museum of American History, Smithsonian Institution; *bottom* Illustration by Patrick Whelan; **xii** *top* From the collections of the Minnesota Historical Society; *bottom left* The Granger Collection, New York; *bottom right* Copyright © 1998 Louis Psihoyos/Matrix; **xiii** *top* Copyright © George Peter Alexandre Healy/Wood River Gallery/PNI; *center* Courtesy, *Soldier* magazine, U.S. Army; *bottom* The Granger Collection, New York; **xiv** *top, Northern Pacific Railroad. The Pioneer Route to Fargo Moorhead Town Bismark Dakota and Montana and the Famous Valley of the Yellowstone* (about 1885), Creator–Poole Brothers, Printers. Broadside. Chicago Historical Society; *bottom* The Granger Collection, New York; **xv** *top* Doubleday, Page and Company, New York, 1906, second issue; *center, Portrait of Queen Liliuokalani,* date and artist unknown. Bishop Museum; *bottom left* The Granger Collection, New York; *bottom right* Culver Pictures; **xvi** *top* Copyright © Stock Montage; *center* The Granger Collection, New York; *bottom* Copyright © Rob Boudreau/Tony Stone Images; **xvii** *top* Corbis-Bettmann; *center* NASA; *bottom* Copyright © Charles Feil/Stock Boston/PNI.

Voices from the Past

xxi The Granger Collection, New York; **xxii** Hulton-Deutsch Collection/Corbis; **xxiii** Library of Congress; **xxiv** Survey Compass, accession number 1982–145. Colonial Williamsburg Foundation.

Themes of American History

xxviii *top* Copyright © 1999 PhotoDisc, Inc.; *center* Photo by Howard Sochrer/*Life* Magazine, Copyright © Time Inc.; *bottom* Michael S. Yamashita/Corbis; **xxix** *top* Library of Congress; *bottom* National Museum of American History/Smithsonian Institution.

Reading to Remember

xxx *left inset* The Granger Collection, New York; *top right inset* The Granger Collection, New York; *bottom* Photo by Sharon Hoogstraten; **xxxi** *top right* Copyright © 1999 PhotoDisc, Inc.; *bottom right inset* Courtesy Commonwealth of Massachusetts Art Commission; *bottom left inset* Colonial teapot, Colonial Williamsburg Foundation *The Battle of Princeton* (detail) by William Mercer. The Historical Society of Pennsylvania *Sons of Liberty raising a Liberty Pole in 1776,* The Granger Collection, New York; **xxxii** *top left inset Portrait traditionally said to be Abigail Adams,* (1795). Artist unidentified, oil on canvas, H: 30 1/4", W: 26 1/2", N-150.55. Photograph by Richard Walker. Copyright © New York Historical Association, Cooperstown, New York; *top right inset* (Detail) *The Death of General Warren at the Battle of Bunker's Hill, 17 June 1775.* John Trumbull. Oil on canvas. Yale University Art Gallery, Trumbull Collection, *bottom right* AP/Wide World Photos; **xxxiii** *top right inset* Stamp (top) and seal (bottom) Rare Books Division, The New York Public Library. Astor, Lenox and Tilden Foundations, *bottom left inset* Copyright © Charles Winters/Stock Boston.

Geography Handbook

2 *top right* Copyright © H. Abernathy/H. Armstrong Roberts; *center left* Copyright © Warren Morgan/H. Armstrong Roberts; *bottom* Copyright © 1996 Denver A. Bryan; **3** *top* Copyright © Nathan Benn/Stock Boston; *bottom right* Copyright © Andy Sacks/Tony Stone Images; **4–5** The Granger Collection, New York; **4** *top* Copyright © 1997 David Noble/FPG International; **5** *top* Copyright © John Coletti/Stock Boston; *center* Copyright © Bill Horsman/Stock Boston; **6** *top* Copyright © George Mobley/NGS Image Collection; *center* Copyright © Lowell Georgia/NGS Image Collection; *bottom left* The Granger Collection, New York; **10** *top* Copyright © T. Algire/H. Armstrong Roberts; *bottom* Copyright © Ken Graham/Tony Stone Images; **11** *top* Copyright © SuperStock; *bottom* Copyright © Tom Dietrich/Tony Stone Images; **12** *top* Copyright © Zane Williams/Tony Stone Images;

bottom Copyright © Eastcott/Momatiuk/Tony Stone Images; **13** *top* Copyright © SuperStock; *bottom* Copyright © F. Sieb/H. Armstrong Roberts; **14–15** Illustration by Ken Goldammer; **16** *top* Copyright © M. Schneiders/H. Armstrong Roberts; *bottom* Copyright © D. Frazier/H. Armstrong Roberts; **17** *top left* Copyright © Ron Levy/Liaison Agency; *top right, center right, bottom right* Copyright © Steve Adams/NGS Image Collection; *bottom left* Copyright © Cathlyn Melloan/Tony Stone Images; **18** *bottom* Copyright © J. Marshall/The Image Works; **19** *left* Culver Pictures; *right* Copyright © Santi Visalli/The Image Bank.

Unit 1

22–23 Copyright © R. Kord/H. Armstrong Roberts.

Chapter 1, 24–25 The Granger Collection, New York; **24** *left* Courtesy of the Ohio Historical Society; *right* Roman horseman (A.D. first–third century). Bronze figurine from Orange, France. Musée des Antiquites Nationales, Saint-Germain-en-Laye, France. Photo © Erich Lessing/Art Resource, New York; **25** *left* © Leonard de Selva/Corbis; *right* The Granger Collection, New York; **26** *top* Werner Forman/Art Resource, New York; *center* Copyright © Aldona Sabalis/Photo Researchers, Inc.; *bottom* Copyright © Stuart Dee/The Image Bank; **27** Courtesy of Rock Art Foundation, San Antonio, Texas; **28** *center left* Courtesy Arizona State Museum, University of Arizona, Tucson, Arizona. Photo copyright © 1996 Jerry Jacka; **29** Copyright © Francois Gohier/Photo Researchers, Inc.; **30** Copyright © SuperStock; **32** *background* Photo of Bill Reid by R. Bettner. Collection Canadian Museum of Civilization, #K96-215 [or K96-216]. Reprinted with permission of Ms. Martine Reid; *foreground* Bear sculpture (1962), Bill Reid. 248 cm x 136 cm x 126 cm, U.B.C. Gift of Dr. Walter Koerner. Courtesy U.B.C. Museum of Anthropology, Vancouver, Canada; **34** National Museum of Anthropology, Mexico City, Mexico/Werner Forman Archive/Art Resource, New York; **35** Smithsonian Institution, Washington, D.C.; **36** *background* Copyright © Richard Saker/AllSport; *bottom left* Copyright © Salamander Picture Library; **39** Copyright © Thomas D. W. Friedmann/Photo Researchers, Inc.; **40** *left* Copyright © Aldona Sabalis/Photo Researchers, Inc.; **41** The Granger Collection, New York; **42** PNI; **43** The Metropolitan Museum of Art, The Michael C. Rockefeller Memorial Collection, gift of Nelson A. Rockefeller, 1972 (1978.412.310). Photograph copyright © 1983 The Metropolitan Museum of Art; **44** Copyright © Stock Montage; **45** Illustration by Alexander Verbitsky; **47** *School of Athens* (1508), Raphael (Raffaello Santi). Stanza della Segnatura, Vatican City, Vatican. Photo copyright © Erich Lessing/Art Resource, New York; **49** Detail of *St. Vincent Polyptych* (date unknown), Nuno Gonçalves. Museu Nacional de Arte Antiga, Lisbon, Portugal. Copyright © Scala/Art Resource, New York; **50** *Portrait of a Man, Called Christopher Columbus* (1519), Sebastiano del Piombo. Oil on canvas, 42" x 34 3/4". The Metropolitan Museum of Art, gift of J. Pierpont Morgan, 1900; **52** Archivio Fotografico del Museo Preistorico Etnografico L. Pigorini, Rome. Photo by Lorenzo de Masi; **53** Cliché Bibliothèque nationale de France, Paris; **55** *bottom* Courtesy of John Goss; **56** Copyright © Francois Gohier/Photo Researchers, Inc.; **57** Photos by Sharon Hoogstraten.

Chapter 2, 58–59 The Granger Collection, New York; **58** *top left* Mask, representing the god Quetzalcoatl or Tonatiuh (about 1500), Aztec. Museum of Mankind, London. Photo © Bridgeman Art Library; *bottom left* © Gianni Dagli Orti/Corbis; *right* © Bettmann/Corbis; **59** The Granger Collection, New York; **60** The Granger Collection, New York; **61** Detail of *Pope Alexander VI Borgia Kneeling in Prayer* (date unknown), Bernardino Pinturicchio. Sala die Misteri della Fede, Appartamento Borgia, Vatican Palace, Vatican State/Scala/Art Resource, New York; **64** Corbis; **65** Aztec mask (early 16th century), artist unknown. Turquoise, pearl shell. Werner Forman Archive/British Museum,

London/Art Resource, New York; **66** The Granger Collection, New York; **67** *top, The Last Voyage of Henry Hudson* (1881), John Collier. Tate Gallery, London/Art Resource, New York; **68** PNI; **69** *Sea Battle between the Spanish Armada and English Naval Forces* (about 1600), Hendrik Corneliez Vroom. Oil on canvas, 91 cm x 153 cm. Landesmuseum Ferdinandeum, Innsbruck, Austria. Photo copyright © Erich Lessing/Art Resource, New York; **71** The Granger Collection, New York; **73** The British Library; **75** PNI; **76** Copyright © The Fotomas Index; **77** Corbis; **78** *left* The Newberry Library, Chicago; *right, Slaves Below Deck of Albanez* (date unknown), Francis Meynell. Copyright © National Maritime Museum Picture Library, London.

Chapter 3, 82–83 Colonial Williamsburg Foundation, Virginia; **82** *top Captain John Smith, 1st Governor of Virginia* (about 1616), English School. Private collection. Photo © Bridgeman Art Library; *bottom Portrait of Akbar and Prince Salim* (19th century), Indian, Mughal dynasty. The Newark Museum, Newark, New Jersey. Photo © The Newark Museum/Art Resource, New York; **83** *left* © Bettmann/Corbis; *right* The Granger Collection, New York; **84** The Granger Collection, New York; **85** British Museum; **87** AP/Wide World Photos; **88** *Pocahontas* (1616), Simon van de Passe. Engraving, 6 7/8" x 4 3/4" (17.5 cm x 12 cm). Published in the *Baziliologia*, London, 1618. National Portrait Gallery, Smithsonian Institution/Art Resource, New York; **89** The Granger Collection, New York; **90–91** Illustration by Ivan Lapper. Copyright © The Reader's Digest Association; **92** The Granger Collection, New York; **93** *The Mayflower in Plymouth Harbor* (1882), William Halsall. Courtesy of the Pilgrim Society, Plymouth, Massachusetts; **94** *top* Copyright © SuperStock; *bottom* Copyright © Andrew J. Martinez/Photo Researchers, Inc.; **95** *bottom* The Granger Collection, New York; **96** *left* Courtesy of American Antiquarian Society; *right* The New York Public Library; **97** *Trial of George Jacobs for Witchcraft, 1692* (1855), T. H. Matteson. Oil on canvas, acc. #1246. Peabody Essex Museum, Salem, Massachusetts. Photo by Mark Sexton; **100** Detail of *Peter Stuyvesant and the Trumpeter (The Wrath of Peter Stuyvesant)* (1835), Asher B. Durand. Oil on canvas, 24 1/4" x 30 1/4", accession no. 1858.28. Copyright © Collection of The New-York Historical Society; **101** Copyright © Tom Dietrich/Tony Stone Images; **103** Brown Brothers; **105** Colonial Williamsburg Foundation.

Chapter 4, 106–107 The Granger Collection, New York; **106** *top* © Joseph Sohm; ChromoSohm Inc./Corbis; *bottom* The Granger Collection, New York; **107** *left* © Bettmann/Corbis; *right Portrait of Nadir Shah Afshar of Persia* (1700–1725), Mughal School. Victoria & Albert Museum, London. Photo © The Stapleton Collection/Bridgeman Art Library; **109** *Sperm Whaling: No. 2, The Capture* (1862), A. Van Best and R. S. Gifford. Lithograph by Endicott and Company, corrected by Benjamin Russell, 16 3/4" x 25 3/4" (43 cm x 65 cm). N.M.A.H., Harry Peters "America on Stone" Lithography Collection; **110** *right* Copyright © Thomas Neill; **112** North Carolina Collection, University of North Carolina Library at Chapel Hill; **114** Detail of *Quaker Meeting* (date unknown), Egbert Van Heemskerk. The Quaker Collection, Haverford (Pennsylvania) College Library; **115** *right* Historic Hudson Valley, Tarrytown, New York; **116** The Granger Collection, New York; **118** Library of Congress; **119** Detail of *George Mason* (1811), Dominic W. Boudet. Oil on canvas, 30" x 25" (76.2 cm x 63.5 cm). Virginia Museum of Fine Arts, Richmond. Gift of David K. E. Bruce. Photo by Ron Jennings. Copyright © Virginia Museum of Fine Arts; **120** *right* Copyright © Chip Henderson/Tony Stone Images; **121** Virginia Historical Society, Richmond, Virginia; **122** The Granger Collection, New York; **124** *bottom left* Smithsonian Institution, Washington, D.C.; *bottom right background* Photo copyright © Dorothy Miller; *bottom right foreground* Copyright © The New York Botanical Garden; **125** *bottom center* Copyright © Old Dartmouth

Historical Society, New Bedford (Massachusetts) Whaling Museum; **126** The Granger Collection, New York; **127** *right* Copyright © Michael P. Gadomski/Photo Researchers, Inc.; **128** Copyright © Mark McGehearty/AllSport; **129** *Catching the Wild Horse* (date unknown), George Catlin. Oil on canvas, 12 1/4" x 16 1/4". The Thomas Gilcrease Institute of American History and Art, Tulsa, Oklahoma.

Chapter 5, 132–133 The Granger Collection, New York; **132** *top* The Granger Collection, New York; *bottom left King William III* (18th century), English School. Photo © Derrick E. Witty/National Trust Photographic Library/Bridgeman Art Library; *bottom right Mary Stewart, Consort of William III* (17th century), William Wissing or Wissmig. Photo © Derrick E. Witty/National Trust Photographic Library/The Bridgeman Art Library; **133** *left King George II* (about 1743–1745), Joseph Highmore. Tate Gallery, London. Photo © Tate Gallery, London/Art Resource, New York; *right* The Granger Collection, New York; **134** Library of Congress; **137, 139** The Granger Collection, New York; **140** Corbis; **141** Detail of *Increase Mather* (1688), John Vander Spriett. Courtesy of the Massachusetts Historical Society; **142** Courtesy of Knox County, Illinois Teen Court; **143** The Granger Collection, New York; **145** *left* Corbis; *right* The Newberry Library, Chicago; **146** Detail of *Braddock's Defeat* (1903), Edward Deming. State Historical Society of Wisconsin Museum Collection; **147** Library of Congress; **149, 151** The Granger Collection, New York.

Unit 2

154–155 Copyright © William Johnson/Stock Boston.

Chapter 6, 156–157 The Granger Collection, New York; **156** *left* Rare Books and Manuscript Division of the New York Public Library, Astor, Lenox, and Tilden Foundations; *right* © Dorling Kindersley; **157** *left The Boston Massacre (The Bloody Massacre)* (1770), Paul Revere. The Granger Collection, New York; *right Louis XVI, King of France* (1770s), Joseph-Siffrède Duplessis. Musée du Château de Versailles, Paris. Photo © Dagli Orti/The Art Archive; **158** The Granger Collection, New York; **159** *James Otis Arguing Against the Writs of Assistance in the Old Towne House* (1901), Robert Reid. Courtesy Commonwealth of Massachusetts Art Commission; **160** *top* Rare Books Division, The New York Public Library. Astor, Lenox, and Tilden Foundations; *bottom* Emmet Collection, Manuscripts and Archives Division, The New York Public Library. Astor, Lenox, and Tilden Foundations; **161, 162** The Granger Collection, New York; **163** Copyright © Stock Montage; **164** Copyright © Collection of The New-York Historical Society; **165** The Granger Collection, New York; **166** *left* The Granger Collection, New York; *right, John Adams* (date unknown), John Trumbull. National Portrait Gallery, Smithsonian Institution/Art Resource, New York; **167** The Granger Collection, New York; **168–169** Copyright © McDougal Littell Inc.; **170** Copyright © Paul Mozell/Stock Boston; **173** Copyright © Charles Winters/Stock Boston; **174** Copyright © McDougal Littell Inc.; **175** The Granger Collection, New York; **176** *Portrait traditionally said to be Abigail Adams* (about 1795), artist unknown. Oil on canvas, 30 1/4" x 26 1/2", N-150.55. Photo by Richard Walker. Copyright © New York State Historical Association, Cooperstown, New York; **177** Detail of *The Death of General Warren at the Battle of Bunker's Hill, 17 June 1775* (date unknown), John Trumbull. Oil on canvas. Yale University Art Gallery, Trumbull Collection; **178** Library of Congress; **179** *top* The Granger Collection, New York; *bottom* Library of Congress; **180** *top* Detail of *The Declaration of Independence, 4 July 1776* (date unknown), John Trumbull. Oil on canvas. Yale University Art Gallery, Trumbull Collection; *bottom* Copyright © R. Kord/H. Armstrong Roberts; **181, 182** The Granger Collection, New York; **187** *bottom* Clement Library, University of Michigan; **88** The Granger Collection, New York;

189 Photos by Sharon Hoogstraten.

Chapter 7, 190–191 The Granger Collection, New York; **190** *bottom left* © Bettmann/Corbis; *bottom right* ©Archivo Iconografico, S.A./Corbis; **191** *top* © Getty Images; *bottom* © Bettmann/Corbis; **192** The Granger Collection, New York; **194** *George Washington in the Uniform of a British Colonial Colonel* (1772), Charles Willson Peale. Washington-Custis-Lee Collection. Washington and Lee University, Lexington, Virginia; **195** *top* From *American Story: The Revolutionaries.* Courtesy of the Jamestown-Yorktown Educational Trust. Photo by Katherine Wetzel. Copyright © 1996 Time-Life Books Inc.; **196** *The Passage of the Delaware* (1819), Thomas Sully. Oil on canvas, 146 1/2" x 207" (372.11 x 525.78 cm). Copyright © Museum of Fine Arts Boston. Gift of the owners of the old Boston Museum; 03.1079; **198** Copyright © Michael Newman/PhotoEdit/PNI; **199** *Two American Flags Flown by John Paul Jones in 1779* (date unknown), unknown Dutch artist. Watercolor. Chicago Historical Society; **200, 201** The Granger Collection, New York; **202** From *American Story: The Revolutionaries.* Courtesy of the Jamestown-Yorktown Educational Trust. Photo by Katherine Wetzel. Copyright © 1996 Time-Life Books Inc.; **205** The Granger Collection, New York; **206** Library of Congress; **207** Defense Visual Information Center, Linda Delatorre, Researcher; **208** Illustration by Bill Cigliano; **210** *Surrender of Lord Cornwallis at Yorktown* (date unknown), John Trumbull. Yale University Art Gallery, Trumbull Collection; **211** Private collection; **212** The Granger Collection, New York; **215** Courtesy of the Massachusetts Historical Society; **216** Private collection.

Chapter 8, 218–219 *The Signing of the Constitution* (about 1940), Howard Chandler Christy. Private collection. Photo © Art Resource, New York; **218** *left* The Granger Collection, New York; *right* © Archivo Iconografico, S.A./Corbis; **219** *left* © Getty Images; *right* © Christie's Images/Corbis; **220** The Granger Collection, New York; **221** Detail of *Daniel Boone Escorting Settlers Through the Cumberland Gap* (1851–1852), George Caleb Bingham. Oil on canvas, 36 1/2" x 50 1/4". Washington University Gallery of Art, St. Louis (Missouri). Gift of Nathaniel Phillips, 1890; **222, 225** *top* The Granger Collection, New York; **225** *bottom* Copyright © Thad Samuels Abell II/NGS Image Collection; **226** *bottom left* Copyright © John E. Fletcher & Arlan R. Wiler/NGS Image Collection; *bottom right* William L. Clements Library, Map Division, University of Michigan; **227** *top* The Granger Collection, New York; *bottom* Courtesy of the Shelby County (Ohio) Historical Society; **228** Corbis; *inset* Library of Congress; **229** Copyright © Joseph Nettis/Tony Stone Images; **230** The Granger Collection, New York; **231** PNI; **234** The Granger Collection, New York; **235** *left, Portrait of John Jay* (c. 1783, 1804–1808), Gilbert Stuart, believed to have been begun by and finished by John Trumbull. National Portrait Gallery, Smithsonian Institution/Art Resource, New York; **235** *right,* **236** The Granger Collection, New York.

Constitution Handbook

242 *left* The Granger Collection, New York; *right* Copyright © Ivan Massar/Black Star; **243** *top* Copyright © Bob Daemmrich/The Image Works; *center* Copyright © Topham/The Image Works; *bottom* Courtesy of The New York *Times;* **244** *bottom* Copyright © J. L. Atlan/Sygma; **245** *top* Copyright © Robert E. Daemmrich/Tony Stone Images; **247** *top* Copyright © 1973 Engelhardt in the *St. Louis Post-Dispatch*/Reprinted with permission; *bottom* Copyright © Patrick Forden/Sygma; **248** *background* The Granger Collection, New York; **248** *inset,* **257** AP/Wide World Photos; **258** *top right* Copyright © Archive Photos; *top left* Culver Pictures; *center right* Copyright © 1972 Magnum Photos, Inc.; *center left* AP/Wide World Photos; *bottom right* Courtesy Ronald Reagan Library; **264** AP/Wide World Photos; **265** Copyright © Collection of The New-York Historical Society; **267** Copyright © Baron Wolman/Tony

Stone Images; **268** *left* Copyright © Jean-Marc Giboux/Liaison Agency; *right* Copyright © Bob Daemmrich/Sygma; **270** Copyright © 1993 Ron Rovtar/FPG International; **272** The Granger Collection, New York; **273** *left* Copyright © 1998 FPG International; *right* Copyright © Cynthia Johnson/Liaison Agency; **274** Franklin D. Roosevelt Library; **277** Copyright © Rock the Vote Inc.

Citizenship Handbook

280 AP/Wide World Photos; **281** *background* Copyright © Bob Daemmrich; *foreground* Copyright © 1994 Mark Harmel/FPG International; **284** Copyright © Bob Daemmrich/The Image Works; **285** Copyright © David Young-Wolff/Tony Stone Images; **286** AP/Wide World Photos.

Unit 3

288–289 Copyright © Marvin E. Newman/The Image Bank.

Chapter 9, 290–291 The Granger Collection, New York; **290** *left* © Lee Snider; Lee Snider/Corbis; *right* © Leonard de Selva/Corbis; **291** *left* © Getty Images; *right* © Charles & Josette Lenars/Corbis; **292** © Joseph Sohm; Visions of America/Corbis; **294** AP/Wide World Photos; **295** *Portrait of Alexander Hamilton* (about 1796), James Sharples (the Elder). National Portrait Gallery, Smithsonian Institution/Art Resource, New York; **297** Copyright © Larry Stevens/Nawrocki Stock Photo Inc.; **298** Chicago Historical Society; **299** *right* Ohio Historical Society; **301** *Execution of Louis XVI* (18th century), anonymous. Colored engraving. Musée de la Ville de Paris, Musée Carnavalet, Paris, France/Giraudon/Art Resource, NY; **303** Mount Vernon Ladies Association; **305** *top* The Granger Collection, New York; *center right* Maryland Historical Society; **306** The Granger Collection, New York.

Chapter 10, 310–311 © Historical Picture Archive/Corbis; **310** © Bettmann/Corbis; **311** *top* © Francis G. Mayer/Corbis; *bottom left* Miguel Hidalgo y Costilla (1895). Engraving from Mexican publication *Patria e Independencia,* Illustrated folio. Antochiw Collection, Mexico. Photo by Mireille Vautier/The Art Archive; *bottom right* © Archivo Iconografico, S.A./Corbis; **313** *left, Thomas Jefferson* (date unknown), Rembrandt Peale. Copyright © Collection of the New-York Historical Society; *right* Boston Athenaeum; **314** The Granger Collection, New York; **315** *center right* Kirby Collection of Historical Paintings, Lafayette College; *bottom background* Monticello/Thomas Jefferson Memorial Foundation, Inc.; *bottom center* Polygraph, 1806. John Isaac Hawkins, Charles Willson Peale. University of Virginia. Photo courtesy of Monticello/Thomas Jefferson Memorial Foundation, Inc.; **316** Boston Athenaeum; **317** Copyright © James Blair/NGS Image Collection; **318, 319** The Granger Collection, New York; **320** *inset* Copyright © Addison Geary/Stock Boston/PNI; **321** *Lewis and Clark at Three Forks* (date unknown), E. S. Paxson. Mural in the Montana State Capitol. Courtesy of the Montana Historical Society. Photo by John Reddy; **322** Copyright © 1998 North Wind Pictures; **323** National Museum of American History, Smithsonian Institution; **324** *center left* Copyright © Stock Montage; *center right, The Surrounder, Chief of the Tribe* (1833), George Catlin. Oto tribe. National Museum of American Art, Smithsonian Institution/Art Resource, New York; *bottom center, bottom right* Peabody Museum, Harvard University. Copyright © President and Fellows of Harvard College. Photo by Hillel Burger; **325** *center left, Mink, a Pretty Girl* (1832), George Catlin. National Museum of American Art, Smithsonian Institution/Art Resource, New York; *center right, Steep Wing, a Brave of the Bad Arrow Points Band* (1832), George Catlin. Teton Dakota (Western Sioux). National Museum of American Art, Smithsonian Institution/Art Resource, New York; *bottom* Whaling Chief's Hat, Makah or Nootka. Cedar bark, bear grass, unidentified mammal hair, remnant feathers, leather thong. H 22 cm, D 27 cm. PM# 99-12-10/53080. Peabody Museum of

Archeology and Ethnology, Harvard University. Copyright © President and Fellows of Harvard College. Photo by Hillel Burger; **326** Detail of *Decatur Boarding the Tripolitan Gunboat* (date unknown), Dennis Malone Carter. Oil on canvas. Courtesy of the Naval Historical Foundation; **327** Library of Congress; **328** The Granger Collection, New York; **330** *left* White House Collection. Copyright © White House Historical Association; *right* The Granger Collection, New York; **332** National Museum of American History, Smithsonian Institution; **334** *top, Thomas Jefferson* (date unknown), Rembrandt Peale. Copyright © Collection of the New-York Historical Society; *bottom* National Museum of American History, Smithsonian Institution; **335** "Ograbme, or, The American Snapping Turtle" (1807), D. Longworth. Negative no. 7278. Copyright © Collection of The New-York Historical Society; **336** *top left* Elk skin bound journal (1805), William Clark. Ink on paper. Missouri Historical Society; *right, bottom* Copyright © 1998 North Wind Pictures; **337** Photos by Sharon Hoogstraten.

Chapter 11, 338–339 © Bettmann/Corbis; **338** *left* © Bettmann/Corbis; *right* © Archivo Iconografico, S.A./Corbis; **339** *top* Library of Congress; *bottom* © Paul Almasy/Corbis; **341** Corbis-Bettmann; **342** The Granger Collection, New York; **343** Illustration by Patrick Whelan; **344** Corbis-Bettmann; **345** Copyright © Stock Montage; **346–347** Illustrations by Randal Birkey; **348** The Granger Collection, New York; **349** Illustration by Patrick Whelan; **351** Detail of *Plantation Burial* (1860), John Antrobus. Williams Research Center, The Historic New Orleans Collection. Photo copyright © Jan White Brantley; **352** Corbis-Bettmann; **353** The Granger Collection, New York; **354** Corbis-Bettmann; **355** *right inset* The Granger Collection, New York; **356, 357** *right inset* Corbis-Bettmann.

Unit 4

364–365 Layne Kennedy/Corbis.

Chapter 12, 366–367 The Granger Collection, New York; **366** © Archivo Iconografico, S.A./Corbis; **367** The Granger Collection, New York; **368** Copyright © Collection of the New-York Historical Society; **369** Redwood Library and Athenaeum, Newport, Rhode Island; **370** *left, John Quincy Adams* (1858), George Healy. Oil on canvas, 62" x 47". White House Collection. Copyright © White House Historical Association; *right, Andrew Jackson* (1845), Thomas Sully, The Granger Collection, New York; **371** The Hermitage: Home of President Andrew Jackson, Nashville, Tennessee. Photo of ribbon by Sharon Hoogstraten; **372** Copyright © The *News-Sentinel,* Fort Wayne, Indiana; **373** *left* The Granger Collection, New York; *right* Culver Pictures; **374** *Sequoyah, Indian Statesman* (date unknown), anonymous, after Charles Bird King. Hand-colored lithograph, J. T. Bowen lithography company. National Portrait Gallery, Smithsonian Institution/Art Resource, New York; **375** Copyright © J. Pat Carter/Liaison Agency; **377** *The Trail of Tears* (date unknown), Robert Lindneux. Woolaroc Museum, Bartlesville, Oklahoma; **378** The Granger Collection, New York; **379** *top, John Caldwell Calhoun* (about 1818–1825), attributed to Charles Bird King. Oil on canvas, 76.2 cm x 63.5 cm. National Portrait Gallery, Smithsonian Institution/Art Resource, New York; **379** *bottom,* **381** *top* The Granger Collection, New York; **381** *bottom* The Museum of the Confederacy, Richmond, Virginia. Photo by Katherine Wetzel; **382** Detail of *Webster's Reply to Hayne* (date unknown), George Healy. Courtesy Boston Art Commission; **384** *top* The Granger Collection, New York; *bottom inset, Nicholas Biddle* (1839), Henry Inman. Oil on canvas [1978.2]. The Historical Society of Pennsylvania; **385** The Granger Collection, New York; **386** Copyright © Collection of The New-York Historical Society; **389** Library of Congress.

Chapter 13, 390–391 National Archives; **390** *left* The Granger Collection, New York; *right* The Granger Collection, New York; **391** *left* © Bettmann/Corbis; *right* © Archivo Iconografico, S.A./Corbis; **392** © Brian A. Vikander/Corbis; **393** *Jedediah Smith in the Badlands* (date unknown), Harvey Dunn. The South Dakota Art Museum Collection; **394** Copyright © United States Postal Service; **395** *inset* Copyright © Ric Ergenbright; **396** Skillet, negative no. OrHi 97119. Oregon Historical Society; **400** The Granger Collection, New York; **401** *top* Broadsides Collection, The Center for American History, The University of Texas at Austin; **402** Copyright © Bob Daemmrich/Stock Boston/PNI; **403** *The Battle of the Alamo* (about 1913), Frederick C. Yohn. Courtesy Continental Insurance; **404** *left* Texas State Library and Archives Commission; **404** *right,* **406** The Granger Collection, New York; **408** *inset,* **412** Courtesy of the California History Room, California State Library, Sacramento, California; **413** Copyright © Collection of The New-York Historical Society; **414** Courtesy of Levi Strauss Company; **415, 417** Courtesy of the California History Room, California State Library, Sacramento, California; **419** *bottom* From the collections of the Minnesota Historical Society.

Chapter 14, 420–421 © Getty Images; **420** *left* © Archivo Iconografico, S.A./Corbis; *right* The Granger Collection, New York; **421** *left, right* The Granger Collection, New York; **422** The New York Public Library; **423** *background* From the collections of the Minnesota Historical Society; *foreground* Copyright © Collection of The New-York Historical Society; **424** *center* The Granger Collection, New York; **427** Michael S. Yamashita/Corbis; **428** The Granger Collection, New York; **429** From *The Headless Horseman* by Natalie Standiford, illustrated by Donald Cook. Illustration copyright © 1992 Donald Cook. Reprinted by permission of Random House, Inc.; **430** The Granger Collection, New York; **432** *background* Photo by Simon Marsden/The Marsden Archive; **433** The Granger Collection, New York; **434** Copyright © Archive Photos; **435** Department of Archives, Oberlin (Ohio) College; **436, 440** The Granger Collection, New York; **441** Chester County Historical Society, West Chester, Pennsylvania; **442** Copyright © 1996 Wayne Sorce; **443** *from left to right* The Granger Collection, New York; The Granger Collection, New York; The Granger Collection, New York; Corbis-Bettmann; **444** The Granger Collection, New York; **445** *The Discord* (1885), F. Heppenheimer. Color lithograph, negative no. 51038. Copyright © Collection of The New-York Historical Society; **446** *center* Sophia Smith Collection, Smith College; *bottom right, bottom left* Copyright © 1998 Louis Psihoyos/Matrix; **447** *bottom* From the Collections of the National Underground Railroad Freedom Center, Cincinnati, Ohio; **450** From the collections of the Minnesota Historical Society; **451** Photos by Sharon Hoogstraten.

Unit 5

452–453 Corbis.

Chapter 15, 454–455 The Granger Collection, New York; **454** *top, bottom* The Granger Collection, New York; **455** *left* © Bettmann/Corbis; *right* © Hulton-Deutsch Collection/Corbis; **456** The Granger Collection, New York; **457, 460** The Granger Collection, New York; **461** Corbis; **462** Hulton-Deutsch Collection/Corbis; **463** *left* The Granger Collection, New York; *right* Corbis-Bettmann; **466** From the Collection of David J. and Janice L. Frent; **467** AFP/Corbis; **468, 471** The Granger Collection, New York; **472** Lloyd Ostendorf Collection; **474** *background* Hulton-Deutsch Collection/Corbis; *inset* Copyright © George Peter Alexandre Healy/Wood River Gallery/PNI; **477** *The Last Moments of John Brown* (1884), Thomas Hovenden. Oil on canvas, 77 3/8" x 63 1/4". The Metropolitan Museum of Art, gift of Mr. and Mrs.

Carl Stoeckel, 1897. Photograph copyright © 1982 The Metropolitan Museum of Art.

Chapter 16, 478–479 The Granger Collection, New York; **478** *left* © Massimo Listri/Corbis; *right* © Museum of the City of New York/Corbis; **479** © Bettmann/Corbis; **480** *top left, top right* Library of Congress; *bottom left, bottom right* The Granger Collection, New York; **482** The Lincoln Museum, Fort Wayne, Indiana. #0-43; **485** Copyright © H. Armstrong Roberts; **486** Copyright © McDougal Littell Inc.; **487** *left* Courtesy of Brian C. Pohanka; *right* Massachusetts Commandery Military Order of the Loyal Legion and the U.S. Army Military History Institute; **488** Bureau of Archives and History, New Jersey State Library; **489** Corbis-Bettmann; **490** Culver Pictures; **491** The Granger Collection, New York; **492** Illustration by Alexander Verbitsky; **493** Library of Congress; **496** U.S. Signal Corps photo no. 111-B-4146 (Brady Collection) in the National Archives; **497** Chicago Historical Society; **498** *left,* Photograph copyright © High Impact Photography. Courtesy 103rd ENG.; *center* Courtesy, Museum of the Confederacy, Richmond, Virginia; *bottom right* Fort Sumter National Park.

Chapter 17, 500–501 Detail of *Cavalry Charge at Yellow Tavern, VA, May 11, 1864* (1871), H.W. Chaloner. West Point Museum Art Collection, United States Military Academy; **500** *left* The Granger Collection, New York; *right* © Paul Almasy/Corbis; **501** *left* The Granger Collection, New York; *right* Library of Congress; **502** *top left, top right, bottom left* Library of Congress; *bottom right* The Granger Collection, New York; **503** Corbis; **504** The Granger Collection, New York; **505** *top* Copyright © Archive Photos; *bottom* Library of Congress; **506** Defense Visual Information Center, Linda Delatorre, Researcher; **507** Culver Pictures; **508** The Granger Collection, New York; **510** American Red Cross; **511** *background* Corbis; *foreground* Massachusetts Commandery Military Order of the Loyal Legion and the U.S. Army Military History Institute; **512** The Pejepscot Historical Society; **513** Copyright © 1994 Kunio Owaki/The Stock Market; **514–515** *background* Illustration by Ken Goldammer; **514** *center* Library of Congress; *bottom left* Courtesy, Gettysburg National Military Park Museum. Photograph by Eric Long; *bottom right* The Museum of the Confederacy, Richmond, Virginia. Photo by Katherine Wetzel; **515** *bottom* Courtesy, Gettysburg National Military Park Museum. Photograph by Eric Long; **516** Library of Congress; **518** *top left* Courtesy of Stamatelos Brothers Collection. Photo by Larry Sherer. Copyright © 1991 Time-Life Books Inc.; *bottom* Courtesy Meserve-Kunhardt Collection, Mount Kisco, New York; **520** Copyright © Robert M. Anderson/Uniphoto, Inc.; **522** National Archives; **526** *top right* Photograph copyright © High Impact Photography. Courtesy, Virginia Military Institute; *bottom right* Collection of Old Capitol Museum of Mississippi History; **528** *left,* Cruz Collection, New Bedford Historical Society; *center* National Archives; *right* Courtesy, *Soldier* magazine, U.S. Army; **529** Photos by Sharon Hoogstraten.

Chapter 18, 530–531 National Archives; **530** © Bettmann/Corbis; **531** *top left* © Bettmann/Corbis; *bottom left* © Corbis; *right* Library of Congress; **533, 534** The Granger Collection, New York; **535** Corbis; **536** *His First Vote* (1868), Thomas Waterman Wood. Oil on board. Cheekwood Museum of Art, Nashville, Tennessee; **537, 538–539** *background* The Granger Collection, New York; **538** *top right,* **540, 541** Corbis; **542** Library of Congress; **544** The Granger Collection, New York; **545** Library of Congress; **546, 547** The Granger Collection, New York; **548** Library of Congress; **551** *bottom* The Granger Collection, New York.

Unit 6

552–553 The Granger Collection, New York.

Chapter 19, 554–555 © Corbis; **554** *left* The Granger Collection, New York; *right* © Corbis; **555** *left* © Bettmann/Corbis; *right* © Bettmann/Corbis; **557** Denver Public Library; **559** *top* The Granger Collection, New York; *bottom* Copyright © Dan Suzio/Photo Researchers, Inc.; **560** *California Vaqueros* (1875), James Walker. Oil on canvas, 31" x 46". Courtesy of The Anschutz Collection. Photo by William J. O'Connor; **561** Culver Pictures; **562** *background* The Granger Collection, New York; *foreground* State Historical Society of North Dakota; **564** *Custer's Last Stand* (1899), Edgar S. Paxson. Oil on canvas, 70 1/2" x 106". Buffalo Bill Historical Center, Cody, Wyoming; **565** *top* The Granger Collection, New York; *center* Culver Pictures; *bottom* Library of Congress; **566** Western History Collections, University of Oklahoma Libraries; **567** Library of Congress; **568** The Kansas State Historical Society, Topeka, Kansas; **569** *top, View of San Francisco [Formerly Yerba Buena]* (1847), attributed to Victor Prevost. Oil on canvas, 25" x 30". California Historical Society, gift of the Ohio Historical Society; *bottom* The Bancroft Library, University of California, Berkeley; **570** *top* The Granger Collection, New York; *center* Courtesy of the Arizona Historical Society/Tucson; *bottom* The Granger Collection, New York; **571** Photofest; **572–573** Wyoming Division of Cultural Resources; **573** *top* Library of Congress; **574** *foreground, Northern Pacific Railroad. The Pioneer Route to Fargo Moorhead Town Bismark Dakota and Montana and the Famous Valley of the Yellowstone* (about 1885), Creator–Poole Brothers, Printers. Broadside. Chicago Historical Society; **575** Solomon D. Butcher Collection, Nebraska State Historical Society; **577** The Granger Collection, New York; **578** Culver Pictures; **579** *Rush for the Oklahoma Land* (1894), John Steuart Curry. Department of the Interior.

Chapter 20, 582–583 The Granger Collection, New York; **582** *top* National Museum of American History/Smithsonian Institution; *bottom* © Hulton-Deutsch Collection/Corbis; **583** *left* © Michael Maslan Historic Photographs/Corbis; *right* © Bettmann/Corbis; **584** The Newberry Library, Chicago; **585** Corbis-Bettmann; **587** Library of Congress; **588** *background* U.S. Dept. of Commerce—Patent & Trademark Office, Washington, D.C.; *left foreground* The Granger Collection, New York; *right foreground* Courtesy of AT&T; **589** *left background* U.S. Dept. of Commerce—Patent & Trademark Office, Washington, D.C.; *left foreground* First Church of Christ, Lynn, Massachusetts; **590** Special Collections Division, University of Washington Libraries. Negative no. 2315; **591** *top* Courtesy Colorado Historical Society; *bottom, The Last Spike* (1869). William T. Garrett Foundry, San Francisco. 17 6/10 carat gold, alloyed with copper. 5 9/16" x 7/16" x 1/2" (shaft including head), 1/2" x 1 3/8" x 1 1/4". Iris & B. Gerald Cantor Center for Visual Arts at Stanford University. Gift of David Hewes, 1998.115; **593** Stamp Designs © United States Postal Service. Displayed with permission. All rights reserved. Written authorization from the Postal Service is required to use, reproduce, post, transmit, distribute, or publicly display these images; **594** Corbis-Bettmann; **595** *left, John Davison Rockefeller* (1967), Adrian Lamb, after the 1917 oil by John Singer Sargent. Oil on canvas, 58 3/4" x 45 3/4". National Portrait Gallery, Smithsonian Institution/Art Resource, New York; *right* National Portrait Gallery, Smithsonian Institution/Art Resource, New York; **596** *left The Hatch Family* (1871), Eastman Johnson. Oil on canvas, 48 x 73 3/8". The Metropolitan Museum of Art, Gift of Frederic H. Hatch, 1926 (26.97). Photograph copyright © 1999 The Metropolitan Museum of Art. *right, Room in a Tenement Flat* (about 1910), photo by Jessie Tarbox Beals. The Jacob A. Riis Collection, Museum of the

City of New York; **598** *top right* Library of Congress; *center left* Chicago Historical Society; *bottom right* Library of Congress; **598** *bottom left,* **599** *center left* Corbis-Bettmann; **599** *bottom* Chicago Historical Society; **600, 601** Corbis-Bettmann; **602** Brown Brothers.

Chapter 21, 606–607 The Granger Collection, New York; **606** *left* The Granger Collection, New York; *right* © Corbis; **607** *top* © Corbis; *bottom* The Granger Collection, New York; **609** Copyright © Collection of The New-York Historical Society; **610** Illustration by Patrick Gnan; **611** The Granger Collection, New York; **613** Corbis-Bettmann; **614** The Granger Collection, New York; **616** Brown Brothers; **617** Michael S. Yamashita/Corbis; **618** Illustration by Ronald Himler. Copyright © 1995 HarperCollins Publishers. Bottom background copyright © Bill Pogue; **619** Corbis; **620** Copyright © Jacques Chenet/Liaison Agency; **621** *top* Joseph Schwartz Collection/Corbis; *bottom* Corbis; **622** Library of Congress; **623** The Granger Collection, New York; **626, 627** Corbis-Bettmann; **628** *top* Lake County Museum/Corbis; *center, bottom* The Granger Collection, New York; **629** Corbis-Bettmann; **631, 632** *top right* The Granger Collection, New York; **632** *bottom left* Culver Pictures; **633** Photos by Sharon Hoogstraten.

Unit 7

634–635 Brown Brothers.

Chapter 22, 636 *top* Family Making Artificial Flowers (about 1910), photo by Jessie Tarbox Beals. The Jacob A. Riis Collection, Museum of the City of New York; *center* © Bettmann/Corbis; *bottom* © Bettmann/Corbis; **637** *top* Library of Congress; *center* © Corbis; *bottom* © Bettmann/Corbis; **638** Brown Brothers; **639, 640, 641** Library of Congress; **642** *bottom* Brown Brothers; *left inset* Doubleday, Page and Company, New York, 1906, second issue; **643** *Theodore Roosevelt* (date unknown), John Singer Sargent. White House Collection. Copyright © 1992 White House Historical Association; **644** *center* Culver Pictures; *bottom left* Copyright © F. Sieb/H. Armstrong Roberts; *bottom right* Copyright © W. Bertsch/H. Armstrong Roberts; **645** *bottom* Copyright © J. Blank/H. Armstrong Roberts; **646** Eugene V. Debs Collection/Tamiment Institute Library, New York University; **648, 649** Culver Pictures; **650** *top, Lillian Wald* 1867-1940, public health nurse, social worker. William Valentine Schevill, 1864-1951. Oil on cardboard, 71.7 x 71.7 cm (28 1/4 x 28 1/4 in.) feigned circle, 1919. NPG. 76.37 National Portrait Gallery, Smithsonian Institution. Gift of the Visiting Nurse Service of New York/Art Resource, NY; *bottom, A Short Cut over the Roofs of the Tenements; A Henry Street Visiting Nurse* (1908), photo by Jessie Tarbox Beals. Museum of the City of New York. Lent by the Visiting Nurse Service of New York; **651** The Granger Collection, New York; **652** *left* Copyright © 1994 FPG International.

Chapter 23, 656–657 *Great White Fleet,* Harry Reuterdahl. Courtesy of the U.S. Naval Academy Museum; **656** *left* The Granger Collection, New York; *right* © Bettmann/Corbis; **657** *left The Mexican Revolution,* Diego Rivera © 2004 Banco de México Diego Rivera and Frida Kahlo Museums Trust. Av. Cinco de Mayo No. 2, Col. Centro, Del. Cuauhtemoc 06059, Mexico, D.F./ Charles & Josette Lenars/Corbis; *right* © Lake County Museum/Corbis; **658** The Granger Collection, New York; **659** Corbis; **661** *Portrait of Queen Liliuokalani,* date and artist unknown. Bishop Museum; **662** The Granger Collection, New York; **663** Chicago Historical Society; **664, 666** The Granger Collection, New York; **667** From *Puerto Rico: A Political and Cultural History,* Arturo Morales Carrion; **668** U.S. Naval Academy Museum; **671** Illustration by Nick Rotondo; *center left* Corbis-Bettmann; **673** Copyright © Caren Firouz/Black Star/PNI; **674, 675** *bottom* The Granger Collection, New York.

Chapter 24, 676–677 The Granger Collection, New York; **676** *top* © Bettmann/Corbis; *bottom* © Swim Ink/Corbis; **677** *left* Library of Congress; *right* © Bettmann/Corbis; **678** The Granger Collection, New York; **679** The Granger Collection, New York; **681** *top center* Copyright © Mike Fizer/Check Six; *top right* Copyright © Hulton Getty/Tony Stone Images; *bottom left* Hulton-Deutsch Collection/Corbis; *bottom right* Copyright © Hulton Getty/Tony Stone Images; **682** The Granger Collection, New York; **684–685** Illustration by Patrick Whelan; **684** *top right,* **686, 687** Corbis; **689** *left* From *The Enormous Room* by E. E. Cummings, Penguin Twentieth Century Classics Edition. Cover painting *Prisoner's Round* (1890), Vincent Van Gogh, after Dore. Pushkin Museum of Fine Arts, Moscow. Photo courtesy Scala/Art Resource, New York; *right* Book cover from *A Farewell to Arms* by Ernest Hemingway. Cover illustration by Cathie Bleck. Reprinted by permission of Scribner, a Division of Simon & Schuster (New York: Scribner/Simon & Schuster, 1995); **691** Wyoming Division of Cultural Resources; **692** Culver Pictures; **693** Panel no. 1: "During the World War There Was a Great Migration North by Southern Negroes" from *The Migration of the Negro* mural series (1940–41), Jacob Lawrence. Tempera on masonite, 12" x 18". Acquired through Downtown Gallery, 1942. The Phillips Collection, Washington, D.C.; **695** Corbis; **696** The Granger Collection, New York; **697** *right,* **701** *bottom* The Granger Collection, New York; **702** Culver Pictures; **703** Photos by Sharon Hoogstraten.

Unit 8

704–705 Morton Beebe/Corbis.

Chapter 25, 706 *top* The Granger Collection, New York; *center* The Granger Collection, New York; *bottom* Photo: comstock.com; **707** *top* The Granger Collection, New York; *center* © Bettmann/Corbis; *bottom* © Bettmann/Corbis; **708** *LIFE* cover (July 1, 1926) Fred Cooper; **709** Brown Brothers; **710** Copyright © 1923 by the New York Times Co. Reprinted by permission; **711** *center right* Copyright © Stock Montage; **713** Underwood & Underwood/Corbis; **714** Culver Pictures; **715** Brown Brothers; **716** UPI/Corbis-Bettmann; **717** Brown Brothers; **718** *from top to bottom* Movie Still Archives; Copyright © Blank Archives/Archive Photos; Copyright © Archive Photos; Photofest; **719** *left* Brown Brothers; *right* Copyright © Albert L. Bresnik; **720** *The Ascent of Ethiopia* (1932), Lois Mailou Jones. Oil on canvas, 23 1/2" x 17 1/4". Accession no. M1993.191. Milwaukee Art Museum, Purchase, African-American Art Acquisition Fund, matching funds from Suzanne and Richard Pieper, with additional support from Arthur and Dorothy Nelle Sanders; **721** *top* Copyright © Stock Montage; *bottom* Book cover from first edition of *The Great Gatsby* by F. Scott Fitzgerald (New York: Charles Scribner's Sons, 1925). Used by permission of Scribner, a division of Simon & Schuster; **722, 723** *bottom* National Baseball Hall of Fame Library, Cooperstown, New York.

Chapter 26, 726–727 The Granger Collection, New York; **726** *top center* © Bettmann/Corbis; *bottom center* © Bettmann/Corbis; *right* © Hulton-Deutsch Collection/Corbis; **727** *left* Leon Carlin/© *Vanity Fair,* The Condé Nast Publications, Inc., *Vanity Fair* October 1, 1933 cover; *right* © Getty Images; **728** From the Collection of Janice L. and David J. Frent; **729** Nebraska Historical Society; **731** Copyright © 1929 Icon Comm./FPG International; **732** From the collections of the Minnesota Historical Society; **733** Corbis; **734** Library of Congress; **735** Photo by Margaret Suckley/Franklin D. Roosevelt Library; **736** *inset* Courtesy of the Tennessee Valley Authority; **738** F.D.R. Presidential Library; **739** Detail of *Mary McLeod Bethune* (1943–1944), Betsy Graves Reyneau. National Portrait Gallery, Smithsonian Institution/Art Resource, New York; **740** *inset* Corbis; **741** *left* Photofest; *center, right* The Kobal Collection; **742** Oscar White/Corbis; **743** UPI/Corbis-Bettmann; **744** Copyright

© McDougal Littell Inc.; **745** Farm Security Administration—Office of War Information Photograph Collection; **746** Library of Congress; **748** *Construction of the Dam* (1937), William Gropper. Mural study, Department of the Interior, National Park Service. National Museum of American Art, Smithsonian Institution/Art Resource, New York; **749** Courtesy Social Security Office; **750** *top* Copyright © 1929 Icon Comm./FPG International; *bottom* From the Collection of Janice L. and David J. Frent; **751** Photo by Dorothea Lange/Library of Congress; **752** Details of *South Texas Panorama* (1939). Warren Hunter. Mural, Alice Texas Post Office. National Museum of American Art, Smithsonian Institution/Art Resource, New York; **753** Photos by Sharon Hoogstraten.

Chapter 27, 754 *top* The Granger Collection, New York; *center* © Bettmann/Corbis; *center right* © Bettmann/Corbis; *bottom* © Getty Images; **755** *top* © Bettman/Corbis; *center* © Museum of Flight/Corbis; *bottom* Yellow star of David patch (1940). Holland. Gift of Mr. and Mrs. Herbert Klaber. Courtesy of the Spertus Museum of Judaica; **757** Photo by Hugo Jaeger/Life Magazine, copyright © Time Warner Inc.; **758** Corbis; **759** The Granger Collection, New York; **761** Corbis; **762** Copyright © 1999 Owen H. K./Black Star; **763** The Mariner's Museum/Corbis; **764** *left*, **765** Corbis-Bettmann; **766** *top* National Archives; **767** Hulton-Deutsch Collection/Corbis; **768** Photo by Margaret Bourke White/Life Magazine, copyright © Time Inc.; **770** Corbis; **772** National Archives; **773** The Granger Collection, New York; **774** U.S. Office of War Information, photo no. 208-LV-38BB-3 in the National Archives; **775** Corbis-Bettmann; **776** Wally McNamee/Corbis; **777** Photo by Dorothea Lange/National Archives; **778–779** *background* Copyright © Photolink/PhotoDisc, Inc.; **778** *bottom left* Corbis-Bettmann; *bottom right* The Granger Collection, New York; **779** *top, Captain America* TM and copyright © 1999 Marvel Characters, Inc. Used with permission; **780** Corbis-Bettmann; **782, 783, 785** *bottom* The Granger Collection, New York.

Chapter 28, 786–787 © Carl Iwasaki/Time Life Pictures/Getty Images; **786** *top* Detail of Image from the Collections of The Henry Ford (64.167.19.243); *center* © Bettmann/Corbis; *bottom* © Bettmann/Corbis; **787** *left* © Hulton-Deutsch Collection/Corbis; *right* Sovfoto/Eastfoto; **788** © Bettman/Corbis; **789** U.S. Army photos; **791** UPI/Corbis-Bettmann; **793** Photo by Walter Sanders/*Life* Magazine, copyright © 1972 Time Inc.; **794** Photofest; **795** AP/Wide World Photos; **797** Corbis-Bettmann; **798** Photo by Hank Walker/Life Magazine, copyright © Time Inc.; **799** Sovfoto/Eastfoto; **800** Courtesy Brunswick Record Corporation; **801** Copyright © Frank Cezus/Tony Stone Images, Inc.; **802** *from top to bottom* Copyright © Archive Photos; Elvis Presley Enterprises, Inc. Used by permission; Copyright © Harold Lloyd Trust/Archive Photos; The Kobal Collection; **804–805** *background* Illustration by Alexander Verbitsky; **804** *top* Copyright © Tom Bean/Tony Stone Images; *bottom left* Curt Teich Postcard Archives, Lake County Museum, Wauconda, Illinois; **804** *bottom right, center left* Copyright © 1996 Terrence Moore; **805** *center right* Copyright © Ferguson & Katzman/Tony Stone Images; *bottom* Copyright © Rob Boudreau/Tony Stone Images; **807** *bottom* Courtesy Ross Lewis and the *Milwaukee Journal*.

Unit 9

808–809 Photo by Francis Miller/*Life* Magazine, copyright © Time Inc.

Chapter 29, 810–811 James P. Blair/National Geographic Image Collection; **810** *top center* © Bettmann/Corbis; *bottom center* © Owen Franken/Corbis; *right* © Getty Images; **811** *left* © Bettmann/Corbis; *top center, bottom center* Photos: comstock.com; **812** © Elliott Erwitt/Magnum Photos; **813** Corbis-Bettmann; **814** AP/Wide World Photos; **815** Black Star/Time Inc.;

816 UPI/Corbis-Bettmann; **818** Corbis-Bettmann; **819** Copyright © 1963 Charles Moore/Black Star; **820** Photo no. KN-C30670 in the John F. Kennedy Library; **822** President Lyndon Baines Johnson Library and Museum; **823** AP/Wide World Photos; **824** Copyright © 1978 George Ballis/Take Stock; **825** Copyright © Robert Fried/Stock Boston/PNI; **826** Corbis-Bettmann; **827** AP/Wide World Photos; **830** *top* UPI/Corbis-Bettmann; *center* Black Star/Time Inc.; *bottom* Photo by Sharon Hoogstraten; **831** *bottom, Freedom* (date unknown), Anthony Gauthier. Property of the Institute of American Indian Arts Museum, no. WIN14.

Chapter 30, 832 *top* © Bettmann/Corbis; *bottom* © Corbis; **833** *top* © Wally McNamee/Corbis; *center* © Bettmann/Corbis; *bottom left* © Reuters NewMedia Inc./Corbis; **832** *bottom right* © Bettmann/Corbis; **835** From *The Unquiet American* by Cecil B. Currey. Photo courtesy of the author; **836** AP/Wide World Photos; **837** *right* Sovfoto/Eastfoto; **838** Corbis; **839** Corbis-Bettmann; **840** Corbis; **841** Corbis-Bettmann; **842** *left* Copyright © Popperfoto/Archive Photos; *center* PNI; *right* National Archives; **843** *left* Copyright © 1999 Jim Pickerell/Black Star; *right* Photo by Larry Burrows/Life Magazine, copyright © Time Inc. Courtesy Larry Burrows Collection, New York; **845** Copyright © 1968 Herblock; **846** Copyright © John Paul Filo; **847** *inset* UPI/Corbis-Bettmann; **848** Copyright © 1998 Nik Wheeler/Black Star; **849** Dave G. Houser/Corbis.

Chapter 31, 852–853 © Bettmann/Corbis; **852** *left* © Wally McNamee/Corbis; *right* © Reuters NewMedia Inc./Corbis **853** *left, right* © Wally McNamee/Corbis; **854** © Larry Voigt/Photo Researchers; **855** Copyright © 1999 Dennis Brack/Black Star; **856** NASA; **858** AP/Wide World Photos; **859** Copyright © Penelope Breese/Liaison Agency; **860** Cartoon by Paul Conrad. Copyright © Los Angeles Times Syndicate; **861** Copyright © 1974 Alex Webb/Magnum Photos, Inc.; **862** AP/Wide World Photos; **863** Copyright © R. Krubner/H. Armstrong Roberts; **864** Copyright © Dirk Halstead/Liaison Agency; **866–867** *background* NASA; **866** *center left* Copyright © 1996 Ariel Skelley/The Stock Market; **867** *top* Copyright © R. Krubner/H. Armstrong Roberts; *bottom right* Photo by Vernon Merritt/Life Magazine, copyright © Time Inc.; **868** From the Collection of David J. and Janice L. Frent.

Chapter 32, 870–871 © R. Ian Lloyd/Masterfile; **870** *left* JSC Digital Image Collection/NASA; *right* © Owen Franken/Corbis; **871** *left* © Brooks Kraft/Corbis; *right* © Jeff Albertson/Corbis; **872** Copyright © 1993 Time Inc. Reprinted by permission; **873** From the Collection of Janice L. and David J. Frent; **874** Courtesy Ronald Reagan Library; **875, 876** *top left* AP/Wide World Photos; **876** *top* Copyright © 1998 The Washington Post. Reprinted with permission; **877** Kevin Kallaugher, Cartoonists & Writers Syndicate/cartoonweb.com; **879** © Michael Ainsworth/Dallas Morning News/Corbis; **880** Copyright © Paul Soulders/Liaison Agency; **881** Photo by Donna McWilliam; **882** *top right* Corbis-Bettmann; *center* Commodore Business Machines, Inc.; *center right* Copyright © Charles Feil/Stock Boston/PNI; *bottom left* Copyright © Ted Kawalerski/The Image Bank/Chicago Core; **883** Copyright © Peter Charlesworth/ SABA; **884** Photo by Doug Hoke; **885** Photo copyright © Marion Ettlinger; **886** Copyright © Robert Brenner/PhotoEdit/PNI; **889** *bottom* Photograph by Kaku Kurita; **890** *top* Copyright © Peter Simon/Stock Boston/PNI; *bottom left* Copyright © Lambert/Archive Photos; *bottom center* Copyright © Henry/TSI Imaging/Tony Stone Images; **891** Photos by Sharon Hoogstraten.

Special Report

893 *top, bottom* AP/Wide World Photos; **895** *top, bottom* © Ahmad Masood/Reuters/Corbis; **896** AP/Wide World Photos; **897** *left* AP/Wide World Photos; *right* © Reuters NewMedia Inc./Corbis.

Historic Decisions of the Supreme Court

898 *top left* Corbis; *bottom left* Copyright © 1994 North Wind Pictures; *bottom center* The Granger Collection, New York; *bottom right* Copyright © 1999 North Wind Pictures; **899** *top* Corbis; *bottom left* Corbis-Bettmann; *bottom right* AP/Wide World Photos; **900** *top left* Corbis; *bottom right* The Granger Collection, New York; **901** Copyright © 1994 North Wind Pictures; **902** Corbis; **903** *left* Culver Pictures; *right* The Granger Collection, New York; **904** *top left* Corbis; *bottom right* The Granger Collection, New York; **905** Copyright © 1999 North Wind Pictures; **906** Corbis; **907** *left* The Granger Collection, New York; *right* Lincoln University Archives, Langston Hughes Memorial Library, Lincoln University, Penn.; **908** *top left* Corbis; *bottom right* The Granger Collection, New York; **909** AP/Wide World Photos; **910** Corbis; **911** Wally Mcnamee/Corbis; **912** *top left* Corbis; *bottom right* AP/Wide World Photos; **913** Corbis; **914** *top left* Corbis; *bottom right* Corbis-Bettmann; **916** *top left* Owen Franken/Corbis; **917** AP/Wide World Photos.

SkillBuilder Handbook

R15 Library of Congress; **R28** Courtesy of the Lloyd Ostendorf Collection.

Presidents of the United States

R40–R42 The Oval Office Collection™ except Clinton AP/Wide World Photos.

McDougal Littell Inc. has made every effort to locate the copyright holders of all copyrighted material in this book and to make full acknowledgment for its use.